W9-CET-600

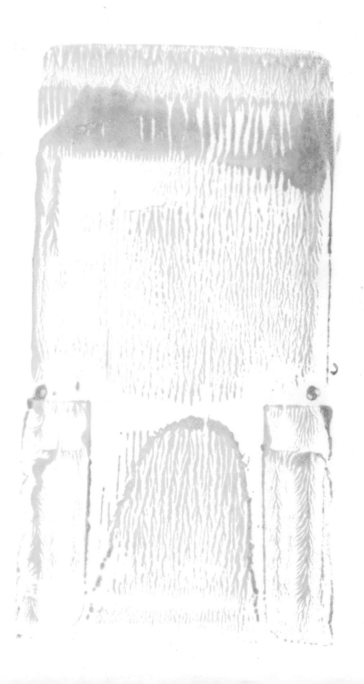

A History of

LATIN AMERICA

◈◈◈◈◈◈◈◈◈◈ *from*

the Beginnings to the Present

A History of
LATIN
AMERICA

 *from*

the Beginnings to the Present

 *by*

HUBERT HERRING

with the Assistance of Helen Baldwin Herring

Third Edition

ALFRED · A · KNOPF
New York

VERNON REGIONAL
JUNIOR COLLEGE LIBRARY

© Copyright, 1968, by Helen Baldwin Herring, Executrix of the Estate of Hubert Herring. © Copyright, 1955, 1961, by Hubert Herring. All rights reserved under International and Pan-American Copyright Conventions. Distributed by Random House, Inc. Published simultaneously in Toronto, Canada, by Random House of Canada Limited.
Library of Congress Catalog Card Number: 67-25977
Manufactured in the United States of America

PUBLISHED 1955, REPRINTED FOUR TIMES
SECOND EDITION, REVISED 1961, REPRINTED NINE TIMES
THIRD EDITION REVISED, ENLARGED AND RESET 1968
98765

This book is for

MARK *and* HUBERT

Foreword

In presenting this third edition, largely revised, of *A History of Latin America,* I again acknowledge my debt to the writers of numerous books and articles, many of whose names are duly listed; to hundreds of Mexicans, Argentines, Brazilians—citizens of all the twenty republics—who have repeatedly welcomed me to their homelands, and shared with me their thoughts on present problems and reflections on past events; and to my associates who have given generous counsel.

My chief debt is to my wife, Helen Baldwin Herring, who has worked with me for years on research and writing. Many parts of the book are as much her work as mine, and the chapter on Africa is hers alone.

I again thank Mary Patricia Chapman for the two fruitful years which she devoted to research for the first edition.

I repeat my indebtedness to those who gave counsel on the first edition: five colleagues read the entire manuscript—Russell H. Fitzgibbon, C. Alan Hutchinson, Irving A. Leonard, Henry Bamford Parkes, and William T. Jones; Wendell C. Bennett read the chapter on the Indian background; Fernando Ortiz, James F. King, Melville J. Herskovitz, and Charles Wagley, the chapter on Africa; William Lytle Schurz, Engel Sluiter, and Paul Vanorden Shaw, the chapters on Brazil; Ysabel Fisk Rennie and Sergio Bagú, those on Argentina; Charles J. Bishko, the chapter on the Iberian background. Others who read various sections of the original manuscript include Frederick Mulhauser, John H. Gleason, Ramón E. Ruiz, David W. Davies, Robert Nugent, and Arthur F. Zimmerman. Margaret L. Mulhauser and Lucile Klotz did much editing.

For valued aid in preparing this third edition, I am indebted to numerous friends. Ambassador Merwin L. Bohan gave generous advice on many points. Ambassador Philip W. Bonsal criticized the chapter on Cuba. Rollie Poppino and John W. F. Dulles gave counsel on Brazil. Donald W. Bray, James R. Levy, and Ronald Dolkart gave advice on Chile and Argentina. Gregory B. Wolfe read and criticized numerous chapters. Kathleen Walker Seegers did valuable research in Washington. Charles Leslie, Betty J. Meggers, and Clifford Evans helped on the revision of the chapter on the Indian background. Virginia Herring Cook did helpful research on Central America. Donald L. Wiedner criticized the chapter on Africa. Howard T. Young counseled on the literary contributions of Latin Americans. Margaret L. Mulhauser prepared the index for the third edition, as she did for the second. Berl Golomb contributed to the preparation of the statistical tables.

I am grateful to Gladys Boggess and Kathryn Milne for the preparation of the manuscript for the three editions. Also helpful on this third edition—in collecting material, checking statistics and bibliography, proofreading, and some typing—were Virginia Esterly Dunbar, Dianne C. Herring, Mark Herring, Hubert B. Herring, Helen M. Huling, Mary K. Manzoli, and Carol Waingrow.

In thanking these numerous friends for help, I make haste to add that none of them are responsible for any errors. On that point, I again express gratitude to students and readers who have caught me in error from time to time—and I hope they will continue to call me to account.

I would also express my appreciation to the editors of Alfred A. Knopf, Inc., especially Peninah M. Blaustein, for their painstaking and skillful work on the manuscript.

Claremont, California   HUBERT HERRING
September, 1967

Contents

Tables

Maps

Planned and executed by Theodore R. Miller

PART I

Foregrounds and Backgrounds

This book is designed to introduce the peoples of Latin America and to trace the course by which they have come to their present estate: their deep roots in Asia and Europe and Africa; their heritage of unreckoned Indian centuries in America; their rule for three centuries by Spain, Portugal, France; their angry political break with Europe; their excursions on the troubled seas of independent life.

The lands and peoples of Latin America have long been banished to the far periphery of our modern world concern. Only in recent years have the people of the United States and other nations awakened to the obvious fact that these twenty sovereign republics will play a strategic role in the clash of rival ideologies. Largely amorphous and underdeveloped, they are the target of the disturbers of the peace from both right and left. Whether they fall prey to the dictatorship of army cliques and would-be Caesars or whether they yield to the blandishments of the emissaries of international Communism, they threaten the democratic health of the hemisphere. Militarily unimportant at the moment, the Latin American world is the "soft underbelly" of our world, carrying promise or threat to stability and peace. We cannot fail to reckon with the problems and the promises of the nations which share our America.

Chapter 1

THIS LAND, THIS PEOPLE

Ours is the story of Latin America, the bulk of that generous span which stretches from the southern border of Texas 7,000 miles south to Cape Horn, 3,200 miles at its widest across Peru and Brazil, an area twice that of all Europe, two and one-half times that of the continental United States. This is Latin America, which shares the Western Hemisphere with the United States, Canada, and the scattered remnants of European colonial power in the Caribbean.

We use the term Latin America for that southern realm, today occupied by twenty sovereign states, knowing full well that the name is awkward and inaccurate. The umbrella word "Latin" can hardly cover the Negro of Haiti, the Aymará on the shores of Lake Titicaca, the Maya of Yucatán, not to mention a half-hundred other Indian groups. Some prefer to speak of "Hispanic America," arguing that the Iberian peninsula was called Hispania from the days of the Romans. Spaniards resent the appellation "Latin America," and agree with Menéndez Pidal, who protests "blotting out our name [Spain] from half the world." Others speak of "Ibero-America," but that as well as "Hispanic America" takes no account of the Indian. Some plead for the term "Indo-America," but that ignores the Spaniard and the Portuguese altogether. And all with one accord forget the African. Were we to be logical, this southern world would be "Indo-Afro-Ibero-America." But, for lack of a better term, we fall back upon "Latin America."

PANORAMA

For the average citizen of the United States, Latin America is still a hidden world. Its varied panorama can best be seen by the modern traveler-by-air who spends a few days or weeks in a swing around the circle of 15,000 miles. We start with a flight over Mexico's burnt northern desert to the high valley of Anáhuac, where we alight at Mexico City (altitude 7,555 feet), whose Spanish palaces and churches are crowded by bold skyscrapers and whose fringes are sprawling Indian villages. We then push south under the shadow of great Popocatépetl and Ixtaccíhuatl, touching briefly at the little Central American capitals—shining Guatemala City, ambitious San Salvador, primitive Tegucigalpa, tropical Managua, modern San José; and we stop by the side of the Panama Canal to visit Panama's capital with its strange assemblage of peoples from every corner of the earth.

From Panama we fly up over Colombia to Bogotá (8,397 feet), bleak but prospering outpost long isolated from the world; and perhaps we stop at busy industrial Medellín and booming Cali. Then we head south over formidable mountain passes to Ecuador, landing on the high plateau to see Quito (9,250 feet), where primitive Indians move placidly through streets boasting some of the finest sixteenth- and seventeenth-century churches and monasteries; and we drop down over the mountain ledge to coastal Guayaquil, from which cargo ships carry off bananas, coffee, and cacao. Flying south we see the swift transition from the drenched coastal lands of Ecuador to the tinder-dry desert of Peru, with occasional oases where sugar and cotton are grown; and we stop in the green valley watered by the Rimac to visit the city of Lima, whose bright showiness cannot hide the surviving monuments to viceregal pride. Continuing south 1,000 miles over the baked nitrate beds of the Atacama Desert, we reach Santiago de Chile, set in a fruitful valley and almost crowded into the sea by the towering Andes.

Leaving Chile, our plane circles over the mountains and heads east, passing so close to Mount Aconcagua, more than four miles above the sea, that it almost seems as though we could lay our hand upon its ice-covered rocks. Then we fly over the Pampa to Buenos Aires, capital of Argentina and metropolis of Latin America, a worldly-wise city whose tree-lined streets, mansard roofs, and sidewalk cafés recall Paris, whose aspiring sky-scrapers imitate New York, and whose stockyards add an odor reminiscent of Chicago. We cross the estuary of the Río de la Plata to visit Montevideo in Uruguay, a solid and architecturally graceless city. Then, if we like, we may fly inland along the sluggish Paraná to Asunción, the isolated and poverty-stricken capital of backward Paraguay; and we can fly still farther into the center of the continent to high Bolivia and its stark cold capital, La Paz (11,920 feet). As we fly north into Brazil, we may stop at São Paulo, brisk and aggressive with its fine office buildings and factories, the center of Brazil's coffee, cotton, and industrial production; and Santos, through which most of the nation's coffee is shipped to the world. But the most beautiful city in all the Americas is Rio de Janeiro. Its island-picketed harbor, its miles of curving beaches which, like ribbons of silver, bind the city together, its mountains of granite thrusting up from the city's very heart—all this is set against the backdrop of the jagged peaks of the Fingers of God and Mount Tijuca.

From Rio de Janeiro we may take a plane that skirts the coast, giving us time to visit Bahia, the Portuguese colonial capital; Pernambuco, where the Dutch created a prosperous colony in the seventeenth century; and dank hot Belém at the broad mouth of the Amazon. Or, we may fly to

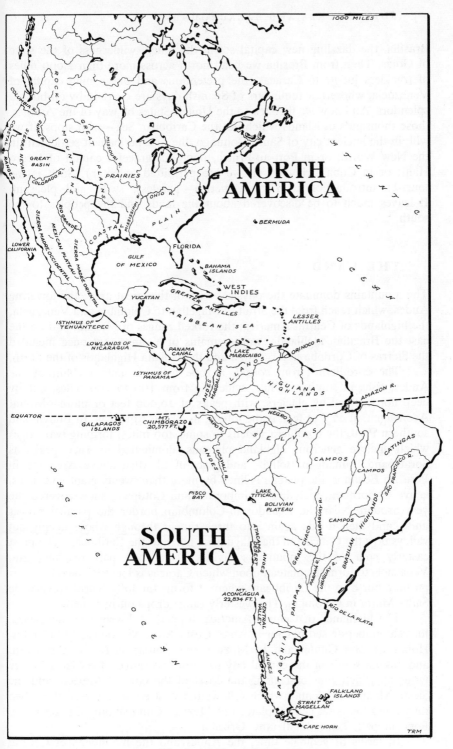

NORTH AMERICA

COLUMBIA R.

ROCKY

SIERRA NEVADA

COASTAL RANGES

SNAKE R.

GREAT BASIN

MISSOURI R.

MOUNTAINS

GREAT PLAINS

PRAIRIES

OHIO R.

COLORADO R.

RIO GRANDE

SIERRA MADRE OCCIDENTAL

MEXICAN PLATEAU

SIERRA MADRE ORIENTAL

COASTAL PLAIN

MISSISSIPPI R.

BERMUDA

LOWER CALIFORNIA

GULF OF MEXICO

FLORIDA

BAHAMA ISLANDS

YUCATAN

GREATER ANTILLES

WEST INDIES

LESSER ANTILLES

CARIBBEAN SEA

ISTHMUS OF TEHUANTEPEC

LOWLANDS OF NICARAGUA

PANAMA CANAL

LAKE MARACAIBO

ORINOCO R.

ISTHMUS OF PANAMA

MAGDALENA R.

LLANOS

GUIANA HIGHLANDS

AMAZON R.

ANDES

NEGRO R.

EQUATOR

GALAPAGOS ISLANDS

MT. CHIMBORAZO 20,577 FT.

NAPO R.

SELVAS

CAMPOS

CATINGAS

ANDES

UCAYALI R.

CAMPOS

SAO FRANCISCO R.

PISCO BAY

LAKE TITICACA

BOLIVIAN PLATEAU

PARAGUAY R.

CAMPOS

BRAZILIAN HIGHLANDS

SOUTH AMERICA

ATACAMA DESERT

ANDES

GRAN CHACO

PARANA R.

URUGUAY R.

MT. ACONCAGUA 22,834 FT.

CENTRAL VALLEY

PAMPAS

RIO DE LA PLATA

ANDES

PATAGONIA

FALKLAND ISLANDS

STRAIT OF MAGELLAN

CAPE HORN

ATLANTIC OCEAN

PACIFIC OCEAN

1000 MILES

TRM

Physical Map of the Americas

Brasília, the dazzling new capital set in the lonely wilderness of the state of Goiás. Then from Brasília we head north across more than 2,000 miles of trackless jungle to Caracas, the pretentious and burgeoning capital of Venezuela, whose few reminders of Spanish days are overlaid by oil-bought splendors. And now we fly back to the United States by way of the Antilles, those thousands of islands which dot the Caribbean Sea—with stops, if we will, in the ancient city of Santo Domingo, the first permanent settlement in the New World; or in Port-au-Prince, poor but graceful capital of Negro Haiti; or in Cuba's Havana (if we are permitted to enter). Such is the tourist's introduction to Latin America—painless, swift, and pleasant. It leaves much to be discovered about the lands and the peoples to the south.

THE LAND

The mountains dominate the physical map of this great area: the towering Andes, which reach from the Strait of Magellan to Colombia and Venezuela; the highlands of Central America; the forked ranges of Mexico; and on the east the Brazilian highlands, worn remains of a range that once included the Sierras of Córdoba in Argentina and the Guiana Highlands of the north.

The cordillera (from *cordel,* a rope), the mountain chain of the Andes, rises in southern Chile, widening from 100 to 200 miles, cut by deep fiords, lined by glaciers, with peaks of 20,000 feet or more—Mount Aconcagua, at 22,834 feet, is the loftiest in all the Americas. In Bolivia and southern Peru, the cordillera widens to some 400 miles, forming two ridges which enclose generous highland plateaus, dominated by such peaks as Sorata and Illimani in Bolivia, and graceful El Misti above Arequipa in Peru. In Ecuador, the plateau is lined by more than twenty giant volcanoes, active or dormant, including Chimborazo and Cotopaxi, snow-covered the year around. Near the Ecuadorian-Colombian border the parallel ranges unite, and then divide again into three ranges through whose deeply cut valleys flow the Cauca and the Magdalena north to the Caribbean. The most easterly spur of the mountains divides again, one part reaching into Venezuela to form the plateau upon which Caracas is located, the other spur pushing north to the Caribbean, where it forms the lofty Sierra Nevada de Santa Marta in Colombia. The westerly range drops off in Panama.

The highlands of Central America, topped by lovely volcanic peaks, furnish temperate settings for much of Costa Rica, Nicaragua, El Salvador, Honduras, and Guatemala. In Mexico, the mountains rise in the south, and unknot south of the capital city to form two ranges, the Sierra Madre Oriental, which runs east along the coast of the Gulf of Mexico, and the Sierra Madre Occidental, which follows the west coast. Between these two ranges lies the great central plateau of Mexico. Commanding this scene are Popocatépetl, Ixtaccíhuatl, and Orizaba.

In terms of geologic time, the Andes and the mountains of Central America and Mexico are young; they are jagged, magnificent, relatively untouched by the storms of time. Their geologic youth is proved by the persistent activity of their many volcanoes, and new ones periodically appear, boiling up out of the plains. In 1770 the volcano Izalco took shape within a few weeks in El Salvador. In 1943 Paricutín erupted from the corn-fields in Mexico's state of Michoacán, reaching a height of 1,500 feet within eight months. This turmoil of the earth along the entire length of the cordillera has brought recurring and costly earthquakes. Guatemala, for example, has had three capitals: the first (Ciudad Vieja) was totally de-stroyed by an earthquake in 1541; the second (Antigua) was laid in ruins in 1773; the third, modern Guatemala City, was shattered in 1917. Indian legends tell of repeated earthquakes during pre-Conquest times. The records since Columbus recite destruction in Lima, Caracas, Santiago, Cuzco, Quito, Concepción, and Mendoza. Within this century, costly disasters have struck Valparaíso in 1906, Costa Rica in 1910, Managua in 1931, southern Chile in 1938, the Ecuadorian plateau in 1949, Cuzco in 1950, El Salvador in 1951, Mexico in 1956 and 1957, Arequipa in 1958, Chile in 1960 and 1965, Colombia and Venezuela in 1967.

The eastern mountains, old and worn by wind and rain, include the highlands which reach from the northern coastal states of Ceará and Pernambuco through Bahia and Minas Gerais to the southern state of Rio Grande do Sul. Here are no such lofty peaks as adorn the western cordillera: the highest are only some 9,400 feet. The Brazilian highlands crowd close to the coast at Santos, Rio de Janeiro, and Bahia, erecting a jagged coastal wall, the Serra do Mar, which long served to confine the population to this scallop fringe on the sea. There is no churning of the earth beneath this eastern range, no smoking volcanoes, no earthquakes.

The mountains and their high plateaus have largely determined the po-litical, economic, and social patterns of much of Latin America. The Andes' high barriers established the boundaries of Chile and Argentina. The plateaus and inaccessible valleys furnished refuge to aboriginal peoples, delayed their conquest by European invaders, and helped to preserve their ancient ways. Furthermore, the existence of great expanses of high plateaus and valleys has gone far toward offsetting Latin America's chief climatic liability —the fact that three-quarters of its total area lies between the Tropics of Cancer and Capricorn. In Mexico, Central America, and the Andean re-publics the majority of the people live on the cool tablelands from 4,000 to 12,000 feet above the steaming tropics at sea level. In Brazil, too, the vigor of the people of São Paulo and Minas Gerais—almost one-third of all Brazilians—may be largely credited to the temperate climate of those highlands.

Rivers have determined much Latin American history. The several regions vary in the usefulness and extent of their rivers. Those of Mexico and Central America are swift flood streams, of little use except for power and irrigation. In the north of Mexico, the Colorado and the Rio Grande are shared with the United States. On the Nicaraguan–Costa Rican bound-ary the San Juan River permits traffic by small steamers, and may one day make way for a second interoceanic canal. But no river north of Colombia is truly navigable. The west coast of South America is similarly ill-favored. Of the scores of streams which feed upon the melting snow of the cordillera and flow toward the Pacific, only one, the Guayas of Ecuador, allows limited use even by light vessels. Southern Chile has racing streams which pour into the sea but are useless for the few people who occupy that forested wilderness. From central Chile to northern Peru stretches the 1,800-mile-long treeless coastal desert, where the rushing streams from the high mountains have created only patches of green oases where cotton, sugar, and rice are cultivated. Little water from these rivers ever reaches the sea.

Into the Atlantic and the Caribbean flow some of the great rivers of the world. There are lesser systems such as the Río Negro and the Río Colorado in Argentina. More important is the São Francisco of Brazil, draining the eastern highland region, 1,800 miles from its source to the sea, and navigable, with interruptions, for some 1,000 miles. But these and other lesser streams are overshadowed by the four chief river systems which dominate South America.

The first is the shallow Magdalena-Cauca, navigable for 900 miles, whose two prongs arise near the Ecuadorian-Colombian border, join where the western spur of the Andes sinks and disappears, and then flow north into the Caribbean. This system drains the valleys between the forked Andes of Colombia, tapping an area of some 365,000 square miles and furnishing for centuries the chief routes of communication for the entire region.

The second is the Orinoco, rising in southeastern Colombia and southern Venezuela and flowing into the Caribbean. One of the great waterways of the world, the Orinoco is little used for navigation above Ciudad Bolívar, 200 miles from its delta. There is no lack of prophets to foretell the day when, with flood control and dredging of the channel, the Orinoco will serve the vast unoccupied hinterland of Venezuela and Colombia.

The third is the sprawling Paraná-Paraguay river system, emptying into the 170-mile estuary of the Río de la Plata, draining an area of about 1.5 million square miles of northern Argentina, Paraguay, southern Brazil, and Uruguay, and serving a population of more than 20 million. Ocean-going vessels (twenty-foot draught) use the Paraná for about 300 miles, to Rosario, Paraná, and Santa Fe. Smaller ships (with draught up to seventeen feet) maintain year-round service to Corrientes and to Paraguay's capital, Asunción, about 1,000 miles from Buenos Aires. Although shorter than the Amazon and its tributaries, the Paraná-Paraguay river system is of first importance in all Latin America, affording shipment of grain and meat from northern Argentina, lumber and quebracho (the source of tannin) from Paraguay.

The fourth is the Amazon, the most fabulous river of the world, a system which, with its uncounted tributaries, spreads a network over the interior of the continent, collecting the waters from melting snow in the Andes and from torrential rains, draining not only the heart of Brazil but

NORTH
AMERICA

SOUTH
AMERICA

ELEVATION
ABOVE SEA LEVEL
(IN FEET)

OVER 6000

3000 TO 6000

1500 TO 3000

SEA LEVEL TO 1500

1000 MILES

TRM

Physical Contour Map of the Americas

also large areas of the three Guianas, Venezuela, Colombia, Ecuador, Peru, and Bolivia—an area of more than 2.7 million square miles, about 40 per cent of all South America. Thousands of little streams racing down the mountainside converge on the floor of the Amazon basin; at Manaus, where the Negro and Amazon converge, over 900 miles from the delta on the Atlantic, the elevation is scarcely 100 feet above the sea. In seasons of excessive rain, the Amazon and its feeders overflow their banks, submerging broad areas of rain forests and swamps. The unreckoned thousands of miles of navigable streams in this river system may one day, when the handicaps of the jungle are overcome by agronomists and sanitary engineers, furnish a royal highway over which many ships will bear their cargoes. It is still a wilderness, however; few people live here, little is produced, and the watery highway is little used. Ocean ships make regular trips to Manaus, and smaller vessels sail a thousand miles farther west to Iquitos in Peru.

For those who would see with their own eyes the making of the greatest river in the world, here are two suggestions. First, start out from the Pacific coast and travel by automobile from Lima up over the high divide, past Oroya and Tarma; then with stout heart and good brakes turn your car into the exceedingly bad road which winds down the eastern slopes to Merced. You have left behind you the bare, baked, shrubless slopes facing the Pacific and now all is green, great trees and vines and shrubbery dripping in the almost incessant rain. You will note by the side of the road a little stream. Follow it. Each minute of each hour the stream grows until by the time you have dropped 8,000 feet it has become a roaring torrent and you have seen the source of one stream that feeds the Amazon. Multiply it by 10,000 (more or less) and you have the story of the Amazon's beginnings. Second, take a ship on the Atlantic coast for the port of Belém at the Amazon's mouth. Some 200 miles out at sea the ocean is muddy with the topsoil of the heart of the continent. You will now readily believe that the Amazon pours into the sea four or five times as much water as the Mississippi.

Great as are these river systems of South America, none of them affords access to such rich areas as are served by the Mississippi, the Missouri, and the Ohio rivers in the United States. Even the Argentine Pampa, most nearly comparable to the grain and cattle lands of the American West, offers no such advantage for commerce and exploitation.

But if the rivers are great and useful, the lakes of Latin America are few and unimportant: Lake Chapala, in western Mexico; a few lovely minuscule crater lakes in Guatemala; steaming Lakes Managua and Nicaragua; glacial pools in southern Chile and Argentina which are as breathtaking as Lakes Neuchâtel and Como. The largest lake in all Latin America is Titicaca, which lies 12,507 feet above the sea in Peru and Bolivia, with an expanse of 3,200 square miles. But none of these compare with the Great Lakes of North America in their contribution to commerce.

Jungle lands are generously scattered over most of the nations. The jungle varies little from the wet forests of Mexico's Isthmus of Tehuantepec to "the green hell" of the Gran Chaco over which Bolivia and Paraguay have fought so fiercely. It is a pattern of heavy forests, tangled foliage, continuing rain, unabated heat. In the jungle all nature seems to have taken up arms against man, his crops, and his domestic animals; a profusion of insects torture man and beast; the serpents kill with venom or strangulation; fish attack with poison, an electric charge, or with teeth to strip away the flesh of animal or man. The warm moisture of earth and air stimulates rank growth; the trees, in competition with each other to reach the sun, create a heavy mass of verdure which effectually shuts out all light. One observer writes of "the relentless fecundity and savagery of the jungle . . . [where] the environment . . . induces melancholy and taciturnity in man. The dark green walls of the rain forest press closely upon him and he lives in a world of deep shadows into which the sunlight trickles all too sparingly. The heavy steaming atmosphere; the sense of futility and inadequacy that comes from the struggle with inexorable forces—floods, the daily inundation of the tide, the drenching rains, the matted vegetation—which dwarf him at every turn; the debilitating effects of malaria and hookworm; the inhospitality of the forest that offers him only such food as he can kill; the discomforts of a half-aquatic existence—all these provide a physical setting for human life in which nearly all the odds are against him who is so bold —or so hopeless—as to challenge its handicaps. People do not laugh or sing in this diabolical world."[1]

The higher lands on the edge of the Amazon basin are lightly populated but rich in promise. The *montañas* of Peru, the *yungas* of Bolivia, the forested slopes of Colombia and Ecuador hold a high potential for future development. Politically, much of this land belongs to the west coast republics; economically, it falls within the Amazon empire. Here are temperate valleys and plateaus, rich soil, heavy forests of mahogany and other fine woods. A few primitive Indians survive precariously; a few hardy migrants have moved in. There is room here for the displaced and landless from other continents, but effective colonization waits upon the opening of roads over the Andes to the west and the development of river traffic to the east. If this is a paradise, as many enthusiasts report, it is still a paradise quite lost.

There are vast stretches of desert in Latin America. Mexico, Brazil, Argentina, Peru, and Chile have great regions where the rain falls fitfully, if at all. The greatest and driest desert is that which stretches for about 1,800 miles along the north coast of Chile and most of the coast of Peru. In the Atacama region of northern Chile, there is practically no rain whatsoever. As you move north to Lima, there may be a little rain in some years, a few drops, no more. There are three culprits in the geographic plot which created this western desert. First, the prevailing trade winds from the east drop their moisture over the warm Amazon basin. Second, the Andean range catches and precipitates moisture which has escaped the jungle. Third, the

[1] From the book, *Latin America: A Descriptive Survey;* new and completely revised edition, copyright, 1949, by William Lytle Schurz, published by E. P. Dutton & Co., Inc.; New York: p. 28.

Humboldt Current[2] wells up in the Antarctic and passes north along the coast, cooling that coast to its welcome comfort[3] and preventing effective formation of rain clouds by precipitating all available moisture at sea.

This pattern of the desert is occasionally interrupted in northern Peru. At irregular intervals, around Christmas time, a vagrant current from the north sweeps down the Peruvian coast. It is called *El Niño*—the Christ Child. *El Niño* brings warm clouds and torrential rains, upsetting the normal rhythm of the desert and of the sea. Fish flee the coastal waters. Birds, cut off from their customary source of food, die from starvation. Houses, bridges, and roads are destroyed. These catastrophic rains have come in almost every decade. Peruvians do not pray for rain. Rain, for them, spells death.

This Chilean-Peruvian desert has its economic virtues. Oases, growing larger from Chile to Peru, yield quantities of sugar, cotton, rice, alfalfa, grapes, vegetables, and fruits. Another economic asset is the centuries-old accumulation of the droppings of sea birds upon the islands and promontories. The lack of rain has permitted this guano to pile up for the use of man. The Incas and their predecessors enriched their fields with it. It was neglected during the colonial years, but after the 1840's it brought profit to Peru. Also, thanks to the rainless desert, the deposits of sodium nitrate in northern Chile and southern Peru were not washed away. Their generous yield brought prosperity to Chile from the 1880's to 1920, and the output is still important.

Latin America has its fruitful plains, producing grains and pasturing cattle. But they are meager compared with the United States' broad expanse of level lands between the Appalachians and the Rockies. The Argentine Pampa, almost as large as the state of Texas, is the fertile heart of Argentina; its level plains, whose flatness has forestalled erosion, are banked high with alluvial soil and constitute the richest agricultural region in Latin America. Other rich and well-watered plains are in Uruguay, Paraguay, and southern Brazil. Elsewhere most of the farming is done on the broken plateaus, in the valleys, and on the oases of the Pacific coast.

Aside from lands for tilling and pasturage, Latin America offers a wide range of resources. There are millions of acres of scarcely touched forests scattered all the way from Tehuantepec to Patagonia; their valuable woods have been slightly exploited. In the tropics, the forests yield rubber,

2 This current is generally so called after the German Baron Alexander von Humboldt, who explored the Americas during the years 1799-1804, and who first made soundings in this Pacific current. Geographers point out that there are actually two currents. First, the Peru Oceanic Current, a cold current, poor in marine organisms and colored a deep indigo, flows fifty to a hundred miles offshore. Second, the Peru Coastal Current, flowing along the shore, is still colder, rich in marine organisms, greenish in color, and moves more rapidly. Feeding upon marine organisms, fish multiply within the Coastal Current, and because there are fish the birds come—pelicans, cormorants, gannets—and devour the fish. These birds in turn, dropping their precious manure upon the islands and the coast, built up the mountains of guano. See Preston E. James: *Latin America* (New York: Lothrop, Lee and Shepard Co.; 1942), p. 174.

3 The annual mean temperature at Lima is 64° F.—about ten degrees cooler than Bahia on the Brazilian coast at the same latitude.

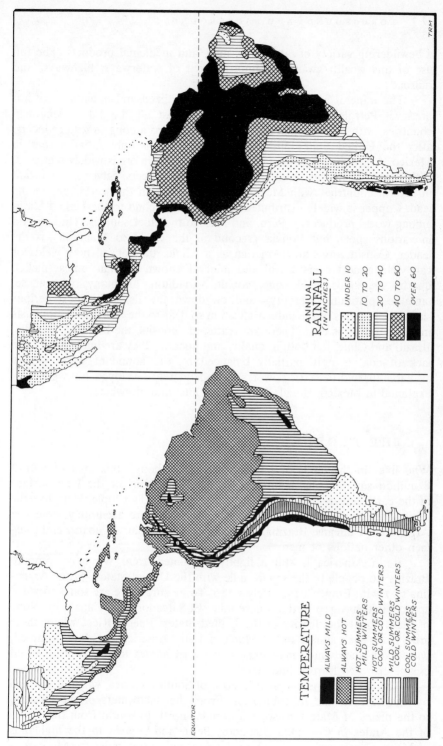

ANNUAL
RAINFALL
(IN INCHES)

UNDER 10
10 TO 20
20 TO 40
40 TO 60
OVER 60

TEMPERATURE

ALWAYS MILD
ALWAYS HOT
HOT SUMMERS
MILD WINTERS
HOT SUMMERS
COOL OR COLD WINTERS
MILD SUMMERS
COOL OR COLD WINTERS
COOL SUMMERS
COLD WINTERS

EQUATOR

Temperature; Rainfall

a bewildering variety of oils, gums, nuts, and medicinal products. The full use of this wealth awaits the improvement of waterways, highways, and railroads.

The mineral assets of Latin America, realized and potential, are impressive. Petroleum has been found in almost all the Latin American countries, with Venezuela in the lead, ranking third among world producers, after the United States and Russia; and there is substantial output in Mexico, Argentina, Colombia, Brazil, and Peru. Iron ore is widely scattered, with Brazil, Venezuela, and Chile the chief producers. Silver is important in several countries, with Mexico (first producer in the world) far in the lead. Copper is widely distributed, with Chile (second to the United States among world producers), Peru, and Mexico the chief sources. Tin is found in various spots, but Bolivia (second in the world to Malaysia) is the leader. Considering Latin America as a whole, the subsoil now yields or can yield almost every metal and mineral known to man: mica, nickel, quartz, diamonds, gold, zinc, cobalt, vanadium, antimony, manganese, tantalite, platinum, mercury—and on down the list. The most serious shortage, in terms of the industrialization so dear to the hearts of nationalists in all countries, is coal. There are scattered deposits, the best in Colombia, Brazil, and Chile, but both in quality and quantity they are inadequate. The lack of coal is only partially balanced by the abundant water supply available for hydroelectric power, still inadequately developed, but vigorously exploited in Mexico, Brazil, Argentina, Chile, and elsewhere.

THE PEOPLE

Who lives in the lands of Latin America? Although this area of almost 8 million square miles comprises some 16 per cent of the land surface of the earth, it supports but 7 per cent of the world's people. Here live the Latin Americans, 245 million more or less; or, more accurately, here live Argentines, Chileans, Brazilians, Mexicans, Colombians, Cubans, and fourteen other nations of men.

Latin America is still a lightly populated area. We may compare Brazil's 26 people to the square mile with the United States' 54; or Argentina's 21 with France's 232, Italy's 446. To be sure there are some crowded spots: Haiti has 419 to the square mile, El Salvador 368, Cuba 177. None of these equal the density of the United States' Puerto Rico, where there are 777 to each square mile.[4] Much of Latin America is lightly occupied, with good lands which may some day afford homes for many who would escape crowded Europe and Asia.

The chief void is the great interior of South America, which is drained by the Amazon and its tributaries. From the headwaters of the Orinoco to the plains of Mato Grosso, 1,800 miles north to south; from the slopes of the Andes in Colombia, Ecuador, Peru, and Bolivia to the highlands of Minas Gerais and the mouth of the Amazon, 2,000 miles west to east—

4 These figures are based upon 1966 population estimates.

in this area which is about two-fifths of all South America, there may not be more than two million people, less than the population of little Connecticut.

Who, then, are Latin Americans? Here are a few, listed at random: a learned judge in Rosario in Argentina bearing an Italian name; a Negro worker in the sugar fields of Pernambuco; a highly intelligent and well-trained statesman of Ecuador, of Spanish blood; an Indian on the road to Otavalo on market day; the wiry *roto*, of mixed Araucanian and Spanish blood, working on the docks in Valparaíso; a distinguished French professor of medicine in São Paulo; an Indian schoolmaster in the village of Tepoztlán; a rich German-Jewish Brazilian, owner of textile mills in São Paulo; a banker in Rio de Janeiro whose name is Dutch; a distinguished editor and newspaper owner in Santiago, who, although his name is English, is a Chilean through and through. These are all Latin Americans.

To tell the story of the Latin Americans, we must start with some 15 to 25 million Indians scattered over the broad area from California to Patagonia at the beginning of the sixteenth century. These Indians were the first Americans, the first Latin Americans. Then Spaniards and Portuguese moved in. And then Negroes arrived from Africa. The importation of slaves was an act of both prudence and mercy: prudence, for shortage of labor prompted recruiting slaves from Africa; mercy, as the missionary friars sought to protect their Indian charges, who, they felt, possessed immortal souls, by substituting African Negroes who, some thought, did not. The chief concentration of Negro labor was in Brazil and the Caribbean, but the trade reached all areas from Mexico to Argentina.

These, then, were the racial origins of the Latin American people—first, Indians; second, Europeans; third, Africans. From the beginning intermingling was common. Whites cohabited with Indians, whites with Negroes, Negroes with Indians. Sometimes the unions were blessed by the Church; usually they were not. Children were born of every shade of color: red, brown, black, and white. This process has continued.

Immigration contributed to the complicated patchwork of Latin America. Throughout the colonial period a few migrants drifted in from northern Europe, legally or illegally, and made their homes in the New World. After independence, and particularly after the 1850's, immigration increased. Spaniards, Portuguese, and Italians came in large numbers, as well as French, English, Japanese, Germans, and Slavs. Over the length and breadth of Latin America we find people who speak no word of the language suggested by their English, French, German, or Dutch names. With few exceptions these migrants became loyal nationals of the lands of their adoption, settled down, and intermarried.

There are today, in the mid-1960's, some 245 million Latin Americans, divided among twenty nations. How then may we classify and describe the varieties of Latin Americans? The southern republics fall roughly into six classifications according to their prevailing racial patterns.

First, there are four nations in which the Indian predominates: Guatemala, Ecuador, Peru, and Bolivia. Second, there are eight nations in which the mestizo[5] outnumbers all others: Mexico, Honduras, Nicaragua, El Salvador, Colombia, Venezuela, Chile, and Paraguay. Third, there are the nations in which Negro blood is important, together with sizable mestizo populations: Panama, Cuba, and the Dominican Republic (as well as substantial areas of Colombia, Venezuela, and the coastal zones of Honduras and Nicaragua). Fourth, there is Haiti, which is almost entirely Negro. Fifth is Brazil, which has a racial pattern distinctly its own; here the population is a mixture of Indian, Negro, and white—perhaps half white, with the balance represented by mixtures of various descriptions. Sixth, there are three countries definitely white European in origin: Argentina, Uruguay, and Costa Rica.

The republics may be classified in terms of political habits. Theoretically, all are constitutional republics, with elected presidents and congresses; all have constitutions akin to that of the United States, with the same theoretical balance between the executive, the legislative, and the judicial branches of the government. The theory is clear; the practice varies greatly. Perhaps we would do well to start with a definition. Let us say, then, that a constitutional democracy is one in which elections are held, in which votes are faithfully counted, in which those who get the votes get the offices, in which those who get the offices are permitted to hold them until the end of their elected terms, at which time they are permitted to retire to their own firesides and in due course to die in their own beds from natural causes. How well do the twenty republics of Latin America measure up to this definition?

The score board on democratic performance for the twenty republics is spotty. First honors, as of 1967, go to Uruguay, Costa Rica, and Chile, where honest elections are the rule, where the military bows to the civilian authority, and where courts and congresses operate in constitutional fashion. Close behind them are several nations in which progress toward democratic control has made hopeful gains during recent years: here we tentatively place Colombia and Venezuela—and to them we hopefully add Peru, although her military has not yet proved that it has really learned its place in a democratic society. At the opposite extreme are nine countries in which dictatorship of various degrees of virulence has been the almost unbroken rule; where elections seldom reflect the will of the people; where executives continue to dominate the congresses and the courts; where military men are reluctant to keep their hands off the civilian authorities: here, with various shadings, exceptions, and emphases belong Honduras, Nicaragua, Haiti, Panama, Guatemala, Ecuador, Bolivia, Paraguay—and, of course, Cuba. El Salvador traditionally belongs with this group, but has now hopefully embarked upon a constitutional course. And among the dictatorships— or quasi-dictatorships—we must today place Argentina and Brazil: both have tacitly confessed defeat of their democratic pretensions by permitting

5 Literally, a person of mixed blood. In Spanish America the term mestizo is usually applied to those of mixed Spanish and Indian blood.

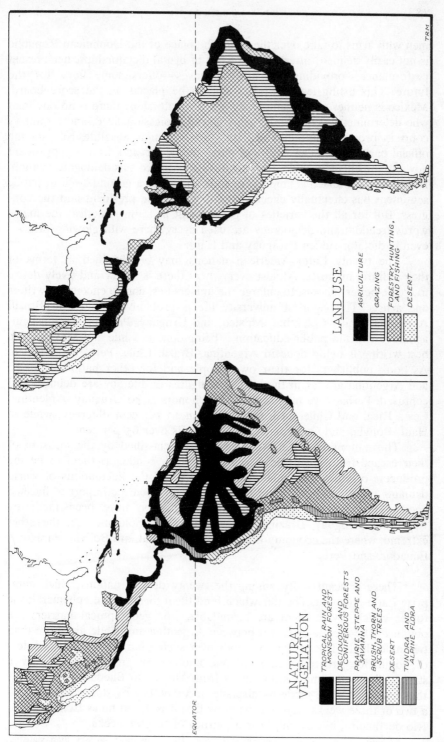

NATURAL VEGETATION

TROPICAL RAIN AND
MONSOON FOREST

DECIDUOUS AND
CONIFEROUS FORESTS

PRAIRIE, STEPPE AND
SAVANNA

BRUSH, THORN AND
SCRUB TREES

DESERT

TUNDRA AND
ALPINE FLORA

EQUATOR

LAND USE

AGRICULTURE

GRAZING

FORESTRY, HUNTING,
AND FISHING

DESERT

TRM

Natural Vegetation; Land Use

men with arms to take over the rule. The place of the Dominican Republic is not easily defined: after a long record of brutal dictatorships, her present performance—providing the army behaves—offers some hope for the future. This listing leaves Mexico still to be placed on the score board. Mexico is neither a free democracy nor a dictatorship: there is no one man who determines its course; the army is well professionalized, and a military coup is probably unthinkable. But the well-nigh absolute rule of the official party, which can and does name public servants from the president down to the village alcalde, scarcely qualifies Mexico as a democratic nation. Nevertheless, Mexico is unique, for time and again a ground swell of public sentiment has effectually checked the power of the president and the congress. But for all the varieties of government in Latin America, the magic words freedom and democracy are used everywhere with glowing pride— even in dictator-ridden Paraguay and Haiti.

The twenty Latin American nations may be classified in terms of their cultural maturity. Almost everywhere there is a new and lively desire to create better schools, to enlarge the universities, and to encourage writers and artists. The vigor of university life is probably strongest in Brazil, Argentina, Chile, Colombia, Mexico, and Uruguay. Perhaps the most imaginative work in public education is being done in Chile and Mexico. The best writing is being done in Argentina, Brazil, Chile, Peru, and Mexico. As book publishers for their own people and for other nations, Mexico and Argentina are far in the lead. The figures on literacy are debated and confused. Perhaps we may say that first honors go to Uruguay, Argentina, Costa Rica, and Chile, each with less than 17 per cent illiteracy; while in Haiti, Bolivia, and Guatemala the illiteracy is over 65 per cent.[6]

The nations of Latin America may be classified by the measure of their escape from the colonial economy which condemns them to be the producers of cheap raw materials, subject to all the fluctuations of world demand and prices, and forces them to depend upon the import of finished goods. Here, notable records in industrialization have been made by Argentina, Uruguay, Brazil, Chile, Mexico, and Colombia. At the other extreme, where the economy is still frankly colonial, are Bolivia, Paraguay, Ecuador, and Peru.

There is scant unity among the twenty diverse nations which comprise Latin America. The ties which bind them together are ephemeral; the forces which divide them are formidable. The geographical barriers are obvious. The mountain passes between Argentina and Chile are more than two miles high. The cartage of goods over such a barrier is costly. Centers of population are removed from one another by great distances. By a straight line it is almost 5,000 miles from Mexico to Buenos Aires. Today that journey can be made by airplane in a day, but by steamship it is still a two or three weeks' trip. As the crow flies it is 2,000 miles from Lima to Rio de Janeiro, but by ship it is a journey of several weeks.

6 Citation of figures on illiteracy is difficult. There are more guesses than statistics. See the estimates in the table on pp. 960–1.

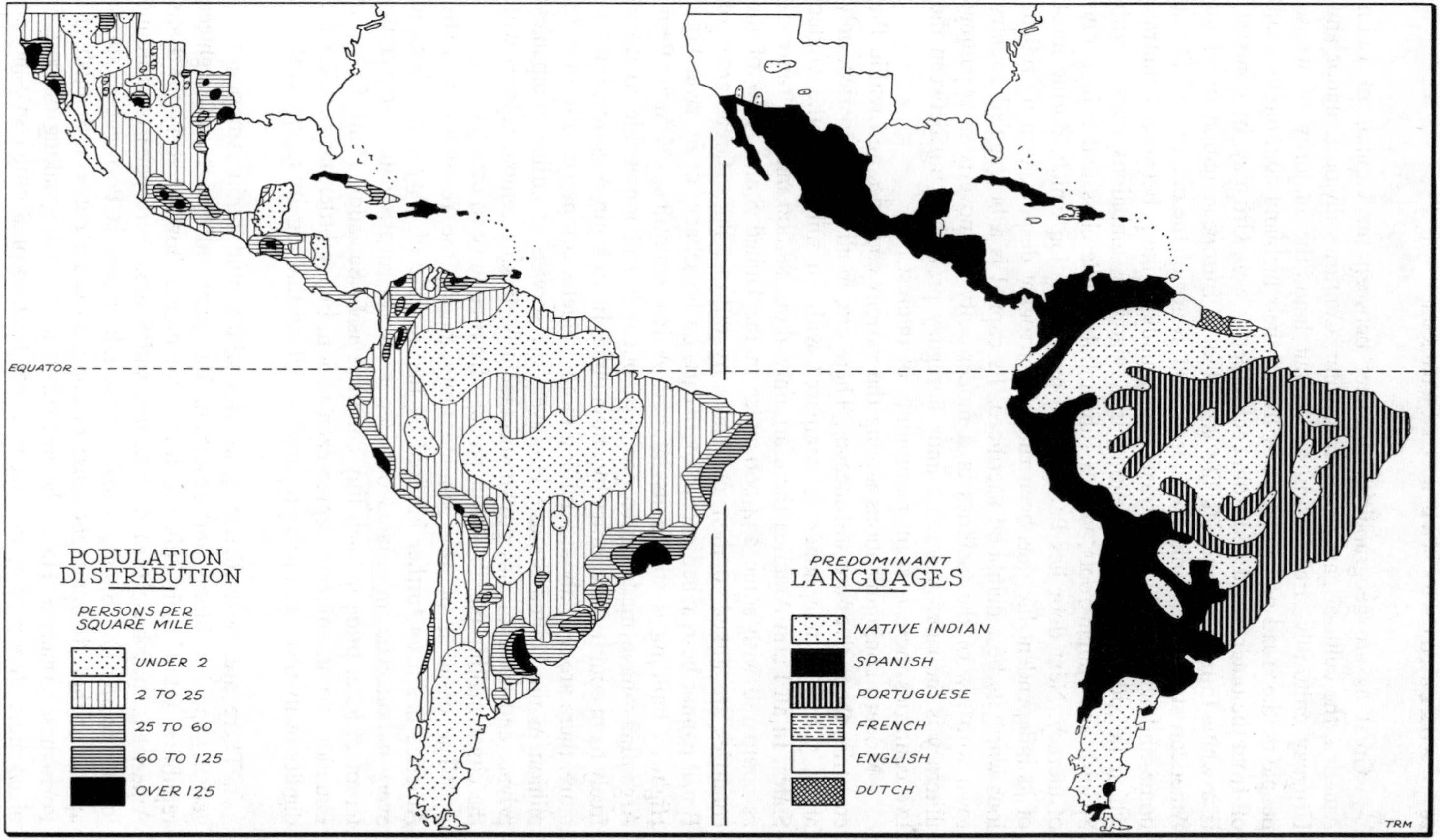

Population Distribution, 1951; Languages, 1951

PREDOMINANT
LANGUAGES

NATIVE INDIAN
SPANISH
PORTUGUESE
FRENCH
ENGLISH
DUTCH

POPULATION
DISTRIBUTION

PERSONS PER
SQUARE MILE

UNDER 2
2 TO 25
25 TO 60
60 TO 125
OVER 125

EQUATOR

TRM

VERNON REGIONAL
JUNIOR COLLEGE LIBRARY

Great as are geographical distances between the capitals of Latin America, the cultural gaps are even greater. Centuries divide Ecuador and Uruguay culturally. Ecuador is an Indian land, the majority of whose people neither read nor write. They live in their highland communities cut off from the outer world and from each other as well. Uruguay, by contrast, is a white European land; its life is that of a European nation or of an American state. Its people are literate and aware of the currents of life at home and abroad. The contrasts are equally striking between countries which lie side by side. Argentina is a vigorous, ambitious nation with Spanish and Italian roots, with a substantial middle class and a high rate of literacy. Next door lies Paraguay, a mestizo nation which, during most of its independent life, has been ruled by arrogant despots, torn by ridiculous wars, its best manhood sacrificed. Its capital is a bedraggled country town with few of the facilities of a modern city. Its poverty is appalling; illiteracy is the rule. Argentina finds Paraguay profitable, but between the two countries there is scant community of interest.

Modern communications among the various countries and within the countries themselves are still meager. There are, in all Latin America, only about 5 million telephones as compared with 89 million in the United States. In all Latin America there are only about 88,000 miles of railroads as compared with some 234,000 miles in the United States. Few of the countries are linked to their neighbors by railroad lines. Great areas of Brazil cannot be reached except by oxcart, on horseback, or by river boat. Highway building is still in its infancy. A few countries—Mexico, Peru, Argentina—have made brave progress, but it is still impossible to travel freely from country to country by automobile. In all Latin America, furthermore, there are only about 6 million motor vehicles compared with some 84 million in the United States.[7] However, the service of airline companies, private and national, has grown spectacularly, linking remote regions with the cities, making possible swift passage from country to country.

The creation of any genuine unity among the republics of Latin America has been further blocked by the increase of lusty nationalism in every nation. The uninitiated outsider is always surprised to discover the fervor of local pride in such tiny countries as El Salvador, Haiti, Cuba, or Ecuador. To an amazing degree each nation, big or little, has developed a dignity of its own, and it is prepared to defend that dignity at any cost.

There are, nevertheless, stout ties which bind Latin Americans together. Spanish blood and tradition, the joint inheritance of eighteen republics, retain their adhesive force. No matter how savagely the Latin Americans may have turned upon *political* Spain, there persists profound loyalty to *spiritual* Spain. Brazil, whose inheritance is Portuguese, stands apart, for there is but slight sense of common cause between Spanish and Portuguese America. Haiti, the last surviving French-speaking outpost, is of no more than passing interest to either Spanish or Portuguese America.

7 Figures for railroad mileage are for 1959; those for motor vehicles and telephones are for 1964.

The common Indian inheritance of Mexico, Guatemala, Ecuador, Peru, and Bolivia, is gradually becoming a cohesive force, as a new, but not yet general, interest in *indianismo* colors the intellectual and cultural life of these Indian lands. The strongest bond among Latin Americans of all countries is loyalty to the Catholic faith. No matter how noisily anticlerical exhorters may attack the priests, the people from humblest peon to most cultured intellectual are profoundly Catholic in sentiment.

Another force uniting all Latin Americans has been the general fear of outside aggressors. In the first days of independence, common fear of Spain held them together in fitful alliance and it flared up later as Spain sought to regain her hold. Then, from time to time, the threats of France and England aroused general outcry. The United States later became the chief target. We will consider in later chapters the steps by which the republic of the north became the specter of imperialism for the republics of the south—the annexation of Texas, the war with Mexico, the Panama incident, the extension of military control in the Caribbean. Common fear of the United States perhaps did more to unite the Latin Americans than all the forces of common blood and inheritance. This fear lessened when a more generous neighborliness emerged in the United States. Meanwhile, other common fears engaged the attention of all Americans, north and south. In World War II most Americans found that their deep interests lay together. And by the mid-twentieth century they were generally united in resistance to international Communism—an issue dramatized by the Cuban missile crisis of 1962.

INTERLUDE

We look back to the beginnings of America—and Latin America.

Who were the ancestors of today's builders of cities, cultivators of corn and wheat and manioc, tenders of herds, miners for gold and copper, handlers of machines in mills and factories, teachers in schools, traders in market places? Where did these Latin Americans come from? The answer leads us into three continents—Asia, Europe, Africa. America is young. It was only the day before yesterday, in terms of geologic time, that America was empty of human life, that no human voice competed with the call of birds, the chattering of monkeys, the wail of coyotes, from Alaska to Cape Horn. On that day-before-yesterday in Asia, Europe, and Africa, man had already been standing erect for hundreds of thousands of years.

Modern Latin America is the product of three migrations. The first came from Asia. Some 30,000 years ago (add or subtract according to your tastes or the books you read) the last glacial ice sheet was slowly melting away across the northern stretches of Siberia. As the ice retreated, the shoots of plants and trees pushed up through the warmed wet earth, animals moved north, roving bands of primitive hunters pursued them. At some unreckoned point of time a company of these nomad hunters reached the shores of Bering Strait, today a fifty-mile tongue of water separating

American Alaska from Russian Siberia. These unknown and undated wanderers were the first American immigrants. We may guess why they left Asia. Perhaps they came in pursuit of game, perhaps to escape enemies bearing down from the rear, perhaps out of curiosity. We may guess as to the fashion in which they made the crossing. Perhaps the strait was still frozen and they walked from Asia to America. Or perhaps so much water was still held captive in the glacial mountains as to lower the ocean's level, and they crossed on dry land. Or they may have come by raft or rough canoe, using the islands as resting spots. Scientists are in general agreement that the peopling of America began in some such fashion 30,000 or more years ago (some would set the date at 50,000 or even 75,000 years ago), and that the migration from Asia by way of Bering Strait continued for some thousands of years, the newest arrivals being the Eskimos of Alaska. We know less about the first comers to American soil than we do of their contemporaries in Europe and Asia, for American archaeology is more recent. But available evidence suggests that the first men to migrate to America belonged to the company of *homo sapiens*: the reconstruction of Tepexpan Man, found in the town of Tepexpan near Mexico City and dated about 11,000 B.C., closely resembles a present-day youth in the tropical forests of the Amazon basin; and nothing has been found to suggest the existence in the Western Hemisphere of a man more primitive than *sapiens*.

From the north these migrants moved south, fanning out over what is now Canada and the United States, moving down into Mexico and Central America and pushing all the way to the southern reaches of South America, a trek of some 9,000 miles from Bering Strait to Patagonia. It took these wanderers thousands of years to filter over the North American continent, and more millennia to reach the southern tip of South America. They lived first by hunting and fishing, later by gathering plants and shellfish. Probably by 5000 B.C. some began the domestication of plants, which marked the birth of agriculture and community living. And in the course of time men learned to make pottery vessels, to spin, and to weave. Meanwhile, these primitive peoples bred and multiplied; spread out over the fields, prairies, mountains, jungles, deserts; divided and subdivided into countless families of men shaped and determined by the kinds of communities in which they lived and worked, and by their adaptation to the various environments. Out of this multiplicity of peoples there arose tribes, nations, empires. Civilizations took form and disintegrated or fell prey to the mightier force of new civilizations. At the dawn of history, the two Americas sheltered peoples speaking hundreds of different languages. . . . Thus the primitive Asian hunter was the ancestor of the American Indian.

The second migration came from Europe, less than five centuries ago. Spaniards and Portuguese led the way, followed by the Dutch, the French, and the English. By the seventeenth century, America—North, South, Central—belonged to Europe.

The third migration came from Africa. The white men, intent upon mining gold and silver and cultivating the rich soil of America, required the supple muscles and the strong backs of Negro slaves. The African came in chains, but by mixing his blood with that of the Indian and the European he contributed to the new people called Americans.

So it has come to pass that young America is the blood child of old Asia, Europe, and Africa.

Chapter 2

THE INDIAN BACKGROUND

The Indian, the first American, is still much alive in the New World. There are today somewhere between 15 and 25 million Indians in the Western Hemisphere; less than a million live in the United States and Canada, and the others are scattered over the nations of Latin America.[1] Indians constitute a large slice of the population in Bolivia, Guatemala, Peru, and Ecuador; and, in mixtures with whites, they outnumber all others in Mexico, Colombia, Venezuela, Chile, Paraguay, and all of Central America except Costa Rica. The conclusion is clear: those who would understand Latin America must reckon with the Indian, whose blood and spirit have had much to do with shaping this New World.

THE INDIAN, THE FIRST AMERICAN

Indian America before Columbus is shadowed in mystery, its monuments and temples overgrown by the jungle, its inscriptions all but erased by sun, wind, and rain. Only during recent decades have archaeologists turned to the study of ancient America. Since the last years of the nineteenth century, skillful and patient men have slashed through the tangled growth of centuries, dug under the banked lava flow, uncovered old cemeteries, temples, cities, villages. They have explored caves where they have found clues as to early migrants in piles of bones and shells, in buried campfires of forgotten men. The scientists have been able to reconstruct something of the story

[1] The question "Who is an Indian?" complicates the problem of classifying and counting the Latin American people. For over four centuries the original Indian stock has been intermingled with European and African peoples from the Old World. Anthropologists therefore discourage classification on a purely racial basis, preferring linguistic and cultural considerations as their criteria. Is the Mexican whose features are eloquent testimony of his Indian ancestry, but who wears shoes and speaks fluent Spanish—is this Mexican still an Indian? An anthropologist would answer "No." Is the Paraguayan, who obviously is descended from the white man as well as the Indian, but who still speaks Guaraní and lives in poverty—is this Paraguayan to be classed as "Indian"? An anthropologist would answer "Yes." There are some "official" estimates, using both race and language as bases for enumeration. Those who enjoy neat figures may look at a careful study by the United Nations in the *Demographic Yearbook, 1956,* Table 7.

of the dispersal of men over the Western Hemisphere, their shaping into distinct tribes, with varied languages, customs, occupations, religions. They report to us in diffidence, frankly admitting their incomplete knowledge. The story of Indian America must be written with soft chalk, easily erased and corrected. The conclusions which yesterday seemed tenable may tomorrow be overruled by the discovery of a handful of bones in a cave or hitherto unknown utensils in volcanic ash.[2] "We are still in the dark," writes J. Eric Thompson. "Occasional archaeological discoveries enable a feeble ray of light to be flashed on the fringes of this impenetrability, but the past . . . is like some distant landscape. Two or three objects detaching themselves from their surroundings stand out prominently, but the rest of the picture is lost in the haze of distance."

Although the rays of light upon the Indians of America in pre-Christian times are indeed feeble, in the past decade archaeologists have uncovered exciting new evidence as to the course followed by the early wanderers, where and how the beginnings of New World civilization took place, in what directions ideas spread from major areas to remote parts of the South American continent. Primitive nomad hunters roamed over North America for many thousands of years before some of their number reached Mexico, where a few remained to become the far distant ancestors of the present-day Mexican. Others crossed the narrow Isthmus of Panama, probably arriving in northern South America at least 10,000 years before the Christian era: beautifully chipped stone points, found in northwestern Venezuela, are similar in shape and workmanship to objects associated in the United States and Mexico with the long-extinct mammoth and pre-historic horse. The southward course of these hunters, for more thousands of years, can be traced through obsidian blades found in highland Ecuador, chipped stones from highland and coastal Peru, and tools of stone from

[2] For example, the archaeologists debate the arrival of the first man in America. For many years the hypothetical crossing of Bering Strait was set at about 15,000 years ago. Then came discovery in a Nevada cave of remains of campfires in which sloth dung was used as fuel, and around which were found bones of extinct sloths, horses, and camels. Further digging uncovered spear-thrower shafts painted green and red. This led to the conclusion that man was walking erect on American soil in the days of those extinct animals, suggesting that the first comers to America arrived 20,000 years or more ago. (See J. Eric Thompson: *Mexico Before Cortez* [New York: Charles Scribner's Sons; 1933], pp. 4–6.) Later, Dr. Frank C. Hibben, excavating in Sandia Cave, New Mexico, encountered five stratified levels. From top to bottom (late to early) there were: (1) Wind-blown deposits with potsherds, *metates,* etc., plus bones of ground sloth, previously thought to be Pleistocene. (2) Crust of calcium carbonate. (3) Folsom layer, with fluted Folsom points, blades, gravers, scrapers; also, bones of horse, camel, bison, mammoth, ground sloth. (4) Sterile layer of yellow ochre. (5) Sandia layer with typical Sandia points; bones of horse, bison, camel, mastodon, and mammoth. Dr. Kirk Bryan, geologist, concludes that the earliest level, No. 5, corresponds to a period of very wet climate, correlated with the last advance of ice in the Wisconsin glacial stage, and must be dated more than 20,000 years ago, suggesting the arrival of man in North America more than 25,000 years ago. Then in 1952 and 1954, excavations at Santa Isabel Iztapán, near Mexico City, yielded tools and artifacts in association with mammoth remains, furnishing further proof that man and mammoth were contemporaries in the Valley of Mexico. (See H. M. Wormington: *Ancient Man in North America* [4th ed.; Denver, Colo.: The Denver Museum of Natural History, Series 4; 1957].) Most archaeologists now agree that men crossed Bering Strait between 30,000 and 50,000 years ago—some guess that it was even much earlier.

caves in Argentina. Eric Wolf suggests that these big game hunters had probably reached the southern tip of South America by 7000 B.C.[3]

Perhaps the most important milepost in man's long march toward civilization was the point in time at which he changed from a food-gatherer to a food-producer. This transition, which marked the beginning of settled life and cultural development, occurred at various spots in the Old World more than 10,000 years ago, and independently in the New World at a later date. The efforts of archaeologists to pinpoint the time and place of the first plant domestication in the Western Hemisphere—particularly the cultivation of corn—have very recently led to fruitful digging in the high valley of Tehuacán near Mexico City. Many of the scientists' questions were answered: they discovered the steps by which an ancient wild grass was converted to small but recognizable cobs of corn some 7,000 years ago; they found evidence of incipient agriculture in the highlands of Mexico by at least 5000 B.C. But most interesting of all, in the Coxcatlán cave just south of Tehuacán they uncovered twenty-eight "occupation levels" from which they have reconstructed an almost complete chronology of the life and activity of the people of this high valley for some 12,000 years—the most extended record so far unearthed in the New World. For the first few thousand years these people were hunters, their chief food being birds, small animals, and an occasional horse or antelope. Their simple tools were made of flaked stone. After about 6700 B.C., for some 1,700 years, there was a gradual shift to the gathering of plant foods as the chief means of subsistence, and new implements—such as stone choppers, grinders, mortars, pestles—tell us something of the preparation of these foods. In this period some domesticated plants appeared—among the first were squashes and avocados; there were probably some temporary settlements; and there is also evidence suggesting the possible existence of witch doctors, or priests, who presided over the burial of the dead. Around 5000 B.C. began another phase during which there was increased domestication and cultivation of such plants as corn, squash, beans, chili, gourds—and also cotton—until by about 3400 B.C. some 30 per cent of the total food supply came from agricultural crops. This conquest of the plant world, increasing man's ability to control and increase his food supply, laid the foundation for all later advances toward civilization. It was at this point in time— something over 3,000 years before the Christian era—that the people of the valley of Tehuacán began to settle in more or less permanent villages, domesticating animals as well as plants. By about 2500 B.C. the making of pottery was begun, giving the archaeologists a new and important source of evidence on the life of the people and the diffusion of culture. About 1500 B.C. village life became more complex, and an elaborate ceremonial-ism appeared which included a figurine cult, perhaps representing a circle of family gods. Sometime after about 850 B.C. hybrid corn was grown in irrigated fields, temple mounds appeared, and artifacts suggest that the people of Tehuacán were in contact with cultures outside their own

[3] Eric R. Wolf: *Sons of the Shaking Earth* (Chicago: University of Chicago Press; 1959), p. 23.

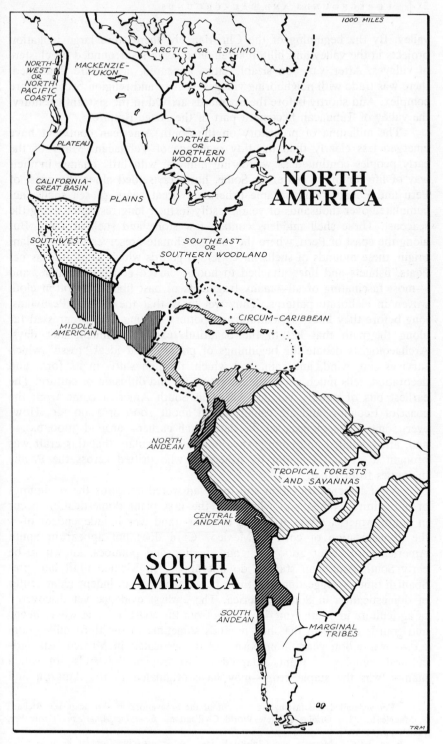

Principal Culture Areas of Primitive America

valley. By the beginning of the Christian era there were large irrigation projects in the valley and hilltop ceremonial centers surrounded by clusters of villages. After A.D. 700 sizable cities appeared, agriculture flourished, there was trade with neighboring villages, society and religion became more complex. And shortly before the Spaniards arrived in the sixteenth century, the valley of Tehuacán became a part of the Aztec Empire.[4]

The millennia of prehistory on the South American continent have emerged less clearly than the tidy sequence of Tehuacán. Many of the early peoples continued as wandering hunters, with little change in their way of life for many centuries. Some, however, settled along the coast of Peru and Ecuador and became fishermen: great heaps of sea shells, accumulated over thousands of years, testify to their long residence along the seacoast. These shell middens contain few stone and shell artifacts. But along the coast of Peru, where the rainless climate preserves items of plant origin, these mounds of shells have yielded gourds which were used as net floats, fishnets and lines attached to hooks, carved gourd containers, and —most fascinating of all—many fragments of bast fiber and cotton cloth woven in elaborate patterns. Thus we know that the coastal Peruvians, long before they knew agriculture and pottery-making, had progressed far along the path that led to the beautiful textiles of much later days. Archaeologists debate the beginnings of pottery, that ideal "fossil" which survives sun, wind, and rain, and which, through shifts in its form and decoration, tells much about the development and diffusion of culture. The earliest bits of pottery yet discovered in South America come from the coast of Ecuador, and are usually dated about 1000 or 1200 B.C. However, some archaeologists set the date much earlier—around 3000 B.C.— and, after detailed and comparative analysis, speculate that this craft was brought to coastal Ecuador by fishermen who drifted across the Pacific in canoes from Japan.[5]

A fundamental question still to be answered concerns the beginnings of agriculture: When and where did the first plant domestication occur in South America? Was it before or after—and was it independent of— the domestication of corn in Mexico? Corn does not appear in South America until about 2000 B.C.; and manioc and potatoes, known to be early South American staples, do not appear in Mexico until late pre-Spanish times—suggesting that there may have been an independent center of domestication in South America. The earliest evidence yet discovered of agriculture in South America comes from the coast of Peru, where beans and gourds appear in the shell mounds sometime in the third millennium B.C.—over 2,000 years after corn was domesticated in Mexico. An agricultural complex of plants adapted to the tropical lowlands—of which manioc was the staple crop—may have originated in the Amazon and

---

[4] For a detailed and fascinating account of the excavations at Tehuacán, see Richard S. MacNeish: "The Origins of New World Civilization," *Scientific American* (November, 1964), pp. 29–37.

[5] See Betty J. Meggers and Clifford Evans: "A Transpacific Contact in 3000 B.C.," *Scientific American* (January, 1966), pp. 28–35.

Orinoco basins, where there was simple village life at an early date. Some remote inland groups, however, remained ignorant of domesticated plants until only a few centuries before the Spaniards arrived; and in the swamps, savannas, and remote forests of the heart of South America, Indians have retained their wandering way of life up to the present day. It was in the Central Andean area that agriculture—and civilization—developed most rapidly. Ancient coastal peoples clustered around the rivers which, fed by the snows of the high cordillera, slice their way down through the foot-hills to the sea. The tribes living in these valleys were isolated from one another by the strips of desert and spurs of rock which divided them, and each was unified by its dependence upon a single source of water—the river. At least by the beginning of the Christian era these people irrigated their farms by a system of ditches which channeled water from the rivers. And there was also irrigation on the terraces which were carved into the steep slopes of the high mountains.

Thus the emergence of civilization in the broad stretch of territory now called Latin America took place in two chief areas: the first was centered in Mexico and Guatemala, the second was the Central Andean region of South America. Although many groups remained isolated, with slight contact even with their near neighbors, almost up to Christian times, there is clear evidence that there was communication by sea among some scattered peoples of Middle and South America as early as 2000 B.C.; and by the beginning of the Christian era there were probably planned trading expeditions and some exchange of ideas.

From Teotihuacán, near present-day Mexico City, south to Lake Titicaca, on the high plateau of modern Bolivia and Peru, the life of the Indians—for some 1,000 to 1,500 years before the Spaniards arrived—begins to come into focus. It now seems clear that by the middle of the first Christian millennium various pre-Aztec peoples were established in central and southern Mexico, and in the heart of the Yucatán peninsula the Maya were building cities; in the Andean region of the south, the Mochica and related civilizations—following the older Chavín culture but antedating the Inca Empire—were spreading through the highland and coastal areas. By the year 1000, the Toltecs had won power in central Mexico and were beginning to extend their influence over the previously autonomous Maya city-states of Yucatán and Guatemala; and the people of the Central Andean highlands were expanding their control northward and to the coastal states. Then, between the year 1000 and the coming of the Spaniards, there arose the dominant civilizations of the Aztecs in Mexico and the Incas in the Andes.

The record of these ancient peoples is based on scattered evidence, some convincing, and some baffling. Only the Maya had a written language developed beyond the pictograph, but few of their codices escaped the fire with which the conquerors thought to erase paganism. However, inscriptions on Maya monuments furnish some tentative dates. The chroniclers of the sixteenth and seventeenth centuries, too, are of service to modern scholars, for they wrote voluminously, reporting what they had seen and heard and gathering up the accumulated oral traditions of the Aztec, Maya, and Inca peoples. But such records are often too spare or too inaccurate to satisfy the curiosity of modern students, and we turn as well to the monuments and relics of the ancient peoples themselves for evidence. The developing complexity of social organization and religion is attested by the priceless remains unearthed and reconstructed by the archaeologists: stone temples dedicated to the gods of rain and fertility; sculpture of remarkable artistry; painted walls uncovered in tombs and buried cities; intricately designed textiles; beautiful pottery vessels, which, because they had no practical use, we know were created for their own sake, or as a part of religious worship. These sculptured stones, jugs, and bits of weaving provide us with a picture of the wars and daily lives, achievements, and defeats of these diverse peoples over a period of more than 2,000 years.

By drawing upon such evidence, modern scientists undertake to classify the various aboriginal peoples. Food is one criterion. Some of the tribal groups continued to live by hunting and fishing, as in the caribou area of present-day Canada, the bison area of the central plains of the United States, the salmon area from Alaska to Southern California, the guanaco area of South America. Other groups emerged from the hunting and fishing stage and relied chiefly upon crops; the most important of these inhabited the corn belt, a 5,000-mile span from the Mississippi Valley to Santiago de Chile. Aboriginal Americans may also be classified by their methods of transport. In the far north the dog served man by drawing his sleds; in the Andean area the llama, a second cousin to the camel, was bred as a carrier and was the only beast of burden for aboriginal man. In the area between the Colorado River of the United States' Southwest and northern Ecuador, freight was carried on the backs of men. People have been further classified by their skill in weaving fibers, making baskets, designing cloth, fashioning pottery, building houses and temples, and contriving musical instruments. And they have been classified by the intricacy and skill of their social and political organizations, by their religious customs, by the growth of their mythology, by the devices employed to control nature and its gods. On the basis of these various criteria, modern scholars have sought to demarcate the chief cultural areas in the Western Hemisphere.

In this general introduction to Latin America, we can pay scant attention to the numerous minor groups of aboriginal Americans. In Mexico and Central America, we will dwell especially upon the civilizations of the Maya and the Aztecs. In South America, we will devote ourselves to the Andean civilizations which culminated in the Inca Empire. But before turning to these three major Indian peoples, we will give brief attention first to the other pre-Conquest civilizations in South America, then to the contemporaries of the Maya in the first Christian millennium.

In South America, by the time the Spaniards arrived in the sixteenth century, the inventions and discoveries of many millennia had been molded by the varying environments into four general cultural types, which are classified in the *Handbook of South American Indians*[6]—a comprehensive work compiled during World War II by a group of anthropologists and archaeologists from the United States and Latin America. The first of these four categories includes the "marginal hunting and gathering tribes of eastern Brazil, the Gran Chaco, the Pampa, Patagonia, and Tierra del Fuego"; these many tribes, while varying greatly in customs and beliefs, lived from hunting, fishing, and the collecting of berries and other wild foods. In the north, their communities seem to have been more stable, and there was some orderly cultivation of the soil with production of manioc, maize, and beans.

Under a second grouping, the authors of the *Handbook* include the tribes living in the tropical forests, a region embracing the Amazon basin, the lowlands of coastal Brazil, the slopes of the *montaña* in Peru and the *yungas* in Bolivia. Here we find reliance upon soil cultivation, with manioc the staple product; we find the effective use of river craft, the use of hammocks as beds, and the manufacture of pottery. These Amazon peoples, never numerous, erected no buildings or monuments to perpetuate their memory; they dwelt in rough thatched houses; and they lived from the crops they raised, the animals they trapped, or the fish they caught. They knew the use of the poison *curare*, and used it against animals and birds. Some were cannibals. Their pottery and basketry was simple. Their tools were of wood; little use was made of stone, and none of metal. They traveled by dugout canoes. They lived in a world of magic, of shamanism, by which they thought to control evil spirits. They left few reminders of their life.

To the north, on the islands of the Antilles, the mainland of Central America, and the northern shores of South America, the authors of the *Handbook* identify a third group of civilizations under the heading of "Circum-Caribbean Tribes," the least known of aboriginal Americans. Easily accessible, these people were overrun by the Spanish conquerors; their lands were taken over, thousands of Negroes were introduced, few Indians survived. The Arawaks and the Caribs, occupying the West Indies when the Spaniards arrived, were soon all but exterminated. The numerous other peoples of this area have been so merged with the Negro as to have lost their identity.

The fourth group, the "Andean Civilizations," include the Araucanians of Chile and contiguous areas in Argentina, the Chibchas of Colombia, and the numerous civilizations which were merged into the Inca Empire. The Incas of the *Central Andean* area we leave for later and more detailed treatment. On their southern fringe were the Araucanians of the *South Andean* area, including numerous tribes scattered over the fertile valley of central Chile. Although they used the same language, they seem to have had little political, physical, or cultural unity. In their earlier history the Araucanians shared the nomadic habits of the Patagonian peoples; they

[6] *Handbook of South American Indians,* edited by J. H. Steward (6 vols.; Washington: Smithsonian Institution; 1946–50).

lived by hunting, fishing, and gathering wild food. Later they seem to have been influenced by the Inca, and perhaps even more by the pre-Inca peoples, for they reflected some of the political and economic habits of those dominant peoples. On the northern fringe of the Inca domain were the Chibchas of the *North Andean* area, whose homeland was along the Cordillera Oriental (the region around modern Bogotá). The Chibchas seem to have been far more numerous, more advanced in political organization, more expert in their handiwork than the primitive peoples hitherto described. In some of their arts and crafts they may be ranked next to the Incas, Aztecs, or Maya.

Survivors of these lesser South American aboriginal peoples are still to be seen. Descendants of the Chibchas—some hundreds of thousands of them, perhaps even a million—are chiefly concentrated in the Colombian departments (states) of Cundinamarca and Boyacá. In the far south, there are still 50,000 or more Araucanians in Chile, and a few thousand survivors of primitive nomad peoples on the Argentine side of the Andes. In the tropical Amazon basin, there are a few hundred thousand sons of the forest peoples (some put the figure as high as 1 million) divided into many tribes, existing precariously in the tropical forests beyond the reach or concern of Brazil and its neighbors, under whose sovereignty they dwell. Some vestigial remnants of the "Circum-Caribbean" peoples are found along the coasts of Central America, Colombia, and Venezuela.

In Middle America we have a few dramatic clues to the early shadowy peoples scattered from the Valley of Mexico to the valley of Oaxaca. Archaeologists have cut through the lava flow of Copilco on the edge of Mexico City, revealing evidence of a people whose life was interrupted by the volcano's overflowing in the first or second century. The ancient cemetery of Tlatilco near Mexico City has yielded pottery vessels and figurines of great variety and aesthetic vigor spanning the period from 2000 to 150 B.C. These Archaic or Formative cultures developed gradually into the Classic civilizations of the first Christian millennium—the era in which the Maya came to their greatest glory. These Classic peoples include the Zapotecs—and later the Mixtecs—of Mitla and Monte Albán, who created notable temples and tombs, pottery, and metal work; the Totonacs of the gulf coast, linguistic cousins of the Maya-speaking peoples farther south, who developed an impressive architecture and sculpture; and the people of the city of Teotihuacán, which, with its great Pyramid of the Sun and its many temples and courts, dominated the central plateau of Mexico.

The Classic Period in Middle American history came to an end with the fall of Teotihuacán around A.D. 900, and the rise to power in the tenth and eleventh centuries of the Toltecs, who founded a dynasty at Tula in a now barren spot in the state of Hidalgo. The archaeologists are wary of dogmatizing about the Toltecs—the very name, according to J. Eric Thompson, "is a concession to nebulous tradition." They may have been one of the Nahua-speaking peoples to which the Aztecs belonged, or they may have been an amalgam of diverse peoples who had drifted into the Valley of Mexico. Toltec, in Nahua, means "master builder," and their architecture, metal and stone work were of high order. The religion of the Toltecs centered around the legendary cult of the feathered serpent Quetzalcoatl (*quetzal*, a bird; *coatl*, a snake), who in Toltec tradition was a king-god, a bringer of civilized arts and crafts like Prometheus, a patron of merchants like Mercury, and a lord of wind and rain. Tradition has it that Quetzalcoatl once ruled in mercy and justice, opposing human sacrifice, encouraging peaceful arts and learning. The name "Toltec" was later used by the Aztecs to evoke visions of just and peace-loving rulers. The Aztec tyrants rationalized their own power by claiming affiliation with the "virtuous" Toltec. However, the Toltecs in fact formed a warrior aristocracy and transformed the cult of Quetzalcoatl into a fierce religion whose ceremonies included human sacrifice and, later, worship of the vengeful sun-god. This religion was to become, by the time of the Spanish conquest, one of the most bloodthirsty in human history. Whether or not Quetzalcoatl was ever a living king, he was certainly a living god to the Toltecs and, after the tenth century, to the Maya. The motif of the feathered serpent, appearing repeatedly upon Toltec ruins in central Mexico, and also upon the sculptured façades of the Maya city of Chichén Itzá, proves that the Toltecs, whoever they were, extended their hold from central Mexico to northern Yucatán. It seems clear therefore that the Maya were greatly influenced by their contemporaries, and that those contemporaries were in their turn indebted to the wisdom of the Maya.

THE MAYA

The Maya peoples, by the time the Spaniards arrived, occupied an area embracing the modern Mexican states of Yucatán, Campeche, Tabasco, part of Chiapas, the territory of Quintana Roo, most of modern Guatemala, the western fringe of Honduras, and all of British Honduras—an area of some 125,000 square miles, larger than all of New England, New York, and New Jersey put together. Here flourished the most brilliant civilization of the New World in pre-Columbian times—its roots going back some 500 years before the Christian era, its period of greatest glory between the fourth and tenth centuries.

Modern interest in the Maya is new. There was brief curiosity on the part of sixteenth-century Spanish conquerors, but the scholarly interests of a few churchmen could not stop the wholesale burning of Maya codices, a wanton attack upon paganism forever to be mourned by students. A few Franciscan fathers left accounts of things they had seen and heard, notably Bishop Diego de Landa in his *Relación de las cosas de Yucatán,* written in 1566. The Maya, conquered in Yucatán by the middle of the sixteenth century, defended their isolated retreat in the jungles of Guatemala until the end of the seventeenth century. Meanwhile, their amazing cities and temples were all but forgotten.

In 1839–41 a young man named John Lloyd Stephens was sent by President Martin Van Buren upon a footless diplomatic errand to the roving government of the United Provinces of Central America. Stephens, bored by diplomacy, found excitement in exploring and actually rediscovering Maya cities overgrown by the green mantle of the jungle, their crumbling walls now occupied by snakes and birds. The publication of his journal, a lively narrative, marks the revival of interest in the Maya. Any modern pilgrim to these cities must understand the ecstasy with which Stephens first looked upon long lost Copán in the wet forests of northern Honduras. "The city was desolate," Stephens wrote. "No remnant of this race hangs around the ruins, with traditions handed down from father to son and from generation to generation. It lay before us like a shattered bark in the midst of the ocean, her masts gone, her name effaced, her crew perished, and none to tell whence she came, to whom she belonged, how long on her voyage, or what caused her destruction—her lost people to be traced only by some fancied resemblance in the construction of the vessel, and, perhaps, never to be known at all."[7]

Seldom has a diplomat more successfully aroused interest in lands to which he was assigned. Stephens's accounts of buried Maya cities turned attention to this region. The English archaeologist A. P. Maudslay spent the years 1881–94 in the Maya country. Harvard University sent repeated expeditions during the years between 1888 and 1915. The Carnegie Institution sent scientists to study and reconstruct these monuments.

What, then, do we know of the beginnings of the Maya? Archaeologists generally agree that their culture evolved from that of the earlier Olmecs in southern Veracruz and Campeche; and that it took on the distinctive characteristics of the Classic Maya civilization at least by the fourth century of the Christian era, with its heartland around Lake Petén Itzá in northern Guatemala and its most active centers the neighboring cities of Tikal and Uaxactun. This argument rests largely upon the testimony of a piece of carved jade (the Leyden Plaque), found near Puerto Barrios in Guatemala, but probably a product of Tikal, which bears a date in the Maya calendar usually translated as A.D. 320; and upon a stone shaft, or stela, found at Uaxactun, which bears a Maya date probably corresponding to A.D. 328.[8]

If Maya civilization was already a going concern in the fourth century, we may then conjecture as to how long that civilization had been in the making. Many archaeologists believe that for perhaps 1,000 years Maya-speaking peoples from the Guatemala highlands had been moving into

[7] John Lloyd Stephens: *Incidents of Travel in Central America, Chiapas, and Yucatán*, edited by Richard L. Predmore (2 vols.; New Brunswick, N.J.: Rutgers University Press; 1949), Vol. I, p. 81.

[8] These are the calendar correlations used by Sylvanus G. Morley: *The Ancient Maya* (3rd ed., rev. by George M. Brainerd; Stanford, Calif.: Stanford University Press; 1957); and by J. Eric Thompson: *The Rise and Fall of Maya Civilization* (Norman: University of Oklahoma Press; 1954). George Kubler uses Spinden's calendar correlations, which put all Maya dates 260 years earlier: *The Art and Architecture of Ancient America* (Baltimore: Penguin Books; 1962).

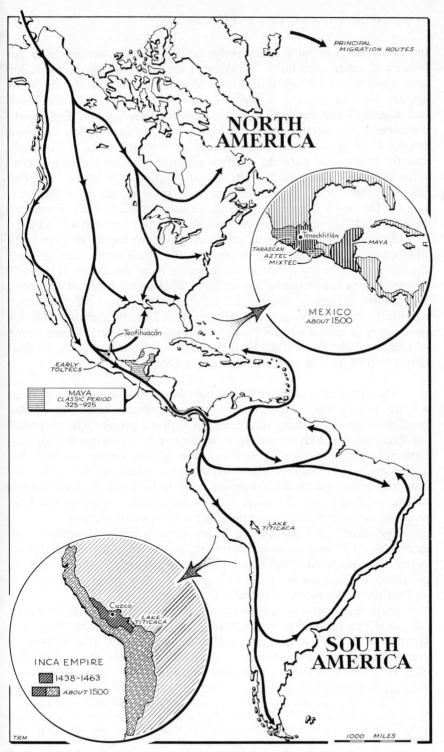

Principal Indian Migration Routes; Mexico, about 1500; Inca Empire, about 1500

the Petén basin, bringing a knowledge of corn culture, burning back the forest wall, establishing farms. We do not know who these people were, nor how many waves of migration came. Morley believes that by the third century B.C.—or perhaps as early as the fourth century B.C.—the Maya had done their mathematical and astronomical pioneering, and had already developed their calendar and chronology, a system "so delicately built and balanced" as to excite the admiration of all students. Thus it is thought that the Maya were pursuing accurate scientific research for several centuries before the first plausible date appears in the fourth century A.D. The home of these pioneer-scientists may have been in the Tikal-Uaxactun region. This early phase of Maya civilization constitutes the Formative Period, which Thompson dates between perhaps 500 B.C. and A.D. 325.[9]

Assuming that the historic period of the Maya begins with the early fourth century, the archaeologists piece together their story, drawing upon the testimony of hieroglyphics on stelae erected in the chief cities at intervals of ten years or less, weighing the evidence of changing forms of sculpture, architecture, designs of pottery, and painting on the walls. All these speak eloquently to those who are trained to hear and enable them to retell for us the story of an extraordinary people reaching from the first known dating of cities by Lake Petén Itzá, down through fourteen centuries to the final destruction of the last capital of the Itzá in 1697.

The Classic Period of the Maya, spanning some 600 years from about A.D. 325 to 925, was the golden age of the most versatile and skillful of the pre-Columbian civilizations of America. Of all the peoples who antedated the Conquest, the Maya were the most creative in architectural sculpture, painting, and such intellectual pursuits as hieroglyphic writing, mathematics, astronomy, and chronology. However, the most skilled and diversified pottery and textiles that remain to us come from the Inca and pre-Inca peoples, and in political power the Maya did not achieve an empire to match in grandeur and complexity the empires of the Incas or the Aztecs.

The record of Maya culture during these centuries is written large and clear upon temple, palace, pyramid; in the painting and design of pottery, baskets, textiles; and above all in the sculptured hieroglyphics of the stelae, on which dates are given with great accuracy, events are depicted, and the life of the people is portrayed.

Maya civilization in the Classic Period was centered in the southern jungles of the Yucatán peninsula, and in the central highlands of modern Guatemala and British Honduras. There were city-states, akin to those of ancient Greece or medieval Italy, with government in the hands of a small class of priests and nobles. Each city was a law unto itself. Few if any political ties bound them together, although many of their rulers were

9 J. Eric Thompson, *The Rise and Fall of Maya Civilization,* pp. 270–71, divides Maya history into the following periods: Formative Period, 500 B.C. (?) to circa A.D. 325; Classic Period, circa A.D. 325 to 925; Interregnum, A.D. 925 to 975; Mexican Period, A.D. 975 to 1200; Period of Mexican Absorption, A.D. 1200 to 1540. This text will follow these divisions. For a somewhat different periodization, see George Kubler, *op. cit.,* who puts the beginning of the Classic Period around the time of Christ.

probably blood relations. The cities were rivals in trade, but an almost total absence of battle scenes upon the stelae suggests that their rivalry seldom led to war. Traffic among them in styles of clothing, pottery, and sculpture was lively. There was great Copán, the astronomical center. There were Palenque with its amazing low relief sculpture and fine stucco modeling, Piedras Negras with its strong carving in stone, Uaxactun with its fine palace, and Tikal with gracious wood carving and the 229-foot temple.[1] The ceremonial life of these city-states was elaborate and exuberant. The prosperity of the countryside flowed into them, building monuments whose dignity and beauty have survived the onslaughts of the jungle.

The culture of the Maya was created and shaped by the planters and harvesters of corn, the chief food of the people. The surplus of corn, whose production was generous and easy, flowed over into the cities and financed the priest-scientists who probed the mysteries of earth and stars, and developed a cosmology, an astronomy, and a system of writing and of mathematics. And this wealth from corn also made possible the building of the great civic and religious centers whose monuments stand as testimony to the skill of the people.

This brilliant civilization reached its apogee in the seventh and eighth centuries. Then, like a chill wind, desolation swept the land. In one city after another, during a period of a hundred years or more, ceremonial centers were abandoned, building ceased, half-finished temples were left to the ravages of the jungle. The collapse of the cities is attested by the latest dates of their stelae: Copán was probably deserted about the year 800; Tikal dedicated its last stela in 869; Uaxactun was active until 889. What caused the fall of the Maya cities—was it shortage of corn, due to soil exhaustion? Was it civil war? Was it a series of deadly epidemics? Was it conquest by foreign foes? There is no clear answer. Thompson suggests the possibility that the peasants, weary of forced labor on temples and palaces and in the cornfields, rebelled against the priests and nobles, driving them away or massacring them; and that city after city, left in the hands of inept peasant leaders, crumbled, and was finally deserted.[2] Whatever the cause, by the early tenth century, all of these once-proud city-states were emptied, never again to be occupied by man.

Into the spiritual and cultural vacuum left by the collapse of the Classic Maya cities, came an invasion from central Mexico—an invasion of people and of ideas. Maya civilization, gone from the lowlands and jungles of the south, would be reborn in the riverless baked plains of northern Yucatán, where man depends for water upon the sacred *cenotes*, the great natural wells which dot the area. Its character forever altered, this new Maya civilization would rise, flourish, and finally decline before the Span-

[1] This temple was an infinitely greater accomplishment, for its time, than the erection of the Empire State Building in the twentieth century. The Maya built without benefit of modern tools, hoisting machinery, or even beasts of burden.

[2] For discussions of the possible causes of the collapse of the city-states, see J. Eric Thompson, *The Rise and Fall of Maya Civilization*, pp. 84 ff., and Sylvanus G. Morley, *op. cit.*, pp. 68 ff.

iards arrived. Thompson divides the almost six centuries of this new civilization into the Mexican Period (975–1200), during which Toltec patterns were imposed upon the Maya by invaders from the Mexican highlands; and the Period of Mexican Absorption (1200–1540), when Maya language and religion prevailed, but culture steadily declined.

During most of the Classic Period northern Yucatán had lain within the periphery of Maya influence. Between the years 475 and 909, at least ten substantial Maya cities had been built there. These cities, notably Tulum, Izamal, Mayapán, Uxmal, and Chichén Itzá, were provincial Maya outposts, "analogous," suggests Morley, "to the Roman towns of Britain during the first and second centuries of the Christian era." Into this area, in the tenth and eleventh centuries, came foreigners who brought with them Toltec religion and culture, and Toltec militarism. Chief among these foreigners were the Itzá, whose origin is unclear, but whose leader, legend has it, was none other than Kukulcán—the Maya name for the Toltec king-god, Quetzalcoatl.[3]

The Itzá—whoever they were, we will call them "Mexicans"—occupied the city of Chichén Itzá around the year 987. They probably also settled in other Maya cities in northern Yucatán, and there is evidence of a triple alliance among Chichén Itzá, Mayapán, and Izamal—with Chichén Itzá the dominant partner—which lasted some 200 years. Here began the renaissance of Maya civilization, which was to take on the coloration of the cultures of central Mexico, chiefly that of the Toltecs. The Itzá—or Mexicans—introduced the religious cult of the feathered-serpent god, Quetzalcoatl, who became Kukulcán to the Maya: the feathered serpent is the recurring motif upon the architecture of Chichén Itzá. The carvings on temples and pyramids in this city also give grim evidence of the cults of militarism and human sacrifice brought by the newcomers, cults which were to transform forever the ways of the Maya people.

The rule of Chichén Itzá ended abruptly shortly before the year 1200, as civil war split the triple alliance. Legend tells of the treachery of Hunac Ceel, head-chief of the city of Mayapán, who played the leaders of Izamal against those of Chichén Itzá, and finally—reinforced by new allies from the west—routed the local rulers and seized control of the alliance for Mayapán. "And thus," writes sixteenth-century Bishop Landa, "he brought the Mexican people into Mayapán and oppressed the poor and made many slaves and the lords would have put him to death but for the fear they had for the Mexicans." The wars left the Cocom dynasty of Mayapán—the descendants of Hunac Ceel—supreme in a despotism which dominated northern Yucatán for some 250 years. Thus was Mexican imperialism brought to the Maya people.

The power of the Cocoms in Mayapán was not broken until about the year 1441, when a liberator named Ah Xupan—who claimed Toltec

[3] Although the possible date of the expulsion of Quetzalcoatl from the Toltec city of Tula (978?) corresponds closely with the arrival of this Kukulcán-Quetzalcoatl in Yucatán (967–87), Thompson, *The Rise and Fall of Maya Civilization*, p. 99, warns us against being too sure that they were one and the same, reminding us that "Quetzalcoatls seem to be as frequent in Mexican history as Roosevelts or Adamses in American public life."

lineage as a member of the Xiu family—united the forces of the other cities against Mayapán and crushed the Cocom tyranny. Rule of the dozen or so city-states of northern Yucatán was returned to the local chieftains, and the empire of the Cocoms fell apart, never again to be reunited. Liberated from the discipline of a central authority, the free cities waged intermittent war upon one another. The cultural decline, which had begun with the end of the Classic Period, continued: no longer were great temples and pyramids erected to the honor of the gods; sculpture and art deteriorated; road-building ceased, and the centuries-old roads of the Maya fell into disrepair. Although the Toltec cult of Quetzalcoatl all but disappeared, and the Maya language and religion finally prevailed, the militarism introduced by the Mexicans became the way of life for these survivors of the Maya of Yucatán. And the avenging gods were seemingly not content with plunging this once-proud and peace-loving people into primitive tribal warfare. In 1464 a hurricane swept northern Yucatán. Then pestilences took their toll, the last of which, in 1515 or 1516, may have been smallpox ("great pustules rotted the body," reports Landa). Civil wars continued; cities and villages were laid waste.

Then, to complete the havoc, the Spaniards came. First, in 1511, a few survivors of an ill-fated expedition were washed up on the eastern shores of Yucatán, and all but two of them were quickly eaten. Of the two survivors, one joined an Indian tribe where he won respect, and the other, Aguilar, was protected by a friendly chieftain and joined Cortés in 1519. These Spaniards may have brought the smallpox, if that was indeed the plague which swept the peninsula in 1515 or 1516. The second expedition, in 1517, was headed by Francisco Hernández de Córdova, whose wars with the Maya brought his death. The third expedition, in 1518, headed by Juan de Grijalva, was marked by a few skirmishes and the collecting of some treasure in gold and turquoises. The fourth expedition, that of Hernán Cortés in 1519, touched on the island of Cozumel, where a few idols were destroyed, a cross was erected, and Aguilar was rescued to serve as a useful interpreter. From there Cortés moved on to Campeche, Tabasco, Veracruz, and the conquest of Mexico. The fifth was a series of expeditions led by Francisco de Montejo and his son during the years 1527–46. Their first attempt, after initial successes, met with defeat. The next campaign, 1531–35, proved the Maya chiefs more than a match for the invaders. The Spaniards were finally victorious in the campaigns of 1540–46, and the conquest of Yucatán was completed. Spanish rule was forthwith consolidated in northern Yucatán and Guatemala,[4] but the Maya still held the area of Lake Petén Itzá. This last stronghold, centering in the Itzá city of Tayasal,

[4] In dealing with the Maya from the beginning of the Mexican Period, we have given major attention to the Maya centers in northern Yucatán. The Mexican conquest of the Maya around Lake Atitlán in Guatemala, and the decline and fall of civilization in that area, parallel the story of Yucatán. The Quiche—who, like the Itzá, boasted Toltec ancestry —brought the cult of Quetzalcoatl to the Maya of the Guatemala highlands, where they established dominance. Their "empire" collapsed about the same time as that of the Cocoms in Yucatán, and a similar cultural disintegration set in. Pedro de Alvarado, companion of Cortés in the conquest of Mexico, conquered Guatemala in 1525.

resisted Spanish power for another century and a half. Repeated efforts of friars and soldiers to penetrate this jungle bastion met with indifferent success. In 1697, after bloody battles, Tayasal was overcome and occupied by Spanish troops. Thus the great civilization of the Maya ended on the spot where it had probably risen many centuries before.

No visitor to the Maya ruins of Yucatán, Guatemala, and Honduras can be deaf to the eloquence of these monuments of a majestic civilization. Copán, Quiriguá, Uxmal, Tikal, Chichén Itzá, and many another dead city speak with living voices across the centuries. Against the background of the most beautiful monuments and sculptured carvings of pre-Columbian America, such as the Palace of the Governor in Uxmal and the temples of Chichén Itzá, one may repeople these cities in imagination and speculate upon the pageantry and splendor of their great days. And then, by way of contrast, we may observe the simple life of their descendants in modern Yucatán and Guatemala.[5] One may well ask, How much do we know of the once great civilization of the Maya?

Thanks to the faithful work of scientists, and to the greater accuracy of Maya records, we know more about the Maya than we do of any of their contemporaries in America. The record of this people is written in their cities. We do not know how many cities there were. Morley lists 116. With the exception of Copán, we do not know the names by which the Maya called their cities in the Classic Period. And of the cities in the Mexican Period only seven names are clear. The names by which we call most of them are of later invention. Some cities were of great size. Tikal and Copán of the Classic Period, and the later cities of Chichén Itzá, Uxmal, and Mayapán may have had populations of 200,000 or more. The Yucatán peninsula may well have had three times as many people in the eighth century as it has today.

Enough remains of the chief cities to suggest their appearance at the time of their glory. At the heart of each city were the civic and religious monuments, temples, ball courts, and meeting places; on the periphery of the city were scattered villages and farms. Tikal was probably the largest and oldest. Its civic-religious center had an area of about one square mile, and within a radius of two or three miles around it were lesser centers. It was dominated by five pyramid temples, the highest about 229 feet. Then there was Copán, which Morley calls "the Alexandria of the Maya world," headquarters of astronomers and scientists in the greatest days. Chichén Itzá in the north, where Mexican influence was most pronounced, was the most sacred city in all Yucatán, a place to which pilgrims journeyed in reverence, and its great natural well was a place for human sacrifice.

In the shadow of the cities lay the cornfields. Everything the Maya did,

5 Two fascinating studies of the modern Maya by Robert E. Redfield are: *The Folk Culture of Yucatán* (Chicago: University of Chicago Press; 1941) and *A Village That Chose Progress: Chan Kom Revisited* (Chicago: University of Chicago Press; 1950). See also Charles Wisdom: *The Chorti Indians of Guatemala* (Chicago: University of Chicago Press; 1940) and Ruth Bunzel: *Chichicastenango: A Guatemalan Village* (Locust Valley, N.Y.; J. J. Augustin; 1952).

everything he believed, was related to the cornfields. His temples and sacrifices were designed to assure a profitable crop. His elaborate theology was an instrument for propitiating the powers and winning abundant harvests. His calendar was devised as a working schedule for the recurring cycle of the cornfield. That cycle has changed very little in 2,000 years. We can understand the ancient corn farmer by observing his modern descendant. The pattern has not changed appreciably. To be sure, the ancient wooden digging stick is now tipped with iron and the stone ax has yielded to the steel machete. But the rhythm is the same—and the calendar still controls it. There is the same ceremonial locating of the field, the assurance of water, the laying out of the fields into the traditional units about sixty-five feet square, the marking of the corners with stones, the cutting and burning of trees and brush, the planting of seed, the weeding from May to September, the bending of the cornstalks after the ears have matured so that the ears point toward the ground, the harvesting from November to March or April, the storing of the corn, the marketing—each of these operations takes on ceremonial significance today as it did a thousand or two thousand years ago. And in the Maya village, as in most of the villages of Mexico, the cadenced tapping of the *tortilla* makers is still the familiar music of the countryside. In every Maya home, as in almost all homes in rural Mexico, there are still found the *metates,* the grinding stones on which the women prepare the daily supply of meal—although in the larger centers the mechanical mill is steadily supplanting the drudgery of hand-grinding.

The government of the Maya was simple. The people seem to have desired as little government as possible. Scholars used to speak of the Old and New "Empires" of the Maya, but the word was discarded as a misnomer, for never at any time was there either empire or emperor. There were simply city-states, each sovereign in its own right, sharing with the others in culture, language, and religion. There is no evidence of confederation between the cities in the Classic Period. Not until the thirteenth century did imperialism emerge under the Cocom dynasty of Mayapán. A hereditary ruler presided over each city-state. His functions were administrative, executive, and probably religious as well. Under him the nobility presided over the smaller municipalities which clustered about the city center. These nobles were *caciques,* in Spanish terms, serving as judges, tax collectors, and guardians of order. There were also soldiers, although war seems to have been unimportant in the Classic Period. There were priests, ranking in importance with lords and nobles and probably allied to them in blood. The high respect for the priests was due to their importance as custodians of learning. They were astronomers and mathematicians, the men who knew how to reckon years, months, and days, who knew when it was time to plant and to harvest. Furthermore, they knew how to control and check the gods of evil and to please the beneficent gods from whom rain and fertility and all good gifts proceeded.

We may conjecture as to the life of the common man. He was usually a corn farmer; he must harvest enough to feed himself and his family, and to pay tribute to rulers, nobles, and priests. Perhaps this could be done in half his time, leaving him free to devote half of his energy to the service of the state. It was in his "leisure" time that the great pyramids, temples, palaces, convents, and ball courts were built. That leisure provided him with time to cut and shape stone from the quarries, to burn lime and prepare the mortar, to fashion wood and stone into sculpture. The labor of freemen was supplemented by that of slaves, who included prisoners of war, those convicted of crimes, and those purchased from other areas or kidnaped. The Maya seem to have been a cleanly people; the daily bath which is the rule today is probably an inherited tradition. For the sick, the Maya could call upon the priest, the medicine man, and the sorcerer, with their varied recourse to herbs and magic.

The religion of the Maya, from its primitive beginnings, reached impressive elaboration through the centuries. Its ritual may have been shaped 300 or 400 years before Christ, when the priests were responsible for the development of the calendar, chronology, and writing. Gradually the list of gods was enlarged, the ceremonial became more complicated, and the demands upon believers more exigent. Their religion was personal and touched the entire cycle of life. An elaborate astrological scheme settled the destiny of each new baby by the day and hour of his birth. Detailed ritual followed the child from the first hours, when the head was compressed for the flattening of the forehead. There was ritual for the ceremonial of puberty, discipline of girls, preparation for marriage, for every phase of life down to the elaborate ceremonies which attended death. Morley concludes that the Maya religion of the Classic Period was "an august stately faith" and that just as this period was "the golden age of Maya culture, so was it also the noblest period of Maya religion before the latter's beliefs and practices had degenerated into bloody orgies." The Mexican Period introduced the new cult of Quetzalcoatl, called Kukulcán by the Maya, and with this cult there was an increasing emphasis on militarism and human sacrifice. This period also brought idolatry, a multiplicity of gods, and a more complicated ritual.

The Maya, like their contemporaries everywhere, had an elaborate explanation of the history of the world. There had been several worlds; each had ended in a deluge, and another deluge was expected. The Maya universe, like that of contemporary Christians, was caught in perennial struggle between the powers of good and evil. The good brought rain, fertility, and abundance; the bad brought drought, hurricanes, and wars. There were heavens of blessedness above the earth, thirteen of them altogether, and hells beneath, nine of them. In the final paradise there was neither pain nor poverty nor heavy burdens to be borne. In the final hell there was hunger and cold and misery.

The Maya had a generous complement of gods. There seems to have remained from some more ancient cult a faith in one supreme god, the creator. But this god was too remote from life, so the Maya contrived intermediaries who would serve every phase of daily life. There was a son of the one true god; this son became the captain of the company of gods with whom man must deal. There were the gods of corn, and of death. There was a ubiquitous god of the north star who watched over the journeyings of merchants. Several gods were charged with oversight of war, human sacrifice, and violent death. There was the god of the winds, possibly Kukulcán (Quetzalcoatl). And there were goddesses as well. One had jurisdiction over floods, pregnancy, and weaving. Another was the goddess of suicides, held in high repute, for suicides were favored as speeding departure to the highest heaven. Separate gods were assigned to each of the storied orders of the upper and lower world. Other gods had special jurisdiction over the chronological periods into which time was divided, still others were assigned to each of the separate days, and for good measure each numeral had its own god. The Maya pantheon had its charming and intimate side. There was a god for every emergency, a god for every need, a god for every period of time. We may conclude that the god to whom the simple corn farmer turned with the most sincere devotion was Chac, the god of rain, whose favors yielded life and happiness and whose anger yielded death.

The Maya's intellectual achievements included a system of writing using glyphs. They alone of all the pre-Columbian peoples had gone beyond the primitive form of writing, the pictograph, in which a drawing conveys a situation. They had not only reached the ideograph, in which characters stand for ideas; but, according to present-day linguists and glyph experts, most Maya glyphs are apparently phonetic, indicating that they had reached the third stage of writing, where symbols stand for sounds. Their system of hieroglyphics was not so old as that of the Babylonians, or the Egyptians, or the Chinese, but the Maya written language may go back at least to the beginning of the Christian era. Many of their hieroglyphics, carved on the stelae, have been preserved, and thanks to Bishop Landa's painstaking labor in the sixteenth century, we are able to read about one-third of them. The stelae tell us the chief dates of Maya history with considerable accuracy. We also know of the Maya's skill in mathematics. It is quite probable that by the fourth or third century B.C. the Maya used a system of numeration by position involving the concept of zero.

"The great theme of Maya civilization," writes Thompson, "is the passage of time—the wide concept of the mystery of eternity and the narrower concept of the divisions of time into their equivalents of centuries, years, months, and days. The rhythm of time enchanted the Maya; the never-ending flow of days from the eternity of the future into the eternity of the past filled them with wonder."[6] Maya chronology was reckoned from some fixed point in the distant past, just as the Christian counts from the birth of Jesus, the Greek from the earliest Olympic festival, and the Roman from the foundation of Rome. Their calendar reaches back to a date usually translated as 3113 B.C. Possibly they thought to tie their calendar to some hypothetical event—perhaps a re-creation of the world after some great catastrophe. There is no question as to the astronomical skill of the Maya. They may have had a more accurate astronomy during the fourth to first centuries B.C. than the Egyptians had during the same period. By

6 Thompson, *The Rise and Fall of Maya Civilization*, p. 13.

the early Christian centuries, their priest-astronomers were predicting eclipses with great precision. They accurately charted the course of Venus. We marvel that those primitive scientists, without the use of instruments or telescopes, their only observatories the high towers of the temples, were able to reach such exact computations. They had evolved the conception of the 365-day year; from the stelae we learn of the 260-day sacred year and of the correlations between the sacred year and the 365-day calendar year. And by the sixth or seventh century A.D., the priests of Copán had worked out corrections on their solar year somewhat more accurately than was done under the aegis of Pope Gregory XIII in 1582, a thousand years later.[7]

The architecture of the Maya seems to have been purely indigenous. However, several responsible scholars argue that it could have been influenced by some trans-Pacific contacts with Asian civilizations. Some art motifs from Palenque and Uxmal around A.D. 800 show similarities with Asian design. The material required was abundant. Limestone was easily cut while fresh from the ground, and could be burned for lime to make mortar. The labor was supplied by corn farmers whose strength and skill show in the handling of stone, the shaping of blocks, the carving of sculpture—all done with stone tools. Here we find baffling evidence of their tenacity and artistry. In the days of the Classic Period, especially between the years 731 and 889, the sculpturing of the stelae reached great distinction. Later centuries yielded abundant sculpture but it became flamboyant, and the purity and strength of that of the Classic Period was lost. A characteristic feature of Maya architecture was the corbeled roof, vault, and arch. The true arch, held together by the keystone at the top, was never used by the Maya.[8]

The pageantry and pomp of Maya splendor are long since spent. The sons of ancient kings live today in thatched huts, tending their flocks, planting and harvesting their corn, working on the flat acres which produce henequen fiber for the world. Temples and altars have been replaced by village churches topped by the cross. Meanwhile, old fashions and old beliefs persist in the life of the Maya family and community. And perhaps to some of these sons of kings a kindling of the spirit comes as they remember their heritage of a race whose skill in counting the stars, in measuring the movements of the planets, in fashioning stone in the likeness of gods and men, places it among the Olympian nations of the past.

[7] Sylvanus G. Morley, *op. cit.*, p. 256, gives these figures:

> Length of the year according to modern astronomy: 365.2422 days
> Length of our old, uncorrected Julian year: 365.2500 days
> Length of our present, corrected Gregorian year: 365.2425 days
> Length of the year according to ancient Maya astronomy: 365.2420 days

(In an earlier edition, Morley points out that "Pope Gregory's correction is 3/10,000 of a day too *long*, while the ancient Maya correction was only 2/10,000 of a day too *short*.)

[8] Thompson, *The Rise and Fall of Maya Civilization*, p. 13, said that the Maya "excelled in the impractical but failed in the practical. What mental quirks (from our point of view) led the Maya intelligentsia to chart the heavens, yet fail to grasp the principle of the wheel; to visualize eternity, as no other semicivilized people has ever done, yet ignore the short step from corbeled to true arch; to count in millions, yet never learn to weigh a sack of corn?"

THE AZTECS OF MEXICO

The Aztec Empire was at the peak of its power when Hernán Cortés and
600 men landed on the Mexican coast in 1519 and founded the city of
Veracruz. Moctezuma II, from his imperial city of Tenochtitlán built upon
an island in Lake Texcoco in the high Valley of Mexico, ruled over a domain
which reached south into Oaxaca, west into Michoacán, east to the Gulf,
an empire of several million souls.[9]

This Aztec civilization, interrupted in its greatness, was painstakingly
described by the sixteenth-century chroniclers, who "read" the manuscripts
in picture writing which were the only written record of the Aztec people.
The Spanish friars were aided in this task by aged Indians who had been
born in Tenochtitlán, Texcoco, or Tula before the arrival of the white man,
and who related the narratives which elaborated upon and explained the
manuscripts—narratives which had been memorized in detail and passed
on from generation to generation.[1]

The Aztecs were a Nahua-speaking Chichimec people whose mythical
home was Aztlán, somewhere far beyond the northern frontier of the
"civilized" world. The name "Chichimec" was used to describe many
diverse groups of nomad barbarians who came from the north to invade the
settled world of the Toltecs in the twelfth and thirteenth centuries. Inconspicuous among these groups were the Aztecs, whose shadowy journeyings
brought them to Tula, on the mountainous rim above the Valley of
Mexico, where they settled to become cultivators of the soil and to learn
the arts of war as mercenaries in the armies of the Toltecs. For countless
generations stretching into the mythical past, the Aztecs had been led by
the god Huitzilopochtli. On all of their wanderings, their chieftain-priests
carried a little idol of this terrible god who drove his "chosen people"

[9] The population figures of pre-Conquest Mexico have long been vigorously debated.
The German scholar Karl Sapper suggested in 1924 that the total population of Middle
America in pre-Spanish times was between 12 and 15 million. Later scholars discounted
the estimates of the Spanish chroniclers as being extravagantly high. See Bailey W. Diffie:
Latin American Civilization (Harrisburg, Pa.: Stackpole Sons; 1945), pp. 180–1, for defense
of the argument that "the population of Moctezuma's empire would not have reached a
million people." In 1948 S. F. Cook and Lesley B. Simpson concluded that the total population of central Mexico was about 11 million in 1519. Eric Wolf suggests that "recent
careful studies of the Spanish records have shown . . . that there is no need to distrust
those most careful of all bureaucratic observers. Modern estimates using these records for
their basis of departure confidently assert population totals running from nine million for
all of Mexico to eleven million for Mexico north of the Isthmus of Tehuantepec alone."
Op. cit., p. 31.

[1] Chief contributor among the Spanish chroniclers was the sixteenth-century Franciscan,
Fray Bernardino de Sahagún, whose *History of Mexico,* translated by Fanny R. Bandelier
(Nashville: Fisk University Press; 1932), is a detailed account of Indian customs, beliefs,
and history. Also, Francisco Javier Clavijero: *Historia antigua de México* (4 vols.; Mexico,
D. F.: Editorial Porrúa; 1958–59); Gerónimo de Mendieta: *Historia eclesiástica indiana*
(Mexico: Antigua Libreria [impresa por F. Diaz de Leon y S. White]; 1870); Toribio de
Benavente (Motolinía): *History of the Indians of New Spain,* translated and edited by
Elizabeth Andros Foster (Berkeley, Calif.: Cortés Society; 1950); Juan de Torquemada:
Monarquía indiana (Mexico, D.F.: Universidad nacional autónoma de México; 1964); and
Fray Diego Durán: *Aztecs: The History of the Indies of New Spain,* translated by Doris
Heyden and Fernando Horcasitas (New York: Orion Press; 1964).

relentlessly to their violent destiny. When Tula was conquered by various Chichimec groups, the Aztecs—still obeying the voice of Huitzilopochtli—joined in the scramble for a share of the spoils, entering the Valley of Mexico in the late thirteenth century. It was a warring valley. Around the shores of Lakes Texcoco, Xochimilco, and Chalco were city-states which had risen to power following the Chichimec invasions—chief among these were Atzcapotzalco, Tlacopan, Texcoco, and Culhuacán. These cities, inhabited by victorious Chichimec peoples, by vanquished Toltecs who had fled from Tula, and by some indigenous tribes, were constantly engaged in battles, intrigues, and fitful alliances. One student of the Aztecs suggests: "A tempting analogy is to compare the Chichimec Period to the European colonization of North America where groups of many conditions and sorts struggled to populate the land and eventually incorporated the sum total of their experience into the North American Republic."[2] According to other observers, the fusion of the "barbarian" Chichimecs with the "civilized" Toltecs, which finally resulted in the Aztec Empire, is to be compared with the Roman conquest of Greece.

When the Aztecs arrived on this battleground, they quickly gained a reputation for cruelty and treachery, and were unwelcome wherever they went. They finally managed to settle on a hill on the western shore of Lake Texcoco called Chapultepec, near the powerful cities of Atzcapotzalco and Tlacopan,[3] where they lived for perhaps a generation. As their numbers and strength increased, they became involved in the feuds of the neighborhood, and in due time they were evicted from Chapultepec by a coalition of the people of Culhuacán and the Tepanecs of Atzcapotzalco. Then, legend has it, the Aztecs were led to an island in Lake Texcoco by their god Huitzilopochtli, who ordered them to settle where they found an eagle sitting on a cactus devouring a snake, and charged them to wage a holy war on their neighbors and to offer their victims to the sun in a bloody sacrificial ceremony. But it was probably less in fulfillment of this sacred mission than as a refuge from pursuing enemies that the Aztecs built their city of Tenochtitlán in the middle of Lake Texcoco, perhaps in 1344 or 1345.[4] Today the heart of metropolitan Mexico City, the new stronghold of the Aztecs was an unpleasant spot: swampy and dank, its buildings resting

[2] George Vaillant: *Aztecs of Mexico: Origin, Rise, and Fall of the Aztec Nation* (New York: Doubleday, Doran & Company; 1941), p. 71. Vaillant's work was for many years the most influential account of Aztec history. More recent studies are: Eric Wolf, *op. cit.*, and Ignacio Bernal: *Mexico Before Cortez: Art, History, and Legend*, translated by Willis Barnstone (Garden City, N.Y.: Doubleday & Company; 1963).

[3] Today we may visit these old cities in their modern setting. Chapultepec, once the home of Aztec kings, now boasts its palace-museum and a great park. Atzcapotzalco is a sleepy suburb. Tlacopan is now the village of Tacuba. Only a vestige of the lakes remains, after their draining in the nineteenth century.

[4] A legend explains the Aztecs' eviction from the mainland. Their chief, seeking "international" recognition and prestige, begged the chief of mighty Culhuacán for his virgin daughter as a wife. The request granted, the girl formally delivered, the Aztecs skillfully skinned her, draped the skin over a priest and invited the girl's royal father to the celebration. When the chief saw what had happened to his daughter—not to mention what had happened to her skin—the Aztecs found it well to move. This is one explanation of the founding of Mexico City.

on piles, it offered security but few resources. All that they lacked in soil and forest, however, the Aztecs were finally to make up for in resourcefulness and cunning. They shared this poor bit of land with the older city of Tlatelolco, with which they established an uneasy truce. Their chief reliance was upon Huitzilopochtli, in whose honor they forthwith erected a substantial pyramid and temple—on the spot now occupied by the Cathedral of Mexico.

Postponing for a time the "holy war" ordained by their bloodthirsty god, the Aztecs allied themselves with Atzcapotzalco, paying tribute as protection from their quarrelsome neighbors. Fighting as mercenaries in the army of that city, they took part in the destruction of Culhuacán in 1367. They proved themselves skillful diplomats when, a few years later, covetous of the Toltec lineage, they requested a ruler from the defeated Culhuacán dynasty, which claimed direct descent from the Tula kings. Under their new king, Acamapichtli, there arose a hereditary nobility who made a tenuous claim to the honored but mythical Toltec name, thus justifying their military aspirations. Atzcapotzalco, under the indomitable tyrant Tezozomoc —and with the continued help of Tenochtitlán—rapidly extended its domain to include the whole Valley of Mexico: this prodigious task was completed with the sound defeat of powerful Texcoco in 1418. The canny little god of the Aztecs perhaps foresaw, and rightly, that this unification of the valley would vastly facilitate further conquests by Tenochtitlán when the proper moment came. It was a diabolical tactic: Atzcapotzalco laid the foundations for the Aztec Empire and, in doing so, burned itself out.

When Tezozomoc died in 1426—perhaps of old age, perhaps at the hand of assassins—the glory of Atzcapotzalco was spent. In 1427 the new king of the Aztecs, Itzcoatl, prudently shifted his loyalties to the formidable heir to the kingship of Texcoco, who had been biding his time in exile since his ouster in 1418. Itzcoatl destroyed Atzcapotzalco in 1430, and Tenochtitlán promptly entered upon a triple alliance with Texcoco and the buffer state of Tlacopan—an alliance which lasted almost a century, until the Spaniards made such compacts unavailing. It was a century of almost unbroken imperial success, during which the Aztecs won reputation as the bravest fighters in the Valley of Mexico. They finally outplayed Texcoco— for many years the dominant member of the triple alliance—and, by the early years of the sixteenth century, reduced that once-mighty city to the status of inferior partner.

Moctezuma I, who mounted the throne of Tenochtitlán in 1440, began the solid expansion of the Aztec Empire. During his reign, Aztec warriors carried the battle south into Guerrero and Oaxaca, east into Veracruz. Moctezuma's successors carried on the imperial tradition until only the neighboring Tlaxcalans and the Tarascans in the west maintained their independence. The apex of imperial triumph came in the year 1487 when the great temple-pyramid to Huitzilopochtli, which had been rebuilt, was suitably dedicated by the sacrifice of 20,000 prisoners of war,[5] the fruit of a successful foray in Oaxaca. The unlucky victims made their last journey up the high steps of the temple-pyramid and were laid on the sacrificial

[5] Some reports put this figure at 80,000—but 20,000 would seem to be enough.

stone, the *techcatl,* where priests tore open their breasts with obsidian knives, ripped out their throbbing hearts and threw them into the living flames. The little god of war, found in a humble cave years before, must have been deeply moved by these pledges of affection.

Young Moctezuma II, who came to the throne in 1502, inherited a great tradition. He had job enough, if he was to hold his refractory vassals, to maintain the flow of tribute into his treasury, and to furnish sacrificial victims worthy of the god of war. His record was fair, although he could not match the prowess of his predecessor in snaring victims for the sacrificial stone. His best record on that score was the occasion when he delivered 12,000 prime males from Oaxaca.[6]

But Moctezuma and his stout warriors were no match for the Spaniards. Even Huitzilopochtli proved helpless against men with horses and guns. The empire itself was weakened by the unresolved jealousies of the city-states around Lake Texcoco, by its tenuous control over angry vassals, by the growing anger of subject peoples faced with mounting demands for tribute and sacrificial victims. But Moctezuma was finally defeated by his own fears. He was a slave to his astrologers, who found grave portents in the stars, in terrifying columns of fire, in comets, in the whisperings of birds. When the word came of mysterious strangers upon the coast, equipped with horses and fire-spitting weapons, all the warnings of the astrologers were confirmed. The empire with tens of thousands of warriors would shortly fall to an enemy whose initial force numbered 600 armed men.

The social and political structure of the Aztecs changed with their changing fortunes. When they were a weak and inconspicuous band making their way to the Valley of Mexico, the lowliest warriors among them probably had a share in decision-making, as members of a council which served as a check on their chieftain-priests. But as their power and prestige increased, they forsook such democratic ways. The *calpulli,* or subgroups of the tribe— of which there were twenty when the Aztecs settled in Tenochtitlán—may originally have been primitive kinship units or clans. But as the Aztec nation took on the aspect of a military and aristocratic state, it ceased to be a tribal society, and the *calpulli* became simply administrative divisions or landholding units. (Some observers have tried to trace the *barrios* or divisions of modern Mexico City back to these *calpulli.*) After Acamapichtli came to the throne in 1376, the whole population became stratified into a hierarchy of classes or castes. At the bottom were the *tlacotli,* or slaves, who were recruited chiefly from among criminals and prisoners of war. At the top was the hereditary nobility which claimed direct descent from the Toltecs. Intermarriage among the castes was rare—although now and then a nobleman found it politically expedient to choose a wife from among the commoners. The Aztecs chose their kings from the immediate family of his predecessors, and all of the kings from the year 1376 to the coming of

[6] Needless to say, these figures and facts are subject to discount. But they come from the Aztecs themselves, and who should know better than they?

the Spaniards were direct descendants of Acamapichtli. The early kings were perhaps not absolute rulers. But as the empire grew in size and strength, the kings—or "emperors" if you will—grew giddy with power, and became more and more autocratic. Moctezuma II was a despot. He became even a kind of god to his people: his subjects were forbidden to touch him or even to look upon his face. But even at its most glorious moment, his "empire" was not to be compared, for instance, with the empire of the Incas. The Aztecs terrorized their subjects into submission, collected tribute from them, but made no attempt to integrate them into the Aztec nation. The vanquished peoples remained vassals, with only hatred in their hearts for their conquerors.

The Aztecs worshiped a vast array of gods, each contributing promise of woe or bliss. Chief among them was the terrible Huitzilopochtli, "Humming Bird on the Left," often identified with the Sun, who had led the Aztecs to their promised Valley of Mexico. They also adopted the gods of their neighbors and vassals, as easily as they later adopted the god of the white man; and distinctions among individual gods became blurred, one often being the reincarnation of another. They worshiped Tezcatlipoca, "Smoking Mirror," chief god of the Toltecs, sometimes identifying him with their own Huitzilopochtli; and the quasi-mythical Quetzalcoatl, "Feathered Serpent," who came to stand for peace and wisdom. There were fertility gods and goddesses who guarded the crops, including Tlaloc, "He Who Makes the Plants Spring Up," ancient god of the Nahua-speaking tribes. There were numerous gods credited with unique powers, one of the more quaint being Tlazolteotl, "Filth Eater," who, by destroying all that is evil, purged men's souls. One of the most highly revered of their deities, especially among the commoner peasants, was Tonántzin, "Our Mother," whose temple was on the hill of Tepeyac, near Mexico City (here the Virgin of Guadalupe appeared in 1531, and the Indian masses transferred to her the devotion formerly accorded Tonántzin). And, of course, there were gods of corn and of maguey, gods of rain and wind and fire, gods of the moon and the stars, gods of death, gods of the earth. By the rites of religion, the gods of death were persuaded to furnish abundant harvests and to safeguard the people from all perils. The gods spoke through the priests, who knew their secrets; and the people held the priests in awesome regard.

The religion of the Aztecs was less spiritual and imaginative than that of the Maya. Its central theme was simple, direct, and violent—it has been called a "doomsday ideology": each age through which humanity had passed had ended in widespread destruction—by flood, fire, or the falling of the sky. The world of the Aztecs was destined to end in crashing earthquakes, and the divine mission of the people was to postpone as long as possible this cosmic catastrophe. To this end the Sun must be kept alive and well and shining in its heaven—and for that, the Sun must be fed the only food fit for its divine consumption: human blood. Thus the ceaseless prodding by the gods—especially the dread Huitzilopochtli —to warfare and human sacrifice. No new phenomenon in the annals of the world's religions, human sacrifice among the Aztecs reached extremes which dizzy the mind and unsettle the stomach. Every year the hearts of thousands of young males were torn from their breasts in bloody ceremonies to propitiate the gods, to feed the Sun. And subject peoples were kept in line by being forced to witness these murderous rites. To be sure, those who departed this world as sacrificial victims won a special place in the next: whether they were Aztec youths, slain enemies, or prisoners of war, they dwelt forever in paradise, honored companions of the Sun. But whatever the symbolism which justified this carnage, the Aztecs themselves perhaps grew weary of bloodshed and longed for an end to the cruel rites. By the time the white man arrived, Eric Wolf surmises that "the will of the gods and the burden of human sacrifice rested heavily upon the land."

Games were a part of religious ritual. Chief among them was a ball game played on special courts called *tlachtli,* the aim being to knock a hard rubber ball, with elbow, hip, or knee, across the center line, preferably through one of two stone rings on the sides of the court. This game was played all the way from Honduras to southeastern Arizona. Another ritual game, which the Spaniards called *volador,* involved a high pole from which men, dressed as birds and attached by ropes, flew out in a wide circle, whirling thirteen times around the pole.

The social life of the people was carefully charted from birth to death. Education was a serious matter. Children of the nobility attended a school called the *calmécac,* where they were subjected to rigorous discipline and trained to suffer, and many were prepared for the priesthood. Commoners went to public schools called *telpochcalli,* where they were trained for war or for the tilling of the soil. Marriage was safeguarded by a vigorous code which permitted polygamy and divorce but protected the rights of women and children. Labor was meticulously organized, definite tasks were assigned the able-bodied, and there was slight tolerance for drones. Slavery was common, the slaves being either purchased or recruited from among prisoners of war and those convicted of crime.

The economic life of the people was based upon communal ownership of the soil. It was chiefly a corn economy. Lands were allotted to the *calpulli* on the basis of their needs—in terms of corn. Many varieties of beans, squashes, peppers, and other plants were developed. The maguey, a species of cactus, furnished the intoxicant pulque from its sap, rope and textiles from its fiber, roofing from its leaves, needles from its thorns. Cotton was cultivated and fine weaving was done. Tobacco was used. The turkey was a prime delicacy, and to this day, Mexicans call the turkey by its Aztec name, *guajalote,* rather than by the Spanish *pavo.* By the time of the Conquest, however, the land was proving inadequate to produce needed crops. Levies were made upon the lands of conquered peoples. Artificial islands were built on floating masses of brush, to make new garden patches along the shores of the lakes.[7] But overpopulation

[7] The visitor to "the floating gardens of Xochimilco"—which have long since ceased floating—may see how well the Aztecs managed this venture.

and land shortage had created a serious situation by the time the Spaniards arrived. The Aztecs supplemented their farming with a substantial trade in textiles, pottery, and metal products. The Aztec economy also relied upon the tribute of outlying colonies. It was chiefly an economy of barter, although cacao beans (chocolate) sometimes served as a medium of exchange. The heart of the economy was the village market. It was the heart of the social life as well, as it still is in the villages of Indian Mexico.

The tools of farmer and craftsman remained much as they had been for thousands of years. Seed corn was still planted with the digging stick. Corn was still ground in the hollowed stone *metate*. Stone chisels, axes, and knives yielded slowly to instruments of copper and obsidian.

The houses of the people ranged from adobe huts with thatched roofs to impressive structures of hewn stone. Their greater buildings were solid and massive, but neither in architectural design nor in sculpture did the Aztecs match the imaginative grace of the Toltecs or the Zapotecs, or that of the Maya.

Intellectually, the Aztecs lived upon the stored capital of those who had gone before them. They made no new contribution to knowledge of the calendar, the movement of the stars, or mathematics. Their writing never went beyond the simplest pictographs.

The one point at which the Aztecs definitely surpassed the Maya was in organization of the state. But on that score their performance was overshadowed by that of the Incas of Peru. The Aztecs never learned that the building of an empire means not only conquest but the winning of the hearts of the conquered. The Aztec "empire" contained the seeds of its own destruction before the Spaniards landed.

THE EMPIRE OF THE INCAS

When Francisco Pizarro, the ex-swineherd of Estremadura, reached Peru in 1530 with 180 men, he discovered the most far-flung and highly organized civilization of ancient America, the empire of the Incas. Here was a domain stretching from northern Ecuador to central Chile, a ribbon almost 3,000 miles from north to south, varying from 100 to 400 miles in width. Here the Incas—writes the English archaeologist Thomas A. Joyce—"had evolved if not a civilization at least a very magnificent barbarism." Here lived some 6 million people[8] who, over a period of many centuries, had been incorporated into the Inca state. Here had

8 Estimates on the number of Indians in the Inca Empire at the time of the Conquest range from 3 million to 33 million. Philip Ainsworth Means thinks there were between 16 million and 32 million (*Ancient Civilizations of the Andes* [New York: Charles Scribner's Sons; 1931], p. 296). More recent estimates by George Kubler and John H. Rowe suggest a figure between 4.5 million and 7.5 million (*Handbook of South American Indians,* Vol. II, p. 185). Modern scholars agree almost unanimously with Kubler and Rowe.

been developed governmental, social, economic, and religious institutions of great skill and wisdom. But the Emperor of the Incas was no match for the Holy Roman Emperor, Charles V. So, says Means, the "Empire of the Incas collapsed in a cloud of golden dust through which flitted away the dismayed ghosts of Incaic aspirations."

Who then were these peoples? Where did they come from, and by what long journeyings? How were they shaped into tribes and kingdoms finally to achieve the regal splendor of the sixteenth century? In answering these questions archaeologists and historians find themselves on less secure footing than in dealing with the ancient Maya. The Incas had no written language such as the Maya had used for more than 1,000 years. Our knowledge of them and of the peoples they conquered is based upon the sculptured and painted records of tens of thousands of pottery jugs uncovered in old cemeteries and cities; upon the testimony of stone walls and ornaments in ancient temples, pyramids, and fortresses; upon the tracery and color of old tapestries and textiles and metal work; and upon the *quipus* (the *quipu* was a device consisting of knotted fiber cords which was used to keep numerical records). And we have the chronicles of sixteenth- and seventeenth-century soldiers, priests, and historians who wrote down with varying degrees of faithfulness what they had heard and seen. Pedro Cieza de León wrote conscientiously. Francisco de Toledo, viceroy in Peru (1569–82), was indefatigable in preparing his *informaciones* for Philip II; under his direction Pedro Sarmiento de Gamboa wrote his *History of the Incas*. Garcilaso de la Vega, born in Peru in 1540 of a Spanish father and a royal Inca princess, published his fascinating but unreliable "royal commentaries" on the Incas during his last years in Spain. The best and most complete work was the *Historia del Nuevo Mundo* by Bernabé Cobo, written about 1653. To these, and many others, we owe the preservation of the traditions handed down by the Incas from father to son for many generations.

Modern archaeologists and anthropologists, although lacking written records on pre-Conquest events, have gathered a wealth of material on the scores or hundreds of peoples, speaking an unreckoned number of tongues, who occupied the area that was finally consolidated into the Inca Empire. The testimony of buried cities, agricultural terraces, bridges, temples, pottery, textiles, and fashioned metal has thrown a flood of light upon the story of these peoples. Their stages of development have become clear: from simple fishing, hunting, and food-gathering peoples there gradually emerged many local cultures, which evolved into more elaborate societies with complex social and political organization and well-developed arts and crafts. Some of these societies reached a high level of civilization—such as the Mochica and Chimú empires on the northern coast of Peru, the Nazca on the southern coast, the Tiahuanaco on the shores of Lake Titicaca. Finally the Inca welded together these widely scattered and varied peoples into a vast empire which stretched from northern Ecuador to central Chile.

Some of the most elequent finds in all of this archaeological probing have been the thousands of pottery vessels—many from the Mochica and Chimú empires in the coastal areas of northern Peru—which were buried in graves, presumably to hold food and drink for the dead. The best examples of these vessels were modeled and painted with an artistic vigor and skill which place their contrivers high among their contemporaries throughout the world. The Mochica pottery is conceived in startling and often brutal realism. Some show scenes of war with bound prisoners. There are portrait-vessels, which seem to be realistic likenesses of important personages. Some are effigies, possibly used to pay off old scores. Others are group portraits, in which community and family life is depicted. Some give the record of daily life, hunting, fishing, harvesting, cooking. Others depict the diseases and the appropriate medical and surgical treatments, or give frank accounts of sexual habits and abnormalities. Others show ceremonials by which the gods were placated, or immortalize mighty deeds of warriors. Some portray landscapes. From these pots, and from the textiles, of which a surprising number have been preserved, one learns how the people lived and loved, sinned and suffered, dressed and labored.

The pottery of the Nazcas of the southern coast is also notable. Here realism yields to conventionalized and abstract presentation. While the Mochica dealt with everyday matters in candid and earthy fashion, the Nazca inclined to an esoteric and symbolic representation of the powers of earth and air. Sculpture is subordinated to painting. Nazca pottery is rich in polychrome brilliance; pots and textiles are gay with crimson, scarlet, orange, yellow, green, and various shades of blue, brown, black, white.

These early peoples had chiefs or kings whose jurisdiction was both secular and religious. War was a constant preoccupation, and the warrior was held in high honor. They had many gods related to the forces of nature and to their daily needs, but there seems to have been a persistent faith in a great creator-god, who appeared under various guises. Viracocha, a name derived from the Tiahuanaco culture, was the most common designation. Supreme over all powers was the Sun. It is probable that Tiahuanaco inspired the subtle, philosophic, exalted, and abstract faith of the pre-Inca peoples, but that this faith degenerated as it spread to the coastal plains. Meanwhile, in the highlands and on the coast, a varied ceremonial which sometimes included human sacrifice was evolved for the propitiation of the gods.

The pre-Inca peoples cultivated the fields of the coastal valleys and the high basins of the sierras; they were skilled in creating great networks of irrigation canals, in the use of fertilizers, in weaving the wool of guanaco, llama, alpaca, and vicuña, in working gold and silver. In the highlands their masons handled the abundant stone with precision and grace. On the lowlands they built with sun-baked bricks, and their handiwork has survived many centuries on the rainless deserts.

These primitive peoples were finally conquered and absorbed by the Incas, their ancient fashions obliterated, their languages forgotten. Few traces remain beyond pictured and sculptured designs on pots and tapestries, a few frescoes on walls. Meanwhile, archaeologists dig, classify, and interpret, seeking new clues to the buried life of peoples who during unreckoned centuries occupied the land before the Inca conquest.

The origin of the early Incas is richly overlaid with myth. The romantic chroniclers of the sixteenth and seventeenth centuries offer delightful explanations of the way in which a handful of obscure people appeared at some dim date in the valley of Cuzco (a word which in the Quechua language means "navel"). Some may favor the account of Pedro Sarmiento de Gamboa (Viceroy Toledo's court historian), who told of four brothers and four sisters who emerged from caves in a hill called the "Tavern of the Dawn," some eighteen miles southeast of Cuzco. These eight, leading several *ayllus* (groups) who had also come out of the hill, set out in search of fertile farm lands on which to settle. They journeyed for several years, during which Manco Capac managed to dispose of his three brothers; and he and his four sisters, together with their company of followers, finally arrived in the valley of Cuzco, where they attacked and routed the inhabitants and founded a city—and an empire. Others will prefer the account of Garcilaso de la Vega, who avowed that the Sun created a son and a daughter, set them down upon an island in Lake Titicaca, gave them a staff of gold and bade them settle where the staff sank into the earth. The brother and sister—Manco Capac and his future sister-queen Mama Occlo—traveled north to the valley of Cuzco, where the golden staff disappeared into the ground. Here they stayed, made friends with the people living there, teaching them useful arts, and together they founded the city of Cuzco. Inca[9] Manco Capac, the legendary hero and founder of the Inca Empire, is an attractive figure; but, as in the case of the Mexican Quetzalcoatl, we cannot be sure that he ever really lived.

For the story of the Incas from this shadowy beginning until the early fifteenth century, modern scholars again must choose from among the accounts of the Spanish chroniclers, who gathered the oral traditions and embellished them. Means favored the version of Garcilaso, who tells an enlivening tale of a procession of emperors—beginning with Manco Capac and his successor, Sinchi Roca—who, from their mountain bastion, expanded their domain to include Lake Titicaca; captured the fortress city of Tiahuanaco; then moved west to conquer some of the coastal peoples. According to Garcilaso, by the beginning of the fifteenth century a large part of present-day Peru and Bolivia had been conquered and incorporated into the Inca Empire. However, more recent scholars, including John H. Rowe, discount these exaggerated tales of extensive conquest by the early Incas, favoring the accounts of Sarmiento de Gamboa and the Jesuit Father Bernabé Cobo, who tell of minor wars in the valley, but no real expansion of the empire until the end of the fourteenth century.

[9] To avoid confusion, note that the word "Inca" describes the little company who launched the new empire; that it is also the title of the chief of state who was *the* Inca; and that finally it was applied to all the people of the empire.

Sometime around the year 1200—according to the currently accepted version of the story—there lived in the high valley of Cuzco various groups of stocky, brown-skinned people with similar language and culture, and the Incas were one of these groups. As far back as memory served, it was a feuding valley, with the various tribes intermittently engaged in plundering, raiding, and collecting tribute from one another. Gradually developing a society superior to those of their neighbors, the Incas shortly gained a position of prestige in the valley; but probably not for some two centuries did they undertake any permanent conquest of neighboring peoples. The Indians who recounted the history of their Inca forefathers to the Spaniards in the sixteenth century remembered the names of their past rulers with some unanimity: now generally considered reliable is a sequence of thirteen emperors, or Incas, each chosen from among the sons of his predecessor, beginning with the legendary Manco Capac and his more real son Sinchi Roca, and ending with the unfortunate Atahuallpa, who was betrayed and executed by Pizarro in 1533. Eighth on this list was Viracocha Inca (he assumed the title of the god as the result of a divine visitation), who has been called the "first true imperialist." Probably around the turn of the fifteenth century, Viracocha Inca expanded the empire to include tribes living some twenty-five miles around Cuzco, and extending his influence as far as Lake Titicaca.

The illustrious Pachacuti, son of Viracocha, probably assumed the high office of Inca in 1438—the first more or less firm date in Inca history. This event marks the beginning of an era of imperial conquest which was cut short less than a century later by the arrival of the Spaniards. Although modern scholars discount tales of Inca prowess prior to 1438, they are well agreed as to the mighty deeds of the ninety-two years from the crowning of Pachacuti to the arrival of Pizarro's little army in 1530. And there is general accord as to the stature of Pachacuti Inca, who was conqueror, builder, civic planner, man of intellect—and tyrant. Clements R. Markham called him "the greatest man that the aboriginal race of America has produced." The sayings of Pachacuti reveal something of his severity, his wisdom, his stern justice:

> When subjects, captains and Curacas, cordially obey the King, then the kingdom enjoys perfect peace.
>
> Envy is a worm that gnaws and consumes the entrails of the envious.
>
> He that envies the good, draws evil from them for himself, as does the spider in taking poison from flowers.
>
> He that kills his neighbour must of necessity die.
>
> It is very just that he who is a thief should be put to death.
>
> Adulterers, who destroy the peace and happiness of others, ought to be declared thieves, and condemned to death without mercy.
>
> Impatience is the sign of a vile and base mind, badly taught and worse accustomed.
>
> When subjects do their best to obey without any hesitation, kings and governors ought to treat them with liberality and kindness; but when they act otherwise, with rigour and strict justice, though always with prudence.

Judges who secretly receive gifts from suitors ought to be looked upon as thieves, and punished with death as such.[1]

In the fifty-five years of their rule, Pachacuti (1438–71) and his son Topa Inca Yupanqui (1471–93), in a burst of imperialism, increased the Inca domain to an area of some 350,000 square miles. These two, according to J. Alden Mason, "rank with Alexander, Genghis Khan, and Napoleon as among the world's great conquerors."[2] Their armies extended their hold over the highlands of present-day Peru and Bolivia; they subdued strong federations of tribes such as the Lupaca and Colla around Lake Titicaca, and the Chancas of the western slopes; they moved south into central Chile and inland as far as Tucumán in Argentina; they conquered the formidable feudal kingdoms of the Chimú on the north coast of Peru and Quitu (modern Ecuador), and subjugated the coastal peoples as far south as the Río Maule in Chile. Their exploits constitute a notable chapter in imperial expansion and organization. Earlier assaults upon the territory of rival tribes seem to have been desultory and inconclusive; but now conquered lands and peoples were integrated into the life of the Inca Empire. It was probably during these years that great fortresses were erected against troublemakers, the most impressive of which was the mountaintop city of Machu Picchu, high above the Río Urubamba.[3] While the early battles against old enemies in the near neighborhood were often brutal, with large-scale murder of the population, later and more distant campaigns were somewhat less ruthless. However, both Pachacuti and Topa Inca were driven by a lust for power; and although the subduing of rival peoples and their absorption into the empire seems to have been done with prudence and dignity, the process was firm as steel, and the subjugation complete.

The successors of Topa Inca—who died in 1493, unaware of the intrusion of a man named Columbus—added little to the extent of the empire. Huayna Capac (1493–1525) conquered with difficulty some territory in northeastern Peru and northern Ecuador; but for the most part his long reign was devoted to problems of administration and the quelling of unrest in his huge domain. Leaving his cumbersome empire to two of his sons— Atahuallpa to rule in Quitu, Huáscar in Cuzco—Huayna Capac died in 1525; and the land was torn by civil war as the brothers fought for dominance. Atahuallpa, whose victory in 1532 was clouded by the news of Pizarro's landing, had little time to enjoy his throne: he was executed by the Spaniards within a year.

.   .   .

[1] Quoted in Garcilaso de la Vega: *The Royal Commentaries of the Yncas,* translated by Clements R. Markham, Vol. II (London: Hakluyt Society, No. 45; 1871), pp. 208–9.

[2] J. Alden Mason: *The Ancient Civilizations of Peru* (Baltimore: Penguin Books; 1957) p. 117.

[3] Most recent scholars place Machu Picchu in this period. However, Hiram Bingham, who headed the expedition of 1912 which rediscovered that lonely fortress, argued that the city may have been "selected perhaps a thousand years ago as the safest place of refuge for the last remnants of the old regime" (*The Lost City of the Incas* [New York: Duell, Sloan & Pearce; 1948, p. 251]). That theory has no support from modern archaeologists.

The Inca Empire occupies a high place among the successful empires of the world. Its military victories were seldom soured by revenge or extermination. Many neighboring groups even avoided bloodshed by yielding to the diplomatic overtures which usually preceded an armed attack; for there were definite advantages in alliance, and virtually no hope of successful resistance. And so by persuasion as well as by compulsion, the Incas incorporated into their far-flung society scores, perhaps hundreds, of diverse groups. By the end of the fifteenth century, the authority of the Inca in Cuzco was supreme in the vast area from northern Ecuador to central Chile—a stretch of some 2,500 miles; from the coast to the highlands; and inland as far as Tucumán in Argentina. Only the fierce Araucanians in southern Chile resisted conquest. The relative calm which pervaded the land was due in large part to the practice of *mitima* (forced colonization) probably begun in the time of Emperor Pachacuti: the more unruly inhabitants of conquered areas were uprooted from their homelands and resettled among faithful followers of the Inca in order to assure their greater loyalty. These *mitimaes* (transplanted persons) were replaced by peasants whose spirit had been broken by long years under Inca rule, and who were not likely to cause trouble in their new and distant homes. There was also reshuffling among the nobility: sons of conquered kings were sent to Cuzco as hostages to assure their fathers' loyalty to their new rulers; they were received as honored guests at the royal court, where they were indoctrinated in Inca ideology—against the day when they would return to their homes to assume responsible posts in local government. This constant intermingling of peoples—nobles as well as peasants—went far toward making the Inca Empire into a huge melting pot, with increasing homogeneity in customs, language, and ideology. According to Father Cobo: "Throughout the length and breadth of the Empire similarity and conformity prevailed in religion and government. All the nations learned and spoke the language of Cuzco [*quechua*], which thus came to be general throughout Peru."[4] The least "conforming" nation was the proud coastal kingdom of Chimú, whose life and customs remained much the same after its submission. The Chimú culture persisted, perhaps enriching, more than it was enriched by, the culture of the Incas.

One secret of the strength of the empire was the concern of the Inca for the well-being—if not the happiness—of his subjects. The physical needs of the people were taken care of by the state: hunger and acute hardship were unknown. This concern may well have been prompted less by benevolence than by the knowledge that a sick and hungry people could not serve their Inca well—either as warriors, tillers of the soil, or builders of roads, temples, palaces. Scholars debate the plight of the Inca peasantry, beyond the basic requirements for health and physical strength. The testimony of the most reliable of the chroniclers varies widely. Cieza de León, though attributing much of the peasants' acquiescence to fear, still asserted that

4 Bernabé Cobo: *Historia del nuevo mundo* (4 vols.; Seville, 1890–93), Vol. III, pp. 156–62; translated and quoted by Benjamin Keen in *Readings in Latin American Civilization* (Boston: Houghton Mifflin Co.; 1955), p. 30.

"the Incas always did good works for their subjects, not permitting them to be wronged or burdened with excessive tribute or outraged in any way."[5] While Father Cobo wrote: "The yoke that weighed down the necks of these miserable Indians was so heavy that I doubt if all the men in the world, joining together to invent a species of subjection and tyranny as oppressive as that in which they lived, could improve on what the Incas achieved to keep these Indians in a state of submission. . . . [The objective of the Incas] was to exhaust the strength of the Indians until they were unable to raise their heads."[6]

The structure of Inca society—political, social, and economic—was based upon the *ayllu*. Far older than the Inca civilization, the *ayllu* was the traditional kin group or subtribe of ancient Peru, differing from a proper clan in that it reckoned descent in the male rather than the female line, and endogamy (marriage within the group) was the rule. The Incas modified the *ayllu* in imperial times, and while kinship remained important, rigid endogamy became impractical, and—especially among the commoners— the community came to be almost synonymous with the *ayllu*. Land was worked communally by the *ayllu*, and its members performed many reciprocal tasks such as tending the lands of the sick and aged, and helping neighbors at harvest time. There were also royal *ayllus,* consisting of the direct male descendants of each Inca. These made up the nobility of highest rank, who filled the most important administrative posts throughout the empire.

A conviction long held by the Indian peoples was that land belonged to the community or to the state, not to the individual. The Incas imbedded this conception of land tenure into the framework of the empire. All land—including that of conquered tribes—became the exclusive property of the Inca himself as trustee for the people. The Inca in wisdom and bounty then divided the land three ways. First, each family, or *ayllu*, was allotted enough land to keep its members adequately fed; for, while under Inca philosophy the individual belonged to the state, the state in turn was pledged to protect and support the individual. A second part was assigned to the gods, its produce being used for religious ceremonies and for the support of the priests. A third part was assigned to the Inca himself, for the support of the royal court, government officials, and warriors. The care of the lands was a communal responsibility, and the people worked first the fields of the gods, then those of the Inca, and lastly their own. The planting and harvesting of crops seems to have been carried out in a spirit of cooperation and gaiety, with much singing and drinking of *chicha* beer. Surplus food was never destroyed—that would have angered the gods— but was kept in great storehouses as a reserve to meet the emergencies of stricken areas and to succor victims of pestilence and drought. We do not know how fairly the system was administered. Some writers have expatiated upon the beauties of Inca "communism"—but it was too class-bound

[5] Pedro Cieza de León: *Del señorio de los Incas* (Buenos Aires, 1943); translated and quoted by Benjamin Keen, *op. cit.,* p. 36.
[6] Bernabé Cobo, *op. cit.;* translated and quoted by B. Keen, *loc. cit.*

a society to fit that definition. To call it a "socialistic empire" would be closer to the truth. Or perhaps it was merely a highly organized theocratic paternalism.

Government was entrusted to a pyramidal hierarchy of officials who were numerous and well disciplined. At the top of the governmental structure stood the Inca himself, final arbiter in matters of law and doctrine, son of the Sun, infinitely removed from those below him. The Inca chose his successor from among the sons of his *coya*, or principal wife, who was theoretically, at least from the time of Topa Inca, his full sister—and thus the purity of the royal line was protected. Next in line was the imperial council of four members ("viceroys" the Spanish chroniclers called them), each assigned to rule over one of the four quarters of the empire—Tahuantinsuyu, or "Land of the Four Quarters," was the official name of the realm. Then came the provincial governors of the provinces, administrative units which usually corresponded to a conquered tribe or state, and thus differed greatly in size. Below the provincial governors were the *curacas,* who were assigned to oversee 10,000, 5,000, 1,000, 500, or 100 families or taxpayers; and lesser officials were in charge of 50 or 10 taxpayers. And, lest some members of this numerous bureaucracy yield to temptation, "inspectors" were appointed to keep a check on all servants of the state.

The ranking of officials was based on a rigid caste system. Members of the imperial council and provincial governors were nobles of high rank, usually members of one of the royal *ayllus,* who were appointed by the Inca. These posts were nonhereditary. The *caracas* were members of the lesser nobility (*hidalgos,* or "gentlemen," the Spaniards called them). The Incas showed their political skill by allowing chiefs of conquered tribes—provided they had shown themselves amenable to the royal will—to serve as *caracas,* elevating them to the status of nobility, with many of the immunities, privileges, and perquisites thereof. Once filled, these posts were passed from father to son, subject, of course, to the approval of the Inca. Officials of the two lowest grades, those assigned to oversee fifty or ten families, were commoners appointed by the *caracas,* and were nonhereditary. The success of the governmental system depended largely upon the zeal of these lesser officials, for they were in immediate and constant contact with the people. They were responsible for ensuring the fruitful labor of their charges. They must see that men had tools with which to work, proper seeds and fertilizer. They must administer justice and safeguard loyalty to the empire. These lower officials also kept records of births and deaths on their *quipus,* and rendered monthly reports on their tiny segments of the empire.

The people paid taxes with their own toil. The working of all the land, as we have seen, was the responsibility of the people. In addition, there was a further labor levy called the *mita*: to discharge this obligation each commoner (within the span of his working years, which was between the ages of sixteen and sixty) served for a specified number of days each year as warrior, miner, builder, runner, or special servant to the nobility.

Exempt from the *mita,* as well as from agricultural labor, were some skilled craftsmen such as sculptors, carvers, goldsmiths, and the *quipucamayacs* who kept accounts: these were supported by state funds. Also exempt were the *yanaconas,* boys who were selected in early youth for special service to the emperor and separated forever from their *ayllus.* They became pages at the royal court and servants in the homes of the nobles (to whom they were given as a reward for loyalty); and, by the time the Spaniards arrived, they were virtual slaves. To the present day the *yanaconas* (the word is still used) are effectually bound by custom to the service of the *hacendados,* the great landholders.

The young girls of the villages were also classified; at about the age of ten, those of special beauty and talent were removed from their *ayllus* to become *acllacuna,* or "Chosen Women"—an institution about which fanciful tales have gathered. Hundreds or thousands of these comely maidens, often lyrically described as "Virgins of the Sun," were sent to "convents"—either in Cuzco or in distant provincial capitals—where they were held inviolate against the world and instructed in religion and also in such domestic skills as spinning, weaving, cooking. Their education complete, they were again divided: some—doubtless the most alluring— became secondary wives of the emperor, or were presented to deserving nobles and warriors; others lived lives of chastity in the temples, weaving fine textiles for the priests; a few were selected to be sacrificed at great ceremonial occasions—and these were the most fortunate, as they were assured of eternal bliss in the world to come.

The life of the common man was simple. Virtually all his necessities were drawn from the soil he worked. His food was the dried meat of the llama, corn, potatoes, and other tubers. His drink was the *chicha* from fermented corn. His narcotics were coca leaves (cocaine) and a little tobacco. His clothing was of cloth woven in the home. His house was usually a one-room, windowless, adobe structure with a thatched roof. He was not allowed to change his residence from his immediate neighborhood, and travel for pleasure was prohibited, so his world was a small one. There was little commerce from community to community, and, since there was no currency, the few exchanges of goods were by barter. Though polygamy was regarded as a mark of distinction among the nobility, it was forbidden among the commoners. And incestuous marriages were rigorously denied to all except the Inca and his heir apparent, who were expected to marry their full sisters.

If life was simple for the common man, it was regal for the Inca and the chief nobles. No visitor to modern Cuzco can fail to see beyond the present shabbiness and to conjecture upon the splendor of the last days of the fifteenth and the first days of the sixteenth centuries. Cuzco was a city of perhaps 100,000 people. It had great palaces and public buildings, chiefly one-storied buildings of hewn stone, their great blocks so finely fashioned that they have stood unmoved for centuries. There was the palace of Inca Roca, 300 feet square; the school for sons of the nobles, 400 feet on one side, 500 feet on the other; the immense palaces of Inca Viracocha and Inca Pachacuti; and the "Convent"—a somewhat inaccurate term—of the

Chosen Women. We can only surmise the grandeur of these buildings in their days of glory and guess at their decorations of gold and silver. The early writers left ample accounts of the luxury of those who lived in these palaces, of the gold and silver vessels from which they ate, of the fine vicuña wool woven into tapestries and clothing, of the fresh fish carried to their tables by swift runners from the sea, of the delicate game brought from the mountains.

The empire was bound together by two systems of roads. One followed the highlands from northern Ecuador to central Chile, and a parallel road lay along the coast from northern Peru to the Río Maule in Chile. These roads were supplemented by transverse roads. They were not roads in a modern sense. The Incas, like the Maya and the Aztecs, had not discovered the wheel; hence there were no carriages or wagons. The roads were for the use of couriers, the swift runners who carried messages and some goods, and for the use of officials on business. Over these roads were borne the ruling Incas. It must have been an impressive sight to see the great Inca setting out upon a trip of inspection, carried in his richly ornamented litter, sheltered by curtains of fine vicuña wool, with thousands of warriors leading the way and other thousands following. Impressive also was the system of couriers, whose relays could cover the 300 miles from the coast to high Cuzco in two days, or the 1,000 miles from Cuzco to Quito in from five to ten days. Post houses were built at regular intervals along the way where fresh couriers waited their turn and where the wearied, at the end of their stint, could rest. There were also inns for the use of official travelers.

These roads were soundly built, often paved and lined with adobe walls, with frequent causeways. Suspension bridges of fiber ropes swung over ravines and canyons, spans of 400 to 500 feet. It is probable that travel in the Inca Empire of the fifteenth century was equal in comfort to that of contemporary western Europe.

The administration of justice was stern and inexorable. It was designed to assure and safeguard the firm loyalty of all subjects. A chief instrument of discipline, we have noted, was the forcible relocation of conquered peoples. This measure made for imperial unity and order. It was also devised to assure the efficient use of land and to strengthen sparsely occupied frontiers against possible enemies. The laws bore down with severity upon the great and the humble. It was justice tempered by mercy: a thief who stole out of greed might be sentenced to flogging, stoning, or death; but a man who stole to satisfy his family's hunger might be acquitted, and punishment imposed upon the official who was responsible for that hunger. According to J. Alden Mason, "the entire village or *ayllu* of a great criminal was held guilty with him, and in the most heinous crimes the village was destroyed and the entire population put to death." The heaviest penalties were reserved for those of high estate who proved faithless. "Imprisonment was unknown," says Mason, "except for one delicate variety reserved for the most egregious traitor: he was placed in an underground dungeon filled with snakes and other venomous, noxious, and dangerous animals. His incarceration was necessarily a brief one."[7]

7 J. Alden Mason: *op. cit.,* p. 200.

In science and abstract learning the Incas were far inferior to the Maya. In astronomy, they had reckoned the length of the lunar month with some accuracy, and—although the chroniclers tell us little about the Inca calendar—it is probable that their year consisted of twelve lunar months with an extra month interjected by imperial decree when the times for planting and harvesting got too far out of step with the seasons. In mathematics, it seems evident from a study of the *quipu* that the Incas used a decimal system with place value, and that they understood the concept of zero. For the actual calculations which were recorded on the *quipus,* it is almost certain that they used a kind of abacus. In medicine, they made use of herbs and roots, including quinine which was a Peruvian gift to the world; they knew the value of purging and bleeding. But medicine was chiefly magic. Today's visitor to a market in Peru or Bolivia will see on display the countless oddities guaranteed to work cures. In surgery, however, the Incas accomplished feats of great skill. Skeletal remains, as well as scenes depicted on Mochica pottery, give evidence that they used bandages, forceps, and the tourniquet; that they set fractures and performed amputations; and that their operations on the skull included the delicate process of trepanning.

The art of the Incas showed great technical perfection. Their jewelry, figurines, plates, and vases in gold, silver, and various alloys, belong among the finest accomplishments of any ancient craftsmen. The designs and coloring of their pottery and textiles were chiefly borrowed from the peoples they conquered. In architecture, they reached their greatest heights: the massive fort of Sacsahuamán, overlooking Cuzco, and the imposing city of Machu Picchu—both probably built in the time of Pachacuti—are but two of the many monuments to this formidable skill. The "Stone of Twelve Angles" in a wall in Cuzco is a striking example of the way in which huge stones were cut with the simplest of tools, and fitted together so accurately that today, after centuries of wind and rain, it is difficult to insert a wedge between them.

Although the Incas themselves offered little that was new in the way of technological advances, they made skillful use of the contributions of the various peoples whose cultures they absorbed; their manipulation of man power for the building of bridges and roads, the terracing of land for agriculture, and the construction of stone architecture, give added testimony to their efficient social and political organization.

The religion of the Incas, rich in ceremony, related to the harvesting of food and the curing of disease. In exaltation of one chief creator-god, eternal and omnipotent, the maker of all other supernatural powers, of animals and of men, the Incas were in effect monotheists. The name assigned that creator, Hispanicized by the sixteenth-century scribes as Viracocha, carried the titles "Ancient Foundation, Lord, Instructor of the World." All other gods and supernatural powers existed by the will and act of the creator Viracocha, and were subservient to him. The Sun, progenitor of the Inca dynasty, was the god assigned to the protection and the maturing of crops; despite his obvious importance, the sun-god was still overshadowed by Viracocha. Following these in order of importance came the thunder-god of weather; the moon-goddess, wife of the Sun; the various gods of the stars; the goddesses of the earth and the sea. In addition, there were numerous local shrines, which included such varied spots as springs, mountains, tombs, caves, with a vast variety of sacred meaning to the people of the various regions. Inca ritual was served by a body of priests in elaborate shrines and temples. Their theology included belief in a future life, with a comfortable heaven for the faithful—but members of the nobility were admitted without question as to their character. There was also a hell—very cold, and lacking in food. Much of the literature of the people, preserved by oral tradition, was concerned with religion. One prayer ran:

> Oh conquering Viracocha!
> Ever-present Viracocha!
> Thou who art without equal upon the earth!
> Thou who art from the beginnings of the world until its end!
> Thou gavest life and valor to men, saying,
> "Let this be a man."
> And to woman, saying,
> "Let this be a woman."
> Thou madest them and gavest them being.
> Watch over them, that they may live in health and in peace.
> Thou who art in the highest heavens,
> And among the clouds of the tempest,
> Grant them long life,
> And accept this our sacrifice,
> Oh, Creator.[8]

Such, in brief, is the record of Indian America. There were, perhaps, from 8 to 15 millions of those first Americans, holders of clear title to the forests and plains and jungles from Hudson Bay to Tierra del Fuego. Some were primitive wanderers living from the game they snared, the berries they picked. Others had created elaborate nations. Some had progressed no further than the making of simple baskets and earthenware. Others had created temples and sculptures which place them high among their contemporaries of all lands. Some lived in a world of fetishism. Others had mastered the secrets of the sun and stars and had counted the days and years. But, simple or sophisticated, they were destined to lose their heritage to mightier men with guns and horses and wheels. Their beliefs, their customs, their languages would be subordinated to those of their conquerors. They themselves would become the vassals of alien kings. And then, in the curious alchemy of time, these conquered peoples would in turn become conquerors as their blood mixed with the blood of the white man and their skills and customs helped to create America.

8 Philip A. Means, *op. cit.,* p. 438. Means translated this from an orison preserved by Father Molina of Cuzco.

Chapter 3

THE IBERIAN BACKGROUND

There can be no understanding of the world called America without a sensitive appreciation of those European peoples who fastened their pattern of life upon it. As no American would venture to explain New England without reference to Old England, so Brazil must be studied against the background of Portugal, the Spanish-speaking republics against that of Spain. The Iberian signature is written clear and strong on all South America and much of North America; it can be seen on faces of creole and mestizo from Mexico to Patagonia, in the languages they speak, in the religious faith they profess, in the customs that shape their daily lives.

It is not easy for the English-speaking outsider to penetrate the life of Spain and Portugal. Tradition has reared a formidable barrier in the *leyenda negra* of Spanish perfidy with which American and English school-boys have long been regaled. This "black legend" perpetuates the conviction that Spaniards (and, in lesser degree, Portuguese) were—and are— wicked, cruel, wanton, bigoted, and foolish. A sagacious Spaniard explains that "Love of tribe made it necessary for England, France and Holland to blacken Spain; for the richest and most majestic empire the world had seen was for three hundred years the quarry out of which England, France and Holland built their own [empires]. Spain had to be wrong so that France, Holland and England, and later the United States, could be right."[1] We are slowly escaping the tyranny of that "black legend," and with better perspective recognize the stature of the conquerors who, with meager bands, brought populous empires into vassalage to the kings of Castile and Portugal. No less impressive was the success of Iberian colonization in America. Spanish and Portuguese administrators followed the conquerors, and organized economic life and civil rule so skillfully that their colonial empires remained intact and faithful for three centuries. Friars and priests came with the civil rulers, often tempering power with mercy, defending the Indian against the white man's rapacity. All these—captains, governors,

---

[1] Salvador de Madariaga: *The Rise of the Spanish American Empire*, p. xvii. Copyright 1947, reprinted with the permission of The Macmillan Company, New York.

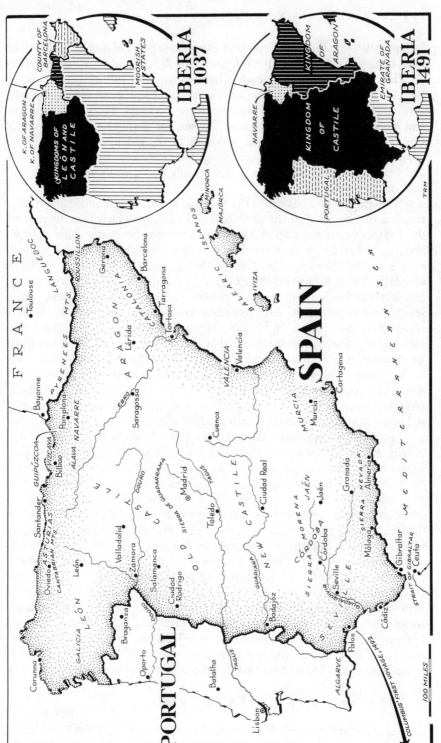

Iberian Peninsula, 1519; Iberian Peninsula, 1037; Iberian Peninsula, 1491

and priests—are the Spaniards and Portuguese whose history and genius must be appraised if we are to understand the life of modern Latin America.

But that understanding comes hard. Spain and Portugal have always been lands apart, aloof from the chief currents of European life. Geography accounts in part for Iberian isolation. The Pyrenees interrupted the free and natural flow of men and ideas between the peninsula and the rest of Europe. On the other hand, the accessibility of Africa, only twelve miles across the Strait of Gibraltar, encouraged easy intercourse with the south, and the Iberian peninsula became historically and socially an African outpost on European soil.

Geography was unkind to the Iberians so far as soil and climate were concerned. The heart of the peninsula is a plateau, which falls away from the Pyrenees and the Cantabrian Mountains on the north. This plateau, about 2,500 feet high, is drained by four rivers which take their southwest course to the Atlantic—the Douro, the Tagus, the Guadiana, and the Guadalquivir. A fifth river, the Ebro, flows parallel to the Pyrenees, southeast into the Mediterranean. This pattern of rivers and mountains, which separates the peninsula into compartments, partly explains the divisive regionalism that marks its history. The mountain ranges also block the rain-bearing clouds with the result that the central plateau, at whose heart lies Madrid, is a windswept and treeless plain blistered in the summer, icy in the winter. The well-watered and temperate mountainous areas of the north and northeast offer only meager valleys for cultivation. The Mediterranean coast, aside from the wastelands of the Sierra Morena, has good soil and a subtropical climate which produce olives, oranges, rice, and sugar.

The Iberian peninsula is, and always has been, a poor land for the farmer. Miguel de Unamuno describes the Spain of Don Quixote, the prototype of the Spaniard of all the ages: "The land that fed Don Quixote," he writes, "is a poor land, so wasted by the downpours of centuries that its granite bones crop out everywhere. . . . Its rivers in winter run squeezed into cuts, gorges, and canyons, carrying to the sea in their muddy waters the rich coating that would have given the earth its verdure. This poverty of its soil made wanderers of its people, for they had either to go to distant parts in search of bread or to drive from pasture to pasture the sheep on which they lived." Then Unamuno, still pondering the career of Don Quixote, adds: "Thus year after year our gentleman saw the herders go by with their flocks, with no definite home, at the mercy of God. And perhaps, seeing them so, he sometimes dreamed of travel and of seeing new lands."[2] Perhaps the experience of Don Quixote reflects the long shifting of populations on Iberian soil and the eagerness with which the Spaniards and Portuguese of the fifteenth and sixteenth centuries journeyed to fairer lands.

BEFORE THE ROMANS

The clear history of Iberia begins with the year 202 B.C., when Rome overcame Carthage and started its six-century rule of the peninsula. Thanks to

2 Miguel de Unamuno: *The Life of Don Quixote and Sancho,* translated by Homer P. Earle (New York: Alfred A. Knopf; 1927), pp. 5–6.

the digging of archaeologists, however, much is known of those who came before the Romans, and we are able to reconstruct their story with fair accuracy. The Iberian soil yields evidence of Cro-Magnon Man and his rough stone tools, of his cousins in the ages of polished stone, copper, bronze, and iron. Then, at some unfixed point in prehistoric time, the invasion of the peninsula began. We call the early comers "Iberians," but we know little about them. They may have been squat, swarthy fellows akin to the whitish Berbers of North Africa. They may indeed have come from Africa, conquering the cave dwellers already in possession, extending their hold over much of the peninsula. The Iberians and their forerunners left eloquent reminders of their life. The Altamira caves near northern Santander have rock walls painted with handsome bison, boar, and deer—the work of men who lived there long before the Iberians. Caves in central and southern Spain have similar paintings. Formidable stone tombs in Andalusia and elsewhere testify to the skill of early peoples. Heavy walls, like those of Tarragona, may be the work of the Iberians or of earlier peoples. Scattered excavations yield stone and metal implements, pottery, and sculptures.

Another prehistoric invasion may have been that of the Celts. This somewhat nebulous family of men, who fanned out over Europe from the Balkans to the British Isles, may have entered Spain about 800 B.C., and again about 500 B.C. These Celts mingled with the Iberians to create the Celtiberians, who then became the target of the dominant Mediterranean powers of Phoenicia, Greece, Carthage, and Rome. Still another group of immigrants were the Basques, as to whose origins there is no agreement among scholars.

The Phoenicians, a Semitic people whose cities of Tyre and Sidon in Syria controlled the trade of the Mediterranean world, early skirted the Iberian coast and found profitable trade in cattle, fruits, fish, and minerals. They may have established trading posts at the site of present-day Cádiz in the eleventh century B.C., and a little later at Malaca (Málaga). The Phoenicians were good teachers, encouraged farming and mining, promoted trade, and introduced writing.

By the year 500 B.C., or thereabouts, the Greeks were competing with the Phoenicians for the trade of the peninsula, and were founding cities. The period of Greek activity in Iberia coincided with Greece's own Golden Age in art. Greece shared her cultural wealth with the peninsula, as is abundantly revealed in scattered remnants of buildings, sculptures, roads, bridges, and aqueducts credited to the Greek period.

Then came the Carthaginians, whose North African stronghold, Carthage, had broken away from the parent Phoenician Empire. In the sixth century B.C., the Carthaginians took Cádiz from the Phoenicians and built it to greater glory. In the third century B.C., they founded New Carthage (modern Cartagena) in Murcia as their Iberian capital. They extended their power over much of the peninsula and laid the foundations for Iberian unity.

THE ROMANS AND THE VISIGOTHS, 202 B.C.–A.D. 711

When Scipio Africanus defeated Hannibal in 202 B.C., Rome expelled the Carthaginians from the peninsula and began two centuries of wars against the tenacious Celtiberians, wars of incredible ferocity and endless reprisals. These Roman campaigns were part of that larger imperial drive which fixed Roman rule upon the Mediterranean world and much of Europe. By the beginning of the Christian era, in the days of the great Augustus, the Iberian peninsula was fully incorporated into the Roman Empire.

Roman contributions to Iberia were varied and far-reaching. The conquerors imposed unity. Roman law replaced the conflicting codes of the several regions. Rome introduced Latin as the common tongue, destined to serve as parent to the varieties of Spanish and Portuguese spoken today. Unity was further expedited by forced colonization, by moving people from one area into another, by breaking old ties, and encouraging common loyalty to the empire. The Romans were city-builders; they regarded the city as the bulwark of order, the training school in Roman citizenship. The Roman period brought buildings, roads, public works. The peninsula is dotted with reminders of their prowess: the amphitheater of Itálica near Seville, the graceful and sturdy aqueduct of Segovia, the aqueducts and bridges of Mérida, the massive walls of León, the bridges of Salamanca, the imperial highways.

The Romans left their mark upon the arts, taking over the gifts of Greeks and Phoenicians, adding their own energy and artistry to create an abundance of sculptured stones, tombs, buildings, walls, pottery, and metal work. The Roman period was intellectually fecund. Sons of Spaniards and sons of Romans who had moved to Spain became notable. The philosopher Seneca and the poet Lucan were born in Córdoba. The master of epigrammatic wit, Martial, was born in Bilbilis. The rhetorician Quintilian was born in Calahorra. These and many other sons of the peninsula gave impetus to intellectual life.

Christianity reached the peninsula during the Roman period. The first missionaries arrived in the second century, possibly in the first. There is a legend that St. Paul himself was among them. Persecution of the first Christians was bitter, but by the early fourth century equal rights were guaranteed to the Christians, and their religion was firmly established on the peninsula. In 400 a Church council at Toledo accepted the creed adopted in 325 by the Council of Nicaea, an action which made clear Spain's loyalty to the Christian world.

The early fifth century brought the collapse of the Roman Empire and a new turn in Iberian history. The waves of Germanic "barbarians" who swept in from the north were more than a match for the luxury-softened Romans, and their intrusion into the Iberian peninsula ushered in the "Visigothic Period" (409–711). The first invaders were the Vandals and the Suevi, who arrived in 409 and occupied various regions from the south to northwestern Galicia. They were followed by the Visigoths, a formidable people who had left Scandinavia several centuries before, spent many years on German soil, then settled for a hundred years by the Black Sea, migrated to the Danube Valley about the year 270, and then a century later had been driven into Roman territory by the Huns. At first they cooperated with the Romans; then they turned upon them and finally sacked Rome itself in 410. Leaving Italy in 412, they shortly arrived in southern Gaul and northern Spain.

The Visigoths brought war to the peninsula. For more than a century and a half the newcomers were in conflict not only with the Romans, but with the Vandals, the Franks (a Germanic people who moved south into Gaul), the Suevi, and the Basques. In 419, after forcing the Vandals to flee to Africa, they established a kingdom with Toulouse as the capital. In 507 they lost most of Gaul to the Franks and moved their capital to Toledo. In 585 they conquered the kingdom of the Suevi in Galicia—and from that date the Visigothic kings were in control of most of the peninsula. Despite Visigothic political supremacy, however, Roman law and culture continued to dominate. Although they had some rulers of ability, the troubles of the Visigoths increased: by the seventh century their ranks were divided by jealous quarrels.

A question of theology was a prime cause of discord between the Visigoths and the Romanized Iberians. The rough Visigoths, during their years under Roman influence, had accepted Christianity but had generally adhered to the Arian doctrine. Arianism was a heresy against official Catholicism rooted in the teachings of Arius, an early fourth-century priest of Alexandria, who had sought to dignify the one true God by subordinating Christ to a secondary position in which "he was neither truly God nor truly man." This deviation had caused vast consternation to the faithful in Rome and was officially banned by the Council of Nicaea in 325. But the Visigoths persisted in their error until 587, when the Visigothic king in Toledo formally renounced his heresy and pledged fealty to the Pope. This prudent change of heart brought a measure of unity to the peninsula. However, the Visigoths' rule of their Iberian domain lacked the cohesion and consistency of that of the Romans. The best intentions of the Visigothic kings were betrayed by the private wars of refractory Visigothic nobles. The increasing confusion during the sixth and seventh centuries prepared the way for invasion by the Moslems.

MOSLEM IBERIA, 711–1031

Moslems from Africa struck in 711. They conquered and occupied most of the peninsula, exerted a profound influence on cultural and economic life, and maintained their hold over a gradually reduced share of the region until their final defeat in 1492. Their stay of almost eight centuries falls into three periods: first, 711–1031, the years of conquest and final consolidation of power under the Caliphate of Córdoba; second, 1031–1276, the recapture of most of the peninsula by the Christian kingdoms; third, 1276–1492, the confining of the Moslems to a small area in the south and the final triumph of Christian forces.

When they first took up cudgels against the dissension-weakened Visigoths, the Moslems represented a religious-political power scarcely a century old. Mohammed, their prophet, had been born in the Arabian city of Mecca in 570. He was about forty when he received the heavenly vision, heard himself appointed prophet of God, heir of Jesus of Nazareth, and leader of his people. The record of his visions was later compiled in the Koran. He proclaimed one all-powerful God, eternal reward and punishment, the end of the world and final judgment, the efficacy of unceasing prayer and works of mercy. His prophetic exhortings evoked derision, hatred, stonings. In 622 he fled from Mecca to Medina—this was the hegira, marking the year 1 of the Moslem calendar. Within a century the Moslems added Asia Minor, much of North Africa, and the Iberian peninsula to their religious empire.[3]

The Moslem invasion was probably expedited by an ill-advised Visigothic claimant to the throne who, in 711, invited Moslem allies to aid his cause. The invaders gave brief help to their host, then evicted him and all other claimants and took over the power themselves. Berbers from Morocco were probably the first arrivals, landing at Gibraltar under the chieftain Tarik.[4] Hard upon their heels came Arabs. The conquest proved easy. By 718, seven years after the initial attack, Moslems controlled much of the peninsula and shortly spilled over the Pyrenees. The fear that all Europe would fall to the infidels was ended at Tours in 732 by Charles Martel and his Franks.

The Iberian peninsula was now ruled by the Caliph, political and religious leader of the Moslem world, at first from Damascus, and after 750 from Bagdad. But dissensions within Moslem ranks had their repercussions in Iberia. In 755 the Emir of Córdoba declared his independence of Bagdad; from that time on, Moslem rule in the peninsula was increasingly detached from outside dictation. By the ninth century, the Caliph of Córdoba dominated Moslem Iberia.

Moslem rule proved surprisingly tolerant. The Christians who had fled to the northern mountains were invited to return, promised security of person and property, and assured full freedom of worship. The Moslems showed little zeal in winning converts to Islam—in marked contrast to their earlier record—and were content with the special but not exorbitant tax imposed upon Christians. Many Christians returned to their homes

[3] We describe these invaders as "Moslems." In popular parlance they are often called "Moors," but that word properly covers only those from Morocco. They are sometimes referred to as "Arabs," but these are only the people of Arabia. During eight centuries of Moslem occupation, successive waves of invaders represented many and diverse peoples for which there is but one inclusive word, "Moslems."

[4] Tarik won limited immortality by giving his name to the great rock, which became *Gebel-al-Tarik*, Gibraltar, "the hill of Tarik."

and lived peaceably with their Moslem neighbors; they were called
Mozárabes, "Arabized folk." On the other hand, many Moslems lived
unmolested in Christian communities and were called *Mudéjares.* The numerous Jews went about their business without interference.

Meanwhile, Christian Spain rallied its forces in the northern mountains
and laid the foundation for the Reconquest, which would make an
intermittent battlefield of the peninsula until the last Moslem stronghold
of Granada fell in 1492. The first center of Christian resistance was northern Asturias, and fresh revolts broke out in Navarre, Aragon, and Catalonia.
Early Christian fervor was probably inspired less by religious faith than
by the desire of nobles, priests, and kings to recapture their lost holdings.

The Reconquest, in its beginnings chiefly a measure of prudence, took
on during the ninth and tenth centuries the aura of a crusade. A mighty
impulse to this crusading spirit came with the discovery of the long-lost
tomb of the Apostle James the Greater. There had been a tradition that
St. James had preached in Spain, returned to Judaea, where he was beheaded, and that his body was returned to Spain and buried in a forgotten
tomb. In the ninth century, according to legend, word spread that a bright
star had come to rest over his lost tomb in northwestern Galicia. This
campus stellae became in Spanish Santiago de Compostela, "the field of the
star of St. James." Pilgrims came by the thousands, from the peninsula
and from all Europe—and they have come ever since.[5] In the eleventh
century the tomb was incorporated in one of the noblest of Romanesque
cathedrals. The pilgrims did much to shape the history of northern Spain.
They introduced new ideas, new goods, and new skills. They spread the
culture of France which influenced northern Spanish development. Santiago
became the patron saint of Spanish knights; time and again he appeared
on battlefields where Christians battled with Moslems. The name Santiago
became the symbol of Spanish piety and pride, the battle cry of courage
and faith.

The first three centuries of Moslem rule (the period during which
they dominated most of the peninsula) were a decided success both for the
invaders and for their victims, despite the continuous quarrels among
the servants of Allah. Arabs settled chiefly in the fertile south, Berbers in
the barren north, taking over lands of intractable nobles, but scarcely
disturbing the daily life of the ordinary man. Prosperity steadily increased,
reaching its high point in the tenth century. The Moslems, few of whom
had won prowess as farmers, proved resourceful in improving upon
Hispano-Roman methods; they extended irrigation, encouraged seed selection, fertilization, and stockbreeding, and introduced rice, sugar, and other
crops to the peninsula. They were skilled metallurgists, with improved
methods for mining and processing of ores. They promoted industry.

The Moslems built new cities and expanded old ones. Ancient
Córdoba became their proud capital; by the tenth century it may have
had, according to the Spanish historian Rafael Altamira, more than 500,000

---

[5] Spaniards call the Milky Way *El Camino de Santiago,* "the Road of St. James," the
many stars suggesting the multitude of pilgrims.

VERNON REGIONAL
JUNIOR COLLEGE LIBRARY

people, 200,000 houses, 600 mosques, 900 public baths—but the figures
are challenged. It was one of the largest and richest cities of the world.
Seville, Granada, Toledo, Murcia, and Saragossa were also populous and
impressive cities.

The Moslems brought intellectual ardor to the peninsula, organized
schools, and won credit as preservers and transmitters of Greek and Roman
culture. They were intellectually cooperative; Arabic, Christian, and Jewish
scholars worked side by side. They produced scientists and mathematicians.
They introduced paper to the peninsula long before it reached the rest of
Europe, and books multiplied. Among their libraries, that of Córdoba
claimed 600,000 volumes; and Andalusia boasted fifty public libraries—
the figures were probably exaggerated. Meanwhile, the Moslems added
their artistic contribution in the shaping and decoration of public buildings
and private houses: their delicate geometric tracery of design and fine color,
their use of tiles, their skill with gold and silver and other metals.

THE RECONQUEST AND THE CREATION OF THE SPANISH NATION, 1031–1516

The year 1031 was fateful. Moslem rule, brilliantly administered by the
Caliphs of Córdoba, had reached its apogee in the tenth century. The
life of the peninsula had never been more prosperous, gracious, and vigorous. But then came family quarrels in Moslem ranks, and there was no
leader strong enough to impose his will upon his rivals; Moslem Iberia fell
apart into rival kingdoms, and the way was cleared for the *Reconquista* by
the leaders of the Christian kingdoms. The two ensuing centuries brought
great changes to the peninsula: the Spanish crusaders, with the battle cry
of *Santiago,* drove the infidels into the far south; the Christian kingdoms
of Castile and Aragon expanded until they practically divided Spain between them; and Portugal withdrew to pursue its separate course. Two
victories were decisive: the capture of the fortress-city of Toledo in 1085
by the soldiers of Castile, and the occupation of Saragossa in 1118 by the
armies of Aragon.

The hero of the battles of the eleventh century was *El Cid Cam-
peador,* the "conquering chief": the fabulous deeds of Rodrigo Díaz de
Vivar furnished the stuff for hero worship to succeeding generations. The
Cid became the prototype, the eternal symbol of the Spanish knight. He
served under two kings in the eleventh century, won a vast reputation, and
evoked the envy of a king who banished him about 1081. Forthwith the
hero sold his military prowess to the Moslem kings of Saragossa and
Valencia and during his last years served as quasi king of Valencia. It
remained for the unknown writer of *The Song of the Cid,* which appeared
in the twelfth century, to assure him immortality.

Meanwhile, the troubles of the Moslems multiplied. After the loss
of Toledo in 1085, the dispirited Moslem kings invited the aid of the
Almoravides, a powerful Moslem people of Morocco, without previous

VERNON REGIONAL
JUNIOR COLLEGE LIBRARY

Iberian experience. These hardy soldiers of fortune arrived about 1090 and took over control of the surviving Moslem kingdoms for themselves. Then further troubles developed. In Morocco, the Almoravides were decisively beaten in 1122 by another Moslem people called the Almohades. These new victors, regarding their rivals' possessions in Spain as fair game, crossed the Mediterranean in 1146 and seized practically all Moslem Spain. These Moslem family disputes made the next victories of Christian Spain easy. Córdoba fell in 1236, Jaén in 1246, Seville in 1248. In the meantime, Aragon had annexed Valencia and the Balearic Islands. The mid-thirteenth century found the Moslems crowded into the mountainous kingdom of Granada. The Reconquest was now all but completed and Spain had gone far toward achieving national consciousness. Her numerous regional loyalties had been largely subordinated to the powerful royal houses of Castile and Aragon. Momentous social and political changes had taken place.

Spain now had a language. Latin had been tossed about, reshaped, clipped, expanded, and diluted—and had finally yielded Spanish. There were wide regional variations upon this Spanish tongue, as there are to the present day, but the literate of Castile and Aragon could understand each other. On the periphery of Spain there were wide and obstinate varieties of speech. In northwestern Galicia and in Portugal, isolated from the heart of the peninsula, a widely divergent dialect had developed, the basis of today's Portuguese and the kindred speech of Galicia. An even more pronounced variant was the language of northeastern Catalonia, its Latin ancestry tempered by long ties with France, and resembling the Provençal. The orphan tongue of Spain is the Basque of the north, its lineage quite unknown.

The Spanish language (and Portuguese as well) was modified by the varied peoples who had come and gone for a thousand years. The Moslems left a clearer mark than any of the others. Arabic words were imbedded into common speech. The ejaculation *ojalá,* "would to Allah," became "would to God." Moslems were builders, so Spanish is studded with such words as *azulejos,* tiles, and *alcázar,* a fortress-palace. They were farmers, so Spanish has *azúcar* (a Persian word adopted by the Arabs) for sugar, *arroz* for rice, *aceitunas* for olives, *aceite* for oil, *acequia* for an irrigation ditch, *alberca* for reservoir. Moslems organized municipal life, so the Spaniards speak of the *alcalde,* the mayor of the city; of the *alguacil,* the constable; of the *alférez* or municipal standard bearer. The Moslems were traders, so Spain uses *almacén* for warehouse, *alhóndiga* for granary, *arroba* for measuring grain, and *fanega* for reckoning acreage. These Arabic words are all reminders of the Moslems' long stay.

The concentration of power in the two royal houses of Castile and Aragon proceeded rapidly during this period. In the early eleventh century, the rulers of little kingdoms and principalities were numerous and weak; by the middle of the thirteenth century, the kings of Castile and Aragon dominated. Their supremacy, the prelude to national unity, was won at the expense of the counts, dukes, and lesser nobles who divided the realm among them, ruled with autocratic power over their lands and serfs, and used their private armies to harry each other. The arrogance and power of these nobles expanded greatly during the period of the Reconquest, as they exacted exorbitant rewards for aiding the greater kings in battles against the Moslems. Then, as the infidels were dispossessed, the kings of Castile and Aragon set about curbing the upstart nobles. Chief weapons to this end were the strengthening of the cities, the enlarging of their middle-class population, and the creation of city militias. The cities were granted new and more generous charters, with extensive immunities and special privileges (*fueros*). This zeal for the building of cities inspired generous hospitality for Jews, Moslems, and foreigners. Toledo, for example, assigned separate districts to non-Spanish elements; within their sanctuaries, Jews were permitted to have their synagogues, Moslems their mosques. This happy tolerance prevailed, with fitful interruption, until the fourteenth century. Meanwhile, the powerful cities, with their *hermandades* ("brotherhoods" for patriotic service) and effective militia, buttressed the royal power against the quarrelsome nobles.

Even the serfs, bound to the lands of their masters, profited from the contest between kings and nobles. By the twelfth century, there were numerous uprisings. The kings found it expedient to bid for their loyalty by decrees which reduced the labor they must render to their lords, barred selling them with the land, guaranteed their right to move from place to place without hindrance and to marry as they chose. Numerous enlightened churchmen used their considerable influence on behalf of these wise laws.

Another instrument for royal control was the launching of parliaments, or the *cortes,* in the several kingdoms by the end of the twelfth century. The *cortes,* representing the nobility, the clergy, and the citizens of the cities, had limited rights often forgotten or overruled, but could at least discuss taxes and initiate petitions to the throne.

Commerce and industry increased. In the north, the pilgrims to the shrine of Santiago de Compostela brought new ideas and skills from France. The great ports of Seville, Valencia, and Barcelona attracted the trade of the Mediterranean world. This new commercial energy owed much to the increasing power of the guilds, which became more numerous after the eleventh century. There were guilds for shoemakers, carpenters, stonecutters, tanners, bakers, merchants, and a wide variety of other craftsmen, traders, and artisans. Their organizations were close-knit, disciplined, and effective. Admission to the several occupations was carefully regulated. Young men were admitted as apprentices, advanced to the rank of craftsmen, finally to positions as master craftsmen. Guilds became important in city government and in some instances named representatives to city councils (*ayuntamientos*). These guilds were later transplanted to the New World, and exercised a potent influence until the nineteenth century.

The Church shared the triumphs of the Christian kingdoms. It was a period in which great cathedrals, churches, and religious houses were built and generous endowments gathered for their support. The clergy grew powerful; their privileges were confirmed and enlarged. Their increased dignities made them a powerful force behind the kings and advanced national unity. Furthermore, the Church, a chief landholder, served the economy of the nation by setting a useful example in progressive farming. By the thirteenth century, the Church reached a high place in spiritual and intellectual leadership, thanks largely to the devotion and energy of the missionary orders. Spain's debt to these orders was of long standing, going back to the ninth century when the French Benedictines had sent to the peninsula missionaries, zealous in the faith, eager in defense of learning. In the eleventh century the French Cistercians sent members of their order, and a century later that same order, under the inspiration of St. Bernard, exercised a powerful influence upon Spain. The two orders destined to have the greatest influence on Spain's religious experience were the Franciscans, founded by the Italian, Francis of Assisi, in 1215, and the Dominicans, founded by the Castilian, Domingo de Guzmán, in 1219. The Franciscans soon became the most effective agency for spreading the faith among common men; the Dominicans, intellectuals and preachers, were the chief protagonists of learning.

It was a period of intellectual ferment. The universities attracted students from all Europe; their curriculums expanded; they became notable in science, philosophy, and the arts. They extended hospitality to Moslem and Jewish scholars and profited from the intellectual stimulus of these unbelievers. By the thirteenth century, Toledo had offered asylum to so many of these displaced intellectuals that it was one of the brilliant intellectual centers of Europe.

The Reconquest was all but complete by the year 1250. The two centuries that followed saw a lull in the fight against the Moslems, but they were marked by violent dynastic contests between the dominant houses of Castile and Aragon, continued battles between kings and nobles, revolts of cities against centralized power, and uprisings of the serfs. During these stormy years Castile and Aragon divided Spain between them, Aragon extending its holdings to include much of Italy and Sicily as well.

A significant step toward unification of Spain was the marriage which linked her two royal houses. In 1474, after the breaking of some heads, the twenty-three-year-old Isabella came to the throne of Castile. She had married Ferdinand, heir apparent to the throne of Aragon, five years before. In 1479 Ferdinand became King of Aragon. Now under "the Catholic Monarchs," *los reyes católicos,* Spain was almost unified. It required careful juggling to allot royal prerogatives to the royal pair. Ferdinand made an abortive attempt to seize the throne of Castile for himself, and even after the two stout-willed monarchs had settled down upon their twin thrones, differences arose. For Castile, it was a dual monarchy, a "diarchy," in which the two sovereigns acted together on foreign affairs, and had both their profiles stamped upon coins of the realm; but Isabella jealously reserved the right to administer internal affairs. In Aragon, Ferdinand ruled alone.

Isabella and Ferdinand ruled for twenty-five years, a period of momentous decisions at home and historic excursions abroad—a period which raised the curtain on Spain's greatest power and glory. The first problem was the perennial squabbling of the refractory nobles. The more powerful still lived in isolated strength upon ancestral lands, protected by private armies. In order to bring the nobles under royal control Ferdinand and Isabella lured them into the cities by granting them titles, assuring them social prestige, and providing generous exemptions. The monarchs brought the military orders under control of the Crown. They created a new national Holy Brotherhood, the *Santa Hermandad,* forerunner of the Civil Guard which has policed Spain for years. The cities, holders of special immunities under their charters, were next brought under royal discipline by the appointment of agents of the Crown to oversee municipal affairs. Another step toward unity was the creation of royal councils for consultation and wider representation, a device which created bureaucracies under Charles I and Philip II in the sixteenth century.

The Catholic faith, so long the one firm tie between warring kingdoms, now became the chief force for unifying the nation. The religious motive was stern and compelling, especially to the highly devout Isabella. Two things seemed clear: the Church herself must be purified and made worthy, and the nation must be purged of elements alien to the faith of Spain—which meant that Moslems, Jews, and all dissenters must go. In other words, the Reconquest must be completed. All that happened during the twenty-five-year reign of Ferdinand and Isabella must be appraised in the light of this determination.

The Spanish Inquisition was devised as the chief instrument for the twofold purging of Church and nation. Castile created it by royal edict in 1477, Rome confirmed it by a Papal Bull in 1483, Aragon accepted it in 1484.[6] Its stern program met stout resistance both in Spain and in Rome, sometimes out of protest against its harshness, more often out of expedient desire to retain Moslems or Jews needed in shops, factories, or farms. Its chief contriver was the Dominican Fray Tomás de Torquemada, a man of passionate religious zeal and devout patriotism who believed that no price was too high to pay for the purity of Spain—a conclusion most dramatic in the light of the fact that Torquemada himself had Jewish blood. The machinery of the Inquisition was powerful and far-reaching. Suspected heretics were subject to trial, torture, confiscation of property, death by burning. The historian Altamira estimated the deaths at about two thousand during the reign of Isabella.

The Inquisition must be judged within the framework of Spanish convictions and realities. It reflected the passion for national unity, so long deferred by the presence of alien Moslems. It struck at the Moslems

6 The Inquisition was not a new creation. Aragon (and Italy) had had it since the thirteenth century, but Castile had never accepted it. The Inquisition of Isabella differed greatly from its predecessor. The older Inquisition had been the tool of the bishops; its operation chiefly delegated to the Dominicans, it had not been enforced with much vigor. The new Inquisition was the instrument of the Crown, with papal consent and blessing. Successive popes proved uneasy over its workings, placing restrictions upon it.

not only because they were infidels, but because they had long disrupted the Spanish state. It attacked the Jews, in part because of their refusal to accept Catholicism, and in part because of their wealth. It also reflected the conviction that man is saved by right thinking, damned by wrong thinking, and that it is worth any sacrifice to protect the weak and ignorant against the contamination of evil doctrine. Spaniards have always been more concerned than their French and Italian neighbors over the heresies which beset the Church, and were determined not to be faithless to their trust. The Inquisition not only punished infidels and heretics, but also assumed many of the functions of a modern police court: it concerned itself with the moral interests of citizens, prosecuted priests who used the confessional for immoral ends, and harried members of the religious orders who were faithless to their vows.

The methods of the Inquisition, cruel as they were, must be judged in the context of the times. Havelock Ellis suggests that "In an age when torture was a recognized part of judicial procedure nearly everywhere, its use by the Inquisition in Spain can only call for special comment if it can be shown that the Spanish Inquisitors went beyond their judicial con- temporaries in its application. This is the reverse of the fact."[7] Salvador de Madariaga, no apologist for the Church, writes: "The idea that it [the Inquisition] was a dark institution bent on denying the human spirit . . . is a superstition of some Protestants and free-thinkers which free-thinking free-thinkers should avoid."[8] He insists that we place the Spanish Inquisi- tion in its historical setting, which included Protestant John Calvin's burn- ing of the Spaniard Servetus, Mary Tudor's measures against Protestants in England, Elizabeth's occasional burning of dissenters, and the witch hunts of England, Germany, and, later, New England. He says: "England hanged proportionately thirty to fifty times more persons for witchcraft than the Spanish Inquisition in the Indies burned for heresy." Madariaga may be exaggerating but modern scholars generally agree that in any com- parison of the Spanish Inquisition's record with that of northern Europe, Spain does not fare badly. Furthermore, as Irving A. Leonard notes: "To the Inquisition's eternal credit, *it kept records*—which is more, apparently, than was done in the Tower of London."

The convictions which created the Inquisition, and which were in turn intensified by it, made the next two steps inevitable—the final expul- sion of the Moslems and the exile of the Jews. The historic Spanish toler- ance which gladly accepted the skills and insights of Jews and Moslems was ended. Isabella and her advisers would accept no compromise. The army of Castile attacked Granada, the last Spanish stronghold of Moslem power, now weakened by internal strife. In 1492 the Alhambra and the kingdom of Granada fell to Castile. The terms of peace were generous: Moslems could remain, retain their property, live under their own laws, and worship as they pleased. But the Spaniards did not honor their prom- ises. The gentler counsels of those who respected the industrious Moslems

[7] Havelock Ellis: *The Soul of Spain* (Boston: Houghton Mifflin Co.; 1908), p. 42.
[8] Salvador de Madariaga, *op. cit.*, p. 37.

could not stand against the crusading zeal of such men as Cardinal Jiménez de Cisneros, who offered the infidels a choice between conversion and exile. The furious Moslem uprisings that ensued were crushed with much bloodshed, and in 1502 a Castilian edict decreed exile for all Moslems who refused to abjure their faith and accept Christianity. Meanwhile, in Aragon Ferdinand yielded to the persuasions of employers of Moslem farmhands and artisans, permitted them to remain, and relieved them from the discipline of the Inquisition.

In the same year that Granada fell, came the edict against the Jews, who were compelled to accept Christianity or leave Spain within four months. Some were baptized, and they and their sons were hounded by suspicion for generations to come. Others sacrificed their goods at forced sales, quit the land which had been theirs and their fathers' for centuries, and established new homes in the Mediterranean world and in Europe. By conservative estimates there were at least 200,000 of those exiles.

The pity of it, seen from the vantage of later years, is as much for Spain as for the exiled Moslems and Jews. Spain could ill afford their loss. For 800 years the finest of Moslem skills had been contributed to the peninsula, and for at least 1,000 years Jews had enriched cultural and economic life. Spain, in one year's folly, lost thousands she could not spare. But it is well to remember that England had expelled her Jews 200 years before Isabella.

Then, still in 1492, an event occurred which was to remake the world. An expedition chartered by Castile and headed by Columbus discovered the New World of America. We deal with Columbus in a later chapter, and simply note here the luster his feat lent the reign of Their Catholic Majesties—and chiefly Isabella, for it was her project, and Columbus was her Admiral.

No account of the reign of Ferdinand and Isabella can omit reference to the towering figure of Francisco Jiménez de Cisneros, whose convictions and vast energy did much to shape the emerging nation of Spain. Born in 1436 and educated at Salamanca, he took holy orders and made his pilgrimage to Rome in 1459, then returned to serve the Church. First repulsed and then given high preferment, he was overcome by a sense of sin and sought release in a Franciscan monastery in Toledo where he observed the most rigid regime of fasting, scourging, and prayer. In 1492 Cardinal Pedro de Mendoza of Toledo, admiring the emaciated friar for the piety which he himself did not possess, nominated him as confessor to Isabella. Jiménez resisted the appointment at first but finally accepted on condition that he enjoy no royal luxury and be free to speak his mind. As titular chief of the Franciscans, he instituted so rigorous a purge of the order as to drive many of its more worldly members from the country. In 1495, informed by Isabella of his appointment by the Pope as Cardinal Archbishop of Toledo and Primate of Spain, he rushed from her presence, muttering (so legend has it): "Only a woman could have thought of that," and refused to return for six months. Finally yielding to the Queen's importunities, Jiménez stripped the archiepiscopal palace in Toledo of its luxurious trappings and enforced the Franciscan discipline;

he himself slept on the hard floor, ate the roughest of food, and wore the coarse habit of his order under the gold brocade of the Cardinal's office.

When in 1499 the Queen ordered Jiménez to take charge of the Christianization of the Moslems in the south, he met the stout resistance of the Archbishop of Granada, who sought to convert the infidels by peaceful persuasion. There was little peace in the tortured soul of Jiménez, who demanded immediate baptism of the unbelievers, thus provoking fresh violence which led to their wholesale expulsion in 1502. It remained for Jiménez to serve his nation during the troubled years following Isabella's death in 1504, twice acting for brief periods as regent and helping to hold the nation together until the accession of Isabella's grandson Charles in 1517. He died that same year at the age of eighty-one. Churchman, statesman, scholar, he was a figure of fanatical integrity at the dawn of Spain's Golden Age.

THE GOLDEN AGE OF SPAIN

Spain's greatest age was the *siglo de oro,* the "Century of Gold," spanning most of the sixteenth and part of the seventeenth centuries. Two great kings, Charles I and Philip II, gave vision and unity during this period. Their captains moved from conquest to conquest until the flag of Spain was raised over the greatest empire the world had yet known. Triumphs abroad excited creation at home: it was the age of the greatest painters, novelists, and dramatists in Spanish history.

Politically, this period brought unity to Spain. Isabella's death in 1504 left the throne of Castile to her twenty-five-year-old daughter Juana, "the Mad," but her uncertain mental state made it expedient for Ferdinand, still King of Aragon, to act as regent of Castile. Meanwhile Juana married Philip, "the Handsome," of the Hapsburg dynasty (and thereby further involved Spain in Europe's dynastic quarrels). In 1506 that ambitious young man pushed his father-in-law aside, and assumed the throne of Castile as Philip I, but died within a year. With Juana's insanity now well advanced, Ferdinand returned as regent, a post which he occupied until his death in 1516. After a brief regency under Cardinal Jiménez de Cisneros, Juana's and Philip's son Charles returned from his schooling in Flanders, and in 1516 the sixteen-year-old boy was crowned as Charles I of united Spain. His dynastic inheritance was generous: from his mother he received clear title to the dual throne of his grandparents Ferdinand and Isabella; through his father he was the legatee of the Holy Roman Emperor Maximilian and received as well the Burgundian possessions of his paternal grandmother. Three years after his crowning as Charles I of Spain, he was elected Holy Roman Emperor Charles V. Thus, as a lad of nineteen, he was the nominal ruler—either through direct inheritance or through his ephemeral imperial title—of much of Europe.[9] These

9 Here the reader is again reminded of that anomalous medieval Holy Roman Empire, with its nostalgic appeal to the grandeur of Rome and to unity in the Catholic faith, which took form in the tenth century and gradually lost all but nominal control over quarreling German princes—a creation not conspicuously Holy, not at all Roman, and only haltingly an Empire.

multiple honors with their unlimited pageantry flattered the pride of Charles's subjects and gave them a new sense of national destiny.

As Holy Roman Emperor, Charles was a dubious success. German nobles outwitted him. Protestant leaders, inspired by Martin Luther, won victory after victory. Popes often opposed him in rivalry for temporal control of Italy. Charles ruled as Emperor for almost forty years; for at least twelve of those years war raged between Spain and France, and the years of peace were little better than periods of armed truce, during which Spain served as the catspaw for the Hapsburgs. Meanwhile, Spanish America's gold and silver paid the bills for Charles's imperial magnificence and costly wars.

But as Charles I of Spain, he had a brilliant reign. Each year brought new triumphs in America. The flow of gold and silver increased. The exacting tasks of Europe did not prevent Charles from giving wise rule to his transatlantic empire. He used able counselors and appointed worthy administrators. He effectively consolidated the victories of his stalwart soldiers and laid the foundation for what was, up to that time, the greatest and the most skillfully governed of imperial domains. But the cares of empire finally worked his undoing. In 1556 he abdicated as King of Spain, retired to a monastery, and committed his throne to his son, Philip II. He renounced his shadowy imperial throne in 1558 and died the same year.

Philip II ruled for forty-two years (1556–98). Under his able but erratic hand Spain found national unity and consolidated her hold upon the American empire. But the treasure of America as well as money expensively borrowed from Europe's bankers were swallowed up by his almost unceasing wars with France, the Low Countries, the Turks, and England. Denied the imperial honors of his father, he was determined to assert Spain's major role in Europe, but his efforts were disastrous. The climax of his defeats came in 1588, when his Invincible Armada was almost completely destroyed by England. His European policy was colored and dominated by the fervor of his Catholicism. Philip thought himself "the right arm of God," ordained to extirpate Protestant error and to restore religious unity to Europe. However, despite his Catholic faith, he could fight and defeat the Pope for mastery of Italy. Within Spain he waged a relentless war of extermination against the Moriscos, the nominally converted Moslems. In 1580 he laid successful claim to the throne of Portugal and inaugurated a joint rule which lasted for sixty years. Despite these distractions Philip's rule of Spain and her American domains was constructive.

In matters of religion, sixteenth-century Spain continued in the spirit of the crusades that had long engaged her. Catholic Spain, quit of Moslem and Jew, now had to contend with a new threat to her spiritual unity. In 1517 Martin Luther nailed his theses on the church door of Wittenberg. The Protestant infection spread through Germany, France, England, and Scandinavia, and finally reached Spain itself. Scattered Protestant groups appeared in Seville, Valladolid, and elsewhere, arousing the lively fears of all devoted Spaniards. "The Latin spirit," writes

Menéndez y Pelayo, "quickened by the Renaissance, protested with un-wonted violence against the Reformation which was the legitimate daughter of Teutonic individualism. . . . It was . . . intolerance, if you will, but a noble and redeeming intolerance."

Spain gave two answers to Martin Luther and the Protestants: one negative, the intensified attack of the Inquisition against all who deviated from Catholic doctrine; the other positive, the zealous spiritual reform within the Catholic Church itself. Antedating by more than a half century the Catholic Counter Reformation, which was given substance by the Council of Trent (1545–63), the reforms within Spain were inspired by Isabella and her intrepid confessor, Jiménez de Cisneros. During the last years of the fifteenth and the first years of the sixteenth centuries, there were heroic efforts to cleanse the religious orders and the secular clergy. After Luther and his followers had appeared, this process of purification was accelerated.

One aspect of this rebirth of religious zeal was the kindling of mysticism in the sixteenth century. Not new in Spanish religious experi-ence, mysticism had deep roots in the dark days of Moslem occupation, when devoted Christians sought a faith which surmounted national humili-ation. Notable among the earlier mystics was thirteenth-century Ramón Lull of Mallorca. He was a poet of insight, a philosopher of daring, and a student of geometry, astronomy, physics, chemistry, and anthropology. He wrote voluminously on all these subjects. His religious experience was profound. He stressed direct communication with God through prayer, demanded renunciation of the world, and found joy in the ecstasy of a purified soul.

Of the mystics who appeared in the sixteenth century, St. Theresa of Ávila (1515–82) was one of the greatest. To her came the vision of the wounded Christ; every worldly ambition died within her; the cross of her rosary was snatched from her hand, then returned to her with jewels more brilliant than diamonds, visible to her alone. She saw the hated Protestants making inroads into Spain, winning converts, establish-ing churches. The explanation for this apostasy she found in the relaxation of discipline within the religious orders. She founded the new order of Barefoot Carmelites, whose discipline required rope sandals, straw beds, spartan cloisters, and dependence upon alms. She established convents and monasteries, which she ruled with a strong hand but a heart of mercy. She brought religion down to common life: "God," she wrote, "walks among the pots and the pans." In Ávila, St. John of the Cross (1542–91) carried on the work which Theresa had begun. Another great mystic was Luis de León (1527–91), a poet whose verses are still treasured, a teacher of theology at the University of Salamanca, a man of intellectual vigor and spiritual insight. His textual criticisms of the Vulgate version of the Bible and the jealousy of his colleagues brought him imprisonment for five years at the hands of the Inquisition. To this day no bride in Spain feels properly married unless her gifts include a fine copy of Luis de León's *La perfecta casada,* "The Perfect Bride."

The Society of Jesus was sixteenth-century Spain's most militant, positive, and effective reaffirmation of faith. It emerged as the fulfillment of the reforming ardor of Isabella and Jiménez, as the vehicle for carrying the new zeal of an aroused Church to the ends of the earth. Here we meet the stalwart figure of Ignatius Loyola (1491–1556), an idler at the court until he was thirty, when he was converted and dedicated to religion. Loyola studied theology, sought unsuccessfully to make a pilgrimage to Jerusalem, donned sackcloth and preached in the streets, thus encountering the hostility of the Inquisition, which opposed all that was new. He gathered six companions, who assumed vows of poverty and chastity and offered their services to the Pope. In 1539 the Society of Jesus was recognized by Rome. Its fight for the faith could not be confined to the cloisters but must be waged in the open streets. The Society's influence spread, despite attacks by other orders, suspicion of the Inquisition, and the hostility of monarchs who did not wish popes exalted above kings. The missionaries of the Society carried the Cross with heroism to India, China, and America and proved themselves the most competent, zealous, and consistent of the emissaries of religion.

The Spain that set its stamp upon America was thus deeply in earnest about religion. Of course, the Spaniards were intent upon conquest and empire, upon winning gold and silver and trade, but they also had a genuine zeal for carrying the true faith to the ends of the world. The conquest and colonization of Spanish America cannot be understood except in the light of this compulsion.

Economically, Spain was a poor and backward land in the sixteenth century. The adding of America to its empire and the quick flow of gold and silver which followed brought a fleeting prosperity which was more than canceled by inflation and the drain of European wars. There may have been about 6 million Spaniards at the beginning of the century and a million more by the end of it, but the lot of all except the most fortunate was meager.

Spain's economy was of the colonial pattern which she transferred to America, an economy dependent upon production of raw materials and the buying of finished goods from industrialized lands. But even as a producer of raw materials, Spain was backward. Her agriculture was the most retarded of western Europe; it was burdened by the unwieldy latifundia, the concentration of land in the hands of a few, with little incentive to effective use or improvement. Another handicap upon agriculture was the monopoly conceded to the *mesta,* the corporation of sheepmen who for centuries had driven their flocks across the central plateau, trampled upon cultivated fields, and, by stripping hillside slopes of protective vegetation, speeded erosion. Even the mines of Spain with their iron, copper, and mercury were worked fitfully. The great landholders blocked mining, and the government did little to encourage it.

Industrially, Spain lagged far behind France, the Low Countries, and England. There was a brief flurry of industrial activity under the first impact of the new American trade. The output of textiles, clothing, leather goods, arms, and other items of common use was stimulated, but the results were unimportant compared with those of the rest of western Europe. Spanish textile production in the sixteenth century never equaled that of the Flemish city of Bruges. Spain continued to export much wool and to buy back finished cloth. Although trade increased, Spain remained a middleman, handling raw materials and finished goods like a merchant and leaving the larger profits to industrialized nations.

All these economic ills were intensified by the shortage of labor for field, mine, and factory. The expulsion of Moslems and Jews had already crippled the economy by removing skillful farmers, miners, artisans, and managers. This shortage of man power was aggravated as the more venturesome abandoned their homeland to seek glory and profit overseas.

It was therefore a poor Spain that took over potentially rich America and transferred its economic policies to conquered lands. Spain, obsessed with the promise of gold and silver, spent her riches on foolish battles and did not learn the hard lesson that lasting wealth must come from fruitful farms, active mines, and busy looms.

Spain's social organization in the sixteenth century was the product of shifts in population and power. The landed nobility, chief holders of power, had gradually been drawn into the cities to constitute the social and economic core of the nation. This powerful handful of dukes, counts, and marquises now found their ranks enlarged by newcomers whose titles were bought to the profit of the Crown. The *hidalgos*, least of the nobles, multiplied at such a pace that in 1541, one out of eight taxpayers in Castile proudly claimed such rank. Meanwhile, the lot of lesser men had improved only a little. The social inequities of Spain provoked exodus to the promised land of America.

The chief cities presented a brave front in the prodigal luxury of the favored classes, the riotous displays on feast days, the enthusiasm of bullfights and carnivals. But Spain was still unkempt and unsanitary. Paved streets were limited to Madrid, Seville, and Barcelona. The water supplies of cities and towns were inadequate. Those who bathed were eyed with suspicion, for only Moslems indulged in that dubious practice.

The Golden Age of Spanish arts and letters was a burst of creative enthusiasm born of national elation. Spain, long a pupil of the Moslems, now became a teacher and a leader. Schools and scholars multiplied. Eight universities existed at the beginning of the sixteenth century; twenty-six were added in little more than a hundred years. Students of law, theology, and medicine flocked from all parts of Spain and all Europe to Salamanca, Alcalá de Henares, and Valladolid. Salamanca, brilliant ever since its founding in the thirteenth century, had almost 7,000 students by 1550. Then came numerous Jesuit colleges which were centers for classical studies. The printing presses turned out many books; great libraries abounded. The century produced Luis Vives (1492–1540), the friend of Erasmus who delved into psychology long before Francis Bacon and Descartes, and who anticipated Bacon's emphasis upon the validity of reasoning from the clear facts of nature and experience rather than from preconceived theories, thereby winning for himself a high place among the first exponents of empiricism. Spain's imperial ventures encouraged new attention to international law, history, geography, and the natural sciences. Spanish scholars showed prowess in all these fields.

Spanish literature reached its peak in this period. It had been acquiring momentum for three centuries. By the twelfth and thirteenth centuries a number of epic poems had celebrated the great deeds of Christian knights, and of these *The Song of the Cid* had helped to give form to the Spanish language. In the early sixteenth century came the flood of romances of chivalry, among which *Amadis of Gaul* lasted longest, traveled farthest, and was most widely imitated. By 1550 more than fifty such romances were eagerly passed from hand to hand.[1] Spain now also developed a national theater, with a host of known and unknown writers of plays. Conspicuous among these was Lope de Vega (1562–1635), notable for exuberance and artistry but also for productivity—almost 500 of his plays survive to this day, probably less than a third of his production.

It was the Golden Age of the novel. The imitators of *Amadis of Gaul* wrote reams of tales of far-off lands, of knights and villains and fair maidens—the "comic books" of their time. Spain's unique contribution to European literature was the picaresque novel, which told of rogues and knaves—*Lazarillo de Tormes* (1554) is a conspicuous example. The picaresque influence is clear in Henry Fielding's *Tom Jones* and Tobias Smollett's *Roderick Random*. The greatest of all Spanish novelists, if not the greatest of the world, was Miguel de Cervantes Saavedra (1547–1616). A son of poverty, Cervantes joined the army and fought the Turks in the battle of Lepanto, where he lost the use of his left hand "for the greater glory of the right," and was captured by the Moslems and held for five years as a prisoner in Algiers. He then wrote plays without collecting royalties, was jailed for debt once or twice, and finally in 1605, at the age of fifty-eight, published *Don Quixote,* a best seller in almost every language of the world ever since. This was Cervantes's ridicule of the novels of chivalry with all their posturings, but it was itself the finest of all novels of chivalry. In fact, Cervantes appropriated and combined the three current types of novel: the chivalrous, the pastoral, and the picaresque. In *Don Quixote* were humor, pathos, and understanding, with deft prickings of the pompous and compassion for the weak, as well as expert delineation of courtesans, nobles, peasants, priests, robbers, and rogues. "It is," writes Havelock Ellis, "a story-book that a child may enjoy, a tragicomedy that only the wisest can fully understand."

1 "The *Four Books of Amadis of Gaul* remained throughout the sixteenth century the favorite of innumerable readers, the manual of good taste, the model of valor and nobility, and the oracle of elegant conversation. To what extent its influence lingers in the ceremonial courtesy and courtly manners still practiced by the cultured elements of Hispanic society on both sides of the Atlantic is an interesting subject for speculation. Of more immediate interest is the certainty that the vista of exotic lands, strange peoples, and hidden wealth offered by the novel to contemporary conquistadores could not fail to lure them on to fantastic adventures abroad in the suddenly expanded world in which they lived." Irving A. Leonard: *Books of the Brave*, p. 17. Reprinted by permission of the publishers, Harvard University Press, Cambridge, Mass.; copyright 1949 by The President and Fellows of Harvard College.

In architecture, sixteenth-century Spain was the rich legatee of Greece, Rome, Islam, France, and Italy. For more than 1,000 years the gifts of other lands had been brought to Spain. The Spain that was now to shape America was rich beyond description in graceful and powerful churches, palaces, and public buildings. Some bore the pattern of the Romanesque, with its rounded arches and massive walls, reflecting the sturdy pride of the first victorious years of the Reconquest. A notable example is the cathedral of Santiago de Compostela, with its *Pórtico de la Gloria*. Others showed the French influence in the Gothic pointed arches and vaults of the churches of Burgos, Toledo, Barcelona, Palma de Mallorca, Segovia, Seville, and León. León's cathedral, the purest Gothic of them all, reflects the spirit of Amiens and Chartres in its airy and lacy grace, its effortless strength. The mark of the Moslem is almost everywhere in the geometric caprices and arabesques, the rich coloring of tile and plaster, the artistry of bare walls relieved by delicate tracery—all characteristic of the *mudéjar* style, compounded of Moslem and Christian elements.

The last influence was the Italian, which produced the plateresque—after *platero*, silversmith—with its delicate handling of decoration in wood or stone or metal. The plateresque echoed the spirit of release of the Renaissance, the freedom to roam and breathe. An American architect describes the plateresque: "Take a bit of Gothic, stir it up with a cup of Renaissance, put in two tablespoonfuls of *mudéjar*, and there you have it. There were no fixed proportions in the recipe, however. Each chef mixed the ingredients according to his own taste. A strictly Renaissance saint can stand under a Gothic canopy beside a Moorish arch and the blend is *Plateresque*. Or a Gothic finial can rise triumphant over a Moorish stalactite cornice while Renaissance cherubs play merrily about among the candelabra and the result is also *Plateresque*."[2]

The mid-sixteenth century brought an architectural interruption. Dour Philip II, intent upon fixing his stern creed on stone walls and turrets, built the Escorial on the slopes of the Guadarrama Mountains near Madrid. This bleak granite pile—combining in one structure monastery, church, palace, and mausoleum—embodied Philip's defiance to the world. In "the deathly solemnity of this ferocious Escorial" (Havelock Ellis's description) Philip renounced all that was graceful and lovely and returned to the Greco-Roman tradition as a symbol of his ascetic faith. But no sooner was Philip's body laid in the crypt of the Escorial in 1598 than Spain broke from the austerity he had imposed. Within a few years new churches were being built and the old ones were being decorated in the baroque style with its ornate facades and altars, with red, blue, and gold angels and saints and cherubs tumbling over each other in joyous confusion. The baroque and its even more riotous stepchild, the churrigueresque, were fixed upon the architecture of all Spain, and were then transferred to America, there to determine the patterns of hundreds of great and little churches from Mexico to Argentina.

[2] Trent Elwood Sanford: *The Story of Architecture in Mexico* (New York: W. W. Norton & Co.; 1947), p. 107.

Sculpture followed architecture. The carvers of wood and stone and metal contributed to the beauty and strength of the great buildings with their figures of saints and angels, carved choir stalls, and the profuse and varied decoration of chapels and tombs. The Golden Century achieved fresh sculptural distinction in the work of such masters as Berruguete and Alonso Cano.

The Golden Age gave the country a preeminent place in painting. Spain's painting had long been a borrowed art, its inspiration coming from the other lands of western Europe. Now, in her great awakening, Spain continued borrowing from the great Flemish, Dutch, and Italian masters —Frans Hals, Rubens, Rembrandt, Michelangelo, Titian, Raphael, and many others. Both Charles I and Philip II devoted much of the profit from American mines to buying the works of these masters with the result that the public and private collections of Spain, notably that of the Prado in Madrid, are among the most distinguished in the world. But there also emerged a definitely Spanish school of painters. The first painter in the new style was Spanish only by adoption. El Greco (1541–1616), "The Greek," whose real name was Domenico Theotocopuli, was born on the Greek island of Crete and did his first painting in Italy under the Italian masters. He came to Toledo in 1575 where he painted until his death forty-one years later. In Toledo, in Madrid, and in the Escorial, the pilgrim finds El Greco's portrayal of the dignity, gravity, pride, tenderness, arrogance, humility, and gallantry of Spanish character. After him came José de Ribera (1588–1656), intensely Spanish despite his debt to Titian and Caravaggio, prime interpreter of Spanish piety with all its mysticism and exaltation and haunting morbidity. Ribera's violent realism, his sculpturesque handling of figures, and his brutal portrayal of human passions later influenced the powerful twentieth-century Mexican painters, José Clemente Orozco and Diego Rivera.

The next giant was Francisco Zurbarán (1598–1661), realist and brilliant colorist notable for his portraits of monks—Carthusian, Mercedarian, Dominican. The student of Spain's gifts to America will find profit in contemplation of Zurbarán's friars and a new understanding of the benignity and wisdom of the men who carried the Cross to far lands. Perhaps the greatest of all Spanish painters was Diego Velásquez de Silva (1599–1660), who stands quite alone in the history of painting, pupil and follower of none, master and teacher of many. His work is marked by a great calmness in which no struggle appears. He was a devout Catholic and painted religious pictures of insight and beauty, with none of the torment and storm of Ribera. He was court painter to Philip IV; he painted his monarch and the various princes and princesses with candid eye, depicting their meagerness and ugliness without rancor. Superb draftsman and colorist, master of detail and mass, a realist always, he could paint the weak Hapsburgs, the drunken loafers from the streets, or the dwarfs and buffoons of the court with cool and precise deftness. He was the last of the giants in this period, although Murillo (1618–82) is still admired for his beauty of color and lively imagination.

SPAIN'S LEGACY TO AMERICA

Spanish America was created out of the bone and blood and muscle of sixteenth-century Spain—a Spain that was economically beggared, with her soil rutted and depleted, her hills stripped of trees, her people poor in goods and promise; but a Spain rich in ideas, mighty in religious conviction, justifiably proud of her place in the world.

Spain gave her language to America. Supple and robust, Spanish is one of the richest and most varied languages of the world and a fine instrument for the tenderness of the mystic or the battle cry of the warrior. It is a language whose strength and grace are attested by the poetry, drama, and fiction of old Spain and of new Spanish America. Spain gave her religion. Never has the faith of one people been transferred to another so swiftly, so generally, and with such answering enthusiasm. Spain gave her fashions of government. It is easy to criticize those fashions centuries later, but the fact remains that the Spanish empire operated with solid success for 300 years. Spain gave her high tradition of valor. One may scoff at the bombast and hypocrisy of the knights of Castile, but their greatness cannot be denied. There was an epic quality to their tenacity, of which Spanish America is a legatee. Spain gave her individualism, manifested in the mother country in obstinate regionalism, in an almost anarchical emphasis upon the separate rights of each tiny community and city. It was an individualism that stimulated a rough democracy. No matter what social distances separated king and peasant, there remained the basic assumption of the integrity of the individual. George Borrow, in 1843, wrote of the Spaniard: "No people in the world exhibit a juster feeling of what is due to the dignity of human nature. . . . [Spain] is one of the few countries in Europe where poverty is not treated with contempt, and, I may add, where the wealthy are not blindly idolized." A modern visitor to Spain can confirm the judgment. The Spaniard, no matter how menial may be his post, carries himself with assured dignity. Servants in home or hotel, underpaid and overworked, have no obsequiousness. Courtesy is given; courtesy is expected. Spain left her mark on the social customs of the people of Spanish America. This is revealed in exaggerated formalism and attention to ceremony, in the stubborn contempt for manual labor. Spain, having learned from the Moslems, hid her women behind walls and screens and Spanish America followed her example.

Spain passed on to America that which she herself had received from Greek and Roman, Visigoth and Moslem, Italian and Frenchman.

PORTUGAL

The story of Portugal parallels that of Spain. Its land has the same contours, the same assets and liabilities. It was peopled and shaped by the same Iberians, Celts, Phoenicians, Greeks, Carthaginians, Romans, Visigoths, and Moslems. Its language and religion were taught by the same Roman teachers. But it early developed its own personality and language. Portugal's separate course was necessitated and encouraged by its exposed position on the Atlantic coast, where it was subject to foreign meddling. For six centuries Portugal's history has been chiefly determined by its great and good friend, England.

Independent Portugal[3] was born of the Christian Reconquest. The parting of the ways began in the eleventh century, a by-product of the dramatic southern thrust of Castile and León. French recruits joined the crusading armies against the Moslems; one of them, Henry of Burgundy, married the daughter of the King of Castile and León and was appointed Count of Portugal—but as a subject of the Castilian kings. The House of Burgundy, thus launched, presided for three centuries over the emerging kingdom of Portugal. The successive Counts of Portugal had two long battles to fight: one with Castile, to win independence; the second with the Moslems, to achieve unity. The Moslems were driven from Lisbon in 1147; and in 1178 the Pope recognized Portugal's king. In 1249 the Moslems yielded southern Algarve. Castile was defeated in 1385 by a Portuguese army reinforced by English recruits. From then on, English influence dominated Portugal. The French House of Burgundy was ousted and John I was installed, the first of the Aviz dynasty which ruled Portugal throughout the two centuries of its greatest glory. King John, mindful of his debt to his English allies, signed the Treaty of Windsor in 1386, assuring "an inviolable, eternal, solid, perpetual and true league of friendship, alliance and union" between grateful Portugal and stronger England. This alliance was confirmed by John's marriage to the daughter of John of Gaunt.

John I's reign (1385–1433) marks the rise of Portugal to power. He imposed order upon his kingdom, fought off the Spaniards, and struck at the Moslems in North Africa, capturing Ceuta in 1415. His impressive success was augmented by the brilliant work of his son, who is known to history as Henry the Navigator (1394–1460). Henry had fought bravely at Ceuta, and at twenty-two he was appointed governor of Algarve. A man of unbounded curiosity, he gathered about him men of many nations to tell of far-off lands. He set out promptly to prepare for the bold expeditions which were to found Portugal's maritime empire: he assembled a staff of geographers, map makers, navigators, and ship designers; and he borrowed enormously from kings, bankers, and merchants. Henry's interest was scientific—he would learn about the world. It was economic—he would gather the wealth of the East. And it was religious—he would strike more blows against the enemies of Christ. His first expeditions fixed Portuguese control on the Azores, the Canaries, and the Cape Verde Islands. He repeatedly dispatched ships down the African coast, a forlorn and stormy waste. By the time of his death his caravels had pushed beyond Cape Verde, and he had convinced his countrymen that there was a way to India around the continent of Africa.

[3] The name comes from Portucalia, which was derived from Portus Cale, a Roman outpost later incorporated into the city of Oporto.

Zeal for exploration outlived Henry the Navigator. Adventurers continued to explore the African coast and to push into the heart of the continent. Trade in gold, ivory, and slaves increased. In 1487 a campaign was launched to discover the fabulous Prester John, a legendary Christian monarch variously reported to reign in the heart of Africa or Asia. One of these expeditions, under Bartholomeu Dias, doubled the Cape of Good Hope, explored the African east coast, and entered the Indian Sea. But at last it was forced by a mutiny to return home.

Meanwhile, an obscure Italian, Christopher Columbus, lingered in the Portuguese court seeking funds with which to finance a westward expedition to India, China, Japan. Portugal, daydreaming of India's treasure almost within its reach by the shorter eastern route, ignored Columbus and permitted him to sail under the Spanish flag. His triumphs for Spain were humiliating to Portugal, but shortly a seemingly greater feat stirred national pride. In 1497 Vasco da Gama, with four ships and 168 men, pushed around the Cape of Good Hope, explored the eastern coast of Africa, collected fabulous tales, fought the Moslems, reached India, and prudently returned to Lisbon in 1499 after a voyage of two years and two months. It was an exploit, the Portuguese thought, which outshone that of Columbus, who returned empty-handed from his American journeys, while Vasco da Gama brought pepper, cloves, nutmeg, cinnamon, and precious stones. But, a year later, in 1500, Portugal also staked out its claim in America by the discovery of Brazil—a chapter to which we will return later. Sixteenth-century Portugal could then boast of an empire reaching more than halfway around the world, from Brazil to the China Sea.[4]

We are here concerned with Portugal's course during the fifteenth and sixteenth centuries, the background against which the settlement of Brazil must be understood. Politically, Portugal's record stands in melancholy contrast to that of Spain. It boasts no such impressive monarchs as Isabella, Charles I, or Philip II. The story of the House of Aviz is one of tragic disintegration and finally disastrous failure. It began well with John I (1385–1433), called "John the Great," a brave soldier, an able administrator, and a sensitive patron of arts and letters. Next came Alfonso V (1438–81), an extravagant fellow whose African adventures beggared the nation and who was overshadowed in popular esteem by Henry the Navigator. Then the throne passed to John II (1481–95), known as "John the Perfect," an astute, arrogant king who magnified his own office by stripping the power of parliament and liquidating the powerful nobles. The Duke of Braganza, master of over fifty cities and possessor of a private army of 300 horsemen and 10,000 foot soldiers, was the most notable of John's many victims. John quarreled with the Vatican, sought greater control of the clergy, but failed to establish such power over the Church as was

---

[4] It is interesting to recall that vestigial remnants of this once vast empire have remained in Portuguese hands down to the present time: the six-square-mile Macao in China, a part of the island of Timor off the northern coast of Australia, the Cape Verde Islands and the Azores in the Atlantic, and the African colonies—almost 800,000 square miles in area—of Guinea, Angola, and Mozambique. (Three pinpoint possessions in western India, including Goa, were lost to India in 1961.)

won by the Spanish kings. John, seizing advantage from Spain's expulsion of the Jews in 1492, invited many thousands to seek refuge in Portugal, collected generous fees for his hospitality, and then mistreated those whom he had succored. There followed Manoel I (1495–1521), "The Fortunate," an energetic, austere, and reasonably successful king, whose reign included some of the more spectacular imperial adventures. He was succeeded by John III (1521–57), also dubbed "The Fortunate," a man of limited mentality, vast extravagance, and passionate piety, who installed the Inquisition in 1536 and brought in the Jesuits in 1540. By the time of his death in 1557 the Portuguese Crown was in low repute.

In 1568, after eleven years of stormy regencies, fourteen-year-old Sebastian was installed for ten years of capricious rule. The boy was an ill-balanced religious fanatic who plumed himself on his role as defender of the faith against Moslem infidels. Physically, spiritually, and mentally, Sebastian seems to have represented the end result of the bad habits of the Portuguese court. Dire diseases kept him in the hands of watchful physicians, but nothing could quench his crusading fire. In order to gather the greatest army Portugal had ever thrown into a holy cause, Sebastian appealed to his uncle, Philip II of Spain, from whom he received much good advice but no gold. He gathered up what money he could find, stripped the national treasury, took funds held in trust for orphans, borrowed from German bankers and from subject kings of India, levied new taxes upon converted Jews, and in 1578—at the age of twenty-four—led an armada of 500 ships with a fighting force of some 20,000 men across the Mediterranean. The Moslem armies, with far less fanfare, were ready for them. The well-advertised crusade ended in a rout. Some 8,000 of Sebastian's men were killed, twice that number were captured and carried into slavery, and among the casualties was King Sebastian himself. This was the Battle of Alcazar-Kebir.[5]

Sebastian's death left the House of Aviz in desperate plight; its only survivor was the decrepit sixty-six-year-old Cardinal Henry, brother of John III. The prelate did what he could to hold the kingdom together and to block the designs of Philip II of Spain to add the Portuguese throne to his own. The Cardinal toyed with the idea of marrying and nursed the wan hope of producing an heir, a project sensibly discouraged by the Pope and the sickly prelate's godly counselors. That debate and the House of Aviz were ended by Henry's death in 1580. Philip II shortly arrived with soldiers to crush opposition, and with gold to buy the nobles' votes; he installed himself as King of Portugal, and the dual rule lasted sixty years. The days of Portuguese glory were done.

There were marked contrasts between Portugal and Spain. Their religion was a case in point. The Church of Portugal had developed alongside that of Spain, but there were marked divergences. The Portuguese

[5] The cult of "Sebastianism" arose from this event. Faithful servants of the crusader-king would not believe that he was dead. At least four impostors later appeared to claim the throne, each purporting to be Sebastian returned from death. For more than three centuries, the cult flourished in Europe and Brazil.

clergy were less vigorous, devout, and intelligent. As compared with the
Castilian, the Portuguese Church had suffered a greater corruption from
the Moslems, the African Negroes, and the various aliens who drifted into
their exposed nation. The astute Brazilian Gilberto Freyre writes that
Portuguese religion was not "the hard and rigid system of the Reformed
countries of the north or even the dramatic Catholicism of Castile itself;
theirs was a liturgy social rather than religious, a softened, lyric Christianity
with many phallic and animistic reminiscences of the pagan cults." In
other ways Portugal followed Spain: it installed the Inquisition in 1536,
welcomed the Jesuits in 1540, shared something of the new vitality which
marked the Spanish Church. But Portugal produced no religious leaders
comparable to Isabella, Cardinal Jiménez, Ignatius Loyola, Theresa of
Ávila, or Luis de León. It rose to no such spiritual or intellectual dignity
as marked Spain's Golden Age.

For Portugal, the sixteenth century was a period of decline—economic, political, social, and spiritual. The reasons were various. First, the
kings of the House of Aviz were mediocre and uninspired. Nor were their
aides men of leadership. Second, Portugal had been weakened by excessive
importation of Negro slaves since the 1440's, until the southern district of
Algarve was more Negro than white and most of the nation depended upon
slave labor. This slavery increased the already too common distaste for
manual labor and discouraged inventiveness and industry. Third, the expulsion of Moslems and Jews by the beginning of the sixteenth century
had, as in Spain, removed the ablest farmers, artisans, and technicians.
Fourth, Portugal, whose economy had been seriously disrupted by the quick
wealth of India and the East, indulged in wanton extravagance, neglected
her own productive fields and used the profits from spices to buy meat,
corn, cheese, and fish from Flanders. The little farms fell into disuse and
speedily passed into the hands of great and lazy landholders. Manufacturing, never important, was almost completely forgotten. By 1530 the
prosperity which had worked such corruption tapered off as profits from
spices failed. Fifth, the meager man power of Portugal—her population in
1500 was probably no more than a million—was depleted by futile and
costly crusades against the Moslems, and by migrations to the newly established colonies in America, Africa, and Asia. A significant commentary
on the energy of the Portuguese is the fact that a common word for "work"
is *mourejar,* "to work like a Moor."

Portugal enjoyed a brief hour of glory in letters and the fine arts.
A few painters, sculptors, and architects exhibited vigor and skill but it
was only in letters that Portugal even remotely kept pace with Spain.
Notable work was done by the dramatist and poet Gil Vicente (1470–
1536), much of whose writing was in Castilian; but the greatest name
was that of Luís de Camões (1524–79) whose epic poem *The Lusiads,*
commemorating the exploits of Vasco da Gama, holds a firm place among
the great works of all the centuries.

Thus Portugal gave shape to the new land of Brazil, transferring to
it the easy indolence and tolerance of the motherland. Portugal was well

equipped by her long experience with Negro and Moslem to make the necessary adjustment to tropical areas, to carry over her good-natured acceptance of all races to a colony that would prove a gigantic melting pot of Indian, Negro, and white. A Brazilian describes the Portuguese settler in America: "In certain respects he resembles the Englishman, in others the Spaniard. A Spaniard without the warlike flame or the dramatic orthodoxy of the conquistador of Mexico and Peru; an Englishman without the harsh lineament of the Puritan. The compromiser type. With no absolute ideals, with no unyielding prejudices . . . [of] greater social plasticity . . . as compared with any other European colonizer."[6]

Portugal had her brief hour of glory, then slipped back into the third rank of European powers. Even that brief hour sufficed to fix her language and habits upon the most extended and most populous nation of the New World. Meanwhile, says Freyre, "Portugal continued to stand on tiptoe in an effort to appear to be one of the great European powers."

[6] Gilberto Freyre: *The Masters and the Slaves* (New York: Alfred A. Knopf, Inc.; 1946), p. 185.

Chapter 4

THE AFRICAN BACKGROUND

Every Brazilian, even the light-skinned fair-haired one, carries about with him on his soul, when not on soul and body alike . . . the shadow, or at least the birthmark, of the aborigine or the Negro. Along the seaboard . . . it is chiefly the Negro. The influence of the African, either direct or vague and remote. . . . In everything that is a sincere expression of our lives, we almost all of us bear the mark of that influence.[1]

The blood of Africa flows in the New World. Brought to western shores in chains, uncounted millions of Negroes have remained to share their culture, their personality, and the blackness of their skin with their English or Iberian hosts. Today 50 million or more citizens of the Americas are of African descent, and their contribution to the culture of the Western Hemisphere must be taken into account.

The black man seized from his home in Dahomey, the Gold Coast, or Angola, shackled and sold to a slaver and packed into the eighteen inches between the decks of his ship in a space little larger than a grave, who survived weeks of disease, stench, and frenzy—such a black man had little sense of a destiny beyond this malignant journey. He would scarcely have styled himself as a builder of a New World—but such he was. From the cotton fields of Georgia to the coffee plantations of São Paulo, he was —to use Gilberto Freyre's description—"the white man's greatest and most plastic collaborator in the task of agrarian colonization."

Acceptance of the Negro as a full partner in the creation of the New World of America is still resisted by racists, especially in the United States; clinging to the conviction of the inherent superiority of what Adolf Hitler called the "Aryan," this slowly decreasing company has persisted in believing that the white man was born to rule the world; that the Negro came to America from savagery with nothing to offer but his brawn; that he did what he was told, learned whatever he knew from the white man; that he had no cultural past or future, and must remain an inferior being. The

[1] Gilberto Freyre: *The Masters and the Slaves* (New York: Alfred A. Knopf, Inc.; 1946), p. 278.

Latin American would seldom phrase it that way; for there is an imponderable difference in the way he feels about the Negro. Among most of the people of the southern republics, a Negro is first a citizen, second a Negro. Ethnologists in Brazil, for example, have sometimes been hard put to it to discover whether a given distinguished artist or intellectual a century or so before was Negro, white, or mulatto—because the person was, first of all, a distinguished Brazilian, and his race seemed of no consequence to the historian. If the "color line" does not quite disappear south of the Rio Grande, at least it loses its sharpness: many Brazilians, Cubans, and all Haitians, know that they have some African blood in their veins.

The roots of this subtle difference in the place of the Negro, north and south, go back to the Pilgrims and the conquistadores. The first Anglo-Saxons brought their women with them, the Spanish and Portuguese did not. English colonists—when they had a choice—tended to choose slaves for animal strength, much needed on the plantations; and they preferred those who had worked in the fields, especially the cotton fields, of West Africa. Spanish and Portuguese added other criteria: some slaves were selected for specific skills, such as techniques in metalworking; others, especially women, were desirable for their comeliness, their gentle and domestic nature—for many of these women were taken as true companions, or were even "elevated to mistresses of the house," and the progeny of these unions were often adopted into the family and into society, their children's children destined to become respected citizens of Brazil or Cuba.

Another difference in the attitude toward Negroes, north and south, derives from qualities and definitions of slavery. Latin America inherited patterns of slavery from Spain and Portugal, where slavery had been established for centuries. In these cultures the slave had legal and social status as a human being, involving certain specific rights and privileges as well as duties; moreover, it was often possible for the slave to improve his status, even to purchase his freedom. This pattern was carried over to the countries of the New World where, from early in their history, there were always free Negroes who had a definite place in society. To the English colonist, whose position as master over slave was a new experience, the imported Negro was no more than a chattel, with no legal and social rights as a human being, and he remained so until the abolition of slavery. There was little place in North American society for the freed Negro, and he remained an anachronism.

In the countries of Latin America the institution of slavery was certainly as cruel as it was in the United States, but perhaps with this subtle difference: while the Spaniard or the Portuguese was cruel to the *slave*, the North American was cruel to the *Negro*. And this may account in part for the somewhat more ready acceptance of the free Negro into the society of Spanish and Portuguese America.

How *much* African blood flows in the veins of Mexicans, Peruvians, Brazilians, Cubans? The search for an answer is difficult. No Latin American census has applied the criterion of race with the rigor of the United

States' tabulators, and the figures reveal little as to racial divisions. The difficulties, over a period of centuries, have been many. Negroes escaped the census whenever possible, having "the natural distrust of exploited beings." When he did not escape, the Negro would try, sometimes successfully, to pass himself as a shade lighter than he was—Negro to mulatto, or mulatto to white. White masters would hide their slaves at census time, admitting to fewer than they actually owned in order to avoid taxation.

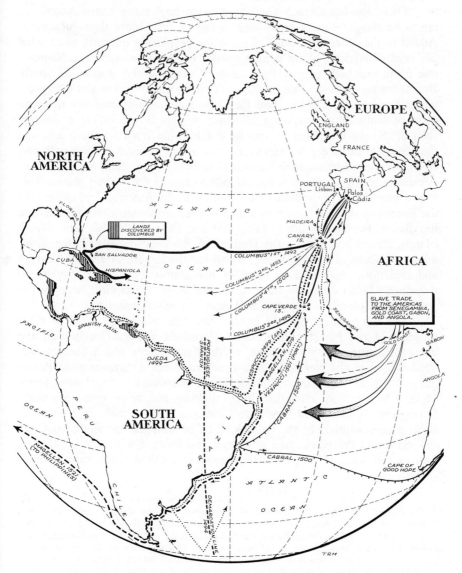

Voyages of Discovery and the Beginning of the Slave Trade

In some countries—Mexico, Colombia, and Chile, for example—census takers were not allowed to question the citizen on his racial origin. Add to these difficulties the custom, which generally prevailed, of counting as Negroes only those who were slaves. More than half the population of Latin America is of mixed ancestry, representing the largest mixture of Mongoloid, Caucasoid, and Negroid to be found anywhere in the world. The various combinations are almost endless: mulatto, mestizo, *pardo, zambo,* and dozens of others. The very problem, then, of determining "who is a Negro" is a baffling one.

There has been much conjecture as to how many Latin Americans are to be classified as Negroes—but it can be little more than guesswork. Added to the other difficulties, there is the perplexing question as to what per cent of African blood a man must have to be reckoned a Negro—one drop, one-half, or just how much? Criteria differ, north and south. But "if we see fit to say that one drop of Negro blood makes you a Negro," writes Rayford W. Logan, "and they [the Latin Americans] say that one drop of white blood makes you white, we should maintain a discreet silence." So the most that we can do is take what few data there are, add the speculations of careful observers, and arrive at some probable figures. In the Western Hemisphere there are probably more than 50 million of African descent, of whom some 20 million live in the United States. This leaves more than 30 million in the twenty Latin American republics and the European colonies and new states in the Caribbean. Certain areas are heavily on the Negro side: Haiti, and the French, English, and Dutch islands, almost completely; the Dominican Republic, largely; Panama, almost half; Cuba, a third to a half. Brazil has the largest *number* of Negroes and mulattoes: one-third or more of her almost 85 million may be so described.[2] Other countries have substantial Negro minorities: here we put Venezuela, Colombia, Ecuador, and most of Central America.

The story cannot be told in statistics. One must look into the faces of some of the fairest and proudest Brazilians and see for himself the curve of feature, the tilt of head, or the flash of eye which betrays "the shadow . . . of the Negro." For a Brazilian is not a "transplanted Portuguese." Nor are the Cubans, Mexicans, or Peruvians "transplanted Spaniards." But rather, into this huge melting pot have gone Spaniard, Portuguese, Indian—and Negro, to form new peoples with their own distinctive personalities. In the nations of Latin America the white man, the red man, and the black man have met and merged with one another to form a new kind of people: José Vasconcelos called it the *raza cósmica* —the cosmic race.

2 In Brazil, especially, is the scholar frustrated in attempts to find the truth about the Negro element. In 1890, after the fall of the empire and the abolition of slavery, Ruy Barbosa, minister of finance, ordered all documents dealing with slavery burned so that "all traces of this loathsome institution which has paralyzed . . . society . . . corrupting and polluting its moral atmosphere," might be eradicated. This was done to the sorrow of later students. The guesses on the total number of slaves imported into Brazil run from 4 million to 18 million. However, perhaps Arthur Ramos's figure of 5 million is the most reasonable estimate.

THE CONTINENT OF AFRICA

Africa, second largest of the continents with an area of 11.5 million square miles, today shelters over 300 million souls—nearly a tenth of the population of the world. This vast tableland averaging some 2,000 feet in height sprawls across the equator, reaching from the Cape of Good Hope at thirty-four degrees south latitude to the city of Tunis at thirty-seven degrees north. Its history through the centuries has been shaped by its great rivers —the Nile, the Congo, and the Zambezi, draining from the high lakes in east central Africa, and the Niger, which drains the grassy Sudan of western Africa; by the deserts and monsoon forest of southern and eastern Africa, and the dense rain forests, or jungles, which straddle the equator in central Africa, hugging the western coast; and by the Sahara Desert, which covers some 3 million square miles across the bulk of northern Africa. The rain forest and the desert were the basic challenges to man in Africa, and their conquest—one by the advent of iron tools, and the other by the camel— were crucial steps in early African history.

Phoenicians colonized the north coast of Africa as early as 1100 B.C., when they sailed across the Mediterranean from Tyre to found the city of Utica on the northern coast of Tunisia. Some 300 years later they built the city of Carthage. Herodotus tells us that these intrepid navigators— the Phoenicians—set sail from the Gulf of Suez some 600 years before the Christian era and actually circled the continent of Africa, passing through the "Pillars of Hercules" (the Strait of Gibraltar) on their way back to the delta of the Nile—a formidable journey that took them three years. Hanno, a Carthaginian, sailed south, perhaps as far as Sierra Leone, about 520 B.C. The Greeks were aware of Negro Africa from the time of Homer, who referred to "the land of the blacks." And later Aeschylus spoke of the "Ethiopians"—the ancient name for the people of mysterious Africa—who fought under Xerxes at Thermopylae in 480 B.C. Both the Greeks and the Romans colonized the north coast of Africa: the Greeks founded the city of Cyrene in about 631 B.C.; Alexander the Great founded Alexandria in 332 B.C.; and Rome conquered the Phoenician city of Carthage in 202 B.C. In A.D. 66 Emperor Nero sent centurions to find the source of the Nile River; they got as far as the land of the Dinka and the Shilluk near the bend of the Upper Nile in the northern tip of Abyssinia. Other legions apparently penetrated to the oasis of Ghadames, 500 miles south of Carthage; but the great Sahara Desert proved an impassable barrier and thwarted all other attempts by the Romans to penetrate southward into the interior of Africa. Then, early in the Christian era, the Romans introduced the camel into North Africa. In the second century A.D., Ptolemy used information gathered from Negro traders in Alexandria to prepare a map of Africa including the great lakes at the source of the Nile, and the Niger River—a map which proved to be more accurate than any to be drawn for some 1,700 years.

The Arabs arrived in Africa in the seventh century. They conquered Egypt, then moved westward to dominate, intermittently, the Berbers and the Latinized peoples of Northwest Africa. Four hundred years later, fresh hordes of Arabs, crusading for Islam, swept into North Africa. Then Moslem converts among the Berber population of Northwest Africa, taking up the banner for Islam, pushed south into the Sudan and the Senegal River basin, overthrowing Negro states along the Niger River. Old Ghana fell in 1056, and Timbuktu became the chief contact between the African and Mediterranean worlds. Thus the law of the Koran began to fuse with the indigenous customs and institutions of the Negro people. This Islamic cultural diffusion from the interior of Africa was beginning to reach the people of the Guinea Coast and the Upper Congo basin by the time the Europeans arrived—by sea—in the fifteenth century.

Henry the Navigator, seeking Portuguese control of Africa, sent expeditions down the west coast in the fifteenth century. As early as 1441, trade had begun with the people at Arguin, an island off the coast at the south edge of the desert. By 1480 the Guinea Coast had been explored, and the first trading post was established at Elmina on the Gold Coast in 1482. The whole African coast was soon known—in 1498 Vasco da Gama retraced in reverse most of the course which, according to Herodotus, the Phoenicians had sailed more than 2,000 years before, rounding the Cape of Good Hope on his way to India. At first the attraction was gold and other valuable items—as suggested by the names given to the newly discovered lands: for example, Gold Coast, Ivory Coast, Pepper Coast, Camaroon or Shrimp Coast. But after the discovery of America, the exploration of Africa was bound up with the lucrative slave trade. Few attempts were made to penetrate the interior of Africa until the middle of the nineteenth century, when Stanley and Livingstone made their historic explorations in South Africa and the Congo basin.

Mystery surrounds the origin of African peoples, as indeed it does the beginnings of peoples everywhere. It was once thought that man was born in Asia; but recent research presents the probability that all human "races" originated in east central Africa, either from common roots or in immediate parallel.[3] Scholars—now clearly separating the development of language and culture from the emergence and distribution of modern biological variations of man[4]—have only begun to reconstruct the history of early peoples. Perhaps among the earliest well-defined groups were the Khoïsan-speaking Bushmen, who penetrated southward, and the related Pygmies (about whose language we know little), who moved west through central Africa. It seems probable that from early times men who spoke Niger-Congo languages were concentrated in the Sudanic and Saharan area, from the Nile to the Atlantic: these people included many local types

---

[3] See Henriette Alimen: *Préhistoire de l'Afrique* (Paris: N. Boubée: 1955) and Sonia M. Cole: *Prehistory of East Africa* (New York: The Macmillan Co.; 1963).

[4] See Joseph H. Greenberg: *The Languages of Africa* (Bloomington: Indiana University Press; 1963).

which have been grouped together and commonly called the Negro "race" —with kinky hair, thick lips, broad nose, and dark skin, although their skin color and other physical traits varied considerably. And Afroasiatic-speaking peoples from remote times inhabited Ethiopia, the Nile valley —including Egypt—and the north coast of Africa: many of these, but perhaps not all, shared "Caucasoid" characteristics with other Mediterranean groups—smooth hair, thin lips, narrow nose, but with skin color varying from near-black to blond.

The Barbary states or Mahgreb of northwestern Africa were probably once inhabited by a people similar to the ancient Egyptians. From remote times their shores were invaded by lighter-skinned Latin- and Germanic-speaking peoples from Europe, and the resulting mixture was a people known to the Greeks and Romans as Libyans, whom we call Berbers. Then came the Arabs, arriving first in the seventh century A.D., and settling in large numbers in the eleventh century. Aside from a slight Negro strain, due chiefly to slaves brought across the Sahara from the south, the racial pattern of the modern states of Morocco, Algeria, Tunisia, and Libya is a blend of Arab and Berber, shading from the Arabs in the east to the virtually pure Berbers of Morocco. The established Sudanic Negro was pushed by the Arabs and the Berbers—and by an increasingly hostile climate—out of the Sahara which he once dominated. By adopting iron tools, however, he conquered the forbidding rain forests of West and Central Africa, thus making possible his occupation, in more recent centuries, of the open grasslands of eastern and southern Africa. The Bushman, who at one time occupied most of southern Africa, was thus finally squeezed by his expanding Negro enemies into the desert hinterland of Bechuanaland and Southwest Africa. And the Pygmy, who originally inhabited a wide strip of tropical Africa from the Atlantic to the east coast, now lives only in small enclaves in the equatorial forests of the Congo basin.

Who, then, is an African? He is the fierce Bushman of the Kalahari Desert, with his stocky build, yellowish skin, tufted hair, flat nose, and slanting eyes, who lives by his bow and poisoned arrow—almost the direct descendant of one of the oldest peoples of Africa. . . . He is the Hottentot, a linguistic relative of the Bushman but taller, with a longer and narrower head, who loads his rude hut on the back of his oxen and follows his cattle over the savannas of South and Southwest Africa. . . . He is the Pygmy of the Congo forests, with his reddish-yellow skin, Negroid features, and average stature of about four and a half feet, who is a hunter and trapper known for his cunning; who has been famed as a dancer from the days of ancient Egypt, when the Pharaohs sent south for "dancing dwarfs" from the "land of spirits" to entertain them. . . . He is the warlike Zulu of eastern South Africa, with his black skin and Negroid features, who lives in a thatched hut and plows his fields, but who wins prestige among his fellows only as an owner of cattle; whose religion is chiefly ancestor worship. . . . He is the tall, handsome Somali of Ethiopia, who is predominantly Afroasiatic with his high cheek bones, high forehead, prominent nose, and long wavy hair; who herds his cows, goats, sheep, treasures his camel, sometimes cultivates corn and coffee. . . . He is the very tall naked Dinka, one of the Nilotic Negroes of the eastern Sudan, who smears himself with white ashes, raises cattle, and practices totemism. . . . He is the proud Egyptian. . . . He is the nomadic Arab of North Africa, who has little interest in the soil, believing that "shame enters with the plow"; whose society is aristocratic, with rule hereditary; and who is a devout Mohammedan. . . . He is the tall, fair Kabyle of Morocco, typical Berber, who is a farmer and cattle raiser, whose society is democratic and sedentary, and who calls himself a Mohammedan. . . . He is the veiled Tuareg, of Berber blood, who rides across the Sahara in his camel caravan raiding his neighbors for more camels, whose ancestors brought Islam to the Sudanese Negroes. . . . He is the Mandingo, intelligent Moslem Negro of the western Sudan, who is a cattle grazer, a keen trader, and a skilled craftsman. . . . He is the Dahomean, Negro of the Gulf of Guinea, who is a skilled farmer, who scarifies his body, whose religion is polytheism and ancestor worship, whose sculpture in bronze and copper has unusual artistic merit.

There is a myth, invented by the white man, that the Negro was brought to the New World from a primitive and savage land, that whatever "civilization" he has attained has been through contact with the superior races of Europe and America—that "the Negro is thus a man without a past."[5] This myth has influenced the black man himself, and the Negro of the Americas, north and south, has tried in heart and mind to turn his back upon that savage land from which he came. The truth is that the word "primitive" cannot with accuracy be applied to the culture of West African peoples if we use it as meaning *simple,* for in their politics and economic institutions, their religious beliefs, their family customs, and their art forms, their vast storehouse of unwritten literature, many of these peoples have developed highly complex societies. Nor is it completely correct to call the Negroes of the past *nonliterate,* for there have recently been discovered significant stores of family and trade records from both the western and eastern coasts. Thus, in the areas from which the slaves came there was much that cannot be dismissed as "primitive." The African peoples, we conclude, have a rich cultural heritage and have transferred this heritage to the New World; the talents, the temperament, the beliefs, the physical traits of the Negro are ingredients in that new company of man—the American.

Which African was brought to the New World? No completely accurate answer can be given—but the question is important, because of the differing cultural heritages of the various regions of Africa. The principal area of slaving operations was the west coast of Africa from the Senegal and Gambia rivers, east to the Guinea Coast, and south to the port of Luanda, in Angola. But we do not know how many slaves came from the core of

5 See Melville J. Herskovits: *The Myth of the Negro Past* (New York: Harper & Brothers; 1941).

that region, how many from the periphery, nor how many were brought from the interior or from distant parts of Africa. The Senegalese, the Mohammedanized Negroes of the northern Sudan, the Bantu tribes of the heart of the Congo region, the people of Angola, and even Negroes from Mozambique in the southeastern corner of Africa and the island of Madagascar—these were all present in some degree. But there seems to be a growing body of evidence to indicate that the vast majority of slaves brought to the New World were gathered perhaps not much more than 200 or 300 miles from the coast: in the densely populated forested belt of the west coast of Africa from the Ivory Coast to the mouth of the Niger River, and in a strip between Lândana, just north of the mouth of the Congo, and mid-Angola. This would point to the importance of studying the cultural background of the Negroes of West Africa and the western Congo.

Let us look—quite arbitrarily—at one of these regions: that section of West Africa between the Sahara Desert on the north and the Gulf of Guinea on the south, from Ghana (the Gold Coast) to Nigeria, since this is the region that has seemed to set the pattern for the Negroes of the New World. This region is slightly north of the equator, well within the Tropic of Cancer. The mean annual precipitation ranges from about fifty inches near the coast to about thirty inches in the more northerly interior, the heaviest rains falling in the summer months. The average temperature is about eighty degrees. Along the coast is a strip of mangrove swamp and dense jungle, rising through a forested zone to the high grasslands of the interior. Except for a very narrow strip along the coasts of Morocco and Algeria, this is the most densely populated region of the entire continent of Africa—supporting over 50 million people.

The African of this section—especially in the southern part, along the coast—is traditionally considered the true "Negro" in culture, language, and appearance, although there is no certain evidence that he is ethnically any more, or less, *pure* "Negro" than many other, somewhat different, dark-skinned peoples throughout tropical Africa who also speak Niger-Congo languages. The typical West African Negro is strong, tallish, heavy-set. He has woolly hair, black skin, and a long head. He has a receding forehead, full lips, and a broad flat nose (which a slave trader in the eighteenth century attributed to "a continued grubbing in their Infancy against their Mothers' Backs, being tied within the Tomee, whether upon Travel or Business, for a year or two, the time of their sucking"). Generalizations about the region cannot be accurate, as the cultures of these peoples vary—the tribes to the north are largely Mohammedanized, while those along the coastal belt have much in common with the tribes of the Congo basin.

When the white man began his invasions in the fifteenth century, this was an area of many kingdoms, great and small. These included the kingdoms of Ashanti, Benin, Dahomey, and Yoruba, which lay near the coast; as well as the actively commercial Hausa city-states to the north and the kingdom of Bornu in northeastern Nigeria—these last two

Mohammedanized. The king ruled over a hierarchy of chiefs and subchiefs, though the smallest unit usually had a considerable degree of local autonomy, and the petty village "king" was often favored with the first loyalty of the people themselves. Authority was further divided, the head of the family group being responsible to the village chief or "king." Stable dynasties, passing either from father to son or through the maternal line, were the rule rather than the exception. The king was usually despotic and ruthless—but he could generally be replaced if he was inefficient; and his subjects enjoyed considerable security, for there were well-organized courts of law to protect personal rights, as well as loyal warriors who stood ready to defend the royal territory. The king supported himself—lavishly, by local standards—by taxing the people on their trade, by taxes on personal wealth and possessions, and by death dues.

The economy of this region was, and continues to be, agricultural, although herding was also important in the grasslands to the north; and there was considerable trade throughout most of West Africa. However, though the soil is fertile and the climate propitious, the native of West Africa has not been pampered by nature to the extent that the crops grow themselves: he has been obliged to work, and work hard, to make a living from the soil. The Negro developed agricultural skills invaluable to the plantations of the New World. He cultivated his fields with a special type of short-handled hoe. Division of labor was well defined, with the men doing the heavy work and the women tending and harvesting the crops. Produce was sold in organized markets, the unit of exchange usually being the cowrie shell. The land was held by kinship groups, and the individual owned only the produce from the plot he cultivated. Division of labor in occupations other than agriculture was evident in the craft guilds, based on family relationships. These occupations included wood carving, basketry, weaving, trading, and iron work. Not surprisingly, the iron-worker clan in the strong tribes—by virtue of its power over the soil as well as in hunting and in war—controlled the kingship or the chieftaincy.

The basis of the social structure was the family. The broad kinship group was the "sib" or clan, and a smaller and more closely related group was the "extended family." The immediate family was usually polygamous, with complex rules of inheritance varying from tribe to tribe: social position and legal rights were usually inherited from the father, and a certain "spiritual affiliation" from the mother—though in some tribes this was reversed. Marriage was an alliance between families, and lineage was carefully traced to prevent marriage between two persons of the same "sib." The immediate family usually occupied a fenced-in group of huts—the man in one, and his various wives in the others, visiting their husband in turn. The children of these unions shared their father with the children of his other wives, and often there developed strong ties between mother and child, as they conspired together to win the favor of the father, especially in the matter of inheritance. Even after death, departed members of the family held power over the living—there was a strong belief in the continuity of a spiritual bond from one generation to the next.

The religions of this area were complex in theology and ritual. Even the Hausa, the Mandingo, and other Mohammedanized peoples to the north held on to many pagan customs which became a part of their brand of Islam. The typical West African Negro worshiped a pantheon of gods representing the forces of nature and the various trades. The gods fell into family groups similar to the kinship groups of the people themselves. The will of the gods was interpreted by "diviners," who had undergone years of training. West Africans were open-minded in accepting new gods —from their neighbors or from their conquerors—providing these new gods had proved useful. Thus it was easy for the Negro to accept the white man's God in America without altering his ancestral beliefs or practices. Priests and priestesses were inducted with elaborate ritual, usually involving the phenomenon of "possession." At the climax of a frenzied orgy of dancing, accompanied by the wild beating of drums, the body of the initiate underwent a violent convulsion, and he was "possessed" of the spirit. Also important was a belief—often described as fetishism—in the power of an inanimate object or image which, having received a "spirit" within it, perhaps by means of a spell cast upon it by the medicine man or witch doctor, became a "fetish" (a word derived from the Portuguese *feitiço,* meaning "charm" or "sorcery"). Properly worshiped, the "spirit" within a fetish has power over the forces of nature, disease, and one's enemies. Other magic charms, especially prepared by the witch doctor, are carried by the warrior to protect him from harm. Some Mohammedans carry on their persons extracts from the Koran which serve as charms.

Secret societies were important in the religious, political, and social life of many Guinea Coast peoples. Only those surviving the ordeal of initiation were admitted to the well-hidden meeting places, and absolute obedience to the prescribed codes was a solemn requirement. Offense against a secret society, whether by members or nonmembers, was punished by torture or death.

Music played a large part in religious worship and aesthetic expression. The drum was the most important instrument, and the chief musical form was the song. The music was highly complex in rhythm, scale, and form, varying considerably in style from one tribe to another. Melodic line was important in the structure of the music, and much of the singing was polyphonal. Music was inseparable from the dance, in all its intricate and varied forms: there were religious dances and recreational dances; there were war dances and dances of the hunt; some dances were improvised, the form of others carefully worked out. Both music and the dance were often characterized by frenzied excitement.

Although the Negroes of West Africa never developed a written language, several major tribes used some Arabic script and employed Sudanic scribes. But even more significant was their accumulated wealth of literature which was passed on from generation to generation by word of mouth. Folk tales, proverbs, and riddles, as well as a rich store of mythology, were important in their education, their recreation, and their religious life.

"African art" has been an inspiration to modern painters and sculptors.

The Yoruba, Ibo, and other Nigerian peoples were masters of wood carving, and the Dahomeans did exquisite iron work and carved brass figures of rare strength and beauty. Many tribes, such as the Ashanti of the Gold Coast, are also known for their handsome weaving. It is interesting to note that some of their works of art were valued by these people not for their usefulness, but merely for their beauty—a phenomenon not often found among "primitive" cultures.

THE SLAVE TRADE

"Oh how fair a thing it would be if we who have come to this land for a cargo of such petty merchandise were to meet with the good luck to bring the first captives before the face of our Prince."[6] The year was 1441, and this youthful captain had been sent down the west coast of Africa for a cargo of skins and oils by Prince Henry the Navigator. The wish of the young captain was fulfilled. He and his men captured a dozen Moors not far from the shore south of Cape Bojador (about 200 miles north of the Tropic of Cancer) and returned with them to Prince Henry. But one of the Moors was a nobleman and pleaded for his release. As ransom for himself and two others, should they be returned safely to Africa, he offered to turn over to the captain "ten Moors, and it was better to save ten souls than three—for though they were black, yet they had souls like the others, and all the more as these blacks were not of the lineage of the Moors but were gentiles, and so the better to bring into the path of salvation."[7]

The bargain was completed and a new age was begun. Now Europeans, for the first time, began to carry slaves from Africa to be sold in the markets of Europe. For four centuries the history of the Western World —the internal and external struggles of the nations of Europe, the development of the New World—was bound inextricably with the African trade. The treasure of Africa included gold, ivory, and spices; but the coveted prize was the storehouse of black human beings, millions of whom were transported to the sugar fields, coffee and cotton plantations, and the mines of the New World, to the enrichment of traders, planters, and the crowned heads of Europe.

It is not known when the first Negro set foot upon the soil of the New World, though it is possible that one or two may have come with Columbus in 1492. In 1502, when Ovando was sent to the island of Hispaniola as governor, he was given permission by the Spanish Crown to take with him a few Christian Negroes born in Spain or Portugal. But the real traffic in Negroes to the New World began in 1510, when Ferdinand acceded to the demands of the colonists for laborers and ordered the Casa

6 Gomez Eannes de Azurara: *The Chronicle of the Discovery and Conquest of Guinea,* translated by C. Raymond Beazley and Edgar Prestage (London: Hakluyt Society; 1896, 1897), ch. XII; quoted by Elizabeth Donnan: *Documents Illustrative of the Slave Trade to America* (4 vols.; Washington, D.C.: Carnegie Institution; 1930), Vol. I, p. 18.
7 *Ibid.,* ch. XVI; quoted by E. Donnan, *op. cit.,* Vol. I, p. 22.

de Contratación to send out 250 Negroes. Cuba probably received its first slaves about 1512, when they were imported by Diego Velásquez, the governor, to work in the sugar fields. In 1517 Father Bartolomé de las Casas gave impetus to the trade when he urged that Negro slaves be substituted for Indians, who were rapidly being exterminated. In 1518 the Crown granted permission for 4,000 Negroes to be shipped to Hispaniola, Cuba, Jamaica, and Puerto Rico. A little later Negroes were introduced into Brazil, though the exact date when the first Negro slave arrived on Brazilian soil is not known. By the early 1530's, at least, plantation owners in Brazil were granted the right by the Portuguese Crown to import a few slaves to work in the sugar fields. By 1540, possibly as many as 10,000 Negro slaves were being imported into the Americas each year, and within the next two centuries the annual importation reached 75,000 —perhaps more. By 1810, according to Alexander von Humboldt, there were some 6,433,000 Negroes in all America, including the United States and Brazil—only 776,000 of them, however, in Spanish America.

For at least the first century of the trade, the Portuguese were well in control of the African coast; while, on the other hand—except for direct trade into Brazil—the Spanish enjoyed a monopoly of the slave markets of the New World. The Spanish Crown established the *asiento* system, by which certain individuals or companies were granted the right to ship slaves for sale in the Spanish colonies. The earliest slaves had to be bought from Portuguese traders, as the Spanish themselves were excluded from activity on the African coast by the Papal Bull of 1493. Competition developed before the middle of the sixteenth century, when both English and French merchants were stopping on the Guinea Coast on their way to Brazil, and the Dutch arrived on this "international battleground" around 1592. (It was the Dutch, incidentally, who brought the first cargo of Negro slaves to Jamestown in 1619.) By the end of the century, Portugal's monopoly of the African trade was a fiction. However—except for the extracurricular forays of Captain John Hawkins in the 1560's and 1570's, who, unauthorized by the British Crown, collected slaves in Africa and sold them in the West Indies—neither the French nor the English traded in slaves until well into the seventeenth century. A native merchant on the Gambia River in 1620 offered slaves to a British trader who was searching for gold, ivory, or spices, and was told that:

> We were a people, who did not deale in any such commodities, neither did wee buy or sell one another, or any that had our owne shapes; he seemed to marvell much at it, and told us it was the only merchandize they carried downe into the countrey, where they fetcht all their salt, and that they were sold there to white men who earnestly desired them . . . we answered, They were another kinde of people different from us.[8]

The scruples of both the British and the French disappeared, however, when their own colonies in the New World demanded slaves. By the 1640's

[8] Richard Jobson: *The Golden Trade or a Discovery of the River Gambia, and the Golden Trade of the Aethiopians* (London, 1623), pp. 88–9; quoted by E. Donnan, *op. cit.,* Vol. I, p. 79.

the French, and at least by the 1660's the British, had entered into the slave trade.

Throughout the eighteenth century, slaves were exported from Africa to the New World by the English, the French, the Portuguese, the Dutch, and the Danes. Around 1790 the annual exportation of these countries was in that order, with the total number of slaves taken out of Africa each year estimated at some 74,000, of which England was responsible for more than half. The Spanish still had control of a large share of the American markets, but Spain never competed for the African end of the trade.

By the end of the eighteenth century, the liberal ideas of the Enlightenment had their effect on the institution of slavery and the slave trade. England—where the Quakers had taken a stand against the slave trade as early as 1727—took the lead among nations in this crusade, although Denmark was the first country to take action, closing her trade in 1802. England herself prohibited, by the Act of 1807, any trade in slaves within her dominions; and her example was followed by other countries: the United States banned the slave trade in 1808 (but it continued on an illegal basis until the Civil War), the Dutch in 1814, the French in 1818, and the Spanish in 1820. The Portuguese in 1815 prohibited the trade in slaves north of the equator, but not until 1836 was there a royal decree prohibiting the export of slaves from any Portuguese possession. Also chiefly under pressure from the British, most of the newly independent nations of Latin America—which were engaging in the slave trade on an informal basis—had, by the 1830's, made the first gestures toward outlawing the trade. Few of the actions were immediately effective, but by the 1830's at least all *legal* trade in slaves was arrested, although contraband traffic continued through much of the nineteenth century.

For almost four centuries, then, the civilized world traded in this human cargo and few voices were raised in protest. The rationalizations used to quiet the conscience are shown in a letter written in 1610 by Brother Luis Brandaon, rector of the Society of Jesus at São Paulo de Luanda, in Angola, to Father Sandoval in Portugal, who had written to inquire whether the slaves brought to Portugal had been "legally captured." Brother Brandaon replied that his Reverence "should have no scruples on this point," because the matter had been "questioned by the Board of Conscience in Lisbon, and all its members are learned and conscientious men." He argued that, even though some slaves were captured illegally, "to lose so many souls as sail from here—out of whom many are saved, because some, impossible to recognize, have been captured illegally, does not seem to be doing much service to God, for these are few and those who find salvation are many and legally captured."[9] It would seem fatuous to define the

[9] Letter from Brother Luis Brandaon to Father Sandoval, March 12, 1610. Printed in José Antonio Saco: *Historia de la esclavitud de la raza africana en el Nuevo Mundo . . .* [4 vols.], Vol. IV (Barcelona: Imprenta de Jaime Jepús; 1879), p. 253; quoted by E. Donnan, *op. cit.,* Vol. I, p. 123.

methods of obtaining slaves in terms of "legality." The ends to be served—
the handsome profit, the genuine need of workers to develop the New
World—dragged "legality" in their wake. How were the slaves obtained?
By every means, both fair and foul—from capture "by the sword" to an
elaborately "legal" system of trade with the natives, and among the natives
themselves. The institution of slavery was not new to West Africa when
the Europeans arrived. But the increase in demand for human merchandise
so dazzled the native trader that, no less a rationalizer than the white man,
he devised new means (and perfected the old ones) of acquiring possession
of his fellow blacks, fitting his methods neatly into his own code of
"legality."

A European trader calling at the ports of Cape Verde, Whydah,
Elmina, Calabar, Luanda—or any one of dozens of other ports on the west
coast of Africa—usually made contact first with the local factor, or trader,
who represented his king and his trading company. The visiting merchant
replenished the factor's supply of goods kept on hand to trade with the
Africans, sometimes loading onto his ship slaves already purchased,
branded with the company's seal, and chained in the vault of the
factory (trading post). More often he was obliged to procure his own
cargo of slaves. The next step was a visit to the native chief, or "king,"
whose good graces he courted with *dashees,* or presents, consisting of
pipes, sealing wax, brandy, and odd trinkets. The king, if properly
cultivated, gave permission to trade in his domain, fixed the prices to be
paid for slaves, as well as the tax to be paid to himself, and appointed
native traders to assist the merchant in procuring his slaves. The king
sometimes sold his petty criminals and debtors, and sometimes even
allowed his own people to be bought as slaves. But more often he forbade
the sale of slaves born in his kingdom, insisting that only prisoners of
war or slaves purchased from a neighboring tribe be sold to the white
man.

Perhaps the most common means of obtaining slaves to sell to the
white trader was the capture of prisoners of war. These included a wide
variety of people: criminals, improvident loafers, women and children,
warriors, priests, tribal chieftains, and even "kings." Although there had
always been wars between African tribes, it has been noted that when the
demand for slaves was acute, fresh wars were waged for flimsy reasons—
or no reason at all. More than one chronicler has suggested that European
traders themselves often instigated these wars. This practice was, of course,
denied; an Englishman writes in 1763:

> It is a mistaken notion, that the company's officers (during their com-
> mand) created wars between the African chiefs, in order to purchase the
> prisoners, which should be made on either side. This falsehood was propa-
> gated also at a certain time, to serve particular purposes. On the contrary,
> slaves are bred in the inland parts of Africa, and sent for sale, according
> to the want those people are in for European manufactures; the same as
> an ox or horse is taken to market, when a farmer in England wants money

to pay his rent, or for other purposes. Every man in Africa is looked upon to be a man of property and power in proportion to the number of Negroes he is possessed of.[1]

Sometimes there was no pretense of "war," and the local chieftain conducted forays for the seizure of slaves from his neighbors. A British trader in 1787 described his experiences with a king in Old Calabar with whom he was allowed to go "up the river" to trade for slaves. "In the day-time," he reported, "we called at the villages as we passed, and purchased our slaves fairly; but in the night we . . . broke into the villages, and, rushing into the huts of the inhabitants, seized men, women, and children promiscuously." Of the factory at Mossula Bay, in the kingdom of Angola, this same trader writes: "I know of no other way of making slaves there, than by robbery." He said that the "traders" from the factory "were al-ways armed when they went out. They took no goods with them, but yet they returned with slaves." He explained the increasing difficulty of find-ing Negroes, for, "when so attacked, [they] immediately leave their habita-tions, and go farther inland. They are continually in a wandering, uncertain state, on account of these frequent depredations." At Cape Palmas he was told that the natives intended to "attack a village" on a certain night. When he asked them if the villagers had "done them any injury," they replied, No, but that "there was a considerable number of fine stout young men belonging to it, who were good for trade." This, he said, was their only reason. Having occasion to sleep, on the appointed night, in the house of a native trader in the vicinity of the proposed raid, this Britisher testifies: "At about two in the morning he awakened me to see the fire. I jumped up instantly from a chest on which I lay, and saw the village in flames. The next day more than fifty young men were brought down, all of whom had been taken during the conflagration."[2]

Often it was necessary for a slaver to call at several ports in order to find enough slaves to fill his quota. Before leaving the African coast, the trader stocked his ship with provisions for the long journey to the New World. Food for the slaves, according to one account in 1795, consisted chiefly of "plantain, bananas, ochro, yams, potatoes, and other ground provision, together with rice, bread, wheat, etc., [which] is so exceedingly moderate, that ten shillings sterling for each slave will be acknowledged a very ample allowance." The horrors of the middle passage were described by a member of the British Parliament who visited a slave ship in 1788. The Negroes, he said, "were chained to each other hand and foot, and stowed so close that they were not allowed above a foot and a half for each in breadth. Thus crammed together like herrings in a barrel, they con-tracted putrid and fatal disorders; so that they who came to inspect them in the morning had occasionally to pick dead slaves out of their rows, and to unchain their carcasses from the bodies of their wretched fellow-sufferers

[1] *Consideration on the Present Peace, as far as it is relative to the Colonies and the African Trade* (London, 1763); quoted by E. Donnan, *op. cit.*, Vol. II, pp. 518-9.

[2] Thomas Clarkson: *Essay on the Efficiency of Regulation or Abolition* (1789), pp. 4-6; quoted by E. Donnan, *op. cit.*, Vol. II, pp. 572-3.

to whom they had been fastened."[3] Mortality was high. There was a macabre name for the slave ships—*tumbeiros,* coffins. Merchants usually counted on losing at least 5 per cent of their slaves, while one account of the Liverpool trade reported 474 slaves lost out of a total of 2,305 which had been loaded onto seven ships—or more than 20 per cent.[4] And in 1723 a captain wrote to his company from Barbados "to certifie you of my Arivall hear haveing seven Weeks Passage from Bony but very Dismall and Mortall for outt of 399 Slaves I brought in hear butt 214 for the Like Mortalaty I think Never was known for Jolly Likely Men Slaves to Eatt thair Diett over Night and the Nex Morning Dead 2 and 3 in a Night for severall Days after Wee Came from Bony as for Managementt I think itt Could Not be Better I allways had their Victtualls in good order and Took that Care to keep them and the Ship Sweet and Cleane allthoyt I Did itt my Self and Nott to Sufer any of them to Wett Their Foott on No Acctt."[5] Sporadic attempts were made to improve conditions and to limit the number of Negroes to be carried on a ship. But, at least so far as the trading companies were concerned, profit was the only consideration. When the British Parliament drew up a bill in 1788 allowing only five slaves to every three tons of the ship's burden instead of two slaves per ton, Liverpool traders figured that even if two-fifths of the slaves regularly lost were saved by the regulation, their profits would be smaller, and they protested that the act would impose "a variety of unnecessary and grievous restrictions upon the African Slave Trade."

What was the price of a Negro slave in Africa? In the first days of the trade, Negroes were bought from the natives for beads and trinkets. In the 1440's, a Portuguese captain reports that the Moors on the Rio do Ouro "sold him a black for the price of five doubloons [something over £8], which he paid them by certain things he gave them in their stead." In 1455 Cadamosto, also in the service of Prince Henry, visited the island of Arguin. "Here," he says, "for woolen and linen cloth, silver, tapestry, and grain, the Arabs gave slaves and gold." As the slave trade prospered, European traders made a study of the items most apt to please the natives, and packed their ships with a motley assortment of merchandise including bars of iron, brass kettles, silk, linen, and cotton cloth of all descriptions (even old sheets), guns and gun powder, "spirits," tobacco, tallow, and hides. The value of these was often reduced to the iron bar, the most common medium of trade on the African coast, estimated to be worth from 2s. to 6s., depending on the time and place. The price of a *pieza d'India* (a term often applied to one black man—or several, depending on their quality) varied greatly, increasing in the seventeenth and eighteenth centuries as slaves became more scarce and the African "middlemen"

---

[3] Sir William Dolben, as quoted by J. K. Ingram: *A History of Slavery and Serfdom* (London: Adam and Charles Black; 1895), p. 152. The treatment of slaves by the Spanish and Portuguese, however, was much less cruel than treatment by the English and the Dutch.

[4] Thomas Clarkson, *op. cit.,* pp. 29–30; quoted by E. Donnan, *op. cit.,* Vol. II, p. 573.

[5] "Captain Edward Hollden to the Owners of the *Grayhound,* Barbados, Aprill the 30th, 1723" (Bristol Public Library, Jefferies mss., p. 52); quoted by E. Donnan, *op. cit.,* Vol. II, pp. 299–300.

learned to bargain. A British trader in New Calabar in 1699 complained of having to pay "thirteen bars for men, and nine for women, and proportionately for boys and girls, according to their ages." In the 1730's, on the Gambia River, slaves sold for forty or fifty—or even eighty—iron bars each. According to one early eighteenth-century journal, a woman slave was purchased at Junk, on the Grain Coast, for:

Two Quarter Barrells of powder at Eight Accis Each
    [An accy was a unit of African currency, worth about 5*s*.]
Foure Trading Gunns at foure Do.
One Challow [coarse calico] at Nine Do.
Thirteen Sheets at One Do.
Two cotton Ramalls at Six Do.

This would be a total of about £15. Thus the cost of a slave purchased on the African coast during the three centuries of the trade varied from a few shillings to as much as £25.

And the price paid for Negroes in the New World after the arduous "middle passage"? In 1517 Genoese merchants, under a contract with the King of Spain which carried the privilege of shipping 4,000 Negroes to the West Indies, were reported to have made a profit of 300,000 ducats on the transaction. This would be at least £15 or £20 a head in profit alone. A Spanish *asiento* around 1530 carried the restriction that a maximum of 45 ducats a head (£9–£13) was to be charged for slaves in the West Indies, and in 1556 the Crown set the top price at 100 ducats (£20–£30). In 1662 the Royal African Company agreed to supply Barbados and the "Caribbee" islands with 3,000 slaves annually at £17—or 2,400 pounds of sugar—each, and in 1664 the Dutch sold Negroes in Martinique for 2,000 pounds of sugar per head. The Governor of Jamaica reported in 1671 that the Spanish were paying up to £40 for a slave. In an *asiento* between England and Spain in 1707, the contractors were instructed by the Spanish Crown that "those they carry to the Windward Island, St. Maries, Cumana and Maracaybo, [they] shall not sell for more than 300 ps ⅜ each [£62 10s.; a "piece of eight" was worth 4*s*. 2*d*.], but less when they can, for the ease of the people, but in other parts of New Spain and Terra firm, they may sell for the highest Prices they can get." An account of the Liverpool slave trade, written in 1795, says that "the price of slaves about the year 1730 was £35 per head; in 1750, about £45; and they have been sold at £100 currency at Jamaica." Fernando Ortiz estimates the profits on one voyage to Havana around 1800:

850 slaves sold at £50 each		£42,500
Expenses of the voyage	£2,500	
Cost of the slaves at £4 each	£3,400	
		£ 5,900
Net profit		£36,600[6]

6 Fernando Ortiz: *Hampa afro-cubana: Los negros esclavos* (Havana: Revista bimestre cubana; 1916), p. 159.

. . .

In the early days of the slave trade the greatest activity was around the Senegal and Gambia rivers. From there merchants ventured west and south along the coast until, at the height of the traffic, England, Portugal, France, Holland, and Denmark had thriving factories (trading centers) along the 4,000-mile stretch from Senegal to Angola. In the last days of the trade, when slaves became scarce, some Negroes were imported from distant Mozambique and the island of Madagascar. The quality of the slaves differed from place to place. One contemporary British account reports that:

> Slaves differ in their Goodness; those from the Gold Coast are accounted best, being cleanest limbed, and more docible by our Settlements than others; but then they are, for that very reason, more prompt to Revenge, and murder the Instruments of their Slavery, and also apter in the means to compass it.
>
> To Windward they approach in Goodness as is the distance from the Gold Coast; so, as at Gambia, or Sierraleon, to be much better, than at any of the interjacent places.
>
> To Leeward from thence, they alter gradually for the worse; an Angolan Negro is a Proverb for worthlessness; and they mend (if we call it so) in that way, till you come to the Hottentots, that is, to the Southermost Extremity of Africa.[7]

The British preferred slaves from the Gold Coast, and they imported many Ashanti and Fanti from this area. An English merchant reports in 1694 that "the Negroes most in demand at Barbadoes, are the gold coast, or, as they call them, Cormantines, which will yield 3 or 4 *l* a head more than the Whydahs [Dahomeans] . . . ; but these are preferr'd before the Angola, as they are before the Alampo, which are accounted the worst of all."[8] The French, on the other hand, did not like the Gold Coast slaves, but preferred the Dahomeans—and many of the Negroes of Haiti are of Dahomean descent. Fernando Ortiz says of the Dahomeans, however, that they were "bad slaves, prone to suicide and nostalgia." The Yoruba of western Nigeria were the favorite slaves of the Spanish and Portuguese planters, and there is evidence that large numbers of these Negroes were imported into Brazil and Cuba. From the Gold Coast came the comely, light-skinned Minas who were favored as concubines and domestic servants in Brazil, especially in the state of Minas Gerais. Even more important in Brazil, however, were the Negroes from Angola, stronghold of Portuguese power. Also brought to Brazil were a considerable number of Mandingo and Hausa, Mohammedan Negroes of the Sudan area who were considered superior in their culture and intelligence. Of the Mandingo, also present in Cuba, Ortiz says that they were "gentle of character, easily taught, skillful and

7 John Atkins, Surgeon in the Royal Navy: *A Voyage to Guinea, Brasil, and the West-Indies* (London, 1735); quoted by E. Donnan, *op. cit.*, Vol. II, p. 282.

8 Thomas Phillips: "A Journal of a Voyage made in the Hannibal of London, Ann. 1693-1694"; from Churchill: *Collection of Voyages and Travels* (1732), Vol. VI, pp. 173-239; quoted by E. Donnan, *op. cit.*, Vol. I, p. 392.

indefatigable traders, generous, frank, hospitable, rather fatalistic, perhaps due to their Moslem background."

The Congo Negroes, also important throughout the New World, were strong and suited to work in the tropics. They were docile and gave their masters little trouble, except for too frequent naps in the sun. Late-comers to Haiti, the Congo Negroes were held in contempt by their fellow slaves as being too complacent in the face of their slave status. The Ibo, or Calabar Negroes, were considered "weak and slothful, but cruel and bloody in their temper"; despondent, and prone to suicide: the Haitians said of them, "*Ibo pend cor' a yo*"—"the Ibo hang themselves." The Negroes of the Cameroons and Gabon were regarded as the least useful. One contemporary report says that "they are purchased so cheaply on the coast as to tempt many captains to freight with them; but they generally die either on the passage or soon after their arrival in the islands; the debility of their constitutions is astonishing."⁹ Many traders believed that the blacker the skin of the Negro, the better he could withstand the hot tropical sun; and for this reason many tribes, such as the reddish Fulani of the Upper Sudan, were considered by some to be inferior. But Ortiz describes the Fulani as "a species superior in intelligence and physical beauty . . . good fighters, industrious workers, though not easily assimilated." And the Fulani women were favorite "companions" of the Brazilians.

WHAT THE NEGRO BROUGHT TO THE NEW WORLD

The African's mark is clear upon the culture of the New World; he had a hand in shaping the political life, the religious institutions, the arts, and the social customs of the lands to which he was forcibly carried.

The first thing that the Negro brought with him was himself—his temperament and his personality: his "unfathomable gaiety," his genial disposition, his love of life, his adaptability, his sense of humor. And withal, his gentle melancholy. The Brazilian owes some of his most distinctive and charming traits to the infectious qualities of his Negro compatriots, if not to his own Negro blood. The typical Brazilian is carefree and uncomplicated —and almost always gay. There is no sullenness in his soul.

The Negro brought with him his religious beliefs and practices. He was forcibly converted to Christianity (indeed, the saving of the black man's soul was the justification for enslaving him); and baptism into the Catholic Church was often required before he was put on the auction block. But among the wretched beings unloaded from the slave ships were African priests, who kept their aboriginal practices alive. The Negro accepted the God of the white man, but the nominal Catholicism of the Brazilian, Cuban, or Haitian Negro is tinged with the hue of African cults. The

⁹ U. B. Phillips: *American Negro Slavery* (New York: D. Appleton & Co.; 1918), p. 43; quoted by M. J. Herskovits, *op. cit.,* p. 37.

belief in magic and the phenomenon of spirit-possession remained strong
in the tradition and lore of the black man, influencing his religious outlook
and behavior.

Wherever African modes of worship have survived, they are a *folk*
religion, occupying an inferior social position. In Haiti, for example, the
religion of the lower castes is Vodun (popularly called Voodoo). The name
"Vodun" is derived from a Dahomean word meaning "spirit" or "god";
and the religion of Vodun is a set of beliefs and practices, West African
in origin, which attempts to solve the mysteries of the universe and man's
relation to spiritual forces. But, according to James G. Leyburn, "few members of the *élite,* however their hearts may yearn for the consoling securities
of Vodun, dare openly . . . to participate in the cult. They must be
Catholics or agnostics. . . . It is because Vodun is a *folk* religion that the
élite cannot permit themselves to adhere to it openly."

The purest forms of worship of African *orishas* or deities are veiled
in secrecy. In Brazil, perhaps the most uncorrupted form of Negro worship is the *candomblé,* a ceremony performed in the remote and inaccessible villages of Bahia. The *candomblé,* derived from Dahomey and Yoruba,
usually begins with the *despacho* or banishment of Eshu (a Yoruban diety),
which is followed by chants, the beating of drums, and exhausting dances
which continue far into the night until the *queda no santo* or possession by
the spirit is attained and his demands for expression fulfilled. The more
familiar *macumba* of Rio de Janeiro (according to Arthur Ramos) involves
the incarnation in the priest of a family spirit, reflecting the ancestor worship of the Bantu peoples of Angola and the Congo region, whence the
ceremony is derived.

The strength of such African religious manifestations as the Vodun
cult in Haiti, and the *candomblé* and *macumba* of Brazil derives in part
from the direct identification made by the Negroes between Catholic saints
and the *orishas* or deities of West Africa. The great Yoruban god Obatala
is identified in Cuba with the *"Virgen de las Mercedes"* and even with Christ
himself. Shangô, the god of lightning and storms, becomes Santa Barbara
or St. Jerome at Bahia, St. Michael the Archangel at Rio de Janeiro, Santa
Barbara in Cuba. Legba, the Dahomean god who guards the crossroads (the
equivalent of the Yoruban deity, Eshu), who is worshiped in the Vodun
ceremony in Haiti, is held by some to be St. Anthony, and by others to
be St. Peter. Damballa, the Dahomean "rainbow-serpent deity," becomes
St. Patrick, "on whose *image* serpents are depicted"; and Moses is the father
of Damballa, because he turned his staff into a serpent before the eyes of
the Pharaoh. Ogun, the deity of war and strife, is identified in Brazil as St.
George, St. Jerome, or St. Anthony; in Cuba as St. Peter. Eshu, in some
places, is synonymous with the devil.

The African brought with him his dances. The favorite pastime of
the Negro slave was dancing, and his white master could not resist the
contagion of his rhythm, his excitement, his sheer joy in the movements
of his body. And so were born the folk dances of Brazil, Cuba, and other
countries, which are performed with equal enthusiasm on village streets

and in ballrooms. The *samba,* the national dance of Brazil, is derived from the *quizomba,* the wedding dance of Angola, and the Angola-Congolese dance called the *batuque.* At a certain point in the *batuque,* one of the dancers strikes another with his belly; and the name *samba* is probably derived from the word *semba,* or belly blow. The *rhumba* of Cuba is African in rhythm and spirit. The Cuban dance, the *son,* is pure African in origin. And so, also, are the *conga* and the *mambo,* dances originating among the Congo Negroes of Cuba. For all of these dances, with their infectious rhythm of motion and sound, caught from the intricate beating of the drums—and for jazz, whose contagion has spread throughout the modern world—the white man is in debt to the African.

The Negro has had a profound influence on all forms of musical expression. Of Brazil, Arthur Ramos says: "In rhythm and melody, the whole process of the nationalization of our music has depended on the Negro." The Afro-Brazilian musical instruments are percussion instruments derived from the drum, or *atabaque,* which is essentially Bantu or Sudanese in origin. The subtle rhythms that haunt so much of typically Brazilian music today, the simple, short melodic line, the repetition of phrases, derive in large part from the chants in the religious rituals of the Sudanese, and from the songs for every occasion of daily life which were so much a part of the African tradition. Brazilian composers have drawn inspiration from Negro folklore, from the rhythm and melody of Negro rituals. Notable among these is the composer Heitor Villa-Lobos, whose *Dansas Africanas* and *Macumba* are both taken from Negro themes. The Negro himself has contributed directly to the development of Brazilian music. José Mauricio, a Negro priest in the colonial period, is considered to be the founder of the first real school of music in Brazil. The history of serious Brazilian music is dotted with the names of Negro and mulatto scholars and composers; these include Francisco Braga, José Raymundo da Silva, Manuel Augusto, and Paulo Silva. Domingos Caldas Barbosa, whose mother was born in Angola, was a famous singer of popular songs in the nineteenth century and "the first representative of typically Brazilian music in the drawing rooms of Europe."

The Negro has left his mark on the literature and folklore of the lands of the New World. The popular tales and legends of Brazil are in large part of African origin, inspired by the unwritten legends, myths, proverbs, poetry, heroic tales, and riddles of the Sudanese and Bantu peoples. The "Uncle Remus" of Brazil was a mythical old Negro called Pae João, "a shuffling figure of mumbling speech and soft eyes," the storyteller of the plantations, who recounted tales of the African past. Not only have Negro themes been the inspiration of much of the literary output, but as the Negro emerged from slavery, his literary talent became more articulate, and both Cuba and Brazil list many Negroes and mulattoes among their eminent poets, novelists, and journalists. A few names in Brazil will suffice: José Basílio da Gama, in the colonial period, famous for his epic poem *Uruguay*; in the nineteenth century, Antônio Gonçalves Teixeira, a novelist, poet, and playwright of romance and fantasy; Antônio Gonçalves

Dias, the great pantheistic poet; Tobias Barreto, eminent writer, as well as scientist and philosopher; Luiz Gama, son of an African princess—poet, journalist, and a great leader in the abolition movement; Cruz e Sousa, "symbolist" poet of the late nineteenth century; and Castro Alves, called the "poet of the slaves," who expresses his nostalgia for Africa where

> All live happy
> A-dancing in de patios,
> Where all God's chillun
> Ain't sol' fuh money.[1]

Eminent among Cuban writers is Nicolás Guillén, who captures in his poetry the rhythm and spirit of African music and dances:

> Negro near the canebrake.
> White man on the canebrake.
> Earth beneath the canebrake.
> Blood that ebbs away.[2]

Jacques Roumain, the Haitian, expresses the pride and the bitterness of his race:

> Your soul is a prism of whispering waters
> Where your ancestors bowed their dark faces.
> Latent rustlings stir, obscure yet perceived,
> And the white man who made you a mulatto
> Is merely a flake of scum, far off, forsaken,
> Like saliva spat in the face of the river.[3]

The Negro came to his new home with a rich heritage in the arts. The museums of the world have preserved many examples of "African art": the metal work, the wood sculpture, the ceramics, and the weaving of West African peoples are universally admired for their strength and beauty. This skill which the Negro slave brought to America has influenced almost every art form. The temples of Bahia are decorated with wooden figures carved by Yoruban Negroes; the churches of Brazil are full of images, sacred vessels, candlesticks, and other religious objects of rare delicacy made by the Negroes out of wood, clay, or metal. Negro subjects have inspired Cândido Portinari and other artists. And Negroes themselves have achieved fame as architects, painters, and sculptors. In the colonial period in Brazil, a whole school of art developed around the mulatto Aleijadinho, who was a designer of churches and a sculptor of rare ability. A Negro slave, Sebastião, received wide acclaim for his paintings on the ceilings of churches in Rio de Janeiro.

The Negro brought qualities of leadership to the New World. Far from being the docile and acquiescent slave of popular mythology, the

---

[1] Quoted by C. M. Lancaster: "Gourds and Castanets: The African Finger in Modern Spain and Latin America," *Journal of Negro History*, Vol. 28 (January, 1943), p. 78.

[2] *Ibid.*, p. 82.

[3] *Ibid.*, p. 84.

Negro displayed his aggressiveness and his talent for organization in the fight for freedom—not only his own freedom, but the freedom of oppressed peoples everywhere. The history of Brazil includes many slave insurrections, big and little, with the fugitive slaves gathering themselves together in well-organized groups called *quilombos*. In the seventeenth century several of these *quilombos* in the northeast of Brazil banded together to form the Republic of Palmares, which flourished for sixty-seven years "with all the trappings of a civilized state." Following aboriginal African patterns, it had its king, who was all-powerful but venerated by his people; it had a complex political structure with ministers of justice and legislative bodies; it had a high degree of social and economic cooperation, its customs chiefly of Bantu origin. It was, as Arthur Ramos has put it, "a monument to the innate ability of the Brazilian Negro to create for himself without outside aid or encouragement the essential implements of a social order." The other notable rebellion of Negroes in Brazil was the religious uprising of the Moslem Negroes—chiefly Hausa—in the state of Bahia in the eighteenth century.

The Negro distinguished himself as leader and soldier in practically all the campaigns for independence in the New World. He brought his talent and aptitude for warfare to the campaigns of both Simón Bolívar and San Martín, in which there were well-organized and well-disciplined troops of Negro soldiers. The history of Haiti is a saga of the leadership of such Negroes as Toussaint L'Ouverture, Dessalines, and Henri Christophe.

The Negro has been called, especially in Brazil, "the principal architect or agent of his own emancipation." He worked diligently and saved money to purchase his own freedom, and he joined organized groups to purchase liberty for his fellow tribesmen. These groups, or brotherhoods, sometimes religious in inspiration, systematically collected funds to free more and more slaves, and became a very important factor in the abolition movement. The names of many heroic Negroes stand out as leaders in this fight for freedom. Chico Rei, an African "king" sold into slavery in the state of Minas Gerais in the eighteenth century, purchased freedom for himself and his son, then worked with other freed Negroes to liberate first his own kin, then slaves of other Negro tribes. This courageous man is known as "the first Negro abolitionist in Brazil." Luiz Gama, once a slave, became one of the great leaders of Brazil. There were many others, but perhaps the greatest of them all was José de Patrocinio, who, as journalist and social leader, was a chief spokesman of the campaign which brought abolition in 1888.

PART II

The Iberians
in the New World

The injection of the Europeans into the shadowy world of the Araucanians, Incas, Chibchas, Aztecs, and scores of other primitive peoples brought one of the major upheavals in the history of mankind. Old civilizations were overturned, and the foundations were laid for the sovereign nations which now occupy the span between Hudson Bay and the Strait of Magellan. Of those European invaders and colonists, the Spaniards and Portuguese arrived first, staked out their claims to the most extensive territory, and held it for three centuries. We turn to the record of the Iberians: their discoveries and conquests; their organization of the political, religious, and economic life of the areas they occupied; and their final eviction.

Chapter 5

DISCOVERY AND CONQUEST

The year 1492 marks one of those exhilarating points in time when a jaded world is given a fresh start, the chance to prove that it is peopled neither by fools nor apes. The Europe of 1492 was unhappy. The Church had reached a nadir of misery by electing corrupt Rodrigo Borgia to the papacy. Henry VII of England, Charles VIII of France, Maximilian I of the Germans, and Ferdinand and Isabella of Spain were surrounded by able men, but their subjects were heavy-laden by the incessant wars of the ambitious monarchs. Europe's unhappiness reflected a deep uncertainty and restlessness. It was a world adrift. The lines lashing it to the old age of blind authority had been loosened, and as yet it had no secure mooring to the modern age. The blame—and the credit—lay with the Renaissance. Its gusty winds were enlivening but they had not brought peace. The Renaissance had spread abroad the most unsettling idea ever to enter the mind of man, bidding him dare to be himself. It had led artists to break with Gothic and Byzantine traditions and to paint pictures, carve sculpture, and build churches in which living figures were suffused in light and color. It provoked philosophers and scientists to seek facts, ever more facts, and to ignore ancient dogmatisms. It encouraged scholars and common men to write and speak in their vernacular tongues and not to be held in bondage to Latin. It spurred printers to make many books. It drove buyers and sellers to new energy, loosing the initiative of the individual from the policing of the state. The Renaissance fostered restlessness in religion and was in part responsible for the Protestant Revolt in Central Europe and the Catholic Reform in Spain and elsewhere. Its spirit was generous and eclectic, prompting men to lay hold upon truth and beauty no matter whence they came, from Greek or Roman or Moslem.

To this restless Europe came the distraction of the discovery of America. Here at last was promise of adventure, gold, and glory. Spain and Portugal would gather the quickest prizes, then England, France, and Holland would claim their share, and all Europe would feel the quickening spirit of a new golden age.

CHRISTOPHER COLUMBUS AND THE CONQUEST OF THE CARIBBEAN WORLD

Columbus was not the first European to step on American soil. The Norsemen of Scandinavia claimed that honor 500 years before Columbus. They were rough fellows who ranged far and loved nothing better than to drink stiff toasts from the scoured skull of a freshly beheaded victim. (Their descendants still cry *skål,* "skull," as they lift their glasses.) They had swift, light boats driven by oars. Their navigators sailed by the stars; the magnetic compass was not yet in use. Norsemen settled Iceland in the ninth century, Greenland in the tenth. In 1000 or thereabouts, Leif Ericsson pushed south from Greenland to the temperate North American mainland, where he found wild grapes. He called the spot *Vinland,* "Wine-Land." Later, another chieftain named Thorfinn Karlsefni tried unsuccessfully to establish colonies in Labrador, Nova Scotia, or New England. Although there were probably further abortive colonial enterprises before Columbus, the evidence is unclear. If Christopher Columbus was not the first finder of America, he had the good fortune to represent a nation which was enterprising enough to follow up the explorer with the farmer, miner, and priest, all equipped to create permanent homes in a new world.

For 500 years men have argued in a dozen languages as to where and when Columbus was born. Books variously contend that he was a Spaniard, a Portuguese, a Catalan, a Jew, a Frenchman, a German, an Englishman, a Greek, or an Armenian. "It only remains," writes Samuel Eliot Morison, "for some American patrioteer to come forward and claim that Columbus was really an Indian, native to these shores, who was 'blown across' . . . and so knew his way home." The best available evidence suggests that he was born in Genoa, probably in 1451, and was baptized with the name of the third-century St. Christopher—"the Christ-bearer." We gather that Columbus was born to poverty, that his father was a master weaver of such improvidence as to make the family's next meal uncertain, that the boy had little or no schooling, and that he worked as a woolcarder in his father's shop until he was twenty-two. We can readily picture the influence upon a restless boy of the bustling port city of Genoa with its great shipyards, its map makers, its docks swarming with traders and navigators from strange places. By 1475 he had served as seaman on various ships in the Mediterranean. In 1476 he was headed for the Atlantic, when raiders intercepted and plunged him into the sea off the Portuguese coast, a fateful accident that led him to Lisbon, then a center of maritime activity. From Lisbon he sailed on several expeditions, perhaps journeying as far as Ireland and Iceland, and then settled in Portugal until about 1485.

It was Portugal that schooled the future Admiral of the Ocean Sea. Here he married a lady of some importance, who, after she had borne him a son Diego, shortly died. Here he learned Castilian, the language of the upper-class Portuguese. He also learned Latin, necessary for reading ancient

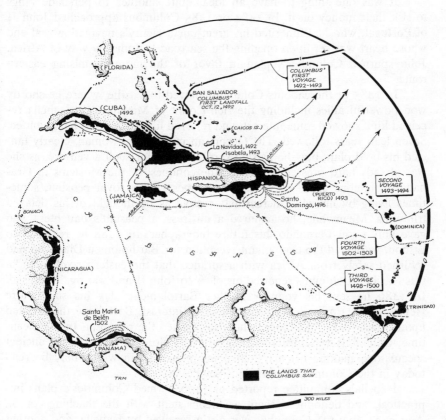

Columbus's Four Voyages, 1492–1503

books on navigation. He learned what there was to know about navigation, thanks to the pioneering work of Henry the Navigator. He learned about the brave new ships developed by the Portuguese in their African explorings, about the caravel with its revolutionary reshaping of hulls and recutting of sails, the most swift and stalwart vessel so far designed. The caravel, the result, writes Morison, of Henry the Navigator's "happy marriage of mathematical learning to practical seamanship," could make 150 miles a day under ordinary conditions, more than 200 when winds were favorable.

It was in Portugal that Columbus's great idea was born—to sail west to Asia. It was not far, he thought, only 2,400 miles to Cipango (Japan), 3,500 miles to Hangchow. He did not know of intervening oceans and continents. We can guess where he got the idea: perhaps from the idle talk of mariners, their tales of islands sighted, driftwood collected; perhaps from conjectures in old books. The idea was not altogether new; geographers and map makers had long been saying that the earth was shaped like a pear or an orange.

It was one thing to have an idea, quite another to persuade kings to risk their money on it. In 1484 or 1485 Columbus approached John II of Portugal, who had inherited his great-uncle Henry's navigating zeal and whose heart was set upon opening the sea road to India by way of Africa. John spurned Columbus's plan in favor of the more promising eastern route.

In 1485 or thereabouts Columbus moved to Castile, where he shortly won powerful allies including the rich Count of Medina Celi. Isabella received him, showed some interest, and referred his proposal to a committee. Seven lean years followed. The Queen, an imaginative woman, clearly fancied his bold plan; but she had no surplus funds for such a venture, as she was already hard pressed to finance the conquest of the Moslems in Granada. Columbus could only wait, sometimes with a royal pension, sometimes living by his wits, increasingly restive as he thought of his delayed triumphs. Meanwhile, he acquired a mistress, a peasant's daughter, who gave him a son Fernando, his future biographer. In 1488 he returned to Lisbon, witnessed the triumphant reception for Bartholomeu Dias who had returned safely from Africa with assurance that the eastern road to India was feasible. Columbus renewed his pleas to John II and was again refused. In 1489 he sent his younger brother Bartolomé to lay his suit before Henry VII of England, who showed slight interest. Bartolomé then waited upon Charles VIII of France, who also rejected the proposal. In the meantime, Columbus was busily reading Marco Polo, Pliny, and other ancient speculators, making his marginal notes in bad Latin which may be read today in the Columbian Library in Seville.

Isabella's committee reported in 1490, termed Columbus's plans impractical, and denounced them as inconsistent with the teachings of St. Augustine. In 1491 Columbus was again received by Isabella, and another committee was appointed, which in its turn reported adversely. Columbus, out of patience, decided to go to France and appeal again to Charles VIII. At this juncture, on January 2, 1492, Granada fell. The Christian prisoners were released from Moslem dungeons and eight centuries of infidel meddling were ended. Columbus again appealed to Isabella. When he was again refused, he set out for France. A last minute intervention of a friend at court brought a sudden change of the royal mind. Isabella sent a messenger who overtook Columbus and brought him back. She then accepted his terms. Columbus was solemnly proclaimed "Admiral and Viceroy and Governor" of all lands he might find; the honors and perquisites granted to him, including one-tenth of all profits, would be assured to "his heirs and successors forever"; and to Columbus were entrusted royal letters to the Grand Khan, to all the kings and lords of India.

The Atlantic village of Palos was the port of embarkation for Columbus's first voyage (August 3, 1492—March 15, 1493). Cádiz, a more logical choice, was too busy with shipping thousands of exiled Jews. Palos, guilty of some unrecorded offense, was ordered to provide two caravels, free of all costs, to the Admiral. Three ships were readied. The *Niña,* Columbus's favorite, and the *Pinta* were each of some sixty tons; the *Santa María* was somewhat larger. Ninety men and boys were enlisted, chiefly careless fellows eager for adventure, also a few veterans of earlier voyages, including the three Pinzón brothers. There was no priest.

Columbus's journals tell the story in detail. The preamble, after the customary verbal obeisance to his monarchs, carefully restates the terms under which he would sail; it reveals him as a sound man of business who would not neglect to write a careful letter of confirmation. He wrote: "Your Highnesses . . . granted me many rewards and ennobled me so that henceforth I might call myself by a noble title and be Admiral-in-Chief of the Ocean Sea and Viceroy and Perpetual Governor of all the islands and mainlands that I should discover and win, or that henceforth might be discovered and won in the Ocean Sea, and that my eldest son should succeed me, and thus from rank to rank forever."

They sailed on August 3. After a call at the Canary Islands for repairs, rerigging, and provisioning, they set sail for the west—and Asia. The winds were propitious, but the crew was troublesome. Muttering and grumbling increased; there was talk of mutiny and of killing the visionary Admiral—but Columbus did not waver, promised that he would "keep on until he found [the Indies] with the aid of Our Lord." On October 12 an island was sighted, a coral bank of the Bahamas (the modern Watlings Island), thirteen miles long and six wide, to which Columbus gave the name San Salvador. Here they found a few simple Arawaks, an "ingenuous and free" people, hardwood forests, strange lovely flowers, but no gold. On October 28 they reached northern Cuba and, cruising along the shore, decided that this was the mainland of China or Japan; but they looked in vain for the splendid cities with gold-roofed palaces which Marco Polo had described two centuries before. Meanwhile, Indians told them that a great capital lay inland, and Columbus dispatched a delegation with Ferdinand's and Isabella's letter to the Grand Khan. They discovered neither Grand Khan nor golden palaces, only a rude Indian village presided over by a naked bronzed chieftain. Columbus faithfully reported to his sovereigns on the "guileless and unwarlike" savages, ripe for conversion to the true faith.

Haiti, to the east, was the next land of promise. Meanwhile, Martín Alonzo Pinzón, a disloyal fellow, disappeared with the *Pinta* on a private gold hunt. On Christmas Eve, Columbus, with the *Santa María* and the *Niña,* reached the northern shore of Haiti and anchored in a harbor which he called San Nicolás, naming the island *La Isla Española*—later Latinized as Hispaniola—the island which would shelter the first permanent European colony in America and which would bring Columbus his greatest glory and finally his greatest sorrow. Troubles began within a few hours. On Christmas morning the *Santa María* was caught on a reef and wrecked. The Indians, led by the chieftain, helped to land the crew and unload its stores, and provided houses and provisions. Columbus's report is eloquent in admiration of these primitive people so "loyal and without greed." They were "most handsome men and women" and not least of their charms were their golden ornaments. At the sight of gold Columbus decided that the island was worthy of royal attention. A considerable quantity of gold was collected by barter, and expeditions sent inland brought back fabulous tales of stores of gold awaiting collection. The fortress and settlement of Navidad was established on Haiti's north coast, and the forty-four men of the wrecked *Santa María* were left with orders to seek gold, to explore the island, to abstain from cruelty, and to leave the women alone.

On January 16, 1493, Columbus was rejoined by the disloyal Pinzón and the *Pinta,* and set sail for Spain. After a stormy trip and a stop at the Azores they reached the river Tagus and Lisbon on March 4. The Portuguese were in an ugly mood, resentful of Spain's success. Some demanded that the upstart Admiral be jailed, but John II, aware of the superior power of Castile, permitted him to sail in peace. The expedition reached Palos on March 15, 1493.

This was Columbus's hour of glory, never again equaled. He was received by his sovereigns in Barcelona with the dignity and pageantry due the Admiral of the Ocean Sea. There were now no scoffers; no one questioned his most exaggerated tales.

Columbus's exploits precipitated a delicate diplomatic dispute between Spain and Portugal. Portugal pressed her claims, based upon prior papal grants on the Guinea Coast of Africa. The case was laid before Pope Alexander VI, the Spanish Rodrigo Borgia who owed his office to Ferdinand and Isabella. The Pope's decision, expressed in successive bulls, divided the uncharted world between Portugal and Spain, set the line of demarcation 100 leagues west of the Azores and the Cape Verde Islands, the line to run from pole to pole. Portugal, not content with this settlement, won the Treaty of Tordesillas from Spain in June, 1494, by which the line of demarcation was set 370 leagues west of the Cape Verde Islands. This imaginary line would finally serve to create Brazil as a Portuguese colony.

On one question all were agreed. Columbus must hurry back, stake out Spanish claims against Portuguese and all other intruders, get gold, win souls, and find the elusive kingdoms of Japan and China. Ferdinand and Isabella provided 15,000 ducats. On September 25, 1493, little more than six months after his return, Columbus sailed for his second voyage (1493–96) with seventeen ships and 1,200 to 1,500 men—soldiers, artisans, nobles, and five priests. They carried a cargo useful for establishing permanent settlements—horses, sheep, cattle, seeds, wheat, barley, fruit, tools, and shoots of sugar cane. No women were included; they could go later.

Columbus chose a southerly route; he sighted first the island of Dominica in the lesser Antilles. He continued north touching various of the islands over which England, France, and Holland would struggle in later years, discovered the Virgin Islands and Puerto Rico. He pushed on to Hispaniola to learn the fate of his settlement of Navidad. The fort was in ruins; the men had disappeared. The Indian chief, still Columbus's friend, told the sorry record of the forty-four dead (the entire crew of the *Santa María*)—their merciless treatment of the Indians, their greed for gold and women, their quarrels among themselves, and finally their slaying by the angered Indians. Columbus now founded a new settlement called Isabella on the north coast of Hispaniola, with elaborate plans for streets, plazas, and public buildings. There were tasks to be done and not enough Indian slaves to do them. Columbus ordered his men to take up tools, to get to work. There were mutinies against such affront; the men were gentlemen, and gentlemen do not soil their hands. Columbus decreed rigid discipline, and his men plotted against him. Sickness took heavy toll; food was unfamiliar, hygiene was primitive, medical skill was lacking. Columbus presided over an angry, miserable company.

Meanwhile, Columbus must deliver gold or lose the support of the Spanish Court. He sent an expeditionary force into the interior under Alonzo de Ojeda, a hot-tempered, ruthless fellow, who compelled the Indians to mine the gold he found, under penalty of death. The good will cultivated by Columbus disappeared. Columbus thought now to satisfy Spanish cupidity by sending 500 slaves to Spain. At least half of them died on the ocean crossing, others died after reaching Spain, and Isabella did not relish the slave business.

In the spring of 1494 Columbus made another effort to discover the Grand Khan and Japan. He sailed to Jamaica, had an inhospitable welcome from the natives, explored a bit of the island, and then moved on to Cuba. He skirted the Cuban coast, sent expeditions inland, found no gold, and concluded that Cuba was indeed the mainland, a mistake which he could have corrected by sailing two days farther to the west. In September, 1494, he returned to Isabella, his settlement on Hispaniola, to find his brother Bartolomé appointed by the Spanish Court as his deputy. Bartolomé had little of the Admiral's genius. He was a hard-working, plodding map-maker, faithful, loyal, courageous, and a believer in stiff discipline. He had borne down upon mutinous Spaniards who would not work and upon Indians who would not dig their quota of gold. The island was distraught. The severity of forced labor, the drain upon meager food supplies, the Spaniards' seizure of Indian women, provoked Indian revolts which were ruthlessly crushed. The Indians fled the seacoast, taking refuge in the mountains. The prospects for Spain's first colony were bleak. Columbus's critics saw to it that all blame was laid on him and that full reports reached the Court. Columbus, eager to defend himself, returned to Spain in June, 1496.

Spain was glad to have the Admiral back but pride in him was dimmed. He had little to show for his labors—a little gold, a few Indians, some trinkets. He had found neither Japan nor the Grand Khan; in fact he did not know what he had found. His one settlement was in anarchy. Humiliated and weary, he took refuge with the Franciscans, assuming their rough habit, and waited. Finally, Ferdinand and Isabella summoned him, received him affectionately, and said little of the complaints against him, but when he asked for money for a third voyage, promising that this time he would find the mainland, they gave scant encouragement. He waited two years before he got his ships.

Columbus's third voyage (1498–1500) led to the island of Trinidad, where he anchored on July 31, 1498. From there he sailed along the Venezuelan coast, finding new tribes, strange animals, and lush forests. In mid-August, 1498, he wrote in his journal: "I am convinced that this is the mainland, and very large, of which no knowledge has been had until now . . . and there is a river so great that it makes a fresh water sea of forty-eight leagues." But his zeal as an explorer was waning. He did no more than probe the coast and take a few notes on the flooded Orinoco.

Now he became obsessed with cosmic speculation, indulged in weird conjectures as to "the earthly Paradise," which he identified with Venezuela. He harked back to ancient books, dreamed of the Garden of Eden, a Paradise perched upon a nodule of earth high above all creation. There are, he recalled, four rivers in Paradise, and he concluded that the Orinoco was one of them.

Meanwhile, he must get on to Santo Domingo, the new capital of Hispaniola founded by his brother Bartolomé and fated to be the first permanent European settlement in the New World. Crippled with arthritis and with his eyes greatly inflamed, he reached the city at the end of August and found the island embroiled in civil strife between Bartolomé's forces and rebels under Francisco Roldán. Roldán had won the support of the Indians, to whom he promised relief from all levies, and also of numerous Spaniards, who were tired of Bartolomé's iron discipline. The disorder was aggravated by an outbreak of syphilis, from which about a fourth of the Spaniards were suffering.

Columbus supported his brother and appealed to the Crown for reinforcements, but finally he made such disastrous concessions to Roldán as to discredit his own leadership. Angry complaints, just and unjust, reached Isabella, who decided that Columbus's usefulness as a colonizer was done. In mid-1500 the Court sent Francisco Bobadilla to Hispaniola as governor, with orders to supplant Columbus and to investigate his record. Bobadilla, on reviewing the evidence, ordered Columbus's arrest and shipped him to Spain in chains. The Admiral wrote to the Queen's confidante: "It is now seventeen years since I came to serve these princes . . . they made me pass eight of them in discussion, and at the end rejected it as a thing of jest. None the less, I persisted therein. . . . I have placed under their sovereignty more land than there is in Africa and Europe, and more than seventeen hundred islands, without counting Hispaniola. . . . In seven years I, by the divine will, made that conquest. At a time when I was entitled to expect rewards and retirement, I was incontinently arrested and sent home loaded with chains, to my great dishonor and with slight service to their Highnesses."[1]

[1] Letter to Juana de Torres, quoted by Samuel Eliot Morison: *Admiral of the Ocean Sea*, 2 vols., Boston, 1942. Vol. II, pp. 309–10. Reprinted with the permission of the Atlantic Monthly Press-Little, Brown & Co.

There was no immediate royal welcome for the chained Admiral. He was released six weeks after his arrival, however, and was received affectionately by the monarchs, who reassured him of his rights. But his days of glory were ended. In February, 1502, Nicolás de Ovando was sent to Hispaniola as governor, and Columbus was not consulted. Nevertheless, he was to have one last chance.

Isabella rid herself of the importunate Admiral by giving him four ships for his fourth voyage (1502–04). Sailing in May, 1502, he made his swiftest crossing, twenty-one days, touching the island of Martinique. He skirted the lesser Antilles and Puerto Rico, heading for Santo Domingo. Governor Ovando, who had taken office a few weeks before, brusquely denied him permission to land. Columbus, lying off shore, sent warning of an approaching hurricane and advised against the sailing of the armada which was preparing to depart for Spain. This advice was not respected; the armada pushed out into the Caribbean and was almost completely destroyed. Columbus, denied the security of the harbor, found refuge in a cove and escaped with slight damage. He now sailed west, continuously buffeted by heavy winds, and on July 30 reached the Bay Islands off the coast of Honduras. For eight months he explored the coast from Honduras to Panama, convinced that he had found the Malay peninsula. The driving storms, skirmishes with hostile Indians, and disease took heavy toll of his men and ships. He himself was a sick man. In April, 1503, heading again for Hispaniola, he was forced to beach his ships at Jamaica, where he remained for a year and five days. When rescuers arrived, he was a broken man. He reached Spain in 1504 and shortly heard of the death of Isabella. Columbus died on May 20, 1506, in the city of Valladolid. Two countries claim to have his bones: one tomb is in the Cathedral of Seville, with an inscription recalling "the ingratitude of America," and another is in Santo Domingo, on the island he discovered and named.[2]

The greatness of Columbus needs no defense. His tenacity, courage, faith, his rough skill, his genius for handling men, his generous instincts in dealing with Indians—these qualities need no laboring. His obvious limitations, his curiously unscientific mind, which often crippled his genius, his ineptitude with scheming politicians, his nagging insistence upon his own honors and emoluments—these things must also be noted.

Columbus died at the age of about fifty-five, an old man by sixteenth-century standards. The tragedy is that he did not die earlier. If he had died at the end of his first voyage or even at the end of the second, few would have questioned his greatness. But as it was, his true stature did not appear until many years had passed.

Had justice been done to the man who found it, the new land would have been called Columbia; but by a fluke it was named America

[2] There is an immense volume of print arguing the rival claims of Seville and Santo Domingo. Morison concludes that Santo Domingo has the better claim. "That is," says Morison, "as it should be. Columbus belongs to America, the New World of his discovery." Morison, *op. cit.*, Vol. II, p. 426.

after a Florentine clerk whose itch for travel led to service in several overseas expeditions. Amerigo Vespucci's claim to glory lay not in his discoveries but in the speed with which he wrote down what he had seen, heard—
and imagined. In 1503 Amerigo's famous letter *Mundus Novus* was circulated over Europe, and his account of the discovery of the New World was
read long before Columbus's journals were made public. In 1507 a German cartographer published a map with the word "America." The
name stuck.

Thanks to Christopher Columbus, the Caribbean Sea became a
Spanish lake. The Admiral had discovered it, but it was left to others to
organize its lands under the Crown. The island of Hispaniola, after six
years under the harsh rule of Nicolás de Ovando, in 1509 welcomed Columbus's son Diego as governor. In that same year the energetic and un-
principled Ponce de León became governor of Puerto Rico, the island he
had ruthlessly subdued the year before. In 1511 Diego Velásquez was
assigned the rule of Cuba as a lieutenant of Diego Columbus. In 1514
Ponce de León, seeking the mythical island of Bimini where Indians had
promised he would find the fountain of eternal youth, discovered the
Florida mainland.

The conquest of the Caribbean coastal lands of Central and South
America was marked at first by costly defeats. Alonso de Ojeda led an expedition in 1509 against northern Colombia, and Diego de Nicuesa led
another to Central America; both were routed by Indians. Success came,
however, when a few survivors of Ojeda's forces, with timely reinforcements, established themselves on the Isthmus of Panama, where under the
wise rule of Vasco Núñez de Balboa they built the city of Darién and laid
the foundation of a colony. In 1513 Balboa and a few companions crossed
the isthmus and looked out upon the Pacific (so named by Magellan in
1520). Wading breast deep into the surf, Balboa raised the flag of Castile,
took possession of the ocean and of all lands it touched in the name of his
sovereign. Balboa, one of the wisest and most merciful of conquerors, was
soon displaced as governor of Darién by Pedro Arias de Ávila (usually
known as Pedrarias), a harsh man who ordered Balboa beheaded and for
sixteen years ruled arbitrarily in Darién and later in Nicaragua.

THE CONQUEST OF MEXICO

By 1515 Cuba had supplanted Hispaniola as the stronghold of Spain
in America. Governor Diego Velásquez had quieted the Indians (and
reduced their numbers in the process), and was ready for new conquests.
He had able aides—Bartolomé de las Casas, Hernán Cortés, and Pánfilo
de Narváez.

Mexico, rumored storehouse of unlimited gold, was the chief target.
Velásquez sent an expedition in 1517 under Francisco Hernández de
Córdova, which landed on the island of Cozumel off Yucatán, explored the
coast of the peninsula, and saw a few abandoned Maya cities which still

revealed the artistry of their creators. Córdova, who was wounded in skirmishes with the Indians, returned to Cuba to die. In 1518 Juan de Grijalva led a second expedition which visited Cozumel and followed the coast north beyond present-day Veracruz. He coaxed a few gold trinkets from the Indians and returned to Cuba.

Then emerged the valiant figure of Hernán Cortés. Born in 1485 in backward Estremadura and educated at the University of Salamanca, Cortés had come to the New World in 1504, later accompanying Velásquez to Cuba. His years in Cuba had been full of reckless, amorous adventures. He was the Spanish gentleman—generous, impulsive, courageous, charming. He was contemptuous of all discipline except that of the king himself, an attitude destined to provoke trouble between him and the governor. Cortés was *alcalde* (mayor) of Santiago in 1519 when Velásquez named him as commander of a new expedition to Mexico. Shortly, remembering his subordinate's waywardness, the governor sought to recall the appointment; but Cortés, in order to forestall such action, had already hurriedly set sail on February 10, 1519, with his fleet of eleven vessels, 550 men, and 16 horses.

Cortés's first stops were in Yucatán and Tabasco, where good fortune gave him interpreters. In Yucatán he picked up Aguilar, survivor of an earlier expedition, who had escaped the cage in which his captors were fattening him for the feast and had lived for several years with the Indians, learning the Maya tongue. Then in Tabasco, Cortés was given a slave named Malinche—Marina, the Spaniards called her—daughter of an Aztec *cacique* (chieftain), who had been sold into slavery among the Maya. Cortés thus acquired excellent aides: Malinche spoke Aztec and Maya; Aguilar spoke Maya and Spanish. Malinche—Cortés's mistress, counselor, interpreter—rendered as great service as any hundred fighting men. Time and again her quick wit saved Cortés from torture and death. Out of love for her master, she told what she knew of Moctezuma's empire, of its vastness and great population and the bitter wars between subject tribes. She told Cortés of the superstitions of priests and rulers, of the legend of long-lost Quetzalcoatl, the fabulous god-king who had promised to return out of the waters of the East. She told of the astrologers who were convinced by heavenly signs that the white strangers in their white-winged ships were the invincible army of Quetzalcoatl. Malinche herself may have believed that her lover and master was indeed that gracious and all-powerful god and king.

Cortés cast anchor in the harbor of San Juan de Ulloa on Good Friday, 1519, landed his men and horses to the bewilderment of the natives, and immediately organized the municipality of Villa Rica de la Vera Cruz, "the rich city of the True Cross." By creation of a municipality, which under Castilian law enjoyed the direct protection of the King, Cortés was appealing over the head of the Governor to Charles I himself. The *cabildo,* or municipal council, immediately named Cortés governor and commander of New Spain. This was Cortés's declaration of independence from Velásquez.

The tale of the conquest of Mexico has been told and retold for four centuries.[3] It is the familiar epic of the toppling of an ancient civilization by a handful of resolute men. Veracruz was the beachhead, held for the King of Spain under the double symbols of Cross and Sword. Then began the skillful juggling of words and deeds by which the scattered tribes of Indians were variously appeased, made allies, or stirred to resistance against Moctezuma. From the capital of Tenochtitlán came emissaries of Moctezuma, burning copal incense in the Spaniards' honor, bearing gifts of cotton fabric, featherwork, and gold ornaments. But they brought also that ruler's demands that the intruders quit Mexican soil and sail away. This royal counsel was acceptable to many of Cortés's men, who plotted against their captain and demanded to return to Cuba. Cortés's reply was characteristic: he ordered his ships burned and thus silenced the mutiny. Then he marched north, won over the chiefs of coastal Cempoala, and gained new allies. Turning inland through the coastal jungle, he pushed up the rough mountain trails toward Tenochtitlán. He reached Tlaxcala, home of the most stalwart resistance to Moctezuma, where he first fought the Tlaxcalans and then won them to an alliance which greatly served the final Spanish triumph. With new Indian reinforcements the Spanish army moved to Cholula, for centuries a holy city of Toltecs and Aztecs. Here outward hospitality cloaked a plot inspired by Moctezuma's agents. Warned by his mistress Malinche, Cortés arranged the wholesale massacre of several thousand Cholulans. His prestige was now high; thousands flocked to his banner as the Aztecs temporarily ended their resistance.

The road now lay open to the Aztec capital. A few days' march brought the Spaniards and their straggling allies to the divide two miles high from which they could look down upon the valley of Anáhuac and Lake Texcoco, its islands crowned with the walls, houses, and temples of Tenochtitlán, the most populous capital of Indian America. The invaders filed down the mountainside and were met outside the city by numerous nobles, headed by the Lord of Texcoco, Moctezuma's nephew. The Aztec noble, wrote Bernal Díaz fifty years later, was "carried in a magnificent litter adorned with green plumes, and enriched with jewels, set in the branched pillars of solid gold. He was borne by eight lords, who assisted him out of the litter, and swept the way by which he was to pass. . . . We then set forward on the road to Mexico. . . . When we beheld the number of populous towns on the water and firm ground, and that broad causeway, running straight and level to the city, we could compare it to nothing but the enchanted scenes we had read of in *Amadis de Gaul,*

---

3 Cortés told the story himself in his letters to Charles I. Numerous contemporaries, or those who came shortly after, left their versions. The most illuminating is Bernal Díaz del Castillo's *The True History of the Conquest of Mexico,* translated by Maurice Keatinge (printed for J. Wright, Piccadilly, by John Dean, High Street, Congleton, 1800), the work of one who served under Cortés. It was an angry answer to Cortes's apologist, López de Gómara, whose account gave most of the credit to Cortés himself. Díaz wrote his book in Guatemala about fifty years after the Conquest when he was more than eighty, blind, and deaf; the *True History,* finished in 1572, clearly and fervently states that Cortés "owed his success, under God, to the stout and valiant captains, and to us brave soldiers." Another classic is William H. Prescott's *History of the Conquest of Mexico* (1843), written by a scholar who was almost blind and had never visited the lands of which he wrote.

from the great towers and temples, and other edifices of lime and stone which seemed to rise out of the water. To many of us it seemed doubtful whether we were asleep or awake; nor is the manner in which I express myself to be wondered at, for it must be considered, that never yet did man see, hear, or dream of anything equal to the spectacle which appeared to our eyes on this day." Nor was the wonder lessened as they were led to lodgings prepared for them "in palaces magnificently built of stone, and the timber of which was cedar, with spacious courts, and apartments furnished with canopies of the finest cotton . . . gardens . . . beautiful and aromatic plants . . . and a lake of the clearest water . . . when I beheld the scenes that were around me, I thought within myself that this was the garden of the world!"[4]

Moctezuma's welcome was outwardly friendly, but Cortés knew that he had led his men into a trap. The courtesy shown them could not hide the fact that a few hundred intruders were at the mercy of a ruler who commanded tens of thousands. Nor were their fears quieted by further inspection of the formidable city. The temple-pyramid of the god of war, topped by the sacrificial altar tended by priests in blood-caked robes, the air heavy with the stench of human blood, was not reassuring. Cortés decided that he must move swiftly, or shortly he would not move at all.

Cortés found pretext for action. Word came that some of his garrison in Veracruz had been killed by officers of Moctezuma, presumably on royal orders. Cortés, after a night of prayer, took two interpreters and six armed guards, crossed the square to Moctezuma's palace, charged him with treason, invited him to move to the Spaniards' quarters, and made him a prisoner in his own capital. The Aztec chiefs responsible for the murders in Veracruz were brought in and burned alive before the emperor's palace. Cortés imprisoned the Lord of Texcoco and numerous other princes, ordered ships built for emergency use, and instructed Moctezuma to assemble a vast store of gold, silver, and precious stones. The spiritless compliance of Moctezuma can probably be explained only by his conviction that Cortés was indeed the avenging Quetzalcoatl. But Cortés's possession of Moctezuma's person was of immense aid to the Spaniards: so long as the Aztec ruler retained his prestige, his subjects would not imperil his life by attack.

Disturbing news then came from Veracruz. Eighteen Spanish ships had anchored with 800 foot soldiers, 80 horsemen, and ample munitions; this expedition, commanded by Pánfilo de Narváez, had been sent by Velásquez to supplant Cortés. Quick-witted Cortés professed joy over this welcome reinforcement, left Pedro de Alvarado in charge of Tenochtitlán, and made a quick descent with a detachment of soldiers to Veracruz. He fell upon Narváez's forces, took the leader prisoner, and persuaded the men to join his command. Meanwhile in the capital city hot-headed Alvarado had murdered some 200 Aztec nobles, unloosing new hatred of the Spaniards. As an added complication, Narváez's expedition brought smallpox, new to America, which swept Mexico, destroying entire com-

[4] Bernal Díaz del Castillo, *op. cit.,* pp. 130–1.

munities and killing so many able-bodied workers that fields went untilled and famine was added to other disasters.

Cortés returned to Tenochtitlán with his augmented forces, including new Tlaxcalan allies. He faced an angry populace, no longer ready to obey their captive emperor. Alvarado's stupidity had undermined what was left of Moctezuma's prestige, for an emperor and nobility so easily subdued had lost all royal dignity. Cortés ordered Moctezuma to the gallery of the palace to make a fresh appeal to the people. The response was a volley of stones. Moctezuma was struck in the head and died three days later. The populace now rallied to a kinsman of Moctezuma, Cuitláhuac.

The Spanish position was no longer tenable. Many had died; many were wounded or sick; food and water were scarce; powder was exhausted. Meanwhile, Aztec forces were increasing ominously. Cortés fixed the night of June 30, 1520, for retreat. The gold, silver, and precious stones were divided among the men. The flight was disastrous, as they fought their way through the city. A movable bridge for use in crossing gaps in the causeways jammed and was abandoned, and each man had to swim for his life. Weighted down with gold and silver, many drowned. A few survivors reached Tacuba and from there fled to friendly Tlaxcala. They rallied to face the Aztecs in the uneven battle of Otumba, suffered further losses, and staggered back to Tlaxcala.

Cortés, refusing to admit defeat, prepared for a new attack. Thirteen vessels were built in sections, these to be carried over the mountains and launched upon the lake. Rigging and equipment were brought from Veracruz. On December 26, 1520, six months after the *noche triste*—the "sad night" of retreat—Cortés reviewed his troops at Tlaxcala, 550 infantry, 40 horsemen, 8 guns, some thousands of Tlaxcalan allies. Two days later they set out for Tenochtitlán, where Moctezuma's successor Cuitláhuac, who had died from smallpox after a reign of only eighty days, had been succeeded by Cuauhtémoc. On December 31, Cortés reached Texcoco, his headquarters for more than three months of further preparation. His jigsaw-puzzle ships were fitted together and launched. In April, 1521, plans were perfected, and the attacking forces were divided among three commanders, Pedro de Alvarado, Cristóbal de Olid, and Gonzalo de Sandoval. They penetrated the heart of the city, climbed the temple-pyramid, but were driven back with the loss of many men. For ten days they watched helplessly the ritual processions to the sacrificial altar, listened to the great drum beating out its hymn of triumph as the hearts of brave comrades were ripped from their living bodies.

Cortés now decided to destroy Tenochtitlán—"the most beautiful city in the world," as he called it—building by building, block by block. He offered the young emperor safety and continued rule in return for surrender; but Cuauhtémoc refused. Fighting continued for almost four months, until a mere fourth of the city was still standing and few Indian warriors survived. On August 13, Cuauhtémoc himself was captured, taken to Cortés, treated with royal honors, embraced; his only response was: "I have done my duty in defense of my city. Take that dagger and kill me." "Cuauhtémoc," Bernal Díaz later wrote, "showed gentle breeding in form and features, a long and cheerful countenance, eyes which looked at one gravely and pleasantly." Cortés ordered him tortured to persuade him to reveal hidden treasure but the Aztec refused to speak.

Cortés, now only thirty-six years old, had won a spectacular success in little more than two years. He had reached Veracruz in April, 1519, entered Tenochtitlán in November, outwitted Narváez in May, 1520, ordered a humiliating retreat in June, returned to the attack in December, and won control of the city by August, 1521. Tenochtitlán was now the capital of "New Spain of the Ocean Sea."

The collapse of the Aztec capital brought quick proffers of allegiance from chieftains who were eager to be on the winning side. In 1522 Cortés was named governor and captain-general of New Spain. He ingeniously consolidated his winnings. He sent expeditions to the high crater of Popocatépetl for sulfur with which to make gunpowder. He fostered mining of copper and tin, and was soon casting bronze cannon. He organized shipbuilding on the Pacific coast. He rebuilt much of the capital city. He dispatched lieutenants on various errands of further pacification, and he himself journeyed far afield. But the Spanish King, grateful as he was to Cortés, did not intend to permit any man to become indispensable, and soon Cortés found his governing powers abridged by new royal officers who had never raised a lance for King or St. James.

In 1529 Cortés sailed to Spain with forty Indian nobles, much gold and silver, strange animals, plants and fruits, and specimens of Mexican handicrafts. He was received with every honor by Charles I, who confirmed his titles, made him the Marquis of the Valley of Oaxaca, and granted him an *encomienda*[5] which embraced about 25,000 square miles south of the capital, with a population of more than 100,000. At Cortés's request, Charles decreed perpetual exemption from tribute to the people of Tlaxcala in recognition of their services to the Crown. Royal provision was also made for the education of the sons and daughters of Mexican nobles, for the building of schools and churches. But when Cortés returned to Mexico, he found his powers as captain-general so limited by the royal *audiencia* (circuit court) as to make his honors empty. In 1535 he was definitely superseded by the first viceroy to New Spain, Antonio de Mendoza.

Cortés's restlessness needed new scope. He organized four expeditions in the Pacific; on one which he himself commanded, he discovered the coast of California. He finally returned to Spain, where he died in 1547 at the age of sixty-two.

The breath-taking tale of Cortés should not lead to the neglect of explorers and fighters who carried the Spanish flag to neighboring lands in North and Central America. In 1528 Pánfilo de Narváez, the earlier rival of Cortés, landed on the coast of Florida with 400 men, most of whom

[5] The *encomienda*, a grant of Indians to deserving soldiers of the Crown, was, in effect, a grant of land upon which the Indians lived. See pp. 186–7 for further discussion.

were promptly killed by Indians or fevers. Four survivors, led by Álvar Núñez Cabeza de Vaca, made an unbelievable journey of eight years along the northern shores of the Gulf of Mexico, across Texas and Mexico to the Gulf of California, and finally reached Mexico City in 1536.[6] In 1539 Hernando de Soto landed in Florida with 600 men, crossed the North American Southeast, and discovered the Mississippi in 1541 before his health broke and he died of fever.

Meanwhile, two lieutenants of Cortés had moved into Central America. In 1523 Cristóbal de Olid sailed to Honduras, where he announced his independence of Cortés, a bit of impudence which brought Cortés on a quick overland march—but Olid died before his captain-general arrived.

Pedro de Alvarado, who struck south into Guatemala in 1523, was a courageous soldier whose quick temper and scant pity had already embarrassed Cortés. Smallpox had swept before him, wiping out entire villages, but Alvarado's attacks were no less devastating. Despite continued resistance of the Indians, mutinies within his own ranks, and the rivalry of Governor Pedrarias of Panama, by 1530 Alvarado dominated much of Central America and had built his capital city in Guatemala. However, Central America, yielding neither gold nor silver, could not hold him, and in 1534 he sailed to Ecuador and entered the contest for the land of the Incas—an area already preempted by Francisco Pizarro. Exacting a high price from Pizarro, he withdrew from Ecuador; he returned to Guatemala and made plans for crossing the Pacific, a project forestalled by his death in an Indian war in Mexico.

Other expeditions probed the northwestern frontier of Mexico. In 1536 Viceroy Antonio de Mendoza received detailed and highly colored reports from Cabeza de Vaca of unbounded wealth in that corner of his realm and sent a Franciscan friar, Marcos de Niza, to ascertain the facts. Marcos returned with glowing tales of "The Seven Cities of Cíbola," whose stone houses of two, three, and four stories were ornamented with gold and turquoises. Mendoza, a godly man with an eye for business, chose his twenty-nine-year-old favorite, Francisco Vásquez de Coronado, to command an expedition for the conquest of cities that promised to rival Tenochtitlán itself. In 1540 Coronado set out with three hundred Spaniards and many Indians, and entered the region now known as Arizona and New Mexico. There he found the "Seven Cities," squat miserable villages of adobe huts quite bare of gold and turquoises. They were the Zuñi villages, as unimpressive then as they are today. Marcos de Niza, it seems, was blessed with more than his share of creative imagination. However, Coronado continued his search. One detachment of his men found the region of the Hopi Indians; another discovered the Grand Canyon of the Colorado, while Coronado himself led an expedition east along the Rio

---

[6] Cabeza de Vaca alternately outwitted the Indians, doctored them, was imprisoned by them, won their affection. He later turned up as governor of Paraguay after a fantastic journey through the jungles of southern Brazil. See Morris Bishop: *The Odyssey of Cabeza de Vaca* (New York: Century Co.; 1933).

Grande. In Texas Coronado was told of another El Dorado called Quivira, whose cities were encrusted with gold and precious stones. He struck northeast across present-day Oklahoma and Kansas, and found a few ragged villages of the Wichita Indians but no treasure. Although he returned to Mexico empty-handed, he had added the area from Arizona to Kansas to New Spain. It would be many years, however, before anyone would take that wind-swept waste seriously.

MAGELLAN PROVES THAT THE WORLD IS ROUND

Columbus and many before him had known that the world was round, but it remained for Fernão de Magalhães—whose name becomes Ferdinand Magellan in English—to prove it. Magellan, son of Portuguese lesser nobility, was born about 1480. He had been nurtured on the adventures of Henry the Navigator, had witnessed the triumphal return of Vasco da Gama from India, and had served in Portuguese India and Africa for nine years. In 1517 he offered his services to the King of Portugal, promising to find the westward passage to Asia. The Portuguese Court again, as in the case of Columbus, failed to recognize genius, and Magellan turned to Spain.

In 1517 Magellan, who had adopted Spanish citizenship, laid his plans before the Casa de Contratación (the Board of Trade). He was granted an audience by Charles I, the youthful monarch just come to the throne, and was eloquent in pressing his case. Magellan's methods of persuasion would do credit to the modern educational technician with his "audio-visual aids." He came to court with a great globe upon which were painted continents and vague routes across the seas. He was indefinite as to how he would pass the land barrier of America, but later it became clear that he expected to find a passage through the Río de la Plata, which had been discovered the year before by Díaz de Solís. He did not know of the Andes, which barred the way. Magellan convinced Charles, who in 1518 gave him a royal commission and the promise of five ships and provisions for two years.

On September 20, 1519, Magellan set out with about 270 men. He touched the coast of Brazil and sailed south to the Río de la Plata, where he found only fresh water, clear evidence that this was no passage to the western sea. In March, 1520, as winter was closing in, he anchored on the Argentine coast at Latitude 49° and provoked mutiny among his men by announcing that they would stay there until spring. A few quick shots quieted the mutiny, and the crew sat out the winter, carrying on a desultory trade with the Indians, whom Magellan called Patagones ("the big-footed"). In August they resumed the journey and reached the strait, now named after Magellan, in October. They sailed thirty-eight days through the winding strait to find a sea which Magellan called the Pacific. Now the way to Asia was open, but they could not know how great was this ocean, across which they boldly struck. Their provisions gave out, water failed, and they were sick and worn when, on March 6, 1521, they found islands which they called the Ladrones (robbers), after the light-fingered natives who boarded their ships. On March 16 they sighted new islands which were later called the Philippines in honor of the infant prince who would one day be Philip II. Here Magellan fell in a skirmish with the natives. His surviving men found their way back to Spain by way of India and Africa. Magellan had proved that Columbus was right.

THE CONQUEST OF PERU

It was now the Incas' turn. Their well-organized empire, despite civil war, was still impressive. Its royal court in Cuzco was lavish with gold and silver; its armies were well trained; its vast and skilled officialdom maintained discipline over millions of workers; the diverse conquered peoples were well assimilated into the empire. The Inca Empire, which had assumed shape within the span of four centuries, was a brilliant success; but it would shortly collapse from dissension within and attacks without.

The story of the conquest of Peru begins with the year 1522 in the city of Panama, over which ruthless Pedrarias still ruled. Three chief actors now appear whose plottings would shortly shake the Inca Empire. The first, Francisco Pizarro, was born in the early 1470's in Estremadura, the bastard son of a poor gentleman; unschooled and illiterate, he allegedly spent his boyhood tending his father's swine. He was about forty when he joined Ojeda's ill-fated expedition to the Spanish Main. Later he was with Núñez de Balboa when the first Spaniards looked out upon the Pacific. He then settled in Panama, receiving an allotment of Indians. The second, Diego de Almagro, born about 1475 to nameless peasants in Castile, had fled from Spanish justice to the Indies. He was illiterate, uncouth, and ugly, but possessed of unlimited energy. The third, Fernando de Luque, was a priest of whom little is known aside from his gift for currying favor with the rich. The three men were partners in sundry enterprises— trading, farming, and mining; they were prosperous and seemingly content to round out their old age in Panama.[7]

The Panama of 1522 was agog with rumors of treasure in Peru, and this greedy triumvirate made a pact for the conquest of that rich land. They found support. Governor Pedrarias gave his blessing in return for a share in the expected spoils. Various important people contributed a total of 20,000 gold pesos to the expedition. The priest Luque seems to have been the chief financier, drawing upon the reserves of his rich friends.

[7] Both Pizarro and Almagro were probably over fifty at the time of the Conquest—a ripe old age in those precarious days. Conquering was chiefly a young man's game: Núñez de Balboa was thirty-eight when he discovered the Pacific; Cortés was thirty-four when he first landed at Veracruz; Magellan was about forty when he discovered the Strait; Valdivia was about forty when he founded Santiago de Chile; and Columbus was about forty-one when he first landed in the New World.

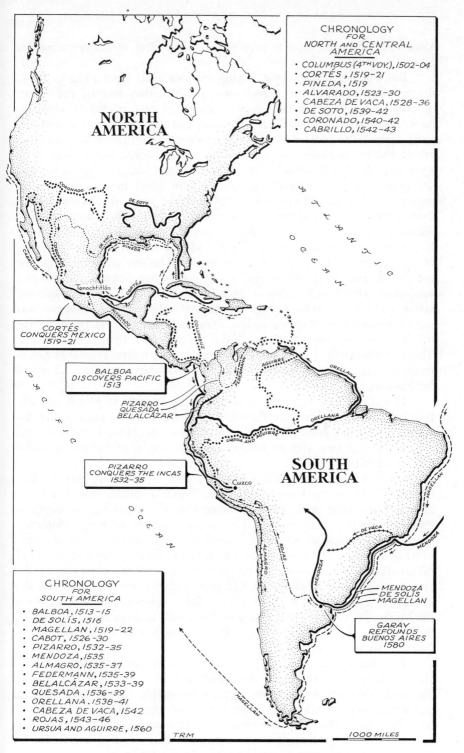

CHRONOLOGY
FOR
NORTH AND CENTRAL
AMERICA
- COLUMBUS (4TH VOY.), 1502-04
- CORTÉS, 1519-21
- PINEDA, 1519
- ALVARADO, 1523-30
- CABEZA DE VACA, 1528-36
- DE SOTO, 1539-42
- CORONADO, 1540-42
- CABRILLO, 1542-43

NORTH
AMERICA

ATLANTIC OCEAN

CORONADO

DE SOTO

DE VACA
PINEDA

CABRILLO

Tenochtitlán
CORTÉS

CORTÉS
CONQUERS MEXICO
1519-21

ALVARADO

COLUMBUS

PACIFIC OCEAN

BALBOA
DISCOVERS PACIFIC
1513

FEDERMANN
AGUIRRE

PIZARRO
QUESADA
BELALCÁZAR

ORELLANA

ORELLANA

URSUA AND AGUIRRE

SOUTH
AMERICA

PIZARRO
CONQUERS THE INCAS
1532-35

PIZARRO

Cuzco

MAGELLAN

DE VACA

ALMAGRO

ROJAS

MENDOZA

MENDOZA

MENDOZA
DE SOLÍS
MAGELLAN

CHRONOLOGY
FOR
SOUTH AMERICA
- BALBOA, 1513-15
- DE SOLÍS, 1516
- MAGELLAN, 1519-22
- CABOT, 1526-30
- PIZARRO, 1532-35
- MENDOZA, 1535
- ALMAGRO, 1535-37
- FEDERMANN, 1535-39
- BELALCÁZAR, 1533-39
- QUESADA, 1536-39
- ORELLANA, 1538-41
- CABEZA DE VACA, 1542
- ROJAS, 1543-46
- URSUA AND AGUIRRE, 1560

GARAY
REFOUNDS
BUENOS AIRES
1580

MAGELLAN

TRM

1000 MILES

Early Explorations, Land and Sea, 1502–60

Meanwhile, sidewalk scoffers pronounced the project arrant nonsense, its promoters madmen.

But whether mad or sane, during the four years from 1524 to 1528, the partners launched two expeditions, in which they reached the shores of Ecuador but were forced back by shortages of men, munitions, and supplies. Their failure excited further derision, and the flow of capital stopped. Solid citizens, including Pedrarias, were through with these elderly knights-errant. Pizarro had one last recourse, the imperial court. In the summer of 1528 he sailed for Spain to carry his petition to Charles I. The scene was dramatic: the ex-swineherd appeared hat in hand before the greatest monarch of Europe, offering trinkets of gold and silver, fine fabrics woven from vicuña wool—and for good measure some llamas, queer sniveling second-cousins to the camel, burden-bearers of the Andes. Pizarro found the king-emperor in amiable mood. Cortés had just arrived with golden proof of the glories of Mexico. Charles was ready to believe anything, hope for everything, and forthwith named Pizarro governor, captain-general and *adelantado* (the king's "advance agent") of Peru for life at a handsome salary—which he could collect for himself. His partner Almagro was named governor of Túmbez at less than half Pizarro's salary—touching off the argument which embroiled the partners and Peru for ten years. These arrangements completed, Pizarro visited his native Trujillo in Estremadura, enlisted the services of four brothers and a cousin, and sailed for Panama.

It was not easy to persuade the idlers of Panama to join a new expedition to Peru. To be sure Pizarro now had royal blessing, but men remembered earlier disasters. Finally, at the end of 1530, Pizarro set sail with about 180 men and 27 horses. Almagro stayed in Panama to enlist further recruits.

After thirteen days' sailing from Panama, Pizarro put into the Bay of San Mateo on the Ecuadorian coast, marched inland, raided a town, and procured some gold, silver, and emeralds. He dispatched the booty to Panama, where Almagro used it to good effect in winning volunteers. Meanwhile, Pizarro's men were forced to settle down for six months, nursing a plague of ulcers. Then followed the jungle march to the Gulf of Guayaquil, the crossing to northern Peru, and the conquest of the Inca stronghold of Túmbez. At this point Pizarro was reinforced by the arrival of troops led by Hernando de Soto (who would later discover the Mississippi), and together they pushed south and founded San Miguel, the first Spanish settlement in Peru. Pizarro was now ready to strike at the heart of the Inca Empire.

Fortunately for Pizzaro, the Inca Empire was already disintegrating. Its last great ruler, Huayna Capac, had died in 1525, after making the disastrous decision to divide his realm between his rightful heir Huáscar and a bastard son Atahuallpa—Huáscar to rule from Cuzco, Atahuallpa to hold the northern kingdom of Quitu. After an uneasy truce a civil war had followed in which Atahuallpa was victor and Huáscar was imprisoned in Cuzco. At this juncture the Spaniards arrived.

Pizarro, camping by the seaside at San Miguel, must now strike at Atahuallpa, sole ruler of the Inca Empire. In October, 1532, he set out with 62 horsemen, 106 foot soldiers, and a few cannon. He scaled the blistered mountain wall to the three-mile-high pass and after fifty-five days reached the city of Cajamarca set in a green valley. The city was deserted, its people had fled to the camp where Atahuallpa was guarded by some 30,000 of his prize troops. Pizarro dispatched his brother Hernando and De Soto with 35 horsemen to bid the Inca visit him in Cajamarca. The envoys rode boldly into Atahuallpa's presence and Hernando from his saddle delivered his invitation, which was then translated into Quechua. The Inca sat motionless, made no reply. De Soto gave telling exhibition of his horse's prowess; he charged, then brought the horse to a dead stop before the Inca. Atahuallpa consented to visit Pizarro the following day.

Hernando returned to Cajamarca, to report on the many thousands of soldiers and on the Inca's promise. Fear spread through the Spanish ranks, but there could now be no retreat. Pizarro, emulating Cortés's example, decided to seize his royal adversary. The night was spent in prayer and polishing of arms. Soldiers and horses were hidden. The following day the royal Inca guard moved slowly toward the city together with thousands of men and hundreds of nobles, with Atahuallpa on a golden throne carried by nobles. Pizarro sent a renewed invitation to the Inca, who finally was borne into the central square, surrounded by some 5,000 of his warriors. Not a single Spaniard was to be seen. Then appeared the priest Valverde, alone, who recited to the imperturbable Atahuallpa that strange proclamation called the *requerimiento*,[8] calling for prompt submission to the king of Castile and to the Pope, and its unfamiliar phrases were awkwardly translated by an Indian interpreter. Out of this strange gibberish the Inca at least understood the demand for submission and replied with haughty contempt. The priest pressed a prayer book into the ruler's hand, and Atahuallpa threw it to the ground. That was enough. A shot rang out. With the shout of *Santiago y a ellos!*, Spain's ancient battle cry, Pizarro's soldiers opened fire. Horsemen charged the undefended Indians, slaughtering thousands, and Atahuallpa was taken prisoner. The decisive battle was over, without loss of one Spanish soldier, with scarcely a wound. It was November 16, 1532.

Defeated Atahuallpa was accorded the deference due a king; he was permitted the solace of his concubines and the services of his nobles. His relations with his captors were as amiable as had been those between

8 This "requirement," the serving of notice upon peoples about to be conquered, was devised to furnish legal sanction to the conquest. It was "full of legal technicalities, began with the Biblical creation of the world, and passing in review the origins of the Roman hierarchy and the donation of Alexander VI, called upon the bewildered aborigines to acknowledge the supremacy of the Pope and of the kings of Castile, on pain of enslavement and confiscation of wives and goods. Every Spanish *conquistador* was required to have it read to the Indians by a notary and through an interpreter, before their territory could legally be taken or hostilities against them be started." C. H. Haring: *The Spanish Empire in America* (New York: Oxford University Press; 1947), p. 9.

Moctezuma and Cortés. He learned to play chess with the Spaniards and recited to them the epic tales of the Incas. Meanwhile, his brother Huáscar had been murdered in Cuzco, probably by his orders. Atahuallpa, having learned the Spaniards' love of gold, made a bid for freedom; he offered to fill the room in which he stood—measuring some twelve by seventeen feet —as high as his arm could reach, with objects of pure gold. A second room would be filled with silver. Pizarro promised him freedom and confirmed the promise in a written agreement. Messengers brought in load after load of golden vessels and ornaments, filling the designated room within two months. The gold was then melted down into bars so that the booty might be more easily distributed; thus Inca handiwork of priceless artistic value was destroyed. There were, all told, about 13,000 pounds of gold and about twice that weight in silver. Everyone, to the last foot soldier, was now rich. Each horseman got about ninety pounds of gold and twice as much silver, a fortune that could have supported him and his family for life. Few kept their treasure; the gamblers soon had most of it. The king's share, the royal fifth, was sent to Spain in the care of Hernando Pizarro.

Pizarro's forces in Cajamarca were now augmented by the arrival of Almagro with 150 foot soldiers and 50 horsemen. All was serene. There were no uprisings of the Indians; the nobles would not imperil Atahuallpa by any plottings; the common people seemed to care little so long as their daily life was undisturbed. The prospect seemed to promise a peaceful completion of the conquest. So it might have been had Pizarro been a little wiser and had he and Almagro been able to work together. As it turned out, the conquest would be long and bitter, stained by useless wars with Indians and by fratricidal struggles among the conquerors themselves.

The royal person of Atahuallpa posed the first problem. He had paid for his release with gold and silver, but Pizarro soon discovered legal grounds for refusing to honor his pledge. The Inca, argued Pizarro, was guilty of treason; he was inciting his followers to revolt. Atahuallpa denied the charge, whereupon Pizarro sent Hernando de Soto to the south to seek evidence of conspiracy. He found none, but Pizarro did not wait for his report. Atahuallpa was tried, convicted, and sentenced to be burned alive; but he was offered the more honorable death by strangling on condition that he accept baptism. He accepted, and his baptism was immediately followed by his execution.

The execution of Atahuallpa left Pizarro in a highly vulnerable position. He had, of course, broken his sacred word of honor as a Spanish gentleman, a fact later used against him in Spain. But, more immediately disastrous, he had destroyed the basis for his authority in Peru. So long as Atahuallpa lived, Pizarro could rule through him. But with Atahuallpa dead, Pizarro was forced to promote another Inca, a son of old Huayna Capac, to serve as a Spanish royal puppet. This new Inca survived only briefly, and his death brought suspicion upon one of Atahuallpa's generals, who was burned alive after he refused baptism, arguing that he "did not understand the religion of the white man." These events compelled Pizarro to move fast, extend his lines, and establish Spanish power against the surging anger of the Inca nobles, who no longer had a son of the Sun to command them.

Cuzco, the Inca stronghold in the south, fell to Pizarro and De Soto in November, 1533—almost one year to the day after the seizure of Cajamarca. The city was stripped; palaces, temples, tombs were looted; the people were treated without mercy; men and women were tortured in hope they would reveal hidden treasure. Pizarro, true to Spanish tradition, organized a municipality, installing a *cabildo* (city council) with a full complement of officials. He raised up a new Inca, Manco, placed the crimson band upon his forehead, and invested him with all rights and privileges— except, of course, the right to rule. The southern flank now seemed secure.

San Miguel, the northern outpost, was reinforced by fresh recruits eager to share in the boundless gold, and was placed in charge of Sebastián de Belalcázar, another son of Estremadura, who had served in Nicaragua and Panama. Belalcázar promptly led an expedition to conquer the Inca kingdom of Quitu—modern Ecuador. He crushed spirited assaults by the Indians and established Spanish power in the cities of Quito and Guayaquil. Here he was shortly confronted by the unlicensed expedition of Pedro de Alvarado from Guatemala. Pizarro, warned of Alvarado's arrival, sent Almagro with troops to aid Belalcázar, and the intruder was bought off and shortly returned to Guatemala.

Belalcázar then completed the conquest of Ecuador and pushed north into what is now Colombia, where he founded the cities of Popayán in 1536 and Cali in 1537, and penetrated the heart of the country to found the cities of Anzerma and Cartago. But his progress was blocked by rival expeditions from the Caribbean.

The conquest of the Inca Empire seemed complete by 1535; Spanish garrisons were firmly in control from Cuzco to Quito. It had been painless —at least to the Spaniards—and profitable beyond golden dreams. It was logical that Pizarro should now build a city, visible symbol of his triumph. He chose a site on the green oasis of the river Rimac for his "City of the Kings," founded in January, 1535—on the day of the Magi, hence the name given to the city. The name Lima (corruption of *Rimac*) soon supplanted the original name. It was Pizarro's city: he planned its cathedral, in which his blackened bones now rest; he laid out its streets and squares. He would make the city worthy of Spain, of Spain's king, and of himself.

The illiterate swineherd of Estremadura had traveled far, but troubles lay ahead. The jealousy of Almagro threatened the peace of their jointly won domain. Pizarro claimed chief honors. As a Marquis of Spain, he was assigned an area reaching 270 leagues south from Quito, while Almagro as *adelantado* was allotted a stretch of 200 leagues south of Pizarro's. The formula was potentially dangerous, for no boundary was fixed. Almagro claimed Cuzco, but Pizarro would not concede the point and prepared to fight.

The fight was postponed by Almagro's ruinous expedition into northern Argentina and Chile, a diversion that occupied him for two years (1535–1537). He set out from Cuzco with 570 Spaniards and several thousand

Indians, and by a semicircular route over the *altiplano*, through northern Argentina, and across the high Andes, he reached northern Chile in the valley of Copiapó. The bitter cold of the Andes and the rigors of the desert brought death to several thousand Indians and broke the health and spirits of the Spaniards. They probed south as far as the river Maule in Chile (the southern limit of Inca power), had fierce brushes with the Araucanians, treated the Indians with gross brutality, and finally withdrew with the conclusion that Chile held no promise for the white man.

During Almagro's absence troubles multiplied for the Marquis. He was occupied in building Lima, Trujillo, and other cities. His forces were scattered. Belalcázar was in the north (modern Colombia). Cuzco, guarded by his brother Hernando, was attacked by an Indian revolt led by the current puppet Inca Manco, who had escaped and rallied the Indians to his support. Manco's indictment of the Spaniards was bitter: "You Christians . . . have made us slaves. . . . You took our wives and daughters for concubines, you stole our property, burning us and tearing us with dogs." The Inca and his Indian followers laid siege to Cuzco and ravaged Spanish settlements far and wide. Manco fled to the mountains but continued to lead sporadic raids on the Spaniards until his death in 1545. When Almagro returned from Chile in 1537 he found Cuzco in the hands of Hernando Pizarro and his brother Gonzalo. He forced his way into the battered city, seized control, and jailed the two brothers of Francisco Pizarro.

Almagro, now master of Cuzco, crowned a new puppet Inca; this affrontery was resented by the Marquis, who considered himself the king-maker. Now Almagro, resolved to settle scores with his unfaithful partner, laid claim to Lima. In 1538 he moved his forces ("the men of Chile," they called themselves) down to the coastal plains and encamped at the point now called Chincha. Here, at Lima and Chincha—less than 100 miles apart—the two aging partners, Pizarro and Almagro, both well over sixty, faced each other in glowering anger. Attempts at conciliation were futile. In April, 1538, their forces met in the battle of Las Salinas. Pizarro's control of the port of Callao, into which munitions were coming from Panama, gave him a clear advantage. Almagro was overcome, taken prisoner, given an impressive trial, sentenced, and strangled. Meanwhile, the heathen Indians pondered the ways of the conquerors: "These Christian captains lie in calling themselves servants of a great lord beyond the sea, for in our country the servants of a great lord do not make war upon one another."

Pizarro was now the undisputed master of the Inca Empire. His lieutenant, Belalcázar, had subdued Ecuador and much of Colombia. Central Peru had thriving cities. Pizarro followed up the victory of Las Salinas by reorganizing and strengthening Spanish power, crushing further Indian revolts, and founding the city of La Plata (present-day Sucre) in Upper Peru (Bolivia). In 1539 he delegated the conquest of Chile to Pedro de Valdivia. Meanwhile, his brother Hernando was dispatched with royal gold to the Spanish Court where he encountered bitter criticism of the

Pizarro brothers' highhanded rule, and was jailed for twenty-two years. In 1540 the Marquis, almost seventy, returned to his City of the Kings, but not to peace. The ghost of his dead partner walked the streets. The "men of Chile," led by Almagro's mestizo son, plotted against him; and in June, 1541, assassins broke into his house and killed him.

The death of Pizarro did not bring peace. For almost ten years the land was torn by strife between his followers and those of Almagro until royal governors sent by Spain gradually restored order. Not until the arrival in 1551 of Viceroy Antonio de Mendoza, fresh from his brilliant fifteen-year term in Mexico, was the Spanish colony of Peru to assume an ordered life.

THE CONQUEST OF CHILE

There remained an unconquered empire in southern Chile. Almagro, to be sure, had found there neither gold nor glory; his only rewards had been wounds and sickness and disillusion. The conquest of Chile waited for an abler and more stalwart leader. Two years after Almagro's attempts, such a leader appeared in Pedro de Valdivia, one of the boldest, most intelligent and charming of conquerors. He was born in Estremadura about 1500, the son of impoverished lesser nobility. He was given a sound education and served in Charles I's army in the Italian campaigns against France. Caught by the fever of the New World, he went to Venezuela in 1535, reached Peru in 1537, attached himself to Pizarro, fought bravely against Almagro's forces, and was rewarded with a grant of Indians and a silver mine on the *altiplano*. Secure in his prosperity and favored by Pizarro, he begged and won the dubious honor of appointment as lieutenant-governor of Chile.

It was not easy to organize a new expedition to Chile. Those with money were loath to risk it upon such a fool's errand. Nor was it easy to enlist men, for Almagro's veterans were still recounting their tales of hunger, thirst, and torture. Valdivia finally gathered 15 men and set out from Cuzco in January, 1540, with about 1,000 Indians to carry tools, seeds, chickens, pigs, and other necessities for fighting and living. Other recruits joined as they marched down through Arequipa to northern Chile until the force included 150 Spaniards.

The obstacles to success were grievous. The journey over the Atacama Desert, a blistered, rainless wasteland, meant a year of torment from heat, hunger, and thirst. Valdivia's unruly company, repeatedly disrupted by mutiny and treason, taxed his patience and diplomacy. And he must face the Araucanians, the most dauntless, cunning, and unyielding foe yet encountered by an American conqueror. A great Spanish writer describes them:

> Beardless men, robust of gesture
> Theirs are full-grown, shapely bodies,
> Lofty chests and massive shoulders,
> Stalwart limbs and steely sinews;

> They are confident, emboldened,
> Dauntless, gallant, and audacious,
> Firm inured to toil, and suffering
> Mortal cold and heat and hunger.[9]

Valdivia's year-long march from Cuzco to central Chile equals, in sheer courage and skillful leadership, the campaigns of Cortés and Pizarro. Valdivia was a man of extraordinary poise and patience. Second only to Valdivia was the Spanish woman whom he loved, his constant companion, Inés de Suárez. The record reveals her dauntless spirit, her indomitable energy, her overflowing sympathy and steady courage, which again and again reinforced the will of Valdivia and his men. She played a man's part in battle, a woman's in nursing the sick and the wounded, a priest's in offering the consolation of religion to the dying. Her presence in the little company was criticized. Valdivia had a wife in Spain and Pizarro was loath to condone any irregularities; but he finally permitted Inés to accompany Valdivia as a *criada,* a domestic servant.

Neither deserts nor mutinies nor hostile Indians stopped Valdivia. Early in 1541 the little band reached the green valley of the Mapocho and camped on an island at the foot of the rocky hill called Huelén ("Sorrow") by the Indians, renamed Santa Lucía by Valdivia. Here he founded the city of Santiago on February 12, 1541.[1] He was shortly elected governor of Chile. Houses were built, fields planted, fortifications erected, and a chapel was built on the slopes of Santa Lucía.

The city was scarcely six months old when the Araucanians, nursing bitter memories of Almagro's cruelties, almost totally destroyed it, killing some Spaniards and burning almost all their supplies. Legend has it that only three hogs, two chickens, and two handfuls of corn escaped. The faith of Valdivia and Inés was not abated. They gathered their forces on craggy Santa Lucía and laid plans for rebuilding the city while still surrounded and outnumbered by Indians. The courage of Valdivia was matched by that of Inés, who rode from outpost to outpost heartening the men, nursing the wounded, confirming their faith in the greatness of Spain and the glory of their religion. For two years the weakened men held their fortified island and rocky hill against repeated attacks. They rebuilt their houses, using adobe as safeguard against fire. They all but starved. The two handfuls of corn were planted, and the first harvest was planted again. Under cover of night, foraging expeditions seized food from the Indians. The hungry and tattered army finally received help from Peru late in 1543. The new-

---

[9] Alonso de Ercilla y Zúñiga: *La Araucana,* Canto I, translated as *The Araucaniad* by C. M. Lancaster and P. M. Manchester (Nashville, Tenn.: Vanderbilt University Press; 1945). This epic poem, "the Aeneid of the Chileans," was the work of a Spanish soldier who had fought against the foe whose bravery he immortalized. Spain's modern critic, Menéndez y Pelayo, calls it "the best of our historical poems . . . the first . . . in which contemporary history was lifted to epic dignity." It is significant to remember that Ercilla's poem, despite its praise of Spain's most stubborn foe, was warmly acclaimed in Spain.

[1] At the time of the conquest the river Mapocho divided to form an island. Later on the current was confined to one channel, and the island no longer exists. Santiago's modern pattern of downtown streets and plazas shows Valdivia's plan.

comers brought word of the assassination of Pizarro and the turmoil of
Peru, news which emboldened Valdivia to assert his unconfirmed title as
governor of Chile. Reinforced by men and supplies, he took steps to extend
his control both north and south of Santiago. But he soon saw that his force
was still inadequate, and in 1547 he returned to Peru to beg aid from the
royal representative, Pedro de la Gasca. He there volunteered his services
and gave decisive help against the rebellion led by Gonzalo Pizarro. He
was confirmed as governor of Chile and he returned with new troops and
supplies.

Meanwhile, a personal tragedy came to Valdivia. The king's envoy in
Lima, Pedro de la Gasca, ordered Valdivia to give up his mistress and
bring his wife from Spain. Valdivia made one last plea to his king: "She
[Inés] is an honored woman in my home. She came with me by permission
of the Marquis. She is a good woman, loved by all." But finally Valdivia
and Inés bowed to the royal command.

He now pushed south, founded Concepción in early 1550, Valdivia
in 1552, and established other southern outposts. But he had reached too
far and too fast. His forces were inadequate against the unwearied Araucanians, now led by the heroic Lautaro. The story of Lautaro, the Araucanian
hero immortalized by the poet Ercilla, is chiefly legend. He may have been
a lad of ten or twelve when he was captured by the Spaniards shortly after
the founding of Santiago and assigned to Valdivia and Inés de Suárez as a
stableboy. Legend has it that they treated the lad with warm affection. He
learned some Spanish and, even more important for his future, learned that
Spaniards were only men, that man and horse were not one creature as
superstitious Indians believed, that their horses tired as men tired. Perhaps
he also learned how to make and use gunpowder. But one day, after a year
or two in the Spanish camp, young Lautaro disappeared and became a
leader of his Araucanian people. Ten years passed. Spanish power had
spread from Serena in the north to Valdivia in the south, but in all Chile
there were no more than a thousand Spaniards, opposed to an Araucanian
population of hundreds of thousands.

In the last months of 1553, Valdivia and Lautaro again met, this time
as leaders of opposing armies. Lautaro had studied Spanish strategy and
devised one of his own. He divided his forces, threw one detachment against
the Spaniards, knowing that it would be destroyed; then he threw another
and still another, wearing the Spaniards down by sheer numbers. Valdivia
and his men were routed and Valdivia himself fell prisoner to the stableboy
whom he had trained and loved. There are many legends concerning
Valdivia's death. One story, colorful but unconvincing, has it that he was
tied to a tree and Lautaro spoke to him: "You came for gold, now we give
you all the gold you can use," and poured melted gold down his throat.
We only know that Pedro de Valdivia died in southern Chile.

The death of Valdivia was followed by disputes among rival claimants
to his post. War with the Araucanians continued; the Spanish forces, augmented by fresh recruits, pushed south to the Chilean lakes, but were finally
compelled to accept the Bío-Bío River as the boundary between them and

the unyielding Indians—and it remained as such for more than 200 years. Meanwhile, in 1561, Spanish troops from Chile crossed the Andes, founded the cities of Mendoza and San Juan, and attached that area of modern Argentina to the Captaincy-General of Chile, an arrangement which lasted until the creation of the Viceroyalty of La Plata in 1776.

SPANISH EXPLORATION IN THE AMAZON BASIN

The conquerors of Peru, occupied in consolidating their hold upon the Inca Empire and in extending their lines north into present-day Colombia and south into Chile, believed that fabulous wealth also lay to the east beyond the wall of the Andes. There was El Dorado—land of spices and gold, both magic words to Spanish ears.

The legend of El Dorado titillated the fancy of the conquerors. There was, it seemed, an Indian king who once a year was generously sprinkled with gold dust and then immersed in a sacred lake. The conquerors were eager to find a king so richly endowed that he could substitute gold dust for bath salts.

Pizarro appointed his brother Gonzalo governor of Quito in 1540 and bade him prepare an expedition to the land of spices and gold. In 1541 Gonzalo set out for the east with some 200 Spaniards, several thousand Indians, herds of swine, dogs and llamas, and generous supplies, for one of the most disastrous journeys on record. Many Indians died in the cold mountains and others in the jungle. They pushed through the jungles for eight months, encouraged by Indians who assured them that fortune lay just ahead, but they found neither cinnamon nor gold. Their supplies had given out and almost all their Indians were dead, when the Spaniards made their camp on one of the smaller streams leading to the Amazon. From there Gonzalo sent his lieutenant Francisco de Orellana downstream with 57 men and some improvised boats in search of food. Gonzalo and his companions, waiting for relief, ate their dogs and horses and all but starved. Finally, giving up hope of Orellana's return, Gonzalo led the few survivors back to Quito in August, 1542.

Orellana, meanwhile, had made his way over 2,000 miles to the mouth of the Amazon. We do not know whether he made an effort to relieve Gonzalo and his starving companions marooned in the jungle. He probably found it easier to drift with the river current than to row back upstream. Orellana's journey furnished plenty of excitement. Amiable Indians were always ready to promise him abundant food and gold five or ten days' journey ahead. He was forever on the trail of mysterious "Amazons," the warlike women living in villages alone, described in the novels of chivalry, the "best sellers" of that period. In August, 1542, after encounters with Indians led by female warriors, they reached the mouth of the Amazon, and three months later, Santo Domingo. They then took ship for Spain to announce their exploration of the Amazon, to encourage

Spain in its contest with Portugal, and to repeat tales of gold, cinnamon, and shapely Amazon women. Orellana then returned for further exploration, but his ship capsized at the mouth of the Amazon, and he and his men were drowned. It was Spain's last futile gesture in the Amazon. Portugal gradually extended her hold over most of the basin.

THE SPANISH MAIN

The conquest of the Spanish Main, comprising modern Colombia and Venezuela, was delayed until after 1535. Fitful efforts had been made before 1530 to establish Spanish control, but the Indians were hostile and the jungles forbidding. In the early 1530's sporadic expeditions into the Orinoco region had met with little success. In return for financial aid to Charles I in his contest for the imperial crown, the German banking house of Welser was granted large concessions in Venezuela. A few German commanders, with Spanish soldiers, attempted conquest of the area, explored the country about Lake Maracaibo, promoted the slave trade with little profit, and finally abandoned the venture by 1550.

The conquest of the area now called Colombia was more successful. Reports on the gold and emeralds of the Chibchas had attracted attention to their homeland on the plateau of Bogotá. Chief honors belong to Gonzalo Jiménez de Quesada, who, with 900 men, started from the Caribbean coast in 1536. The expedition toiled through the rain forests and fought hostile Indians, built vessels on the Magdalena, finally reached the upper highlands after an eight months' journey, penetrated the Chibcha country, captured the stronghold of Tunja, and marched into the valley of Bogotá. Here Jiménez was confronted by two rival claimants: Belalcázar, fresh from triumphs in Popayán and Cali, and a German named Federmann. They refrained from fighting it out on the spot and agreed to submit their case to Madrid. The Crown appointed Belalcázar governor of Popayán and gave Federmann nothing. Jiménez de Quesada apparently made no demands; he returned peacefully to the land he had so brilliantly conquered, contented himself with an honorary title, and lived to the age of eighty, organizing vain schemes for the conquest of mythical El Dorado, winning distinction, in heaven if not on earth, as the least quarrelsome of the conquerors.

THE LANDS OF THE RÍO DE LA PLATA

The basin drained by the rivers Paraná, Paraguay, Uruguay, and Pilcomayo, which converge in the Río de la Plata—an area now divided among Argentina, Uruguay, Paraguay, Bolivia, and Brazil—was still the undisturbed home of nomadic Indians long after Spanish power had been secured in the Caribbean, Mexico, Peru, and the Spanish Main. Spain had made several excursions into the region. In 1516 Juan Díaz de Solís sailed into the broad estuary and landed on the Uruguayan side, only to be eaten by the Indians. Magellan explored the estuary in 1520. Sebastian Cabot, Venetian-born but long a resident of England and now an employee of Spain, arrived in 1526, penetrated to a point north of Rosario and fixed upon it the name Río de la Plata in the mistaken notion that there were silver deposits nearby. In 1535 Pedro de Mendoza landed with a substantial force and founded the city of Santa María de Buenos Aires, which was soon destroyed by the Indians. Mendoza set out for Spain in 1537 but died at sea. Meanwhile, some of his aides pushed 1,000 miles up the river Paraguay, and in 1537 built a fort called Asunción, the first permanent settlement in the La Plata area, for many years the stronghold of Spanish power in the region. The governor of Asunción was Domingo Martínez de Irala, an able but unscrupulous fellow who exercised dictatorial powers until his death in 1556. He extended Spanish power, conquered and pacified the Indians. In 1542 Álvar Núñez Cabeza de Vaca, hero of the amazing march from Florida to Mexico, reached Asunción with 400 men, and with royal appointment as governor, but he was soon deposed and Irala was reinstated.

Meanwhile, other attempts to conquer and colonize La Plata came from Peru. A preliminary expedition explored present-day northern Argentina in 1543–46. In 1553 an expedition from Potosí founded Santiago del Estero, the oldest city in Argentina. In 1565 Tucumán was founded; in 1573, Córdoba. The refounding of Buenos Aires by Juan de Garay in 1580, with forces from upriver Asunción, completed the cycle of Spanish conquest in the New World.

PORTUGAL STAKES OUT HER CLAIM

During the century of Spanish conquest of America—from Columbus's first journey in 1492 to the establishment of Buenos Aires in 1580— Portugal had also been staking out her claims. For much of this time Portugal was preoccupied with what seemed greater treasure in the East. While Columbus had returned empty-handed from his American expeditions, Vasco da Gama, on his epochal journey to India in 1497–99, had brought back pepper, cloves, nutmeg, cinnamon, and precious stones; and King Manoel had triumphantly added to his titles "Lord of the Conquest, Navigation and Commerce of Ethiopia, Arabia, Persia, and India." However, Portugal, by the Treaty of Tordesillas, had established her claim to a share in the unknown lands Columbus had discovered. Now the problem was to discover what land lay "within 370 leagues west of the Cape Verde Islands," the territory conceded to Portugal.

In 1500, six months after Vasco da Gama's return, a fleet of thirteen ships with 1,200 men set out under Pedro Alvares Cabral, bound for India. According to the official account, the ships were blown far off their course, and on April 22, 1500, the coast of Brazil was sighted. The truth is unclear. Portugal had long been secretive in regard to her maritime adventures, with a standing rule against maps and chronicles that might give away her secrets. It is possible that Portuguese explorers had already touched upon American soil and that Duarte Pacheco Pereira had found Brazil in 1498. It is also possible that a Spanish expedition under Vicente Yáñez Pinzón, one of Columbus's lieutenants, had reached the mouth of the Amazon a few months before Cabral and that he deserves credit as the true discoverer of Brazil. But the *official* discoverer is Pedro Alvares Cabral and the date, April 22, 1500; and let those who will, argue rival claims.

Portugal's development of her undefined American empire was to follow a very different course from that of Spain. Portugal's attention was still fixed upon the spices of the East. Cabral, in 1500, after formally claiming Brazil and sending a report back to his King, had sailed on around Africa to India, established settlements, and laid the permanent foundation for an empire that within fifty years reached east to Burma, Siam, and China. With Portugal thus preoccupied, the settlement of her American possessions progressed slowly. That record we will leave to a later chapter.

Chapter 6

INTRODUCING THE SPANISH
COLONIAL PERIOD

In practically every part [of the New World] the valiant Spaniards have conquered with invincible courage innumerable provinces, kingdoms, and nations, winning them for the monarchs of Spain; in all of which the Holy Gospel has been preached with such success for the Church and the monarchy of Spain that . . . the very Catholic and puissant King of Spain has sheltered, extended, and upheld the Holy Catholic Faith through the great valor and effort of his Spanish vassals, in consequence of which at every hour without pause praise is continually offered to God and agreeable sacrifice made to Him; and thus His Divine Majesty will be served, that all may come to real knowledge of Him.[1]

Any proud Spaniard would have agreed with the itinerant missionary who wrote these words in the early seventeenth century. The Spanish conquest and settlement of America was the most brilliant feat of imperial expansion the world had ever known. "The innumerable provinces, kingdoms, and nations" that lay within the span of some 8,000 miles between the Golden Gate and the Strait of Magellan, conquered by the bravery and cunning of a few thousand men, were the proud outposts of Spain for more than three centuries. During those years Spain fixed her governmental patterns upon the scattered peoples of that area, transferred to it her language and faith, her economic fashions and skills, her social and political ideas. It is obvious that we cannot understand the life of *Spanish* America of today, from great Argentina to little El Salvador, without reckoning with those 300 years of schooling by the mother country. We speak here of *Spanish* America, for we postpone to a later chapter parallel events in *Portuguese* America, Brazil. They had much in common, but there were palpable divergences as well.

In approaching the colonial era of Spanish America, we start with some tentative generalizations. First, this period cannot be dismissed as a tidy chapter in history in which conquerors marched in, took control of lands and people, and were then evicted. Too many years, too vast an area,

[1] Antonio Vázquez de Espinosa: *Compendium and Description of the West Indies,* translated by Charles Upson Clark (Washington, D.C.: Smithsonian Institution; 1942), p. 3.

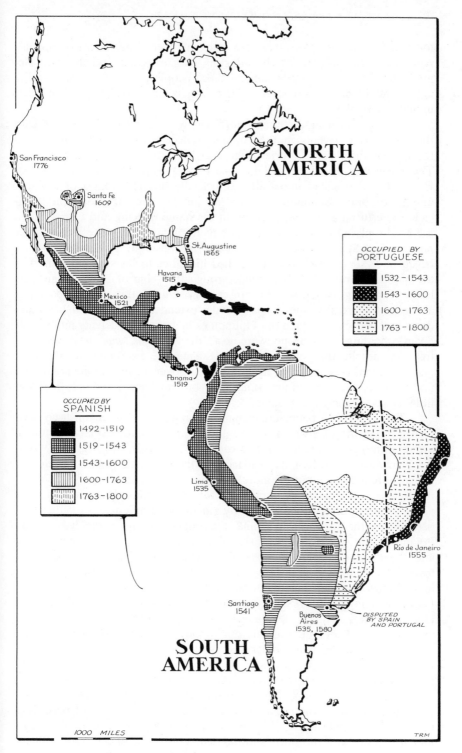

NORTH
AMERICA

San Francisco
1776

Santa Fe
1609

St.Augustine
1565

Havana
1515

Mexico
1521

Panama
1519

OCCUPIED BY
PORTUGUESE

1532 – 1543

1543 – 1600

1600 – 1763

1763 – 1800

OCCUPIED BY
SPANISH

1492 – 1519

1519 – 1543

1543 – 1600

1600 – 1763

1763 – 1800

Lima
1535

Rio de Janeiro
1555

Santiago
1541

Buenos
Aires
1535, 1580

DISPUTED
BY SPAIN
AND PORTUGAL

SOUTH
AMERICA

1000 MILES

TRM

Expansion of Colonial Settlements, 1492–1800

too diverse and numerous a people were involved. The record of Spanish America is complicated by the mingling of Europeans, Indians, and Negroes; by the endless clashes among those peoples, as well as the rivalries among the Spaniards themselves. The canvas is large, its lights and shadows infinitely complex.

Second, Spanish America's fortunes were inextricably bound with those of Spain. Events in the colonies reflected those of the homeland throughout the three centuries, which divide into three separate periods. The first was a period of exultation—discovery, exploration, and conquest. Every ship that sailed into Cádiz and Seville brought tidings of new triumphs, of brave Spaniards penetrating jungles, leaping mountain barricades, overturning old empires—all in the name of King and Christ. Then followed a period of caution, in which their claims were contested by other powers, and Spain slowly lost her exclusive position. This second phase began in 1556 when Charles I resigned his office to his son and retired to the monastery of Yuste. It carried through the reign of Philip II and the lesser Hapsburgs of the seventeenth century. During this period Spain was alternately aggressive and defensive: she extended and fortified her kingdoms in America, occupied the Philippines in 1565. But defeats multiplied: Spain's holdings in Europe were lost; the Armada was destroyed; the treasury, despite the gold and silver of America, was emptied. The final phase covered the period of new energy in government and economic life under the eighteenth-century Bourbons, but an energy too late and too little to save America for Spain.

Third, we shall better understand our reading of the Spanish colonial record if we rid ourselves of the Anglo-Saxon fervor for explaining human events in terms of villains—in this case the Spaniards. "In history," writes the provocative Salvador de Madariaga, "there are no villains. There are but men, bad enough but far more complex than devils can be." Of course, the Spanish conquest was unpleasant for the Indians. But conquests are never pleasant, are seldom marked by amenity and mildness—whether perpetrated by the Japanese in China, the English in India, the Russians in Poland, or the Americans in Mexico. Conquerors are inevitably unwelcome and the Spaniards were no exception. They often behaved abominably toward the Indians over whose souls and lands they had assumed an uninvited custody. Such men as Nuño de Guzmán, Pedro de Alvarado, and Diego de Almagro were guilty of unspeakable cruelty. Others, such as Hernán Cortés, Núñez de Balboa, Antonio de Mendoza, Jiménez de Quesada, and Pedro de Valdivia could show magnanimity of first order. The modern reader will temper his judgment by recalling that he deals with events in the sixteenth and seventeenth centuries; that the British, Dutch, and French behaved equally badly—when they had an opportunity.

Fourth—to continue the necessary rebuttal of the Black Legend—Spain did not topple the Indian peoples from an Elysian state of perfection to one of abysmal misery, despite the lyricists who dwell upon the communal happiness of the Incas and the democratic joys of the Aztecs. Spain did not destroy great Indian populations: there never were great populations. Spain did not bring hunger and poverty to Indian America: life was meager and hunger was general before the conquerors came. Spain did not introduce cruelty and war: exploitation was an old story to the Indians. Spain did not destroy human freedom: it had never been enjoyed by Maya, Aztec, Inca, or Chibcha. Spain did not destroy ancient systems of noble moral standards: the Indians were masters of gluttony, drunkenness, sexual excesses, and refined torture. Spain brought changes to the Indian world, some for ill, some for good. It is possible that the Indians of Mexico and Peru had more to eat under Spanish rule, more protection against each other and against their masters, more security of life and happiness than they had had under Indian nobles and priests. The shift was undoubtedly distasteful, always disruptive, frequently cruel, but it was not a shift from paradise to torment.

Fifth, the record of Spain's rule in America was finally a success or a failure in the degree to which it furthered the material well-being of all the peoples of America—Indian, mestizo, Negro, white. It is easy to over-emphasize the pomp of kings and viceroys and to forget the much greater importance of the price of corn. All imperial glamour becomes insignificant when compared with the fate of the cornfields and the men who tilled them. Spain prospered in America as long as all prospered; she lost her colonial empire when accumulated economic ills beggared both crown and vassals.

◆¦◆¦◆¦◆¦◆¦◆¦◆¦◆¦◆¦◆¦◆ [*Chapter 7*]

SPAIN'S GOVERNMENT IN AMERICA:
KINGS, VICEROYS, AND
OTHER IMPORTANT PEOPLE

Spanish power over America was vested in the Crown, and, during the first decades, in the Crown of Castile. The royal court of Castile made the decisions that determined the fate of the millions of whites, Indians, and Negroes who lived in the empire stretching from California to Patagonia.

America from the beginning was Castile's concern: Columbus was Isabella's man; his triumphs were hers. There was a standing agreement that Aragon should look east for expansion, that Castile should look west. Furthermore, there were practical reasons for transferring to the colonies the governmental patterns of Castile rather than those of Aragon. The kings of Spain preferred to pass on the extensive royal powers of Castile rather than the political liberties of Aragon, whose stout regionalism had curtailed royal prerogatives and emboldened the *cortes* (parliament) to withstand the king.[1] It was established that the lands overseas were the personal and private possessions of the king. They belonged, not to Castile, but to the Crown of Castile. They were not properly colonies but kingdoms added to the congeries of kingdoms united in the exalted person of the king. Successive kings would speak of *estos reinos,* "these kingdoms" of the peninsula, and of *esos reinos,* "those kingdoms" of America. This emphasis was rooted in respect for the earlier Roman policy of incorporating new realms into the empire on a basis of equality. The fine distinction between colony and kingdom kept alive a sense of dignity in the Spanish domains of the New World, and created a feeling of regional integrity which crystallized in the idea of nationality in the nineteenth century.

---

[1] Roger B. Merriman: *The Rise of the Spanish Empire in the Old World and in the New* (4 vols.), Vol. II, p. 221. Copyright 1918–34, reprinted with the permission of The Macmillan Company, New York. Merriman cites "the unwillingness of the sovereigns to permit any of the political methods of the eastern kingdoms to percolate to the Indies . . . lest the new territory would be contaminated by coming into contact with the Aragonese liberties which they had not been able wholly to subvert."

THE HIERARCHY OF AUTHORITY IN SPAIN

The theory of the divine right of kings, so dear to Ferdinand and Isabella —and magnified by the Hapsburgs who followed them—was fixed upon Spanish America to a degree never accepted in the homeland. According to this theory the king was the supreme ruler; men acting in his name carried out his will. The land was the king's: the right to exploit its fields, pastures, and mines was a grant of royal favor revocable at will. The Church, her hierarchy subject to royal patronage, was an instrument of royal control. All agencies of government merely echoed the voice of the king.

Theoretically, the king was supreme. Actually there were sharp limitations upon his powers. Sheer distance was not the least of these. The sailing ships that carried orders back and forth were slow and uncertain links between Madrid, Mexico, and Lima. Furthermore, the new kingdoms speedily developed obstinate resistance reminiscent of the experience of the homeland. The royal powers of the kings of Spain had long been tempered by the chartered cities, the stout nobility, and the powerful clergy. Against such challenges the Hapsburgs, beginning with Charles I, struck with vigor. But in America the cities and the transplanted nobles and clergy clung to the older habits, and disputed the king's will time and again. Willful and disobedient officials, far removed from royal control, often ignored royal decrees. They could easily argue that a given royal edict was impractical, that it would promote strife; or they could fall back upon the classic Spanish formula: "I obey but do not enforce" (*Obedezco pero no cumplo*).

The first established instrument of imperial control was the Casa de Contratación (the Board of Trade), organized in 1503 and charged with overseeing the growing commerce between the homeland and the American colonies. Seville, an inland port on the Guadalquivir River, was chosen as the seat of the Casa, according to Clarence H. Haring, "not because of superior maritime facilities, for Cádiz had much the better harbor, but probably because Seville happened to be the wealthiest and most populous city of Castile of which the Indies were considered to be the exclusive possession." Seville was also beyond the reach of pirates. Practical Isabella had recognized the necessity for such supervision shortly after Columbus's triumphant return in 1493 and had appointed her chaplain, Juan Rodríguez de Fonseca, to oversee Columbus's further expeditions, an intrusion which galled the petulant Admiral. By 1503 it was clear that the job was too onerous for one man and the Casa de Contratación was devised. Fonseca, active in founding the Casa, continued as its director and as chief colonial adviser until his death in 1524.

The functions of the Casa multiplied rapidly. It was charged with licensing ships, ordering their activities on the high seas and abroad, the collection of taxes, and the care of the royal share of treasure remitted from the New World. It became a training school for navigators, makers of maps, and devisers of nautical instruments. It maintained archives of charts, maps, and logs. It was a court with jurisdiction over all cases incidental to American trade. In 1717 under the Bourbons the seat of the Casa was shifted from Seville to Cádiz, and it was finally abolished in 1790. We will consider its activities later in connection with Spain's commercial policies.

The chief agency for directing colonial affairs was the Royal and Supreme Council of the Indies, created by edict of Charles I in 1524. Subject only to the king, with brief interruptions it exercised large authority over the colonies until it was abolished in 1834. Its president enjoyed high prestige; its corps of councilors, four or five in the early years, numbered eighteen or nineteen by 1700. The Casa de Contratación became its agent in dealing with shipping. It acquired a numerous bureaucracy. During most of its life, the Council of the Indies was an able and hard-working body, and its high prestige survived even the corruption of the later Hapsburgs. Its powers were frequently abridged and at times some of its functions were transferred to other agencies; but during most of its existence its authority was well-nigh absolute—always as the instrument of the Crown—in making laws, administering justice, controlling finance and trade, supervising the Church, and directing armies.

From the beginning the American "kingdoms" were inundated with laws and edicts drafted by king and council for the control of the colonists down to the last detail of daily life. These laws reflected the royal desire to hold the Indies firmly in hand, to assure profit to the Crown, to safeguard the interests of the colonists, and to protect their Indian charges. There was commendable effort to incorporate the ancient practices of the Aztecs and Incas into the new body of Spanish law. A conspicuous instance is revealed in advice given Spanish administrators by an adviser of Viceroy Toledo in Peru. He urges them not "to try and change the customs abruptly and make new laws and ordinances, until they know the conditions and customs of the natives of the country and of the Spaniards who dwell there. . . . One must first accommodate oneself to the customs of those one wishes to govern and proceed agreeably to them until, having won their confidence and good opinion, with the authority thus secured one may undertake to change the customs."[2] Minute regulations sought to assure justice to the king's vassals. Although much of the legislation was ignored, its production never slackened. The task of a conscientious lawyer or judge was an onerous one. By 1635 more than 400,000 edicts were in force. In 1681, after years of labor, a *Compilation of the Laws of the Indies (Recopilación de las leyes de las Indias)* was issued, which reduced the number of laws to a mere 6,400.

ROYAL GOVERNMENT IN AMERICA

Columbus's discovery of the New World had caught Spain unprepared. She had anticipated no such accession of new territory and had given no

[2] Juan Matienzo: *Gobierno del Perú* (Buenos Aires, 1910), p. 118; quoted by C. H. Haring: *The Spanish Empire in America* (New York: Oxford University Press; 1947), p. 110.

thought to its organization and rule. A chaotic period followed in which the advance agents of the Crown occupied the lands of the Caribbean, Mexico, Peru, Chile, and La Plata.

The first Spanish adventurers were notable exponents of private enterprise. They were given the royal blessing and sometimes a limited subsidy, authorized to stake their own fortunes and lives in the conquest and colonization of unmapped lands. The Crown offered them a business contract: they were to get what they could, then share their winnings with the king. They were, in modern commercial parlance, salesmen on commission, guaranteed nothing—and they took all the risks; it was a thrifty arrangement for the Crown. These advance agents were often called *adelantados* (from Spanish *adelantar,* to advance). It was no new title. For three centuries Spain had appointed *adelantados* as the king's proconsuls in lands recaptured from the Moslems. This office was merely transferred to the New World. The term *adelantado* in Spanish America describes all the first discoverers, conquerors, and colonizers, although not all bore the title. Probably the first to be so designated was Bartolomé Columbus, appointed to rule Hispaniola in 1497. Ponce de León was an *adelantado* when he set out in search of Bimini, as were Alvarado in Guatemala, Almagro in Chile, and many another. About half of the threescore early explorers and colonizers were honored with the title. Few collected the promised rewards; all were quickly pushed aside when the time came to make way for the officialdom of an ordered government.

The organization of the government of Spanish America, which prevailed with few modifications throughout the colonial period, was chiefly a product of the Hapsburgs of the sixteenth century. The structure of government framed by Charles I and Philip II and their appointment of its officials were designed to fortify royal power in America, curb anarchic forces, and buttress the political unity of the scattered kingdoms. The chief instruments to these ends were the *cabildos,* the *audiencias,* the viceroys, the captains-general and their lesser aides.

The basic instrument of royal authority was the *cabildo,* or city council. The Spaniards, true to the Roman tradition, had long exalted the city (more accurately the city-state, with a considerable area dominated by the municipal center); Spanish America followed the same tradition, magnifying the city to a degree unfamiliar to those of English heritage. This difference is described by Bernard Moses: "In the English colonies of America the town grew up to meet the needs of the inhabitants of the country; but in the Spanish colonies the population of the country grew to meet the needs of the town." It was therefore consonant with Spanish character that Columbus, after landing upon Hispaniola, should lay out the ill-fated settlement of Navidad; that Balboa should found Darién; that Cortés should establish Veracruz; that Pizarro should celebrate victory by erecting The City of the Kings—Lima; and that Valdivia, while still threatened by the Araucanians, should organize the city of Santiago. The municipality was the one firm legacy of the *adelantados.*

Appointment to the *cabildo* was a coveted honor: its *regidores* (councilors) and *alcaldes ordinarios* (magistrates) were mighty men within their little spheres. The viceregal cities of Mexico and Lima had twelve or more such officials, lesser cities as few as one or two. As cities grew, the city fathers appointed constables, collectors of taxes, inspectors of weights and measures, and notaries. The tasks of these expanding city governments included policing, jailing and fining, sanitation, supervising of building, justice, tax collecting, and the drilling of municipal armies. Numerous royal decrees were designed to assure efficient and honest rule by the *cabildo*. Its officers were forbidden to work for private gain, and their official acts were periodically reviewed. At their occasional best the *cabildos* were public spirited and honest; at their frequent worst they looted city treasuries and preyed on citizens. Municipal government was seldom more than an indifferent success and reminds us of certain unhappy chapters in the history of New York, Chicago, and San Francisco.

However, with all its failures, the *cabildo* was the one governmental body in which the American-born Spaniard occasionally made his voice heard. The first *cabildos* were appointed by the founders of the cities. In 1523 Charles I decreed that they should, in a few instances, be elected by the landholders. This enlightened promise proved chimerical, for the king had too many deserving friends for whom he must provide lucrative posts. Later, beginning with Philip II, the kings were so impoverished by costly wars and royal display that they found it expedient to sell offices in the colonies, a measure which inflicted many useless men upon the *cabildos*. In some instances the purchaser of a place in a *cabildo* had the right to bequeath his seat as a part of his estate. Despite these handicaps, the membership of the *cabildos* included numerous creoles (American-born Spaniards), to whom other important government posts were barred. Furthermore, some of its places were occasionally filled by the election of landed citizens, subject to the confirmation of the viceroy. The *cabildo* proved more American in composition than any other political instrument, but, notes Clarence H. Haring: "As a repository of the people's liberty, a training school for the democratic system to be set up after independence, the *cabildo* possessed no potency at all."

Not least of the *cabildo*'s contributions to Spanish American history was its sponsoring of the *cabildo abierto,* "the open town meeting," to which chief citizens were occasionally bidden when matters of moment impended. These meetings were later to be the rallying center for the secessionists who severed American ties with Spain.

The *audiencia* was an early instrument for royal control. It was a court, whose functions in the colonies were roughly equivalent to those of a modern American circuit court—so Charles Upson Clark describes it, and he goes on to say: "It was not a Supreme Court, cases being appealed, e.g., from the *Audiencia* of Guatemala to that of Mexico City and from there to Spain or Rome: and the Justices did actually go on circuit." It was not new, for Spain had used the *audiencias* to enforce royal discipline in territory reconquered from the Moslems. Now transplanted to America, they were designed to curb the *adelantados* and their turbulent henchmen. The first *audiencia* was installed in Santo Domingo in 1511, followed by that of Mexico in 1527, Panama in 1535, Lima in 1542, Guatemala in 1543, New Galicia (Guadalajara) in 1548, and Bogotá in 1549. By the end of the colonial period the original seven *audiencias* had been doubled.[3]

The American *audiencia* was primarily a court, as it was in Spain. Its members were judges (*oidores,* "they who hear"), three or four of them being assigned to each of the first *audiencias,* a number doubled and redoubled as time went on. As a court representing the king, it was superior to all other courts within its jurisdiction. In addition to judicial duties, the *audiencia* was the mouthpiece of the king. Its decisions had final authority subject only to the king's veto, hence it became in effect a legislative agency. Furthermore, the *audiencia* had administrative and consultative functions. Although later overshadowed by viceroys, the *audiencia* remained the constant core of royal authority. It had continuity; its plural membership assured the presence of royal authority no matter what might happen to the viceroys. When a viceroy died or was removed, the *audiencia* automatically took his place. Membership in the *audiencia* was jealously restricted to *peninsulares,* Spaniards from Spain, but with the passage of time an increasing number of its judges became so identified with the American "kingdoms" as to lose their exclusively Spanish point of view. Many founded families which became influential in subsequent colonial and independent history.

The *audiencia* early proved inadequate. The conquerors and their heirs were difficult to handle, and the disputes which multiplied among them and the clergy and the civil authorities required a sterner discipline than any court could impose. Some of the *audiencias* were corrupt, more were inefficient. The *audiencia* of Santo Domingo was not strong enough to compel Governor Diego Velásquez and Hernán Cortés to compose their differences. The first *audiencia* of Mexico, appointed in 1527, could not overawe Cortés; it could not or would not take effective measures to protect the Indians, a failure which embroiled it with the clergy. In Peru the *audiencia* appointed in 1542 failed to quiet the strife between followers of Almagro and Pizarro. The Crown's answer was to appoint viceroys, and relegate the *audiencias* to a subordinate position.

The viceroy (the vice-king) represented the prestige and power of the sovereign. His dignity was attested by the luxurious welcome accorded him, the triumphal arches erected in city streets, the display of fine robes of judges and churchmen, the feasting and the pageantry. His all but royal position was made clear by an impressive corps of private guards, a numerous retinue of servants, a palace with Gobelin tapestries and gold plate, a princely salary and expense account—large enough, it was hoped, to put the incumbent safely beyond temptation. The viceroy was a man apart

---

[3] Additional *audiencias* were established as follows: Charcas, 1559; Quito, 1563; Manila, 1583; Santiago de Chile, 1609; Buenos Aires, 1661; Caracas, 1786; Cuzco, 1787.

from common men; he was the king's man. He was expected to hold office for three years (a rule to which there were numerous exceptions), but was subject to instant recall; he was enjoined against intimacy with the vassals whom he ruled, forbidden to marry within his realm, and barred from all private business.

The viceroy's powers were great. Madrid was far away and he was given wide latitude in interpreting the royal will. He was automatically president of the *audiencia* within his viceroyalty. He possessed generous powers of appointment to civil and ecclesiastical posts. When he was a man of force and ingenuity, he could outplay priests and judges; he could temporize with royal commands or disregard them. However, his powers were subject to constant and irritating checks. Although he was president of the *audiencia,* the judges of that court could report directly to the king. Theoretically, he had power over numerous officials, but many of these were royal appointees who had the right of appeal to the king. He largely controlled the Church, in theory, but time and again the chief clergy went over his head to the Crown. Nominally sharing the power of the king himself, he was actually at the mercy of the latest caprice of the king or of the king's inner circle. There was always a candidate for his office quick to spread rumors for his undoing. He was subject, as were all chief officials, to the periodic check of a royal *visitador* who could come when he chose, inspect the financial records of the viceroyalty, and hold hearings to which any vassal might bring complaints. At the end of his term the viceroy must subject himself to the *residencia,* a judicial review conducted by a judge appointed by the Crown and before whom his entire record was exposed to public view. In some cases the *residencia* served the cause of justice, in others it facilitated the revenge of lesser men, and in still others corrupt viceroys were able to buy a favorable verdict from complacent judges.[4]

From the standpoint of the kings, the viceroyalty was a success. The viceroys were usually the kind of men they wanted, the sort described by one historian: "The utmost care must be taken to make sure that the new official did not follow the same course as the *conquistadores* and defy the authority of the monarch who sent him out. The Hapsburgs did not, as a rule, take kindly to subordinates of the brilliant or the inventive sort who wanted to strike out on lines of their own. The official whom they preferred was the hard working, competent, but obedient type, who would faithfully discharge the duties laid upon him and send back for fresh instructions if they had a case of doubt."[5] The viceroys who ruled Spanish America for 300 years in general met those requirements. A few were brilliant, many were competent, some were honest, and some were scoundrels; but with scarcely an exception they were loyal to their kings.

The history of colonial Spanish America chiefly gathers around the

---

[4] It was often said in colonial days that a viceroy (and other high officials) must make "three fortunes" while in office—the first to pay for his appointment, the second to support him during his term, and the third to bribe the *juez de residencia.*

[5] Roger B. Merriman, *op. cit.,* Vol. III, p. 649.

1000 MILES

SPANISH

PORTUGUESE

FRENCH

DISPUTED

BRITISH
NORTH AMERICA

CLAIMED BY
ENGLAND,
UNITED STATES,
RUSSIA,
SPAIN

LOUISIANA

UNITED STATES

Mexico

VICEROYALTY OF
NEW SPAIN

VICEROYALTY OF
NEW GRANADA

Bogotá

GUIANA

VICEROYALTY OF
BRAZIL

Lima

VICEROYALTY
OF
PERU

Rio de
Janeiro

LOUISIANA
• FRENCH BEFORE 1762
• TO SPAIN, 1762
• TO FRANCE, 1800
• SOLD TO U.S., 1803

Buenos Aires

VICEROYALTY OF
LA PLATA

LOUISIANA

NEW FRANCE

ENGLISH
COLONIES

NEW SPAIN

CENTRAL
NORTH AMERICA
1755

TRM

Western Hemisphere, 1784; Central North America, 1755

varying fortunes of the two viceroyalties of New Spain and Peru, which between them had sovereignty over most of that extensive domain until the eighteenth century, when there was a further division of authority under the Bourbon kings. The Viceroyalty of New Granada was established in 1717, abolished in 1724, and restored in 1740, with jurisdiction over the region of modern Colombia, Ecuador, and Venezuela. In 1776 the Viceroyalty of La Plata was created, with jurisdiction over the area now divided among Argentina, Paraguay, Bolivia, and Uruguay. However, the colonial record chiefly deals with the forty-one viceroys in Peru and the sixty-two in New Spain (Mexico) between the years 1535 and 1824.

The first and perhaps the greatest of the viceroys was Antonio de Mendoza, who was sent to Mexico in 1535, where he ruled for fifteen years. He was then transferred to the Viceroyalty of Peru, where he died after a year in office. Mendoza was about forty-five when he reached Mexico; he came from a proud lineage of great soldiers, clerics, and statesmen, and he himself had already won honors as a soldier and diplomatist. He found tasks enough in Mexico to tax his ability. The first *audiencia* (1528–30) with Nuño de Guzmán as president had ruled with such cruelty as to arouse the wrath of honest citizens and to stir the clergy, led by the newly appointed Bishop Zumárraga, to denounce its members to the King.[6] The superior second *audiencia* of 1530, including Bishop Fuenleal and the humanitarian Vasco de Quiroga, had been unable to control Hernán Cortés, who took his title of captain-general seriously. In western Mexico, meanwhile, the unsavory Nuño de Guzmán ruled as governor of New Galicia, but he was finally ordered back to Spain in 1536. Following this disorderly period, Mendoza ruled for fifteen years with moderation and wisdom. The limits of New Spain were extended further in the west and northwest, and in the east to Yucatán. He held a tight line on the overreaching *encomenderos* who exploited the Indians "entrusted" to them. His palace doors were open to all suppliants. He encouraged the friars in their works of mercy and education. He fostered better agriculture and stock raising. Churchmen, city dwellers, and the humble Indians respected him.

Second only to Mendoza was Francisco de Toledo, who served in Peru from 1569 to 1581. Like Mendoza, Toledo represented one of the great houses in Spain and had a distinguished career behind him when, in his middle fifties, he was named to Lima with jurisdiction over all of Spanish South America with the exception of the coast of Venezuela. Peru was an onerous assignment. Nerves were still raw from the long and bloody struggles between Pizarro and Almagro. The *audiencia* and the high clergy were in no mood to accept Toledo's guidance. The landholders, rich from despoiling the Indians, feared his humanitarian intentions. The last of the Inca rulers was stirring up trouble on the frontier. Toledo's task was further complicated by Philip II's desire to dictate each detail of his viceroy's course. Despite all handicaps, Toledo did much to consolidate Spanish discipline over his domain. Shortly after his arrival he set out on a

---

6 Zumárraga's great letter to Charles V is in Lesley Byrd Simpson: *The Encomienda in New Spain* (Berkeley, Calif.: University of California Press; 1950), pp. 214–29.

journey of inspection, traveling more than 5,000 miles in five years and visiting most of the important points of Peru. He had two chief concerns: the state of mining and the welfare of his Indian wards. The silver deposits of Potosí in Upper Peru (Bolivia) were yielding handsomely. Toledo encouraged improved methods of mining and extraction, and drew up wise codes to govern mining and the treatment of miners. The flow of silver increased. He took measures to protect the Indians against both mine operators and *encomenderos*. He found thousands of Indians in the indescribably dirty slums of Lima and created a special suburb for them to be ruled by their own chieftains under the guidance of the Jesuits.

Toledo was appalled by the wretched condition of the Church. The gold and silver of Peru attracted many unworthy clergy who neglected their flocks to pursue wealth, clung to the cities, and avoided the villages. Toledo, with the support of devout Philip II, enforced salutary reforms upon the clergy, required them to learn Indian tongues so that they might more effectively instruct their charges, and welcomed the Inquisition as an aid to reform.

Toledo's activities included the building of aqueducts for bringing pure water into the chief towns, the establishment of inns and hospitals, and the erection of forts to protect the highways. In his dealings with the Indians he often made use of the ancient organization of the Incas. But he made the mistake of uprooting large groups of Indians and forcing them to live in villages unsuited to their traditions and needs. Garcilaso de la Vega was caustic in his denunciation of Toledo on that score.

His record was marred by the execution in 1571 of the last of the Inca line, Tupac Amarú. This Inca ruler had maintained his independent court in the inaccessible mountains northeast of Cuzco, from which he harassed the Spaniards. He was finally captured by Toledo's men, given a summary trial, and executed. Philip A. Means writes: "It is pitiful to reflect that they whose only crime was that of endeavoring to rid their country of tyrannical and oppressive invaders were subjected to unspeakable humiliations and tortures." And Means goes on to say that Toledo showed his further animus against the Incas by "a systematic perversion of traditions relative to the Incas and their history all to the end that the Incas might be made to appear before the world as a set of ruffians, blackguards, bastards and usurpers."[7] But Means scarcely does justice to the Viceroy.

In Toledo's *Memorial,* his concluding advice to his successors, he reveals a sagacity and human comprehension which entitle him to a high place among Spanish administrators. However, his services did not earn him the gratitude of the Crown. In 1581 he was recalled to Madrid, where he was charged with unlawful enrichment and the illegal execution of Tupac Amarú. Perhaps Philip was jealous of his viceroy's popularity or was sincerely outraged by the execution of the last Inca. The indefatigable Toledo died in 1584 "of a broken heart."

Not until the last decades of the colonial period do other names of

7 P. A. Means: *Fall of the Inca Empire and the Spanish Rule in Peru* (New York: Charles Scribner's Sons; 1932), pp. 123-4.

importance appear. Two deserve mention. Antonio María Bucareli was appointed viceroy of New Spain by the enlightened Charles III; he ruled from 1771 to 1779, a period of notable progress. The greatest of the last viceroys was the younger Count Revillagigedo, who was appointed by corrupt Charles IV and served in Mexico from 1789 to 1794. He was one of the four (out of a total of 170) American-born viceroys in the colonial period. His father was governor-general of Cuba and later viceroy of New Spain. When the son was named to New Spain, he had already acquired prestige as a soldier. He was a man of energy and quick intelligence who had come under the influence of the French Enlightenment. Revillagigedo served Mexico well, made extensive administrative reforms, improved the courts, regularized finance, and gave impetus to agriculture, mining, industry, education, and the arts. He consolidated Spanish power on the California coast and recommended extension of that power to Alaska. He improved the Mexican capital, which he found to be "so many filthy dunghills, not excluding the space in front of the palace in which there was a veritable gypsy camp of sheds and huts made quite without order since each one built as his fancy directed; and these sheltered by day as well as by night an endless number of folk of both sexes who committed all sorts of excesses without it being possible to watch over what went on in that confused and disorderly place."[8] He urged completion of the canal for the draining of Lake Texcoco, a project not completed until the days of Porfirio Díaz. He improved the water supply, extended paving, and organized the police. He even refurbished the local theater and its stock company of actors. His motives in launching these laudable reforms were mixed: not the least of them was to deflect the minds of the people from the revolutionary ideas that were spreading, especially from France. But Charles IV cared little for such reforms; also, Manuel Godoy, his chief adviser, had a brother-in-law named Branciforte who coveted the Mexican post. Revillagigedo was recalled, and arraigned on trumped-up charges of inefficiency and corruption, of which he was finally cleared. He was the last able viceroy.

We retrace our steps to consider the lesser officialdom. The great viceroyalties of New Spain and Peru were early subdivided into smaller administrative units, chiefly *presidencias* and captaincies-general. All were nominally subordinate to the viceroys; but the great distances, slow communication, and the jealousy of the deputies curtailed the viceroy's power. The presidents, who were less important and often more accessible, were usually subject to greater viceregal control than the more remote captains-general, who became largely independent of the viceroy and were in effect "little viceroys." Both captains-general and presidents were direct appointees of the king; both reported to the king and received orders directly from him, often paying no more than lip service to the viceroy. For ex-

---

[8] Revillagigedo: *Instrucción Reservada,* Art. 244; quoted by James F. King: *The Reforms of Viceroy Revillagigedo, the Younger, in the City of Mexico* (Master's thesis, University of California, Berkeley, Calif.; 1935).

ample, at the end of the colonial period the viceroy of New Spain (Mexico) exercised a considerable control over the *presidencia* of Guadalajara in the west but had slight control over the Captaincy-General of Guatemala, which included most of Central America, and over the Captaincy-General of Santo Domingo, which included the Spanish West Indies. In South America the viceroy of Peru, who was supreme in Lima, was held responsible for the *presidencia* of Cuzco, but paid only fitful attention to the remote and relatively unimportant Captaincy-General of Chile.

It was a cumbrous mechanism in which the theoretically powerful viceroys were checked by the ambitions of *audiencias,* presidents, and captains-general. All these exercised their right to send petitions and complaints directly to the king. One concludes that the Crown enjoyed the discomfiture of its viceroys under this clumsy system of checks and counter-checks. It was a system of planned intimidation by which the several royal authorities were kept in a salutary mood of frightened dependence. As an instrument for regularity and loyalty, it worked well; but as an instrument for the service of the kingdoms overseas, it proved awkward.

Under the viceroys, presidents, and captains-general, there were minor officials—governors, *corregidores,* and *alcaldes mayores*—who presided over municipalities and other administrative units of varying size and importance. Their titles and duties shifted in various regions; but it is important to understand the critical role of those officials who were usually called *corregidores.* In the beginning the *corregimiento* (administrative unit for governing remote communities) was devised to protect the Indian, to hold distant and scattered communities in subjection, to collect taxes, and to preserve the peace. It was obviously impossible for higher officials to supervise thousands of villages hidden in distant valleys. The *corregidores* assigned to Indian communities, who were given virtually absolute power over their wards and were usually quite unchecked by higher officials, were responsible for the greatest scandals of colonial rule. The *corregidor* was tax collector, policeman, and magistrate, and it was easy for him to use his power for his own enrichment. He could collect as he was able, pocket as much as he pleased, commandeer the services of Indians, and farm out their labor to contractors near or far. He could acquire the best land for himself and rob the Indian of his water rights at will. He could buy the Indians' wares at whatever price he chose to pay, and he could sell manufactured goods to them under threat of slavery or excommunication. We read of *corregidores* who forced their villagers to buy silk stockings, eyeglasses, and other preposterous items. The *corregidores* often used Indian chieftains as aides in their nefarious schemes, and many of these outdid the Spaniards in defrauding the simple Indians. Even more corrupt than the *corregidores* were the *alcaldes mayores,* who were assigned to lesser communities and seldom received any salary.[9]

·   ·   ·

[9] L. E. Fisher: *The Intendent System in Spanish America* (Berkeley, Calif.: University of California Press; 1929), p. 5. A gloomy parallel may be suggested between the *corregidores* of Indian villages and later administration of Indian affairs in the United

The last of the seventeenth-century Hapsburgs had ruled abominably, selling viceregal and lesser posts to the highest bidders. The Bourbons, and especially Charles III (1759–88), brought refreshing new ideas. A capricious disciple of the French Enlightenment, Charles III magnified royal power and dignity, centralized authority, brought greater unity between the Crown and the kingdoms overseas, and injected welcome humanitarianism into the control of his subjects. His zeal was partially explained by desire to quiet restive elements at home and abroad, as well as by the need to set Spain's house in better order to meet British competition.

Charles III's economic reforms reduced the shackles upon trade, opened the way to freer movement of goods, and provoked a marked revival in prosperity both in Spain and the colonies. His chief ecclesiastical reform, the expulsion of the Jesuits in 1767, had disastrous results, as we shall see in a later chapter. His creation of a colonial militia, while responding to demand from overseas, was a measure of prudence against the English who were encroaching upon Spanish holdings, especially in the Caribbean area.

Charles III's chief political reforms divided Spanish America into *intendencias* under officers known as *intendentes*. This system, a French device, had been installed in Spain in the early eighteenth century, and Charles now extended it to America. The advance agent of this reorganization, José de Gálvez, was sent as *visitador general* to Mexico in 1765. Returning to Spain as minister of colonies, he reorganized the colonial government according to Charles's plan. Governors, *corregidores,* and *alcaldes mayores* were displaced and their tasks were allotted to the *intendentes*. In New Spain, some 200 *corregidores* and *alcaldes mayores* lost their posts and their domains were divided into 12 *intendencias*. By 1790 all Spanish America was thus apportioned. The *intendentes* were charged with the administration of justice, the overseeing of communities, the collection of taxes, the promotion of business and trade, and the organization of the provincial militia. The new system provoked angry criticism. Some viceroys regarded it as inimical to their own powers, some *audiencias* resented the transfer of judicial functions, and all displaced officials were unhappy. By the time the new system was fixed upon Spanish America, Spain had lost her last able king. In 1788 Charles III died, leaving the throne to his son Charles IV, a weak and vacillating fellow who undid the work of his distinguished father. The new system never had a fair chance. The forces were already at work which would undermine the royal hold upon the colonies and would lead within two decades to successful outbreaks against the power of the Spanish Crown in America.

States. There were abundant instances of Indian agents who behaved no better in the nineteenth century than did the seventeenth-century Spanish *corregidores*. The Indian agent, long the local guardian and provisioner of the reservation Indians of the United States, was the poorly paid despot of his charges, selected in order to pay off political debts and given opportunity to enrich himself out of the funds and goods he handled. Investigations during the last half of the nineteenth century revealed an abuse of power unpleasantly reminiscent of the *corregidores*. Abraham Lincoln said, "It needs more than one honest man to watch one Indian Agent."

THE CHURCH IN SPANISH AMERICA

It is not without mystery that in the same year in which Luther was born in Eisleben . . . Hernando Cortés saw the light in Medellín . . . the former to upset the world and bring beneath the banner of Satan many of the faithful who from fathers and grandfathers and times far back had been Catholics; and the latter to bring into the folds of the Church an infinite multitude of people who for years without number had been under the domination of Satan, immersed in vice, and blinded with idolatry.[1]

The historian, after due celebration of Spain's explorers, con- querors, and civil rulers, approaches the grateful task of describing the churchmen who accompanied the soldier and the ruler to Spain's new home in America. The conquest of America was launched in violence and consummated in a degree of mercy. The man with the Cross finally proved mightier than the man with the Sword. The soldier won battles, but the friar won hearts. The last Spanish flag in America has long since been hauled down, but the faith of the mother country remains as the most tenacious bond among Spain's former vassals. The Cross is silhouetted against the sky from Mexico to Argentina.

For time out of mind the history of Spain in the New World has been told to American and English readers by men obsessed with the Anglo-Saxon Protestant tradition. The belittling of Catholic Spain at last yields to more serene judgment: Spain and Spain's Church should be ap- proached not in search of polemics in national or religious controversy, but as rich chapters in the history of ideas.

The Church of Spanish America faithfully mirrored the shifting spiritual forces of the Church at home. The priests who came with the conquerors were afire with the crusading zeal of a Spain which had rid itself of unbelieving Moslems and Jews and had gone far in cleansing itself of timeserving priests, a Spain which, under the ardor of Isabella and

---

[1] Gerónimo de Mendieta: *Historia eclesiástica indiana* (Mexico: Antigua librería [Impresa por F. Díaz de León y S. White], 1870), pp. 174–5. Quoted by B. W. Diffie: *Latin American Civilization*, p. 247. Copyright 1945, by permission of the publisher, The Stackpole Company, Harrisburg, Pennsylvania.

Jiménez de Cisneros, had recaptured much of the religious fervor lost since the thirteenth century. Then, as colonizers followed conquerors, the Church in America was influenced by Charles I's battles for the faith, waged in his international role as Charles V—battles against the Moslems in Africa, against France in league with the Turks, and against the Protestant powers of northern Europe. During the sixteenth century the Church gained spiritual refreshment from St. Theresa, Luis de León, and St. John of the Cross; and militancy from the newly launched Society of Jesus. This spiritual climate gave zest to the friars who were pouring out their energy and devotion upon the hard frontier of America. However, after the sixteenth century, religious devotion lessened both in Spain and America. The religious orders —notably the Jesuits—continued with energy, but the secular clergy who had flocked to the colonies seldom shared the zeal of the first missionaries.[2] Institutionalism triumphed over devotion. Thousands of great and little churches appeared, hundreds of convents and monasteries were built, the Church became rich in land and gold. The many noble-hearted priests were outnumbered by those who found America comfortable and secure. This was the Church in Spanish America under the later Hapsburgs.

The Church suffered further changes under the eighteenth-century Bourbons. Frenchmen dominated the imperial court, dictated decisions, chose men to serve in viceregal offices and ecclesiastical posts. Cynical ideas supplanted the warm devotion with which the Church had been translated to America during the first decades after the Conquest. There was little room for crusaders and mystics in an empire ruled by Charles III and his brilliant minister, the Count of Aranda—Grand Master of the Freemasons, and friend of Voltaire.

The Spanish Church came to America with the conquerors. Beginning with Columbus's second journey in 1493, probably every expedition carried missionaries to the New World. The friars came first—the Dominicans, Franciscans, Mercedarians, Augustinians, and others. The learned Dominicans were prominent in the first days, preaching, converting, defending the Indian's rights. Then the Franciscans, and finally the Jesuits, became the great crusaders of the colonial age.

The soil of Indian America was well prepared for the seeds of the gospel. The religions of the aborigines made them hospitable to the teachings of the friars. To be sure, the Indians served many gods, but they tended to exalt one above all the others. The Incas subordinated lesser deities to the creator-god Viracocha. The Aztecs were also attracted by the idea of one supreme power: we have the testimony of Aztec King Nezahualcóyotl, who believed that "these idols of wood and stone can neither hear nor feel, much less could they make the heavens and the earth and man the lord of it. Some all-powerful unknown god is creator of the universe on whom alone I must rely for consolation and support."[3] The Indians were

2 The *secular* clergy were those living in the world, as distinguished from the *regular* clergy, who belonged to a religious or monastic order or community.
3 C. S. Braden: *Religious Aspects of the Conquest of Mexico* (Durham, N.C.: Duke University Press; 1930), p. 23.

not only prepared for monotheism but also for the promise of life after death: many of them held theories on heaven and hell, on rewards and punishments beyond the grave. Furthermore, both Aztec and Inca found the Spaniard's ecclesiastical organization not unfamiliar, for they too had convents and a hierarchy of priests. They were familiar with the symbol of the cross. They had their feast days and their fast days, all readily transferred to the new faith. Some of their ancient sacraments were similar to those of the Spaniards; baptism with water was widespread, and the Aztecs had a rite of confession followed by penance.

So there was a minimum of strain in the transition from the primitive faiths of Aztec and Inca to the discipline of Catholicism. The Indians found it simple to shift their temporal loyalty from their own rulers to the king of Spain, and to accept new priests in the place of the old. The friars showed wisdom in permitting this seeming continuity of faith. It is significant that the Shrine of Our Lady of Guadalupe on the edge of Mexico City occupies a site long dedicated to the Aztec goddess, Tonántzin ("our Mother"). In Cholula the high pyramid of the Toltecs and Aztecs is now topped by a church and cross. In Cuzco, ancient Inca capital, the foundation stones of the temple of Viracocha now support a Christian church. To this day, the Church often permits the ritual dances of forgotten centuries and finds it neither blasphemous nor incongruous when Indians bring their ancient ceremonies before the high altar.[4]

The religious conquest of the New World was a triumph. The friars baptized tens of thousands of Indians—in fact some sixteenth-century accounts tell of more baptisms than there were Indians, an easy exaggeration considering the uncritical judgment of the times and the pride of the crusading friars.[5] The Indians generally found it expedient to accept the white man's God as well as his king. Credit belongs to the friars, who by their generous service made their God so convincing.

If it was relatively easy to persuade the Indians to accept mass baptism, it was more difficult to compel them to abandon their pagan habits.

[4] This writer recalls two humble priests whose way with the Indians entitles them to commemoration. He found one of these in the village of Ysleta in New Mexico. To the question, "Are your Indians faithful?" the old priest replied: "Yes, they attend mass regularly. Then," he added with a smile, "they go to the stone altar of their ancestors at the far end of the village and observe the rites which have survived four centuries of alien rule. But," and the priest smiled again, "who am I to tell them that the flesh and blood of the eternal God appears in the wine and wafer of the mass but that God cannot also incarnate himself in the stones of their ancient sacrifice?" And a second priest, long serving in Guatemala's Chichicastenango, told this writer with affectionate pride of the way in which his Indians carried their ancestral dances to the steps of the church itself, and then entered the church under the shadow of the high altar. These two priests, typical of thousands, bear witness to the human sympathy of the Church.

[5] In 1531 Bishop Zumárraga reported that the Franciscans alone had baptized more than a million. Motolinía says that some Franciscans baptized as many as 1,500 in one day. Pedro de Gante in 1529 reported 14,000 baptisms in one day. By the middle of the seventeenth century, according to another chronicler, 10 million had been baptized by the Dominicans and Franciscans alone. See C. H. Haring: *The Spanish Empire in America* (New York: Oxford University Press; 1947), p. 186; and B. W. Diffie, *op. cit.,* p. 252.

Idolatry, chief affront to the conscience of the friars, still flourished. Each Indian home had its household idol, which was invoked at times of planting or harvest or when sickness threatened man or beast. In 1538 Fray Motolinía boasted: "The idolatry of the masses was blotted out . . . the Indians had so far forgotten their idols as though a hundred years had passed." He was overoptimistic. The idols simply went "underground," ready to come out of hiding when needed to stop the corn borer or ward off the plague. Human sacrifice, repugnant to the Spaniards, yielded more readily, at least in accessible regions. Polygamy presented a harder problem. To Indians it was natural to love their multiple wives and the children of all of them. Furthermore, a generous supply of women and children was an asset in those pastoral days. The friars were stern in denouncing polygamy, but they were not greatly helped by the example set by their countrymen—the conquering captains, horsemen, and foot soldiers frankly enjoyed the well-shaped, bronzed Indian women in spite of the dour warnings of ascetic friars.

Meanwhile, the Church was the right arm of the king. Wherever the king's agents journeyed, they represented not only the imperial court but the Church as well. "Spain in America," writes Clarence H. Haring, "reflected the indissoluble union of the altar and the throne." The king was secular head of the Church by direct commission of the pope. This delegation of authority was implicit in the bulls of Alexander VI in 1493, by which the New World was divided between Spain and Portugal. It was made explicit in the bull of 1501, by which the king was assigned all tithes collected in America, the money to serve as a sacred trust for winning the Indians to Christ. The king's powers and tasks were enlarged by the bull of 1508, which conferred upon the king the right of patronage over the Church in America, including all decisions as to the building and location of churches and monasteries, and the appointment of clergy to all posts high and low. This "royal patronage of the Indies" (*real patronato de las Indias*) gave the king greater powers than he possessed over the Church in Spain itself. This grant of power precipitated debate between the "regalists," who exalted royal prestige, and the "ultramontanists" (i.e., those from beyond the mountains, in other words, the upholders of the Vatican). Sovereigns, including devout Isabella, Charles I, and Philip II, were jealous of any meddling by the pope. The popes, though grateful for the devotion of the Spanish Crown, were properly suspicious of royal pretentions. The regalists steadily won the argument. The king's power over the Church increased throughout the colonial era, his supremacy finally proved by Charles III's successful expulsion of the Jesuits in 1767.

The royal will in matters of the Church was executed during the first century after the Conquest through the Council of the Indies. Its onerous duties were somewhat lightened by the creation in 1600 of the Cámara de las Indias (the Chamber of the Indies), charged with supervision of the Church in America. This division of responsibility provoked some jealousy between the Council and the newly organized Chamber, introducing one more element of discord on the sore point of patronage which already involved the rival claims of various civil and ecclesiastical officials at home and abroad.

The Church in America was early organized with an ecclesiastical hierarchy which paralleled the political ranks of viceroys, *audiencias,* and captains-general. In 1511 the first bishops were installed, two in Hispaniola, one in Puerto Rico. Other appointments followed: in Darién in 1513; in Cuba, 1522; in Mexico, 1527; in Colombia, 1529; in Peru, 1534. By the end of the sixteenth century, there were five archbishops and twenty-seven bishops. By the end of the colonial period the number had increased to ten archbishops and thirty-eight bishops. Under them a growing army of secular clergy manned great and little churches scattered over Spain's American domain. The special Church courts, so long a jealously treasured privilege of the Church in Spain, were transferred to America, where the clergy continued to enjoy immunity from civil courts.

But the religious orders contributed most of the early missionaries, whose records are the Church's chief glory.

SOME NOTABLE FRIARS

One of the most diligent friars was Antonio de Montesinos, a member of the first Dominican group in Hispaniola. In 1511 Montesinos, aroused by the abuse of the Indians, arose in his pulpit and, using the text "I am a voice crying in the wilderness," denounced his well-fed congregation: "You are in mortal sin . . . for the cruelty and tyranny you use in dealing with these innocent people. . . . Tell me," he cried, "by what right or justice do you keep these Indians in such cruel and horrible servitude? . . . Are these not men? . . . Have they not rational souls, are you not bound to love them as you love yourselves? . . . Be certain that, in such a state as this, you can no more be saved than the Moors or Turks."[6] Anger flared against the presumptuous priest. The colonists were of no mind to forego the fat profits from exploited Indian labor. A deputation called upon Fray Pedro de Córdoba, the Dominican vicar, to demand that Montesinos be returned to Spain. Córdoba refused, replied that Montesinos spoke for the Dominicans, and bade them listen. On the following Sunday Montesinos made his indictment even more clear. The brave friar was recalled to Spain and laid his case before King Ferdinand; beyond that we know little of him. Henríquez Ureña, distinguished son of Hispaniola, describes Montesinos's moral indictment as "one of the greatest in the spiritual history of mankind."

Another epic figure among the early friars was Bartolomé de las Casas. Born in Seville in 1474, educated in law at Salamanca, Las Casas came to Santo Domingo as a gentleman soldier of fortune in 1502. He was successful, won lands and Indians, and mined gold with untroubled conscience. In 1510, when he was thirty-six, he was ordained to the priesthood,

6 Lewis Hanke: *The Spanish Struggle for Justice in the Conquest of America* (Philadelphia: University of Pennsylvania Press; 1949), pp. 17 ff.

but he continued his money-making. He was one of the colonists whom Montesinos denounced, and he resented the friar's impudence as soundly as any. He shortly joined Governor Velásquez in Cuba, where he got more land and more Indians. However, in 1514, at the age of forty, Las Casas suddenly awoke to the iniquity of the system under which he profited, gave up his lands and Indians, and for fifty-two years fought for the Indians of America.

Las Casas journeyed to Spain in 1516 and presented the case for the Indians to the Regent, Cardinal Jiménez de Cisneros. The two men understood each other. The Cardinal knew full well that Christian Spain had no right to sleep while helpless vassals were done to death. He named Las Casas "Protector of the Indians," a title he wore with distinction until his death at ninety-two. Las Casas's pleas were heeded. The Cardinal ordered inquiries into the abuses reported, but they brought little relief for the oppressed natives. The inefficacy of these attempts at reform is explained by Peter Martyr, member of the Council of the Indies, who wrote: "All these instructions have been thought out by prudent and humane jurisconsults and sanctioned by religious men. But what of that? When our compatriots reach that remote world, so far away and so removed from us, beyond the ocean whose courses imitate the changing heavens, they find themselves distant from any judge. Carried away by love of gold, they become ravenous wolves instead of gentle lambs, and heedless of royal instructions."[7]

When Las Casas returned to Hispaniola to belabor his former companions, he was ordered to leave. He went to Spain again in 1517 and presented his complaint to Charles I, freshly come to the throne. The young king and his ministers were sympathetic, but being hard-headed men, they demanded that Las Casas be practical, that he suggest a plan. Las Casas had two solutions. The first was to import Negroes in order to save the Indians. The judgment of history has been harsh on Las Casas for this counsel, blaming him for the slave trade; but the truth is that Negro slaves had been imported into Spanish America fifteen years before Las Casas's proposal. Moreover, the friar soon repented this advice. His second plan was a cure for the evils of the *encomienda*[8]: Spanish farmers would be organized, for effective colonization of the New World, into villages of forty families each. An allotment of Indians would be held in sacred trust by each village (instead of by an individual, as in the *encomienda* system); and the land would be worked in common under the rigid supervision of friars. The councilors of Charles I were convinced, and Las Casas was authorized to put the scheme into effect. But his plans miscarried. The feudal landlords of Spain, short of labor, blocked enlistment, and the farmers secured were lazy fellows whom no one else wanted. Las Casas led an expedition to Venezuela where the poor quality of the colonists was soon evident. Furthermore, the civil authorities refused to keep hands

---

7 Quoted by Lewis Hanke, *ibid.*, p. 49.

8 See pp. 186–7 for discussion of this device for allotting Indians to deserving soldiers.

off, led raids upon the Indians, and Las Casas's colony never had a chance. In 1520 Las Casas, discouraged by failure, retired to a monastery in Santo Domingo and became a member of the Dominican Order; he spent about ten years writing his *History of the Indies* and taking no part in active life.

In the 1530's Las Casas quit the monastery and resumed his fight, proposing a new method of conquest through persuasion, which he elaborated in a tract, *The Only Method of Attracting Men to the True Faith.* His argument was concise: we have erred, he said, in seeking to convert by force. All men are ready for the faith. They can be won by persuasion, by affection, by patient repetition. They can be convinced if they are taught "as rain and snow falls from heaven, not impetuously, not violently, not suddenly like a heavy shower, but gradually, with suavity and gentleness, saturating the earth as it falls." In 1537 he was given the chance to test his method. There was a mountainous area in Guatemala which the Spaniards, after three futile efforts to conquer it, called the Land of War. Las Casas agreed to subdue the unwilling Indians with no arms save those of the true faith. His two conditions were accepted: there should be no seizure of Indian land, and for five years no Spaniards except the friars should be allowed to enter the region. His first step was to compose ballads in the Maya tongue which recounted the mysteries of the Christian faith from the beginning of the world. He picked four Christian Indian traders, taught them to sing the ballads, and sent them into the Land of War. There, before an audience of curious Indians, the traders sang the ballads over and over again, day after day. When the Indians demanded more knowledge of these strange affairs, they were told of the friars who traveled without guns, who sought no treasure, asked no land. Fearfully the Indians invited the Dominicans to visit them. The audacious experiment worked for a time. The Land of War was renamed by Las Casas the Land of True Peace. And so it might have remained had rival priests and settlers not forced their way into the region. Finally the Indians revolted and the Land of True Peace was again the Land of War. Meanwhile, Las Casas was named Bishop of Chiapa, his diocese including the Land of True Peace; but the opposition was more than he could overcome.

While these events were transpiring in America, Las Casas's arguments had persuaded Charles I to promulgate the New Laws of the Indies in 1542. These were brave but quixotic blows at the greedy *encomenderos* who were reducing the Indians to slavery from New Spain to Chile. Although these laws failed miserably before the resistance of the strongly entrenched soldiers of fortune who had preempted lands and Indians, they stand as eloquent testimony to the clear conscience of Las Casas.

In 1547 Las Casas—then about seventy-two—quit America for the last time and spent the remaining twenty years of his life in Spain writing a series of spirited polemics on behalf of his Indian protégés. His most famous tract was his *Very Brief Recital of the Destruction of the Indies,* printed in 1552 and crowded with gruesome description of the treatment of the aborigines. His bitter critics, including most of the clergy, could not refute his indictments. To be sure, he exaggerated and his statistics were absurd. He claimed that 15 or 20 million Indians had been killed by the Spaniards—perhaps as many Indians as lived in America in the early sixteenth century. But few tracts in history had more far-reaching effects. It aroused the humanitarians to fresh energy, although even the devout deplored his excessive indictments. It evoked the fury of the colonists and stiffened their determination to defeat the meddlesome priest. It furnished fuel to Spain's enemies, who forthwith made capital of Spain's iniquities for their own ends. It laid a solid foundation for the "Black Legend" which has colored the writings of the English, Dutch, Germans, and Americans ever since. It was an instant success in the bookstalls of Europe and within two centuries there were three Italian editions, three Latin, four English, six French, eight German, and eighteen Dutch. A London edition of 1689 carried the title: *Popery truly Display'd in its Bloody Colours: Or a Faithful Narrative of the Horrid and Unexampled Massacres, Butcheries, and all manner of Cruelties, that Hell and Malice could invent, committed by the Popish Spanish Party on the Inhabitants of West-India . . . Composed first in Spanish by Bartholomew de las Casas, a Bishop there, and an Eye-Witness of most of these Barbarous Cruelties; afterwards translated by him into Latin, then by other hands into High-Dutch, Low-Dutch, French, and now Taught to speak Modern English.*[9] And so Las Casas's tract takes its place in history with such polemics as Harriet Beecher Stowe's *Uncle Tom's Cabin* and Emile Zola's *J'accuse.*

Controversies raged around the head of the old priest until his death. He challenged the most eminent humanist of his time, Juan Ginés de Sepúlveda, author of arguments justifying further wars on the Indians and proving that Nature and Nature's God had ordained certain men to be slaves. Las Casas was despised by the colonists, rejected by most of the clergy, denounced as a "quarrelsome and turbulent fellow." There is still debate as to whether he finally served the cause so dear to his heart or helped to defeat it by stiffening the opposition. There is no debate as to his courage.

The Franciscan Juan de Zumárraga, first Bishop of Mexico, was less spectacular than Las Casas but no less brave a defender of the Indians. Zumárraga was already a man of sixty when he arrived in Mexico in 1528 to face a colony torn by strife between the first *audiencia* and the conqueror Cortés. The Indians were losing their land and were being forced to labor at cruel tasks. They saw their daughters dragged off at the pleasure of the white men and their sons impressed into slavery and carried to distant areas. The new bishop was powerless against Nuño de Guzmán, president of the *audiencia*. Zumárraga decided upon an appeal to Charles I; but knowing that his letters were not safe from Nuño de Guzmán, he made the hard journey to Veracruz, entrusted his letter to a sailor who embedded it in a ball of wax which he placed in a barrel of oil, and so carried it safely to the king. This letter reveals the calm dignity and the moral passion of the Franciscan. It was not an appeal but rather a command that the king

[9] Lesley Byrd Simpson: *The Encomienda in New Spain* (Berkeley, Calif.: University of California Press; 1950), pp. 2–3.

appoint a new *audiencia* of honorable men, that he protect the Indians even under the *encomienda* system, and that all enslavement cease. Zumárraga cited the rumor that the king had given permission to enslave the Indians and charged his sovereign: "If it is true that your Majesty gave such a license, for the reverence of God do very great penance for it."[1]

The king heeded the bishop's advice. Nuño de Guzmán was dismissed. A new *audiencia* was sent, manned by the admirable Bishop Fuenleal and Vasco de Quiroga. Zumárraga returned to Spain to face his critics, was duly acquitted, and returned to Mexico in 1534. Then with the cooperation of the new *audiencia,* and in 1535 of Viceroy Mendoza, the bishop at last had a chance to effect some of the reforms for which he had hoped. He established schools for Indians. He brought to Mexico in 1537 the first printing press in the New World. He carried on his fight for the dignity of the Indians: he argued against branding them, opposed their use as beasts of burden, received them freely, listened to their complaints. When his friends warned against receiving such foul-smelling fellows, Zumárraga rebuked them: "You are the ones who give out an evil smell according to my way of thinking. . . . These Indians have a heavenly smell to me: they comfort me and give me health, for they exemplify for me that harshness of life and penitence which I must espouse if I am to be saved."[2] Zumárraga died in 1548 at the age of eighty, loved and respected by both Indians and Spaniards.

Zumárraga is also remembered for his grudging acceptance of the miraculous apparition of Our Lady of Guadalupe and the founding of the shrine which bears her name. On December 9, 1531, an Indian, Juan Diego, was passing the hill of Tepeyac on the northern outskirts of the Mexican capital when an Indian maiden appeared in a half-moon of dazzling light, announced herself as the Mother of God and the mother of all Indians, and bade Juan Diego carry a message to the bishop begging that a shrine be built upon the spot. Zumárraga was properly cautious. The virgin appeared to the Indian a second and a third time. On the third occasion she gave him a miraculous sign: roses suddenly appeared on the slopes of barren Tepeyac. Juan Diego wrapped the flowers into his mantle and hurried to the bishop. When he unfolded his mantle, the roses had disappeared, leaving in their place the painting of the Virgin of Guadalupe, which now hangs over the high altar of the basilica near Tepeyac. The story, long debated by churchmen, conveyed the dramatic message that the religion of the Spaniard was not an alien faith, that it belonged to Indian Mexico, that the Mother of God could rightfully appear with the dark hair, golden skin, and somber eyes of a Mexican maiden. It was no coincidence that three centuries later, when they took up arms against the Spaniards, the Indians of Mexico marched behind the banner of Our Lady of Guadalupe.

Among other memorable churchmen mention should be made of

[1] Lesley Byrd Simpson, *ibid.,* pp. 214–29. Simpson reprints most of the famous letter in translation.

[2] Gerónimo de Mendieta, *op. cit.,* pp. 631–2; quoted by Lewis Hanke, *op. cit.,* p. 175.

Pedro de Gante, a Flemish Franciscan, who founded a school for Indian boys on the outskirts of Mexico City in 1523. Another devoted Franciscan in Mexico was Toribio de Motolinía who sought to reform the *encomienda* system. The highminded Vasco de Quiroga came to Mexico as a member of the second *audiencia* and was appointed Bishop of Michoacán, where, inspired by Sir Thomas More's *Utopia*, he gathered the Indians into sheltered villages organized on communal lines. In Peru in the early days there were fewer notable friars and priests than in Mexico, but some names stand out, including the Franciscan Francisco Solano and Archbishop Mogrovejo y Robles—both of whom were later canonized. Beyond the names of those who won fame lies a great company of forgotten friars and secular priests who worked in faithful affection and devotion to lay the foundation for the Church in America.

THE INQUISITION IN AMERICA

The Holy Office of the Inquisition, almost a century old in Spain, was formally introduced to America by royal edict in 1569, the first inquisitors reaching Lima in 1570, and Mexico the following year. To be sure, the early bishops in America had been used as deputies by the Holy Office fifty years before. But after 1570 the Inquisition took its important place in colonial life and held it as long as Spanish power prevailed in America.

We must again remind ourselves that the Inquisition, unpalatable as it is to our modern taste, mirrored the deep convictions of the sixteenth century. The devout regarded heresy as a cardinal sin and the condoning of error as an affront to God. It was the bounden duty of believers to destroy those who fouled the springs of faith. There was complete unanimity among the great-spirited clerics and the civil leaders of the colonies in welcoming the stern discipline of the Holy Office. It was just and good in their eyes that punishment be meted out to all enemies of the true faith: to Jews who, because of Portuguese laxity, were slipping into Brazil and from there into Spanish America; to Protestants introduced by Dutch and English freebooters; to heretics, skeptics, and all dalliers with holy doctrine.

The Inquisition was also welcomed by conscientious bishops and viceroys as a scourge against self-seeking and lustful priests. The cleansing begun by Isabella and Jiménez de Cisneros was continued in the New World (even before the installation of the Holy Office in 1570): in the first half of the sixteenth century by Bishop Zumárraga, whose heart was troubled by the "immorality and corruption" of many priests; by Viceroy Mendoza, who described many priests as "wicked and motivated by self-interest"; by Archbishop Montúfar, who complained of the clergy's sinful luxury; and later, under the Inquisition proper, by Viceroy Toledo, who sought to curb priests who "went to enrich themselves at the expense of the Indians, shearing them of all they could." Many of the sentences imposed throughout the life of the Inquisition were upon priests who dishonored their office. The Inquisition in America, as in Spain, became a sort of police court for tracking down bigamists, robbers, seducers of youth, and other undesirable people. As an extension of its police duty, it acted as a censor of books, with its chief animus directed against heretical writings. It also gave attention to the theater, barring plays which were deemed lewd or irreverent.

The inequities of the Inquisition are obvious to the modern eye: damning suspicions cast upon thousands of innocent people by jealousy and malice; the choking of new ideas by fear; the seizure of men's liberties and properties on scant evidence. However, justice dictates the reminder that the Spaniards were no more intolerant than their contemporaries in Europe: Charles I was less harsh with dissenters than Henry VIII of England; Philip II was no more relentless in crushing heresy than his contemporaries, Charles IX and Henry III, on the throne of France. The Holy Office was fully as merciful as John Calvin. The witch-hunting and hanging in Germany, England, and New England were not morally superior to the *autos da fé* of Lima and Mexico with their commitment of Protestants, Jews, and sinful priests to the flames.

The Inquisition rested more lightly on the colonies than on the homeland. In 250 years there were only thirty culprits burned at the stake in Lima, and it is doubtful whether there were more than one hundred victims in all America during the colonial period. It must also be gratefully remembered, and to the eternal credit of Spain, that the Indian was early released from the burden of the Inquisition. During the early decades, a few Indians were burned for the sin of idolatry: in Yucatán Bishop Landa tortured some Maya, and in Texcoco an Indian *cacique* was executed for bowing to gods of stone. But these isolated instances aroused a storm of protest both in Spain and in the colonies, and there was general agreement that Indians could not rightly be judged by Spanish standards. After 1575 the Inquisition was ordered to leave the Indians to the discipline of the bishops, since they were "so new in the faith, so frail a people, and of so little substance." The Indians were but children, uncouth, irresponsible, not subject to the judgments applied to grown men. It is significant that Philip II showed the same tolerance with Moslem vassals in the Philippines, ordering the authorities not to enslave them: "But you shall endeavor to convert them . . . by good and legitimate means."

By the last decades of the eighteenth century, the inquisitors had largely lost their crusading fire against heretics and clerical sinners, and the Holy Office had become the whip used by the Bourbons to flay those who had learned from Voltaire and Rousseau to laugh at the divine pretensions of kings.

THE MISSIONS

The ardor of the early friars left an impressive monument in the mission villages[3] into which they gathered the frontier Indians to protect

---

[3] These villages were usually known as *reducciones,* conveying the idea of "reducing" Indians in one center, of concentrating them so that they might be conveniently trained,

them against slave-hunting colonists, to nurture them in the faith, and to train them in tilling the soil and in simple crafts. "The missions were born," writes Fernando de los Ríos, "as a religious aspiration and protest against the covetousness of the *conquistadores*." That ideal was maintained with rare fidelity throughout the colonial years, even though the missions gradually assumed the character of political and military outposts against Spain's rivals—Portugal, England, and France.

The mission village was paternalism flavored with theocracy, a benevolent communalism for the glory of God and the salvation of souls. Its origins can be seen in the efforts of the Jeronymite fathers who were sent to Hispaniola after 1512 to save the decimated Indians by gathering them into villages; in the ill-fated colonization of Venezuela by Las Casas, and in his quixotic Land of True Peace in Guatemala; in Vasco de Quiroga's "communities of innocents" on the shores of Lake Pátzcuaro. The religious orders, notably the Franciscans and the Jesuits, organized missions in great number and variety from California to Argentina, many of which continued in strength to the last days of Spain in America.

The most dramatic and successful missions were those of the Jesuits in the La Plata basin, the area now covering Paraguay, Uruguay, northern Argentina, and southern Brazil. Spanish Jesuits settled in Asunción in 1605, and from that center created the missions of the La Plata area, whose century and a half of history were both tragic and impressive. These missions were harried by the raids of the Brazilian *paulistas* (people of São Paulo, at that time militant slave hunters), by the ceaseless opposition of planters and civil and religious authorities, and by involvement in the territorial disputes of Portugal and Spain. But the number of missions increased: by the mid-eighteenth century there were about thirty, with some 100,000 Indian charges. Whether the Indians in these missions enjoyed a state of a tranquil "Arcadia"—as Cunninghame Graham described it—may be questioned, but certainly they shared in one of the bravest, most ingenious, high-spirited and pure-hearted ventures in all the white man's dealings with primitive peoples.

Jesuit rule in the La Plata missions was benevolent but despotic. The Indian was cut off not only from the greedy Europeans but from his own kind. His daily life was ordered with rigid provision for religious training, daily labor in the fields, play, and pageantry. The missions prospered, produced generous surpluses of cotton, hides, yerba maté, and tobacco, the sale of which filled the mission treasuries. The Indian was content; he probably fared better than any Indian of America before or since. But the training by the friars did not prepare the Indian to stand alone. He had no practice in self-government, no responsibility for his economic life, and small opportunity to learn new skills. Baron von Humboldt visited the missions after their greatness was spent and wrote of the Indians: "They have progressively lost that vigor of character and that natural vivacity

---

utilized, and protected. They were sometimes called *congregaciones*, "congregating" centers; and often simply *pueblos de indios*, villages of Indians.

which in every state of society are the noblest fruits of independence." In 1767 the Jesuits were expelled from the Spanish empire and were replaced by other friars and civil rulers, and the missions fell apart. The new administrators generally lacked both economic skill and character, and the untrained Indians were powerless to defend themselves against their despoilers. The one permanent result of the missions of La Plata was to fix the power of Spain upon the territory now shared by Uruguay and Paraguay, and to lay the basis for the creation of those nations as buffer states between Argentina and Brazil.

The last outthrust of the mission builders fixed Spanish power upon northwestern Mexico and California. In the late seventeenth century the Jesuit, Eusebio Kino, laid the foundation for missions in Sonora, Arizona, and California, and another Jesuit, Juan María Salvatierra, moved into Lower California. A century later the work of these pioneer Jesuits was inherited by the Franciscans, headed by Junípero Serra, who took over the posts of the expelled Jesuits and founded many of the missions that lie in the 600-mile span between San Diego and the Golden Gate. There was no lack of enlightened mercy in these California missions, but they were primarily military bastions charged with defense of that lightly populated wilderness against Spain's rivals. Ruins of the fortified *presidios* remind us today that the mission existed not only to rescue the Indian from sin, but also to safeguard Spain's hold upon her far-flung empire.

So the mission village ran its course from early experiments in Hispaniola to the last outpost founded in 1823 in northern California; and then it quietly disappeared. "The idea of the missions was as artificial as it was noble," writes Fernando de los Ríos; "it was impossible to maintain them in isolation nor was it possible to suppress every sort of human impulse . . . it was a city-convent without place for the initiative of the individual man, without place for adventure."

THE JESUITS

The large credit due the builders of the Church in America must be fairly apportioned among the numerous devoted secular priests and the various orders of monks and nuns. But in terms of the entire colonial period, the greatest chapters were written by the militant and tireless Society of Jesus, with whose activities in the La Plata area we have already dealt.

The Jesuits lived under an inflexible discipline. From their founding to modern days, no sustained charge has been brought against their financial integrity or their personal character. In days when many other priests were growing rich by extortion, the Jesuits personally profited not at all. In days when the clergy shared with the laity the careless sexual liberties of the times, the Jesuits kept their record clean. The reports of Antonio de Ulloa and Jorge Juan, sent by the Spanish king to investigate Peru in the 1740's, had much to say about the lax habits of the clergy; but of the Jesuits they wrote: "One does not see in them the lack of religion, the scandals and the loose behavior so common in the others."

The Jesuits, first and last, were defenders of the Indian. By 1750 their villages in all Spanish America harbored over 700,000 Indians. Jealous critics accused them of exploiting their helpless wards, but the record shows that while they were inexorable in their rule of the Indians, they were no less hard masters of themselves. They asked no more than they gave.

They were the custodians of learning. They were active in multiplying printing presses. Their leadership in the study of native languages, in reducing them to print and preparing grammars, encouraged the effective communication of ideas. They were the chief builders of schools, colleges, and universities. They were responsible for spreading the new learning of Europe. They gave currency to the work of Descartes, Leibnitz, and Newton. They gathered famous libraries and laid the foundation for some of the best collections of books in Spanish America.

The Jesuits prospered. The rigid discipline of the order and the undeviating austerity of its members inspired confidence and attracted endowments from the wealthy pious. They accumulated land. Their skill in farming was celebrated. They knew how to make the earth produce, how to organize the labor of Indians, how to extract the largest profit from the soil. They were among the chief holders of Negro slaves, and like other citizens found no incongruity in the practice. They organized industries. Their flour mills and bakeries supplied the cities. They manufactured lime, made rope, pottery, and textiles, tanned leather, built ships, and for a time held a virtual monopoly on drugs and medicines. Their success was the reward of unfaltering consistency. Under their strict regime there was little time for recreation and none for sinning. Generation after generation they built up their power and accumulated their reserves. They became the bankers, the chief traders, the dominant economic power in all Spanish America.

The Jesuits inevitably aroused the jealousy of the less successful, of their rivals for power and wealth, and thus accumulated the enemies which finally destroyed them. They incurred the wrath of civil authorities when they fought the Indian's battles against extortionate *corregidores,* when they opposed viceroys and governors and carried their appeals to Madrid or Rome. They angered bishops by appealing over their heads to king or pope, and were often on bad terms with the other religious orders, none of which matched them in consistency and zeal. There was constant strife with the great landholders, both creoles and Spaniards, who clamored for Indian slaves and resented the obstinacy of the Jesuits. The landholders also resented the unfair economic competition of the Jesuits, charging them with undue advantage in the markets, thanks to the tax exemptions they enjoyed. The Jesuits finally ran afoul of the kings. From their inception, they were dedicated to the overarching power of the pope, a doctrine distasteful to the kings. Philip II was uneasy over their extreme ultramontanism and the seventeenth-century Hapsburgs were too weak to make effective protest; but when Bourbon Charles III came to the throne in 1759, he was of no mind to brook competition, to tolerate a state within a state, or to permit appeals over his head to the Holy Father in Rome.

The long-developing forces which finally destroyed the Jesuits were given fresh impetus by the teaching of Voltaire, Rousseau, and D'Alembert. Voltaire's slogan, *Écrasez l'infâme!*, was a battle cry directed at the Church, and the Jesuits were the inevitable target as the most formidable, incorruptible, and able arm of the Church. In France the Jesuits refused absolution to the king's mistress. In Portugal they would not bow to the dictator Pombal. In Spain they appealed to God and the pope, while the king rested upon his own competence and saw no reason for tempering his royal will.

So the end came to the Jesuits. Civil governors denounced them and landholders rose in wrath against them; rival orders and secular clergy often joined in the abuse or at least refused to plead the Jesuits' cause. In Madrid the Count of Aranda persuaded Charles III that the Jesuits were plotting against his royal person. And, more eloquent than arguments, the rich fields and ample bank accounts of the Jesuits attracted a court beggared by war and facing new European contests.[4] The king signed the edict of expulsion in 1767. Officers of the law gathered in the Jesuits from Mexico to Argentina; they were placed aboard ships, handled with scant courtesy, and returned to Spain. Their expulsion aroused the deep resentment of many devout Catholics and many of their Indian charges. The mission villages, turned over to other orders or to civil authorities, fell apart. Their schools, the best in America, declined sharply. Hospitals and houses of charity were crippled. Their lands passed into the hands of rich planters. Their industries languished. The Church, robbed of its most stalwart defenders, lost prestige. There had been only 2,200 Jesuits in all Spanish America, a small company to wield such influence. But by their expulsion the empire lost perhaps its strongest cohesive force.

THE CHURCH AT THE END OF THE COLONIAL PERIOD

The Church in Spanish America was still a prosperous enterprise in 1800. Ten archbishops and thirty-eight bishops supervised its activities. Secular clergy manned the parish churches in cities and larger towns. Catechists instructed the semicivilized Indians in outlying villages. The religious orders conducted the mission villages on the wild frontier.

4 Pope Clement XIII, upon demanding of the king reasons for the expulsion of the Jesuits, received this devious reply: "In order to keep from the world a great scandal, I shall conceal in my breast the abominable machination which has been the motive of this severity. Your Holiness must believe me on my word: the security and repose of my existence require of me the most absolute silence on this subject." Bernard Moses: *Spain's Declining Power in South America* (Berkeley, Calif.: University of California Press; 1919), p. 106.

Churches and cathedrals dominated the sky lines of the chief cities and towns. Convents and monasteries were everywhere.[5]

The ancient faiths of Inca and Aztec had theoretically been rooted out. There was no longer a high *teocalli* with blood-caked altar for the praise of Huitzilopochtli in Mexico, no Temple of the Sun in Cuzco. The great majority of the Indian peoples had been drawn within the orbit of Spanish faith as well as of Spanish law. There has been long debate as to how soundly the Indian had been indoctrinated. Juan and Ulloa, reporting on Peru in the middle of the eighteenth century, were highly critical, insisted that the so-called converts usually learned no more "than parrots would obtain if they were so taught." Humboldt, visiting Mexico at the beginning of the nineteenth century, remarked that "the natives knew nothing of religion but the exterior forms." Viceroy Revillagigedo, writing at the close of the eighteenth century, judged that "the Indians are still very ignorant and uncultivated in religious matters." A bishop, reporting from Chile in 1787, said that the Araucanians "continue to practice their barbarous rites." The modern student, with longer perspective, concludes that the wonder is not that the Indians received so little of the imported faith, but that they absorbed so much. We still may marvel that Spain was able within three centuries to instill so much of the devotion as well as the forms of her faith into so great a company of untutored men.

By the end of the colonial period, the Church had grown too large, too unwieldy, too expensive. Churches, convents, and monasteries had multiplied beyond the need for them. As early as 1644 the *cabildo* of Mexico begged the king to put a stop to the founding of new convents and monasteries. There was vast inequality among the clergy. An archbishop might have a salary equivalent to $100,000 or more in modern terms, while many priests serving on the hard frontier were fortunate to get the equivalent of $75 or $100 per year.

By 1800 the Church was too rich for her own good, a fact which disturbed many devout Catholics, including the historian Lucas Alamán, who reported that: "The total property of the secular and regular clergy [of Mexico] . . . was not less than half of the total value of the real estate in the country." It was inevitable that the Church should amass wealth under a system in which generous tax exemptions made it easy to pyramid her holdings, and in which the faithful found satisfaction in giving or willing their property to the Church. The Church in Spanish America was simply doing what churches of all persuasions, colleges and universities, hospitals, and numerous other institutions do today—accumulating whatever endowments they can in order to further their several causes.

The Church remained largely Spanish to the end of the colonial period. In religious as in civil control, the kings theoretically limited appointments to those born in Spain; but there were exceptions. Some creoles

---

[5] In fact, the building of churches outran the need for them, and laid an onerous load upon Indians who were impressed for their construction. As early as 1556 Archbishop Montúfar of Mexico protested the excessive building, charging that battalions of 500 or 1,000 Indians were being used without wages, even without provision for their food and housing.

were named to bishoprics after the middle of the seventeenth century, but the most and the best appointments went to the Spanish-born. Slowly the priesthood was opened to the creole, and then to a few mestizos. Some Indian converts were given limited appointments as missionaries on the frontier. These exceptions were unimportant. The Church remained a thoroughly Spanish institution in days when the great majority of the people she served were thinking of themselves as Americans.

Chapter 9

MAN, HIS LAND, AND HIS
LABOR IN SPANISH AMERICA

We will now consider the men who made up the American empire of Spain, the classes to which they belonged, the parceling out of the land among them, the labor of one for another. Man, his land, and his labor are inextricably bound together.

The story of the creation of the Spanish American population has already been told. It is the story of the men who came to America, the Spaniards; of the people they found there, the Indians; of the men they brought in chains, the Negroes; and of the mixtures of blood among them. Thus was created in Spanish America a mixed people with Asiatic roots in its Indians, African roots in its Negroes, and European roots in its Spaniards.

Spanish America from the beginning developed a rigidly stratified class society, as inflexible as that of Spain itself but with new variations. The arrangement of the several classes became clear within a few years after the Conquest. At the top stood the Spaniards born in Spain, the *peninsulares,* or "men of the peninsula," derisively known in Mexico as the *gachupines,* "the men with the spurs," and in South America as *chapetones,* "tenderfeet." Throughout the colonial period the *peninsulares* maintained the top position in society, held the chief offices, and received the best salaries from state and Church.[1] The second class comprised the creoles, those of pure Spanish blood born in America. They were holders of less important offices, landholders, business and professional men, and artisans. The creoles, no matter how proud their lineage, were relegated to a social position far below that of the *peninsulares.* These two top classes, increasingly antagonistic, included the dominant and wealthy families of Spanish America.[2] It was in harmony with Spanish tradition (and European, as well) that a few thousand families should hold the chief

---

[1] Of a total of 170 viceroys between 1535 and 1813, only 4 were American-born; of 602 captains-general and presidents, 14; of the 706 bishops, 105—but their dioceses were usually the less important ones. B. W. Diffie: *Latin American Civilization* (Harrisburg, Pa.: Stackpole Sons; 1945), p. 488.

[2] Not all *peninsulares* and creoles were wealthy. Their ranks included numerous shiftless fellows who lived no better than many Indians. In 1574 there were some 160,000

positions, collect the major rewards, and dominate the social life. Protagonists for this ordering of society found justification in the teachings of thirteenth-century St. Thomas Aquinas and even in Aristotle. In 1544 the Dominicans avowed that "in a well-ordered Commonwealth, it is necessary that there be rich men who can resist the enemy in order that the poor of the earth may be able to live under their guardianship."

The third social class was that of the mestizo, issue of the mingling of Spaniard and Indian, heir of Castile and Andalusia, of Cuzco and Tenochtitlán. These were chiefly the progeny of unblessed unions, who bore the stigma of their illicit birth, were fully recognized by neither the Indian nor white worlds, and were torn between their rival loyalties. The mestizo was denied his birthright to ownership of land in either world, learned to fend for himself, and laid the foundation for a middle class of small traders, schemers, and promoters. Flanking the mestizo were the various mixtures of white and Negro, and Indian and Negro. The fourth class comprised the two groups of Indians, those tamed and nominally Christianized, living under the shadow of the white man's world, and the wild Indians of the frontier. At the bottom of the social scale came the Negro. It was an infinitely complex ethnic pattern, the principal groups already described splitting into numerous variations. But the very multiplicity and variety of social groups played into Spanish hands. The effectiveness of the policy of "divide and rule" has never been more successful.

This social organization was not altogether inflexible. There were many creole families who, because of honored ancestry or economic power, outranked most *peninsulares*. There were, in the course of time, families with marked admixture of Indian blood who, because of their accumulated wealth, achieved a place with honored creoles. Racial lines steadily yielded to economic realities, and society was willing tacitly to overlook Indian ancestry where a family had won distinction and wealth.

Of such varieties were the men of America. Each had his own idea of what he wanted out of this new world. The Spaniard came to gain fortune. "I came to get gold, not to till the soil like a peasant," said young Hernán Cortés when he first landed in Cuba, a remark often quoted but probably overworked, for the Spaniard came to win not only gold but also land, for land meant power, prestige, and a new home. The Indian, offered little choice, desired only to be permitted to enjoy the land which was his father's before him, to tend his cornfields, and to serve his ancient gods. The mestizo, his loyalties divided between the world of his Indian mother and that of his Spanish father, struggled for whatever advantage he could get from either, and often ended as an outcast from both of those worlds. The Negro—but few cared what the Negro wanted.

The Spaniard, dominant in the unequal partnership, finally got

---

Spaniards and creoles in Spanish America, and only about 4,000 of them held *encomiendas*. Throughout the colonial period the New World attracted thrifty, industrious peasants from Spain, and many of these bettered their lot, as peddlers and petty merchants. Some acquired substantial properties, married into good creole families, and helped to break down the class barriers transferred from the peninsula.

what he wanted. He wanted land, much land, as much as he could get. He wanted it for the crops it would yield and for the social distinction it conferred upon its holder. And closely allied to desire for land was demand for Indian labor to till it. The Spaniards were too few in number to plant and harvest the crops even had they wished to. But the will to labor was not in them, for the great majority of the migrating Spaniards regarded themselves as gentlemen (no matter how humble their rank may have been in Spain), and Spanish gentlemen did not dirty their hands. There were, of course, many in Spain who dug, sowed, fertilized, and harvested with their own hands, but the grandees of Spain saw to it that such hardy fellows stayed at home to look after their masters' fields. So it was inevitable that Spaniards transplanted to American soil demanded land *and* Indians. The one was useless without the other. The first conquerors expected both as their rightful due. Those who came later continued to clamor for the same generous treatment.

Thus debate was inevitable, always wordy and often bloody, between the partisans of two opposing views. On the one hand were the planters and mine operators, who swore that the land and the treasure which lay under it belonged to the Spaniards by right of conquest and that the Indians were bound to serve their conquerors. On the other hand were the enlightened friars, some civil authorities, and the kings, who argued that the landrights of the Indian should be respected and that the Indian himself deserved treatment as a man and could not be enslaved. Theologians enlivened the discussion by arguing whether the Indian was indeed a man, whether he had a soul. During the first decade after Columbus landed on Hispaniola there was no clear royal policy on these fine points. The first colonists reduced the Indians to slavery. Generous Queen Isabella, who accepted responsibility for the souls of her primitive subjects, sent Ovando as governor to Hispaniola in 1502, with strict orders against despoiling and enslaving the Indians. Ovando faithfully obeyed Isabella's instructions, whereupon the Indians fled to the mountains, dug no gold, cultivated no corn, did not answer when the church bells summoned them for religious instruction. Such idleness and disdain for the gospel provoked Isabella to action. In 1503 she ordered the introduction of the *encomienda* as the royal solution for regulating land and labor in America.

The *encomienda* (from *encomendar,* to entrust), a word for which there is no adequate English equivalent, was the legal device under which the Crown "entrusted" specified numbers of Indians to deserving Spaniards, the *encomenderos,* who thereby won definite rights over their Indians and incurred equally specific obligations to them. The *encomendero* was entitled to certain definite days of labor from his charges and was duty bound faithfully to serve their physical and spiritual wellbeing. The plan, based upon earlier Spanish experience with conquered Moslems, was devised to serve both practical and ideal ends. It rewarded devoted soldiers by assuring them of fruitful fields and productive mines. It also fulfilled the Crown's pledge to the pope, guaranteeing the conversion of the savages to the Christian faith and their protection against rapacious conquerors. It was specifically designed as a cure for the brutal *repartimiento* (from *repartir,* to divide up), by which the first settlers had seized Indians at random and put them to work in the mines or shipped them to distant points as slaves.

The royal intention in establishing the *encomienda* was merciful, and royal intentions continued to be good under the kings of the sixteenth century. Unfortunately for the Indians thus "entrusted," the *encomiendas* were managed not by kings but by planters and mine operators who thought much of the wheat, corn, gold, and silver the earth produced, little of the health and happiness of the Indians who garnered that wealth, and even less of the salvation of the hypothetical souls of their charges. It was therefore inevitable that the *encomienda,* despite its safeguards, brought seizure of Indian lands—theoretically not included by the *encomienda*—and the reduction of the Indians themselves to a state of slavery. The granting of *encomiendas,* begun in 1503, continued and spread from Mexico to Chile. Cortés was given some 100,000 Indians in a domain of about 25,000 square miles. Pizarro fared equally well. Lesser captains received princely allotments. Even foot soldiers and cavalrymen were remembered, each receiving Indians—and, in effect, the lands they occupied.

The abuses of the *encomienda,* glaring from its inception, aroused the stormy protest of many churchmen. The kings joined in the effort to save the Indian. In 1512 the Crown issued the Laws of Burgos, confirming the *encomienda* but laying down new ordinances for the protection of the Indian. In 1520 Charles I ordered an end to the *encomienda* but soon rescinded his action in the face of protests from overseas. In 1526 he issued new regulations designed to safeguard the Indians "from the rapacity and cruelty of the Spaniards." Pope Paul III ruled in 1537 that the Indians were "truly men," possessed of immortal souls, fit for conversion, and under no circumstances to be enslaved. The New Laws "for the governing of the Indies . . . and the protection of the Indians" were promulgated by Charles I in 1542. The Indians were declared free vassals of the Crown, never to be slaves. The *encomienda* was to be outlawed, no new *encomiendas* were to be granted, and those existing were to lapse upon the death of their holders. The New Laws incited revolts in Mexico and Peru, and within three years they were revoked. The life of the *encomienda,* chief instrument for holding the Indian in virtual slavery, was extended and inheritance was permitted from generation to generation; it was not finally outlawed until the last days of the eighteenth century. By that time most of the best land was concentrated in the hands of the great plantation owners (*hacendados*) and of the Church. And the Indians, save for those in more remote villages, were chiefly peons with scant rights as free men.

There were other devices for enslaving the Indian. The *repartimiento* (called the *mita* in Peru) was revived after 1550; Indians were seized and carried far afield for work on plantations, in mines, or in the building of churches and roads. This meant the dividing of families, interminable labor, cruel treatment, short rations, and bad housing. Fray Motolinía describes scenes around the mines of Mexico: "It was hardly possible to walk except over dead men or bones and so great were the numbers of the birds and the buzzards that came to eat the bodies of the dead that they cast a huge shadow over the sun." The inhumanity of this forced labor was aggravated by the use of Indian bosses (called *caciques* in Mexico, *curacas* in Peru) as foremen. These Indian bosses often treated their kinsmen with even greater cruelty than did the Spanish overseers. And in Peru (including present-day Bolivia) unbelievable cruelties attended the mining of silver and mercury. Equally barbarous was the lot of the textile workers. *Corregidores,* conniving with Indian bosses, sold Indians to conscienceless employers who treated them as virtual slaves. In relating these ugly events, we remind ourselves that the Spaniards held no monopoly on the exploitation of the defenseless. The Spaniard simply added his part to the cruelty of early industrial enterprise, amply shared by the English, the French, and the Germans. To Spain's credit there was protest from brave statesmen and churchmen, who never tired of demanding with Padre Montesinos: "Are these not men?"

The traffic in Negro slaves aroused only slight moral censure. The Spaniards with few exceptions regarded the Negro as a "natural slave," as a man of such "innate wickedness" that he should be grateful for being permitted to work for Christians. Although they left to others the gruesome task of seizing Negroes from their African homelands, the Spaniards had no scruples in buying and selling the slaves delivered to them. The institution of slavery was accepted as necessary and just. Las Casas himself, we have noted, urged the importation of Negro slaves as a measure of protection for the Indians, a counsel which he shortly repudiated in his *History of the Indies*: "It is as unjust to enslave Negroes as it is to enslave Indians, and for the same reasons." There were other protests from time to time. In 1560 Archbishop Montúfar of Mexico appealed to Philip II, arguing that the Africans "receive the Holy Gospel with good will and do not make war on the Christians." But the majority of churchmen kept silent. Even the Jesuits, so clear in their conscience on the score of Indian slavery, did not question the enslaving of Negroes; they owned Negroes in large numbers, perhaps as many as 1,200 in Chile alone.

We have dealt (in Chapter 4) with the abominations of the slave trade; of the seizure of victims in Africa, of their shipment and sale in the New World. But Spain's record of dealing with the Negro was more humane than that of England, Holland, and France. Under Spanish law the Negro could purchase his freedom or could seek out another owner when ill used. We may reasonably conclude that these generous promises were often, perhaps usually, unredeemed. However, the fact that Spain made the gesture stands to her credit. But in Spanish America, as in English America, slavery was brutal. It is eloquent that the royal edict of 1784, which prohibited the branding of Negro slaves, was reckoned a humane step.

Negro slavery failed to fulfill the promises made for it. It failed to relieve the pressure upon the Indians. It introduced an element of turbulence and revolt. Negro outbreaks were frequent throughout the colonial period, beginning in 1522 in Hispaniola, and in 1550 in Venezuela. Bands of Negroes frequently fled their masters and established independent communities in the backlands. Within the cities the Negroes proved quarrelsome, a constant tax on the discipline of the police. As early as the sixteenth century, Negroes in Mexico City became successful racketeers, collecting tribute from the whites and Indians. The Negro was striking back at the white man who had enslaved him.

Population figures for the colonial days are of doubtful validity but an estimate suggests that Spanish America in 1823—the year in which Spain finally lost her chief colonies—had about 17 million people, of whom about 44.5 per cent were Indian; 19.4 per cent, white; 31.5 per cent, of mixed bloods; and 4.6 per cent, Negro.[3]

3 B. W. Diffie, *op. cit.,* p. 458. His figures are based chiefly upon those of Humboldt.

Chapter 10

THE GETTING AND THE SPENDING:
THE ECONOMIC LIFE
OF SPANISH AMERICA

Colonial Spanish America was a business venture which paid dividends to the Crown, enriched the merchants of Seville and Cádiz, and furnished a livelihood to the Crown's American vassals. Profits came from gold and silver, the varied crops, the herds of cattle, the output of factories and mills, and the flow of trade. There are two ways of looking at this abundant economic activity: through the eyes of the king in Madrid, or through those of the colonists.

ROYAL CONTROL OF SPANISH
AMERICAN ECONOMY

The economic fortunes of Spanish America were controlled by the Crown. For the king, the American colonies constituted a glorified monopoly ordained to serve the congeries of kingdoms united under him. This theory of monopoly was simple: Spain would get the silver and gold of America and in return would sell the processed goods required by Peru, Mexico, and the other colonies. Spain would thereby pile up bullion wealth, recruit mightier armies, build larger vessels of war and peace, and increase the power and prosperity of Spain at home and abroad.

Sixteenth-century Spain, in common with all Europe, was enchanted with the economic theory of "mercantilism," which had triumphed over the anarchic feudalism of quarreling lords, each of whom pursued his own irresponsible course. The getting and the spending of the mercantilist was subordinated to the interests of the nation. The votaries of this new economic gospel devoutly believed that the prosperous nation sells more than it buys, always enjoys a comfortable balance of trade, and piles up gold and silver in national vaults. (Fort Knox's stored bullion is a modern fulfillment of the mercantilist's dream.) The mercantilists espoused free trade within national boundaries and tariffs against all foreigners. The Spaniard, a robust individualist, now found his unruly spirit bound by a regimented economy which made all producers and traders servants of the state. Not until the late eighteenth century would this exaggerated

[*190*]

"statism" be challenged by the doctrine of laissez faire—the impatient economic cry of "Don't bother me," with its protest against public meddling with private enterprise.

The mercantile theory did not work. It seemed simple enough that gold and silver—then sugar, hides, tobacco, cotton, and chocolate—should be shipped to Spain and that Spain should send back to the colonies silk gowns, woolen suits, and iron hoes. But the theory finally miscarried for a variety of reasons. The influx of precious metals provoked disastrous inflation in Spain. Prices doubled and redoubled, and the buying power of the treasure was reduced.[1] The flow of easy money discouraged prosaic enterprise at home. Spanish agriculture, never efficient, waned as the barren farms were increasingly neglected. Industry, already outstripped by that of England and the Low Countries, steadily deteriorated. And worse, the flow of American treasure emboldened the kings to fight new wars in the futile hope of maintaining and increasing Spain's hold in Europe; the wars consumed most of the gold and silver, and brought Spain into heavy debt to the bankers of Europe by the time of the death of Philip II in 1598. By 1700, Spain had lost her military and naval supremacy. She had fallen behind other nations in productive capacity, and her people were hungrier than ever. Furthermore, the monopoly theory ran afoul of the individualism of the Spaniard, who found it more profitable to bypass the strict codes of the monopoly. So mercantilism did not pay off. Spain got the gold and silver (what was not diverted to illegal channels) but could not produce the promised manufactured goods. By the early seventeenth century, industrialized northern Europe was furnishing five-sixths of the manufactured goods consumed in Spain and nine-tenths of the goods Spain shipped to America. American bullion was dissipated in paying for wars and for industrial goods to satisfy the colonies. By the early eighteenth century, perhaps nine-tenths of American gold and silver was quickly passing into the hands of foreign processors and traders.

Spain's chief reliance for enforcing her monopoly over American economy was the Casa de Contratación (the Board of Trade), founded in Seville in 1503. The Casa was the royal agency for fostering, encouraging, and protecting the flow of precious metals and other goods from America to Spain—and in reverse for overseeing the export of manufactured goods to the colonies. The Casa was tax collector, court of appeals, board of arbitration, and custodian of the royal interest. It controlled every detail and item of the trade and served as a sedulous watchdog upon the business of the New World. Closely associated with the Casa was the *Consulado* of Seville, a trade association of the merchants of the chief trading center.[2]

Spain reinforced her monopoly system by designating certain "mo-

---

[1] Earl J. Hamilton: *American Treasure and the Price Revolution in Spain, 1501–1650* (Cambridge, Mass.: Harvard University Press; 1934), pp. 189, 215, 271, 390–2. In New Castile (Madrid), the price of grains in 1650 was about thirteen times that of 1504, while wages had increased but five times. The over-all price of key commodities more than doubled in the first half of the sixteenth century, doubled again in the last half, and increased by 50 per cent in the first half of the seventeenth century.

[2] There is no exact English equivalent for *Consulado* in this usage. It was somewhat like a modern Chamber of Commerce, but with definite powers delegated by government.

nopoly ports." Seville was usually the port from which all ships had to sail, to which all ships had to return, and in whose customhouses all taxes had to be paid. Seville held this monopolistic position until 1717 when Cádiz, near the mouth of the Guadalquivir, took its place.[3] There were monopoly ports in America through which all ships were required to clear their cargoes: Cartagena, in what is now Colombia; Nombre de Dios, and later Portobello on the Isthmus of Panama, from which goods were carried across the isthmus on muleback and transshipped to Peru and Chile; and Veracruz, chief distributing feeder for all Mexico. These monopoly ports, both in Spain and in America, were devised to facilitate supervision and collection of taxes and to block illegal trade. Later, when pirates and privateers became active at sea and along the coast, the monopoly ports were a measure of security.

Spain early encountered competition. Neither France nor England nor Holland would concede that the pope's openhanded concession to Spain and Portugal could shut them off from so rich a prize. The seas were soon alive with pirates, buccaneers, freebooters, privateers, openly or secretly in the service of their respective sovereigns. This piracy was regarded as thoroughly honorable business. After all, it was war; Spain was conspiring against England; England, with inferior strength at the beginning, waged a naval guerrilla warfare which finally wore down Spanish resistance. The bold men who scuttled Spanish ships, murdered Spanish seamen, and ravaged Spanish ports were held in high regard by their kings. The French began by seizing some of Cortés's ships in 1523 and continued their profitable sorties throughout the sixteenth century. The English did much bloody plundering during Elizabeth's reign, and Sir Francis Drake and Sir John Hawkins were knighted for their prowess. In the seventeenth century, Sir Henry Morgan won fame and fortune. Their harrying and burning of Spanish settlements, their spirited fights at sea, served England and embarrassed Spain; they furnished exciting tales still read by small boys. Drake's winnings on one lucky raid amounted to several million dollars in gold and silver, plunder dutifully laid at the feet of the Virgin Queen. The Dutch and others also took a turn, but the English threat lasted longer and proved more costly than any other. Closely related to the work of the pirates and freebooters was the immense company of contraband traders who slipped in and out of Spanish ports selling their wares and taking on illicit cargo; their profitable enterprise continued throughout the colonial period.

Spain's answer to the pirates was the organization of the fleet system. By 1526 all ships were required to travel in groups. By the 1560's

---

The parent organization in Seville was copied in the creation of the *Consulado* of Mexico in 1592, and that of Lima in 1613. By the end of the eighteenth century, there were similar *Consulados* in Caracas, Guatemala, Buenos Aires, Havana, Cartagena, Santiago, Guadalajara, and Veracruz.

[3] There were various shifts in this arrangement, and Cádiz was from time to time a subsidiary port. There was also a brief period under Charles I in the early sixteenth century when ships were permitted to sail from northern ports but were required to return to Seville.

regular convoys had been arranged: there were usually two fleets each year, one bound for Veracruz, the other for Panama. The two fleets, after disposing of their wares and taking on fresh cargo, united at Havana and made their way home to Spain under the protection of warships. By 1700 there were sometimes ninety merchant ships in this impressive procession. The number thereafter decreased, partly because of larger ships and partly because of the inroads of smugglers. The protection given traders by these convoys was costly and was covered by taxes on exports and imports, sometimes as low as 6 per cent but at times as high as 30 per cent. The fleet system, maintained with diminishing effectiveness down to the close of the Hapsburg period in 1700, lapsed under the eighteenth-century Bourbons.

The introduction of the Bourbon dynasty in 1700 brought shifts in economic control. The chief means of imposing a state monopoly on American trade was the creation of monopoly companies modeled after the East India companies, among which the English company lasted longest and was most profitable. The Bourbons founded a number of such companies. The most important were the Honduras Company, founded in 1714; the Caracas Company, 1728; the Havana Company, 1740; the Santo Domingo Company, 1757. The Caracas Company, given great powers in Venezuela, was the only profitable venture of this series, and continued to the last years of the eighteenth century, paying generous dividends and laying the foundation for the prosperity of Venezuela; it delivered much chocolate, cotton, indigo, tobacco, and dyewoods at reduced prices to Spain, at the same time lowering the prices of necessities in Venezuela and greatly reducing contraband trade.[4]

The last and most intelligent chapter in Spain's control of American economy was written by Charles III (1759–88). The humanitarianism of the French Enlightenment had provoked a demand for more generous treatment of the colonies. A notable exponent of this attitude was the early eighteenth-century economist, José Campillo, a convinced mercantilist who viewed colonial wealth as the natural possession of Spain but who nevertheless denounced the failure to make the Indian a positive asset to the empire. He recommended that the Indian be given lands of his own and be guaranteed his rights as a man. He further urged freer trade within the empire, an end to the monopoly of Cádiz, the lifting of the prohibition against trade between the colonies, and reduction of taxes. Such a course,

---

4 See Roland D. Hussey: *The Caracas Company* (Cambridge, Mass.: Harvard University Press; 1934). While the Spanish monopoly companies were being planned, England launched the English South Sea Company in 1711, loaded upon it the entire national debt of some £10 million, and as an offset granted the company exclusive rights of trade with all Spanish territories from the Orinoco to Tierra del Fuego, and also with the Pacific coast of both North and South America. The Company gained a limited advantage from the Utrecht Treaty of 1712 under which Spain conceded to England a share in the trade with South America, especially in slaves. The Company's course was riotous: the price of a share of stock multiplied in value 14 times between 1711 and 1720. Spain, now under more able leadership, was able to check its activities. Profits were slight and fraud was common. The bubble burst in 1720. In 1716 the French organized the French Mississippi Company, but it met a similar fate.

he averred, would make trade more profitable and would reduce smuggling. It remained for Charles III and his astute ministers to put some of these revolutionary principles into practice. In 1765 the Caribbean islands were opened to almost unlimited trade with nine chief Spanish ports. The same concessions were extended to Louisiana in 1768, to Campeche and Yucatán in 1770, to the ports of New Granada (Colombia) in 1776–77, and in 1778 to all Spanish America with the exception of New Spain and Venezuela. Meanwhile, taxes were sharply reduced to a mere 6 per cent ad valorem duty. During this same period trade lines between the colonies were gradually opened, and by 1790 traders from any port in Spain could buy and sell anywhere in Spanish America. This liberalization of the Crown's policy brought swift increase of business. Prices of manufactured goods fell in the colonies, and those of raw materials were reduced in Spain; the activities of smugglers diminished; and prosperity was widely shared by colonists and the mother country. On the eve of the final break with Spain, Spanish America was enjoying the greatest prosperity it had ever known.

THE DEVELOPMENT OF SPANISH AMERICAN ECONOMY

The economic activities of the colonies were many and various: digging for gold and silver, planting and harvesting crops, breeding cattle and horses, building textile mills and other industries, and trading with Asia and Spain.

The migrants to Spanish America—we repeat—had a twofold ambition, to get gold and to win land. The desire for gold was obvious, but it is well to remember that Columbus, on his second journey, brought boatloads of colonists, seeds, plants, and domestic animals. The newcomers, weary of Spain's barren soil, were seeking new homes in the land of promise as surely as were the men of the *Mayflower* a century later. Nevertheless, gold was the magic word.

Spanish America was born of a gold rush, just as were, in later years, Australia, California, South Africa, and the Klondike. Men sold all they had, left their families, and journeyed to lands of treasure.

They got some gold, but finally much more silver. They little knew that this new-found fortune would beggar the conquering nation by breeding ruinous inflation, discouraging sound enterprise, and provoking costly wars. But while gold and silver proved a curse to Spain, which got most of it (and kept almost none of it), it proved a boon to America, which kept little. Hunger for precious metal was the propulsive force which cleared the way for the Spanish American empire. Had America offered no other lure than fruitful valleys, the few migrants would have gone no farther than the valley of Anáhuac and the green oases of the Pacific coast. But gold beckoned men across cruel deserts, through savage jungles, and over forbidding mountain passes. Gold led Coronado into New Mexico,

Texas, and Kansas; drove Orellana over the Andes into the Amazon jungles; led Belalcázar through Ecuador and Colombia; and summoned Valdivia into Chile. Gold built hundreds of cities and surrounded them with farms.

The gold rush began with plunder. Under the prick of Spanish swords, Moctezuma and Atahuallpa filled rooms with gold. These gleaming heaps did not assuage the appetite of the conquerors. Temples and old tombs were looted for further treasure. The plunderers gathered the treasure accumulated over many centuries. The untutored Indians, unversed in the virtues of gold reserves, valued the precious metals "only for their beauty and splendor for ornaments," as Garcilaso reports. The simple natives liked to admire and handle ornaments of gold, silver, and precious stones, and could not comprehend the white man who melted down their precious jewelry into solid bars to be locked in the strongboxes of kings. After plundering, came mining. We hazard the guess that Spaniards mined more precious metals during their first half century than had the Indians in 1,000 years. Mining began on the island of Hispaniola, where it continued with diminishing success until about 1515. Then Cuba and Puerto Rico enjoyed a brief gold boom. After 1531 Peru and Mexico yielded the chief profits, Peru leading for over 100 years and Mexico then becoming chief producer of minerals in the eighteenth century.

The pursuit of gold and silver was the driving force which lengthened and broadened the lines of empire. Wherever mines were dug, cities grew and prospered. Farms multiplied to supply food for miners. Textile mills and small industries sprang up. Trade increased. A middle class had its beginnings. In Mexico prospectors moved north and west; they opened the mines of Zacatecas in 1548, of Pachuca in 1552, and of Guanajuato in 1558, baring the veins which yielded rich profits throughout the colonial period. In the high Andes of Upper Peru (Bolivia) mining scouts discovered in 1545 the most fabulous pile of silver ever uncovered by man, a 2,000-foot hill of silver resting on the bleak and inhospitable plateau 13,000 feet above the sea. From that mountain of Potosí some 400 million pesos of silver were hacked out within fifty years after the first shaft was sunk. By the end of the colonial period, it had yielded over 60 million troy pounds of silver (worth about $900 million today). Beside the mountain of silver was built the city of Potosí, with a population of 160,000 by the middle of the seventeenth century—the largest city in all America, outstripping even the Mexican capital. It was a city of baroque churches, costly palaces, a fine theater, and gambling houses, and to it were drawn daring speculators, hardy frontiersmen, and glamorous courtesans, who vied with each other in amassing and wasting fortunes. Potosí's showy glory passed, and by 1800 it had shrunk to a village of only 8,000. It had served its turn, furnished much of the silver to finance Spain's wars, and fixed Spanish power upon the *altiplano*. Had it not been for the mountain of silver, the Spaniards might have clung to the gentle climate of the coastal oases and the lower valleys, and left the frozen, wind-swept highlands to the Aymarás and Quechuas.

It was logical and inevitable that the Spanish Crown should sedulously encourage mining, for in it were royal rewards. The Crown, owner of all mines, took its accustomed fifth of all precious metals.[5] Miners were under royal protection. Their tools, slaves, and supplies were exempt from legal attachment or foreclosure. They were accorded special leniency by courts and officers of law. Royal agents fostered improved processes of extraction and refining. The first process, that of simple smelting, was wasteful, utilizing only the richest ores. In 1556 the patio process was introduced at the Real del Monte mines of Pachuca in Mexico. This process, with mercury used as an amalgam, revolutionized the industry by making possible the use of low grade ores, and gave strategic importance to mercury, of which Spain possessed the chief world source in the mines of Almadén. In 1559 mercury was made a royal monopoly in order to conserve supplies and increase royal profit. In 1563 "a mountain of extremely hard rock soaked in mercury" was discovered at Huancavélica in Peru, and its mines were operated as a royal monopoly.

The fortunes of mining fluctuated. The boom days of Peru (including Bolivia) were over by 1650. In the eighteenth century, Mexico took the lead. In both areas, silver dominated. Colombia was the chief source of gold. Pedro de Heredia's expedition in 1533 yielded more gold than Pizarro and Cortés together had seized. By the close of the colonial period, Colombia had produced some 30 million fine troy ounces of gold—equivalent in 1967 values to more than $1 billion. Interest in other metals was slight throughout the colonial period although some copper was mined in Chile, Cuba, Hispaniola, and Venezuela.

Mining in Spanish America was a distinct success. By 1800, Spanish America and Portuguese Brazil were producing about 90 per cent of the world's supply of precious metals. The estimates of the total yield of American mines from Columbus's time to the nineteenth century are all conjectures. Official figures could not reckon the smuggled gold and silver. The early nineteenth-century figures of Baron von Humboldt are interesting, although hardly dependable. He estimated that Spanish and Portuguese America had yielded up to that time the following (in terms of pesos, probably worth more than 1967 dollars): Mexico, 2,028,000,000; Peru and Bolivia, 2,410,200,000; New Granada, 275,000,000; Chile, 138,000,-000; Brazil, 855,500,000; a total of 5,706,700,000 pesos. In any event, the mines paid.

The soil finally yielded more profit than all the mines—a lesson which the Spaniard might have learned from the Indian, had he asked for advice. On the score of fruitful fields and rich pasturelands, the Indian, willing or unwilling, was the white man's benefactor. The Indian furnished the land and the labor to work it. The Spaniard was also indebted to the Indian for unfamiliar crops and products which added to the joy of life in America and enriched the national larder of the homeland. These Indian gifts to the white man's dinner table included Indian corn (maize), numerous

---

[5] The fifth, the *quinto,* was the usual toll the Crown exacted from mining. In actual practice, the Crown's share was often larger.

varieties of potatoes and yams, tomatoes, manioc (which yields tapioca), new species of nuts and melons, vanilla, and cacao (chocolate). The Indian contributed useful fibers for the making of textiles. And he contributed medicinal plants: cinchona (quinine), coca (cocaine), ipecac, sarsaparilla, cascara, and a drug called tobacco which shortly made grateful slaves in all continents. Mexico contributed the maguey, a species of heavy spined agave (the century plant), described by the early historian Acosta as "the tree of marvels . . . it furnishes water, wine, oil, vinegar, honey, syrup, bread, needles, and a hundred other things." Mexico also gave the turkey, which flew wild in generous flocks.

The Spanish farmer found much to emulate in the agricultural practices of the Indian. The Incas had irrigation systems which made possible the use of terraces on steep mountain slopes. Fertilizers were generally used, notably by the Incas, who utilized human manure, fish, and guano, the bird droppings banked high on the coastal islands of Peru.[6] The Incas had developed skill in the storing of surplus grains and potatoes against periods of drought. Furthermore, it is probable that Indian farmers had, in the course of the centuries, learned about the breeding of plants, notably corn, and had by some rough methods of trial and error discovered means of selection, crossing, and hybridizing.

However, little of Indian America was developed for intensive agriculture. Fruitful lands were chiefly confined to the central plateau of Mexico, the highlands of Central America, the high valleys of the Andes, and a few oases on the Pacific coast. The more primitive peoples lived mainly from hunting and fishing, with fitful reliance on the potato and manioc.

The Spaniard gave to America all that he knew of farming. He brought new ideas on fertilizers and irrigation, on the choice of seeds and the improvement of stock, much of which he had learned from the Moslem. He brought knowledge of the handling of metals. He introduced the wheel, unknown to the Indians of America, and the wheel made possible the cart. He brought draft animals—the horse, the mule, oxen—to peoples who had long used the backs of men for the bearing of burdens and whose one draft animal was the llama of the Andes. The Spaniard brought animals for food—chickens, hogs, sheep, goats, and cattle. Stock raising spread rapidly to all parts of the growing empire.

The story of the horse in America is a dramatic saga. The horses of the conquerors, first regarded by the Indians as one creature with the rider, had struck almost as much terror among them as had the guns. The horse

6 An early seventeenth-century Spanish visitor to the coast of Peru reported on "a mine of wealth. . . . The fact is that . . . all the wheat and corn and other crops are guano'd, i.e., fertilized with guano, both before and after planting, in order to bear abundantly and profitably." They get this guano, he continued, from offshore islands; "it is yellowish white, smelling like shellfish, and not very heavy . . . all the farmers buy it for their crops and the Indians freight it on their llamas. In fact, they would rather go without eating than without buying their guano, for with its use, a fanega [1.6 bushels] of grain usually yields 300, 400, or 500 fanegas, but without it, yields no more than with us . . . some say that it is soil that God put there for that purpose, and others that it is the excrement of sea birds." Antonio Vázquez de Espinosa: *Compendium and Description of the West Indies,* translated by Charles Upson Clark (Washington, D.C.: Smithsonian Institution; 1942), p. 1418.

made it possible for man to move farther and faster, and speeded the extension of the Conquest. The horse finally became one of the most effective aids in conquering the frontier. Horses broke loose from their owners, disappeared into the wilderness, and bred and multiplied, producing great wild herds; the frontiersmen pushed farther afield to capture the horses and the lands over which they roamed.

The Spaniard brought new crops to America. The first and most revolutionary was sugar, perhaps introduced by Columbus in 1493. Sugar culture spread over the Caribbean, into Mexico and South America. It required the labor of many hands, speeded the destruction of Indians in the Caribbean region, and quickened the African slave trade. It was a chief export throughout the colonial period. Spain also introduced cereals, wheat, barley, rye, and oats. Silk culture was early introduced into Mexico—perhaps by Cortés himself—and Viceroy Mendoza took pride in promoting it. The Spaniard imported his familiar fruits: bananas, oranges, limes, peaches, apricots, apples, and pears. He introduced the grape, and the making of wine became profitable, especially in Peru. Coffee came late; it assumed importance in the eighteenth century, first in Haiti and then in all the Caribbean region, Brazil, and Peru.

The Spaniard fostered production and marketing of the indigenous crops of America. The European demand for chocolate grew, and the cultivation of cacao spread over Ecuador, Venezuela, and the Caribbean islands. The Spaniards early acquired a taste for corn, beans, potatoes, and other unfamiliar foods, which they transplanted to Spain. Tobacco was an instant success and was made a royal monopoly. Cotton production multiplied.

The areas of intensive development in farming, as in mining, were Mexico and Peru. However, in the less favored outposts of the colonial empire—that is, in the areas where gold and silver were not found—the farmer and the stock raiser became the trail blazers of Spanish civilization. In Chile, later found to be rich in minerals, agriculture dominated throughout the colonial period. There, despite a scanty Spanish population and serious shortage of labor, agriculture soon flourished in the fertile central valley. Valdivia introduced wheat, and the first flour was ground in 1553. Grapes were produced by 1555, olives by 1561.

The lands of the Río de la Plata, including present-day Argentina, Uruguay, and Paraguay, lacking in gold and silver, were chiefly developed by the stockmen. Cattle were introduced into Asunción, first Spanish stronghold, in 1555. When Juan de Garay sailed down the river from Asunción and founded Buenos Aires in 1580, he took with him about 500 cattle and 1,000 horses. The animals got out of hand; many wandered off onto the broad Pampa where they multiplied and ran wild in the lush grass. The roving cattle attracted new settlers, and thus the stock industry of Argentina, Uruguay, and Paraguay got its start. There was no market for meat in the early years; only the hides were taken, the carcasses left to the vultures. By the eighteenth century, the open pasturelands were the concern of the half-breed Gauchos who fought bloody battles for their rights over the roaming horses and cattle. The last colonial years brought fine profits. In 1778 Buenos Aires shipped 150,000 hides; in 1780, 800,000; and in 1783, 1,400,000. During the last days of the eighteenth century, the cattle farmers of Argentina and Uruguay began to preserve the meat in salting factories (*saladeros*) and to ship it to distant markets. Thus cattle raising became the foundation for the business enterprise of Argentina, Uruguay, and Paraguay.

In Venezuela and Colombia the hot, wet coastal plains produced cotton, tobacco, cacao, and tropical fruits. Some wheat was grown on the higher plateaus. A stock industry developed on the grassy plains (the *llanos*) of the Orinoco.

It was, then, chiefly the farmer and cattle raiser, rather than the miner, who developed the Spanish empire in America. However, the impressive success of agriculture was won in the face of grave handicaps. The first was the shortage of arable land. The land surface is so sliced and spotted by mountains, deserts, and jungles as to be largely useless. The only farming area comparable in utility to the Mississippi Valley is the broad expanse of plains in Argentina, Uruguay, and southern Brazil. A second handicap was the impossibility of marketing such perishable products as fruits and fresh meat. A third was the paucity of roads and the resulting high cost of transportation. A fourth was the perennial shortage of labor— there were never enough workers to meet the demand. The fifth handicap was the concentration of land in a few hands. The great plantations profited those who owned them but impeded the colonial economy. The plantation system kept the masses in varying degrees of serfdom, stifled inventiveness, retarded technical advance, and held back production. Sixth, slavery undermined vigorous enterprise, intensified the Spaniard's distaste for manual labor, and postponed the adoption of laborsaving devices. Nevertheless, the Spanish American farmer proved that the cornfield finally offers more security than the silver mine. By 1800, according to Humboldt, "The value of the gold and silver of the Mexican mines is less by almost a fourth than the value of the agricultural produce."

Manufacturing made surprising progress in the Spanish colonies, in the face of dogged opposition by the peninsular monopolists. Those shortsighted traders sought to force their overseas kinsmen to buy only wares bearing the stamp "Made in Spain," down to the last carpet tack, saucepan, and pocket handkerchief. It was a fatuous demand, calculated to make life in America intolerably expensive. Furthermore, Spanish factories, never efficient, steadily declined as American bullion created the illusion of prosperity. Spain's traders became mere middlemen, passing American raw materials on to factories in northern Europe, buying back the processed goods, and selling them to the colonists.

The economic formula of the monopolists is epitomized in the sad tale of a fine handkerchief. A Spanish broker bought a pinch of good cotton at the fair in Portobello; a Spanish ship carried it to Seville; a broker sold it to the agent of a mill in Flemish Ghent; after another ocean voyage the cotton was carded, the thread spun, the fabric woven, the handkerchief fashioned; the delicate confection journeyed again, first to Seville, then to Portobello, then overland to Panama, then by sea to Callao and Lima; in due course it was sold to a fine lady in the viceregal court of Peru, or even in Tucumán or far-away Buenos Aires. The pennyworth of cotton had become a two-dollar handkerchief, and the mercantilist's cycle had been completed. Such was the true tale of much Spanish American trade, but common sense steadily triumphed over theory and the colonists made their own handkerchiefs—and almost everything else they required. Only the few rich could buy goods from Europe. The common man used American shoes, glassware, iron shovels, and kitchen chairs. The opposition of the monopolists finally subsided, and by 1800 the colonies had a more extensive and effective industrial system than Spain itself. However, the factories and mills of the Spanish empire at home and overseas were insignificant compared with those of northern Europe and of the newly independent United States.

Colonial industry was built upon the craftmanship of the Indians, who wove cloth of cotton and wool, used durable and beautiful dyes, fashioned pottery, carved stone for temples and palaces, and shaped metals for beauty and utility. The expanding industry made use of all these skills. Textile making developed first and became the most widespread and successful of all industries. Woolen and cotton mills multiplied in Peru and Mexico. The silk industry got an early start in Mexico and flourished until 1580, when the competition of cheap Chinese silk caused its decline. Mexico and Peru—and to a lesser degree Chile—manufactured furniture, iron tools, shoes, harnesses and saddles, porcelain, and glass. Mexico made fine tile. Peru cast cannon and church bells. Ecuador made leather articles. Food processing was of major importance almost everywhere, with generous output of flour, butter, lard, and cheese. Almost all regions made soap and gunpowder. Tobacco was widely grown and processed. Shipbuilding early became an important industry, at first in Havana and Panama, then in Guayaquil, and toward the end of the colonial period in Buenos Aires.

The growth of factories and mills affected the social development of Spanish America. Craft guilds, fashioned after European models, enlisted industrial workers: their masters, journeymen, and apprentices constituted a sort of middle class which exercised some influence on commercial and political life.

By 1800 Spanish American industry was well established, third in importance in the colonial economy after agriculture and mining.[7]

Spanish American industry, while paying dividends to its promoters, further exploited the Indians. An eighteenth-century eyewitness account of the textile mills in Peru tells how Indians were delivered to the mill operators by faithless *corregidores*; how they were worked twelve to fourteen hours a day, miserably fed, housed in filth, flogged and sometimes

---

[7] Baron von Humboldt, reporting on Mexico in the first days of the nineteenth century, estimated agricultural production at about 30 million pesos, mineral output at about 25 million, and industrial output at between 7 million and 8 million.

tortured when they failed to perform the stints assigned them; and how they often died from exhaustion and disease in factories which were no better than prisons.[8] Baron von Humboldt visited the mills of Querétaro in Mexico in 1803 and found that conditions there were no better than in Peru.[9] Such barbarity was no monopoly of Spain. As late as the 1830's, the condition of textile workers in England was deplorable: "The hand loom weavers . . . still continue a very extensive class, and though they labor fourteen hours upward daily, earn only from five to seven or eight shillings per week . . . ill-fed—ill-clothed—half-sheltered and ignorant:— weaving in close, damp cellars, or crowded in ill-ventilated workshops, it only remains that they should become, as is too frequently the case, de-moralized and reckless, to render the portraiture of savage life."[1] Other abuses included fines (as much as a half week's wages) for trivial infractions of rules, compulsory purchase at company stores, and extensive child labor —with most of the children starting work between the ages of six and eight, some as early as five. Inhuman as were conditions in mills and factories, those in the mines were even worse. Against such abuses Sir Robert Peel and many another raised their voices in the 1830's, but decades passed before substantial reforms were enforced. England, one concludes, was in no position to criticize Spain on this score.

Trading was a major concern for three centuries. Merchants in Mexico, Lima, and other cities made their annual trips to the great fairs, either in Portobello on the Isthmus, or in Jalapa, inland from Veracruz. These fairs were the distributing centers for wares brought by the fleets from Spain.[2] Small merchants came to buy from the greater ones, and

[8] This was the description of the mills (*obrajes*) of Peru by Jorge Juan and Antonio de Ulloa, who were sent by Philip V of Spain in the 1740's. Their report, *Noticias secretas de América,* was not made public until 1826. Quoted by Bernard Moses: *South America on the Eve of Emancipation* (New York and London: G. P. Putnam's Sons; 1908), pp. 178–80.

[9] "On visiting these workshops," Humboldt wrote, "a traveler is disagreeably struck not only with the great imperfection of the technical process in the preparation for dyeing but . . . also with the unhealthiness of the situation, and the bad treatment to which the workmen are exposed. . . . All appear half naked, covered with rags, meager and deformed. Every workshop resembles a dark prison. The doors which are double remain constantly shut, and the workmen are not permitted to quit the house. Those who are married are only allowed to see their families on Sundays. All are unmercifully flogged if they commit the smallest trespass." Alexander von Humboldt: *Political Essay on the Kingdom of New Spain,* translated by John Black (4 vols.; London: Longman, Hurst, Rees, Orme, and Brown; 1811), Vol. III, pp. 463–4.

[1] James Phillips Kay: *The Moral and Physical Condition of the Working Classes Employed in the Cotton Manufacture in Manchester* (London, 1832), p. 27; quoted by Jürgen Kuczynski: *A Short History of Labour Conditions Under Industrial Capitalism* (London: F. Muller; 1942), Vol. I, p. 19.

[2] "The exchange took place at Portobello during a forty-day fair on which occasion this otherwise quite desolate and unhealthy place was for a time enlivened. . . . Small booths were rented for 1,000 pesos or more and single houses for 4,000 to 6,000 pesos. The remaining larger portion of the year was characteristically enough called the dead time of the year." Wilhelm Roscher: *The Spanish Colonial System,* translated by E. G. Bourne (New York: Henry Holt & Co.; 1904), pp. 33–4; quoted by C. E. Chapman: *Colonial Hispanic America* (New York: The Macmillan Co.; 1933), p. 163.

humble peddlers, to fill their mule packs for their journeys from village to village. There were commission men dealing in large or small amounts of sugar, cotton, wool, cereals, hides, and cacao. The lowliest traders were the Indians, who sold their produce in the public markets, which were, and still are, the business centers of Indian America. Out of this varied trading emerged a quasi middle class—creole and mestizo.

The trading of Spanish America owed almost nothing to Indian practice. There had been little exchange of goods even between close neighbors in Indian America and virtually none between widely separated communities. For example, in Aztec days there had been little intercourse except for war between Tenochtitlán (Mexico City) and Tlaxcala, fifty miles apart. Spain's rule extended the range of trading by leveling ancient political barriers which had blocked passage of goods between neighboring political rivals. Money now took the place of barter. Communications were improved. Rough trails were opened, over which mules and sweating human carriers bore their loads. Such a trail led from Buenos Aires, through northern Argentina, over the *altiplano* to Lima, almost 3,000 miles away. Rough carts drawn by oxen served some of the shorter trade routes. Coastal shipping carried many goods between the colonies, linking Acapulco, Panama City, Callao, and Valparaíso. Small ships plied along the Mexican coast of the Caribbean and served the islands and the coast of the Spanish Main. Rafts and small craft carried produce from Asunción to Buenos Aires.

There was, then, much legitimate business—conducted under the rules of the Crown, with proper licenses, inspections, and taxes. In addition a large but untabulated clandestine trade, carried on by English, French, Dutch, and Portuguese—and plenty of enterprising Spaniards as well—furnished abundant and often cheaper goods to the colonists, graft to greedy officials, and profits to the nimble operators. No one knows how much business was done in this colonial "black market," how much silver and gold slipped through without registration and payment of taxes to the Crown. At various times in the colonial era it may have equaled or even exceeded legal trade. The slave trade was a juicy plum for enterprising traders, whose operations were sometimes legal, often contraband. The Negro was a prime article of commerce, which fetched high prices. Many of the first families of Cartagena, Havana, and Lima (as of Savannah and Boston) owed their excellent social and economic position to profits from the slave trade.

Trade with the Orient was important in colonial economy after 1550. The Spanish Crown early sought to establish control of the Pacific and to furnish outposts against the Portuguese by encouraging Cortés in his first ill-fated attempts to establish trade lines with the Philippines and China. In 1565 the first of the Manila galleons made the crossing from Acapulco in Mexico to the Philippines. For two and a half centuries, until the final trip in 1815, the galleons made their annual crossings, carrying the silver pesos of America (until recent days the "Mexican dollar" was a popular monetary standard in China), together with iron articles, cochineal, cacao, wine, and wool. They returned from Manila with cargoes of silk, precious stones, and spices for the rich colonists of Mexico and Peru, as well as for Spain. This trade provoked an auxiliary exchange between Acapulco and Callao in Peru, sometimes legalized but always flourishing. This China trade (most of the goods collected in Manila came from China) brought profits to colonial and peninsular merchants: it fixed Spanish political control on the Philippines and extended it over California, where exploration was incidental to these journeyings. It also aroused the jealousy of the Mexican silk producers, whose promising enterprise was wrecked, by the end of the sixteenth century, by the competition of cheap Chinese silk.

Chapter 11

THE FORMATION OF
SPANISH AMERICAN CULTURE

The cultural birthright of the colonies was Spanish, its forms and spirit modified in the fresh air of America, enriched by the Indian and the Negro. Spain gave all she had to the colonies: as a mother transmits life, Spain passsed on governmental patterns, social and economic fashions —and cultural gifts as well. Spanish America was favored by being born in the golden days of her mother country's greatness, when Spain was alive with religious fervor and the flowering genius of painters, writers, sculptors, and architects.

The transfer of genius from parent to child is never automatic. Spanish America could not be expected to inherit all Spain's creative talent. Spain did not send America the thinkers Luis Vives and Luis de León, nor the painters Zurbarán and Ribera, nor the writers Cervantes[1] and Lope de Vega. Spain indeed sent men of epic stature—brave soldiers, noble churchmen, a few able statesmen—but chief credit for carrying the love of letters, learning, and beauty to the New World must be given the churchmen.

The cultural achievements of the colonial years are impressive. In perspective, the wonder grows that with all the handicaps of the rough frontier, Spain succeeded so admirably in passing on her spiritual and cultural gifts. The appraisal of her success must take account of Spanish America's schools and universities, men of learning and letters, creators in the fine arts, and the circulation of her books.

SCHOOLING IN SPANISH AMERICA

The provision for educating the people was meager and haphazard. Learning was chiefly a privilege accorded the sons of the more prosperous Spaniards, creoles, and mestizos (daughters, of course, were not generally regarded as educable). This restriction of privilege reflected Spain's practice at home, where illiteracy was general, and differed only in degree from seventeenth-century England, where probably not more than a third of the

---

[1] It is recalled that Cervantes applied for a post in America, but was refused.

people could read and write. While the Spaniards denied universal education to those of white parentage, they also found solid reasons for withholding it from the Indian and Negro; substantial citizens believed that schooling of subject peoples produced subversive thoughts, unbelief in religion, and social commotion. As a result, Spanish America was largely illiterate at the end of the colonial period. José Ingenieros, the Argentine social historian, puts the figure for illiteracy in the area of La Plata at 99 per cent. The situation was better in Mexico.

An important factor in the popular schooling of Spanish Americans was the generous importation of books from the mother country. Fiction and nonfiction, some of it trash and some of it of serious worth, found eager readers in the overseas kingdoms. These books in Castilian fixed that tongue upon all of Spanish America. Although Basques, Catalans, and Galicians were numerous, they were forced to read Castilian, which became the universal language of Spanish America to a much greater degree than it was in Spain.

An early effort to broaden the base of education was made by the Franciscans in Mexico with the support of Viceroy Mendoza. They believed that sound schooling would lift the Indians to an appreciation of Spanish culture. The first school for Indians was established at Texcoco in 1523 by Pedro de Gante, a Flemish Franciscan. He directed the school for more than forty years, enrolling every year from 500 to 1,000 Indian boys; he taught them Spanish and manual arts, and trained them as artists and artisans for the decoration of the churches. Other schools were organized for sons of Indian chieftains, still others for Indian girls in preparation for motherhood. In 1547 Viceroy Mendoza founded the school of San Juan de Letrán, where unclaimed mestizo children were entrusted to the Franciscans. This school, early supported by the sale of wild cattle, had an unbroken history of more than three centuries. Similar schools, although less successful, were organized in Lima. Such ventures provoked the fears of landholders and some churchmen (especially the Dominicans), who opposed them as corrupters of the Indian. These experiments in popular education were generally abandoned by the end of the sixteenth century, and schooling was limited chiefly to the sons of privileged families.

Spain's most distinguished contribution to education in the colonies was the university: she founded ten major and fifteen minor institutions of higher learning during the colonial period. They were chiefly modeled after the venerable University of Salamanca. In the thirteenth century Salamanca had ranked—with Paris, Bologna, and Oxford—as one of the four chief centers of learning in medieval Europe. By the mid-sixteenth century, Salamanca had reached its greatest glory, with some 7,000 students enrolled from all Europe. Its charter and numerous immunities made it all but independent of kings. It had an almost international character and brought Spain enviable prestige throughout the world. Second only to Salamanca in influence upon American educational life was the University of Alcalá de Henares, founded in 1498 by Cardinal Jiménez de Cisneros.

The founding of Spanish American universities began in 1551 when Charles I authorized the creation of "royal and pontifical" universities in Mexico and Lima and granted them charters patterned after that of Salamanca. The University of Mexico opened its doors in 1553, that of Lima in 1572.[2] These two institutions were the chief inspiration to the other universities which sprang up over Spanish America. Of the twenty-five greater or lesser institutions organized by the end of the eighteenth century, those designated "royal and pontifical" were creations of the Crown and the others were founded by the Church. All were dominated by the clergy and were, at least until the eighteenth century, little more than training schools for priests—just as Harvard and Yale were devoting themselves to the training of Protestant clergy.

Each university was controlled, as in Spain, by a faculty made up of professors and resident scholars. The rector, or president, held a position of much honor but received no salary; he was usually elected annually and rarely served for more than two years. The university community often lived under its own laws and administered justice to its members. At times some universities dropped racial and class bars and admitted a few Indians and an occasional mulatto. Under the eighteenth-century Bourbons, lines were tightened and enrollment was limited to those who could prove "purity of blood." The routine costs of instruction were low, but the fees and incidental expenses of acquiring degrees were enormous, sometimes aggregating several thousand dollars.

The highest distinction in university education was reached by the University of Mexico in the seventeeth century. At that time it boasted twenty-three chairs (*cátedras,* platforms), the majority in theology and canon law, and others in medicine, surgery, anatomy, astrology, rhetoric, and the Aztec and Otomí languages. During the last quarter of the seventeenth century, the university was graced by the chief intellectual of the Spanish colonial period, Carlos de Sigüenza y Góngora, for twenty years its professor of mathematics. Sigüenza was mathematician, critic and poet, astronomer and historian, archaeologist and philosopher. A modern Spanish scholar writes of him: "The appearance of such a man in the days of Charles II is enough to exalt a university and a country, and is proof that the shadows of ignorance in which we had enveloped our colonies were not so thick nor was the predominance of theology in the schools which we founded there so despotic."[3] Sigüenza's restless search for truth, his empirical method, his ranging versatility, all set their stamp upon the university and won it recognition in Europe as well as in America.

[2] Claims to being the first university in America are hotly debated. Lima argues that the royal decree establishing her University of San Marcos was the first to be signed. However, the University of Mexico was the first to offer courses. Santo Domingo claims priority by citing the papal bull of 1538 which accorded university rank to the Dominican school in that city. John Tate Lanning: *Academic Culture in the Spanish Colonies* (New York: Oxford University Press; 1940), pp. 12–14.

[3] Marcelino Menéndez y Pelayo: *Historia de la poesía hispano-americana* (2 vols.; Madrid: V. Suárez; 1911–13), Vol. I, pp. 70–1; quoted by Irving A. Leonard: *Don Carlos de Sigüenza y Góngora* (Berkeley, Calif.: University of California Press; 1929), p. 1.

The effectiveness of the Spanish American universities was uneven: some had periods of distinction; others were never more than mediocre training schools for priests; still others were little more than secondary schools. Despite their generous charters, they were all at various times subject to the interference of royal officials. The University of San Marcos in Lima, earlier a center of vigorous intellectual life, by the middle of the eighteenth century had become—according to one Peruvian historian—"an institution for purely literary exhibitions without serious study in any departments." They all shared one common weakness: faculties were recruited chiefly from among members of the religious orders, the professors devoting only a few hours each week to their students and receiving trifling fees. In naming instructors and in ordering the curriculums, there were intermittent disputes between the rival religious orders and, in the eighteenth century, between ecclesiastical and secular factions. Faculties were under constant pressure not only from civil authorities, but from successful men of business; time and again they found it expedient to grant degrees to unworthy men.[4]

There was a quickening of university life by the close of the colonial period. Ecclesiastical control was yielding to secular. Scientists were speaking their minds with unaccustomed freedom. Exponents of new philosophical trends, influenced by the French Enlightenment, were making themselves felt. Mexico now definitely led the intellectual life of the colonies. Mexico's School of Medicine was founded in 1768. Her Botanical Gardens for scientific study of plants and flowers were laid out in 1788. The Mexican School of Mines was organized in 1791.

THE MAKERS OF BOOKS

The Spanish colonial period produced writers, numerous and varied. The first books dealing with America were the chronicles and histories written by early explorers and churchmen, which reflected the mood of exhilaration of the period. They were chiefly factual reports of events and impressions, and, although seldom of literary distinction, were marked by rough vigor and penetration. They include Columbus's reports to his sovereigns, the Italian Peter Martyr's assembling of early reports, and the letters of Cortés to Charles I. In 1552–53 there appeared López de Gómara's *History of the Indies and the Conquest of Mexico,* a sober recital of events, although criticized for its adulation of Cortés. López de Gómara was answered by Bernal Díaz del Castillo, one-time soldier under Cortés, then living in retirement in Guatemala, in his naïve and spirited *True History*

4 In perspective, it is wise to remember that higher education in the United States was not brilliantly successful in the late eighteenth century. Francisco de Miranda, precursor of Spanish American independence, visited Harvard in the 1780's, found few books, and wrote that "the natural history room hardly deserves the name . . . it seems to me that this establishment is better calculated to turn out clerics than skillful and educated citizens . . . there is no single chair of living languages." He visited Yale, and noted that "the book collection is unimportant."

of the Conquest of New Spain (published fifty years after his death) in which he sought to capture deserved credit for the common soldier. His book, despite its rude syntax and verbosity, remains the chief literary and most readable account of the conquest of Mexico.

The first critical historian was Gonzalo Fernández de Oviedo (1478–1557), whose extended journeyings in America yielded his *General and Natural History of the Indies,* published in 1535. Bartolomé de las Casas, more crusader than historian, wrote his ponderous and unreliable *History of the Indies,* published in 1575–79. More impartial was Cieza de León, whose *Chronicle of Peru,* published in 1553, contributes much to our knowledge of the Inca Empire. Chief in literary distinction as well as in content was the *Royal Commentaries of the Incas,* published in 1609, the work of Garcilaso de la Vega, called "the Inca," the most distinguished mestizo of the sixteenth century. Garcilaso was born in Peru in 1539, son of a Spanish soldier and an Indian mother who was a granddaughter of one of the last of the Inca rulers. After a boyhood spent in Peru, at twenty Garcilaso went to Spain and spent fifty years on his writing. In Garcilaso we have the first opportunity to fathom the soul of the mestizo and to understand the clash within him between the two worlds which gave him life. His writing, the first distinguished work of an American-born man of letters, reveals him on the defensive against both races whose blood he shared. He strikes at his father's world by painting an idealized picture of the Inca Empire of his mother. Then he seems to turn against his mother's heritage in praise of the Spain of his father. Although Garcilaso's account of Inca history is not regarded highly by modern anthropologists and archaeologists, he still holds a firm place as an interpreter of the mestizo. His *La Florida,* describing the conquest of that region, is readable and exciting.

We are indebted to numerous other chroniclers and historians. The Jesuit José de Acosta published his *Natural and Moral History of the Indies* in 1590, the source of much of our knowledge of the social and economic patterns of Mexico and Peru. The Franciscan Bernardino Sahagún wrote his *General History of the Events of New Spain* in the middle of the sixteenth century (though it was not published until 1829); he gave minute details of the daily life, and religious customs and beliefs of the Aztecs. Another Franciscan, Bishop Diego de Landa, wrote on Yucatán, adding greatly to our knowledge of the later Maya. One of the most illuminating reports, recently uncovered in Rome and published in 1942, is the *Compendium and Description of the West Indies,* the work of the Carmelite missionary, Antonio Vázquez de Espinosa, who came to America about 1600, spent some twenty years in Mexico and Peru, and wrote detailed notes on the crops, weather, customs, abuses of Spanish rule, church organization, wages, and countless other aspects of life in early colonial times.

In the early seventeenth century, a few substantial histories were written. Notable among these were Jerónimo Becker's *Histories of New Granada and Venezuela;* Bernabé Cobo's *History of the New World* (not published until the late nineteenth century), throwing much light on the Inca past of Peru; Juan de Torquemada's *Indian Monarchy,* dealing with pre-Conquest Mexico; and Alonso de Ovalle's *History of Chile*. The most comprehensive historical work of this period was Antonio Herrera's *General History of the Deeds of the Spaniards in the Isles and Tierra Firme of the Ocean Sea*.

Little history was written after 1650. The glamour of exotic Indian lands had dimmed. Interest revived in the eighteenth century, whetted by the reports of scientific explorers, the most notable of whom was Antonio de Ulloa, commissioned by the king to report on Peru and Ecuador in the 1730's. Ulloa, collaborating with Jorge Juan, delivered scathing indictments of the abuses of colonial rulers and the savage treatment of Indians in field and factory, and helped to provoke the belated reforms of Charles III.

A chief contribution of the friars was their indomitable activity in reducing the Indian languages to written form. Their zeal, always scholarly, was chiefly inspired by a desire to pass on the blessings of religion and Spanish civilization to their Indian charges. By 1800, no less than ten languages of Mexico, and four or five languages of South America, had been mastered. The Jesuits and other missionaries preached to the Indians in their own ancient tongues, a feat which won respect and affection.

Poetry, a hardy perennial wherever Spanish is spoken, was produced in abundance. There was continuous enthusiasm for celebrating the valiant records of history in epic poems. A notable exception to the general tediousness of such poems was *La Araucana* by Alonso de Ercilla y Zúñiga, a Spanish soldier who came to Chile after Valdivia's conquest, and whose verse celebrated the bravery of the Araucanians—and thereby helped lay the foundation for the idea of "the noble savage." Few of the poets are remembered. Most of them were under the spell of the curious baroque style called *gongorismo* after the Spaniard Luis de Góngora (1561–1627). His artificial, exaggerated, obscure, and precious style had many imitators, whose output is described by a competent critic: "Pompous, affected, and heavily freighted with classical and mythological allusions, strained conceits, and a distorted syntax, the metrical productions of this era are, in general, difficult to decipher as to their meaning if, indeed, they possessed any."[5] Welcome relief from such bombast came from writers of satirical verse—notably Juan del Valle Caviedes of seventeenth-century Lima, whose earthiness and salty good sense delighted those surfeited by *gongorismo*.

A brilliant exception among the followers of Góngora in Mexico was the greatest poet of the colonial years, Sor Juana Inés de la Cruz. Born in 1651, she read Latin when she was five; and at fifteen she was a girl of radiant beauty and such rare intelligence as to confound the scholars. Denied admission to the University, which barred women, even when she offered to don men's clothes, she found her chief satisfaction in books. At sixteen she quit the world and became a nun—an unhappy love affair is the conventional explanation—and there continued her reading, her music, and her scientific observations. She wrote some plays and many poems. Her profound interest in mathematics was the basis of friendship with her great contemporary, Sigüenza. Her imagination was restless, her power of ob-

[5] Irving A. Leonard, *op. cit.,* p. 20.

servation untiring. So far as we know, she wrote nothing on science, but she was continuously pondering physical forces, from the spinning of a top to the mixture of ingredients in the kitchen. She wrote: "If Aristotle had known how to cook, he would have written even more than he did," an observation recalling the homely wisdom of St. Theresa of Ávila. Her appearance in that arid period of poetry "partakes of the supernatural and miraculous," writes a modern Spanish critic. Sigüenza wrote of her: "There is no pen that can rise to the eminence which hers o'ertops." Much of her poetry shows the influence of *gongorismo,* but she broke from its fetters, wrote sensitively, and, unlike most of her contemporaries, used words to express ideas rather than conceal them. Her poems of love are described by Menéndez y Pelayo as the "gentlest and the most delicate that have come from the pen of a woman." But her versatility rested uneasily with her somber ecclesiastical superiors, and she was finally ordered to put away her books and to devote herself to religion. She sold her substantial library of several hundred volumes, an extraordinary collection for the seventeenth century, gave the proceeds to charity, and devoted herself to good works; she died in 1695, at the age of forty-four.

DRAMA, MUSIC, AND THE FINE ARTS

Drama flourished throughout the colonial period, reflecting the popularity in Spain of Lope de Vega, Tirso de Molina, and Calderón de la Barca. The chief cities had theaters in which the luxury of trappings and wealth of offerings mirrored the varying fortunes of their mines. Potosí at the peak of its wealth had a theater which vied with the most pretentious in Spain. The viceroys of Mexico and Lima installed private theaters in their palaces. The plays of the Spanish masters were staged, as were many others written in America, most of which are long since forgotten.

The most popular early dramas were religious allegories, thoroughly Spanish in tradition and designed to convey the truth of the gospel to unlettered Indians. Their pageantry and color were effective in conveying the lessons of creation and salvation, as well as the record of Spain's greatness. Indian pageantry was amalgamated with the Spanish to produce a hybrid folk drama in which Indian dances and music were overlaid with Christian and Spanish legend. To this day, a traveler in Mexico may see Indian festivals in which the ancient conflict between Christians and Moors is reenacted, with much heroic posturing, crackling of fireworks, and the final destruction of the hated Moors. If the traveler asks an Indian the identity of the Moors whom he belabors so assiduously, he receives no clear answer.

Spanish America produced dramatists, but few were more than pallid imitators of the Spanish immortals. Sixteenth-century Mexico boasted González de Eslava (1534–1601), whose allegorical comedies were so simple, direct, and well contrived as to give the Mexican stage brief distinction. González is remembered for his imagined insults to a pompous viceroy who promptly ordered his arrest. Spanish America's sole dramatist to win international acclaim was Juan Ruiz de Alarcón (1580–1639), who left Mexico at twenty, studied at Salamanca, returned briefly to his native land, and spent the bulk of his life in Spain. Alarcón, a creole hunchback tortured by the jeerings of the *peninsulares,* wrote sensitively and brilliantly, and his twenty-three plays gave him a firm place among Spanish men of letters in *el siglo de oro.*

Meager in quantity and quality as was Spanish colonial literature, it was superior in both respects to that of the English and French colonists in the New World.

Spanish America made but slight contribution in music. The music of Castile and Andalusia was introduced to America, there to be modified by the rhythms of Indian and Negro, yielding a large volume of popular songs. The plaintive songs that came from these mingled sources were sung by the common people to the accompaniment of the Spanish guitar or the African marimba. Meanwhile, well-born and proper daughters of the wealthy *peninsulares* and creoles picked out traditional melodies on the harp or clavichord. The chief cities boasted orchestras. The churches continued the Spanish tradition of sacred music.

The architects, painters, and sculptors of Spanish America had a superb heritage from the Spaniards who, for more than 500 years, had been building some of the most splendid churches in Christendom; carving wood and stone figures for their façades, choirs, and altars; and painting glowing canvases to add a final touch of glory. The soldiers, civil rulers, traders, and farmers who settled America brought memories of the cathedrals of Seville, León, Toledo, and Ávila; of the delicate grace of the Giralda and the Alhambra; of the sculptured power of the Pórtico de Gloria at Santiago de Compostela; of the tombs and altars of Valladolid, Saragossa, and Salamanca; and of the paintings of El Greco, Zurbarán, Ribera, and Velásquez. This was the heritage of even the humble builders of America.

The colonists brought a love of beauty with them, and throughout the colonial period they sought to emulate the Spanish tradition. They, too, would have churches enriched by noble sculptures and paintings. However, the sculptors and painters of Spanish America were imitators, seldom creators. There is beautiful carving of stone and wood in the choir stalls, finials, pediments, reredos, corbels, and cornices of churches in Puebla, Morelia, Guatemala Antigua, Lima, Quito, Sucre, and Arequipa; but their grace is generally a borrowed grace. Over altars and in sacristies are smoky paintings of saints, virgins, angels, cardinals, and bishops. Many of these canvases were brought from Spain, and an obliging sacristan is always ready to tell the visitor that this is an authentic Murillo, that a Titian, the other a Zurbarán. Some are genuine, but many are poor imitations. The borrowings continued as American painters made pale copies of the masters or, painting on their own account, followed the styles of Ribera and Murillo. There were a few painters of considerable technical skill, among them the Mexicans Juan Herrera, José María Ibarra, and Miguel

Cabrera, and the Ecuadorian Miguel de Santiago. Artists never lacked support. Schools of fine arts were established toward the end of the colonial period. Mexico's Academy of Fine Arts, organized in the late eighteenth century when Goya was renewing the prestige of Spanish painting, was well housed, amply financed—in fact, it had everything except artists.

In architecture, Spanish America made best use of its cultural heritage. The wealth of mine and field and the labor of docile Indians were early dedicated to the rearing of palaces and religious edifices. Some few fine examples of secular buildings have survived, but Spanish America is spotted from end to end with cathedrals, churches, and monasteries of such symmetry and power as to attest the fervor and artistry of their creators. They are, however, unevenly distributed. Such regions as Chile and La Plata, yielding neither gold nor silver and producing only prosaic grain and cattle, built only modest temples. Peru, Ecuador, and Mexico boasted the finest and most richly ornamented churches and cathedrals, but with Mexico far in the lead.

The architecture of the thousands of churches and monasteries built in the colonial years faithfully recapitulates the development of architecture in Spain. Moslem motifs appear almost everywhere—in geometric caprices of decoration and, above all, in the thousands of varicolored tiled domes of Mexico. Eleventh-century Italian influence is clear in the constantly recurring sculptured and rounded arches of the Romanesque. Thirteenth-century French Gothic is widely represented; the more than 400 fortress-churches and monasteries built by the Franciscans, Augustinians, and Dominicans in Mexico are usually Gothic in feeling, although with frequent addition of Romanesque arches, Moslem designs in decoration, and plateresque details. Sixteenth-century Italian Renaissance appears in the jewel-like plateresque; the cathedral of Morelia in Mexico, perhaps the loveliest church in America, is a splendid example; the façade of the convent of Acolman is another instance. Philip II's late sixteenth-century retreat to classicism, represented in Spain by the gloomy Escorial, had its influence upon the cathedrals of Mexico City, Puebla, and Lima. Seventeenth-century Italian baroque (sometimes described as the child of Michelangelo's exuberance), which was elaborated in Spain and exaggerated by the Salamanca architect Churriguera, dominated American builders during the late seventeenth and eighteenth centuries, yielding big and little churches adorned with tumbling angels, riotous fruits, and tossing flowers on their pediments and façades; Taxco, Tepozotlán, and Ocotlán are a few of the many instances in Mexico; the churches of the Jesuits and the Franciscans in Quito are among the finest in South America. The late eighteenth century brought a brief burst of creative imagination in architecture, chiefly in Mexico; there Francisco Eduardo Tresguerras built the lovely Carmelite church in Celaya, and Manuel Tolsa elaborated the exterior of the cathedral in Mexico City.

Chapter 12

THE PORTUGUESE EMPIRE
IN BRAZIL

Portugal also had a stake in the new world of America—a stake recognized in the bulls of Pope Alexander VI, confirmed by the Treaty of Tordesillas, and formally claimed by Pedro Alvares Cabral in 1500. By the early sixteenth century, Portugal had a tenuous legal claim to a thin slice of what is now Brazil, the line of demarcation cutting through Pará in the north and modern Santa Catarina in the south. Time, and Spanish preoccupation with the silver of Peru, permitted Portugal to push far west of that line and to assemble a domain embracing almost half of South America. Much that has been said of Spanish America can fairly be repeated of Portuguese Brazil. Although their common Iberian ancestry and tutelage account for the similarities between Spanish and Portuguese America, there are marked contrasts as well. The differences are elusive but substantial; they can scarcely be crowded into the words of the Spanish proverb: "Strip a Spaniard of all his virtues and you have a Portuguese." The Portuguese has his own virtues; he has special gifts and an overflowing charm. He is a quite different creature from his blood cousin of Spain, and his distinctive traits have left their mark on Brazil.

THE BEGINNINGS OF BRAZIL, 1500–80

Pedro Alvares Cabral (according to the official record) was blown off the sea road to India by vagrant winds which brought him to the coast of America in the year 1500. Cabral raised Portugal's flag over a land so vast and varied that neither he nor those who followed him could know what it held. Cabral's men probed the jungle and found a strange tree, its wood red as a live coal; it was similar to the dyewood imported from the Far East since ancient times, long known as "brazil," and the name was now applied to the wood found in America. The name was thus fixed upon Brazil, later the chief colony of Portugal.

It was a preoccupied Portugal that suddenly found herself with an American empire, and for thirty years she gave it only fitful attention.

[*213*]

The Court of Lisbon was engrossed in reckoning the profits from India's silks, jewels, and spices and in collecting tribute from the fabulous cities of the east which now made their obeisance to the king of Portugal. India's magnificence cast into the shadow a Brazil devoid of cities and palaces, peopled by naked cannibals. However, Portugal did not wholly neglect her new possession: in 1501 she sent three ships to explore the coast south of Natal, an expedition reported by Amerigo Vespucci. In 1503 another expedition under Gonçalo Coelho—with Amerigo as one of his captains—spent five months probing inland here and there, making notes on the rude Indians, collecting parrots and monkeys, and gathering dyewood.

Portugal's initial indifference toward Brazil later yielded to active concern. Four factors contributed. The first was the discovery that there were profits in dyewood: Europe's expanding textile industry clamored for dyes. In 1502 a royal commission authorized Fernão de Noronha, a converted Jew of Lisbon, to gather the red brazilwood, carry it to Lisbon, and pay the Crown a royalty. The concession appears to have paid the king well; at least it helped to assure royal hold upon the colony by establishing armed outposts.

Second, the French exhibited a lively interest in Brazil: Francis I was contemptuous of Spanish and Portuguese claims to monopoly in America and declared that he "had never seen a clause in the last will of Adam conceding such exclusive control to Kings Manoel and Charles." His interest was echoed by many of his subjects, including the aspiring Protestants who thought to strengthen their ranks by sending missionaries overseas. French ships skirted the Brazilian coast, cut some brazilwood, and raided Portuguese shipping. Portugal's fleets attacked the French and placed a small garrison in Pernambuco in 1521. The French struck back, destroying the Pernambuco post in 1530. French designs whetted Portugal's desire for firm control.

The third element in Portugal's new concern for her American empire was her uneasy fear of Spanish ambition. Spain was stronger than Portugal and was united at last under ambitious Charles I. By the mid-1520's Spanish garrisons held most of the Caribbean islands, Hernán Cortés had conquered Mexico, and Francisco Pizarro had made his first journeys toward Peru. Navigators carrying the Spanish flag were already sailing close to the Brazilian coast—Díaz de Solís in 1516, Magellan in 1519, and Cabot in 1526. Spain's success was intoxicating, and no one knew how far she would go. Portugal had the solemn guarantees of the Treaty of Tordesillas, but her long experience with Castile made her cautious.

Fourth, Portuguese trade with India was languishing by 1510. Shiploads of pepper and cloves had yielded fabulous profits but at a cost in human lives that Portugal could ill afford—"every grain of pepper" was costing "a drop of blood." Furthermore, the European market was glutted (there is a sharp limit on the appetite for cloves and pepper), and prices fell. By 1530 the rich India trade could not meet the increasing deficits of the spendthrift Court, and the king was borrowing right and left from the usurers of Europe. Brazil's promise became brighter as reliance upon India waned.

In 1530 Martim Affonso de Souza set sail from the Tagus with five ships and spent two years covering the 3,000-mile coast from Maranhão to Rio Grande do Sul. He seized some French ships and captured the French fort at Pernambuco. In 1532 he founded São Vicente—near modern Santos—the first permanent settlement in Brazil. Inland he established Piratininga, near the site of the modern city of São Paulo.[1] Portugal now had two chief outposts: northern Pernambuco, the center of the dyewood industry, and southern São Vicente, a spearhead aimed at the Spanish wealth of Peru.

In 1533 John III, seeking further consolidation of Portuguese control, installed the system of captaincies, a type of concession used to good effect in the Madeira and Azores islands. The captaincy was a grant of land carrying economic and political privileges and responsibilities. The recipient of this favor was the *donatario*—the concessionaire. His responsibilities were explicit: he must enlist settlers, promote farming and trade, look after the spiritual welfare of the people, and protect his area against marauders. He must pay his own bills with little or no subvention from the Crown. Each captaincy was a strip from twenty-five to more than sixty leagues wide along the coast and extending inland to the line set by the Treaty of Tordesillas. This property was, in part, the private possession of the *donatario* but most of it was reserved for settlers. The scheme was protected by an elaborate code with provisions for generous tax exemptions. Of the twelve original captaincies, two proved definitely profitable before 1549—those granted in Pernambuco to Duarte Coelho Pereira and in São Vicente to Martim Affonso de Souza.

The captaincy system soon revealed serious flaws. Theoretically, the *donatario* had ample powers. He could rule as a monarch within his own domain; but before he could rule he must make himself master of his land. Duarte Coelho stated the problem: "We are obliged to conquer by inches the lands Your Majesty granted us by leagues." The success of the *donatario* also depended on an adequate supply of labor; the Indian was not easily enslaved and the Negro did not come until later. And in fighting the French, the *donatario* got little help from Portugal, a weak nation with about a million people, whose scant man power was being spent in maintaining her foothold in India. In fact, the system of captaincies was a confession of Portugal's weakness. Her very poverty dictated a policy under which private initiative of gambling captains took the place of royal enterprise. Alexander Marchant suggests that the captaincy system is properly described as rugged private enterprise and trader capitalism; others note the presence of substantial feudal ingredients.

The captains of the new empire were further handicapped by the peopling of the colony by exiles unwanted in the homeland. The Inquisition,

[1] It is interesting to remember that Affonso de Souza, after his exploits in Brazil, earned further glory as governor of Portuguese India, and had the honor of conducting the Jesuit missionary St. Francis Xavier to the Far East.

established in Portugal in 1536, provoked many Jews to emigrate to Brazil. Portugal's criminal code emptied jails of their *degredados,* banishing them to Brazil. But it is misleading to conclude that Brazil was settled by "criminals" in a modern sense. A murderer or a rapist in Portugal might get off with a fine, but let anyone deny God or affront the state and he could have his tongue ripped out, be burned alive—or be exiled to Brazil. The *degredados* summarily packed off to Brazil included some criminals, but also many others who were merely dissenters and nonconformists, men who scoffed at rules. They were mostly a virile and unruly lot ("Unbridled stallions is what they were," says Gilberto Freyre), who bred riotously with Indian and Negro women in the warm air of Brazil. Whether criminals or not, they were arrant egoists who made life unhappy for the *donatarios.*

The French continued to plague the Portuguese captains. It was clear that the threat of powerful France could not be blocked by a dozen weak *donatarios,* each driven by his own hope for profit, dependent upon the cooperation of unruly exiles, and without any powerful sense of unity in a common cause. It was again clear that Portugal must act or Brazil would be lost.

In 1549 John III took two steps: he sharply limited the political powers of the *donatarios* by appointing a captain-general, Tomé de Souza, who had won fame in Africa and India, and he named Bahia as the capital of a united Brazil. A formidable expedition brought the new captain-general to his post: 6 vessels, 320 "persons in the king's pay," and 400 exiles. Important for the future of Brazil were six members of the Society of Jesus, headed by Father Manoel da Nóbrega, of whom Robert Southey writes: "There is no individual to whose talents Brazil is so greatly and permanently indebted." The new captain-general and the Jesuit fathers, in the judgment of historian Calógeras, were the "founders of Brazil." Tomé de Souza, who served four years, did much to unite the colony. Father Nóbrega's ministry lasted until his death in 1570. After an interval came another able captain-general, Mem de Sá, who ruled for fifteen years (1557–72). His efforts to protect the Indians and to abolish cannibalism were vigorous. "A great outcry," writes Robert Southey, "was raised against these measures not by the natives themselves but by the settlers, who could not bear to see the Savages considered as human and reasonable beings. . . . They inveighed against his proceedings as violations of the liberty of the Indians . . . said it was absurd to dream of forbidding tygers to eat human flesh; that the more they warred with each other, the better it was for the Portugueze; and that to collect them in large settlements, was to form armies with which they should ere long have to contend."[2]

By 1580 Brazil had eight well-established captaincies; a capital city in Bahia; sixty sugar mills; a population of between 17,000 and 25,000 Portuguese, 18,000 "civilized" Indians, and 14,000 Negro slaves. Sugar, brazilwood, and cotton were the chief exports. The exhibit was unimpres-

---

[2] Robert Southey: *History of Brazil* (3 vols.; London: Longman, Hurst, Rees, and Orme; 1810–19), Vol. I, p. 268.

sive as compared with that of Peru or Mexico, but nevertheless Brazil by 1580 was an established and prosperous colony.

THE SPANISH INTERLUDE, 1580–1640

While Portugal had been slowly extending her hold upon Brazil, Spain had been closing in. Spanish explorers continued to sail uncomfortably close to the Brazilian coast. Mendoza founded his ill-fated fort at Buenos Aires in 1536, and his lieutenants established Asunción in 1537. Orellana crossed the Andes from Peru, sailed down the Amazon in 1541, and staked out Spain's claim to the Amazon basin west of the line of Tordesillas. These were threats enough, but more serious was Spanish Philip II's seizure of the Portuguese throne in 1580. That event was made possible by the ending of the Aviz dynasty, which had ruled Portugal for two centuries: in 1578 fanatical Sebastian had died dramatically in battle with the Moslems; in 1580 his successor, Cardinal-King Henry, died, leaving no heir to the Portuguese throne. In the turmoil that ensued, Philip, basing his claims on his Portuguese mother, invaded Portugal and bribed the nobles into electing him king. That fervid zealot, ruling as Philip II of Spain and as Philip I of Portugal, was now titular chief of the whole Iberian peninsula and of the vast Spanish and Portuguese colonial empires in Africa, Asia, and America. However, Philip, arbitrary as he was, usually respected his promise that Lisbon would continue to administer her colonies.

The sixty-year dominance of Spain yielded one substantial advantage to Brazil. Spain, on the theory that Brazil was hers forever, was lax in blocking Brazilian occupation of the frontier beyond the line of Tordesillas. Spain's chief disservice to Brazil in this period was to demand monopoly rights to her trade and to put an end to Brazil's profitable dealings with Holland. And Spain, having embroiled Brazil's relations with the Dutch, did little to help her against the enemy. The net result of the sixty-year bondage was to deepen Brazil's dislike for Spain, arouse Brazilian contempt for a Portugal that could not hold her own, and create a faint sense of Brazilian nationalism among the colonists. In 1640, thanks to Spain's preoccupation with European wars, Portugal regained her freedom under John IV, the first of the Braganza dynasty.

OTHER COMPETITORS—ENGLISH, FRENCH, AND DUTCH

It was Portugal's good fortune that gold and diamonds were not uncovered in Brazil for almost 200 years after Cabral's landing. Had there been such allurement, Brazilian territory might have passed permanently into the hands of the English, French, or Dutch. Each of these powers gave attention to Brazil and made gestures toward taking the colony into its own imperial sphere, but the stakes never seemed high enough to warrant the expenditure of the wealth and man power required to detach the colony from Portugal.

The English caused less trouble than the others. A few English traders from Southampton worked up and down the Brazilian coast during the early sixteenth century, perhaps left a few traders and soldiers at Bahia and Santos. English privateers did some plundering: Cavendish burned Santos in 1591, Lancaster pillaged Recife (Pernambuco). There was intermittent English exploration of the Amazon. In 1595 Sir Walter Raleigh searched for El Dorado in the Orinoco basin, waxed lyrical over Guiana— "a country that hath yet her maidenhead, never sacked, turned nor wrought." His enthusiasm was chiefly responsible for an abortive English settlement at the mouth of the Amazon in 1630, the last British attempt to occupy Brazilian soil.

The French were not so easily warded off. During the first three decades of desultory Portuguese control, French corsairs harried Portuguese shipping and trading posts, made alliances with Indians, and organized their own posts in Bahia and Pernambuco—all of which, as we have seen, was partially responsible for the tightening of Portuguese control by the creation of captaincies in 1533 and the appointment of a captain-general in 1549. The French persisted. In 1555 a company of several hundred colonists, led by Nicolas Durand de Villegagnon, established themselves in the bay of Rio de Janeiro with the avowed purpose of creating "Antarctic France"—a chilly designation for the hot, wet climate of Rio de Janeiro. The group, divided between Catholics and Protestants, had the support of the Huguenot leader, Admiral Gaspar de Coligny, who hoped the quarreling religionists could work together. The hope proved vain: soon the opposing factions were breaking each other's heads and in 1560 the Portuguese, led by Governor Mem de Sá, were able to evict the survivors. In 1567 the city of Rio de Janeiro was founded. But the French signature remains: an island in the bay bears the name of Villegagnon. After this fiasco, the French sailed north, captured Recife, promptly lost it, then occupied northern Maranhão —an important step in the colonization of the Amazon delta—and were not finally evicted until 1615.

The Dutch were more successful. They had long served as carriers for the Portuguese between Brazil and Lisbon, but Spain put a stop to that profitable business in 1605. Brazil was now caught in the current war between Holland and Spain, and offered an excellent target for Dutch gunners. In 1604 a Dutch fleet attacked Bahia. In 1621 the Dutch West India Company, modeled after the Dutch East India Company (1602) which had bested the Portuguese in Asia, was chartered as a colonizing and trading agency with a monopoly of trade (as against other Dutch nationals) on the American coast from Newfoundland to the Strait of Magellan—and with the specific purpose of supplanting the Portuguese in Brazil. In 1624 the Company's fleet, commanded by Piet Heyn, captured Bahia, but was unable to hold it. Then, in 1630, the Dutch seized Recife and Olinda in Pernambuco. They finally held the territory from the present state of Sergipe and the mouth of the São Francisco River north to Maranhão and almost to the mouth of the Amazon, a span of some 1,200 miles—a feat which cast into the shade their purchase of insignificant 22-square-mile Manhattan Island in 1626.

The Dutch had staunch allies in Brazil. The Jews, now subject to the Spanish Inquisition (always more thoroughgoing than the Portuguese), befriended the Dutch, who had a reputation for fair dealing with the Jews in Holland. Many Negroes and Indians were also convinced of the superior generosity of the Dutch. The Dutch were fortunate in their choice of John Maurice of Nassau as their Brazilian administrator. Distinguished soldier and nobleman, Maurice proved himself a skillful conciliator and executive. During his seven-year rule (1637–44), many Portuguese colonists, who had fled upon the arrival of the Dutch, returned under his guarantee of their property rights and freedom of worship. Life was orderly, streets were clean, houses and public buildings were erected, and schools were established. Dutch Brazil prospered from its brazilwood, its tobacco, and above all from its sugar fields and refineries. Slave ships unloaded their useful cargoes at Recife. The Dutch, the most scientific farmers of their time, proved their skill with seeds and soils, and introduced the most improved methods of harvesting and refining. The West India Company flourished, paying regular dividends of 25 per cent or more each year.

The Dutch occupation exerted a profound influence upon the colonists. As Brazilians and as sons of Portugal, they resented seizure by an alien power. Their protest was political, for the Dutch were outsiders. It was economic, for the Dutch were taking profits from them. It was also religious, for the Dutch were introducing Protestantism into a Catholic land. When news came in 1640 that Portugal had struck against Spain and that a Portuguese king again ruled in Lisbon, there was a burst of loyal pride. Hard upon that news came word of a truce with Holland whereby Portugal recognized the validity of Dutch Brazilian claims in return for Dutch aid against Spain. Brazilian anger then flared up against the mother country which had betrayed them, and in 1641 revolts against the Dutch broke out from Maranhão to Sergipe. The colonists were fighting as Brazilians for the soil of Brazil, without help from Portugal. Meanwhile, the Dutch were facing war with England and the threat of war with France. In 1642 Portugal and England signed a treaty of peace and commerce, confirming and continuing the alliance which dated from the fourteenth century when John of Gaunt fought with Portugal against Castile. In 1654 the Dutch withdrew from Pernambuco. They took their tools, slaves, and technicians to the West Indies, where their superior skills and command of shipping gave them a decisive lead in the competition for world markets.

So passed from the Brazilian scene the trespassers upon Portuguese territory. Each left its mark on the northern periphery. There, in an area which stout Brazilians occasionally covet, lie French Guiana, Surinam, and Guyana, reminders of the thwarted dreams of the French, the Dutch, and the English.

PORTUGUESE COLONIAL GOVERNMENT, 1640–1808

Portugal's break with Spain and the seating of the Braganzas on the Lisbon throne brought slight change of status to Brazil. Fitful and largely ineffective efforts were made to tighten the royal hold on the colony. A viceroy took the place of the captain-general, but the new designation was quickly dropped and was not restored until 1763. An Overseas Council, modeled after the Spanish Council of the Indies, was assigned large powers over Brazil. There were numerous changes in the lines of the original captaincies, the most important of which came as a result of the discovery of gold: the captaincy of São Paulo, including Minas Gerais, was created in 1710; the captaincy of Minas Gerais was detached as a separate unit in 1720.

In the far north, after the final expulsion of the French in 1615, the areas of Maranhão and Pará—and temporarily Ceará—were organized as the state of Maranhão, independent of the authority of the captain-general in Bahia and directly ruled from Lisbon. It was a realistic measure, for the prevailing trade winds made communication with Portugal easier than with Bahia. This northern outpost, embracing the territory between Cabo São Roque and the Amazon, went its separate way until 1774 and was an effective base for extending Portuguese hold upon the jungle lands of Amazonia.

Portugal's last burst of imperial imagination came during the reign of Joseph I (1750–77). The king himself was of slight importance, certainly not the equal of his contemporary, Charles III of Spain; but he had wit enough to accept as his prime minister the Marquis of Pombal, who ruled as a dictator from 1751 to 1777. Calogeras describes Pombal as "energetic . . . of iron will . . . with a pathological spirit of suspicion . . . vindictive . . . frightfully cruel." His abounding energy led him to drastic measures, wise and unwise, at home and in Brazil. He shared the anticlericalism which dominated the courts of both Lisbon and Madrid. His chief target was the Jesuits: he stripped them of much of their land and wealth and in 1759 banished them from Portugal and Brazil. He compelled the Inquisition to accept rules prevailing in civil courts, and removed education from the control of the clergy. Pombal reorganized public services, promoted schools, reformed agriculture, and encouraged industry. Enlightened beyond his time, he saw that slavery was an evil both in Portugal and in Brazil, abolished all slavery in Portugal and theoretically ended Indian slavery in Brazil. "His generous intentions were admirable," writes Southey; he meant "to emancipate the Indians from servitude, to reclaim them from their brutal manner of life, civilize their habits, cultivate their faculties, and blend them with the Brazilian Portuguese, so that they might become one people, enjoying equal rights. The project was worthy of his ambition . . . but in destroying the Jesuits he deprived himself of the only agents by whom it could have been effected."[3]

[3] *Ibid.,* Vol. III, p. 513.

After the earthquake of 1755 in Lisbon, Pombal rebuilt much of the city—with Brazilian gold. Meanwhile, thousands of his critics spent unhappy years in jail. In Brazil, he kept alive the boundary dispute with Spain (theoretically settled by the Treaty of Madrid in 1750), moved the capital from Bahia to Rio de Janeiro in 1763, established a new system of courts, and vigorously promoted trade by substituting monopolistic trading companies for the older fleet system. "Mistaken as he often was," concludes Southey, "and too frequently careless of justice and humanity, his mind was capacious and his general views would have been worthy of a better man."

Comparison of Portuguese rule in Brazil with that of Spain in Peru and Mexico suggests that the Portuguese were seldom as thorough and consistent as the Spaniards. The Brazilians largely enjoyed that "salutary neglect" upon which Edmund Burke congratulated England's colonists in America. Portugal's colonial rule never affected the life of her colonists to such degree as did that of the Spanish. The captain-general's (later the viceroy's) court in Bahia—and after 1763 in Rio de Janeiro—was far less effective than its counterparts in Lima and Mexico. Portugal's tenuous, and often indifferent, control was explained in part by Portugal's increasing poverty and weakness, in part by the impossibility of policing Brazil's meager population scattered in isolated settlements over so vast an area. Brazil was finally ruled, not by king or viceroy, but by the great plantation owners (*fazendeiros*), who exercised over their lordly domains the power of life and death. Brazil's affairs were administered by the municipal councils (the *câmaras,* roughly equivalent to the Spanish *cabildos*), whose members were partly hereditary, partly appointed, partly elected. By the end of the colonial period, the cities had developed prestige and power reminiscent of the feudal cities of Portugal, each with its special rights, exemptions, and privileges. And Brazil's local communities were at the mercy of the lesser administrative and military officials (*capitães móres*) who, having won appointment, were largely free from interference because of their isolation and their control of the militia.

THE CHURCH IN BRAZIL

Priests came with the conquerors, but there was little energy or order in the Brazilian Church during the first half century after Cabral's landing. The arrival of six Jesuits in 1549 marks the true beginning of organized religious activity in the colony; and two years later a bishop was appointed to Bahia, with responsibility for supervising the few priests scattered over the sparsely populated domain. In 1551 the pope designated John III and his successors forever Grand Masters of the Order of Christ; he made them responsible for propagating the faith, naming bishops, collecting and spending Church funds, and supervising Church courts. By comparison with the Spanish American colonies, the extension of Church organization lagged in Brazil. More than a century passed before more bishops were added. In 1676 Bahia became the seat of an archbishop, and by the end of the colonial period bishoprics had been established in Rio de Janeiro, Pernambuco, Maranhão, Pará, São Paulo, and Minas Gerais.

The record of the Brazilian Church rests chiefly upon the work of the Jesuits. There were representatives of the other orders, Franciscans, Mercedarians, Benedictines, Capuchins, and Carmelites, as well as numerous secular clergy; but the Jesuits were the most effective and, until they were expelled by Pombal in 1759, they dominated religious life in the colony. Three members of the order are memorable in the story of Brazil: Manoel da Nóbrega and José de Anchieta in the sixteenth century, Antônio de Vieira in the seventeenth.

The first concern of the Brazilian Jesuits, as of their Spanish contemporaries, was to protect the Indian. Under Nóbrega, Jesuit missionaries pushed south to São Paulo and north to Pernambuco. In 1553 Nóbrega established a school near the site of the present city of São Paulo; Anchieta, placed in charge of it, reported to Ignatius Loyola in Spain: "Twenty of us are in a little hut of wickerwork and mud, roofed with straw . . . this is the school, this is the infirmary, dormitories, refectory, kitchen and storeroom. . . . I serve as physician and barber." Anchieta mastered the Tupí language, reduced it to writing, prepared a grammar and a dictionary, and made that tongue the *lingua franca* or common language linking diverse Indian peoples. As defenders of the Indians, the Jesuits encountered the hostility of planters clamoring for slaves. Yet the fathers extended their work rapidly south, north, and west; baptized Indians by the thousands; and gathered them into fortified mission villages (*redução* in Portuguese, *reducción* in Spanish) where they received instruction in the truths of the Gospel, were taught to farm more expertly, and were trained in simple crafts.

The fathers had difficulty in uprooting pagan habits. The numerous cannibals found it hard to overcome their craving for human flesh; Robert Southey describes a Jesuit's encounter with an old Indian woman about to die: "Having catechised her, instructed her . . . in the nature of Christianity, and compleately taken care of her soul, he began to enquire whether there was any kind of food which she could take . . . [asking] . . . if I were to get you a little sugar now, or a mouthful of some of our nice things which we bring from beyond the sea, do you think you could eat it? . . . Ah . . . said the old convert, my stomach goes against everything. There is but one thing which I think I could touch. If I had the little hand of a little tender Tupuya boy, I think I could pick the little bones; . . . but woe is me, there is nobody to go out and shoot one for me!"[4] Polygamy offered another evil to overcome. Nothing in Indian philosophy made clear why one wife is better than five. The Jesuits were firm and persuaded a few Indians to retain one wife and to let the others go. Such decisions created embarrassing problems of unemployment for surplus and veteran wives. Nor were the fathers' arguments fortified by the example of promiscuous Portuguese males with Indian and Negro women, "begetting offspring with procreative fervor."

4 *Ibid.*, Vol. I, p. 223.

The Jesuits' fight against Indian slavery lasted 200 years; the fathers pitted against governors, planters, and slave-hunting bands. With rare exceptions, the Jesuits were faithful to their trust. They had support from the Portuguese Court, which, corrupt and ineffective as it was, usually leaned toward decent treatment of the Indians. Royal decrees against Indian slavery were issued by Sebastian in 1570, Philip I in 1580, and Philip II in 1605 and 1609. But kings were far off; their words did not carry well nor fast. Royal edicts bade Jesuits defend their charges, but royal governors protested when Jesuits sought to obey their kings. In 1611 the captain-general complained to his king: "It is necessary for you to reprimand them and to take the villages from the Jesuits . . . if the fathers wish to teach the Indians to be Christians there will always be opportunity for them to do so." In 1640 the reading of a bull of Pope Urban which forbade traffic in Indian slaves provoked riots in Rio de Janeiro, Santos, and São Paulo. The Jesuits were actually expelled from São Paulo and were not permitted to return for fifteen years. In northern Pará and Maranhão, after the expulsion of the Dutch in 1654, the contest between planters and Jesuits resulted in a brief exile for the fathers. It was during this period that Father Vieira preached his powerful sermons against Indian slavery.

For two centuries, the Jesuits were one of the chief civilizing and unifying forces in Brazil. During that time they made enemies who finally caused their expulsion in 1759. The *fazendeiros,* the great landholders, hated the fathers for keeping tens of thousands of trained Indians barricaded in the missions, safe from slavery. They also resented the economic competition of the Jesuits who used Indian labor on their own sugar plantations. Governors and civil authorities deplored the ease with which the fathers could appeal directly to Lisbon and Rome. Secular priests and the other orders had complained that the Jesuits were too rich, excited envy, and were self-righteous. The final argument of planters, civil authorities, and other churchmen was that the Jesuits were entirely too powerful, an argument which determined Pombal to expel them in 1759.

Temperate judgment upon the Jesuit record in Brazil is not simple. Gilberto Freyre admits that: "From the point of view of the Church . . . the padres acted heroically; they were admirably firm in their orthodoxy, loyal to their ideas." He cites Joaquim Nabuco: "Without the Jesuits, our colonial history would be nothing other than a chain of nameless atrocities." But Freyre is critical: "It was the entire rhythm of social life that was thus altered for the Indians; for peoples accustomed to a scattered and roaming life are always degraded when concentrated into large communities and forced to adopt an absolutely settled mode of existence." The Jesuit village was, he continued, "the regime of a boarding school kept by priests. Or of an orphan asylum . . . while admirably efficient, it was a regime that was destructive of any animal spirits, freshness and spontaneity and combativeness of mind."[5] The Jesuits were finally expelled not because they were bad men—no serious critic makes such a charge—but because their single-

5 Gilberto Freyre: *The Masters and the Slaves,* translated by Samuel Putnam (New York: Alfred A. Knopf; 1946), pp. 108–9.

minded fidelity was bad for business. They were expelled not for their failures but for their successes.

The Church's influence extended throughout the colony under the direction of bishops, the orders, and the secular clergy. It was the Portuguese Church transplanted to Brazilian soil, a Church which itself had been modified by Moslem influence and was now further shaped by the primitive beliefs of slaves from Africa and of Indians. The resulting synthesis, according to Freyre, was a religion which was not "the hard and rigid system of the reformed countries of the North or even the dramatic Catholicism of Castile itself; theirs was a liturgy social rather than religious, a softened, lyric Christianity with many phallic and animistic reminiscences of the pagan cults."[6] The less rigid character of the Brazilian Church was evidenced by the failure to install the full machinery of the Inquisition in Brazil. The colony was indeed subject to the Inquisition in Lisbon, but its administration —according to F. A. Varnhagen, ablest historian of Brazil's colonial period —was mild as compared with the Holy Office in Mexico and Peru. The Catholic Church was the most important cohesive force in Brazilian life. "This solidarity," notes Freyre, "was splendidly maintained throughout the whole of our colonial period, serving to unite us against the French Calvinists, the Reformed Dutch, the English Protestants. To such an extent that it would in truth be difficult to separate the Brazilian from the Catholic; Catholicism was in reality the cement of our unity."[7]

THE PEOPLING OF THE LAND

There was no such creature as a Brazilian in the beginning. There were a few hundred thousand Indians; then a few thousand Portuguese; a few French, Dutch, and English; and finally, a host of Negro slaves. The mixing of these various bloods produced the Brazilian; his eyes, skin, hair, stature, and habits betray his varied ancestry.

The intermingling of white, Indian, and Negro was rapid. "The milieu in which Brazilian life began was one of sexual intoxication," writes a Brazilian sociologist; and he quotes Father Anchieta: "The women go naked and are unable to say no to anyone but they themselves provoke and importune the men . . . for they hold it to be an honor to sleep with the Christians." When Negroes arrived after 1530, promiscuity increased. Where privileged males have economic power over underprivileged females, there is always promiscuity; it is the inevitable concomitant of slavery. It was true in the North American cotton belt and true in Brazil. There was, however, a marked difference between Brazilian and North American attitudes toward mulatto offspring: the North American concealed his parenthood; the Brazilian was proud of it as proof of his virility. Slight stigr was attached to miscegenation: white children, black children, and brow children played happily together under the shadow of the plantation house. The mixture of Indian and white was called the *mameluco*; of Negro and

6 *Ibid.,* p. 30.
7 *Ibid.,* p. 40.

white, the mulatto; of Negro and Indian, the *cafuso*. These were all Brazilians, as were the white children born in Brazil of Portuguese fathers and mothers.

At the end of the sixteenth century, Brazil was still an empty land. The scattered settlements were chiefly on the coast; only a few hardy pioneers ventured inland. An early historian wrote: "The Portuguese . . . are content to scrape along the seaside like crabs." There were sound reasons for staying near the coast. Portugal could not spare man power to police the interior. The produce of inaccessible settlements would yield no returns to the Crown. Furthermore, the Crown feared that colonists removed from easy commerce with the homeland might lose their loyalty to Portugal.

The seventeenth and eighteenth centuries brought expansion of the occupied territory. The frontier was pressed back by farmers in search of broader fields and richer pastures. These pioneers followed rivers inland; settled the island of Marajó in the mouth of the Amazon; moved up the Uruguay and Paraguay rivers to colonize Mato Grosso, Rio Grande do Sul, and Santa Catarina; and explored the long course of the São Francisco. They took horses and cattle with them, and many of the animals broke away and multiplied, luring those who would recapture them to further penetration of the frontier, just as in Mexico and Peru.

Other trail blazers helped to open the frontiers. Perhaps the boldest of all were the missionaries, whose remote mission villages became political and economic outposts of the expanding colony. Then the diggers for gold did for Brazil what the "forty-niners" did for the United States; they pushed back the frontier, built cities, established communications, and consolidated political control. The last, but not the least, of the makers of Brazil were the slave-hunting *bandeirantes* (members of a *bandeira,* a military company) of São Paulo—the *paulistas.*

The *bandeirantes* of São Paulo, whose bloody slave raids furnished the epic tale of seventeenth-century Brazil, finally did more to establish Portuguese rule in the uncharted backlands than any other group. These sons of Portuguese and Indian parents (whose leaders were often pure-blooded Portuguese) were the toughest and most enterprising of Brazilians, but they had insufficient outlet for their energy. Their soil was undeveloped and there was no market for the goods they could produce. Gold and diamonds had not yet been discovered. They therefore hit upon the profitable, if unpleasant, idea of hunting Indian slaves. It was regarded as a soundly patriotic project: they would extend Portuguese power and ward off the Spaniards; they would reinforce Brazilian economy with new labor— and they would make money. The *bandeirante,* aside from his pioneering, had little in common with the North American frontiersman, the man in the covered wagon piled high with furniture and plows, with his wife and children, driving west in ambition and the fear of God, to Iowa and Kansas, California and Oregon. The Brazilian frontiersman, the *bandeirante,* followed the rivers which led into the jungles, traveling with companions of like tastes, with slaves to help, with rifle, water bag and manioc flour, and no women—plenty of those were to be had in the jungle. These bands of fifty, a hundred, five hundred, or several thousand set out on their search for Indians for the slave markets. Often they were gone a year or more, stopping here and there, sometimes long enough to plant and harvest crops. They established settlements and built roads; they made alliances with one tribe of Indians against another, and often ended by enslaving both.

The Spanish Jesuits in the La Plata region of the south inadvertently made the task of the *bandeirante* easier by concentrating Indians into villages, exposing them to capture. In 1629 the twenty-one mission villages in the region of the Upper Paraná were attacked by a *bandeira* of 900 *paulistas* and 2,000 Indian allies, headed by Antônio Raposo. Some 2,500 Indians were captured, of whom more than half reached the slave markets of São Paulo. The raids continued. The Jesuits transferred their villages further south and west, and armed their Indians for defense. The struggle between the *bandeirantes* and the Jesuit missions, begun during the period of Spanish control of Brazil, finally sharpened the contest between Portugal and Spain for supremacy in the La Plata basin. The lawless ranging of the *bandeirantes* had profound influence upon Brazilian history. The immediate results were obvious: huge profits for the slave hunters, death or misery for the captured Indians. The political result of their activities was to push the frontier far beyond the treaty lines of Tordesillas, to fix Brazilian control upon territory given by the pope to Spain, and to furnish the legal basis for the domain of modern Brazil.[8] The economic fruits of their marauding finally included the opening of fertile areas for the production of cotton, coffee, and cattle; the establishing of towns; and the opening of roads. The discovery of gold and diamonds in the broad path cleared by the *bandeirantes* yielded profits which led directly to the industrialization of Brazil. These tough frontiersmen who feared neither God nor man begot the modern *paulista,* the citizen of São Paulo, who represents the most vigorous element in the Brazilian population today.

Meanwhile, the traffic in Negro slaves was flourishing. It had soon become clear that Indian labor would not suffice, and by the 1530's slave ships from Africa were unloading their cargoes in São Vicente. The Negro slave traffic was no new thing to the Iberians. Father Nóbrega, who arrived in 1549, condemned Negro slavery with vigor; but the Jesuits finally accepted the institution, even had slaves of their own. Their task was to protect the Indians. The slave trade prospered. By 1585, according to Father Anchieta, there were more than 14,000 Negro slaves in Brazil. By the end of the colonial period, there were a million or more.

The Negro was not always docile. Thousands escaped into the backlands. Many were captured, brought back, and branded. Settlements of fugitives existed throughout the colonial period; the most famous was "the Republic of Palmares," named after its great forest of palm trees. For more

---

[8] The international lawyers of Brazil, among the ablest of America, had ample exercise for their legal cunning in the endless debates over national territorial limits. The juridical principle of *uti possidetis* (Latin, as you possess), assigning to the actual holder of a given area the right to retain it, was brilliantly defended by the jurists.

than fifty years this refuge in the northeastern state of Alagôas resisted attack. The Dutch sought to dislodge the truants but failed. The slaves had a capital city, a king, an organized government. In 1687 the governor of Pernambuco hired the leader of a formidable *paulista* band to clean out Palmares. In 1697, after several failures, the *paulistas* destroyed this community of some 20,000 Negroes, who were carrying on their business and government in a capable manner.

Thus was the Brazilian people created, and its regional pride developed. Men of all colors came to regard themselves primarily as Brazilians, not Portuguese. The process was hastened by the struggles they had shared against intruders and against the jungle. There were 3 million or more Brazilians in 1800, their long roots deep in Europe, Africa, and Asia. Perhaps this was the "cosmic race" of which the Mexican José Vasconcelos writes.

PRODUCTS OF FOREST, FARM, AND MINE

The economic balance sheet of colonial Brazil lists exported products— dyewood, sugar, chocolate, cotton, tobacco, gold, and diamonds. The colony's economic health suffered two chronic complaints: lack of sufficient man power and lack of diversified production, with overdependence on one or another item. Its economic record is of recurring failure to improve production and processing of such profitable crops as sugar and cotton, and the resulting failure to hold advantage in the world's markets.

Most important, first and last, was sugar. Bailey Diffie concludes that: "The total value of sugar exports for the whole colonial period was more than double that of all other products combined, including gold and diamonds." The Portuguese brought sugar to São Vicente in 1532; its cultivation spread north to Bahia and Pernambuco so that by 1600 Brazil was the chief world exporter of sugar. Pernambuco, chief producer, prospered under the Dutch but languished when they were driven out. The Portuguese lacked the agricultural skills of the Dutch: they burned over the lands, destroying the forests and robbing the soil of its fertility; they knew little of fertilization or of choosing seeds; and they failed to use sugar waste for restoring their soil. They were backward in developing water power for their mills. They failed to learn the usefulness of combining stock raising and crop culture, and lost the fertilization from such a system. The decline of sugar prosperity was also due to increased competition with the English, Spanish, French, and Dutch growers on the scattered islands of the Caribbean.

Then came the discovery of gold. The Portuguese, envious of Spain, had long hoped for it. In 1542 the *donatario* of Pernambuco had assured his king: "As to gold, My Lord, I never cease to inquire . . . but . . . it would be necessary to go through sections of very perverse and bestial people" to reach the lands where gold was supposed to exist. The delay in finding gold was providential. "God did not wish," writes Varnhagen, "that gold be found until Brazil was well established . . . expeditions failed, and this was well, for otherwise there would not have been enough people on the coast to defend the land against the French." After almost two centuries the dream, long thwarted, was realized.

The year 1693 marked the beginning of the gold rush to Minas Gerais. Sugar planters closed their houses, abandoned their fields to weeds, and took their slaves to the gold mines. By 1711, said a chronicler of the time, 30,000 men were digging and other thousands lived by trading with the miners. They came from all over Brazil, from Portugal, from all Europe; every manner of man, white, brown, black, red; priests, nobles, merchants, farmers. It was, says a modern writer, Caio Prado, "the blackest period in Portuguese colonial administration." Negro and Indian slaves were driven into the mineshafts, sometimes 3,000 feet below the surface. Slaves passed buckets of ore from hand to hand. The human cost was not reckoned; only gold counted. Father Vieira wrote gloomily that Brazil was "well nigh ruined . . . we shall shortly relapse into the savage state," and a bishop noted that "just when our sugar mills had obtained a condition of marked improvement . . . gold mines were discovered which led us to neglect our true agricultural wealth." The gold rush brought wild inflation and reckless speculation. It provoked a civil war, in which *paulistas* fought unsuccessfully to establish exclusive claim to Minas Gerais. The gold rush did not stop with Minas Gerais. The *paulistas* pushed west and found more gold in Mato Grosso and Goiás. In 1728 diamonds were discovered in Minas Gerais, or, more accurately, the glittering stones long used as chips in games of chance were then recognized as diamonds, and the fevered search for more of them began.

All this brought joy to royal hearts in Lisbon: this was wealth they could understand. However, royal agents found it difficult to collect the king's share, a fifth,[9] in the face of the ingenuity of smugglers. We do not know what part of the gold and diamonds was registered, what part passed through illegal channels. Production boomed from 1693 to 1760, then declined. Calogeras estimates the production of gold for the entire eighteenth century at 983,000 kilograms (more than $1.1 billion in current United States dollars but worth several times that amount in eighteenth-century purchasing power). He puts the yield of diamonds at 3 million carats. But, whatever the figures, Lisbon's Court had a holiday. John V aped Louis XIV of France, built atrocious palaces, and wasted money on his greedy favorites. Meanwhile, in Brazil dour realists were saying that the gold boom had inflated prices, lifted the cost of living to fantastic figures, and brought neglect of agriculture; in short, that gold and diamonds had brought little if any prosperity to the Brazilian people. However, it was one more step in the "moving frontier." The boom brought settlers and created such cities as Villa Rica (modern Ouro Preto) with 100,000 people in the eighteenth century, and Tijuca (modern Diamantina) with 40,000 people during the diamond rush.

[9] Although the king's share was consistently called the *quinto,* or a fifth, the percentage varied from one-fifth to one-twentieth, generally declining as the output of the mines declined.

Cotton, too, had its era of prosperity. It had gotten an early start in Bahia, Pernambuco, and Maranhão. During most of the eighteenth century, Brazil was the chief world exporter of cotton. But here again, as with sugar, Brazil lost her advantage. In 1793 Eli Whitney perfected his cotton gin, which could pick out seeds at less cost than could slaves. Brazil, failing to modernize its methods, lost the lead to the United States and has only in recent years regained a significant share in the world's cotton trade.

There were other products. Tobacco prospered, chiefly in Bahia. Chocolate showed steady production and sales. A little coffee was grown, but its production was unimportant until the mid-nineteenth century. Hides and a variety of other items such as rice, vanilla, spices, and indigo were substantial exports by the end of the colonial period.

Brazilian trade throughout the colonial period was theoretically under monopoly control from Lisbon, but the system was less rigid than Spain's. Trade was a cutthroat game in which Portugal had to contend with the English, Dutch, and French. Monopoly companies were organized to offset those resourceful competitors. The first, the Company of Brazil, founded in 1649 and inspired by Father Vieira, had a monopoly on the wine, oil, codfish, and flour trade of Brazil which continued until 1721. The second, the Maranhão Company, prospered from 1678 to 1684, handling slave traffic and commerce in the north. The third, the General Company of Pará and Maranhão, launched by Pombal, lasted from 1755 to 1778. A similar company operated in Pernambuco and Paraíba during Pombal's term of office. These monopoly companies served Portugal, but England was usually an active partner.

SOCIAL AND CULTURAL PATTERNS

The vigorous heart of Brazilian life was the ruling country family who lived on the *fazenda*, the plantation. These *fazendas*, often vast in area (one was larger than Portugal itself), were privately owned. Within his domain the *fazendeiro* ruled as king, dispensing justice, commanding his own private army, acting as banker and merchant. He and his family lived in the *casa-grande*, the "Big House," which became the symbol of the ruling class of Brazil. Under the shadow of the Big House was the *senzala,* the slave hut. Brazil was created out of the contest between them. This is the theme of Gilberto Freyre's epochal *Casa-grande e senzala*. Freyre writes: "The social history of the Big House is the intimate history of practically every Brazilian; the history of his conjugal life under a slave-holding and polygamous patriarchal regime; the history of his life as a child; the history of his Christianity, reduced to the form of a family religion and influenced by the superstitions of the slave hut." And, Freyre continues, from the sixteenth century on "the lord of the manor was almost the sole dominating figure in the colony, the true lord of Brazil or nearer to being than either the viceroys or the bishops." The *fazendeiro* dominated the Church and the secular priests. Only the Jesuits dared to denounce his sins. And, adds Freyre: "These country squires were the lords of the earth and of men . . . but all this pomp had long since turned to dust, and when all is said, it was the churches that survived the Big Houses."

Contrasted with Big Houses there were little churches, literally and figuratively. The Brazilians built few such towering temples as Spain scattered profusely in cities and towns, from Mexico to Tucumán and Córdoba. Colonial Brazil's one distinctive builder and decorator of churches was the crippled mulatto, Antônio Francisco Lisboa, called Aleijadinho. During the last half of the eighteenth century, he created in the villages of Minas Gerais some of the loveliest churches of Brazil. The Church in Brazil, aside from the work of the Jesuits, never had the moral and political stature of the Church in Spanish America. The typical Brazilian church, architecturally and spiritually, bowed its head to the Big House.

The Big House towered over the cities, which were unimpressive even in 1800. In that year Rio de Janeiro may have had 80,000 people; Bahia, 70,000; Pernambuco, 25,000; São Paulo, 15,000—but their streets were unlighted and unpaved, sewage trickled down rutted gullies, water supply was inadequate, and policing was meager. The cities did not count; they were servants of the plantations. The people of the cities packed and shipped the sugar, cotton, hides, chocolate, and tobacco that the *fazenda* produced. Cities furnished errand boys, hucksters, no more; the lords of Brazil lived inland. This was true even of Rio de Janeiro, seat of the viceroy since 1763. Here was little of the pomp of the viceregal courts of Lima and Mexico, for the true rulers of Brazil paid scant attention to viceroys.

Brazil's was a class society, theoretically rigid. Actually it was "a combination of aristocracy, democracy and even anarchy." The class lines were roughly drawn after this fashion. At the top were "men of the kingdom," the Portuguese-born, appointed as governors, judges, and chief officials. Next came those born in Brazil of Portuguese parents, including most of the *fazendeiros*. Third, *mamelucos* of Portuguese-Indian parentage, workers on *fazendas*, foremen, and artisans. Fourth, tamed Indians, farm hands, and house servants. Fifth, Negro slaves, chief reliance for field and mine. Sixth, wild Indians of the back country. But the system was often elastic. Caste lines were more economic than racial. Brazil shared "the greater social plasticity of the Portuguese as compared with any other European colonizers." Brazil was able to absorb a considerable number of English, French, Florentines, Genoans, Germans, Jews, and Spaniards. There was little animus against foreigners as such, unless they were heretics. Theoretically, there were high barriers against the Negro, but actually Brazil shared Portugal's easy acceptance of men of all colors, a lesson acquired from long association with the Moslems. Time and again, Brazil found it convenient to regard sons of Negro women as white. Men with Negro blood came to high positions in Church and state. The winning of wealth or political preferment automatically gave the fortunate individual white status. It is therefore impossible to compare a Brazilian's and an Alabaman's figures on race: the Brazilian counts as Negroes those who are economically Negro; the Alabaman judges by blood alone.

The Brazilian's attitude on the status of women revealed his Iberian inheritance, colored by Moorish tradition. The Brazilian woman of standing was locked away out of sight. She became a shadowy figure in the background, jealously protected but seldom respected as an equal; even her sons were early taught to regard her as unworthy of confidence or companionship. The dominance of the male, taken for granted by the Spaniard, was further exaggerated by the Portuguese. Woman's abilities were utilized neither by the family nor by the state. She was not expected to have a mind.

By the end of the colonial period, there had been definite physical degeneration in the white stock of Brazil. The explanation lay partly in his faulty diet. He ate too much sugar and not enough fresh vegetables, fruits, and milk. He used too much manioc—a tuberous root that grows easily and widely and still serves as the staple food for most Brazilians. Slavery had also undermined the vigor of white Brazilians. The boy of good family could not demean himself with physical labor. Both his physical and moral health were corrupted. Brazilian boys were denied physical exercise and grew up as "flabby males." They shared the sexual libertinism of a slave society in which the dominant male could choose as he would from the women in the slave huts. Promiscuity spread; syphilis became a scourge. By contrast, those with Negro blood fared better. Bad diet was not new to the Negro; his African fathers had survived centuries of it. Furthermore, deficiencies in diet were offset by life in the open air and vigorous exercise. The ravages of syphilis were mitigated by labor in the sun and the rain.

The intellectual life of colonial Brazil was meager. Life in the Big House did not encourage intellectual excitement. The Church provided a few schools for the privileged. For those with money and ambition, there was Portugal's University of Coimbra. But no university was established in Brazil during the three colonial centuries in which Spain had founded institutions of distinction in Mexico, Lima, Córdoba, and a score of other cities.

Books and the printed word were all but unknown. There was no printing press until 1808, while Spanish Americans had been printing books for almost 300 years. Brazil imported few books. The Spanish American clergy had been reading widely, even sampling the forbidden works of Voltaire and Rousseau, but the Brazilian clergy indulged in few such digressions. It was part of the isolation of Brazil. The security of a slave society was safeguarded by the absence of universities and presses and by the scarcity of books. Brazil's *fazendeiros* would have found themselves in hearty accord with Virginia's mid-seventeenth-century Governor William Berkeley: "I thank God there are no free schools nor printing, and I hope we shall not have any these hundred years, for learning has brought disobedience and heresy and sects into the world and printing has divulged [them] and libels against the best government. God keep us from both."

In literature, the Brazilians continued to glory in the great Camões, whose *Lusiads* celebrated the feats of Vasco da Gama. Colonial Brazil produced few writers whose work is remembered. The early chroniclers wrote pungent reports. The Jesuit fathers wrote memorable letters and records. Anchieta, described by Afrânio Peixoto as "the founder of our Brazilian literature," wrote letters, reports, and poems. Nóbrega left commentaries. Vieira's fifty-year ministry yielded a great number of sermons—rotund, tempestuous, great in moral passion, but hardly supporting Afrânio Peixoto's enthusiastic description of "his gentle, flowing style"; Vieira was as gentle as Niagara. One of the great documents was André João Antonil's *The Culture and Opulence of Brazil in its Produce and Mines,* published in 1711. A few writers in the late eighteenth century broke with the sonorous tradition which Góngora had fixed upon the literature of both Spain and Portugal: Basílio da Gama in his epic poem *Uruguay*; Santa Rita Durão in his tempestuous *Caramurú,* in which the conflicts of the Indians were dramatized; Tomaz Antônio Gonzaga in his love poems—"the most nearly perfect idealization of love to be found in all of our poetry," says the modern Erico Verissimo. These marked the beginnings of a Brazilian literature.

BRAZIL IN 1800

By 1800, 300 years after Cabral, Brazil's colonial days were drawing to a close. Portugal's vigor was long since spent. The colony she had created had outstripped her and would soon assume its place as an independent nation. So we may ask what sort of a nation Brazil was by 1800, how life went on.

Colonial Brazil was a land apart and quite unlike colonial Spanish America. Theoretically, there were the same harsh lines of cleavage between man and man; actually there was a greater tolerance—or sense of humor—in Brazil, which made it possible to transfer a Negro to the white lists by the vote of the brotherhoods, possible for the slave to buy his way to freedom, and for the nation to assimilate all sorts of alien elements which Spain's greater consistency repudiated. In government, the same hierarchy of officialdom had the same theoretical powers; actually Brazil enjoyed a lax control which left the colony free to develop in its own haphazard fashion. Both Spanish and Portuguese America had the same Church with the same arrangement of bishops and clergy, regular and secular; actually the Brazilian Church had drawn within itself so much of the spirit of the Negro and of the Indian that it was infinitely more elastic than the Church of Peru and Mexico.

This was a quite different land from English North America. Perhaps the explanation lies partly in climate: there was a great dissimilarity between the ice and snow of Massachusetts and the cloying warmth of Bahia. Perhaps it lies in religion: the Puritans claimed freedom of worship but saw no inconsistency in cutting off the ears of Quakers, dragging women dissenters through icy waters, and expelling Anne Hutchinson because she believed in an "inner light." Colonial Brazil was more patient, more amiable—even the Jew was usually safe. Compare seventeenth-century Cotton Mather with his Brazilian contemporary, Father Antônio de Vieira: both were strong in conviction, both commanding in invective, both great in religious works and political action. Perhaps Vieira knew as much of the mercy of God as did his Boston contemporary: Mather could condone, albeit uneasily, the hanging of witches; Vieira fought bravely for his Indians. Or compare the two colonizing powers in their relations with subject races. The English formula was liquidation; the Portuguese, assimilation. The Englishman, in the name of his God, shot his Indians; the Portuguese, with a slight nod to his God, slept with his Indians. English planters in Virginia behaved as Portuguese planters did in Pernambuco. They chose the fairest of Negro wenches. The English, out of a sense of sin, refused to recognize the offspring of such irregular alliances. The Portuguese, in warm affection, took pride in their brown children, often trained them, and now and then sent them to school in Portugal. There were likenesses and there were differences. Perhaps the moral of the tale is that there should be a moratorium on Anglo-Saxon self-congratulation.

The year 1800 marks the end of an age for Brazil. The sleepy life of this sprawling empire, dramatized in the indolence of its *fazendas,* was about to be shaken. The turmoils which had torn North America and which were now raging in France and all Europe were about to reach the soil of Spanish and Portuguese America.

PART III

The New World
Breaks with the Old

The severing of the ties between the Iberian kingdoms and their American colonies was inevitable. It is not within the nature of man to accept forever the status of a dependent. The wonder is not that the emergence of the free nations of America came so soon, but rather that it came so late.

Neither Spain nor Portugal has ever understood why her American colonies broke away. Injured pride is betrayed by the inscription on Columbus's tomb in Seville, which refers to "ungrateful America." The Iberians argued with good conscience that they had poured their best blood and treasure into their kingdoms overseas, that the colonies were morally beholden to the motherlands and had no right to abandon them so abruptly. But in reality there was nothing abrupt about the wars for Latin American independence. The blows which were finally struck reflected the accumulated angers and ambitions of three centuries.

 [*Chapter 13*]

THE TUMULT OF REVOLUTION

WHO REVOLTED AND WHY

When the break came, all races and classes had a hand in it. Of these, the Indian had most grievances. Shouldered with the heaviest physical burdens, yet denied any voice in shaping his own fate, he was seldom more than a slave in his ancestral homeland—a treatment no worse, however, than that accorded him by his Aztec and Inca masters. From the days of Columbus's first settlement on Hispaniola down to the end of Spanish power in America, the Indian had protested sporadically against these wrongs. The outbursts were unorganized and ineffective, and are given little space in the recorded history of those three centuries. Nor did the Indian play a major role in the final battles against the Spaniards. But behind those who pushed the Spaniard into the sea stood the angry figure of that first American, whose elemental human rights had been so brusquely denied.

The restless mestizo, product of the illicit love of the conqueror for the Indian woman, emerged as an explosive social force. From the early days of the Conquest, the bronzed children of these irregular unions began to appear in the streets of Mexico, Lima, Caracas, and Havana. Offspring of both white and Indian worlds, the mestizo was accepted wholeheartedly by neither. His soul was torn on the one hand by pride in his father's power, and on the other by resentment of the slight against his mother. Economically, he was denied full privileges in either the Indian or the white community. Spiritually and materially, he was an outcast, compelled to create his own new world, obliged to live by his wits. The mestizo multiplied until he formed a sizable segment of the colonial population which was consciously American, with no loyalty to European kings.

The chief leader of the final revolt was the creole, the pure-blooded Iberian born in America. For 300 years the creole fretted at the superior privileges of the "men of the peninsula"—the officials sent out from Lisbon and Madrid. These *peninsulares* (or *gachupines,* "the spurred ones," as the Mexicans called them) held most of the high positions: they were viceroys, captains-general, governors, judges, bishops; they dominated the political, religious, and social life of the colonies. The creoles, who soon outnumbered the small company of the *peninsulares,* were denied easy jobs and quick profits; and, toughened in the process, they used their wits to win a place in the New World.

While the interlopers from Spain were enjoying the luxury of vice-regal courts and episcopal palaces, the creoles were extending their fields and organizing businesses—in short, they were completing the conquest of America. In this struggle the creole developed "the robust consciousness of being no longer a Portuguese or a Spaniard, but an American"; and as the colonial years wore on, he even learned to laugh at the strutting officials sent to rule over him. But the resentment of the creole steadily increased, and by the end of the eighteenth century it was clear that he would no longer consent to play the role of a Cinderella on the colonial hearth. This was his America, and the time was coming when he would fight for it.

And so all Americans—creole, mestizo, and Indian—joined in the clamor against the abuses of colonial rule, with the creole the most vocal. Their grievance was more economic than political: the sons of the New World had little complaint against the authority of kings (even when they were as stupid as Ferdinand VII), but they did not wish to have the profits of American fields and mines drained off to support the waning magnificence of the courts of Lisbon and Madrid. They were even more insistent that the special economic privileges of the *peninsulares* should be ended—to their own enrichment. To be sure, the rule in America was no worse than that in Portugal or Spain. As E. G. Bourne puts it: "All things considered, Spanish America was quite as well governed as was Spain and on the whole more prosperous." And specific injustices might have been ameliorated. But the colonists of Latin America, like those of North America, had long passed the point where they could reach agreement. By the first years of the nineteenth century, their tempers were strained to the breaking point.

The decision to break the ties with their Iberian masters was in large part due to the new and disturbing ideas which had been spreading over the Western world during the eighteenth century. The accession of the French Bourbons to the Spanish throne in 1700 had extended the influence of France and French ideas and provoked a lively desire in all enterprising young creoles to see Paris before they died. The sons of rich landholders, merchants, and operators of mines used part of their profits to taste the glories of France. Here they saw with their own eyes the unhealthy splendor of kings. Here, too, they were exposed to the exciting ideas of Voltaire, Raynal, Montesquieu, and Rousseau, who were boldly ridiculing kings and clerics. Of course, their books were periodically burned or banned in France, Spain, Rome, and America. But the censor proved, as always, the most effective salesman.

The colonists were as eager as any other people to delve into the proscribed books, which were always included among the contraband goods of the freebooters when they landed at Veracruz, Callao, or Buenos Aires. Thus dangerous ideas were given currency. Americans learned of Raynal's

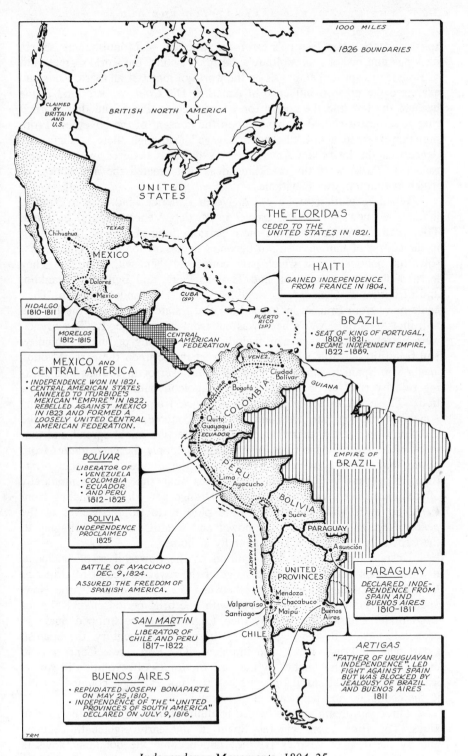

1000 MILES

1826 BOUNDARIES

CLAIMED BY BRITAIN AND U.S.

BRITISH NORTH AMERICA

UNITED STATES

THE FLORIDAS
CEDED TO THE UNITED STATES IN 1821.

Chihuahua

TEXAS

MEXICO

Dolores

Mexico

CUBA (SP)

PUERTO RICO (SP)

HAITI
GAINED INDEPENDENCE FROM FRANCE IN 1804.

HIDALGO 1810-1811

MORELOS 1812-1815

CENTRAL AMERICAN FEDERATION

BRAZIL
• SEAT OF KING OF PORTUGAL, 1808–1821.
• BECAME INDEPENDENT EMPIRE, 1822–1889.

MEXICO AND CENTRAL AMERICA
• INDEPENDENCE WON IN 1821.
• CENTRAL AMERICAN STATES ANNEXED TO ITURBIDE'S MEXICAN "EMPIRE" IN 1822. REBELLED AGAINST MEXICO IN 1823 AND FORMED A LOOSELY UNITED CENTRAL AMERICAN FEDERATION.

VENEZ.

Ciudad Bolívar

GUIANA

BOLÍVAR

Bogotá

COLOMBIA

Quito

Guayaquil

ECUADOR

BOLÍVAR
LIBERATOR OF
• VENEZUELA
• COLOMBIA
• ECUADOR
• AND PERU
1812-1825

PERU

Lima

Ayacucho

EMPIRE OF BRAZIL

BOLIVIA
INDEPENDENCE PROCLAIMED 1825

BOLIVIA

Sucre

PARAGUAY

Asunción

SAN MARTÍN

BATTLE OF AYACUCHO DEC. 9, 1824.
ASSURED THE FREEDOM OF SPANISH AMERICA.

UNITED PROVINCES

PARAGUAY
DECLARED INDEPENDENCE FROM SPAIN AND BUENOS AIRES 1810-1811

Mendoza

Chacabuco

SAN MARTÍN
LIBERATOR OF CHILE AND PERU 1817-1822

Valparaíso

Santiago

Maipú

Buenos Aires

CHILE

ARTIGAS
"FATHER OF URUGUAYAN INDEPENDENCE", LED FIGHT AGAINST SPAIN BUT WAS BLOCKED BY JEALOUSY OF BRAZIL AND BUENOS AIRES 1811

BUENOS AIRES
• REPUDIATED JOSEPH BONAPARTE ON MAY 25, 1810.
• INDEPENDENCE OF THE "UNITED PROVINCES OF SOUTH AMERICA" DECLARED ON JULY 9, 1816.

TRM

Independence Movements, 1804–25

spirited attack upon Europe's errors in America, of Montesquieu's satires on kings and bishops, of Voltaire's diatribes against the world's great, and of Rousseau's spirited emphasis on the worth of man. Of all these, Rousseau exercised the greatest influence in America. His *Contrat social* and *Emile* became the law and the gospel for young creoles. From him they learned that government should be based upon the consent of the governed. From him they learned about "the noble savage" (although there is slight evidence that the lot of the American "savage" was bettered by Rousseau's readers). These were the crackling ideas that created the atmosphere in which revolution was inevitable.

When revolution broke out in North America, and then in France, it was good news for restless creoles in Mexico, Venezuela, and La Plata. They read the words which northern patriots flung at George III: "When in the course of human events it becomes necessary for one people to dissolve the political bands which have connected them with another." They learned of Thomas Jefferson and Thomas Paine and Benjamin Franklin, and of battles at Concord, Lexington, Bunker Hill, and Yorktown. Then came news from France; in 1789 the Third Estate struck, and the Bastille fell; in 1793 Louis XVI's head was cut from his royal body. The French were marching to strange new melodies, were talking of liberty, equality, and fraternity—words which fell like sweet music upon the ears of young idealists in Spanish America. Then came the Terror in France with shifting rule by rival factions; and finally Napoleon with his imperial ambitions. These events shook Hispanic America from end to end. But the American creoles, the only element that counted, recoiled against the turbulence in France; they feared that the infection might spread and that mobs of Indians and mestizos might not only topple the *peninsulares* from power, but might even destroy the creoles themselves. Such sober afterthoughts generally persuaded the creoles that the Spanish monarchy offered them more security than all the strange new ideas emanating from Paris. So even while the creoles were plotting to rid themselves of the *peninsulares* and to inherit their power and wealth, they were clinging to the Crown as a buttress against anarchy at home.

Despite the new mood of caution of the powerful creole element, it was obvious that the waning prestige of the royal houses of Madrid and Lisbon was leading on to a break between the Old World and the New. Spain's position had worsened sadly, with one brief period of revival after 1759 under Charles III. But by then England had outstripped Spain in economic power. By the beginning of the nineteenth century, the Spanish Court was bankrupt, venal, and impotent. The Portuguese Court was in even more melancholy state. By the time the forces of revolution in America had reached full strength, neither Spain nor Portugal counted greatly in the economic and political life of Europe.

Three peripheral groups helped to diminish the dignity of the Iberian kings. The Freemasons entered Spain in the early eighteenth century, and by the time of Charles III they had become the dominant advisers to the Bourbon kings. They imported the ideas of the French Enlightenment; they injected the catharsis of a robust criticism; and their influence finally proved hostile to the pretensions of kings. The Jesuits contributed to the disquiet. After their expulsion by 1767 from Spain, Portugal, and the American colonies, they gathered in their various refuges in western Europe, forming centers of disaffection toward the kings who had betrayed them. These well-trained and able priests now became willing allies of those who would destroy the royal establishments which had dared to attack the Society of Jesus. The Jews, expelled from Spain in 1492 and from Portugal a little later, had also taken refuge in all parts of Europe and the Mediterranean world. These outcasts, including some of the ablest and richest leaders of the time, continued as bitter critics of both the Spanish and the Portuguese royal houses.

The final outbreak in Spanish America came as the direct and inevitable result of Spain's involvement in the dynastic struggles of Europe. By the eighteenth century, Spain had been far outdistanced by England. Charles III (1759–88) sought to meet England's onslaught on Spanish trade in America—as, for example, the War of Jenkins's Ear (1739–41), the Seven Years' War (1756–63), and the occupation of Havana (1762) —by signing in 1761 the "family compact" between the Bourbon houses of Spain and France, an arrangement which gave more advantage to the French branch of the Bourbons than to the Spanish. In order to harass England, Charles gave comfort to the English rebels in North America, despite the warning of his most astute counselor, the Count of Aranda, who saw clearly that demands for liberty in New England would incite similar demands in New Spain. Charles did not heed Aranda's caution on the perils inherent in helping to create a great North American republic so close to Spain's colonial domain. Deaf to all arguments, Charles aligned Spain with France in war on England in 1779, thereby giving moral— though not military—aid to the North Americans in their unequal struggle with England. When his dull-witted son Charles IV came to the Spanish throne in 1788, even greater mistakes were made. In 1793 Spain briefly united with England against France and lost Santo Domingo as a result. In 1796 Spain again joined France in attacking England and as one result lost the rich island of Trinidad. The English defeat of France and Spain at Trafalgar in 1805 convinced Charles IV's chief minister, Manuel Godoy, that Spain would do well to cultivate an alliance with England. This mood quickly changed as Napoleon's triumphs increased, and Godoy decided to make his peace with the Corsican.

It was Napoleon Bonaparte who finally and most effectively upset the uneasy loyalty of Spain's colonists in America. Unconvinced by Godoy's turncoat diplomacy, Napoleon decided that the time was ripe to unseat the Bourbon line in Spain, and for good measure the Braganzas of Portugal. At this point Napoleon's strategy was primarily directed against England; by occupying Portugal, he would keep the British off the Continent. His armies marched into Portugal in 1807, arriving on the hills above Lisbon just in time to see the English navy carry off mad Queen Maria and her numerous court to Brazil. Then, in 1808, Napoleon's forces took

Charles IV, who had abdicated, and his son Ferdinand VII into custody, occupied Madrid, and placed Napoleon's brother Joseph on the throne. It was this situation in Spain that finally served to provoke the outbreaks in Spanish America. The citizens of Caracas, Buenos Aires, Santiago, and Mexico were still sound royalists, ready to stomach even the ill-favored Ferdinand. But they would not bow to the upstart Napoleon. So when Spanish America struck out for liberty in 1810, the target was not Ferdinand but Napoleon.

THE PRECURSORS OF REVOLUTION

Many protested against Iberian rule during the three colonial centuries, but few struck hard enough or shouted loud enough to be remembered by the chroniclers. We cite four chief rebels, precursors of the wars of independence. One was a Peruvian Indian, the second a Haitian Negro, the third a Venezuelan creole, the fourth a Brazilian.

The first was Tupac Amarú, the lineal descendant of the great Inca Tupac Amarú who was executed by Viceroy Toledo in 1571. He was born in 1742 in Upper Peru, and baptized José Gabriel Condorcanqui. The royal authorities early recognized him as the legal heir of the Incas and named him Marquis of Oropesa, the title granted by Philip II to the Inca line in the sixteenth century. But the young Indian preferred to be known as Tupac Amarú, taking the name of his great ancestor. Carefully educated by the Jesuits, accorded honors and wealth by the Crown, Tupac Amarú made common cause with the poorest of his Indian kin. There were no more dejected and bitterly driven Indians in all the Spanish realm than those of high Peru. The outrageous mistreatment of them, reported by Juan and Ulloa a few decades earlier, had not markedly improved. Extortionate *corregidores* still grew rich from forced sales of useless goods to the Indians, beggaring them, stripping them of their lands, and compelling them to work as virtual slaves in mines and factories. Many unworthy priests conspired with the civil rulers, using the confessional and the sacraments as instruments of coercion.

Tupac Amarú, identifying himself with the victims of this iniquitous system, boldly presented his case to viceroys and governors, but without success. Finally, in November, 1780, he called the Indians to his banner and enrolled an "army" (few of whom were armed) numbering some 70,000 or 80,000 men. Within a few months he controlled much of what is now southern Peru, most of Bolivia, and some of Argentina. In his innocence Tupac Amarú was sure that the Spaniards would recognize the justice of his petitions and yield to the fair claims of an abused people, and that whites and Indians could then live happily together in mutual respect. The representatives of the Spanish Crown were in no such conciliatory mood, and they summoned reinforcements from Buenos Aires and Lima. Within six months Tupac Amarú was captured, together with his wife, his sons, and members of his family and staff. Punishment was pitiless. Tupac Amarú witnessed the execution of his wife, sons, and aides. Then his tongue was cut out, and he was torn to pieces by horses attached to his arms and legs. The bleeding members of his body were fixed on poles and exhibited in the villages which had supported him. The grim news spread from village to village, and thousands of new Indian recruits joined the revolt, plundering Spaniards wherever they were to be found. Murder and rapine swept the countryside for many months, until the victims on both sides numbered not less than 80,000.

The second was that strange and tragic figure, Toussaint L'Ouverture, the slave grandson of an African king, who became the leader and the banner-bearer of the Negro slaves against the few thousand French planters on the island of Hispaniola. France's most lucrative colony in the eighteenth century, accounting for more than half of its colonial trade, was Saint Domingue—modern Haiti—on the western third of the island. When the French Revolution struck in 1789, Saint Domingue suffered immediate repercussions of the events in Paris. The island was already torn among three classes: at the top, a few thousand whites, mostly French; at the bottom, the driven mass of some half million Negro slaves; and in between, those of mixed blood, despised by Negroes and whites alike, and themselves divided by their various degrees of whiteness into mutually antagonistic groups. The French Revolution set off the explosion by outlawing slavery. This incited violence, first of all by the mulattoes. Soon all groups were involved and the island was torn by riots. Slaves began to desert their masters and to organize bands which ranged up and down the countryside pillaging and burning.

In 1791 Toussaint emerged as the leader of the Negroes. He had been born a slave in 1743; but, thanks to his own considerable ability and the generosity of his French master, he had prospered until he could boast a private fortune amounting to several hundred thousand dollars. When revolution came, he first saw to the safety of his French master's family and then threw in his lot and his private fortune with the Negro group to which he belonged. For ten years he led his straggling armies of illiterate Negroes, ill-equipped and largely unarmed, over the mountains and valleys of Hispaniola, striking now at the French, then at the British and the Spaniards who intervened, and again testing his strength with the various mulatto groups who confused the issue. He had scant munitions and his army lived from the country as they marched. But by 1801 he controlled not only French Saint Domingue (modern Haiti) but also the eastern end of the island—the colony of Santo Domingo, which had been ceded to France by Spain in 1795. Assuming dictatorial powers, he promulgated a constitution, theoretically emancipating all slaves and, curiously enough, providing for the further importation of slaves from Africa.

By this time Napoleon dominated France and it was clear that he would not accept Toussaint's self-appointed rule of France's rich colony. When Napoleon was presented with Toussaint's constitution, he snapped:

"Never again will I leave an epaulette on the shoulder of a Negro," and he dispatched an expeditionary force of 54 ships and 23,000 men under General Leclerc, his brother-in-law. Despite this impressive force, Leclerc was hard put to it to defeat Toussaint. Not least of Toussaint's allies was yellow fever, which decimated the French ranks. However, the French superiority in man power and munitions finally forced Toussaint's surrender. Leclerc invited the Negro leader to his camp with the words: "You will not find a more sincere friend than myself." But Toussaint was seized, chained, thrown on a ship, and consigned to a French prison, where he died the following year, in 1803—"free at last." He had lost the battle, but a year later General Jean Jacques Dessalines defeated the last of the French forces and declared the independence of Haiti, the first area in all Latin America to cut its ties with the Old World.

The third rebel was Francisco de Miranda, born of Spanish parents in Caracas in 1750, who was destined to prepare the way for the liberator, Simón Bolívar. Miranda has been variously eulogized and execrated. He has been denounced as a libertine, waster, opportunist, and coward, and praised as an untiring patriot who spent his life pleading the cause of Spanish American liberty. His was a bizarre career. At twenty-two he went to Spain, with money enough to buy a commission in the army. At thirty he was back in America, fighting with the Spanish against England. Then he withdrew from the Spanish army and visited the newly independent United States, where he talked with Alexander Hamilton and other leaders. By 1785 he was in London, where he spent most of the years until 1810, plotting the liberation of America from Spain.

Although England was not minded to provoke colonial revolts against Spain, her prime minister, the younger Pitt, astutely foresaw that such outbreaks might come, and that it would be wise to harbor, though not to encourage, this spirited revolutionist. Miranda was given a modest subsidy from the Royal Treasury—a comfortable arrangement, which he enjoyed during most of his long stay in London. He found time to wander on the Continent, making fresh friends for himself and his cause. He was a brilliant conversationalist in most of Europe's languages and was everywhere a welcome guest. By now he bore the title of "Count," although the source of that honor is unknown. Women found his charm irresistible. Even the great Catherine of Russia, to whose court he journeyed, smiled upon him, furnished him with funds, of which he was always in need, and grieved when the handsome young man quit her land.

In 1790 Miranda was expounding to Pitt his grandiose plans for creating one great free new nation in South America, presided over by a native prince of the Inca line. Then the French Revolution interrupted his career. He served briefly in that fervid crusade, became a full-fledged French general, then was caught in one of the war's swift overturns, and found himself in a French jail. This debacle would have ended the career of anyone less nimble than Miranda: Spain despised him as a turncoat, England resented his aid to France, France herself was through with him, and even Catherine did not like to see her young friend dabble in radicalism. But Miranda talked his way out of jail and back upon the payroll of England.

Miranda's house in London now became the rallying center for all plotters against Spain. The English paid the bills for food and drink but equipped no expeditionary forces for attacks upon Spanish America. In 1806 Miranda turned to the United States, found a few volunteers and a small vessel, the *Leander*, and actually landed at the Venezuelan port of Coro. There he discovered to his chagrin that the villagers had not the slightest desire to attack Spanish garrisons. From this abortive expedition, Miranda returned to London; but when the Caracas *cabildo* created an independent junta in 1810, he returned in triumph to his native Venezuela, where he was proclaimed commander in chief of the revolutionary army and dictator of the country. His long-postponed glory was short-lived. The first tests of strength with royalist troops brought defeat. Miranda capitulated in July, 1812; and, taking the funds of the revolutionary junta with him, he fled to La Guaira, where he planned to catch a ship for England. But the younger hotheads—including Simón Bolívar—denounced him as a coward, seized him and turned him over to the Spanish authorities, who shipped him first to Puerto Rico and then to Spain. He died in a Cádiz prison in 1816. With the perspective of the years, one must consider this last episode a blot on Bolívar's record. Despite his poor showing as a military strategist and his instability of character, Miranda had proved constant in his chief conviction. He had blazed the way for the liberators of Spanish America.

The fourth precursor of the wars of independence was the Brazilian known as "Tiradentes," leader of the first serious outbreak against Portuguese rule in 1788, in the rich mining state of Minas Gerais. This man, whose true name was Joaquim José da Silva Xavier, was variously amateur physician, small merchant, minor army officer, and dentist—this last occupation giving him the popular name, Tiradentes, "the tooth-puller." (He was a good dentist, if we may believe a contemporary record: "He drew teeth with the most subtle lightness and ornamented the mouth with new ones made by himself.") The *mineiros*, as the citizens of Minas Gerais are called, had real grievances. When the output of gold and diamonds declined, Portugal had sought to exact more profit by raising taxes and lowering wages. The workers' protests attracted support from a few soldiers, priests, and lawyers, but Tiradentes was the active leader of the conspiracy which ensued. That man of many skills, while primarily voicing the grievances of the workers, enlarged his demands to include an appeal for a university (there was, as we have already noted, none in Brazil), the abolition of slavery, the establishment of factories, and the complete independence of the nation. The armed uprising which he led was quickly crushed, and the leaders were captured. Tiradentes faced the court, refused to retract or to implicate his confederates, and demanded that he alone be punished. He was beheaded on April 21, 1792, his head raised on a pole so that all might take warning. His name is honored by all Brazilians. The hall of Congress in Rio de Janeiro is called the Palacio Tiradentes.

These four were among the brave souls who dared to speak out for the freedom and the independence of the people of America. They laid the foundation upon which the emancipators built.

The year 1810 marked the formal outbreak of revolution in Spanish America. France's chief colony, Haiti, was already free. Portuguese Brazil would wait another dozen years. But in 1810 the *cabildos* of Spanish Caracas, Buenos Aires, Bogotá, Quito, and Santiago took their stand, registering their contempt for the upstart Joseph whom Napoleon had placed on the throne in Madrid and avowing their allegiance to the rightful Ferdinand VII. All these were municipal revolts, led by the wealthy creoles in opposition to the *peninsulares*. Only in Mexico did revolt start outside the capital city, led by a poor priest commanding an army of ragged Indians and mestizos. No master plan united all these first sporadic uprisings, but they were the prelude to the wars of independence which rocked Spanish America for more than a decade. These wars divide into three chief campaigns: first, the Mexican war for independence; second, the struggles in northern South America led by Simón Bolívar; and third, those in southern South America led by José de San Martín.

 [*Chapter 14*]

MEXICO'S WAR FOR INDEPENDENCE

When news came of Napoleon's usurpation of power in Madrid in 1808, there was considerable excitement in Mexico City. The creoles of the *cabildo*, eager to prove Mexico's loyalty to the deposed Ferdinand, entreated Viceroy Iturrigaray to form a junta which would hold New Spain in trust for Ferdinand. Iturrigaray wavered, and seemed inclined to assent; whereupon the Spanish contingent, fearful that the creoles would gain advantage, ousted Iturrigaray and installed their own man, Garibay. Further confusions and shifts in office ensued, but by the fateful year 1810 the Spaniards—the *gachupines*—were in undisputed control of the Mexican capital. Mexico was fated to be the one country in which revolt started not in the capital city but on the periphery—although the region in which revolution started was the center of profitable mining, and may be described as the economic heart of the country.

The standard-bearer of the Mexican Revolution was Father Miguel Hidalgo y Costilla, the parish priest in the village of Dolores some 100 miles northwest of the capital city. Hidalgo was a poor farmer's son. He was educated at the Colegio de San Nicolás (founded by the revered Vasco de Quiroga in Valladolid—now called Morelia), where he made an enviable record and won respect for his ranging and curious mind. He became rector, or president, of that institution and was widely known for his scholarship and good works. Then as an ordained priest he served in several curacies. However, by 1800 his reputation was clouded: he was an avid reader of the French philosophers, especially Rousseau; he was rumored to have spoken approvingly of the French Revolution; furthermore, he had fathered two daughters, whom he sheltered in paternal pride within his own home. Hidalgo was denounced to the Court of the Inquisition and charged with heresy and moral lapses: speaking disdainfully of the pope, questioning the virgin birth, and making his home and church a center for spreading dangerous ideas. He escaped conviction but was virtually banished to the unimportant village of Dolores. However, no matter what his irregularities may have been, his ministry at Dolores was a robust success. His passion for scholarship never lagged; he read volumi-

[247]

nously and mastered a number of Indian dialects. In his zeal to serve his humble parishioners, he taught them to improve their vineyards, to plant mulberry trees for the feeding of silkworms, and to operate a pottery works, a tannery, and a brickyard. He organized an orchestra for the Indians. He shared the deep conviction of Mendoza, Vasco de Quiroga, and the other great founders of the Church in Mexico, that the Church has a mission of social redemption for the poor. The poor of Dolores loved and respected him.

Hidalgo's convictions inevitably involved him in politics. He instinctively took sides with the underdogs of Mexican society—the Indian and the mestizo. His reading of the French philosophers had made him impatient of the slow-moving leaders of both Church and state, and prepared him for active participation in revolt. In the nearby city of Querétaro, a full-fledged conspiracy was under way which enlisted many important people, the Spanish *corregidor* himself as well as a wealthy young creole named Ignacio Allende. Hidalgo found this company congenial and immediately took an active share in the plotting. In early September, 1810, word reached Hidalgo that the Spanish authorities had discovered the plot, were about to strike, knew the names of the principal conspirators, and that it would be well to move without delay.

On Sunday morning, September 16, 1810, the priest distributed weapons to his trusted workmen, opened the jail, armed the prisoners, and then proceeded to the parish church, whose bells had summoned the people. The church and the churchyard were soon crowded with Indians armed with machetes. Hidalgo addressed his motley audience from his pulpit: "My children, this day comes to us a new dispensation. Are you ready to receive it? Will you be free? Will you make the effort to recover from the hated Spaniards the lands stolen from your forefathers 300 years ago?" The crowd shouted their approval, and then Hidalgo cried: *"Viva Nuestra Señora de Guadalupe, muera el mal gobierno, mueran los gachupines!"* This was the *grito de Dolores*, the battle cry of the Mexican Revolution—"Long live our Lady of Guadalupe, down with bad government, death to the Spaniards!" The Mexican Revolution was thus consecrated in the shadow of the altar.

The marching began. Father Hidalgo was followed by a crowd of ill-kempt, ragged, barefoot Indians, some mestizos, and a few creoles. They were armed with bows and arrows, clubs, pikes, machetes, and a few guns. The Indian women—the *soldaderas*—followed their men, foraged for supplies, and when night came cooked meals for them around 10,000 campfires. There may have been from 50,000 to 60,000 men in this "army." They carried banners bearing the image of the Virgin of Guadalupe, the symbol of Indian faith, the eternal proof of the identification of the Indian with the Mother of God. Other banners bore the inscriptions, *Long Live Religion, Long Live Ferdinand VII, Long Live America,* and *Down with Bad Government.* This was the kind of army that delighted the exuberant soul of Father Hidalgo. But it was not so pleasing to such careful and calculating men as Ignacio Allende. There was little discipline; supplies were scanty, and the men seized what they could from villagers along the way.

It was a war of revenge in which every Spaniard was a target for the pent-up fury of generations. Typical was the attack upon Guanajuato, for three centuries source of gold and silver for the Crown. When Hidalgo, "Captain-General of America" by his own appointment, approached that prosperous city with his unruly army, the Spanish *intendente* prepared to resist. Barricades were piled up in the principal streets, and the Spanish garrison of some 500 men occupied the Alhóndiga de Granaditas, the massive royal granary. Hidalgo's men occupied the city without difficulty, but met stout resistance from the soldiers who guarded the Alhóndiga; finally the patriots, by sheer force of numbers, overcame the Spanish forces and killed them to the last man. Terror swept the city and several thousand were killed. Such was the fashion in which Hidalgo's army ravaged as far west as Guadalajara, and then returned to the conquest of the capital itself.

Ill-defended, Mexico City might easily have been taken by a surprise attack, but Hildalgo stopped on the mountain road high above the city. His reasons were never explained. Was he fearful of the risks, or did he hesitate to turn loose his unruly mob upon the city? Whatever the explanation may be, Hidalgo turned back north toward Querétaro. Many adventurers deserted him, but more than 40,000 men remained to face the Spanish forces. On December 15, 1810, Hidalgo issued a proclamation from Valladolid (modern Morelia):

> Let us establish a Congress composed of representatives of all the cities and villages . . . which will enact mild and beneficent laws appropriate to the circumstances in each community. These representatives governing with the kindness of fathers, treating us all as brothers, will exile poverty, moderating the devastation of the country. . . . Crops will be stimulated, industry will come to life; we shall make free use of the intensely rich products of our fertile land and in a few years its inhabitants will enjoy the benefits which the sovereign author of nature has poured over this vast continent.[1]

Hidalgo's chief triumph came in the western city of Guadalajara, where he received a royal welcome and was granted the title of Serene Highness. But he was shortly evicted by the Spanish troops and driven north to Saltillo. Here news reached him that the Spanish royalist parliament meeting in Cádiz had decreed pardon for all rebels, and had invited Hidalgo to prove his loyalty to the exiled Ferdinand. Hidalgo, now stripped of most of his army, returned his indignant reply:

> In the discharge of our duty we will not lay aside our arms until we have wrested the jewel of liberty from the hands of the oppressor. We are resolved to enter into no arrangement which has not for its basis the liberty of the nation, and the enjoyment of those rights which the God

---

[1] Quoted by Lucas Alamán: *Historia de México* (Mexico: Victoriano Agueros y Comp.; 1883), Vol. II, App. Doc. 8.

of nature has granted all men—rights inalienable which must be sustained
by the shedding of rivers of blood if necessary. . . . Pardon, your excellency, is for criminals, not for defenders of their country.[2]

But Hidalgo's time was up. In March, 1811, he was captured by trickery,
tried and convicted by a military court, and stripped of his priestly robes.
He faced a firing squad on July 31, ten months after the *grito de Dolores*.
Inept as organizer and commander, Hidalgo had settled nothing. Nevertheless, he is remembered as the first hero of Mexican independence.
September 16, the day of Hidalgo's *grito de Dolores*, is Mexico's Independence Day.

Another leader was ready. José María Morelos was a squat mestizo
who had worked as a farm hand until his twenty-fifth year and then, after
a hurried schooling, had been ordained to the priesthood. He had little
intellectual curiosity and no such imagination and daring as had Hidalgo.
As a priest in the humble parish of Carácuaro near Lake Pátzcuaro, he had
a salary of sixteen pesos per month. He had won high praise for patience
and reliability, and he had never been accused of harboring dangerous
thoughts. Joining Hidalgo early in his campaign, Father Morelos had become one of his chief lieutenants. A skillful organizer, he had collected
a few volunteers, gathered more as he marched, and had won numerous
victories between Mexico and Acapulco. He was forty-six years old when
he took up the sword which Hidalgo laid down. In November, 1813, now
in control of most of southern Mexico, Morelos convened a congress at
Chilpancingo which declared Mexico's independence and drafted a constitution which was promulgated in 1814. Morelos proved himself a soldier of amazing capacity and an administrator of genius—"the most
extraordinary man produced by the war of independence," as the Mexican
historian Orozco y Berra describes him. However, the Spanish forces were
too powerful. Morelos was captured, taken to the prison of the Inquisition
in Mexico City, tried, convicted, stripped of his priestly robes, and shot
on December 22, 1815. His bones lie beneath the Monument of the Revolution in the Mexican capital, and a heroic statue of him stands on the island of Janitzio in Lake Pátzcuaro.

The Mexican Revolution floundered for five years after the death
of Morelos. In the south the guerrilla leaders, Vicente Guerrero and
Félix Fernández (popularly called Guadalupe Victoria), carried on their
fitful battles. Events in Mexico now mirrored events in Spain. Ferdinand
VII, restored to his throne in 1814, immediately rescinded the liberal
Constitution of 1812 and reimposed an absolutist regime—and the response of Mexican patriots was to shout more lustily for independence.
Then, in 1820, the liberals in Spain rose in revolt against Ferdinand, forc-
ing him to restore the 1812 instrument and to convene the parliament.
This step went far toward persuading Mexican conservatives that they
could no longer trust the mother country, which seemed to be falling into

<hr/>

[2] Emilio del Castillo Negrete: *México en el Siglo XIX* (28 vols.; Mexico, 1875–91),
Vol. III, p. 75; quoted by Ernest Gruening: *Mexico and Its Heritage* (New York: The
Century Company; 1928), p. 32.

the hands of dangerous liberals. The result was a rapid switch of wealthy Mexican creoles to the cause of independence, on the theory that a break with Spain would permit them to take over the mines, lands, banks, and sundry businesses owned by the hated *gachupines.* Only the *gachupines* remained faithful to Spain. Many of the principal clergy and landholders favored establishment in Mexico of an independent kingdom, and hoped that Ferdinand (whom they regarded as the unwilling prisoner of Spanish liberals) might be persuaded to come to America and rule over them. Out of this confusion of counsels emerged the man who was to lead Mexico into independent life—Agustín de Iturbide, one of America's most spectacular rascals.

Augustín de Iturbide was born in Valladolid in 1783, of a Spanish father and creole mother, into a family of wealth and social position. In 1810 Hidalgo invited the twenty-seven-year-old Iturbide to join him, but the young man, who avoided unpopular causes with a sure touch, refused. Instead, he enlisted in the Spanish army and fought with much bravery against Hidalgo and Morelos. "I have always been successful in war. . . . I never lost an action," he later admitted. With the cooling of revolutionary ardor after 1815, Iturbide settled down to enjoy the ease of the capital city. During the years from 1816 to 1820, that astute opportunist saw the gradual change of mind of the rich creoles, and reached the conclusion that it was only a matter of time until they, too, would espouse independence. He moved warily, with due regard for the Spanish authorities, and petitioned Viceroy Apodaca to name him commander of the Spanish armies in the south, where the rebel guerrillas of Guerrero were still active. Iturbide was appointed and marched south with 2,500 men, but instead of fighting Guerrero, he joined forces with him and made a compact to fight for the independence of Mexico. In order to finance that considerable undertaking, Iturbide raided a caravan transporting silver from Mexico to Acapulco and seized a half-million pesos.

Thus allied with Guerrero and financed by brigandage, Iturbide proclaimed his *Plan de Iguala,* a fervent appeal to "Americans . . . and under this name I include not only those born in America but also Europeans, Africans and Asiatics who live here." In lieu of a battle cry, he called his forces "The Army of the Three Guarantees": these guarantees were *religion,* which meant allegiance to the Holy Apostolic Roman Catholic religion; *independence,* preferably under a monarchy and with Ferdinand VII as king; and *union,* which promised equality for those born either in America or in Europe. This formula commended its author to all practical politicians everywhere, for it was designed to please everyone—or, more accurately, everyone who counted; of course it said nothing about the rights of Indians and poor mestizos. The program was an instant success. Numerous royalist generals turned to the support of Iturbide; the victory over loyal Spanish forces was soon won; and on September 27, 1821, Iturbide entered the city of Mexico in triumph. Independence had been won and Mexico was free. However, she still had Iturbide to deal with, not to mention numerous other shabby fellows.

Meanwhile, Central America, loosely joined to Mexico in the Vice-royalty of New Spain, had halfheartedly followed Mexico in asserting its independence. Guatemala City, seat of authority for the captain-general who presided over the entire region, created an independent junta in September, 1821; then the area was briefly annexed to Mexico—but in 1823 its people went their own way.

Chapter 15

THE INDEPENDENCE OF SPANISH
SOUTH AMERICA

The story of the liberation of Spain's empire in South America covers a period of fourteen years, beginning with the first gestures, a few "town meetings" in 1810, and ending with the decisive battle of Ayacucho in 1824. The story has scores of heroes, but they are overshadowed by the two commanders who are rightly called the liberators of South America: Simón Bolívar in the north and José de San Martín in the south. The debate as to their relative stature still continues. Each earned his place among the great soldiers of history. Nevertheless, the analysis of their likenesses and differences continues to be absorbing.

Bolívar and San Martín were alike in their zeal for winning the freedom of America, alike in their ability to command men and plan campaigns, and alike in the possession of personal courage. But two more utterly different men never lived and worked on one great assignment. Bolívar was emotional and glowing; his every word and gesture was vivid and dramatic. San Martín used few words and made no gestures. Bolívar never forgot that he walked a stage that was floodlighted for posterity. San Martín cared little what men said or thought, arranged no pageants for their titillation. Bolívar gloried in adulation and was warmed by the titles and decorations showered upon him. San Martín brusquely refused honors and gifts, and let others have credit which was due him. Bolívar, despite his repeated disavowals of personal ambition, enjoyed his role as creator of nations and may indeed have hoped for still greater honors and powers in years to come. San Martín, when confronted with Bolívar's jealousy, sailed away to a European exile, never complaining, never accusing. Both these disparate leaders succeeded in their central purpose—to sweep the Spanish garrisons into the sea, to banish the Spanish flag from the continent of South America. Both failed to influence greatly the political destinies of the lands they had freed. Both finally shared major credit for the emancipation of South America.

SIMÓN BOLÍVAR'S CAMPAIGNS
IN THE NORTH

On April 19, 1810, the *cabildo* of Caracas ousted the Spanish captain-general and organized a junta to rule in the name of the deposed Ferdinand VII. Thus were launched the fourteen years of wars that gave freedom to Venezuela, Colombia, Ecuador, Peru, and Bolivia. The first uprising in Caracas was no madcap revolt; it was the considered act of wealthy creoles who thought to serve their sovereign. But there were also hotheads in the movement, young men who insisted upon complete independence; a young aristocrat named Simón Bolívar was the leader of these intransigents.

Simón Bolívar was born in Caracas on July 24, 1783, to a family rich in land and slaves. Both his parents died during his childhood; and when he was seven, his education was turned over to tutors. One of these was the learned Andrés Bello; but the best beloved of his teachers was the erratic Simón Rodríguez, an ardent disciple of Jean Jacques Rousseau, who found in *Emile* the guide for the education of his young charge. Rodríguez's fiery persuasiveness was later acknowledged by Bolívar: "You have molded my heart for liberty, justice, greatness and beauty. I have followed the path you traced for me. You were my pilot. . . . You cannot imagine how deeply engraved upon my heart are the lessons you taught me." At seventeen, Simón was sent to Spain for more schooling. His wealth and position made him welcome in circles close to the profligate court of Charles IV. At nineteen, he married the niece of the Marquis of Toro and took her back to Caracas, where she died within a year. The grief-stricken Simón, vowing never to marry again, took refuge in the gay madness of Paris, seeking forgetfulness in a wasteful libertinism. He had now come into control of his patrimony, the equivalent of several million dollars in modern terms. In 1804 he was a delighted spectator when Napoleon proudly fixed the crown upon his own head; this was the sort of pageantry that he would emulate in his own days of triumph. But the young Bolívar was more than an idler, more than an onlooker. In 1805, with his old tutor Rodríguez as companion, he visited Rome. There he climbed the Aventine Hill, and fell upon his knees and called God to witness that he would never rest nor permit peace to his soul until he had broken the chains that bound his nation to Spain.

In 1810 Bolívar, leader of the rebels in Caracas, was dispatched to London in a vain attempt to secure British aid. While there, he persuaded that versatile advance agent of liberation, Francisco de Miranda, to return and help in the rebellion. By the end of 1810 both men were in Caracas: Bolívar, just twenty-seven and at the beginning of his career; Miranda, now sixty. A congress was then assembled, and a constitution was drafted and promulgated. On July 5, 1811, this congress declared Venezuela independent of Spain, "in the name of the all powerful God . . . appealing to the Supreme Being as witness to the justice of our demands and the rectitude of our intentions." Miranda was named commander in chief of the newly organized patriot army, and by early 1812 he was the virtual dictator of Venezuela.

Initial successes were followed by two cruel blows. On March 26, 1812, one of the most disastrous earthquakes in American history convulsed the country around Caracas, killing some 20,000 in the region where the patriots were strongest, but scarcely touching the centers of royalist power. In June the patriot army met a crushing defeat at Puerto Cabello. Then Miranda, after signing a humiliating capitulation, fled to the port of La Guaira where he planned to take ship for London. Simón Bolívar, who had become increasingly jealous of his superior, now accused Miranda of treachery and joined others in turning him over to the Spaniards. Bolívar, given a passport by the grateful Spaniards, sailed off to the Dutch island of Curaçao. Bolívar never attempted to justify his betrayal of the older man. The first round in the fight had been lost; in its further development, Simón Bolívar would play the title role.

The bitter reverses of 1812 did not break Bolívar's valiant spirit. Exiled from his country by the royalists, he stopped briefly in Curaçao, then went on to New Granada (modern Colombia) where the patriot struggle had followed much the same course as in Venezuela. There in high Bogotá other brave patriots were keeping up the fight. Among them was Antonio Nariño, just returned from a Cádiz prison where he had spent twelve years for his temerity in printing a translation of the French Assembly's *Declaration of the Rights of Man*. Here again Bolívar offered his services; but he soon felt compelled to return to Venezuela. He gathered a few hundred volunteers and started back, reaching Venezuela in March, 1813. There, with bloody thoroughness, he retaliated against the Spaniards' terrorism, proclaimed "war to the death," and butchered all Spanish prisoners. Bolívar's dramatic return to his fatherland evoked impetuous response from hitherto lethargic countrymen. Fresh recruits flocked to his aid as he marched toward Caracas; he occupied the capital in August. The patriot cause now seemed irresistible. In October, 1813, Bolívar was solemnly acclaimed as the Liberator, and in January, 1814, he was named dictator.

Meanwhile, Ferdinand was again on his Madrid throne, proclaiming rule by divine right and sending reinforcements to stamp out rebellion in America. But a change had come among solid citizens in Venezuela. They had originally struck at Napoleon in order to uphold Ferdinand. Now they were reluctant to follow Ferdinand as he attempted to restore royal absolutism. However, despite the increased zeal for independence, there were not enough men and munitions on the patriot side to withstand the better-armed royalists, and Bolívar's forces suffered costly defeats. In September, 1814, he had no choice but to admit that the enemy was too strong for him and to flee again to Curaçao, and from there to Cartagena in New Granada. The patriot forces of New Granada were also fighting a losing war with the augmented Spanish armies. With renewed hope, they welcomed Bolívar and appointed him their commander in chief, but even Bolívar could not restore the uneven balance. Spanish victories spread, and Bolívar left New Granada to find asylum on the English island of Jamaica.

It was a restless Liberator who was now forced into inaction for more than six months on an island whose English masters would not, or dared not, show sympathy for the cause he represented. But he was not idle. He tried to persuade the British that their future greatness and security depended upon the freedom of Spanish America. But his hosts, upon orders from London, kept silence. Meanwhile, he received reports of new reverses to the patriot cause in Venezuela and New Granada. He had moments when he thought the revolution was dead, that his life had been futile. He was now only thirty-two, but he was old beyond his years. His face was pale, but his black eyes still burned; he was far from beaten. He spent the days in writing. In his famous Letter from Jamaica, he poured out his diagnosis of the ills of Spanish America and the possible lines of its redemption. He wrote to his unnamed (and probably nonexistent) correspondent: "We are threatened with the fear of death, dishonor, and every harm; there is nothing we have not suffered at the hands of that unnatural stepmother—Spain. The veil has been torn asunder. We have already seen the light and it is not our desire to be thrust back into darkness."[1]

He summarized the situation in the various parts of Spanish America, revealing profound insight into political realities. He analyzed the dire lack of political schooling among the colonists: "The role of the inhabitants of the American hemisphere has for centuries been purely passive. Politically they were non-existent. We are still in a position lower than slavery, and therefore it is more difficult for us to rise to the enjoyment of freedom. . . . We find that America was denied not only its freedom but even an active and effective tyranny." He continued: "We have been harassed by a conduct which has not only deprived us of our rights but has kept us in a sort of permanent infancy with regard to public affairs. If we could at least have managed our domestic affairs and our internal administration, we could have acquainted ourselves with the processes and mechanics of public affairs." Spain, he said, had denied positions of responsibility to American-born creoles: "We were never viceroys or governors, save in the rarest of instances; seldom archbishops and bishops; diplomats never; as military men, only subordinates; as nobles, without royal privileges."

He dwelt upon his hopes for the future government of Spanish America: "I desire," he wrote, "to see America fashioned into the greatest nation in the world, greatest not so much by virtue of her area and wealth as by her freedom and glory. Although I seek perfection for the government of my country, I cannot persuade myself that the new world can, at the moment, be organized as a great republic. Since it is impossible, I dare not desire it; yet much less do I desire to have all America a monarchy because this plan is not only impracticable but also impossible. Wrongs now existing could not be righted, and our emancipation would be fruitless. The American states need the care of paternal governments to heal the sores

1 This and following quotations are taken from *Selected Writings of Bolívar*, compiled by Vicente Lecuna, edited by Harold A. Bierck, Jr., translated by Lewis Bertrand (New York: Colonial Press; 1951), Vol. I, pp. 103–22. Reprinted by permission of the Banco de Venezuela.

and wounds of despotism and war." He then debated the possibility that some one country—possibly Mexico—might take the lead as a presiding parent. He suggested that the future might be safer with a number of small republics: "The distinctive feature of small republics is permanence: that of large republics varies, but always with a tendency towards empire. Almost all small republics have had long lives. Among the larger republics only Rome lasted for several centuries, for its capital was a republic."

He conjectured on the fate of various parts of Spanish America. Of Chile he wrote: "If any American republic is to have a long life, I am inclined to believe it will be Chile. There the spirit of liberty has never been extinguished; the vices of Europe and Asia arrived too late, or not at all, to corrupt the customs of that distant corner of the world. . . . In a word, it is possible for Chile to be free." Of Peru, he said that it "contains two factors that clash with every just and liberal principle: gold and slaves. The former corrupts everything; the latter are themselves corrupt. A soul of a serf can seldom really appreciate true freedom. Either he loses his head in uprisings or his self-respect in chains." Mexico, he thought, would "establish a representative republic in which the executive will have great powers." He noted how easily such power in a single person might degenerate into tyranny or into an absolute monarchy, and remarked that "Only a people as patriotic as the English are capable of controlling the authority of a king and of sustaining the spirit of liberty under the rule of scepter and crown."

He speculated on the future of the New World as a whole: "It is a grandiose idea to think of consolidating the New World into a single nation, united by pacts into a single bond. It is reasoned that, as these parts have a common origin, language, customs, and religion, they ought to have a single government to permit the newly formed states to unite in a confederation. But this is not possible. Actually, America is separated by climatic differences, geographic diversity, conflicting interests, and dissimilar characteristics. How beautiful it would be if the Isthmus of Panama could be for us what the Isthmus of Corinth was for the Greeks! Would to God that some day we may have the good fortune to convene there an august assembly of representatives of republics, kingdoms, and empires to deliberate upon the high interests of peace and war with the nations of the other three-quarters of the globe."

Bolívar had no dogmatic prescription for the future government of Spanish America. He was skeptical of the federal system. "It is over-perfect, and it demands political virtues and talents far superior to our own. For the same reason," he continued, "I reject a monarchy that is part aristocracy and part democracy although with such a government England has achieved much fortune and splendor." So he noted: "Since it is not possible for us to select the most perfect and complete form of government, let us avoid falling into demagogic anarchy or monocratic tyranny. These opposite extremes would only wreck us on similar reefs of misfortune and dishonor; hence, we must seek a mean between them. I say: do not adopt the best system of government, but the one which is most likely to succeed."

After a six months' interlude among the indifferent residents of Jamaica, Bolívar impulsively set off for Cartagena but shortly was deterred by news of royalist strength. He then decided to try his fortunes in the friendly ex-slave republic of Haiti. There President Alexandre Pétion had been providing food and housing for numerous patriot refugees from the mainland; and he now helped to equip Bolívar for his proposed assault upon Venezuela. Bolívar's expedition was ready by March, 1816; it consisted of some 250 officers and supplies for the army of 5,000 which he expected to recruit once he had established himself on the mainland. He succeeded in landing on the northwestern coast of Venezuela; he announced his plans to the lethargic population, who dutifully hailed him as "Supreme Chief of the Republic" but did not enlist with the enthusiasm he had expected. He fulfilled a pledge made to Pétion by decreeing freedom to all slaves. Then, with Spanish forces converging on his small company, he sailed back to Haiti.

Three events contributed to Bolívar's final success in Venezuela during the years 1817–20. The first was alliance with José Antonio Páez, the brilliant leader of the *llaneros*—rough, illiterate horsemen who feared neither God nor man. In the earlier phases of the revolution, the *llaneros,* then commanded by a brutal Spaniard named Boves, had served the royalist cause. Páez finally won their support, persuading them that the enemy was Spain and that they should fight for their *patria.* Páez and his *llaneros*—whose stronghold was in the valley of the Apure, a tributary of the Orinoco in the far south—definitely turned the tide against the Spaniards. The second was the decision to postpone the contest for possession of the heavily populated Caracas area and to concentrate upon the Orinoco basin, which had abundant cattle, water communications both with the outside world and with New Granada, and plenty of fighters among the *llaneros.* The third was the arrival of reinforcements from England, a few in 1817, and over 4,000 in 1819. These welcome volunteers proved to be Bolívar's best fighters and his useful aides in drilling raw recruits. That motley crowd of English, Scottish, Irish, and German adventurers acquitted themselves with honor in the difficult campaigns that finally assured independence to both Venezuela and New Granada.

Thanks to these various reinforcements, Bolívar's strength mutiplied. He held firmly the eastern and southern areas, establishing a temporary capital in Angostura (now Ciudad Bolívar) near the mouth of the Orinoco; Spaniards commanded by Morillo held most of the north. Bolívar's efforts to dislodge the Spaniards were costly and ineffective; and his alliance with Páez, though invaluable, proved exceedingly difficult: Páez time and again would decide to act independently, without reference to Bolívar's plans. Nevertheless, by February, 1819, enough of the country was united under the patriot banner for Bolívar to justify convening a congress in Angostura. The Liberator gave sage advice to that body about the need for strong centralized authority and the wisdom of following British experience.

Meanwhile, even though the war was far from won in Venezuela, Bolívar decided he must strike in New Granada. He started out from the hot lowlands of the Apure valley with an army of more than 2,000, including some British allies. They pushed across the tropical jungle with its torrential rivers; they clambered up the jagged granite trails of the Andean wall and over icy passes two miles above the sea. The men suffered from the cold and from *soroche,* mountain sickness. Almost all the horses died. The battered army finally had a breathing spell on the plains near Bogotá, where they shortly met the enemy at Boyacá on August 7, 1819; there they won the victory which assured the independence of New Granada. Simón Bolívar entered Bogotá with the fanfare so pleasing to him, and was acclaimed Liberator of New Granada. Then, leaving Santander as vice-president at the head of a provisional government in Bogotá, he returned to Angostura in Venezuela.

After quieting factional disputes in the congress there, he used that body as a sounding board to announce, in December, 1819, his grandiose scheme for uniting Venezuela, New Granada, and the still unconquered Ecuador into a new state called Gran Colombia. This was essentially the ukase of a dictator and betrayed both the audacity and the impracticality of its author. Neither New Granada nor Venezuela had given evidence of desiring to live with the other, and few Ecuadorians had even heard of the project. Furthermore, the three areas thus yoked in Bolívar's imagination were separated by jungles and mountains and had little in common economically or culturally. To be sure, they had been united in the Viceroyalty of New Granada, but there had never been much traffic in ideas among them. Bolívar imposed his plan upon peoples who did not understand what it meant and did not care.

With the dawn of 1820, it was still necessary to rid Venezuelan soil of its last Spanish troops. This achievement was hastened by the liberal revolt in Spain, which resulted in the seating of a new government. General Morillo was ordered to reach an understanding with Bolívar; in November, 1820, the two men signed an armistice and Morillo returned to Spain. Two months later the patriot armies broke the armistice by marching toward the royalist stronghold on Lake Maracaibo. On June 24, 1821, Bolívar's army of 6,500 men defeated a somewhat smaller Spanish force at Carabobo. This victory assured the freedom of Venezuela, although the last royalist garrisons were not dislodged from Maracaibo and Puerto Cabello until 1823.

Bolívar next decided that his unrealistic creation, Gran Colombia, must have constitutional status. Soon after the victory of Carabobo, a constituent congress representing Venezuela and New Granada was summoned to meet at Cúcuta, near the border between the two nations. Despite inadequate representation of the peoples involved and general apathy, Bolívar dictated a constitution, which provided for strong centralized power, a capital in Bogotá, and a bicameral congress with senators and deputies from Venezuela, New Granada, and Ecuador. Bolívar, stoutly protesting, was elected president; Francisco de Paula Santander, acquiescent, was named vice-president, with the understanding that he would do the actual ruling while Bolívar did the fighting. It was an awkward formula certain to provoke discord between the two men.

The close of 1821 saw the pattern of disjointed Gran Colombia all neatly cut out—at least on paper. It pleased almost no one: certainly not Santander, who immediately schemed to separate New Granada from the union; certainly not Páez, who was dashing about with his rough *llaneros,* inventing new schemes for Venezuela that would never fit into Bolívar's plan. But it was characteristic of the robust enthusiasm of Simón Bolívar that he could ride roughshod and with clear conscience over indifference and hostility. He still had much work to do.

Bolívar was eager to carry his campaign south, to notify Quito and Guayaquil that Ecuador—the ancient Inca kindom of Quitu—was now a part of Gran Colombia. And still further south, he must expel the Spanish garrisons from Peru, the last royalist stronghold in South America. To be sure, his great contemporary, José de San Martín, had already been in Peru for more than a year and had proclaimed its freedom in July, 1821; but for a man like Simón Bolívar, the job would not be well done until he himself took charge.

In December, 1821, Bolívar was at last free to start. He marched overland, crossing the spurs of the cordillera which lie between Bogotá and the Cauca valley, encountering here and there nests of stubborn royalists. Months before, he had sent José Antonio de Sucre, his ever-faithful friend and general, south by sea with an advance force. Sucre had bolstered the patriot cause in the port city of Guayaquil and had then climbed the mountains to 9,250-foot-high Quito, where he routed the Spanish army on the slopes of Pichincha on May 24, 1822. Shortly thereafter, Bolívar and his men arrived and made their triumphal entry into the ancient Inca stronghold. Against the backdrop of snow-capped volcanoes, down streets lined with superb colonial churches and palaces, through crowds that shouted their joy and praise, came the procession of the Liberator. Here was pageantry and imperial splendor: Simón Bolívar had not forgotten Napoleon's lessons in pomp. Here, too, was romance: as Bolívar rode beneath a balcony in Quito, he caught the eye of a spirited girl who threw him a wreath of flowers; that evening the Liberator and the girl met at the ball—and from that hour to the day of his death, the story of Simón Bolívar was intimately bound with that of the lovely, quick-tempered Manuela Sáenz.[2] But there were tasks to be accomplished. He must persuade the

[2] Manuela Sáenz offers rare material for the biographer. Of the many women in Bolívar's life, none held his loyalty and affection longer than she. The wife of a Briton, she was high-spirited, brilliant in conversation, and reckless in her exuberance and refusal to conform. She brought Bolívar joy and embarrassment. Time and again he would banish her, only to call her back to his side. We have his letter to her from Bogotá: "Your kindness and grace dissolve the frost of my years . . . your love gives back life which is expiring. I cannot live without you. . . . I have not as much strength as you, not to see you; an immense distance hardly suffices. I see you, though I am far away. Come, come, come now. My soul is yours."

We learn something of Manuela from the letter to the husband who implored her to return. "No, no, no, never again, man, so help me heaven . . . Señor, you are excellent, you are inimitable, I shall never say anything else about you; but you, my friend, to leave you for General Bolívar is something: to leave another husband without your qualities, would be nothing . . . and do you believe I, after being the beloved of this general for seven years, with the certainty of possessing his heart, would choose to be the wife of the Father, the Son or the Holy Spirit. . . . I know very well I can never be joined to him with what

leaders of Quito and of Guayaquil to cast in their fortunes with Gran Colombia. Guayaquil, the more vocal of the two cities, inclined toward union with Peru. Bolívar's charm—and armed forces—persuaded them to join Gran Colombia. Bolívar's dream had been realized—or so it appeared.

There must now be a shift of scene. We have traveled with Bolívar through the campaigns of Venezuela, New Granada, and Ecuador. We leave him in torrid, fever-ridden Guayaquil in July, 1822, on the eve of his fateful meeting with the Liberator of the South, José de San Martín. Only against the background of San Martín's experiences in Argentina, Chile, and Peru will it be possible to understand that strange meeting of the two men who shared the honor of emancipating Spanish South America.

SAN MARTÍN AND THE LIBERATION
OF THE FAR SOUTH

While Bolívar fought in the north, San Martín fought in the south. The southern wars began with the defiant pronouncement of the Buenos Aires *cabildo abierto* (open town meeting) in 1810; San Martín carried the banner of La Plata over the Andes to reinforce the losing battle of the patriots in Chile; and from there he led the men of La Plata and Chile north to Lima, the citadel of Spanish power in South America, setting in motion the forces which finally, under Bolívar, assured liberty to Peru and Bolivia. It was there in the land of the Incas that the liberating armies won the final victory over Spain.

In approaching the story of José de San Martín, we must first recount the events which led to Buenos Aires's break with Spain in 1810, and the course of that struggle during the four fateful years before San Martín took command of the army of liberation.

Two sets of circumstances dictated the course of Buenos Aires's first moves toward independence. Internally, the tempers of the enterprising *porteños,* "the port dwellers," had reached the boiling point over their economic grievances. Throughout most of the colonial period, Buenos Aires had been treated as the neglected stepchild of Spain. For almost three cen-

---

you call honorable love. Do you think me less honored because he is my lover and not my husband? Ah, I do not live by the social preoccupations invented for mutual torment. In heaven we shall marry again; but not on earth. In paradise we shall pass an angelic life, one wholly spiritual (because as a man you are heavy). Everything there will be in the English manner, since monotonous life is reserved for your people . . . love is arranged for them without pleasure, conversation without grace, the walk is hurried, the salutation is without reverence, they get up and sit down with caution, they do not laugh at their own jokes; all these are sacred formalities; but I, miserable mortal, who laugh at myself, at you, at these English seriousnesses, how I shall suffer in heaven! As much as if I had to go and live in England or Constantinople. . . . Have I bad taste? Enough of jokes: formally and without laughing . . . I shall tell you that I shall never join myself to you again. That you are an Anglican and I a pagan, is the strongest spiritual obstacle; that I am in love with someone else is still better and stronger. Don't you see with what precision I reason? Your invariable friend, Manuela." This letter is quoted by Hildegarde Angell: *Simón Bolívar, South American Liberator* (New York: W. W. Norton and Co.; 1930), pp. 243–4.

turies her port had been closed and all trade had been routed through Lima, some 3,000 miles overland by a trail over which mule trains made the journey in three months. (At least in theory trade was to follow that route; in practice, the La Plata basin enjoyed profitable contraband trade with Portuguese, English, and other freebooters.) In 1776, under the pressure of the encroaching Portuguese from Brazil, the administrative unit of the Viceroyalty of La Plata was formed (including the area now divided among Argentina, Uruguay, Paraguay, and Bolivia), and Buenos Aires became the seat of the viceregal court. That city was a straggling, unpaved, unlighted, unpoliced town of some 24,000 people when this honor came to her. Now brighter days appeared.

In 1777 Spain made peace with Portugal and the pressure from Brazil was removed. The port of Buenos Aires was opened for direct trade with Spain and the other Spanish colonies. During the years 1792–95, forty-seven vessels sailed from the port, and fifty-three entered; exports and imports aggregated more than $8 million. Streets were paved, houses and public buildings were constructed, and by 1800 the population had reached 40,000. But the *porteños* now realized that it was rich England, not impoverished Spain, that constituted the most profitable market for hides and salted beef. Unofficially, the contraband trade continued and increased. Officially, the demand for free trade grew, the first official petition for that concession being forwarded to the Crown in 1793. The clamor for free trade increased during the Napoleonic Wars, when all economic grievances were aggravated. This was the troubled mood of the traders of Buenos Aires during the first years of the nineteenth century. They had tasted the sweets of profit and wanted more.

Then, the broils of Europe reached Buenos Aires. In England, William Pitt, watching Napoleon stamp up and down the Continent and aware that he might soon appropriate not only Spain but some of Spain's colonies, decided that England must take a hand. Pitt's reasoning was clear: the Napoleonic Wars had cut off much of his nation's trade; England needed Spanish America as a source of bullion and an outlet for industrial goods. Pitt toyed with the idea of fomenting revolts in the Spanish colonies (as his subsidized friend, Francisco de Miranda, had long urged), or of seizing for England a few strategic ports in America. Pitt's death in 1806 did not end such thinking.

On June 27, 1806, an English squadron commanded by Sir Home Popham appeared in the Río de la Plata and landed 1,700 men under Colonel Beresford, who quickly occupied the city without meeting more than token resistance. The Spanish Viceroy, surprised while viewing a play, fled precipitately to Córdoba. Beresford proclaimed British sovereignty, named himself governor, and demanded allegiance to George III. He attempted to calm the *porteños* by promising full respect for their Catholic faith, the sanctity of private property, evenhanded administration of justice, and—most eloquent of all—free trade. He also borrowed a million pesos from the royal coffers—a consignment of bullion earmarked, it was thought, for the Spanish treasury—and sent it to England with a request for reinforcements. Sir Home's audacious *coup d'état,* unauthorized by London, was so far a complete success. He immediately wrote Francisco de Miranda, with whom he had discussed projects for joint action against Spain in America, reporting his success and inviting that mercurial genius to use Buenos Aires as his base in any plans he might undertake. Unfortunately for Popham, his mentor Pitt was now dead and he was acting on his own initiative, a circumstance which prompted his government to recall him for stern reprimand. A year later, however, the government, under a new cabinet, sent another naval expedition to Buenos Aires.

Meanwhile, events in Buenos Aires proved that the British did not understand the temper of their unwilling hosts. No matter how the *porteños* may have wearied of Spanish rule, it did not follow that they would welcome another imperial overlord in the person of George III. A British officer in Beresford's occupation forces noted how few able-bodied men appeared in the Buenos Aires streets and discovered too late that all the healthy males were drilling assiduously outside the city. In August this citizen army, led by Santiago Liniers, a Frenchman in the service of Spain, evicted the British intruders. Emboldened by their success, the *porteños* gathered in a *cabildo abierto* and named Liniers their supreme military commander. When the British, with typical pertinacity, appeared again with augmented forces in June, 1807, the *porteño* army made short shrift of them. And when one of the British vessels failed to catch the tide and got stuck in the mud, *porteño* horsemen dashed out through the shallow water and boarded her.

The chief result of these skirmishes was to give the *porteños* such assurance of their own competence that when the time came they would not truckle to any alien interloper. And then, too, they had experienced briefly the blessings of free trade. Liniers, in expedient mood, permitted many English traders to remain after the soldiers were ousted and made no effort to end the enlarged contraband trade. Liniers was the hero of the day: he was named acting viceroy by the Spanish Crown and managed to hold his office until 1809, when he was supplanted by Hidalgo de Cisneros, who faced the growing demands of the *porteños* for free trade.

In September, 1809, a tract appeared from the pen of Mariano Moreno, a thirty-one-year-old creole lawyer, advocating free trade for a two-year trial period. His arguments were reminiscent of Adam Smith. A prosperous people, Moreno argued, will not revolt. Illicit trade with England, he continued, is already general and lucrative; now let it be legalized, and all will prosper. Such argument could not be ignored, for it was tenaciously held by the influential creoles; and the creoles controlled the civil militia which had been organized to drive off the British in 1806-07. Furthermore, even the *chapetones* (the "tenderfeet," as the *peninsulares* were derisively called in Argentina), who represented Spanish monopolistic policy, reluctantly admitted that it might be well to concede free trade to the *porteños,* as the least dangerous way of escape from serious economic crisis. In November, 1809, the viceroy capitulated and decreed a limited freedom of trade with nations allied to Spain or neutral in the Napoleonic Wars. These concessions, generous as compared with the niggardly treatment in the past, resulted in increased trade but did not satisfy the patriots.

The immediate occasion for the final break was furnished by the turn of the political wheel in Europe. Napoleon's unseating of the Bourbon king in Madrid in 1808 excited anger throughout the Spanish world. For two years the forces of Ferdinand still held part of Spain; then in 1810 French forces swept south and seized Seville and Cádiz, the centers of Bourbon resistance. The news of this final affront reached Buenos Aires in May, 1810, and inspired the summoning of a *cabildo abierto* on May 22 to discuss the future course of the colony. Spokesmen for the various sectors voiced their convictions: the Bishop of Buenos Aires demanded loyalty to the viceroy; other conservative citizens urged that the legal *cabildo* assume power in Ferdinand's name; and the influential creoles demanded a ruling junta composed of members chosen by "the people."

Three days later the dignified members of the regular *cabildo* met to consider these demands; and, after a second look at the well-drilled militia of the creoles, they found it expedient to create a "provisional junta of the Provinces of the Río de la Plata, governing for Ferdinand VII," and to name as members those nominated by the creoles. The junta was headed by Cornelio Saavedra as president and Mariano Moreno as one of the secretaries; it included Manuel Belgrano and Bernardino Rivadavia. They were a strangely disparate group. Saavedra was a pompous man who viewed his new position as tantamount to that of viceroy. He, too, would have a court, would be accorded the homage due a ruler, and would drive over the rough streets of Buenos Aires in a rich carriage drawn by finely caparisoned horses (eight of them to his carriage, one eyewitness reported). Belgrano was a studious, honest, and devoted patriot, whom ill fortune sent into battle as a general when he would have served better as an administrator. Rivadavia was a versatile and exasperating genius, with the appearance of a gay dandy but with a varied and inventive ability which made him a useful public servant for almost twenty years. But the dynamic leader of that "provisional junta of the Provinces of the Río de la Plata, governing for Ferdinand VII" was the fiery young *porteño* lawyer, Mariano Moreno.

Mariano Moreno, "the soul of the revolution" and author of the economic broadside of 1809, was the most able and energetic member of the junta during its first months. Despite the dislike of the pretentious Saavedra and the unpredictable Rivadavia, Moreno seems to have dominated the junta—a triumph explained by his hold upon the creoles. He was largely responsible for exiling the viceroy and the *audiencia* to the Canary Islands; for easing trade restrictions, founding a national library, and organizing a census bureau; and for reforms in the army and negotiations with the Vatican to define the patronage issue. He also edited the official newspaper, *La Gaceta de Buenos Aires*. Moreno, in common with his colleagues, at first professed loyalty to discredited Ferdinand. But it became abundantly clear that for many solid citizens this was sheer Machiavellian strategy. Moreno really stood for complete independence. When an attempt was made to secure recognition by the junta of the pro-Ferdinand Council of Regency in Spain, Moreno opposed it and won his point; by this he gave impetus to the movement for complete separation.

Opposition to Moreno gained momentum. It came to a head when Saavedra forced the seating of a group of reactionary provincial delegates in the central junta, an action vigorously opposed by Moreno. This was the first round in the long struggle between the *unitarios*, protagonists of centralized power, and the federalists, who would permit each province to chart its own anarchic course. Confronted by the strength of his federalist opponents, Moreno resigned after seven months in office; he accepted a diplomatic mission to England and died at sea on his way to London. This was a crippling loss to the junta, as was the departure of Belgrano at about the same time for military duty in Paraguay. Without these two men, the junta lost its popular support, and in September, 1811, it was replaced by a triumvirate of uncertain powers and rapidly shifting personnel which lasted another two years. (The one leader of consequence to outlast the junta and to serve in the triumvirate was Rivadavia.) By 1814 rule by committee had proved so futile that all sectors welcomed one-man rule under a supreme director, but the mediocre politician who got the office lasted little more than a year. By mid-1815 the "united" provinces were splitting apart, and it was with difficulty that a majority were cajoled into sending delegates to a congress in northern Tucumán in 1816. There a constitution was adopted, independence was at last declared (on July 9, 1816), and a national executive, Supreme Director Juan Martín Pueyrredón, was chosen. We will not tarry here to describe the difficulties under which he struggled for three years in office, the strident disunity which blocked his efforts to create a nation, or the general anarchy and confusion of the 1820's. That story properly belongs to the record of independent Argentina. It is sufficient for our present narrative to note the background of divided counsels and the jealous rivalry of the provinces during the period of the wars for independence.

During the six years from 1810 to 1816, there was a general breaking up of the region which Spain had called the Viceroyalty of La Plata. Immediately after its appointment in 1810, the junta had invited allegiance from the outlying areas. Moreno and Belgrano attempted to hold the widely separated provinces together, and were the chief protagonists of centralized authority in Buenos Aires. The junta, thinking to use both persuasion and compulsion, sent a small force under Manuel Belgrano to Asunción. There the stiff-necked Paraguayans had already decided that they would rule their own affairs and not bow to Buenos Aires. They easily brushed off Belgrano's small force early in 1811 and continued to repulse all overtures from the central junta. Finally in 1813, under José Gaspar Rodríguez Francia, one of the shrewdest and most durable dictators in Latin American history, the Paraguayans declared their independence not only of Spain, but also of Buenos Aires.

Buenos Aires also had trouble with the Banda Oriental (the "East Bank," i.e., modern Uruguay). It had long been disputed territory between Spain and Portugal, but its Spanish status had finally been settled by treaty in 1777–78. The *porteños* invited the Banda Oriental to join them in 1810, but the Uruguayans (the *orientales*) found themselves embarrassed by the presence of the newly appointed Spanish Viceroy Elío, who, spurned by

Buenos Aires, had established his court across the Plata in Montevideo. That royalist spokesman (so cavalierly treated by the *porteños* who professed to love Ferdinand) now became the target for attack by a rough crew of Gauchos led by José Gervasio Artigas, the man remembered as the hero of Uruguayan independence. Elio solicited aid from the Portuguese Court, which had been transferred from Lisbon to Rio de Janeiro in 1808, and found an eager listener in Carlota Joaquina, wife of Prince Regent John. That sister of Spain's deposed Ferdinand VII regarded herself as the guardian of her brother's threatened domain in La Plata. Through her influence a small Portuguese force moved south into the Banda Oriental in 1811 to protect Elio and the royalists against both Artigas and Buenos Aires. The three-way fight continued, with Uruguay the battleground between Brazil and Buenos Aires. Artigas repulsed the Brazilians and then dallied with Buenos Aires for two years, offering to unite the Banda Oriental with the junta if he were promised complete autonomy for his domain. In 1813 Buenos Aires, obsessed with zeal for centralized authority, refused such concession, and Artigas and his horsemen decided that Uruguay must be a separate and sovereign state. In 1814 *porteño* soldiers occupied Montevideo; and in 1815 Artigas threw them out. In 1816 the Portuguese returned in greater force, carried on a running fight with Artigas for four years, and by 1820 were in virtual control. Not until 1828, after an inconclusive war between Brazil and Argentina was terminated by British mediation, was the independent status of Uruguay finally assured.

Upper Peru (modern Bolivia) was also a part of the Viceroyalty of La Plata. Its rich mines, a chief source of Spanish colonial wealth for three centuries, were guarded by strong Spanish garrisons. The *porteños* ordered General Manuel Belgrano, who had failed to subdue Asunción but who had won victories in northern Tucumán and Salta, to carry the war to Upper Peru. Belgrano obeyed; but his troops were hopelessly outnumbered, and he was compelled to fight at a disadvantage on the *altiplano*. His defeat in 1813 postponed the liberation of Upper Peru until 1825, when Bolívar and Sucre would drive out the last Spanish soldiers and give it the name of Bolivia. Failure in this last mission brought undeserved reproach to the gallant Belgrano and prepared the way for the emergence of José de San Martín.

The figure of José de San Martín has grown in stature with the years. The people of Argentina gave him scant support while he fought their battles, rewarded him with contempt when he returned from his triumphs, and ignored him during his last twenty-eight years of retirement and exile; but finally, long after his death, they gave him the honors due him. Today almost every village boasts a plaza or a street bearing his name; and Argentine school children study the life of their hero as Americans study that of Washington. The life of San Martín—according to his biographer Ricardo Rojas—falls into three chief periods: the years from 1778 to 1817 were the "initiation"; from 1817 to 1822, the "achievement"; from 1822 to 1850, the "renunciation."

San Martín was born in 1778 in Yapeyú, a Jesuit village on the northern frontier of Argentina in what is now the province of Misiones. His father was a Spanish officer, and when the boy was seven the family returned to Spain. The young José began his military career at the age of eleven and worked his way up in the ranks until, after twenty-two years of service, he was a lieutenant colonel. When Ferdinand VII was pushed out by Napoleon, the young officer resigned his commission and returned to his native land. In 1812 he offered his services to the government of Buenos Aires, thereby expressing his conviction that the time had come to sever all ties with Spain. He made his stand even clearer by joining the Lautaro Lodge (named for the Araucanian lad who fought Valdivia), a secret order modeled after the Freemasons and made up of militant believers in independence. San Martín was first and last a soldier; he never pretended to competence in statecraft, although he expressed fear of chaotic federalism and preference for constitutional monarchies. His chief business was to fight Spaniards until America was free.

After the shelving of General Belgrano, San Martín was appointed to fill his place in 1814, and he was immediately ordered to enlist a force for fresh attack upon Upper Peru. But he was convinced that such an attack could not be successful and, pleading illness, he resigned his post. He then begged to be made governor of the province of Cuyo, under the shadow of the Andes in the far west. His health, he explained, would improve in Mendoza's clear air; his true plans, which he discreetly hid, covered more than his health. San Martín's strategy was based upon conviction that the stronghold of Spanish power, both in royalist sentiment and in strength of garrisons, was in Peru, and that until Peru was liberated there could be no freedom for Spanish America. This conclusion was not new, for Belgrano had thought to attack Peru through Bolivia: what was new was San Martín's strategy. His plan was to establish his headquarters in western Argentina, gather his forces, store up material, then move over the Andes into Chile; there he would reinforce the patriots who were waging a losing battle with the Spanish garrisons; and then, with Chilean reinforcements, he would move north for the emancipation of Peru. San Martín got the appointment to Cuyo upon which his project depended, and he proceeded to carry out his plan step by step during the eight years that followed.

For three years, from 1814 to 1817, San Martín organized his forces in Cuyo. He had scant support from the confused leaders of Buenos Aires, who were torn by divided counsels, opposed by outlying provinces, and powerless to speak for a united nation. He was compelled to seek out his own recruits and to gather materials as he could. One of his first tasks was to enlist refugees from Chile. The Chilean struggle for independence, begun in 1810, had been marked by fierce contests between factions headed by Bernardo O'Higgins and his rivals, the Carrera brothers. By 1814 the divided patriots had lost to the Spanish garrisons, and now many of the rank and file made their way to Mendoza. San Martín had to choose between the rival Chilean contestants and decided upon O'Higgins, thereby angering the Carreras. With recruits from Chile and soldiers of fortune and patriots who drifted in from Buenos Aires and the provinces, San

Martín increased his nucleus of 180 men to a force of some 5,000. But he was still desperately short of clothing, munitions, guns, and supplies of all sorts. His young wife, forced by ill health to spend most of her time in Buenos Aires, persuaded women of fashion to contribute their jewels, and the government of Pueyrredón helped a little. Invaluable aid was given by the priest Luis Beltrán, who had served in the revolutionary army of Chile and had then joined San Martín in Mendoza. He was a versatile genius with considerable knowledge of mathematics, physics, and chemistry. He now set up foundries and factories where church bells were melted down to make guns and bullets; bayonets and swords were hammered out; and portable suspension bridges were contrived.

Meanwhile, in 1816, delegates representing all areas of the old viceroyalty were summoned to a congress in the northern Argentine city of Tucumán. This congress took some steps toward national unity, and elected Juan Martín Pueyrredón as supreme director with theoretically extensive powers. Pueyrredón favored San Martín's strategy and gave him what little backing he could. But San Martín was not greatly admired by the leaders of Buenos Aires and was alternately abused and neglected. He wrote to a friend: "In fine, my friend, I do not feel the shots fired against me at all, but their repetition bores the most stoic of men." San Martín was more than bored: he was continually embarrassed by the vacillating rulers of Buenos Aires who could not decide whether to return to allegiance to Spain, to import a king of their own, or to establish a republic. He wrote of them: "This does not seem to be a revolution of men but of sheep." Meanwhile, Ferdinand had returned to his throne, and his uncertain defenders were confronted with a fact and no longer a theory. By the time the Tucumán congress convened in 1816, the sentiment of loyalty to Ferdinand, never very real, had been largely dissipated. San Martín helped to clarify the issue by the letter he wrote to one of the delegates:

> How long must we wait to declare our independence? Don't you think it is ridiculous to mint coins, have a flag and coat of arms, and to make war against the very government that is supposed to rule over us? What is there to do but to say it? Besides what international relations can we have when we act as minors under a guardian and the enemy (with perfect reason) calls us insurgents, inasmuch as we still call ourselves vassals? Be sure that nobody will help us under these conditions. Besides, the system would gain fifty percent with this step. Courage! Great undertakings are for men of courage. Let us see clearly, my friend: if this is not done, the Congress will be invalid in all it does, inasmuch as if it assumes sovereignty, this would be an usurpation against him who believes himself the true sovereign, that is, little Ferdinand.[3]

The congress was finally persuaded to declare complete independence of Spain, an action which was heartening to San Martín and his little army on the frontier.

[3] Ricardo Rojas: *El Santo de la Espada* (Buenos Aires: Editorial Losada; 1940); translated by Herschel Brickell and Carlos Videla, as *San Martín, Knight of the Andes* (Garden City, N.Y.: Doubleday & Company, Inc.; 1945), p. 91.

January, 1817, found San Martín prepared for the next phase of his plan: the precarious trip over the high Andes to Chile. He sent out scouts to prepare for the crossing. He divided his army chiefly between two detachments, one to go over the pass of Los Patos, the other over the pass of Uspallata. We have San Martín's own description of this extraordinary trek over passes more than two miles above the sea:

> The difficulty that had to be overcome in the crossing of the mountains can only be imagined by those who have actually gone through it. The chief difficulties were the lack of population and roads, the lack of game, and especially of pastures. The army had 10,600 saddle and pack mules, 1,600 horses, and 700 head of cattle, and despite the most scrupulous care there arrived in Chile only 4,300 mules and 511 horses in very bad condition. The rest either died or were rendered useless during the crossing of the mountains. Two six-inch howitzers and ten four-inch field pieces, which went through Uspallata, were transported by 500 wheeled carriages, although a great part of the way they had to be carried by hand, with the help of block and tackle, when reaching the higher peaks. Food supplies for the twenty days the march was to last were taken on muleback, inasmuch as there was no house or town between Mendoza and Chile by way of Uspallata, and five mountain ranges had to be crossed. The greater part of the army suffered from lack of oxygen, as a result of which several soldiers died, besides others who succumbed to the intense cold. Everyone was convinced that the obstacles which had been overcome did not leave the slightest hope for a retreat; but, on the other hand, there reigned a great confidence among the ranks, which carried out their tasks heroically, in the midst of keen rivalry among the different units.[4]

The Spanish forces in Chile were taken completely by surprise. On February 12, 1817, San Martín's army met and routed the Spanish at Chacabuco. The city of Santiago hailed San Martín as a deliverer and elected him governor of Chile, an honor which he refused in favor of the hero of Chilean independence, Bernardo O'Higgins. For a year San Martín strengthened his army. In March, 1818, his troops were badly defeated at Cancha Rayada, but rallied bravely. Three weeks later, on April 5, San Martín threw his forces against the remaining Spanish garrisons at Maipú, where he won the decisive battle for the independence of Chile. The city of Santiago gratefully presented him with 10,000 pesos, which he gave to a hospital. Chile voted to give him an elaborate set of silverware and allotted him a salary of 6,000 pesos a year, but San Martín refused all gifts. He spent two more years making ready for the next leg of the journey. Not the least of his labors during this period were his seven trips across the Andes and two to Buenos Aires, made in an untiring effort to secure needed support.

By 1820 San Martín was prepared to move north and to attack the Spaniards in Peru. The organization of a navy to transport his forces, ably begun by the Chilean Blanco Encalada, was completed by Lord Cochrane, who arrived in 1818 to offer his services. That officer had been dismissed in disgrace from the British Navy (historians still argue the justice of the

[4] *Ibid.,* p. 108.

indictment), and had then embarked upon a spectacular career of assisting, for a price, the battlers for liberty in the New World. The Admiral was a complex blend of adventurer and idealist, vain and overbearing. He and O'Higgins worked happily together, but his relations with San Martín were always strained. Difficult as he was, Cochrane proved useful to the patriot cause: he collected small ships by purchase and cajolery and fitted them out in the harbor of Valparaíso; he ranged up and down the Chilean coast, destroying Spanish supply ships; and, finally, he assembled the makeshift navy which carried San Martín's army north to Peru.

Peru presented grave obstacles to San Martín. No area of Spanish America was more unready for revolt. Peru was dominated by wealthy families, creoles and *peninsulares*, who had been granted privileges by the Crown. These ruling Peruvians had suffered the insidious corruption of easy money, and their vigor had been sapped by the abundance of slave labor. To none of her American domains had Spain more effectively transferred her rigid class system. Peru had fewer men of independent mind than had Argentina and Chile. San Martín, knowing that he could count on few allies among influential citizens in Peru, moved cautiously. Instead of landing at Callao, the port of Lima, and risking his small army of ill-equipped troops against royal garrisons, he landed at Pisco on the southern Peruvian coast. He reached there in September, 1820, and lingered for several months while recruits joined him. Then, with his men rested and their numbers increased, he sailed north to Callao, where he waited again until further volunteers enlarged his ranks. Hotheads denounced him and accused him of cowardice, but San Martín explained his plan:

> The people are asking why I do not march on Lima immediately. I could do it and I would do it right now if it were convenient to my plans; but it is not convenient. I do not seek military glory, nor am I ambitious for the title of conqueror of Peru: I only wish to free it from oppression. What good would Lima do me if its inhabitants were hostile politically? How could I further the cause of independence if I should take Lima militaristically, or even the entire country? My views are very different. I want all the people to think as I do and not to take one single step ahead of the progressive march of public opinion; since the capital is ready now to show its feelings, I shall give it the opportunity without danger. In the certain expectation of this moment, I have delayed my advance until now; and for those who understand the variety of methods at my disposal, sufficient explanation for all these delays which have taken place will be apparent.[5]

While San Martín was warily approaching Lima in late 1820 and early 1821, the liberal outbreak in Spain forced Ferdinand to restore the Constitution of 1812 and to promise defense of Spanish liberties everywhere. This new turn of events compelled the viceroy in Lima to attempt conciliation of San Martín. The negotiations that followed were futile, for San Martín would accept nothing short of complete independence. Mean-

[5] *Ibid.*, p. 179.

while, the creoles of Lima were slowly being persuaded of the utility of independence, not, one suspects, out of admiration for democratic institutions, but rather out of hopes for greater profits once the Spaniards were ejected. The viceroy, whose subjects were divided between those who favored the liberal Constitution of 1812 and royalists who deplored any abridging of the king's powers, was hard put to it in his handling of the secessionist disciples of San Martín. He temporarily eased his situation by quitting Lima and moving into the interior. The *cabildo* of Lima was then emboldened to invite San Martín to enter the city in July, 1821. There, on July 28, 1821, assured that Peru was ripe for freedom, José de San Martín formally declared the independence of Peru.

But independence was still to be won. San Martín's small forces held Lima and a few miles of coastline. Most of Peru and all Upper Peru were still controlled by royalist garrisons. Even in Lima, where San Martín had been assured of popular support for independence, the great landholders, high ecclesiastics, and other recipients of Spanish bounty feared any move that might annoy the king. San Martín had few men of ability and patriotic integrity on whom to rely for counsel and cooperation. His army was small, not more than half the strength of the enemy. In this crisis, Lord Cochrane failed him. Shortly after San Martín's occupation of Lima, Cochrane demanded the rewards due him and his men. When San Martín begged for patience, Cochrane seized gold and silver from the government treasury, made off with the ships, and sailed north along the Mexican coast and finally back to Chile, where he spread tales of the perfidy of San Martín. There was grumbling in San Martín's ranks, as the campaign lagged and the promise of glory and profit dimmed. These events explain his next steps: in order to exercise a greater control over unruly elements, he assumed the post of dictator of Peru; and, convinced that only joint action with Bolívar could dislodge the Spaniards, he sought alliance with the northern Liberator, whose forces were now occupying Quito and Guayaquil in Ecuador. That Bolívar shared the conviction of the necessity for concerted action is indicated in a letter written to San Martín in November, 1821: "We should draw closer together and agree to engage with the new enemies and with the new means they employ." In June, 1822, Bolívar wrote offering San Martín troops to help him in Peru. On July 13 San Martín replied: "Peru will receive with enthusiasm and gratitude all the troops that Your Excellency can spare."

THE MEETING OF THE LIBERATORS

One can conjecture as to the confused emotions of the two extraordinary men who would soon be brought face to face: Simón Bolívar and José de San Martín. There was admiration, certainly, on both sides. Was there also jealousy, fear lest the other seize credit beyond his due? Was each one's ambition threatened by the other's power and prestige? The rival partisans of Bolívar and San Martín have long debated these questions.

At any rate the proprieties were observed, as may be seen from the somewhat orotund letter from Bolívar received by San Martín on the eve of his entry into Lima. Bolívar had written:

> I have been looking forward to this moment all my life; and only the moment of embracing Your Excellency and joining our flags can be more satisfactory to me. The victor of Chacabuco and Maipú, the first son of his Fatherland, has forgotten his own glory when he addresses his exaggerated praise to me; but it does him honor, because it is the most shining evidence of his goodness and of his selflessness. . . . I am on my way to fulfill my promise of uniting the Empire of the Incas to the Empire of Freedom. Doubtless it is easier to enter Quito than Lima; but Your Excellency will be able to accomplish with more ease the difficult task than I the less difficult one, and soon Divine Providence, which has so far protected the banners of Law and Liberty, will bring us together in some corner of Peru, after having trampled upon the trophies of the tyrants of the American world.[6]

In July, 1822, San Martín sailed north from Callao to meet Bolívar in Guayaquil. When he entered the Guayas River, he received a message from Bolívar expressing pleasure at the prospect of embracing San Martín "on Colombian soil," a studied bit of discourtesy in which Bolívar made explicit his claim to Ecuador, instead of leaving the question open to further discussion. Bolívar's greetings were phrased in the exuberant prose so characteristic of him. He wrote:

> With the utmost satisfaction, most respected friend, I give you for the first time the title which my heart has granted you. I call you friend, and this is the name we should carry through life, because friendship is the only bond that should unite brothers in arms, in enterprise and in opinion. I would regret as much your not coming to this city as the loss of many battles; but you will not leave unsatisfied the wish I have of embracing on Colombian soil the foremost friend of my heart and my country. How would it be possible that you should come from so far away without letting us in Guayaquil see the great man that all are anxious to know, and if possible to touch? It is not possible. I am waiting for you and will meet you wherever you indicate; but without desisting from the honor of having you visit this city. A few hours, as you say, are enough for a discussion between soldiers; but they would not be enough to satisfy the passion for friendship, which is going to begin to enjoy the happiness of knowing the dear object of its affection, which it loved only through opinion, only through fame.[7]

The two men met in Guayaquil on July 26 and 27, 1822. Bolívar met San Martín at the dock, and after a public reception the two men conferred for an hour. Then at a banquet attended by the chief aides of the two generals, Bolívar proposed the toast: "To the two greatest men in South America—General San Martín and myself"; and San Martín re-

6 *Ibid.*, p. 198.
7 *Ibid.*, p. 202.

sponded: "To the early end of the war; to the organization of the republics of the continent and to the health of the Liberator of Colombia." The following day the two men were closeted alone for four hours; and that evening San Martín quietly slipped away from a ball given in his honor and boarded his ship, which set sail that night for Peru. The secret of what was said was locked away in the memories of the two men. Both Bolívar and San Martín later wrote a few letters giving some details. Our chief source of information is a letter to Bolívar written by San Martín as he was sailing south. This letter was not released by San Martín until ten years after the death of Bolívar, and the original was not found among Bolívar's papers. San Martín wrote:

> The results of our interview have not been those I promised myself for the quick termination of the war. Unhappily I am profoundly convinced either that you did not believe my offers sincere to serve under your orders with my troops, or that my person is embarrassing to you. The excuses you gave me, that your delicacy would never permit you to command me, and that even if this difficulty could be overcome, you were sure the Congress of Colombia would never consent to your absence from the Republic—permit me to say, General, that they have not seemed plausible to me. . . .
>
> My decision is irrevocably made. I have convoked the Congress of Perú for the twentieth of next month, and the day following its installation I shall embark for Chile, convinced that my presence on this soil is the one obstacle which keeps you from coming to Perú with the troops under your command. It would have been the height of felicity to me to have finished the war under the orders of the general to whom America owes her liberty. Fate wills otherwise, and one must conform. . . .
>
> I have spoken to you frankly, General; but the sentiments which this letter expresses will remain buried in the most profound silence; if they should come to light, the enemies of our liberty could make use of them to jeopardize it, and intriguers and ambitious men to sow discord.
>
> With Major Delgado, bearer of this letter, I send you a fowling piece and a pair of pistols, together with the riding horse, which I offered you in Guayaquil. Accept this remembrance, General, from the first of your admirers.[8]

This letter and others support tentative conclusions as to what transpired in Guayaquil. San Martín accepted as a *fait accompli* Bolívar's annexation of Guayaquil to Colombia. He offered to serve under Bolívar in the final campaign against the Spaniards, but Bolívar refused. Bolívar offered a certain number of troops to reinforce San Martín's threatened forces, but San Martín regarded the offer as inadequate. San Martín argued the unfitness of Peru for republican government and urged the importation of a European prince who would reign under a constitution, but Bolívar vetoed all such plans as alien to the spirit of America. And so San Martín, seemingly persuaded that his continued presence on the scene would lead to strife, quietly withdrew.

[8] Quoted by Hildegarde Angell, *op. cit.*, p. 181.

During his brief stay in Lima on his way south, San Martín found new plots. In August he wrote to Bernardo O'Higgins, the dictator of Chile:

> Believe me, my friend, I am tired of being called tyrant, and of having it said in all quarters that I wish to become a king, an emperor, or even the devil. Further, my health has become much poorer; the climate of this country is bringing me to my grave. Lastly, as my youth was sacrificed in the service of Spain and my middle age in the service of my native land, I believe that I have the right to dispose of my old age.[9]

He presented his resignation to the Congress of Peru in September, 1822. The delegates formally thanked him, and voted him a life pension of 12,000 pesos. He sailed to Chile, where he lingered briefly, and then moved to his farm near Mendoza, where word reached him of the death of his wife in Buenos Aires. San Martín was a prophet without honor in his own country; and he could find no peace in a land torn by fresh strife between provincials and *porteños*. In 1824 he sailed for England with his small daughter, María Mercedes; then settled in Belgium. In 1829, drawn by love of his fatherland, he sailed for Buenos Aires. But he was met on shipboard with word of the fierce dissensions that were tearing the country and of the continued vilification of his name, and he returned to Europe without setting foot on Argentine soil. He lived until 1850 as an exile largely dependent on the bounty of friends, first in Paris and finally in Boulogne. Not until thirty years after his death did the lawmakers of Argentina give adequate recognition to the Liberator of the South: in 1880 San Martín's remains were moved to Buenos Aires, and he was given his final burial in the capital's cathedral.

THE FINAL ACT

We now retrace our steps to Guayaquil and 1822. Simón Bolívar at last dominated the grand stage, free to direct the final act in the drama of emancipation. But his authority was illusory: from all quarters of Gran Colombia came reports of dissension. In Venezuela, renewed attacks by the royalists had finally been suppressed by Páez; but it was a restless and discontented Venezuela plotting for separation from Colombia, and Bolívar could do little but plead. In Bogotá, under Santander's control, the New Granadans were increasingly resentful of Bolívar's long absence and of his drain upon the funds and man power of their land. From Peru came delegations to tell of the disintegration of government, of the betrayals of public trust by Riva Agüero and Torre Tagle. And in the country back of Lima, the Spaniards still boasted an army which outnumbered any force Bolívar could muster. For over a year after San Martín's withdrawal, Bolívar made his uneasy headquarters in Guayaquil. He repeatedly asked permission of the Bogotá congress to march into Peru, to stabilize that govern-

[9] Quoted in William Spence Robertson: *Rise of the Spanish American Republics,* p. 260. New York; copyright 1936, used by permission of Appleton-Century-Crofts, Inc.

ment, and to fight the inevitable battle with Spain. The grudging permission finally came, and in September, 1823, he sailed to Callao.

The entrance into Lima was a grand triumph in the royal manner. The exuberance of the populace seemed to prove that their long apathy was ended. The Peruvian Congress gave him the title, "Man of Liberty," and voted him powers as supreme dictator. Behind the pleasant façade, Bolívar found a government rotten with graft and idleness. There was no money in the treasury. There were few men on whom he could rely. His one faithful lieutenant was the twenty-nine-year-old Antonio José de Sucre, the hero of Pichincha. He seems not to have had a single confidant among the Peruvians. Many of his closest friends were the English officers on his staff.

His task was to deliver the *coup de grâce* to the Spaniards. The honor of commanding what would prove the decisive battle fell to Sucre. The rival armies met on the high plateau near Ayacucho on December 9, 1824. In the lull before the fight, many officers and men left their ranks and crossed over to the enemy lines to embrace brothers and friends—a poignant reminder of the tragedy of civil war, which for fourteen years had driven its cruel wedge between men of the same blood and faith. The patriot victory was complete, despite the fact that the royalists had a superiority of at least 3,000 men and not less than ten times as many guns. The royalists were routed with the loss of some 2,000 men; their viceroy and chief generals were taken prisoners. Ayacucho marked the virtual end of the wars for Spanish American independence.

The victory of Ayacucho brought Bolívar another burst of acclaim. He may have been tempted to leave Peru and return as a hero to Gran Colombia, but first he had to finish his task by wiping out a few small garrisons and by carrying the battle to Upper Peru, where 4,000 Spanish soldiers still hung on. Furthermore, Bolívar was delayed by his enjoyment of the easy luxury, the good food and drink, and the charming women of Lima. In 1825 he was again on the march, south to Arequipa, inland to Lake Titicaca, and then on to the fabulous city of silver, Potosí. There in Upper Peru came the first rift between Bolívar and his beloved Sucre. Bolívar would have bound Peru and Upper Peru together into one great republic. But under pressure from the patriots of Upper Peru who wanted independence from both Spain and Peru, Sucre had already given his blessing to the creation of a new and separate state. Bolívar's wrath seems to have been mollified when the new state was given the name República Bolívar, later to be Bolivia. He then helped prepare a constitution for this new republic on the *altiplano,* a document duly accepted by the congress in Lima. Sucre, the true author of Bolivian independence, was named the first president.

Bolívar returned to a faction-torn Lima at the end of 1825. It was clear that he had failed, as had San Martín before him, to establish a stable and responsible government for Peru. He lingered on for ten months, a weary and disillusioned man at the seeming apogee of his success, now desperately attempting to discipline his corrupt government, and then seeking forgetfulness in the excesses of social life. At last, in late 1826, news of factional disputes in Bogotá and Caracas persuaded him to return north. On November 14, he entered Bogotá after an absence of five years. Here all was confusion, with Vice-President Santander the chief plotter against his titular chief. Even worse news came from Venezuela, where Páez was scheming to withdraw from the union with Gran Colombia, while blandly suggesting that Bolívar be crowned as king. Again Bolívar started out with his troops for the hard march over the mountains. That he had not lost his warm eloquence, appears from a letter he wrote to Páez on the way: "I have come to Colombia to save both you and our country from the greatest of all catastrophes. No personal ambition brought me here. . . . I want no throne, no presidency, nothing. . . . I seek only tranquillity for Venezuela so that I may resign my office." In January, 1827, Bolívar entered Caracas, Páez reaffirmed his loyalty, and Bolívar shortly left Venezuela for what proved to be the last time.

Bolívar returned to New Granada at the end of 1827 to deal with the refractory Santander, who was unwilling to idolize the mercurial Liberator. In June, 1828, the delegates to the congress again succumbed to the spell of Bolívar and named him dictator. He sought briefly to rally his strength and impose his will, but he was a feverish, ailing man. He was bitter and vindictive, convinced that he had no friends whom he could trust. Santander was the chief target of his scorn. In September, 1828, a night attack by armed men almost brought his death, and he was saved only by the quick wits of Manuela Sáenz. From then on there was no glory for Bolívar, no lift for his spirit. He wrote: "There is no good faith in America, nor among the nations of America. Treaties are scraps of paper; constitutions, printed matter; elections, battles; freedom, anarchy; and life, a torment." The Gran Colombia that was his dearest creation now fell apart: in September, 1830, both Venezuela and Ecuador withdrew.

Meanwhile, on May 8, 1830, Simón Bolívar, near to death from tuberculosis, left Bogotá for the last time, planning to sail for exile in Europe. He got as far as Santa Marta on the Caribbean coast, where he died on December 17. "America," he had said shortly before, "America is ungovernable. Those who have served the revolution have plowed the sea."

Chapter 16

THE INDEPENDENCE OF BRAZIL

       The clipping of the ties that bound Brazil to Portugal was a gentle operation, almost bloodless. There were no heroic liberators, no forced marches over high passes; with simply a declaration of independence, a few mild skirmishes, Brazil emerged a sovereign empire. In Spanish America, independence was won in defiance of kings; in Portuguese America, the heir apparent to the Braganza throne himself raised the cry of freedom.

       Portugal at the beginning of the nineteenth century was impotent. The days of her glory had long since passed. Her empire had shrunk and she no longer counted among the powers of Europe, although she continued to enjoy a tenuous liberty under England's protection. The brilliant dictator-premier Pombal had briefly revived national ambition; but his fall from power in 1777 had left Portugal without a leader. Queen Maria, quite mad, was on the throne, and her son John was regent. John was a fat, sluggish fellow, not unintelligent. His wife, the wanton Carlota Joaquina, sister of Ferdinand VII of Spain, was his chief liability. These were the legatees of the tradition of Henry the Navigator, Vasco da Gama, and Camões. The thoughtful people of Portugal were heartily ashamed.

       Brazil, the only remaining colony of importance in the once spacious Portuguese empire, had far more vigor than her mother country. Brazil also had serious weaknesses. Her sprawling immensity was spongy, inert. Her population was more than 3 million, but the effective population— those who could read and write, who were politically conscious, who had ideas about their Brazilian destiny—consisted of a few hundred thousand at most. About two-thirds of the people were slaves; many others were virtually serfs. Brazil was culturally retarded; there were few schools and few books. It was a land with a name but without unity; a land of little cities, tiny towns, and great plantations. Royal and viceregal rule meant little; the planter was still king on his own domain. The Church was a cohesive force, but her stature had suffered by loss of the Jesuits.

       But over against the weakness and disunity of Brazil stood a growing sense of nationalism which promised to draw the scattered land together into an effective whole. The process had begun in the seventeenth century, when the Brazilians themselves evicted the Dutch. It was encouraged by the indifference with which the Portuguese supervised their richest overseas domain. Frontier struggles had toughened the Brazilians and had taught them to rely upon their own ingenuity and strength. Brazil had grievances against Portugal which were almost identical with those nursed by the colonies of Spain. But the Brazilian grievances were on the whole less bitter, owing in part to the gentler quality of the Portuguese character, in part to the fact that Portugal, although imposing stringent economic controls upon the colony, was never so exigent in political control as Spain. There had been a few flare-ups against Portuguese rule, of which the most serious had been the revolt of Tiradentes in Minas Gerais in 1788. By the first years of the nineteenth century, it was clear that Brazil would not tolerate much longer her status as an appendage to bankrupt Lisbon. The people were no longer Portuguese; they were Brazilians.

Napoleon was the catalyst that set off the chain reaction which finally split Brazil from Portugal. Even before he unseated the Bourbons in Madrid, he had turned his attention to the Braganzas of Lisbon. In November, 1807, a French army under General Junot moved into Portugal; whereupon the British Minister, Lord Strangford, and Admiral Sir Sidney Smith, who had a British fleet ready in the Tagus, told Prince Regent John that the time had come to pack up his mad mother and get out. So the royal court, numbering more than 1,000, with servants and hangers-on, crowded into some forty merchant ships and eight men-of-war and sailed down the Tagus as the French army reached the hills above Lisbon. Escorted by British ships, they set out on November 29, 1807. With them went the jewels and gold of the royal treasury. It was a hard two months' journey; water gave out, the ships were dirty and verminous, seas were stormy, and everyone was sick.

The welcome in Bahia in January, 1808, was friendly. It was royalty's first visit to American soil. The people of Bahia opened their homes, hunted clothes fit for princes, and prepared their best food. But the visitors were not in a pleasant mood. They were weary, sick, filthy. Proud Carlota had her head shaved to be rid of vermin.[1] Mad Maria went about muttering: "I am going to hell." The nobility and attendants were arrogant. John behaved better than the others; he greeted Brazilians with a smile and made friends. After a few weeks' rest they sailed south to the capital city.

Now the princes of Portugal had their first sight of Rio de Janeiro, the city whose loveliness brings a catch to the throat of every visitor. They saw the sweeping bays, the shining beaches, and the jagged peaks of the Cariocas thrust from the heart of the city. The most beautiful city in the world, they said—which it was, and is. They looked more closely and saw rutted streets down which sewage drained, meager public buildings, and crowded slums. Then, perhaps, there was a stirring of conscience over a colony so long neglected—John, at least, had traces of conscience.

---

[1] There is a tale, possibly apocryphal, that the good ladies of Bahia, thinking that a shaven head was the latest European fashion, followed Carlota's example, to the considerable annoyance of her arrogant majesty.

The hospitality of the *cariocas*[2] overflowed. They opened their homes and hearts, shared food and clothing. John responded with generous enthusiasm. He liked Brazil and the Brazilians, and they liked him. Not so much could be said for the nobility and their toadies who, while they took over houses, clothing, finery, and food, ridiculed their Brazilian hosts and continued to demand more. Carlota was the most ungracious of all. (The Princess had lost her hair, and what lady can be gracious with a shaved head?)

Now Rio de Janeiro and Brazil received overdue attention from the Portuguese Crown. The city, said John, must be made fit for kings. Under British prodding, he ordered Brazilian ports opened to the trade of the world, with special privileges granted to English merchants. Industries were encouraged, immigration was invited, and the judiciary was enlarged. Other innovations followed: a national bank, a military academy, a medical school, a printing press, a national library, and an art museum. A National Institute was created, and invitations were sent to European men of science, art, and letters. Meanwhile, British traders, salesmen, and clergy were moving in. Full liberty of worship was allowed the British, provided their chapels were inconspicuous and their clergy abstained from proselyting. England had every advantage, every privilege, but it was a one-sided arrangement: the British sold much, but they did not buy enough to satisfy the Brazilians. Impatience with England steadily increased. A Brazilian historian writes: "Once more the dynasty sold the kingdom as Esau had sold his birthright; once more the house of Braganza, to preserve its throne, sacrificed the nation." England might have pertinently retorted that had it not been for her, Portugal would long since have lost both empire and homeland. Alan K. Manchester describes Brazil's status: "In 1808 the colony was emancipated economically from the decadent mother country; in 1810 it acquired a rich stepmother."

In December, 1815, John signed an edict giving Brazil dominion status within the empire; in 1816 the mad queen died and John was crowned "John VI of the United Kingdom of Portugal, Brazil, and the Algarves."[3] With new dignity came new pomp. Palaces and public buildings were built. The city drew into itself the great families of the land. The *fazendeiros,* the plantation owners, long contemptuous of city dwellers, flocked to the capital, built homes, and divided their time between their plantations and Rio de Janeiro—later between Brazil and Paris. This royal pageantry served to unite Brazil, but it was also a long step toward the destruction of the *fazendeiro:* the landlords absented themselves from their plantations, entrusting the supervision of their sugar and cotton fields, and their herds of cattle to underlings; and, drawing upon the profits from these ventures, the *fazendeiros* basked in royal favor in the capital and began to build homes in Paris, increasing their neglect of the lands that furnished

2 The name given to the residents of Rio de Janeiro, after the mountains which end in rocky Corcovado and Pão de Açúcar at the water's edge.

3 The Algarves is the name of the southernmost province of Portugal, the last to be taken from the Moslems (1249); it has long regarded itself as set apart from the rest of the nation.

their luxuries. The King turned their vanity to his royal ends. Titles, honors, and decorations were distributed lavishly; barons, counts, and marquises multiplied. Some titles were given outright; others were sold. The inequities of a class society were increased.

Joy over these events was not unconfined. Many simple citizens found the dandies of John's court a sorry lot who took the best houses and demanded more than their share of food. The air was thick with intrigue. Carlota Joaquina, now Queen of Portugal and Brazil, aspired to further royal honors and encouraged monarchist factions in Buenos Aires to elect her queen of a united La Plata, in the absolutist fashion of the Bourbon line; but the British vetoed that scheme. Carlota was at one time accused of plotting her husband's death. Meanwhile, her lovers furnished titillating gossip for idlers in coffee shops. John did what he could to counteract his queen's baleful course; he worked indefatigably and won respect. He even gave Brazil a brief taste of imperial expansion when he seized French Guiana in 1808 and annexed the Banda Oriental (Uruguay) in 1816. Nevertheless, restlessness was in the air as the idle Portuguese outstayed their welcome and squandered money Brazil could ill afford. In 1817 a sizable revolt flared up in Pernambuco, but it was quickly suppressed, the leaders were hanged, and more martyrs were added to the score against the Portuguese.

Events in Portugal finally dictated Brazil's course. In 1820 rebels ousted the regency in Lisbon, which was holding power in the name of the absent Braganzas, and convoked a parliament which adopted almost line for line the liberal Spanish Constitution of 1812. The new government, liberal in domestic affairs, was imperialistic in its zeal to hold Brazil. It condemned John's opening of Brazilian ports, bade Brazilian provinces ignore their king, countermanded many of John's decrees, and ordered Portuguese officers in John's army to disobey his commands. This flurry of liberalism in Lisbon was reflected in revolts in northern Pará and Bahia. John was in imminent danger of losing both his Brazilian and Portuguese crowns. At this point England, intent upon holding Portugal within the British orbit, advised John to hurry back to his threatened throne. In April, 1821, John, after prudently collecting all the gold in the treasury, sailed with 3,000 of his court, leaving his son Pedro, a youth of twenty-three, to rule as regent. With sound prescience, he advised: "If Brazil demands independence, grant it, but put the crown upon your own head."

"Pedro was a grand fellow," writes the Brazilian novelist Erico Verissimo, "at least from the fiction writer's angle—sentimental, impulsive, romantic, sensual and spoiled." His education had been haphazard; he had been detested by his mother, neglected by his father, and left to the companionship of stableboys. Despite such an inauspicious start, Pedro displayed firmness and sound sense. Shortly after his father's departure, he received a peremptory summons from the Lisbon parliament to return immediately for the completion of his education. Deputations from São Paulo and elsewhere waited upon him, begging him to stay. Pedro replied: "I stay." A few months later came another ultimatum from Lisbon. This time he was in São Paulo, and, standing by the Ypiranga River, he ripped the Portuguese colors from his uniform and shouted: "Independence or death!"—this was the *grito do Ypiranga,* Brazil's declaration of independence, September 7, 1822. He had good advisers: his father, whose parting counsel was fresh in memory; his chief counselor, José Bonifácio de Andrada e Silva, who urged this course; and his wife, Leopoldina, who wrote: "The apple is ripe; pick it now, or it will rot."

Independence it was, almost without bloodshed. But not quite. A substantial Portuguese garrison held Bahia. Brazilian volunteers attacked, but they were thrown back. Then the ubiquitous Lord Cochrane, whom we have met before as the ally of San Martín in Chile and Peru, appeared in Rio de Janeiro with a tiny squadron manned by Brazilians, English, French, and a few Americans. While Brazilians attacked Bahia again by land, Lord Cochrane struck from the sea, and the Portuguese took off in great disorder. Cochrane then cleared the Portuguese out of Maranhão, and one of his lieutenants did the same for Pará. By 1823 Brazilian independence was secure, and the following year Lord Cochrane again served Brazilian unity by putting down a revolt in Pernambuco.[4] John's advice had proved useful. The son was crowned on December 1, 1822, Pedro I, Emperor of Brazil by the grace of God—not to mention the grace of England.

[4] A queer combination of crusader for liberty and frank freebooter, this Scottish Lord Cochrane. He drove a hard bargain with Pedro, whom he detested, collected an ample salary, and was promised possession of any ships he might capture, but failed to collect on that account. See C. Lloyd: *Lord Cochrane* (London: Longmans, Green & Co.; 1947), pp. 161 ff.

Chapter 17

FROM WAR TO PEACE

With the soldiers of Spain, Portugal, and France all but ejected from American soil by 1824, the independence of Latin America was a reality. European flags now flew over little of the New World south of the Canadian border, although England, France, and Holland still held a few islands and some stretches of the mainland; and Spain retained Cuba and Puerto Rico, which she would not lose until 1898. The war was won, but the problems of the free peoples had only begun.

Recognition by the major powers was the first requirement of the weak and unformed nations of Latin America. Without such acknowledgment of their independent status, they would labor under serious economic and political handicaps. Great Britain's full and prompt recognition in 1783 of the seceding United States had been an object lesson in good sportsmanship; the fight was lost, and the contestants smiled grimly and shook hands. The Latin American states fared less well. France recognized Haiti in 1825, twenty-one years after the French had been finally expelled. Portugal did better, recognizing Brazil in 1825, but only under the prodding of England. Spain stubbornly postponed acceptance of the obvious: she did not recognize Mexico until 1839, eighteen years after the fight was finished; and she made her other ex-subjects wait even longer; Honduras, the last, was not recognized until 1895.

The United States was the first to welcome the newcomers to the company of free nations. The earliest reports of rebellion in the south had stirred the enthusiasm of the northern Americans. When the first scattered juntas were organized in 1810, Washington sent "agents for seamen and commerce" and in the following year, even a few consuls; these were measures little short of formal recognition. But when, in 1815, patriot reverses everywhere in Latin America made the outcome less secure, Washington prudently withdrew some of these representatives and steered a neutral course. This attitude was designed to placate Spain, from whom the United States was seeking to buy the Floridas. But public sentiment applauded the flagrant breaches of neutrality: a Venezuelan agent "borrowed" guns and powder from the United States Ordnance Department; other

South American agents outfitted privateers in New Orleans and Baltimore and enlisted American crews. There was no doubt that the American people were on the side of the patriots. When the Florida treaty was finally confirmed in 1821 and there was no further need to appease King Ferdinand, Washington extended full recognition: in 1822 to Gran Colombia, Mexico, and Argentina; in 1823 to Chile; in 1824 to Brazil and Central America; and in 1826 to Peru.[1] The American example was followed by England and other powers. The Latin American nations were thus given formal acceptance, without which they could not assume their place in world life.

Security against attack from European powers was a prime concern of the weak nations which were parceled out from the former colonial empires of Spain, Portugal, and France. However, their fears were ill-founded. France did indeed continue to interfere in Haiti. Portugal was too weak to seek recapture of Brazil; in any event, as we have noted, England exercised an effective veto upon Lisbon. Spain, demoralized and suffering the rule of weak monarchs, was incapable of effective reprisals; her repeated thrusts, during the ensuing half century, in Mexico, the area of the Río de la Plata, Peru, and Chile proved unavailing. During the early 1820's the Holy Alliance of European absolutists authorized France to intervene in Spain on behalf of Ferdinand VII; and discussed the recapture of Spain's American colonies, but this move was countered by the cooler decisions of England's Canning. The English, despite their preference for monarchical institutions, found it wise to accept the new state of affairs in America and to extend their trade. The United States, by Monroe's pronouncement of "Hands Off" in 1823, gave moral encouragement—there was little more that she could give—to the newly created states. Thanks largely to Europe's preoccupation with internal conflicts, the new Latin American nations were permitted to develop their political life with a minimum of outside interference.

Security against each other early became a clear need of the Latin American countries. The territorial demarcation of the several states was indefinite, provoking border conflicts which began early in the independent life of Latin America and have continued down to the present time. Simón Bolívar revealed wise statesmanship when, at the conference in Panama in 1826, he sought to create an instrument for inter-American cooperation; but such concerted action was then no more than a pious hope.

The social chaos left by the wars for independence was an ugly problem. In almost all the nations (Brazil was a notable exception), much of the best young manhood had been sacrificed in battle. Then, when troops were mustered out, hordes of homeless and penniless men were turned adrift to augment the confusion. The discipline of the agents and garrisons of the Crown had been removed; the new governments had few trained

---

[1] Uruguay was recognized by the United States in 1834, Venezuela in 1835, Ecuador in 1838, Bolivia in 1848. The slavery issue delayed American recognition of Haiti until 1862 and of the Dominican Republic until 1866. Cuba, taken from Spain in 1898, was recognized as independent in 1902. In 1903 Panama was detached from Colombia and recognized by Washington.

leaders on whom to depend for building stable political institutions; many of the *peninsulares,* including trained jurists and administrators, were exiled; and few creoles and mestizos had experience to fit them for governmental posts. As a result, lawlessness prevailed throughout Latin America, the disorder continuing in some cases for many years.

The Church suffered in the general disintegration of the postrevolutionary days. Many of her ablest and best-trained leaders had come from the peninsula; and the revolt against Spain brought refusal by Spanish America to accept priests who had been trained abroad. The Church had always been active in maintaining hospitals, orphanages, and other agencies of mercy. Her endowment in land and mortgages, which financed such useful works, was greatly reduced during the years of disorder. Education, long a monopoly of churchmen, suffered a marked decline. Furthermore, the Church, whose chief clerics had inclined toward royalist sentiment, lost prestige as the masses espoused republican ideas.

Economic havoc had been wrought by the revolutionary years. Rich mines and productive plantations, often the properties of *peninsulares,* fell into disuse. Lack of security in country districts discouraged careful farming and provoked a flight to the cities. Much of the chief business in banking and trading had been in the hands of *peninsulares* who were now banished.

Political chaos inevitably descended upon the newborn states (and has remained with some of them down to the present hour). The people of Latin America were catapulted at dizzy speed from a governmental pattern in which they had almost no voice of their own, into an unfamiliar political system that required them to elect their own rulers and lawmakers. These new voters were a mass of miserably poor and illiterate people. To judge from the scattered notes of Humboldt or the later conclusions of José Ingenieros, one may hazard the guess that not one in ten Latin Americans in the early nineteenth century could read or write, and that not one in twenty earned enough to live in modest comfort and security. Such men were now expected to conduct the intricate affairs of sovereign states.

There was no lack of wise men to caution against precipitate action in erecting republics and to urge emulation of the English example of constitutional monarchies. Brazil heeded such counsel and enjoyed almost fifty years of constitutional liberty under wise Pedro II. The Spanish Americans, instead, spurned the various proposals for installing kings (most of the nominees, it seems in retrospect, were either dull or vicious) and declared for republics. They wrote constitutions fashioned chiefly on the model of the United States, calling for free elections, congresses with upper and lower houses, courts, and presidents. The words were carefully written, but they had slight applicability to current realities.

The peoples of Latin America in those years did not lack political consciousness. The chief lack was political maturity; this resulted in a dangerous oversimplification of many issues. Consider for example the glib division between conservatives and liberals. The conservatives of the royalist-landholding-clerical tradition were confronted by liberals who had learned to quote Rousseau without understanding the purport of his words.

The conservatives cried: "No change; the old was good." The liberals answered: "Change everything; the new is always better." The conservatives were dull but often competent; the liberals were bright but untried. The results were unpleasant and unprofitable. Another major quarrel arose between exponents of the rival theories of centralism and federalism. The

Later Independence Movements

centralists wanted all power lodged in the national government, while the federalists insisted upon large autonomy of the component political units (variously called states, provinces, or departments). Often, in one nation or another, conservatives and liberals found themselves opposed on this issue; but such alignments shifted easily, and what was the liberal side yesterday became the conservative today. The centralist-federalist debate produced many broken heads in Mexico, Colombia, Venezuela, Brazil, and Argentina, and in the other republics to a lesser degree. It was a debate that strengthened the hand of the caudillo, "the boss," and fixed the curse of *caudillismo* on Latin America. If the caudillo proved mighty enough, he believed in centralism—or at least practiced it. If he was a minor boss, he fought for federalism in order to justify his misrule of his own state or province.

The result of this riotous political scramble was inevitable. The caudillo, or strong man, whether he was the man on horseback or the man in the countinghouse, won. He became the dictator, taking advantage of the preoccupation of the sovereign electorate with the specious issues between liberals and conservatives or centralists and federalists. He cared little for such fine distinctions, using them only when expedient. The dictator manipulated elections, seeing to it that ballots served his cause and that his favorites were awarded key positions. He treated the public treasury as though it were his private purse, and regulated the activities of citizens, rewarding those who were obedient and striking down those who rebelled. All the Latin American republics have had such dictators part of the time, and some of them almost all the time. Some of these national bosses were reasonably amiable and wise, others were brutal killers, but in neither case did the people have a voice. Such was the governmental lot of most of the Latin American republics during the first decades of their independent history; such is the lot of some of them in 1967.

PART IV

Mexico

The story of large and populous Mexico is of lively concern to its neighbors in the United States. This is the Latin American republic which Americans know best, visit most frequently, enjoy most heartily—and it is a nation with which their government has had numerous and bitter disputes. If Mexico and the United States can live peaceably side by side and cooperate to their mutual advantage—as they have done with increasing success since 1927—the achievement will give substance to the vision of all-American solidarity voiced by Simón Bolívar in 1815.

 [*Chapter 18*]

INTRODUCING MEXICO

Mexico, second largest in population and third in area of the Latin American republics, is a land of bewildering variety and haunting beauty. It is dominated by its heaped mountains: the Sierra Madre of southern Mexico divides into two high spurs reaching to the northwest and the northeast, crowned by the peaks of Orizaba (18,701 feet), Popocatépetl (17,887 feet), and Ixtaccíhuatl (17,342 feet). More than half of Mexico lies within the tropics, and its climate is varied by altitude: there is the *tierra fría,* the cold land, the central plateaus where most Mexicans have their dwelling places 6,000 to 9,000 feet above the sea; the *tierra templada,* the temperate zone, on the lower tablelands and valleys; and the *tierra caliente,* the hot lands, of the coastal plains and steaming Isthmus of Tehuantepec. Mexico's earth is stored with rich treasure: gold, silver, lead, petroleum, copper, and zinc; but the nation has little tillable, well-watered soil. Only about 12 per cent of Mexico's land surface is developed for the growing of corn and other foods. The fabulous wealth of Mexico is an ancient and exploded myth. This is a bitterly poor land, pleasant for those who can afford leisure, but hard for those who must work.

Mexico's 44 millions (1966) inherit the blood of the Maya, Toltecs, Tarascans, Zapotecs, Mixtecs, Aztecs, and an unreckoned number of other varieties of men whose battles for mastery stretch back far beyond recorded history; they inherit the blood of those indomitable conquerors who began to arrive in 1519; and a few of them inherit the blood of African slaves imported to work in mine and sugar field (although the mark of the Negro is far less pronounced in Mexico than in other parts of the Caribbean world). Today's Mexican is an amalgam of these diverse strains, but he is still predominantly Indian. About 30 per cent of Mexico's people are racially and culturally Indian, many speaking Indian languages (thirty-three of these are officially listed, with fifty or more other tongues not tabulated by the census). About 60 per cent fall roughly into the mestizo category, many of them living nearer to the Indian's than to the white man's world. About 10 per cent are whites, or regard themselves as such, including substantial numbers of Americans, English, Germans, French, Spaniards, Italians, and other European peoples.[1] Mexico's people are mostly country folk, living in thousands of villages which dot the plains and valleys.[2] But here, as everywhere, there is a steady drift toward the cities, which mushroom out at disastrous pace: in 1965 Mexico City and its suburbs had a population of some 5.5 million; Guadalajara had 1,048,351; Monterrey 821,843; Ciudad Juárez, 385,082; Puebla, 338,685.

Mexico has much to excite the interest of the wayfarer, whether he be historian, sociologist, economist, archaeologist, or an innocent tourist. More than any other nation of the Americas, Mexico has preserved eloquent remains of the successive civilizations that have formed her polymorphous life. The ancient Maya still seem alive in their holy cities of Chichén Itzá, Uxmal, and Mayapán; the Zapotecs and Mixtecs speak through the ruins of Monte Albán and Mitla; the Toltecs, Aztecs, and others, through the pyramids and temples and courts of Tenayuca, Xochicalco, Teotihuacán, and Tula. The Spaniards of the colonial centuries left the grim but graceful fortress churches of central Mexico and the abundant temples which show what their builders had learned from Spain, France, and Italy. And the builders of modern Mexico have also left their mark, sometimes exciting, in adaptations and imitations of things seen in Paris, Berlin, and New York.

Mexico's beginnings as an independent nation in 1821, when she cut her last ties with Spain, were inauspicious. Because of the lack of self-rule under Spain, the general poverty and illiteracy of the inert masses, and the preponderant economic and political powers of the army and the Church, Mexicans were unprepared to rule their own house. The shift from colony to republic (after a brief imperial interlude) meant to the common man little more than a new set of rulers: yesterday the Spaniards with their hierarchy of officials; today the creoles with home-grown bosses of various grades. The tensions merely shifted, and the struggle between *peninsular* and creole was replaced by that between creole and mestizo.

The task of creating a republic was confused by injection of a quite unreal clash of ideas. From the first days of independence, there was confused talk of conservatism and liberalism: the conservatives were authentic enough, holding firmly to the faith and practice of the past, torn only

[1] Nathan L. Whetten: *Rural Mexico* (Chicago: University of Chicago Press; 1948), pp. 52–4. Whetten believes "that statistics on race represent little more than crude estimates and have very little reliability or utility. The latest data available on race are from the 1921 census and give the racial proportions for the total population as follows: whites, 10.3 per cent; mestizos, 60.5 per cent; and Indians, 29.2 per cent." Ethnologists increasingly suspect attempts to count the Indian population; the most workable test is whether a given individual lives in the social milieu of an Indian, not whether he is of undiluted Indian stock—a point impossible to verify. Robert Redfield estimated that at least 75 per cent of Mexicans have more Indian than white blood. For another analysis of racial composition see Howard F. Cline: *Mexico, Revolution to Evolution, 1940–1960* (New York: Oxford University Press; 1963), p. 90.

[2] Although only about one-half of all Mexicans are technically classified as rural—meaning those who live in communities of less than 2,500—in Mexico a village of 5,000 or even 10,000 may be made up largely of families who till the soil. Few farmers live on their own plots. They live in the villages and travel out to their fields every day.

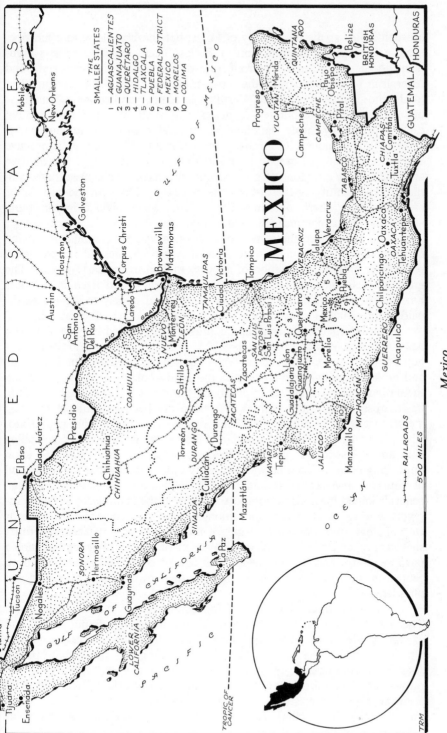

MEXICO

on such issues as the desirability of kings; but the liberals were often doctrinaire Jacobins, split on a score of issues. There was also endless argument about centralism (the strong rule of the national government) and federalism (the autonomy of the separate states). On such issues the electorate chose sides. The creole, Castilian in temper and training, usually—but with notable exceptions—espoused conservatism and made common cause with clergy, army, landholders, and later with the foreigner who came to invest money. Centralism was natural to him, for an impressive and powerful national executive looked something like a king. The mestizo approached the questions of government with dark suspicions of affairs in the capital, identifying the pretensions of new leaders with the bad habits of viceroys; the liberal doctrine of federalism, which divided responsibility among the states, commended itself to him.

Contention over these fine-spun theories was to continue for many decades. Those who fought over them may have represented a twentieth part of the nation's population of about 7 million in the early 1820's. The great masses toiled, ate meagerly, dressed in rags, and lived in floorless hovels. Their participation in politics was limited mainly to serving as ill-paid or unpaid conscripts in wars whose issues they never understood.

Such internal weaknesses and confused ideas served the caudillo, who has dominated Mexico from the days of Iturbide almost down to the present hour. When one man proved powerful enough, he became a national boss and broke the wills—and sometimes the heads—of the little bosses. When the national boss (usually the "president") was not strong enough, the little bosses rose against him. Politics in Mexico has been government by *coup d'état*; that was the rule in the 1820's and it prevailed at least until 1920. The procedure was almost standard: first some stalwart soldier, calling God and the swinging planets to witness, issued a *pronunciamiento* upon impending reforms; then he was joined by other redoubtable warriors (and of course a few lawyers), and together they drafted a *plan*.[3] If enough generals joined the conspirators, there followed the *cuartelazo,* or barracks-revolt, during which a few opposition leaders were consigned to exile or eternal glory, and a new crowd moved into the national palace. Sometimes such a turn of events was dictated by men of high conscience and noble purpose, sometimes by evil men whose talk of conservatism or liberalism, centralism or federalism, was a blind for their own pursuit of power and plunder.

The more than 130 years of independence fall into six chief eras. The first (1821–55) was dominated by the formidable Santa Anna, and except for a few brief outbursts of liberalism, a creole-conservative-centralist bloc held sway. The second (1855–76), the age of the Indian Benito Juárez, saw the balance of power shift to the mestizo, with liberalism the rallying cry. The third (1876–1910) was the era of Porfirio Díaz, who, with a strong clique of mestizo and creole henchmen, fortified Mexican unity under an able dictatorship. The fourth (1910–20) was a period of revolu-

---

[3] *Plan* in Spanish is "plan" in English, but a "plan of this-or-that" becomes vastly impressive in Mexican usage.

tionary convulsions, during which a succession of caudillos fought for control of the national government. The fifth (1920–40) was marked by strongly policed national government, in which usually powerful presidents imposed their will upon minor national and state bosses. These strong men invariably made loud protestations of their generous intentions; in some instances, these protestations cloaked a tasteless scramble for spoils; in other cases the promises seemed honest, and their fulfillment substantial. The sixth (1940–   ) marks Mexico's swing to the right.

Meanwhile, Mexico has gone hungry. It was hungry under the Aztecs in 1500, hungry under the Spaniards in 1600 and 1700 and 1800; it remained hungry under Santa Anna, Juárez, and Díaz; it is still hungry in the 1960's. The rapid increase in population (over 100 per cent from 1910 to 1967) and the crowding of the cities have aggravated that hunger. This is the basic and continuing tragedy. All other issues, whether of the Church, the school, or the army, seem unimportant beside the sober fact that there is never enough corn to go around.

Chapter 19

THE ERA OF SANTA ANNA,

1821-55

In 1821 began Mexico's frantic efforts to create a nation from the torn fragments of the once proud Viceroyalty of New Spain. For more than three decades the figure of Antonio López de Santa Anna dominated. But before we introduce Santa Anna, we must dispose of the shabby dictator, Iturbide.

AGUSTÍN DE ITURBIDE

Judgment on Iturbide, who reigned briefly as Agustín I, first Emperor of Mexico, is almost unanimous. The American Herbert Priestley calls him "that vain, dissolute, young coxcomb"; and the Mexican José Vasconcelos describes him as "an irresponsible military *caudillo,* the precursor of that system of government which brought ruin to the country for more than a century."

Agustín de Iturbide, unfortunately for Mexico, had looked too long upon the image of Napoleon and had detected subtle likenesses between himself and that redoubtable warrior. This discovery prompted the Mexican to reach for a crown. Iturbide, as we have already noted,[1] marched triumphantly into the capital on September 27, 1821, calling himself the father of Mexican independence. When his congress met in May, 1822, the creole majority favored a king and would gladly have translated Ferdinand VII from Madrid to Mexico; but Ferdinand had just sense enough to stay where he was. The mobs of *léperos* (beggars and other riffraff) filled the streets and plazas, crying *Viva Agustín I*; soldiers, whose economic state could not be worsened by any turn of events, joined the clamor; and prosperous creoles added their blessing. And so Iturbide got his crown. He and his empress were invested with their new glories in a ceremony of synthetic splendor, and their court was given a dazzling pomp such as no viceroy had ever enjoyed. Decorations and honors were scattered among the ward heelers of the new emperor. The Order of Guadalupe was formed, and numerous

---

[1] See p. 251.

knights sported their new dignity. There was one weakness in this royal display: the treasury was bare,[2] and Iturbide could not meet the prime requisite for staying in power—he could not pay the army. Within a few weeks after the coronation, unpaid generals were fretting, and no Mexican ruler lasts long when generals fret. The emperor also met resistance in his congress, where a brave minority of republicans, Freemasons, and liberals denounced his wasteful course. One of his most devastating critics was the priest, Servando Teresa de Mier, of whom we shall hear more. In August, 1822, Iturbide became so aroused by censure and ridicule that he ordered the imprisonment of fifty members of congress, including Fray Servando. But attacks against him continued, and in October he dissolved congress and named a governing junta more amenable to his royal will.

By the last days of 1822, the air was electric, and the explosion could not long be delayed. The faction-torn country awaited someone to lead the revolt. The prayers of generals, angry liberals, and Freemasons were answered by the appearance of the curious savior-on-horseback, General Antonio López de Santa Anna. That soldier, detailed by the emperor to capture the fortress of San Juan de Ulloa from the Spanish forces, used his position in Veracruz to consolidate his own power over Iturbide's forces. Apprised of this conspiracy, the emperor went himself to Veracruz, took his refractory aide into custody, and started back to the capital. Santa Anna escaped his royal escort, returned to Veracruz, and in December pronounced against the emperor. He was quickly joined by disaffected generals, including the intrepid revolutionist Guadalupe Victoria, and together they issued the *Plan de Casa Mata* in February, 1823. This federalist *pronunciamiento* called for the end of the empire, the creation of a republic, a new congress, and a new constitution. In March, 1823, less than ten months after the anointing of Augustín I, the unlucky emperor reconvened his abused congress, mumbled remarks designed to be conciliatory, and then offered to abdicate. The proposal was refused on the ground that he had not been legally crowned, and he was summarily removed from office. Mexico's tragicomic digression in monarchy thus ended, she was ready to continue the "labored gestation" of her political institutions.

Iturbide was exiled to Italy; but he tired quickly of that pleasant land and went to England, where he issued fresh *pronunciamientos*. Early in 1824 he returned to Mexico, landing near Tampico, and called upon loyal patriots to rally to his banner; but instead he was taken into custody and shot. In 1838 devout royalists dug up his bones and buried them in the cathedral of Mexico City. Thus "the new nation was born," as Ralph Roeder puts it, "but under such conditions as to raise the question whether it was a birth or an abortion." Mexico had still to prove herself as a nation.

2 Spanish garrisons held the island fortress of San Juan de Ulloa off Veracruz after the mainland had won freedom, and they were not finally evicted until 1825. This gave them control of commerce, and prevented the customs officials from collecting their toll, an item which bulked large in the national revenue.

THE NATION GETS UNDER WAY

The thirty-two years following the fall of Iturbide were marked by the floundering efforts of the unformed nation to develop constitutional government. They were years in which presidents appeared and disappeared in bewildering number: Santa Anna himself was formally president six times, less formally on five other occasions; while more than twenty other men occupied the post for periods ranging from a few days to a few years. They were years disturbed by a Spanish invasion in 1829, the defection of Texas in 1836, a French raid in 1838, war with the United States in 1846–47, the loss by treaty of Mexico's northwestern territories in 1848, and the sale of the Mesilla valley to the United States in 1853. They were years of violent shuttling between Liberal-federalists and Conservative-centralists; of congresses which were summoned and quickly dissolved; of three separate constitutions. Throughout this period, the public treasury was drained by greedy rulers and costly wars, while successive administrations were forced to conclude disadvantageous bargains with foreign bankers or to levy upon the Church. Mexico continued to be chaotic and lawless, with bandits making every country road a way of terror. It was the perfect setting for bosses who sought to manipulate the army and the hungry masses to their hearts' desire. In this period Mexican political life was fixed with the curse of *personalismo,* a doctrine which discards constitutions, political parties, and ideals, and exalts the anarchic rule of the demagogue who can outshout reasonable men. Of all such demagogues in Mexican history, Santa Anna was the archetype.

Antonio López de Santa Anna was born in the state of Veracruz in 1795. A creole of inherited wealth and position, the young Antonio was early drawn "towards the glorious career of arms," enlisted at the age of fourteen in the royal army of New Spain, and fought against Hidalgo and Morelos. His boyhood hero was the great Bonaparte, and he never outgrew the ambition to be the Napoleon of the West. He pondered the triumphs of that conqueror and imitated his every pose and gesture. Army life, the parading of troops, and the fanfare of victory possessed him, though as a strategist he had little distinction, and as a warrior he proved himself of uneven valor. As an actor, Santa Anna was unsurpassed: he was master of the dramatic entrance and the commanding exit; he had the figure, the eyes, and the voice that gave his movements a touch of greatness not in his soul; and his extravagant display of personal glory eclipsed even that of a Napoleon. He was the supreme egotist: he made vanity a profession, bombast a fine art, treachery a specialty; he was faithless to men, women, and causes. He betrayed Spain for service with Iturbide; he betrayed Iturbide for his own ends; he betrayed the Liberals who gave him power, then betrayed the Conservatives who used him. Later he betrayed Mexico to the United States and, after taking money from Washington, betrayed his northern friends for his own profit at home. His vices were shabby and gross: he indulged his passion for cockfighting even in the national palace. For almost thirty years Mexico, for lack of political maturity and a literate citizenry, was the victim of this fellow who made and unmade presidents, seized the top office for himself time and again, mismanaged his country's pathetic wars, and stole the savings of the peasants and the Church.

The congress which deposed Iturbide in March, 1823, was strongly conservative and monarchist in sentiment, but it was aware of the popular support for the federalist doctrines of the *Plan de Casa Mata.* It therefore prudently favored the federalist cause, called a constituent congress for the writing of a constitution, and named a military triumvirate to perform the executive functions while the new charter was being drafted. The triumvirate then discreetly assigned Santa Anna (who had proclaimed himself "Protector of the Federal System") to military service on the frontier. The new congress assembled in November with a federalist majority, and the debate began between the two rival factions.

The chief spokesman for the Liberal-federalist cause was the aggressive, plump, and voluble delegate from Coahuila, Miguel Ramos Arizpe. An ex-priest and a Freemason, he had had a varied and highly spiced career. He had been sent to Spain in 1812 as one of the Mexican delegates to the Cádiz *cortes* (parliament), where he had shared in its liberal exuberance in drafting a new constitution; then, when Ferdinand returned and suppressed liberal troublemakers, Ramos Arizpe went to jail. Finally released, he returned to Mexico in time to join the clamor against Iturbide in 1822 and to preach republicanism and federalism. To him fell the task of writing a preliminary draft of the proposed constitution. On November 20, five days after the task had been assigned him, Ramos Arizpe presented his draft, the *Acta Constitutiva.* It was strongly federalist: "The Mexican nation," it read, "adopts for its government the form of representative, popular, and federal republic . . . the integral parts of the nation are free, sovereign, and independent states." Ramos Arizpe made an eloquent plea for his document, argued that the states wanted federalism, and that "the enormous differences between the provinces would thus be recognized, and the rights of man realized."

The Conservative-centralist opposition was directed by Servando Teresa de Mier, deputy from Nuevo León, the leading intellectual of the convention. Fray Servando, a Dominican priest, had run afoul of the Inquisition in 1794 by preaching a sermon at the shrine of Our Lady of Guadalupe in which he suggested that the Virgin had arrived in Mexico on the cape of the apostle Thomas, who, he believed, was the first Christian missionary to the Indians. Fray Servando was punished for his doctrinal waywardness by commitment to a Spanish prison; he escaped, took part in various subversive movements looking toward the independence of Mexico, and was captured again by the Spaniards. He escaped a second time but was recaptured and imprisoned in the island fortress of San Juan de Ulloa in the harbor of Veracruz. The Spanish officer in charge of that last citadel against Iturbide was inspired with a brilliant idea for tormenting the emperor: he released the bothersome priest, who straightway won a seat in the congress, where he castigated Iturbide with such venom that the emperor ordered him off to jail again. Fray Servando was an austere and slender aristocrat, who spoke for the centralists in the debate with the ebullient federalist Ramos Arizpe. He stated the case against the federalist charter: "Federalism," he said, "was designed to unite that which had hitherto been divided—as was the case in the United States—but the provinces of Mexico have always been united; there is nothing here to federate." He argued further from the experience of the United States noting that Ramos Arizpe's draft assigned a greater degree of sovereignty to the several provinces than did the United States Constitution to the several states. His plea for national greatness was eloquent: "Sovereignty rests in the nation. . . . This congress seems to represent the aims of the provinces rather than those of the nation."

The Conservatives, outvoted 70 to 10, lost their fight for a centralized government. The victory for federalism was inevitable from the beginning of the congress—or, for that matter, from the hour when Santa Anna had called upon the provinces to organize a federalist government. The detailed constitution was finally drafted, and the ceremony of signing was held in October, 1824. Fray Servando wore a mourning band upon his sleeve as he signed, remarking: "My country died the day the *Acta Constitutiva* was accepted. Today we observe its funeral."[3]

The Mexican Constitution of 1824 is often described as a pale copy of the Constitution of the United States. The final document was much like the American, but it showed the influence of the liberal Spanish Constitution of 1812 and of the French intellectuals. The Mexican Constitution provided for nineteen states and four territories, with each state empowered to elect its own governor and legislature: it called for an executive elected for four years, a bicameral legislature, and a judiciary. Federalist emphasis was clear in the clauses empowering state legislatures to choose the president and vice-president, the senate, and the judges. The lower house—the chamber of deputies—was to be named by the direct vote of the electorate, one deputy for each 80,000 inhabitants. The illiberality of the times accounted for the lack of provision for religious tolerance, for trial by jury, or for adequate safeguards for civil rights. The central government was given a firm check on state expenditures and the right to impeach state governors. The powers of the president were carefully delimited.

But despite the good intentions of its drafters, this constitution did not have its roots in Mexican reality: it took no cognizance of the inequitable distribution of land; it said nothing about education; it made no provision for the inarticulate Indians; it ignored the need for fundamental economic reform. And its checks upon the executive were a gallant but futile gesture in a nation where, as Ramón Beteta puts it: "The ever-present tradition of personalism in Mexico made the executive not only the popular hero, but also an omnipotent political being, who could exercise his extraordinary powers, regardless of the nature of the constitution under which he held office."

---

[3] Fray Servando died three years later, after asking his political opponent, Ramos Arizpe, to administer the last rites of the Church—a commendable instance of brotherly love between political foes.

In the first national election in 1824, the state legislatures gave the presidency to the Liberal-federalist Guadalupe Victoria, a stalwart soldier of the revolution whose refusal to accept a Spanish pardon after the death of Morelos had endeared him to patriots. The vice-presidency, by a clumsy constitutional device borrowed from the United States, went to the candidate with the second largest number of votes, Conservative-centralist Nicolás Bravo, also of revolutionary fame. The two war heroes could not work together in peace, a lesson that taught later presidents to dispense with vice-presidents who might plot against them. Victoria, for all his virtues, was no administrator and lacked both the force and the cunning to discipline his scheming colleagues. Nevertheless, he established two records quite unusual in Mexico's first decades of independent life: he served out his full term (1825–29), and he never turned a dishonest centavo.

His inauguration was carried through in an atmosphere of general optimism. For the first time since Father Hidalgo's *grito de Dolores,* the country seemed on the road to peace. Writing in 1827, Henry G. Ward, the British chargé d'affaires, was struck by the progress the country had made since an earlier visit in 1823. "There was an appearance of settled habits," he said, "and there seemed more respect for civil authority." Ward noted that at least in Puebla an honest effort was being made to furnish jobs for the milling throngs of beggars who cluttered the streets of Mexican cities. He compared that hopeful effort with what he had seen earlier in Mexico City: ". . . 20,000 of these *léperos* [beggars] infested . . . the streets, exhibiting a picture of wretchedness to which no words can do justice. In addition to the extraordinary ugliness of the Indian race . . . all that the most disgusting combination of dirt and rags could do to increase it was done . . . they were nothing but a public nuisance."[4]

Optimism, however, was premature. Renewed quarrels between self-styled Liberals and Conservatives shattered the tranquillity. The loyalties of these new factions crystallized around two branches of Freemasonry: the Scottish Rite Masons (the *escoceses*) were rapidly becoming the militant core of the Conservative-centralists and their allies, the die-hard monarchists; the newly established York Rite Masons (the *yorkinos*) represented the Liberal-federalists. This strife between the Masonic rites involved many of Mexico's top leaders. President Victoria and some of his Liberal cabinet members, Ramos Arizpe among them, were *yorkinos,* while Vice-President Bravo was a grand master of the Scottish Rite.

Meanwhile, the civil confusion was complicated by rivalry between the United States and Great Britain for trade advantages. The English, ably led by Foreign Minister Canning, were cultivating the affections of Mexico and other erstwhile Iberian colonies. England recognized Mexico in 1825 (three years after the United States) and sent H. G. Ward there to press the British case. "The British," writes J. Fred Rippy, "considered Mexico the key to their policy of checkmating the United States in Hispanic America." The United States, somewhat less experienced in such matters, sent Joel R. Poinsett, "a flaming evangelist of republicanism" who

---

[4] H. G. Ward: *Mexico in 1827* (London: H. Colburn; 1828), Vol. II, p. 236.

had previously (1809–16) served Washington as a roving trade commissioner in Chile and the far south, to be minister in Mexico (1825–29). Ward was a nimble advance agent of empire; he entertained the right people with ample food and wine, and won a trade treaty in 1827. Poinsett had no such good fortune; he only succeeded in being declared *persona non grata* and was recalled to Washington—and the United States did not get a trade treaty until two years after he had left. To be sure, Ward had a fatter expense account with which to garner friends; he spent about £10,000 in two years, whereupon he was called home by his government, criticized for his extravagance—and commended for his success. The American Poinsett, "an imprudent man of good intentions" in Fred Rippy's phrase, was given scant expense funds and furthermore suffered the disabilities of "a flaming evangelist of republicanism," forgetting that an exported evangelism often incites resentment in its alien recipients.[5] In Poinsett's case the evangelism was Masonic: for he had secured charters for the Mexican York Rite lodges. Ward, on the other hand, was a supporter of the Scottish Rite Masons. The injection of international jealousies and of the family quarrels of Freemasonry served to deepen and widen the rift between Liberals and Conservatives.

The spark that set off the inevitable explosion was a debate over the public debt. The English bankers who had floated a substantial loan went into bankruptcy, with money still owing to the Mexican treasury. The Victoria government (predominantly *yorkino*) then suspended service on the debt. Vice-President Bravo, abetted by his Scottish Rite colleagues, launched an armed revolt against Victoria in 1828; its failure brought exile to Bravo and his coconspirators, and loss of prestige to the *escoceses;* and Victoria managed to complete his term despite the empty treasury. In the meantime, however, the *yorkinos* split among themselves over the question of presidential candidates in the election campaign of 1828, with the result that Masonic rivalry was much reduced as a factor in Mexican politics.

The elections of 1828 and the four years that followed set a pattern of unconstitutionality and violence that was to become endemic in the body politic: the losing presidential candidate was unwilling to accept the verdict and was seated by force; whereupon he and his vice-president had a falling out and the latter was placed in office; and then a minister in the cabinet assumed actual power in a virtual dictatorship—all accomplished with the aid (or at least by the leave) of Santa Anna. In the election of 1828, Vicente Guerrero, veteran aide of Morelos and a staunch *yorkino,* was opposed by Gómez Pedraza of the "Impartials," who refused allegiance at that time to either of the Masonic groups. Guerrero lost the election to Gómez Pedraza and resorted to arms; at this point Santa Anna charged upon the scene and forced Guerrero's seating in April, 1829, with the Conservative Anastasio Bustamante as vice-president.

[5] The debate was not ended by Poinsett's retirement to private life in South Carolina. Strident Mexican historians have had much to say of *poinsettismo,* an ugly word used to cover all manner of Yankeephobia and directed at American meddling in Mexican affairs. Americans remember Poinsett for introducing the plant called the poinsettia.

Guerrero got off to a bad start by expelling many Spaniards, thousands of whom had remained after independence under the promise of the "three guarantees." This ill-advised act resulted in a great loss to the nation. "The Spanish," notes Lesley Simpson, "were the thrifty middle class of Mexico and their expulsion cleared the way for other foreign exploiters who were not readily assimilated and who usually sent their money abroad." The President justified his action by citing Spanish plots against the republic. He showed praiseworthy but dangerous generosity in pardoning the rebellious Bravo and permitting his return. He outlawed slavery, a measure designed to make Texas less enticing to American migrants. But honest Guerrero's good intentions were obscured by a new tumult of applause for Santa Anna. That soldier of ill fortune was inadvertently given a new boost to glory by Spain. Ferdinand, waiting for a chance to recapture his former domain, had sent an expedition in 1829 which landed troops on the coast near Tampico. When his soldiers seized a fort, they were promptly laid low by yellow fever, and the few weakened survivors were suddenly attacked and overcome by the ever-dramatic Santa Anna. As the "hero of Tampico," Santa Anna returned in vast pomp to the capital, where he unseated the hapless Guerrero and placed Vice-President Bustamante in the national palace. That latest legatee of Santa Anna's bounty was permitted to remain in office for three years. But the real power during that period (1829–32) was in the hands of Bustamante's minister of foreign affairs, Lucas Alamán.

Lucas Alamán, leader of the Conservatives for almost thirty years and chief spokesman for centralized government, was one of the more honorable representatives of the era of Santa Anna. Alamán was born in 1792 in the rich gold and silver center of Guanajuato and was educated as a mining engineer. He was eighteen when Father Hidalgo led his butchering mob into that northern city; a year later, he saw the heads of Hidalgo and his chief aides fixed upon the corners of the royal granary. His contempt for the excesses of that early patriot force (of whose overtones he was never quite aware) flows in blazing torrent from his later *History of Mexico,* an indispensable record of the revolutionary years. He spent most of those years in Europe: in 1819 he served as a Mexican deputy in the Spanish *cortes,* where he sought to enlist capital and technical aid for mining in Mexico; and he became a warm admirer of British political and economic institutions. He returned to service in Guadalupe Victoria's cabinet, and from then until his death in 1853, in and out of office, he was the accepted champion of Conservative interests.

Alamán was the aristocrat in politics; he was short and plump, cleanshaven and bespectacled, austere and arrogant. Few of his political enemies failed to credit him with personal and political integrity. As Victoria's minister of foreign affairs, he had a decisive influence on those formative years. His admiration for England made him the natural ally of her representative, H. G. Ward; thanks to Alamán, England lent the money Mexico needed (at usurious rates, perhaps justified by the gamble involved), and a trade treaty with England was signed in 1827. His respect for the English was accompanied by an equally fervent dislike of the Americans. Minister Joel Poinsett evoked his intense hostility. Alamán blocked efforts to open the Santa Fe trail (leading from Missouri into the heart of Mexico's northern territory); he impeded the flow of Americans into Texas, and he postponed conclusion of a trade treaty with Washington until 1831. During Bustamante's presidency (1829–32), Alamán, his chief minister, became the virtual dictator. Despite provisions of the Constitution of 1824, Conservative-centralist rule was supreme, with the army and the Church as chief allies. The blackest deed of those years—and a major blemish on the record of Alamán—was the seizure and execution of the patriotic ex-President Guerrero.

Alamán had bold plans for strengthening Mexico. He sought to reform education by expanding and revivifying the schools, but there was neither time enough nor money. His program of economic reform fared better. He established a national credit bank for agriculture and industry. A trained engineer himself, Alamán had made futile efforts in the early 1820's to restore the mining industry. Later, in a position of power, he continued his efforts, and also sought to establish such industries as textile mills and iron foundries. He anticipated the demand that became articulate in the twentieth century: he dreamed of an industrialized nation freed from economic ties with any foreign land, a nation able to appropriate technical skills from other lands without falling into the hands of alien interests. His numerous critics charge that Alamán, driven by zeal for political and economic centralism, sought to impose the industrial revolution before Mexico was ready for it.

THE LIBERAL INTERLUDE, 1832–35

In 1832 the restless Santa Anna found it expedient to utilize the current anger against Bustamante's reactionary regime. He led his forces into the capital, unseating the President he had illegally imposed; then, after a brief breathing space, he permitted himself to be elected by a grateful citizenry, with the Liberal Gómez Farías as his vice-president. However, when the day of his investiture came, Santa Anna had already ridden off to his Jalapa plantation in the midst of gardenias and mimosas, leaving the Vice-President to handle the affairs of government. This sudden flight may have represented the prudent decision of Santa Anna to escape responsibility for the liberal course to which Gómez Farías was committed.

Valentín Gómez Farías, the *doyen* of Mexican liberalism from the 1820's until his death in 1858, was a physician from Guadalajara. He belonged to that numerous company of young Spanish Americans who had caught the infection of the exciting new ideas from France. An intellectual of ranging curiosity and a man of warm human sympathy, Gómez Farías exercised profound influence upon independent Mexico in its formative years. His brief command of the nation in 1833–34 brought one of the most controversial periods in Mexican history. He is unfairly remembered as a "fierce enemy of the Church" (as the Jesuit historian Mariano Cuevas describes him), an appraisal which must be tempered by cooler analysis. He indeed favored sharp curtailing of the powers of the Church, but he never was an intransigent critic who denied the clergy due credit for their moral and spiritual contribution. The violent anticlericalism associated with his name may be traced to some less irenic spirits among his colleagues in Liberal ranks. Among these were the ex-priest José María Luis Mora, a man of considerable learning, and Lorenzo de Zavala, an explosive little mestizo from Yucatán, whose lack of moderation—and lack of character— proved embarrassing to the wiser Gómez Farías.

The liberal interlude of 1833–34 brought sweeping changes. On taking over the presidency, Gómez Farías made a searching diagnosis of the ills of the immature nation: there was need for more and better schools, especially primary schools; for reform of the courts and the assurance of justice; for the cleansing of the prisons, which were in lamentable state; for the colonization of the empty lands in the north—in Texas, where the Americans were already gaining the mastery, and in California, where the Russians were suspected of imperialistic designs. Gómez Farías antagonized the army by reducing the excessive number of generals, by ending the special privileges of the military, and by creating civil militias for keeping order. He angered nationalistic Mexicans by adopting a generous course toward Spaniards living in the country, permitting those who married Mexicans to remain. He aroused the ire of dishonest officials by reforming the customhouses and abolishing the tobacco monopoly.

His course with the Church evoked most of the fury against him. He transferred the control of the California missions from the Spanish regular clergy (who generally refused to take the oath of allegiance to the new nation of Mexico) to secular priests who would work under the supervision of the state—the expenses to be paid out of the "pious funds," endowments collected through the years for the support of the missions. He closed the ancient University of Mexico, clerically controlled and almost moribund, and proposed to create six institutions of higher learning in its place. Church control of education was ended. He favored the complete severance of Church and state, but was blocked by his Liberal colleagues who wished the Mexican government to assume Spain's *patronato*—the right of the state to name incumbents of ecclesiastical posts. With his full consent, two laws were passed: the compulsory payment of tithes was rescinded, and the members of religious orders were made free to retract their vows. Over his opposition, a law to grant the state the old Spanish right of patronage was adopted.

These acts brought uproar from the generals, the clergy, and the landholders. Santa Anna, nominally president but taking no hand in these drastic measures, rode up now and then from Jalapa, fidgeted for a week or two in the presidential office, and rode back again to the peace of his plantation. "Santa Anna and Gómez Farías," wrote a contemporary historian, "alternated in power like two theatrical impresarios; one, with his retinue of ignorant soldiers, bullies, usurers and disorderly office seekers; and the other with his train of Freemasons, spread-eaglists . . . each with . . . his unique plan for quick regeneration."[6] Santa Anna, the perfect weathercock, was waiting to see which way the winds blew. If the people wanted to fight the army and the Church, he would cheer them on. If not, he would shift to meet their demands. He heard the shouts of the poor and ignorant for *religión y fueros* —the *fueros* were the numerous special privileges of the clergy, notably their protection by Church courts. Then, a scourge of cholera swept the capital, emptying the streets except for the carts carrying away the dead. The faithful thronged the churches and were assured that the plague was a divine visitation upon a faithless nation. Santa Anna saw a great light, and in April, 1834, he made another famous entrance into the city, ousted Gómez Farías, assumed the presidency with dictatorial hand, and revoked the hated laws. Santa Anna was again hailed as the savior of the country.

Gómez Farías, honest but precipitate, bore the brunt of popular abuse. He fled from Mexico with his family, while a newspaper remarked:

> Yesterday the execrable Gómez Farías finally left the capital, overwhelmed with the just imprecations of the leading city of Columbus's new world on which his terrible acts weighed so heavily. . . . Gómez Farías attracted, like an ill-fated comet . . . cholera and misery; immorality and tyranny; espionage and treason; ignorance and sacrilege; the promotion of delinquents and the demotion of the honorable; the triumph of the worthless canaille and the debasement of the select people; terror and mourning in families; banishment, sorrow and death in a thousand horrible forms.[7]

Zavala and Mora also went into exile; and these two Liberals were never to return. That was the end of the "liberal housecleaning of 1833," a small dress rehearsal of *La Reforma* two decades later. The net result of the brief rule of Gómez Farías was to bewilder the devoutly religious masses, to isolate and discredit the Liberals, and to furnish Santa Anna with excuse for deserting his erstwhile allies and riding to victory with the Conservatives. The Gómez Farías digression temporarily ended the liberal movement, and for the next twenty-five years the Conservatives were on top save for brief interludes.[8]

Santa Anna professed the integrity of his political about-face: "It is very true that I threw up my cap for liberty with great ardor, and perfect sincerity, but very soon found the folly of it. A hundred years to come my people will not be fit for liberty. They do not know what it is, unenlightened as they are, and under the influence of a Catholic clergy, a despotism is the proper government for them, but there is no reason why it should not be a wise and virtuous one."[9] But the new despot was neither wise nor virtuous:

[6] Guillermo Prieto: *Memorias de mis tiempos* (2 vols.; Mexico: Vda. de C. Bouret; 1906), Vol. I, p. 100.

[7] Narciso Bassols: *Valentín Gómez Farías* (Mexico: Impr. de la Secretaría de relaciones exteriores; 1933), pp. 36–7; quoted in W. H. Callcott: *Santa Anna* (Norman, Okla.: University of Oklahoma Press; 1936), p. 110.

[8] The author acknowledges his indebtedness to C. Alan Hutchinson of the University of Virginia, who has done much useful research on Gómez Farías.

[9] Clarence R. Wharton: *El Presidente; A Sketch of the Life of General Santa Anna* (Houston: Printed by C. C. Young Printing Co.; 1924), p. 64; quoted in W. H. Callcott, *op. cit.*, pp. 108–9.

Santa Anna dissolved the Liberal congress, then proceeded to rule with such high hand that he alienated his new allies. When the new military-clerical congress, convened in January, 1835, proved unmanageable, Santa Anna slipped away to his plantation to bide his time. He was destined to remain on the sidelines for almost seven years, during which fresh military adventures brought him varying degrees of discredit and acclaim.

In the meantime the government Santa Anna left behind formally abolished the federal system in October, 1835, a move bitterly resented by the states, in several of which there was now open revolt. In Zacatecas, the uprisings were so frequent that Santa Anna was sent to administer bloody reprisals. And the people of Texas took up arms "in defence of their rights and liberties."

TEXAS

The turmoil over Texas, which finally provoked war, began when the United States bought Louisiana in 1803 and pressed the debate over the line of demarcation between her new territory and what was then New Spain. The quarrel was sharpened in 1821 when Stephen Austin and other promoters were granted concessions by a harassed Spain to settle American homesteaders in Texas, which at that time had a population of about 2,000 whites and a few scattered Indians. Independent Mexico, legatee of this empty wilderness and of Spain's commitments, watched the Anglo-Saxon invasion with mixed feelings. Many federalists innocently thought that thereby a rich and populous state would be added to the Mexican union; but they failed to reckon with the bellicosity of the American frontiersmen, who had already tasted the heady brew of manifest destiny. The northern mood was later expressed by Waddy Thompson, American minister to Mexico: "That our language and laws are destined to pervade this continent, I regard as more certain than any other event which is in the future." Minister Poinsett embroiled relations in the 1820's by suggesting that the United States purchase Texas; this gave the English minister, Ward, an excuse for warning President Victoria against the nefarious Yankees.

The threat to Mexican retention of the area was real, for some 25,000 Americans had settled in Texas by 1830, and the language generally heard was English. Belated precautions were taken: in 1829 President Guerrero abolished slavery, a blow aimed at settlers from slave states; in 1830 Alamán ordered a stop to further migration and a customs barrier against goods from the United States—but Mexico had neither guns nor soldiers to enforce her will. Meanwhile Texas was joined to the state of Coahuila, a wise move on Mexico's part, an exasperating one for the colonists. In 1833, after the triumph of Gómez Farías and the federalists, Austin and other Texans appeared in the capital to argue that Texas simply desired self-rule as a loyal state of the Mexican union. When Santa Anna's government abolished the federal system in 1835, the Texans revolted—but even then the majority of Texans opposed any move toward independence, avowing that their quarrel was not with the Mexican nation but with the centralist government which had overthrown the Constitution of 1824, and offering "their support and assistance to such of the members of the Mexican confederacy as will take up arms against military despotism."[1] But the hoped-for alliance with the Liberals did not materialize. Meanwhile, the laws limiting immigration were flouted, and fresh contingents of colonists arrived daily.

Early in 1836 Santa Anna, whose popularity was waning, decided to play the hero and bring the Texans to their knees. He started north with an army of Indian conscripts, whose shoddy equipment had been furnished by his corrupt contractors. In the meantime, a constituent convention of Texans meeting on March 2 formally declared Texas independent and named David Burnet as president, and Lorenzo de Zavala as vice-president.[2] On March 6 Santa Anna led an attack upon some 150 militia who had taken their stand in the Franciscan mission of the Alamo in San Antonio, killing the Americans to the last man; the cry "Remember the Alamo!" echoed across Texas. Two weeks later Santa Anna shocked even his own subordinates by ordering the massacre of more than 300 prisoners held by the Mexicans at Goliad. Giddy with success, he then pursued the fleeing Americans east to the San Jacinto River, where a Texan army of about 800 faced a Mexican force of twice that number. When the doughty Sam Houston ordered an attack on April 21, the overconfident Mexicans were caught off guard: some 600 were killed, more were taken prisoners, and Santa Anna himself was captured. Hot-headed Americans were eager to string up Santa Anna, but they yielded to wiser counsel—and to the blandishments of the wily Mexican. Santa Anna made treacherous promises to confirm Texan independence, first to Houston, and then —when sent to Washington—to President Jackson. But when he was finally released, he said: "You have kept me too long. The presidency will have passed into other hands; and on my return I shall have to retire to my hacienda shorn of all power, and incapable, however desirous, of carrying out my pledges."

Upon his return to Mexico late in 1836, Santa Anna was greeted with suspicion and distrust, which he countered with customary eloquence:

[1] A convention in Texas in November, 1835, formally declared that the people of Texas "do not acknowledge that the present authorities of the nominal Mexican republic have the right to govern within the limits of Texas . . . but that they will continue faithful to the Mexican government so long as that nation is governed by the constitution and laws that were formed for the government of the political association." For the full text of this declaration see Ethel Zivley Mather: "Recognition of the Republic of Texas by the United States," *The Quarterly of the Texas State Historical Association*, Vol. XIII, No. 3 (January, 1910), p. 156.

[2] This was the same Zavala who had worked with Gómez Farías in 1833 and who shortly afterward went into exile with Gómez Farías and Mora. The plottings of Zavala and his acceptance of the post as vice-president of Texas exposed him to the charge, by Mexican patriots, of treason. Conservative Mexicans argue to this day that the Liberals were essentially traitors who were ready to sell out to the United States; but it should be remembered that Gómez Farías, when confronted with the issue of Texas, was always a good Mexican.

Santa Anna, whether conqueror or conquered, whether free or in chains, yea, I swear it before the world, did not in Texas debase the Mexican name in which he glories and takes pride. . . . It is a great consolation to me . . . that the prejudice of my fellow citizens should rest in part on false appearances that I myself have partially been obliged to create. But by assuring them, now that I am free, that I am not bound by dishonorable treaties against my country, I have dissipated those appearances by confirming the truth. . . . In brief, I offered nothing in the name of the nation. In my own name, I pledged myself to acts that our government could nullify, and I received in exchange the promise of being set free without delay. Where is the treason? . . . The end of my public career has arrived.[3]

And he continued to avow his willingness to bare his breast for the defense of Mexican soil. But the state of Texas was lost to the Mexican union.

CENTRALISM AND DICTATORSHIP, 1835–45

The congress that Santa Anna deserted in 1835 drafted a new constitution, highly centralist and conservative. It was not promulgated until December, 1836, by which time Santa Anna had lost face in the Texas campaign. The new document, besides abolishing states as separate entities, showed a distrust of caudillos in general, and of Santa Anna in particular: it established an inner clique of five members called the *Poder Conservador,* which was designed to dominate congress, the president, and the courts; and was granted plenary powers to unseat the chief executive, nullify laws, and override judicial decisions. The compliant Bustamante, recently returned from exile in Europe, was elected in January, 1837, to serve as president under this "conserving authority." There followed a lull of almost two years in the fortunes of Santa Anna, who professed loyalty to the new regime, as he dramatically pronounced his own career at an end.

But Santa Anna's sun had not yet set, for late in 1838 he acquired a new claim upon the gratitude of his country. A French army, seeking satisfaction for wrongs, real or fancied, against French nationals, occupied Veracruz. Santa Anna, always the first to scent the field of glory, undertook to evict the intruders, a task which he accomplished with tremendous commotion, and some losses—the most momentous, one of his own legs, shot off by French gunfire. That was, perhaps, the most important result of the "Pastry War."[4] Santa Anna, his prestige as the hero of Tampico

---

[3] "Manifesto which General López de Santa Anna addresses to his fellow-citizens Relative to his operations during the Texas Campaign and his Capture. 10 of May 1837." Carlos E. Casteñada, ed.: *The Mexican Side of the Texan Revolution* (Dallas: P. L. Turner Co.; 1928), pp. 7 ff.

[4] So it has been called ever since. A French restaurateur in a suburb of the capital had lost many cakes to a group of drunken Mexican generals, and his claim had been included in the demand for settlement.

eclipsed by the Texas fiasco, was now the hero of Veracruz, and with this new honor he made a jubilant visit to the capital—minus one leg—to be hailed once more as the savior of his country. For the next two years the triumphant Santa Anna and the worried Bustamante jockeyed for position, the unspectacular President playing a losing game.

Popular wrath was mounting against Bustamante and the high-riding Conservatives; the press was demanding restoration of the Constitution of 1824. The Liberals, led by Gómez Farías, recently returned from exile in the United States, made various attempts to recapture the government. Their efforts reached a climax in the summer of 1840, when a miniature civil war raged in the capital for several days, with soldiers shooting "at each other from behind parapets and from the tops of houses and steeples," as eyewitness Mme. Calderón de la Barca reported. She noted the "tranquillity" of the populace; "shops shut, workmen out of employment, thousands of idle people, subsisting Heaven only knows how, yet no riot, no confusion, apparently no impatience." But where the honorable Liberals failed, the dishonorable Santa Anna succeeded, just a year later, in his next dramatic coup. Together with General Mariano Paredes, he staged a military revolt in July, 1841, which was inspired by "disloyalty, hypocrisy, and the most sordid calculations." They attacked the despotic *Poder Conservador* and demanded that the presidency be entrusted to "some citizen worthy of confidence," who of course could be none other than Santa Anna. At the eleventh hour the despairing Bustamante renounced centralism and declared for the Constitution of 1824, but this only inspired the hero of Veracruz to denounce the President as a traitor. By October, 1841, Santa Anna's triumph was complete, and he accepted appointment by a hand-picked "Junta of Notables" as provisional president. But popular emotion was spent, and when the hero entered the capital not a *viva* was heard in the streets.

The rule upon which Santa Anna now embarked lasted off and on— with much time out for rest in Jalapa—from 1841 until the end of 1844. When in 1842 a congress was elected which represented the federalists, Santa Anna retired, leaving a trusted puppet to disband that body and reassemble the more amenable Junta of Notables, who promptly drew up a new dictatorial and highly centralist constitution—the *Bases Orgánicas* of 1843. That instrument legalized Santa Anna's position, permitting him to be suitably elected on January 2, 1844.

Santa Anna's dictatorship was more unashamedly kingly than anything Mexico had known before. His officers were everywhere—six colonels stood at attention behind his chair while he dined. The greatness of the nation's hero was dramatized when his glorious leg—victim of the Pastry War —was dug up from the gardens of his Jalapa plantation and given a solemn reburial in the capital's cathedral. Such official pomp and ceremony was costly, but Santa Anna was adept in both filling and emptying the public treasury. He accepted loans and gifts from the Church and pressed for more. He increased import duties and sold mining concessions. It worked out fairly well until these sources began to run dry, and his numerous army officers and hangers-on found their salaries in arrears. And then—as always in Mexico when paychecks fail—revolt came. Late in 1844 Paredes, long neglected by his one-time ally, struck at the dictator. And in December the congress, which had been quiescent as long as Santa Anna paid the bills, named the mild José Joaquín Herrera as chief executive. The city's mob dug up Santa Anna's leg and dragged it through the streets. Santa Anna himself was driven from the city, found refuge in the mountains of Vera-cruz, and was finally exiled to Havana in the summer of 1845.

Meanwhile, the outer world was crowding in upon Mexico.

WAR AND THE AFTERMATH, 1845–55

The defection of Texas had united Mexicans in anger against the United States, anger which mounted when Washington recognized the Lone Star Republic in 1837. Santa Anna voiced the unanimous sentiment of loyal Mexicans when he said, in 1842, that he "would war forever for the recon-quest of Texas. . . . To sign a treaty for the alienation of Texas would be the same as signing the death warrant of Mexico . . . by the same process [the United States] would take one after the other of the Mexican provinces until [it] had them all." Mexico listened uneasily as Americans debated annexation. It was a confused war of words, the North opposing admission of another slave state, Washington fearing that the British would get Texas if the United States failed to act. Both England and France urged Mexico not to yield. Mexico announced in 1843 that annexation would mean war and meanwhile added fuel to the flames by discontinuing payments on Amer-ican claims against her.

President Polk was elected in 1844 by the adherents of manifest destiny who wanted Texas, California, and the desert that lay between. The Texas question was quickly settled. Texas was annexed by the United States in 1845; and eyes were turned to California, the next goal—and the object of ominous British interest. Polk, a man of hard sense but inexperienced in the niceties of diplomacy, sent John Slidell as minister and presidential agent to persuade President Herrera to sell California and the entire South-west. The approach was awkward. Herrera could not receive a United States minister while Mexican feelings were still exacerbated by the annex-ation of Texas, nor could he openly discuss the sale of Mexican soil. Her-rera's attempts at conciliation were denounced as craven by Mexican patri-ots, who rallied around the belligerent Paredes in January, 1846, as he evicted Herrera, repulsed Slidell, and prepared for war. Polk regarded the United States case as complete: Mexico had refused to pay claims and had expelled the American minister. Polk ordered Zachary Taylor into the de-bated area between the river Nueces and the Rio Grande—and that, said Mexico, constituted invasion. In April, 1846, Mexican forces attacked Tay-lor's men—and that, said Polk, was war. In May Polk advised Congress that war existed, by act of Mexico.

It was a war for which neither the United States nor Mexico was prepared. The American forces were untried, and numerous Europeans confidently prophesied victory for Mexico. But Mexico, riddled by internal strife and corruption, poor in arms, and with an undisciplined army, had no chance. The United States ordered Taylor to march south, and after minor battles he reached Monterrey and Saltillo. Meanwhile, a small force led by the ubiquitous American explorer and sometime soldier John Charles Frémont, together with a small naval detachment, occupied California in July, 1846. These events provoked an overturn in the Mexican capital: a popular revolt returned the Liberals to power, and with them came restoration of the Constitution of 1824. Gómez Farías then turned in desperation to Santa Anna, whose unreliability he knew so well, as the one man who could rally the Mexican army. That scarred hero, now in exile in Cuba, responded to the call, and persuaded President Polk to grant him safe conduct through the American blockade, promising that he would settle the war to the satisfaction of Washington. In August, 1846, Santa Anna landed in Veracruz where, despite his pledge to Polk, he undertook the task of recruiting an army, and actually persuaded several thousand men to follow him. He then marched north to meet Zachary Taylor. The two armies met near Saltillo, where the Mexicans fought bravely against the better-armed Americans. After the considerable battle of Buena Vista in February, 1847, Santa Anna, thinking it wiser not to press fate, started back to the capital. He had two captured American flags, enough to prove him victorious. Taylor reported to Washington that *his* victory was complete, and he returned to his capital, to a hero's acclaim—and to the presidency two years later.

In the meantime, the quandary of Gómez Farías, who had become president in December, 1846, was daily becoming more desperate. In order to pay the bills for Santa Anna's heroics, he levied upon the Church, whereupon the clergy and their supporters vowed to get rid of him. The answer to their prayers now rode into the city from his debatable victory in the north. Santa Anna unseated Gómez Farías in March, 1847, just as he had done in 1834, replaced him with a compliant nonentity, and paid the bills by borrowing 2 million pesos from the Church, promising (as he always did so engagingly) that he would never ask for another centavo. Then he turned toward Veracruz to meet Winfield Scott and the second expeditionary force of the United States.

General Scott was Polk's choice; the President knew that Zachary Taylor was an indifferent soldier, and furthermore suspected that he had his eye on the presidency. Scott's forces landed near Veracruz in March, 1847. They captured the seaport city, marched inland, defeated Santa Anna at Cerro Gordo, and pushed through Puebla to the valley of Anáhuac and Mexico City. Foreign pressure united the Mexicans, while distrust of Santa Anna divided them. Nevertheless, men of all political faiths rallied under that discredited general and fought bravely against the Americans who entered the capital in September, 1847. The streets were ordered cleared, but

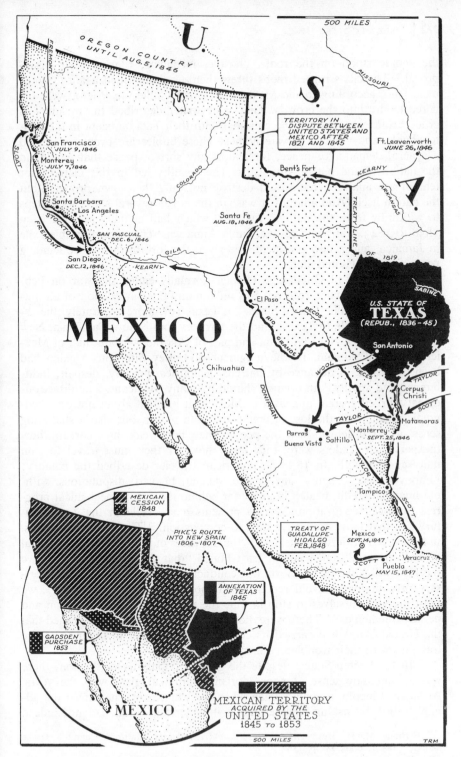

Mexican–United States War, 1846–47; Mexican Territory Acquired by the United States, 1845–53

the people stood on the roofs, "hostile, menacing, roaring their disapproval." The city's ragged mobs threw themselves unarmed against Scott's men, who, according to the Mexican historian Guillermo Prieto, were ordered to fire into the crowds. That same writer described the invaders as crude brutes who entered the churches with their hats on, slept in the confessionals, and violated private homes. These unpleasant events prompted a general demand for peace, for almost any sort of peace that would rid the nation of the hated Americans. The wealthy led in this clamor, for fear of the anarchy that would destroy not only their own property but the nation itself. And anarchy it was: in the north, several states took steps to withdraw from the nation; Yucatán, which had actually seceded from 1838 to 1843, was again restive. Santa Anna was sent to comfortable exile in Jamaica, and a new president was given the forlorn task of concluding peace with the United States.

The Treaty of Guadalupe Hidalgo formally ended the war on February 2, 1848. Mexico received $15 million and the cancellation of all outstanding claims. The United States got Texas (or, more accurately, the assurance of her title to Texas) and the territory that is now California, New Mexico, Arizona, Nevada, Utah, and part of Colorado—about half of Mexico's national domain. In the judgment of Lesley Simpson, Mexico had been "defeated in advance by hatreds, jealousies, poverty, despair, indifference and apathy," an opinion shared by many Mexicans. The disastrous defeat worked a great upheaval in Mexico. It brought about not only economic chaos, with the loss of credit and man power, but also a shattering sense of moral defeat. Now the people knew how weak, how corrupt, how inexpert their leaders were; they knew how far they must travel to gain unity and strength. In 1850 an American traveler described the country: "Impoverished, haughty, uneducated, defiant, bigoted, disputatious, without financial credit, beaten in arms, far behind the age of mechanical progress or social civilization, Mexico presents a spectacle in the 19th Century . . . that moves reflective men to compassion."[5] Thoughtful Mexicans, in honest self-criticism, considered "the disgraces of the war and the scandal of civil discord," and some at least hoped "that the hard lesson that we received will serve us to reform our conduct, obliging us to take the necessary precautions to avoid repetition of those disgraceful events; . . . we must prepare ourselves to stop in time the blows with which ambition and perfidy threaten us."[6] There were, however, many Mexicans who wished that the United States had carried its conquest even further in order to assure tranquillity to their troubled country.

In the United States, despite the general popularity of the war, there was an unhappy sense of poor sportsmanship that grew with the years. Abraham Lincoln, a congressman when the war began, challenged the administration by asking whether the first American blood had not indeed

[5] Brantz Mayer: *Mexico; Aztec, Spanish and Republican* (Hartford, Conn.: S. Drake and Co.; 1851), Book IV, p. 156.

[6] Ramón Alcaraz, ed.: *Apuntes para la historia de la guerra entre México y los Estados Unidos* (Mexico: Tip. de M. Payno [hijo]; 1848), p. 1.

been shed on Mexican soil. Ulysses S. Grant, in his last years, described the war as "the most unjust ever waged by a stronger against a weaker nation." Robert E. Lee expressed himself in similar fashion. American historians generally regard it as one of the less glorious episodes in the history of the United States, although they accept it as a step in the inevitable American expansion to the Pacific.

Mexico's political course in the postwar years was wavering and weak. Herrera (president from 1848 to 1851) and his successors were hard put to it to bring back rebellious states to loyalty, to impose order upon the country, and to gather funds. Lucas Alamán, editing a promonarchist paper *El Universal,* urged a return to the days of kings and clergy; in 1853 he and the Conservatives again came to power. This standard-bearer for old causes, taking counsel of desperation, conceived the idea of again summoning Santa Anna, whom neither he nor anyone else trusted but who seemed the only man strong enough to rally Mexicans for their task. The Conservatives had one overreaching ambition, to "destroy the federal system so closely identified with *poinsettismo* and to restore the respect for authority"; and Santa Anna was the tool by which Alamán hoped to work his last great reform.

But Santa Anna had just been installed in 1853 when Lucas Alamán died. The one powerful check thus removed, Santa Anna's rule became a brazen despotism, resembling but dwarfing that of Iturbide himself. Like Iturbide, Santa Anna depended for his power upon the army and the Church; and he emulated the emperor's example of lavish pageantry. His palace was the scene of profligate luxury, dirty intrigue, and criminal waste. His old love of cockfighting still occupied him. Drunken with adulation, he was titled, by congressional action, "His Most Serene Highness." The Order of Guadalupe, instituted by Iturbide, was refurbished, and Mexico was infested with knights whose spurs were won by pandering to this tyrant. Such antics drained the national treasury, but again Santa Anna saved himself by betraying his own nation. Washington was eager to acquire a strip of some 45,000 square miles in the Mesilla valley (now incorporated into Arizona and New Mexico), as the best route for a railway to the Pacific. Santa Anna sold it for $10 million. This was the Gadsden Purchase of 1853, useful for the United States, but humiliating to Mexico.

Nevertheless, Santa Anna's time was up. The Liberals, who had been maturing during the years of confusion, were now gathering their forces. Santa Anna struck at them, first imprisoning and then exiling Benito Juárez of Oaxaca and Melchor Ocampo of Michoacán, both soon to be notable leaders of the movement called *La Reforma.* By 1855 all signs pointed to Santa Anna's end: generals and politicians deserted him and foreign powers refused to support him. In August he took ship for exile in Colombia, never to trouble Mexico again.[7]

7 His Most Serene Highness's last years were unimportant. He later returned to serve the Emperor Maximilian, who brusquely denied him entrance to the country. He tried again in 1867 and was again expelled. He was finally allowed to enter Mexico in 1872, and lived on charity until his death at eighty-one in 1876.

THE ERA OF BENITO JUÁREZ,
1855–76

Mexico now embarked on twenty-one years of tumult in which the Liberals launched and defended their laws curtailing the traditional privileges of the Church and charted a new economic and social course for the nation—this was the period called *La Reforma*. That stormy era comprised the popular uprising that unseated Santa Anna in 1855; the anticlerical edicts of 1855 and 1856; the rewriting of the constitution in 1857; civil war between Liberals and Conservatives from 1858 to 1860; a breathing space under Juárez in 1861; the intervention of France and the imposition of a foreign monarch from 1862 to 1867; the reconstruction presidency of Juárez from 1867 until his death in 1872; and the rule of Sebastián Lerdo de Tejada until 1876.

LA REFORMA

"The Reform" began with the uprisings of guerrilla bands in the southern mountains in 1854; their chief organizer was Juan Álvarez, an illiterate Indian caudillo who had been fighting alien and domestic tyrants for forty years. Rough but patriotic, Álvarez was the first effective military spokesman for the scattered Liberals united only in distaste for Santa Anna. The Liberals—chiefly middle-class mestizos—were determined to break the hold of the aging cynics who had permitted Santa Anna to ride roughshod over their liberties, and whose blindness had facilitated the loss of half the national domain. They demanded new rulers, a new government, and a new constitution; in short, a second revolution aimed—in Justo Sierra's words—at "an emancipation from the colonial regime, as the first was an emancipation from Spain." They believed that Mexico could be saved from anarchy and further dismemberment by the United States only through subordination of the army and the Church to civil authority. Their leaders were mostly civilians, a tougher lot than those who contrived the reforms of 1833. Benito Juárez had been seasoned by long political experience in his native state of Oaxaca. Melchor Ocampo, lawyer and scientist, and Santos Degollado, professor of law, had worked together in Michoacán for the modernization of agriculture, the cleansing of government, and the reduction of clerical privileges. The brothers Lerdo de Tejada—Miguel and Sebastián—were astute theoreticians of government. The movement had its men of letters, including Guillermo Prieto, the poet, and Ignacio Ramírez, "the Voltaire of Mexican literature." Their ranks had been strengthened by the *moderados,* the fence-sitters of the dismal forties, who were driven into the Liberal camp by the final absurdities of Santa Anna. The mediocre creole Ignacio Comonfort was one of these.

The Liberals' declaration of war upon Santa Anna was a manifesto called the *Plan de Ayutla,* issued in March, 1854. It was a temperate document designed to satisfy the *moderados,* and called for the final ouster of Santa Anna and the convening of a congress to draft a new constitution. This *Plan* hastened the final desertion of Santa Anna's supporters and that hero's flight into exile in August, 1855. In November, 1855, the Liberals occupied the capital city without gunfire, their ranks headed by Álvarez and his Indian bodyguard—a shocking sight for cultured city dwellers. A provisional government was formed, with Álvarez as president and Juárez as minister of justice. They quickly issued an edict, the *Ley Juárez,* which clipped the powers of the long-criticized military and ecclesiastical courts, and ended their jurisdiction in purely civil cases. This attack upon special privilege provoked the general outcry of *religión y fueros* (religion and privileges), and the furor prompted the bewildered Álvarez, already uncomfortable among city people, to turn over the presidency in December to the habitual compromiser, Ignacio Comonfort, who quickly alienated Juárez and other forthright Liberals.

Nevertheless, further edicts gave force to the principal Liberal objectives. In 1856 new anticlerical measures were announced, including the suppression of the Jesuits. The *Ley Lerdo,* drafted by Miguel Lerdo de Tejada, required the Church and all of her orders to divest themselves of lands not devoted to religious purposes, such lands to be sold on easy terms, with a heavy sales tax payable to the national treasury. This drastic measure reflected current Liberal emphasis on the virtue of individual ownership of land. While the law was aimed at the Church, holder of about half of all land in use, it also struck at the communal lands of the village *ejidos.* Its sponsors hoped that the measure would not only replenish the national treasury but would also divide the great estates among many small farmers. The plan miscarried. Church lands were bought by men who already had large holdings, or by others eager to establish themselves as *hacendados.* The helpless peasants, benefited not at all, were simply transferred as so many chattels from their clerical overseers to new secular lords. The Church, although she lost her estates, acquired large money reserves with which she continued as chief banker of the nation.

The new Constitution of 1857 was drafted by a congress dominated by the more moderate Liberals. It reaffirmed the time-honored Liberal principle of federalism, but largely nullified its doctrine of states' rights by assigning almost dictatorial powers to the congress. It struck at the Conservatives by creating a one-chamber congress, eliminating the upper house of senators who had usually been spokesmen for the Church, the army, and the landholders. It rigorously curtailed the president's powers, but contradicted itself by granting him discretionary authority "to defend the independence and integrity of the national territory, and to maintain law." The structure of the new instrument resembled that of the Constitution of the United States, but in its details it incorporated the fighting principles of mid-nineteenth-century liberalism: the anticlerical tenets of the *Ley Juárez* and the *Ley Lerdo* were reaffirmed; the military was subordinated to civil authority; personal liberty was emphasized and was defined to include the right of monks and nuns to renounce their vows; hereditary titles were abolished; and imprisonment for debt was banned. It was a faithful statement of French bourgeois reform, but utterly failed to reckon with the imperative Mexican problem of the landless Indian and his incorporation into national life. The constitution was signed on February 5, 1857, in the presence of the ailing seventy-five-year-old Gómez Farías, who was carried into the hall to witness the triumph of a cause to which he had devoted his life.

The new constitution aroused noisy contention. The Church ordered excommunication for all who swore allegiance to it. Army officers protested its affront to the military. Many Liberals, on the other hand, regarded it as too mild. Melchor Ocampo, condemning its failure to transfer land to small independent farmers, refused to sign. Ignacio Ramírez, an agnostic, denounced its failure to insure full religious tolerance. Comonfort the *moderado* did not (in the words of the Mexican historian Ignacio M. Altamirano) "accept the Constitution in his heart." Despite such dissent, the Constitution of 1857 became—and long remained—the banner of liberalism. The Liberals had indeed matured: in the 1820's, out of hatred for kings, they had been obsessed with federalism; in the 1830's they directed their blows against the Church; but in the 1850's Liberals, while still confusing anticlericalism with progress, were at last dimly aware of the need for fundamental social and economic reforms, although their efforts proved ineffectual. They sought to reform the land system and create a body of small middle-class farmers, but they failed miserably. The large haciendas increased in number and size. The *ejidal* lands of the Indian villages were annexed by their powerful neighbors. For all their good intentions, the reformers succeeded only in increasing the number of the landless and in accentuating the evils of multiplied latifundia. The weakness of liberalism in 1857, as in 1824 and 1833, was preoccupation with political rather than economic reform.

The elections of 1857, held in an atmosphere of high tension, confirmed Comonfort in the presidency and named Benito Juárez vice-president and head of the Supreme Court. Two weeks later General Félix Zuloaga, representing the army, issued a Conservative *pronunciamiento* against the constitution and ordered Comonfort to work out a more acceptable code. Poor Comonfort floundered between vain efforts to appease the Conservatives and to satisfy the Liberals; and then in January, 1858, he resigned and fled to the United States for rest, leaving the capital in the control of Zulo-aga, who assumed presidential powers. Meanwhile, as their answer to the absent Comonfort and the aspiring Zuloaga, seventy Liberal deputies estab-lished their rump congress in northern Querétaro, where they declared Benito Juárez president of the nation. Mexico now had two presidents and a civil war.

BENITO JUÁREZ

Benito Juárez, deeply revered by his countrymen, had much in common with his contemporary, Abraham Lincoln. Both were of humble birth, sons of poverty on the far frontier. They were alike men of few and homely words. Both were reticent men with many admirers and detractors but with few friends. Both were honorable men who held public office as a sacred trust and against whom no word of scandal has ever been proved. Both espoused and served the cause of the poorest of their countrymen. Both were adjudged failures by many of their contemporaries. Of both, it might be written: they were despised and rejected of men . . . men of sorrows and acquainted with grief.

Benito Juárez was born on March 21, 1806, in the village of San Pablo Guelatao, near Oaxaca, a full-blooded Zapotec whose ancestors had occupied the region for at least 2,000 years. His family lived, as other Indians lived, from their tiny corn plot, their few sheep and chickens, and from the few cents a day that were the current wages for Indian labor. The boy lost both mother and father when he was three, and was left to the care of an uncle. When he was twelve, after little schooling and much hard work, a twist of fate brought abrupt change. Some wanderers stole one of the sheep he was tending. Fearful of his uncle's wrath, he set out on the long journey afoot to Oaxaca. There the somber little Indian found employment in the home of a Franciscan lay brother, who gave him warm friendship, books, and an introduction to exciting ideas. His schooling was sporadic. For a time he considered entering the priesthood and studied some moral theology and Latin grammar. Then he turned to the Institute in Oaxaca, founded by the Liberals in the mid-1820's, and was quickly absorbed in the study of science and law. By 1831, then twenty-five, he knew enough law to win a clerkship in a law office. There followed ten years of patient struggle, with little money but with increasing respect from his neighbors. Many of his clients were poor Indians whose small rights to land and water were constantly threatened by neighboring *hacendados*. He fought their cases before judges whose venality was matched by their contempt for all Indians. In one famous case on behalf of an illiterate Indian against a greedy curate, Juárez so angered the Church court that he was imprisoned for a time. But by 1843 his social and financial position enabled him to marry Margarita Maza, daughter of a substantial family. We have her description of the thirty-seven-year-old bridegroom: "He is very homely, but very good."

After a term in the national congress during the war with the United States, Juárez returned as governor of his native state and served from 1847 to 1852. One of his first official acts was to deny the refuge of Oaxaca to Santa Anna, in flight from the capital. That dictator later explained the repulse: "[Juárez] could not forgive me because he had waited on me at table in Oaxaca in 1829, with his feet bare on the floor." Juárez took over an empty treasury, with wages of public servants in arrears; he left it five years later with a surplus of 50,000 pesos—a record for Mexican officeholders. He injected new energy and honesty into public administration, discouraged *empleomanía*—the clamor for jobs on the public payroll. He did a little to extend popular education, even opening the schools to women, in whom he saw "the fertile seed of social regeneration." He continued to fight for his wronged Indian kin, but did not have, then or later, any clear program for improving their economic lot. He sought to better the isolated economy of his state by beginning a road north to Tehuacán and one southwest to the Pacific. He opposed without success the customs barriers which blocked free exchange between the states. He did a little to improve the techniques of mining and farming. He dealt in conciliatory fashion with the Church, and found enlightened priests ready to cooperate for the good of the people. He ended his term as one of the best governors of any Mexican state and then retired to his law practice and to teaching in the Institute.

Santa Anna finally helped to make a national leader of this Indian whom he despised. When that dictator returned in 1853 for his last term as chief executive, one of his first victims was Juárez, who was arrested, jailed, and then banished. He made his way to New Orleans, where Melchor Ocampo and other expatriates were busily plotting, there to spend months making plans, earning his living as a printer and a cigar worker. Meanwhile, in 1854, Juan Álvarez had defied the one-legged hero of lost battles. In 1855 Juárez journeyed by way of Panama to Acapulco, offered his services to Álvarez, and joined in the march to the capital. There he served in the cabinets of Álvarez and Comonfort and finally came to the presidency by the verdict of the penniless rump congress in Querétaro.

CIVIL WAR, 1858-60

In January, 1858, Mexico had two presidents and two governments, a situation which continued through three years of civil war. Félix Zuloaga ruled briefly in the capital, and was then supplanted by Miguel Miramón, backed by the Church, the regular army, and prosperous citizens. Benito Juárez ruled fitfully in the outlying states, supported by a few loyal congressmen and a ragged ill-armed militia. For five months Juárez presided over a government in flight. Naming Santos Degollado commander in chief of his meager army, Juárez set out with his trusted aides, Ocampo and Prieto, in a retreat from Querétaro to Guanajuato, to Guadalajara, and on to the Pacific coast. They traveled rapidly, with the curtains of their carriage tightly drawn—the "sick family," Mexicans called them—only a few steps ahead of their pursuers. Prieto himself later described their journey as that of a "company of stranded actors." From the state of Colima, they took ship to Panama and transshipped to Veracruz, where they set up the capital of the "constitutional" government in May, 1858. The choice of Veracruz was strategic: they could control the customhouse and thus cut off revenue from the capital. And Veracruz had always been a stronghold of Liberalism.

In the civil war which followed, the Conservatives enjoyed the initial advantage: they had a few trained troops and some ammunition, and won most of the early battles over Juárez's untested men. But the Liberals had political advantages: they had the widespread support of the masses; and the Liberal President, Juárez, had excellent aides in Ocampo, Prieto, Ramírez, and the Lerdo de Tejada brothers. Both factions were short of money and arms. The Conservatives could tap the wealth of Church and landholders, which gave them an advantage over the Liberals. This situation prompted the Laws of Reform, issued by Juárez in 1859, which called for the immediate confiscation—without compensation—of all Church property except temples used for worship; for the suppression of monasteries; and for the nationalizing of cemeteries; and which also made marriage a civil contract. These laws were devised as a fiscal measure, to legalize seizure of Church funds, lands, and chattels; and as an expedient war measure, to make clear the ideological line between Liberals and their Conservative foes.

Both Liberals and Conservatives made repeated bids for foreign aid. The Conservatives courted royal support from Europe and managed to float some bonds. The Liberals gained a hearing in the United States, and Juárez's government was recognized in 1859. Juárez, seeking further support from Washington, gave his approval to negotiations which yielded the McLane-Ocampo Treaty of 1859, by which the United States would pay $2 million for a right of way across the Isthmus of Tehuantepec, with the privilege of maintaining troops to police the zone. Although the treaty was rejected by the American Senate, it proved the political death warrant for its negotiator, Melchor Ocampo, and gave critics grounds for branding Juárez "an American . . . one who despoiled the Church with one hand, and sold his country with the other." "Juárez's headquarters," his enemies said later, "were in Washington."

The tide turned for the Liberals in 1860. Their amateur general, Santos Degollado, after losing most of his battles, was replaced by the abler González Ortega. The Liberal armies, augmented by numerous volunteers, closed in and finally occupied the capital city in December, 1860.

Juárez returned to the national palace without fanfare; the bronzed Indian in his invariable black suit was carried in solemn triumph in his black carriage to the seat of the government he had defended. The champions of the Constitution of 1857 had won, and the union was for the moment secure, but the nation was scarred and still bleeding. The year

1861 in Mexico may be compared with the year 1865 in the United States: there were similar hates and losses; but in 1865 the United States was without Lincoln, while Mexico in 1861 still had Juárez, now fifty-five and as homely, simple, and stubborn as ever. Juárez, too, had the ideals of peaceful reconstruction later stated by Lincoln—"with malice towards none, with charity for all"—and he removed all fetters on free press and speech, opening the dikes for a flood of abuse from both Conservatives and Liberals. Some denounced his generous amnesty to recent foes. Many of his ablest lieutenants were dead and others now proved faithless. The congress, permitted a free debate, rare in Mexican political history, was dominated by an anti-Juárez bloc of his erstwhile friends who claimed to speak for the Reform in its pristine purity. In the fall of 1861 it came within one vote of ousting him in favor of General González Ortega.

THE FRENCH INTERVENTION, 1862–67

But Juárez's chief concern was neither the attack of Conservatives nor the anger of Liberals, but the threat of intervention from Europe. The draining of the Mexican treasury was a major cause of the final blow. Taxes upon the prostrate people yielded little revenue. The Church coffers were all but empty; perhaps the wealth had never been so great as described by the anticlericals, or perhaps it had been hidden or dissipated during the civil war. In July, 1861, Juárez ordered suspension of all service on the foreign debt—a measure which struck at Spain, France, and England. Juárez had already provoked a break with Spain by expelling her proclerical minister. France and England now severed relations with Mexico. In January, 1862, expeditionary forces of the three powers put into Veracruz harbor, the first act in an intervention which dragged on for five years.

Various considerations provoked European intervention. Mexican royalists had been plotting in Paris and other capitals ever since the days of Iturbide, making plans to transfer one or another unemployed prince to a nonexistent Mexican throne. The victory of the Liberals and the seating of Juárez in 1861 revived their ardor, and they courted the aid of Napoleon III. That ambitious monarch was pleased with the prospect of regaining an American colonial empire, a project worthy of the name of Napoleon. The hour was propitious: Mexico was torn with dissension; and the United States, fighting for its national unity, could not intercede. Then came news of Juárez's suspension of payments on the foreign debt, an affront to all bondholders, who believed that the flag follows the dollar (or the pound or the franc). Representatives of France, England, and Spain agreed in October, 1861, to take concerted action against the Juárez government, meanwhile solemnly denying any attack upon Mexican autonomy or territorial integrity. While these pious resolves were being recited, Napoleon's agents were coaxing Archduke Maximilian of Austria, the younger brother of Emperor Franz Joseph, to accept the evanescent Mexican throne.

The arrival of the Europeans in January, 1862, was followed by noisy disagreement among the three parties to the compact. Spain and England, discovering that they were inadvertently abetting Napoleon's private ambition, shamefacedly withdrew. The French, basing their case upon the defaulted Jecker loan of 1859,[1] marched inland and were defeated at Puebla on May 5, 1862;[2] they were then sent reinforcements from France, and they triumphantly entered Mexico City a year later, in June, 1863. Benito Juárez, again forced to abandon his capital with a few followers, was driven north to the Texas border, where he established his headquarters in the city later named Ciudad Juárez (across the Rio Grande from El Paso, Texas). The scattered troops loyal to Juárez and the constitution fought on in guerrilla fashion, ill-supported, largely unpaid, and without unified command. The political issue seemed clear, at least to the Liberals: the Conservatives had stooped to treasonable alliance with a foreign foe; the Liberals were the defenders of the republic, the constitution, and the liberty of the nation—and Benito Juárez was the living symbol of their stand. But the Conservatives, supported by French soldiers, were again in control. There had always been numerous royalists among them, and their hopes for a king had been kept alive by the spirited arguments of Lucas Alamán. Now at last they were to receive an emperor, a gift from the weak hand of Napoleon III.

The Mexican reign of Maximilian, with his Empress Carlota, was a tragic interlude for all concerned. This grandson of the last Holy Roman Emperor was a warm-hearted youth of little ability, raised in the shadow of his proud Hapsburg family, who yearned to combine royal power with knightly service to humanity. Napoleon convinced him that the Mexican throne offered such a promising combination. His bride, daughter of arrogant Leopold of Belgium, saw "the hand of God" in their marriage and elevation to the throne. Maximilian's hesitation was overcome by reports of well-nigh unanimous clamor of Mexicans for his services—a clamor expressed in a plebiscite which had been easily arranged by the Conservative junta in Mexico. The thirty-two-year-old Emperor and the twenty-four-year-old Carlota set out for their empire in the spring of 1864. He had written ahead begging Benito Juárez for cooperation, and had received a disheartening reply: "It is given to men, sir, to attack the rights of others, to take their property, to attempt the lives of those who defend their own liberty, and to make of their virtues a crime and of their vices a virtue: but there is one thing which is beyond the reach of perversity, that is the tremendous verdict of history. History will judge us." And history is still judging Maximilian—and Juárez. The biographer Corti describes the course of the young emperor: "He attempted to realize an utopian dream in the spirit of an amateur. . . . The task was undertaken by a man of weak physical constitution and fantastic mind, good natured and kindly at

[1] A Swiss named Jecker floated a loan of some $15 million for Juárez's Conservative opponents in 1859, but actually paid over less than one-tenth of the total. Jecker later assumed French citizenship, and his adopted country now demanded payment in full.

[2] The battle of "Cinco de Mayo" stands as almost the only military victory against foreigners, and Mexicans are very proud of it.

bottom, but also somewhat self-willed and inclined to overestimate his own powers, with a young wife who was primed with the ambitious ideas of her father."[3]

The welcome in Veracruz was chilly, but the reception in the capital was reassuring. The clergy, *hacendados,* and generals rallied to their new monarchs with warm unanimity. Maximilian soon made clear his intention to serve no special interest; he proposed "to be before all else a Mexican, and to place the interests of his people above all others." He traveled widely, talked with men of all stations, was appalled by what he saw of the courts, the clergy, and the army. "None of them," he wrote, "are familiar with their duties, and they live for money alone. The judges are corrupt, the officers have no sense of honor, and the clergy are lacking in Christian charity and morality." His clerical-Conservative sponsors now repented their choice of monarchs. Far from restoring their privileges, Maximilian confirmed the laws of *La Reforma* in January, 1865. He prided himself on his liberalism, flaunting the red tie which was the badge of the Liberals and privately referring to the Conservatives as "crabs"—a derisive epithet employed by the critics of the Conservatives. On his first Independence Day, September 16, he traveled to Dolores, rang the liberty bell, and gave a patriotic speech at the scene of Hidalgo's *grito.* These gestures may have shown him a good Mexican, but they did not soften the heart of Juárez; and they commended him neither to the clergy, the landlords, the generals, nor to the French, who had crowned him.

The royal show soon grew stale, and its supporters fell away. Napoleon was harassed by domestic turmoils, the threat of German invasion, and the pointed advice of Secretary William H. Seward that the United States (with the Civil War ended, free to act) did not relish France's violation of American soil; in 1865 the troubled Napoleon began to withdraw his troops and to reduce the subventions that paid the bills for Maximilian's extravagant court. When Maximilian talked of abdication, the plucky Carlota stiffened his will. But the skies darkened, as Juárez's troops closed in upon the imperial forces. Carlota decided upon a bold step to save her consort's throne: she impulsively set out for Paris, made a futile appeal to Napoleon, then carried her petition to the Pope himself; when the Vatican could not or would not help, Carlota's mind snapped, and she was fated to live on in insanity for another sixty years. Meanwhile, Maximilian, his troops meeting defeat on every side, his French support withdrawn, and his Conservative allies deserting him at home, finally took over the command of his weakened army and marched north, only to be beaten by Juárez's forces near Querétaro. The Emperor was himself taken prisoner and, despite appeals for mercy from thousands at home and abroad, was shot on the Hill of the Bells on the morning of June 19, 1867, while he prayed "that my blood now to be shed may be for the good of the country. . . . Long live Mexico! Long live independence!"

[3] Egon Caesar Corti: *Maximilian and Charlotte of Mexico* (New York: Alfred A. Knopf; 1928), Vol. I, pp. vii–viii.

THE LAST DAYS OF LA REFORMA, 1867–76

Juárez returned to the capital in July, 1867, but his triumph was dimmed by the rivalries and jealousies of his own companions-in-arms. He was welcomed by Porfirio Díaz, the general who more than any other had turned disaster into victory; but the returning President had only a curt nod for that hero. Juárez, whose term of office had already expired, now called for an election, in which he was again chosen president. This action, generally described as dictatorial, angered many Liberals. A lonely and ailing Juárez now undertook the tasks of reconstruction. Almost all his supporters were dead or had deserted him. The financial situation was desperate; there was little money for the reforms to which he was committed. He wanted free public schools and organized an ineffective ministry of education under Gabino Barreda, a devout disciple of the positivist Auguste Comte. Juárez declared a general amnesty, provoking further rancor. He reduced the army by two-thirds, with not even a word of thanks to the dismissed men and officers. His rule, increasingly highhanded, was that of a national caudillo who maintains his position by manipulating elections and forcing congress, generals, and governors to accept his will without debate. He realized that such a course was a repudiation of his liberalism and democracy, and was unhappy in it. He was a realist who could write: "When a society like ours has had the misfortune to pass through years of intense upheavals, it is seamed through with vices whose profound roots cannot be extirpated either in a single day or by any single measure." He did what he had to do in order to fend off anarchy.

Meanwhile, the grievances of both Liberals and Conservatives piled up as preparations were made for the election of 1871. Juárez, stubborn as always, refused to withdraw, and faced the rivalry of two long-time companions, Sebastián Lerdo de Tejada and Porfirio Díaz. In a closely contested election, marked by frauds in which he probably shared, the decision was finally made by Congress, which again gave the presidency to Juárez. Díaz promptly led an armed revolt with the slogan of "no reelection," but was defeated by government troops. Juárez, worn and sick, served a few months and died on July 18, 1872.

Sebastián Lerdo de Tejada, who had assumed office as vice-president and who served until 1876, was honest and able, competent in the theory of government but lacking in political dexterity. He won reelection in 1876, but it was an empty victory. Porfirio Díaz, granted amnesty in 1872, was again at large, organizing his forces from the United States as a base, enlisting the aid of such various malcontents as ex-soldiers of the Reform, disgruntled Liberals and aspiring office seekers. In November, 1876, proclaiming the new era of "effective suffrage and no reelection," he entered Mexico City with his rebel army and drove Lerdo into exile. The era of Juárez was ended, and the era of Díaz was begun.

It was also the end of *La Reforma,* no matter how vigorously Díaz might continue to wave its banner. Mexicans still argue the failures and successes of the stormy chapter that closed in 1876. The failures were serious: the agrarian reform was a fiasco, leaving great landlords more numerous and more wealthy than before, and landless peasants poorer and more miserable; progress toward democratic control was negligible, with elections still corrupt; education of the common people had made little progress; and there was little if any improvement in the living conditions of the Mexican masses. But *La Reforma* also had successes to its credit: the scattered peoples of the Republic were united by their common sufferings into one nation; the unbending reactionaries, discredited by their support of a foreign foe, were for the time quieted; the clamor for a king was ended; and the principle of separation of Church and state was not only written into the basic law of the land, but was generally accepted by the Mexican people.[4] By 1876 liberalism, ill-defined and still naïve, had become the integrating force of Mexican nationality.

[4] In 1874, during Lerdo's presidency, the constitution was amended to incorporate the Laws of Reform of 1859, which disestablished the Church and guaranteed religious liberty for dissenters.

Chapter 21

THE ERA OF PORFIRIO DÍAZ,
1876–1910

Porfirio Díaz seemed an answer to the prayers of a people wearied by a half century of turmoil. The praetorian peace he gave them was the longest period of calm the nation had known since the day Father Hidalgo rang the bell at Dolores.

Díaz was a mestizo born in Oaxaca in 1830; his Indian blood was of the Mixtec peoples, who for centuries had fought the Zapotecs, who fathered Benito Juárez. Díaz, born to poverty, had little schooling; to the end of his eighty-six years, he never learned to write proper Spanish. He considered entering the priesthood but decided against it and at seventeen joined the army. A year later he returned to Oaxaca, entered the Institute, listened to the lectures of Benito Juárez, learned a little law, and joined the Liberal movement. In 1855 Díaz, now twenty-five, joined the guerrillas who were fighting Santa Anna. He fought bravely during the civil war, served in the national congress in 1861, and then fought against the French invaders and was taken prisoner. He made a dramatic escape and rejoined Juárez, who appointed him commander in the south. Captured again by the monarchist forces, he escaped and joined the fighters in the southern mountains, becoming the most formidable of Juárez's generals. He retook Oaxaca, restoring its civil government, and shared in the recapture of Mexico City, where he welcomed the triumphant Juárez in January, 1861.

There was never warm understanding between soldier Díaz and civilian Juárez. After 1867 Díaz grew increasingly resentful of the President, who denied both credit and privileges to the army. In the election campaign of 1871, Díaz entered the contest as an army candidate. Defeated at the polls, he led a revolt which was crushed within four months. After Juárez's death in 1872, Díaz was included in the general amnesty proclaimed by Lerdo, but he continued to plot for seizure of the presidency. He curried favor with the Church, whose leaders resented Lerdo's attempts to enforce the anticlerical laws of the Reform. He pleased the United States by advocating the admission of northern capital, while Lerdo urged his favorite formula—"between weakness and strength . . . a desert"—as an argument against railroads linking Mexico with the United States. Texas

[*325*]

was the base from which Díaz organized his final plot which demanded restoration of the Constitution of 1857, "effective suffrage and no reelection," and the ejection of Lerdo de Tejada. In November, 1876, Díaz led his forces into Mexico City, where he staged an election under his control, and was formally seated the following May. So began his Augustan reign, which (with one four-year interregnum) lasted until 1911.

The Mexico of 1876 was worn by the sixty-six years of almost unrelieved strife since Hidalgo had raised the banner of Guadalupe. There had never been more than brief snatches of peace in which to develop a true national life. The office of chief executive, under different names, had changed hands more than seventy times since independence; some incumbents had been scoundrels, some dullards, and not more than two or three had been men of stature and character; Juárez, the ablest, had never had time or peace enough to carry through his plans. Cultural life had floundered. The Church, traditional defender of schools and learning, had not recovered from the crippling blow of a revolution which stripped her of many priests. The universities were all but dead; there were few schools. The Mexico of 1876 was lawless and chaotic; the broad stretches of countryside and even the streets of substantial cities afforded slight protection for life or property. The economic well-being of the nation had progressively worsened since independence. The mines, source of wealth in colonial days, suffered from neglect and violence; and fields and pastures languished, as Mexico failed to keep step with the technical advances of other lands. Industry, especially the processing of cotton textiles, had made some gains. Mexico's small trade (in 1876 the total of exports and imports was little more than 50 million pesos) was chiefly with England. In 1876 there was one railway line, that connecting the capital with Veracruz; and the roads were rutted trails. It was obvious that little progress could be made until protection for life and property was assured and until new railways and roads were opened.

Díaz's first task was to impose order. The anarchy of earlier decades had produced a plethora of big and little caudillos, who dominated their several regions. Presidents, even Santa Anna and Juárez, had been compelled to come to terms with these lawless rulers. Porfirio Díaz quickly brought the caudillos of all categories to book. Some were won over by honors and decorations, others by largess from the public treasury. The lesser offenders were easily handled—a shot in the back on a lonely road sufficed; the well-known and highly placed required more refined treatment. One such was Ignacio Mejía, Juárez's trusted colleague; he brusquely refused the bribes held out by Díaz, who then charged him with peculation of funds and hounded him to death by piling up false charges. Díaz's effective formula for compelling order was *pan o palo,* "bread or the club"— those who obeyed ate bread, those who resisted felt the club. The instrument for such coercion was the corps of *guardias rurales,* the well-paid and flattered rural police, who made Mexico's lonely roads as safe as any in the world. Into this elite company of guardians of the peace, Díaz sardonically inducted some bandits who had hitherto slit the throats and emptied the purses of travelers.

Opposition melted away. A few sporadic uprisings were swiftly crushed. Critics found it wise to keep silence, and the numerous officeholders learned to praise their benefactor. The press was muzzled—some editors were given subsidies to assure loyalty; but a few editors were ready to risk imprisonment or death by writing their minds. The most conspicuous of such brave spirits was Filomeno Mata, editor of *El Diario del Hogar,* who was jailed more than thirty times; Carleton Beals remarks that Mata "kept a bed permanently in Belén," the national penitentiary.

THE ALLIES OF THE DICTATOR

The phenomenal success of the Díaz regime—and it was successful, no matter how heavy-handed it may have been—was due chiefly to the fruitful partnerships the dictator maintained throughout his long reign. Chief among these were his compacts with the politicians, the army, the Church, foreign capital, and the great landholders. Let us look at each of these.

With the politicians, the *pan o palo* formula worked smoothly, if not always painlessly. Díaz gradually brought every office under his direct control; he paid lip service to the Constitution of 1857 and saw to it that proper elections were held, but made sure that he himself finally named all "elected" officials, from governors and congressmen down to the mayor of the least village. All this was done with scrupulous respect for the letter of the law.

So sensitive was Díaz to the fetish of constitutionality that he would not ask for reelection in 1880 but placed Manuel González in office for the term 1880–84. This seat-warmer proved not unintelligent, continued the policies of Díaz, and turned the office back to his benefactor in 1884. González and his friends enriched themselves during this interlude—a fact which Díaz promptly advertised; this quieted González's political ambitions. After 1884 Díaz arranged to continue himself in office: in 1887 his servile congress amended the constitution to permit one reelection; in 1890 another amendment permitted further reelections. However, as each election year rolled around one or another of Díaz's intimates—discreetly encouraged by the great man himself—expressed the hope that his own shoulders might bear the toga; but he soon discovered his mistake. Even Romero Rubio, Porfirio's father-in-law, dallied with the idea, only to discover that Díaz was tactfully encouraging other rivals to enter the lists.

The year 1892 marked a turning point for Díaz. The able men who surrounded him—and he always had capable ministers—declared that the time had come to create a political party which would disabuse the world of the notion that Díaz was just another Latin American dictator. The *Unión Liberal* was organized, and from then on served as the façade for Díaz's personal rule; needless to say, no rival party was allowed to disturb the Olympian calm. From 1892 on, new faces appeared in the inner circle around Díaz, chiefly creoles in place of the mestizos upon whom he had earlier relied, men who were popularly called *científicos,* scientists. Their political and economic faith owed much to the positivism of Auguste Comte, and they accepted his naïve conclusion that society could be saved by the techniques of the "social" sciences uncorrupted by metaphysics and theology. They called themselves liberals, but dismissed the liberalism of Juárez as visionary and prided themselves upon a tough practicality. The *científicos,* never more than a score in number, were often men of considerable idealism, and favored honest administration, impartial courts, and a measure of freedom of speech and press. They accepted Porfirio Díaz as a bulwark against anarchy—an attitude shared by many honorable citizens. They agreed with the dictator that Mexico's future lay with the white man, that the Indian was useful only as a burden bearer.

The intellectual leader of this palace guard was José Yves Limantour, son of a French migrant who had prospered during the Reform days. He came to the front as minister of finance in 1893 and served as the dean of the cabinet to the last days of Díaz. Limantour was the apostle of positivism in government, exacting hitherto unknown efficiency from public servants, while his colleague Justo Sierra preached the positivist gospel of scientific education. Sierra's substantial learning furnished an attractive front for the Díaz administration. Historian, lawyer, educator, reviver of the moribund National University, Justo Sierra could dilate upon the joys of liberty, while heralding the prior claims of "order and progress." He rejoiced that a "spontaneous Caesarism" had united the country in peace and given it a place of dignity before the world.

The *científicos,* whose activities spanned the last two decades of Díaz's reign, were responsible for the prestige of the regime. They were inventive, thorough, and diligent. To be sure, most of the inner circle enriched themselves (Limantour and Justo Sierra were exceptions): they awarded contracts for public works to companies they controlled and collected generous legal fees for their services. Nonetheless, they remained faithful to Díaz, although some, especially Limantour, entertained the ambition to succeed him. Despite his indebtedness to the *científicos,* Díaz found them uncomfortable companions: they were gentlemen; they were well educated and prided themselves upon their ties with the culture of Europe; while Díaz was never more than a half-literate intruder in the society of Mexico. Meanwhile, the people, whenever they became restless, directed their fire at the *científicos,* while Díaz posed as the friend of the masses.

Díaz, president by grace of the army, never forgot that whoever controls the army controls Mexico. He was adept in keeping his generals faithful; his formula, long to be standard practice in Mexico, was to provide them with salaries and expense accounts to cover such necessities as handsome mounts, shining uniforms, good food and drink, and smart mistresses. And he saw to it that the generals did not forget to whom they were beholden: no longer was a general allowed to retain one regiment as his own, thereby building up a body of troops whose first loyalty was to him; he was constantly shifted from regiment to regiment, from region to region. The device worked: few generals entertained presidential ambitions.

The rank and file soldiery was a driven rabble of conscripts, just as it had been since independence. Men were paid three or four pesos a month, given miserable food, compelled to supplement their scant rations from their small pay or by pillage. Their women, the *soldaderas,* were with them in camp or on the march. Few men entered military service of their own free will; many were thrown into the army by the *jefes políticos* of the various states; it was a convenient way of getting rid of criminals, beggars, and agitators. The power to conscript was a source of handsome profit to the *jefes;* if an industrious worker managed to save a few pesos, the threat of conscription would persuade him to part with fifty or a hundred pesos in order to escape that fate. The atmosphere of the army barracks was little better than that of a prison. The generals, given a per diem allowance for the men's food, stole at will, leaving little for the common soldier. Conditions were bad enough in the populous centers, but they were worse in such outlying territories as Quintana Roo, where an army of several thousand held down the rebellious Maya. There the common soldiers lived in filth and semistarvation—the general who directed that operation for three years after 1900 accumulated a private fortune of 10 million pesos.

Díaz's army, probably never larger than 50,000, was justified by the dictator as protection against Yankee invasion; but its true role was to secure Díaz against possible rivals.

Porfirio Díaz, in spite of his long association with the anticlerical reformers, won the invaluable help of the still powerful Church. A thirty-third degree Mason and only a nominal Catholic, the dictator was understandably suspected by the faithful, but he was finally accepted by them. His animus against the Church was softened by his second wife, Carmen (the daughter of his chief aide, Romero Rubio), whom he married in 1883. Her warm faith modified his acerbity against the Church, and she constantly supported the pleas of churchmen. A typical clerical appeal was made in 1884: "The Catholic Church is much greater than you; in spite of the fact that your flatterers deny it, this will always be a truth. It does not ask protection of you; it demands and wishes with eternal right that which it is your duty to give it . . . liberty."

But Díaz did not forget that the baiting of the Church and her priests is always sound politics in Mexico. He therefore played a double game. He pleased the anticlericals by fitful enforcement of the Reform laws: in 1885, and again in 1889, he suppressed some of the monastic orders; in 1898 he restated the right of the religious to seek release from their vows; and in 1901 he reaffirmed the Reform laws which forbade Church ownership of property not required for purposes of worship. On the other hand, he pleased the clergy by repeatedly warning them through Doña Carmen of impending action against convents and monasteries; by permitting the organization of new orders to take the place of those banned; by encouraging the creation of seven new bishoprics; by permitting increase of the clergy from about 1,600 in 1878 to some 5,000 in the first years of the new century; and by tacitly allowing extension of the Church's landholdings. The letter of the law was not changed—a sop to the anticlericals; but the Church was encouraged to regain much of its lost prestige and wealth. Díaz's way with the Church was generally acceptable. The anticlericals found comfort in the continuance of the Reform laws; the clerics enjoyed their new freedom; and the dictator's life was not troubled by any considerable outcry from either contingent.

The foreigner, with his desirable dollars and pounds, proved a major ally of the dictator. Díaz, despite his Indian blood, had little faith in the indigenous peoples of Mexico. His distaste for the Indian, and even for the mestizo, accounted for his increasing appointment of creoles to posts in his cabinet. Díaz agreed with the *científicos* that Mexico was to be a white man's country and that foreign money should be welcomed.

The railroads, of which there were less than 500 miles when Díaz assumed office in 1876, were increased to more than 15,000 miles by 1910; this was largely the result of American, British, and Belgian enterprise. Thanks to Limantour's boldness, much of this railroad empire was consolidated into a national system in 1910, but the underlying bond issues were still held abroad, chiefly in the United States. These railways served the already productive areas rather than opening up the frontiers and encouraging settlement.

The mining industry, quiescent since the colonial period except for a brief burst of energy by British interests in the 1830's, received new impetus from Díaz. Foreign capital had been chary of investing in Mexican mines because of the Spanish legal tradition that subsoil wealth is the inalienable property of the Crown—that is, of the nation. The mining laws of 1884 (enacted during the González regime) and of 1892 quieted the argument by granting full subsoil rights to the owner of the surface. With that and other encouragement, venture capital—about three-fourths of it American and most of the balance English—revived the mining industry. The production of gold and silver increased more than fourfold during the Díaz years; that of copper, unimportant in 1876, increased until Mexico stood second among world producers in 1910.

Exploitation of petroleum came with the turn of the century. Díaz welcomed both the Briton Weetman Pearson (later Lord Cowdray) and the American Edward Doheny, pioneers shortly followed by others of their countrymen. The race for concessions was on, as British and American rivals fought the sort of battle familiar to Texas and Oklahoma. There followed lawless grabbing of promising oil lands, with a highhanded dispossessing of numerous Indians who thought cornfields more desirable than greasy oil fields. It was a contest pleasing to Díaz, who saw profit for his treasury in the pitting of one set of alien rivals against the other. He first favored the English, then switched his major concessions to the Americans, and during his last years again gave the advantage to the British.[1] The oil industry was a spectacular success: production of 10,345 barrels of oil in 1901 increased to almost 13,000,000 barrels in 1911 (in 1921 it would reach 194,755,710 barrels).

Foreign capital was thus welcomed by Díaz until it dominated the economic life of the nation. The Americans and the British owned the oil wells and mines. The French controlled most of the growing textile business and many of the large shops. The Germans controlled the trade in hardware and drugs. The Spaniards (and especially the *gallegos* from Galicia) were grocers and other retail merchants. The public utilities—trolley lines, power companies, water companies—belonged to the English, the Canadians, the Americans, and various other outsiders. The Mexicans, untrained in modern techniques, were, in effect, aliens in their own land.

To make matters worse, foreigners had preempted much of the best land of the nation. Americans (William Randolph Hearst among others) held millions of acres in the north. Spaniards, with numerous great haciendas, controlled the tobacco fields, whose workers were cruelly exploited. And in almost every test of strength, aliens were given favored treatment by Díaz's courts. Díaz, who admired the outsider and his money, laid the foundation for the violent antiforeign storm that broke loose after his abdication.

Díaz's partnership with the land barons finally proved his strongest bastion. The nation over which he presided was parceled out chiefly among a few thousand great *hacendados,* while the generality of the Mexican people were landless, the ill-paid burden bearers of the lamentable system.

The roots of this unjust division of land went back to the colonial days, when Spanish kings endowed faithful soldiers with *encomiendas,* which conveyed vast rights over the Indians living within their confines. The *encomienda* was the forerunner of the hacienda of later centuries. The honest efforts of kings and viceroys, notably those of enlightened Charles III late in the eighteenth century, availed little in correcting this uneconomic concentration of land in a few hands. At the close of the colonial period, some 4,944 *hacendados* owned most of the best fields and pastures of Mexico. Independence brought no improvement, although Morelos and a few others urged some land reform. Numerous Spaniards were dispossessed, but their holdings passed into the hands of wealthy creoles. The Church, always rich in land, became richer until by 1840 she held at least half of the land in use. Nor did *La Reforma,* for all its good intentions, succeed in breaking up the lands of the Church among small holders. There were, according to the geographer George M. McBride, not less than 40,000 transfers of title after the reform laws of the 1850's, but most of these either enlarged existing haciendas or created new ones.

When Díaz came to power, his program served the scattered *ha-*

[1] It has been argued that Díaz's final partiality to the English explained the willingness of the United States to permit Díaz's archenemy Madero to organize his revolt in Texas in 1910. This has not been proved.

cendados. They sought security for their lives and properties: Díaz gave them the *rurales* (the federal police), who shortly made the most distant and lonely roads safe from bandits. They sought wider markets for their wares: Díaz, with the aid of foreign capital, created a network of railroads that gave them access to the markets of Mexico and the outer world. The provision of security and communications increased the value of land and provoked demand for more. Again Díaz served the ambition of the *hacendados.* There was still unappropriated a great public domain embracing unclaimed and unoccupied desert lands in the west, dry plains in the north, and hot forest lands on the mountain slopes facing the Gulf of Mexico and in the Isthmus of Tehuantepec. There was also an immense area occupied by little farmers and by communal Indian villages (the *ejidos*), unprotected by clear and registered titles; the simple Indians and mestizos who worked this land had lived there for uncounted years, their claims uncontested but never legally confirmed. Such lands, both public and private, were an easy target for Díaz in his search for ways to serve the *hacendados.*

Díaz's compliant congress gave him legislation by which he could transfer large areas to the *hacendados.* By the land law of 1883, revised and extended in 1894, he was empowered to organize "surveying companies" licensed to discover and survey all types of available lands. The charters of these companies were generous: they would receive one-third of all public lands surveyed, and they could acquire additional lands on easy terms. They were permitted to search at will for lands not covered by legal titles, and to "denounce" and seize them. Díaz picked his close friends for such lucrative concessions, and they in turn welcomed foreign entrepreneurs as partners in pillaging the nation's preserves. The limitations written into the law of 1883 were largely nullified in 1894, so that lands recaptured from the national domain and from helpless Indian communities whose titles were nonexistent could be sold in great blocks to the *hacendados.* By 1910, almost a third of the national area (over 180 million acres) had been surveyed by seventeen companies, to their handsome profit. The lands had been sold for a pittance to new and old *hacendados;* some 5,000 Indian villages had lost their ancient *ejidos;* and the concentration of land in a few hands had greatly increased as the result of Díaz's partnership with the landholders.

The hacienda, chief economic and social unit in Díaz's Mexico, represented a little world within the larger nation. Its broad acres converged on the great manor house, to which its owner brought his fine city friends on a few festal occasions each year; clustered around were barns, shops, and stables; next to the house stood the church, and sometimes the schoolhouse; trailing off from the center were the peons' adobe quarters, windowless and floorless. It was a self-contained community: the cornfields furnished the food; the maguey (agave), the drink; the forests, the charcoal, which was the chief fuel; and the cotton fields, the clothing.

Economically, the hacienda was a laggard in a nation that boasted of progress. It clung to outmoded farming methods: the scratching of the surface with a heat-hardened wooden plow, the hand labor of men with machetes, the crude flail for harvesting, and the use of oxen as beasts of burden. Little machinery was used; man power was cheap and plentiful. Modern techniques were almost unknown: soil erosion went on unchecked, fertilization was neglected, and the quality of seeds and the scientific breeding of stock received little attention. The production of corn—staple food crop of Mexicans—dropped steadily throughout the nineteenth century; one Mexican scholar estimates that the yield per acre in 1910 was only one-seventh of what it had been a hundred years before (perhaps an exaggeration, although we cannot know). The fact remains that agricultural Mexico, during the last two decades of Díaz's vaunted prosperity, was a steady importer of basic foodstuffs—in 1910 the bill came to 15 million pesos. Meanwhile, the hacienda fed its own people and furnished an income to its owner, but failed lamentably to serve as provisioner for the nation.

The hacienda had other grave weaknesses. It was the chief tax dodger: the little farmer paid in full, but the big farmer—the *hacendado*—escaped with trifling amounts. It had a privileged credit position: the little farmer, when he could secure credit at all, paid interest of 20 or 30 per cent; the big farmer, friend of the bankers, got his money at a mere 7 or 8 per cent. It was the water-hog of the nation, monopolizing the meager streams whose flow should have been divided with lesser farmers.

The hacienda gave prestige to its owner. To be sure the *hacendado* seldom visited the lands which gave him such distinction. He left their care to an administrator, while he maintained a fine house on the Paseo de la Reforma in the capital, and—if his income sufficed—a house in Paris or on the Riviera.

Economically retarded but socially impressive, the hacienda survived at the cost of the underpaid and abused peons who did the work.[2] The peon's cash wage was almost unchanged from the last days of the eighteenth to the first days of the twentieth century—25 centavos was the price of a man's labor for a full day in the hot sun. His real wage (measured by its purchasing power) shrank steadily. During this hundred-year period "the price of corn rose . . . by approximately 179 per cent, rice 75 per cent, flour 711 per cent, wheat 465 per cent, beans 565 per cent, and chili 123 per cent."[3] To be sure, the peon had perquisites: a permanent job, so long as he obeyed; a hut to live in; his own plot of ground to work; sometimes a small allotment of corn each week; a church and the occasional services of a priest; and, rarely, a school. He also had the dubious boon of the hacienda store, which forced goods upon him at exorbitant profit, extended him credit which kept him forever in debt, carried the debts of the fathers over to the sons—and served as a principal instrument for the perpetuation of the peonage system.

There were some high-minded and generous *hacendados* who made

[2] The word *peón* is used in Spanish for the pawn on the chess board, the least of the battlers in that courtly game—the fellow who is permitted to edge along his narrow line, never looking back, and is denied the gallant sorties of knights, bishops, castles, and queens.

[3] Eyler N. Simpson: *The Ejido: Mexico's Way Out* (Chapel Hill, N.C.: University of North Carolina Press; 1937), pp. 37–8.

brave efforts to improve the lot of their workers—but these were exceptions. More often, overbearing masters treated their men as slaves (which they were in fact, though not in law), working them for unconscionable hours, flogging them for infraction of petty rules, shooting down rebels in cold blood, and appropriating the more comely daughters and wives for their casual pleasure. There were neither police nor courts of appeal for such victims; the benefits of civilization were reserved for the masters.

The land tenure in four chief states in 1910 illustrates how well Díaz served the *hacendados.* In the state of Mexico, 84 per cent of the people were engaged in farming but 99.5 per cent were landless; 64 haciendas— each with over 2,500 acres—comprised the best land; the largest included some 247,000 acres. In the western state of Michoacán, 83.6 per cent were farmers but 97.3 per cent were landless; there were 102 haciendas, averaging 40,000 acres—one boasted 365,000 acres, and another 250,000. In little Morelos, "the sugar bowl of Mexico," where 99.5 per cent of the people owned no land, 41 haciendas held most of the best land—one with 96,000 acres, another with 75,000. In southern Oaxaca, where 99.8 per cent of the families had no land whatsoever, there were 88 principal haciendas ranging from 2,500 acres up to 193,000 acres. The net result of Díaz's agrarian program was that by 1910 most of the occupied lands of the nation belonged to the *hacendados,* and the Mexicans were virtually landless.[4]

SUCCESS AND FAILURE—THE DÍAZ BALANCE SHEET

The Díaz regime seemed to be a brilliant success. When Don Porfirio took office, the treasury was empty, service on the foreign loans was in default, salaries were unpaid, mines were neglected, the farms were stagnant, industry was floundering, there was one short stretch of railroad, and disorder ruled the land. Under his hand order was established, honesty was imposed upon public servants (with a certain latitude permitted the more highly placed), and the country was made safe for investors. Foreign capital poured in. Steady but slow improvement was made from 1876 to 1894. In 1893 José Yves Limantour—the dean of the *científicos*—became minister of finance; from then on he was largely responsible for the triumphs of the Díaz regime. In 1894 the Mexican budget was balanced for the first time. In 1896 the *alcabala,* the sales tax imposed upon goods passing from state to state (an impost inherited from colonial days), was abolished. From then on, Mexican credit stood so high in world markets that old loans could be rewritten and national bonds yielding 5 per cent sold at a premium. In 1905 Mexico adopted the gold standard. By 1910 Limantour had outplayed

[4] McBride estimates that in 1910 the percentages of landless heads of families were as follows: in Guanajuato, 97.1 per cent; in Guerrero, 98.5 per cent; in Jalisco, 96.2 per cent; in Mexico, 99.5 per cent; in Michoacán, 97.3 per cent; in Morelos, 99.5 per cent; in Oaxaca, 99.8 per cent; in Puebla, 99.3 per cent. George M. McBride: *The Land Systems of Mexico* (New York: American Geographical Society, 1923), p. 154.

the American railroad wizard, E. H. Harriman, and had bought up enough railroad shares in the name of the government to consolidate most of the lines into a national system.

Public and private business prospered together. By 1910 the sum of exports and imports reached the grand total of 500 million pesos—almost ten times what it had been in 1876. The mining of gold, silver, copper, and other metals was returning astonishing profits; the petroleum industry was booming; factories and textile mills were multiplying—and only here and there a few sour voices complained that most of the profit went to foreign owners, the United States alone holding an investment of more than $1 billion. Under Limantour there was almost always a balance in the treasury, a happy event which made possible the improvement of the chief harbors, the drainage of the Valley of Mexico, the creation of a national banking system, the erection of a few pretentious schoolhouses, and the adornment of the national capital with public buildings patterned on Parisian models. But the prosperity of these years did not reach down to the barefoot masses. While the rich grew richer (perhaps 5 per cent of Mexicans were better housed, fed, dressed, and amused than ever before), the inarticulate body of Indians and poor mestizos had no share of the bounty: their few centavos a day bought even less corn, chilis, and beans.

Nor was the financial success of the Díaz regime matched by a corresponding advance in cultural life. When Díaz assumed office, he inherited a school system with some 8,000 schools providing for about one-sixth of the nation's 2 million children, but it was ill-financed and ineffective. Díaz paid lip service to the cause of education and actually opened a few new schools in the cities—but almost none in the villages. The census of 1900 showed that about one-sixth of the total population of 13.6 million could read and write; in that same year there were, at least theoretically, schools available to about 30 per cent of the children. But the quality of teaching was poor, the equipment inadequate, and there was little effort to do more than provide for the sons and daughters of the favored urban classes. What little kindling of national conscience there was for this cause, came from the *científicos,* with the brilliant Justo Sierra as the prime mover. Sierra also deserves credit for reestablishing, in 1910, the National University, which had been inactive for almost a hundred years.

Intellectual life during the Díaz years sought its inspiration in Parisian models instead of finding it in the life of the Mexican nation. Poets Gutiérrez Nájera and Amado Nervo were stylists of distinction. Justo Sierra, historian, essayist, and novelist, wrote with charm and learning, but belied his own genius by slavish apology for the dictatorial regime he served. Perhaps the most characteristic was Francisco Bulnes, who used his indisputable ability to serve Díaz by belittling Juárez. Similarly, the fine arts lacked distinction. Díaz's Mexico produced almost no first-rank painters, sculptors, composers, or architects.

The world applauded Porfirio Díaz for his successes and ignored his failures. In 1907 Elihu Root, visiting Mexico on a diplomatic errand, admitted that he "looked to Porfirio Díaz . . . as one of the greatest men to be held up for the hero worship of mankind." In 1908, C. M. Flandrau wrote in his delightful book *Viva Mexico* that a "military Díaz-potism" existed but that the President was both patriotic and enlightened. This judgment was generally shared by Mexican citizens, even by many who deplored Díaz's highhanded measures but who supported the dictatorship because they feared the anarchy which would scourge the land were he removed.

It seemed altogether fitting that Díaz's admirers at home and abroad should join him in celebration of the centennial of the *grito de Dolores* and his own eightieth birthday. Thousands came by ship and train for the happy event in September, 1910. Díaz was a genial host, spending some 20 million pesos of the nation's money on fine food, French champagne, and the best music of the world. The guests discovered in Mexico City a new, if not lovelier, Paris; its Paseo de la Reforma was a worthy counterpart of the Champs Élysées; its unfinished National Theater,[5] an audacious copy of French models. The guests also had abundant opportunity to see how cultured, well-dressed and well-fed the Mexican people were—for the city's riffraff and the barefooted Indians were barred from the central paved streets.

But the Indian was to have the last word.

THE FALL OF PORFIRIO DÍAZ

The beginning of the end of Porfirio Díaz was his decision to seek reelection in 1910. By the time he was inducted into office for his eighth legal term, the storm clouds of revolt were threatening. The rebellion—led by Francisco Madero, of whom we shall hear more—was rooted in the accumulated furies of abused workers, outraged intellectuals, and the voiceless Indian masses. These groups became articulate during the first decade of the twentieth century.

Workers in factory and field found agents to voice their complaints. For more than a dozen years various European troublemakers, mostly Spanish, had entered Mexico to preach the stormy precepts of anarchosocialism. They had organized strikes among henequen workers in Yucatán, textile operatives in Veracruz, and copper miners in Sonora—all bloodily crushed by Díaz's efficient *rurales*. In 1900 a group of these agitators formed a new Liberal party in the capital and launched their newspaper, *Regeneración*. The paper was promptly suppressed and its editor, Ricardo Flores Magón, was jailed. Flores Magón escaped and joined his brother and other comrades in the United States, where they fitfully published their paper first in San Antonio and then in St. Louis, constantly hounded by private agents of Díaz aided by American police. Meanwhile, Liberal clubs

---

[5] This theater of solid marble and bastard architecture stood as an unfinished ghost for thirty years after Díaz disappeared, each year sinking lower into the muck of the ancient lake whose waters Díaz had caused to be drained away. Finally shored up and finished after a fashion, it was renamed the Palace of Fine Arts.

multiplied within Mexico, and in 1906 the clandestine Liberal party issued a manifesto demanding overthrow of Díaz, reform of the Church, the army and the schools, a program for labor, and land reform. Flores Magón and others organized an abortive revolution in Texas, were jailed, then escaped, and were finally recaptured in Los Angeles.[6]

Some Mexican intellectuals also criticized the dictator, directing their bitter logic against the complaisant cynicism of the *científicos.* In 1909 a group of young intellectuals founded the *Ateneo,* a center for free discussion; a year later many of the same men supported Justo Sierra—the best of the *científicos*—in the reopening of the National University. But the high mark in intellectual protest against Díaz was the publication in 1909 of *Los grandes problemas nacionales* by Andrés Molina Enríquez, a classic in revolutionary literature. Molina Enríquez analyzed the tortuous course of the land laws since *La Reforma,* presented a detailed and documented indictment of the hacienda system, and condemned the Díaz regime as a reversion to viceregal government. He called for the breaking up of the distended landholdings in the cereal zone. "It will come," he wrote, "whether in peace . . . or by revolution." The book was suppressed, but not until many copies had been distributed.

The abused peasantry, chiefly Indian, finally found a spokesman in Emiliano Zapata, a tenant farmer on a sugar plantation in Morelos. His anger was first aroused, according to tradition, by the contrast between the hovels assigned to his kin and the tiled stables of his master's race horses. While Díaz was serving caviar and champagne to his fine friends in September, 1910, Zapata was leading his guerrilla horsemen against the haciendas of Morelos and Guerrero, burning houses and sugar refineries, killing owners and foremen who resisted, and taking horses and guns from the *rurales.* ("I never bought a gun," Zapata boasted.)

The uniting of these diverse forces of rebellion was the work of Francisco Madero, a mild little man whose family owned much land in the north. A dreamy spiritualist, vegetarian, teetotaler, and amateur stargazer, he was utterly honest and quite naïve. This strange messiah entered the scene in 1908 with a thin volume called *The Presidential Succession in 1910,* which he was emboldened to publish by Díaz's protestations of democracy and his promise (given currency by an American journalist's account of an interview with Díaz in 1908) that he would not run for office again. Madero's mild argument went no further than to urge that in the event Díaz *did* choose to run the people should have a hand in picking the vice-president. This innocuous suggestion had pith: Díaz had revived

6 Ricardo Flores Magón continued his lonely agitation against Díaz in the United States, and after many bouts with American police was jailed in Leavenworth prison, where he died in 1922. He there defended his uncompromising course: "My comrades of that epoch today are generals, governors, secretaries of state, some even have been presidents. They are rich, famous, and prosperous, while I am poor, unknown, sick, almost blind, with a number for a name, branded as a felon, rotting in this human herd. . . . But my old comrades were practical men, and I am but a dreamer . . . which I prefer to be." Quoted by Carleton Beals: *Porfirio Díaz, Dictator of Mexico* (Philadelphia: J. B. Lippincott Co.; 1932), p. 406.

338] MEXICO

the long moribund vice-presidency in 1904, filling the office with General Ramón Corral, who was detested for his barbarity in selling Yaqui Indians from Sonora into slavery on the henequen plantations of Yucatán. Madero's thesis was understood and applauded: there must be a worthy man to take over when, in divine mercy, Díaz would finally die.

But when Díaz announced in 1909 his intention of again running for office in 1910, Madero announced his own candidacy, sounding the shopworn slogan *Sufragio efectivo; no reelección!* Varied dissidents took their places at his side—those who hated Díaz for good reasons or for bad, those who detested Ramón Corral, the vice-presidential candidate, and those who cherished their own political ambitions, including supporters of the powerful General Bernardo Reyes. *Maderista* clubs sprang up everywhere, and in April, 1910, an informal convention of his supporters named him as their candidate.

Meanwhile, Díaz, contemptuous of this upstart, prepared for the fall election by eliminating possible claimants to the vice-presidency: Reyes, long powerful in the north and ambitious for the presidency, was banished to Europe; Limantour followed him; and Díaz selected the hated Ramón Corral for reelection. Then followed the gay Centennial celebration, the triumphant reelection, and the inauguration of Díaz and Corral. In the meantime, Madero, after a brief jailing by Díaz's orders, went to Texas where, in October, 1910, he published the *Plan de San Luis Potosí,* demanding the resignation of Díaz and honest elections. This was the spark that ignited —according to Jesuit historian Cuevas—"the crowded cellar of dynamite . . . under Díaz. It exploded and wrecked his edifice." It was a worn and outmoded edifice. There had been neither new men, new ideas, nor new techniques for almost two decades. His governors, cabinet members, and chief intimates were men around seventy. His artful policy of "divide and rule" had long blocked any desire of his followers to unite against him; it now prevented their uniting behind him. His army, a beggarly collection of conscripts, had no morale; the generals, constantly shifted from regiment to regiment, could not control their men. Even the rabble no longer shouted for him.

The cornered Díaz recalled Limantour from Europe, but that aged wizard had no magic with which to exorcise Madero. On May 24, 1911, the mobs milled through the capital's streets; 5,000 strong they surrounded the dictator's home, shouting their demands. The next day, troops fired into the crowd in the Plaza de la Reforma. Díaz, mourning his peoples' ingratitude, signed his resignation, made his way to Europe, and died in Paris in 1915.

There are no monuments to Porfirio Díaz in all Mexico—except in his native city of Oaxaca. The nation, by common consent, has erased the name of the man who, for all his faults, worked his considerable miracles for thirty-six years.

REVOLUTION, 1910–20

The plots of 1910, the angry outbreaks against the patriarchal Díaz, and his flight in 1911 introduced a terrifying decade in which the nation was torn from end to end and new leaders, some idealists and some rogues, pursued their visions or their ambitions. A century had passed since Father Hidalgo had rung the bell in Dolores, and now Madero called for a new revolution against the political and social ills which had piled upon the unhappy land.

FRANCISCO I. MADERO

When Francisco I. Madero triumphantly entered the Mexican capital on June 7, 1911, the hopes and prayers of a bewildered people were fixed on this aristocrat "with bulging forehead, flattened nose, black beard, sallow skin, and burning eyes . . . combining in his single under-sized person the triple role of prophet, Messiah and apostle."[1] No conquering hero, not even Benito Juárez, had been accorded such ovation as Madero now received. "He could have walked," wrote an eyewitness, "over a corduroy road of the faithful from the Rio Grande to the capital. . . . Every town he entered was as a Jerusalem, and he entered it literally to the waving of palms and the shouting of Hosannas."[2] The sick, borne on the backs of their kin, lined the streets, seeking healing at the touch of his garments. Surging mobs shouted, *Viva Madero! Viva el Inmaculado! Viva el Incorruptible! Viva el Redentor!* Their instincts were sound, for their hero was indeed "immaculate" and "incorruptible," but those unfamiliar virtues hardly qualified him as a "redeemer." Numerous observers were unconvinced; one such, the American ambassador, retired to his chancellery and dictated a dour dispatch to Washington predicting the early fall of Madero.

Mexico's redemption was overdue, but Madero proved a frail instrument. He had the assurance of tapped-out messages from the spirit

---

[1] Edith O'Shaughnessy: *Intimate Pages of Mexican History* (New York: George H. Doran Co.; 1920), p. 149.
[2] *Ibid.,* p. 153.

world that he was foreordained to the task, but the spirits had failed to warn him that national salvation does not always attend the Australian ballot. He promised free and honest elections to a people whose bellies clamored for food, democracy to a people who wanted land. He was a political theorist who knew little economics. He was a weak man in a nation which demanded strong leadership. And he brought with him rapacious brothers and other kin whose zeal for their own profit discredited him.

Madero's election was inevitable. A caretaker regime under Francisco de la Barra (the constitutional device under which Díaz had abdicated) ruled uneasily through the summer of 1911, and in November Madero moved into the national palace with inept Pino Suárez as his vice-president. Then all the stored-up angers of four decades converged upon him. Agrarian reformers, shouting *Tierra y libertad* (Land and liberty), beset him, while harassed *hacendados,* whose fields and houses were being burned, jammed his offices. Bernardo Reyes, long-time aide—and rival—of Díaz, joined Félix Díaz, the dictator's nephew, in armed revolt; the two rebels were overcome and jailed in the capital city, there to continue their plotting from prison cells. In the north, Venustiano Carranza and Pascual Orozco stirred up further trouble. Meanwhile, Madero was besieged by foreign diplomats, the American Henry Lane Wilson the most insistent, arguing the protection of their nationals' lives and property. Madero was timid and awkward in meeting the hammer blows from within and without. His aides, contemptuous of their leader's dreams, were little help. His commanding general, Victoriano Huerta, was an able fighter but an opportunist without loyalty to Madero.

The inevitable collapse came in February, 1913, fifteen months after Madero's assumption of office. For ten days (*la decena trágica*), Mexico City was raked by cannon fire; the rebels, incited by Reyes and Félix Díaz, who had been released from their prison cells, gave the city a blood bath such as it had not seen since Hernán Cortés leveled the Aztec capital house by house. Out of the welter of plots and counterplots, Huerta emerged the master of the scene; on February 19 Madero's brother Gustavo was killed, the President and Vice-President were imprisoned in the national palace, and Huerta assumed the provisional presidency. Leading citizens breathed more freely. The American ambassador, dean of the diplomatic corps, voiced the general satisfaction in this happy augury of law and order. Madero and Pino Suárez signed their resignations on Huerta's promise of safe conduct from the country; Madero's wife and many others appealed to the American ambassador to persuade Huerta to keep his promise—but without success, for that diplomat had become one of the most fervent supporters of the new regime. On February 22 Madero and Pino Suárez were murdered by guards who were transferring them to the penitentiary.[3]

---

[3] Mexicans generally charge Ambassador Wilson with moral responsibility for the final tragedy of Madero's murder. That he was indiscreet is clear. Secretary of State Philander Knox warned him to use "circumspection." His colleague, the Cuban ambassador, reported that Wilson convened the diplomatic corps after Madero's arrest and proudly informed them: "Mexico has been saved. From now on we shall have peace, progress and prosperity. I have known about the plans to imprison Madero for three days. It was slated

VICTORIANO HUERTA

The restorer of Porfirian calm, Victoriano Huerta, was gratefully welcomed to the presidency in February, 1913, by conservative citizens. He had seen much service during his fifty-nine years. Under Díaz he had proved useful as a general who could kill rebellious Indians without qualms; then under Madero he had struck ruthlessly at the agrarians led by Zapata. During his seventeen months in the presidency, his favorite haunt was a mean saloon, its walls streaked with dirt and pockmarked by the bullets of drunken officers; from one of its back rooms, over a bottle of cognac, Huerta issued decrees which were often enforced by gunmen without recourse to judges and juries.

All signs favored Huerta as he undertook the quieting of the nation. His *de facto* presidency was recognized by Great Britain and the other chief European powers, and by Japan and China. Churchmen praised him and raised a loan of a million pesos. English bankers, with an eye to their oil wells and mines, floated a bond issue which netted Huerta's treasury 7 million pesos. The first discord was struck by President Woodrow Wilson, inaugurated a fortnight after Huerta's *coup d'état*. The American President, deaf to Ambassador Henry Lane Wilson's assurance that Mexico was now united, sent his personal agent, whose sour report on the Ambassador's support of Huerta led to that diplomat's recall. Then Woodrow Wilson, through another agent, demanded Huerta's retirement and the election of a new president—promising that, once these steps were completed, the United States would support a loan to set the government on its feet. In response Huerta summoned Congress, hustled 110 of its members off to prison, and had himself elected by those who survived the purge. In February, 1914, Woodrow Wilson—as obstinate as his Mexican adversary —lifted the embargo on arms, thereby inviting Huerta's enemies to evict him.

Huerta's enemies closed in upon him. In the south Emiliano Zapata and his guerrillas—still crying *Tierra y libertad*—struck at the plantations, burning, wrecking, and killing, until the wiry Indian was master of the rich area south of the capital. Zapata had thrown in his lot with Madero in late 1910, but when Madero failed to grapple with the land problem, he had refused to disband his forces and had continued to pillage the sugar, corn, and wheat lands which furnished much of the nation's food. The northeast was dominated by Venustiano Carranza of Coahuila, a shrewd opportunist who had grown rich as a senator under Díaz, who had backed Madero halfheartedly, and who believed that Mexico's prime need was an energetic middle class. Challenging Huerta in the interests of order, he called himself First Chief of the Army of the Constitution. In northern Chihuahua and Durango, the capricious Pancho Villa (whose real name was Doroteo Arango) and his private army were attacking haciendas and villages, raping, looting, and murdering. He had backed Madero, and he now fitfully made common cause with Carranza; but Pancho Villa never served any cause but his own. From northwestern Sonora emerged the astute Álvaro Obregón, destined to outlast all the other enemies of Huerta, to become the chief ally of Carranza, and to reach the presidency in 1920.

The temper of those riotous years has been captured by two Mexican novelists, who themselves shared in the bloody struggles. Martín Luis Guzmán, who fought first under Villa and then under Carranza, wrote *El águila y la serpiente,* the eagle symbolizing the revolution, and the serpent, the politician. Villa is realistically portrayed; he was "a jaguar whose back we stroke with trembling hand, fearful that at any moment a paw might strike out at us." Carranza is described with contempt, as one "who tried to be like Don Porfirio [and] at the same time wanted to be like Juárez."[4] Mariano Azuela, a physician who served under Pancho Villa, wrote *Los de abajo,* in which he described the "underdogs" revolting against ills they cannot describe and fighting for causes they never understand. The novel's hero is the typical revolutionist: an ignorant peasant who has been made an assassin and outlaw by the caudillos who used him for their own ends. All the characters are entangled in a meaningless war. "The revolution," says one, "is like a hurricane; if you're in it, you're not a man . . . you're a leaf, a dead leaf, blown by the wind." When the hero of the tale learns that Villa and Carranza have split, he decides to go on fighting. When asked, "On which side?" he scratches his head and answers: "Look here, don't ask me any more questions. I never went to school, you know. . . . You gave me the eagle I wear on my hat, didn't you? All right, then; just tell me . . . do this or do that, that's all there's to it."[5]

Disorder spread during 1913 and early 1914. Huerta held the capital, while great and small caudillos rose against the central power, united only by hatred of Huerta. This was "the Revolution," a term covering some idealism and much zest for adventure and plunder. Recruits were drafted from the fields, the mines, and the prisons. The policed security of Porfirian days had given way to anarchy. The "constitutionalists"—followers of savage Villa, idealist Zapata, opportunist Carranza, and capable Obregón—won control of about three-quarters of all Mexico by April, 1914, confining Huerta and his forces to the central region embracing the capital and Veracruz.

Woodrow Wilson finally had the last word. In April, 1914, when American naval forces were seeking to head off a German merchantman bringing arms for Huerta, some American marines landed in Tampico and were arrested by Huerta's agents; but they were soon released. The American President, not content with the apologies of Huerta, ordered the fleet to Veracruz, where the marines again landed, seized the city, proclaimed martial law, and shot a few Mexicans. The incident, mirroring Woodrow Wilson's quixotic determination to "teach the Latin Americans to elect

4 Martín Luis Guzmán: *The Eagle and the Serpent,* translated by Harriet de Onís (New York: Alfred A. Knopf; 1930), pp. 12, 66.
5 Mariano Azuela: *The Underdogs,* translated by E. Munguía, Jr. (New York: Brentano's; 1929), p. 196.

good men," aroused the wrath not only of Huerta but also of many who opposed him. Nevertheless, American aid was decisive in putting an end to Huerta's rule—by withholding recognition, blocking trade, and by permitting his enemies to get arms from the United States. The forces of Carranza and Obregón marched into the capital in July, 1914, while Huerta fled to Veracruz and then to exile.[6]

VENUSTIANO CARRANZA

Venustiano Carranza, self-styled First Chief of the Army of the Constitution, moved into the national palace in July, 1914, thanks chiefly to Álvaro Obregón, ablest military strategist of the era. Carranza had troubles aplenty. From Washington, Woodrow Wilson sent abundant advice, warned him that he would be held strictly accountable for damage to Americans, urged him to make peace with Zapata, and sent another special agent with pure intentions and slight comprehension of Mexican realities. Within the country, Carranza continued a running battle with Pancho Villa in the north and Emiliano Zapata in the south. Villa would settle for nothing less than confirmation of his own reckless power, while Zapata would not lay down arms until Carranza would adopt his program of agrarian reform.

In hope of quieting the disputes among themselves, the rival leaders (in the face of Carranza's opposition) summoned a convention in November, 1914, in Aguascalientes. The adherents of Zapata, Villa, and Carranza were immediately at loggerheads—whereupon Villa's troops occupied the convention hall. Villa then made the ironical suggestion that he and Carranza break the deadlock by both committing suicide, but the First Chief decided instead to seek safety in Veracruz. Zapata and Villa marched into Mexico City and for five months moved in and out of the capital, taking brief turns in the presidential chair; meanwhile Carranza issued decrees from Veracruz. Anarchy ruled the country as rival generals printed their own paper money, tore up railroad tracks, raided lonely haciendas, and shot overseers and strung up their bodies for vultures to eat. Life in the capital was a prolonged horror, as first one faction and then another had its way with quaking citizens.

By the first days of 1915 the contest had narrowed to war between Carranza and Villa. The advantage lay with Villa, whose allies, now including the reluctant Zapata, held almost two-thirds of the country, and whose troops outnumbered Carranza's. But Carranza held the revenue-producing customhouse of Veracruz, controlled the northeastern frontier across which guns came from the United States, and had the inestimable help of Obregón. Carranza's final triumph was due to the sagacity of his aides. Obregón did the fighting, with the tough Yaquis from Sonora as the core of his forces. Luis Cabrera (a brilliant lawyer and early foe of Díaz and then of Huerta), together with Obregón, furnished the ideas;

[6] After a brief stay in Europe, Huerta found refuge in the United States. In 1916 he plotted an attack upon Mexico from Texas, was arrested, and died while in the custody of American police.

they both knew better than their chief that Mexicans wanted a social revolution—which Carranza, who had slight comprehension of such matters, now undertook to give them. Beginning in December, 1914, Carranza signed a series of decrees from Veracruz which called for distribution of idle national lands. Other decrees abolished the *jefes políticos,* petty local tyrants, and created self-governing municipalities. Still other edicts closed the dungeon prison of San Juan de Ulloa, legalized divorce, outlawed peonage, and provided for protection of workmen in industry. Carranza even espoused the cause of organized labor, just then beginning to find voice, and promised further social legislation. These new ideas and Obregón's fighting won the argument; by March, 1915, Villa was in full retreat, and Carranza entered the capital.

The victorious Carranza assured his countrymen that the Revolution was ended, while his advisers argued that the Revolution had only begun. Troubles continued. Zapata still marched, burned haciendas, and distributed land among his Indians. Villa still harried the north. In Washington, Woodrow Wilson still played the schoolmaster, lecturing Carranza on his duties. Then in March, 1916, Villa, seeking to involve the United States in order to embarrass Carranza, crossed the border into New Mexico, shot up the town of Columbus, and killed a few Americans. This provoked Woodrow Wilson to dispatch a punitive expedition under General John J. Pershing, whose forces made futile attempts to catch the elusive Villa.

The confusions under which Carranza floundered led to the calling of a constitutional convention. The elections of delegates were fraudulent: only "constitutionalists" (those who followed Carranza) were eligible; and all churchmen and *hacendados,* as well as agents of Zapata and Villa, were barred. The convention met in Querétaro in December, 1916, and its members, despite their nominal loyalty to Carranza, ignored his plea for greater powers for the chief executive. The most effective spokesmen were Obregón, representing the northern advocates of agrarian reform, General Francisco Múgica, speaking for the central and southern generals who believed in labor and land reforms, and some lonely intellectuals who spoke for Zapata. Molina Enríquez, intellectual father of the agrarian revolt, although not a delegate, drafted important articles of the new instrument. The constitution was completed in two months, and it was promulgated by decree on February 5, 1917.

Much of the Constitution of 1917—like the earlier codes of 1824 and 1857—followed the American and French models. It reaffirmed the principles of representative government; continued the classic division of executive, legislative, and judicial functions; decreed the local integrity of state and municipal governments; and guaranteed the security of the individual and of his property. But it went further, adding the revolutionary doctrine that the common welfare takes precedence over the parochial rights of the individual. The Mexican Constitution of 1917 stands as the most radical document up to that time of any American government, and it is well to note that it antedated the Russian Revolution.

The Constitution of 1917 enunciated a revolutionary doctrine of property. Article 27 announced: "The ownership of lands and waters . . . is vested originally in the nation which . . . has the right to transmit title thereto to private persons . . . [but] the nation shall have at all times the right to impose upon private property such restrictions as the public interest may require . . . in order to conserve and equitably distribute the public wealth." Furthermore, "In the nation is vested direct ownership of all minerals or substances [in the subsoil], solid mineral fuels, petroleum, and all hydro-carbons—solid, liquid or gaseous. . . . The ownership of the nation," it continued, "is inalienable"; all concessions to exploit national resources were subject to definite restrictions; individuals or corporations granted such concessions had either to be Mexicans or to agree to be regarded juridically as Mexicans in their operations, waiving all right of appeal to foreign powers for protection. It was further provided that "no foreigner shall under any conditions acquire direct ownership of lands and waters" within a one-hundred-kilometer zone on the frontiers, or within fifty kilometers from the seacoast. The radicalism of this doctrine of property was softened by a provision that no measure should be applied retroactively, but this word of comfort was canceled by a clause that permitted "revision" of old concessions and empowered the president "to declare those null and void which seriously prejudice the public interest."

This doctrine of property rights, so frightening to domestic and foreign owners of haciendas, mines, and oil wells, had its roots in Spanish law, which vested ultimate title to all lands in the Crown; the king in benign wisdom might concede rights of occupation and exploitation to his vassals —but titles thus conveyed were always clouded by the overriding prior claims of the Crown. What the king gave, the king could take away. No grant was inalienable; every concession was revocable. Use, rather than possession, fortified the particular title. When Charles III and Charles IV confiscated the properties of Jesuits and other Church bodies, their actions were generally accepted as consonant with royal prerogatives.

The Constitution likewise stated a new doctrine for labor. Article 123, the Mexican worker's new charter, promised the eight-hour day, control of wages, equal pay for equal work, the end of child labor, and the responsibility of the employer for occupational accidents and diseases. It gave workers the right to organize freely, to bargain collectively through spokesmen of their own choosing, and to strike. These and many other provisions were written into the basic law, although it was left to the legislatures to implement them with specific statutes. Such guarantees to labor, generally accepted by democratic nations, were new to Mexico, whose labor movement was in its infancy. Operatives in mines and factories, little more than chained slaves under Díaz, were still worked from nine to fourteen hours a day, seldom paid more than 50 centavos a day, and housed in company houses at exorbitant rents; they had no recourse against the perils of obsolete machinery, and their families were without protection in the event of the accidental injury or death of the wage earner.

Drafted by anticlericals, the new Constitution confirmed the Reform laws of the 1850's which stripped the Church of her landed wealth, and went further by declaring temples for worship the property of the state. Article 130 excluded the Church from any share in public education, made marriage a civil contract, and limited the activities of priests. Henceforth all priests were required to register with the civil authorities; each state could limit the total number permitted to officiate within its borders; no foreign priests could serve; all priests were deprived of their right to vote and to hold public office, and were denied freedom to criticize "the fundamental laws of the country, the authorities in particular or the government in general."

The Constitution of 1917, hailed with delight by revolutionists who had followed Madero and Zapata and Obregón, was a declaration of war upon the clergy, the *hacendados,* and the employers of labor. It was also a warning to the United States, Great Britain, and other alien states whose nationals exploited Mexican land, oil wells, and mines. Its bold provisions exercised a profound influence upon subsequent constitutions in Chile, Colombia, Bolivia, and other republics.

Carranza took little pride in the document he had theoretically fathered. He was content with the honors and perquisites of office, and had little taste for crusades. He left the shouting to the honest idealists who took their causes in deep seriousness, appeasing them now and then with a fervid speech or an edict advertised to cure one or another abuse. Meanwhile, the practical generals and the political chieftains (usually the same men) looted the state and federal treasuries, and used the agrarian laws to enlarge their private domains and the laws directed at aliens to enrich themselves. Villa continued his scourging of the north, and scores of lesser caudillos kept the land in anarchy. Carranza placed a price upon the head of Zapata, and in 1919 one of his officers collected the blood money for treacherously capturing and shooting that honest revolutionist.

In the meantime, Carranza carried on a continuous debate with the United States. Early in 1917, when war with Germany appeared inescapable, Woodrow Wilson took steps to end his futile six-year bout with Mexico: in February he withdrew Pershing's discouraged men from their man hunt of Villa and stopped all export of arms and munitions to Mexico; and in March he extended full recognition to Carranza. But Wilson's truce did not silence the outcry of landholders, oil companies, and churchmen against "godless and socialistic Mexico." Carranza counterattacked in 1918 by decreeing that Article 27, with its threat to foreign interests, was retroactive. He also gave some evidence of friendliness to Germany but had the good sense to repulse her proposal of January, 1917, that Mexico join Germany to recapture Mexico's "lost provinces" from the United States.

By 1919 Carranza's control of Mexico was slipping. The agrarians, even after Zapata's death, daily grew more exigent. Labor, now controlled by the blatant Luis Morones, turned against him. Obregón, the general who had put Carranza in office and kept him there, had retired to his farms in Sonora; but early in 1920 he was again on the march, this time against

Carranza. Obregón proved an eloquent champion of all the causes betrayed by his one-time ally, and Carranza could find no troops willing to take up arms against him. Carranza, aware that his time was up, filled a special train with sacks of bullion from the treasury; with his family and cronies, he set out for Veracruz and freedom abroad. But one of his erstwhile supporters arranged an attack upon the train, and Carranza escaped into the mountains only to be trapped there and murdered. The first phase of the Revolution thus ended in May, 1920.

Chapter 23

RECONSTRUCTION: THE ERA OF OBREGÓN, CALLES, AND CÁRDENAS, 1920–40

The entry of Álvaro Obregón into the capital with 40,000 troops gave a new turn of the wheel to luckless Mexico. His subsequent election to the presidency, after a few months of interim rule by Adolfo de la Huerta (not related to Victoriano Huerta), marked the beginning of reconstruction after a bloody decade. During the ensuing fourteen years, the nation was to be ruled by Obregón, Plutarco Elías Calles, and three puppet presidents who did Calles's bidding; it was a period in which the land was forcibly pacified and strong men gave limited fulfillment to the promises of the Constitution of 1917. It was not the millennium. Presidents enriched themselves from the public treasury; generals padded payrolls and pocketed money withheld from ignorant soldiers; regional caudillos took their toll. Democracy remained a myth: elections were rigged, and repression was still an instrument of executive control. An American historian, writing later, made a statement which applies to this period: "The President is the government, and all discussion of Mexican politics must assume that fact. . . . The President of Mexico must be able to do everything he wants or he will be unable to do anything he wants. He has either all the power or no power; there is no middle ground."[1] But despite betrayals of public trust, citizens were given grounds for faith in the ultimate redemption of their country.

All that happened, good or ill, was now celebrated by political orators in the name of the Revolution; they pulled all the stops and released a swelling diapason in praise of the new reign of justice—a few even meant what they said and tried to carry out their promises. The long-bandied slogan *Sufragio efectivo; no reelección* was typed on every official document and letter. The shout *Viva la Revolución!* was used to drown out debate and to justify whatever the government did: the seizure of haciendas and the transfer of their broad acres, sometimes to landless Indians, sometimes to landed generals; the exile of hapless nuns; the suppression of newspapers whose editors wrote as they believed; and the closing of factories, some-

---

[1] Frank Tannenbaum: *Mexico, the Struggle for Peace and Bread* (New York: Alfred A. Knopf; 1950), p. 84.

times for the protection of workmen, sometimes for the collection of black-mail by labor leaders.

ÁLVARO OBREGÓN, 1920–24

Álvaro Obregón was the ablest man yet to appear from revolutionary ranks. He was forty when inaugurated in December, 1920, and had already proved his tactical skill on the battlefield, his capacity for handling men, and his canny trader's sense. Born in the northwestern state of Sonora, he had his first practical experience as a small farmer. He understood the land hunger of the Mexican. He described himself as a revolutionary, but any Iowa banker would have called him a capitalist: at twenty, Obregón had a few fertile acres; at forty-eight, when he was assassinated, he controlled more land than had many of Porfirio Díaz's favorites, and had virtually cornered the national market in *garbanzos* (chick-peas). Unlike common plunderers, Obregón gave as well as took, and he effectively served the nation by his understanding of economic realities. He was the businessman in politics: he indulged in no vain flights of romanticism and (in Henry Bamford Parkes's phrase) "thought in prose and not in poetry."

Obregón imposed peace by methods not unlike those of Díaz. He quieted clamoring politicians by making them cabinet ministers, governors, mayors, congressmen, or generals; and made it clear that they must eat humbly from his hand or disappear from public life. His formula for rule had proved its efficacy under Díaz: it was *pan o palo* in modern dress, although Obregón was more suave and restrained. The press had considerable freedom, and the dealing out of summary justice was curtailed. It was a dictatorship, but a bland one. He consolidated his power over three chief groups of potential rivals—the army, organized labor, and the agrarian reformers. He kept the army content by increasing the number of generals and by allowing their flagrant pilfering. When General Francisco Serrano, his minister of war, lost 80,000 pesos in one sitting at the gaming tables, Obregón approved payment of the sum from the treasury. While permitting such largess to the generals, he wisely decreased the number of enlisted soldiers.

Organized labor burgeoned under Obregón. The powerful CROM (*Confederación Regional Obrera Mexicana*), which, dominated by able Luis Morones, had helped Obregón to power, was repaid with political favors and aid in crushing rival unions. Morones, buttressed by the CROM's inner council (*Grupo Acción*) and defended by his private guards, exercised a power second only to that of the president. Armed with Article 123 of the Constitution and supported by Obregón's courts and police, Morones's CROM exercised the power of life or death over every factory, mill, and shop. The threat of a strike brought almost any employer to his knees. The CROM's ranks swelled from 50,000 in 1920 to 1.2 million in 1924 (so Morones said, although few believed his claims), but only a handful paid dues—that revenue was not necessary so long as employers paid tribute.

Further afield, Morones had a good friend in Samuel Gompers, President of the American Federation of Labor.

The agrarian reformers, still under the spell of the betrayed Zapata and now led by Antonio Díaz Soto y Gama, were given limited encouragement. Obregón created state agrarian commissions supervised by a national commission, and empowered them to satisfy the demands of landless villages by expropriating adjoining haciendas (their owners to be given twenty-year bonds in payment). But Obregón was cautious, for he feared that sudden uprooting of the hacienda system would dislocate the national economy. During his term a total of about 2.8 million acres was thus transferred—no great amount compared with the more than 300 million acres held by the *hacendados,* but nevertheless a token of his genuine, if restrained, enthusiasm for land reform. Unfortunately his efforts were largely nullified by the corrupt officials who administered his laws.

Obregón's revolutionary ardor found its purest expression in his school program. His minister of education was the brilliant and erratic José Vasconcelos, whose printed words had won him intellectual and spiritual leadership of youth not only in Mexico but in all Spanish America. Now, as the leader of Mexican education, he gave substance to the promises of the Revolution. He possessed a lively sense of the cultural heritage from both the Iberian and Indian past. A classicist, he circulated Spanish translations of Plato and Aristotle among his teachers; but he was also a firm believer in the future of the Indian masses and was convinced that through the blending of many peoples America would have a strong and resilient "cosmic race."

With Obregón's loyal support and a budget of unprecedented generosity (35 million pesos at its peak), Vasconcelos created a new type of rural school, which he called *La Casa del Pueblo* (The House of the People), designed to serve the entire life of the village in which it was placed. Within four years he had established almost 1,000 such schools, which offered a program of the three R's, music, painting, sports, theater, and practical instruction in sanitation and scientific agriculture. Few teachers were prepared to give such varied instruction, but Vasconcelos proved ingenious in uncovering talent in unlikely spots and in transmitting his own imagination to this company of recruits. His teachers, many of them scarcely literate, learned as they taught, and worked with zeal at day laborers' wages. Vasconcelos also appointed itinerant teachers with better training, whom he sent among the schools to share their skills with rural teachers.

During this period a new school of artists emerged to paint upon the walls of public buildings their interpretations of Mexico's epic struggles. Vasconcelos gave them contracts at artisans' wages to paint murals in the Secretariat of Education, the National Preparatory School, and the Agricultural School in Chapingo. Their names, especially those of Diego Rivera and José Clemente Orozco, were soon known to the world. Vasconcelos likewise commissioned Carlos Chávez to compose music for a ballet, thus launching the public career of Mexico's most distinguished musician.

Meanwhile, the continuing quarrel between politicians and clergy embroiled the nation. Obregón himself made little effort to enforce the anti-clerical articles of the Constitution, but his unruly laborites, agrarians, and generals continued to bait the clergy and to exact toll from prosperous churchmen. The expanded federal school system alarmed the churchmen, and many rural teachers were roughly handled. The conflict reached a crisis in January, 1923. The immediate provocation was the dedication of a monument to "Christ, King of Mexico" upon a hill in Guanajuato; 50,000 gathered from all Mexico, and the ceremonies, rich in pageantry, were graced by the participation of four archbishops, eight bishops, and the Pope's representative. Obregón, interpreting the event as a challenge to the government, ordered the expulsion from the republic of the apostolic delegate, Archbishop Filippi. This affront to the Pope loosed a storm of anger from the faithful, who immediately placarded their houses in city and village with the fighting slogan, *Viva Cristo Rey!* (Long live Christ the King!).

Not the least of Obregón's burdens was the unceasing debate with the United States. Washington pressed its charges, often justified, that American life and property were not adequately protected. The oil companies denounced as confiscatory Article 27, which vested ownership of the subsoil in the state; and they had the active support of President Harding's corrupt secretary of the interior, Albert B. Fall. Obregón sought to mollify his critics by repeated declarations that the law was *not* retroactive (as Carranza had announced)—that it did not apply to those who had worked their claims before 1917. Washington meanwhile withheld recognition, always a threat to any Mexican president, and asked that Obregón sign a treaty explicitly confirming his verbal pledges. Obregón refused on the ground that his word was enough. American clamor increased; demands for strong measures, even for armed intervention, were voiced by William Randolph Hearst and other editors, by some spokesmen for oil interests, and by a few hot-headed Catholic churchmen—with Albert B. Fall their constant friend in high places. The Harding administration, thanks largely to the moderation of Secretary of State Charles Evans Hughes, kept its temper,[2] and in 1923 sent commissioners to confer with Obregón. The ensuing Bucareli Conference (so called after the street in Mexico City where sessions were held) yielded agreements which temporarily quieted the storm: Mexico tacitly pledged not to apply the Constitution retroactively against the oil companies; and Obregón was recognized in August, 1923.

The tranquillity of Obregón's term was broken by one final explosion. In late 1923 Obregón made clear his choice of Plutarco Elías Calles as his successor in the coming election of 1924. This choice of a man generally described as a hard-hitting leftist and a partisan of the CROM and of the agrarian extremists angered conservatives who wanted a swing to the right, moderates who wanted a policy of conciliation, and sincere liberals who

[2] Public support for a conciliatory course came from the American Federation of Labor, which had assumed a quasi protectorate over the CROM; also from some self-appointed Protestant spokesmen who were variously animated by laudable desire for peace and by an unpleasant desire to assail the Catholics.

viewed Calles as inimical to democratic progress. Various anti-Calles factions settled upon Adolfo de la Huerta, Obregón's minister of finance—the same man who had served as acting president in the summer of 1920—as their leader in revolt. It was a *cuartelazo* (barracks-revolt) in the time-honored pattern; influential generals declared for De la Huerta in Vera-cruz, Jalisco, and Oaxaca, and the fight began in December, 1923. Obregón's agent rushed to Washington and got the promise of arms from President Coolidge—aid which proved decisive, bringing victory within three months.

Mexico had again been subjected to the ruinous cross fire of civil war, and the treasury was drained. The incident was closed with the execution of many chief plotters, but De la Huerta found asylum in Los Angeles. The one happy result of the rebellion was replacement of De la Huerta by Alberto Pani as finance minister. That able businessman strengthened the treasury; he founded a national bank of issue which would shortly over-shadow the foreign-controlled private banks, and he created a government monopoly on silver exports, a device which brought profit to the government. Meanwhile, Obregón finished out his term of office in peace, saw to it that Calles was elected with the customary unanimity, and turned over the cares and honors of office to his long-time brother-in-arms on December 1, 1924.

CALLES AND HIS HENCHMEN, 1924–34

Plutarco Elías Calles ruled for a full decade, first as titular president for a four-year term and then for six more years through three men whom he named and dominated. His inauguration on December 1, 1924, was staged in the presence of thousands of peasants and workers fetched at public expense from all Mexico—from the hot lands of Tehuantepec and from the deserts of Sonora. The scene was splashed with varicolored Indian serapes, the white pajamas of farm workers, and the blue denim of factory laborers. Two men shared the spotlight—Obregón and Calles; and with them stood Samuel Gompers, the seventy-five-year-old veteran President of the American Federation of Labor, who with several hundred American labor leaders had been brought by special trains to share the triumph of Mexico's "labor government," whose cause they had defended in the United States.

The stocky, iron-jawed Calles, then forty-seven, was a son of Sonora, born to poverty. He had taught school briefly, been a bartender, entered the army and fought at Obregón's side during the Carranza days, and then had served in the cabinets of both Carranza and Obregón. His courage had been proved in battle and in politics, but he lacked Obregón's ability to conciliate. The "labor government" he now initiated was big with promises: clean government, emancipation for all workers, schools for children, and land for 12 million peasants. There was no doubt as to his energy and ability. His political housecleaning was impressive. Numerous underpaid public servants found it expedient to cease their pilfering and get to work. The shifts in the higher official echelons were less reassuring; most of Obregón's favorites were eased from office and their places given to new men with equally expensive tastes.

Labor's massive (300-pound) Luis Morones, powerful under Obregón, became more powerful than ever under Calles. As leader of the government-protected CROM—whose roster of 1,200,000 members in 1924 increased to 2,250,000 in 1927 (both figures much exaggerated)— Morones ruled from his Ministry of Labor and Industry, administering rough discipline to those who debated his decisions. Buttressed by the courts, the army, and the police, Morones was the unchecked master of economic life. Any businessman, shop manager, or factory owner who challenged his power was promptly subjected to a strike, the closing of his plant, interminable delays before official boards of arbitration, and bankruptcy—unless he reached understanding with Morones. His rule paid him well: big diamonds flashed from his pudgy fingers, he had fine homes and the fastest cars, and he acquired excellent city real estate. But labor profited from the costly Morones: workers won the right to organize and strike; they gained somewhat better wages and a limited security against the hazards of accident and death.

Calles, self-styled "heir of Zapata," was under bond to fulfill his promise of land to the peasants. In retrospect, there is reason to question how deeply his heart was committed to that cause. Shortly after entering office, whether from expediency or conviction, he ordered expropriation of some hacienda lands and their allotment to villages under the communal pattern of the ancient *ejido,* but with the clear intimation that such joint holdings would shortly be divided into small plots for individual families. He chose as minister of agriculture and chief purveyor of this bounty a young orator named Luis León, who launched these reforms with loud fanfare (and soon began to build a house of many rooms and tiled baths on the heights of Chapultepec). Land, announced Calles, would now be taken from the rich and given to the poor—and 7.5 million acres were expropriated by 1928. Calles decreed that the little farmers should be furnished with seeds, fertilizer, and tools, and that irrigation projects should be launched to make their fields prosper. Agricultural credit banks were organized to finance the growing and harvesting of crops. As months passed, skeptics said that few peasants were getting land, credit, or seeds, but that an undue share of these benefits was going to deserving *callistas,* now endowed with fine stands of waving grain and pastures grazed by blooded stock. Nevertheless, some peasants experienced the new dignity of owning their own corn plots.

Calles, still playing Robin Hood, boldly defied the American and British oil companies. In December, 1925, his congress ordered the oil companies to exchange their holdings for fifty-year concessions—and specifically included operators who had been in business before the Constitution of 1917. Although Calles prudently delayed enforcement of this law, it was denounced by British and American interests as a betrayal of the gentlemen's agreement with Obregón in 1923, which guaranteed operators against retroactive action.

And then Calles, inviting further troubles at home and abroad, renewed the conflict with the Church. The Catholic hierarchy, exercising the right of protest which is accepted as a matter of course by free peoples, published a statement in January, 1926, which read: "The code of 1917 wounds the most sacred rights of the Catholic Church . . . we therefore protest against similar transgressions against religious liberty and the rights of the Church; and . . . we disavow any act or manifesto . . . contrary to . . . this protest." It was signed by all the archbishops and bishops of Mexico. Calles angrily met this and subsequent protests by deporting foreign priests, closing Church schools and convents, ordering priests to register, and accusing the hierarchy of treason. In July, 1926, a group of Catholic laymen announced a boycott on unnecessary purchases in order to cripple the national economy and thereby weaken Calles. On July 31, 1926, all the priests withdrew from their altars, and for the first time since Cortés landed at Veracruz in 1519, no public Mass was celebrated in all Mexico. The "strike" of the clergy lasted three years. Meanwhile, the churches remained open, guarded by their unpaid custodians; the faithful came for prayer, while vandals continued to loot the temples of paintings and sculptured saints.[3] It was war. Outraged believers banded under the name of *cristeros* (followers of Christ the King) and, especially in the isolated villages around Lakes Pátzcuaro and Chapala, burned public schools, murdered federal teachers, and finally dynamited a train killing several scores of persons. Calles retaliated by forcing six bishops into exile, and many priests followed them. The fury of the conflict was increased by irresponsible generals who used the strife as excuse for murderous attacks upon prominent Catholic families and for the confiscation of their houses and lands. In the meantime devout Mexicans found solace in the silent churches, telling their beads, repeating their prayers, and often weeping for the shame of their nation; while many of those with larger houses smuggled in priests in lay garb for the celebration of the Mass behind drawn curtains. (The wives of leading revolutionaries, including Calles, enjoyed this luxury.)

Calles's sorties against landholders, employers of labor, oil companies, and the Church evoked acrimonious attacks from the United States, which gathered force throughout 1925, 1926, and on into 1927. Oil companies released tons of printed argument charging that Mexico had broken her pledged word, that the legislation was confiscatory, that foreign interests could expect no justice from Mexican courts. The Knights of Columbus raised funds, organized protest meetings, and published appeals in the press. The Hearst newspapers printed documents purporting to prove that Calles had paid four American senators and several lesser men over $1 millon to defend his course before the American public. Some Protestant groups, with marked anti-Catholic animus, defended

---

[3] Many fine homes in Mexico have collections of such treasures. Their owners did not steal the images of the Virgin and of the saints—but bought them from those who did.

Calles; and a few Masonic groups added to the clamor against intervention. The American Federation of Labor continued to uphold the right of Mexico to order its domestic affairs as it saw fit.

The American outcry against Calles was encouraged by official statements from Washington. In June, 1925, Secretary of State Frank B. Kellogg issued a declaration deploring the lack of protection accorded American interests and said: "I have seen the statements published in the press that another revolutionary movement may be impending in Mexico. I very much hope this is not true." Kellogg concluded: "The Government of Mexico is on trial before the world." Calles promptly issued a rejoinder: "If the Government of Mexico . . . is now on trial before the world, so too is the Government of the United States as well as those of other countries." The American press, with few exceptions, called Kellogg's words a serious blunder, an incitement to revolt, and an instance of diplomatic discourtesy.[4] Meanwhile, American Ambassador James R. Sheffield proved awkward. When American visitors suggested that the time had come for a diplomat to take sympathetic thought for the welfare of the land to which he was accredited, Sheffield replied: "My business here is to protect American lives and property—and nothing more." The American case against Mexico was serious and well founded, but it was not ably defended either from Washington or from the American Embassy in Mexico City.

In November, 1926, the American Department of State added more fuel to the flames. An assistant secretary confided to the press that he was "morally certain . . . that a steady stream of Bolshevist propaganda . . . [was] filtering from Mexico down through Central America, aimed at property rights and designed to undermine society and government as now constituted"—and he asked the newsmen to print the warning without involving the State Department. Kellogg then enlarged upon the alleged Bolshevik conspiracy; his warning was countered by the conservative *New York Times* in an editorial headed "Too Easily Scared," suggesting that Kellogg revealed a "singular lack of perspective," an opinion supported by many other editors.

By January, 1927, a diplomatic break between the two countries seemed imminent. On January 9, Calles assured a group of visiting Americans that he was ready to submit the issues of land and oil to the review of the Hague court. This statement brought a widespread demand in the United States that the dispute be submitted to arbitration. Meanwhile, the case of the American advocates of intervention was prejudiced by the findings of the Supreme Court against two of their number, Edward L. Doheny and Harry F. Sinclair; the later trial and jailing of Albert B. Fall added to their discomfort. The presence of these men on the American side of the argument did not prove that the Mexicans were perforce pure in heart and purpose, but it persuaded many Americans to reconsider.

Mexico's relations with the United States took a happier turn in the fall of 1927 when President Calvin Coolidge recalled Ambassador

4 See Ernest Gruening: *Mexico and Its Heritage* (New York: The Century Co.; 1928), p. 603, for editorial opinion on this subject.

Sheffield and replaced him with Dwight W. Morrow of J. P. Morgan and Company. Wise in the law and banking, Morrow was equally wise in knowledge of men. In accepting the post, he confided to a friend: "I do not know what I can do in Mexico, but I can like the Mexicans." He went to Mexico, as had his predecessor, to "protect American lives and property"; but he also resolved to help Mexico and the United States to understand each other. His mission to Mexico marked the beginning of a new sort of American diplomacy vis-à-vis Latin America, later called the Good Neighbor Policy. He cut through the niceties of protocol, conducted his discussions with Calles face to face, and became a friend of the man whom so many Americans hated.[5] He did not confine his friendships to men in power, but filled his house with artists, teachers, and others in many fields. The air of distrust was cleared, and by 1928 the two nations were on better terms than ever in their history.

The fruits of Dwight Morrow's diplomacy soon ripened. He created an atmosphere in which both Calles and the American government could break the deadlock without loss of face. In November, 1927, two months after his arrival, the Mexican Supreme Court (under orders from the president) reaffirmed the principle of national ownership of the subsoil but declared unconstitutional any application of the law to companies whose activities began before 1917. Morrow then turned his attention to the troubled land dispute, suggesting to Calles "that Mexico had already taken more land than was needed for peons available to go upon it and that the Mexican Government without definitely changing its policy could now stop taking new lands and devote its energy to improving the land already taken."[6] Morrow won this point with Calles, and the distribution of land slowed down. The United States was pleased, and Mexico breathed more easily now that the threat of intervention had passed. While many Mexicans honestly believed that Morrow had simply proved a more convincing salesman for the United States and that his mission had wrecked their Revolution, other Mexicans felt that Morrow had served their country by persuading Calles to proceed more gradually.

As Calles came to the end of his elected term in 1928, another armed revolt broke out and the generals who led it were summarily shot and forgotten. He prepared to turn over his office to Álvaro Obregón, who was duly elected in July (the Constitution had been amended to permit a second term and to extend the term to six years), but a fanatic's bullet killed Obregón two weeks after the election. The assassination was officially described as Church-inspired, but the charge was never substantiated. In September Calles convened his congress, and made an impassioned speech in which he announced the termination of dictatorship and promised the

[5] A sincere liking grew between Morrow and Calles. The writer remembers an evening spent with Morrow in late 1930, not many months before his death. Again and again, he would begin: "You have no idea what a fine man Calles is"—and then tell some incident of his three years in Mexico.

[6] Harold Nicolson: *Dwight Morrow* (New York: Harcourt, Brace & Co.; 1935), p. 335.

end of rule by "persons," the beginning of rule by "laws." Congress, at his order, then named the ex-governor of Tamaulipas, Emilio Portes Gil, as provisional president for one year.

Portes Gil served (1928–29) under the watchful eye of Calles, although he proved capable of standing up to his mentor—now the self-appointed *jefe máximo de la revolución* (supreme chief of the revolution) —rather more forcefully than was expected. Portes Gil actually speeded the land program, giving away twice as many acres in twelve months as had Calles in his last year. He enforced the labor codes, although limiting the power of Morones. He worked with Calles to coax all political factions into one imposing party, the *Partido Nacional Revolucionario*; the PNR, financed by a "kickback" from the pay envelope of every government employee, would (under various names) dominate elections for years to come. Others were free to organize parties as they pleased, which they did with frequency and futility.

The Church imbroglio was now eased. Under the tactful mediation of Morrow, Portes Gil met the representatives of the Church, and an agreement was reached by which the clergy called off their strike and resumed their places in the churches, while the government pledged itself to recognize the preeminence of the Church in spiritual matters and to permit religious instruction within church walls. In June, 1929, the priests were again at their altars, administering the sacraments to the faithful. Within a few months the *cristeros* ceased their troubling, and Mexico enjoyed a lull in the war between Church and state.

But Portes Gil, despite his first bold gestures, was little more than a front for the powerful Calles. Despite fine words about democracy and the rights of man, Mexico's political and economic life was ruled by a small group around Calles—a new band of *científicos* whose science was that of business enterprise. These men were suave and astute, possessed of good economic sense, and, paradoxically, they combined ability to seize private profit from the Revolution with a measure of loyalty to the interests of the nation. These new *científicos* established their informal court in the flower-banked village of Cuernavaca, in the valley just over the mountain rim from the capital. There they built stucco houses draped with purple bougainvillaea, at generous cost and in dubious taste, on the street irreverently described by taxi drivers as that of "Ali Baba and the Forty Thieves."

In 1929 an election was held for the man to serve out the five remaining years of Obregón's term. The delegates to the PNR's nominating convention were generally agreed upon an intelligent industrialist named Aarón Sáenz; but Calles overruled them and gave the honor to Pascual Ortiz Rubio, whose chief qualification for high office was the fact that few people had heard of him. "Pascualito," little Pascual, as Mexicans derisively called him, was credited with more than a million votes in the election that followed, while his opponent, the embittered José Vasconcelos, received about 20,000.

Ortiz Rubio was admirably qualified for the role of an absent-minded puppet whose strings were pulled by the Supreme Chief from Cuernavaca. He warmed the presidential chair for three years (1929–32), signed the edicts Calles dictated, and appointed the men Calles chose. This was "normalcy," and the shouts of Revolution sank to a hoarse whisper. Calles returned from a trip to Europe in June, 1930, and announced that the agrarian program was a mistake, that the peons did not know how to use their land, and that production of foodstuffs was steadily declining. His indictments were true, but he did not confess how much of the fault lay with the corrupt officials he had named. Distribution of land had slowed down: in 1933 less than one-fifth as much acreage was allotted as under Portes Gil in 1929. Union labor was stripped of its power: Portes Gil had begun the dismantling of Morones's CROM; Ortiz Rubio finished it. The independent unions, used to bedevil the CROM, were then smashed in turn. The war on the Church, momentarily quieted by Portes Gil, passed into a new phase; the states enacted laws severely limiting the number of registered priests, until by 1933 only about 200 were permitted to serve the entire nation. The government had again broken its pledged word. Anger flared into violence, with fresh reprisals by the government against the persons and property of the devout.

In September, 1932, after Ortiz Rubio had ventured to make some appointments without consulting the Supreme Chief, Calles announced that the President was about to resign, a prediction promptly fulfilled by Ortiz Rubio, who retired to the United States for a rest, confiding that "being president is very difficult, very, very difficult." Congress, under orders from Calles, then named Abelardo Rodríguez to fill out the remaining two years of the term that was originally Obregón's. Rodríguez, grown wealthy from gambling casinos built in partnership with Calles and other revolutionists, completed the transmutation of the "labor government" into a regime for the benefit of the *callistas*. But Rodríguez had brains and imagination, and knew that it was idle to build factories, textile mills, and processing plants (as he and his friends were doing) unless the purchasing power of the masses could be enlarged; some must have money enough to buy shoes and cotton dresses and beer. In expediency, and perhaps with a measure of patriotism, he gave some support to the demands of labor and distributed a little land to the peasants.

Storm signals now indicated growing dissatisfaction with the Calles policies. Agrarian reformers were impatient: by the end of 1933 less than 18 million acres had been distributed, leaving some 300 million acres in private hands, four-fifths of it held in large haciendas. New labor leaders, notably Vicente Lombardo Toledano, had created unions whose pronouncements were Marxist in tone. New leaders of education, including the leftist Narciso Bassols, voiced impatience with the stumbling progress of the schools. To be sure, the official roster showed some 6,000 new rural schools founded since Calles had assumed office, and the national illiteracy had been reduced (according to overcheerful official reports) to 59 per cent. The new apostles of enlightenment indulged in a plethora of talk about "socialist education," a phrase whose meaning was unclear.

Meanwhile, humble teachers lived on wages of twelve to fifteen dollars a month, while politicians took their tithe from the meager allotments for schoolbooks and crayons.

The monolithic *Partido Nacional Revolucionario,* assembled in 1934 to name a candidate for the coming six-year term, faced popular demand for a more vigorous president. The older leaders bowed to the will of their younger colleagues and adopted a six-year plan (with a vague genuflection to Moscow) calling for diverse miracles in land distribution, labor reform, school building, and industrialization. They accepted Calles's choice for the presidency: Lázaro Cárdenas, who had a reputation for honest service in the army and in civil administration in his native state of Michoacán. In due course Cárdenas was elected.

LÁZARO CÁRDENAS, 1934–40

Lázaro Cárdenas, fourth to receive the accolade from Calles, was inaugurated in December, 1934, amidst the cheers of peasants, factory hands, and politicians. He was popularly regarded as a well-meaning man who would do as Calles bade him, a conclusion supported by the new president's pledge of "confidence and affection" to his master, and by his appointment of a cabinet dictated by the Supreme Chief. But Calles already had grounds for uneasiness. Cárdenas had conducted a five-month electoral campaign such as Mexico had never known, covering more than 16,000 miles by train, automobile, and horseback, appealing for votes in remote villages. This was an ordeal beyond the call of duty, for nomination by the PNR was tantamount to election. Cárdenas's ambition was novel: he proposed to be president of the *people* of Mexico.

The thirty-nine-year-old Cárdenas had served a tough apprenticeship since his birth in the village of Jiquilpan in western Michoacán; he had fought ably in the revolutionary armies of Carranza and Obregón, served honestly as governor of his state, and risen to cabinet rank under Calles. But unlike the elders of the Revolution, Cárdenas had never forgotten the village where he was born—its rutted roads, its adobe houses with thatched roofs and dirt floors, its lack of a school and of a physician. Cárdenas's father, unlike the 97.3 per cent who were landless under Díaz, had a tiny corn plot of his own—"a bunch of rocks," the son described it to the author—and one horse. His father died when Lázaro was twelve, leaving him as chief support of his mother and seven brothers and sisters. He remembered the weight of the water carried from the central plaza, the long hours his mother spent grinding the family's corn in the hollowed *metate,* and the meager furrow cut by the wooden plow in the exhausted soil. Out of such memories he constructed his informal theories on the duties of government.

The qualms of Calles over this quixotic villager-president were quickly justified. One of Cárdenas's first acts was to close the profitable casinos of the *callistas.* One of these, the Foreign Club in the capital, had

10,000 at its wheels and tables on a Saturday night—an ill-clad, under-fed, feverish crowd of petty officeholders and lower middle-class Mexicans, whose tiny earnings (clerical wages in government offices averaged about $25 a month) were raked in by the croupiers. This attack upon Calles and his friends was impudence enough, but worse followed as Cárdenas resumed distribution of land to the villages and encouraged labor unions to strike against the industrial concerns in which Calles and his partners held a substantial stake.

Cárdenas, to the general surprise, proved an adept politician. Mexican politics, we have noted, is the art of elimination; and Cárdenas was as adroit an "eliminator" as ever sat in the presidential chair—with the marked difference that his victims continued to eat and drink, and were assured the luxury of dying in their own beds from natural causes. Calles was first to go. By the spring of 1935 the cleavage between him and the President was complete, and political wise men were becoming either *cardenistas* or *callistas*. In June, when Calles received a congressional delegation in Cuernavaca, he warned them against troublemakers and reminded them of the summary fate administered to disobedient Ortiz Rubio in 1932. The puzzled lawmakers rushed back to Cárdenas, only to be told of the "perverse intentions" of certain "unfaithful revolutionaries." Every chief job-holder was under immediate compulsion to choose his side; telegraph messengers busily delivered assurances of loyalty to one or the other contestant, and the future was dark for any who chose unwisely.[7] The debate was soon over, with Cárdenas the winner. A presidential messenger informed Calles that he was leaving by plane for the United States; and the Supreme Chief did leave—with a copy of Hitler's *Mein Kampf* under his arm.[8] Cárdenas was now president in fact as well as in law.

Next to fall was Tomás Garrido Canabal, the Calles-imposed minister of agriculture. Garrido had long ruled his state of Tabasco in disdain of law. A violent anticlerical, he solved the Church question by closing all churches. An exuberant revolutionist in his own description, he protected his fellow *hacendados* and distributed no land. He boasted a private army of Red Shirts through which he imposed his will in Tabasco, and he took them with him to Mexico City when he was appointed to the cabinet in 1934; these ruffians were a nuisance in the capital, entertaining themselves on Sunday mornings with raids on religious shrines. When Cárdenas broke with Calles, Garrido retreated to Tabasco, continuing his sanguinary attacks upon critics. Cárdenas then blandly appointed him to head an agricultural mission to Puerto Rico; Garrido got as far as Guatemala, where a presidential order overtook him, calling off the mission and suggesting that he need not return.

The next political head to roll was that of ex-President Emilio Portes Gil, titular chief of the PNR and close friend of Calles, who was gently

[7] The author recalls one such official who wrote two telegrams, one pledging fealty to Calles, the other to Cárdenas, and then kept them side by side on his desk for two exhausting days. He finally guessed right, and rose steadily in official favor.

[8] Calles spent six years in Southern California and was then permitted to return to his Cuernavaca home, where he lived unmolested and died unmourned in 1945.

eased from his official post into the tranquillity of private law practice. Later, in 1938, Cárdenas reorganized the official party, by now purged of all *callistas,* introduced numerous labor and farmer delegates, and renamed it the PRM, *Partido de la Revolución Mexicana.* The new party, like its predecessor, permitted only slight debate at the polls.

The next victim was General Saturnino Cedillo, whom Cárdenas had named minister of agriculture after Garrido's departure. Long the governor of his state of San Luis Potosí, Cedillo now enjoyed the luxuries of a cabinet position, but did little to enforce Cárdenas's agrarian measures. The President prudently shifted a few generals and troops in Cedillo's state and then dismissed him. Cedillo did some blustering, then took to the mountain with his private army. There the old general was presently shot down by federal troops—a bit of rough justice not condoned by Cárdenas.

There was no question of Cárdenas's power after June, 1935. No president in Mexico's history, not even Díaz, had such complete mastery of the nation. He had won it by outplaying politicians and generals, by generous use of patronage, by balancing agrarians against labor leaders, and by making all officeholders answerable to him; but these familiar devices were buttressed by a popular support such as no president, not even Benito Juárez, had ever enjoyed. Cárdenas's rule could scarcely be called democratic; but by giving the masses an opportunity to voice their hopes it served as a training school for the democracy Cárdenas hoped for. Cárdenas was unspoiled by power. He lived simply in a modest house, and his office was as open to a serape-clad peon in *huaraches* as to an influential politician. His speech was lean, stripped of the overworked slogans which had fallen into disrepute. His example worked its leaven among the mass of officeholders: men worked harder, lessened their pillage of the treasury. It was still necessary to overlook the carelessness of powerful generals in their accounting of funds, and some of the President's relatives and intimates still laid away substantial savings for their old age; but the "conspicuous consumption" of other days had decreased. Numerous undersecretaries and bureau chiefs wisely sold their long sleek automobiles and now drove to work in rattling Fords.

Cárdenas, with tough realism, knew how meagerly the promises of the Revolution had been fulfilled, a conclusion confirmed by the 1930 census, the first to give authentic data on the nation's economy. Orators had promised better wages to peons in the fields, but by 1934 they were averaging about 10 cents a day (34 centavos)—their real wage was perhaps a fifth better than in 1891. In 1934 the average annual income of the individual farmer—whether working for wages or for himself—was about $42 (157 pesos). Industrial laborers had more pesos to spend, but few had more purchasing power than in 1910. The land program had lagged. By 1934 about 20 million acres had been distributed and about 20 per cent of the people lived in *ejido* villages; a full half of all Mexicans were still ill-paid workers on the lands of others, chiefly on the haciendas which had escaped partition. The program of education, despite progress under Obregón and Calles, and the creation of 12,000 new rural schools, still fell far short of caring for the children of Mexico.

Cárdenas, in zeal for reform, had a new approach: he thought in terms of the neglected village, not of the brightly lighted capital. The Mexico he knew and understood was the Mexico of his native Jiquilpan— the village Mexico where men neither read nor write; where the poor are usually hungry; where the sick have recourse only to the *curandero* whose castor oil and herbs and magic charms are all equally ineffective; where anywhere from one-eighth to one-third of all babies do not live to blow out even one candle on a birthday cake; where the only water supply is an uncertain and often contaminated trickle. From such villages—of which there are still thousands—Cárdenas ruled his nation. He spent little time in the capital city, for which he had slight respect, but kept almost constantly on the road, shifting his informal headquarters from village to village. On one day he would be in a shabby oil camp in the tropical Isthmus of Tehuan-tepec; a few days later, after hours on horseback, in a tiny village in the mountains of Oaxaca; a week later, in Guerrero. His energy exhausted his aides, who tried to smile while they kept up with his pace. Wherever Cárdenas was, there was the government of Mexico. Seated at his desk in a village plaza and flanked by secretaries, the President would receive delegations of farmers, miners, or factory workers. Through a long day and often far into the night he would listen to their petitions, then dictate orders to his ministers in the capital—orders for a teacher to be sent to one village, a doctor to another, an engineering crew to install a water system in still another; for a new leg for a crippled veteran, schooling at government expense for a needy orphan, or hospital care for an invalid; for the ejection of a tyrannical caudillo; and repeated orders for the restoration of hacienda lands to the villages.

The results of this paternal rule were spotty because of lack of public funds and the shortage of technicians willing to serve the isolated villages. Cárdenas, neither an able administrator nor a competent economist, made more promises than he could fulfill. Many men charged with execution of his plans were faithless or incompetent. But thousands of villagers had their first experience with a government that cared.

Cárdenas encouraged organized labor. Morones's CROM was by now in disrepute, but in 1936 the new CTM (*Confederación de Trabajadores Mexicanos*) emerged under the leadership of the more able Vicente Lombardo Toledano, with a program of industrial unionism patterned after the CIO (Congress of Industrial Organizations) of the United States. Lombardo leaned to the left, using phrases which sounded vaguely Russian although there were few orthodox Communists among his henchmen. Cárdenas used this new labor machine to encourage strikers and to improve wages for the 250,000 factory and mill workers, 90,000 miners, 17,000 petroleum workers, and 80,000 employees of railroads and other transports. But their gains were evanescent; the rise in commodity prices promptly canceled out their nominal gains.

The restitution of land to the villages was Cárdenas's chief enthusiasm. He personally supervised hundreds of transfers of land from hacienda to *ejido*. During his six years he gave the villages almost 45 million acres,[9] twice as much as had been transferred by 1934. When he left office, more than half of all Mexicans were members of *ejido* communities with lands of their own embracing almost half of the cropland of the nation. The dreams of Zapata had at last been given substance. But Cárdenas was not content, for more than 200 million acres remained in private hands, much of it in undivided haciendas, and about 35 per cent of all Mexicans still labored at meager wages on the lands of others. His bold agrarian program encountered inevitable obstacles; the economic pattern of a numerous and poor people could not be remade in a day. The peasants who had been given land were inexperienced and unskilled. Cárdenas's measures for furnishing governmental credit for buying machinery, seeds, and stock were neither adequate nor well administered; there was never money enough, and too many blunderers and grafters handled the funds. Cárdenas was charged, and with some justice, with having moved too far and too fast.

Cárdenas's economic innovations stirred fresh fears among foreign holders of mines, oil wells, lands, and factories. He warmly invited foreign investors to share Mexico's future, then dropped words that chilled them to the bone. When the owners of heavy industry in northern Monterrey deplored a Cárdenas-approved strike and cited their failure to earn dividends, Cárdenas said to them: "If employers weary of the social struggle, let them turn over their plants to the government or the workers. That would be patriotic." He launched repeated excursions into government or union ownership, including an ambitious sugar refinery in Morelos. In 1937 he expropriated the National Railways, sadly deteriorated during the revolutionary years; he consolidated their bonded indebtedness with the national debt, which was chronically in default, depriving American and other bondholders of any voice in management. But such diversions were overshadowed by his renewal of the old battle with the foreign-owned petroleum companies.

Cárdenas's clash with the oil companies, chiefly American and British, began in May, 1937, when the 17,000 oil operatives struck for higher wages, better living and working conditions, numerous social services including medical care, vacations with pay, and insurance against accident and death. In June the men returned to work on the promise that their demands would be submitted to an "economic investigation" by the Labor Board to determine whether they were just and whether the companies could afford to meet them—the procedure prescribed by law. The Board's report in August upheld the chief contentions of labor. It asserted that while *real* wages of American oil workers in the United States had increased 8.75 per cent since 1934, corresponding wages in Mexico had

9 About 7.2 million acres in 1935; 8.2 million in 1936; 12.5 million in 1937; 8 million in 1938; 4.3 million in 1939; 4.2 million in 1940.

decreased almost 23 per cent; that while oil operations in the United States yielded an average profit of but 1.44 per cent in 1935, those in Mexico returned 17.82 per cent. And the Board awarded the workers increases in wages and social services which it estimated would cost the companies 26.3 million pesos. The companies denounced the report as "clearly prejudiced and impassioned" and tried to refute the figures on wages and earnings. They said the award was designed to hand management over to the unions, argued that compliance would cost not 26.3 million but 41 million pesos, and offered to compromise with increases aggregating 21 million pesos.

It was an angry deadlock. The companies appealed to the Mexican Supreme Court and lost on every count. They then appealed over the head of the President and the courts in full-page advertisements in the Mexican press. The deadline for compliance, set for March, brought no easing of tension. Last-minute efforts at conciliation proved futile, and on March 18, 1938, Cárdenas decreed the expropriation of the properties of the seventeen companies. (The British owned roughly 60 per cent of the total and the Americans, about 40 per cent.) The next day the foreign operators were dispossessed from plants and offices, and the Mexican government was in the oil business.

The legal arguments were unclear. Mexico relied on the historic claim of the nation to ownership of all subsoil wealth, based upon the tenets of Spanish law stated by Charles III in 1783: "The Mines are the property of My Royal Crown . . . [including] all bitumens and juices of the earth," a principle written into the Constitution of 1917. Mexico cited her constitutional obligation to subordinate private rights to public usefulness and to administer natural resources for the welfare of the people. The oil companies countered by declaring the appeal to Spanish law a subterfuge, suggesting that the code of 1917 was an afterthought, and pointing out that neither the Constitution of 1824 nor that of 1857 had mentioned sovereignty over the subsoil. They cited Obregón's promises of 1923 against retroactive measures and the Supreme Court's decision of 1927 which declared such retroactive application unconstitutional. The oil companies took their complaints to the American State Department and to the British Foreign Office, while Cárdenas laid his case before the Mexican people, who were jubilant over their defeat of "foreign imperial powers."

But the niceties of law were less important for an understanding of the imbroglio than were certain imponderables. The resistance of the oil companies was quite understandable in the light of their sorry experiences with venal labor leaders (whose American kin in the building trades of New York, Chicago, and San Francisco had proved no less corrupt) and their well-justified lack of faith in the Mexican courts. Their actions during the emergency said in effect: "We will buy our way out as we have always done." But when they tried, they discovered that Cárdenas was not for sale. On the Mexican side, there were other imponderables. The petroleum industry in Mexico (as in the United States) had, since its beginnings in 1900, been a rough and tumble, often lawless enterprise. Especially during the first years, many deeds and leases had been acquired by trickery or murder. Laborers in the oil fields were conscripted by Díaz's *rurales* and treated as slaves, with little protection from the police. Mexicans remembered these wrongs and sought to redress them. Cárdenas himself had memories of a certain General Manuel Peláez who, after breaking with Carranza, used his troops in 1917–19 to terrorize the oil workers in Veracruz, accepting generous pay from foreign oil operators, while Cárdenas commanded the federal troops against him. Such memories did not soften the heart of Lázaro Cárdenas toward foreign oil operators who appealed for relief in 1938. In his view, the oil reserves were an irreplaceable resource of the nation and had to be conserved; the oil operators had been lawbreakers in a land not their own, had shown contempt for the president, the law, and the courts of a nation whose favors they courted, and had defiantly appealed to their own governments. Such convictions prompted Cárdenas's final decision, made in the face of earnest argument from several of his ablest advisers who thought that nationalization would be economic suicide.

The effects were disastrous. Petroleum production plummeted. Foreign oil companies boycotted sales of Mexican oil in the world market, blocked the purchase of oil machinery, and for a time scared off tourist traffic. But so far as the United States was concerned Cárdenas had two advantages: first, Franklin D. Roosevelt's Good Neighbor Policy was in full swing, and his Latin American decisions were made largely by Under Secretary Sumner Welles who was a convinced noninterventionist; second, the ambassador in Mexico was the much-loved Josephus Daniels who was sympathetic to Cárdenas's program—"too sympathetic," according to some Americans. (Daniels, who as secretary of the navy had been officially responsible for the occupation of Veracruz in 1913, was received with hostility when appointed ambassador in 1934, but his kindliness finally disarmed his critics.) Furthermore, the timing of Cárdenas's edict was lucky. War loomed, and Washington was determined to have good relations with potential allies. President Cárdenas announced that Mexico would pay all just claims, and the crisis passed.[1] Mexicans celebrate March 18 as the anniversary of their "Declaration of Economic Independence."

Cárdenas, closing his six-year term in 1940, had written one of Mexico's more enlivening chapters. His detractors were numerous and vocal, charging him with sentimentalism and loosely contrived panaceas. His admirers regarded him affectionately as one of the country's greatest presidents. He had bearded the petroleum colossus—and had got away with it. He had eased the friction with the Church. He had distributed immense amounts of land—although careful observers were not convinced of the efficiency and honesty of the governmental agencies which distributed the land and provided credit, seeds, fertilizer, and guidance to the

[1] Final settlement was reached early in 1942. Mexico agreed to pay $23,995,991 to cover "actual sums invested, less depreciation incident to their various operations." This did not satisfy the companies, which claimed about $450,000,000, but the exigencies of war made acceptance wise. Later settlements with the Sinclair interests and with the British companies put an end to the controversy.

newly emancipated farmers. But Cárdenas was credited with considerable personal integrity, though some carping critics continued to ask why Mexican presidents—including Cárdenas—accumulated so many fertile acres in their own names (not to mention the names of brothers and other kin).

 [*Chapter 24*]

MEXICO TURNS TO THE RIGHT,
1940–

      The retirement of Cárdenas brought relief to those who were weary of crusades and crusaders. After 1940, Mexico settled down to a course of political stability carefully policed by the all-powerful official party, and marked by some competent and often brilliant excursions into industrialization. All that was said and done was still blessed—as in 1920 —by the invocation of the Revolution. But the new "revolutionists" were busy with their money-making: generals and politicos took no time out to disturb the peace—at least for the quarter of a century up to 1967. Mexico in 1967 appeared the most stable and prosperous—at least in the upper echelons of its population—of all the twenty nations of Latin America.

ÁVILA CAMACHO AND WORLD WAR II, 1940–46

There was slight popular enthusiasm for Manuel Ávila Camacho, elected in 1940. Undistinguished, heavy in person and speech, and a political unknown, the new president was "as interesting as a ham sandwich," according to the ubiquitous journalist John Gunther. His first words and acts after taking office were reassuring to cautious citizens. When questioned on the delicate Church issue, he replied: *"Soy creyente"* (I am a believer). When asked his opinions on land reform, he expressed doubts as to the future of the communal *ejidos* and preference for individual landholdings. When pressed for pledges by labor leaders, he said that he would rule for all the people of Mexico, and not for any special class. In choosing cabinet members, he picked several men of marked ability, including some who were honest. His most serious blunder was appointment of his unsavory brother Maximino as minister of communications, an office whose incumbent could make millions from highway contracts.

      Foreign affairs, rather more than internal debates, dictated the course of Mexico during the presidency of Ávila Camacho. World War II had been on for a year when he took office, Germany was winning on land

and sea, and die-hard nationalists, admirers of Hitler and Mussolini and Franco, were outspoken in condemning any cooperation with the Allies and the United States. The few but noisy Communists took the same stand until the Berlin-Moscow pact was ended by German invasion of Russia in June, 1941. Nevertheless, in the face of much opposition, Ávila Camacho from the first days of his administration denounced fascism, expressed sympathy for the Allies, and friendship for the United States. As Washington took steps to aid the Allies, especially by the extension of Lend-Lease to Britain in March, 1941, he made it clear that Mexico would stand with the United States.

The decision to cooperate with the United States marked radical departure from Mexico's historic course. Memories of old grievances, real and fancied, still rankled. But the Mexican President braved the general anti-United States sentiment in openly aligning his nation with the northern power. He had some popular support from sectors where fascism was disliked, and this was augmented by the Communists when Hitler's troops marched into Russia. There were practical reasons for partnership with the United States; that rich neighbor had money to lend and give away, guns and planes and powder to share, machinery and parts useful to keep the wheels of factories and mills turning. When Japan struck at Pearl Harbor in December, 1941, Mexico was one of the first to pledge help to the United States. A month later, at the Rio de Janeiro conference of the foreign ministers of all the American republics, the eloquence of Mexican Foreign Minister Ezequiel Padilla helped to win support for the recommendation that all the republics sever diplomatic relations with the Axis.

Mexican support of the Allied cause was constant and substantial. In May, 1942, the nation declared war on the Axis powers. Meanwhile, her navy had been sinking some German vessels, and her police had been tracking down spies and helping to enforce the American "black list" against traders with the enemy. The United States reciprocated by making loans to buttress Mexican economy against the shocks of war; by extending more loans to modernize the railways and sending technicians to assist in the task; and by giving Lend-Lease aid to strengthen the Mexican army, navy, and air force, and a generous allotment of scarce machinery for Mexican industry. In return Mexico speeded up production of vital materials: mercury, zinc, copper, graphite, antimony, arsenic, steel, cadmium, and henequen. Mexico also furnished man power to United States farmers; under careful agreements, Mexico undertook to furnish migrant labor for the cotton, vegetable, and sugar fields of Texas and the American southwest. The plan was generally well handled; Mexican agents picked men for the task, and American officials usually saw to it that they were decently housed and paid the prevailing wage. The agreement called for 200,000 *braceros* (literally, "arms"), but there were seldom more than 75,000 at any one time. Finally, Mexico was the one Latin American nation, aside from Brazil, to take an active part in the fighting. Mexico furnished an expeditionary air force, and 300 of her fliers served first in the Philippines and then in Formosa. And some 250,000 Mexicans living in the United States enlisted in the American services.

Mexico's participation in the war had a profound influence upon the nation. Psychologically, it helped dispel the traditional isolationism of the people. Economically, it brought an influx of much money; this influx, in turn, provoked inflation, and by 1946 the index of the cost of living stood at 440 (as compared with 100 in 1929). The major profits went to a few thousand speculators, promoters of new businesses, and black market operators. The easy money incited a speculative boom: city real estate sold at fantastic figures and expensive houses multiplied. Official corruption became flagrant: lesser employees, their poor pay even more inadequate under inflation, turned to the *mordida* (literally, "the bite") to supplement their income; top officials, taking toll on the contracts which passed over their desks, built fine houses on Chapultepec Heights. Nevertheless, the war served Mexican economy. Subventions from Washington modernized and enlarged her industrial plant.

Cut off from adequate supplies of goods hitherto imported, Mexico produced more textiles, steel products, cement, processed foods, and many other items. The war also gave incentive to expanding production of foodstuffs—neglected coastal lands were put into use, fertilizers and machinery increased, and irrigation extended. Impatience with the *ejidos,* whose 2 million participants held about half of the cropland of the nation, increased as they proved laggard in feeding the country.

The war sharpened the clash of ideas. From the reactionary right emerged the movement called *sinarquismo,* which appealed for the restoration of Mexico "to its traditional patterns—the Catholic faith; Spanish tradition, home and village; and a Christian social order." Under the banner of "order," a million villagers (more or less) denounced the "godless" Revolution. Although the Church disavowed the movement, the *sinarquistas* were as fanatically religious as the *cristeros* of Calles's day. Some *sinarquistas* were able and devoted, and the charges they leveled against the government were often well founded—especially those involving the shameless misrule of the little municipalities by the petty tyrants appointed by party chieftains. The *sinarquistas,* hating the Mexican government and its allies, became ready tools of Axis agents, and their control remained a major problem for Ávila Camacho and his successors.

Social gains under Ávila Camacho were substantial. The school system continued to expand, slowly but with moderate efficiency. An elaborate Social Security Institute was devised, assuring benefits for the aged, the sick, and the unemployed. By 1948 the Institute boasted eleven clinics, three sanitariums, sixty-four medical posts, eleven laboratories, and eleven maternity centers.

MIGUEL ALEMÁN, 1946–52

The year 1946 brought another rebaptism of the official party, which was the true master of the nation. Under Calles it had been the PNR, *Partido Nacional Revolucionario*; in 1938 it was renamed the PRM, *Partido de la Revolución Mexicana*; now in 1946, it became the PRI, *Partido Revolu-*

cionario Institucional—the party of revolutionary institutions. This juggling of words was designed to prove that the Revolution was won, and that now Mexico would enjoy the gains so bravely fought for.

The winner of the 1946 election was Miguel Alemán. Not only was it inevitable that the party's candidate should be victorious, but it was also clear that his chief rival never had a chance: the former foreign minister Ezequiel Padilla was too ardent a partisan of the United States to suit the tastes of Mexicans; and his fervid orations on the solidarity of the Americas, so pleasing to Washington, now evoked ribald laughter from his countrymen.

Miguel Alemán seemed an admirable choice: he was young (only forty-four) and energetic; he was handsome and *muy macho,* "very much a male," as Mexicans like their heroes to be; he was a civilian, the second to serve as president since Madero; and he had had an excellent record as an administrator, first as governor of Veracruz, and then as minister of the interior under Ávila Camacho. His first steps were encouraging: he demanded honesty and efficiency in government, the reform of the judiciary, and the modernization of state government. He proved to be as good a friend of the United States as either his predecessor or his defeated rival, Padilla, had been. President Truman flew to Mexico, was elaborately fêted, and laid a wreath on the monument to the cadets who fell while defending Chapultepec against United States troops in 1847. When President Alemán returned the visit, he was given full honors in Washington and granted a doctorate by Columbia University. In the aura of such pleasantness there could be no strain between the two nations. When the outbreak of hoof-and-mouth disease obliged the United States to close the border to Mexican cattle in 1946, the two nations cooperated in rooting out the disease at a cost of about $125 million: 680,000 head of cattle, sheep, goats, and pigs were slaughtered and the border was again opened in 1952—although another outbreak of the disease brought a brief reimposition of the quarantine.

The friendly alliance between Mexico and the United States made possible prosecution of public works projects. During the 1940's, loans of almost $400 million, chiefly from the Export-Import Bank of Washington, financed many measures for the improvement of agriculture and the extension of industry. Hydroelectric projects, including reclamation of large areas by irrigation, were avidly promoted. In addition to small projects for harnessing streams, two enterprises similar to the TVA (Tennessee Valley Authority) were given priority: one in the Tepalcatepec basin in western Mexico, and the other in the Papaloapan basin on the Gulf side—each with provision for great dams, development of power, irrigation, and opening of lands to farmers. Another major task, also financed by American loans, was the rehabilitation of the railroad system, which had so deteriorated that it could meet no more than half the need for freight transportation. Work begun during the war was pushed with vigor, heavier rails were laid over many lines, and modern equipment was ordered. In 1951 the government bought the bankrupt west coast subsidiary of the Southern Pacific Railroad.

The national petroleum monopoly, PEMEX (*Petroleos Mexicanos*), responded to Alemán's vigorous treatment. Antonio Bermúdez, an energetic and capable industrialist who was named director general of that ailing industry, made valiant attempts to discipline venal labor leaders and to eliminate unneeded workers from the payroll; but the powerful unions largely blocked these reforms. However, when Bermúdez made it clear that he would welcome the cooperation of United States interests, some California operators agreed to drill under terms which promised to profit them as well as Mexico. Production of petroleum steadily increased: the total output in 1952 was almost double the figure for 1940.[1] By the end of 1951 there were some 1,200 miles of pipelines, a modern lubricant plant, many new wells, and a shipyard at Veracruz for oil tankers which would carry Mexican oil to foreign markets.

The injection of life into Mexico's laggard farming was a major theme in Alemán's program. Various presidents, notably Cárdenas, had taken land from the large holders and distributed it among the people—but the land, no matter who owned it, was still failing to produce the food needed by the people. In 1948 a leading Mexican agriculturist said that there were "sixteen million hungry Mexicans"—and this was probably not an overstatement. Though corn was the mainstay of the Mexican larder, a comparison of Mexican corn production with that of other countries was sobering: in 1940 the average yield per acre of corn in Mexico was less than one-third that in the United States. The showing on wheat was a little better: the yield per acre in Mexico was about three-fourths of the figure for the United States.

Alemán's government pressed various remedies. Irrigation was needed, and the numerous hydroelectric and irrigation projects were a partial answer. Deeper plowing was essential, and called for education of the farmers. Fertilization was important, for most of the cropland was depleted. By a combination of private and public financing, three plants for the manufacture of fertilizer were opened, and in 1952 the total output was 93,000 metric tons, twice that of the year before. The improvement of the seed supply was all important, for seed corn had long been degenerating. In 1944, at the suggestion of Henry Wallace, Ávila Camacho had accepted the technical aid of the Rockefeller Foundation in the development of hybrid corn. In 1946 Alemán created the Mexican Corn Commission to further development of the hybrids suitable for various regions. The progress of the program was rapid: the seed was developed in laboratories; the corn was distributed to reliable farmers under contracts which required them to sell back to the Commission half of the corn produced; this seed was then distributed to other farmers on similar terms. The increasing use of hybrid seed brought substantial improvement in yield per acre.[2] The methods which h'd proved their use with corn were now applied to such other staples as cotton, wheat, beans, and rice.

But industry was the magic word for Alemán and his friends. Continuing the work of Ávila Camacho, the promotion of new mills and fac-

[1] See p. 379 for figures on oil production, 1921–64.
[2] See p. 380 for figures on corn production.

tories became a major concern. *Nacional Financiera,* a government agency roughly comparable to the Reconstruction Finance Corporation of Herbert Hoover, used national and foreign funds (chiefly from the Export-Import Bank) to shore up existing enterprises such as the National Railways, and encouraged new ones by extending credit to them or buying their bonds. By 1950 there were an estimated 53,000 industrial concerns, as compared with 6,916 in 1935; these included steel works, sugar refineries, paper factories, fertilizer plants, electrical equipment plants, cotton mills, cement works, and scores of other types of establishments. Meanwhile, vigorous attention was given to the ailing mineral industry: concentration plants were built near the mines, machinery was modernized, and freight service was somewhat improved.

Miguel Alemán will also be long remembered for the impressive University City built on the edge of the capital, its campus of three square miles boasting some of the most exciting buildings in the Western Hemisphere. The building of a graceful stadium, with seats for more than 100,000 spectators, suggests that Alemán had learned from certain American universities the importance of the football team. Costing more than $25 million and designed to accommodate 25,000 students, the new university has a spectacular plant, a slowly growing library, a few full-time professors, and many part-time teachers drawn from professional groups in Mexico. The brave and pleasant façade which the University turns upon the world is impressive, and there has been steady strengthening of the work done within its classrooms and laboratories.

As the people prepared to vote for a new president in 1952, there were disquieting rumors that the government's treasury was overextended, that industrial enterprise and public works had been bought at the cost of an inflation which made the poor poorer. There was also restlessness over the conspicuous wealth of the Alemán coterie, and it was hinted that certain members of that inner circle owned more than their share of the fine enterprises that now abounded. Despite these gloomy thoughts, there was no question but that Alemán could pick his successor—for that is one of the ground rules by which the game of Mexican politics is played. But rumors spread that certain strong men in the PRI, including Cárdenas, were insisting that Alemán pick an honest man.

ADOLFO RUIZ CORTINES, 1952–58

The austere and soft-spoken Adolfo Ruiz Cortines, named to the presidency in 1952 at the age of sixty-one, was pallid compared with his predecessor. His career had been prosaic. Son of a customs official in Veracruz, he had quit school at sixteen and taken a job as a bookkeeper's assistant. For years he continued as a checker of figures, first as a paymaster in Carranza's army, then as a clerk in government offices, and finally as chief of the government's statistical bureau. After 1936 he served as an aide to Alemán, who in 1943 had him elected as governor of the state of Veracruz. When he entered Alemán's cabinet in 1948 as minister of the interior, Ruiz Cortines continued as poor as ever, driving his own car, and living in a modest house.

Elected by the customary majority of votes, despite the popularity of his principal opponent General Henríquez Guzmán, the new president took the oath of office in December, 1952. Flanked by Alemán's men, Ruiz Cortines gave his inaugural address: "Government monopolies must end," he said. "I shall demand strict honesty from all." One of his first official announcements required federal employees to submit detailed statements of their assets, with another accounting to be made when they retired. The President was the first to comply with his own order, as he reported his house, car, and furniture worth about $30,000. Then came a vigorous reshuffling of the generals, many of whom had been shameless in misappropriating funds; twenty-nine were dismissed or transferred. In choosing his cabinet, Ruiz Cortines included none of Alemán's men. Meanwhile, charges were aired in the press, alleging that Alemán and his friends had collected millions for themselves. Mexicans generally decided that their new president, if not interesting, was at least honest.

The Ruiz Cortines administration faced serious handicaps. Government funds had been overpledged for public works, and the treasury surplus claimed by Alemán turned out to be a deficit. There were further calamities: the end of fighting in Korea decreased the demand for raw materials and prices dropped; a drought in 1953 reduced agricultural output; and the tourist business, which had yielded as much as $400 million a year, was cut in half. By early 1954 the speculative boom seemed over. The plight of the treasury forced the devaluation of the currency from 8.60 pesos to the dollar to 12.49—a measure designed to relieve some of the pressure from the overcommitments inherited from Alemán, and to improve Mexico's trading position in foreign markets. Ruiz Cortines's thrifty and honest handling of the Mexican economy had won for him, by the time he retired in 1958, warm respect at home and abroad.

ADOLFO LÓPEZ MATEOS, 1958–64

The election of 1958 was dominated, as always, by the official party (PRI); its slate won a full 80 per cent of all votes. An element in this election was that, for the first time, women enjoyed full suffrage: some prophesied that the women's vote would give the advantage to the candidate of the clerical party (PAN—*Partido Acción Nacional*). That it did not do so may be explained by the Mexican woman's tendency to follow her husband's example, or by the obvious fact that votes are not yet counted with the precision which prevails in Montclair, New Jersey, and Beverly Hills, California. The PRI's successful candidate for the presidency, Adolfo López Mateos, was the choice of Lázaro Cárdenas and Ruiz Cortines; he was picked for his record of competent government service, his reputation for honesty, and his ideological position somewhat to the left. A handsome and compact man of forty-seven, the son of a village dentist, he had worked his way through the University by teaching and had been minister of labor under Ruiz Cortines. In the latter post, he showed dexterity in handling labor disputes; although he was feared by many employers as being too pro-labor, he was credited with fairness by most parties to the disputes.

On entering the presidency, López Mateos was confronted by a prickly strike of railroad workers which tied up the nation's communications in April, 1959. The President, despite his sympathy with the railroad employees whose wages had not kept pace with the spiraling cost of living, decided that this particular strike was engineered by Communist elements, and used the army to end it. Obdurate leftists did not applaud such rough handling of the striking railroadmen. Nor were they pleased when López Mateos—with the help of the always obedient courts—consigned many strikers to jail, to be held for months without bail and without trial. This the President did under the "social dissolution" law which provided heavy fines for those charged with "agitation." (Another victim of this law was Mexico's widely acclaimed muralist and ardent Communist, David Alfaro Siqueiros, who noisily belabored López Mateos and was jailed in August, 1960. The ebullient painter, cut off from the opportunity to agitate, proceeded to paint some excellent canvasses, which fetched fine prices, before he was released in 1964.[3]) The highhanded tactics of López Mateos in disciplining his critics—while stoutly insisting that he stood on "the extreme left within the Constitution"—served to point up the fact that the distinction between left and right in Mexico is often fictional.

López Mateos completed the nationalization of the electric power industry, about 70 per cent of which still remained in private hands when he assumed office. There had been continuing friction as consumers demanded lower rates and producers sought to protect their profits. In 1960, Mexico bought control of the properties of American and Foreign Power (a subsidiary of Electric Bond and Share): the company named its price, and got it. Then followed purchase of the Mexican Light and Power Company (Belgian, Canadian, and American capital). By the end of 1961 the electric power industry was completely Mexican, and almost everyone was happier.

On the land problem, López Mateos outdid all of his predecessors—except Cárdenas—by distributing some 25 million acres. But the pattern of land allotment was changing. Many of the well-advertised *ejidos* were in trouble: due to bad management and the lack of adequate technical and financial backing by the government, they were less productive than private farms. The new trend was toward the allotment of land to individuals. López Mateos won deserved credit for carrying through token movements of citizens from the central plateau and from ineffective *ejidos* to largely untenanted lands in Quintana Roo, Tabasco, Baja California, and the Isthmus of Tehuantepec.

[3] Americans do well to recall the Sedition Act of 1798, under which ten critics of President John Adams were jailed and fined for saying milder things about the American President than Siqueiros said about López Mateos.

Mexican relations with the United States improved under López Mateos, in spite of the persistent bad feeling between the two countries on the Cuban question (López Mateos continued the long-time Mexican policy of nonintervention in the affairs of other states, refusing to go along with the United States in boycotting Cuba in the OAS). A visit to the Mexican capital by President and Mrs. Kennedy in June, 1962, helped to quiet the clamor—very full-throated at that time—against the "colossus" of the North. The American President announced a $20 million loan to Mexico (part of the Alliance for Progress program), which, in Kennedy's words, was "to help the small farmer buy equipment, improve irrigation, increase storage, and gain access to those resources he so desperately needs to improve his income and raise the production of the land."

GUSTAVO DÍAZ ORDAZ, 1964–

In 1964, the presidential office went to Gustavo Díaz Ordaz, a fifty-three-year-old lawyer whose entire career had been spent in government jobs. Named by López Mateos, with the consent of all six living ex-presidents, Díaz Ordaz was duly elected by more than 89 per cent of all votes cast. Remembered chiefly for his role in crushing the railroad strike of 1959, when he was López Mateos's minister of the interior, the new President excited little enthusiasm among workers in factories and on farms. It is significant that Díaz Ordaz did not find it politically wise to label himself a "leftist," as had his predecessors, but rather described himself as a "conservative." No matter how meaningless the terms might be, this decision marked recognition of the obvious fact that the ruling group in Mexico was now made up of the entrepreneurs, the bankers, the industrialists, the large-scale farmers, and their economic kin. Orators still invoked the spirit of the Revolution when it served their purpose—but Mexico had turned to the right, as it had been doing, with various pullings and haulings, since 1940.

APPRAISAL: 1967

To the vast surprise of those who have watched Mexico from the days of commotion after 1910, the republic stood, in 1967, as the most stable, politically and economically, of all the Latin American republics.

Politically, there was *almost* complete serenity. Since 1934 there had been an orderly procession of duly elected presidents, each man serving out his full term; and since 1946, only civilians had sat in the presidential chair. This record, when compared with the convulsions in almost every other spot in Latin America, is commendable. Furthermore, the integrity and ability of the national government had shown some improvement: presidents and cabinets had become more responsible and more honest —this had begun under Cárdenas, continued under Ávila Camacho, suffered a set-back under Alemán, and definitely improved under Ruiz Cortines, López Mateos, and Díaz Ordaz. To be sure, the price paid for such political stability was high: although Mexican orators never ceased to proclaim Mexico a democracy, most of the articulate segments of the population, by tacit consent, agreed to postpone true democracy to a more convenient season. Elections continued to be meaningless, with the official party, the PRI, picking office holders and making all decisions. The genius of the party (which is neither "revolutionary" nor a "party," but a formula that works for the moment) is its ability to shelter within its ranks the most diverse elements: men of the left like Lázaro Cárdenas and men of the right like Miguel Alemán; tycoons of business and labor leaders; the armed forces and the churchmen. There is even a place for political opposition: the PRI sees to it that the PAN, the wan upholder of traditional conservatism, as well as various little splinter groups, shout lustily—and unsuccessfully—for their several candidates; the PRI also welcomes a show-case minority in the Chamber of Deputies, graciously allotting 11 per cent of the seats to the second party in the national elections.

The PRI, through its ruling hierarchy, is a stern and persuasive disciplinarian; the factions which wrought disaster in most of Mexico's history from the 1820's to 1910, and which have plagued most of the other Latin American republics, have been reduced to meek compliance. The generals, long the chief trouble-makers, have been tamed. Not since Cárdenas brought Garrido Canabal of Tabasco and Saturnino Cedillo of San Luis Potosí to their knees has any general been permitted his private army. Today's generals in Mexico are as quiet and ingratiating as Siamese kittens—the explanation is simple: they are well fed. By common consent, generals are permitted to pad their regimental payrolls and to collect pleasant profit. It is a rare general who does not have a fine home or two, expensive automobiles, a private airplane, and money for a trip to the Riviera. Nor does trouble come from organized labor; the unions are fitted carefully into the power structure of the PRI: they are properly subsidized and rigidly controlled. Labor has its constitutional right to organize and to bargain collectively, but the prudent labor leader knows in his bones exactly how far he can go. The president, spokesman for the party, decides what is best for the worker, and the worker bows his head. Nor does the economic elite cause any disquiet: ever since Cárdenas, these owners of profitable factories, businesses, and industrialized farms have been closely leagued with those who exercise political power (in fact, business and political leaders are often identical), and almost all roads have been clear for them. Occasionally, there have been alarms about excessive government control of business enterprises, and clashes between bureaucrats and private corporations. As for the Church, target of abuse since the days of Juárez and center of commotion during the years after 1910, it is no longer an element of dissension: the well-fed "revolutionaries" of today have outgrown the noisy anticlericalism of earlier leaders. Or consider the role of the press which, when able and fearless, can compel attention and quicken the democratic process (as, for example, in New York, Washington, London, Buenos Aires, Santiago, and Bogotá): the Mexican press is at worst venal, at best timid, and, in the words of Cosío Villegas, has "denied to the people of Mexico . . . all guidance and all light." Subsidies for newspapers are common, and in some cases the PRI has been suspected, on rather solid grounds, of financing opposition journals, thereby cutting the edge of their criticism.

Thus it is that the PRI has worked out a pleasant consensus in which almost everyone is content—almost everyone, that is, except perhaps the 60 per cent or more of Mexicans who have gained little from the new affluence. For the most part these bitterly poor people are weak, unorganized, ineffective, and easily cajoled by circuses and parades and fine orations about the glorious triumphs of the Revolution. The most articulate among this 60 per cent probably live in the villages, and it is perhaps here that one should look for signs of effective protest, as a new and more literate generation raises its voice against the stranglehold of the ruling clique around the national palace in Mexico City. Sporadic demonstrations have broken out in scattered villages since the 1950's, with demands for an end to the PRI's power to name, without debate, not only presidents and members of the national Congress, but also governors of states and mayors of even the smallest municipalities. But dissidents are held in line by the military and the police, who are fiercely loyal to the PRI. While there has been increased integrity and ability in the national government, state governors are still subject to the spoils system, and most of the states suffer from incompetence and graft. Weakest of all, however, is municipal government: the office of *alcalde* (mayor) is merely a reward for political service; the traditional *cacique* pattern is perpetuated for the sake of the control of the reigning party; taxes are assessed and collected with flagrant dishonesty; public improvements are neglected; and the villagers have slight check upon their local rulers. Although it was clear to all observers in 1967 that the PRI still exercised the whip hand over all of Mexico, there were fitful evidences that the depressed 60 per cent of Mexicans—perhaps led by the villagers, whose grievances are more immediate and more personal—would not long remain acquiescent. There was hope that, although Mexico was not to be reckoned a working democracy in 1967, she might soon be on her way.

Economic enterprise flourishes in a climate of political calm, and Mexico boasts a stable and growing economy, which puts her at the head of the list of Latin American nations. The Mexican money market is free, with foreign capital moving in peacefully and taking home its profits without artificial hindrance. Mexico's monetary unit, the peso, has remained stable (at 12.49 to the dollar) since 1954; and this strong currency position is buttressed by "liquid" reserves—gold, foreign exchange, and IMF (International Monetary Fund) commitments—which at the end of 1966 stood at $557 million, over seven times the figure for 1948. The cost of living rose only a modest 23 per cent between 1958 and 1966—in pleasant contrast to exhibits offered by Brazil (2,900 per cent), Uruguay (1,130 per cent), Argentina (920 per cent), and Chile (532 per cent), during the same period. Production was keeping ahead of population, the annual per capita growth rate reaching 2.6 per cent for the years 1960–65, topping the goal of 2.5 per cent set by the Alliance for Progress. The per capita annual income of Mexicans had increased from about $54 in 1929 to some $413 in 1965—a figure, however, which must be assessed with diffidence: by the mid-1960's there were a few thousand families whose revenue from business enterprise, large-scale agriculture, and industry enabled them to build fine homes in Mexico City and elsewhere; while at the other extreme were the ill-paid workers on the farms. The prosperity which made so brave an exhibit in the capital city had no more than trickled down to the men who toil in the sun.

Industry has been the pet enthusiasm of all presidents since Cárdenas. The government has kept a watchful and paternal eye on all basic industry, channeling development funds through the *Nacional Financiera,* intervening from time to time to assume management or even ownership of some companies. Although much industry is still in *private* hands (notably the cement industry), there has been a move toward the "Mexicanization" of industry which started in 1944 when President Ávila Camacho announced the official goal of 51 per cent ownership by Mexican nationals in all companies. The steady progress toward this end has been made possible by the phenomenal generation of investment capital: by 1965 about 85 per cent of such capital was produced within the country—an achievement unique in Latin America. One fine psychological effect of this "Mexicanization" of industry has been to lessen the threat of expropriation. Figures for industrial production show an over-all increase of 61 per cent from 1958 to 1964: manufacturing was up about 64 per cent, petroleum production 44 per cent, mining 23 per cent.

Mexico takes special pride in her steel industry, which began in 1903 in the Fundadora mill in Monterrey, today the second largest plant in the country, the top place going to the state-owned Altos Hornos de México, which began production in 1944. Although Mexico is still far from self-sufficient in steel, production in 1960 was over ten times that of 1940. The automobile industry, one of the fastest growing in the country, produced more than 90,000 units in 1965, and optimists expected the yearly figure shortly to exceed 100,000. Also important, many manufacturers of automobiles reached the goal of 60 per cent domestic content required by the government.

The cement industry, which is still almost entirely in private hands, is of increasing importance in the Mexican economy, production in 1963 amounting to more than four times that in 1948. Also important was the continued expansion of chemical and petrochemical plants. Mexico's 400-year-old textile industry—begun when the Spaniards built a cotton mill in Puebla in 1535—has been undergoing large-scale modernization, especially since the early 1950's. The manufacture of a large number of consumer items—refrigerators, washing machines, stoves, electrical appliances, garden tools, etc.—was given impetus by Sears, Roebuck & Co., which started operations in Mexico in 1947. By 1966 Mexican factories were supplying about 98 per cent of the merchandise sold in Sears' stores in Mexico.

The petroleum industry, which has been operated as a national monopoly since the expropriation of foreign properties in 1938, had made uneven but steady progress by 1967. The national monopoly company, PEMEX, created by Cárdenas in 1938, languished for some years under poor management. From 1938 to 1940 its success was blocked by the boycotts of American and British companies which had lost their properties. Powerful labor unions demanded and won excessive pay increases, and insisted upon loading the company down with superfluous workers (featherbedding); and pressure from the public kept prices for domestic sales at an unprofitably low level. Antonio Bermúdez, director of PEMEX from 1946 to 1958, improved its administration: labor unions were forced to be more realistic about wages and the wasteful duplication of jobs; the artificially low prices for gasoline and petroleum products were increased; contracts were made with foreign companies to drill new wells and explore for new fields. Pascal Gutiérrez Roldán, director of PEMEX since 1958, has continued these policies. To be sure, there is no promise of return to the large production of earlier years: Mexican wells had reached a peak in 1921 when 194.8 million barrels were pumped—about one-fourth of world production. But there had been marked improvement: from some 44 million barrels in 1940, production had increased to 72 million barrels in 1950, and 116 million in 1964.

Mining, in colonial days the chief economic boon of Mexico, has steadily fallen behind. In 1960, only 1.2 per cent of the workers were in mining (and this includes those engaged in petroleum production). The silver and gold mines, which yielded solid profit down through the nineteenth century, were inundated and neglected during the revolutionary tumult after 1910. The mines have been rehabilitated in recent years, and today Mexico is the world's largest producer of silver, but gold output has decreased. In the period 1948–62, copper production was slightly down in volume; lead held its own, zinc production was up about 40 per cent; the output of manganese, coal, and petroleum almost doubled; and, most important for the thriving steel industry, the production of iron increased fourfold. Meanwhile foreign capital has shied off from substantial commitments to Mexican mining, especially since 1961, when the mining law was amended to require 51 per cent Mexican ownership of all mining enterprises—in line with Ávila Camacho's 1944 decree. Mining is at best highly speculative, and foreign money has shown little eagerness to participate on that basis. In 1967 hopes were entertained that the Díaz Ordaz regime might ease that law.

Vitality has been injected into Mexican industry—as well as agriculture—by the bold and, on the whole, farsighted developments akin to the Tennessee Valley Authority in the United States. Streams have been dammed, opening up lands for irrigation and providing increases in hydroelectric power. The production of electric energy increased more than fivefold between 1937 and 1962.

The Mexican agricultural scene in 1967 furnished ground for hope. Mexico must be credited with more consistent attention to the interests of the agricultural sector than any other country in Latin America. The government has invested large sums in the improvement of agricultural technology; irrigated croplands increased some 70 per cent between 1950 and 1960; mechanization has proceeded rapidly on some of the *ejidos* and large private farms—Mexico now boasts more tractors than Argentina. Between 1952 and 1963 over-all agricultural production showed an increase of over 90 per cent, while per capita production was up almost 40 per cent—an exhibit which places Mexico at the top among nations of the hemisphere (comparable figures for the United States during the same period: over-all agricultural production increased some 13 per cent, but per capita production *decreased* almost 4 per cent). Cotton production, by 1963, had increased more than sevenfold since the mid-1930's; despite depressed world prices, cotton had become Mexico's chief export, and Mexico stood second only to the United States as a world exporter of cotton. Coffee production in 1963 had more than doubled since the 1930's. The production of corn, chief food crop of Mexico, had increased from some 66 million bushels a year in the mid-1930's to about 122 million bushels a year in the period 1948–53, and 237 million bushels in the crop-year 1962–63. Equally heartening, the yield of corn per acre had increased from 8.9 bushels in the mid-1930's to 11.9 bushels in the period 1948–53, and then to 15.0 bushels in 1962–63. Despite these striking improvements, the yield per acre was still far lower than the United States figure of 64.2 in 1962–63, or the Argentine figure of 26.3 in the same year. Sugar production was increasing: Mexico had been selling sugar in the world market since the 1950's, and was demanding that the United States give her a larger allotment in the national quota.

Mexico has the good fortune not to be dependent upon sales of one or two products in the world market, as are Venezuela (petroleum), Cuba (sugar), Colombia (coffee), Bolivia (tin), Chile (copper), and Brazil (coffee). For example, while in 1964 petroleum accounted for almost 95 per cent of Venezuela's export revenue, and coffee some 72 per cent of Colombia's, Mexico exported a wide variety of products of which cotton, coffee, zinc, lead, and copper made up less than a third of the total. In 1966 Mexico imported items amounting to about $1.6 billion (largely farm and industrial machinery, railroad and automotive equipment) and sold only some $1.2 billion worth of goods; but the gap was more than made up by the blessed asset of *turismo*. The flood of tourists, chiefly American, who spread out over Mexico every year, filling hotels and buying folkcraft, have been a boon to the Mexican economy. During the early 1960's they were spending some $700 million each year (an amount which was more than two-thirds of the export revenue), and in 1966 the figure reached $860 million. It is debated, however, whether the American tourist, profitable as he is for Mexico, makes for amity between the two countries: the brilliant Mexican historian Cosío Villegas has a harsh word on that point: "The Mexican, who endures the continuous presence of the Yankee tourist, comes to consider him a new Croesus, a conscienceless wastrel in a poverty-stricken country."[4] (If the Mexican government should ask one such

---

[4] Daniel Cosío Villegas: *American Extremes*, translated by Americo Paredes (Austin: University of Texas Press; 1964), p. 30.

"conscienceless wastrel" for advice, he might suggest that Mexico could probably double her tourist income by drafting a few thousand Swiss inn-keepers and restaurateurs and turning over to them the business of housing and feeding the "wastrels." A few Mexican hotels and restaurants are very good, some are passable, most are dreadful.)

Mexico, whose Revolution got off to an enthusiastic start in 1910, has not forgotten Zapata's battle cry, *Tierra y libertad.* The big holdings have been split up at various paces: Cárdenas (1934–40) distributed some 45 million acres; López Mateos (1958–64) holds second place, with distribution of some 25 million acres. The total distribution of land by 1964 amounted to some 132 million acres. However, the earlier enthusiasm for the communal grant, the *ejido,* has been dampened. By and large, the *ejidos* failed to produce as generously as did the privately held lands— many of them were too small to be economically fruitful, and much of the land given to them was quite worthless. Furthermore, the government banks organized to finance the *ejidos* have not had a good record of honesty and competence. Some of the best advertised *ejidos* went sour. A conspicuous instance was the Gran Ejido of Yucatán, embracing some 395,000 acres of henequen lands. World demand for henequen (used for making rope) has fallen off as the manufacture of synthetic cordage increased, leaving Yucatán in deep trouble. Another much-praised experiment, La Laguna, embracing some 6,000 square miles in the states of Durango and Coahuila, has suffered from years of drought, as well as from faulty management. The sorry plight of the *ejiditarios* of La Laguna led many to migrate to the United States to work as *braceros* or to join the overcrowded ranks in the rapidly growing Mexican cities. The government sought to alleviate their condition by transferring workers from La Laguna to areas in the south newly opened up by irrigation. Meanwhile a new generation of *hacendados* has arisen with large and well-run farms of generous size. Throughout the years of revolutionary fervor, the more agile of the political leaders found it pleasant to extend their own private holdings. Calles did this during his years of power, and so did Obregón. Even Cárdenas, for all of his revolutionary zeal, accumulated fine properties. Alemán acquired much land (and a bit of almost everything else). Numerous powerful men on the fringes of the ruling clique indulged their taste for land. These large holdings are by all odds the best operated of all the farms in Mexico, producing most of the export crops, including cotton. Land reform, the endowing of all citizens with their share in the national patrimony, is still a prime article of national faith. But there is a growing tendency to encourage more private holdings rather than to create new *ejidos.* However, there is not enough land to go around, and there are millions of Mexicans who have slight chance of enjoying any of the better land of the republic.

In drawing up the balance sheet on Mexican prospects, perhaps the most somber fact is the population explosion. There were 19.8 million Mexicans in 1940; 25.8 million in 1950, and an estimated 44.1 million in 1966. The annual rate of increase in the population between 1958 and 1966 was about 3.4 per cent. President Ruiz Cortines, in lyrical vein, described the more than a million new babies each year as "Mexico's greatest treasure," but bystanders wondered what the "treasures" would eat. With the population increasing at a rate which would double the population in less than twenty-one years, it is doubtful whether food production can keep pace. The stark fact is that Mexico is short on arable land: about 1.34 acres per capita, compared with about 2.12 acres in Argentina, and 2.33 acres in the United States. Furthermore, the yield per acre of corn still lags (see figures on p. 380).

The increase in population has speeded the flight of Mexicans from the country into the cities. Those who know rural Mexico can understand why people leave the farms: wretched housing, lack of sanitation, poor communications, lack of social advantages, starvation wages—in 1957 a minimum farm wage of 84 cents a day had been decreed, but even that modest level had seldom been reached; furthermore, many found employment for not more than a third of the year. The figures on urbanization are dramatic. In 1900, less than 5 per cent of the population lived in the only two cities of 100,000 or more—Mexico City and Guadalajara. In 1963, over one-fourth of the population lived in cities of 100,000 or more —of which there were now twenty-two. In 1900, the Federal District (Mexico City and its suburbs) had only some 542,000 people; by 1930 it had passed the million mark; in 1965 it had an estimated 5.5 million— over one-eighth of the country's population.[5] This influx of farmers into the capital city caused grave problems. The newcomers were not prepared for jobs in industry (there were never jobs enough anyway), and the strong labor unions erected barriers against them. Unemployment and underemployment increased; slum areas in and around the capital multiplied. The capital city not only dominated the national economy; it also had almost complete power over the country politically: its ruling clique named almost all officials from the president down to the municipal *alcaldes*.

Mexico's burgeoning population, together with the meager lot of the Mexican farm laborer, provoked a frantic exodus of workers to the United States. Migrants left in such numbers as seriously to deplete the labor force in Mexico. This caused dislocation of the farming industry: for example, so many able-bodied men left southern Chiapas during recent years that there were not enough hands to harvest the coffee crop, and as a result workers were imported from Guatemala. The steady drift of farm workers to the United States (chiefly to California, Arizona, New Mexico, and Texas) fell into three classes. First, some sought entrance into the United States as permanent residents; applications piled up in the American con-

[5] The official figures for Mexico classify as "urban" all localities of 2,500 or more. Using this definition, the nation was 35.1 per cent "urban" in 1940; and 50.7 per cent "urban" in 1960. The growth of Mexico's four largest cities—next to the capital—is shown in these approximate population figures: Guadalajara: 101,000 in 1900, and 1,048,000 in 1965; Monterrey: 62,000 in 1900, and 822,000 in 1965; Ciudad Juárez: 7,000 in 1895, and 385,000 in 1965; Puebla: 94,000 in 1900, and 339,000 in 1965.

sulates, but processing was slow, and there was much resentment over what appeared to be a lukewarm welcome by the northern neighbor. Second, many swam the Rio Grande (hence the term *mojados,* "wetbacks"), or slipped across the lightly policed border into the United States southwest. The number of these illegal entries has been variously estimated at from 200,000 to 1 million each year. Third, some 200,000 to 500,000 *braceros* (literally, "arms") were admitted legally each year for stipulated periods of a few months to work in the orchards or vegetable fields of the southwestern states.

Mexican migration into the United States did not improve Mexican-American relations. The permanent migrants, whether legally or illegally admitted, distended slum communities in the American southwest. The Mexicans who sought refuge in the United States, usually drawn from the least privileged and least educated classes, were often exploited, and their treatment stirred resentment in Mexico. The fate of the illegal migrants, the "wetbacks," was especially unfortunate: lacking legal status in their new homes, they were forced to accept whatever pay was offered and to live in miserable hovels. The *braceros* had better treatment: the American authorities and many employers saw to it that these transient pickers of fruit and weeders of vegetable fields had an adequate wage, and that fairly decent housing was provided. However, the *braceros* also had their grievances, against their own countrymen as well as against the Americans. On the Mexican side of the border, the migrants charged that three successive levels of national officials demanded bribes before permitting them to cross into the United States. On the American side, the *braceros* claimed that some employers treated them shabbily. Nevertheless, many *braceros* were delighted with their excursions and felt well paid: it is estimated that in recent years the "take-home pay"—the money that went back home with the workers—had been about $35 million annually. However, under pressure from organized labor in the United States, who demanded that the picking of fruit and the cultivation of vegetables be turned over to unemployed Americans, the *bracero* program was terminated at the end of 1964. This evoked bitter outcry from large-scale farmers in the American southwest, especially those in the Imperial and Ventura valleys of California, who prophesied ruin for their properties unless Mexican workers were made available. (California agriculture is a $3.9-billion-a-year industry.) The Mexican has been willing to do the "stoop-labor" required for tending such low-growing crops as lettuce, strawberries, asparagus, broccoli, and cabbage—for much of the time at a substandard wage of 60 or 70 cents a day. Organized labor insists that if living conditions are improved and wages increased (the target in 1965 was $1.40 per hour) unemployed Americans can be found to take up the slack. The dispute is angry and the answer is not clear. "There is never any shortage of labor in America," one labor man says, "only a shortage of pay." Spurred by the angry protests of large operators in California, the American Department of Labor temporarily relaxed the ban in 1965 and permitted a few thousand *braceros* to enter.

. . .

By 1967, the clash between the state and the Church, which had embittered Mexican life for more than a century, had largely subsided. Under Cárdenas and his successors a more amiable spirit prevailed. The priests went about their business, and almost all were content. A significant sign of the new mood came in 1955 when churchmen were permitted to buy nineteen acres on the outskirts of Mexico City and to build a new monastery, an act that would have been unthinkable in the days of Calles— or even of Cárdenas. To be sure, there were occasional outbursts of anti-clericalism. For example, in 1956 the Church's hierarchy issued a pastoral letter urging Mexicans to vote for candidates who would serve both the nation and the Church; this set off a blast of protests against clerical inter-ference in politics. But in general there was now little friction between civil and ecclesiastical authorities. This happier state was due in part to the good sense of some political leaders, who had decided upon the folly of priest-baiting. Credit also goes to the clergy, who have shown increased concern for social reform, and to the Church schools, which in many cities and towns were making a vital contribution to the education of Mexican children. In spite of the improved situation, it remains a curious fact that a good politician in Mexico must upon occasion assume a hostile stance toward the Church. For example, President Díaz Ordaz, although a con-fessional Catholic, found it wise to stand outside the church temple in which his daughter was being married. This offers interesting contrast with the folkways of Washington: an American president attends church services as a part of his political ritual; a Mexican president stays away for the same reason.

Culturally, Mexico had grounds for pride by 1967. Now, at last, there were schools for most of the children in the larger cities and towns, and for many in the villages. The figures reported by the national statistical agency were eloquent: in 1950, there had been primary schools available for 48.5 per cent of all children in the primary age bracket; by 1960, this had increased to 65.5 per cent. That spelled progress, although it was still true that many, if not most, of the children stayed in school no more than a year. The development of the school system had been uneven. As we have noted, it was launched with fervor and imagination by José Vas-concelos in the early 1920's, then carried on until 1930 under the brilliant Moisés Sáenz. During the 1930's the excitement over new ideas yielded to the dull methodology of the pedagogues; but devoted teachers toiled conscientiously despite meager pay and inadequate equipment; and school buildings multiplied. The third great figure in Mexican education was Jaime Torres Bodet, a leader with much creative energy, who was minister of education under Ávila Camacho and again under López Mateos. Solid evidence of national concern for education was the allotment in the na-tional budget to the Ministry of Education: it had stood at but 5 per cent of the total in 1921, then it had climbed rapidly until in 1965 it reached a level of 24 per cent. The results had been solid: the official estimate of illiterates in 1960 stood at 34.6 per cent, a dramatic gain from the estimated illiteracy of about 75 per cent at the end of the Porfirio Díaz regime in 1910.

There had been hopeful increase in enrollment in secondary and higher education. In 1960, there were about 432,000 students in secondary, technical, and teacher training schools; and about 94,000 in colleges, universities, and professional schools. Chief among the national institutions were the National Autonomous University and the National Polytechnic Institute, both in the capital city. The National Autonomous University, housed in the pretentious University City created by Miguel Alemán, enrolled over 34,000 in 1954 and more than 73,000 in 1965. The National Polytechnic Institute was also growing rapidly, with an enrollment in 1965 of over 53,000. There are a dozen state universities, whose quality is spotty; but the two chief institutions in Mexico City have improved greatly during recent years. There are a few private institutions which have won deserved plaudits: most successful is the Institute of Technology and Advanced Studies in Monterrey, with an enrollment of 8,000 in 1965.

In literature and the arts, Mexico has won hearty respect. Writers of novels, poetry, essays, and history have contributed significant work, much of it showing deep concern for social problems. Mexico has taken the lead in the development of the novel, exerting influence throughout Latin America. In the nineteenth century Latin American fiction was an imitation of French models, chiefly Balzac and Zola. Martín Luis Guzmán and Mariano Azuela, in the wake of the Mexican Revolution, introduced a realistic treatment of indigenous themes, creating for the first time an authentic Latin American novel (see p. 342). In the mid-twentieth century, as the Mexican Revolution becomes less self-conscious, Mexican writing has acquired subtlety and the novel has become more universal; and among the younger generation there has been much experimental writing and psychological analysis. Two novelists have written searchingly on the contemporary scene: Juan Rulfo, in *Pedro Páramo,* pictures the life of the *cacique* in the style of Faulkner; Carlos Fuentes satirizes the new plutocracy in his *La región más transparente,* somewhat in the manner of Huxley and Dos Passos, and has won reputation abroad. Other writers of fiction today include Juan José Arreola and Rosario Castellanos. Octavio Paz, one of the chief poets writing in Spanish today, has also written a perceptive study of the Mexican character, *El laberinto de la soledad.* In the printing of books, Mexico City has vied with Buenos Aires in the variety and volume of output. The Fondo de Cultura Económica, a publishing house founded in 1934 with the chief purpose of translating books on economics, today provides distinguished translations in all fields, in addition to publishing original works, and has had much influence on the cultural development of Mexico.

Carlos Chávez, who organized the National Symphony Orchestra in 1928 and won world renown as a conductor and a composer, went far toward creating a truly national music. Drawing upon Italian tradition, he incorporated into his compositions themes from Mexico's primitive past.

Mexican art, from primitive times to the present day, offers a record of more continuous vitality than perhaps any other single civilization, as anyone who has seen the great exhibition of Mexican masterworks, recently on world tour, can testify. From the charming and humorous figures of the early pre-Classic period which began some 3,500 years ago; through the folk-art, sculpture, and architectural monuments of the Maya, Toltecs, Aztecs, and numerous other Indian peoples; to the architecture of colonial Mexico which fused the genius of sixteenth-century Spain with that of the Indian; down to the mid-twentieth century which has given us Diego Rivera, José Clemente Orozco, David Alfaro Siqueiros, and Rufino Tamayo, whose frescoes and paintings have earned them world acclaim, and a new group of artists including Ricardo Martínez, Juan Soriano, Pedro Coronel, José Luis Cuevas, and many others—all these are evidence of the boundless artistic vigor of the Mexican people.

Mexico offers a confusing exhibit of affluence and poverty. The casual visitor to Mexico's capital is impressed by the pretentious new office buildings, apartments, and hotels. He drives along the graceful Paseo de la Reforma. He looks at the fine houses which adorn Chapultepec Heights and the Pedragal. He sees the best of American and European automobiles. He dines in restaurants as fine as those of New York or Paris. Yes, Mexicans are rich: at least those who own factories and large farms are rich, and so are the bankers, the businessmen, the generals—a few thousand in all. And at last there is a Mexican middle class, aggregating perhaps a fifth of the population—the managerial and professional men, who live comfortably; and the school teachers and clerical workers, who live less comfortably. At the bottom of the economic pile, perhaps 60 per cent of the population—those who work for beggarly wages in fields, shops, and factories, and those who have no jobs at all—still live in bitter and largely unrelieved poverty. Documentation is almost impossible. The most dramatic and authentic interpreter of the poverty of Mexico is the anthropologist Oscar Lewis. In *The Children of Sánchez: Autobiography of a Mexican Family,* Mr. Lewis lets the members of the Sánchez family tell their own story of life in a *vecindad,* a walled slum only a ten-minute walk from the Zócalo, the capital's central plaza, in an area of urban misery marked by murder, drunkenness, and savage delinquency. There are 157 one-room windowless apartments within its walls, the homes of some 700 people who are crowded more than four to each one-room cubicle. Water is carried from a common tap. There is an ill-kept public bath. There are dirty common toilets. But that particular *vecindad* is a haven when compared to other slum areas in which most of Mexico City's 5.5 million live. And to the wretchedness and filth of city slums must be added the misery of rural life in the thousands of villages that dot the nation. There are no statistics on the lot of this 60 per cent—or whatever the true figure is— of the Mexican poor. Their fare is meager: some corn, chilis, unreliable milk, very little meat. Their housing is savage. When they are sick, there is rarely a doctor. At least a third of the children have no schools. The social pattern has been recut since the days of Porfirio Díaz, but no one can say whether the Mexican poor are much better off.

Here is the stuff of which rebellion is made. But the Mexican poor have few spokesmen, and there is little sign of revolt. Oscar Lewis quotes Jesús Sánchez, the father of the family from the *vecindad:*

> If we ever got a really tough government here, and it called up everyone who had been a president and said, "You go to the Zócalo and pile up ail the millions you've robbed from the people," why, there'd be enough to build another capital.

Sánchez then goes on to tell how things are done in Mexico:

> Here the PRI runs everything, so if there's another candidate they stick a gun in his face. So who won? Well, the PRI candidate. That's all there is to it. . . . Things must be different in the U.S. Well, maybe it's better that we have just one gang running the country here, because it's got a pistol in each hand. Don't you know this story about two fellows who were playing cards and one had two aces and the other fellow asks him, "What do you have?" "Two aces. And you?" "Two pistols." So he says, "O.K., you win." And that's the way the PRI is here: it's got the pistols and anybody who objects, well, he gets run over by a car.[6]

Although Mexico's relations with the United States were generally good in 1967, sporadic arguments during recent years had indeed put a strain on friendship between the two nations. The brief renewal of the American quarantine against Mexican cattle in 1952, prompted by a fresh outbreak of hoof-and-mouth disease, had been resented. There were intermittent disputes over fishing rights within the nine-mile limit over which Mexico claimed sovereignty. Other sources of irritation were the rumors that Washington would increase tariffs on zinc and lead; while these were not imposed, in 1958 Washington fixed a quota upon the import of those metals, reducing purchases by 30 per cent; this measure, Mexico claimed, threw 9,000 miners out of jobs. Another element of discord was the dumping upon the world market by the United States of much surplus cotton, a measure which cut the price that Mexico would receive for her crop. A source of great unhappiness between the two countries was the flow of migrant labor across the American border (which we have discussed above). Also irritating to Mexico was the United States effort to persuade Mexico to sign a military pact: this aroused the anti-Yankee sentiment which is always just under the surface in Mexico.

A continuing source of bad blood in United States–Mexican relations was Mexico's policy toward Cuba and its Castro government. Washington pressed its demands that all Latin American governments exclude Cuba from the Organization of American States, but Mexico finally stood as the only holdout. Mexico's firm stand on this issue had three roots. First, it

6 Oscar Lewis: *The Children of Sánchez: Autobiography of a Mexican Family* (New York: Random House; 1961), pp. 497–8.

reflected to some degree the perennial determination of Mexicans to be free from coercion by the United States. Second, the principle of nonintervention in the internal affairs of other states—continued faithfully by López Mateos—had been firmly imbedded in Mexico's foreign policy by Genaro Estrada in 1929: the Estrada Doctrine calls for immediate and automatic recognition of any government that wins control. And, third, the position was buttressed by considerable elements within Mexico which applauded Fidel Castro; the most conspicuous and vocal spokesman for this segment was ex-President Lázaro Cárdenas. Some Americans denounced Mexico for playing into the hands of the Communists by her "softness" toward Castro. On the other side, many Mexicans accused Washington of lack of realism. James Reston of *The New York Times,* reporting in December, 1962, quoted López Mateos as calling the United States handling of Fidel Castro a "clumsy bit of diplomatic blundering" and intimating that "the United States forced Fidel Castro into the Communist camp." But López Mateos was no apologist for Castro: after the revelation of Soviet missiles in Cuba in October, 1962, he wrote the Cuban President that "the government of Mexico cannot view with indifference a Latin American country establishing facilities for the most destructive weapons of all times."

A turn for the better in United States–Mexican relations came with the settlement in July, 1963, of the old and knotty problem of El Chamizal. That patch of some 437 acres between El Paso and Ciudad Júarez was part of the Mexican city until 1864, when the capricious Rio Grande changed its course, shifting El Chamizal to the American side of the river. Debate over this vagrant bit of real estate raged for almost a century. The American case in the dispute was badly damaged in 1911: Washington agreed to arbitrate the matter, but when the Canadian arbiter ruled for Mexico, the United States refused to accept the decision, and El Chamizal continued as part of El Paso. By the terms of the 1963 agreement, the debated area was restored to Mexico, and the United States agreed to resettle the 3,500 American citizens living on the tract and to purchase their properties. This happy solution, for which President López Mateos deserved considerable credit, was applauded in Mexico.

Another important step toward more amicable relations between the United States and her southern neighbor was President Kennedy's frank handling of the angry question of the salinity of the Colorado River water. A 1944 treaty had allotted Mexico 1.5 million acre-feet of water from the Colorado to irrigate the farmlands of northwestern Mexico (an acre-foot is water one foot deep covering one acre). Since then, salty water from the Welton-Mohawk irrigation project near Yuma, Arizona, had been drained into the Colorado, threatening to poison some 50,000 acres of Mexico's richest soil and end the growing of cotton in the Mexicali valley —a crop which Mexicans valued at some $73 million a year. President Kennedy promised that Washington would take prompt and vigorous action in the matter; and after Kennedy's assassination, President Johnson (with the effective help of Assistant Secretary of State for Latin America Thomas Mann) pressed toward a solution. In March, 1965, Washington announced that an agreement had been reached under which the United States, at a cost of $5 million, would dig a thirteen-mile extension of the drainage canal to carry off the offending waters from Arizona and divert them into the Gulf of Mexico.

By 1967 Mexico had, in a century and a half, traveled a long, rough road. She had suffered under scoundrels who had betrayed her and well-meaning men incapable of saving her; she had smarted under vexing clashes over the Church, over land ownership, and the determination of foreigners to exploit her wealth as they saw fit; she had been humiliated by the United States and by France. Only occasionally had leaders of sound head and pure heart given her grounds for hope. But there was now healthy optimism among intelligent Mexicans as they reviewed the momentous changes of recent years. There were now schools, not enough to be sure, but increasing each year. The national soil, long the monopoly of a few, was now widely distributed—in spite of the collapse of the *ejido* system. That soil was yielding a little more each year, as irrigation ditches multiplied, more fertilizer was used, and better seeds were sown. And an expanding industry was gradually rescuing Mexico from her ancient colonial economy. Political control of the nation, although still far short of the democratic ideal, was slowly passing into the hands of more people. Mexico was still a poor land, her people were still ill-served, but the progress since 1910 gave promise of better things to come. The promise, however, hung on Mexico's success in holding population in line with the production of food.

PART V

◈⟐◈⟐◈⟐◈⟐◈⟐◈⟐◈ *The Caribbean*

and Central America

The Caribbean lands constitute a world of their own, reaching 2,000 miles from the Central American states east to the arc of the Lesser Antilles. Over this tropical region fly the flags of fourteen independent nations and four alien powers. In this study, we leave Venezuela and Colombia for later discussion; and we omit the possessions of England, France, Holland, and the United States, as well as the newly independent governments within the British Commonwealth (Guyana, Jamaica, Trinidad and Tobago), as having slight bearing on the history of Latin America. We now turn our attention to nine republics: Cuba, Haiti, the Dominican Republic, the five states of Central America, and Panama.

These lands and peoples of the Caribbean world have much in common: a tropical climate, tempered in the highlands of Central America; a population variously compounded of Europeans, Negroes, Indians, and a few Asiatics—with Haiti almost completely Negro, Guatemala largely Indian, and Costa Rica predominantly white European. Economically, these are the lands of sugar, coffee, cotton, bananas, tobacco, and cacao. These nine republics are superficially much alike, but each has developed a distinct national personality.

Chapter 25

CUBA

The lush charms of the "Pearl of the Antilles" have been fully reported by delighted tourists, of whom Columbus was the first. Nothing but pleasant things can fairly be said of this fruitful island which stretches west to east some 760 miles but measures barely 100 miles at its widest, with its broken 2,000-mile coastline and fine harbors, with its rolling plains, dense forests, and mountains rising to more than 8,000 feet.

Cuba's population of about 7.8 million (1966) is an amalgam of many peoples. The full-blooded Indian has long since disappeared, leaving no more than a glint in the eye of the modern Cuban. The first of the foreign invaders were the Spaniards who came in search of gold and plantations, and occupied the island after the beginning of the sixteenth century. Next came Negro slaves, about a million of whom were brought in during the colonial period to work the sugar fields. French and British freebooters attacked the island from time to time, and in 1762–63 a British force occupied Havana. French refugees, fleeing Negro revolts in Haiti after 1790, settled in Cuba. In the nineteenth century many additional Negro slaves were smuggled into the country. During the nineteenth and early twentieth centuries, Cuba attracted many thousands of migrants from Spain, but few from other European countries. In the same period Chinese, other Orientals, and some Indians from Yucatán entered and stayed. Today's population is a blend of all these peoples. Exact racial analysis of Cuba's population is impossible, but we may guess that roughly one-fourth of the people are Negro, one-half white and mostly Spanish, and one-fourth a mixture of European, Negro, and Oriental. "The vast blend of races and cultures," writes the Cuban Fernando Ortiz, "overshadows in importance every other historical phenomenon."

During the almost five centuries since Columbus landed, Cuba has been dominated by foreign powers: for more than 400 years her destiny was shaped as a colony of Spain; then the island fell under the overshadowing political and economic power of the United States (whose Florida Keys are only ninety miles from Havana); and since 1959 Castro's Cuba has become the target of the Communist powers.

Economically, sugar has ruled the island. The tobacco crop, long important, has declined to a poor second place. The island is the chief vendor of cane sugar in the world market, and its economic and social health has risen and fallen with the fluctuating price of that commodity. The culture of sugar cane, begun in Cuba in the 1520's, created great plantations, prompted the importation of Negro slaves, furnished profit to the Spanish Crown, and attracted marauders. The nineteenth century brought increase in production: in 1817 the output was about 70,000 short tons; in 1894, over 1 million. With independence and the influx of American capital in the twentieth century, the sugar crop reached an average of 5.4 million short tons in the years 1925–29, declined to a low of 2.5 million in 1934, and increased to almost 8 million in 1952. Three-fourths or more of Cuba's export revenue has been from sugar. There has been no lack of warning against the island's monoculture. In 1883 the Cuban hero José Martí wrote: "A people commits suicide the day on which it bases its existence on a single crop," and Cuban experience confirms his wisdom. When world demand is lively and the price is high, the Cuban treasury is filled, businessmen sell goods, and almost everyone eats. When markets contract and prices fall, distress is general. Sugar dictates the life of every citizen. There was prosperity during World War I when the price was pegged at 5.5 cents a pound, feverish speculation in 1920 when it briefly touched 22.5 cents, dismay by the end of 1920 when it dropped to 3.75 cents, and in the 1920's and early 1930's the price tottered and finally fell to a new low of .57 cents a pound in June, 1932. Strict production controls, international marketing agreements, and United States quota arrangements steadied the price at about 4 cents a pound, more or less, until 1960, when Cuba lost her American market.

Although sugar dominates, Cuba has rich resources scarcely tapped: 3.5 million acres of fine forests, rich grazing lands for cattle, substantial deposits of iron, copper, nickel, and manganese. Tobacco, best in the world for cigars, for many years furnished about 7 per cent of the export revenue.

SPAIN'S "EVER FAITHFUL ISLE"

While the wars for Spanish American independence swept from Mexico to Argentina between 1810 and 1824, only Cuba and Puerto Rico remained faithful to the Iberian motherland. A few lonely Cuban dissenters were easily silenced. The masters of land and trade were loyal Spaniards, and their ranks were augmented by royalist refugees from Mexico and Gran Colombia. Cuba's insular position and the presence of strong Spanish garrisons blocked intervention by Simón Bolívar's forces. Cuba indeed had grounds for complaint against Spain, and these increased as the homeland floundered under reactionary Ferdinand VII, inept Isabella II, and the weaklings who followed. Colonial rule grew more incompetent and tyrannical (despite brief periods of reform), stifling the island's economy. It must be noted in retrospect, however, that Cuba prospered during the first

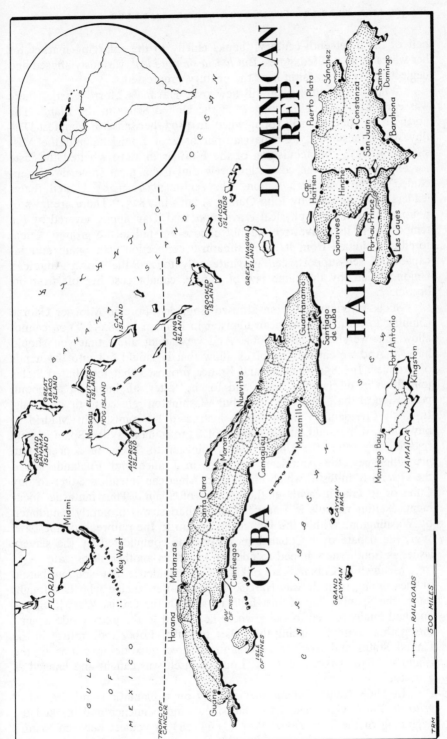

Cuba, Haiti, and the Dominican Republic

half of the nineteenth century, thanks chiefly to the enlarging market for her wares in the United States. But *la isla siempre leal,* variously abused and neglected, grew less faithful as the century progressed.

While the Spanish flag still flew over Havana's Morro Castle, there was early evidence of the interest of the United States in the island. The northern republic was still young when, in 1803, her sense of Manifest Destiny was intensified by the bargain-purchase of Louisiana and the Mississippi Valley. The acquisition of the Floridas in 1819 whetted the taste for expansion, and the conviction grew that Cuba must some day be included in the American nation. The sentiment of many United States leaders was expressed by John Quincy Adams in 1823: "There are laws of political as well as of physical gravitation, and if an apple, severed by the tempest from its native tree, cannot choose but fall to the ground, Cuba, forcibly disjoined from its own unnatural connection with Spain and incapable of self-support, can gravitate only toward the North American Union, which, by the same law of nature, cannot cast her off from its bosom."[1]

Such American ambition aroused England's Foreign Minister George Canning to warn the American minister in London in 1825: "You cannot allow that we should have Cuba. And we cannot allow that you should have it. And we can neither of us allow that it should fall into the hands of France." In 1852 England and France proposed that the United States join them in disclaiming "now and for hereafter, all intention to obtain possession of the island of Cuba," but Washington refused to tie its hands. In 1853 President Franklin Pierce instructed his minister in Madrid to buy Cuba, if he could, at a top price of $130 million. When Spain angrily rejected this offer, the United States minister to Spain, in concert with his colleagues, the American ministers in France and England, issued the Ostend Manifesto, which announced American intention either to buy Cuba or to take it "without the consent of Spain." That fantastic document, exciting ridicule in European chancelleries, was promptly repudiated by Washington. Within the United States, up to the outbreak of the Civil War, the debate over Cuban annexation was complicated by the slavery issue, as Southerners hoped to add the island as another slave state.

Meanwhile, Cubans were talking of independence. An eloquent herald of the coming struggle was Narciso López, a Venezuelan who had fought under the Spanish flag against Bolívar, then in the Carlist Wars in Spain, and had finally moved to Cuba where he shifted to the patriot side against the mother country. Fleeing the police in Cuba, López took refuge in the United States and from there organized three quixotic invasions of the island in 1848, 1850, and 1851; López himself was caught and hanged as a traitor.

In 1868 young Cubans met secretly on a plantation and drafted *el grito de Yara,* which called for the island's independence and marked the beginning of the Ten Years' War (1868–78), a contest between Spain's

---

[1] Adams to Nelson, April 28, 1823. *House Executive Documents,* 32nd Congress, 1st session, No. 121 (serial 648), p. 7.

troops and the poorly armed guerrillas which cost not less than 200,000 lives and some $700 million in property loss. Recent Spanish immigrants played a major role in this struggle. This seemingly futile war, however, fixed the determination of Cubans to be free, trained thousands of young men in defense of their land, and produced heroes whose names are great in the island's history—the mulatto Antonio Maceo, the Dominican Máximo Gómez, and Calixto García. In the final settlement Spain, now in the hands of more sensible rulers, promised administrative reforms, amnesty for rebels, and emancipation of all slaves. The pledge on slavery was fulfilled in 1886, but the other promises proved chimerical. Colonial rulers continued to be highhanded and feckless. And, most eloquent of all arguments, Spanish rule was bad for business. By this time the island's economy depended largely on marketing its tobacco and sugar in the United States. Spain imposed new taxes and restrictions and finally in 1894 arbitrarily canceled the trade agreement between the islanders and the Americans. The results were disastrous: Cuban sales to the United States declined from $89 million in 1889 to $56 million in 1897—a loss partly explained by the depression of 1894 in the United States. Such losses persuaded Cuban businessmen that the hour had indeed come for *Cuba libre.*

The war for Cuban independence, which broke in 1895, was the continuation of the Ten Years' War. A government-in-exile had been maintained in New York, headed by Tomás Estrada Palma and aided by other expatriates. Most tireless of these was José Martí, poet and journalist, affectionately remembered by his countrymen as "the apostle." Born in Havana in 1853, Martí early joined the revolutionists, and at sixteen he was jailed and served on a chain gang. Then followed years of exile in Mexico, Guatemala, and Spain. Returning to Cuba after the Ten Years' War, he was again banished to Spain for his outspoken criticism. In 1881 he found refuge in New York, where he worked to enlist his countrymen, to win friends among the Americans, and to raise money for guns and powder. More than any other Cuban, Martí helped to create the atmosphere which later prompted American intervention.

In 1895 there were uprisings of patriots in eastern Cuba, inspired and armed by the New York junta. Martí, Maceo, and Gómez landed with recruits gathered in the United States, Mexico, Central America, and the Caribbean islands. Martí was one of the first to be killed in battle; but arms and men continued to reach the island, as some sixty volunteer expeditions eluded the neutral American authorities. The army of emancipation scored initial successes and seemed about to push on to Havana itself. Then Spain bestirred herself, ousted incompetent officers, and appointed General Valeriano Weyler commander in chief, who quickly earned himself the epithet of *Carnicero,* butcher. He immediately herded several hundred thousand men, women, and children into concentration camps (*reconcentrados*), where bad and inadequate food and lack of sanitation brought death to many thousands—some 50,000 in Havana province alone. Crops and cattle in disaffected areas were systematically destroyed in order to starve out the patriots, who retaliated by burning Spanish-owned sugar plantations. By the end of 1896 the tide had turned against the revolutionists, and within a few months Weyler had driven them back to the eastern end of the island. The battle for liberty seemed lost, but the United States was to have the last word.

The forces provoking American intervention were various. Some were economic: Americans had invested money in sugar, had drawn profit from Cuban trade, and wanted more. The shrinking of the United States industrial profits in the early 1890's prompted expansion of foreign markets, lessened enthusiasm for the traditional isolationism, and gave impetus to the idea that the nation must assert its place among world powers. There was a strategic motive: the leaders in Washington had already decided on an isthmian canal and thought it unwise to leave Spain in control of the island which dominated the Caribbean. Other motives were humanitarian: the public deplored the savagery with which the Cuban patriots were treated. The American press fanned the flames; in New York, Joseph Pulitzer's *World* and William Randolph Hearst's *American* seized upon the Cuban imbroglio as ammunition in their campaigns for selling papers. Unscrupulous reporters vied in invention of Spanish atrocities and gave only scant attention to Spain's recall of Weyler in late 1897, the ending of the *reconcentrados,* and the offer of home rule to Cuba.

Early 1898 brought the rival editors fresh material for arousing the American electorate. Hearst published a personal letter written by the Spanish minister in Washington, describing President William McKinley as "weak, a pot-house politician, catering to the rabble." On February 15 the U.S.S. *Maine,* anchored in the harbor of Havana to protect American citizens in case of emergency, blew up with the loss of 266 American seamen. What happened to that warship is still unclear. A United States Naval inquiry fixed blame upon a submarine bomb but did not declare its source. A Spanish investigation charged the accident to internal explosion. Some commentators argued, without evidence, that Cuban patriots had blown up the battleship in order to provoke intervention. But the cry, "Remember the *Maine!*" echoed across the land, with newsmen beating the tom-toms, and on April 11 McKinley laid the case before Congress and called for armed intervention—despite last-minute word from Madrid that the Spanish government was ready to accept almost any peaceful settlement.

The war was brief, glorious, and inexpensive. Heroism of a sort flourished—and not the least heroic in the popular mind was Theodore Roosevelt, who, according to some accounts, won the war singlehanded. ("Mr. Dooley" suggested that T. R.'s telling of the tale might well be entitled "Alone in Cubia." [sic.]) American forces on land and sea expelled Spain from Cuba, Puerto Rico, and the Philippines. And Cuba was free, under the tutelage of the United States, which had pledged its word (by the Teller Amendment of April, 1898) that she had no "intention to exercise sovereignty, jurisdiction, or control over said Island except for the pacification thereof, and asserts its determination, when that is accomplished, to leave the government and control of the Island to its people." This pledge, incorporated in the Treaty of Paris (December 10, 1898), was regarded by skeptical European statesmen as an amiable but empty promise. Sensible nations, they said, do not abandon conquered lands, especially lands as rich as Cuba.

AMERICAN MILITARY RULE, 1898–1902

The United States army, charged with pacifying and organizing Cuba, had task enough. Fields lay in weeds, houses and sugar mills were gutted, and tens of thousands were homeless and starving. Of the 3 million cattle at pasture in 1895, scarcely one-tenth had survived. Public business was at a standstill, courts and police forces were not functioning, and the departing Spaniards had stripped island offices—not a single centavo stamp was left in the post office tills. Bandits ruled country roads. The patriot army was ragged and hungry, and had grown by 20,000 men after the shooting was over.

After a brief administration by John R. Brooke, the office of Military Governor was filled by Dr. Leonard Wood, a thirty-nine-year-old army surgeon who had shared the martial adventures of Colonel Theodore Roosevelt and his Rough Riders, and who combined sound discipline with a lively imagination, traits which later made him effective in the Philippines. "Wood," writes Russell Fitzgibbon, "will undoubtedly rank as one of the great colonial administrators in history, comparable to Britain's Curzon and France's Lyautey."

The Army's housekeeping was thorough. A census taken in 1899 reported a population of 1,572,845, of whom 185,393 were born in Spain. Food and clothing were furnished to thousands of families. A rural police was organized. The patriot army was disbanded, its members sharing a $3-million bonus from the American treasury. Courts, municipal governments, and customs services were reorganized. Prisons were cleaned up and many political prisoners released. The Church, many of whose properties had been seized or damaged, was propitiated by a settlement of almost $1 million. Landholders were aided in getting their fields into cultivation, and sugar production increased rapidly. Cattle were imported and sold on easy terms to farmers. Harbors were dredged and docks built. Highway and railroad projects were begun. Public schools, almost nonexistent under Spain, increased in number. The University of Havana, founded by the Dominicans in the eighteenth century but moribund during the nineteenth, was reopened under the revered Enrique José Varona.

The most spectacular benefit was the extirpation of yellow fever, which had been a scourge for four centuries and since 1855 had caused an average of 751 deaths a year in Havana alone. Thanks to the American Walter Reed and other physicians—notably the Cuban Carlos Finlay—the offending species of mosquito was identified and its breeding places cleared out. Within three years the disease was virtually eliminated.

Despite the brilliant success of Leonard Wood's rule, there was popular clamor for American withdrawal. Many landholders, however, including influential Spaniards, feared anarchy if American troops were removed and favored outright annexation to the American Union. But the Cuban people had been promised national independence and the majority would be content with nothing less. In 1900 Wood, under orders from Washington, announced the election of an assembly to draft a constitution for the government into whose hands he could transfer his authority. While this body was framing the new instrument of state, communications from Washington laid down some American demands.

Washington's stipulations for an independent Cuba, delivered to the constitutional assembly, were in the form of the Platt Amendment (named for Senator O. H. Platt of Connecticut). This famous document, largely drafted by Elihu Root and adopted by the American Congress, was designed to place such limits upon the island republic's activities as to make her a safe and tractable neighbor. Under its terms the Cuban government was limited in its power to make treaties with foreign nations and in its freedom to contract public debts; it was pledged to continue the campaign against "epidemic and infectious" diseases; it promised "coaling or naval stations" to the United States; and it left the final disposition of the Isle of Pines, an island of 1,182 square miles off the southwestern coast, to later decision. The most galling provision, and the one which clearly described Cuba as a protectorate of the United States, read: "Cuba consents that the United States may exercise the right to intervene for the preservation of Cuban independence, the maintenance of a government adequate for the protection of life, property, and individual liberty." Washington's demand that the Amendment be incorporated into the Cuban constitution was denounced by the assembly as final proof of American insincerity, but all attempts to soften its terms were rejected. The Cubans yielded and added the Amendment to the constitution which was adopted in June, 1901.

Thus the road was cleared for the election of a president. The first choice was clearly the honored hero of two wars, General Máximo Gómez, but he refused with the words: "Men of war, for war . . . and those of peace, for peace." The choice then fell to Tomás Estrada Palma, of long service in the independence cause. In May, 1902, Governor Wood turned over the government to the President, and sailed with his aides for New York. There was general rejoicing, although cautious men shook their heads with foreboding, saying that the Americans had left too soon.

THE REPUBLIC UNDER THE PLATT AMENDMENT, 1902–34

Cuba was now free—but not free to make her own mistakes. That was the meaning implicit in the Platt Amendment, under whose protection, or threat, Cuba lived for thirty-two years. The rereading of the record suggests a clear lesson on the education of nations, as of children: that none learns to order its life unless granted the privilege of going wrong as well as of going right. In Cuba's case, the well-meant policy of the United States imposed a split personality on the presidents of the newborn republic, who were under bond to serve two masters, the Cuban electorate, and the government in Washington. In the futile effort to propitiate both masters, they could please neither.

Yet the republic got off to a good start under the new president. Sixty-seven and robust, Estrada Palma in his first term (1902–06) gave grounds for faith in Cuba's future.[2] He won a reciprocal trade treaty from the United States in 1903, under which Cuban sugar was given a 20 per cent reduction in tariff duties—an arrangement which, with some modifications, prevailed until 1960. Such a favorable advantage stimulated a rapid increase in sugar production. He also persuaded Washington to renounce its claim to an indefinite number of coaling and naval bases and to be content with Guantánamo Bay and one lesser site, which was relinquished in 1912. In domestic matters Estrada Palma was beset by greedy generals and patriots-for-profit who opposed his efforts to abolish the standing army, fought his economy measures calling for reduction of civil employees, and undermined his efforts to improve municipal administration. In the face of such opposition Estrada Palma developed a surprising degree of honesty and efficiency in public servants, reduced graft in the army, enlarged the public school system, and increased the treasury balance from the mere $689,000 inherited from Leonard Wood's administration to $25 million by 1906.

The year 1906 brought the first test for the Platt Amendment. Estrada Palma had been reelected for another four-year term in a contest in which his "Moderate" party and his "Liberal" opponents were both guilty of fraud. Within a few months after the election, the Liberals, led by José Miguel Gómez and Alfredo Zayas, provoked a revolution which spread over the island. There was little shooting—it was more "a war of bulletins than of bullets"—but it offered Estrada Palma an excuse to appeal for help to President Theodore Roosevelt. The American president sent William Howard Taft to persuade the quarreling Cubans to compose their differences. When that pacific effort failed, Roosevelt—appealing to the Platt Amendment—named Charles Magoon, a Nebraska lawyer, as governor to supplant the elected president. The awkward but assiduous Magoon quieted the stormy contestants, enforced some measures of reform upon public administration, and supervised a reasonably honest election which gave the presidency to José Miguel Gómez in 1909. Magoon then withdrew.[3]

Scrutiny of Cuban politics after 1909 makes sorry reading. There was increased venality in public offices, betrayal of trust by presidents, re-

[2] But many Cubans still regard Estrada Palma with disfavor, charging him with excess of zeal for serving the United States.

[3] Magoon is a target for abuse by Cuban writers, who have called him "gross . . . rude . . . he falls like a buzzard on the Treasury of Cuba, and devours it." Such charges are unsubstantiated. Magoon was honest and reasonably efficient. See Charles E. Chapman: *A History of the Cuban Republic* (New York: The Macmillan Co.; 1927), ch. X.

sort to violence by disaffected factions, and finally, gross rule by violence. Washington intervened time and again, sometimes by sending a battleship, landing marines, or appointing an "adviser"; more often by a discreet warning delivered to the Cuban president by the American ambassador.

José Miguel Gómez (1909–13) was indubitably popular. "In all my life," he confided, "I have been jovial in spirit, with a smile on my lips." With a smile Gómez emptied the treasury and allowed Cuban and American cronies to fatten on concessions. His successor, Mario García Menocal (1913–21), a graduate of Cornell University, seemed a happier choice, but he too succumbed to the infection of easy money for himself and his friends. His fraudulent reelection in 1917 provoked a revolt which was put down by a brief visit of American troops. When the United States declared war on Germany in 1917, Menocal's congress obediently did the same. Concurrent with the accession of Alfredo Zayas (1921–25), Cuba was caught in the postwar collapse in sugar prices; local banks were closing their doors, the national treasury was empty, and the new president's rule by plunder offered no hope for the citizens. Meanwhile, President Woodrow Wilson had devised a new and, it was hoped, less painful form of intervention. In January, 1921, while Menocal was still in office, General Enoch Crowder had been sent by Washington as an adviser without formal diplomatic status. Zayas was forced to accept Crowder with what grace he could summon. For two years Crowder dictated cuts in the budget, uncovered crooked contracts, and finally imposed an "honest cabinet"; this last step was the price for Washington's consent to a $50-million loan from a New York bank. Crowder's work, heatedly denounced by most Cuban historians, wrought a considerable recovery. In 1923 he was named American ambassador, and the painless intervention was theoretically over. Zayas, now feeling strong enough to play his own hand, dismissed the "honest cabinet," named his own cronies to principal posts, and reverted to the shady practices temporarily blocked by Crowder.

The next president, Gerardo Machado (1925–33), was welcomed by solid citizens, who said he was a businessman and would bring order out of chaos. His first measures were reassuring. He launched a successful campaign for crop diversification, a needed corrective to the treacherous dependence upon sugar. He encouraged mineral production and expansion of industry. Drawing upon the easy loans which New York banks were pressing upon all Latin American governments in the 1920's, Machado began numerous public works—some useful but expensive, such as the 700-mile highway from end to end of the island; and some foolish, such as the $20-million marble capitol.

Meanwhile, evidence accumulated that Machado, despite an increase in government efficiency, was not averse to making a profit for himself and his favorites. Inevitably attacked by his political rivals, he created a personal political machine more effective than any his predecessors had devised. He secured the obedience of congress by passing out *colecturías* (agencies) for the National Lottery, each worth $2,000 or $3,000 per month to the lucky holder. While imposing unwonted honesty upon minor officials, he rewarded his inner circle with handsome incomes from concessions and contracts. By 1928, when he was reelected, the opposition was noisy and determined. Students organized demonstrations against him, whereupon he closed the University. Students and professional men organized the ABC, a society with 30,000 to 40,000 members, and there ensued a contest in terror. Machado's gunmen, the *porristas,* shot down students in the streets and invaded private homes without warrant. The ABC collected machine guns, operated a secret radio for the taunting of the dictator, and even dropped a bomb on the national palace.

The Cuban tyranny presented an unpleasant dilemma to the Herbert Hoover administration. Intervention was the obvious solution, but Washington had learned the futility of that course. Nonintervention, the course elected, incited angry denunciation from Cubans and many Americans. Harry Guggenheim, Hoover's ambassador, could urge Machado to be decent, but he could not enforce his requests—and was noisily damned by American liberals. Such was the deadlock in 1933 when Franklin D. Roosevelt became president. In May astute Sumner Welles was sent as ambassador with instructions to apply discreet pressure to effect a change. Emboldened by Washington's support, the ABC and other opposition groups became more active, and in August they called a general strike. Business was at a standstill, and the army demanded a change. On August 12 Machado took a plane for the Bahamas, and the Havana mobs looted the homes of "the butcher" and his friends. Order was quickly restored by a provisional government headed by respected Carlos Manuel de Céspedes, but this new regime, "made in Washington," was only twenty-one days old when it was overthrown by "the sergeants' revolt."[4] This was led by Sergeant Fulgencio Batista, who, after deposing almost 500 of his superior officers and naming his fellow conspirators to their places, promoted himself to the grade of colonel and chief of staff and became overnight the most powerful man on the island. Batista appointed Ramón Grau San Martín, physician and university professor, as provisional president. Grau's government, refused recognition by Washington, lasted but four months.

The fall of Machado marked the end of an era for Cuba. The one lesson thoroughly learned by Washington was the futility of the Platt Amendment, a conclusion strengthened by Sumner Welles's role as president-maker in the tumultuous summer of 1933. That able diplomat returned to Washington, where he was instrumental in the abrogation of the Platt Amendment in 1934.

FULGENCIO BATISTA, 1934–59

By 1934 Cuba had passed from the era of the Platt Amendment to the era of Batista. The one-time sergeant, after his decisive part in the martial events of 1933, gradually emerged as the arbiter of the island's destiny,

4 The author recalls reporting to Sumner Welles, after a conversation with a leader of the ABC: "They say they are going to throw out *your* man Céspedes and put in Grau San Martín." To which Welles spiritedly replied: "They will do no such thing." But they did.

in a dictatorship "mild, suave, and sweet," as he later described his rule. Until 1940 he ruled through puppets, seven of them in seven years, with Carlos Mendieta, Miguel Mariano Gómez, and Federico Laredo Brú the principal incumbents. In 1940 he assumed the presidency in his own name. In 1944, with commendable regard for legality—and, according to rumor, in deference to a personal request from Franklin D. Roosevelt—he permitted the election of his old ally, now a rival, Dr. Ramón Grau San Martín. In 1948 he withheld his hand as Carlos Prío Socarrás was chosen. In 1952, by a plot of his contriving, Batista again seized the presidency and sent Prío into exile. He was not ousted until New Year's Day, 1959.

Fulgencio Batista was only thirty-two when he led the coup of September, 1933, by which he flouted the seasoned politicians of the island, the entire corps of commissioned officers, and the prestige of the United States as represented by Ambassador Sumner Welles. The story of Batista's rise from poverty to riches furnishes inspiration of a sort to small boys in Cuban streets. Born on a farm in eastern Cuba in 1901, he had started out as a cane cutter, banana picker, bartender, and barber; at twenty, he joined the army, studied shorthand, and acted as stenographer to officers. By 1933 he had attracted a considerable following among noncommissioned officers and enlisted men, and with their help he carried through the overturn of 1933.

He ruled as dictators have always ruled in Latin America, by grace of the army. By 1934 almost all the principal officers owed their commissions to him and were not allowed to forget it. He did not neglect the enlisted men: he raised their pay, built fine barracks, furnished good uniforms and excellent food, provided recreation fields, and established pension funds; the 30,000 men in the army, navy, air force, and police became and continued to be his first reliance. Colonel Batista did not neglect other sectors. He knew full well the appetite of middle-class Cubans for public office, and he used his patronage to full effect, granting and withholding appointments in a fashion to strengthen his grip upon the island. Organized labor was cultivated with skill, and thousands of workers profited from the dictator's improvements in wages and working conditions. With the backing of the military forces, the civil servants of the republic, and the organized workers, Batista could face the grumblings of the intellectuals with a smile.

Up to 1944, Batista gave Cuba better government than it had ever had. Country roads and city streets were safer. Public business was conducted more expeditiously. Civil servants worked harder and engaged in less minor pilfering. The school system was enlarged, and entrusted to the direction of army officers. Public works—roads, bridges, harbor installations, and power plants—increased amazingly. With steady sugar prices, the national treasury was filled. The nagging ills of the Machado dictatorship scarcely appeared. The press enjoyed a considerable freedom much of the time. Political murders were infrequent. Critics of the government were not hustled off to jail—not so many, at least. Graft was reduced, or at least regularized. Batista himself grew rich from commissions on contracts, kick-

backs on customs, and percentages on the National Lottery. When he retired in favor of Grau in 1944 and went to live in Florida, he was able to
settle a fortune upon his divorced wife. Cautious observers said that he
had other millions invested in Florida apartment houses and like ventures.

Cuba's experiences with Grau San Martín (1944–48) and Prío Socarrás (1948–52) persuaded many worthy citizens that Batista was indispensable. Grau came to the presidency with the prestige of a distinguished
physician and an effective fighter against Machado, holding the affection
of several generations of university students. As president, he disappointed
the hopes of his admirers. He could not control the grafters who surrounded him, nor could he persuade his congress to adopt his reforms.
There was steady deterioration in public services and increased corruption
in high places and in low. The record of Prío Socarrás was even worse.
Thievery reached new heights, and the President himself was able to build
a remarkable house in nearby La Chata at a cost of some $2 million or $3
million—on his salary of $25,000. The breakdown of police forces, courts,
and public administration was so complete as to threaten profitable business
and scare off foreign investors.

There was, therefore, general relief when Batista made his spectacular and illegal return to power in March, 1952. It was done in the best
cuartelazo (barracks-revolt) tradition: the careful planning of twenty-seven
conspirators, the signal at 2:43 in the morning, the seizure of the army barracks at Camp Columbia, the exile of President Prío, the complete triumph
of Batista. The dictatorship he imposed was thorough. The press was muzzled, the University closed; some critics escaped into exile and others were
jailed. Within a few months an armed rebellion was put down swiftly,
Congress was indefinitely dissolved (but its members kept on the payroll),
and military law was declared.

Batista's last seven years in the presidency (1952–59) were marked
by growing repression, terrorism by the police, and violent reprisals from
angry citizens. Meanwhile, the island's economy boomed, sugar averaging
more than 75 per cent of export revenues, with scattered profits from
tobacco and mineral products. The Havana skyline was proud with fine
new hotels and public buildings. A tunnel was bored under Havana harbor
to a new subdivision promoted by cronies of the dictator. Never were the
Cubans richer—at least, those Cubans who held office, who were granted
concessions, who owned land and fine businesses—and the richest of them
all was ex-sergeant Fulgencio Batista. In fact, under Batista Cuba had
everything—except liberty.

REVOLUTION

The concerted attack upon the Batista dictatorship began among university
students. On July 26, 1953—little more than a year after Batista had seized
office—some 165 youths stormed the Moncada Army Barracks in Santiago: more than half of them fell before machine-gun fire, while the

survivors fled. Their leader was twenty-six-year-old Fidel Castro, a law student and the son of a wealthy sugar planter; he and his brother Raúl had been plotting for many months. Fidel Castro and other survivors of the Barracks incident managed to escape from Batista's police, while official gunmen wreaked vengeance upon citizens of doubtful loyalty. Castro then decided to surrender in order to put an end to the ruthless slaughter. On August 1, Fidel and Raúl gave themselves up and were sentenced to fifteen-year prison terms. Eleven months later, under pressure of public opinion, Batista extended amnesty to the Castro brothers and others. Fidel Castro fled to Mexico, where he gathered new and old allies around him, and planned his next attack upon Batista. On December 2, 1956, he landed with eighty-two men on the southeastern coast. Though most of them were shot by a detachment of Batista's army, a bare dozen, including Fidel and Raúl, found safety in the rugged jungles of the Sierra Maestra, west of the city of Santiago.

There followed a two-year siege of Fidel Castro's Sierra Maestra jungle hideout, which he managed to hold against all the weight of Fulgencio Batista's army, navy, and air force (and, shall we add, against the planes, tanks, and assorted oddments contributed by the United States of America to the cause of "hemispheric defense"). For sheer audacity, the saga of those young men deserves a place with Cortés's conquest of Tenochtitlán and Pizarro's march on Cajamarca. That little band of bearded youths, daily augmented by volunteers who pushed through the armed lines, got food, clothing, and arms from friends all over the island, and from sympathizers in Mexico, the United States, and elsewhere. They also sent out raiding parties to collect supplies from nearby plantations. When Batista's army and air force seemed about to wipe them out, Castro's men began to burn sugar fields. The movement spread underground until there were rebel units throughout the island. In March, 1957, twenty-one young men forced their way into the presidential palace and almost succeeded in killing the dictator.

At each step in this drama the Batista government declared that Castro was dead, and the rebellion ended. In February, 1957, Herbert L. Matthews of *The New York Times* scored a journalistic triumph by making his way through the army lines to Castro's jungle hideout and bringing back word to the world that the young man was alive, and he had photographs to prove it.

In November, 1957, a meeting was held in Miami at which the followers of ex-Presidents Grau San Martín and Prío Socarrás pledged to make common cause with Fidel Castro—a move promptly repudiated by Castro, who proposed to have no traffic with those discredited leaders.

The year 1958 was marked by a running fight between the rebels and the government. Castro and his men continued to burn, pillage, rob, and terrorize. Batista retaliated with wholesale torture and murder of suspected rebel sympathizers. In February unexpected encouragement came to the rebels from the Roman Catholic Church: a pastoral letter from the bishops called for "a government of national unity which can restore our country to normal and peaceful political life." In that same month, the news of the overthrow of Venezuela's Pérez Jiménez brought cheer to the fighters in the Sierra Maestra. By plane and by ship, fresh recruits and new supplies of arms reached Castro's camp. In March the United States placed an embargo on shipment of arms to the government of Batista—but the illegal flow of materiel to the rebels continued.

In April Fidel Castro called for a general strike against Batista; when it failed to materialize, Batista again announced that Fidel was dead and that the battle was over. Meanwhile, Raúl Castro had established another rebel stronghold in the Sierra del Cristal in the eastern province of Oriente. As the result of this running battle between Castro's forces and Batista's there was anarchy in the eastern end of the island, with practically all communications paralyzed. Castro's tactics included kidnapping of American employees of sugar plantations and of mines; these measures brought sharp words from Washington. Castro also took reprisals against British-owned enterprises in the area, when England continued to sell planes and arms to the Batista government. Meanwhile, Batista, despite the defeats which he was suffering from Castro's guerrillas, went ahead with the presidential election of November, 1958, and his candidate was handsomely elected— although most of the voters refused to vote. By December it was clear that Batista's time was up. "Batista didn't fall," write two astute reporters, Karl Meyer and Tad Szulc, "he collapsed. His army wasn't really beaten; it was eroded away by corruption, low morale, and staggeringly incompetent leadership."

New Year's Day, 1959, marked the end of the long era of Batista. Word spread that morning that the dictator, his family, and scores of his aides had fled by plane and ship—Batista had joined the growing colony of unseated tyrants in Santo Domingo. The rejoicing was not confined to the ragged mobs: sober citizens generally applauded the end of Batista. The red-and-black flags of the "26 of July" movement appeared on buildings, automobiles, trucks; portraits of the bearded Fidel Castro were placarded on walls everywhere. The young rebel was Cuba's messiah.

FIDEL CASTRO: THE FIRST PHASES

As the ragged and gaunt young men of Fidel Castro's victorious army straggled into Havana during the first week of January, 1959, some bystanders may have recalled a remark made by Batista nine years before: "This island would be a paradise if it were properly governed." At this writing (1967), we ask how properly the island has been governed by Fidel Castro. Certainly it has been a one-man rule: many who had stood by Castro during the years in the Sierra Maestra were eliminated when they dared to argue with Premier Fidel. A conspicuous victim was Castro's hand-picked president, the incorruptible Manuel Urrutia Lleó, eliminated in July, 1959, because he mildly criticized Fidel's measures. He replaced Urrutia by the little-known Oswaldo Dorticós Torrado, who proved a valuable and durable aide. Closest to Fidel, and his two ablest colleagues, were his brother Raúl, chief of the armed forces, and Ernesto "Che" Guevara, the Argentine-born physician who served as Fidel's chief economic adviser from the first days in the Sierra Maestra until his mysterious disappearance in 1965. As a basis for judging Fidel Castro, after almost nine years in office, we have both his words and his acts. Castro has proved the most talkative of messiahs: during many hours on television, he has delivered himself of millions of words for the consumption of his followers and for the confounding of his enemies. And there has been plenty of action.

Fidel Castro ordered swift punishment for the "criminals" of Batista's regime (and, let it be freely admitted, many of them were criminals): by the end of March, 483 persons (by official count) had faced firing squads after trials notable for their brevity and levity. Thousands of Batista's aides were jailed. And the roll of those executed and jailed was steadily augmented by followers of Castro who were guilty of disagreeing with him. When the American press suggested that Fidel's pattern of justice was not in the highest Anglo-Saxon tradition, Cuban spokesmen countered by asking: "Why had not the squeamish American public been outraged by the bestial cruelty of Batista's police?"

Castro made a clean sweep of government departments, placing his faithful servants in all key positions. Announcing that Batista had plundered to the tune of $200 million (which may have been true), he demanded scrupulous honesty from all public servants—with substantial success.

Land reform was the spearhead of Castro's program. The Agrarian Reform Law, hailed as the Magna Charta of the revolution, went into effect officially in June, 1959, although as early as February Castro had begun to seize the lands of the *batistianos*. The great estates—Cuban, Spanish, American—were to be sliced up; the owners were to be permitted to retain certain minimum properties and were to be compensated with 4¼ per cent national bonds; each peasant family was to receive two *caballerías* (about 66.3 acres). The handling of this land reform was entrusted to the National Institute of Agrarian Reform (INRA), to which Fidel Castro dedicated much of his attention. During the years 1959 and 1960 there was wholesale expropriation of sugar, tobacco, and cattle lands. Machinery, cattle, and agricultural equipment were taken over without compensation. Many large holdings—Cuban and foreign—were seized from families which had worked them for several generations. The United Fruit Company, whose holdings of some 270,000 acres had been scientifically developed for sugar cane and cattle raising, and which had combined effective management with prudent social services, was stripped of its properties. Meanwhile, the promises of the land reform bill were not fulfilled. The owners of land received no bonds, nor were the bonds even printed. And the landless peasants, instead of receiving those 66.3-acre plots, found themselves drafted to work on great cooperative farms managed by the Institute.

Alongside the expropriation of land came seizure of other properties, both Cuban and foreign. Hotel and country club properties were seized. The two leading newspapers in Havana were confiscated. The banks were nationalized. American mining operators with concessions to dig iron ore, sulfur, nickel, cobalt, and other minerals soon found their operations hampered and their properties seized. In mid-1960, the three American-owned oil refineries, after their owners had refused to process Soviet petro-leum, were taken over by the Cuban government; and United States-owned sugar mills were confiscated. "Our hardest fight," announced "Che" Guevara, then president of the Banco Nacional de Cuba, "is against the North American monopolies."

In the first weeks of 1959 Washington was disposed to be hopeful about the new Cuban "revolution." There was belated recognition of the fact that the United States had upheld the hand of the dictator, Batista, and an inclination to give Fidel Castro the benefit of every doubt. To be sure there was some alarm, first in reaction to the summary trials and executions, then to the seizures of American properties. But official Washington con-tinued to give proof of its friendly attitude toward Cuba by appointing intel-ligent and liberal Philip Bonsal as ambassador to Havana in February, 1959. Bonsal, one of the ablest career officers, had won laurels as a foe of dictators in his brush with Rojas Pinilla in Colombia. Upon reaching Havana, Bonsal made clear to Fidel that the United States sought to cooperate with the new government fully and generously. When Castro prepared to visit Washington in April, 1959, Bonsal learned that Castro's suite of fifty included his prin-cipal economic advisers; the Ambassador endeavored without success to learn what they hoped to accomplish in the American capital, and he sought to make it clear to the Cuban leader that the United States was disposed to discuss any or all issues with candor. Castro, however, continued to describe his trip to Washington as purely unofficial and to insist that he asked no favors. As it turned out, it was an entirely friendly visit, the Cuban lunching with the Secretary of State, among others. Though there was no intimation that the visitors had any ulterior motives, it was quite clear—at least at this stage—that the American government was quite willing to extend financial aid to the new regime on the island. But by this time the American press had angered Fidel by its denunciation of his highhanded ways, and the mild-mannered Bonsal was subjected to repeated slights and insults from Castro and his aides: Castro himself refused to see Bonsal for three months.

The United States was now the chief target of Castro's invective. The American press was accused of being subsidized by pro-Batista elements. The American State Department, scrupulously adhering to a policy of moderation, was subject to fervid abuse. When the Eisenhower administra-tion, despite Castro's brusque treatment, assured Cuba of its "interest in, and sympathy for, agrarian reform," affirming its "full support of soundly conceived programs for rural betterment, including land reform," the over-ture was angrily repulsed, and Castro continued to treat the American Ambassador as the agent of an aggressive power. Castro's reaction is under-standable: he did not realize that the American government in 1960 was quite different in temper from that of Philander C. Knox in the days of "dollar diplomacy." In interminable harangues on television, Castro accused the United States of aggression and hostile plotting. When small planes, flying from private fields in Florida, made trips over Cuban territory, Castro charged that these trips constituted a deliberate invasion of Cuban privacy by the United States. When Washington ordered strict control of such flights—very difficult to achieve, since there are over 200 pint-sized airfields in Florida—Castro was still not satisfied and continued to accuse the American government of bad faith. When Washington sought to persuade its European allies to refuse arms and planes to the Castro government, there was fresh outburst of anger. In March, 1960, a French ship, *La Coubre,* carrying munitions from Belgium blew up in Havana's harbor, killing some seventy men: Castro immediately went on the air to denounce this outrage as still another instance of American "sabotage," and the State Department's protest was dismissed by Castro as "insulting." Further patient notes from Washington were met with further outcries of vituperation.

The United States, castigated almost daily by the Cuban Premier, maintained notable restraint for more than a year. By early 1960, however, angry congressmen were calling for punitive measures against the Castro government, and in June Washington finally struck back. Empowered by Congress, President Eisenhower decreed an end to all American purchases of Cuban sugar for the balance of the year, intimating that this cancellation would stand for 1961. This was a body blow to Cuba, in spite of "Che" Guevara's branding of the American quota system as "economic slavery"— a curious term for a system by which the United States paid some $150 million a year *more* for Cuban sugar than Cuba could have got for it anywhere else. Then the State Department warned tourists against visiting Cuba. And the administration clamped an embargo upon all exports to Cuba, except for food and medicine. Critics of the Eisenhower policy, both in and out of the United States, denounced these measures as calculated to throw Cuba more conclusively into the Communist orbit, arguing that the United States would have been wiser to invite multilateral action by the OAS.

Fidel's reply to Washington was a fresh torrent of abuse. His program of expropriation (or more properly, perhaps, of confiscation) of American properties was speeded up. By November, 1960, almost all American-owned properties, including lands, mining companies, oil refineries, banks, mercantile enterprises, hotels, industrial plants, utility concerns—with assets valued at more than $1 billion—had been seized.

Fidel Castro's cold war on Washinghon was marked by his courting of the Communist powers. After a visit by Russia's Mikoyan, in February, 1960, the U.S.S.R. granted the Castro government a credit of $100 million, also agreeing to buy 5 million tons of Cuban sugar over a five-year period —at the world price (about 2 cents a pound below the price paid by the Americans). In April came a trade pact with Poland: in exchange for sugar, Warsaw promised Cuba sundry industrial goods, including helicopters— those last seemingly designed for attacks upon Castro's enemies in the Caribbean area, including the Trujillo government in the Dominican Republic. (When Washington protested, Fidel charged the United States with fomenting revolt.) In July Cuba signed a barter agreement with the People's Republic of China by which China would buy 500,000 tons of Cuban sugar annually, to be paid for mostly in rice.

Meanwhile formal diplomatic relations were inaugurated with the U.S.S.R. in May, 1960, and the Russian Embassy in Havana was opened with much fanfare. The ebullient Khrushchev supported Fidel Castro's denunciation of the United States by promising that "rockets would fly" to protect the sovereignty of Cuba. And in September Castro announced that Cuba would recognize the People's Republic of China and break relations with Formosa—and Cuba became the first Latin American republic to recognize the Peking regime.

Meanwhile, Fidel Castro's agents in all the Latin American capitals busily provoked outcry against the "imperialistic" United States. In Panama Cuba's diplomats joined hands with those of the United Arab Republic in inciting demands for the seizure of the Panama Canal. In Guatemala, Honduras, and Costa Rica they stirred up local attacks upon the United Fruit Company. In Venezuela the *fidelistas*—including many university students—conspired with the Communists to embarrass the constructive regime of Rómulo Betancourt. Castro's admirers in Mexico united with the Communists in organizing demonstrations against Washington. In Bolivia the *fidelistas* yoked their efforts with those of Juan Lechín and his perpetually angry tin miners to harass President Paz Estenssoro. In all the other republics *fidelista* sentiment was strident among university students, and even sober and reasonable citizens were inclined to regard Fidel as the instrument for releasing Latin America from "the tyranny of American imperialism." The force of this appeal became clear at the meeting of the Organization of American States in San José, Costa Rica, in August, 1960; in the resolution deploring Communist inroads in the Western Hemisphere, the Latin American states refused to name Cuba.

The Communist label had been fixed upon Fidel and his cohorts within six months after they seized power. In June, 1959, a Cuban high in Castro's councils defected and made his way to Washington, where he testified before the Senate Internal Security Committee that the Castro regime was indeed "Communist." In July, Senators Keating and Mundt repeated the charge in the Senate. From then on the label stuck, in spite of the warnings of such men as Senator Fulbright, chairman of the Senate Foreign Relations Committee, who advised "patience" with Cuba and avoidance of the "Communist tag." Ambassador Bonsal had steadily been giving the same advice to the President. Query for the record: Was Fidel perhaps driven into Communist ranks by this early barrage of charges?

Fidel Castro carried his indictment of the United States to the United Nations in September, 1960. His stormy days in New York were climaxed by a four-hour speech at the UN, in which he loudly declaimed the sins of the United States and decried the crimes of colonialism everywhere—words which were cheered by the new Asian and African states, as well as by some Latin Americans.

The inevitable break in diplomatic relations between the United States and Cuba came in January, 1961. The redoubtable Fidel ordered the American Embassy to cut its staff to eleven—not enough men and women to run the elevators, to handle the air conditioning, and to sweep out the hallways of that impressive building. President Eisenhower, in one of his last official acts, responded by the formal severance of relations with the island republic.

CUBA, THE UNITED STATES, AND SUGAR

We digress briefly to consider the two fundamental weaknesses of Cuba's position throughout its unhappy history—the tyranny of sugar over the island's economy, and the smothering nearness of the United States—and to assess their responsibility for the plight of Fidel Castro in the 1960's.

Cuba's indictment of the United States over the years should be met with candor. Much can be said for Washington's fair treatment of Cuba: we did set Cuba free in 1898; we withdrew in 1902, and made the withdrawal unequivocal by the abrogation of the Platt Amendment in 1934; after 1934 we sedulously refrained from interfering in the island's affairs; and despite the provocations by Fidel Castro, punitive measures were not taken against the Havana government until 1960. The charge of imperialism against the United States is specious. But it should be freely conceded that the overshadowing power of the United States, with money to be invested, was largely responsible for some of the island's ills, and, specifically, for the concentration of land in a few hands. Under the generous trade relations established after Cuba became independent, there was an inevitable flood of American capital into the sugar business of the island, and this caused mischief. "It is a striking paradox," wrote the authors of the Foreign Policy Association's report (1935) on the island's economy, "that, as a consequence of its struggle for political independence, Cuba lost control over its economic resources." This did not represent a gigantic American conspiracy against the island; it was simply the result of a poor, weak nation living under the shadow of a rich and powerful one.

There were several steps by which Cuban farmers lost control of the lands which yielded sugar and lesser crops. The traditional Spanish *comunera* system of landholdings, under which a large part of the Cuban land was owned collectively (and worked inefficiently), was ended by the American military authorities after 1898, and the way was cleared for the increasing concentration of ownership in the hands of mill owners and large corporate interests. During the same transition there emerged thousands of *colonos* (usually tenant farmers, but often outright owners of small plots) who lived by their contracts with the mills and corporations which dominated the sugar industry. The *colono* was often a self-respecting operator, although he was at the mercy of the large operators, who in turn were at the mercy of the fluctuating world price of sugar. In fact all who were dependent upon sugar—the large mill operators, the numerous *colonos,* and the great body of day laborers who worked in the fields—were chronically buffeted by shifting world supply and demand, over which they had no control. Almost all nations sought and often achieved self-sufficiency in sugar production. And Cuba, chief world producer, alternately profited and suffered under the varying fortunes of the world market. For Cuba, there was "boom," and then there was "bust." The most dramatic chapter in Cuba's sugar experience came at the end of World War I in 1919. European markets were a shambles; production of almost all crops had suffered cataclysmic upsets—and sugar was one item much in demand. Cuban sugar producers had boundless optimism: a hungry Europe would buy all they could produce. The mills went into debt to the banks to extend their fields. The *colonos* went into debt to the mill operators to finance their operations. This reckless process (assuring the output of more sugar than the world could buy) reached its peak in 1920, when sugar prices soared to an all-time high of 22.5 cents a pound—whereupon the people squandered their paper profits in an orgy of high living which observers called "The Dance of the Millions." But the "dance" was short-lived. Within six months, the price of sugar crashed to 3.75 cents a pound. Many of the mill owners, mortgaged to the banks, lost their holdings. Many of the *colonos,* in debt to the mills, lost whatever equity they had. Much of the mortgaged land, large units as well as small, was thrown upon the open market, and the stronger corporations were able to extend their hold over the best land of Cuba. Then, this increase of latifundia was speeded up during the desperate depression years 1924–33 (the Great Depression reached Cuba five years before it struck the United States), when the price of sugar dropped to an all-time low of 0.57 cents a pound in the summer of 1932. With each turn of the screw, the well-financed outsiders had their advantage in adding new acres to their handsome holdings.

Sugar was thus responsible for fixing the latifundia pattern upon Cuba —a pattern which afflicts much of Latin America. By 1946, about three-quarters of the nation's farm acreage was concentrated in 8 per cent of the holdings; and, even more significant, a mere 0.5 per cent of the farms embraced more than one-third of all farm land. A further weakness in the land pattern was the immense, but unreckoned, amount of good soil withheld from cultivation, maintained as a reserve for future growing of sugar.

This was the pattern of land tenure which confronted the new and untested leaders of Cuba in 1959. But to say that the United States was the villain who had foisted this inequity upon the island proved too much; for the American share in the control of the sugar industry had dropped steadily even before Fidel took over: it was about 70 per cent in 1928, and was down to about 24 per cent in 1958. And the Cuban-owned share in the sugar industry rose from 22.4 per cent in 1939 to 60.2 per cent in 1950; and 62.1 per cent of the sugar mills were Cuban-owned in 1959, with Cuban minority interests in some of the American-owned mills making the Cuban share even larger. And so the colonial status of the Cuban economy was gradually lessening well before Fidel Castro made his spectacular moves.

Ever since Cuba emerged as an independent nation, the United States has sought to encourage Cuban economic health (and also to tie the Cuban market to that of the United States). By the Commercial Convention of 1903, Washington gave Cuba a 20 per cent tariff advantage on sales of her products in the American market, and Cuba reciprocated by giving equal preference to American goods. This arrangement gave great advantages to both parties: during the 1920's Cuba furnished about 50 per cent of all the sugar consumed in the United States, and the United States furnished about 75 per cent of all Cuba's imports. A major blow to this mutually profitable trade pattern was the Hawley-Smoot tariff bill of 1930 with its increased duty on sugar: this was instrumental in cutting down Cuba's sales of sugar to the United States from the previous rate of about 50 per cent of American consumption to about 30 per cent. However, by the Jones-Costigan Act of 1934, we adopted the quota system under which our sugar purchases would be allocated among the various countries; from 1934 to 1960 about one-third came from Cuba.[5] Furthermore, we artificially maintained the domestic price of sugar in the United States at roughly 2 cents a pound above the world price: while this was designed primarily to protect American sugar producers, the favored treatment was extended to Cuban sugar. Washington's policy tended to eliminate the more drastic fluctuations in the price of sugar, and also yielded a bonus to Cuba of some $150 million annually.

Cuba's economic fate is inevitably linked with sugar—as Fidel Castro has belatedly begun to realize. As a producer of sugar for export, Cuba stands first among all the nations. During 1948–58 her fields yielded an average of 5.5 million tons annually—about 13 per cent of all the sugar produced in the world. But reliance on sugar is also the Achilles' heel of the Cuban economy. In almost all nations there has been progress toward national self-sufficiency in sugar, even though, as in the United States, domestic production is costly and can survive only behind tariff barriers. As a result of this world situation, Cuba has never been able to sell as much sugar as she could produce, as was shown by the experience of 1952 when Cuban production reached about 8 million tons—more than the world would buy. Castro's ambitious program for increasing sugar production —even if it should succeed—will have to be matched by a no less ambitious search for new markets.

FIDEL CASTRO: THE STORY CONTINUES

Cuba's tortuous course after the breaking of ties with Washington in January, 1961, was complicated by further dealings with the United States, the U.S.S.R., and the People's Republic of China—as well as by Cuba's own internal problems. The first major incident was the Bay of Pigs affair in

[5] Under this system the American Secretary of Agriculture sets the total requirement of sugar in the United States. After allowing for domestic production, the balance is allocated to the various sugar-producing countries, their quotas fixed by acts of Congress at irregular intervals amid a feverish spate of lobbying. One of the complaints of Cuban nationalists was that the Cuban quota was decided unilaterally by the U.S. Congress, not by agreement between two sovereign nations.

April, 1961—an invasion attempt manned by Cuban exiles, and directed and financed by the United States. This bizarre and disastrous adventure may not stand as one of the chief military coups of history, but it can at least be put down as one of the most inept: Theodore Draper accurately describes it as a "perfect failure."

In May, 1960, the Eisenhower administration decided to entrust to the Central Intelligence Agency the task of rounding up Cuban refugees who wanted to unseat Fidel Castro; some 1,400 candidates were forthwith gathered into camps in Florida and Guatemala and trained for an attack upon Cuba. President John F. Kennedy inherited this plan when he came to office in January, 1961, and there followed weeks of unhappy debate within his administration: some would have canceled the plan outright, but their counsel was outweighed by the testimony of top advisers who argued that the plan was justified, and by the assurances of the CIA and the Joint Chiefs of Staff that it was workable.[6] The humiliating and total defeat of the brave Cuban band who landed at the Bay of Pigs on April 17, 1961, and were completely routed within seventy-two hours will long be remembered and variously explained. Some tentative observations are inescapable.

The crashing failure of the invasion raises the nagging question as to the wisdom of entrusting such a project to a secret agency—the question whether a democracy, with a free press and a congress free to speak its mind, can or should embark upon such a "cloak and dagger" operation. The innocent bystander may conjecture that this sort of huggermuggery should be left to police states whose leaders need neither explain nor consult. Furthermore, the secret agency involved in this instance seems to have been awkward: the leaders of the CIA were honorable men, but their secret planning was based on faulty intelligence sources and inadequately checked with the President; and not only did they show slight comprehension of the political and social realities within Cuba itself, but also—curiously—they seemed to have little understanding of the elementary techniques of subversion. The debate on the Bay of Pigs affair gives weight to the demands in Congress that the "watch dog committee" for overseeing the CIA should include representatives of the Senate Foreign Relations Committee, as well as of the Armed Services Committee and the Appropriations Committee.

The blunders of the CIA seem almost incredible. First, there was the inclusion in the expeditionary force of some well-known *batistianos,* men who were remembered for their share in the savagery of Batista's rule. (It is to be noted that President Kennedy ordered that the *batistianos not* be included.) And the most effective and dedicated group opposing Castro—the non-Communist People's Revolutionary Movement, led by Manuel Ray— was barred from any responsible share in the enterprise: Ray and his agents in Cuba were well organized for action, but even up to the day of the landing, Ray had not been informed that the invasion was under way. Strategically, it seems to have been a prime blunder to concentrate the attack on one spot

---

6 Useful testimony on this discussion, as well as on the whole affair of the Bay of Pigs, is given by Theodore C. Sorensen: *Kennedy* (New York: Harper & Row, 1965); and Arthur M. Schlesinger, Jr.: *A Thousand Days* (Boston: Houghton Mifflin Co., 1965).

rather than upon several targets. And then there are those who charge that the final defeat was due to Kennedy's refusal to furnish air cover for the operation—but most observers incline to the opinion that the venture was doomed before it began. Also, of course, there was no true secrecy at all: the expeditionary forces were honey-combed with Castro agents; newsmen in Miami knew most of the details of the plan (but most refrained from publishing them, for patriotic reasons);[7] Fidel Castro himself knew when and where the invaders would land and had his troops, tanks, and guns ready to receive them.

And so it came to pass that the 1,179 survivors of this quixotic band were rounded up, herded into prison, and duly exhibited to the press and interested friends. It gave Fidel special pride to point out some 100 of Batista's henchmen—"butchers" he called them—among the "fighters for freedom." (Castro's figure of 100 was probably an exaggeration.)

This was Fidel Castro's finest hour. He had won an immense propaganda weapon: had he not defeated the all-powerful U.S.A.? The fiasco was a bitter blow to United States prestige everywhere: we had spent much time and many millions of dollars on a shabby failure. Specifically, it may have persuaded the U.S.S.R. that the United States was a "paper tiger," thus encouraging the foolhardy placing in Cuba of thermonuclear weapons a year later. And certainly Castro's agents throughout Latin America were emboldened to carry out campaigns of terror against governments in power. Not only had the United States been humbled, but Cuba's powerful allies renewed their pledges of support: from Moscow came exultant congratulations and warm assurances of Russia's continued loyalty; and a note from Peking brought the comforting word that China "firmly supports the sober and just attitude adopted by the Cuban government to safeguard its independence and sovereignty," stating that Cuba's victory over the United States "stimulates the fighting will of the peoples of America and all the world in their struggle against imperialism." "We Are Not Alone" was emblazoned in neon lights over Havana.

The pleasant aura of elation pervaded the domestic life of Cuba. Schools were being built, state farms were being extended, industries were being launched under the active hand of "Che" Guevara. Castro's Cuba was a going concern, even though dependent upon the continued largess from Moscow. True, there were crippling shortages of foodstuffs, a critical lack of spare parts to keep American-made machinery and automotive equipment running, a dearth of adequate housing in the cities, and the workers had to work long hours—but none of these things could depress the spirits of the rulers of the island. Emboldened by this sense of mastery, Fidel cracked down with new vigor upon his critics. In April, 1961, some 300 priests who had dared to protest the inroads of Communism—largely Spaniards and foreigners—were jailed, quickly released, and most of them left Cuba. Then,

7 At a White House meeting shortly after the Bay of Pigs affair, President Kennedy scolded top representatives of the press for "premature disclosures of security information." He then remarked in an aside to the executive editor of *The New York Times*: "If you had printed more about the operation you would have saved us from a colossal mistake." Reported by Clifton Daniel in *The New York Times*, June 2, 1966.

in October, in reprisal for fresh assault from the clergy, 1 bishop and 135 priests were expelled from the island—and this contingent included 46 Cubans.

Cuba's Communist sorties and continued subversive tactics in Latin America finally provoked the wrath of her neighbors: at a meeting of American foreign ministers at Punta del Este in January, 1962, Washington's spokesmen sought the expulsion of Cuba from the OAS. There was spirited resistance from many Latin Americans, motivated in part by long distaste for any "intervention," in part by a prudent awareness of the strong support Fidel Castro enjoyed within all the countries involved. The United States proposal to expel Cuba was accepted by a bare majority of 14, with 6 states refusing to vote. The holdouts—Brazil, Argentina, Chile, Mexico, Ecuador, and Bolivia—represented 139 million people out of less than 200 million Latin Americans. But even so it was a spirited slap at Fidel Castro. Cuba was now clearly marked as a Communist state. After months of hedging, Fidel had finally made his stand clear: on December 2, 1961, he had given the answer for which the world was waiting: "I am a Marxist-Leninist, and I will be a Marxist-Leninist until the last days of my life." That seemed explicit enough—but perhaps it was too neat. Many cautious or cynical observers continued to wonder: Exactly who is this Fidel, and just where is he going?

In October, 1962, came the missile crisis, in which the United States confronted the U.S.S.R. with an ultimatum so sharp as to carry the risk of a major war. The timetable of that affair will long be studied by historians.

Perhaps the whole thing began with Raúl Castro's visit to Moscow in July, 1962. It was then, in all probability, that the decision to install Russian nuclear missiles in Cuba was reached. Russia had trusted none of her allies or satellites with such weapons—not even China. But now Moscow decided to give them to an ineffectual and highly unreliable little friend 6,000 miles away. Why this Russian folly? The obvious explanation is that, after the Bay of Pigs affair, Khrushchev believed that the United States was weak and, confronted with a nuclear threat, would do nothing about it.

Shipments began in late July, 1962. Intelligence reports confirmed the arrival of Soviet "specialists" and new equipment, and the start of new military construction. On August 29 a report from U-2 flights brought word that surface-to-air missile sites were being built. To Kennedy's warning, Khrushchev replied that Washington's worries were ill-founded, that the U.S.S.R. had such powerful rockets and nuclear warheads that there would be no point in planting them beyond Soviet boundaries. Then Khrushchev went on to issue a warning of his own: the United States should refrain from aggression against Cuba. Continued U-2 flights over Cuba did nothing to allay Washington's forebodings, but still there was doubt that Khrushchev could be so foolhardy. Then on October 14, a U-2 returned with new photographs of western Cuba which revealed not only a launching pad and buildings for the housing of missiles, but even one ballistic missile in full view on the ground.

THE CARIBBEAN AND CENTRAL AMERICA

The news brought Washington up short. There was a chance that Cuba could strike at any moment, and that her borrowed thermonuclear weapons could destroy much of the United States—and much of Latin America. Under tight secrecy, President Kennedy met almost steadily for a week with his aides, the Joint Chiefs of Staff, and congressional leaders. There were divided counsels: some (notably the military) favored an immediate attack upon Cuba; others favored further diplomatic approaches; still others, an immediate blockade of the island to stop the flow of materiel and men into Cuba. The blockade course—a "quarantine," it would be called—won. Meanwhile, more messages were exchanged between Kennedy and Khrushchev. On October 22, barely eight days after the U-2 had brought its frightening evidence, President Kennedy went on the air to tell the American people what was happening: it was a somber and eloquent warning to Americans, to Cubans—and to Russians. The next day Kennedy issued his proclamation on the quarantine, for which he had secured a pledge of support from the OAS: as of 2 P.M., October 24, American forces would intercept ships carrying "offensive weapons and associated materiel" to Cuba. Khrushchev ordered all masters of Cuba-bound Russian ships to stay out of the interception zone—temporarily. Meanwhile the armed forces of the United States were put on the alert: some 40,000 marines were ready in Florida, another 5,000 on the base in Guantánamo; the Army brought some 100,000 troops to Florida; the Air Force readied the many airfields of Florida, and tactical fighter aircraft was flown in from bases all over the United States.

And the world sat before television sets—and waited.

It was a test of wills between Kennedy and the Russian leader. Kennedy was tough and quiet—he had his congress, the American people, and the hemisphere behind him. Khrushchev was tough and noisy—but he had met his match. After further exchange between the two world leaders, the Russians gave in: on October 29, just two weeks after the issue had been clarified by the U-2 flight, Khrushchev sent a message to Kennedy announcing that work would be stopped on "weapons construction sites," that weapons would be dismantled, crated, and returned to the Soviet Union.

The crisis was over—almost. The lethal machinery was packed up and shipped home. Many of the Russian "technicians" withdrew. But the inspection of Cuban missile sites by a UN agency, promised by Khrushchev, did not take place. When Castro threatened to shoot down American U-2 planes still watching the island, Khrushchev advised him to hold his hand. Fidel was beside himself with fury at Moscow for so ignominiously letting him down, but there was nothing he could do about it.

In the midst of the turmoil over Russian guns, there was another bit of international business to be cleaned up: the Cuban prisoners captured at the Bay of Pigs. President Kennedy and many other Americans felt morally bound to effect their release from the foul prisons to which Fidel Castro had committed them: after all, they were there because of the folly of the Washington government. In May, 1961, Castro had offered to exchange them for 500 heavy bulldozers, valued at some $28 million. Although Kennedy could not act for the government, unofficially he had a hand in organizing a Tractors for Freedom Committee, headed by Eleanor Roosevelt and enlisting stalwart Republican Milton Eisenhower; but its drive for funds was bogged down by politically inspired attacks spearheaded by former Vice-President Richard M. Nixon. Meanwhile the poor fellows rotted in their jails, abominably treated and often tortured, and in March, 1962, they were tried and sentenced to long terms in prison. Fidel Castro then raised the price for their ransom to $62 million, an impossible figure. At this point there entered upon the scene a New York lawyer, James B. Donovan, who was suggested by Attorney General Robert Kennedy. Donovan flew to Havana, conferred with Castro, and after weeks of fantastic and determined negotiation persuaded him to accept a lesser sum in food and drugs instead of dollars. On December 2, 1962, President Kennedy greeted the first detachment of gaunt and sick survivors in the Orange Bowl in Miami. By July, 1965, practically all who had survived the Bay of Pigs were freed. Castro got his food and drugs, valued at some $53 million. And the Cuban refugees were restored to their families. The whole episode was a miracle of tact, persuasion, and unflagging energy—and unsparing credit goes to Donovan, the Kennedys, the drug companies, and many others.

The Cuban economy, in 1962 and 1963, underwent some drastic convulsions involving, first, the program of industrialization which was "Che" Guevara's pride and joy; and, second, the belated discovery that sugar was, after all, Cuba's principal asset.

Since the early days of the Castro administration, "Che" Guevara and others had preached the doctrine of industrialization for Cuba's economic salvation; and Castro's great and good friends in Russia, China, and Eastern Europe had fed this dream by promises of equipment and technicians: the U.S.S.R. would build 100 industrial plants and send technicians to install and operate them, these to include a steel mill, electric generating units, and oil refineries; China would contribute 24 factories, Rumania 15, Bulgaria 5, Poland 12, and East Germany 10; Czechoslovakia offered an automobile plant. Under the spell of their fine vision of a Cuba spouting smoke and turning out everything from carpet tacks to locomotives, the Cuban leaders decided that cane sugar was scarcely worthy of their attention: when the United States stopped buying Cuba's sugar, some Cubans decided that the matter was unimportant. But the industrial dream soon went sour. Cuba's friends in Moscow, Peking, and other way stations forgot to send most of the promised gifts: by mid-1963 few of the well-advertised factories had been installed. And the Cubans discovered to their astonishment that factories are not useful without raw materials; and that it was costing more to make plowshares and machetes than it would have cost to import them.

Somewhat disillusioned by the industrial chimera, Cubans took a hard look at their farm lands and at their chief product, sugar. By 1962 there had appeared dark doubts about Castro's proud agrarian reform. The little plots promised to all landless peasants by the measures of early 1959 had not been delivered, and "cooperatives" had become the magic word for Castro and his aides. But there were never any true cooperatives in which responsibility was shared among all concerned: there were, instead, "state farms," owned and managed by the nation, with no real participation by the individuals who worked them. All management and marketing was in the hand of INRA, which set both wages and prices. This formula caused deep unhappiness, and the farmers, working for long hours at low wages, started to peddle their produce in the open market—that is, the black market—for higher prices, thus bypassing INRA. The worst offenders on this score were the "medium farmers," those with holdings ranging from 165 to 995 acres, the most experienced and resourceful operators. Under government pressure, the little farmers and the medium farmers began to lose their acres to the nation, enlarging the state farms. This shift was the "second agrarian reform" which was in full swing by mid-1963: under the 1959 agrarian formula, about 40 per cent of farm land was state-owned and operated; by 1963, some 70 per cent was in state farms; and it was freely prophesied that the ideal allotment would be 95 per cent state lands, and 5 per cent private.

Meanwhile, Cuban leaders belatedly awoke to their error in downgrading sugar—the one product which the island could turn out more cheaply and more abundantly than any other spot on earth. This downgrading had been going on before and during Castro's regime: in 1939 there were 7.56 million acres in sugar cane; by 1958 this had been reduced to 6.12 million acres; and in 1963—more than three years after Castro assumed power—the figure was down to 2.89 million acres. The official notice of the shift in emphasis from industry to agriculture came on August 10, 1963: No longer, Castro announced, would there be a futile effort to diversify and to industrialize: "We are going to develop the cane fields primarily and then the cattle industry. These will be the pillars of our economy until 1970." He went on to prophesy that Cuba would lift its sugar production to 8 or 9 million tons, and that cattle production would double or quadruple. Sugar, however, offered a disappointing exhibit by 1966. Production had stood at about 6.8 million metric tons in 1960, then dropped to a low of about 3.5 million in 1963. In 1965 it climbed to almost 6 million metric tons—but in order to make this good showing Castro's government had recklessly cut a lot of young cane which should have been allowed to mature. As a result, the 1966 crop fell to about 4.5 million tons —a drop of some 25 per cent from the 1965 figure. This decrease in production, together with a drop in the price of sugar on the world market, served to dampen the Cubans' faith in sugar as the savior of the nation's economy.

Cuba continued to make the headlines after 1963, but the attention of the United States was diverted to Vietnam, and in 1965 to the intervention in the Dominican Republic.

Various anti-Castro refugee groups continued to harass Cuba, destroying shipping bound for the island: sometimes they operated from Florida bases (without American permission), sometimes from the Bahamas, whose 700 islands afforded secrecy. But the official Cuban Revolutionary Council, organized by the CIA in connection with the Bay of Pigs affair, had little to say: in April, 1963, José Miró Cardona, its leader, denounced the United States for failing to give proper backing at the Bay of Pigs, and resigned his office; and the United States withdrew its support of the Council, a matter of more than $100,000 per month.

Castro did not cease his troubling in Latin America. Thousands of young men from Venezuela, Colombia, and elsewhere journeyed to Havana for training in guerrilla warfare, and returned to create centers of subversion in their homelands. A principal target was Venezuela, where Castro hoped to unseat that sound democrat, Rómulo Betancourt. In November, 1963, the Venezuelans discovered a large cache of arms buried on the coast which were designed for use by Communists in their campaign of terror against the Venezuelan President. The OAS took cognizance of the affair and adopted a resolution against Cuba's "policy of aggression."

Castro persisted in his courting of Moscow, and the U.S.S.R. continued to support the Castro regime—at a cost of some $1 million each day (a mere guess, of course). Whether Russia regarded it as a sound investment we do not know. In May, 1963, Castro went to Moscow seeking more aid, and valiantly defended his Russian allies from the Chinese charge that Moscow had let Cuba down in the missile affair.

The bad blood between Washington and Havana did not lessen. In July, 1963, the United States froze all Cuban accounts in American banks; and in that same month, Castro expropriated the handsome American Embassy in Havana. In February, 1964, Cuba charged that American forces had high-handedly arrested peaceful Cuban fishermen off the Florida coast, and retaliated by cutting off the water supply from the base at Guantánamo. Washington countered by ordering a drastic reduction in the number of Cuban workers at the base, replacing them with Jamaicans, and installed a desalting plant (which was completed in mid-1965), thus freeing the base from dependence upon the Cubans for water. Some faint gestures were made to ease the tension. When Senator Fulbright suggested in April, 1964, that Cuba, although a "nuisance," was not "a major menace to the U.S.," his placid words evoked little enthusiasm in Washington—but Castro was prompted to suggest that Cuba might be ready to soften its acerbity toward the United States, tentatively proposing that his nation might cease fomenting revolt in Latin America if the United States would quit supporting subversive activities in Cuba.

In October, 1965, Fidel Castro made the startling offer to permit Cubans who had relatives in the United States to leave the island and join their families. He attached conditions: no one could take with him more than a minimum of clothing; no one could take any money; and everyone who signed up for the flight would immediately be dropped from the payroll of government agencies or state-operated industries. Applicants poured in: by April, 1966, more than 14,000 had flown to Miami (the American government paid that bill), and several hundred thousands had their names on the list for future flights. Castro's motives in permitting this exodus were unclear: perhaps he was glad to be rid of more critics, perhaps he welcomed reduced pressure on the inadequate food supplies of the island.

In January, 1966, there convened in Havana the "First Conference of the Solidarity of Peoples of Asia, Africa, and Latin America." That not modestly named meeting brought some 600 delegates and observers from 82 countries, with the announced purpose to "consolidate the front of struggle against imperialist aggression." Planned in Moscow—but, *mirabile dictu,* with Chinese support—the conference was aimed against "imperialism, colonialism, and neo-colonialism, headed by the U.S. capitalists," and expressed "fraternal solidarity with the armed struggle being waged by the Venezuelan, Peruvian, Colombian, and Guatemalan patriots against the stooges of imperialism." It was a rousing challenge, not only to the guerrillas operating in those four countries, but also to all those living under the tyranny of military despotisms in Brazil, Ecuador, Bolivia, and elsewhere. There was a great deal of orating and organizing: Havana was made the headquarters for the continuing movement, and Cuba was encouraged to enlarge its training of guerrilla fighters in Latin America. American newsmen paid little heed, but the press of Latin America and Europe gave it some attention. The council of the OAS denounced the whole affair.

But even while that conference was under way in Havana, curiously enough the government of Peking announced that it had canceled half of its barter agreement, which called for the exchange of rice for Cuban sugar. On February 6, 1966, after close of the "solidarity" conference, Fidel bitterly assailed China, made it clear that "We are not and never shall be satellites of anyone." He accused the Chinese of dumping tons of printed propaganda on Cuba and of basely repudiating their pledge to furnish rice to his islanders. (Cubans, who like rice rather more than they like anything else, were to find their monthly ration of rice cut from six pounds per person to three.) Two days later, Raúl Castro, Deputy Premier, charged that the Chinese were enlisting Cuban soldiers as spies.

So ended one chapter on brotherly love. Fortunately for Fidel, Moscow was still faithful.

Meanwhile, one question puzzled all. Ernesto "Che" Guevara had dropped from sight in early 1965, and had not appeared by mid-1967. Where was he: dead, imprisoned, exiled, working at subversion somewhere in Latin America or Africa? There was no answer. (See note p. 425.)

In August, 1967, Castro made a major play for stepped-up intervention in Latin America by staging a second "Conference on Latin American Solidarity." Delegates came from all Latin America, from the United States, from Europe, from Vietnam. The oratory was immense and vociferous. The American civil rights leader Stokely Carmichael added heat to the sessions by promising "a fight to the death" against the United States white power structure; "the United States is going to fall," he prophesied, "and I hope I live to see the day." There were glowing reports on the activities of guerrilla bands in Bolivia, Peru, Guatemala, Colombia, and Venezuela. But Castro faced discouraging news as well: Moscow warned that the Soviet Union did not favor his subversive plots in Latin America. And Communist Party leaders in Venezuela, Colombia, and Chile made clear that they were not backing Castro's scheming. "We will have to fight alone," was Castro's conclusion.

WHERE GOES CUBA? SOME OBSERVATIONS IN 1967

Ever since Fidel Castro and his brave young men arrived in Havana in January, 1959, there has been a flood of books and articles, alternately extolling and vilifying the Cuban Premier. Washington's ban on travel in Cuba has hampered fruitful study of Castro's revolution by journalists and scholars. Appraisal of Cuba in mid-1967 is difficult.

Observers are generally agreed that Cuba has become a Communist police state. Personal liberties are sharply curtailed, the press is subservient, the right of peaceful assembly and popular protest is denied. Hundreds of critics have been sent to the firing squad with or without decent trials; thousands have gone to prison without fair opportunity to defend themselves. Property rights, so dear to "capitalistic" peoples, have been rudely canceled: most of the foreign-owned land and business, as well as much of that held by Cubans themselves, has been expropriated. Some 70 per cent of the agricultural lands have been gathered into state farms which are operated by a distended and often incompetent bureaucracy. Hotels, banks, industries, mines, refineries are now state enterprises. These things are true.

But there are other things which are also true. There are more schools for the children, and the rate of illiteracy has been drastically reduced. Public health campaigns reach further and deeper than ever before in Cuba's history. There has been marked improvement in rural housing, and if little has been done about urban housing, it is also true that Havana and the chief cities of Cuba are cursed with almost no abominable slums such as those of Cali, Lima, Santiago de Chile, Buenos Aires, Rio de Janeiro, and Caracas. Progress has probably been made in lifting *annual* incomes for farm laborers. And there has been progress toward eliminating racial discrimination against those with Negro blood. Furthermore, although most observers report fantastic incompetence in the handling of government affairs, those same observers report a remarkable increase in the honesty of public officials—an honesty which stands in sharp contrast to the gross knavery of successive governments since the island was freed from Spain.

In the attempt to curb Cuba and to contain her Communist subversion in Latin America, Washington has noted mournfully—and sometimes angrily—the lack of cooperation by her allies both in Latin America and in Western Europe. Washington, time and again, has sought an all-

American front against Cuba's injection of international Communism into the hemisphere, and she has met with repeated rebuffs. The latest anti-Castro measure—mandatory sanctions, proposed at the OAS meeting of foreign ministers in Washington in July, 1964—met the opposition of Bolivia, Chile, Uruguay, and Mexico. By September, Bolivia, Chile, and Uruguay—persuaded by Washington—had fallen into line. But Mexico held out, and still refuses to have anything to do with sanctions against Cuba. The reasons for Latin American distaste for strong measures against Cuba are understandable: the Latin Americans, at various times the target of United States pressure or intervention, have no liking for external coercion of any nation; a more practical and immediate reason is the fact that *fidelismo* is ardently supported by sizable minorities within all Latin American nations. However, on the score of giving aid and comfort to Castro, Mexico's record is the most serious. Mexico still permits free access by air to Havana, and that makes possible the constant flow of Castro agents from Venezuela, Colombia, Ecuador, Peru, Bolivia, and other countries. Cuba is reported to have some two dozen camps for training guerrillas—and Mexico bears the onus of keeping the airlines open for them. Washington resents this lack of cooperation by Mexico, but finds it unwise to do anything about it.

Washington also suggests periodically that the nations of Western Europe should make common cause with the United States in its defense of freedom. In 1964, the Leyland Motor Company of England agreed to sell 400 heavy buses to Cuba for some $11 million, payable over a five-year term; and that contract was shortly increased by the promise of an additional 1,000 buses. A French company promised to sell Cuba 20 locomotives. Spain undertook to build ships for Cuba. And there were others. These agreements aroused deep resentment in Washington: Congress retaliated by cutting off military aid to England, France, Yugoslavia, Spain, and Morocco—all in trivial amounts, but causing ill feeling between the United States and her allies.

Fidel Castro's future depends upon his success in creating a Communist utopia in Cuba. This he has not yet done. Statistics on the island's economy are shaky and unreliable. *The New York Times* reported (January 16, 1966) that beef production had dropped from 200,000 metric tons in 1959 to 135,000 in 1964; that milk production had fallen off slightly; that corn production had dropped from 195,000 metric tons in 1959 to 70,000 in 1964; that rice production had fallen from 280,000 metric tons in 1959 to an estimated 50,000 in 1965. The only hopeful exhibit seemed to be sugar—but the harvest of some 6 million tons in 1965, as we have seen, robbed the 1966 crop, which dropped to some 4.5 million tons. But even if production of sugar should climb, one wonders to whom the Cubans would sell it. Herbert L. Matthews, in *The New York Times* (February 7, 1966), cites a report on Cuba from Barclays, a leading London bank: "Present situation—economy weakening. . . . Development dependent on aid from the Soviet bloc. Continued trade deficit. Reserves very low.

No difficulties with payments for exports to Cuba, but position should be kept under review. Outlook: bleak."

Bleak? Yes, Cuba's outlook is bleak in mid-1967. But it must be remembered that the rules of logic break down when one deals with revolutions and revolutionaries. Just who is this Fidel Castro—who has been variously identified as Fidel the Messiah, Fidel the Communist, Fidel the Clown, and Fidel the Villain—and what does he want? Theodore Draper furnishes a useful thumbnail portrait: "Fidel Castro—as much demagogue as idealist, as much adventurer as revolutionary, as much anarchist as Communist or anything else—was suddenly catapulted into power without a real party, a real army, or a real program." In reflecting upon Fidel Castro's course, two things seem reasonably clear: Cuba was indeed overdue for a revolution, and revolutions are seldom mild and gentlemanly.

NOTE: On October 8, 1967, Ernesto "Che" Guevara was captured in a remote mountain hamlet in southeastern Bolivia. The next day he was shot to death by an officer of the Bolivian army. Thus two mysteries were solved: the whereabouts of that wandering revolutionary, and the puzzling question as to the leadership of the guerrillas in the Bolivian highlands in the spring and summer months of 1967. The death of Guevara (who had hoped that the Andes would become "the Sierra Maestra of South America") and the rout of Bolivia's National Army of Liberation were called, by one observer, "Fidel's Bay of Pigs."

(These things happened after this book was typeset.)

Chapter 26

HAITI

Hispaniola was the island chosen by Christopher Columbus for his first settlement. He called it La Isla Española, which was latinized into Hispaniola; others have called it by its Indian name, Haiti ("place of mountains"), or Santo Domingo after the first city in America. Today, Hispaniola's almost 30,000 square miles of mountains, valleys, and plains—about the size of Maine—belong to two nations, the eastern two-thirds to the Dominican Republic, the western third to Haiti.

Ill fortune has been the lot of the islanders ever since the day Columbus disembarked from the *Santa María*. He found Indians living in idyllic contentment: "So lovable, so tractable, so peaceable are these people . . . ," he wrote his sovereigns, "there is not in the world a better nation nor a better land. They love their neighbors as themselves; and their discourse is ever sweet and gentle, and accompanied with a smile; and though it is true they are naked, yet their manners are decorous and praiseworthy." Within thirty years most of these lovable Indians were dead. Nor did the quarreling Spaniards find contentment here, for the veins of gold were soon exhausted, and the British, Dutch, and French took turns in molesting them. By 1550 the Spaniards had lost interest in the island, having found richer kingdoms to exploit in Mexico and Peru, and Hispaniola was left to the mercy of Spain's rivals. Buccaneers, chiefly French, settled on the island of Tortuga (turtle) off the northwestern coast and spilled over onto Hispaniola. In 1697 Spain ceded the western end of the island to France, and Haiti—then called Saint Domingue—became France's most prosperous colony. Throughout the eighteenth century, slave ships unloaded their cargoes from Africa, and slave labor made possible the generous production of sugar, cotton, coffee, and indigo. Then in the 1790's, echoing the drum beats of the French Revolution, civil war broke out, involving mulattoes, Negroes, French, Spanish, and English, with the intrepid ex-slave Toussaint L'Ouverture as Haiti's most dramatic figure.[1] Out of a dozen years of bloodshed, free Haiti emerged in 1804 in control of the western end of the island. Meanwhile the Spanish colony of Santo Domingo

[1] See pp. 243-4.

on the eastern end of the island, sluggish and unproductive during the eighteenth century, was ceded to France in 1795. Half a century later, after turns of domination by France, Spain, and Haiti, the colony gained freedom in 1844 under the name of the Dominican Republic. But the curse of anarchy fixed upon the island was never lifted and seems to have dogged each step of the two little nations which divide the island between them.

HAITI'S BEGINNINGS, 1804–43

New Year's Day, 1804, was a proud independence day for the ragged Negro army of General Jean Jacques Dessalines. Napoleon's expeditionary force of 43,000 men had been defeated, more by yellow fever than by bullets, and only 8,000 had escaped. The years of fighting had brought great changes: in 1790 most of the land and almost all the 500,000 Negro slaves had been owned by 30,000 Frenchmen; by 1804 most of the French had fled or been killed, slavery had been abolished, and the Negroes and mulattoes had inherited the land. Dessalines, named governor general for life, was an ex-slave about fifty years old, illiterate, arrogant, and brutal. He had no aides with experience in statecraft. Most of the few whites that were left were butchered at Dessalines's orders. There were about 30,000 *gens de couleur,* the mulattoes who had been freed under French rule, including some who could read and write. There were half a million Negroes, almost entirely illiterate and possessed by two ideas: to be rid of everything that reminded them of their serfdom—even the church bells that used to call them to the fields were ripped from their moorings—and never to work again. The sugar fields which had enriched France for a century were overgrown with weeds.

Over this ravaged domain, the illiterate ex-slave Dessalines was formally appointed to rule by his companions-in-arms: "We swear," ran their declaration of allegiance, "entire obedience to the laws he shall deem fit to make, his authority being the only one we acknowledge. We authorize him to make peace and war, and to appoint his successor." A constitution was drafted, abolishing slavery forever, forbidding ownership of Haitian soil by any white man, and making the word "Negro" synonymous with "Haitian." Imitating the Napoleon whom he hated, Dessalines was crowned as Emperor Jacques I. Urged to create a peerage, he refused: "I, only I, am a noble." But his deserving friends were given high posts in army and government, and were placed in charge of the one-time great French plantations. Aware that Haiti could be saved only by hard work, he drafted the now theoretically free peasants and assigned them to tasks and disciplines as onerous as any they had ever known. Under his cruel but competent hand, there was marked recovery for two years; then the populace turned against him, and he himself was shot. There was little mourning for Dessalines in 1806, but today an iron statue of the Father of Independence holds a proud place in the Champs-de-Mars in the Haitian capital, Port-au-Prince.

The death of Dessalines in 1806 was followed by disruption of the little nation. North and south parted company for a time, under separate and very different rulers. In the north, from the city of Cap-Haïtien, Henri Christophe, last of the revolutionary generals, ruled from 1808 to 1820. An ex-slave and quite unlettered, Christophe had been one of the 800 Haitians to volunteer for service under Lafayette in the American Revolution and had fought at the battle of Savannah. Then he had been one of the most intrepid fighters in the Haitian war for independence. Now, supreme in northern Haiti, he ruled for twelve years with rough competence. In vainglory and with desire to impress his simple followers, he had himself crowned King Henri I. He filled his court with an imposing company of barons, counts, and knights; and built the elaborate royal palace of Sans Souci, and then, upon a mountain top, the citadel of La Ferrière, whose ruins are still among the sights of America. The labor of thousands was conscripted for these monuments to his, and to Haiti's, glory. Like Dessalines, he permitted none to be idle. All able-bodied men were assigned to the fields and worked under military discipline. Profits from the long-neglected coffee trees increased. Some sugar fields were returned to cultivation. The "Black Caesar" enforced a regime which brought more security to his people than they had ever known before. Unschooled as he was, Christophe had profound respect for learning and invited scientists, especially from England, to visit his kingdom. His harsh discipline provoked grumbling and finally revolt. In 1820, after twelve years of benevolent despotism, Christophe, paralyzed from the hips down, killed himself—with a silver bullet, according to legend.

Meanwhile, in the south, Alexandre Pétion was the president of "the republic of Haiti" (1808–18). Pétion, a mulatto educated in France, had caught the infection of liberalism; he disliked tyranny, admired democracy to a degree, and gave his people a liberty of action which they had never hitherto enjoyed. He took over the great French plantations and parceled out the land in tiny plots to soldiers. The results of his indulgent course were disastrous. With compulsion removed, the peasants idled, gathered the untended coffee, planted a few crops which required little exertion, and lived meagerly. The national treasury received little from taxes or customs; a few foreign loans were negotiated at usurious rates; and unsupported paper money was issued to pay the bills. Pétion's government was under constant threat from Christophe's armies in the north and from disaffected generals in the south. Although his ten-year rule had slight success, Pétion stands as the most attractive of Haitian presidents, much beloved by a people whom he served little. In the larger Spanish American record, Pétion is remembered for the aid he rendered Simón Bolívar in 1815–16 when the Liberator sought refuge in Haiti after defeats in Venezuela. In return for arms and food, Pétion exacted a pledge that Bolívar would end slavery in all the lands he liberated—a pledge Bolívar sought but failed to redeem.

Haiti was reunited under Jean Pierre Boyer, who succeeded Pétion in 1818 in the south, took over rule of the north after Christophe's suicide in 1820, and then, for good measure, annexed the eastern end of the island in 1822, when the people of Santo Domingo successfully evicted the Spaniards. A mulatto educated in France, Boyer had not joined the revolutionists until after the capture of Toussaint. He had served under Pétion and shared his "liberal" principles, which he now applied by continuing the distribution of land in small plots. His generosity contributed, as had Pétion's, to the general inertia and misery. Jonathan Brown, a visitor in the 1830's, described what he saw: "Poverty and degradation stare one in the face wherever he goes . . . the population . . . is without sustenance or a disposition to make exertions to obtain it." The nation, he observed, was declining: "and no obstacle seems to exist to prevent their descent into barbarism." The members of congress, he reported, were so illiterate that few could sign their names.

The well-meaning Boyer, with an empty treasury, could do little to maintain order in the nation which now included the angry Spanish-speaking people of the eastern end of the island. Nor did the coveted French recognition in 1825 improve his chances, for it was bought by pledging payment of a 150-million-franc indemnity in annual installments and by agreeing to grant French traders a 50 per cent reduction in tariff duties. The inevitable defaults upon the indemnity led to embroiled relations with France. As the internal situation steadily worsened, Boyer abandoned his moderate rule of his idling citizens, resorted to the harsh tactics of Dessalines and Christophe, and compelled the peasants to plow and harvest under armed guard. Boyer continued his ineffective rule until 1843, when a conspiracy of urban mulattoes—the class to which he himself belonged—drove him into exile. In the confusion the people of Santo Domingo broke away and founded their own Dominican Republic. The mulatto conspirators, after futile efforts to establish stable government, soon lost their hold to illiterate Negro leaders. So ended the twenty-three-year rule of the occasionally honest, slightly democratic, and moderately intelligent mulattoes.

THE YEARS OF TUMULT, 1843–1915

The story of Haiti during the seventy-two years following the exile of Boyer is one of almost unrelieved gloom, incompetence, and tyranny. Twenty-two dictators rose and fell, repeated civil disturbances shook the country, and the masses sank to new depths of misery. The Negroes were in almost complete control, with the better educated mulattoes furnishing presidents for only eight of the seventy-two years. The most fantastic period was the twelve-year rule of the ignorant and superstitious Faustin Soulouque (1847–59), expensively installed as Emperor Faustin I (his crown, still to be seen in Port-au-Prince, cost $100,000), who butchered numerous mulatto leaders, appointed illiterate Negroes to public posts, made two unsuccessful attempts to recapture Santo Domingo, and finally had to flee the country. Among all those who occupied the presidential palace, only three proved more than mediocre. Fabre Geffrard (1859–67) cut the army by one-half, built a few schools, organized a school of medicine, promoted public works, signed a concordat with the Vatican which brought some order to the demoralized priesthood, and won recognition from Washington in 1862. The well-educated Lysius Salomon (1879–88) created a national bank, lowered tariffs, opened some rural schools, imported a few French teachers, and brought Haiti into the International Postal Union. Florvil Hyppolite (1889–96) won fame for his bridges, docks, public buildings, telephone and telegraph lines.[2]

It was a period of economic and social stagnation. The eroded and ill-tended soil yielded less and less. Coffee from the trees growing wild on the mountainsides furnished the one cash crop. The national treasury was chronically in default on its foreign obligations. The Church, which had suffered from neglect until relations with the Vatican were restored in 1860, furnished a little leadership in education. As late as 1915, more than 90 per cent of the people were illiterate.

THE CASTE SYSTEM

We now digress to take account of the hardening of the lines between the two classes in Haitian society, the *élite* and the masses—the rigid caste system which was fixed upon the little nation in the nineteenth century and continues to dominate in the twentieth.[3]

The *élite*, never more than 2 per cent of the people, are the legatees of the *gens de couleur,* the freedmen of colonial days. After the murder or exile of the French colonial aristocracy, the mulattoes took over much of the wealth of the erstwhile owners of the land and claimed the political and social supremacy which the whites had held. Under Pétion and Boyer, they held the upper hand. After 1843, as we have noted, they lost control to the Negro leaders, whose followers outnumbered the *élite* by fifty to one. The *élite* were then forced to comfort themselves with the sense of social superiority. Under the shadow of the Negro tyrants, the *élite* became a complacent aristocracy. The *élite* are usually mulattoes, although some pure Negroes win status in their ranks. They pride themselves upon the purity of their French and upon their prowess in music, poetry, and painting. They regard physical labor as demeaning and seek positions in government, or careers in law, medicine, or business. Their sons seldom become teachers or enter the priesthood, for such professions are ill-paid and bring their practitioners uncomfortably close to the masses. They cling to Catholicism as a spiritual symbol of their cherished French tradition, although Voodoo is undoubtedly practiced in secret by many of the privileged upper classes. They live in the best houses in Port-au-Prince, Cap-Haïtien, Pétionville, and other towns. They take pride in the seemli-

[2] James G. Leyburn: *The Haitian People* (New Haven: Yale University Press; 1941), p. 99.

[3] The word *élite* is used by the Haitians themselves to describe members of the upper class.

ness and grace of the Parisian way of life which they claim as their own; their ranks include talented and charming men and women. But their indubitable grace is matched by bland arrogance: between them and the unwashed masses there is a deep gulf, almost as unbridgeable as that which long separated the untouchables of India from their more favored country-men. Few of the *élite* have taken a stand for the education or the social regeneration of the Negro masses. They have withdrawn to the shelter of their own superiority, seemingly indifferent to the general misery of their land.[4]

The masses, numbering more than 4 million, live much as their slave progenitors lived in the eighteenth century. They are almost entirely illiterate, although a few schools are available to those who reside in or near the larger centers. Their language is creole, a blend of French, Spanish, English, and Dutch shaped during the chaotic sixteenth and seventeenth centuries, to which were added many words of African root as slaves filled the land in the eighteenth century. Creole is the Haitian language, no matter how fondly the *élite* cling to their Parisian French. Presidents, businessmen, and lawyers must speak creole in order to be understood. Catholicism is the official religion, but Voodoo is the secret and powerful religion of the Negroes, a religion imported from Africa (where it is called Vodun) and further de-veloped in Haiti. It is a true religion, with a full complement of gods and spirits, and with a ritual for the propitiation and control of supernatural powers. There are magic rites, sacrifices, beating of drums, ceremonial dances, incantation of priests, and the casting of spells to influence the course of birth and death, sickness and health, love and hate.

The Haitian masses constitute a peasant society. Few great plantations remain, and the bulk of the land in the valleys and on the mountain slopes is held in tiny plots, which grow ever smaller as holdings are divided with each generation among an increasing number of heirs. Few peasants hold regis-tered titles to their patches of poor soil, but their boundaries are subject to mutual consent. Only in such spots as congested Puerto Rico, Java, and the Nile valley is there such overcrowding of an agricultural population. There are today more than 400 Haitians to each square mile of valley and moun-tain slope. With little land, most of it sadly eroded, with little fertilization and use of scientific methods, it is no wonder that the Haitian peasant is among the poorest in the world. Estimates during the American occupation set the average annual income of the Haitian at $20, but more recent esti-mates run as high as $70. Such statistics, however, mean little in a land whose people subsist directly from the soil. Not only is the Haitian poor; he is also sick. Malaria, hookworm, yaws, and intestinal infections take their toll. The mortality rate, especially of infants, is fantastically high, although no reliable statistics exist. But the high birth rate exceeds the number of deaths, and the overpopulation of the island is aggravated.

4 There are grateful exceptions. A few *élite* intellectuals have denounced the failure of their class to recognize the worth of their African inheritance, their proneness to worship French culture, and their refusal to take responsibility for national redemption. See his-torian Jean Price-Mars: *La Vocation de l'élite* (Port-au-Prince: Impr. E. Chenet; 1919).

HAITI UNDER AMERICAN OCCUPATION, 1915-34

The American marines were landed in Haiti in 1915, and they stayed for nineteen years. This was the United States answer to the breakdown of orderly government during the violent period 1908-15. During that period seven men had seized the presidency—usually by revolution initiated among the rough *cacos* or mountaineers of the north—and held office briefly; some had then escaped into exile, one was killed by an explosion in the palace, another probably died from poison, and the last was hacked to pieces by an angry mob. Such confusions could not be tolerated in the Caribbean, where the United States held the new Panama Canal; hence President Wilson decided to extend the American police power to Haiti.

The international situation in 1915, with Germany winning by land and sea, also influenced Washington's action. It was rumored that Germany was seeking control of a naval base on Haiti's Mole St. Nicholas. German merchants on the island, principal holders of some $2.5 million of temporary loans floated to finance the seven years of *caco* revolts, were appealing to Berlin for help. The French owners of Haitian securities were pressing their claims, and actually occupied Cap-Haïtien briefly. Woodrow Wilson was not minded to permit any European power to gain new foothold in the "American Mediterranean."

Furthermore, Americans had a financial stake in Haiti's national bank and railroads. In 1910 American interests had taken over the national railways, of which only eighty miles of track had been laid after years of plundering by various alien promoters. The new owners had been given a fifty-year concession for completing the line between the capital and Cap-Haïtien and had been guaranteed a 6 per cent return on their investment; but little had been accomplished by 1915. The fiasco was variously blamed on managerial incompetence, civil wars, and the failure of the evanescent Haitian governments to pay what they owed. The Banque Nationale de la République d'Haïti, organized in 1910, also concerned the Americans. The National City Bank of New York, although it held only 5 per cent of the shares, represented so much of the predominant German and French interest as to give it virtual control of the Haitian bank. There was an intimate relationship between the New York bank, the Haitian bank, and the Haitian national railways; the New York concern lent a half million dollars to the railways; and one of its vice-presidents served as president of the railroad company. Meanwhile, the Haitian bank had taken over virtual control of the republic's national finances, floating a loan of $16 million, collecting all customs receipts, paying off amounts due to bondholders, and turning over the remainder to the Haitian treasury. By 1915 American financial interests controlled the nation's banking and railroads, and were understandably apprehensive lest the anarchic confusion wipe out their investment. Fairly or unfairly, they were charged with a large share of responsibility for inviting American armed intervention.[5]

[5] See L. L. Montague: *Haiti and the United States, 1714–1938* (Durham, N.C.: Duke University Press; 1940), ch. XII.

The landing of the American marines in 1915 came as the climax to months of tension. During 1914 there were repeated visits of American warships to Haitian harbors. In December, 1914, alarmed by news of fresh *caco* revolts, an American ship anchored in the harbor of Port-au-Prince and landed a few officers and men who called upon the Haitian bank and withdrew $500,000, which they carried off to New York for safekeeping in the National City Bank. Bank officials in Haiti justified their surrender of the funds by citing their obligation to protect foreign bondholders against the irresponsible island government. Patriotic Haitians described the act as highhanded theft.

Then in January, 1915, a *caco* army under Vilbrun Guillaume Sam moved south to capture the capital. At this point American intervention took a new turn. American Admiral William B. Caperton, standing by in coastal waters, informed Sam that there was to be no looting or violence; and lest he forget, the Admiral sent aides to remind the Negro leader at each seaport through which he passed. By March, Sam was installed in the presidential palace, his serenity clouded by the presence of American war-ships on the horizon and by news that a rival *caco* army under a chieftain named Bobo was on its way to oust him. In July, when Bobo's men were fighting their way into Port-au-Prince, Sam filled the prisons with his out-spoken critics. On July 27 Sam barely escaped capture by Bobo and took refuge in the French legation. That night, probably by Sam's orders, there was a mass butchery of political prisoners—about 167 were killed, includ-ing numerous honored citizens of the *élite* class. The next morning an angry mob headed by grave and respected citizens appeared at the French legation and demanded delivery of Sam. They brushed aside the French minister's protests, found the shabby president under a bed, dragged him out, and threw him over the wall to the mob which literally tore him to pieces and paraded his several parts through the streets. At this point the U.S.S. *Washington* dropped anchor, and Admiral Caperton landed with his marines.

Descriptions of the nineteen-year rule by American marines range from official panegyrics on the blessings conferred upon Haiti, to vitriolic denunciations of the "imperialistic" United States. Neither verdict is alto-gether fair. There was good in the American occupation, and there was bad. It may be concluded that military occupation, though perhaps some-times necessary, is never palatable to the occupied.

The American military authorities took the necessary steps to regu-larize their position on the island. They chose as president the *élite* mulatto Sudre Dartiguenave and installed him in the face of popular demand for the Negro *caco* leader Bobo, giving him a puppet role uncomfortable for him and angering to the Haitian people. They put through a treaty reduc-ing Haiti to a political and economic protectorate of the United States; and stipulating that American citizens were to be appointed by the Haitian president to collect customs, advise the treasury, head the constabulary, and direct public works, health programs, and an agricultural training cam-paign. This treaty, to be in force for ten years (later extended for another ten years), was thrust upon an angry Haitian congress. The next step, adoption of a constitution, provoked fresh indignation. The occupation officials presented the draft prepared in Washington,[6] and when the Haitian congress refused to ratify it, they ordered President Dartiguenave to dissolve that body. The constitution, "made in the U.S.A.," was then submitted to a national plebiscite, conducted by American marines, and was accepted almost unanimously. Its most dramatic innovation was a provision permitting white foreigners to own land, a privilege denied by every previous constitution.

There was general protest among Haitians against all acts, good and bad, of the invaders. Politicians and army officers, cut off from their accustomed profits, found reasons to resist every measure. Honest patriots, understandably outraged by the denial of Haitian sovereignty, wrote spirited indictments. The marines, whose number averaged about 2,000 during the period of occupation, were accused of every crime. Most of the charges were unsubstantiated, and on the whole the record of the Americans was good. The most serious error committed by the occupation forces was the revival of the old *corvée* law, under which peasants were drafted for road building. The officers in charge of the road program overreached themselves, transferring workers to road projects far from their homes (an act expressly prohibited by the *corvée* law itself); this incited a *caco* revolt in 1920, whose suppression cost the lives of some 2,000 Haitians. That and other grievances were promptly aired in the United States and led to several investigations, official and private, into real and alleged abuses. But in truth it was not the abuses, but the occupation itself, which rankled. There was also a racial aspect; these were white intruders in a Negro nation. Some of the Americans aired their own racial antipathies. The *élite,* cultured and proud, found themselves excluded from certain hotels, clubs, and restaurants. There was a general tightening of racial lines in the fashion familiar to Washington and the American South but unknown to Haiti since its independence.

Under the puppet presidencies of Dartiguenave (1915–22) and Louis Borno (1922–30), American officials controlled the treasury, collected taxes, disbursed funds, effected wise economies, and eliminated graft. Americans organized and directed the Garde d'Haïti, a national constabulary of 3,000 men, the best army Haiti ever had. American engineers supervised the building of roads, wharves, lighthouses, water systems, and irrigation projects. American physicians organized a public health program with hospital clinics and training schools for doctors and nurses; they launched effective campaigns against syphilis, yaws, malaria, and hookworm. American agricultural technicians opened a school for farm leaders and extended the program to rural centers. The successes of the American occupation were substantial, but the complaints of the people were not stilled.

The first step toward ending the occupation was taken in 1930 when

[6] The author of the draft—according to a report which is still debated—was a young Assistant Secretary of the Navy, Franklin Delano Roosevelt.

President Herbert Hoover appointed a commission to meet with leading Haitians. That group recommended that Borno resign in favor of an interim president, who in turn would supervise a free election. The result was the choice of able Stenio Vincent for president (1930–36). Meanwhile, Hoover appointed a wise minister to Haiti, Dana Munro, placed all occupation officials under his direction, and charged him with the task of terminating the stay of Americans as rapidly as he could. The liquidation of the occupation was well under way when Franklin D. Roosevelt came to the American presidency in 1933; responding to the appeal of Vincent, Roosevelt ordered withdrawal of the marines in 1934. Only a financial mission was left to safeguard American holdings, and that was finally withdrawn in 1941.

INDEPENDENT HAITI, 1934–

The departure of the marines in mid-1934 was celebrated as Haiti's second emancipation, and politicians and army officers prepared to recapture their long-lost privileges. During the years that followed, friends of Haiti have had opportunity to assess the results of the nation's tutelage under marine rule. Politically, the island republic seems as far from democracy as it was during the chaotic days before the marines landed. The Americans had imposed a shift of political responsibility away from the illiterate Negroes to the relatively enlightened mulatto leaders such as Dartiguenave, Borno, and Vincent. After the removal of the marines, momentum kept Vincent in power until 1941, when he passed the office on to another mulatto, Elie Lescot, who ruled rather intelligently until 1946. In that year the black masses (especially in the cities), restive under mulatto rule, struck for a return to Negro leadership, ousted Lescot, and put Dumarsais Estimé in the presidency. It was now clear that the effective rulers of Haiti were the black troops of the Garde d'Haïti, who had been trained by the Americans and held in leash since 1934. It was these troops, especially the 500 men of the Palace Guard, who—with the clamor of the masses behind them—brought return to Negro leadership. The "revolution" of 1945 paid slight attention to the ills and needs of the peasantry: it was chiefly a political revolution, investing the Negroes—especially the Negroes of Port-au-Prince—with the power enjoyed by the mulatto *élite* for more than thirty years.

Estimé sounded the old battle cries, talked of the inevitable clash between the *authentiques* and the *nonauthentiques,* making clear that the Negroes were the "authentics." He purged the administration of mulatto officials, replacing them with blacks, and for the first time in history the *élite* were made to pay an income tax. While belaboring the city *élite,* however, he made some use of their technical abilities. He launched reforms aimed at improving the lot of the urban workers: during his administration the minimum daily wage was increased from 40 cents to 70 cents, and Haiti's first social security laws were enacted. (The reader must remember, however, that laws in Haiti are never more than fitfully enforced.) Sensitive to the plight of his country's agriculture, Estimé sent specialists to Puerto Rico to study farming techniques, and collectivized some farms as production show cases. Estimé stirred up fresh disputes with his more powerful neighbors, Trujillo in the Dominican Republic and Batista in Cuba. He made flamboyant speeches in denunciation of "American imperialism," but wisely recognized that the United States offered the surest market for the coffee, sugar, sisal, and bananas that Haiti produced. He showed touches of genius, especially in his proposal that the United States aid Haiti in the development of a "Haitian TVA" in the valley of the Artibonite River, which cuts midway across the country from east to west. The source of much wealth to the French in the eighteenth century, this valley had been wasted by ruinous floods and overcultivation. The plan called for great dams which would control floods, yield 40,000 KWH of electric power, and open some 80,000 acres for settlement. The project was launched by a loan from the Export-Import Bank, and canals irrigating some 30,000 acres were opened in 1949. The cost of the plan soon exceeded the $14 million allotted to it, and finally the bill was more than $40 million—paid chiefly by grants and loans from the United States. By 1960 the dams were built but further work bogged down, with a deadlock between Washington and Haiti, and United States aid for the project was suspended. In 1967, three giant generators were on the site, but no one knew what to do with them.

In 1950, Estimé was ousted from office by Colonel Paul Magloire, another Negro leader and strong man of the army, who was promptly "elected" for a six-year term. The coup had the tacit if not open support of the *élite,* who regarded Estimé's social digressions as a threat to their way of life and saw in Magloire a savior from what they regarded as Estimé's economic recklessness. Magloire came into office with much fanfare: a handsome and impressive figure, he captivated the Negro masses and was hailed abroad as a statesman of high promise. His noisy anti-Communism yielded handsome dividends in American aid. He persuaded Washington to speed up appropriations for the Artibonite River project, health programs, schools, and improved agricultural methods. The economy was bolstered by this aid, by increased exports, and by the brief but spectacular success of tourism—all of which created an atmosphere which encouraged foreign investment. Magloire also succeeded in creating an appearance of national unity by his conciliatory attitude toward the *élite* and by his demagogic appeal to the Negro masses. But it gradually dawned upon thoughtful citizens that he was despotic and corrupt, that his "black revolution" was a fake, that the interests he best served were his own—he was especially skillful in taking toll on all contracts, in laying up a nest egg against the day of his inevitable eviction. (It was rumored with some solid evidence that not less than $10 million to $15 million found its way into his private purse and finally went with him into exile.) In December, 1956, a general strike brought about the overthrow of Magloire. During the next nine months, seven makeshift governments rose and fell, with increased disorder tormenting the nation. And in September, 1957, a little country doctor named François Duvalier was installed as president after an election of dubious legality.

. . .

François Duvalier is likely to win first honors among Haiti's long list of corrupt, incompetent, and savage tyrants. Born into the poor black middle-class of Port-au-Prince, Duvalier was a lonely, studious—and hungry—youth. After receiving a medical degree from the University of Haiti, he studied Public Health briefly at the University of Michigan, then worked in the Public Health Service in Port-au-Prince, winning credit for his share in the campaign against yaws. He made intellectual excursions into ethnology and folk culture, and early became bitter against the domination of the country by the mulatto *élite*. A follower of Estimé, Duvalier refused to bow to Magloire in the coup of 1950, which he considered a betrayal of Estimé's "revolution," and went into hiding until 1957. When he was elected president, he was generally regarded as unassuming, honest, idealistic, and the admiring masses affectionately called him "Papa Doc." But it was soon clear that Haiti was now ruled by a bitter and vengeful demagogue.

Upon assuming office, Dr. Duvalier was theoretically subject to the check of the parliamentary system and the Garde d'Haïti, but he outwitted them both. "Elections" go to his own men. And the Garde has been shoved aside by various devices: its officers were either clubbed into acquiescence, murdered, or forced into exile; and it was replaced as keeper of the public order by the creation of a "militia," or political police, numbering probably more than 10,000 men—twice the size of the Garde. Then Papa Doc devised another refinement: he organized his private gang of hoodlums into the Tontons Macoutes ("bogeymen" in the creole patois), a secret force of gun-carrying ruffians, wearing no uniforms, who preyed upon good citizens, collecting "contributions" for Duvalier's "good works"; who spied and levied blackmail; who terrorized city and countryside, killing, robbing, torturing, raping. Duvalier drove thousands of the more respected leaders of the nation into exile: the schools, pathetic as they were, were stripped of their better teachers who—along with physicians, lawyers, technicians, and able businessmen—found it expedient to seek asylum abroad: some 5,000 managed to reach New York alone, and many found jobs in the Congo. Once something of an intellectual himself, Duvalier now trusted only the ignorant and the lowly. As one of his former teachers put it, "He feels that nobody less educated than he could ever deceive him, so he believes them. And now they are the only people he has around him."

The Catholic Church was one of Duvalier's chief targets. In 1959 he undertook to discipline the clergy, who had criticized his dictatorship: two priests were expelled from the island for "reasons of internal security"; and when about a thousand clergy, nuns, and other faithful churchmen dared to meet for protest, Duvalier's police arrested sixty of them; then, when Archbishop François Poirier denounced the President, an order was issued for his arrest—but the outcry was so great that for a time Duvalier gave up his battle with the Church. In 1960, however, the Archbishop himself was charged with organizing a Communist student plot and was banished from the country. The Vatican then appointed an apostolic administrator whom Duvalier refused to recognize. In January, 1961, another bishop was forced to leave; in November, 1962, one more bishop and three priests were expelled—and the Pope excommunicated Duvalier and all Catholics involved in the deportations. Attacks on the Church continued: in 1964, the Jesuit radio station, seminary, and retreat house were closed by the Tontons Macoutes.

Meanwhile there were rumors, perhaps authentic, that Duvalier himself was more loyal to Voodoo ritual than to the Pope. This enthusiasm may have been genuine, or it may have been simply an appeal to the ignorant masses. Duvalier always dresses in black, to identify himself, some say, with Baron Samedi, the Voodoo god of death—thus increasing his hold on the people through fear as well as through affection.

Duvalier has proved adept at retaining his job. In 1961 the parliament was formally dissolved; a new congress consisting of fifty-eight of the President's most trusted friends was "unanimously" elected; and Duvalier had himself reelected for another six-year term (though he still had two years to go on his previous term). On May 22, 1961, he was inaugurated with fine pomp, with 200,000 peasants brought to the capital for the ceremony. Then in June, 1964, he announced that his presidency was "for life." His obedient congress proclaimed its chief as "the Renovator of the Haitian Nation," and Papa Doc made his divine appointment even more clear:

> I am the personification of the Haitian people. I don't have to take orders from anyone, no matter where he comes from. Twice I have been given power, and I will keep it. God is the only one who will take it from me. No foreigner will remove me against the will of the people.

The years since 1934 have brought continued trouble between Haiti and her near neighbors, the Dominican Republic and Cuba. The lack of adequate employment in Haiti caused an exodus of workers to the better paying labor markets of the other republics. Haitians had long flocked to Cuba to work in the sugar fields: during the 1930's as many as 40,000 to 50,000 went each year, and many remained. Then strong man Fulgencio Batista, hostile to the increase of Negro blood in Cuba, put an end to the immigration. Meanwhile other thousands were crossing the border into the Dominican Republic, earning better pay in the cane fields of that more prosperous country, and many of these casual migrants settled down on the Dominican side. In 1937 Dictator Trujillo was confronted by the presence of some 60,000 Haitians who had settled permanently on Dominican soil and unreckoned thousands who had moved in as harvest hands. Determined to make the Dominican Republic a "white" nation, Trujillo resorted to a pogrom as the quickest way to rid his country of this Negro incubus: in 1937, in a series of butcheries, from 10,000 to 20,000 Haitians were killed in cold blood. Under pressure from Washington, the Dominicans paid the Haitians an indemnity of $750,000.

Haiti's troubles with her neighbors were far from ended by the ouster of Dictator Batista in 1959 and the assassination of Dictator Trujillo in 1961. Cuba, after the accession to power of Fidel Castro in January, 1959, has been an ever-present threat. Castro's crusading zeal found Haiti a ready target. The first attack upon Haiti from a Cuban base came in August, 1959. Since 1959, there have been recurring rumors of attacks from Cuban soil, and Fidel Castro's agents have conspired busily in Port-au-Prince—but no serious incidents have occurred. The Cuban dictator has been preoccupied by troubles at home.

President Juan Bosch of the Dominican Republic, elected in 1962, viewed the terror in Haiti as a threat to any hope for democracy in his own beleaguered land. There were rumors of a plot by Duvalier together with members of the Trujillo family to overthrow Bosch. The Dominicans permitted various bands of anti-Duvalier Haitian patriots to launch attacks from Dominican soil: these brave fellows struck at Duvalier's troops, but were soon tracked down and killed. Dominican nationals in Haiti were savagely treated—some were jailed and tortured, others just disappeared. Matters reached a crisis late in April, 1963, when Haitian police broke into the Dominican Embassy in Port-au-Prince in search of twenty-two Haitian refugees who had found asylum there. Bosch cried, "An invasion of our country!" and massed some 4,000 Dominican troops on the Haitian border, threatening to attack if the refugees were not given safe conduct out of the country, and proclaiming that "the protection of human rights must be beyond any other principle in the hemisphere, even beyond nonintervention." But this hot-headed plan of the Dominican President was effectively discouraged by Washington and the OAS; and, after ten precarious days, Bosch reluctantly backed down. Under the same pressure, Duvalier ceased his harassment of the Dominican Embassy, which was then turned over to the Colombians as caretakers. But in a savage gesture of revenge, Duvalier cleared a strip of territory along the Dominican border, with wholesale burning of hundreds of Haitian farmhouses, creating a no man's land of desolation to bar intruders and prevent the escape of refugees. Haitian and Dominican troops faced each other sullenly along this 193-mile frontier. And, as one Dominican soldier told a reporter, "the Tontons Macoutes shoot at anything that moves in that strip and its ghost villages."

HAITI'S PROSPECTS

As of 1967, some obstinate questions on Haiti persist. How can more than 4.5 million Haitians, crowded over 400 to each square mile in a land about the size of Maryland, about 90 per cent illiterate, earning perhaps $70 per capita each year, with neither industry nor organized farming and almost no trained technicians—how can these people get enough to eat from the exhausted soil of its narrow valleys and steep mountain slopes? The United Nations sent a commission to Haiti in 1949, which reported: "The fundamental economic problem of Haiti derives from the relentless pressure of a steadily growing, insufficiently educated population upon limited, vulnerable, and—so far as agricultural land is concerned—alarmingly shrinking natural resources." This diagnosis of 1949 applies with increased force in 1967: the pitifully small ranks of educated leaders have been decimated by the flight from Duvalier's confused tyranny; and, if present trends continue, in scarcely more than thirty years the population of this little nation will double to some 9 million, or over 800 to the square mile. Statistics on today's Haiti are unreliable, but some facts are clear. Hunger is growing: when a newspaper reports a "rat problem," citizens understand that cats are scarce, because they have been eaten by starving people. Medical care is pathetically inadequate: there are probably some 11,000 persons per physician in Haiti—more than twice as many as in El Salvador, which shares with Haiti the bottom place among Latin American nations on this score. The products which Haiti sells in the world market have suffered: misman-agement and recurrent hurricanes have severely damaged the coffee planta-tions; and the world price of sisal (used to make twine and bags for coffee) has dropped—due partly to the increased substitution of plastics. Public services are incompetent and corrupt. Schools are inadequate. One problem common to most Latin American countries—latifundia—is *not* present in Haiti: there are few large landholdings; almost every peasant family owns its plot—a half acre, more or less—on which he grows his meager crops of corn, rice, beans, yams, manioc, avocadoes, mangoes, and other fruits. Any attempt to industrialize is a wan hope: the consumers' market is too thin—at least three-fourths of the people live almost entirely outside the money economy. The plight of Haiti, as Raymond E. Crist has put it, is that it "has neither a one-crop economy nor a self-sufficient economy—rather it has a bite-your-nails economy."

How can this little nation, about 95 per cent of whose people are ignorant, superstitious, and quite unaware of life in the cities, let alone the world beyond the Haitian border—how can this nation move into the twenti-eth century? Duvalier has his answers. First of all, before Haiti can have a present and a future, it must have a past; and Duvalier, with a curious sense of history, has evoked the dream of Haiti's Negro past: he has called up the brutal spirit of Jean Jacques Dessalines who, with his cry of *"Brûle tête, brûle kay"* (burn heads, burn houses), led black slaves to massacre their masters, redeeming the country from the scourge of the white man; upon occasion he has dressed his militia in the red coats and tricornes of that hero, glorifying his legacy of violence and terror with a "pathetic pageantry" which, as Tad Szulc puts it, "provides for the masses their only sense of excitement and release from the misery of their daily lives."

Duvalier has also evoked the African tradition, and his answer for the twentieth century is to identify Haiti—the first Negro republic in the modern world—with the new African nationalism. He has made overtures to the new governments of Africa, making it clear that Haiti is identified with the resurgence of the Negro everywhere. When Haile Selassie—some-thing of a father figure to the new African nations—visited Haiti in the spring of 1966, Duvalier rolled out a $14,000 red carpet, lavished $300,000 in tinseled gifts and champagne on the Ethiopian Emperor.

The Duvalier dictatorship in Haiti has posed knotty problems for Wash-ington. What, precisely, is the United States to do when an evil little man turns an ostensibly free republic into a place of murder, torture, thievery? Nothing—that is one answer; that was our answer to Trujillo's thirty-one

years of horror in the Dominican Republic; and it was our answer to Rojas
Pinilla in Colombia, to Pérez Jiménez in Venezuela. Or, do we intervene,
knock heads together, force gentlemanly behavior upon evildoers? We did
that in the Dominican Republic, 1916–24; in Haiti, 1915–34; and then we
tried it again in the Dominican Republic in 1965—and, for our pains, we
aroused the wrath of most of the Latin American republics, who shouted
"Yankee imperialism!" and demanded the end of intervention. In the case of
Duvalier, we watched uneasily as he pursued his bloody course after assuming the presidency in 1957, and we protested from time to time. When he
announced his "reelection" for six years in 1961 (though he still had two
years to go on his first "elected" term), we bade our ambassador come home
for consultation, and we were not represented at his inauguration. Then we
sent our ambassador back to Port-au-Prince with orders to maintain an icy
silence, to have no conversations with Duvalier's officials. President Kennedy
made no secret of his distaste for the Haitian dictatorship, and in 1962 he
cut off virtually all aid (which had averaged some $13 million a year) when
Duvalier rejected the United States conditions—which included plans for
early elections, curtailment of Duvalier's secret police, and the publication of
nonfiscal accounts. In the spring of 1963, when the Dominican President
Juan Bosch begged the United States to support an invasion of Haiti to topple
Duvalier, we refused—which angered Bosch and prompted one Haitian
citizen to remark: "We thought that the United States might overthrow
him [Duvalier], but all you did was cut off your aid. You know there is resentment here against the United States, for if you really wanted to overthrow him you could." In May, 1963, while the Haitians and Dominicans
glowered at each other across the border, we withdrew the families of Americans in Haiti, and suspended relations briefly. Then when our ambassador
returned in June, he was promptly withdrawn, at Duvalier's demand—his
only crime being the sympathy he had shown for the dictator's victims.

In January, 1964, with the installation of the Johnson administration,
the mood of Washington changed: a new ambassador was appointed with
orders to be affable, to attend official ceremonies, to have no contacts with
the oppressed, and to express no disapproval. The chief result of this policy
was to anger the honest opponents of Duvalier, who could no longer get
even sympathy at the American Embassy. Duvalier, quite naturally, welcomed the new United States line, expressed confidence in Lyndon Johnson
—while voicing his resentment against President Kennedy, who, he said,
had not addressed a single communication to him, Duvalier, in his three years
in office. (It is possible that Washington's new stance reflected the consoling
argument that Duvalier—no matter how brutal he might be—was, after all,
anti-Communist.) Papa Doc countered with a new mood of his own, made
a play for the resumption of American aid and a revival of the languishing
tourist trade—but in neither of these ambitions has he proved successful, as
of mid-1967: for almost five years, there has been no financial aid from the
United States, aside from support for an anti-malaria program and shipments
of food for the poor; and the tourist trade has been reduced to a trickle.

Perhaps a wan hope is that the Haitians themselves will rid their country of the tyrannical Duvalier. This hope is nourished by some thousands of Haitian refugees in New York, Chicago, Washington, and Montreal. One of the activities of these émigrés is a radio program broadcast from New York each morning at 6 A.M.: this daily bombardment of anti-Duvalier arguments directed at the Haitian people is called the "Black Mass" in Haiti, and Haitians greet their fellows with the query, "Have you been to Mass today?" There are repeated attempts by émigré groups to land on Haitian soil, but these are met by instant capture, torture, and death.

The nagging question for all concerned is what will happen when Duvalier is finally eliminated—as he must be, and will be. Will there be a repetition of the Dominican experience of 1965, with unilateral intervention by the United States? Or, will there be joint action by the OAS? Official Washington hopes that this last solution may be possible, but there is strong resistance in most of Latin America to the creation of an Inter-American Peace Force. Meanwhile the Haitian people—in fact the whole hemisphere —carry the burden of François Duvalier's bestial rule.

THE DOMINICAN REPUBLIC

The Dominican Republic, which shares the island of Hispaniola with Haiti, has almost twice the land area of her western neighbor, but houses fewer people. The 3.8 million Dominicans (1966) are predominantly a mulatto people, with ambition to be reckoned white. With more land and fewer mountains than Haiti, the Dominicans have enjoyed some prosperity from sugar, coffee, cacao, rice, corn, and tobacco.

THE WINNING OF FREEDOM

The Dominicans' half-century fight for liberty is the most protracted and painful in the record of the emancipation of Spanish America. The nation was first caught in the upheavals of Haiti and was fought over by the French, Spanish, English, mulattoes, and Negroes during the years 1791–1803. Haiti finally ousted the French in 1803, but the Dominicans remained under the control of Napoleon's forces six years longer. After evicting the French in 1809, the Dominicans tried to establish a free republic, but in 1814 Spain was again in possession of the territory where Bartolomé Columbus had established the city of Santo Domingo in 1496.

Spain, with Ferdinand VII restored to his throne in 1814, proved inept and tyrannical. Disillusioned, the Dominican patriots rebelled in 1821, proclaiming the freedom of "Spanish Haiti,"[1] and sent envoys to Simón Bolívar asking admittance to Gran Colombia. But Haiti's President Boyer, getting the news before Bolívar could, led his Negro army over the mountains, marched upon Santo Domingo, and in 1822 declared the union of the island under the rule of Port-au-Prince. The Dominicans yielded; they had no choice, for they numbered only 54,000, as compared with Haiti's 650,000.

Haitian rule (1822–44) was brutal. Negro troops occupied the country and ex-slaves filled the principal offices. The white minority, owners of

---

[1] The reader is reminded that the entire island was variously called La Isla Española, Hispaniola, Haiti, and Santo Domingo. "Spanish Haiti," or the eastern end of the island, is now the Dominican Republic.

the more productive plantations, fled before this Negro invasion. The Haitian government, intent upon enforcing Negro supremacy, settled Haitians upon Dominican soil and introduced colonies of freed slaves from the United States. Young men were impressed into the Haitian army. Taxes were onerous, as Haiti sought funds with which to meet the exorbitant claims of France. The University of Santo Domingo, one of the first universities in America, was closed. The Church, boasting the first bishopric in the New World, was cut off from papal supervision, foreign priests were rejected, and the clergy deteriorated. The production of sugar and tobacco decreased, and misery spread. Out of this general confusion emerged a secret revolutionary society called La Trinitaria, dedicated to "God, Fatherland and Liberty," whose genius and mentor was Juan Pablo Duarte, a young Dominican educated in Paris. Their chance to strike came in 1843, when Haiti was torn by the civil war which overturned Boyer. In 1844 the Dominican Republic was at last free.

CONFUSION AND TYRANNY, 1844–1916

The Dominicans were ill-equipped to profit by their hard-won freedom. For seventy-two years, they floundered under corrupt, incompetent, and cruel dictators. The Dominican record during these years was as dismal as the Haitian.

When the last Haitian garrison was finally evicted, the new nation was torn by the argument as to whether it should assert its full dignity as a free republic or seek protection of some foreign power. Duarte and his aides stood for complete independence; the generals, aware of the threat from Haiti, favored a protectorate under Spain, France, England, or the United States. In the initial struggles following the ousting of the Haitians, Duarte and his young men lost to General Pedro Santana and his confederates. The idealists went into exile, and the generals ruled.

Nowhere else has *personalismo*—the rule of the boss—been more persistent and malign than in this weak nation. From 1844 to the end of the century three men dominated Dominican history. The first, Pedro Santana, was soon joined by Buenaventura Báez; in the beginning they worked together and took turns in the presidency, but by the 1850's they were open enemies. Santana dominated most of the time until his death in 1864, and Báez lived, to the further distress of the country, until 1882. Both were brazen opportunists, quite ready to betray their country for their own ends. A few better men served brief terms but contributed little. The century was rounded out by the bestial seventeen-year rule of Ulises Heureaux (1882–99), perhaps the most pitiless tyranny in the history of Latin America.

The recurring theme of the nineteenth century was the desirability of exchanging national sovereignty, total or partial, for greater security under some foreign flag. Fear of Haiti, learned by sad experience, was chiefly responsible. The rise of the braggart Faustin Soulouque in Haiti

(1847–59) and his repeated attacks upon the Dominicans encouraged such proposals. France, Spain, England, and the United States were approached, but until 1859 all refused to be embroiled. In that year Santana made one of his periodic returns to the presidency and found Spain ready to entertain the idea of recapturing some of her lost glory in America. The season was propitious: England and France were convalescing from the Crimean War, and the United States was on the eve of civil war. Santana's zeal for reunion with Spain had two roots: national security against Haiti and assurance of power for himself against the opposition of Báez.

In 1861 Santana ordered the lowering of the Dominican flag and the raising of the Spanish. And with Santo Domingo now a colony of Spain, Pedro Santana served as captain-general, well protected by Spanish troops transferred from Puerto Rico and Cuba. But the pleasure of being ruled by Isabella II was short-lived, both for Santana and for his Dominican subjects. Business languished, as Spain manipulated the island's affairs for her own profit. Churchmen raged, as a Spanish bishop imposed reforms upon the disorderly island priests. Aspiring Dominicans complained when the better posts were reserved for Spaniards. Foreign residents chafed under numerous discriminations; Americans, in particular, were outraged when Spanish officials showed open partiality for the Confederate cause. Santana himself, after a year as captain-general, resigned in protest against slights by Spanish underlings—and was promptly granted a royal title and a handsome pension by Queen Isabella. The Spaniard appointed to replace him as captain-general was an irritating despot and provoked fresh protests. Meanwhile, yellow fever killed some 9,000 of the 21,000 Spanish soldiers introduced for the defense of the colony. During 1863 and 1864, revolts spread throughout the colony. By 1865, it was clear that Spanish rule was a failure, and Isabella ordered the withdrawal of Spanish troops.

Once rid of the Spaniards in 1865, the witless rulers of the republic blundered into various schemes for surrendering all or part of the republic's sovereignty to the United States. In 1866–67 President José María Cabral, a disciple of Santana, sought to secure desperately needed funds by leasing or selling part of northeastern Samaná Bay to the United States as a naval base. The negotiations were greeted with a loud Dominican outburst against "despoiling the *patria*." In 1868 Buenaventura Báez seized the presidency for the fourth time, with denunciation of those who would peddle Dominican soil. In order to replenish the treasury he made a ruinous contract with London bankers for a loan of about $3,750,000. But the bankers, as tricky as Báez, paid over little of the money received from the sale of the republic's bonds. Nimble Báez, in a swift change of mind, then resolved to sell the United States what it wanted on Samaná Bay and even to annex his republic to the United States. This proposal to add a Dominican state to the American union was so awkwardly pressed by President Ulysses S. Grant, and so involved with some of the shady characters of his official family, that it was repudiated by the American Senate. Credit for defeat of the plan belongs to Senator Charles Sumner, whose denunciation was convincing: "The resolution before the Senate," he told the Senators, "commits Congress to a dance of blood. . . . Báez . . . is sustained in power by the Government of the United States so that he may betray his country. . . . The Island . . . can never become a permanent possession of the United States. . . . It is [the Dominicans'] by right of possession; by their sweat and blood mingling with the soil; by tropical position . . . their independence is as precious to them as is ours to us and it is placed under the safeguard of natural laws which we cannot violate with impunity." The fiasco, a rebuff to Grant, brought discredit to Báez. But that durable general made one more comeback and was elected for the fifth time in 1878, only to be evicted by fresh revolt.

The seventeen-year dictatorship (1882–99) of the Negro Ulises Heureaux is one of the most monstrous episodes in Dominican history. Tall, erect, and handsome, Heureaux was well educated, fearless, and versatile. He was an unscrupulous master of men; by bribery, bullying, and murder he cowed all opposition. He maintained an impressive spy ring, using his current mistresses to report on the careless words of his subjects and assigning his former mistresses to similar service in foreign capitals. His considerable army, his personal luxury, and his numerous servitors drained the treasury; he tried to replenish it by exacting forced loans from leading citizens, printing unsupported paper money, and floating ruinous bond issues in Europe. Under his eye, enterprising Americans organized the San Domingo Development Corporation, which bought up some European claims against the republic and extended further credits to the dictator; it was given control of the customhouses. Heureaux made unsuccessful efforts to reopen the project of selling Samaná Bay. In 1899 assassination ended his tyranny.

The seventeen years 1899–1916 brought anarchy, a swift succession of short-lived and usually corrupt presidents, and the repeated intervention of foreign powers. Debts amounting to some $32 million were owing to nationals of France, Belgium, Germany, Italy, Spain, and the United States. Threats of occupation and demands for control of customs revenue came from interested governments. In 1904 the United States, in support of the exaggerated claims of the San Domingo Development Corporation, took over the customhouse in Puerto Plata. In that same year President Theodore Roosevelt, seeing the threat of European powers gaining a fresh foothold in the Caribbean, told Congress: "The adherence of the United States to the Monroe Doctrine may force the United States, however reluctantly, in flagrant cases of . . . wrongdoing or impotence, to the exercise of an international police power." This "Roosevelt Corollary" of the Monroe Doctrine was applied to the Dominican Republic in 1905, when Roosevelt appointed an American receiver of customs to take over all customhouses, collect duties, divide 55 per cent of the proceeds among the foreign creditors, and turn over the remaining 45 per cent to the republic's treasury.[2]

---

[2] Roosevelt did this by executive order, without sanction of his Congress but with the approval of the Dominican government then in power. Two years later the American Congress belatedly approved Roosevelt's plan and ratified a treaty which gave the United States right to intervene in defense of its agents.

The plan worked admirably for a time. Foreign creditors shared fairly; and the Dominican treasury got more from its 45 per cent share than it had previously from a full 100 per cent, a grim commentary on the honesty of its tax collectors. Under President Ramón Cáceres (1908–11), one of the ablest leaders in the republic's history, there were encouraging signs of unity. But when he was assassinated, civil war again broke out, with three ex-presidents leading their factions. Emissaries from the United States finally brought agreement among the contenders; Archbishop Adolfo Nouel assumed the presidency, but after sixteen months retired in frustration. Again there were outbreaks, and again there were warnings from Washington. These disorders continued until 1916, when American marines were sent to occupy Santo Domingo and other principal centers, and began an eight-year military rule.

AMERICAN INTERVENTION AND THE AFTERMATH, 1916–30

Rule by American marines was unpleasant, both for the Dominicans and for their uninvited guests. The American occupation officials, in contrast to those in Haiti during the same years, governed directly, rather than through puppet presidents,[3] and named American officials for all except inferior posts. It was, in the terms of the Navy's official order: "military occupation . . . military government . . . military law." Under American officials a national constabulary was trained and armed, the building of roads and other public works was expedited, sanitation projects were initiated, the public treasury was organized, useless employees were dropped, and the budget was balanced. Despite the excellence of much that was done, popular resentment spread. Clashes recurred between the marines and unruly elements—those who opposed the Americans were called "bandits." Grave abuses of power by the occupying forces were later uncovered by a congressional investigation in Washington; it revealed rough treatment of citizens, some cases of careless shooting, and more cases of incompetent handling of uncooperative nationals by both officers and men. A few editors who criticized the occupation officials were court-martialed. When a Dominican poet, Fabio Fiallo, was sentenced to jail for denunciation of the United States, indignation was widespread and his case was trumpeted all over Latin America as an instance of American arrogance. Altogether, the American rule of the Dominicans seemed needlessly irritating, and both countries were relieved when it ended. In 1922 Sumner Welles, one of the wisest of American diplomats, was sent to arrange the final withdrawal of American forces. Under his leadership an election was held in 1924, Horacio Vásquez was installed as president, and the marines departed; only a financial adviser remained to handle customs receipts in the interests of the island's creditors.

3 Dominicans still laud the patriotic refusal of the scholar Dr. Francisco Henríquez y Carvajal, who was acting president when the marines arrived, to accept a puppet role himself.

It soon became clear that the political habits of the Dominicans had undergone no radical change under American tutelage. Vásquez proved reasonably competent but marred his record by seeking illegal reelection. The final arbiter was now the American-trained constabulary; when revolt broke out again in 1930, the leadership of the country was inevitably seized by the head of that well-equipped force, Rafael Leonidas Trujillo Molina.

THE ERA OF TRUJILLO, 1930–61

There is precedent for the use of the phrase "era of Trujillo." The man who ruled the republic as president, or master of presidents, from 1930 to 1961 used it himself. Here is a sample, the promulgation of a law in 1947:

> Given in Ciudad Trujillo . . . this 14th day in the month of June in the year 1947, the 104th year of our Independence, the 84th year of the Restoration of the Republic, and the 18th year of the Trujillo era.
> Rafael L. Trujillo

The Generalissimo was not modest. There was, in fact, no reason why he should be. His record was impressive.

An act of God gave Trujillo his first chance to prove his prowess. A few days after his installation in 1930, a hurricane swept the land, killing some 2,000 people and leveling most of ancient Santo Domingo. Forthwith he organized relief for the wounded and the homeless, found food for the hungry, and set about the rebuilding of the city. Six years later, at the spontaneous demand of his grateful people (or so runs the official record), the 440-year-old city of Santo Domingo was rechristened Ciudad Trujillo. A loyal congress conferred on him the title *El Benefactor de la Patria*.

No other Latin American ruler offers a more eloquent record of material achievement—or a more savage record of repression of human rights. He took over in 1930 a nation in which lawlessness, banditry, and civil strife had prevailed since its birth in 1844; he made it into a tranquil land whose country roads were as safe as Iowa's. In 1930 the republic was bankrupt and poverty-ridden, with a foreign debt of more than $20 million and a total national income of about $7 million; by 1957 foreign and domestic debts had been liquidated, and by 1960 the national income had increased to $529 million. During most of Trujillo's regime the national budget was balanced, and in 1960 it stood at $147.3 million. In that same year, sales in the world market were more than $174.4 million, about 51 per cent from sugar, 13 per cent from coffee, 12 per cent from cacao.

Impressive buildings and public works further attested Trujillo's skill. The capital city was smartly modern and boasted excellent public buildings. New highways gave access to the interior, modern docks and harbor equipment invited trade, hydroelectric plants furnished power and light, and modern water supply systems delivered pure water to the larger cities.

Progress in industrialization was seen in the new assembly plants, factories for processing food, distilleries, cement works, and sugar mills.

There was a well-advertised social program. New schools were built, illiteracy was reduced. The ancient University of Santo Domingo, believed by patriotic Dominicans to be the oldest in the Americas,[4] was housed in a sparkling new University City on the edge of the capital. Hospitals and clinics multiplied. Campaigns to eradicate hookworm, yellow fever, malaria, and other ills were notably successful.

But these blessings were bought at the price of liberty. Trujillo's constitution gravely described the government as "civil, republican, democratic and representative"; the standard division of powers was made among the legislative, executive, and judicial arms; elections were held in accordance with the rules. But in practice Trujillo exercised all power—even when a brother or other stooge was president. Congress was held on a short leash. Judges interpreted the master's will. Elections were all but unanimous. There was only one political party, the *Partido Dominicano,* dedicated to "sustaining and fostering" Trujillo's creed. Newspapers said no unpleasant word about the dictator. Schools used textbooks in which the era of Trujillo was extolled. The University faculty included no dissenters. One of Trujillo's vice-presidents struck the correct note by erecting a neon sign over his home with the legend *Dios y Trujillo.*

The republic's serenity was won by a long drawn-out purge as thorough as any devised by Stalin or Hitler. Critics of the Benefactor were shot in lonely side streets or jailed without trial, or escaped into exile. "There is no known Communist in the Dominican Republic!" boasted Trujillo in full-page advertisements in *The New York Times*—by which one inferred that not a solitary critic of his regime remained. Critics were all Communists —this was Trujillo's formula.

It was also widely believed that Trujillo's vengeance pursued his critics onto foreign soil. Instances were cited of mysterious deaths or disappearances of his enemies in Puerto Rico, Mexico, and even the United States. A notorious case was that of Dr. Jesús Galíndez, a Basque who had lived in the Dominican Republic for years and then moved to New York City, where he taught in Columbia University and wrote critically about the Dominican dictator. On March 12, 1956, Galíndez disappeared on the streets of New York; rumors spread that he had been abducted by Trujillo's agents, flown back to the Dominican Republic, and murdered. The report could not be substantiated, but its truth is still widely credited.

The "era of Trujillo" was pleasant and profitable for Trujillo and his numerous kin. There were 1,870 monuments to him in the capital city, many others elsewhere. Scores of his relatives were on the national payroll. His brother Hector served a term as president. A son who flunked out of an American military school (he spent too much time with lovely girls in Hollywood) was chief of staff of the armed forces. Another son was vice-president. But Rafael Trujillo *was* the government of the Dominican

---

4 But, with due apologies to the Dominicans, it must be noted that the University of Mexico and the University of San Marcos at Lima have better claims.

Republic. The profit in solid dollars was substantial. His fortune, according to men close to the dictator, amounted to some $800 million (a sheer guess, of course). It was said—but again, nothing can be proved—that he and his family controlled 65 per cent of the sugar production, owned 35 per cent of all cultivable land, operated twelve of sixteen sugar mills. Other holdings, it was believed, included the principal import companies, which gave him a virtual monopoly on the sales of automobiles, machinery, and electrical goods; they also included cattle ranches, meat-packing plants, dairies, radio and television stations, printing, cigarette factories, coffee exports, cement, construction, shipbuilding, breweries, flour mills, textile mills, cotton plantations, and lands with deposits of petroleum and minerals. It was also said that the Benefactor took a toll of 20 per cent or more on all contracts for public works. Trujillo, a common soldier, whom the American marines taught to drill and shoot, had gone far.

By 1960 signs multiplied that the Benefactor had perhaps gone too far and too fast. The ousting of Pérez Jiménez in Venezuela and Batista in Cuba set loose protests everywhere against all dictators—with Trujillo the chief target. In June, 1959, an expeditionary force of Dominican exiles, aided by Cubans, landed on the Dominican coast; most of them were promptly killed, although a few found safety in the interior. This group was the nucleus of the "14 of June" movement, a guerrilla band of great bravery and dedication, aligned with Castroism but attracting support from Dominican leftists, undoubtedly including some Communists—a group which was to play an influential role in the convulsions of the country in the spring of 1965. Trujillo promptly appealed to the Organization of American States, charging that both Cuba and Venezuela were lending aid to disgruntled Dominicans who sought to unseat him. Then followed a frantic increase in the Dominican armed forces at a cost of $50 million. In January, 1960, Trujillo's secret police unearthed a plot which involved many prominent professional men. Mass arrests followed; according to the government, hundreds of men and women were jailed, but leaders of the underground charged that the prisoners numbered 2,000 or 3,000. Prison sentences of twenty and thirty years were given by courts which moved swiftly and permitted no opportunity for defense. Charges that prisoners were being foully tortured were widely circulated. So grievous were these charges that the six Roman Catholic bishops intervened. On Sunday, January 31, 1960, their joint pastoral letter was read in all churches. It was a message of sympathy over "the grievous blow that has afflicted many Dominican homes," a restatement of the Church's belief in "the inviolable dignity of the human person," the insistence that defense of human rights constitutes "a prior and higher law than that of any state whatever." The bishops reasserted "the rights of all men to freedom of conscience, of the press, and of assembly." They condemned, by inference, the current acts of the dictator as "a grave offense against God, against the dignity of man . . . ," and appealed to "the highest authority of the country" to end such excesses. The government's reply was to dismiss the churchmen's protest as "insincere" and inspired by anger against the Trujillo regime for permitting Protestants to operate freely within the nation. As if in retaliation, the government decreed that the sect called "Jehovah's Witnesses," which had long been banned at the demand of the Church, could now operate without restraint.

Hard upon these events came demands from various countries of the Caribbean area for action against the tyrannies of Trujillo. The government of Venezuela asked the Organization of American States to investigate "the denial of human rights" in the Dominican Republic. The OAS assigned the task to its Peace Commission, made up of representatives of the United States, El Salvador, Mexico, Uruguay, and Venezuela. This commission gathered evidence and submitted a report in June, 1960, charging the Dominican government with "flagrant and widespread violation of human rights" which had aggravated tensions in the Caribbean area. Shortly after issuance of this report came an almost successful plot to assassinate President Betancourt of Venezuela, with clear evidence that the attack had been executed by Trujillo's men.

The case of the Dominican Republic then came before a meeting of the representatives of all the American republics, summoned by the OAS in San José, Costa Rica, in August, 1960. It was now clear that all the nations were minded to call a halt to the despotism of Trujillo. The United States, long uncomfortable in its role as quasi-protector of the Benefactor, was at last ready to take forthright action. However, the spokesmen for Washington, smarting under the onslaughts of Cuba's Castro and aware of how easily an overturn in the Dominican Republic might prepare the way for a Castro-like regime in the Dominican land, sought backing for a plan under which the OAS would supervise elections and furnish a caretaker force during the period of Dominican reconstruction. This proposal was angrily rejected by the Latin Americans—an action reflecting the continuing suspicion of intervention. Agreement was finally reached upon a resolution accusing the Trujillo regime of "acts of aggression and intervention" against Venezuela, urging all member states to break diplomatic relations with the Dominican Republic, and recommending limited economic sanctions including a ban on all shipments of arms to the guilty government.

By November, 1960, almost all the nations of the Americas, including the United States, had severed diplomatic relations with Trujillo's government. And in January, 1961, the OAS passed a resolution calling for limited economic sanctions against the Dominican Republic. However, Washington's attitude was ambiguous: President Eisenhower insisted that the United States put teeth into its condemnation of Trujillo by cutting off the Dominican share in the United States sugar allotment, and by refusing to increase it out of the share formerly allotted Cuba. (This arrangement for sale of sugar to the United States carried a tidy premium of 2 cents on each pound.) But Eisenhower's prudent suggestion was blocked by ardent admirers of the Dominican dictator in the American Senate; typical of these was Senator Allen J. Ellender of Louisiana, who said: "I wish there were a Trujillo in every country of South and Central America." He and others carried the day by not only refusing to cut the Dominican allotment, but by increasing it by 332,000 tons. This odd largess reminded critics that the United States had supported that shabby tyrant for three decades.

By early 1961 there were ominous signs that the dictatorship was beginning to crack. The rebuff by the OAS, the threat of invasion from Cuba, the recurring quarrels with Haiti—all these put Trujillo on the defensive; and his bellicosity and lack of confidence were reflected in his mounting expenditures on armaments. The business community was alarmed by the drop in foreign exchange reserves in the Central Bank from $48 million at the end of 1957 to $8 million in March, 1961. The nervousness of the dictator was revealed in his summary handling of the Church. The priests were the pipe-line to the people, and the lives of those who were bold enough to speak out against terrorism were threatened, and more than fifty priests were expelled from the country. An assault on the Church—as will be noted in the record of almost all Latin American dictatorships—is the final sign that all is not well. The atmosphere was one of low morale and waning public confidence, with all signs pointing to the end of *El Benefactor de la Patria*.

On May 30, while the sixty-nine-year-old Trujillo was driving on a country road to meet one of his numerous mistresses, a car drew up along-side, and its occupants opened fire with machine guns. Twenty-seven bullets put an end to the thirty-one-year rule of the durable Caesar of the Caribbean. The assassins had rendered overdue justice.

THE DOMINICAN REPUBLIC SINCE TRUJILLO, 1961–

Trujillo's death left a vacuum in the island republic. The carefully devised structure of government was entirely dependent upon one man, and that man was dead. There was the army, but no general had ever dared call his soul his own. There was the cluster of Trujillos—son Rafael, Jr., three brothers, sundry others—but not one of them had ever ventured to con-tradict the head of the clan: they were puppets granted temporary position and power, a sadistic, degenerate, and corrupt lot whom Trujillo in moments of rage would slap and kick. There was the band of petty office holders, miserably paid, cowed by their superiors, all trembling in the shadow of the Benefactor. Perhaps the best man in the Trujillo entourage was Joaquín Balaguer, who had been adorned with the presidential sash on the firm understanding that he must truckle to the dictator.

The immediate reaction of the Dominican masses to the assassination was stunned terror. There was little popular rejoicing. For three decades anyone so bold as to affront the dictator had been dragged off to prison, to unspeakable torture, or thrown to the sharks. (Various guesses have been made as to how many were murdered—5,000, 10,000—but no one knows.) And now it seemed that God might strike down any who shouted with relief at the tyrant's death. Under this spell, puppet President Joaquín Balaguer assumed control. From Paris came Rafael Trujillo, Jr. ("Ramfis"), thirty-two-year-old heir apparent. (His chartered plane cost $28,000: there was money in the family.) Ramfis became chief of the armed services, and he and Balaguer settled down to rule the country together. A manhunt was launched to avenge the assassination, but the bloody deeds (perhaps hundreds were killed) were chiefly chargeable to Ramfis, who for the moment seemed to have assumed his father's mantle. Balaguer decreed nine days of mourning, and said the proper words on the day after the killing: "The death of such a great man represents an irreparable loss for the republic which he had dignified with his exemplary patriotism and which he enriched with his lasting works." But whether prompted by conscience or expediency, Balaguer soon began to talk softly about the new era of democracy which was about to supplant the old tyranny, and sought to persuade the United States and other nations that he offered the "bridge" to this democracy. Even Ramfis seemed to see the wisdom of a more moderate course, joining Balaguer in promising free elections and amnesty for political prisoners and exiles, a few of whom returned during the summer. But Ramfis was not pleased when, in October, Balaguer spoke words designed to cleanse his own record of slavish obedience to the dead dictator: appearing before the United Nations General Assembly he freely confessed the "decades of terror" under Trujillo, pled for the lifting of diplomatic and economic sanctions by the OAS, arguing that the sins of the dictator should not be visited on his people.

In November, 1961, all seemed set for a military coup to oust Balaguer. The chief instigators were Ramfis and two brothers of the slain dictator, the "wicked uncles," who had had a hand in the long butchery of the Trujillo days. After all, their interests were involved: they thought they owned the republic, and did not propose to lose their patrimony. At this point Washington despatched twelve warships to stand guard off Santo Domingo, with some 1,200 marines prepared to land should the Trujillos attempt a come-back. The hint was enough: Ramfis got the point and sailed off to Paris; and the "wicked uncles" gave up and left the island.

Although Balaguer had weathered the attempted coup, his position was shaky. As the numbness of the people wore off their anger had gradually begun to express itself, and for months there had been riots and strikes. By the end of 1961 it became clear that the Dominican people would not tolerate any holdovers from Trujillo days in positions of power. The many monuments and statues to the Benefactor had been torn down, the capital city had returned to its historic name of Santo Domingo—but Balaguer was still there, the dictator's servile man; and by his side was General Rodríguez Echevarría, head of the air force and rough personification of the armed men who had long done the dictator's bidding. These men would have to go. In December, Balaguer announced a plan for a provisional Council of State, promising to resign as its president when the OAS lifted its sanctions. The Council, sworn in on January 1, 1962, curiously included the two survivors among Trujillo's assassins, who thought to capitalize on their share in that affair (though it soon became clear that the "regicides" had no popular following): one of these was Antonio Imbert Barreras, who was later to play a key role in the Dominican crisis of 1965. The OAS soon voted to end the sanctions. But there was stormy weather ahead: anti-Balaguer rioting broke out in mid-January; Echevarría staged a coup and almost succeeded in seizing power for a military junta; a counter-coup rescued the Council, and Balaguer was replaced as its president by Dr. Rafael Bonnelly, a reasonably able man. Balaguer found it prudent to seek asylum with the Papal Nuncio, and in March both he and Echevarría were exiled to Puerto Rico. Bonnelly and the Council, promising elections not later than December, maintained their tenuous hold throughout the year, with generous grants in money from Washington. But the man who emerged as the leading figure was the adroit Antonio Imbert, in charge of the police force, which grew in power and prestige.

Then in December, 1962, the clouds seemed to part, as the Dominicans flocked to the polls in the first free election in thirty-eight years. The victor, with some 60 per cent of the vote, was Juan Bosch, a fifty-four-year-old intellectual who had spent most of the Trujillo years in exile, plotting and writing against the tyrant. Bosch was inaugurated in February, 1963, supported by a groundswell of enthusiasm at home and abroad. He had the firm backing of the United States: President Kennedy was particularly friendly, placing high hopes in the new regime as a showcase for the Alliance for Progress. Incorruptible but contentious, Bosch had brave plans for the rescue of his homeland, and he worked hard to establish his reforms. Several million acres of Trujillo-owned lands had been taken over by the government, and Bosch proposed to establish 70,000 families upon their own small farms. But Bosch had serious handicaps. He had to depend upon the services of the distended bureaucracy inherited from Trujillo—greedy, incompetent men. He had to deal warily with the armed forces, who were of no mind to cooperate in this new democratic digression. Of these the air force, dominated by Colonel Elías Wessin y Wessin, and the national police force headed by Antonio Imbert were the most truculent. The air was heavy with charges that Bosch was "soft on Communism," that he was too lenient with outright Communists and Cuban agents. There seem to have been slight grounds for such charges: Bosch, an idealist and a sound democrat, simply wished all to move in freedom. But the slander stuck; after all, Bosch was talking of fresh bold moves in organizing the economic and social life of the republic, and this sounded like dangerous heresy to men who controlled business and agriculture, many of them relics of the Trujillo days. His enemies proved too strong for him, and his presidency lasted but seven months. In September, 1963, he sought to curb the military by removing Wessin y Wessin, thus uniting against him the military leaders, who closed in upon him, arrested him, dissolved Congress, outlawed all Communists and alleged Communists, and closed the schools. Bosch was sent into exile, Imbert's police hustled some 500 "subversives" off to jail, and once again the United States suspended recognition and cut off all aid.

Thus, in September, 1963, the Dominicans were again ruled by a committee. But the new three-man junta, as everyone was well aware, ruled only by grace of the military—chiefly Antonio Imbert and General Wessin y Wessin. The "Committee," however, soon slipped into the background, and by December there emerged as the actual president one Donald Reid Cabral, a long-time dealer in automobiles. And in the midst of strikes and riots, Reid Cabral maintained an uneasy control for sixteen months. The United States, after its brief spurt of indignation following the September coup, resumed relations and aided generously, actually putting some $100 million into the Dominican Republic during the Reid Cabral period, more than had been granted to the constitutionally elected Juan Bosch. Reid made a few gestures toward orderliness and honesty, but almost all Dominicans were thoroughly unhappy with the makeshift arrangement. And then, in April, 1965, came the great explosion.

The Dominican revolt, which began on April 24, 1965, proved one of the most tortuous and bloody episodes in the annals of inter-American relations. Many of its phases are still unclear, and historians will long debate the rights and wrongs in this bizarre and tragic affair. It must be considered as a delayed reaction to the assassination of Trujillo on May 30, 1961: the Dominican people had never properly settled their score with the dead dictator.

The uprising was the work of a loosely organized company of rebels, whose central idea seems to have been the restoration to office of the legally elected President Juan Bosch. When the rebels seized two army posts and the chief radio station in Santo Domingo on Saturday, April 24, everyone was apparently caught off balance. The regular armed forces, well equipped with planes and tanks, promptly rallied under the label of the "loyalists," although it was unclear to whom they were loyal—certainly not to Reid Cabral, who resigned within twenty-four hours under pressure from both sides, went into hiding, and finally found asylum in New York. The American Embassy was totally unprepared: the Ambassador was in Georgia visiting his ailing mother; eleven of the thirteen military attachés were attending a routine conference in Panama. Almost the only people—at least the only Americans—who knew that trouble was in the making appear to have been a handful of newspaper correspondents, who had been apprehensive for weeks.

This general disarray continued on Sunday, April 25, with almost everyone contributing to the confusion. The rebels were distributing weapons to citizens at random, including heavy guns to teenagers and gasoline for the making of "Molotov cocktails." The loyalists were appealing to the American Embassy for intervention by United States troops, arguing that they could not protect the lives of the 2,500 Americans in Santo Domingo. Meanwhile Elías Wessin y Wessin, commander at the San Isidro air base— now a self-appointed brigadier general and shortly to emerge as the dominant figure among the loyalists—was sending out planes to bomb the beleaguered city, with special attention to the National Palace, now occupied by the rebel leaders.

The position of the United States was ambiguous from the outset.

For days Washington loudly proclaimed its neutrality, insisting that the protection of American lives was its only concern (a concern which all agreed was justified). But the record suggests that Washington's public pronouncements in the early days of the conflict were in sharp contrast to the actions and decisions of United States government personnel. President Johnson was to announce on the radio on May 2 that the rebellion had begun "as a popular democratic revolution, committed to democracy and social justice." But the fact is that U.S. Embassy officials and military attachés identified themselves almost immediately with the loyalist cause, and the "popular democratic revolution" was scarcely twenty-four hours old when messages to Washington warned that the return of Bosch would mean an eventual Communist takeover. The evidence—or lack of it— upon which this conclusion was based will long be a subject for debate. Just what, exactly, was the "policy" of the administration at this juncture? Was it, perhaps, no policy at all, but rather a series of impromptu reactions to the hasty judgments of lesser officials—judgments which were based largely on rumor, prejudice, or panic? Or, as Theodore Draper suggests, does this "image of a pure, innocent Washington and an incompetent, frightened embassy seem somewhat fanciful"? And is it perhaps true that "a Washington that had pursued a different policy before April 24 would have discouraged the kind of advice that came from Santo Domingo"? These are questions for the future historian.[5]

The frantic telegrams sent to Washington by the Embassy[6] on Sunday, April 25, warning of the Communist danger, were followed on Monday by messages including the suggestion that the United States should give at least logistical support to the loyalists, who had put in an urgent request for walkie-talkies and other communications equipment. The walkie-talkies soon arrived and were turned over to General Wessin. Early Tuesday morning (while the United States was still "neutral") it seems that the 82nd Airborne Division at Fort Bragg was given a briefing in preparation for a "parachute assault" on the Dominican Republic—the details of which would indicate a plan not merely to protect American lives but to give direct aid to the Wessin forces. Also on Tuesday, April 27, a meeting took place between Ambassador Bennett, who had now returned to his post, and Lieutenant Colonel Francisco Caamaño Deñó, commander of the rebel forces. The rebels, it seems, had despaired of victory and had asked the Ambassador to negotiate a settlement. Bennett refused: his response, according to the Colonel, was that "this is not the time to negotiate, this is the time to surrender"; while the Ambassador himself claimed, curiously, that "mediation" would have meant "intervention"—for which he had no authorization. The rebuff spurred the rebels to renew the fight.

[5] Helpful information on the Dominican crisis will be found in: Theodore Draper: "The Dominican Crisis; A Case Study in American Policy," *Commentary* (December, 1965); Senator J. William Fulbright: speech before the U.S. Senate, September 15, 1965; Philip Geyelin: "Dominican Flashback; Behind the Scenes," *The Wall Street Journal*, June 25, 1965; Dan Kurzman: *Santo Domingo: Revolt of the Damned* (New York: G. P. Putnam's Sons, 1965); and Tad Szulc: *Dominican Diary* (New York: Delacorte Press, 1965).

[6] The officer in charge of the Embassy, in the absence of the Ambassador, was William B. Connett, Jr., who had been in the Dominican Republic only five months.

On Wednesday the loyalists, with the aid and counsel of the U.S. Embassy (and with at least the blessing of the administration in Washington), quickly assembled a junta, choosing for its head an obscure air force officer, Colonel Pedro Bartolomé Benoit, who would serve as a front for General Wessin y Wessin, who had an unsavory reputation among the Dominican people as a would-be dictator. Wessin, however, remained the dominant leader of the loyalists, with Benoit the paper head of a paper government.

Also on Wednesday, Ambassador Bennett cabled Washington that "while leftist propaganda will fuzz this up as a fight between the military and the people, the issue is really between those who want a Castro-type solution and those who oppose it," stating that he favored immediate landing of the marines. Washington replied that it was reluctant to intervene unless "the outcome is in doubt." A further message from Bennett recommended that "serious thought should be given to armed intervention to restore order beyond a mere protection of lives. If the present loyalist efforts fail, the power will go to groups whose aims are identical with those of the Communist Party. We might have to intervene to prevent another Cuba." In the meantime, President Johnson went on the air on Wednesday evening to announce the landing of the marines (a process which continued until there were some 22,000 Americans in the occupying force). Mr. Johnson described this as a step which was necessary "to give protection to hundreds of Americans" in the Dominican Republic, also stating that "the Council of the OAS has been 'advised' of the situation." (The fact that the OAS was "advised" of the landing after it had begun was to cause resentment throughout Latin America.)

On Thursday, Ambassador Bennett gave newsmen a colorful account of rebel atrocities (which later proved to be almost groundless); and while repeating that the United States was neutral in the conflict, he expressed his own concern about the rebel leadership, handing the reporters a list of fifty-three Communists allegedly identified in rebel ranks. (This was the first of the famous "lists" which the administration was to use to justify its actions.)

By Friday, the seventh day of the rebellion, both the marines and the paratroopers of the 82nd Airborne Division had been involved in military actions which could only be interpreted as having a political purpose—that of defending the Benoit junta and the Wessin forces against the rebels.

And now new actors appeared on the stage. John Bartlow Martin, U.S. ambassador during the Bosch days, came as a special emissary from President Lyndon Johnson to consult with Ambassador Bennett. The Papal Nuncio, Msgr. Emanuele Clarizio, worked tirelessly to effect a cease-fire. José A. Mora, the Secretary General of the OAS, came as a representative of that organization. Then a new chapter was added. It had become clear that the alliance with Wessin y Wessin was a handicap, for he was regarded as simply a continuance of the Trujillo tradition. Bennett and Martin began conferences with Brigadier General Antonio Imbert Barreras looking toward a new loyalist junta to replace the paper junta headed by Benoit, in the hopes that Imbert would be strong enough to eventually get rid of Wessin.

The theory behind the choice of Imbert seems to have been that because he was one of the assassins of Trujillo he would have popular following—a theory which was proved groundless: Imbert had never been a hero in the eyes of the Dominicans, but was regarded rather as an opportunist, eager for power, who had played both sides of every game. The United States was thus put in a peculiar light: within one week, Washington had lightly espoused the cause of three reactionary military leaders—Benoit, then Wessin, and now Imbert—none of whom had any genuine popular appeal.

By May 1, while Washington was still insisting officially that the United States was neutral, the rebels and their friends were loudly declaring that the military junta, with United States cooperation, was leading the Dominican Republic back into a dictatorship. American officials, meanwhile, seemed more and more determined to identify the rebels as Communists and Castroites. On Sunday, May 2, Ambassador Martin announced to newsmen that the rebels were now completely dominated by Communists—his best evidence seems to have been that "many of these men" had been seen at rebel headquarters. He added that "Bosch must feel as heartbroken as I do at what has happened to the movement in the last three or four days." President Johnson went on the air Sunday evening to announce: "The American nations cannot, must not, and will not permit the establishment of another Communist government in the Western Hemisphere." He then continued: "We support no single man or any single group of men in the Dominican Republic"—this at the very time that Martin and Bennett were busily promoting Imbert to head the new government. On May 5 the State Department in Washington released a list of fifty-four "known Communists and Castroites" involved on the rebel side. (This list—a new version of the "list of fifty-three" given to the press in Santo Domingo on April 29, which was reportedly compiled by the Embassy *after* its declaration that Communists were in control of the rebellion—was regarded with skepticism by critical newsmen who tracked down the men charged, found that some were dead, some were in prison, some were outside the country. It reminded some irreverent observers of the days when Joe McCarthy was announcing wild figures on the Communists in the State Department.)

The OAS entered the picture on May 5, taking action (under pressure from Washington) to relieve the United States from the onus of unilateral intervention by creating an Inter-American Peace Force. This plan was adopted by a vote of 14 to 5 (with Venezuela abstaining, and with Mexico, Uruguay, Chile, Ecuador, and Peru voting against the measure). On May 7 Washington proposed that a commission consisting of former Presidents Betancourt of Venezuela and Figueres of Costa Rica, and former Governor Muñoz Marín of Puerto Rico be sent to study the situation: this hopeful suggestion was shelved because of the conviction in some quarters (notably Brazil and Paraguay) that the three men were too "liberal." Also on May 7, in Santo Domingo, Bennett and Martin completed negotiations for the Imbert government, theoretically a junta with some civilian members, but actually a regime completely dominated by Antonio Imbert. On May 8,

Juan Bosch declared that "the United states is now openly committed to the destruction of the rebel movement." And on May 9, the United States Agency for International Development (AID) turned over $750,000 to Imbert to begin payment of government salaries.

When the civil war was three weeks old there was a subtle shift in United States policy. There had been growing demands, from within both the United States and the Dominican Republic, that Trujillo elements be purged from the loyalist forces. Eight officers were actually expelled, and there was increasing pressure to eliminate Wessin y Wessin, who stubbornly resisted. General Imbert was arrogantly announcing plans to wipe out the entire rebel contingent: the choice of that rough gentleman had clearly been a bad one. Furthermore, it was beginning to dawn on some Washington officials that the excitement over Communists in the rebel ranks had been an oversimplification, and that perhaps the United States had blundered in siding with the loyalists. And so Washington suddenly shifted its policy and decided to consult Bosch, the spurned leader of the rebel cause, in its search for a figure acceptable as provisional president not only to Bosch but to the loyalists as well. On May 16 there arrived in Santo Domingo a formidable team: McGeorge Bundy, special assistant to the president for national security affairs; Thomas C. Mann, under secretary of state for economic affairs; Jack Hood Vaughn, assistant secretary of state for inter-American affairs; and Cyrus R. Vance, deputy secretary of defense. They had come from Washington by way of Puerto Rico, where Bundy had conferred with Bosch. Out of their deliberations, which included talks with Caamaño Deñó, came the suggestion that Silvestre Antonio Guzmán, who had been minister of agriculture under Bosch, was a hopeful choice. The rebels accepted the idea, though of course Imbert resisted, for it was made clear that he must resign. For ten days this plan, ably pushed by Bundy, was discussed. But while Bundy and Vance remained in Santo Domingo to negotiate with Guzmán, Mann and Vaughn returned to Washington; and it was soon apparent that the administration was not ready to accept the shift from cooperation with the loyalists to cooperation with the Bosch-selected Guzmán. Then came the printing in *The Washington Daily News* of a report that Guzmán had been guilty of manipulating the affairs of the Dominican Agricultural Bank during Bosch's term in office. This charge—shortly to be proved false—was used as an excuse to torpedo the Guzmán plan. On May 26, Bundy returned to Washington, admitting that there was no hope in the Guzmán formula. It was a major setback. Bundy's instincts were sound: it was clear that the only hope for the war-torn country was to build a new government around a man who could command the respect of loyalists, rebels, and all sensible people. Guzmán had seemed the ideal choice.

The defeat of the Bundy mission marked the end of a phase in the Dominican conflict. An uneasy truce—the third in the month of fighting—was in effect; but violence continued to flare up, and no real solution to the problems of the tormented country was in sight. The Inter-American Peace Force had been formally inaugurated with Brazilian General Hugo

Panasso Alvim as its head, and already included 450 Hondurans, Nicaraguans, and Costa Ricans. On May 25, 200 Brazilians arrived (the first of the Brazilian contingent, which eventually numbered 1,250), and the United States marines began to leave the country. José Mora was still on the job representing the OAS, which was nominally to conduct all further negotiations toward a settlement; and José Antonio Mayobre had arrived to represent the United Nations. Thus, technically—with its troops now under OAS command—the United States had extricated itself from the role of policeman. But actually Washington continued to make the decisions.

The summer months saw further vacillation in United States policy. Ellsworth Bunker, the U.S. ambassador to the OAS, was sent to the Dominican Republic as head of a new OAS committee. But this able statesman was buffeted by shifting instructions which seemingly reflected a deep rift among Washington officialdom: one faction still wanted to crush the rebels; another would cut off all aid and comfort from Imbert, who continued to pursue his bloody course, arresting, torturing, and executing enemies—or suspected enemies; and Joaquín Balaguer—who was distrusted by many as an "unreconstructed *trujillista*"—was pushed by some as the head of a new government.

At last, more than three months after the collapse of the Bundy mission, Washington policy came full circle, and a solution almost identical with the Guzmán plan was adopted—a solution for which Bunker deserves chief credit. Again the choice for provisional president fell upon a civilian, Héctor García-Godoy, a respected Dominican who had been foreign minister under Juan Bosch. The rebels accepted him. Imbert and his cronies angrily rejected the idea, but were finally brought into line when the United States refused to pour any more money into their purse. On August 30, 1965, the Imbert junta resigned. Four days later, on September 3, García-Godoy was inaugurated. And on September 9, Wessin y Wessin was packed up and shipped to Miami where he was given the decorative and harmless post of Dominican consul.

García-Godoy took over a country whose spiritual and psychological health had been seriously corrupted by the violence and disillusion of almost five months. Not only had the efforts of the United States to eliminate the Communists failed miserably; it is more than likely that their number had increased; after all, the United States had been responsible for foisting a dictatorship on the Dominican people by buttressing and financing General Imbert, whose performance, according to Tad Szulc, "may well go down in history as a prime reason for a surge of Communist strength in the Dominican Republic."

García-Godoy's handling of his office was encouraging, constructive, calm. But trouble continued, and his efforts to end the dispute between rebels and loyalists were frustrated by periodic outbursts: the worst was on December 19, when rebel leaders were attacked—some wantonly murdered—by government troops while they were attending a breakfast meeting in a hotel in the city of Santiago de los Caballeros (ninety miles northwest of Santo Domingo). Rebel sympathizers angrily demanded that the President punish those responsible for the assault, condemning him for permitting a refractory group in the armed forces to ignore civil authority. But García-Godoy refused to take stern measures. He had his plan—which had the invaluable backing of Ellsworth Bunker and the Inter-American Peace Force—and he stuck to it. In January, 1966, his plan became clear: the chief figures on both the rebel and loyalist sides were to be appointed as military attachés in Washington, London, and elsewhere (meaningless jobs, of course, constituting little more than political exile, but well paid). Washington gave firm support, with Bunker now the chief spokesman—Ambassador Bennett and former Ambassador Martin seem to have been pushed into the harmless background. In the Dominican Republic there was angry outcry from both sides, the leaders of each refusing to be the first to leave, the rebels fearing the return to dictatorship, the loyalist crowd still shouting the dangers of Communism. After much argument and intermittent gunfire, Caamaño Deñó and sundry aides were the first to obey the order, leaving for London on January 22, 1966. Late January and early February brought more violence: demands that the military leaders—especially Francisco Rivera Caminero, minister of the armed forces—follow García-Godoy's orders and get out were marked by student demonstrations, police shootings, and the call for a general strike (in which Juan Bosch joined). Finally, in early February, Rivera Caminero and his family sailed off to Washington, where the intransigent navy commander became military attaché.

Once again the Dominican people eagerly looked forward to free elections, scheduled for June. The campaign was spirited. The contest for the presidency was chiefly between Juan Bosch and Joaquín Balaguer; the third candidate, Rafael Bonnelly, did not count. Balaguer labored under the handicap of long service as a henchman of the dead Trujillo—a record somewhat redeemed by his good performance during the months after the dictator's assassination, and by general agreement that he really had not shared in Trujillo's bloodthirstiness. Bosch—favored to win the election —had factors working against him. His eight months in the presidency in 1962 had been disappointing: his goals were worthy; but as an administrator he proved unwise and irascible. And when revolt broke out in Santo Domingo in April, 1965, Bosch clung to his secure home in Puerto Rico and did not return to join the brave fighters for his cause in the Dominican Republic. Then, when the campaign got under way, Bosch barricaded himself in his house in Santo Domingo behind a heavy guard; only twice did he venture outside that house, and then only in secret and at night. Bosch's "image" suffered from this show of timidity: people everywhere like their heroes to be fearless, and on that score Bosch came out a poor second to Balaguer, who campaigned tirelessly in the villages and byways—though he also was a target for assassins. To Balaguer's further advantage, the issue of *trujillismo* had faded: the ordinary peasant in the open country remembered the days of Trujillo for their peace, tranquillity, and relative prosperity (and so they had been, save for those who got in the dictator's way). Also, it must be noted that Balaguer promised most of the reforms to which

Bosch was committed: land for the landless, better pay, peace, and order.

And so on election day, June 1, 1966, some 56.3 per cent of all votes cast went to Balaguer, whose clear lead in almost all rural areas easily overcame Bosch's majority (143,000 to 85,000) in the capital city. And Joaquín Balaguer, with all his liabilities, won the presidency, assuming office on July 1. The situation was fraught with danger, but Balaguer's position was fortified by the withdrawal of American, Brazilian, and other foreign troops —by September, 1966, the last men of the Inter-American Peace Force were withdrawn, and the Dominicans were on their own.

Balaguer's first year in office brought some reassurance. Quietly and with considerable skill he spurred agricultural reforms, won limited success in rescuing the sugar economy, while imposing unwelcome austerity upon all classes. But Balaguer was confronted by troublers from left and right. Some Communists, including active agents of Peking, angrily attacked him. The followers of Juan Bosch denounced him for failure to install their men in government jobs; and when Bosch himself went into exile in Spain, his protégés continued to assail Balaguer as a puppet of Washington. But more serious was the threat from the far right, firmly allied with the armed forces, which continued to be the stronghold of the cronies of the dead Trujillo. Balaguer made some effort to curb the generals, but it was clear that the military held the whip hand. There was sporadic violence, sometimes from angry leftists, more often from highhanded army leaders. The Dominicans had not found peace, although President Balaguer had won considerable respect by mid-1967.

APPRAISAL: 1967

The future of the Dominican Republic hangs upon its success in quieting the turmoil which has rocked the land ever since the killing of Trujillo in 1961. It is impossible to gauge with accuracy the full impact—on the island and on the hemisphere—of the civil war launched in April, 1965, and the events that followed. In the Dominican Republic itself, it is probably safe to say that—in addition to the savage dislocation of the social and economic fabric of the nation—all of the extreme leftist elements, including Communists and Castroites, have been strengthened: the ills which the United States thought to ward off by intervention of its armed forces have actually been fortified, and the angry passions of the opposing groups were not stilled by the free elections of June, 1966. The country will need wise leadership in the days ahead.

The Dominican Republic will also need the moral and financial support of the United States. Washington is committed to generous aid to bolster the Dominican return to economic and social health. But the American government must also use all the tact and wisdom at its command in dealing with its neighbor—and this may mean some mending of its ways. Washington's record during the months of the Dominican crisis was marked by some grievous blunders: the administration misjudged people and misinterpreted evidence; and there was lack of candor regarding the motives of its actions. But there are broader implications: the events since April, 1965, have cast dark shadows on the United States' relations with all of Latin America—indeed perhaps with all the world—because of the underlying policy considerations which they have raised. Revolution in Latin America is inevitable. Situations such as the crisis of April, 1965, in the Dominican Republic may confront Washington many times. What is the role of the United States to be? The nagging doubts of many Americans were best expressed by Senator Fulbright in his speech to the Senate on September 15, 1965, in which he warned the United States against misreading "the prevailing tendencies in Latin America," reminding Washington that "any reform movement is likely to attract Communist support. . . . If we are automatically to oppose any reform movement that Communists adhere to, we are likely to end up opposing every reform movement, making ourselves the prisoners of reactionaries who wish to preserve the status quo."

 [*Chapter 28*]

CENTRAL AMERICA AND PANAMA

The land of bananas and coffee once ruled by captains-general of Guatemala under the Viceroyalty of New Spain is today split among the five republics of Guatemala, El Salvador, Honduras, Nicaragua, and Costa Rica. Severed from Colombia in 1903, Panama falls geographically and economically into the same group. Taken together, these six minor nations occupy the narrow ribbon of land that stretches southeast from the Mexican border about 1,200 miles to Colombia, embracing almost 200,000 square miles, roughly equal to New York and California combined. There are rugged mountains and high plateaus in most of the area, affording temperate climate for the principal cities of Costa Rica, Honduras, and Guatemala.

There are over 14 million people in the six republics (1966): about 4.6 million in Guatemala; 3.0 million in El Salvador; 2.4 million in Honduras; 1.7 million in Nicaragua (1965); about 1.5 million in Costa Rica; and 1.3 million in Panama. Most Costa Ricans are of white European stock, chiefly Spanish, while the majority of Guatemalans are Indian. The inhabitants of the other four countries are largely of mixed blood—Spanish, Indian, and Negro. A disturbing fact is that this area with six little nations is probably the fastest growing spot in the world, its population increasing each year by some 3.3 per cent. Barring adoption of contraceptives or a rain of bombs, its people would multiply twenty-five times in a century, and it would then have some 1,800 persons for each square mile.

Each of these six little nations has a personality of its own, but some generalizations on the area have cogency. Consider the region as Latin America in microcosm, its ills the epitome of the ills of the twenty republics: the stark contrast between the few who are rich and the many who are destitute; the frustration of little farmers who eke out a bare subsistence from their rocky plots; the mounting anger of urban slum dwellers who fight unemployment, and of noisy demonstrators in the universities; the impatience with the poor and insufficient schools. Costa Rica fares better on all of these scores.

The political life of Central America and Panama has been dominated by privileged groups, usually an alliance between wealthy families and the military, clinging tenaciously to the past—with only an occasional digression when groups representing the middle classes and the workers held power. Dictatorships of various degrees of virulence have been the rule. There has been a succession of clashes between the several states, as one dictator or another sought to extend his powers. Again, Costa Rica stands as an exception: for more than a half-century that peaceful country has enjoyed a comparatively orderly and constitutional rule.

The economic life of the region must be spelled out in terms of coffee, bananas, and lately cotton. In 1948 coffee accounted for 53 per cent of the export revenue of the six countries, bananas 27 per cent. Attempts to diversify the products of the soil have had some success, with new emphasis upon rice, cacao, sugar, cattle raising, and especially cotton: by 1965 cotton was in second place furnishing 16 per cent of exports, coffee and bananas dropping to 35 per cent and 14 per cent respectively. All three of these chief products are highly vulnerable to shifting prices and world demand. Coffee (most important to Costa Rica, El Salvador, Guatemala, and Honduras) has suffered riotous fluctuations in price. It touched a low point of about 10 cents a pound in 1940, rose to 80 cents in 1954, then dropped down to figures between 40 and 50 cents. After 1964 the International Coffee Organization, through a system of quotas, stabilized the price at around 49 cents. (These figures are based on the prices of Colombian "milds," nearly comparable to Central American coffees.) By 1967, the quota system was threatened by severe competition and overproduction, not only in Brazil, the leading American producer, but also in Africa. Bananas have been important since the 1870's, when they were introduced into Costa Rica. But the banana industry (important today in Costa Rica, Honduras, and Panama) has suffered from blights, only imperfectly controlled, and from competition from Taiwan and Southeast Asia. Cotton (increasingly important in Nicaragua, El Salvador, and Guatemala) is also beset by world overproduction.

The burgeoning population is largely rural: 60 to 75 per cent of Central Americans are country dwellers. The vast majority of the people are isolated in their rural communities, economically deprived and politically inert. They work the land, but the land belongs to a handful of the rich: Guatemala offers an extreme exhibit of latifundia, with 0.1 per cent of the landholders owning about 41 per cent of the cultivated land. The inequities of this social pattern consign the majority to hovels, to deficient diet, to diseases which shorten their span of life. The wage for farm workers ranges from 50 cents to $1 a day. The tax system usually lays its heaviest burden upon the poor, with too large reliance on consumer taxes, not enough on the income of the prosperous. Two types of farming prevail: subsistence farming is the way of life for about 88 per cent of the farmers, who work some 14 per cent of the cultivated land; commercial farming, with its large-scale operations, is more productive. The subsistence farmer raises his corn, rice, and beans, and consumes them. The commercial operator, better equipped with machinery and technical knowledge, produces export products—coffee, cotton, bananas. The large farmer has access to credit, but the little farmer can borrow money only at usurious rates.

Long an important factor in the economic life of most of Central America have been the American fruit companies—especially the United Fruit Company, which took over many of its competitors in 1899 and became one of the most important economic forces in the area (as well as in Colombia and Ecuador). Its success was spectacular, its service to the several countries solid, and its problems knotty. United Fruit brought technical skills and good management. A notable contribution was its founding and financing of the Pan American Agricultural School near Tegucigalpa, Honduras, long directed by Wilson Popenoe, which renders distinguished service in training leaders for scientific farming in all of Central America. United Fruit paid its workers two to three times as much per day as they could command in other national enterprises. The company built hospitals and schools and conducted them ably, provided housing for its workers, and built roads and highways. But United Fruit became the favorite whipping boy for fervid nationalists everywhere, who accused the company of exploiting the workers, suborning local governments, and draining off exorbitant profits to the United States. The company was dubbed *el pulpo* (the octopus). The abuse heaped upon it in the earlier years of the century (which was partly deserved) applies with less force today, for in recent years the company has shown an increasing awareness of its social responsibility. A significant development has been the Associated Producers Program, under which the company has been transferring ownership of its land to individual farmers, assuring them credit and easy terms, and further assisting them in the changeover by providing technical help and acting as selling agent to the world. It seems to be an intelligent formula, designed to improve relations between the company and the growers, and also to ease the tension between the company and the various governments involved. Each year a few more farmers are working their own land and gaining a sense of new dignity. However, the company's withdrawal from operation of its own lands has been slow. And it requires time for these independent operators to acquire the requisite skills.

A hopeful development in economic cooperation is the Central American Common Market (CACM) in which, by 1965, all five of the Central American republics had agreed to participate. (Panama, though sharing most of the same difficulties, is not yet included.) Adopted under the General Treaty of Economic Integration signed in Managua in 1960, this plan seemed to be operating successfully in 1967. Under its terms, almost all products made in any one nation are exempt from all trade duties in the other four nations. Duties have been eliminated on 95 per cent of all imports originating in the area (although a few agricultural items will retain tariff protection for a time); and common tariffs have been applied to 98 per cent of all imports from outside the area. The premise underlying the plan is that no one of the five countries presents a satisfying market for any manufactured product, but that by leveling tariff barriers it will be possible for a given country to turn out processed foods, textiles, or any of numerous consumer goods which can find a profitable market in the region as a whole. Many of the details are still being worked out. In 1966, it was provided that

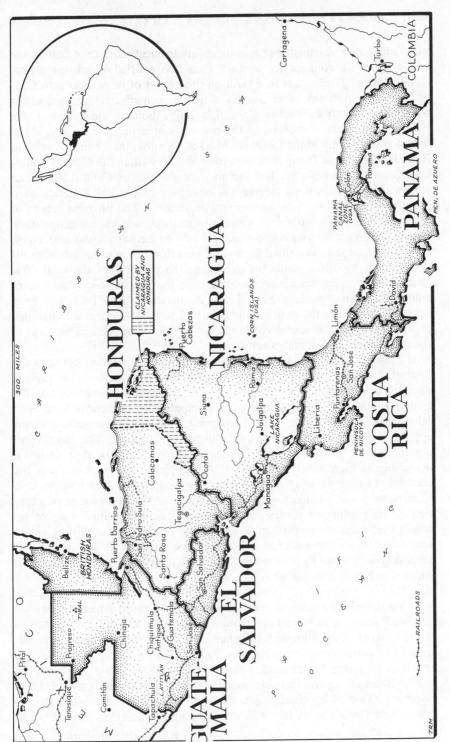

Central America and Panama

Map labels:

COLOMBIA

Cartagena
Turbo

PANAMA

Panama
Colón
PANAMA CANAL ZONE (USA)
PEN. DE AZUERO

David
Limón

CORN ISLANDS (USA)

CLAIMED BY NICARAGUA AND HONDURAS

HONDURAS

NICARAGUA

Puerto Cabezas

San José
Puntarenas
Liberia

COSTA RICA

PENÍNSULA DE NICOYA

Rama
Juigalpa
LAKE NICARAGUA

Siuna

Managua
Ocotal

Calacamas

Tegucigalpa

San Pedro Sula
Puerto Barrios
Santa Rosa
San Salvador

BRITISH HONDURAS
Belize
TIKAL

GUATE-MALA

EL SALVADOR

San José

Progreso
Pital
Comitán
Tenosique
Chinaja
Chiquimula
Antigua
Guatemala
LATITLÁN
San José
Tapachula

300 MILES

RAILROADS

TRM

when any national industry proves its ability to meet more than half of the whole area's demand for its product, then it is entitled to ask for a protective "outer" tariff—that is, a tariff on the import of its product into Central America from any other country. Already such effective protection has been given makers of window glass, light bulbs, bottles, and machetes. An Economic Council, composed of the ministers of national economy, is the policy-making body of the Common Market. In 1961, the Central American Bank for Economic Integration was installed, as well as the Central American Clearing House—this last "to provide the use of Central American currencies in transactions among the countries of Central America as a means of accelerating their economic integration." The progress report of the CACM in 1965, after four years of operation, was encouraging: trade among the five countries more than quadrupled between 1960 and 1965, the increase largely accounted for by the growth of trade in industrial products, which, by 1966, made up more than 70 per cent of the total. The success of the plan, more pronounced than that of the larger and more ambitious Latin American Free Trade Association (LAFTA), has been achieved in spite of the political instability of some of the member nations, proving perhaps that sound economic cooperation can proceed in spite of sporadic upsets in national control.

This bold and hopeful venture in economic cooperation between the Central American states holds promise for future cooperation in various directions. Education, for example, may be enlarged and improved as the leaders of the five states compare their experiences and learn from each other. Schools are still meager, ill-equipped, and poorly manned—and this applies to primary, secondary, and university education. The crucial importance of the universities as training schools for technical and professional leadership is increasingly recognized. A significant step forward was the creation of a regional educational council, the *Consejo Superior Universitario Centroamericano,* charged with responsibility for the interchange of experience, the pooling of professional academic talent, the furthering of research and publications on higher education. The *Consejo,* enlisting representatives of all the national universities, is effective in persuading the several governments to give more serious attention and increased financial support to higher education.[1]

Meanwhile the cultural contribution of the Central American nations has been scant, with few of their numerous novelists, poets, and essayists winning more than a limited audience. The most widely known and admired of Central American writers is the poet Rubén Darío (1867–1916), in whom all Latin America takes pride. His explosive verses expressed the common anger against outside meddlers with the sovereignty of Latin America. (One of his chief targets was the "imperialist" Theodore Roosevelt.) And Darío's work has won delighted and unanimous praise both in

[1] See Barbara Waggoner, George Waggoner, and Gregory B. Wolfe: "Higher Education in Contemporary Central America," *Journal of Inter-American Studies,* Vol. VI, No. 4 (October, 1964), p. 445.

Latin America and in Spain for his enthusiastic appeal to *hispanidad,* "Spanishness." A lesser name is that of Miguel Angel Asturias of Guatemala, whose novel *El señor presidente* is a spirited analysis of the political ills of the early twentieth century.

THE UNITED PROVINCES OF CENTRAL AMERICA, 1821-38

Of the million people who lived in the Captaincy-General of Guatemala in the early nineteenth century, the majority were apathetic Indians in the highlands; many were of mixed Spanish-Indian-Negro blood, on the coastal plains; and there were a few thousand creoles and *peninsulares.* Long neglected by Spain, both its economic and cultural life had lagged; there were few schools except for the better families in the cities. The University of San Carlos in Guatemala, while inferior to that of Mexico, had trained some intelligent priests and civic leaders. But compared with Mexico, Buenos Aires, Santiago, and Bogotá, Central America lacked vigorous young men with understanding of current world affairs. And the Church was chiefly served by an ill-trained priesthood.

Central America's independence came as the backwash of the Mexican Revolution. The handful of rich creoles in Guatemala, landholders, high clergy, and their friends, watched Iturbide's success in Mexico and decided that separation from Spain would pay them as well. Even the Spanish captain-general, Gabino Gainza, reached the same conclusion, although he prudently stipulated that he be continued in high office. On September 15, 1821, spokesmen for the favored classes met in Guatemala City to declare "the absolute independence" of Central America, dating their declaration: "297 years, 3 months, and 19 days, after June 2, 1524 when Alvarado arrived with 300 Spaniards."

The initiative in creating a new government was taken by the leaders of Guatemala, while those of outlying El Salvador, Honduras, Nicaragua, and Costa Rica were apathetic. Meanwhile, events in Mexico shaped those in Central America. Iturbide, crowned Agustín I, invited the Central Americans to join his Mexican empire. In January, 1822, the governing junta in Guatemala accepted the invitation, and Iturbide sent an army of 600 men to make sure that there was no change of mind. The news aroused protests. El Salvador, stronghold of republicanism, sent an emissary to Washington asking admission to the American union, but Iturbide's soldiers occupied the city of San Salvador and put a stop to such ambition. The Mexican general sent by Iturbide maintained tenuous control for a year. The union with Mexico ended when Iturbide was deposed in February, 1823.

In July, 1823, a constituent assembly in Guatemala City declared the formal existence of "The United Provinces of Central America . . . free and independent of old Spain, of Mexico, and of every other power." A constitution was drafted which provided for a federal president ruling from Guatemala and for provincial presidents in each of the five constituent

470] THE CARIBBEAN AND CENTRAL AMERICA

states, restricted suffrage so as to fix control in the hands of the educated and propertied classes, affirmed the exclusive position of the Catholic Church, and ordered emancipation of all slaves.

From the beginning the United Provinces were far from united, and soon the quarrels began. Conservatives, who believed in the Church and strong central government, were confronted by the Liberals, who believed in federalism and were against the priests. Manuel José Arce, elected president, was caught in the cross fire; he tried to agree with everyone and pleased no one. By 1827 rival bands of guerrillas were fighting each other in the jungles. Victory fell to the Liberals, who occupied Guatemala City in 1829 and imposed their leader, the thirty-year-old Honduran Francisco Morazán, as president. They celebrated their triumph by a plethora of anticlerical laws outlawing the religious orders and ending state support of the Church. The rich and well-born denounced Morazán and the priests incited the Indians to revolt. The outlying states were rebellious. In 1834, in order to reduce the influence of the aristocracy of Guatemala City, Morazán moved his capital to San Salvador, but the federation was already falling apart. An outbreak of cholera in 1837, blamed by the priests on the "godless Liberals," increased the disquiet.

The enemies of Morazán found their deliverer in Rafael Carrera, a twenty-five-year-old Guatemalan of Indian blood. An illiterate fanatic, Carrera commanded the loyalty of the humble Indians. With a horde of his worshipful followers armed with "rusty muskets, old pistols, fowling pieces, some with locks and some without . . . clubs, machetes and knives," Carrera occupied Guatemala City in 1838 with the battle cry "Long live Religion, and Death to the Foreigners." Carrera's victory marked the end of the United Provinces; the Conservatives, who favored centralism, had become the instruments of disunion. By 1840 Morazán's forces were destroyed and their leader exiled. Meanwhile, in 1838, the helpless federal Congress had voted that each constituent state was now free to choose whatever form of government it preferred.

THE REPUBLICS GO THEIR SEPARATE WAYS

Before turning to the records of the several states, we note two points in the history of the area after the breakdown of the federation. The first was the repeated attempt to revive the federation. Time and again, one or another country offered projects for reunion; the debate was still going on in the mid-twentieth century. It would seem as though the Central Americans, split among five weak nations, suffered a bad conscience and sought repeatedly to do something about their disunion, but could not. Although reunion proved impossible, there was continued interference across the new national lines. Since 1838 scarcely a year has passed without one state meddling in the internal affairs of another. Again and again the Liberal dictator of one country has imposed a ruler of like mind upon a nearby land; or a Conservative has compelled a weaker neighbor to accept a president of his own political faith. It need hardly be said that the terms "conservative" and "liberal" have slight meaning in the Central American political lexicon.

A second source of contention has been foreign intervention. The first to cause discord were the British, who had maintained a tenuous hold on the Central American coast since the seventeenth century, in spite of Spanish efforts to dislodge them. British buccaneers harried the coast, collected dyewood, and established trading posts. In the early seventeenth century, one such pirate expedition founded Belize (today the capital of British Honduras). In 1678 the British, without invitation, assumed a quasi protectorate over the miserable Mosquito Indians on the Caribbean coast of Honduras and Nicaragua. After Central American independence was declared, England occupied the Bay Islands off the northern coast of Honduras and formally claimed British Honduras as a Crown colony. During the 1830's and 1840's the Britsh extended their hold upon the Mosquito Coast. In 1848, acting in the name of the "king" of the bewildered Mosquitos, they occupied San Juan del Norte (which they rechristened Greytown) at the mouth of the San Juan River, the boundary between Nicaragua and Costa Rica. This affront to those nations was also a direct challenge to the United States. That northern power, having just annexed California, was taking lively interest in a future transisthmian canal, with either Nicaragua or Panama the probable site. The rush of gold hunters to California focused attention on the very spot in Nicaragua which was now in British hands.

Harbinger of the contest between the two English-speaking powers was the launching of a transit company, headed by Commodore Cornelius Vanderbilt (of New York Central Railroad fame), which by 1849 was ferrying prospectors across Nicaragua on their way to California. We shall meet the Commodore again in the story of Nicaragua. The conflict of interests at Greytown led to negotiations between Washington and London which ended with the signing of the Clayton-Bulwer Treaty of 1850, by which the two nations agreed that, when and if a canal was dug, "neither . . . will ever obtain or maintain for itself any exclusive control over the said ship canal . . . that neither will erect or maintain any fortifications commanding the same . . . or occupy, or fortify, or assume, or exercise any domain over Nicaragua, Costa Rica, the Mosquito Coast, or any part of Central America." The British then withdrew from Greytown; after some debate they finally conceded the Bay Islands to Honduras in 1859 and abandoned most of their claims to the Mosquito Coast in 1860, although they did not completely relinquish their protectorate for another thirty years. Thus the more grievous issues were settled with Great Britain, leaving as the only sore point British possession of British Honduras, an 8,900-square-mile patch of swamps and forest (in 1966 supporting some 109,000 people by its output of chicle and lumber), to which Guatemala still lays claim.

But after 1838 the record of Central America is the story of five separate republics.

GUATEMALA, 1838–

Guatemala, somewhat smaller than North Carolina, falls into three regions. The northern waste of Petén, about 45 per cent of the national territory, is inaccessible, undeveloped, and unpopulated, with only about 1.1 persons to each square mile. The Pacific coastal plain, 10 to 25 miles in width, with rich soil for tropical products and cattle raising, is also lightly populated. The highlands—with altitudes ranging from 4,500 to 9,000 feet, and with Guatemala City (altitude 4,927 feet) at their heart—house most of the people; here are most of the roads and railroads, almost all of the industry; here are produced the chief crops, including the all-important coffee.

Indians of Maya stock account for about 54 per cent of the population. Isolated in their villages—largely illiterate, speaking their Indian dialects, and dressing and living much as did their primitive forebears—these Indians are cut off from the effective life of the republic. Scratching the worn-out soil, planting a few food crops, depending for jobs upon the coffee *fincas,* they play no part in the making of national decisions. Most of the remaining 46 per cent of the people are mestizos (or *ladinos,*[2] as the Guatemalans call them), largely of mixed Spanish and Indian blood. To these must be added a few thousand who boast their pure Spanish ancestry. The white Guatemalans, together with some *ladinos,* are the "privileged" citizens, who constitute the managerial and professional class, who own and operate most of the businesses and industries, and who own most of the land—some 70 per cent of the land is owned by only 2 to 3 per cent of the people. Meanwhile the population increases at a swift pace—about 3.1 per cent each year. And too many hopeless souls crowd into the cities, creating new slums: the capital city now houses over one-tenth of the total population. Provision for education, especially in the rural areas, remains meager; illiteracy still stands at about 70 per cent.

For an unforgettable picture of turbulent Guatemala and Central America in the late 1830's, we are indebted to John Lloyd Stephens, author of the finest travel record in American literature.[3] Appointed minister to Central America by President Martin Van Buren, the thirty-four-year-old explorer, more interested in Maya cities than in politics, finally caught up with Rafael Carrera (the Conservative caudillo who had bested Liberal Morazán) in 1839 and gave us his picture of the man: "five foot, six inches in height, with straight black hair, an Indian complexion and expression, without beard, and did not seem to be more than twenty-one years old." He recorded Carrera's description of his campaigns and told how he had started his revolt with "thirteen men armed with old muskets, which they were obliged to fire with cigars." Stephens was impressed by the man's sin-

2 The word *ladino,* used chiefly in Guatemala and El Salvador, officially covers all who do not live like Indians. The well-born white Guatemalans, however, would not accept the word as descriptive of themselves, equating it rather with the word *mestizo.*

3 John Lloyd Stephens: *Incidents of Travel in Central America, Chiapas, and Yucatán,* edited by Richard L. Predmore (2 vols.; New Brunswick: Rutgers University Press; 1949).

cerity: "I told him that he had a long career before him, and might do much good to his country; and he laid his hand upon his heart, and with a burst of feeling that I did not expect, said he was determined to sacrifice his life for his country."

For good and ill, Rafael Carrera controlled Guatemala most of the time for twenty-seven years (1838–65). An illiterate Indian counterpart of his intelligent Ecuadorian contemporary, Gabriel García Moreno, he proposed, like García, to make his nation a living witness to the glory of the Catholic faith. In 1852 he signed a concordat with the Vatican, the first to be concluded with any nation cut from Spain's former empire. The anticlerical legislation of Morazán was repealed, the Jesuits and other orders were reinstated, and the clergy were placed in charge of the few schools. The Indians regarded Carrera as their messiah, hailed him as *Hijo de Dios,* "Son of God," and *Nuestro Señor,* "Our Lord." He was decorated by the Pope for his services to the faith and by Santa Anna of Mexico for his fidelity to conservatism. The creole landowners, the foreigners, and the high clergy, while privately deploring his gross ignorance, supported Carrera because of his firm stand on religion and property rights and his firm control of the masses. He maintained peace and security within his nation, improved roads, encouraged efficient farming, handled public money honestly, and reduced the national debt. But he was despotic, ruthless with all who opposed his will; under him Guatemalans learned nothing of self-government. And he was responsible for continued turmoil in El Salvador, Honduras, and Nicaragua, as he intervened again and again to place fellow Conservatives in power.

Carrera's death in 1865 was followed by a fierce Liberal reaction. From 1871 to 1885 Justo Rufino Barrios was dominant most of the time. Guatemala's ablest ruler of the nineteenth century, Barrios was intelligent, thorough, and harsh. A man of charm and vitality, he commanded general loyalty. Although professing zeal for constitutional government, he "did not observe the fundamental law," as one contemporary naïvely writes; "the Constitution was no more than an ornament in Guatemala, as a bouquet of flowers might be." The Church was subjected to harsh legislation. The Jesuits were again evicted, the archbishop and bishops were exiled, tithes were suppressed, convents and monasteries were closed, and the properties of the orders were confiscated. Priests were forbidden to wear clerical garb, and were barred from teaching. Religious processions were proscribed. Civil marriage was declared obligatory. His anticlerical laws so crippled the Church in Guatemala that she has never recovered her influence.

In his conduct of internal affairs Barrios resembled his contemporary, Porfirio Díaz of Mexico. He exalted the powers of local governors, the *jefes políticos,* charged them with maintaining order, made them accountable for forcing priests to obey the laws, gave them oversight of farms and laborers, and judged them by the productivity of their respective regions. He promoted public works, extended roads, expanded telephone and telegraph services, and enlarged the postal service. He encouraged coffee and banana production but argued for diversification, offering inducements to those who would plant rubber and cacao. He organized the treasury with skill, balanced the budgets, restored national credit abroad, and founded banks. Like Porfirio Díaz, Barrios had no respect for the Indians, did little to improve their lot, and urged immigration of white Europeans as the cure for his nation's ills.

In international affairs Barrios won credit for the peaceful settlement of the long-debated boundary question with Mexico: Chiapas, claimed by both countries, was finally conceded to Mexico. He was less successful in his relations with the other Central American states. Persuaded that "we shall never be a great country until we are a united country," he argued for revival of the federation and in 1882 visited the United States to seek support for his plans. In 1885 he decreed the union of Central America, named himself its supreme chief, and set out with an army to impose his will upon his uneasy neighbors. He got as far as El Salvador, where he was one of the first to fall in battle.

The death of Barrios in 1885 left Guatemala firmly in the hands of the Liberal Party machine. His two successors carried on his program, although with less vigor, until 1898. Barrios's organization of the country and the Spartan discipline which he exacted of the workers had greatly increased the production of coffee and bananas. His plea for white immigrants had brought few recruits; even in 1896 there seem to have been few foreigners in the country—1,303 Americans, 532 Spaniards, 453 Italians, 399 Germans, 349 English, and 572 French.[4] Few as they were, the foreigners were already influential: Germans had gained control of rich coffee lands and had introduced scientific methods. The nineteenth century closed with the assassination of the incumbent president in 1898 and the coming to power of Estrada Cabrera.

Manuel Estrada Cabrera's twenty-two-year dictatorship (1898–1920) was an ugly period. "Reelected" time after time, always "unanimously," Estrada Cabrera devoted himself (according to his own description) "solely and exclusively, with sacrifice of his own interests, to the advance of the Fatherland." Adulation reached such a pitch that the dates of his various reelections, his birthday and his mother's, were all declared national holidays. Apologists find few good things to say about him. They cite the few schools he built; they quote the gratifying increase of receipts from coffee and bananas, for which German coffee-growers and the United Fruit Company deserved much credit; or they boast of the improvements in sanitation and public health, for which the Rockefeller Foundation should have been thanked. Responsible critics declared him "a robber and a murderer," and blamed his administration "for keeping the Indians in peonage, for debauching the public treasury, for starving the army, and for pocketing wholesale the public revenues."[5] The few liberties won by the Guatemalans during the nineteenth century were lost as Estrada Cabrera's army of informers and secret police consigned moderate critics to jail or the firing squad. The overthrow of Estrada Cabrera in 1920 by his disillusioned

[4] Chester Lloyd Jones: *Guatemala, Past and Present* (Minneapolis: University of Minnesota Press; 1940), p. 271.
[5] *Ibid.*, p. 65.

subjects, with moral encouragement from President Woodrow Wilson, brought a little relief. The presidents of the 1920's ruled more circumspectly, but with the customary struggles between rival factions. In 1931 another "strong man" came into office.

Jorge Ubico (1931–44), the next dictator of Guatemala, was ruthless, thorough, intelligent, and effective. He imposed rigid honesty upon public servants and exercised moderation in his own takings. Frugal and canny, he managed the national treasury with skill, kept the budgets balanced, restored national credit in the outer world, financed new roads and other public works, built hospitals, and directed campaigns for public health. His National Police maintained order, supervised the workers on the plantations, and enforced sanitation laws. He posed as the friend of the abused Indians and theoretically ended their state of peonage. There was, of course, no trace of democratic practice: political opposition was banned, elections were controlled, and dissidents either remained silent or found safety in other lands. When the revolts instigated by army men and university students finally broke out against him in 1944, the dictator thought to quiet the situation by withdrawing in favor of a puppet president. But within a few months there were fresh uprisings, the puppet was unseated, and Guatemalans had their first turn at what was officially described as "social revolution."

Guatemala under Juan José Arévalo (1945–50) and Jacobo Arbenz (1950–54) had a new experience in government, one that finally provoked sharp protest from the United States and armed uprising in the summer of 1954. For more than a century successive governments had been the tools of the military, of creole and other landlords, and of foreign interests. The overturn of 1945 was the work of a hitherto unrepresented segment of the population—the group which lies between the financially powerful upper class and the masses of unscrubbed and unlettered Indians. This middle group, scarcely a middle class in the usual sense of the word, includes industrial workers, the lower ranks of civil servants, many soldiers and police, the more articulate farm workers, and the numerous nimble fellows who live by their wits in the cities. These men, who can usually read and write, who are always ready to parade and shout, furnished the backing first for Arévalo and then for Arbenz. They had plenty of grievances upon which their new leaders could play. The rights of labor, whether in factory or field, had never been honored. Labor unions, civil liberties, and freedom of speech and the press had long been proscribed. Foreign interests had been sacrosanct, enjoying monopolistic privileges. Too much of the land had been owned by too few people. Schools had been provided for less than half the children.

The new leaders of the country addressed themselves to the correction of these abuses with much energy. A new constitution was adopted in 1945, its provisions resembling those of the Mexican instrument of 1917, with generous guarantees for all the basic rights of labor and free institutions, and including authorization for land reform. Up to this point the course of events seemed reasonable, but in 1950 the Communist Party injected the slogans and the tactics which have proved so disruptive else-where. In many ways the scene resembled that of Mexico in the 1920's and 1930's, but with one important difference: Mexico's revolutionists had been purely Mexican; Guatemala's bore the markings of Moscow.

American-owned enterprises were the principal targets of the Com-munist attacks. They were, primarily, the "Big Three": the United Fruit Company, with an investment of from $50 million to $60 million, The In-ternational Railways of Central America, with about $50 million, and the Empresa Eléctrica, subsidiary of American Foreign Power, with approxi-mately $15 million. These became the whipping boys of the Communist press. It was futile for thoughtful citizens to cite the benefits the alien companies had contributed to the economy and general welfare. Little heed was paid to the fact that these companies paid higher wages than national employers. United Fruit was paying an average daily wage on its plantations of about $1.25 a day, three times that paid on privately owned coffee *fincas;* Empresa Eléctrica was paying about $4 a day, three times the prevailing industrial wage; and the railroads were paying about $3 a day. Such considerations were smothered by clamor about the bigness of the com-panies, the vast landholdings controlled by United Fruit, the monopolistic charters under which foreigners operated, the special tax favors they en-joyed, and the high rates charged for electric service and freight. When the companies professed willingness to meet the government halfway and to adjust their contracts in equitable fashion, their proposals were ignored.

The situation presented a sobering instance of the power of a willful and determined minority to control a weakly led government and an amorphous state. Competent observers set the Communist Party member-ship somewhere between 500 and 2,000 in 1954, but Communist leaders knew how to insinuate themselves into key positions; how to intimidate presidents, legislators, judges; how to bring the press into line; how to get unlimited time over the radio; how to use the labor unions for their own purposes; and how to play upon the grievances, real or fancied, of farm workers. Above all, they knew how to twist valid demands to their own purpose, and they knew the power of the "Big Lie."

The Agrarian Law of July, 1952, aroused the protest of the foreign companies. Its chief aim was defensible: the recapture of lands withheld from cultivation and their distribution among small holders, thus creating a body of sturdy yeomen whose varied crops would contribute to the stability of the nation. The provisions of the law seemed fair. Owners of expropriated lands would be paid in thirty-year 3 per cent bonds, and buyers of the land would repay the government in small installments. Holdings of less than 667 acres were exempt, and even larger holdings were not subject to seizure where the land was fully cultivated. The United Fruit Company was, of course, the principal target, for its acreage was vast, and much of it was held in reserve for future development. The officials of the com-pany argued that the banana industry of Guatemala—second producer of export revenue—could not survive without such reserves of land since banana culture must be constantly shifted from field to field to prevent soil exhaustion and the threat of the Panama disease. But appeals for moderation, for reconsideration of contracts and tax arrangements, were ignored, and the ax fell. The Fruit Company's holdings at Tiquisate on the Pacific coast were the first to suffer; about 234,000 acres were expropriated, leaving the company about 61,000 acres. The government allotted $594,572 as compensation, at the rate of $2.54 an acre, for land valued by the company at $4 million. Steps were then taken to expropriate 174,000 acres of the company's holdings near the Atlantic coast, to the tune of Communist orators declaiming upon the utopian beauty of thousands of farmers surrounded by tiny clumps of banana trees, selling their produce through cooperatives to the world market.

Guatemala presented puzzling issues to the United States in 1954. Understandably alarmed by the presence of what seemed to be an effective Communist drive on Central America, Washington sought ways to counter and defeat it. But the old solutions had proved futile. Armed intervention on behalf of American interests has only served to unite nations of the Caribbean against the United States. Diplomatic intervention and efforts at persuasion seemed the only answer. At the Pan American Conference in Caracas in early 1954, the United States delegation won lukewarm support from the representatives of the American republics for a resolution against Communism and any attempt of Communist leaders to sieze power in the Western Hemisphere. It was still unclear as to what could be done in Guatemala. When word came in May, 1954, that Russian arms were being delivered to the Arbenz government, Washington expressed its displeasure —and dispatched some guns and other war goods to Honduras and Nicaragua. Meanwhile, the inevitable uprising of Guatemalan malcontents took shape.

Arbenz and his Communist backers were finally ousted in June, 1954. Various malcontents, operating from Honduras and Nicaragua, found planes with which to drop bombs on military installations in Guatemala, and armed invasion followed. Arbenz and some 700 others found asylum in the various Latin American embassies in Guatemala City. In July the capital was formally taken over by a military junta dominated by Colonel Carlos Castillo Armas who was shortly installed as president. There were angry charges throughout Latin America that the United States had bypassed the United Nations and the Organization of American States, had virtually invited rebellion, and had furnished arms to the opposition. Whether justified or not, these charges were believed even by good friends of the United States, and created considerable ill will.

Castillo Armas's government proved awkward, incompetent, and unpopular. Firmly supported and handsomely subsidized by Washington, Castillo Armas returned most of the expropriated land to the United Fruit Company, while making fitful allotments of vacant lands to small farmers. He cracked down upon numerous Communists, although the suspicion grew that he regarded all critics as "Communists." His official family were generally described as grafters and cutthroats. For almost two years he ruled by decree, but in March, 1956, he reluctantly permitted the election of a new congress. Rioting and bombing continued to express the general discontent. In July, 1957, Castillo Armas was assassinated.

In February, 1958, after six months of wrangling makeshift governments, General Miguel Ydígoras Fuentes was installed as president. Ydígoras had served under Ubico before 1944, and soon began to act like a dictator himself. Despite loud protestations of democratic principles, the press was tightly controlled and dissenters were punished. He picked quarrels with Mexico over fishing rights off her coast, claiming that Guatemalan sovereignty extended twelve miles out to sea. He revived the long feud with Great Britain over British Honduras, announcing that Belize (as the Guatemalans call it) must be taken "by reason or by force." He denounced the United States, despite the fact that Washington had given $54 million in loans, grants, and technical assistance to Guatemala during the five years 1954–59. In October, 1959, Ydígoras's government ended the joint Guatemala–United States technical assistance program (for the improvement of rubber, coffee, cacao, fibers, and other agricultural commodities), into which the American government was putting about $500,000 per year. Meanwhile, Ydígoras had expropriated sizable German holdings in coffee and sugar lands on somewhat flimsy grounds, and had taken over the railroad system, in which United Fruit had a 40 per cent interest. There were sporadic attacks upon the President, with bombings and riots: Ydígoras intimated that in some fashion the United States was involved. Observers watching the behavior of the leftist splinter parties concluded that Ydígoras was organizing some of these parties on his own initiative, seemingly with the purpose of splitting the opposition; the net result of these tactics, some observers agreed, was the building up of a much stronger Communist or quasi-Communist sector.

In 1960, Ydígoras's government, with a sudden change of heart, found it expedient to cooperate with the United States Central Intelligence Agency in setting up a hidden base, equipped with an airstrip, for the training of anti-Castro Cubans who would later invade Cuba. Washington evidently made it financially profitable for Guatemala to turn over some 3,000 acres on the western edge of the country, near the Mexican border, which was elaborately sealed off against the outside world. (There was nothing very secret about it: Paul P. Kennedy told *almost* all about it on the front page of *The New York Times* of January 10, 1961.) To be sure, Ydígoras had expressed his dislike for the United States, but money talked, and anyway he hated Fidel Castro. So Ydígoras became a partner in the sorry episode of the Bay of Pigs.

There was no question now but that Guatemala was a protégé of the United States. For good reasons or for bad, Washington had to shore up the shaky Ydígoras regime, which was threatened by repeated revolts— the most formidable of these was in November, 1962, when a faction of the national air force defected and bombed the capital city—and even the presidential palace. Of course, the chief shakiness was in the internal affairs of the country: the 54 per cent of the people who are Indians had received no lessening of their burdens since the United States had had a hand in ousting the more-or-less-Communist government of Arbenz in 1954. Ydígoras's government was a shabby affair: the presidential powers were virtually absolute, subject only to the pleasure of the army. It was big

business for the President and his cronies: Ydígoras's tax-free salary was
$144,000, and he controlled annual confidential funds in excess of $1
million. Added to all these perquisites, the inner circle pilfered at will
from the national treasury, while salaries of lesser officials fell into arrears,
school teachers were unpaid, and the National University of San Carlos
had difficulty in keeping its doors open. The only government employees
who could count with assurance on their monthly paychecks were those in
the armed forces.

The inevitable ouster of Ydígoras came in March, 1963. It was a
purely military affair, directed by Colonel Enrique Peralta Azurdia, the
President's fifty-five-year-old minister of defense. Peralta took over the
presidency, announcing that he would "exercise the executive and legislative functions." The Constitution was suspended and Congress dismissed.
The political atmosphere was troubled at this moment by the return of ex-
President Juan José Arévalo, who announced that he would enter the
contest for the presidency; but Peralta was in no mood to admit that there
was any contest—he had the post, and he would hold it. The military coup
posed difficulties for the United States, which was freshly determined to discourage all such informal shifts in government; but after indignant speeches
in Congress and soul-searching in the Department of State, Washington
finally recognized Peralta within a month after his seizure of power.

So far as the constitutional niceties were concerned, Peralta differed
little from his predecessor, although there was commendable lessening of
graft in high places. But economic factors treated Peralta kindly. The price
of coffee rose, and coffee production increased handsomely, too handsomely, in fact: by 1965 Guatemala had more coffee to sell than the
market would absorb. Peralta was able to persuade various foreign companies—Arrow Shirts, Colgate-Palmolive, International Nickel, General
Mills, Texaco, and others—to enlarge their plants. Sales of automobiles
increased. By 1964 there was a small-sized boom. All this pleased the few
people who had money and land, but did nothing for the great mass of
unintegrated Indians.

Meanwhile the perennial debate with Great Britain over the possession
of British Honduras plagued all concerned. That unfruitful patch of 8,867
square miles of swamp and forest, held by England since the early seventeenth century, had been claimed by Guatemala since the early nineteenth
century. By 1963, it became clear that England would now grant limited
autonomy to the 90,000 people of its ragged and unprofitable colony, and
that it would soon confer upon them absolute independence. In July, 1963,
Peralta broke diplomatic relations with Britain, and the argument simmered
during 1965 and 1966. The United States entered the dispute in 1965,
and appointed a mediator. But the whole effort seemed futile. England had
slight interest in holding the area, and the vocal People's United Party in
Belize would be satisfied with nothing short of immediate independence.

The chief thorn in the side of the military government of Peralta was
the growing threat from the guerrilla bandits who exploited the nagging
discontent of the peasants. Generally described as "Communists" (and perhaps the term fitted some of them), they were not a numerous company—

a few hundred altogether—and, fortunately for the government, they were split into two rival factions. But their activities were costly, accounting for numerous cases of sabotage and taking heavy toll of the soldiers who pursued them. As part of their strategy, they kidnapped members of rich families—in some cases actually seizing them on the streets of the capital city—and collected large sums as ransom. No figures were available on this terror, but probably fifteen or twenty victims were involved, with hundreds of thousands of dollars actually paid to the kidnappers—not to mention other thousands paid in extortion money to buy protection. There was a wholesale flight, to the United States and elsewhere, of families who were threatened. The conspiracy was usually charged to emissaries of Fidel Castro, but it is probably more correct to lay the blame upon a government which had done practically nothing to improve the lot of the poor Indians.

In mid-1965, there came the welcome announcement from Peralta that the days of government by decree would soon be at an end. A constituent assembly was at work on a new constitution, and on September 15 it would be put into force; there would be an election in March, 1966, and the new president, members of Congress, and municipal authorities would be installed in July. Furthermore, Peralta said that under no circumstances would he be a candidate for the presidential office. The news was received with apathy, for there was no precedent in Guatemalan history for the willing abdication of a dictator. But, to the general surprise, the government's promises were kept. A fair and open election took place on March 6, 1966: a record 450,000 Guatemalans went to the polls, where they rejected two military candidates in favor of Julio César Méndez Montenegro, dean of the law school of the University of Guatemala, leader of the moderate Revolutionary Party. There was an honest recount of the ballots which confirmed Méndez's election; further, his party was given an absolute majority in the new congress. The new government assumed office on July 1, 1966. It all seemed too good to be true—perhaps it was, only time would tell.

Meanwhile the fact remains that Guatemala's chief peril is from the irresponsible military and their far-right sympathizers who resist liberal change—rather than from a few hundred Communists who roam the mountainsides.

HONDURAS, 1838–

Independent Honduras, a nation about the size of Pennsylvania, poorest of the Central American states, has taken shape despite the repeated interference of aggressive Guatemala and Nicaragua. It is thinly populated with only some 55 persons to the square mile (1966); perhaps 87 per cent of its people represent various mixtures of Spanish, Indian, and Negro blood, with a few who may be reckoned as more or less pure white, Indian, or Negro. Its economy rests upon the export of bananas, coffee, and a little silver and hardwood.

Honduras's political history has been much like that of more powerful Guatemala. Presidents, succeeding each other with startling rapidity, have won and lost office by military coups. Dictatorships have been the rule, but scarcely ever so harsh and extreme as those of Guatemala. Hondurans seem a gentler and less volatile people than their western neighbors. Ten constitutions have been drafted, promulgated, and ignored. The nation has produced few leaders of consequence: Policarpo Bonilla (1894–99) was the ablest nineteenth-century president. Tiburcio Carías Andino (1932–1948) was the strongest in the twentieth century. Conservatism and Liberalism have been the banners under which the Hondurans have fought in civil war and which they have used as shields for their political and economic opinions. The Church, caught in the intermittent clash between clericals and anticlericals, has suffered much the same fate as in Guatemala.

The Conservative Tiburcio Carías, the most durable of the nation's dictators, president for sixteen years, did more for his country than any of his predecessors. A little progress was made in road building, in the modernization of agricultural methods, in the promotion of stockbreeding, and in the building of schools. But it was a praetorian rule: Carías imposed his will by the customary suppression of free speech and by exercise of the police power over all critics.

In October, 1948, Carías yielded to public clamor and held an election of sorts: the presidency—predictably—went to his candidate, Juan Manuel Gálvez, who served for six years. But Gálvez proved to be no puppet for the old caudillo. Traditionally a "Conservative" himself, he ridiculed the label: "How can there be Conservatives in a land where everything remains to be done?" he asked. "Conservers of what? Of ignorance, of backwardness?" Gálvez's term in office was marked by a political tolerance and a respect for constitutional government quite unfamiliar to the nation. Furthermore, his material accomplishments were not inconsiderable: he stepped up the school construction program and adopted various health measures; his attempts to diversify the economy, thus freeing the nation from its reliance on bananas, met with some success: coffee, which had accounted for less than 4 per cent of total exports in 1948, provided almost 26 per cent of export revenue in 1954, while in the same period bananas dropped from over 74 per cent of total exports to about 52 per cent. Gálvez, a firm anti-Communist, gave aid and comfort to the plotters against Jacobo Arbenz in Guatemala in 1954, thus ingratiating himself with the United States, which rewarded him with generous financial aid. But this angered Honduran Liberals, who bested the Conservatives in the elections of 1954. The outcome, however, was inconclusive, and the Liberal candidate was not seated. After a noisy two-year interim, elections were again held, and the victor was the Liberal pediatrician Dr. Ramón Villeda Morales.

The regime of Dr. Villeda, installed by as honest an election as Honduras had enjoyed for many years, should have been a success. But Villeda proved politically inept and vacillating, immediately losing control of both executive and legislative branches of the government and offering little leadership to his beleaguered nation. He did push plans for extending the highway system, of key importance to a nation where much of the best land could not be reached either by railroads or by highways. He enacted advanced labor legislation, and put through Honduras's first social security law, and launched an agrarian reform measure, but it was poorly projected, and chiefly served to arouse the fears of conservative citizens. His most disastrous error was in failing to keep the powerful armed services in line. In his zeal for giving some semblance of democracy to Honduras, Villeda permitted large freedom of expression and activity to leftist groups, allowed the small contingent of Communists to act as they would, and permitted Castro's agents to operate without repression. These policies laid him open to the charge of being "soft on Communism": although he refused to take part in the Bay of Pigs invasion of Cuba, he was no Communist, but he did give a longer rein to troublemakers than was good for the health of the little republic.

It was something of a miracle that Dr. Villeda almost succeeded in completing his full term in office. On October 3, 1963—only ten days before the scheduled election of his successor—he was ousted by the armed forces,[6] which were headed by Colonel Oswaldo López Arellano. Villeda and his family were despatched by a Honduran air force plane to San José, Costa Rica. The coup was applauded by Conservative politicians and businessmen, who charged Villeda's candidate—Modesto Rodas Alvarado—with irresponsibility. Furthermore, the coup presented another challenge to the United States, which was seeking to follow the policy of the Alliance for Progress in its commitment to constitutional niceties. President Kennedy angrily severed diplomatic relations, refused to recognize López, and withdrew financial aid. But the new Johnson administration, in January, 1964, accepted López's promise that fair elections would be held, and restored recognition. Then, in February, 1965, López conducted congressional elections, and his Nationalist Party won handily by the formula which had so long proved effective—a brave display of fairness in city elections, and high-handed coercion and violence in the rural areas. López's hand-picked congress proceeded to elect him constitutional president for a six-year term. López was the boss of the army, and the army bossed the nation. And the reforms launched by Gálvez were well forgotten. So Honduras returned to her "normal" state, and her familiar troubles persisted: frequent uprisings and riots were bloodily suppressed by the military; there was continuing conflict with the United Fruit Company over wages and division of profits; intermittent border disputes with Nicaragua and Guatemala disturbed the peace; and there were angry attacks upon the government from Communists and Castroites.

On every count—social, economic, and political—Honduras is still the most retarded of the Central American states. Politically, it is a laggard, with an arrogant army (semiautonomous in its powers) holding the whip hand over the civil authorities. Socially, it is ill-served on the score of education: illiteracy still stands at about 55 per cent; primary schools are available to only half the children, and few of them go beyond the third

---

[6] The armed forces were well equipped with military hardware, thanks to the perhaps unfortunate proneness of the United States to bolster Latin American armies.

grade; secondary schools are few; the University is ill-prepared to train technical and professional leaders. Economically, Honduras depends largely upon agriculture: over 75 per cent of the people live in rural areas, where unemployment is high. On land tenure, we find the pattern familiar in most of Central America: 57 per cent of the landholdings (occupying 8 per cent of all land held) were in plots of 12.4 acres or less; while about 0.1 per cent of all holdings (aggregating 21 per cent of total land held) were in units of 2,471 acres or larger. There has been slight effort to provide land for the landless. Meanwhile, the population continues to increase at the rate of about 3.3 per cent annually, swelling the ranks of the jobless both in the cities and the open country. Incomes of small farmers and of farm laborers are probably below $100 per year. The few who work in the minuscule industries fare a little better. The farm laborers who work for United Fruit and Standard Fruit enjoy more favorable treatment, although bananas prove an uncertain reliance, as pests increase and crops decrease.

Despite political instability which makes continued national planning difficult, Honduras has some solid successes to its credit. Since 1955, a new power development program has brought electricity to most of the nation, reducing by one-half the cost of power in Tegucigalpa and San Pedro Sula. New roads between Honduras and El Salvador have facilitated trading between the two countries, reducing the cost of living for the isolated western area of Honduras. A new highway is being completed between the capital and San Pedro Sula which will open up sluggard rural areas. Much of the countryside is still isolated, but progress in communications is being made.

Furthermore, Honduras has enjoyed generous cooperation from international agencies: the United States alone furnished grants and loans totaling $45 million between 1945 and 1963, and has continued a liberal program of technical assistance. And although progress in development has been laggard, the national resources of Honduras are substantial: rich but hardly tapped deposits of gold, silver, copper, and other metals; hardwood forests; large undeveloped but fertile lands capable of producing more bananas, coffee, tobacco, cotton, sugar, and other items; fine grazing lands which could be used for greatly extended herds of cattle.

In short, Honduras may be poor today, but her potential for the future is sound.

EL SALVADOR, 1838–

El Salvador, with an area of 8,260 square miles (about the size of New Jersey), is the smallest of the Central American states. Perhaps 75 per cent of its more than 3 million inhabitants are mestizos, 5 per cent whites, and 20 per cent Indians—but El Salvador's Indians, in sharp contrast to those of Guatemala, have given up their Indian dialects and their Indian way of life, and are well integrated into the life of the nation. With a hard-working, progressive, and homogeneous population, El Salvador has made some progress toward meeting the challenges of the twentieth century; but it also offers a glaring exhibit of the twentieth century's most ominous problem—that of overpopulation: with some 368 persons to the square mile (1966), it is one of the most densely populated spots in the hemisphere. And almost every hectare of this beautiful and fruitful land is under cultivation: its fertile plains and valleys, its precipitous mountain slopes where fine coffee flourishes—these dauntless people plant their crops right up to the edge of active volcanoes.

The Pan American Highway crosses the country from border to border, and there are a few secondary roads; but the ox-cart is still an important means of heavy transport. The Salvadorans are a rural people: the workers on the farms constitute some 60 per cent of the labor force. Traditionally second to Guatemala among Central American states in exports to the world, El Salvador has held first place since 1957 (with the exception of the single year 1963). Coffee has for many years been its principal crop, furnishing some 75 per cent of the export revenue in 1958, but dropping to 51 per cent in 1965. A hopeful sign of diversification has been the increase in cotton production, which in 1965 accounted for about 20 per cent of exports. (Salvadorans take pride in the fact that their cotton production per acre exceeds that of the United States.) Some gold and sugar are also sold on the world market. El Salvador runs true to the Latin American pattern in its concentration of land and wealth in the hands of a privileged few—but the well-born Salvadorans are among the more enlightened aristocracies in Central or South America.

In politics El Salvador has usually reflected the shifting moods of Guatemala, whose strong men have repeatedly intervened. The words "liberal" and "conservative" have been loudly trumpeted, but personalities have been more influential than ideas. Presidents come and go, civil wars rage briefly, and moderate dictatorships are the general pattern. When the first families manage to agree, there are periods of calm; a notable instance was the domination of one family from 1913 to 1930, a period in which coffee production was much increased, the government was rather efficient, and roads and other public works were extended. When coffee prices crashed in 1930, a revolution brought to power the dour Maximiliano Hernández Martínez, whose fourteen-year dictatorship was mildly paternalistic and whose faith in spiritualism led him to accept vague advice from occult powers. In 1944 a strike of students and soldiers unseated Hernández Martínez, and the military forces seized control of the government, with the consent and blessing of the chief families. A period of wrangling among political factions culminated in the Revolution of 1948, in which power was seized by a group of reform-minded army officers who announced a bold and revolutionary program of change for their country.

The armed forces of El Salvador have been something of a maverick compared with their opposite numbers in other Latin American nations. The increasing concern of the army, since the 1940's, for the economic and social well-being of the country reflects some stirring of conscience among able and honest military leaders. Another explanation is prudence, for it was obvious to the more intelligent that the spirit of revolt was in the air; and rather than let control slip from their hands they would meet the threat of Communism and leftist agitation, not with increased repression, but with a program of reform which would undercut the demands of the agitators. Edwin Lieuwen writes: "Here is the only country in Latin America in which the armed forces organization is both leading and supporting the nation along the pathway of democratic, evolutionary, social revolution."[7]

The Revolution of 1948 led to the organization of an official party bearing the pretentious title "The Revolutionary Party of Democratic Unity" (PRUD), which dominated the country during the 1950's through two presidents—Major Oscar Osorio (1950–56) and his hand-picked successor, Colonel José María Lemus (1956–60).

The ambitious program of the two PRUD administrations met some success on the economic front: agricultural development and diversification were stimulated; highways were projected; housing needs received attention; dams and power plants were built on the Lempa River; Lemus actually found capital with which to expand a cigarette plant, a sugar refinery, and a variety of small industries; and Lemus and his associates were active in promoting the agreement with El Salvador's neighbors to organize the Central American Common Market, which they hoped would relieve the Central Americans from some of their dependence upon the fitful prices of coffee and other commodities on the world market.

But the social pattern of El Salvador remained undisturbed. No nation in Latin America presented a greater contrast than that between the few Salvadoran families who lived in luxury, sent their sons to schools abroad, and drove fine sports cars—and the masses who were ragged and ill-fed. The chief families—the "fourteen families," they were popularly called, although there were more than fourteen—owned the most land and the best land: it was estimated in 1961 that less than 0.1 per cent of the land-holders owned some 16 per cent of the farm land, in haciendas of 2,471 acres or more; while at the other extreme about 85 per cent of the farmers, holding less than 15 per cent of the farm land, were hard put to it to make a living from their meager plots of 12.4 acres or less, working without machinery or scientific handling of seeds and fertilizers. The great plantations were efficiently run, but the humble workers on those plantations were lucky to get the equivalent of 50 to 60 cents a day, plus meager rations of tortillas and beans. And the military leaders were not ready to break their long alliance with the country's elite which had been effective in throttling social legislation. They had agreed to keep the poor in their place; and although the poor were beginning to awake—some turning to Communism, which flourished in a few labor unions—the PRUD administrations still found it unwise to push social security, public health measures, and agrarian reform.

But the real deterioration of the proud aims of PRUD was political. Osorio had ruled in a mild dictatorship, resorting to shady tricks to stay in power and managing the elections of 1956 so efficiently that his candidate,

7 Edwin Lieuwen: *Generals vs. Presidents: Neo-Militarism in Latin America* (New York: Frederick A. Praeger; 1964), p. 92.

Colonel Lemus, was elected over the opposition of two strong contenders, with the near-unanimity which marks elections in dictator-ridden lands. (After the election Lemus brought criminal prosecutions against the men who had dared to challenge him.)

Even more flagrant was the flaunting of constitutional procedures by President Lemus. His four-year term was marked by angry opposition, an assassination attempt, and numerous strikes and riots, which were officially described as "Communist-inspired"—and his answer was to crack down on all free expression, to curtail the right of peaceful assembly, and to jail dissidents on slight evidence and without fair trial.

By 1960 little El Salvador, which had long been regarded as the least volatile of Central American republics, seemed in explosive mood. The decline in the economy was the fundamental factor: the fall in the price of coffee entailed a $40-million loss in governmental revenue during the years 1957–59, reducing wages and profits for virtually all classes and increasing unemployment. Cotton, now important to El Salvador's economy, had also dropped in price.

But the growing unrest was also political and social: workers on farms and in the cities were rebelling against the long domination by the rich families and the military. Especially angry was the denunciation of the official party's handling of the congressional elections of April, 1960; a new electoral law had been so framed as to make it virtually impossible for any effective political opposition to make itself felt. In September, Lemus banned all political parties. And he quelled student protest demonstrations with a brutality that even the army could not stomach.

On October 26, 1960, the Lemus regime was overthrown by a group of leftist army officers and civilians (many, including the American ambassador, called them "pro-Castroites"). But the six-man junta which they installed was too radical for the majority of El Salvador's military, and it was deposed by a counter-coup on January 24, 1961.

The new junta, headed by Colonel Julio Adalberto Rivera, was recognized by President Kennedy after it promised early elections and a speedy return to constitutional government. Now came action, much action, to the delight of those who had demanded vigorous grappling with the social ills upon which Communists and Castroites fatten. During the first 270 days of the junta's reign, 325 decree-laws were promulgated, and they attacked many of the obvious inequities in El Salvador's ill-balanced society. These measures—many of which were inspired by the objectives of the Alliance for Progress, of which Rivera was a staunch supporter—included an income tax decree fixing a top levy of 76.5 per cent on incomes above $78,000. This law also tackled the knotty problem of the flight of capital, by providing tax exemption for money used for private investment in El Salvador, while taxing uninvested capital at a higher rate. The income tax law was a sensational move, evoking throaty charges of "Communism" against the highly respected military junta; and the American Embassy in San Salvador was accused of urging its adoption. There was a furious exchange of manifestos between defenders and opponents of the measure. The ruling junta defended its course by saying that its policy was inspired by the obvious ills of the citizenry—"malnutrition, illiteracy, high index of infant mortality, bare feet, seminaked bodies, filthy tenements, long and exhausting working hours, and wages of hunger." This was indeed strange talk from a military junta.

April, 1962, brought the promised election, but with Colonel Rivera the sole candidate. Opposing groups, numerous and noisy, denounced the election as fraudulent, and refused to enter candidates—but the truth was that no group had a chance against the popular Rivera. So Rivera and his National Conciliation Party (PNC) were triumphantly and "unanimously" elected, with Rivera to serve for five years, until 1967.

Forthwith the reforms launched by the junta began to take shape. High priority was given to agrarian reform: although densely populated, El Salvador has little available land for colonization; some state-owned land plus some privately held farms would furnish about 135,000 acres to be distributed to some 3,500 families in plots ranging from 5.25 acres to 14 acres; it was not a very bold program, but at least it was a beginning. There were various measures for easing the burden on the poor: Sunday rest with pay; minimum wage laws; reduction of rents on tenements; provision for more generous food allowances for workers on the large farms. The new income taxes were enforced with considerable success. Banking laws were reformed, making credit more easily available to small farmers. And government operations were honest.

The inequities of a feudal society had not been extirpated, but Rivera had consistently addressed himself to that goal, enforcing his social legislation with some vigor. Furthermore, the economy of El Salvador had prospered during the early 1960's: the per capita product of the nation rose from $253 in 1960 to $314 in 1964. There had been solid gains in export agriculture, diversification and increase of industry, much enhanced by the success of the Central American Common Market.

There was pressure for change as El Salvador looked forward to a presidential election in March, 1967. Citizens who had hitherto been silent began to demand that military rule, in force since 1931, yield to civilian control. The popular Rivera was an odd target for this distaste of the military, as he had governed with admirable constitutional restraint and was certainly the ablest and most honest of all the military men who had occupied the presidential office. In fact almost all agreed that Rivera could easily win in 1967 if the constitution did not forbid such reelection. Fears were being expressed that the less liberal army elements might come to power. But all such fears were quieted in March, 1967, when Colonel Fidel Sánchez Hernández won the presidency for a five-year term in an honest election. Sánchez made clear his determination to continue the policies of Rivera. His reputation as a moderate liberal, firmly committed to sound democratic practices, augured well for El Salvador's future.

El Salvador's root problem, however, was the baffling problem facing the world in the twentieth century: overpopulation. With too many people and too little land, Salvadorans were beginning to talk of despatching some of their citizens to less crowded countries nearby, where they would have a better chance to earn a living. Such a step would reduce the heavy load of unemployment and underemployment in El Salvador, where about one-third of farm laborers—the most numerous group of workers in the country—are idle except at planting and harvesting time. President Rivera has negotiated with the government of Honduras in an effort to legalize the status of thousands of Salvadorans who have crossed the border and settled in Honduras illegally. And Rivera has discussed with leaders of Nicaragua the possibility of Salvadorans migrating to that uncrowded land. But no matter how intriguing we may find the idea of exporting surplus people, it is doubtful that the specter of a teeming world can be banished by such a simple device.

NICARAGUA, 1838–1909

The Republic of Nicaragua (about the size of Michigan), covering some 54,000 square miles of lakes, swamps, mountains, jungles, and plains, has developed under serious handicaps. Most of its citizens live in the tropics; its principal cities are on the moist lowlands by Lakes Nicaragua and Managua, regions which until recent years were ravaged by yellow fever and malaria. During colonial days this region attracted fewer energetic Spaniards than the settlements on the salubrious highlands of Guatemala and Costa Rica. And it had the ill luck to be placed astride an obvious site for a transisthmian canal, a location which repeatedly involved the nation in the ambitions of greater powers. These disabilities help to explain the tortuous course of this nation which now numbers 1.7 million (1965), made up of about 75 per cent mestizo, 3 or 4 per cent Indian, more than 10 per cent Negro, and some whites. Its ample resources, still largely undeveloped, include reserves of gold; lands which produce coffee, cotton, sugar, rice, and corn; forests of hardwood; and pasturage for many cattle.

Nicaragua's induction into self-government was stormy. The little country was torn by rivalry between the city of Léon, the Liberal stronghold, and Granada, headquarters of the Conservatives. Then came the further complication of the British occupation of San Juan del Norte (Greytown) on the Nicaraguan Caribbean coast, the entrance of Commodore Vanderbilt's transit company to ferry prospectors across Nicaragua, and the bloodless clash of British and American interests. While the little nation was thus involved in larger international affairs, the feud between Léon and Granada continued. In 1855 the Liberals of Léon invited an eccentric American soldier of fortune, William Walker, to come to their aid against the Granada Conservatives.

The William Walker episode set to music would outdo the best of Gilbert and Sullivan. Born in Nashville in 1824 and schooled in law and medicine, this little man of about a hundred pounds set out in 1850 for San Francisco, where he wrote furiously on America's Manifest Destiny. Restless and persuaded of his own calling to heroic duty, he led a little band into Mexico's Lower California in 1853, declared that region and neighboring Sonora an independent republic, was jailed, and escaped with difficulty to California. In 1855, invited by Nicaragua's Liberals, he set out with an expeditionary force of fifty-eight men, reached Nicaragua, seized one of Vanderbilt's lake steamers, captured the Conservative stronghold of Granada, and made himself commander in chief of the Nicaraguan army. In 1856 he was "elected" president of his adopted country and prospered amazingly for a few months until Vanderbilt persuaded other Central Americans, especially the Costa Ricans, to take up arms against him. Meanwhile, Walker was aided by powerful elements in the United States; he was applauded by those who wished to embarrass the British; and he was encouraged by the southern states in the hope that Nicaragua might be added to the Union as another slave state. Despite the addition of several hundred American adventurers to his army, Walker's enemies were more than a match for him. In 1857 he prudently surrendered to an American naval officer and got back to the United States. He made two further attempts to invade Central America but was finally captured in Honduras in 1860 and was shot.

After this *opéra bouffe,* Nicaragua's turbulence was quieted by the Conservatives, who seized and held control for thirty years (1863–93); they named presidents, put down occasional uprisings, and gave the country a somewhat stable rule. Coffee production increased, bananas were introduced, and the gold mines were worked fitfully. A few Germans and other Europeans entered the country, bought land, and contributed to the moderate prosperity of the era.

A Liberal revolt in 1893, made possible by quarrels among the Conservatives, brought the unscrupulous José Santos Zelaya to the presidency. His sixteen-year rule was a brutish tyranny. He hounded many of his Conservative opponents to financial ruin, suicide, or exile. He betrayed his Liberal colleagues and broke every promise his party had made. He and his cronies fattened on monopolies, collected toll on almost every governmental operation, and sold reckless concessions to foreigners. Under his spies and police, human liberty became a mockery; critics were jailed, tortured, driven from the country, or assassinated. Yet he was responsible for the extension of railroads, the launching of new steamers on the lakes, the enlargement of the coffee plantations, and a slight increase in the number of public schools. In spite of his peculations, the nation prospered as it never had before.

Zelaya's shameless performances at home were matched by no less reprehensible activities abroad. He stirred up repeated revolts in other Central American republics and was the noisiest protagonist of reunion for Central America—with himself as the indispensable ruler. Incited largely by Zelaya's arrogance, the United States and Mexico took the initiative in calling the Washington Conference of 1907, out of which came the Central American Court for adjudicating disputes in the area; created in 1908, the Court survived for ten years. That same Conference exacted from the five nations of Central America a pledge that they would henceforth refrain from stirring up revolutions on their neighbors' premises. Zelaya signed the agreement but continued to make trouble.

By 1909 Zelaya was heartily despised at home and abroad. His enemies organized a revolution to unseat him. When two American adventurers were executed by Zelaya's orders, Secretary of State Philander C. Knox expelled the Nicaraguan representative from Washington, publicly describing Zelaya as "a blot on the history of his country." The tawdry despot sought safety in exile.

NICARAGUA AND AMERICAN INTERVENTION, 1909–33

The American Secretary of State's blunt words in 1909 marked the beginning of United States intervention, diplomatic and military. The flight of Zelaya left the country in a state of near-anarchy. The treasury was empty, and European creditors were clamoring for payments on their bonds. The Conservatives appealed for help to Washington, and able Thomas C. Dawson, fresh from advising the Dominican Republic, was sent to draft a program for the restoration of order in Nicaragua. He called for agreement between the rival political factions on a presidential candidate; for the installation of an American collector of customs, who would apportion receipts between the local government and foreign creditors (as had been done in the Dominican Republic); and for the floating of a loan by New York bankers (with the tacit guarantee of the United States), the proceeds of which would be used to retire British loans and furnish working capital for the government of Nicaragua. The Nicaraguan government, now in the hands of the Conservatives, accepted the plan, but the American Senate refused to ratify the necessary treaty. However, President William Howard Taft, by an executive agreement which did not require Senate action, appointed a collector of customs, and the New York bankers made several small loans, taking as additional security a controlling interest in the National Bank and the state railways.

Such was the anomalous situation of Nicaragua in 1912; a supposedly sovereign republic had become the virtual ward of New York bankers, acting informally for the American government but without Senate authorization. The Conservatives, bolstered by foreign interests, placed Adolfo Díaz in the presidency. Then, with the slogan "Down with Yankee Imperialists," the Liberals revolted. At this juncture American warships landed marines, put down the rebellion, and kept Díaz in office. For nineteen of the twenty-one years that followed, American marines remained on Nicaraguan soil, although usually the occupying force was no more than a "legation guard" of about a hundred men. The motives behind this occupation have been variously described. Nicaraguan critics, with most Latin Americans concurring, called it another instance of "dollar imperialism," by which American guns protected her citizens' investments in gold mines, loans, plantations, the bank, and railroads. Apologists for the United States justified intervention on humane grounds: life and liberty had to be safeguarded; and on strategic grounds: the Panama Canal had to be protected. They upheld the American financial protectorate as defense against intervention by European creditors.

In 1914, the year in which the first ship cleared the Panama Canal, the United States undertook to establish its claim upon a future canal route by Lake Nicaragua and the San Juan River. The Bryan-Chamorro Treaty, finally ratified by the American Senate in 1916, conceded rights over that route to the United States in return for $3 million to be paid to Nicaragua. This mutually profitable treaty released unexpected furies. Costa Rica protested that Nicaragua could not concede exclusive rights on the San Juan River, which was Costa Rica's boundary as well as Nicaragua's. El Salvador denounced a provision which permitted the United States to build naval bases on islands in the Bay of Fonseca, threatening her territory. These protests were presented to the Central American Court, which rendered verdicts in favor of El Salvador and Costa Rica. The United States, refusing to honor these decisions, helped to destroy the court which she had helped to create—it survived until 1918, discredited and impotent. The Bryan-Chamorro Treaty also served further to inflame Nicaraguan wrath against the United States. When the $3 million was paid, American commissioners superintended the disbursal of the funds, determining what sums should be allotted to foreign creditors and what should be spent within the country. This emphasized the obvious fact that the Managua government was a puppet of Washington.

By 1925 the New York bankers had recovered the funds risked in Nicaragua, and Washington decided that it was safe to withdraw the marines, but optimism proved premature. No sooner had the last marine embarked than civil war broke out again. The Liberals, long barred from power and plunder, resumed the contest. The American minister used his influence to reinstate the trusty Conservative Adolfo Díaz in Managua, but the determined Liberals countered by establishing a rival government on the east coast, with Juan B. Sacasa as their president. This defiance of the United States was further complicated by Mexico's president, Plutarco Elías Calles, who now harassed Washington by extending moral and military support to Sacasa.[8] The informal alliance between Sacasa and the Mexican troublemakers stiffened the determination of President Calvin Coolidge's administration, and their next step was directed at Mexico as well as Nicaragua.

In 1927, when the American puppet, Adolfo Díaz, seemed about to lose to the Sacasa forces, American battleships again steamed into Nicaraguan waters, landed 2,000 marines, delivered arms and powder to Díaz's army, and brought promise of new loans to bolster the Conservatives. On the heels of the marines came President Coolidge's personal mediator, respected Henry L. Stimson. Stimson persuaded almost all factions to surrender their guns and accept the decision of an American-supervised election. Meanwhile, as further surety of order, the Americans undertook to train a national constabulary to replace the unruly army. Liberal José María Moncada was fairly elected in 1928, and ruled under the continued vigilance of the marines. Only one discord marred the general har-

---

[8] The amount of aid given Sacasa by Mexico has never been uncovered. The activities of Sacasa's "ambassador" in Mexico and of Luis Morones, the labor leader detailed by Calles to convey help to the Nicaraguan Liberals, were well known to all observers (this author included) in Mexico during 1925–27.

mony. General Augusto César Sandino refused to accept the official accord and with a few ill-equipped men continued his guerrilla attacks. Regarded by many Nicaraguans as their sincerest patriot, Sandino was applauded by Latin Americans generally, who took puckish satisfaction in the "bandit" who eluded the American marines. In 1934, after Sandino had finally laid down his arms, he was treacherously shot by officers of the Guardia Nacional.

The year 1933 brought liquidation of the American occupation, so long the object of virulent Latin American criticism and a source of embarrassment to Washington. Another honest election gave the victory to Juan B. Sacasa, the Liberal whom the Americans had earlier opposed. With the withdrawal of the marines, the Nicaraguans were again free to rule themselves. But hopes for orderly government soon yielded to the realization that the most tangible contribution of the Americans was the Guardia Nacional, trained by the marines. Against its superior discipline and arms, would-be revolutionists had little chance of success. When the Americans left in 1933, Nicaragua was at the mercy of the Guardia and its adroit leader, General Anastasio Somoza.

NICARAGUA: THE SOMOZA DYNASTY, 1933-

Rid at last of the American marines, the government of Juan B. Sacasa ruled with moderate competence, and Nicaraguans dared hope that the days of barracks-revolts, dictators, and guerrilla bands were done. But it soon became clear that the true master of the nation was not the president whom they had elected, but Anastasio Somoza. Sacasa had ruled uneasily for three years when Somoza used the Guardia to unseat Sacasa and clear the way for his own election and inauguration in 1937. From then until his death in 1956, either as president or as commander in chief with a puppet in the presidency, Somoza was supreme.

Somoza proved one of the more competent Latin American dictators. Born in 1896, schooled in the United States, and trained by the marines, Somoza was a man of such exuberant good nature, of such dexterity in handling men by force or persuasion, and of such varied abilities as to confound his critics. Never so ruthless as Zelaya or Machado or Trujillo, Somoza so enforced his will that no rival managed to survive very long in Nicaragua. His enemies, numerous and noisy, found it safer to denounce him from Mexico City or New York. His hand-picked congress and courts confirmed his decisions without debate.

None could praise democracy more fervently than Somoza. "I would like nothing better than to give [the Nicaraguans] the same kind of freedom as that of the United States," Somoza told a reporter in 1953, but he went on to say: "It is like what you do with a baby. First you give it milk by drops, then more and more, then a little piece of pig, and finally it can eat everything. . . . You cannot give a bunch of five-year-olds guns. . . . They will kill each other. You have to teach them to use freedom, not to abuse it." When asked what percentage of freedom he had given to Nicaragua, Somoza replied: "Oh, by now 100 per cent . . . the baby is full-grown and healthy!" When asked what he thought of the charge that he was a dictator, he replied: "Dictatorship! The Opposition knows how kind I am. I pardon them. We have no political prisoners here. I am getting to the point where I think the word is just a title."[9]

Foreign observers of Nicaragua in the early 1950's concluded that Somoza could probably win an honest election, if he ever risked such a test. Somoza had done much for his retarded land; he built schools and hospitals, extended roads, modernized agriculture, erected hydroelectric plants, expanded cattle raising, and spurred mineral production. Long dependent upon exports of coffee and bananas, today Nicaragua relies chiefly on sales of cotton, coffee, and gold. To be sure, the President's fine roads usually led to one or another of his own farms, and much of the produce sold in world markets came from those same farms. But by 1954 Nicaragua was paying its bills, balancing its budget, and showing a trade surplus (about $11.6 million in 1952). Under Somoza, Nicaragua had been the firm friend of the United States, doing as Washington bade and receiving the generous loans which make easy the life of a Central American despot.

Of course, dictatorships are expensive. Sour critics charged that Somoza owned a full tenth of the productive land, owned or controlled many of the more lucrative businesses and industries, and had handsome reserves beyond the reach of rival politicians. Like his good friend Trujillo of Santo Domingo, Somoza was creating a family dynasty. One son, Luis, was president of the National Congress, and another, Anastasio, Jr., was chief of staff of the Guardia Nacional. But by the mid-1950's there were signs that Somoza thought it expedient to relax the lines of dictatorial power. In 1955, when rumors spread that he was about to offer asylum to the ousted Argentine dictator Perón, the opposition press protested noisily. Perón was not invited, and the journalists were neither jailed nor exiled. In 1956 the same critical newspapers warned that the opposition would not participate in the reelection of Somoza or of any member of his family. The indomitable "Tacho" went ahead with his campaign, but in September, 1956, was struck down by an assassin's bullet. Congress promptly elected son Luis as president until May, 1957, and then a well-policed election formally gave the office to the thirty-five-year-old heir by a handsome 89 per cent of the votes. His brother, Anastasio, Jr., continued as chief of the Guardia Nacional.

Luis Somoza's six-year term in the presidency (1957–63) brought some slackening of the dictatorship. Less able and forceful than his father, Luis also seemed to have acquired some democratic ideas from his education in the United States. But perhaps the young President's somewhat liberal stance was dictated more by prudence than by idealism: he was well aware that feudal dictatorships were out of date—change was the order of the day, and to forestall violent upheaval, disgruntled elements must be appeased. For whatever reasons, Don Luis announced that his regime would serve as a "bridge to democracy" and professed concern for the social and economic welfare of his people. Critics were permitted more latitude in expressing their opinions, the press was allowed some liberty

9 Sydney Gruson in *The New York Times,* Nov. 16, 1953.

and members of the cabinet exercised more authority. In 1958 the President actually suggested that Congress bar his reelection—or the succession of any member of the Somoza family—to the presidency until 1967: Congress obeyed, and Luis showed no signs of reneging. In the early 1960's the young Somoza made some gestures toward social reform: a mild agrarian reform program was proposed, and the labor code was extended to include farm workers. Labor was permitted to organize, subject to the restraining hand of the Guardia Nacional. Furthermore, Don Luis played down the role of the military, curtailing its budget. But whatever liberalism there was in the hearts of Luis Somoza and his brother Anastasio, Jr., lessened as plots inside and outside the country imperiled their regime. There was a series of brushes on the Honduran border. The hostile attitude of Costa Rica continued. An ever-threatening cloud on the horizon was the Caribbean Legion—an amorphous assortment of young firebrands united by a desire to rid the area of dictators. And the agents of Fidel Castro stirred up continuous trouble in Nicaragua. There were numerous jailings of critics and troublemakers, who were indiscriminately dubbed "Communist"—and undoubtedly some of them were properly so described.

The Somoza brothers lent a sympathetic ear to plotters against Fidel Castro, who, in the words of the rebel leader José Miró Cardona, were seeking the help of the "democratic countries" of South America in their fight against the Cuban dictator. And Luis Somoza cooperated enthusiastically with the United States in the Bay of Pigs invasion of April, 1961. The Somozas were rewarded for their staunch anti-Communism by generous aid from the United States, which helped to perpetuate their rule.

The economy of Nicaragua, which had been sagging in 1956, took a turn for the better during the administration of Luis Somoza. After 1960 the nation's goods and services suddenly shot up, registering an annual average increase of 8.3 per cent from 1960 to 1965, the per capita product in the same period advancing by an annual average of 4.6 per cent—well above the minimum target of 2.5 per cent set by the Alliance for Progress. The prosperity was largely due to the continued expansion of cotton. A negligible item in 1950—when coffee was all-important— cotton had been elevated to first place among Nicaragua's exports by 1954 (it slipped to second place only in 1957 and 1960). And large-scale production and efficient techniques increased the yield until in 1965 cotton accounted for 46 per cent of total exports. But both coffee and cotton prices are subject to wild fluctuations on the world market, and the Somoza administration gave serious attention to the diversification of agricultural products, stimulating the expansion of such potentially exportable items as cacao, rubber, tobacco, and bananas.

With the cotton boom came fresh impetus to industrialization. Textile factories multiplied, as did plants for food processing, metal construction, and furniture making. Manufacturing increased its contribution to gross domestic product from 10 per cent in 1953 to 14 per cent in 1965. Much of the credit for the industrial boom goes to the Central American Common Market, of which Nicaragua is one of the most enthusiastic

members. With the growth of manufacturing came an expansion of all related businesses. And this in turn enlarged the middle class of white collar
workers, businessmen, and entrepreneurs, who furnished a growing market
for the products of a growing industry. Sleepy and bedraggled Managua
suddenly came alive: the streets were crowded with new automobiles, the
Central Bank erected a twelve-story building (the highest in Central
America), and the shops exhibited the best of wares from abroad. It was,
of course, a somewhat bogus prosperity, scarcely reaching below the 10
per cent, more or less, who had new privileges. Even Managua (grown
from 109,000 people in 1950 to 249,000 in 1964) was no showcase:
its squalid slums spread out in the fashion of most other Latin American
cities. Sixty per cent of the people still lived on the farms, managing
precariously on the 85 cents a day (supplemented by a food ration) which
was the legal minimum wage—although even this was not always enforced. And almost all of the best land was owned by a few people.

It was something of a surprise when Luis Somoza kept his promise
and stepped down from the presidency at the end of his allotted term,
backing the candidacy of René Schick Gutiérrez in the elections of February, 1963. It was no surprise, however, when Schick, a long-time employee in the Somoza empire, won an overwhelming victory, thus keeping
the presidency in the family. Although it was as near an honest election as
Nicaragua had ever known—a fine gesture in the direction of democracy—
the Somoza brothers controlled the all-important rural vote, by gentle
coercion, and the outcome was never in doubt. Furthermore, most of the
opposition parties withdrew, when Somoza firmly refused to allow supervision of the elections by the OAS. Nevertheless, it was a reassuring gesture,
for Schick was indubitably an honest man, widely respected, and even
inclined to be a bit independent of the dictation of the Somozas. There
was a general sense of loss when the fifty-six-year-old President René
Schick Gutiérrez died suddenly in August, 1966.

Through all of these changes the Somoza dynasty was still supreme:
Anastasio "Tachito" Somoza, who had remained chief of the armed forces,
was handsomely elected to the presidency in February, 1967. On April
13, two months after his brother's election, Luis Somoza suddenly died
from a heart attack at the age of forty-five. This left "Tachito" not only
the presidency, but control of the sizable Somoza fortune, which embraced
perhaps 10 per cent of all the arable land and a large share in the profitable
new industries—a fortune which was variously reckoned at anywhere from
$100 million to $300 million (all pure guesswork, of course).

But the air of Nicaragua was freer in the 1960's. The press was
surprisingly free, although editors knew there were limits beyond which
they dared not step. *La Prensa,* for example, with the largest circulation
of any newspaper, was consistently critical of the Somoza regime: its
editor and publisher, Pedro Joaquín Chamorro, was a dauntless young
man inspired by a devout ambition to end the Somoza dynasty. But the
Somozas were credited with some new improvements: they had accepted
tax reforms, long overdue, including a new federal income tax and high

taxes on land (even the Somozas were paying their taxes—a novel idea); a few gestures toward land reform, though nothing substantial was accomplished; a few halfhearted provisions for easing the burdens of the poor. But the Somozas had always been skittish on social legislation.

The death of Luis did not quiet the growing opposition to the Somoza dynasty. To be sure, there was almost none of the outcry which had animated the Dominicans under Trujillo or the Venezuelans under Pérez Jiménez—the Somozas had never been bloodthirsty. But the overwhelming power and wealth of the family caused bitter resentment in every quarter. The affluent deplored the high taxes imposed by Luis and Schick, accusing them of disloyalty to their class. The new merchants and entrepreneurs, restive under the Somoza paternalism, demanded a voice in the government. The long-inert masses of workers in agriculture (some 59 per cent of the labor force) were beginning to find spokesmen—including some Communists and Castroites—who talked about better wages and working conditions.

The Nicaraguans were growing up: each month they were less willing to come to attention and to salute at the bidding of a dictator.

COSTA RICA, 1838–

The Republic of Costa Rica, a little smaller than West Virginia and with a population of 1.5 million (1966) offers numerous contrasts to its Central American neighbors. This is the one white European people in the area, with about 80 per cent of the population so classified. Cut off by mountains from its northern neighbors, Costa Rica has usually remained indifferent to projects for uniting Central America. Costa Rica's high literacy rate of almost 85 per cent sets it apart culturally from the other Central American states. For years Costa Rica has boasted that she had more school teachers than soldiers. Politically, this state has matured in constitutional government more rapidly than any of her neighbors.

When the United Provinces split apart after 1838, Costa Rica went its separate way. It was a peaceful region with pleasant farms, inhabited by some 80,000 people (census of 1844), among whom were many hardworking Basques and Galicians. Our most accurate contemporary description comes from John Lloyd Stephens, the American diplomat whose reports on Guatemala we have already noted. He found in Costa Rica an orderly and hospitable people, with neat houses and rich sugar fields; "every house has its own *trapiche* or sugarmill." On the plateau, the little capital of San José was surrounded by thriving coffee plantations. The Costa Ricans, he reported, had little thought of being a nation; they were indifferent to their neighbors and asked only to be let alone. Stephens concluded that Costa Rica was "not like the rest of Central America, retrograding and going to ruin, but smiling as the reward of industry."

Costa Rica's early ventures in government were little more than informal pacts between the principal families, by which they named moderately competent presidents who protected the interests of the landowners. Indicative of their pacific intentions was a provision included in the Constitution of 1848 which provided for the abolition of the army as a permanent institution and substituted a civil guard. This commendable stand did not prevent occasional armed contests between partisans of rival politicians, nor did it block Costa Rican intervention against the filibuster William Walker in Nicaragua. Aside from a few such clashes, the life of Costa Rica was far more orderly than that of any of its neighbors. A few migrants entered the country, chiefly Spaniards and refugees from other Central American states, and by the 1860's the population had increased to 125,000. Although a few families had sizable farms, most of the cultivated land was distributed among small farmers. Coffee continued to be the principal cash crop.

Costa Rica's first experience with strong-arm government of the typical Central American pattern came in 1870. Tomás Guardia, president or master of presidents from 1870 to 1882, was an undisguised dictator in a land which has shown slight liking for dictators, and has not tolerated them for long. He seized power from the oligarchy of first families, whose authority had seldom been disputed for thirty years. High-handedly exiling numerous leading citizens, thereby crippling some efficient plantations, he brought the nation firmly under his control. He broke up the old political parties, installed his friends in office, ended political discussion, spent money lavishly, and loaded the republic with heavy debts. Under his strong hand, production of sugar and coffee increased, trade was enlarged, public schools multiplied, railroads were begun, and the nation of Costa Rica received more attention from the outer world than it ever had.

The most important event in Tomás Guardia's rule was the arrival of Minor Cooper Keith, American adventurer, railroad builder, and pioneer in the banana industry. Guardia, eager for a railroad linking San José and the Caribbean coast, sent emissaries to Henry Meiggs, whose railroad building in Chile and Peru had brought him fame, and begged him to undertake the task in Costa Rica.[1] Guardia met Meiggs's greedy terms and awarded him a contract for seventy-one miles of track; then Meiggs entrusted the task to his nephew, Henry Meiggs Keith. But it was the younger brother, Minor, who did the work. The story of laying the rails from coastal Limón to the capital is memorable in railroad history: the frantic scramble for funds, the floating of loans at usurious rates in London, the scourge of yellow fever on the coast, the tragic fate of laborers imported from the United States and Italy, the final success with Negroes from Jamaica who were immune to the fever, and the boundless energy of Keith himself.[2] The line, finally completed in 1890, cost about $8 million and not fewer than 4,000 lives.

The astute Keith soon saw that his railroad could not prosper without freight, so he turned his attention to bananas, which were just beginning to come into the American market. While laborers were constructing

---

[1] We meet Henry Meiggs again in Peru (pp. 597–8) and in Chile (p. 653).
[2] The story is told by Charles Morrow Wilson: *Empire in Green and Gold; The Story of the American Banana Trade* (New York: Henry Holt and Co.; 1947), pp. 36 ff.

the first miles of track through the jungle, Keith was laying out banana plantations along his right of way. From Costa Rica, he extended his ventures into Guatemala and El Salvador. During the last three decades of the century, twenty rival companies entered the banana business, but Keith maintained his lead. In 1899 most of the competing interests were consolidated into the United Fruit Company.

Indicative of the range of Keith's interests in Costa Rica, of the services he rendered, and of the price he exacted, was his contract with the Costa Rican government in 1884. Under its terms Keith agreed to fund the national debt and to build an additional fifty-two miles of railroad. In return, he was granted all rights for a term of ninety-nine years to the railroad tracks already laid; and in addition received "800,000 acres [an area the size of Rhode Island] of undeveloped national lands along the railroad line or in any other part of the country" exempt from taxes for twenty years.[3] Such were the steps by which Keith earned the title, used by some critics, of "the uncrowned king of Central America."

The first sign of political maturity in Costa Rica—and, for that matter, in all Central America—was the election of 1889, in which for the first time there was full freedom of speech and press, frank discussion of issues by rival candidates, and honest counting of votes. "From this time on," writes Chester Lloyd Jones, "popular interest in political developments and the influence of popular opinion on elections were to be real factors in the life of the republic."

Subsequent political evolution in Costa Rica gave that country a place of honor not only among the retarded Central American states but in the entire company of the twenty Latin American republics. Not that all elections have been completely fair, nor that political parties have eclipsed *personalismo;* but the heartening resistance to dictatorships, the concern of citizens in national issues, the desire to elect honest men, and the proper subordination of the executive to the judicial and the legislative authorities have marked the development of Costa Rican political life. There have been lapses. In 1917 Federico A. Tinoco seized the presidency by force, ruled arbitrarily, throttled the press, and angered the people, but he was forced to withdraw within two years. In 1932 an attempted revolution failed.

The most recent crisis in constitutional procedures came in 1948, following the administrations of Rafael Angel Calderón Guardia (1940–1944) and his hand-picked successor. Seeking reelection in 1948—allegedly with some Communist backing—Dr. Calderón was defeated by Otilio Ulate. A *calderonista* revolt—an unlikely brew of die-hard rightists and determined leftists—sought to prevent the seating of the legally elected Ulate; whereupon a civilian uprising was led by farmer José "Pepe" Figueres. A minor civil war ensued, in which the *calderonistas* were supported by

[3] C. D. Kepner, Jr., and J. H. Soothill: *The Banana Empire* (New York: The Vanguard Press; 1935), p. 45. American readers may remember that railroad promoters at home fared generously in this same epoch. The builders of the Union Pacific got 12,800 acres for *each* mile of track laid, while builders of the Northern Pacific received twice as much.

dictators Somoza of Nicaragua and Carías of Honduras, while Figueres and his followers were aided by President Arévalo of Guatemala. Figueres's scrub "army" quickly disposed of the *calderonistas,* and the victorious Don Pepe installed his own junta, which ruled for eighteen months, and then turned over the presidency to Ulate, who held office until 1953. Figueres himself, a socialist who disliked Communism and dictatorship with equal fervor, was elected president in 1953, announcing his belief in "the American conceptions of the stability of representative government, the fundamental freedoms, and the respect for human dignity." Figueres rallied behind him reformist elements born of the depression of the 1930's, whose political influence had increasingly made itself felt. Although Figueres had championed the cause of Otilio Ulate in 1948, this was more a defense of constitutional ways than an evidence of political affinity: the more conservative Ulate did little in his four-year term to further the revolutionary program of Figueres; and in 1952 Figueres broke with Ulate to form the National Liberation Party (PLN), which attracted strong support from moderate and left-of-center liberals.

José Figueres's years in office—both as head of the junta (1948–49) and as president (1953–58)—were fruitful. One of the junta's first acts was to dissolve the army, leaving only the police force to preserve the national order. In 1949 a new constitution gave women the vote, provided for expansion of education and social welfare. A successful farmer himself, Figueres did much to spur better agricultural methods, to diversify products, to develop hydroelectric power, and to improve the schools. The temporary rise in the price of coffee, Costa Rica's chief export, made possible increased expenditures on public works. Figueres inherited Costa Rica's long quarrel with the United Fruit Company, whose bananas constituted the country's second largest export item. But practical "Pepe" Figueres, unlike Arbenz in Guatemala, knew the folly of undermining United Fruit, thereby destroying the banana industry which must depend upon large-scale scientific production. With patience and logic, he persuaded United Fruit to allow the government a 30 per cent share of the profits instead of the 10 per cent which had long prevailed—thereby establishing a precedent which served the interest of Honduras, Guatemala, and other banana producers.

Fundamental to Figueres's program was the idea that government should be an instrument of economic as well as political power, and should organize and encourage production of items basic to the economy. It was socialism, his enemies said, and so it was—socialism in the fashion of Sweden and Switzerland. Figueres expanded state ownership and control beyond the traditional areas of transportation, telecommunications, and insurance, to include banking, electric power, and public housing. There were further digressions designed to fortify the agricultural production of this land of little farmers: the use of revenue from the liquor monopoly to finance grain storage facilities, flour mills, feed and fertilizer plants; the marketing of farm machinery; to set up a chain of retail food stores, and fish-freezing and meat-packing plants. At each step, the government asserted that private enterprise would be free to compete. It was all very expensive, which furnished ammunition for the opposing parties, both right and left.

An outspoken critic of all dictatorships, Figueres made bitter enemies; the current dictators of Cuba, Venezuela, Colombia, the Dominican Republic, and Nicaragua denounced him as a "Communist," and in January, 1955, his enemies struck; planes appeared over San José, and a small invasion force crossed the Costa Rican border from Nicaragua. Figueres's government appealed to the Organization of American States, which within a matter of hours sent a commission to investigate; this commission reported that there was indeed an invasion from the north—i.e., from Nicaragua—and the OAS asked the United States to sell some fighting planes to Costa Rica for her defense. Washington promptly flew down four F-51 Mustangs, and the little war was over. It was an admirable instance of inter-American cooperation.

Figueres—and Costa Rica—won plaudits for the conduct of the 1958 election. Figueres invited three United Nations observers to oversee the balloting. In a scrupulously fair election, Figueres's candidate lost to Conservative Mario Echandi (due to the defection from the PLN of wealthy businessmen, who were weary of Figueres's socialistic reforms). Figueres, with good sportsmanship, said: "I consider our defeat as a contribution, in a way, to democracy in Latin America. It is not customary for a party in power to lose an election."

President Mario Echandi (1958–62) proved unpopular and ineffective. A devout believer in free enterprise, he was blocked by a hostile congress in his attempts to reduce the role of government in business and industry, and to halt the expensive program of public works to which Figueres had committed the country. The economy which had prospered in the mid-fifties suffered from the fall in the price of coffee after 1957, and from the decline in income from bananas. Despite substantial loans from Washington's Export-Import Bank and other sources, Costa Rica was hard put to it to keep her budget in balance. However, it was during Echandi's administration that Costa Rica broke from her traditional isolation to join the Central American Common Market.

The election of February, 1962, brought a swing back to Figueres's PLN, whose candidate was Francisco Orlich. His chief opponent was former President Calderón, who enlisted a motley lot of Communists, Castroites, and other malcontents who were dubbed "Caldero-Communists." Election day brought sound defeat for Calderón, with Orlich collecting some 57 per cent of the votes.

Francisco Orlich (1962–66) reverted to the program inaugurated by Figueres. He consolidated the various projects effectively, and little Costa Rica took on the coloration of a quasi-socialist state; in these undertakings he got the blessing of United States and international agencies, with loans and grants aggregating more than $100 million after 1961.

In mid-1964, Orlich visited Washington, and gave his advice to the Johnson administration: "Democracy," he told the Americans, "is paralyzed by its fear of Communism. Instead of being a dynamic, revolutionary force, democracy has been put on the defensive." He warned against the placid acceptance of tyranny in various countries of Latin America (not naming them, but obviously referring to Brazil, the Dominican Republic, Nicaragua, and Honduras), and suggested that the American nations might well use military force "to restrain those who do not understand the strength of law." Some bystanders commented that this was brave talk from a Costa Rica which had no army at all.[4]

Orlich's regime had more than man-made problems to disturb the calm. Throughout the years 1963, 1964, and 1965, Costa Rica's prize little volcano, 11,300-foot-high Irazú, fifteen miles southeast of San José, blazed in a series of eruptions, spewing clouds of volcanic ash and rocks which blanketed more than 100,000 acres of the nation's richest farm lands. These eruptions, intermittently making life intolerable for the nation's capital city and much of the surrounding area, destroyed some $10 million worth of coffee, killed cattle, reduced the milk supply by two-thirds. As the aftermath of the eruptions, came the rains which washed immense amounts of volcanic ash, compounded in thick mire, over the countryside, blocking highways. There were a few deaths in the wake of these torrents of mire, and some 5,000 families lost their homes. These lashings of nature dealt savage blows to the already lagging economy of the little nation: the loss of cattle and crops caused severe food shortages, cut export income, and laid new burdens on the budget.

The election of February, 1966—in typical see-saw fashion—brought another shift in power from Figueres's PLN to the conservative opposition. The Figueres group had put forward Daniel Oduber, who had served ably as foreign minister under both Figueres and Orlich. The successful candidate (by a minute margin of only 4,200 votes) was José Joaquín Trejos, professor of mathematics and economics at the National University, who had the support not only of the various conservative parties, but also of the leftists of Calderón's faction. This disparate coalition won by hurling charges of "creeping socialism" against the Figueres-Orlich tradition, and by labeling Oduber a "Communist"—their campaign slogan was "A vote for Daniel is a vote for Fidel." But when the election returns were announced, many of the opposition—in true Costa Rican spirit of good will—joined the crowd in singing Trejos's theme song, "Cielito Lindo."

President Trejos confidently announced that forthwith the government would quit interfering in private business, that social welfare projects would be more moderate. But it was unlikely that his administration could—or would even try to—erase the reform measures of the PLN. Trejos, while narrowly elected to the presidency, did not win control of the Legislative Assembly, which was still dominated by the PLN. Furthermore, in the various shifts since 1948, there had been a remarkable continuity of policy: the somewhat leftist measures of Figueres had never been canceled out—just as the Republicans in the United States, when they had a chance, never really discarded the innovations of the New Deal.

4 But Orlich evidently meant what he said. When the Inter-American Peace Force took control of the Dominican Republic in 1965, Costa Rica sent 20 stout policemen to bolster the 22,000 Americans and the 1,200 Brazilians who were defending democracy in the hemisphere.

In mid-1967, it seemed clear that neither the flow of lava, nor the eruptions of politicians, nor budget deficits, nor a decline in trade, nor a stagnant economy could disturb the complacent Costa Ricans, who *know* that their little nation is the most civilized spot in Central America.

PANAMA, 1903−

The Republic of Panama is an anomaly among nations. Independent and sovereign, with the full panoply of a free government, Panama is dominated economically and politically by the American-controlled Canal. No matter how sincerely the United States may guarantee the little state its dignities and privileges, the fact remains that Panama exists only because of the Canal. The result is a nondescript state unlike any other in the world.

For many years a part of the national territory of Colombia, Panama by geographic position and economic habits belongs with the Central American states. A little smaller than Maine, Panama has a span of over 400 miles between the borders of Colombia and Costa Rica. It is a land of dense forests, fertile plains, and thick jungles, most of it drenched by torrential rains. About 150 rivers flow into the Caribbean, twice that number into the Pacific.

It is still a largely untenanted land. Of its 1.3 million people (1966), more than one-third live by the side of the Canal, in the capital city of Panama and in the Caribbean city of Colón. The rest are spread thinly over the balance of the national area. A cluster of small towns and some great plantations producing cattle, corn, and rice lie on the Gulf of Panama, to the west of the Canal Zone. The largest outlying settlement centers in the small city of David near the Costa Rican border, where good farms produce cattle, corn, and sugar. The northwestern Caribbean coast is devoted to bananas. In the unoccupied areas, much good land awaits use, but agricultural interests lag, for energetic young men turn to more profitable employment in the Canal Zone. Panama's dilemma is not uncommon in Latin America. Although 46 per cent of its labor force are farm workers and agriculture accounts for 39 per cent of the gross domestic product, there is underproduction and underconsumption of food stuffs. Unemployment of nonfarm workers is 20 per cent or more. The dietary standard of the average Panamanian is low, and medical attention is scant in the rural areas. Schools are substandard, especially outside the chief cities; despite this fact, the rate of illiteracy has been reduced from about 75 per cent to about 27 per cent during the past fifty years.

The people of Panama are a conglomerate of many races. Statistics are conjectural; perhaps three-quarters of the people are a mixture of white and Negro, with Oriental and other bloods added for good measure. About 10 per cent are reckoned as white, about the same number as Negro, and about 5 per cent, Indian.

Panama embarked upon independent life as a protectorate of the United States, a status defined by the Hay−Bunau Varilla Treaty of 1903 and confirmed by the constitution adopted the following year. The United States was granted possession in perpetuity of the ten-mile strip across the Isthmus "as if it were sovereign"; it was empowered to appropriate whatever other lands or waters of the Republic it deemed necessary for the construction and maintenance of the Canal, and was authorized to intervene for the protection of the Canal and to exercise complete control over the sanitation and policing not only of the Zone itself but also of the cities of Colón and Panama. In return for these concessions, the United States undertook to "maintain the independence of the Republic of Panama" and to pay $10 million in gold and an annuity of $250,000 "in like gold coin," beginning nine years after the ratification of the treaty. (See pp. 547–9.)

A government was duly installed under the Constitution of 1904, with the usual delegation of powers and responsibilities to executive, legislative, and judicial authorities. These democratic processes proved meaningless, for a handful of principal families assumed charge of public affairs, indulged in fatuous debate over conservatism and liberalism, and promoted the fortunes of their favorite candidates. The inevitable uprisings were put down by a show of American bayonets. As one contribution to tranquillity, the United States persuaded the Panamanians to disband their quarrelsome army and to substitute a national police corps. Subsequently, the national police has often proved as unmanageable as the former army.

Meanwhile, the digging of the Canal got under way. After three years of fumbling by Washington, including arguments over the rival advantages of locks or a sea-level route, Colonel George W. Goethals was given complete charge in 1907. A major triumph, largely credited to Dr. William C. Gorgas, was the eradication of yellow fever and malaria. The digging and construction took seven years. Three locks were built at each end of the fifty-mile waterway; the 164-square-mile Lake Gatun was created eighty-five feet above sea level; and the Canal was opened in 1914, at a total cost of $366 million. The success of the undertaking, "the greatest liberty man has ever taken with Nature," as James Bryce described it, is beyond debate. In the year 1965, 12,201 ships passed through it, paying tolls of $67.3 million.

Since 1914 the Republic of Panama, its politicians, its officeholders, and many of its people—certainly all who dwell beside the great waterway —owe their incomes largely to the Canal and the business that has resulted from it. Washington's annual payment is the least item in the account. Ship crews and passengers have spent millions in Panama City and Colón. Thousands of Panama's citizens have drawn wages and salaries from the administrators of the Canal. Despite the profit which the Panamanians have gained from the Canal, its presence has occasioned prolonged and bitter controversy with the American government, for which neither side can be cleared of responsibility. While Panama was intent upon being a free and sovereign nation, hurling endless vituperative charges against the United States, she also played the role of a colonial appendage to a great power, continually demanding favors. On the other hand, the unimaginative and heavy-handed actions of some of Washington's representatives are a mark against the United States, who only very gradually learned to take cognizance of the psychological factors which aligned the Republic of Panama against her.

Panama's political course since 1904 has been halting. The little country embarked on its separate life with neither experience in government nor competent leaders. Political decisions have been dictated by a few powerful families, by shifting political cliques, by the policies of American authorities, and by the intervention of the national police. Popular elections have meant little. Until 1918, the armed intervention of the United States was the rule, but in recent years pressure by American diplomats has been substituted. The national police, created in deference to American wishes, has been corrupt and arbitrary; by the 1950's its chief was making and unmaking presidents. Panama has had a few intelligent and patriotic leaders; notable was Ricardo J. Alfaro, former minister to Washington, provisional president in 1931–32, and representative of his country at numerous international conferences. Perhaps least useful to his country— and to the United States—was the Nazi-admiring Arnulfo Arias, elected in 1940. Author of the quasi-fascist Constitution of 1941, Arias defied President Franklin D. Roosevelt by refusing to concede the bases asked by the United States during World War II and by banning the arming of merchantmen flying the Panamanian flag. (Many American ships were registered as Panamanian in order to evade the neutrality laws which blocked Washington from giving direct aid to the allied powers.) At this point of American-Panamanian exasperation, Arias flew to Havana for a visit to his oculist (or so he said), whereupon his cabinet declared the office vacated and named as president a man more compliant with Washington's wishes. Arnulfo Arias emerged again in 1948 and was almost reelected to the presidency; the following year, with the help of the chief of police, José Antonio Remón, he actually got the position but shortly lost it when Remón found him uncooperative.

It was now clear that Remón was the actual ruler: he seated and unseated four presidents in five years, and then in 1952 he had himself legally elected. Intelligent Panamanians regarded him as an unhappy choice and cited charges that he used the police force to organize shabby rackets. But these gloomy forebodings were soon dissipated. Remón, formally installed in the presidency, imposed order, improved government services, compelled public employees to work hard and to cease pilfering, handled national finances so thriftily as to reduce the national debt, and set an excellent example himself as a hard worker and an honest administrator. When he was assassinated in January, 1955, Panamanians mourned him sincerely as their ablest president. After a year of confusion, Ernesto de la Guardia, Jr., was elected, and the little republic slipped back into its customary habits.

In April, 1959, Panama felt the impact of current Caribbean disorders. Eighty-seven men, mostly Cubans, landed at Nombre de Dios on Panama's Caribbean coast; Fidel Castro seemed to be implicated, although he promptly disavowed all responsibility. In any event, the abortive invasion was designed to unseat De la Guardia in favor of Roberto Arias. However, the choice of the next president was settled in the moderately peaceful election of May, 1960. The winner, Roberto F. Chiari, representing elements of the oligarchy definitely unfriendly to the United States, presided over Panama during the stormy period in United States–Panama relations which culminated in the angry outburst of January, 1964. And in the midst of the debate that followed that violence, a new president took over the disorganized little country: Marco Aurelio Robles was inaugurated on October 1, 1964, after defeating the obdurate Arnulfo Arias. Robles had tasks enough: wages and salaries were far in arrears, unpaid bills amounted to some $20 million, and unemployment stood at about 20 per cent. But he showed some vigor: new and higher taxes were collected; suits were filed for the collection of back taxes; large corporations were suddenly faced with audits of their tax records—all quite new. A cynical bystander commented: "Most un-Panamanian, un-Latin, and unbelievable."

The steady deterioration of Panama's relations with the United States goes back to the days of the building of the Canal. Panamanians cite the agreement under which tens of thousands of Jamaican and other West Indian Negroes were originally introduced for work on the Canal, and the American promise that these would be withdrawn when the work was completed—a promise which was never kept. Furthermore, Panamanians bitterly resented the imposition of "Jim Crow" racial discriminations, under which all employees in the Canal Zone were divided between "gold" and "silver" categories—the former covering citizens of the United States, the latter everyone else, white or Negro. Not only were those on the "gold" list paid about twice as much for the same tasks as those on the "silver" list, but there was further irritating discrimination carried to ridiculous lengths: for example, post offices in the Canal Zone had separate windows for "gold" and "silver" categories, and the whitest citizen of Panama was obliged to join the queue with a Jamaican Negro. The American commissaries in the Canal Zone, organized to sell all kinds of goods to employees —and to make life more tolerable for the many Americans transplanted to the Zone—have long irked the merchants of Panama and Colón. A further source of irritation—which has continued to the present day—was what Panamanians regarded as the insolent sense of superiority of the little colony of American citizens who lived in the seclusion of the Canal Zone ("Zonians," they are called), enjoying a variety of special privileges and showing little interest in their Panamanian neighbors. Of course, there was continual pressure on the American government to raise the amount of the annuity paid to Panama. And, beyond all other complaints, there was angry grumbling against the protectorate status of the Republic.

Faced by determined protest, Washington yielded point after point. A new treaty, drafted in 1936 but not ratified by the American Senate until 1939, formally released Panama from its status as a protectorate. By that treaty the United States ended its guarantee of Panama's independence, canceled its right to police Colón and Panama City, gave up its option to appropriate lands and waters at will, limited the use of commissaries to bona fide residents of the Zone, and forswore the right to intervene in Panamanian affairs. Instead of unilateral intervention, there was now to be consultation and joint action between Washington and Panama against any threat to the safety of the Canal. (The American Senate ratified the treaty only after assurance that, in case of any serious threat to the Canal, the United States would be free to shoot first and consult later.) But Panama was not content, and in 1955, another treaty (negotiated by President Remón, but not ratified until after his death) brought further concessions. The American annuity was increased from $430,000 to $1,930,000. (In 1933, when Washington devalued gold, the annuity had been raised from $250,000 to $430,000.) A uniform wage scale was assured to American and Panamanian workers in the Zone. Valuable property in the heart of Panama City, formerly owned by the Panama Railroad, was ceded to the government. Panama won the right to tax some 17,000 Canal Zone employees who lived outside the Zone.

When Egypt seized the Suez Canal in 1956, big and little politicians in Panama decided that it was high time they justly share in the glory and the profits of *their* Canal. When the powers met for conference on Suez in London, Panama protested—she had not been invited to sit at the table with England, the United States, and the other powers. Then President De la Guardia confided to newsmen that Panama proposed to "resume complete sovereignty" over the Canal Zone; and, referring to the original lease to the United States, the President remarked that the word "perpetuity" was purely academic, that "only God makes eternal things: men make treaties." In the midst of this discussion there were serious proposals from both inside and outside the United States that it might be wise to turn the Canal over to some international agency, perhaps the United Nations or the OAS; this view was defended by the argument that the Canal was no longer militarily or economically vital to the United States and, furthermore, that it was no longer defensible. Such arguments provoked sharp debate.

Meanwhile, official Panamanian demands grew larger weekly: that the United States further increase its annuity and give Panama a share of the gross collections of the Canal; that Panama be conceded all rights to oil or minerals uncovered in the Zone; that the United States refrain from building radar stations on Panamanian soil; and that Panamanian sovereignty be extended twelve miles off the coast. The debate was further enlivened by the protest of the International Transport Workers Federation against the growing use of Panamanian registry for all manner of ships, including many owned by Americans, a device which enabled the ships' owners both to ignore American safety and sanitary requirements and also to pay far lower wages than were paid on ships registered in the United States—and which permitted Panama to collect $2 million annually for registration fees, although many of the ships so registered never visited Panamanian ports.[5]

[5] The reader should give attention to the arguments of the American corporate users of such ships sailing the flags of Panama, Liberia, Honduras. See: "Foreign Flags are 'Flags of Necessity,'" *The Texaco Star* (published by Texaco, Inc.), Vol. LII, No. 1 (1965).

In June, 1962, President Chiari made a state visit to President John F. Kennedy, with all the usual fanfare. Kennedy was conciliatory, and agreement was reached that more Panamanians would be employed in the Canal Zone, that wages would be increased, that the Panamanian flag would be flown side by side with the American at certain points in the Zone, and that the American authorities would withhold income taxes from Panamanian and non-United States workers in the Zone, and turn the money over to Panama.

But these concessions were not enough: the Panamanians had learned that the baiting of Washington was good politics—and much fun—and their demands became more strident. They saw the United States collecting fat fees from ships which used the Canal—$67.3 million in 1965, for example—and they saw no reason why they should not share in this abundance. It was useless for Washington to argue that the United States was not making any money out of the Canal, and that the original cost had not yet been amortized. But, Panama insisted, the United States could double or treble the tolls on ships, bringing its revenue from the Canal up to a fine annual total of $200 million or more; and then the United States could give Panama a 20 per cent cut, and Panama would be in a position to improve its agriculture, build houses for the poor, extend education and health services. It was futile for Washington to point out that raising the tolls would inflict irreparable damage upon all nations making use of the facility —Chile, Peru, and Ecuador, for example, about 80 per cent of whose foreign trade passed through the Canal. (As for Panama's concern for her deprived citizens, the United States could have answered that Panama's own ruling families had shown slight concern for the plight of the poor.)

Throughout Panama in the early 1960's there were outbursts of nationalism. Panamanians were now saying, "The Canal is ours." In Panama City this discontent was fanned by the ubiquitous diplomats in the service of the United Arab Republic and Cuba. Nasser and Fidel Castro were making their voices heard by the volatile mobs on the edge of the Canal. It was increasingly clear that the Panamanians would not be satisfied with more money from the United States, greater equality of payment for Panamanian and American workers, skilled or unskilled, or recognition of Panamanian sovereignty over the Zone. Their final goal was Panamanian ownership of the Canal.

January, 1964, brought a savage outbreak of mob violence. It was precipitated by an exuberant band of American high school students who raised the American flag over the Balboa High School in the Canal Zone; this display of teenage patriotism provoked youths from Panama to raise their own flag over the same school. Then angry mobs of adults from the Panama side entered the fray, and there was much throwing of rocks and Molotov cocktails, all of which brought the American soldiers into the contest. The terror spread into Panama City, and the rioters wrecked the buildings of some American concerns—Pan American World Airways, Sears Roebuck, Goodyear, and others. The American Embassy was attacked, its windows broken. There was shooting by American military, and sniper fire from Panamanians. After three days of this savagery, twenty-four Panamanians and three United States soldiers had been killed, several hundred were in hospitals, and other hundreds had been jailed. It was impossible to assess the blame for this little war. Certainly, President Chiari had done little or nothing to hold his people in check. The American soldiers had probably done no more than their duty, although one might hazard a guess that they could have controlled the rival mobs without gunfire. And it was not explained why, for five months before the outburst, the United States had had no ambassador in Panama—this was a serious blunder on the part of Washington.

The Panamanian reaction was swift. President Chiari broke off diplomatic relations with the United States, accusing Washington of "unprovoked aggression." The United States moved its embassy staff over to the Canal Zone. Emissaries from Washington went to Panama to discuss matters with Chiari. Panama demanded that the UN Security Council and the OAS conduct an investigation—but these agencies furnished no solution. Panama's bar association made an appeal to the International Committee of Jurists, based in Geneva, asking them to rule on the question of whether the United States had been guilty of an act of aggression in meeting the mobs with military power and gunfire. The Jurists' committee—a Dutch lawyer, an Indian lawyer, and a Swedish judge—reported that the United States had indeed been careless; that Washington should have yielded more gracefully on the knotty problem of flying Panamanian and American flags side by side; that the United States had been remiss in not eradicating the double living standards in the Zone; and that the American military had been precipitate in "extensive use of high fire power" during the riots. But the committee also concluded that the riots were premeditated, that Panamanian authorities had actually encouraged violence, that Panama's National Guard ignored appeals for help, and that Panamanian sniper fire justified American retaliation.

The discussions between Panama and Washington were plagued by semantics as much as by issues. It became clear that President Chiari's chief demand was for a complete renegotiation of the Panama Canal Treaty of 1903. As the weeks went on, the debate settled down into a hassle as to whether Washington would agree to *negociar* (negotiate) or to *discutir* (discuss). President Johnson was firm: he would *discuss* but he would not *negotiate*. Many Latin Americans felt that Johnson was too stiff-necked, that renegotiation was imperative and that the United States might as well face it; and some American critics made the same charge. By the end of January, the Johnson administration agreed to a "full and frank review and reconsideration of all issues affecting both countries, including those deriving from the existence of the Panama Canal"—but Johnson still refused to use the word *negotiate*.

In April, after three more months of argument, diplomatic relations were resumed. But neither side had made any concessions, and tempers continued to run high. The tension was somewhat eased by the election in May, 1964, of Marco Aurelio Robles after a bitter contest with the firebrand Arnulfo Arias. Although Robles was uncompromising in his demand for renegotiation of the 1903 Canal treaty, his language was more temperate than that of either Chiari or Arias, and there seemed to be a better chance for reaching agreement with Washington.

Then in December, 1964, the Johnson administration made its long-awaited decision. Yes, said Washington, we are now ready to "negotiate" a new treaty with Panama—and meanwhile we are planning a *new* canal. The present canal is obsolete, the statement continued: more than 300 ships already built or on the drawing boards could not pass through it; and it requires too large a labor force. There must be a new sea-level canal, and there are four possible sites: in Panama, about 150 miles east of the present canal; in northern Colombia; on the border between Nicaragua and Costa Rica; or on the site of the present canal, which would have to be widened and deepened. And then when the new canal is completed, the present canal will be turned over to Panama. At first there was jubilation in Panama: they would get their canal. Then dismay, as they realized that the old canal would be hopelessly expensive to operate in competition with a new sea-level canal.

There was no quieting of the debate over the canal question. President Robles ruled his refractory little country with some wisdom, but he was faced by the perpetual clamor of the chief opposition group headed by the long-time troubler, Arnulfo Arias, who lost no opportunity to remind his followers that they must not permit Robles to sell out to the iniquitous Americans. The canal issue obscured all others: there could be no sensible grappling with economic issues until satisfactory agreements were reached on the present canal and any future canal. The irascible Panamanians were quite right that the decision to dig a sea-level canal in Colombia or on the Costa Rican–Nicaraguan border would plunge Panama into utter bankruptcy. In December, 1965, the president of Nicaragua told newsmen that his country would not be content to have the canal built there without Costa Rican consent, and that, anyway, Nicaragua had no interest in the project. Colombia's government said nothing about the issue, but it seemed clear that it would not be averse to entering into an agreement with the United States. But the Panamanians, to a man, knew that it must be constructed in Panama. Robles managed to keep his people from demonstrations against the United States. (On the first anniversary of the violence of January, 1964, he took every precaution against any celebration of that grisly affair.) But under the surface, anti-Americanism grew in virulence.

Meanwhile negotiations between the Robles government and Washington continued (chiefly in secret), and in September, 1965, President Johnson announced that five "areas of agreement" had been reached: (1) that the 1903 treaty would be replaced; (2) that Panama's sovereignty over the Canal Zone would be recognized; (3) that the new treaty would automatically terminate after a specified number of years or on the day that a proposed sea-level canal opened, whichever came first; (4) that the primary objective of the new treaty was to achieve "the political, economic, and social integration" of the Canal Zone into the Republic of Panama; and (5) that both United States and Panamanian employees of the canal should be dealt with "fairly." These points seemed reasonably acceptable, but then followed the statement that "the new treaties will provide for the defense of the existing canal and any sea-level canal which may be constructed in Panama. United States forces and military facilities will be maintained under a base-rights and status-of-forces agreement" (i.e., a treaty for each base).

Parenthetically, as an American official in Panama was quoted by a reporter for *The National Observer* (November 12, 1965), "One of the sweet little ironies in this situation is that every time there's a little news about negotiations for a new treaty the hard line conservatives at home cry that Johnson is selling the United States out of the Canal Zone, and down here [Panama] the nationalists scream 'traitor' and 'sell-out' at Robles."

June 26, 1967, brought word from President Johnson and Panamanian President Robles that agreement had finally been reached, and that mutually acceptable treaties were ready for confirmation by the congresses of the two nations. The exact text of the treaties was withheld, but the scope of the agreements was revealed. The first treaty dealt with the present canal. In effect it meant complete abrogation of the controversial treaty of 1903. The old canal would now be a joint concern of the two nations—administered by a board of nine, five Americans and four Panamanians. The United States-dominated Canal Zone would be abolished and Panama's sovereignty recognized. And Panama would get a larger slice from canal tolls—although no figure on that sensitive item was revealed. The second treaty concerned future sea-level canals, whether on the site of the present canal or on Panamanian soil 200 miles to the east of the present canal—in either case to be under joint United States–Panama control. The third treaty assured the United States the right to defend any canal.

The announcement of this arrangement between the two presidents evoked much applause as well as spirited criticism from both nations. Numerous Panamanians denounced it as a sell-out by Robles, with demands to know exactly how much Panama would get. From Washington came demands from congressmen who viewed with alarm any concessions on United States control of the Canal Zone. It seemed likely that the debate would be bitter, both in Washington and in Panama.

But Washington held one all-important trump card: the United States had still not explicitly promised to build the new sea-level canal in Panama. Surveys continued for the Nicaraguan–Costa Rican border route and also for the route in northwestern Colombia; and although such possibilities were tactfully not mentioned in the announcement of June, 1967, realistic Panamanians were uncomfortably aware that, should the United States and Panama not peaceably agree on a sea-level canal in Panama, Washington could easily turn to one or another of these alternatives (probably Colombia), bankrupting the old canal and delivering a body blow to Panamanian economy. No responsible spokesmen in Washington were talking of such a course, but President Robles and many others in Panama were aware of this threat. Diplomacy still had big battles to fight.

PART VI

◇⦂◇⦂◇⦂◇⦂◇⦂◇⦂◇⦂◇⦂ *The Lands of the Spanish Main*

The Caribbean coast of South America from Panama to the delta of the Orinoco was the Spanish Main of pirate legend, harried and pillaged for three centuries by English, French, and Dutch freebooters. Spain retained her hold on the continent, but her enemies raised their flags on the offshore islands, and in the Guianas on the mainland; although Spain finally lost to her unruly sons, the Dutch, the English, and the French remained in the Caribbean area. Slightly valued and usually neglected by the Spanish Crown, the Spanish Main was divided between the free republics of Venezuela and Colombia. Much alike in racial inheritance, the two nations have gone their separate ways since Simón Bolívar's Gran Colombia fell apart in 1830.

Chapter 29

VENEZUELA

Little Venice, Venezuela, was the name given to the region of Lake Maracaibo by the explorers who first sailed in from the sea and saw native huts on stilts in the shallow, brackish waters. Today Venezuela is one of the treasure-troves of the earth, with buried wealth whose extent no one can guess: lakes of petroleum whose present yield puts Venezuela in third place as world producer, behind only the United States and the U.S.S.R.; mountains of iron ore which are barely tapped; and rich reserves of other minerals and metals. This wealth is in weak and immature hands; only a few thousand of the 9 million Venezuelans have an adequate share in the national bounty and participate in the decisions which shape their lives. Only in the Americas, under the restraining shadow of the United States, could so rich a nation and so defenseless a people have retained sovereignty against nineteenth-century imperialism.

There are four Venezuelas. In the northwest there is the low spur of the Andes, upon whose plateaus rest the cities of Caracas, Valencia, and Mérida. West of that spur lies the Maracaibo basin with its rich oil deposits. In these two regions, covering about one-fourth of the national area, live more than 90 per cent of the population. To the east and south stretch the sprawling *llanos,* the plains of the Orinoco, a span of 600 miles from west to east, a land of lush grasses and swamps in the wet season (April to October), and of parched ground for the rest of the year. East and south of the *llanos* are the Guiana highlands, unoccupied and largely unexplored wasteland. The *llanos* and the Guiana highlands, almost three-quarters of the national domain, contain less than 10 per cent of the people. The Venezuelans are predominantly a mestizo people; perhaps 10 per cent are whites, 10 per cent Negro, and 5 or 6 per cent Indian—but these figures are conjectural. There are a few thousand Germans, Italians, and other Europeans.

Oil is the magic word in modern Venezuela: over 90 per cent of her export revenue comes from petroleum products; oil has filled the national treasury, often wiping out all domestic and foreign debt; oil has enriched the fortunate few in Caracas, and has corrupted public officials.

Long one of the least regarded of Spain's colonies, Venezuela had scant tutoring in self-government and her first years of independence were disastrous. Of the 800,000 people who lived within her borders in 1810, only a few thousand were literate. From 1810 to 1830, she furnished many of the men who followed Simón Bolívar to New Granada (Colombia), Ecuador, Peru, and Bolivia. She paid dearly for liberty, for by 1830 she had lost at least one-fourth of her population, including a large proportion of her able young men. Not until 1850 did the population equal that of 1810.

Only against the background of such initial confusions can the anarchic development of the nation be appraised. More than twenty constitutions have been drafted, promulgated, and then ignored; more than fifty armed revolts have taken toll of life and property. Dictatorship has been the rule. Political parties have meant little, political principles even less. The caudillo has dominated Venezuela during almost all of her troubled history; the present (1967) constitutional and democratic regime is a grateful exception.

JOSÉ ANTONIO PÁEZ

The first of those chieftain-presidents was José Antonio Páez, who was either president or the master of presidents from 1830 to 1846, returning as outright dictator in 1861–63. Páez was a *llanero* by birth and training. As a boy he rode the range, and by the time he was twenty he owned much land and fine cattle. Physically powerful, utterly fearless, and a master of guerrilla tactics, Páez cast his lot with Simón Bolívar, recruited a band of his fellow plainsmen, and carried on a war of extermination against the *llaneros,* led by the ruthless Boves who was in the pay of Spain. As Bolívar's chief Venezuelan aide, Páez shared the credit for the decisive victory at Carabobo in 1821. In 1823 he dislodged the last Spanish garrison from Puerto Cabello.

Many parallels may be drawn between the career of Páez and that of his contemporary, Rosas, in Argentina. Both were trained on the cattle range, both were expert herdsmen; both commanded the unfaltering loyalty of their comrades, both had the gift of making friends, both used their command of the frontiersmen for political purposes. But comparison favors Páez, who was less ruthless than Rosas, less unscrupulous in his use of power, and more respectful of law. From 1830 to 1846, his course was restrained: the constitution which he had promulgated in 1830 was often honored, the press was allowed some freedom, and there were few such savage reprisals against detractors as marred the record of the boss of Buenos Aires. Despite the interruption of five armed uprisings, Páez made some progress in organizing the country, providing funds for the national treasury, encouraging agriculture and industry, promoting a little immigration, and building a few schools. Páez handled the problems concerning the Church with moderation and skill, maintaining the state's right to patronage and abolishing tithes and special ecclesiastical courts, while assuring national support of the clergy and respect for their services to

South America and the Caribbean

the nation. Venezuelans accord him a place second only to Bolívar among national heroes.

The fall of Páez in 1846 was followed by a fifteen-year period of distress under the dictatorship of the two Monagas brothers, José Tadeo and José Gregorio. Páez, after unsuccessful attempts to regain power, was imprisoned and then exiled to New York. In 1861, then seventy-one years old, he returned, raised a new army of *llaneros,* and after getting rid of his rivals ruled as dictator for two years (1861–63). The moderation of his earlier years was replaced with censorship of the press and severe treatment of political dissidents. The clergy regained their ascendency and the country signed a concordat with the Vatican. In 1863 the Liberals—a word of slight meaning in Venezuelan history—finally ousted the founder of the nation.[1]

The seven-year period from 1863 to 1870 was a chaotic interlude between dictatorships. Intermittent civil war laid waste the countryside. The populace was treated to the first full-scale debate between partisans of rival political opinions. Young Liberals, infected by current European revolutionary talk, shouted against the Church and the clergy, demanded regional autonomy in place of strong central government, and denounced dictatorship. Conservatives replied in defense of religion, order, and property. Neither party boasted such respected leaders as were active in Mexico, Argentina, and Chile. The Conservative chiefs were the caudillos of earlier days, still intent upon plunder. The Liberal spokesmen were uninformed and unconvincing. Several men of reasonably good intentions held power briefly but proved incapable of restoring order.

ANTONIO GUZMÁN BLANCO, 1870–88

The principal figure to emerge during this confused period was the nimble Antonio Guzmán Blanco, who in 1870, at the age of forty-one, was installed as president. For eighteen years, either as president or through puppets of his choice, he was the master of the nation. Unlike Páez, Guzmán was a gentleman, schooled in law and medicine and conversant with the larger world of Washington, London, and Paris. In dealing with his quarrel-torn country, he resembled his contemporary, Porfirio Díaz of Mexico, in his ruthless handling of antagonists, the suborning of generals and public officials, and the imposition of order by the armed forces. Skillful and magnetic, Guzmán strengthened the halting government of his country through stern discipline of government officials, securing a hitherto unknown efficiency. Under his rule, the material prosperity of the nation increased. Coffee became the principal item of export, and wise tariff reductions cleared the way for enlarged trade. In nostalgia for Paris, Guzmán beautified Caracas, laying out generous boulevards and adorning them with an opera house, a presidential palace, and a pantheon for the illustrious dead.

---

[1] On his return to New York, Páez wrote his life story. He later visited Argentina, where he was fêted as a hero, and then returned again to New York where he died in 1873 at the age of eighty-four.

While Guzmán demanded scrupulous honesty from lesser officials, as proper and deserved adjunct to his high position he took a personal cut on every public contract and foreign loan. A sybarite, a waster, and a profligate, he gathered about him a court glittering with luxury such as no other Latin American ruler had enjoyed. He spent long periods in Paris, leaving puppets to rule in Caracas. A Grand Master of the Freemasons, Guzmán was a stout foe of the Church. His anticlericalism was touched off when the Archbishop of Caracas refused to celebrate a Mass in his honor. The dictator retaliated by abolishing convents and monasteries, confiscating Church property, decreeing state control of education, and finally attempting to establish a national Church. These measures provoked such widespread indignation among the loyal Catholic population that he found it expedient, after 1876, to temper his course.

Guzmán Blanco's vanity was boundless. He delighted in his titles, "Illustrious American" and "National Regenerator." The national universities conferred high degrees on him. Foreign governments decorated him. Venezuelan books were dedicated to the "Illustrious American." His portrait hung in public buildings and private offices, and statues of him graced every park and plaza.

The atmosphere of Guzmán's Venezuela was murky. The press was throttled and men were jailed for an idle word. But, despite the suppressed anger, the plump despot might have equaled Don Porfirio's span of years had he eaten less, drunk more moderately, been more discreet in his philanderings, and stuck to his post in Caracas. In 1888, during one of his frequent stays in Paris, it finally became apparent that a dictator cannot rule by telegraph. His puppet president suddenly refused to jump when the strings were pulled, and Guzmán's power soon ended. The populace was waiting to settle several scores. Guzmán had aroused bitter criticism by attempting to prevent transfer of the bones of his hated rival, Páez, to the national pantheon. An even greater storm was raised by the charge that Guzmán was selling out national rights in the controversy over the boundary line between Venezuela and British Guiana.

In 1888 the people finally struck. University students broke up the statues of the "Illustrious American," looted his mansion, and threatened death to the dictator if he dared to return. Guzmán Blanco, comfortably rich after his years of pilfering, wisely remained in Paris, where he lived until his death in 1899. History reluctantly acknowledges some benefits of his regime. To his credit were some new schools, a limited impetus to cultural life, and an improvement of the universities. He furthered the national economy, opened the ports to freer trade, built railways and highways, strengthened national credit, and tightened the lines of federal administration. He was confident that Venezuela was embarked upon "an infinite voyage toward an infinite future." Regarding his personal interests as identical with those of the nation, he viewed his own wealth and honors as fitting.

The decade which followed the fall of Guzmán Blanco brought new revolts and short-term presidents, with one four-year period of comparative tranquillity under Joaquín Crespo (1894–98). The long smoldering dispute with Great Britain over the Venezuelan–British Guiana boundary now flared up. President Cleveland, invoking the Monroe Doctrine, demanded that the issue be submitted to arbitration. The British, ruling the waves and many lands washed by the waves, refused to yield. In 1895 Cleveland's Secretary of State Richard Olney delivered his bellicose ultimatum: "The United States is practically sovereign on this continent." The British yielded, the issue was arbitrated, and in 1899 the line of demarcation was established, Great Britain winning most of the disputed territory although not the coveted delta of the Orinoco.

CIPRIANO CASTRO, 1899–1908

Cipriano Castro added another tainted chapter to Venezuelan history. Born in 1858 in the Andean highlands, he had never gone to school; he had worked as a cowboy, gone into politics, fought in various civil wars, and been exiled to Colombia, where he recruited a private army with which he captured Caracas and the presidency in 1899. For nine years he exercised a more absolute control than any of his predecessors. In 1902 his truculence provoked a blockade by British, German, and Italian naval units, with demand for a settlement of the claims of their nationals against Venezuela. After some blustering—to which President Theodore Roosevelt contributed his full share—the issues were submitted to arbitration and amicably settled.

Internally, Castro's rule was more corrupt and dissolute than any the country had known. With his toll from all government operations, he accumulated sizable balances in New York and London banks. A drunkard, a glutton, and an unrestrained libertine, he lived in frivolous luxury, surrounded by sycophants. Critics of the regime were jailed, murdered, or exiled. He demanded servile adulation, and was hailed as "Supreme Chief of the Liberal Revolutionary Restoration" and "the Moses of the Republic." Portraits and statues of him were everywhere. May 23, the day on which he had seized Caracas in 1899, was declared a national holiday. In 1908, broken in health, he placed the government in the hands of his trusted lieutenant, Juan Vicente Gómez, and sailed for Paris for medical care. But Gómez proved faithless, seized power for himself, and Venezuelans never saw Castro again (although he spent the next sixteen years, until his death in Puerto Rico in 1924, in plotting a return to the presidency).

JUAN VICENTE GÓMEZ, 1908–35

The twenty-seven-year dictatorship of Juan Vicente Gómez gave the nation the ablest—and the most savage—rule that it had yet known. Born in 1857 in the Andean region, Gómez had almost no schooling; he worked as a cattle hand and had already made himself master of numerous acres before he entered politics. After joining Castro's rebel army in 1899 and helping him to seize the government, Gómez was rewarded with the vice-presidency. When Castro left for Europe in 1908, Gómez declared martial law and seized the presidency for himself. From then until his death in 1935, Gómez ruled as president or through stooges, holding a firm hand upon the army, which is the final arbiter in Venezuela. During his twenty-seven years, six constitutions were drafted and promulgated, each guaranteeing all basic liberties but concentrating more and more power in the hands of the chief executive.

Gómez's reign took place in auspicious times. The United States had money for foreign investment. There was an eager market for Venezuelan exports. Increased coffee production resulted in treasury balances that made possible a mechanized army with which Gómez could maintain his hold. Then the discovery of petroleum in the Lake Maracaibo basin brought a flood of gold. From 1918 on, American, British, and Dutch companies were drilling, pumping, and piping out oil. In dealing with foreign oil companies, Gómez proved a shrewd trader, playing American and British-Dutch interests off against each other to the benefit of Venezuela. His Petroleum Law of 1920 was realistic; the companies paid substantial taxes, and the nation retained ample oil reserves for the future.

In contrast to his predecessor, Gómez was indifferent to titles; he ate sparingly, drank little, and worked assiduously. He never married, but provided generously for his scores of bastard sons and daughters, many of whom he loved devotedly, endowed handsomely, and permitted to use his name. He followed his predecessor's example by collecting his share on all governmental operations, and was reputed to be the richest man in South America, owning productive farms, numerous businesses, and various industries. His bank balances abroad were a subject of envious curiosity. On one of his many farms, "Maracay," he built a thousand-foot-long palace with some one hundred rooms, flanked by gardens which would have excited the jealousy of an eighteenth-century Bourbon prince. Aside from such peccadilloes, there was much to be said in praise of Juan Vicente Gómez. He won and maintained good relations with foreign powers. The domestic peace he imposed encouraged production on the farms. Skillful in public administration, he paid off the entire external debt, built roads and other public improvements, extended sanitation measures, and even built a few schools. He rallied around him some able men who accepted him as the only hope for their confused nation. These described his system of governing as "democratic Caesarism," whatever that may mean.

But Gómez's rule was harsh. A powerful army, numerous police, and ubiquitous spies scrutinized the acts and words of every citizen. Jails and dungeons were crowded with thousands of political prisoners, committed without trial and held without appeal. Tortures reminiscent of the Dark Ages were applied. Thousands escaped to Paris, Mexico, New York, and elsewhere, there to spend their days retelling with due exaggeration the terrors they had experienced. Gómez could ignore such publicity, for he and his nation were rich, his army had the finest guns and planes, his subordinates were faithful and well paid, and Venezuela owed not a copper centavo to any man or nation.

In 1935 the death of Gómez, at the age of seventy-eight, released the pent-up resentments of the populace, who stormed through the streets of Caracas sacking and firing the houses of Gómez's numerous sons and henchmen. The man whom Congress had declared *El Benemérito* ("the well-deserving") was now described as *el bagre* ("the cat fish"). Prison doors were opened, and the victims of his hate staggered out into the sunlight.

THE MOVEMENT TOWARD DEMOCRACY, 1935–48

The Venezuelan people, rid of Gómez, were without leaders. The generals, masters of great estates, and businessmen, tainted by long alliance with the dictator, continued in power. Eleazar López Contreras, a tuberculous general who had been minister of war under Gómez, assumed the presidency, made a few fumbling gestures toward democracy, evicted some spoilsmen from their offices, and announced a "three-year plan" of public works. His performance was not convincing; in 1937 he exiled forty-seven of his noisier critics on a flimsy charge of Communism; in a rigged election in 1940 he seated another army officer, Isaías Medina Angarita, as president.

Medina (1941–45) governed with moderation, permitting considerable freedom to the press and faithfully cooperating with the United States in World War II. Opposition parties were allowed to organize, the largest and most authentic being AD (*Acción Democrática.*) On the eve of the presidential election of 1945, AD—convinced that Medina was about to force the reelection of López Contreras—rose in revolt and placed a seven-man junta in control. The man named as provisional president was Rómulo Betancourt, a thirty-seven-year-old leftist intellectual who had helped to organize the new party.

The victory of AD was exhilarating to the people, who had now spoken for the first time in the history of Venezuela. The new leaders were civilians, middle-class professional and businessmen, democratic in conviction, and mildly leftist—but not Communist—in political philosophy. They incorporated their principles in a new constitution, which provided for moderate social legislation, the right to expropriate oil properties, and the election of the chief executive by direct popular vote. In the congressional elections of 1946 AD polled three times as many votes as all other parties. Betancourt's government brought action to recapture the ill-gotten wealth of Gómez's companions, in one case actually seizing property worth $12 million. It initiated a program of land reform, proposing the division of large estates into small farms. Such measures, faintly reminiscent of recent Mexican acts, worried both domestic and foreign investors.

In December, 1947, Betancourt helped to bring about the peaceful election of AD's candidate Rómulo Gallegos, famous novelist and popular hero.[2] Gallegos was chosen by a 4 to 1 majority in the first popular and honest presidential election in the nation's history. At his inauguration in February, 1948, his pledge of full democracy and his promise that all parties would be "allowed an open eye and a loose tongue" heartened those who had deplored the nation's wanton course. Their hopes proved abortive when ten months later the honorable but woefully impractical Gallegos was ousted by an army *coup d'état* and replaced by a three-man military junta. Gallegos had been less successful as a politician than as a novelist. He had ideas and ideals, but he was in a hurry, and he forgot to reckon with the corrupt army officers, the obstinate landowners, and the masters of business. He angered the generals by ordering an end to their plundering of the treasury, alarmed business leaders by proposals to increase the government's royalties on oil, and frightened landowners by mild proposals for division of their holdings. Gallegos and Betancourt were exiled, and the brief experiment in democracy was ended. There were loose and probably unfounded charges that foreign oil companies backed the military coup. There were also rumors that the agents of Argentine Dictator Perón were involved. Seasoned observers saw in the coup the familiar hallmarks of traditional Venezuelan political behavior.

THE ARMY TAKES OVER, 1948–58

The three-man junta installed in late 1948 proclaimed its love of democracy, its purpose to rescue the nation from the "Communistic" AD. As the price for recognition of the new regime by the United States, the junta pledged itself to honor all international obligations and to submit to free elections. That these new guardians of democratic order constituted a new dictatorship became clear as strict censorship was imposed upon the press, opponents were jailed without trial, tear gas was used against student demonstrators at the Central University of Caracas, and labor leaders were imprisoned.

The junta maintained its hold, despite sporadic revolts, for four years (1948–52). Oil profits kept the treasury filled, paid the army, suborned generals and other important people, and maintained a high level of prosperity for the favored minority. Delgado Chalbaud, leader of the 1948 coup, was assassinated in 1950 but another officer took his place. AD, outlawed from political activity, organized an undercover resistance with secret cells in labor unions, farm communities, and even in the army. Ten underground newspapers in the form of mimeographed bulletins were widely circulated, despite the fact that the mere possession of one was enough to send its holder to prison. The country had returned to the ways of Gómez.

In November, 1952, the long-deferred presidential election was held. Two factors persuaded the junta to submit their case to the electorate. They thought it safe to risk an election, for they had created a powerful

2 It should be noted that Rómulo Gallegos is far and away the best known of Venezuelan writers, and his novels (*Doña Barbara* and others) have won wide acclaim.

government party financed from the central treasury, and they had outlawed opposition parties except for the hitherto innocuous URD (Democratic Republican Union) and COPEI, the party of the Christian Democrats.
Also, the junta had been informed by the American State Department that
the United States would not favor holding the Tenth Pan American Conference, scheduled to meet in Caracas, under the shadow of a dictatorial government which failed to assure honest elections. The outlawed AD sent
out word through its grapevine that votes should be cast for COPEI in
Conservative rural sections and for the URD in the cities. The first returns
showed a 2 to 1 lead for the opposition over the government. The junta
responded in traditional fashion. Marcos Pérez Jiménez, its dominant
member, rid himself of his two associates, imposed a tight censorship on
election returns, announced that he had won an overwhelming majority
of votes, and took office as provisional president in December, 1952.

The Pérez Jiménez regime moved with speed and with smooth autocracy. In January, 1953, the constituent congress adopted a new constitution under which the president was assigned almost unlimited powers. In
April, Congress named Pérez Jiménez for a five-year term.

The new despotic regime was as thorough and as brutal as any that
Venezuela had ever suffered. Pedro Estrada, as vicious a man hunter as
Hitler ever employed, was made chief of the national security forces. Thousands of the adherents of AD, URD, and COPEI were rounded up, jailed,
or consigned to a concentration camp in the jungle, where many were tortured and murdered, or died from disease. Other thousands escaped into
exile. Leaders of the labor unions were arrested, and their organizations
were either abolished or put under officials appointed by the government.
The public schools were stripped of teachers who had shown signs of independent mind. The Central University of Caracas was closed. The press
was fettered and the few brave editors jailed or exiled. Foreign journals
which criticized Pérez Jiménez were barred from the mails.

Meanwhile, Pérez Jiménez governed with the loyal help of a little
coterie of friends. He called his new dispensation the "New National Ideal."
With the unprecedented flow of money from oil, Pérez embarked upon a
program of public works: he built a fine freeway connecting the capital with
the port of La Guaira; a petrochemical plant, hotels, office buildings, model
apartment houses for workers, power plants, steel works, dams. Caracas
flowered with proud boulevards and impressive modern buildings. Some
millions of dollars went into a club house for officers of the armed forces,
the most ornate and luxurious in the Americas. Pérez and his confederates
collected fat commissions on every operation. But the hardworking President and his chosen friends had time for pleasure. They had a retreat on an
island in the Caribbean, to which planes brought comely prostitutes from
Havana.

Honored and richly endowed as Pérez Jiménez was by his grateful
country, he was not neglected by friends abroad. He exchanged visits with
his like-minded colleague, President Rojas Pinilla of Colombia. When he
visited Washington in 1954, he was given an enthusiastic welcome, and

President Eisenhower conferred upon him the Legion of Merit. And, later, when he was finally ejected, the United States permitted him to settle in Miami.

By 1957 it became clear that the abused Venezuelans would no longer tolerate the psychotic and plundering Pérez. In December Pérez held a "plebiscite" (to take the place of a promised election) which continued him in office for a new term. Meanwhile, there was rumbling of anger from all sectors. The underfed masses were confronted with increased prices, which wiped out raises in wages and left them more destitute than ever. University students were plotting. The Church, through Archbishop Rafael Arias, spoke out against the "subhuman" conditions under which most people lived. In January, 1958, Pérez jailed five priests, whereupon the ecclesiastical authorities protested. The political parties—AD, URD, and COPEI —made an alliance against their common enemy. The Communists, first coddled by Pérez and then hounded, added their denunciation. The literate middle class, suffering from inflation and angered by the denial of liberty, grumbled. Even the army, well paid and indulgently courted, finally revolted—junior officers venting their resentment against the favored generals who got most of the perquisites. The navy and the air force took a hand in unseating the dictator. On New Year's Day, 1958, the first blows were struck when planes dropped bombs on Caracas. After three weeks of rioting, the coalition of opposition parties called a general strike. On January 23, Pérez Jiménez fled to Miami.

With the ouster of Pérez Jiménez, the armed forces took control and named a junta of five members from their ranks. The spokesmen of the allied AD, URD, and COPEI protested against such monopoly by the military, and they compelled the addition of two civilians to the junta, with the provision that the cabinet should be made up entirely of civilians. The measures of the junta—headed by Admiral Wolfgang Larrazábal, an able navy man—were swift and admirable: the press was freed; political prisoners were released; exiles were invited to return; the universities were reopened; the property of Pérez Jiménez and his cronies was seized. But the treasury was almost empty, and there were obligations of about $500 million—Pérez Jiménez having made off with $200 million, more or less. In order to ease the financial crisis, the junta served notice upon the oil companies that the old fifty-fifty division of profits between the government and the oil companies would no longer stand, that the ratio would now be 60 per cent for the government and 40 per cent for the companies.

December, 1958, brought an orderly and honest election. The three parties, despite their alliance, could not agree on one candidate: AD named Rómulo Betancourt; URD, Admiral Larrazábal; COPEI, Rafael Caldera. At the last minute Larrazábal accepted the support of the Communists, a move which so angered COPEI, the party of the Christian Democrats, that many of that group added their strength to AD. The result was victory for AD and Betancourt, who was inaugurated in February, 1959.

RÓMULO BETANCOURT, 1959–64

Rómulo Betancourt's five-year term in the presidency constituted a miracle in Venezuelan history. For the first time an honestly elected president was able to stay in power for his full term, then turn his office over to another man in an honest and peaceful election.

Betancourt the man was unique in the nation's history. Born into a poor middle-class rural family in 1908, he was educated in public schools and the Central University in Caracas. As a boy of twenty, he joined other hot-heads in protest against the tyrant, Juan Vicente Gómez, for which he was rewarded with a brief stay in a Gómez dungeon and a seven-year exile in Costa Rica. In the hospitable air of San José, reading, writing, talking with men of generous learning, he joined the Communist Party, but wisely left it almost immediately. After the death of Gómez in 1935, Betancourt returned to Caracas and joined the plotters against López Contreras. Once more he had to seek safety in exile, this time in Chile and Argentina, not returning to Caracas again until 1941. We have seen how Betancourt shared in the creation of *Acción Democrática,* serving as that party's provisional president for two years after Medina was ousted in 1945 (when he put through such drastic reforms as the law by which the oil companies would divide their profits with the government on a fifty-fifty basis— measures which prompted conservative elements to denounce him as a Communist); and how he helped to elect Rómulo Gallegos, then shared that patriot's exile—Betancourt's third—when the military took over in 1948. When, after nine years of senseless dictatorship, Pérez Jiménez and his unsavory gangsters were unseated in 1958, Betancourt came back to his ravaged country to piece together the torn remnants of AD. And in February, 1959, he was again president.

Now fifty-one, Betancourt was seasoned and disciplined. Still convinced that Venezuela needed the purge of social and economic revolution, he had nevertheless become tough and realistic. He admitted past mistakes, said that he and his party, in their earlier turn in power, had made "psychological errors. There was a certain arrogance, a certain intolerance with minorities. Some say we tried to do too much too fast." He assumed the heavy burden of his country's need with chastened spirit.

And the need of the nation committed to Betancourt's hands was great. To the chronic problems of illiteracy, a too rapidly growing population, meager housing, and the tragically unequal distribution of the nation's land and wealth, was added the special legacy of Pérez Jiménez: that gentleman had overspent, overrobbed, and undermanaged, leaving bankrupt a national treasury which, during the fourteen years 1943–56, had received $5.3 billion from the fabulously prosperous oil wells. Furthermore, agriculture had long been neglected, and the nation did not feed itself: in 1959, almost $200 million went abroad for wheat, corn, rice, meat, and eggs. And there was the immediate menace of the ragged, hungry, and perpetually angry mobs in the city of Caracas. Living in the filthy hillside slums (*ranchos,* the Venezuelans call them), which housed one out of three *caraqueños,* most of these bitterly poor and ignorant people had fled the open country to find jobs and security; but few were really employed, and they were a natural prey for leftist orators. Always ready to parade, riot, bomb, they had spat upon Richard Nixon in 1958 and were now largely against Betancourt. To these unruly mobs were added the troublemakers in the Central University; by some curious quirk, many faculty and students had been converted to the Communist gospel; but the University held its autonomous position, and this barred the intervention of the army and police.

Betancourt's first task was to build a viable democratic political life, into which he hoped to incorporate the "faceless" poverty-ridden masses: "A feeling of social responsibility," the President told his congress in March, 1961, ". . . converts the man in the street into a citizen." With skill and patience he created a bloc in which his own *Acción Democrática* could make common cause with two minority parties: COPEI, led by able and idealistic Rafael Caldera, and the URD; but this united front crumbled in November, 1960, when the URD group in Congress broke with Betancourt because of his firm stand against Fidel Castro. *Acción Democrática* itself suffered defections: a group of the younger men, charging Betancourt with foot-dragging on land reform, quit the party to form the MIR (*Movimiento Izquierda Revolucionaria*), which moved toward the Communists. In January, 1962, another group called *Grupo ARS,* also impatient with the President's slow progress in reform, broke off, crippling Betancourt's control of Congress.

From the outset Betancourt was firm but conciliatory with the armed forces. He knew that his government would not survive overnight if the generals and the admirals decided to oust him—that was, and still is, an obvious fact in Venezuelan politics. For a century and a half the military has had the final word: fattened up with high pay checks and fringe benefits, the "brass" has put presidents in and turned them out. Although it galled him, Betancourt spent too much on the army, navy, and air force, and he permitted their continued pilfering of the national treasury. He spent long hours explaining his policies to the leaders of the armed forces, and he made some converts; but the most intransigent among them were moved to diplomatic posts abroad. Despite his best efforts, however, there were two major uprisings and rumors of many more. But Betancourt held the military in line.

Agrarian reform was the cornerstone of Betancourt's program for remaking the nation. The extent of latifundia in Venezuela is clear in these figures for 1950: in that year, farms of over 1,236 acres each—or only 2.4 per cent of the total number of farms—accounted for 64.2 per cent of all the land in use; and, at the other extreme, 53.7 per cent of all agricultural and livestock units had less than 12.4 acres each. Betancourt's Agrarian Reform Law, adopted in March, 1960, created a National Agrarian Institute empowered to expropriate the great estates, with provisions for full indemnity to owners and the distribution of their acres to landless farmers—the goal being eventually to settle the 350,000 landless families on their own plots. (The law wisely exempted from expropriation productive farms up to 370 acres.) But the program had wider objectives than the mere parceling out of land: a central aim was to boost agricultural output so that Venezuela might become self-sufficient in foodstuffs— Betancourt announced that the government was "not trying to substitute for the unproductive latifundia the equally unproductive minifundia." Furthermore, it was hoped that raising the living standards in rural areas would halt the drift of misery-bound farmers to the cities, where they added to the rolls of the unemployed and the swollen mobs of angry agitators; and would discourage the destructive migration of the *conuqueros,* the squatters, who settled for a year or two on mountain lands, stripping the forests and speeding soil erosion, then moved to fresh areas, there to continue their disastrous course. The scope of the agrarian legislation was impressive, and the performance substantial. Various agencies were created to finance new farmers, to provide technical training, machinery, seed, fertilizer, etc., to build schools and roads, to enlarge health services.

Betancourt was a devout believer in planning for his country's economic and social progress. His four-year plans were carefully examined each year, with shifts to meet new conditions. Fortunately for Venezuela, there was money, mostly oil money, with which to pursue the many-sided programs of land reform, education, industrialization, health, public works —at this point, Venezuela stood in marked contrast to her less affluent neighbors. Oil alone furnished over half of the national budget. In addition to money, Venezuela boasted a growing body of responsible leaders. Her universities, which had contributed little under the dictators, were forging ahead, turning out competent technicians and managers; and many of the richer families were sending their sons abroad for education. Also important was the solid contribution made by the technicians of foreign oil and mining companies.

Betancourt's planning did not disguise his fidelity to the socialist faith—socialism of the Swiss or Swedish variety, rather than that of the Russian. He hoped for eventual government ownership not only of petroleum, but also of electric power facilities: and he was firm in demanding that the government should maintain a strong hand in basic manufacturing industries, especially iron and steel, petrochemicals, and aluminum.

Not all of Betancourt's plans had clear sailing. In 1960–61 a sharp recession slowed down many programs. The blame for this recession was chiefly leveled against the inherited extravagance of the Pérez Jiménez days. Aside from his wanton pilfering, the dictator had erected public and private buildings of dubious utility, including a silly hotel on a mountain top outside Caracas, committing the nation to vast expenditures; and Betancourt had undertaken to pay off Pérez's reckless debts. In 1960–61 the oil boom slackened, and the treasury felt the pinch. But Betancourt's administration weathered the storm, and by 1963 the President was able to announce that the GNP (gross national product) had registered an average yearly increase of 4.5 per cent since 1958. Honesty and hard work had paid off handsomely.

Betancourt's troublers were of both the right and the left. The ranks of the right had been steadily augmented by those dependent upon the oil industry, mining, and business, many of whom still labeled Betancourt a Communist. In the election of 1958 the voters of Caracas voted 5 to 1 against Betancourt: while part of that vote came from the Communist-Castroite left, a significant part came from the unconvinced right. Some partisans of Betancourt charged that leaders of the oil interests (both Venezuelans and foreigners) withheld cooperation from Betancourt because he had increased the government cut on petroleum receipts, denied new concessions to existing companies, and espoused a national petroleum corporation (*Corporación Venezuelana de Petroleo*) which would ultimately inherit all existing concessions. In this connection it is well to bear in mind that the foreign oil interests—chiefly powerful American elements—have faced a perplexing task in dealing with a Pérez Jiménez one year and a Betancourt the next. Also it is well to remember that after the swift and complete expropriation of all foreign oil properties by Mexico's Cárdenas in 1938, foreign oil companies—in Venezuela and elsewhere—pondered the experience, faced their mistakes, and adopted new policies. By and large the foreign oil companies operating in Venezuela have, through generous and intelligent social and economic cooperation, been successful in establishing a considerable measure of mutual confidence with the leaders of Venezuela. And Betancourt himself was able to win the esteem of many of the leading oil operators.

The battle was drawn with Betancourt's enemies on the left when, in his inaugural address of February 13, 1959, he made clear his unwillingness to concede anything to the Communist Party, although recognizing its legal existence. There was a hard core of Communists who were increasingly fortified by the sympathizers with Fidel Castro in Cuba. The Castroites in Venezuela presented a special problem. During the months before Castro entered Havana on New Year's Day in 1959, Betancourt and his friends had helped Fidel's guerrillas in their fight against Batista; but as Castro began to play with the Communists, Betancourt's group turned against him. In 1961, Betancourt supported the OAS expulsion of Cuba, and in November of that year, Venezuela broke off relations with the Castro government. Meanwhile, in 1960, the Communist Party had officially pledged loyalty to Fidel and promised to wage guerrilla warfare against the Betancourt regime.

This league of Communists and Castroites did their best to plague Betancourt. Together with the MIR (left-wing dissenters from *Acción Democrática*), they took part in marine revolts at the naval bases of Carupano and Puerto Cabello in May and June of 1962. When Betancourt suspended civil guarantees, hardline Communists, in alliance with some extreme rightists, organized the terrorist group called FALN (Armed Forces for National Liberation), using Communist and MIR congressmen as a front: these gentlemen, having been legally elected, enjoyed immunity against prosecution. During 1962 and 1963 these terrorists ranged the countryside and reached even into the capital city itself. They destroyed property, national and foreign: a Sears Roebuck warehouse was blown up, pipe lines of the oil companies were damaged, and a bomb was thrown into the United States Embassy. Despite the best efforts of the army—which was largely faithful to the government—there was wanton murder and sabotage. When the President finally cracked down in September, 1963, arresting all Communist and MIR members of Congress, there were loud outcries that he had betrayed the democratic cause; but sober Venezuelans upheld his hand. The case against Castro intervention became abundantly clear in November, 1963, when a three-ton cache of small arms, mortars, and grenades was discovered buried in a lonely stretch of Caribbean beach. The Caracas government entered a charge with the OAS that agents of Castro had delivered the arms for the use of the FALN in a campaign of terror designed to prevent the presidential election of December, 1963; the evidence was convincing, and the foreign ministers of the American republics, called together in Washington, voted to impose sanctions against Cuba (with Chile, Uruguay, Bolivia, and Mexico abstaining—but by mid-1967 only Mexico was holding back).

Besides the continuing nuisance of the disciples of Fidel Castro, Betancourt was harried by other outside forces. The durable dictator of the Dominican Republic, Rafael Trujillo, made clear his hostility to Betancourt's democratic regime. Trujillo's hand appeared in most of the plots uncovered in Venezuelan military circles. And when a bomb exploded beside Betancourt's car on June 24, 1960—killing his military aide, wounding the minister of defense, and inflicting painful burns on Betancourt's hands and face—the almost successful assassination attempt was promptly and accurately traced to Trujillo agents: representatives of the other American states, called to confer in San José, Costa Rica, voted to condemn the Dominican government and to impose economic sanctions against it.

The election of December 1, 1963, to choose Betancourt's successor as well as members of Congress marked the final triumph of Betancourt's years in office. Almost 90 per cent of the qualified voters turned out on election day. Raúl Leoni, standard bearer of *Acción Democrática,* a founder and leading figure in the party, led with 33 per cent of the votes (not as good a record as that of Betancourt, who got 49 per cent in the election of 1958). Rafael Caldera, leader of COPEI, came in second with 20 per cent of the votes, and his party increased its seats in Congress. The other five candidates divided the balance of the vote between them. The election was carefully policed, there was almost no violence or fraud. Venezuela had again proved its democracy by permitting peaceful succession in the presidency.

RAÚL LEONI, 1964–

March 11, 1964, was a proud day for Leoni, Betancourt, and all who hoped for effective democracy in Venezuela. Members of Congress, political leaders, and the representatives of fifty nations watched as the outgoing president placed the presidential sash on the shoulders of Raúl Leoni. The two men presented contrasts: the ebullient, stocky, always dramatic

Betancourt made way for the tall, somewhat colorless—and never dramatic —Leoni. Long the efficient political wheelhorse in the shadow of Betancourt, Leoni had little popular appeal, and many glumly prophesied that he would be unable to hold the country together.

Leoni made the early mistake of abandoning the alliance between AD and COPEI. Almost all observers considered COPEI under Rafael Caldera. to be a responsible and able party, standing for most of the policies proclaimed by AD; and Betancourt was outspoken in calling upon Leoni to preserve the alliance. (After all, both Betancourt's election to office and his administration had been made possible by the cooperation of COPEI.) But Leoni would not yield, regarding COPEI as a threat to the dominance of AD. He refused to give COPEI adequate representation in the new cabinet, buttressing his minority position in Congress by appointing 12 out of 14 cabinet members from splinter groups.

Leoni inherited most of the turmoils which had beset Betancourt. Communists still demonstrated, Castroites were noisy, and FALN terrorists ranged through the back streets of Caracas and in the open country, despite the valiant efforts of the army to corner them. Rightist elements still clamored against the "socialistic" measures of AD; and the spurned Christian Democrats of COPEI cooperated only fitfully with Leoni.

But if Leoni inherited Betancourt's enemies, he also inherited a nation which was a going concern: most of Pérez Jiménez's debts had been liquidated, and the upturn in the economy had continued since 1962. A conspicuous proof of this happier state was afforded in May, 1964, when Leoni presented a four-year, $850-million public works program which was to be financed almost entirely by commercial loans within the country and by foreign banks, with little help needed from Alliance for Progress funds. The program was directed primarily at the serious problem of unemployment (which stood at 13 to 14 per cent in 1964), and included new schools, electric power projects, and irrigation and flood control designed to bring 3 million acres into production by 1980—and, hopefully, to end the drain on the nation's economy caused by the heavy importation of food. A high place was given to opening up the back country by feeder roads, airports, and docks.

Leoni continued to tackle his stiff task of realizing the program established by Betancourt. At the end of his first year in office he confidently bade his nation tighten and buttress its economy, strike for an annual increase of 7.2 per cent in the total GNP, set a goal of 8 per cent expansion in agriculture and 11 per cent in industry. He was confident that potable water would be available for 90 per cent of the people by the end of his term in 1969, that 6,000 miles of new roads would be built, that electric energy would increase 50 per cent, and that over 4 million acres of new land would be opened up by irrigation. He promised more schools and a drastic reduction in illiteracy. Although Leoni's promises were overoptimistic, there was no doubt as to his tenacity and skill, and he rendered a better account of himself in his first three years of office than had been anticipated. There was no inflation; the currency maintained its stability; there were moderate increases in the GNP; and at the end of 1966 the monetary reserves stood at $776 million.

But Leoni faced formidable obstacles. He, like Betancourt, was caught in the cross fire between left and right. On the right was the firmly entrenched military, many of them unwilling to give more than token assent to Leoni's "socialistic" measures. There were repeated rumors of military revolt, and in October, 1966, the officers of one garrison staged a futile *coup d'état* which was swiftly ended with the court-martial of a few highly placed officials. And leftist elements were a continuing threat to Leoni's program. The Communist Party, not large but always active, embarrassed him at every turn. The adherents of Cuba's Castro were even more difficult to handle. Guerrilla bands, probably never enlisting more than a few hundred men, played havoc with life and property in rural communities, and occasionally struck with fire and terror in Caracas itself. The Communists, after brief yoking of power with the Castroites, turned against the agents of Fidel as irritating attacks by Cuban expeditionaries aroused the ire of all Venezuelans. Finally the Communist Party severed all ties with the Castroites and announced that it would push for its reforms through constitutional channels. The fact remained that all leftist factions had rich soil in which to thrive: misery was still the lot of a full half of the Venezuelan people; much of the backland was a rotting rural slum, and a third of Caracas's population lived in the rabbit warrens (the *ranchos*) on the hills around the dazzling capital city.

The most dramatic answer of Leoni to the guerrillas and terrorists came on December 14, 1966, with the seizure by the army of the Central University of Caracas—an action demanded by the armed forces, and reluctantly accepted by Leoni. The inescapable fact was that that institution was a refuge for the leaders of angry leftists of all categories—although it may fairly be said that the troublemakers were no more than a minority of the students and faculty. The University had for years enjoyed autonomous status, running its own affairs as it pleased, and was legally not subject to intervention by the army or police. During the years since Fidel Castro seized power in Cuba, many of the leaders of the Castro faction—and most of the Communist Party as well—had entrenched themselves in the faculty and student body of the University. (The autonomous character of the Central University was matched in many other principal Latin American universities, but the Caracas institution seems to have been burdened with more Communists and their fellow-travelers than any of the others.) Now in December, 1966, Leoni ordered an end to the University's autonomy, and detachments of police and soldiers occupied the seven-acre campus. Hundreds of students were arrested and a few guns and ammunition were collected. There was excited protest not only from the extreme leftists but also from moderate liberals who denounced Leoni's measures as highhanded. But Leoni defended his course by describing the University as "a terrorist base of operations for armed subversion."

Leoni promised that nothing would be done to block the legitimate exercise of the University's functions. But the intervention in December had so disorganized the University that, as one professor put it, "It was impossible to teach and it was impossible to learn." There was general demoralization of the faculty, as new appointments were blocked, as the flow of public funds for the support of the institution slowed down.

A dramatic and unexpected development was the return to Venezuela in April, 1965, of the former dictator, Pérez Jiménez. Since his flight from Caracas in January, 1958, Pérez had been living in fine luxury in Miami. Then came demands from Betancourt's government for his extradition; and Washington finally gave its approval—not on the various charges of murder and torture, all well documented, but on the charge of embezzling some $13 million. He was delivered to the Venezuelan authorities, who jailed him in comfort, and proceeded to a leisurely trial in which Leoni assured that all justice would be done.

Leoni's job, as of mid-1967, was a tough one. With another year and a half to go, a dozen volunteer statesmen were preparing for the next election in December, 1968.

VENEZUELA IN 1967

It is difficult to draw up an accurate balance sheet for Venezuela in 1967: the assets are so great, the handicaps so serious, and the possible threats to progress so real.

On the asset side we list, first, the abundance of good soil, which is still largely potential wealth; for agriculture was neglected after oil was first exported in 1917, and only now is attention being paid to the improvement of the nation's farms, which employ some 32 per cent of the labor force. But there is soil enough, and it is rich enough, to feed the people well with a large surplus for export.

Then oil, the magic word in Venezuela, which accounts for over 70 per cent of the government revenue and 92 per cent (1964) of all exports. Petroleum production has increased more than a thousandfold since the 1920's, reaching 1.3 billion barrels in 1965, and today Venezuela is the largest petroleum-exporting country in the world and the third largest producer (after the United States and the U.S.S.R.). The companies which pump and sell the oil are almost all foreign: the major producers are Creole (subsidiary of Standard Oil of New Jersey), with about 40 per cent of total production; Shell (British and Dutch), with about 25 per cent; Mene Grande (subsidiary of Gulf, American), with some 13 per cent. Sixteen smaller companies also participate. Before World War II almost all the petroleum was refined on the Dutch islands of Aruba and Curaçao; today more than one-third is refined in Venezuela. Petroleum has brought fine profits: from 1943 to 1956 the industry's profits averaged some $293 million a year, government revenues some $379 million; and in 1961 the industry's take was $734 million—a handsome 32.3 per cent return on its net invested capital of $2,272 million *after* the government took its share of $881 million. The Venezuelan government, quite naturally, has tried to take as large a slice of the oil revenue as possible without killing the industry. In 1946 the Betancourt administration had increased the government's share to 50 per cent; the provisional junta of 1958 lifted that share to 60 per cent; and various shifts in tax schedules have raised the figure further until in 1964 the government collected about 66 per cent, leaving the companies 34 per cent. In his last term in office, Betancourt repeatedly warned against exorbitant demands upon the companies, lest initiative be threatened; but he did frighten the foreign companies by announcing that no new oil concessions would be granted and that lapsing concessions would go to the newly launched *Corporación Venezuelana de Petroleo*. There was no immediate threat of outright expropriation (as had been the case in Mexico). On the whole, there had been surprisingly little turmoil considering the size of the stake—both the government and the companies had kept their tempers. But all were agreed in opposing the quota system limiting exports of oil to the United States, which had been imposed by Washington in 1959. This quota system, designed to protect American oil producers at home, was especially resented in Venezuela, inasmuch as oil from Mexico and Canada (which Washington argued would not be interrupted in time of war) was allowed to enter the United States without restriction.

Also on the credit side is the immense potential wealth of the jungle lands of the Orinoco. The boom city of Guayana, on the banks of the Orinoco near its junction with the Caroni River, 350 miles southeast of Caracas, has all the promise and all the squalor of the boom cities of the Golden West in the days when Americans were streaming to California. This area, with its rapidly developing industrial complex, has often been called the Venezuelan Ruhr of the future. Its endowments are prodigious: heavy forests, vast reserves of high grade iron ore, coal, petroleum, substantial deposits of aluminum, manganese, sulfur, gold—and a greater hydroelectric potential than Niagara Falls. With justifiable pride Betancourt described Guayana as "the cornerstone of Venezuelan development," and in his planning assigned it $2 billion over a thirteen-year period. Enough has already been done to make the dream seem feasible: a $350-million steel mill and a 350,000-KWH hydroelectric plant have been completed, and various small industries launched; seven ports have been built between Guayana (a deep seaport accessible to ocean-going ships) and the mouth of the Orinoco on the Caribbean; sixty miles up the Caroni, work is under way on a 330-foot dam, one of the highest in the world, which will yield electric current for the area. Control of the development of mineral resources is divided between the state *Corporación de Guayana* and various foreign companies—chiefly, U.S. Steel, Bethlehem Steel, and Reynolds Metal Corporation—with the government offering the foreign companies limited rights under concessions.

But Venezuela in 1967 faced vast problems. First and fundamental was the political confusion inherited from its stormy past. For more than a century the usual pattern of government had been vicious, wasteful, despotic, with the unwieldy growth of an incompetent and distended bureaucracy, and little tradition of trained and honest public servants.

And the overshadowing power of the military time and again helped to establish new tyranny. Rómulo Betancourt struggled against these handicaps, and did more than any leader in Venezuela's history to impose constitutional order. But the evils were still there.

Then there was the burden of the population explosion: with the total population of over 9 million increasing at some 3.6 per cent each year, Venezuela was the fastest growing nation in South America in the 1960's. This rapid increase was partially explained by the influx of foreigners attracted by the quick profits in enterprises linked to the production of oil and minerals. But Venezuela also had one of the highest birth rates in the hemisphere. Together with a high death rate, the result was that more than half the population was under twenty years old—"a nation of teenagers," one Venezuelan remarked. Each year some 80,000 youths were thrust into the labor market. "Their demands for a place in schools and universities, industry and society, have the force of an avalanche," said Leoni in July, 1965. "Industrial development, agrarian reform and mass education are therefore necessities that cannot be postponed." Also there was the serious question as to how all of these people would find food enough to eat and homes in which to live. As it was, the farm lands of Venezuela did not feed the people; and housing was woefully inadequate: one-third of all the people in Caracas lived in hillside slums, and most rural families had to make do with hovels.

The glaring inequity in the distribution of land and income continued to plague the nation. The generous annual per capita income of $761 (1965)—the highest in Latin America—is deceptive. Averaged into that figure are the ample incomes, derived from oil and other industries, which go to foreigners, a thin slice of affluent Venezuelans, and the lawyers, doctors, and managers who serve the wealthy. The numerous generals and admirals are overpaid. As for labor—skilled and unskilled—there is the anomalous situation of the petroleum industry, which produces some 70 per cent of the government income, accounts for about one-fifth of the GNP, but employs scarcely 1.3 per cent of the workers. And despite the valiant efforts of recent years the nation's land was still unequally divided: a handful of the aristocracy still held most of the best land; a large number of farmers wrung a meager living from small plots; and almost 300,000 farm families still had no land at all, working as laborers for others for a pittance.

By 1967 Venezuela had made a brave start toward solving its problems. The program of agrarian reform launched by Betancourt in 1959 and continued by Leoni was still under way in the mid-1960's, despite the noisy opposition of conservatives, who wanted no land reform at all, and leftists, who demanded everything at once. In 1965 President Leoni could report with accuracy and pride that "since 1959, the National Agrarian Institute has distributed 1,465,000 hectares (about 3.7 million acres) to nearly 80,000 peasant families." Venezuela had embarked upon its program of land reform with more wisdom than had Mexico in the years after

1910, or had Bolivia in 1952: unlike those two countries, Venezuela had proceeded with restraint, paying for the land taken from the great plantations; furthermore, Venezuela, with its vast oil wealth, was able to invest over $100 million to help the new farmers make their land more productive.

Industry in Venezuela had been enlarged, especially since World War II. In 1941 workers in industry made up less than 5 per cent of the national labor force; in 1950 they made up more than 10 per cent; in 1962 more than 12 per cent. And from 1950 to 1962 the manufacturing index increased almost 300 per cent. Venezuelans increasingly produced their own textiles, leather goods, paper products, chemicals, tires, and many other items. The generation of electricity (for public use) increased tenfold between 1948 and 1964, but was still inadequate.

Foreign capital was a powerful element in the economy: 65 per cent of it was American; 23 per cent, Dutch; 10 per cent, English. Oil profits have also encouraged the rapid growth of state investment. The Venezuelan government was the chief banker, the largest landholder, the principal distributor of foodstuffs, the manager of slaughterhouses, the owner of grain warehouses, the operator of cattle ranches, the marketer of sugar and rice, the owner of a steel mill and great hydroelectric plants. For good measure, the government also owned some textile mills, sugar refineries, canneries, construction companies, and hotels. It owned the state railroad system, with only one small line still in private hands. It owned two of the three principal airlines. It had a merchant fleet. It owned the telegraph system, and most of the telephone, radio, and television systems. An interesting joint venture of state capitalism and private industry was the Venezuela Basic Economy Corporation (of which Nelson Rockefeller was the chief designer): this partnership pioneered in food distribution, establishing supermarkets, experimental farms, fish-processing plants, and dairy products concerns.

Education had long been neglected: in 1958, at the close of Pérez Jiménez's nine-year term, there were no schools at all for over half the children of school age. Under Betancourt the budget for education increased until it was second only to that for public works; and schools—primary, secondary, university, teacher-training—have multiplied rapidly. Between the school years 1957–58 and 1962–63 the enrollment in primary schools almost doubled, and secondary students increased threefold. President Leoni optimistically predicted that illiteracy—which in 1950 was about 51 per cent—would be down to 5 per cent by the end of his term. But his promise was rash.

By 1967 Venezuela was again solvent. Of the more than $1 billion in floating debts left by Pérez Jiménez, only some $30 million remained unpaid. And Venezuela had held the line on inflation: the cost of living rose only 9 per cent between 1958 and 1966 (compared with 12 per cent in the United States, 532 per cent in Chile, and some 2,900 per cent in Brazil); and Venezuela had one of the most stable currencies in South America.

A perceptive Venezuelan remarks that his country did not enter the twentieth century until the death of that durable dictator, Juan Vicente Gómez, in 1935. Only then did there begin to emerge an honest national purpose. The brave progress since 1935 has been achieved against formidable odds. But today there is a new generation of Venezuelans, with a sense of national responsibility and with the skills required for leadership. All weather is not fair in 1967, but the nation has a sense of direction and a body of dedicated citizens—which bodes well for the nation's future.

Chapter 30

COLOMBIA

Colombia is a fortress nation, her bastions in the high valleys and broad plateaus of the interior and her back turned upon the outer world. A green girdle of tropical coast extends along the Pacific and the Caribbean, but the port cities of Buenaventura, Cartagena, and Barranquilla are little more than the ground entrances to the country which towers above the sea.

There are two Colombias: a grim wilderness of plains, forest, and jungle, whose waters drain into the Orinoco and the Amazon, occupying almost two-thirds of the national domain but containing scarcely 2 per cent of the population; and the towering Andean region, little more than one-third of the country, which is the effective Colombia. The cordillera of the Andes unknots itself on the southern borders and spreads out three finger-ranges toward the north. Between the eastern and the central ranges flows the 1,000-mile Magdalena River, and between the central and western spurs the Cauca winds, joining the Magdalena on its way to the Caribbean. These mountain ranges, valleys, and plateaus, together with the narrow coastal belt, contain the farms, factories, mines, and businesses of the Colombian people.

Colombia's politics, economy, and culture have been shaped by her awkward geography. Jungles and high mountain passes have blocked the normal passage of men, goods, and ideas from the capital city to the other centers of population. Bogotá's access to the sea and the outer world was long dependent upon the clumsy boats which ride the Magdalena. The building of highways and railroads has scarcely begun. Exaggerated regionalism has been the inevitable result. An excellent network of airlines, begun in 1920, has finally brought quick communication among the scattered cities.

Colombia's land area of 439,513 square miles—more than Texas and California combined—had a population of 18.1 million in 1965, of which roughly 20 per cent were whites, 70 per cent mestizos, 5 per cent Indians, and 5 per cent Negroes. The Negroes are chiefly on the coast, and the Indians in the jungle and forest lands of the south and east. The whites,

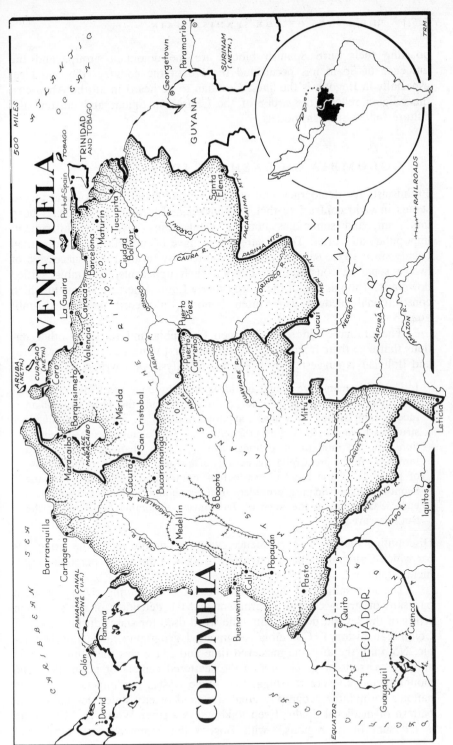

Venezuela and Colombia

boasting their pure Spanish blood, are the dominant group, and the influence of Spain has permeated the life of the country: the language, especially in Bogotá, is the finest Castilian to be heard in all the Americas; the religion reflects the ardor of the Church in Spain; and custom and culture follow Spanish models.

COLOMBIA'S CLASHING IDEAS

Enthusiasts for democracy find comfort in Colombia. Her political record stands in vivid contrast to that of Venezuela. Elections have always been important, and sometimes honest; dictatorships have been infrequent, unpopular, and brief. To be sure, there have been civil wars, more than twenty since 1830. Riotous political controversy resulted in a succession of twelve separate constitutions. Despite such upheavals, Colombia settled down after 1909 as one of the more orderly Latin American states, in which constitutional pledges were often honored, a record maintained until 1948.

The dramatic difference between Colombia and the four other nations that owe their freedom to Simón Bolívar (Venezuela, Ecuador, Peru, and Bolivia) is suggested by a Peruvian analyst, who writes:

> In Colombia men have fought for ideas; anarchy there has had a religious character. . . . A Jacobin ardor divides mankind; the fiery Colombian race is impassioned by vague and abstract ideas. . . . These sanguinary struggles have a certain rude grandeur. . . . In Colombia exalted convictions are the motives of political enmities; men abandon fortune and family, as in the great religious periods of history, to hasten to the defense of principle. These hidalgos waste the country and fall nobly, with the Semitic ardor of Spanish crusaders. Heroes abound in the fervor of these battles. Obedient to the logic of Jacobinism, Colombia perishes but the truth is saved.[1]

Discounting that writer's eloquence, we may inquire as to the principles for which Colombians have fought each other. Two of the perennial arguments stand out.

The first subject of dispute has been the continuing rivalry between partisans of strong central government and the defenders of the sovereign rights of the several departments (the word used for states during much of Colombian history). Colombia's segmented geography made this inevitable. Not until the airplane mastered time and space was there much traffic either in persons or goods among the scattered centers of population; the mountain passes were too high, the jungle wastes too impenetrable. The nation's formidable geography created a land of city-states not unlike the pattern of medieval Spain. Even today, says Arthur Whitaker, "Colombia is the sum of its regions," with Bogotá the commercial, cultural, and

---

[1] F. García Calderón: *Latin America, Its Rise and Progress,* translated by Bernard Miall (London: T. F. Unwin; 1913), p. 202.

political center; Medellín the industrial stronghold; Cali and Popayán the important agricultural centers; and Barranquilla the Caribbean outlet to the world for coffee, oil, and other commodities. Living for years in pocketed isolation from one another, each region developed its local pride, way of life, and even its variation on the common tongue. Jealous regional loyalties produced civil wars and postponed national unity. Of the ten nineteenth-century constitutions, six called for strong centralization, four for regional autonomy. National unity meant little until Rafael Núñez imposed his will upon the warring states in the 1880's. Jealousy still exists among the several regions, and those who live on the coast have a lively contempt for the "cliff dwellers" of Bogotá, a contempt generously reciprocated.

The second issue over which heads have been split is the status of the Catholic Church. Religion has been a prime source of discord between Conservatives and Liberals. The Conservatives, self-appointed custodians of order, have stood for highly centralized government and the perpetuation of traditional class and clerical privileges, and they have opposed extension of the voting rights of the people. The Liberals have stressed states' rights, universal suffrage, and complete separation of Church and state. In no other Latin American republic except Mexico has the Church-state imbroglio been more angry and obstinate. From 1830 to 1849, there was inconclusive sparring between the two factions. After 1849 the Liberals held power most of the time until the 1880's. From the 1880's until 1930, the Conservatives were in command. From 1930 until 1946, the Liberals again had their turn. In 1946 the Conservatives returned to vindicate their principles of order, with the Church issue again in the foreground. By 1967, anticlericalism had lost much of its fury, especially in the cities. In the isolated villages there were still angry clashes between clerical Conservatives and anticlerical Liberals.

Colombian internal tumult, costly as it has been, has a morally impressive side. Resistance to strong central government, carried to fantastic extremes, demonstrated a zeal for liberty and impatience with would-be dictators. The Church argument, for all its fury, reflected deep conviction. Colombian churchmen, perhaps spiritually more akin to their colleagues in Spain than those in any other Latin American republic, have been impelled by the belief that Colombia was and must continue to be dedicated to the service of the true faith, and that all unbelievers and heretics are enemies of the nation. They have revealed the tenacity of a Jiménez de Cisneros or an Ignatius Loyola. At the other extreme, the Liberals have shown no less ardor in defense of *their* principles, which took on the aura of a new religious faith—although they looked to Voltaire, Rousseau, and Montesquieu rather than to the apostles, prophets, and saints. The bystander concludes that the force of ideas, either right or wrong, has made an immense and continued appeal to the Colombian people.

THE FOUNDATION OF THE NATION, 1819–42

The battle of Boyacá settled the independence of New Granada in 1819, but for a decade the land to be called Colombia[2] was involved in the costly campaigns of the irrepressible Simón Bolívar, as he led his armies along the 3,000-mile battle line from the tropical *llanos* of Venezuela to the frosty *altiplano* of Bolivia. Throughout the 1820's Colombia suffered alternately from the Liberator's erratic rule and from his preoccupation with other regions. Nor was Colombia's tranquillity furthered by the intermittent clashes between Bolívar and his vice-president, Francisco de Paula Santander. Theirs was an unhappy team. Bolívar wanted an empire uniting the scattered and dissimilar peoples in the 2,000-mile span between the mouth of the Orinoco and the river Guayas of Ecuador, an unnatural union of mutually suspicious people without common heritage or economic ties. Bolívar, accurately gauging the hazards of democracy for his ill-prepared people, favored a strongly centralized nation commanded by a president chosen for life. "Pure representative government," he warned, "is not suited to our character, customs and present conditions." Against such regal ambition, the cautious Santander, loyal to his homeland of New Granada, foretold the futility of Bolívar's schemes, affirmed his faith in the rule of law, demanded the separation of New Granada, and urged respect for the autonomy of the several departments.

The clash between Bolívar and Santander involved New Granada throughout the 1820's. Bolívar, with much of the best manhood of Colombia in his army, pursued his campaigns in Ecuador, Peru, and high Bolivia. The admiration of his northern supporters soon turned to resentment as many Granadans, as well as Venezuelans, tired of his theatrics and bitterly opposed his steady drain upon man power and funds for support of "foreign wars." These criticisms were made openly when Bolívar returned triumphantly from the south in 1826, fresh from his creation of independent Bolivia. Santander, still vice-president in charge of New Granada, became the spearhead of this opposition and the spokesman for a people who were weary of empire builders.

Santander, an unbending legalist, had little in common with the mercurial Bolívar. "Arms," Santander said, "have given us independence; laws will give us freedom." To his credit stood solid achievement during Bolívar's long absence in the south. He had gone far toward imposing order over the scattered regions of New Granada with its population of scarcely more than 1 million. The recognition of Gran Colombia by the United States in 1822 and by Great Britain in 1825 was a tribute to Santander

2 The country will be designated by its modern name in order to ease the perplexity of the reader. *Gran Colombia* was the name given to Bolívar's short-lived union of New Granada, Venezuela, and Ecuador. In 1830 the region now called Colombia was given its viceregal name, New Granada. In 1858 it became the Granadine Confederation. In 1861 it was rebaptized as the United States of Colombia. In 1886 it emerged as the Republic of Colombia.

as well as to Bolívar. When Bolívar was reelected president and Santander vice-president of Gran Colombia in 1826, the relations between the two men were tense. When the Liberator answered his critics at the convention of Ocaña two years later by declaring himself dictator, his highhandedness provoked a plot to assassinate him. Bolívar charged Santander with complicity and jailed him for a time, but later permitted him to go into exile. However, Bolívar's power was slipping from him. The Peruvians rose in a revolt which he put down with difficulty. There were outbreaks against him in Popayán and Medellín. In 1830 Gran Colombia fell apart, as Santander had prophesied, with Venezuela and Ecuador seceding. Bolívar, entrusting the presidency of New Granada to Joaquín Mosquera, withdrew to the Caribbean coast ostensibly bound for Europe, a move sometimes interpreted as the last dramatic bid for a vindicating recall to Bogotá. But tuberculosis, which had long been weakening him, brought his death near Santa Marta in December, 1830. The first chapter in the history of Colombia was closed.

   .Santander, recalled from exile in New York in 1832, stands as the true founder of the Colombian nation. Freed by Bolívar's death from the constant threat of his interference, Santander undertook the presidency with vigor and intelligence. Despite his loyalty to democratic institutions, he imposed firm discipline upon his unruly country. Although he had earlier defended the cause of regional autonomy, he knew that the authority of the central government must be assured. Under his hand the country was largely pacified, finances were organized, and trade increased. Although this "man of laws," as he is gratefully remembered by Colombians, was much of a martinet, he proved a wise conciliator in the thorny contest between churchmen and their opponents which had been provoked by Bolívar's earlier anticlerical measures. Although a loyal Catholic, Santander pleased the Liberals (as the anticlericals were now called) by curtailing the jurisdiction of Church courts, providing non-Catholic cemeteries, and promoting secular schools. He angered some Conservatives by demanding for the government the right of patronage over ecclesiastical appointments, a privilege long claimed by the Spanish Crown. Meanwhile, his warm loyalty to the faith went far toward allaying the fears of the clergy. A victory for his moderation was the Vatican's recognition of the new nation in 1835.
   When one considers the perplexing problems which Santander inherited, his success seems clear. He lost much of his popular following when he accepted as a national responsibility one-half of the accumulated war debt of defunct Gran Colombia. His earlier grievances against Bolívar prompted his unflagging hostility to all who had remained faithful to the Liberator. In 1836 Santander sought to impose as president one of Bolívar's bitter enemies, General José María Obando, the man generally accused of responsibility for the murder of Sucre. The Colombians, who revered the name of Sucre, refused Santander's nomination and elected a civilian, José Ignacio Márquez (1837–41). On the whole Márquez con-

tinued the constructive work of Santander, although he proved less tactful on questions of the Church. He aggravated the problem by closing some missions and monasteries and diverting their properties to the use of the public schools. His term was disturbed by a civil war which waged intermittently from 1839 to 1842 over issues partly regional, partly clerical, and partly personal, Obando being the most active conspirator.

POLITICAL STRUGGLES, 1840–80

The gap between Conservatives and Liberals had widened by 1840. The Liberals were charged with making blasphemous attacks upon religion and with fomenting disorder by asserting the right of each state to rule itself. While civil war still raged, the Conservatives gained power as defenders of order, godliness, and strong national government. Under Pedro Alcántara Herrán (1841–45) and his father-in-law Tomás Cipriano de Mosquera (1845–49) the nation prospered from the vigorous alliance of landlords, high clergy, and army officers. Their intellectual mentor was Mariano Ospina, able defender of the doctrine of orderliness through Christian discipline. The Conservatives' doctrine of the state was incorporated in the Constitution of 1843, a somewhat Draconian instrument which invested almost absolute powers in the chief executive. The Church regained most of her traditional dignities; her special courts were restored, the schools were entrusted to the clergy, and the Jesuits (banished since 1767) were recalled.

The nation prospered in the 1840's. The population had doubled since 1810 and reached 2 million in 1850. Trade increased substantially. Coffee production, to whose extension Ospina devoted tireless exhortation, was expanding. The increased population gave impetus to settlement of the immense public lands; in distributing them to farmers, the government wisely allotted them in modest parcels—a procedure in marked contrast to the reckless grants made to the *hacendados* in Mexico, Chile, and Argentina. Of first importance was the introduction of steam navigation on the Magdalena River, bringing the farms of the interior closer to their foreign markets. In Colombia's Panama, thanks to the feverish rush of gold hunters to California, American engineers began work on a transisthmian railroad, which linked the Atlantic and the Pacific in 1855.

In international affairs the Conservatives won diplomatic laurels in the Bidlack Treaty of 1846, by whose terms the United States guaranteed Colombian sovereignty over the Isthmus of Panama, which was threatened by the encroachment of England on the Central American coast.

Meanwhile, the Conservatives were targets for the numerous Liberals. Liberal clubs were formed in Bogotá, Cali, and other centers; their exuberant young leaders, reflecting the revolutionary ardor of contemporary Europe, wrote reams of poetry and prose in defense of democracy, equality, freedom of speech, and popular sovereignty. The Conservatives, despite the dictatorial powers they had conferred upon the president, exercised commendable restraint, permitted much noisy debate, and administered no discipline beyond exiling an occasional orator.

The most dramatic figure of this era was General Tomás Cipriano de Mosquera. Born in southern Popayán, stronghold of clerical influence, Mosquera was the son of a family which for more than two centuries had produced statesmen, clerics, intellectuals, and soldiers. He had served under Bolívar at fifteen and become a brigadier general at the age of thirty. Domineering, unscrupulous, and unpredictable, he was an unreliable friend and an implacable enemy. Elected president in 1845, he was accepted by the Conservatives with misgivings. Even his brother, the Archbishop of Bogotá, warned against him. Nevertheless, he served the Conservatives faithfully, instituted wise fiscal reforms, reduced the public debt, opened steam navigation on the Magdalena, concluded the contract with American interests to build the Panama railroad, and generally furthered economic progress. While favoring the Church, Mosquera roused clerical fears by abolishing tithes and by reducing the state's subsidy to the clergy. Despite his conservatism, he was aware of the growing power of the Liberals, and made friends in that camp.

By 1849 the Liberals were strong enough—especially in Bogotá where their perorations were most effective—to outvote the Conservatives and to place José Hilario López in the presidency. It was a victory for the extremists in Liberal ranks, and marked the beginning of a tempestuous decade. For four years the "radicals" enjoyed a Roman holiday. Intensely anticlerical, López evicted the Jesuits, proclaimed full religious liberty, assigned the appointment of parish priests to municipal authorities, transferred state support for the Church from the central government to the provincial authorities, disbanded ecclesiastical courts, outlawed tithes, and legalized divorce. When Bogotá's Archbishop Mosquera and two bishops protested, they were summarily exiled. Slavery, persisting in spite of Bolívar's edicts against it, was finally ended. Trial by jury was provided in criminal cases, freedom of the press was guaranteed, and the death penalty was abolished. Suffrage was extended to all males; and governors and judges were chosen by popular election. All these provisions were incorporated into a new constitution in 1853, which returned to the divisive principles of federalism.

But the Liberals had moved too far and too fast. Sharp cleavages on economic policy developed. Conservatives and moderate Liberals demanded tariff protection for new industries, while Liberal extremists favored free trade. The free traders won the first rounds and boasted that they would root out the evils of colonial economy. But their measures proved disastrous; for the confiscation of Church property, the abolition of the state tobacco monopoly, and the outlawing of slavery upset the economic balance without providing a workable substitute. The central treasury was empty and efforts to obtain funds from the departments were unsuccessful. Liberal promises proved chimerical. Liberals had torn down the old house but had not built a new one. Their attacks upon the Church had united Conservative opposition. Fresh revolts broke out and for seven years there was no peace. The Liberals succeeded in seating their leaders for brief and ineffective terms. Meanwhile, enthusiasts for regional rights made the most of their opportunity.

By 1857 the hot-headed Liberals were discredited, and the Conservatives were able to impose a president and in 1858 to promulgate a new constitution. But the Conservatives, cowed by the still powerful Liberals, were opportunistic, espoused the doctrine of states' rights, and renamed the country the Granadine Confederation, more federalist in structure than any Liberal had dared demand. This Conservative expedient did not work the promised miracle. As the several states grew more exigent, the government placed new limits on the army, thereby angering the Liberals, whose chief support was in the armed forces. The government then attempted to bring the state militias under control, and this antagonized the state bosses, who regarded these militias as their private armies. By 1860 a full-scale civil war was again in progress, its most conspicuous leader the ubiquitous Tomás Cipriano de Mosquera, one-time darling of the Conservatives who was now outshouting the Liberals with his radicalism and professions of faith in the "full sovereignty of states." In July, 1861, he led his army into Bogotá and proclaimed himself provisional president.

For two decades (1861–80) the Liberals ruled without successful challenge. In 1863 a new constitution stated in its preamble: "The sovereign states [there were now nine of them] . . . unite and federate . . . to form a free, sovereign and independent nation under the name of *The United States of Colombia.*" Under this constitution each state was virtually a law unto itself. Anticlericalism reached new extremes. Not only did the Constitution of 1863 reaffirm separation of Church and state and full freedom of worship, but it also called for suppression of religious orders, prohibition of corporate ownership of real property, and the right of the government to exercise "supreme inspection over public worship." For the first time (except for a makeshift instrument of 1861), a Colombian constitution failed to start off with the words, "In the name of God, legislator of the universe," or some similar phrase. Such was the Constitution of 1863, which represented "the pinnacle of achievement for the Liberals. Extreme localism seemed securely established in the fundamental law. The powers of the president, the national government, the Catholic Church, and all the other sources of Conservative power were, it was thought, so completely weakened and circumscribed that the Conservatives would never again be able to regain any influence in Colombian politics."[3] But the Liberals who cherished that delusion failed to reckon with the profound Catholicism of the Colombian people.

Fear of Mosquera's ambition inspired the drafters of the new constitution to limit the presidential term to two years with no immediate reelection, and, as a further check upon a leader whom they distrusted, they limited his first term to a single year. But he was elected again in 1865, and

---

[3] William Marion Gibson: *The Constitutions of Colombia* (Durham, N.C.: Duke University Press; 1948), p. 272.

the forebodings of his opponents were fully realized as he imposed one of the few dictatorships in Colombian history. At his whim, he exiled bishops, confiscated the goods of convents, sought to create a national church, shot or jailed his critics, revived agitation for a reconstituted Gran Colombia, waged victorious war against Ecuador, and angered the theoretically sovereign states by repeated incursions into local affairs. In 1867 a coalition of Liberals and Conservatives sent him into exile, ending the second dictatorship of Colombia.

For thirteen years after the fall of Mosquera, the Liberals continued in power, naming a succession of presidents who proved unable either to subdue the wrangling states or to unify their Liberal ranks. Repeated uprisings retarded prosperity and confirmed the dire prophecies of Conservatives. The Liberals finally signed their own death warrant in 1879 by electing Rafael Núñez.

RAFAEL NÚÑEZ AND
THE CONSTITUTION OF 1886

The induction of Rafael Núñez in 1880 marked the beginning of a full half century of uninterrupted Conservative rule. Núñez was a very different man from the shifty Mosquera. Núñez was a poet, an intellectual, a civilian, and an honorable patriot. Unlike Mosquera, who entered public life a Conservative and became a Liberal, Núñez began as an eager Liberal and ended as an intense Conservative. Born in Cartagena in 1825, he was active in Liberal clubs as a young man, writing poetry, and dabbling in politics. As a member of Congress in 1853, he helped draft the first Liberal constitution and served in several cabinets, including that of Mosquera. In 1863 he entered the consular service and sailed to Europe for a stay of thirteen years, there to study governments and peoples, writing profusely upon many subjects. In England, under the spell of Herbert Spencer, he abandoned his earlier radical ideas and learned to believe in the slow evolution of national institutions. For Colombia, this meant political centralization, religious tolerance, stringent economic controls, and Catholic morality as the cornerstone of progress. In 1875 Núñez returned to Colombia. After an unsuccessful bid for the presidency, he served briefly as governor of the state of Bolívar and then as president of the national senate, where in 1878 he attracted attention by warning that Colombia's future held either "regeneration or catastrophe."

At the time of Núñez's return to political life the nation was wearied and distressed. The attacks upon the Church had angered the people. The weakness of the central government, a result of the constitutions of the 1850's and 1860's, had provoked recurrent strife and retarded prosperity. Production and sale of tobacco, coffee, quinine, and other products had fallen off disastrously. No political faction, neither Liberal, Conservative, nor moderate, had any cure for the confusion. Núñez was elected in 1879 by the moderate Liberals, with the aid of many Conservatives, and he took office for his first term, 1880–82. Barred from immediate reelection, he imposed his own man as his successor. In 1884 he was again elected, this time primarily by the Conservatives. For ten years, until his death in 1894, Núñez was the undisputed master of the nation, sometimes as actual president but more often delegating his powers to aides while he sought quiet on his farm near the Caribbean coast.

Núñez's dramatic role as the "Regenerator" began with his second administration in 1884. With wise moderation, he at first included both Liberals and Conservatives in his government. But it soon became clear that his policies called for fulfillment of the long deferred hopes of the Conservatives. Another civil war raged through 1884 and 1885, after which Núñez emerged as the leader of the National Party, a coalition of Conservatives and moderate Liberals. New leaders and new policies resulted in the Constitution of 1886, the tenth in Colombia's history. The nation was rebaptized as the Republic of Colombia. Centralized government was now assured: "Sovereignty resides essentially and exclusively in the nation, and from it emanate all the public powers which shall be exercised within the limits prescribed by this constitution." The president was to be elected by a direct popular vote for a period of six years (later amended to four) and he was given the right to issue decrees which had the force of legislation. The "sovereign states" created by the Constitution of 1863 were demoted to the status of "departments" headed by governors appointed by the president. Despite such concentration of power in the central government, the drafters of the constitution made concessions to the stout spirit of localism which, as we have seen, has always been a strong force in Colombia. Falling back upon the formula "political centralization and administrative decentralization," the constitution permitted some latitude in the local application of national laws.

Núñez restored the power of the Church. By the Constitution of 1886 and by a concordat signed with the Vatican in 1887, most of the anticlerical legislation was revoked. Symbolic of this change in spirit was the fact that the new constitution began with the words: "In the name of God, supreme source of all authority." Catholicism was again made the national religion and the nation was charged with the protection of the Church. No longer would civil authorities supervise Church affairs: "The Catholic Church will enjoy complete liberty and independence of the civil power, and consequently there shall be no intervention of this power in the free exercise of its spiritual authority and ecclesiastical jurisdiction."[4] The Church's right to acquire and hold property of all sorts was reestablished, and, although properties previously seized were not restored, the Church was assured that "similar abuseful alienations will not be repeated in the future." The nation, in partial atonement for the earlier seizures, agreed to make annual contributions to the Church's treasury. Religious orders, proscribed by the Liberals, were again welcomed. Education was entrusted to the clergy, to be "organized and directed in conformity with the dogmas

4 J. Lloyd Mecham: *Church and State in Latin America* (Chapel Hill, N.C.: University of North Carolina Press; 1934), pp. 157 ff.

and morals of the Catholic religion." Ecclesiastical authorities were to inspect and revise textbooks. The Liberals, defeated on most points, found a
little comfort in the assurance of full liberty of worship for dissenters.

The rule of Rafael Núñez was the third dictatorship in Colombia's
history. The press was muzzled, political dissidents were exiled, and the
dictator's decisions prevailed. "And what were the achievements of his long
rule?" asks an American historian; he gives an answer: "They were the
Constitution of 1886; the restoration of the wealth and privileges of the
clergy; an era of peace without liberty; a few internal improvements; a
backward and very inadequately supported educational system; millions of
pesos of depreciated currency; inevitable petty graft on the part of distant
agents; a low credit rating abroad; and sycophancy, adulation, and monuments."[5] Such judgment is rejected by many of his countrymen who still
describe Núñez as the "Savior of Colombia," the "Regenerator" who
united Colombia and created a harmony of liberty, order, progress, and
stability.

Núñez's death left the Conservatives firmly in control of governmental machinery, but with no leader strong enough to withstand the
anarchy that again swept the country. The inevitable civil war broke in
1899, and for three years federal troops fought the forces of the Liberals.
The Conservatives won, but at the cost of not less than 100,000 dead, destruction of much property, and the demoralization of national life. Thoughtful Colombians of all parties were sobered by a sense of profound humiliation. And then, in 1903, came further humiliation in the loss of Panama.

THE LOSS OF PANAMA, 1903

We digress to consider Colombia's bout with the United States in November,
1903, by which Colombia lost Panama. President Theodore Roosevelt,
described by Henry Adams as that "man of pure act," decided that the
United States could no longer delay cutting a canal between the Atlantic
and the Pacific. Such a canal had long appeared desirable, and the Spanish-
American War proved that it was imperative that the United States fleet be
able to move from the Pacific to the Atlantic and back again without delay.

It was Colombia's misfortune that she had never been able to incorporate Panama into her national life. Cut off from the main body of the
republic by impenetrable jungles, Panama could only be reached by sea.
Throughout Colombian history Panama, with an area roughly the size of
Maine and with a population of not much more than 200,000 in 1903, had
run its own disorderly house with little effective control from Bogotá. For
four centuries the Isthmus had provided a well-traveled highway between
the oceans. The digging of a canal had long been discussed. As early as the
sixteenth century, Charles I had sent explorers to survey possible routes.
Vague discussions continued during the sixteenth, seventeenth, and eight-

5 J. Fred Rippy in *South American Dictators,* edited by A. Curtis Wilgus (Washington:
The George Washington University Press; 1937), p. 383.

eenth centuries. At the beginning of the nineteenth century, Baron Alexander von Humboldt explored Mexico, and Central and South America. His five years of journeyings (1799–1804) yielded voluminous reports, including a recommendation for a canal across Panama. Humboldt's words were read in 1827 by the aged Goethe, who wrote enthusiastically of the duty of the United States to open such a waterway, adding: "Would that I might live to see it!" Nor was Colombia unaware of her stake in neglected Panama. The Santander government in 1833 negotiated fruitlessly with various foreign agents in the hope that capital for the project might be forthcoming.

The 1848 gold rush to California inspired thousands of treasure hunters to take ship to the Isthmus, where they traveled overland through the steaming jungle, and transshipped to California. The people of the Isthmus, and especially those in the city of Panama, collected profitable toll from the pilgrims. In 1848 Colombia granted a concession to three American citizens, who incorporated a railroad company in New York, sold stock, and actually completed the forty-seven miles of track across the Isthmus in 1855. The railroad was one of the most prosperous ventures of those speculative days; in 1868, for instance, the dividend was 44 per cent.

Meanwhile, debate over the inevitable canal involved Great Britain, who was comfortably aware that her navy ruled the seas and who had no mind to give a free hand to the United States. In 1850 the United States, in trouble at home, signed the Clayton-Bulwer Treaty, which provided that the two powers would exercise joint control over any future canal, guaranteed equal treatment to Great Britain and to the United States in any such venture, and provided that there would be no fortification, colonization, or exercise of sovereignty over the area by either party. But when neither Great Britain nor the United States made a move, a French company was organized by Ferdinand de Lesseps of Suez Canal fame and began digging in 1878. After years of financial skulduggery, engineering incompetence, and bad luck, the project was abandoned in 1889. A new French canal company took over the concession and the rusted machinery, not to dig a canal but to sell its concession to the highest bidder.

The Spanish-American War had convinced the United States that she was now a world power and that she had to be able to defend her new possessions in the Atlantic and the Pacific. By the second Hay-Pauncefote Treaty with Great Britain in 1901, the Roosevelt administration won the right to build, own, operate, fortify, and defend a transisthmian canal. In January, 1903, the Hay-Herrán Treaty was drafted, by which Colombia would lease for a hundred years a strip ten kilometers wide across the Isthmus of Panama, for which the United States agreed to pay $10 million plus an annual rental of $250,000. However, the Colombian Congress in Bogotá, smarting under the humiliation of the civil war which had just ended—and also in the hope of more generous terms—refused to ratify this treaty. The impetuous Theodore Roosevelt was in no mood to wait. Meanwhile, the lobbyists for the French company, after unsuccessful efforts to sell their concession first to the Russian, and then to the British government, were exerting eloquent pressure in New York and Washington, persuading American lawmakers to abandon thought of the Nicaraguan route, and to pay the $40 million demanded by the stockholders in the French concern.

On November 3, 1903, a miniscule revolt broke out in Panama City and the independence of the Republic of Panama was noisily declared. By curious coincidence, naval forces of the United States appeared on the Atlantic side at this opportune hour to prevent landing of Colombian troops sent to quell the revolt. On November 6, three days after the "revolution," Washington formally recognized independent Panama, and on November 18 a treaty was signed with that country for the digging of the canal. By another coincidence the diplomatic agent of Panama who signed this treaty was none other than Philippe Bunau-Varilla, a French citizen, chief lobbyist for the French canal company and now the accredited minister of the Republic of Panama. It was a grateful triumph for Theodore Roosevelt, who had won a ten-mile strip (instead of the ten-kilometer strip asked earlier from Colombia) in return for the guarantee of the independence of the new republic. Cool rereading of the record suggests that if the bellicose Colonel had exercised a little patience, an equally good bargain could have been concluded with Colombia, thereby avoiding much bitterness. Eight years later, in 1911, Theodore Roosevelt boasted: "I took the Canal Zone," and proceeded to elaborate his position: "Every action taken was not merely proper but was carried out in accordance with the highest, finest and the nicest standards of public and governmental ethics." The affronted Colombians did not accept this simplified account of the events, and Latin Americans generally found in it fresh reasons for fearing the United States.[6]

CONSERVATIVE RULE, 1904–30

A distraught Colombia now demanded a leader strong enough to rebuild the nation after the ghastly losses of civil strife and the wounding of national pride by the United States. The Conservatives, still in firm control of the army and the ballot boxes, promptly installed Rafael Reyes (1904–09) who proved a more absolute dictator than had either Mosquera or Núñez.

At the risk of offending Colombian pride, it may be noted that Rafael Reyes bore striking resemblance to Theodore Roosevelt, whose name is still execrated in Colombia. Born in 1850, Reyes had led the "strenuous life" to which Roosevelt dedicated his robust prose. Like Roosevelt, he was a man of furious pride, unbounded egotism, and burning energy; always impatient of dissent, he was vitriolic in denunciation of critics and ready to take a

6 An American minister in Bogotá described the reaction: "By refusing to allow Colombia to uphold her sovereign rights over a territory where she had held dominion for eighty years, the friendship of nearly a century disappeared, the indignation of every Colombian, and millions of other Latin Americans, was aroused and is still most intensely active. The confidence and trust in the justice and fairness of the United States . . . has completely vanished, and the maleficent influence of this condition is permeating public opinion in all Latin American countries." DuBois to Knox, December 30, 1912, *Senate Executive Document*, No. 1, 65th Congress, Special Session, p. 35, quoted by J. Fred Rippy: *The Capitalists and Colombia* (New York: The Vanguard Press; 1931), p. 103.

short cut in order to win his ends. He, too, heeded "the call of the wild."
At the age of twenty-four, he and two brothers had set out to explore the
jungle lands of the Putumayo River, which links Colombia with the Amazon.
They wandered for many months, encountered hostile cannibals, and suffered incredible hardships; but they succeeded in laying out a water route
from the Colombian jungle to Brazil and discovered resources of rubber,
quinine, and other tropical products. Reyes's sorties into the jungle continued for a dozen years, in the course of which one brother died from fever
and another was eaten by the Indians. At last persuaded that he could not
earn a living from the hostile jungle, he turned to politics in 1885, joining
Núñez and becoming that dictator's most valiant commander against troublemakers in Panama and Cartagena. He was rewarded with various political
posts and was drafted for further military service in repeated civil uprisings,
but he found time to write voluminously upon his ideas and exploits. He
headed the expeditionary force sent to quell the revolt in Panama in 1903,
but, as we have already noted, he was prevented from landing by United
States forces. He was then sent to Washington on a futile mission to secure
compensation for the wrong done his nation. In 1904 he was made president at the age of fifty-four.

Rafael Reyes's five-year term was stormy. National life was disrupted,
the treasury was empty, and the populace was bitter. When his congress
failed to cooperate, he dissolved it, jailed some members, and exiled others.
Then he declared martial law and assumed full dictatorial powers. Finally,
in order to give the aura of legality to his procedures, he summoned a
hand-picked national assembly, whose only function was to ratify his decisions. His stern measures worked for a time. He reorganized the national
finances, restored Colombia's credit in world markets, floated some loans,
speeded the building of railroads and highways, and encouraged coffee production. But the growing opposition to his dictatorship crystallized in 1909
when he attempted to conclude a treaty under which the United States
would pay $2.5 million in return for Colombia's recognition of the inde-
pendence of Panama. Reyes resigned in the face of popular fury against
such compromise with Washington, wandered in the United States, Europe,
and Africa, and finally returned to Colombia in 1919, where he died a
year later.

Five Conservative presidents followed Reyes during the twenty years
until 1930, when Conservative rule ended. This period saw a marked advance in realism and cooperation: elections became freer and more honest,
and Liberals secured more seats not only in congress but in most of the
cabinets. The press was largely freed from censorship, and political issues
were openly discussed.

American businessmen and statesmen were agreed in deploring the
rupture in relations between the United States and a land so rich in oil,
metals, and coffee. In 1914 a treaty was signed by which the United States
expressed "sincere regret" and offered $25 million as proof of repentance.
However, the United States Senate refused to ratify a pact which Theodore
Roosevelt and his friends denounced as "blackmail." Finally, under Presi-

dent Harding, the treaty was rewritten, the "regrets" were eliminated, and provision was made to pay the $25 million in annual installments of $5 million each from 1922 to 1926.

Though Colombian memories were still bitter, relations with the United States steadily improved as businessmen of both countries found how much they had to gain in dollars and pesos. Coffee, Colombia's chief export since 1880, was the most important source of foreign exchange; by 1920 Colombia was furnishing more than a quarter of the world's supply of *mild* coffee. The $25 million of United States "conscience" money went into the building of ports, highways, and railroads. Oil companies invested about $45 million. American bankers lent the Colombian government, departments, and municipalities more than $200 million. This tidal wave of easy money brought an extension of coffee and other agricultural production, textile mills and other industries, railroads, and power plants; it also corrupted public officials, encouraged ill-advised expansion, and provoked inflation. By 1929 a severe break in the price of coffee brought the worldwide depression to Colombia; the Conservatives, who had ruled for fifty years, were discredited, and a split in their ranks permitted a Liberal victory.

THE LIBERALS, 1930–46

The peaceful transfer of power to the Liberals in 1930 stood in pleasant contrast to the violent overturns elsewhere in Latin America in that depression year. The Liberals took office at a time of general distress; the price of coffee, the chief export, had dropped about one-third since 1928; the flow of money from the American bankers had stopped; and business was paralyzed. Responsibility was pinned upon the Conservatives, who had indeed borrowed too much, spent too freely, and failed to halt inflation. But the blanket indictment of the Conservatives was obviously unfair: neither they nor the Liberals could do anything about the world price of coffee, the all-important factor in Colombian economy.

The victorious Liberals of 1930 bore slight resemblance to their nineteenth-century progenitors. Dead and almost forgotten was the old argument over states' rights. Almost dead—but not buried—was Liberal clamor against the Church. The hostility to the clergy had shifted to indifference and to the assumption that the faithful and the faithless could live peacefully together. Twentieth-century Liberals were more concerned for economic and social reforms which would protect the interests of workers in textile mills, oil fields, and factories. Enrique Olaya Herrera (1930–34), first of the new Liberal presidents, was a happy choice. Scholarly, irenic in spirit, personable, witty, and warmhearted, Olaya satisfied Liberals but reassured Conservatives by the restraint of his reforms. Thanks to Olaya, the Colombian nation survived the depression with better temper and more sense of national unity than even the most optimistic could have anticipated.

International disputes plagued the new administration. Colombia had been troubled for years by debates over the boundaries of the ill-defined and sparsely settled jungle lands of the Amazon where Colombia touches Venezuela, Brazil, Peru, and Ecuador. The dispute with Venezuela had been settled by the arbitration of Switzerland in 1922. Another dispute with Brazil had finally been settled in 1928. There remained the question of the Colombian frontier facing Ecuador and Peru, a region in which there was much rubber but few people. In 1911 Peru's rubber collectors had invaded what Colombia regarded as her lawful territory, and there was some gunfire. Ecuador, the weakest party in the dispute, came to terms with Colombia in 1916, but the line of demarcation with Peru was not determined until 1924. In 1932, Peru, now in the hands of the swashbuckling dictator, Sánchez Cerro, violated the agreement with Colombia and seized the outpost of Leticia. Small Colombian and Peruvian forces were dispatched to the scene and there was some bloody hand-to-hand fighting; the issue was finally settled in 1934 by direct negotiation, and agreement to restore the earlier settlement of 1924.

Alfonso López Pumaréjo, president from 1934 to 1938, was a more outspoken reformer than his predecessor. Wealthy, able, and with a realistic grasp of the social and economic ills of the country's masses, López embarked upon a social program similar to the New Deal in Washington. Convinced that the Liberals were now strong enough to put their ideas into effect, he was responsible for drastic changes in the Constitution of 1886. These amendments, ratified in 1936, were frightening to business interests, both domestic and foreign. One provision empowered the nation to expropriate property "for motives of public utility and social interest"—words reminding American oilmen of the Mexican Constitution of 1917. Another amendment stated that "labor shall enjoy the special protection of the state"; another announced that "property is a social function which implies obligations"; still another said that "public assistance is a function of the state." However, López's critics were reassured by the relatively mild legislation which was enacted. Labor was belatedly given workmen's compensation, a forty-eight-hour week, and unemployment benefits. The public school system was enlarged, and new attention was given to public health services.

Eduardo Santos (1938–42), thoughtful and conciliatory, had the respect of the moderates in both parties. Publisher of El Tiempo, Colombia's best newspaper (and one of the three or four distinguished journals in all Latin America), Santos was a scholar and recluse. Kathleen Romoli says of him: "Public life is to him something between an exile and a dedication." More interested in national unity than in high-sounding reforms, Santos concerned himself with the improvement of agriculture, the development of industry, the extension of education, and the moralization of public business. As a measure to ease the tension between the Church and her critics, Santos in 1942 concluded a new pact with the Vatican which modified the Concordat of 1887, ended clerical control of education, and stipulated that bishops must be Colombian citizens, approved by the government. This reasonable compromise, freely accepted by Rome and most of the Colombian hierarchy, was applauded by moderates of both parties but was vigorously denounced by two bishops ("They are more Catholic than the Pope," ex-President López commented to the author), and by intransigent Liberals who wanted no agreement of any sort with the Vatican.

Happily for the cause of world democracy, Santos was in office when World War II broke out in 1939. The Panama Canal, so vulnerable from Colombian airfields, made Bogotá's friendship of major importance. Santos, outspoken in his sympathy with the Allies, made his position clear: "The security of the Panama Canal is indispensable to the welfare of Colombia and all South America . . . no one will be permitted to menace the security of the Canal from Colombian soil." Santos's stand on the war made trouble for him at home. Alfonso López warned against reckless commitments to the Allied powers. Jorge Eliécer Gaitán, left-wing Liberal firebrand, shouted for Colombian neutrality. Laureano Gómez, powerful spokesman for the ultra-right wing of the Conservatives, admirer of Hitler and of Franco, denounced all concessions to the United States. From Madrid, Franco's government warned Colombians against granting bases to the United States. Berlin's agents worked through Germans living in Colombia to sabotage Santos's pro-Allied policies.

A sore point was the presence of the German-owned airline, SCADTA, whose pilots, many of them reserve officers of the Reich, flew over the 4,000 miles of Colombian air lanes. The company, organized in 1920, was a brilliant pioneer in South American aviation and had served Colombia well. In 1940, shortly after the war's beginning, Santos ousted the German company and all its foreign personnel and replaced it with AVIANCA, joint property of the Colombian government and Pan American Airways. This measure, critically important to the United States, brought credit to American Ambassador Spruille Braden. In September, 1941, President Franklin D. Roosevelt pointed out that there were in Colombia "secret landing fields within striking distance of the Panama Canal," a statement which roused a storm of abuse from some Colombians who described it as another instance of United States meddling. The American President had the facts: one German-owned tract of 7,500 acres lay near Cartagena, one hour by air from the Canal. President Santos, braving much popular outcry, took steps to end the menace.

When Pearl Harbor brought war to the American hemisphere, Santos led his nation into a break of diplomatic relations with the Axis. In July, 1942, opening the new congress, Santos declared that it was "impossible to adopt political or spiritual neutrality. . . . Weak nations cannot remain indifferent or fail to realize that their future is at stake in the light of totalitarian principles. We have associated ourselves with the democratic cause and we can never repent this action, for the survival of this cause is yoked with our own survival as a sovereign people."

Meanwhile, Colombia's ties with the United States were tightened by the increased community of economic interest; the northern nation was not only the source of continued loans and investments but was the chief buyer of Colombia's coffee, petroleum, and bananas. An important factor in the improvement of relations was the work of American scientists, financed by the Rockefeller Foundation, in fighting yellow fever, a campaign which, in the description of a *New York Times* correspondent, "had done more to make friends between Colombia and the United States than all the goodwill tours, congresses and trade missions together."

The election of Alfonso López Pumaréjo for a second term (1942–46) proved a disservice to the man and to the nation. Liberal ranks were split, Conservative opposition was angry, and López was blocked in his legislative program. The pro-Allied policy was continued, culminating in a declaration of war on the Axis powers in November, 1943, which elicited fresh cries of rage from extreme leftists as well as from ultra-Conservatives. It now became clear that López, popular during his first term, had outstayed his time. Serious scandals in his official and personal family served to undermine his reputation. Plots were rife in army circles, and in mid-1944 López was actually seized by malcontents in the south but was quickly released when the coup failed to enlist support. A focal point of disaffection was the body of governmental employees whose low salaries had not been increased to meet the runaway inflation; of a total of 27,682 public servants, only about 500 were receiving enough to live on. In July, 1945, López yielded to public pressure and resigned.

Alberto Lleras Camargo, provisional president from August, 1945, to August, 1946, made a spirited attempt to restore national unity. Brilliant and honorable, Lleras had already at thirty-nine won deserved praise as writer, cabinet member, and diplomat. Although he adopted a moderate position, using men of all parties in his cabinet, he still represented the Liberals, who had lost their prestige. When the statutory election was held in 1946, the Liberal vote was split between a moderate candidate and the left-wing demagogue, Jorge Eliécer Gaitán, and although the two Liberal candidates received a majority of the votes, the split enabled the Conservatives to elect their candidate. Lleras Camargo shortly moved to Washington, the first Latin American to serve as director general of the Organization of American States, the reorganized Pan American Union.

THE CONSERVATIVE RESTORATION, 1946–57

The choice of Conservative Mariano Ospina Pérez (1946–50) seemed a happy augury for peace. Intelligent, moderate, wealthy, and honored, the fifty-five-year-old Ospina appeared qualified to bind up the political wounds of the republic. His failure to do so was explained by his tendency to become panicky when confronted by a crisis, but even a stronger man might have lost his head in the political anarchy which kept the nation in virtual civil war from the day he assumed office. Liberals denounced the Conservatives, charged them with responsibility for the lawlessness which spread over the nation, and Conservatives blamed the Liberals. The impartial observer concluded that responsibility for this unhappy condition must be charged against two groups: the demagogic left-wing Liberals and the fanatical ultra-Conservatives.

Upon entering office, Ospina made an honest effort to utilize the services of both moderate Liberals and Conservatives, but he was blocked on one side by intractable Laureano Gómez, whose ideas of government had progressed little beyond the days of the sixteenth-century Philip II, and on the other by rabble-rousing Gaitán, intent upon winning overnight a socialistic utopia. The result was a deadlock in congress, a constant shift in cabinets, and the sharpening of hostility between rival factions. Liberal revolts inspired by Gaitán broke out in outlying departments and were put down by government forces. Ospina's chief cabinet minister made an inflammatory speech in congress: "The government will control the situation with blood and fire." Gaitán's followers cried out against "political murders." In 1947 Ospina declared a state of siege in some disaffected areas.

Such was the setting in April, 1948, when the Colombian government was host to the Ninth International Conference of American States and the city of Bogotá was gay with the flags of the twenty-one American republics. The air was oppressive as rumors of plots and counterplots multiplied. Laureano Gómez—admired by the extreme rightists, and detested by all others—was the principal spokesman for Colombia. The assassination of Jorge Eliécer Gaitán on April 9, ignited the powder keg. Angry mobs stormed through the streets, burning, shooting, pillaging; some 2,000 were killed, and much property was destroyed. It was easy to place all the blame on the Communists. However, while a few Communists had taken part and had used the incident to further their own ends, the later and cooler conclusion was that final responsibility lay with the extremists in the two major parties. Laureano Gómez, popularly charged with complicity in the murder, sought asylum in Spain. The dead Gaitán, a glorious martyr in the eyes of the worshiping masses—and the man they had proposed to elect president in 1950—became the symbol of the struggle which spread over the nation. Evaluation of Gaitán is difficult. There is no doubt of his appeal as a rabble-rouser. Certainly not a Communist, he had as a student in Italy come under the spell of Mussolini, and he had used the lessons learned there in organizing Colombian workers. No matter how pure may have been his zeal, a point still debated, Gaitán was responsible for a blood battle between Liberals and Conservatives—*la violencia*—which was to plague the countryside, with varying degrees of terror, for eighteen years.

As the voters looked forward to the elections of November, 1949, sporadic revolts were put down by the army, and thousands of country people sought safety in the cities. Ospina extended martial law. The sole contestant for the presidency was Laureano Gómez; the Liberals, badly split and expecting coercion at the polls, had refused to put up a candidate. Ospina tightened the state of siege, posted troops in public buildings, imposed strict censorship on the press, and denied the Supreme Court its constitutional right to pass upon his edicts. Gómez was elected and took office in 1950.

Laureano Gómez (1950–53) personified the clerical-authoritarian tradition of Spain. Contemptuous of democracy, he was an open admirer of Hitler in the earlier years and a devoted friend of Franco. His triumph saddened many intelligent Conservatives. A correspondent of *The New York Times,* interviewing Gómez in 1941, reported that he freely admitted "his spiritual affinity with General Franco in Spain and Franco's followers. . . . He saw in them . . . the reincarnation of the Catholic Empire of Ferdinand and Isabella." Gómez bitterly denounced the United States, which he said supported an anti-Catholic regime in Mexico and might support similar anti-Catholic forces in all Latin America. "Your Anglo-Saxon culture and our Latin one are different," said Gómez. "They can live together, but cannot mix. Whenever the two have met, the North American culture has destroyed the Latin."

The Gómez regime earned a place in Colombian history comparable to the dictatorships of Bolívar, Mosquera, Núñez, and Reyes. Congress, disbanded in late 1949, was not reconvened. The press, long free and able, was throttled. Even *El Tiempo,* Eduardo Santos's respected journal, was bludgeoned into silence on national problems. Censors occupied editorial offices, exercising authority over news, editorials, and even advertisements. On one occasion *El Tiempo* was closed for twenty-four hours as punishment for printing an advertisement of cough drops with the legend "Silence! Do Not Cough!" The courts, whose prestige had increased since 1909, bowed to the executive will. Meanwhile, intermittent civil war tore the country. "Thousands of country people, leaving their lands, their cattle, their homes . . . have had to seek refuge in the neighboring cities," wrote Germán Arciniegas in 1951; "as a result village after village has been deserted. The number who have lost their lives in the last two years runs into the tens of thousands." Meanwhile, the nation was ruled by edict from the home of ailing Laureano Gómez, while his deputy, the "president-designate," occupied the palace. It was a minority government at best, for Gómez represented only one segment of the Conservatives, but such a consideration did not trouble the conscience of Gómez, whose ideas on governing were hardly Jeffersonian.

Freedom of worship, a privilege guaranteed to non-Catholics for a full century, also virtually disappeared. Missionaries representing American Protestants claimed some 25,000 adherents. These alien cults had long been generally resented as an affront to Colombian religious tradition, but they had been permitted to operate without interference. However, as civil strife spread after 1946, Protestant chapels became targets for fanatical mobs. The Liberals, few of whom belonged to the alien sects, now became defenders of the Protestants. Conservatives used attacks upon the dissenters as a means of expressing their nationalism, their scorn for the United States, and their allegiance to the *hispanidad* in which their souls delighted. There was no lack of simple people to join in singing the doggerel *No queremos protestantes,* of which one stanza ran:

> We don't want Protestants,
> They have come to Colombia to corrupt us,
> We don't want Protestants,
> Who soil our fatherland and our faith.

Although Laureano Gómez seemed intent upon reverting to the political fashions of the sixteenth century, he was quick to adapt himself to the international realities of the postwar world. Upon assuming office he promptly tried to erase his record of sympathy for Hitler and distaste for the United States. He became an outspoken proponent of the United States and offered protection to American capital; when the United Nations intervened in Korea in 1950, he sent a token force of a corvette and 1,000 men, and Colombia became the one Latin American country to send a force to Asia. Gómez's action was variously interpreted: some discovered in it an honest change of heart; others averred that Gómez used the Korean war to get the American guns and planes he needed for the suppression of rebellion at home; still others said that the Korean expedition served to remove certain potentially dangerous Liberal officers.

By 1953 Laureano Gómez had worn out his welcome. The country was torn by civil war, with guerrillas variously labeled "Conservatives" and "Liberals" killing each other at the rate of more than 1,000 each month. Gómez's declaration of a "state of siege" had inflamed the passions of all elements. In June, 1953, a strong coalition of Liberals and moderate Conservatives, with the support of the armed forces, deposed Gómez, who fled to Spain. There was general relief when he was replaced by General Gustavo Rojas Pinilla: it was at least a change, although it was soon clear that it was a change from bad to worse.

The four-year rule of Rojas Pinilla (1953–57) may be described as one of the most savage, venal, and altogether incompetent administrations in the history of the nation. It was rule by decree: even the evanescent constituent assembly of Gómez was not permitted to meet. It was rule by terror: Rojas was a sadist whose police murdered and looted. His most barbarous act was staged in the Bogotá bullring in February, 1956: interspersed with the thousands of spectators were secret police; when the banner of Rojas Pinilla was raised, the police used knives and clubs upon all who failed to applaud—no one knows how many were killed and injured. A stern censorship was placed on the press: *El Tiempo* was forced to suspend publication; and when Rojas later announced that he would permit *El Tiempo* to reopen, Santos replied from Paris that he refused to be "a king of clowns" subject to the whims of Rojas's censors. Other newspapers, Liberal and Conservative—including even Gómez's ultra-rightist journal—were closed down, fined, or intimidated. Rojas decreed a law of *descato,* under whose terms anyone speaking in "disrespect" of the President could be fined or jailed. Violence against Protestant churches and schools increased. Meanwhile, until 1954 economic life withstood the shocks of political anarchy, for coffee (which usually accounts for about 80 per cent of Colombia's export revenue) was bringing increased prices: Colombia's coffee had sold for about 14 cents a pound in 1939; then there was a surge upward until in 1954 the price was more than 96 cents a pound. After 1954 the drop in coffee prices brought depression. Meanwhile, Rojas used the money he pilfered on government contracts to buy great stretches of fine grazing lands, which he stocked with the finest of cattle. (He was less forehanded than his thrifty friend Pérez Jiménez of Venezuela, who put his gold and silver where neither moth nor rust—nor rebels—could corrupt: in Swiss and New York banks.) Colombia paid dearly for Rojas, who left the nation with a foreign commercial debt of $498 million.

The end came for Rojas Pinilla in May, 1957, when he found it expedient to resign. There was but one good thing to be said for Rojas: his shameless abuse of both Conservatives and Liberals had finally driven these two parties, angry enemies since the 1830's, to cease their feuding in order to make common cause against him. It was a miracle of sorts when Alberto Lleras Camargo, leader of the Liberals, and Laureano Gómez, the most uncompromising and extreme Conservative, finally sat down together in Spain to rescue Colombia. They had wide support. The Church's leaders, Cardinal Luque and the bishops, expressed themselves repeatedly and frankly against the bestialities of Rojas. The leaders of the armed forces gave their backing to the new coalition. And citizens generally welcomed the plan: a constitutional plebiscite in December, 1957, approved the formula by which the presidency would go alternately to a Liberal and to a Conservative for the next sixteen years, and national and departmental posts would be divided between the two parties for the same period. The wonder of it was that the coalition plan was actually put into effect: the Liberal leader, Lleras Camargo, was chosen as the candidate for the new National Front; Lleras was elected in May, 1958, and installed in office in August.

THE NATIONAL FRONT, 1958–

Alberto Lleras Carmargo (1958–62), lean and energetic, fifty-three years old on assuming office, was a scholar by background, but with varied experience as provisional president (1945–46), minister of education, ambassador to Washington, director general of the OAS, and rector of the University of the Andes. He faced a task of great political delicacy as he assumed office under the Liberal-Conservative coalition. He had to reckon not only with the biting distrust between the two parties, but also with the factional strife within each of those parties. His own Liberals were divided between the moderates, of whom ex-President Eduardo Santos was a distinguished leader, and the extremist faction MRL (*Movimiento Revolucionario Liberal*), directed by Alfonso López Michelson, son of ex-President Alfonso López Pumaréjo. The Conservatives, for their part, were divided into three factions of which the largest was dominated by Laureano Gómez. Riding herd over these disparate contestants, Lleras was impartial and conciliatory, and his congress (the first to be freely elected in ten years) responded in good temper. Out of the wreckage of the Rojas Pinilla days Lleras brought orderly constitutional government, and his term in the presidency went far toward proving that the National Front was workable.

Lleras had job enough. The economy was a shambles, thanks to the looting of Rojas Pinilla, the piling up of debt, and the dislocation of the national currency. Lleras imposed austerity, cut imports, stabilized the peso, and installed an able National Planning Council for the charting of Colombia's economic future. Thanks to the vigor of the administration, Colombia's ten-year plan for economic and social reform was ready for presentation to the Alliance for Progress in December, 1961—the first program to meet the requirements laid down by the Alliance at the Punta del Este Conference in August of that year. This program, setting the objective of an annual economic growth rate of 5.6 per cent, evoked warm praise from the United States and international lending agencies (although formal approval did not come until Lleras was out of office). In coping with the economic problems bequeathed by Rojas Pinilla—including a $498-million accumulated commercial debt and the disordered exchange rate for the peso—Lleras found prompt cooperation in the United States: the Export-Import Bank loaned $87 million, and private banks, $103 million. Furthermore, the United States continued to cooperate with Colombia on the technical assistance program—with projects involving education, agriculture, health, industrial management, and civil aviation—furnishing about $1.7 million each year.

A prime target of Lleras Camargo's program was land reform. For in Colombia, as in most other Latin American nations, a few owned too much land and the many starved on inadequate plots—or owned no land whatever. According to the latest agricultural census (1960), 62.6 per cent of all landholdings were in farms of less than 12.4 acres each, and occupied a scant 4.5 per cent of the land in use; while a mere one-half of one per cent of the holdings embraced 40.4 per cent of the total farm land of Colombia. This disparity provoked angry discontent. The little farms (minifundia) would not support a family.[7] The large farms (latifundia), while often productive, also encouraged wasteful neglect of good land. Earlier attempts to rectify this maldistribution, notably that of Alfonso López Pumaréjo in 1936, had failed.

On the face of it, Colombia was in a good position to satisfy the land hunger of her people. About three-fifths of the national territory is thinly settled, and almost all of that three-fifths is the property of the nation. Much of this land is good, although adequate exploitation waits upon the building of railroads and highways, upon drainage of swamps and control of floods, and upon the clearing of jungle lands. Lleras proposed that 50,000 families from the crowded urban and rural areas of the Sierra be resettled on the unused land. But the plan encountered two chief difficulties—the first, of course, was the need for funds with which to develop the region. The second obstacle was the resistance of the peasants themselves to being moved from their familiar surroundings, a resistance stiffened by the angry issue of *la violencia:* many rural communities were well marked as Conservative, others as Liberal, and there was continuing bloody war between them; as a result, many rural families were loath to give up the tenuous security of their homes. And so the small farmers continued to demand that the larger holdings right next door be divided and shared with them.

Thus Lleras was caught in the crossfire between the little farmers who

---

[7] However, the small farmer who can produce coffee is in a better position than those who rely upon other crops. It is significant that one-half of Colombia's coffee is grown on farms of 25 acres or less.

did not want to move, and the noisy resistance of the large farmers to any plan which threatened their holdings. His attempts to ease the pressure by the colonization of state lands met with only limited success: some 2,000 peasant families were resettled in the unoccupied river valleys in south central Colombia. But any hope of drastic land reform had to wait upon the enactment of a new agrarian law. This law, finally passed in November, 1961, provided for a new agency, INCORA (*Instituto Colombiano de la Reforma Agraria*), to administer its program. INCORA was authorized to expropriate lands not efficiently worked or land in units of more than 720 acres, to borrow money to pay for these lands, and to allot them to landless peasants on easy terms. It seemed a moderate and sensible policy: there was none of the highhandedness of the land measures in Mexico, Bolivia, or Cuba—there was full provision for orderly procedures and for adequate compensation for lands taken. But it nevertheless aroused a storm of anger: the leftist elements among the Liberals denounced the plan as cowardly and inadequate; and the more reactionary among the Conservatives pronounced it revolutionary and communistic. INCORA got off to a slow start and there was little progress by the end of Lleras's term in office.

Adequate housing, high among the objectives of the Alliance for Progress, was stressed by Lleras. Due to the crowding of the cities, the proliferation of filthy slums—*tugurios,* as the Colombians call them—around Bogotá, Cali, Barranquilla, and other cities, the continued congestion on the small landholdings, some 300,000 families lacked decent housing. Thanks to Lleras, there was created the Territorial Credit Institute, subsidized by the Inter-American Development Bank and other agencies. A good beginning was made by the end of Lleras's term in 1962: by the end of 1963, some 64,000 new housing units had been built.

The provision of adequate water supply and sewers, urged by the Alliance for Progress, also received vigorous treatment by Lleras. It was estimated that only 37 per cent of Colombians had access to adequate and safe water systems, and only 26 per cent had sewage disposal facilities. Colombia's high death rate, about 10 per 1,000, was largely chargeable to contaminated water. Financed by the Inter-American Bank, Washington's AID, and others, Lleras's program was well under way by 1962.

A chief emphasis in Lleras's program was the improvement of education. Officially, the rate of illiteracy stood at 38.5 per cent of those over ten years of age; actually that figure was probably optimistic. There was weakness in all levels of education, but Lleras and his associates decided that primary schools should have the first attention. Some 8 million Colombians—more than half the population—were under eighteen years of age; but of these 8 million only about 1.8 million were in primary schools and about 150,000 in secondary schools. Lleras's four-year plan called for 22,000 new school rooms and the training of 38,000 teachers.

A continuing problem was the brigandage and violence which had cursed the countryside of Colombia ever since the outbreak of 1948, when Eliécer Gaitán was killed by a mob in Bogotá. Lleras's government moved with vigor and skill against those who were responsible, but the killing continued.

Lleras closed his term in 1962 with generous plaudits from his people and from leaders in the larger American fraternity. He had made the best of an almost unworkable political situation. He had been able, conciliatory, and honest. Despite the excesses of the Rojas years, he had brought the economy of the nation back into line: thanks to his stabilization program and a devaluation of the peso in 1961, the currency remained steady and inflation was slowed down. Production had increased: by 1962 the per capita economic growth rate had almost reached the goal of 2.5 per cent set by the Alliance for Progress. The output of industrial goods, especially aluminum wares and textiles, gained handsomely, with growing sales to Venezuela and Ecuador. Petroleum and banana sales increased. Cotton was a major success: in 1959, for the first time, Colombia had surplus for sale in the world market. Of course much remained to be done, but Lleras had at least made a start on needed economic reforms, and he brought a return of confidence to the nation: Colombia once again had the will to survive and prosper. His four years in office stand as one of the brightest periods in Colombia's troubled history.

The election of Guillermo León Valencia (1962–66) was the first severe test of the workability of the National Front. Valencia, a distinguished Conservative and son of Colombia's honored poet—but with little experience in public office and lacking the prestige of his predecessor—was far from the unanimous choice of the National Front. According to the agreement of 1957, and to the amended Constitution, the president in 1962 had to be a Conservative; and Valencia was chosen as the official candidate of the National Front over the bitter opposition of dissenters among the Conservatives led by Laureano Gómez. But he had opposition at the polls. The extreme rightist Jorge Leyva ran independently, receiving 12 per cent of the vote. The Liberal Alfonso López Michelson broke away from the Front and ran as a candidate for the MRL, polling 24 per cent of the vote.[8] An ominous note in the election was the attempted comeback of the dictator Rojas Pinilla. After returning from exile in 1958, Rojas had been stripped of his political rights. But in 1960 he organized the ANAPO (*Alianza Nacional Popular*), a movement which appealed to the frustration and discontent of the masses, proposed the abolition of the National Front, and called for an end to United States influence in the affairs of the nation. Rojas became involved in plots to overthrow the government and ran as an illegal candidate for the presidency in the 1962 elections, receiving more than 54,000 votes. Loyally supported by Lleras Camargo, Valencia received about 62 per cent of the vote, and won a narrow majority in Congress. Colombians rightly congratulated themselves upon an election which was honest and peaceful.

Valencia, aged fifty-three, assumed the presidency in August, 1962, with much good will from citizens at home and friends abroad. There were

8 Leyva's candidacy was legal because he was a Conservative. López Michelson's candidacy, as a Liberal, was unconstitutional, but he contended that if he were elected it would reflect the will of the people, and the constitution would, *de facto*, stand amended, thus nullifying the National Front.

encouraging omens during his first few weeks in office. In September, the experts of the Alliance for Progress gave their blessing to the ten-year plan proposed by Lleras, applauded Colombia's "solid and rapid advance," noted that the gross national product was increasing about 4.1 per cent annually, and estimated that the nation needed about $270 million each year from abroad. They congratulated the nation on the promising start on agrarian reform, but warned that at least 35,000 families should be settled on their own lands during 1962–65, and that another 100,000 families should be settled in the period 1965–70. Another encouraging note was an agreement between the United Fruit Company and a Colombian subsidiary for the development of a 25,000-acre tract of tropical rain forest, in the far northwest near the Panama border on the Gulf of Uruba, for banana production.

But Valencia was riding on the momentum of Lleras Camargo's program, and it soon became clear that this son of a poet had little sense of drive and no taste for economics. Two of the projects which Lleras had pursued with skill, and which had been praised by the leaders of the Alliance for Progress, were now largely ignored by Valencia. The Planning Council, expert and indefatigable in its efforts to plot Colombia's economic future, got no help from the President: he did not meet with them, nor did he fill the vacancies as some of the ablest members resigned. Nor did Valencia evidence any interest in the Agrarian Institute, or in the program of land reform so bravely launched. He seemed to bow to the demand of the Agricultural Society (the "trade union" of the great landholders) for repeal of the reform law which set the top figure that could be paid for expropriated farms at 30 per cent above their assessed value (and in Colombia—as in Peru, Chile, Argentina, and Brazil—the large landholders, to avoid taxes, had always held down such assessed value to comfortably low figures).

Valencia's choice of a finance minister was a happy one: Carlos Sanz de Santamaría, an economist highly regarded at home and abroad, served in that post until March, 1964, when he resigned to become chairman of the Inter-American Committee for the Alliance for Progress. In December, 1962, Sanz devalued the peso from 6.7 to 9.0 to the dollar—a bit of financial realism encouraged by the World Bank. But Sanz's proposals for new taxes met with hostility in Congress, which, instead, voted an inflationary increase in the minimum wage. Rising prices followed (the cost of living increased 50 per cent between the fall of 1962 and the spring of 1964); and the inevitable printing of too much paper money came next. Furthermore, the price of coffee dropped in 1962 and 1963, with the usual devastating effect on the economy. But if Sanz, in spite of his best efforts, was unable to hold the economy in line, he did maintain the respect of the international agencies: in February, 1964, the World Bank and others gave firm promise of $200 million immediately, with a more indefinite proposal of a total of $2 billion within ten years—with conditions attached: stiff tax reform, firm control on the spiral of wages and prices.

Valencia had worries enough. With bandits still stalking the countryside, his able war minister, General Alberto Ruiz Novoa, proceeded with vigor against the troublemakers—and actually lessened the terror. But the valiant general's success went to his head, and through 1963 and 1964 he made speeches criticizing the President and indicating that he himself might be the man who could bring order out of the chaos into which Valencia was plunging the country. At least he was right about the chaos.

To compound Valencia's unhappiness, Rojas Pinilla was again stirring up trouble. The sometimes amiable Colombians had permitted that worthless fellow to live in peace for five years after his return in 1958—bad judgment, certainly, on their part. After his illegal bid for the presidency in 1962 he had continued to plot against the government. In August, 1963, he was arrested and shipped off to a frontier concentration camp, but his exile was brief: the ubiquitous Rojas soon returned to plague his countrymen.

The congressional elections of March, 1964, uncovered the tragic weakness of Valencia. Some 70 per cent of the voters did not bother to cast a ballot, 10 per cent voted against Valencia's candidates, and only 20 per cent voted for the National Front. The dissident Liberals of López Michelson scored increased victories, as did the candidates put up by Rojas Pinilla. Valencia could now muster a thin majority in Congress, but he could not count upon them for bold action. But there was no boldness about Valencia, anyway.

By January, 1965, Valencia—and Colombia—were in deep trouble. The refractory but able war minister, Ruiz Novoa—the "reformer in uniform" who was outspoken in his criticism of the laggard Valencia—was suspected of trying to engineer a military coup to take over the presidency. A general strike to protest a recently imposed sales tax was called for January 25. The strike, backed by Ruiz Novoa, fortunately did not materialize; and Ruiz was finally dismissed as war minister on January 27. In the meantime the threat of inflation was ominous: prices continued to rise, the free peso had slipped to 13 to the dollar, and reckless printing of paper money grew apace. Contraband trade with Venezuela and Ecuador was rampant, causing large drains on the economy. The government faced a severe deficit: all aid from the United States had been suspended in December, and some $64 million in foreign loans promised in 1964 had been withheld; and the internal indebtedness limit had run out. "I am doing all I can," said Valencia. "I am a poor bullfighter with a bad troupe and a very demanding audience."

The threatened strike and the rumors of plots against the government finally brought Valencia to heel. In May, 1965, he sent a commission to Washington to plead Colombia's case. For the moment he seemed to agree to the demands of the International Monetary Fund, the World Bank, and other lending agencies that Colombia set its economic house in order; but before an accord could be reached, word came that Valencia had changed his mind—he would not permit "foreign dictation." And at home in Bogotá, where fierce student riots were protesting rising prices, Valencia imposed a state of siege, and ruled by decree—an obvious confession of weakness by the President. The gross incompetence and vacillation of the government further confounded the already chaotic political situation. Carlos Lleras Restrepo, the white hope of the more moderate Liberals for the 1966 presidential election, but bitterly attacked by the Conservatives as well as splinter groups in his own party, announced his withdrawal from the presidential race—and the National Front seemed to be doomed.

After the collapse of Valencia's appeals for international aid and his cowardly retreat from constitutional government, there came a turn for the better for ailing Colombia. Valencia's finance minister had resigned in June, after seventy-eight frustrating days in office. And after various candidates had turned down the thankless job, Valencia prevailed upon the able Joaquín Vallejo to accept it, announcing that Vallejo had his full support "to do whatever is needed to save the nation."

Vallejo moved swiftly and with a sure touch. Taking advantage of the state of siege which was still in effect, he bypassed the reluctant and divided congress and enacted his reforms by decree: new and higher taxes, and stern measures to collect the old ones;[9] a curb on imports; preferential exchange rates, which were a thinly disguised devaluation; and other austerity measures designed to please the lending agencies. In November the United States and other international agencies, impressed by Colombia's belated tackling of her problems, had a change of heart, and agreed to a package loan of some $322 million—placing Colombia among the three countries which were accorded favored treatment under the Alliance for Progress. In this agreement there was a happy innovation in United States policy: there were the familiar conditions placed upon Colombia; but this time Colombia would be answerable, not to the United States, but to the World Bank—this reliance upon a third party as watchdog promised to be psychologically effective.

And so Colombia was again in the good graces of the financial world. This happier state was largely due to the determination of Vallejo to convince his government that the desperately needed aid would not be forthcoming unless Colombia took drastic steps in her own behalf. As one observer put it: "From last December until late July, it was a matter of seeing who could stare hardest [the foreign aid groups or Colombia]. Then Vallejo reluctantly took the finance ministry post and managed to persuade the government that Colombia would have to blink first."

Also in November came the announcement from Liberal Carlos Lleras Restrepo that he had reconsidered his earlier decision not to run for the presidency, and that he would indeed be the candidate in 1966—a decision which aroused hopes for the survival of the National Front. This improved political climate, plus the leveling off of the dreaded inflation, put a stop to military talk about a coup to remove Valencia and made it possible for the President to complete his term in office.

The 1966 elections were orderly, but the voters were apathetic. The congressional elections in March, in which less than half of the 7.1 million

---

[9] Valencia proudly unveiled a new computer which would be used to facilitate tax collection. A survey made by Bogotá newspapers revealed that less than 30,000 of the city's 80,000 businesses had even registered with the tax office.

voters bothered to cast their ballots, was a victory of sorts for the old troublemaker, Rojas Pinilla, whose hand-made political party, ANAPO, was bolstered by a motley lot of disgruntled Conservatives and angry Communists. Rojas's most valiant aide was his daughter, Doña María Eugenia —"little mother of the poor," as the Rojistas called her—who sold rice, yucca, and corn at half price in village streets, with the blithe promise, "This is what they will cost after we win." ANAPO received nearly a fourth of the votes, and the National Front fell short of the two-thirds majority needed to push their measures through Congress. Then on May 1, the presidential election gave about 60 per cent of the votes to the National Front's Liberal candidate, Carlos Lleras Restrepo. His opponent was an almost completely unknown stooge of Rojas Pinilla, named only a month before the election, who actually got almost a third of the votes.

The new president, fifty-eight-year-old Carlos Lleras Restrepo, assumed office on August 7, 1966, for a four-year term, the third to serve under the National Front formula. Lleras Restrepo—a distant cousin of ex-President Alberto Lleras Camargo—was a professor of economics, one-time editor of *El Tiempo,* president of the National Committee of Coffee Growers (which was arbiter of Colombia's most important source of revenue). Long a dominant leader in the Liberal Party, Lleras had been the object of violence and abuse: in 1948, when Eliécer Gaitán was murdered, Lleras's home in Bogotá was burned, and he himself found it wise to spend some time as an exile in Mexico. He was known as the most militant of Liberals: at one point, when *la violencia* was at its most bitter, Lleras had forbidden his fellow Liberals to greet Conservatives with "Good morning." This excessive partisanship had not endeared him to his Conservative neighbors. Now he proposed a "national transformation," to be wrought by "political harmony and continuity."

Although no one questioned the ability and energy of the new president, there were many who wondered whether a man who had been so belligerent a Liberal could bring peace to tumultuous Colombia. But, upon the completion of his first year in office in August, 1967, such doubts had yielded to a general admiration for the fearless Lleras. Despite grudging support from his congress, he turned boldly to the economic program of Alberto Lleras Camargo. The distribution of land, launched in 1961 but neglected during Valencia's term, was pushed with vigor, and by mid-1967 the government could boast that 50,000 hitherto landless families now had lands of their own. The land program got welcome support from the Church: two bishops transferred title to lands long held by the Church and turned them over to the nation's distribution agency.

Furthermore, Lleras had won respect abroad. The international lending agencies recognized—in the words of one spokesman for the United States—that "Lleras Restrepo is a genuine developmentalist. He has put together the best government Colombia has had in years. What's more, he has the public behind him and the political initiative in congress."

Lleras Restrepo also dared to speak frank words to the U.S.S.R. In April, 1967, when Soviet negotiators came to Bogotá to discuss a trade

THE LANDS OF THE SPANISH MAIN

treaty, Lleras's government warned them that Moscow would be wise to put a brake on it's satellite's (i.e., Cuba's) support of the guerrillas in the Colombian backlands. The warning was explicit: "Either the Russians keep the Communist Party here out of the support apparatus for the guerrillas, or we do not recognize good faith in a trade agreement." (Parenthetically, this warning was given shortly before Mr. Kosygin told Fidel Castro that Moscow viewed with disfavor any support for subversion in Latin America.)

Nor did Lleras Restrepo mince words in dealing with his refractory congress. In July, 1967, he went on television to demand that Congress look to its behavior, calling it a threat to the nation's democracy: "I am deeply convinced," said the President, "that if Congress does not adopt measures to reform itself, if it continues to present a spectacle of incapacity to make decisions, its prestige will diminish, and democracy with it." And the people generally applauded their President.

COLOMBIA: HOPES AND PROMISES

Colombia is rich in human and natural resources. From its formative days under Bolívar and Santander down to the present time, this nation has had more than its share of competent leaders, and, except for brief lapses, has suffered little from dictatorships. But still there is the baffling reminder (to quote Alberto Lleras Camargo) that Colombians are driven by "an intense preoccupation with public life and political passion almost without limits, oscillating from disinterested sacrifice to the most cruel crimes," making the nation "a privileged zone for the liberty of men and at the same time a theater of turbulent battle."

The present political, social, and economic chaos in Colombia must be interpreted against the background of the class structure of the nation. The aristocracy has always been an intelligent and charming company. Complacent in the conviction that Bogotá was the "Athens of America," these patricians of the New World have meant well by their country, with all the good will in the world for the hewers of wood and the carriers of water— but theirs has been a paternalistic outlook and class lines have been powerful. There was much arrogance in the attitude of this favored aristocracy— those who spoke the purest Castilian heard in America, who owned good lands, who dominated the professions and sought to control political and social life, who produced poets and writers.[1] Nowhere in Latin America was there more devout reverence for *dignidad,* which has always meant more than the English word "dignity" can convey. Locked away in their mountain fastness of Bogotá—ten or twelve days distant from the outer world until the airplane ended their isolation—these "better" people created

[1] No other nation in Latin America has had more writers than has Colombia—but few of them have been internationally recognized. A notable exception was José Eustasio Rivera, whose novel *La vorágine* (1924, translated as *The Vortex*)—a powerful portrayal of the life of rubber gatherers in the Amazon valley and a study of man's disintegration in the jungle—is among the best that Latin America has produced.

a little world which was a faithful copy of an earlier Spain, in which the *hidalgos (hijos de algo,* sons of something) lorded it over those who were sons of no one in particular. Colombia's esteem for *dignidad* was not unlike that of Peru and some other lands in Latin America, but the remoteness of Bogotá served to perpetuate that curious resurgence of the Spanish temper. And in Colombia, as in Spain, there was a deep gulf between those who ruled and those who served. The slum dwellers in the cities and the workers on the farms—while their misery was less abject than that of the Indian masses in Peru and Bolivia—had to content themselves with crumbs from the national table. The life of the Colombian peasant has always been peculiarly bleak. "Other poor cultures have art, stories, music, rituals," a Bogotá psychiatrist remarks. "This culture has nothing. . . . There is no life in the villages. There is only Liberal-Conservative."

As Colombia moved into the twentieth century, its isolation began to break, and new and dangerous ideas spread among the landless or near landless, and among industrial workers: the Liberals were the first to break the spell; then came a variety of others, more radical than the Liberals had ever been. Important in the shifting of social classes has been the increased social mobility; here the role of higher education has been a strong factor, for the universities—long the private domain of the aristocracy—have increasingly encouraged the sons of the underprivileged to aspire to a place in the professional and business community of the republic.

Against that background of clashing social groups must be understood the strange and violent outrages of recent years. *La violencia,* born of the bloody massacre in Bogotá in 1948 when the popular Eliécer Gaitán was murdered, has raged ever since, taking a toll variously estimated between 200,000 and 300,000. It has been a senseless conflict: rooted in the old clash between Conservatives and Liberals, it has set neighbor against neighbor, village against village. In the name of Conservatism, the homes, fields, and villages of Liberal farmers have been sacked and burned: and a Liberal might murder a stranger who was merely rumored to be a Conservative. Also rooted in the angry demands of the nation's underprivileged millions, the conflict has crystallized into guerrilla warfare, with armed bands ranging far afield. From this terror, many thousands have fled the farm areas and distended the cities—seeking security, seeking jobs, but quite unprepared for the few jobs available.

The latest side-product of the insane burst of violence has been a rash of kidnappings; without the somewhat fictitious excuse of the battling of Conservatives with Liberals (or vice versa) kidnapping is simply good old-fashioned private enterprise of a sort—the grabbing of a child or an adult for the sake of a ransom of a few or many dollars. The operators of this unpleasant business find their victims in both the villages and the cities; even proud Bogotá is not exempt. City matrons take lessons in shooting pistols; businessmen protect themselves by taking burly bodyguards in their cars and having them stand watch over their offices; communities hire special guards to patrol their streets. During 1964, official reports listed twenty-nine men, women, and children who had been captured, some of them killed, their abductors collecting more than $100,000—and probably many more cases were not reported.

This general breakdown of law and order reflects the low morale of the Colombian people and serves to spread chaos in the social and economic life of the nation. Some more affluent citizens have found it prudent to move themselves and their families to safer spots in the United States and Europe.[2]

The optimism of the Alliance for Progress experts who saw in Colombia an enormous potential for development was based largely upon the nation's inventory of untapped resources—chiefly land. Colombia boasts an abundance of land in relation to its population. Most of the Colombian people are huddled into two-fifths of the national area: the high mountain slopes, though broken up by jagged ranges which block free movement from one region to another, have much good soil and water—and it is here that the Colombian people live. The remaining three-fifths of the nation is an almost empty wilderness, akin to the "Wild West" of the United States in the nineteenth century, and much of this area has great potential for future development. In the northwest there is the unoccupied jungle land up against Panama. And the valley of the Magdalena River has other untamed jungles and swamps which can be brought under control, opening perhaps 2.5 million acres to cultivation. But the great untouched areas of Colombia are the *llanos,* the plains which fall off from the high cordilleras of western and central Colombia and dip down toward the Orinoco and the Amazon. In the upper reaches there are great expanses of treeless grassland; at the next lower level there are scrub trees and grass; still lower, little above sea level, there are impenetrable jungle lands. Cutting down through the *llanos* are rivers bound for the Orinoco and the Amazon—the Meta, the Guaviare, the Coquetá, and the Putumayo—which begin as tiny streams high in the mountains and become mighty torrents when they reach the jungles below. The *llanos* embrace some 243,000 square miles—more than half of all Colombia—but in that whole area there is only about one inhabitant to each square mile. Not all of this land is good, but with the clearing of jungles, the draining of swamps, and the discipline of rivers, there is hospitable space for the raising of cattle, the growing of cotton, sugar, and rice—thus increasing the diversification of Colombia's agriculture. And, above all, there is land for the landless—provided the obstacles can be overcome.

The opening up of this great expanse of unused land hangs upon better communications. The recent completion of the railroad linking the high plateau of Bogotá with Santa Marta on the Caribbean coast—a project requiring nine years, generously and wisely financed by the World Bank—was an engineering feat of skill and pertinacity, a triumph of wise planning. Until this was done, Bogotá and other chief centers had been dependent upon the slow traffic of barges over some 500 miles of the Magdalena River,

2 In fairness to Colombia it should be remembered that she is not alone in lawlessness: The race riots of 1967—and earlier—must persuade the United States to avoid self-righteous judgment upon Colombia.

a ten- or twelve-day journey. Also hopeful is the road building program: road mileage increased about 50 per cent in the 1950's. The chief cities are now linked by highways, although many of them are not yet paved. But much of the country is almost inaccessible; and there is a sore lack of feeder roads to connect richly productive areas to main arteries sometimes only a few miles away. Air transportation, meanwhile, has expanded rapidly. AVIANCA (jointly owned by the Colombian government and Pan American Airways), which replaced the German-operated SCADTA in 1940,[3] is now one of the most generously used of any airline service in the world.

The yield of the land is bountiful and varied, thanks to the richness of the soil and the varying climates determined by altitude. Products grown chiefly for the domestic market include rice, sugar, corn, potatoes, plantain, yucca, wheat, barley, tobacco, bananas—although the export of tobacco and bananas is increasing. Cotton production, newly launched, is large enough to supply the growing textile industry with a surplus for sale abroad.

Coffee, of course, is the chief export crop, accounting for over 60 per cent of export income,[4] and therein lies at once Colombia's greatest strength and greatest weakness—a weakness shared with some other Latin American nations which rely too heavily upon one or two products (Chile—copper and nitrates; Brazil—coffee; Bolivia—tin; Venezuela—oil). The price of coffee, rudely buffeted on the world market, strikes at the very life of the Colombian economy. "For Colombia," writes Pat M. Holt, "every cent of variation in the New York price means an increase or decrease of $7.5 million in annual income. This is equal to 50 cents for every man, woman, and child in the country—a country where the annual per capita income is equal to about $250."[5] In 1940, premium Manizales coffee sold at 10 cents a pound; in 1954, the price soared to an all-time high of 80 cents a pound; and it was down to 40 cents in 1962 and 1963. The decline in coffee prices between 1956 and 1961 cost Colombia about $950 million. By 1964 the International Coffee Agreement with its quota system had steadied the price at about 49 cents. About one-third of the land in permanent cultivation in Colombia is in coffee, and coffee accounts for about one-third of the entire agricultural output of the country. It is this imbalance, plus the uncertainty of world demand, which makes clear the importance of diversification of the nation's output. Cattle raising, cotton, tobacco, and bananas, hold promise for the future. The diversification of agriculture, however, is complicated by the fact that few crops can be grown satisfactorily in the mountainous terrain where coffee thrives. Furthermore, farmers are loath to give up coffee, which is the most profitable crop they can produce. Thus diversification also waits upon the strengthening of mineral output and the enlargement of industry.

The mineral wealth of Colombia is varied, generous, and only slightly

3 See p. 553.

4 In 1950, Colombia sold $307.9 million worth of coffee, which accounted for 77.8 per cent of her total exports; in 1954 (when the price of coffee reached its peak) the figures were $550.2 million and 83.7 per cent; in 1960, $333.5 million and 71.6 per cent; and in 1965, $343.9 million and 63.8 per cent.

5 Pat M. Holt: *Colombia Today—and Tomorrow* (New York: Frederick A. Praeger; 1964), p. 101.

exploited. Petroleum, widely scattered with new fields being opened, is more than enough for national use: in 1965, petroleum sales on the world market brought in $88 million, accounting for 16 per cent of total exports. Iron reserves are important, but not yet adequate to satisfy national needs. Coal deposits (estimated at 40 billion tons) are probably the greatest in South America. The Colombian soil is inlaid with other minerals: gold, silver, copper, lead, mercury, manganese, emeralds, uranium, and the largest deposit of platinum in the world—but these treasures have scarcely been tapped.

Industrially, Colombia stands fourth among Latin American nations (after Argentina, Brazil, and Mexico). Textiles and brewing got off to a good start early in the twentieth century. Centered in Medellín, the textile industry uses homegrown cotton and wool, produces almost all the textiles for national consumption, and exports some $30 million worth of textiles or clothing each year. But the real industrial boom came after World War II. The chief pride is the steel plant at Paz del Río, 110 miles northeast of Bogotá. Built by the government in the early 1950's with money borrowed in Europe (the World Bank regarded it as a poor investment), it is now largely owned by private investors. After initial halting performance, the plant now provides almost one-half of the national demand for steel.

An element of strength in Colombian industrial development is the wide dispersal of industries. Among the industrial centers are Medellín (textiles, cigarettes), Cali and Bogotá (tires, chemicals, and pharmaceuticals), Cartagena (chemicals, oil refining, petrochemicals), Manizales (metalworking, cotton textiles), Barrancabermeja (oil refining), Bucaramanga (metalworking, food-processing, tobacco), and Palmira (food-processing). Automobile assembly plants, owned by European and American companies jointly with Colombian corporations, are being projected and built. In 1965, industry accounted for 19.6 per cent of the total national product—small compared with coffee's share, but a hopeful sign of diversification.

One potential and only partially realized asset is hydroelectric power. The numerous and substantial rivers promise an almost unlimited source of energy. During the years 1949–58, the production of electric energy increased at an annual rate of 11.7 per cent. In the Cauca valley, a public corporation fashioned after the United States Tennessee Valley Authority has scored a magnificent success.

Colombia's fiscal health since World War II has been fortified by the steady flow of loans and grants from abroad: during the years 1946–67 this aid amounted to more than $1 billion. These international contributions have been offset by the crippling drain of Colombian capital which has sought safety in the banks of Western Europe and the United States. No one knows the volume of this fugitive capital, but various estimates place it as high as half a billion dollars—roughly equal to the total received from the United States, a disturbing item for American taxpayers, buttressing the arguments of those who would cut off all foreign aid.

A serious social problem in Colombia is the rapid growth of the urban population. Fleeing from *la violencia*, the peasants have flocked to the cities in alarming numbers. In 1945, the proportion of people living in urban centers (those with population of over 1,500) stood at 33.4 per cent; by 1965 it stood at 53.2 per cent; and if the present trend continues, the urban population will exceed 58 per cent by 1970. The results are terrifying: urban congestion, high unemployment, more violence, and the growth of sprawling slums—*tugurios*—around Bogotá, Cali, Medellín, and other chief cities. Cali, second largest city of Colombia and center of the richest agricultural area, is the chief offender with the worst slums in the nation, slums comparable in misery to those of Lima and Rio de Janeiro. Cali's growth has been formidable: its population was 101,900 in 1938; 812,810 in 1964. People are attracted by the booming industrialization of the city, but jobs in industry require skills which few of the peasants possess. No one knows the unemployment rate in Cali, but guesses run between 40 and 50 per cent of the labor force. Furthermore, there is little available housing—none, in fact, for the very poor—so the newcomers build their shacks on the edges of the city, and get along with no sewers, little water, slight police protection.

The changing role of the Catholic Church is important. Colombia has long been dominated by a Catholicism as intransigent as that of Spain. But each year more of the clergy reflect the new mood of elasticity which has been increasingly powerful ever since the days of Pope Leo XIII. And the leavening influence of American Catholics has had its effect. To be sure, the quality of the priesthood—especially in the rural communities—has been inadequate. But by and large the Colombian Church has developed a new fervor for social improvement which is refreshing and hopeful. A significant voice is that of Msgr. José Joaquín Salcedo, whose efforts to increase literacy in rural areas have been distinguished.

Theoretically, Colombia takes education with great seriousness. Actually there are critical gaps. There has never been money enough or trained teachers enough. It is understandable that Lleras Camargo, when president, made the decision to give major attention to primary education, for the great majority of the children, especially in rural areas, had slight chance to learn. But secondary education is still pitifully inadequate. The need for technicians and intellectual leadership has prompted a large effort to provide institutions of higher learning. There are twenty-two institutions, public and private, at the university level. Two private universities in Bogotá, the University of the Andes and the Jesuit Xaverian Pontifical Institute, are conspicuous for their scholarship and equipment. The state-supported universities have made solid progress, but like many universities throughout Latin America, they are overdependent upon part-time faculties, and they lack adequate library and laboratory facilities.

Two projects for the preparation of technical and managerial leaders are hopeful. The first is the Overseas Technical Specialization Institute, an autonomous government agency charged with responsibility for encouraging, directing, and financing the training of technicians for service to the state. Applicants for study both at home and abroad, after careful scrutiny, are granted loans at low interest; and during the years 1953–63 such loans, over 1,700 of which were for foreign study, were made to almost 7,000 men and women. A second important project is the National Apprentice-ship Service, organized in 1957, which has a nationwide program for train-ing young workers and adults in agriculture and industrial crafts.

By mid-1967 there were hopeful signs of recovery. President Carlos Lleras Restrepo was vigorous and able, and he had some excellent men in his cabinet. He had inherited troubles enough. General Ruiz Novoa con-tinued to pursue the presidency. The old ex-dictator Rojas Pinilla was still busily contributing confusion, and his followers were numerous and active. Congress was still deadlocked between bellicose Liberals and Conservatives, each seemingly intent upon preventing the other from getting anything done. But there had been one highly encouraging turn of events: in 1966 and 1967 the armed forces had captured some of the abler leaders of the bandits who had been harassing the countryside and even carrying their terror into the cities. The problem of *la violencia* was not eradicated, but there was now more hope that that festering sore might be cured. Furthermore, sober citizens were having second thoughts about violence, were talking less about Communism and Castroism, and were becoming more aware that the social ills of their country would yield only to a more generous and intelligent handling of national problems.

PART VII

The Indian Lands of the Andes

T hree modern republics share a million square miles of the Andean area in which the Incas once ruled over Chimus, Nascas, and scores of other aboriginal peoples. Of the more than 21 million who live in modern Ecuador, Peru, and Bolivia, fully 80 per cent are either pure Indian in their ancestry or of mixed Indian and Spanish stock; 10 to 15 per cent are officially described as white, chiefly Spanish in inheritance; a few thousand are Negro, mulatto, Chinese, and Japanese.

Under the shadow of the commanding cordillera, the sprawling communities of these Indian lands are scattered on the coast, on the high plateaus, in the valleys which slice east and west, or in the tropical jungles whose waters drain into the Amazon. The history of each of these three republics has been marked by political instability and recurring dictatorships. Yet each of them has developed its own proud national life and is quick to resent any affront to its sovereignty.

 [*Chapter 31*]

ECUADOR

The little republic of Ecuador should have been called Quito (in Inca usage "Quitu"), the name by which it had been known for a thousand years—first by scattered Indian tribes who lived on its high plateaus, then by the Incas who incorporated it into their empire, and finally by the Spaniards who created the *Audiencia* and later the *Presidencia* of Quito. But when independence came, geography rather than history dictated the name: it is *La República del Ecuador*, "the republic of the equator."

Ecuador is a tiny land that has grown smaller with each redrawing of the map. In Spanish days Quito claimed some 400,000 square miles. After the creation of a free republic in 1830, Brazilians, Peruvians, and Colombians took turns in trimming bits from its frontiers until by the mid-twentieth century it had been reduced to 109,483 square miles— roughly the size of Oregon.

Ecuador has four parts. The first is the Sierra, a region of high plateaus and valleys lying astride the snow-crowned Andes with Chimborazo (20,577 feet) and Cotopaxi (19,344 feet) dominating the skyline. Here are important cities—Quito, Ambato, Riobamba, Cuenca, and Loja —and the homes of more than one-half of the Ecuadorian people. The second part is the coast, the 500-mile ledge on the Pacific, a drenched tropical land in which about 48 per cent of the nation's people live. (The Humboldt Current, responsible for the southern desert, flows out to sea off northern Peru, yielding to the warmer currents from the north which bring heavy rainfall to the Ecuadorian coast.) Guayaquil, on the broad Guayas River, is the principal port and largest city of the republic. The third region is the Oriente, an uncharted and sparsely occupied jungle land on the eastern slopes of the Andes, where live a few primitive Indians. Fourth is the Galápagos Archipelago, more than sixty little islands lying athwart the equator 500 to 700 miles offshore, the home of a few hundred people (they cast 63 votes in the 1948 election). Less than 2 per cent of the Ecuadorians live in the Oriente and the Galápagos. Of those four Ecuadors, only two are important, the Sierra and the coast. The Oriente supplies travel writers with material for fanciful nonsense. The Galápagos Islands, sheltering strange tortoises and birds, furnished arguments to Charles Darwin in support of his thesis on the origin of species and provided bases for American military forces during World War II.

There are over 5 million Ecuadorians (1966); perhaps one-half may be roughly described as pure Indian, 5 to 10 per cent as Negro, a few as Asiatics, 10 to 15 per cent as whites, the rest as of mixed bloods. About 33 per cent of the people over the age of fifteen can read and write. The whites and the "almost whites" own most of the best land, run the principal businesses, publish the newspapers, and dominate the government. A small middle class is emerging in the cities, especially Guayaquil. The majority of the people continue to live in a world that bears few marks of the twentieth century. The Indians of the Oriente are little removed from the Stone Age. A few Indians, notably those of the Otavalo valley, show, according to recent studies, a heartening "vitality that is breaking the bonds of their traditional poverty, making them into a society of prosperous and independent citizens." But Indian (and much of mestizo) Ecuador is a world far removed from what we call civilization; its people live in isolated communities, toil long hours on the lands of others, and are cut off from a share in the national life. Their isolated state is described by a sympathetic writer who tells of his encounter with an Indian:

> I told him I was a foreigner. He said he had heard of France. Not France, the United States, I said. He said, was that in Peru?
>
> José Manuel's idea of the world was a valley in which he lived, an outer world consisting of Cuenca, Oña, Quito, Loja, and Saraguro, and beyond them, France on the one side and Peru on the other.
>
> France was the country to which wealthy owners of large pieces of land sent their sons for an education. Peru was the country of great wealth which lay to the south. It developed, as I pursued the line of questioning . . . that his political ideas were fully as vague. He had not heard of any of the last three Presidents of Ecuador. It was not clear to me whether he thought of himself as an Ecuadorian or not.[1]

Ecuador's history has been tempestuous from 1830 to the present hour. Fifteen constitutions have been drafted, published and usually forgotten. Forty-seven chief executives have been elected or brought to power by military coups, but only ten have served their full terms. Political platforms, whether called Conservative or Liberal, have been overshadowed by *personalismo*. This clash between caudillos has been further complicated by the long rivalry between the highland capital of Quito and the port city of Guayaquil. The history of Ecuador, says Arthur Whitaker, is "a tale of two cities."

Quito, 9,250 feet above the Pacific, with a population of 401,811 (1965), isolated under gleaming Chimborazo, is Ecuador's historic fortress of conservatism and Christian faith. Its noble churches, finest of Spain's architectural gifts to South America, stand in eloquent defense of a way of

[1] From *Ecuador: Portrait of a People* by Albert B. Franklin; copyright 1943 by Doubleday & Company, Inc.; pp. 200–1.

life fixed in the days of the Hapsburgs. Long dominated by wealthy landlords and powerful clergy, Quito has been the citadel of those who favored
kings and viewed all change as apostasy. Guayaquil, a sprawling, unlovely
city of 651,542 people (1965) built on the banks of the turgid Guayas
River, is the port through which the nation's cacao, fruit, balsa wood, and
rice pass to the outer world. Long rotten with yellow fever and shunned by
traders, it is now rid of that incubus, thanks to the help of foreign sanitary
engineers and the Rockefeller Foundation. A port in which ships of all
nations drop their anchors, Guayaquil has been host to varied guests—
labor agitators, Communists, anarchists, German and Italian agents—
who have made their converts and sailed on. Guayaquil thus became the

Ecuador, Peru, and Bolivia

spawning ground for revolutionary ideas on government, labor, and religion. From there have come attacks upon the *hacendados* and the clergy.

Ecuador's economy has always been colonial, dependent upon the sale of cheap raw materials in world markets and the purchase of costly manufactured goods from industrialized nations. Its bananas, coffee, rice, and cacao, laboriously produced by workers under conditions of virtual serfdom, are traded for the steel rails, hydroelectric equipment, trucks, and tractors which the modern nation demands.

THE INITIAL CONFUSION, 1830–60

When Bolívar's ill-starred Gran Colombia fell apart in 1830, a *cabildo abierto* in Quito declared for the independence of Ecuador, called a constitutional convention in Riobamba, and named Juan José Flores civil and military chief. Inferior in brains and patriotism to Venezuela's Páez and New Granada's Santander, Flores was a brave soldier who had been one of Bolívar's principal aides but had little else to recommend him as the leader of a new republic. Illiterate and capricious, Flores imposed the autocratic Constitution of 1830. The odds against him were numerous. There was little money in the treasury. The army was overmanned and split by rival factions. The followers of Flores in Quito and the leaders in Guayaquil eyed each other with distaste. There was slight common purpose among the people; some favored annexation to New Granada, others preferred union with Peru, while a steadily increasing number wanted complete independence. Everywhere, there was abuse for the "foreigners"— Venezuelans, New Granadans, British, Irish—whom Bolívar had left in key positions. Flores, a "foreigner" born in Venezuela, ruled with a rough hand, jailing or exiling his critics. He led an army against New Granada in an attempt to establish Ecuadorian claims upon the Cauca valley, but failed to do so. In 1832 he occupied the Galápagos Islands (whose principal inhabitants were oversized tortoises, some tipping the scales at 500 pounds), a feat more conducive to national pride than to prosperity.

Flores's tyranny excited vigorous opposition from the self-styled Liberals, who shouted for honest government, free speech and press, and curbs upon the Church. Vicente Rocafuerte, ablest of the agitators, was a wealthy young aristocrat who had lived in the United States, England, Mexico, and France, and now found support for his views in Guayaquil. After briefly jailing this formidable opponent, Flores came to terms with him. In a spirit of pleasant reciprocity, which Machiavelli would surely have applauded, Flores and Rocafuerte agreed to take turns in the presidency; and for a time this preposterous scheme actually worked. In 1835 Rocafuerte became president, while Flores contented himself with being commander in chief of the army. Rocafuerte forthwith wrote a new constitution, complete with the anticlerical and democratic articles of faith so dear to the Liberals. He granted amnesty to political exiles, invited immigration, and built a few schools. Flores returned to the presidency in 1839, while Rocafuerte retired to Guayaquil as governor of the coastal province of Guayas. Flores's second term was moderately successful. In 1840 Ecuador's independence was recognized by Spain. Internal peace was maintained, although there were sporadic clashes with New Granada and Peru. In 1843, when he was pledged to exchange places again with Rocafuerte, Flores suddenly drafted a new constitution and had himself reelected for an eight-year term. Liberal Rocafuerte was bought off with a high-sounding title and money enough to live in Paris. Flores held on until 1845, when the Guayaquil Liberals again revolted and the new government exiled him to Europe—with titles and a pension.

Thus rid of the two rivals, Ecuador had fifteen years of anarchy (1845–60): eleven presidents or juntas ruled fitfully, usually under the banner of Liberalism; three new constitutions were adopted; civil wars were frequent, and border wars with Colombia and Peru continued; and the conflict between the clergy and their opponents became more savage. The one bright spot was the final ending of Negro slavery. By 1860 there was no semblance of national government. Local bosses ruled their several regions by grace of guns. The caudillo Guillermo Franco of Guayaquil finally provoked popular anger by signing a treaty which ceded that city and the southern provinces to Peru. At this juncture the ubiquitous Flores rushed back from Europe and joined forces with Gabriel García Moreno to oust Franco and put down revolts in other sections. After this incident Flores was forgotten, and García Moreno came to power.

THE AGE OF GARCÍA MORENO: THE THEOCRATIC STATE, 1860–95

Unique not only in Ecuador's chaotic history but in all the annals of America, Gabriel García Moreno has been variously described by his votaries as "a Christian Hercules," and by his enemies as "a Jesuitical despot." The ebullient García Calderón says of him: "Indefatigable, stoical, just, strong in decision, admirably logical in his life, García Moreno was one of the greatest personalities of American history. He was no tyrant without doctrines, like Guzmán Blanco or Porfirio Díaz. . . . A mystic of the Spanish type, he was not content with sterile contemplations: he needed action: he was an organizer and a creator."[2]

Born in Guayaquil in 1821, Gabriel García Moreno was trained in law and theology at the Central University in Quito, and by the 1840's attracted attention by his brilliant polemics against liberalism. A trip to Europe, where he watched the revolutionary uprisings of 1848, deepened his conviction that conservatism and the Catholic faith offered the only hope to his distressed country. Returning to Ecuador in 1850, he fought the Liberals with new fury, espoused the cause of the Jesuits evicted from Colombia, and was exiled to Europe. After his return from his second stay

2 F. García Calderón: *Latin America, Its Rise and Progress* (London: T. F. Unwin; 1913), p. 220.

in Europe, he was elected mayor of Quito and rector of the University, and was recognized as the leader of the Conservatives against the "anarchic and godless Liberals." Seizing power in 1860, he dictated the Constitution of 1861, served as president from 1861 to 1865, and then, with some difficulty, dominated the two men who followed him for brief terms. He returned to office in 1869 and drafted a new constitution, which provided for a six-year term and unlimited reelection. In 1875, shortly after he was chosen to succeed himself, he was assassinated.

García Moreno's religious fervor determined his course. Reading daily in Thomas à Kempis's *The Imitation of Christ,* García was persuaded that his nation would find safety only in an "unshakable attachment to the Holy See," with an "education based on morality and faith." Admiring Philip II as the greatest of all Catholic kings, he was certain that "civilization is the fruit of Catholicism." He proposed to reshape Ecuador into a theocratic state in which the Church would exercise moral and spiritual authority in the name of the Almighty. His Constitution of 1861 pledged the government to defend Catholicism as the exclusive religion; and in the Concordat of 1863, he conceded to the Vatican more privileges than the Church had enjoyed in the days of the Hapsburgs: undisputed control of all education, freedom to publish papal bulls without state interference, and restoration of ecclesiastical courts. He further strengthened the Church's position in his Constitution of 1869 by limiting citizenship to practicing Catholics and stripping all others of their civil rights. "It is necessary," he said in defense of this measure, "to raise a wall of division between the lovers of the true God and those who serve the devil." When the Italian government stripped the Vatican of its temporal domain in 1870, García Moreno not only protested to King Victor Emmanuel II but appealed to the other Latin American states to join their voices with his, but no one heeded the suggestion.

Meanwhile, he was tireless in efforts to rescue the Church from the low estate to which it had fallen during the chaotic years since the break with Spain; he purged it of many unworthy priests; and brought in successors, notably Jesuits, from Europe. He espoused the Church's cause in other American nations, hailing Maximilian as Mexico's deliverer from the "excesses of a rapacious, immoral and turbulent demagogy" and intervening in Colombia when the Church was attacked by Mosquera. He persuaded his congress to vote money to the Vatican. The crowning proof of his devotion came in 1873, when the congress solemnly dedicated the Republic of Ecuador to "The Sacred Heart of Jesus," an action which, according to Catholic historian Richard Pattee, "perpetuated in visible fashion the ties between the Ecuadorian community and the outward symbol of divine mercy . . . the highest manifestation of devotion to the Catholic faith."

Although García Moreno is chiefly remembered for his preoccupation with religion, he contributed more to the economic and cultural well-being of his nation than any other president of the nineteenth century. His range of interests was immense; his intelligence and skill were impressive. He gave the nation its first efficient treasury, improved its credit position abroad, introduced a uniform currency, built roads, spurred foreign trade, attracted foreign investment, and improved agricultural methods. A wagon road from Quito to Guayaquil, a considerable engineering triumph, was a step toward national unity. Schools, from elementary to scientific and technical institutions, increased in number, chiefly under the guidance of the Jesuits. One Jesuit, Theodore Wolf, is gratefully remembered for his writings on the geology and geography of the country.

It was a dictatorship, although cast in a mold all its own. Freedom of speech and press were sharply curtailed. Congress was chiefly used to approve the president's decisions. Constitutions were not always honored. Critics still sought refuge outside the country. Meanwhile, the fury of the Liberals grew. The most powerful polemicist was Juan Montalvo, a fervent Christian and a good democrat, who fought with barbed words from the safety of Colombia. When García Moreno accepted reelection in 1875, Montalvo answered with a tract, *La dictadura perpetua*, which was widely distributed despite the alertness of the police. In August, 1875, the dictator was cut down by an assassin's knife. Montalvo, hearing the news in exile, exclaimed: "My pen killed him."

García Moreno left no heir who could continue his policies. For twenty years, Ecuador floundered through civil war, brigandage, and economic stagnation as several short-lived presidents tried their hand at ruling. Three of these were men of moral courage and intellectual capacity, and only one was a would-be dictator; all of them proved ineffective as the bitter Conservative-Liberal battle tore the nation, with the Liberals steadily gaining the upper hand. Another revolution in 1895, originating in the storm center of Guayaquil, brought Eloy Alfaro and the "Radical Liberals" to power.

THE RULE OF THE LIBERALS, 1895–1944

The entrance of Eloy Alfaro in 1895 marked the end of García Moreno's theocratic state and the beginning of a half century of control by the Liberals. Under twenty-eight presidents, three new constitutions were drafted, religious orders were banished, and the privileges of the Church were curtailed. However, the Liberals' promises of free elections and honest government proved empty.

Eloy Alfaro, still a magic name for Ecuadorian Liberals, dominated the nation for sixteen years, occupying the presidency from 1895 to 1901 and again from 1906 to 1911. Alfaro had won Liberal recognition by bold plots against García Moreno, for which he had been imprisoned and then exiled. Recalled from Nicaragua in 1895, the "Old Campaigner," as his admirers still refer to him, quickly put down disorders and seized the presidential office, which he held against various revolters until 1901. He then imposed the admirable Leónidas Plaza Gutiérrez for four years, after which he returned for a second term (1906–11). The puppet whom he then named died after a few months in office, whereupon Alfaro raised an army in 1912 and sought to seize office without recourse to an election. Overcome by the regular army, Alfaro was locked in the penitentiary in Quito, from which an angry mob dragged him, murdered him, and burned his body.

Alfaro's activities were not notable. He did a little for education, restored a degree of order which gave impetus to increased agricultural production, and carried through the project for a 290-mile railroad between Guayaquil and the capital. Perhaps his best gift to his nation was Leónidas Plaza, who was president from 1901 to 1905, and again (after Alfaro's death) from 1912 to 1916. An honorable soldier, inspired by firm respect for law, he achieved more solid results than those of the better-known Alfaro.

During these years, Ecuador, too weak to resist the superior forces of her neighbors, lost much territory. In 1904 Brazil compelled her to concede debated lands in the Oriente. In 1916 Colombia won control of a region long claimed by Quito. Subsequently, after a forty-year quarrel, Peru in 1942 acquired disputed land in the south.

There was prosperity of a sort in the 1910's, "chocolate prosperity." The cacao pods, exported profitably for 300 years, returned handsome incomes to great landholders, enabling them to spend much time in their fine homes in Paris. The men who gathered the pods still got their few cents daily pay and lived in mud-thatched huts. Meanwhile, a blight appeared and the unmatured pods began to drop, and many of the best families had to come home to live on reduced incomes. The Liberals, squandering their energy on fighting the Church and each other, did little for the nation during this period.

Political, social, and economic crises multiplied during the 1920's and 1930's. Presidents—fourteen of them from 1931 to 1940—moved in and out with startling rapidity. Foreign investors in mines and oil wells became targets for nationalistic pot shots. By the mid-1930's numerous German agents were inciting the populace against United States "imperialism." The German-owned airline SEDTA, whose planes hopped between the tiny airfields of inland cities, was an effective instrument for Hitler's plotters. Anti-Semitism flared briefly when a short-term dictator in 1938 banished all Jews who were not working on the land.

Carlos Arroyo del Río (1940–44), a Liberal representative of the Guayaquil plutocracy, was an attractive and able spokesman for the wealthy Ecuadorians who believed that their country should cling firmly to alliance with the United States—a doctrine highly unpopular with large segments of the populace. Arroyo proved consistent in that stand. In 1941 he ousted the German operators of the nation's airline (SEDTA) and turned the enterprise over to Pan American Airways. In January, 1942, immediately after Pearl Harbor, he led Ecuador in a break with the Axis powers; and he permitted American forces to build and occupy bases on the Galápagos Islands and at Salinas on the mainland. These pro-United States policies of Arroyo aroused a storm of protest from nationalistic Ecuadorians; furthermore, his domestic policies exposed the President to sharp criticism—

in this case, well deserved. He proved repressive in his handling of critics, cracked down upon refractory newspapers, and used crooked elections to maintain himself in power. While he was thus angering many of his fellow citizens, a savage guerrilla war broke out with Peru over possession of great stretches of Ecuadorian jungle land in the Oriente. The not too competent Peruvian forces were more than a match for the quite incompetent Ecuadorians who were poured in to die from disease and gunfire. The United States, now deeply involved in war with Germany and Japan and concerned that international plans should not be embarrassed by bloodshed in South America, moved to end the Peruvian-Ecuadorian affair at the conference of foreign ministers at Rio de Janeiro in January, 1942. Pressure from the United States, Argentina, Brazil, and Chile forced Ecuador to sign a treaty which yielded to Peru some 77,000 square miles of territory reaching into the Amazon basin; this staggering loss aroused violent criticism of Arroyo, criticism which was far from stilled when the President journeyed to Washington and was loudly hailed as "the apostle of Pan Americanism." But Washington continued to uphold Arroyo by financing a campaign to rescue the cacao industry of Ecuador from a disastrous blight, by furnishing money for the modernization of the decrepit railways, for highway construction, for hydroelectric plants and other public works, and for agricultural and industrial projects. Other American loans financed rehabilitation of Ecuador's southern province, which had been ravaged by Peruvian troops. Meanwhile, the war brought some prosperity to Ecuador as demand increased for balsa wood (used in airplane construction and lifesaving equipment) and cinchona bark (quinine). But Arroyo del Río was soundly hated for his "delivery of the nation into the hands of the imperialistic United States." His supine acceptance of the Rio "Treaty of Peace, Friendship and Boundaries" is still regarded as one of the marks of shame in national history.

1944 AND AFTER

Mid-1944 brought a return to confusion. José María Velasco Ibarra, who had previously ruled in highhanded fashion for one year (1934–35) and had since kept at a safe distance in Colombia, returned to Guayaquil and announced that "the government of Arroyo has been an interminable orgy of crime, thievery and infamous mistakes which have brought ruin to the country." These charges against Arroyo had the almost unanimous backing of Ecuadorians, who applauded Velasco Ibarra's return to power in May, 1944. "The Great Absentee" created his own party, the Ecuadorian Democratic Alliance, which guaranteed peace and abundance. A professor of law in his more relaxed moments, Velasco liked to be called "the National Personification"—whatever that may mean. He had the artistry of the perfect demagogue. A witness (quoted by George Blanksten) who had lived under Hitler and Mussolini testifies: "I have been mesmerized by experts, and I rank Velasco Ibarra high among them." His charm worked for a time, but rival politicians, army officers, and the public finally wearied of his theatrics. In August, 1947, the army again sent him into exile. Those who had ousted him had no cure for the disorder, and three presidents came and went in one year. But finally, in 1948, Ecuador had one of her infrequent turns of good fortune in the election of Galo Plaza Lasso.

Galo Plaza (1948–52) was that rare specimen among the rich landholders of Ecuador, a "dirt farmer" who knew all about soils, seeds, fertilizers, hogs, and cattle. Tall, solid, energetic, charming, and wise, Plaza was a phenomenon in Ecuador's bizarre history. Contemptuous of politicians, he won office without the support of the army; and, equally remarkable, he held it until the end of his elected term. His chief disability in Ecuadorian eyes was his admiration for the United States. He was born in New York in 1906, son of ex-president Leónidas Plaza, and had later returned to the United States to complete his education at the universities of California, Maryland, and Georgetown. When his academic performance failed to match his prowess in football, his father cut off his allowance, whereupon he sold apples on the New York streets and then worked his passage back to Ecuador. After much farming and some politics, he went to Washington as ambassador, enjoying himself hugely and making friends for his little-known country.

Plaza's term was refreshing. Indifferent to the pompous jargon of the old parties, he set out to increase the production of bananas, cacao, coffee, and rice, and to clear the way for more industry and mining. Indulging in no loud promises, he balanced the budget, serviced the public debt, and raised the reserves in the treasury to hitherto unknown levels. Within three years receipts from coffee and cacao doubled and the output of bananas increased by one-half. Meanwhile, Ecuador was one of the few Latin American republics in which democratic practices were honored. Editors wrote as they pleased, citizens assembled freely and denounced at will, and malcontents were neither jailed nor exiled. A few barracks-revolts were put down without difficulty.

As the election of 1952 approached, Plaza's only counsel was that the people should respect the constitution, vote peacefully and honestly, and accept the verdict of the polls. The winner turned out to be the perdurable José María Velasco Ibarra, already twice ejected from the presidency and now returned without hindrance from his latest exile in Argentina. The old mesmerism had again served "the Great Absentee," as had the quasi-fascist clique, who had taken lessons first from Hitler's agents and then from the envoys of Argentina's Perón. The choice disturbed thoughtful Ecuadorians, who found solace in the hope that Velasco Ibarra had been mellowed by time and exile. But it became clear that "the National Personification" had learned nothing from his travels. Public administration settled back to its old patterns of plunder and sloppiness. In 1955 Velasco Ibarra picked an argument with the United States by seizing two American fishing boats which were operating within the 200-mile offshore zone over which Ecuador claimed sovereignty. In classic dictatorial temper, he proceeded to crack down upon three newspapers in Quito and Guayaquil which showed disrespect for his policies. His police indulged in thuggery against respected journalists in Guayaquil ("Communists," Velasco Ibarra labeled them), and protests were unheeded. Yet, despite his poor performance, the momentum of Galo Plaza's tutoring of the nation carried Velasco Ibarra through his term in relative peace.

In 1956 Camilo Ponce Enríquez, a conservative unjustly attacked as a "clerical rightist," won the presidency in an honest election. While there was little popular enthusiasm for him, Ponce proved competent in furthering the agricultural reforms of Galo Plaza: production of bananas, rice, and cacao increased. In 1957 he won credit for the completion of the 230-mile railroad from Quito to San Lorenzo on the northern coast—this sizable triumph, made possible by loans from the United States and France, was designed to open up a large area of good farming lands as well as a region containing rich deposits of minerals.

The election of May, 1960, to the surprise of many, returned the sixty-seven-year-old José María Velasco Ibarra to the presidency for the fourth time. The reentry of "the National Personification," with his customary trumpetings and hosannas, was humiliating to thoughtful Ecuadorians, but heartening to the shouting mobs. Velasco Ibarra, as always, promised everything: land, houses, and fat wages—and the hungry and ragged citizens forgot that the demagogue had never yet fulfilled a promise. In his inaugural address on September 1, 1960, Velasco formally renounced the hated Treaty of 1942, by which Ecuador had been stripped of some 77,000 square miles of her national territory by the Peruvians. Thus, in effect, the idol of the people declared war, of a sort, not only on Peru, but on the nations which guaranteed that treaty—the United States, Argentina, Brazil, and Chile. As the people cheered, it became clear that the Eleventh Inter-American Conference, scheduled to meet in Quito but already postponed once, would be postponed again.

Velasco cultivated strange friends: the little Communist Party was coddled; Fidel Castro's most vocal admirer in Ecuador, Manuel Araújo Hidalgo, was appointed as interior minister; and when Vice-President Carlos Julio Arosemena made a pilgrimage to Moscow and came back extolling Communism, Velasco applauded. But for all his forensics, Velasco was a practical man: when Adlai Stevenson, representing Washington, arrived in Quito in June, 1961, the President had ready a formal request for $140 million in aid. Meanwhile Velasco sought to persuade the depressed masses that he was serious about economic reforms to bring them comfort; but this presidential affection lacked tangible proof, as new taxes were imposed on thirty-seven categories of consumer goods, striking heavily against the least privileged and hitting the wealthy scarcely at all. The nation was disaffected by November, 1961, just fourteen months after Velasco's inauguration: the air force rose in rebellion, Arosemena was arrested and briefly jailed, the cabinet resigned, and Velasco Ibarra, feeling the winds at his back, quit the presidential palace and again headed for asylum in Argentina.

It was now Carlos Julio Arosemena's turn to be president—by grace of his popular appeal and the support of the air force, who considered him the least of possible evils. On taking the oath of office on November 11, 1961, Arosemena made a few remarks indicating that Ecuador would welcome help from any quarter—Cuba, Russia, the United States: "We will trade with the devil if he has money," announced the rich, forty-two-year-old Guayaquil lawyer and banker, who a few weeks earlier had been indulging in pleasant banter with Comrade Khrushchev in Moscow. From Havana came word that Fidel Castro was chortling with joy over the discomfiture of Washington. And of course all talk of holding the Pan American conference in Quito was shelved: few American nations wanted a conference in which Fidel Castro would play a stellar role.

Arosemena's dalliance with Communists and Castroites lasted for some five months. But the nimble President saw a great light by April, 1962: he broke relations with Cuba, accepted the resignation of leftist officials, reorganized his cabinet on safe centrist principles—and set out for Washington in July, 1962, in search of funds. Given a heart-warming reception by President Kennedy, he continued to demand revision of the Treaty of 1942 —but more than Amazonian jungle lands he wanted money, and this he was assured that he would get. The fraternal affection between the two presidents was somewhat dimmed with the revelation that President Arosemena had a not very secret weakness: he was a dedicated alcoholic who was often incapacitated for two or three days at a stretch; in fact, he arrived for a conference with President Kennedy with neither his legs nor his head thoroughly under control. (The American press was courteous, scarcely mentioning this pecadillo until later.)

July, 1963—twenty months after Arosemena's inauguration—brought an end to that gentleman's term of office. A four-man military junta seized power, and Arosemena was out. Drunkenness was the official charge; in resentment Arosemena described his critics as "Creole Calvinists who have a brilliant future behind them" and bragged that he was a man who did his job "despite masculine passions and vices."

The junta took over with the maximum of good taste and little violence. After packing Arosemena off to Panama, the junta forbade the press from further discussion of the expelled President's "passions and vices," and even censored outgoing news stories on that score. Furthermore, the junta —made up of the commanders of the army, navy, and air force and the secretary general of the National Defense Council—behaved most circumspectly, with no one member showing signs of political ambition. They made it clear that they would turn over their powers "sometime" to whoever was chosen by a constituent assembly (and in December, 1965, they actually announced that elections would be held the next June). There was a general atmosphere of euphoria as the junta settled down to rule together with vigor, honesty, and even some intelligence. As they made the customary promises—land reform, tax reform, penal reform, customs reform, and so on—one member remarked, with refreshing candor: "We who have no political futures can make the reforms they [the politicians] would like to make but cannot." The initial reaction to the junta was mildly favorable. Recognition by the United States came three weeks after the coup.

On the whole, the rule of the junta proved moderate. Some critics were jailed, but most of them were quickly released, and some were permitted to find asylum abroad. The most highhanded action was the raid by the police on the Central University of Quito in January, 1964, the arrest of trouble-makers, and the junta's announcement that they would reorganize the University. Meanwhile the promised reforms faltered. A land reform meas-ure was finally adopted in early 1964, but it was so mild and meaningless that the chief applause came from the large farmers—about 0.4 per cent of all landholders—who owned about 45 per cent of the nation's arable land.

A comic-opera flourish came with the visit of .France's de Gaulle in September, 1964. *Le grand Charles,* who had been distributing medals to sundry presidents in South America, reached Quito, was enthusiastically fêted, and pinned the golden sunburst of the *Grand officier de la Légion d'honneur* upon each of the four junta members. There was a momentary glow of pride until it was discovered that de Gaulle had given a medal a peg more glamorous—the *Grand-croix de la Légion d'honneur*—to the rulers of other countries. Confronted with this slight to the dignity of Ecuador, it was explained that France could hardly allot four top honors to Ecuador when other countries had got but one. Whereupon the junta members packed up their medals and returned them to the French Embassy.

Storms of discontent were rising by mid-1965. In July the junta, alarmed by demonstrations, jailed ex-President Camilo Ponce, leader of the Christian Democrats, together with several score leaders of other rival parties. The center of the opposition, briefly united under the title National Patriotic Junta, was in Guayaquil, where antijunta sentiment was powerful among businessmen, planters, students, and practically everyone else. The *guayaquileños* felt, with some justice, that the rulers in Quito always acted with more diligence for the interests of the Sierra than for Guayaquil and the coastal area, which furnished about 75 per cent of the national revenue. Curiously enough, the unrest in Ecuador did not discourage outside agencies from committing aid to the junta and its ten-year plan of development: in May, 1965, the Inter-American Development Bank announced the forma-tion of a "consultative group" of foreign countries which would undertake the financing—to the tune of some $173 million—of the social and eco-nomic program of Ecuador. This "group" included five Latin American states—Argentina, Brazil, Chile, Colombia, and Mexico. For good measure it also included the OAS, various agencies of the UN, Israel, Belgium, Great Britain, Canada, France, West Germany, Italy, Japan, the Netherlands, South Africa, Spain, Switzerland, and the United States. It was a curiously complicated situation: practically all the "free" world seemed intent upon rescuing an undemocratic military dictatorship which was losing control at home.

By the year's end, signs multiplied that the junta was coming unstuck. Telephone calls to the presidency were still answered by a gentle feminine voice: *La Junta Militar.* But in December one of the four members was dropped, and then there were three. Early 1966 brought new reforms to meet the economic stringencies which were closing in upon them (especially the disastrous drop of income from bananas in 1965). New taxes were decreed, and spartan efforts were made to streamline the archaic tax collection system—to the distress of the merchants of Guayaquil, who traditionally carried their tax burdens lightly. Price controls were increased. And when certain import duties were doubled in February, Guayaquil's Chamber of Commerce closed down most business establishments and called for a general strike. Then followed demonstrations by university students and labor unions—in Guayaquil alone some 800 students and professors were jailed. The game was up: the weary junta was neatly overturned by the air force on March 29, 1966.

The provisional president, chosen largely on the advice of the business oligarchy of Guayaquil, was sixty-one-year-old Clemente Yerovi Indaburu, a leading businessman, banana-grower, and economist who had served on the cabinet of President Galo Plaza. The prosperous and able Yerovi, sworn into office on March 30, had no liking for his new post, and made it clear that he would get out as soon as elections could be held. He made the proper promises—austerity for the rescue of the economy, amnesty for political prisoners, the opening of the universities and the schools. The populace showed no enthusiasm for the new president: he was inaugurated against a chorus of student voices chanting, "The people, yes! Yerovi, no!" And noisy demonstrators charged that "the oligarchs were replacing the oligarchs," and Yerovi was denounced as a "military stooge."

November, 1966, brought another shift in the political spectrum. Yerovi Indaburu was dismissed, and a constituent assembly named as president a political nonentity, Otto Arosemena Gómez, a cousin of the "alcoholic" Arosemena (1961–62).

No one was very happy in Ecuador in 1967.

ECUADOR: ITS ASSETS, PROMISES, AND PROSPECTS

Only a hardy prophet would dare to project the future of a country so chaotic, so unmanaged and unmanageable, so economically indefensible, so poor and hungry as little Ecuador. Such gloomy thoughts dissolve in the presence of the beauty of the land and its mountains, in the charm of the people from the well-born to the humble Indian. But the sober onlooker can see faint hope of a pleasant future.

Politically, Ecuador seems absurd. One can list fifteen or more "parties" which have names, leaders, slogans. But the party system is largely meaningless: Velasco Ibarra wrote in 1938: "In Ecuador there is not a single political party, a single true political program, a single ideological school which deserves that name"—and Velasco Ibarra, if anyone, should know. To be sure, Conservatives are always conservative, exuberantly clerical, and never trifle with dangerous ideas. And the Communists— are Communists. But such words as "democracy" and "liberalism," which adorn sundry parties, mean little. Such political chaos makes concerted and continued political action difficult.

On the score of management, the Ecuadorian government has almost always stood as one of the least competent in South America. A reporter for *The New York Times,* writing in 1963, described a tax office in one large city, where auditors had uncovered 50,000 delinquent tax accounts: it was lighted by three twenty-five-watt bulbs and its machinery consisted of two broken-down calculators. When Guayaquil sought to modernize its tax office in 1964, the American consultant brought in to supervise the job found that back taxes stood between $4 million and $6 million. The customs service, which should yield half of the national budget, is so incompetent and dishonest that smuggling is a major enterprise, and a subsidiary industry in the south manufactures special leather boots to protect the feet of cattle that are driven over mountain trails to be smuggled into Peru. The traveler in Ecuador is constantly beset by peddlers of cigarettes and other wares upon which no duty has been paid. This general sloppiness exists in the universities and in the public schools. Even the armed services, which seem smart enough on parade, fell down disastrously in the border war with Peru which wound up in the sad treaty of 1942.

Despite national poverty and disruptive politics, Ecuador has made brave efforts to educate its children and youth. Official figures, probably optimistic, indicate that illiteracy was reduced from 43 per cent in 1950 to 33 per cent in 1962. Theoretically there were schools for 77.5 per cent of the children between six and twelve years old in 1964–65. Actually the dropout rate was so great that only about one out of seven finished primary school; and of these, about 17 per cent attended secondary schools. In 1965 there were some 12,000 students enrolled in seven universities and two polytechnic institutes. There are some good schools and some able teachers, but estimates suggest that 68 to 70 per cent of elementary teachers have not had even a secondary education. Salaries are pitiful; secondary schools and universities rely upon part-time teaching by lawyers, doctors, and other professional people; and in the elementary schools, only repeated protests and strike threats brought an increase in the monthly wage to $35. Meanwhile the universities and the normal schools turn out more teachers than can be hired even at that beggarly wage.

The Indian is Ecuador's most serious and continuing problem. Of Ecuador's present population of more than 5 million, almost half are reckoned as Indian. The line between Indian and mestizo is a thin one, with the Indian slipping over into the mestizo world by learning Spanish, substituting western dress for Indian garb, and moving from distinctly Indian communities. But even mestizo Ecuador is far nearer to the Indian world than to the world of western civilization.

There are a wide variety of Indians in Ecuador. First, the Indians of the Oriente, the jungle lands lying south and east of the Sierra, who get little attention from the government. These simple people include the docile Yumbos, the hardy Jívaros famed for their macabre skill in shrinking human heads to the size of an orange, and the savage Aucas (who murdered five Protestant missionaries from the United States in 1956).

Second, the coastal Indians. Traditionally cut off from their brothers in the highlands, their numbers have been steadily augmented by migration of landless Indians from the Sierra. Enjoying the fruits of the rich soil of the 500-mile shelf along the Pacific, earning better wages than the Sierra affords, they increasingly enter the money economy, and in the process, they slip over into the mestizo world. Racially, they appear to be Indians; economically and socially, they tend to be mestizos.

Third, the Indians of the Sierra. Crowded onto the high tablelands between the two parallel mountain ranges are some 2.4 million people, of whom perhaps half are definitely Indian in race and culture. These are the Indians who constitute the "Indian problem" of Ecuador. The Indian peoples of the Sierra are little pockets of many peoples, some of whom may have drifted down from the north a thousand years or more ago, while others moved up from the south—and there is little sense of unity between them: the Indians of this area never felt the unifying force of the Incas, who held dominion over what is now Ecuador for less than a century. Most of the Sierra Indians are a shabby, ill-fed, unimpressive lot. But one group—the Otavalos living north of Quito—stands as the aristocracy among the Indians of Ecuador. Handsome, clean, able, the Otavalo Indians are a stalwart lot. They do some of the most skillful weaving in all South America, and their fabrics are not only sold in Ecuador, but peddlers carry them over northern South America, to Colombia and Venezuela.[3]

The "Indian problem" is primarily the land problem. Ecuador's pattern of land tenure is the familiar Latin American pattern. A national agrarian census (1954) revealed that on the lowest rung of the economic ladder some 251,700 holdings, 73.1 per cent of the total, were in plots of 12.4 acres or less; at the other extreme, some 1,400 holdings, 0.4 per cent of the total, were in haciendas of 1,236 acres or more. On the crowded Sierra there is simply not room enough, not soil enough, for the burgeoning population. And the lot of the Indian depends inevitably upon his relation to the land. Worst off is the landless Indian employed on the great hacienda, who works for a few cents a day and is given the use of a tiny plot called the *huasipungo* (literally "house-door," indicating the smallness and the nearness to the hut in which the Indian lives). There have been numerous enactments to protect these fellows, to raise their pay, to protect their rights—but laws passed by the congress in Quito seldom have any discernible effect upon the lives of these illiterate Indians. Little better off is the Indian who owns a plot too small to provide food for the family and who must depend upon getting jobs on neighboring haciendas. And the Indian lucky enough to own any land at all usually has only a patch of worn out soil on the mountain slopes, while the richer lands of the fertile valleys are largely preempted by the great haciendas. Best off are the energetic Otavalos, who make and save their money, and put it into the only wealth they can understand—precious land: each year they manage to buy more and more good land from the *hacendados*.

[3] For a somewhat ecstatic, but highly interesting, account of the Otavalos, see: John Collier, Jr., and Aníbal Buitrón: *The Awakening Valley* (Chicago: University of Chicago Press; 1949).

Despite the crowding of the Sierra, there is still room in Ecuador for those who would work the soil. The jungle lands of the Oriente are largely untenanted, and the Ecuadorian government has been making fitful attempts to open up that area for settlement. There is a road pushing east from Ambato to Puyo and toward the Napo River, and a few enterprising farmers from the highlands are moving in, and raising cattle, coffee, citrus fruits. But the coastal shelf on the Pacific is still the great attraction. Here the fertile and well-watered soil produces bananas, cacao, rice—the export crops which sustain the national economy.

But as the desperate Sierra Indians are lured by the relative affluence of the coastal area, too many of them crowd into Guayaquil and find themselves in some of the most miserable slums in all of South America: much of Guayaquil is flooded from time to time, and the shacks of the poor are built on stilts; there is little or no sanitation, little or no water supply.

Economically, Ecuador stands among the poorest nations in the world. Her all-time high national budget for 1965 was about $186 million—less than half of the municipal budget of Chicago. Between 1960 and 1965, the per capita gross domestic product grew by only 1.2 per cent annually. And the per capita income in 1965 was estimated at some $185. (This is an average figure: the per capita income in the coastal area is more than twice that in the Sierra.) These gloomy figures reflect the paucity of income from mining and petroleum; the backwardness of industry, which has suffered from inefficient operation and lack of a local market; the beggary of the Sierra Indians. But the fundamental weakness of the Ecuadorian economy is its overdependence upon agricultural products for export: in 1964 about 83 per cent of all export revenue came from sales of bananas, coffee, cacao, and rice. All these commodities are highly vulnerable—to pests and floods at home, to international competition abroad. Take bananas as the prime exhibit: since 1959, Ecuador has been the world's leading banana exporter, her banana sales accounting for 60 to 64 per cent of export revenue in the years 1959–63. Since 1964 bananas have fared unevenly, with a sharp drop in sales in 1965, and some recovery in 1966. This was not Ecuador's fault: too many people were producing too many bananas. For example, until 1963, Japan had bought most of its bananas from Ecuador; after 1963 Japan bought its bananas from Taiwan. And Western Europe, by 1965, found it cheaper to bring bananas from Central America than from Ecuador (remember the tolls on the Panama Canal). Furthermore, the price of Ecuador's bananas dropped steadily after 1957.

Misfortune also befell other chief products: heavy rains washed out much of the 1964 rice crop, and Ecuador had to buy rather than sell rice; a blight attacked cacao, cutting shipments for 1964 by 22 per cent from 1963.

The obvious answer to this imbalance in Ecuador's economic output was industrialization. But the industrial exhibit in 1966 was not encouraging. Textiles were in the lead: 20 textile factories, with about 100,000 spindles and less than 2,500 looms, employed only some 7,000–9,000 people—and one report stated that the machinery was obsolete, and that the whole operation could be run in one modern mill by 500 workers. Other industries include food-processing, beer, cigarettes, cement—but industry is still only a hope for the future in Ecuador.

A constructive step has been taken at Guayaquil on the Guayas River. As the principal port for the nation, Guayaquil has been handicapped by the fact that the river is so burdened with silt that it is all but impossible to maintain a channel deep enough for larger ships to enter. This is now being corrected by the building of a port at Puerto Maritimo, five miles south of Guayaquil, on an estuary thirty-six miles from the open sea, which will be connected by a five-mile canal to the Guayas River. Protected against deposits of mud and differences in tide, this canal will offer freer access for large ships.

But for Ecuador all progress—in land reform, tax reform, customs reform, the enlargement and improvement of industry—hangs upon stability in government. All reforms come to nothing so long as the central government is at the mercy of an endless shifting of power between rival caudillos.

Chapter 32

PERU

Of all the nations carved from Spain's American empire, the Republic of Peru clung most tenaciously to the traditions of the Iberian motherland. There was little popular clamor for independence, which finally came through the intervention of Argentine San Martín and Venezuelan Bolívar. Lima, dedicated by Pizarro as "The City of the Kings," remained a city in which kings would feel at home. When Simón Bolívar finally defeated Spanish forces and established himself as dictator, the attitude of the populace was voiced by an irreverent priest in vulgar doggerel:

> When, at Ayacucho, we
> broke our fetters with Spain,
> it was no more than the swapping
> of a dirty nose for a drooling mouth.
> Yes, we changed our condition,
> passed from the power of Don Fernando [Ferdinand VII]
> into the hands of Don Simón.[1]

The mantle of colonial viceroys, captains-general, and royal judges fell upon the shoulders of landholders, bishops, and political chieftains.

Modern Peru is a land of 496,233 square miles, twice the size of Texas, fourth largest in area of all the Latin American republics; it has a coast line of 1,410 miles and a maximum width of 800 miles. In the geographer's reckoning, there are three Perus: coast, Sierra, and Selva. Coastal Peru, a narrow ribbon, is a windswept desert bare of all vegetation save on the oases watered by more than forty little rivers which slice their way down from the snowbanks; about 11 per cent of the national domain, the coast houses some 40 per cent of all Peruvians and accounts for more than 50 per cent of the national product. Lima, a modern and ornate city with 1.4 million people (1964), dominates coast and nation. The Sierra, framed by the three-pronged Andes, occupies about 26 per cent of the land mass of the nation and is the home of 52 per cent of the people. Its tablelands (*punas*) and valleys are topped by snow-crowned peaks, nine of them ex-

1 Quoted by Jorge Basadre: *Historia de la República del Perú* (2 vols., 3rd ed.; Lima: Editorial Cultura Antártica; 1946), Vol. I, p. 52.

ceeding 19,000 feet. Here are cities two miles above the sea: Cuzco, Puno, Ayacucho, Juliaca. In this Indian world the aborigines work on their ancient communal plots or serve the masters of the great plantations. It is a bleak world, in whose thin air the wayfarer from the coast easily falls prey to the annoying soroche, mountain sickness. The Selva, lush jungle land of dense forests and swift rivers lying on the eastern slopes of the cordillera, accounts for 62 per cent of the republic's territory and is occupied by less than 9 per cent of the total population. Iquitos, Peru's port on the Amazon, prospered lustily from rubber from the 1880's to 1912 and is today a city of over 58,000, the outpost of an inland empire which counts little in the national economy.

If any visitor would sense the drama of the three Perus, he can start out in the morning from Lima (choosing a car with trustworthy brakes), push across the hot sand of the coastal desert, climb the fine highway to the 15,680-foot divide, drop down to Oroya where copper smelters blanket the mountains with sulfur fumes, continue to Tarma, and find the road which leads to the Amazon valley. That downward passage to the village of Merced gives the taste, the smell, the feeling of the Selva, with its heavy rain clouds, its dripping vegetation, its forests of mahogany and other hardwoods. Little streams are everywhere, growing in volume with every mile traversed, until at Merced they have gathered into a roaring river, the Perené, one of the many which feed the Amazon. The traveler will have seen the three Perus between dawn and dusk.

There are over 12 million Peruvians (1966); almost half are Indians, a third or more, mestizos (*cholos,* Peruvians call them), and perhaps a tenth, whites. White Peruvians, proud of their Spanish blood, own the best land of coast and Sierra, and control business and politics. European immigration has been scanty, but a few thousand of German and Italian descent are powerful in commerce and finance. The German-Swiss in Lima have contributed greatly to business and industrial development. Some 90,000 Chinese, imported between 1849 and 1874 for their cheap labor, have intermingled with the coastal population. About 30,000 Japanese entered the country after 1900, and many have remained.

The Peruvian economy is broadly based. Mineral wealth is abundant and diversified, with rich deposits of petroleum, lead, copper, zinc, silver, gold, and vanadium; and the output of the mines has increased generously in recent years. Agriculture, support of more than half the people, lessens in relative importance: for example, sugar and cotton accounted in 1958 for 39 per cent of total exports, but by 1965 the proportion had dropped to about 19 per cent. A newly important item in the export column is fishmeal: the phenomenal increase in the output of that commodity, whose sales on the world market multiplied fourteen times between 1958 and 1965, put it in first place with 21.5 per cent of Peru's exports. (See pp. 614–5.) Foreign interests—American, British, and others—dominate petroleum, mines, railroads, and public utilities, and have a considerable stake in large-scale farming. A few hundred Peruvian families control most of the fruitful plantations. The masses, Indian and mestizo, are an ill-nourished, illiterate proletariat.

Peru's political history has been sterile: parties have meant little, and electoral contests have usually been settled by gunfire. However, the nation has been free of two acrimonious disputes which long troubled Colombia, Ecuador, Mexico, and other lands: the argument as to whether power should be vested in the central government or divided among the provinces was settled by the supremacy of the capital city, Lima; and the contest between Church and state has never, until recent years, been voiced in more than a whisper, the Church retaining many of her privileges and most of her wealth and authority.

FOREIGN LIBERATORS AND DOMESTIC TYRANTS, 1822–45

Freedom from Spain was imposed on Peru by outsiders. José de San Martín, with his shiploads of Chileans, Argentines, and various soldiers of fortune, anchored in the harbor of Callao in 1821, occupied Lima, and proclaimed himself the "Protector" of independent Peru. A first congress met in Lima in 1822, while Spanish troops, encamped nearby, taunted the separatists with burlesque verse:

> Little Congress [*congresito*] . . .
> Are you going—or coming?
> Or are we?

San Martín, after failing to reach an understanding with Bolívar at their famous meeting in Guayaquil, withdrew and sailed south. The victories of Bolívar's forces at Junín and Ayacucho in 1824 put an end to Spanish hopes in America and gave Bolívar a free field in Peru and Bolivia.

Bolívar's rule in Lima was abruptly ended in 1826, when the quarrels of his jealous subordinates in New Granada summoned him north. The *limeños*, the people of Lima, were glad to see him go: jealous nationalists resented him as an outsider; the populace disliked the presence of his "foreign" Colombian troops; those of democratic leanings deplored his regal ways; the clergy viewed his interference with the convents (some of whose properties he had transferred to the support of hospitals and orphanages) as attacks upon the faith; and ambitious army men saw him as an obstacle to their own success. With Bolívar's withdrawal, the contentious "marshals of Ayacucho" could make their bids for power. Andrés Santa Cruz served a brief term (1826–27) and lost to José de la Mar (1827–29), who in turn was supplanted by Agustín Gamarra (1829–33). Intent upon undoing the work of Bolívar, Gamarra attacked Bolivia in 1828, unseated Bolívar's aide, Sucre, and ousted Colombian troops from both Bolivia and Peru; a year later he and La Mar struck at Bolívar's forces commanded by Sucre in Ecuador, but failed to establish Peru's claim to that territory.

By the early 1830's, the struggle for power involved four principal contestants. Gamarra, an unlovely despot, yielded office to Luis José Orbegoso in 1833, but that more honorable patriot was helpless against the continued plottings of his predecessor. Then the charming Felipe Santiago Salaverry revolted in the south. And to complete the confusion, Santa Cruz, now dictator of Bolivia, marched into Peru in 1835 at Orbegoso's invitation, defeated the insurgents, killed Salaverry, and imposed his rule over united Peru and Bolivia.

Naming himself "Protector" of the Peruvian-Bolivian Confederation (for a life term, and with a provision that the office be inherited by his son), Andrés Santa Cruz retained his high-sounding title from 1836 to 1839. Under him served two presidents of Peru, one in Lima, the other in the south. There was much grumbling, although *hacendados* welcomed security under Santa Cruz's firm hand. Outsiders, not insiders, checked this Napoleon of the Andes. Argentina sent an army which was easily turned back. Chile's more formidable army defeated Santa Cruz at the battle of Yungay in January, 1839. The Confederation was ended and the Protector fled to Europe. Meanwhile, the hated Gamarra recaptured the presidency in Lima and launched a new war designed to reverse the action of Santa Cruz by annexing Bolivia to Peru. But before his plan had succeeded, the ambitious caudillo fell in battle in 1841.

THE AGE OF GUANO AND ITS AFTERMATH, 1841–1900

The martial scufflings of the caudillos left Peru prostrate. Unpaid soldiers turned brigands and ravaged the countryside. Once prosperous farms were ruined, their fields neglected, their cattle driven away. Mines, long a source of wealth to Spain, were unworked. Anarchy reigned until 1845. In that year Ramón Castilla seized the presidency and held power until 1862 (except for the interval 1851–54); he proved the ablest ruler of nineteenth-century Peru. His earlier record seemed no better than that of the other war heroes who had scourged the nation for twenty years. Born in 1797, Castilla had fought under the Spanish flag in Chile, had been captured and imprisoned by the patriots, and had later appeared in Peru, where he joined San Martín and then Bolívar, fought bravely in the battle of Ayacucho, and then allied himself with Gamarra during the early 1830's. But, happily for Peru, Castilla proved a skillful ruler. He organized the nation's business and quieted the discordant voices of rival leaders. Himself a Conservative, he made wise concessions to the Liberals: he abolished Negro slavery, ended forced tribute from the Indians, and built a few schools. Though a strong churchman, he pleased the anticlericals by moderate reforms, the closing of Church courts, and the abolition of tithes. He took no such drastic measures against the Church as were current in Mexico, Colombia, Venezuela, and Ecuador.

The true economic liberators of Peru at this critical period, however, turned out to be not men, but birds. For unreckoned centuries millions of pelicans, cormorants, and gannets had been feeding from the abundant fish of the Peru Coastal Current (see p. 12) and dropping their excrement upon the uninhabited offshore islands. Undisturbed by rain, this bird dung had accumulated in vast mounds. Long before the arrival of the Spaniards, the Indians had collected the manure, carrying it on their backs up to the terraces cut into the high mountains. Obsessed by the quick profit from silver mines, the Spaniards paid no attention to this prosaic treasure. When Alexander von Humboldt visited the Peruvian coast during the first years of the nineteenth century, he made notes on this neglected wealth, but no serious effort was made to exploit it until scientists announced, in the early 1840's, that this bird manure was rich in nitrogen (from 14 to 17 per cent). The Peruvian government, with uncontested control over the islands, declared the exploitation of guano a national monopoly. For forty years the national treasury profited as ships of many nations carried the fertilizer to the depleted lands of Europe.

While the gift of the birds was thus being appropriated, explorers found rich deposits of sodium nitrate (source of fertilizer and gunpowder) on the arid southern desert. Lacking capital and engineers, Peru entrusted the development of this treasure to foreign concessionaires, chiefly British operators in league with the Chileans, who blasted, crushed, and refined the ore, and shipped it to Europe. The lonely oasis of Tarapacá became a booming center, and the port of Iquique the loading point.

Castilla's relatively benign rule of almost twenty years ended in 1862. In 1860 he had been responsible for a new constitution, the fifteenth in the nation's history, which concentrated powers in the hands of the president, sharply limited the franchise, and recognized the Catholic Church to the exclusion of all others. The twenty-three years following his retirement (1862–85) were a period of almost constant tension; of the nine presidents who were elected or who seized power, only two served their full four-year terms. The best of them was Manuel Pardo (1872–76), the first civilian president and the founder of the *Partido Civilista*. Paradoxically, the calamities which overtook the nation during these years—the war with Spain, the corruption of officialdom and business, and the costly War of the Pacific—were all direct results of the prosperity of the period.

The first disaster, Spain's war on Peru from 1862 until 1866, was the mother country's last tragicomic effort to recapture her lost glory in America. It was a treasure hunt, as became clear when Spanish troops seized the Chincha Islands with their heaps of guano. Peru was weak, but Spain's forces were even weaker, and the invaders withdrew.

The corruption of Peruvian politicians and businessmen was a direct result of the abundant money from guano, mineral nitrates, and loans floated in Europe. The most garish incidents accompanied the building of railroads by an American soldier of fortune, Henry Meiggs. That strange plunger, after making and losing a fortune in gold-drunk San Francisco, had spent thirteen years constructing tracks and bridges in Chile; he finally turned to Peru in 1868, to work new miracles there for nine years. "In 1868," notes his biographer, Watt Stewart, "Peru was as ripe for pillage by a daring and able foreigner as it had been when Francisco Pizarro entered the country." Peru was clamoring for railroads, and Meiggs built them—at a price. He found a willing conspirator in corrupt President José Balta (1868–72). Contracts were drawn; rails were laid from the southern port of Mollendo to Arequipa, later to Puno and Juliaca on the way to Cuzco; and then, in central Peru, from Callao up the high divide toward Huancayo. Meiggs was adept in managing labor; when he found that Peruvians would not work, he imported *rotos* (common laborers) from Chile and used many Chinese coolies who had been dragooned from their homeland, treating them all with unusual consideration. He was adroit in handling the politicians who controlled the public treasury; each contract included funds for bribery of presidents and politicians.

His luck held for a time; the railroads were built and he had his profit. But by 1872, when Balta was murdered, profits from guano had declined, European bankers were demanding payments on their loans, and the treasury was depleted. Meiggs died in 1876, almost penniless, his name execrated. His story epitomizes the state of public morals. As González Prada wrote:

> Riches served as an element of corruption, not of material progress. The sale of guano, the floating of loans, the building of railroads, the emission of bills and the expropriation of nitrate beds gave opportunity for the most scandalous frauds. . . . No means of acquisition seemed illicit. The people would have thrown themselves into a sewer if at the bottom they had glimpsed a golden *sol*. Husbands sold their wives, fathers their daughters, brothers their sisters. . . . Meiggs had a seraglio among the directing classes of Lima. . . . He built many bridges and tunnels in the Andes, but wrecked many homes and reputations in Lima.[2]

The disastrous war with Chile (the War of the Pacific, 1879–83) was the logical result of the mushrooming prosperity and the irresponsible politics of nineteenth-century Peru. We will have more to say on that conflict in dealing with Chile. The weakness of Peru and Bolivia had facilitated the penetration of Chilean interests (with British backing) in the nitrate-rich desert. Chile's armed occupation of Bolivia's Antofagasta in 1879 immediately involved both Bolivia and Peru. Chile was victorious on land and sea. Efforts to halt the fighting in 1880 were abortive, and the Chileans occupied Lima, turned the halls of ancient San Marcos University into a barracks, and pillaged the City of the Kings. Not until the Treaty of Ancón in 1883 was Peru rid of her unwelcome guests. Bolivia lost her coastal territory. Peru lost Tarapacá, while the border provinces of Tacna and Arica were committed to Chile for a decade, when the final decision was to be submitted to a plebiscite of the inhabitants of the contested region.[3]

2 Manuel González Prada: *Propaganda y ataque* (Buenos Aires: Ediciones Iman; 1939), pp. 225–6; quoted by Watt Stewart: *Henry Meiggs: Yankee Pizarro* (Durham, N.C.: Duke University Press; 1946), p. 244.

3 The plebiscite was never held, and this "Alsace-Lorraine" controversy of South America plagued inter-American relations for almost half a century. After tedious and repeated negotiations, the deadlock was finally broken in 1929 by a proposal from President Herbert Hoover, under which Arica was assigned to Chile, and Tacna to Peru; and Chile paid an indemnity of $6 million and promised to build a railroad from Arica to Tacna and to provide a free port for the passage of Bolivian goods.

Peru's recovery was slow. Thousands had been killed, much property had been destroyed, and the nation's pride had been wounded. A seven months' civil war added to the misery. The country's economic state was deplorable: government revenue had fallen to one-third of what it had been in the 1870's, an external debt of more than $200 million had piled up, her nitrate lands were lost, and the guano deposits were almost exhausted. A reasonably intelligent dictator, Andrés Caceres (1886–90), made brave efforts toward reconstruction. In 1890 British interests incorporated the Peruvian Corporation in London, which assumed the entire external debt of Peru; in return, the government in Lima assigned to the Corporation all the railways, the steamship line on Lake Titicaca, a lien upon 3 million tons of guano for a term of sixty-six years, the free use of seven ports, and an annual subsidy of £80,000 for thirty-three years.

After further flounderings there were thirteen years of relative peace (1895–1908) under *civilista* presidents, of whom the most successful were Nicolás Piérola (1895–99) and José Pardo (1904–08). A measure of order returned to the country, production and trade increased, and the government gave some attention to education. Meanwhile, Manuel González Prada, the most authentic liberal voice in nineteenth-century Peru, continued his denunciation of the "colonialism, traditionalism and clericalism" which had the upper hand in his nation.

TWENTIETH-CENTURY PERU

The major event of the new century was the rule of Augusto B. Leguía, president from 1908 to 1912, who later seized power for eleven years of dictatorship (1919–30). Energetic and able, he imposed order upon public administration, gave impetus to agriculture and mining, and restored his nation's credit in world markets. During the 1920's, when American bankers were thrusting ill-secured loans upon almost all Latin American governments, Leguía's government got more than $90 million[4] of the easy money, with which he extended railroads and highways, improved ports, installed irrigation projects, modernized the sanitary facilities of thirty cities—and built an ornate marble presidential palace for himself. An ardent admirer of American engineers and financiers, he encouraged such companies as Cerro de Pasco (copper and other metals), the Vanadium Corporation, Standard Oil, and W. R. Grace and Company (shipping and miscellaneous activities) to expand their operations, with the result that British investment was now overshadowed by that of the United States.

Leguía preened himself as a humanitarian. An astute opportunist, and perhaps with generous intentions, he organized many schools, imported teachers from the United States, espoused the cause of the neglected Indians, officially (but not actually) ended the serfdom under which they toiled, and proclaimed them full citizens of the republic. His reforms were

---

[4] An unsavory incident, later unearthed by a congressional investigation in Washington, was the payment by an American banking house of a $415,000 "commission" to Leguía's son for his services in persuading the dictator to accept a loan.

incorporated into the new Constitution of 1920, which for the first time provided for direct election of the president and members of Congress, and extended the franchise to all literate males over twenty-one. But Leguía's practices belied his protestations. In open disregard of his constitution, he was twice illegally reelected. The Bill of Rights of his constitution was nullified by flagrant throttling of the press, wholesale jailing of critics, closing of the University of San Marcos when students staged a protest, and the iron rule of army and police.

Under the shadow of this new tyranny, more oppressive than any Peru had known, there were now stirrings of the first authentic liberalism. In the venerable University of San Marcos, students formulated demands for constitutional government, the end of dictatorship, and the reform of education. Manuel González Prada (1848–1918), their mentor, had long been a lonely and unflagging critic of presidents, priests, and landlords during the years of waste and betrayal. "In Peru," he had written, "there exist two great lies: the republic and Christianity. We talk about civil rights . . . and most Peruvians have no security in their freedom or their lives. We talk about Christian charity . . . and stand by consenting to the crucifixion of a race. Our Catholicism is an inferior paganism, without greatness in its philosophy or magnificence in its art; our form of government should be called an extension of the Conquest and Viceroyalty."[5]

Conspicuous among the disciples of González Prada were José Carlos Mariátegui and Víctor Raúl Haya de la Torre. Mariátegui, a cripple who died in 1930 at the age of thirty-five, was a polemicist who accepted Marxism, writing brilliant essays on the communal delights of Inca days, and denouncing the concentration of land in a few hands as Peru's major economic sin and *gamonalismo* ("bossism") as her cardinal political error. This man, who (as Jorge Basadre puts it) "gave answers to the questions González Prada had raised," exercised a profound influence upon his generation of students, swaying many of them to Communism.

Haya de la Torre repudiated the Communist gospel and became an influential political figure in Peru. An attractive and energetic leader of twenty-four when Leguía seized power in 1919, Haya was exiled the following year, and spent years in Mexico, the United States, western Europe, and Russia. In Mexico in 1924, he announced formation of an international party, APRA (*Alianza Popular Revolucionaria Americana*), whose activities have complicated Peruvian politics ever since. Quixotic and confused, this new political dogma borrowed from Russian models (although it rejected Lenin's dictatorship of the proletariat), from the Mexican agrarian revolution, and from European socialism. It called for the nationalization of land and industry, the united front of workers and intellectuals, the unity of Indo-America (as Haya would rename Latin America) against the imperialism of the United States, and, for good measure, the internationalization of the Panama Canal. Unimportant elsewhere, in Peru the party

[5] Manuel González Prada: *Prosa menuda* (Buenos Aires, 1941), p. 156; quoted by William Rex Crawford: *A Century of Latin American Thought* (Cambridge, Mass.: Harvard University Press; 1944), p. 181.

immediately attracted a large following of middle-class liberals, young intellectuals, and intelligent workers. Its bold platform offered hope to idealists who were wearied by the venality of Peruvian politicians. Haya became a demigod to his ecstatic followers and a target for virulent abuse from almost everyone else. Leguía consigned suspected *apristas* to prison or exile. Communists, inspired by Mariátegui, attacked Haya's character and program. Foreign capitalists and domestic landholders denounced him as a Communist. The press, led by *El Comercio,* mouthpiece of the *civilistas,* berated the dangerous upstart. Meanwhile, the imperturbable Haya, roaming comfortably in enforced exile, extended his power in his native land as his friends organized cells in labor unions, government offices, the army and navy, and middle-class circles.

By 1930 the grievances of the Peruvian people were numerous. Sound democrats could not stomach Leguía's terrorism. Fervid nationalists resented his acceptance of the 1929 compromise on Tacna and Arica, his pacific settlement of Colombian claims to disputed Leticia, and his co-operation with American financial interests. Anticlericals, by then a considerable body, disliked his favors to the Church. Then the force of world depression struck Peru, lowering the value of copper, oil, cotton, and sugar; this was all that was needed to crystallize opposition. Colonel Luis Sánchez Cerro led the inevitable revolt. Leguía resigned and took ship for England, but he was overtaken by a warship and imprisoned on an island off Callao, where he died in 1932.

Sánchez Cerro, another caudillo, after ruling without legal warrant, submitted to a regular election in 1931. Haya de la Torre, back from exile, was his principal rival. The balloting, according to impartial observers, resulted in a clear victory for Haya, but Sánchez Cerro and not Haya controlled the urns. Despite the fraudulence of the election, APRA won twenty-three seats in the convention for the framing of a new constitution, whereupon Sánchez Cerro jailed Haya and many of his adherents, exiled others, and outlawed APRA. Public debate was silenced and sporadic revolts were ruthlessly crushed (in Trujillo several thousand *apristas* were shot down). In foreign affairs, the dictator truculently repudiated Leguía's settlement with Colombia and sent troops to Leticia for some bitter fighting. In April, 1933, Sánchez Cerro was assassinated, presumably by an *aprista.*

Marshal Oscar Benavides, president from 1933 to 1939, ruled with "dictatorial moderation." He came to terms with Colombia, chose wise ministers, improved public administration, promoted trade and industry, built roads, encouraged education and sanitation, and gave the workers some good laws for their protection. He released Haya from prison but soon sent him off for another period of exile. When other *aprista* leaders failed to keep silent, they were either imprisoned or exiled. When the first returns in the presidential election of 1936 gave an overwhelming majority to an obscure candidate who, while not an *aprista,* was evidently backed by that party, Benavides ordered a stop to the tallying and persuaded Congress to extend his term for three years. Meanwhile, the *apristas,* officially out-

lawed as an "international" party and with most of their leaders in exile
or in jail, still had a strong hold on all sectors of Peruvian life.

Manuel Prado's administration (1939–45) was conciliatory and relatively enlightened. Happily for the United States and her allies in World
War II, Prado cooperated with the democracies. Washington made an
early blunder by ordering the seizure in New York of eighteen bombers
bought by Peru from Norway and Holland; the episode touched off violent
criticism from the Peruvian press. Despite the protests of firebrand nationalists, Prado dislodged many suspected Germans, policed the more than
20,000 Japanese in Lima and vicinity, and reorganized the powerful Banco
Italiano, long in control of more than half the banking of the country,
and renamed it Banco de Crédito del Perú. After Pearl Harbor, Peru severed relations with the Axis powers early in 1942 and declared war in 1945.
The United States was permitted to build an air base in northern Talara,
which was returned to Peru when the war was over. In 1942 Prado visited
Washington; he was properly fêted, given the customary honorary doctorate by a great university, and returned with the promise of subventions
from the Export-Import Bank. American dollars were used to modernize
the army, navy, and air force; to spur collection of rubber in the Selva;
to increase the output of quinine; to enlarge the yield of zinc, copper,
vanadium, and other much-needed metals; to bolster Peruvian currency;
and to build irrigation projects, hydroelectric plants, model housing, highways, and better schools.

Meanwhile, the *apristas* were extending their influence. Haya de la
Torre, permitted by Prado to return, lived in Lima under police surveillance
but unmolested. His foes thought that APRA's force was spent, but their
error became clear in the presidential election of 1945. A politician of the
traditional caudillo type had the support of the oligarchy of planters, generals, and high clergy; a moderately respected lawyer, José Luis Bustamante, represented the amorphous liberal factions. The *apristas,* changing
their name to *Partido del Pueblo* (People's Party), threw their weight
behind Bustamante, held enormous mass meetings (on one occasion an
estimated 200,000 met in the fields outside Lima to yell themselves hoarse
for Haya), and elected their candidate.

Bustamante (1945–48) ruled by grace of the *apristas,* and knew it.
Three of Haya's lieutenants sat in the cabinet, *apristas* presided over the
Senate, the Chamber of Deputies, and the University of San Marcos. Haya,
now fifty, held court in his party's headquarters and dominated the government. *Aprista* leaders drafted bold proposals for public works, the increase
of mineral production, and measures for social amelioration, but they faced
the determined opposition of the powerful financial and military elements.
In pressing their program, it became clear that they were less effective as
political contrivers than as propagandists. By 1947 the brief day of the
apristas was over. The murder of the editor of a virulent anti-*aprista* newspaper was blamed on Haya's men, and in the resulting uproar the *apristas*
were compelled to resign their cabinet posts. When sailors and civilians revolted in Callao in October, 1948, and seized some warships, the uprising

was charged against APRA. The hard-pressed Bustamante sought to ingratiate himself with the powerful oligarchy by outlawing the *Partido del Pueblo* and by denouncing Haya. The inevitable *putsch* now materialized; a junta headed by General Manuel Odría forced Bustamante to resign and jailed several hundred *apristas*.

Manuel Odría, after two years of illegal rule, was formally elected president in 1950 and proved himself an effective administrator. According to one critic, Germán Arciniegas, Odría "restored the order and balance that the forty most influential families of Lima have been aiming for under the most varied forms of dictatorship." Pretense of democracy was abandoned, a hand-picked congress did Odría's bidding, a disciplined press refrained from criticism, and the army ruled.

Odría's principal wrath was directed at the *apristas*. Many were imprisoned; others escaped into exile. A few leaders found asylum in the Cuban Embassy and after a stay of eight months escaped to Cuba—whereupon Odría severed diplomatic relations with that island republic. Haya de la Torre, hounded by the police, found refuge in the Colombian Embassy in Lima in January, 1949. The International Court of Justice at The Hague was asked to decide whether Haya had the right to such asylum, and whether Colombia or Peru had the right to decide the merits of his case. In their decision the judges dodged the issue by declaring Haya a political refugee, but they refused to recommend safe conduct out of the country. There the matter rested, and Haya continued as the guest of Colombia until early 1954, when Odría finally permitted him to leave the country.

Aside from his rough handling of political critics and his denial of democratic processes, Odría rendered good account of himself in the conduct of national affairs, the promotion of trade, the building of roads and a great hydroelectric plant, the beginning of a steel mill, and the improvement of Peru's international credit position. On the whole, Peru's prosperity now offered a pleasant exhibit. Its exports exceeded imports by a comfortable margin. Bank reserves were growing, and the fluctuating currency was stabilized. The output of cotton and sugar showed steady gains. Oil wells were yielding more than 13 million barrels each year. Copper production had dropped, as old veins had been worked out; but energetic American mining companies were seeking new veins, as well as deposits of lead, zinc, iron, tungsten, bismuth, manganese, vanadium, antimony, and many other minerals for which industrialized nations clamored.

As Peru awaited the presidential election of 1956, it was generally expected that Odría would either extend his own term illegally or impose a stooge whom he could dominate. Then came his firm promise to retire, while backing his own man for the office. To the general surprise, Odría finally permitted an honest election. The voters chose between three men: Odría's candidate Lavalle, ex-President Manuel Prado, and Fernando Belaúnde. The last of these, Belaúnde, entered the lists only six weeks before the election. A brisk young architect, who represented the new generation of intelligent professional and businessmen, Belaúnde evoked a groundswell of popular enthusiasm. His election seemed quite likely until the ever active *apristas* took a hand in the contest: they first made overtures to Belaúnde, who refused to make them any promises; whereupon their leaders reached agreement with their old foe, Prado, who won handily with their help.

Manuel Prado's new term of office (1956–62) got off to a poor start. His intentions seemed honorable, but he was not strong enough to hold the now shaky economy in line. Furthermore, Prado, indebted to the *apristas* who had elected him, bore the incubus of that group, which was now more conspicuous for scolding than for statesmanship. There were rumblings of discontent in labor ranks, in the armed forces, and among university students. The armed forces won repeated pay increases and in 1957 bought four submarines in the United States at a cost of $32 million (what they were to be used for—or against—was not clear). The national currency, which had been held firm at about 19 soles to the dollar by Odría, began to slip under Prado, and by the summer of 1958 it reached a low point of 31.50 to the dollar. As inflation spiraled, strikes broke out and in some cases were put down by force. In 1958, after long argument, the American government imposed a quota on the purchase of foreign zinc and lead—two important items on Peru's export list—which reduced United States purchases by about 20 per cent, costing Peru about $20 million per year. The measure was held up temporarily when Czechoslovakia offered to buy Peru's surpluses of those two metals.

In May, 1958, Vice-President Richard Nixon of the United States visited Lima. In the course of his tour of the ancient University of San Marcos, some 2,000 students staged an angry demonstration. This was unexpected, for Peru and the United States had always been on fairly amicable terms. The incident was dismissed by many American commentators as Communist-inspired, and there were undoubtedly Communists in the plot. But the espisode revealed a growing animosity toward the United States, compounded of resentment against American cutbacks on purchases of zinc and lead, the lessening of American loans and grants to Peru and other Latin American lands as compared with American aid to Europe and Asia, and anger against large American enterprises in Peru. This last vexation, important in understanding anti-United States sentiment in Peru, applied chiefly to International Petroleum Company (Standard Oil of New Jersey), Cerro de Pasco Company, and W. R. Grace and Company. Peruvian criticism of the mining companies is that they extract wealth and leave nothing except wages—an argument which has a certain weight in Peru, where there is no export tax on minerals such as Chile thriftily imposes. However, the American companies operating in Peru deserve credit for paying better than prevailing wages, and for providing good housing, medical care, and numerous social services. Fernando Belaúnde, the unsuccessful candidate of 1956, made an interesting comment after visiting the International Petroleum Company's installations at Talara and after seeing the houses provided for workers: "If this is foreign imperialism, what we need is more, not less of it." (This remark, incidentally, was very impolitic on the part of Belaúnde.)

By 1959 Peru was dangerously close to economic collapse. Prado was weak and vacillating, his allies quarrelsome, his foes noisy; and confronted with strikes and riots, he virtually abdicated by appointing Pedro Beltrán as premier and minister of finance. A rich cotton rancher, owner and editor of the able newspaper *La Prensa,* the sixty-two-year-old Beltrán had studied at the London School of Economics, had served as ambassador to Washington 1944–46, and as a representative to the founding session of the United Nations in 1945. As citizen and editor, he had denounced Odría's dictatorship, and had actually been jailed for twenty-six days in 1956. He supported Prado, but was forthright in criticizing his weakness. Despite his birthright in one of the "forty families," who owned rather too much of Peru's land, he had accepted Prado's appointment in 1956 as president of a commission to study agrarian and housing reforms. To the dismay of his wealthy friends he argued that Peru would never find security and peace until land was found for the peasants. This stand pleased neither extreme rightists nor impatient leftists.

Beltrán assumed his new post in July, 1959, and public confidence was speedily restored; inflation was slowed, the sol was stabilized at 27.70 to the dollar. Beltrán imposed austerity, cut luxury imports, lifted uneconomic price controls, cracked down on corrupt government officials, enforced stiffer collection of taxes. He played no favorites, and was heartily damned as well as respected. "Like missionaries who go among savages, and who must be prepared to face being eaten," said Beltrán, "we independent newspapermen and honest politicians should be prepared for the worst." And there were times when Beltrán might have been "eaten": one such was a visit to heavily Communist Cuzco for the dedication of a new housing project, where Beltrán was bombarded with stones by a hostile throng. Beltrán knew some things which must be done to rescue Peru from its feudal state: the people must have houses instead of hovels; the landless must have land; and the Selva—the fertile but undeveloped trans-Andean jungle—must be opened up for colonization. Beltrán's plans were well considered—but his appeals to Congress fell on deaf ears: the intransigent followers of Odría would have none of such "radical" ideas; not even the *apristas,* who had been chattering about land reform for forty years, would go along with him.

Such was the background for the presidential elections of June, 1962. There were three candidates: Odría, ex-dictator; Haya de la Torre, veteran chief of the *apristas;* and Fernando Belaúnde Terry, a forty-nine-year-old architect who had almost won in 1956. Haya emerged with the most votes, but short of the one-third required for election; Belaúnde was second; Odría a poor third. By law, the decision should have been made by Congress, with Haya de la Torre the logical choice. But the army, long-time foe of the *apristas,* made clear that they would never permit Haya to be president. Haya first attempted to make a pact with Belaúnde, who promptly denounced the election as "fraudulent" (which it probably was not), and refused to have any dealings with Haya. Then Haya agreed to join his bitter former enemy Odría, with the understanding that Odría would serve as president, but that APRA would control the cabinet. This settled the question for military leaders: they would not allow Haya to get that near to the throne. On July 18—five weeks after the election—army tanks appeared outside the ornate presidential palace (that marble confection built with easy loans from American banks in the days of Calvin Coolidge); and, after due warning, an American-made Sherman tank crashed through the iron gates, and officers arrested seventy-three-year-old Manuel Prado, whose presidential term still had ten days to run—although of course the army was not striking at Prado, but at Haya.[6] At the last minute, Cardinal Landázuri had pleaded, "In the name of Our Holy Mother, the Church, I beg of you not to break the legal order," but General Pérez Godoy had answered, "It is too late. The prestige of the army is at stake." So, after dispatching President Prado to a prison ship in the harbor of Callao, the four who had arranged the coup—General Ricardo Pérez Godoy and three fellow officers—knelt together before a crucifix in the Palace and swore themselves into office. (It was a delightful Peruvian gesture: at their most lawless, the Peruvians never forget the proper genuflection.) The junta promptly suspended constitutional guarantees, dissolved Congress, clubbed angry demonstrators—and promised "clean and honest elections" for June 9, 1963.

The reaction abroad was dismay. Nine Latin American countries cut diplomatic relations. The United States broke relations, canceled $81 million in Alliance for Progress aid, stopped military aid which was running at the rate of $5 million a year. President Kennedy called it a "serious setback" to democracy. The members of the junta were hurt and astonished that the United States did not understand that they were acting "to protect democracy," and a representative of the junta in Washington, pleading the case with Latin American diplomats, was reported to have told them, "You must make Kennedy repent." Meanwhile, in Lima, the junta formally elected General Pérez Godoy as "constitutional president," and embarked upon a brazenly dictatorial rule: some 1,500 to 2,000 citizens were hustled off to jail and held for months without trial. Washington, after much gulping, managed to swallow its distaste for the whole performance, and on August 17, 1962 barely a month after breaking relations, restored recognition and resumed economic aid—but military aid was withheld.

The rule of the junta was inept. At first, in zeal for castigating the *apristas,* they yielded to the blandishments of the Communists, permitting them to strengthen their hold in the labor unions. Then, when a rash of strikes broke out in the mines of Cerro de Pasco, on the docks, on the sugar plantations of the coast, the junta used army battalions to put down violence. In January, 1963, the military police arrested about 1,000 ring-

---

[6] Outside observers, puzzled by the bitter anti-*aprista* stand of the Peruvian military, must be reminded of the deep-seated conviction—not only of the military and of the economic oligarchy, but also of many of the more moderate elements—that any victory for APRA and Haya de la Torre meant ruin for the nation. This antagonism was based not only on the alleged radicalism of the *apristas,* but also upon the poor performance they had rendered when given a chance to share the rule in 1945–48.

leaders in what was described as a "Red Plot" to overthrow the government. The military proved particularly clumsy in dealing with peasants' revolts in the valley of Convención, near Cuzco, whose leader was a Communist named Hugo Blanco who preened himself as the "Fidel Castro of Peru." By March, 1963, the junta itself was falling apart. Its members turned against Pérez Godoy, accused him of acting like a dictator, and removed him from the presidential palace. General Nicolás Lindley López took his place.

To the surprise of many, the promised presidential election of June 9, 1963, actually took place—perhaps because the junta had felt the sharp distrust of the public, and were cowed by the American government, which could both give aid and take it away. The elections gave the office to Fernando Belaúnde Terry, now fifty, with about 39 per cent of the votes; the perdurable Haya de la Torre got 34 per cent, and ex-dictator Odría got 26 per cent. The Christian Democrats voted for Belaúnde because he promised reforms, the Communists voted for him because he promised everything, and many cautious citizens voted for him in order to stave off the election of Haya de la Torre.

Belaúnde, duly installed for the term 1963–69, was still a baffling figure after four years in office. There was no questioning his boundless energy, his magical charm, and the bewildering array of reforms he espoused. To some he was a conscienceless demagogue; to others, a Galahad destined to rescue his people. There was a hit-or-miss quality to his leadership which was enlivening. Intent upon being president of all the people, he would visit the slums of Lima one day, a group of new settlers in the Selva the next, and he was quite at ease with the bankers and big planters, whose economic skills he respected.

But Belaúnde was engaged in a tug of war with his political opponents which was still being waged at this writing (mid-1967). Aligned with Belaúnde were his own *Acción Popular* and the small but dedicated Christian Democratic Party, which together controlled about 75 votes in Congress. Opposing him were Odría and his National Union Party and Haya de la Torre's *apristas,* together commanding 110 votes, who fought the popular Belaúnde with venom and skill. It was easy to understand Odría's hostility, for he and his followers represented Viceregal Peru, the Peru that had fought all change for more than four centuries. It was less easy to fathom Haya's refusal to go along with Belaúnde: they agreed at many points, but the two men heartily detested one another; and the *apristas,* who had been bold dreamers in earlier days, were now "tired radicals," and supinely allied themselves with Odría (who had imprisoned scores of *apristas* and had driven Haya to seek refuge in the Colombian Embassy from 1949 to 1954). Belaúnde was able to win sporadic and grudging support from both opposition groups, but month after month his opponents consumed his energy, forced cabinet shifts, undermined his hold. Five months after taking office he pulled off a tour de force: Belaúnde called for municipal elections in 1,400 cities, towns, and villages throughout Peru— the first such election in forty-five years—and his candidates got more than half of all the votes; this showing had its chastening effect upon both Odría and Haya.

By persuasion, coercion, and cajoling, Belaúnde worked political miracles: described by some as the "Peruvian Lyndon Johnson," during the first half of his allotted term he rammed some 500 bills through Congress. These included measures to stimulate education, to enlarge the social security program, to provide housing. One of Belaúnde's most imaginative programs was *Cooperación Popular,* under which dwellers in remote villages—aided by some 1,000 university students who served as a sort of Peruvian Peace Corps—used materials furnished by the government to build houses, schools, roads, parks, community centers, churches. (The Odría–Haya de la Torre contingent in Congress, however, said that Communists had infiltrated that project, and in April, 1966, canceled the small budget assigned to it.)

But most surprising was Belaúnde's success in pushing through his Agrarian Reform Law, which was enacted in May, 1964, after stormy debate in Congress. The people must have land, said Belaúnde, to give dignity and a decent living to each family. A survey in 1965 revealed that there were about 240,000 landless rural families, plus another 719,000 families with plots of land too small to provide minimum subsistence for five persons. The inequity in land distribution was also shown by these figures for 1961: 88 per cent of all farms accounted for only 5.2 per cent of the total cultivated land, while 0.2 per cent of the farms covered some 73 per cent of the farm land. Furthermore, the total amount of land under cultivation must be increased: more crops must be grown to provide more food for hungry Peruvians and for sale abroad. Belaúnde announced, "We have only one-half acre under cultivation, per capita. We must double that to one acre."

Belaúnde's agrarian program was comprehensive: it called for expropriation of some privately owned lands which—together with publicly held properties—would be distributed to the landless; it also covered water rights and struck at the evils of the old system of sharecroppers holding small plots in return for a stipulated amount of labor; it included plans for colonization of new areas; and it made provision for watering the vast stretch of desert on the coast: drawing upon the experience of the Incas— who, centuries ago, had led water from over the rim of the Andes by viaducts to the valleys in the Sierra—Belaúnde planned to divert this water by tunnels to the coastal desert.[7] But the program—despite the bellicose opposition of the "forty families"—was moderate. Expropriated lands were to be paid for; and Belaúnde sought to appease the large landholders by exempting from expropriation the efficient and scientifically run sugar and cotton plantations on the coast, and the profitable cattle-raising haciendas of the Sierra. From study of Mexico's experiences, he knew the folly

---

[7] As of 1967, plans are in progress for diverting three rivers through tunnels which would open up great stretches of desert land. Engineers are at work on ten miles of tunnels which will channel the waters of the Chotano River to the region of Chiclayo where, hopefully, 200,000 acres will be made productive.

of breaking up the latifundia into minifundia—plots too small to support a family. He proposed to apply his law to large farms that were unproductive and badly run, chiefly on the Sierra; and to the lands which could be opened up for settlement in the Selva.

The Selva (some 62 per cent of the national territory), whose jungle lands fall away from the stark rim of the Andes and extend east to the Amazon basin, is a region of heavy rainfall, raging rivers to be harnessed for power, untouched stands of fine timber, fertile soil enough to yield all the foodstuffs that Peru needs for consumption and export. This vast paradise—still a "paradise lost," as any wayfarer can attest, with only some 2.8 inhabitants to the square mile—constituted Belaúnde's chief hope for colonization. But the region had few roads, no railroads, and was reached chiefly by air. Belaúnde's most dramatic proposal was for a Marginal Highway to be built along the eastern slopes of the Andes from Peru's border with Bolivia north to Ecuador. This highway, to be linked by feeder roads to the Peruvian coast, would open up the Selva, providing markets for the goods to be produced there (and it would also link Peru with Bolivia to the south, and with Ecuador, Colombia, and Venezuela to the north). The plan had popular appeal, reminding all of the Royal Inca Highway (for runners only) which linked Cuzco with Ecuador. But the business aristocracy in Lima had no relish for the recapture of jungle lands, dreaming rather of a Peru transformed by industry. The $500-million Marginal Highway, still on the drawing board, had no assurance of financial support by 1967.

Belaúnde's land program was denounced as "communistic" by the oligarchy and as inadequate by the explosive *apristas* (who, it seemed, had no liking for reforms which did not carry their label). The obstacles were familiar to those who have watched agrarian reform in Mexico and Bolivia: the resistance of the landowners to expropriation; the lack of money to pay for the land and to pay for training and equipping the newly independent farmers. But Peru labored under an added handicap: unlike Mexico and Bolivia, Peru was a constitutional government and could not execute its programs by decree. However, Belaúnde succeeded in taking over a limited number of properties, and actually began to distribute some lands, especially in the province of Convención near Cuzco. By the end of 1965 something over 500,000 acres had been distributed by Belaúnde's government.

Belaúnde fell afoul of the Communist-baiters in his handling of terrorists in the Sierra who—in the name of land reform—not only seized lands, but robbed, murdered, and looted. Belaúnde dismissed them as "cattle rustlers" and "gangsters," thus angering those who would call all troublemakers "Communists." It was not until after nine of his policemen had been ambushed and killed that he admitted the seriousness of the situation, signed a law providing the death penalty for terrorists, and called for an increase in the military budget of $10 million.

Although Belaúnde continued to be denounced as a "Communist," the Communists were among his most pestiferous opponents. One instance

of their hostility involved Belaúnde's dealings with the International Petroleum Company (a subsidiary of Standard Oil of New Jersey), which operated rich fields in its 643-square-mile property in northern Talara, furnished
about 80 per cent of the nation's petroleum products—and was a natural
target of the Communists. In his preelection oratory Belaúnde had courted
the leftist vote by promising expropriation of the company's properties.
But in the calmer days that followed he judiciously hedged: knowing that
Peru was dependent upon foreign capital, he sought to work out a compromise whereby the oil properties would ultimately be nationalized, but
with a working arrangement between the nation and the company, which
would assure a mutually satisfactory sharing of profits. Now all leftists
angrily accused him of selling out the nation to Standard Oil.

Mid-1967 brought two major crises, both of which involved Belaúnde's government in clashes with the United States—an unfortunate
development, inasmuch as Belaúnde had many admirers in Washington,
and he himself was warm in appreciation for his North American neighbor.
The first was the revival of clamor from both leftists and ultranationalists—
and from within his own party as well—for expropriation of the Talara
oil properties, an issue which had long troubled United States–Peruvian
relations. Belaúnde was forced to accept the mandate of Congress to move
towards the expropriation of the surface rights of the American-owned
company. The issue put Belaúnde into a tight box: the American Congress
(by the Hickenlooper Amendment of 1962) had committed itself to cut off
aid to countries expropriating American property "without prompt and
adequate compensation"—and Peru needed American aid to further Belaúnde's brave social and economic program. But there was still hope for a
compromise which would settle the affair amicably.

The second storm was caused by the decision of Peru to buy super-
sonic jet fighters from France—a measure dictated by the Peruvian military,
but one which evoked angry outcry at home and serious protest from the
United States government: Washington did not relish having aid money
used to step up the arms race. Belaúnde, harassed by critics in his congress,
was forced to use his considerable powers of persuasion to mollify Peru's
strong northern neighbor.

By August, 1967, as President Belaúnde began his fourth year in
office, there was general admiration for the intrepid fifty-five-year-old
architect-turned-politician who refused to admit defeat. He was still hammered viciously by his foes of the Aprista-Odría coalition in Congress, but
he came out of every contest smiling and confident. He continued to fight
for his policies no matter how many roadblocks his opponents put up in
his way. His agrarian program, subjected to sabotage from right and left,
made slow but steady gains. There was solid improvement in government
administration. Schools multiplied, roads were built, housing projects took
shape.

The genius of Belaúnde lies in the fact that he was the first to think
in terms of a plural society. He refused to follow the line of earlier radicals,
including Mariátegui, who rang the changes on the idealized Indian of

the Sierra who would redeem the nation (a faint echo of Rousseau's "noble savage"). Nor did he join in the refrain of damnation of the oligarchy, "the forty families" who have a first lien on the property of the nation. He has recognized the solid contribution of coastal agriculture, even though it is dominated by a few men and corporations. He has given credit to the American oil operators who have acquitted themselves ably in the fields around Talara. He has not invited the Sierra Indians to impose their pattern upon the coast, nor the operators on the coast to extend their pattern to the Sierra.

Belaúnde's hold was firm in 1967, and most Peruvians (even many who had voted against him) regarded him as the ablest president the nation had ever had.

PERU: PROSPECTS AND PROMISES

Few spots in the world can surpass the scenic beauty, the archaeological fascination, the abundant charms of this land of the Incas. But Peru is an anachronism in the twentieth century, for it remains the most obstinately feudal society in all the Americas. The clear-eyed Mexican educator Moisés Sáenz tells in his classic *El indio peruano* of an encounter with an old Indian and his daughter on a road in the Sierra. Sáenz asked them, "In what village do you live?" Their answer was: *"Somos de don Guillermo Pacheco* (We belong to Mr. Guillermo Pacheco)." "They know," writes Sáenz, "to whom they belong, but not where they live."

At the top of the ladder in Peru are the "forty families" (a tag, not a statistic) who offer granite resistance to any change in this feudal pattern. These are the rich who live in fine houses filled with rare collections of art, mainly on the best streets of Lima; who own sugar and cotton plantations on the coast, great haciendas in the Sierra, banks, factories, and businesses. Chiefly of white Spanish extraction, these are the rulers of the nation, who, like their fathers before them, continue to ignore the workers in field and mine.

Next, on the score of affluence, come the middle classes. Generously interpreted, perhaps 15 per cent or more of the Peruvians fall into this category. At the top level are professional men, business entrepreneurs, large and small, teachers, skilled industrial workers. But also to be reckoned in the middle classes are the farmers who have entered the money economy. The increase in the middle classes has been speeded by the shift of population from the poverty-ridden Sierra to the farms and cities of the more prosperous coast, where there are better-paying jobs. (The urban population increased from 35 per cent in 1940 to 47 per cent in 1961.) Also, the opening of the universities to sons and daughters of the poor has brought increase in professional groups. This new "white collar" population includes many who live on meager wages and whose white collars are frayed.

And there are the poor—9 million of them, more or less. There are the landless *peones* on the great haciendas of the Sierra, traditionally although not legally attached to the land of the *patrón*: each family is required to furnish a worker for the *patrón* for three days a week and is allotted a patch of land for its own crops. Then there are the independent farmers living in indigenous communities in the Sierra, most of whom have such small patches that eking out a living for a family is difficult. Then, those who are detached from the land and work in mines, as servants, or as migrant workers. Of this group, a careful analyst reports, "It is a rare laborer in the Sierra whose cash earnings for a year exceed $75: the income of the majority probably falls within the range from $25 to $50 per year."[8]

For most of the poor who live in the rural areas of the Sierra, the conditions of life include shacks with dirt floors, meager diet, almost complete lack of medical attention, few schools, and hopelessness from generation to generation.

A fourth group of the poor are the dwellers in the city slums, the *barriadas,* which are crowded with migrants from the bleak Sierra, who seldom find the jobs they hope for and who now must live on the few cents a day they can get from odd jobs.[9] Consider the proud city of Lima, with its lovely boulevards, its fine remnants of colonial architecture, its pretentious houses—where a fourth of the people, something over 400,000, live in the *barriadas* on the hills around the city, in ravines which slice the city's edges.[1] (One *barriada* is built on top of a garbage dump, where, until recently, the people dug into the garbage for what bits of food they could find.) Housing in the *barriadas* consists of shacks made of bits of cardboard, discarded metal wired together to make a roof—nothing more. With no sewers, there is no sanitation. The pervasive smell of rotting food and unwashed flesh settles down under the fog and clings—and the wanderer through the *barriadas* carries that smell with him when he leaves. And water—that story is eloquent testimony to the futility of life in the *barriadas.* Water carriers had long come in with a burro or a cart to sell five-gallon cans of water at 2 centavos each. As the demand increased, trucks replaced the burro, and the water carrier raised his price to 20 or 30 centavos. In the meantime the government installed a few pipelines and a few taps, and the grateful women stood in line for their share of the precious water—until, in January, 1965, the water "mafia" came with trucks and rammed the pipelines in seven *barriadas,* ripped out

---

[8] Thomas R. Ford: *Man and Land in Peru* (Gainesville: University of Florida Press; 1955), p. 93.

[9] The metropolitan complex of Lima and its port city, Callao, had about 601,000 people in 1940, and about 1.6 million in 1961—the rapid growth due largely to migration from the Sierra.

[1] The *barriadas* are not confined to Lima-Callao. All the larger cities have their own. For example, of Arequipa's 135,400 people, 63,200 live in the *barriadas*; of Chimbote's 66,800 people, 45,000 live in the *barriadas*; of Iquitos' 58,100 people, 36,000 are *barriada* dwellers; of Trujillo's 100,100, 34,500 live in *barriadas* (all figures for 1961). The Social Progress Trust Fund (Inter-American Development Bank), *Fifth Annual Report* (1965), p. 516, reports these figures, and notes that in eleven cities of more than 25,000 population, the increase between 1940 and 1961 was largely accounted for by migration from the Sierra, and that in 1961, the "marginal population"—i.e., the *barriada* dwellers—bulked some 657,600 people. Some careless writers report blithely about "millions" of *barriada* dwellers. There are not "millions," but 657,600 would seem to be enough to deserve attention.

water mains, and the price of a can of water went up to 40 centavos. When police came to arrest the water carriers the people turned on them with stones and shouts: "If they arrest the water carriers and the government does not give us new taps, what will we do for water?" While the authorities stood helplessly by, the water carriers refused to enter some *barriadas,* parking outside and forcing the women to come and get their water. On the sides of some trucks were the legends: "See me and suffer." "Wait and don't complain."[2]

A tragicomic note was added when the Peruvian Tourist Corporation suggested in 1964 that the façades of the *barriadas* be painted so that they would not be so depressing for tourists. "With tricks and cheap masks," reported *El Comercio* of Lima, "the Tourist Corporation is trying to put a low-cost pretty face on the dwellings—if you can call them that—which rage like an epidemic through our city."

The world of the poor is largely the Indian world, although it also includes many mestizos. But the line between Indian and mestizo is a dim one. The biological line is blurred by the mingling of centuries. The cultural line is clearer: it is determined by dress, language, manners. The Indian wears homespun, chews coca, speaks Quechua or Aymará, and his misery is the most abject. The mestizo speaks Spanish, does not chew coca, wears western dress, and is first to break the chains of poverty. Some villages are predominantly mestizo, others Indian. The mestizo predominates on the coast and in the chief cities; the Indian, in the Sierra.

Not all ears are deaf to the miseries of Peru. In Lima numerous groups—including churchmen, both Catholic and Protestant—seek to alleviate the suffering in the *barriadas.* Over the country there are new projects each year, representing the government, the education ministry, the Indigenous Institute, the United Nations, AID of the United States. At Vicos in the Sierra, 250 miles northeast of Lima, Cornell University in cooperation with the Peruvian government has undertaken a pilot project of some significance. A 35,000-acre hacienda—one of two or three hundred which have long been the property of the nation, leased for terms of years to a *patrón*—was taken over by the Peru-Cornell project in 1952. The hacienda produced corn, potatoes, barley, wheat, beans, quinona; the higher slopes afforded almost unlimited grazing for cattle and sheep. The more than 1,800 Quechua-speaking Indians (about 300 families) who lived on the hacienda had served their *patrón* in familiar feudal fashion, working their tiny plots and affording free labor and services for the *patrón.* Virtually nothing had been done to protect the health of these *campesinos:* parasitic diseases had taken heavy toll; diet was meager and badly balanced. There was only one school—a miserable shack with an untrained teacher; and not a single primary pupil could read or write, either in Spanish or in Quechua. There was practically no community organization among the Indians, except for religious festivals. The Peru-Cornell project took over

2 This account of "The Water Mafia" was reported in *Expreso,* Lima, and reprinted in *Atlas* (April, 1965).

the lease, ended the forced labor in the fields as well as the hated levy upon the Indians for household servants, and embarked upon a program to increase production and raise the level of living of the *campesinos.* Despite the early suspicion of outsiders—two of the four who managed the program were Peruvians, but Lima was as "outside"as Ithaca, New York— the *peones* gradually yielded to persuasion. Improved methods of plowing, fertilizing, seeding, were slowly accepted. The potato crop increased four-fold until by 1960 there were not only enough potatoes for the people to eat, but a surplus for sale outside the hacienda. The people of the com-munity joined in building a school, and, with the cooperation of the Na-tional Education department, better teachers were brought in. The people responded: in 1951 there had been only 14 to 18 pupils with 1 teacher; by 1958, enrollment was some 250, with 8 teachers. In 1957 the hacienda lease was formally transferred to the people, represented by a loose but effective community organization. The response was enthusiastic. Agri-cultural products doubled within a year after the transfer; and plans were laid and work begun on roads and water supply. The Vicos experiment was not perfect, but it presented a hopeful exhibit of what might be done with a small group of Indians in one hacienda.[3]

Peru's economic health is attested by the diversity of its products. In 1965 about 20 per cent of the GDP was from agriculture, slightly less from manufacturing, some 7.5 per cent from mining. In terms of exports, the chief items in 1965 were as follows: fishmeal, 21.5 per cent; copper, 18.2 per cent; cotton, 13.1 per cent. Peru has thus escaped the ravages of the monoculture that afflicts Chile, Bolivia, and some other nations.

Peru's mines render a good account of themselves. Copper, silver, and lead together yielded 29.8 per cent of export revenue in 1965. The output of all of these nonferrous metals had been expanding for over a decade. The marked increase in the production of copper (which multiplied three and one-half times from 1956 to 1964) and silver (which increased fourfold from 1948 to 1964) was largely due to the great Toquepala mine (the American-owned Southern Peru Copper Company). The success of Peru's largely foreign-owned mining companies is due chiefly to favorable treatment by the government: lower taxes, fewer restrictions on exporting profits, and other concessions.

The most spectacular boon to the Peruvian economy has come from the little anchovy, which, by 1963, had raised Peru to the top place among the fishing powers of the world. Running in closely packed schools in the Peru Coastal Current, feeding on the plentiful marine organisms (zoo plankton), these anchovies had once before had a part in rescuing the Peruvian economy: in the mid-nineteenth century it was discovered that the birds which ate the fish deposited manure—guano—upon the coastal

[3] Allan R. Holmberg, professor of anthropology at Cornell University, describes the Vicos project in "Changing Community Attitudes and Values in Peru: A Case Study in Guided Change," in Richard N. Adams and others: *Social Change in Latin America Today* (New York: Council on Foreign Relations; 1960).

islands, and this guano was collected and sold to the world for fertilizer at a handsome profit. Scientists a century later pondered those bird droppings and posed the question: why depend upon the birds to turn the fish into manure? Why not grind up the anchovies directly? After all, birds' stomachs are inefficient fertilizer-factories: for 1 ton of guano the birds must swallow 20 tons of fish; whereas 1 ton of machine-ground meal requires only 5.5 tons of fish—and used as food for poultry and hogs it fetches higher prices. The venture was a huge success. Hundreds of seiners, pushing out to sea, harvested billions of anchovies; and by 1964 there were some 140 processing plants grinding up the fish, packing the meal into sacks for export. This new industry not only brought fat profits to its promoters, but furnished new jobs for several hundred thousand people, many of them poor migrants from the Sierra: some did the seining, the processing, and the packing; others manufactured nylon nets, plastic net buoys, steel hulls, pumps, manila cordage, and sacks. This influx of workers jammed the fishing communities and wrought swift social changes: Chimbote, for example, was a sleepy town of 20,000 in 1950, but had 120,000 people by 1964. Wages were relatively high. The newcomers demanded schools for their children, and got them. The insignificant anchovy was responsible for sales of some $143 million in 1965: since 1962 fishmeal had been the chief item on Peru's export list. But there were danger alarms: Peru might produce more fishmeal than the world would buy; or the anchovies might quit running. Meanwhile, fishmeal was Peru's leading export. And as the world's teeming population puts increasing pressure on the one-eighth of the earth's surface that produces crops, man is again reminded that he must look seaward for food.

Housing offered stern demands in 1967. Faced by the miserable housing allotted to some 90 per cent of the nation's people, Belaúnde installed a National Housing Board dedicated to building 100,000 new housing units by 1970. But even this optimistic goal—toward which the government made a brave start—fell far short of the nation's need. The 1961 census had reported that 68 per cent of rural homes consisted of one or two windowless rooms each, these often shared by human beings and animals. Only 21 per cent of the nation's houses had piped water, and more than 55 per cent had no sanitary facilities of any kind.

On the score of health, Peru's record is among the poorest in Latin America. There has been some improvement, especially in the urban centers. The general mortality rate was reduced from 13.6 deaths per 1,000 population in 1951 to 8.9 deaths in 1964, and the rate of infant mortality was reduced a little—but the fact remained that in 1964, out of 1,000 babies born alive, 84 died in their first year. Malnutrition was one explanation: the caloric intake was about 20 per cent less than the accepted minimum; and hunger haunts more than half the people. Lack of medical services, especially in the rural Sierra, was serious: of Peru's 5,061 physicians, 3,279 were in the municipal metropolis of Lima-Callao. It was clearly almost impossible to persuade trained physicians to settle down and practice in the bleak villages of the Sierra, much less the lightly populated Selva.

Education presents a hopeful picture in 1967. Illiteracy was reduced from about 57 per cent in 1940 to about 40 per cent in 1961. In 1960, the national budget allotted 16 per cent to education, and in 1965 this figure had increased to more than 24 per cent. Universal free education from the kindergarten to the university was made an article of national policy by Belaúnde; and although there have not been enough buildings, teachers, or books to make it a workable policy, the schools are improving —slowly in the remote villages of the Sierra, more rapidly on the coast and in the cities. Universities have multiplied: in 1940 there were seven universities enrolling 3,839 students; in 1964, there were thirty universities, 48,000 students. Not that all university education is first-rate, but Peruvian youths are demanding access to the modern world by training for leadership in the professions, in business. Thanks to fellowships from the government, sons of the poor increasingly take their places beside the sons of the well-born in the University of San Marcos in Lima—the oldest university in the Americas (a claim, by the way, which is challenged by the National University of Mexico). Thus education makes its contribution to social mobility.

Peru's cultural contribution has been meager, but a few voices have been raised to dramatize the tragic needs of the disinherited. Here the earlier writers Manuel González Prada and José Carlos Mariátegui deserve a high place. (See pp. 598–601) In the twentieth century the poet César Vallejo—a Communist of wide influence, whose work has been translated abroad—is known for his *Los heraldos negros.* Highly respected is the novelist Ciro Alegría, whose *El mundo es ancho y ajeno* (translated as *Broad and Alien is the World*) is a realistic and straight-forward portrayal of Indian life.

An interesting development has come from the armed forces. Peruvian officers have often been extremely reactionary; but, by a curious quirk, the military in late years has taken a lively part in social reforms. And— again curiously—it was one-time dictator Manuel Odría who was responsible for organizing the *Centro de Altos Estudios Militares,* where officers pursue social studies and plan for the growing "democratization of the military." Detachments of the military are actually active in helping rural communities build schools and social centers, improve roads, disseminate agencies for public health.

Another hopeful element is the Church. Traditionally, the Peruvian Church has been one of the most reactionary in all of Latin America, following the tradition of the Church in Spain rather than that in France, England, and the United States. But there has been a shift in spirit and temper, largely accounted for by the increasing sense of social responsibility evidenced by Pope Leo XIII and his successors. Quotations from two eminent Peruvian churchmen give vivid evidence of the change. In 1937,

Lima's Archbishop Pedro Pascual Farfán made this revealing statement: "Poverty is the most certain road to eternal felicity. Only the state which succeeds in making the poor appreciate the spiritual treasures of poverty can solve its social problems." Twenty-two years later, in 1959, Cardinal Archbishop of Lima, Juan Landázuri Ricketts had this to say: "The Church sees that the present economic and social order must be reformed and improved. . . . A living wage must be paid to workers and there must be a better distribution of wealth: private selfishness must be curbed, for there is no longer an excuse for the miserable conditions in which rural laborers and the urban proletariat live."

 [*Chapter 33*]

BOLIVIA

The Republic of Bolivia has been called "the American Tibet." Locked away on the bleak roof of the continent, it is one of the world's most hapless nations—its economy dependent on mines of doubtful future, its people hungry and diseased, its political course a continuing torment. Surveying his nation's history, the Bolivian historian Alcides Argüedas writes of his "sick people" (*pueblo enfermo*) and notes that since independence "the barracks was the schoolroom," and that "the cult of force dominated a nation which was without culture, economic wealth and moral principles."

Bolivia's 424,163 square miles, roughly equal in size to Texas and California combined, lie athwart three spurs of the Andean cordillera. Almost half of her original area—including a strip on the Pacific coast—has been taken from her by Brazil, Paraguay, Argentina, Chile, and Peru. This landlocked domain has two principal regions, the *altiplano* and the lowlands. The lofty tablelands, 12,000 to 14,000 feet above the sea, comprise about two-fifths of the territory and house some four-fifths of the people. Here is the *de facto* capital, La Paz, with 352,912 inhabitants (1962), lying in an icy pocket some 12,000 feet above the sea in the shadow of Mount Illimani (21,185 feet); and here are Sucre and the mining cities of Oruro and Potosí. Here also is Lake Titicaca (12,507 feet), shared with Peru, the highest navigable lake in the world. On the lower lands, where three-fifths of the national area furnishes homes for one-fifth of the people, are the *yungas,* deep valleys that slice down the mountainside, the *selvas,* forest lands with untouched stands of mahogany and other hardwoods, and the prairies which face Brazil and Paraguay. Bolivia looks to the *yungas,* the *selvas,* and the prairies for grain, meat, fruit, rubber, and other products; but there is a lack of workers, and railways and roads are inadequate.

Of 3.7 million Bolivians (1966), nine-tenths are Indian or mestizo (*cholo*) and one-tenth white or "whitish." Only about 31 per cent can read and write. The rugged Aymarás, unruly and vindictive, predominate around Lake Titicaca and La Paz, while the more docile Quechuas are scattered over the nation. The Indian of the *altiplano* farms the exhausted soil, herds a few animals, lives in a stone or mud hut, eats dried potatoes, parched corn, and fried beans, and dulls his appetite by chewing coca leaves. Ignorant and lethargic, the Indian counts for little in the life of the nation.

"Bolivia's prospects are bleak," wrote Arthur Whitaker, as he contemplated the collapse of the nation's short-lived tin prosperity after World War II. Observers agree that Bolivia suffers from the "metal-mania" which bankrupted Spain, the madness which persuades its victims that all problems will be settled by an abundance of gold, silver—or tin. For three centuries, colonial rulers relied on the silver of Potosí rather than on the grain of the *yungas*. In the mid-twentieth century, Bolivia imports much of her food.

Bolivia's political anarchy is the counterpart of her economic and social misery. During the century and a quarter since Simón Bolívar gave the nation independence, there have been over sixty full-scale revolutions, more than a hundred lesser uprisings, and some forty presidents, of whom eight were assassinated. Political parties, platforms, and slogans have meant little. "Conservatism," "liberalism," "democracy," "social justice" have been invoked, and in their defense men have died; but, with a few grateful intermissions, Bolivian political history is the inglorious saga of rival chieftains in struggle for power and profit.

THE BIRTH OF THE NATION, 1825–29

Bolivia's independence was a vague afterthought of the wars of liberation. Its territory, called Upper Peru in colonial days, was an appendage of Lima until 1776, when it was transferred to the Viceroyalty of La Plata. After the people of Buenos Aires struck for independence in 1810, their junta made repeated attempts to include Upper Peru in the new nation of Argentina. But the ending of Spanish power on the *altiplano* had to wait for Bolívar's victories in Peru. In 1825 the Liberator sent Antonio José de Sucre to free Upper Peru and to create the "Republic of Bolívar," a name shortly changed to Bolivia. Simón Bolívar himself was then summoned and named as dictator. His Constitution of 1826 provided an awkward three-chambered congress and a life term for the president, who was given the right to name his successor. In drafting the constitution, Bolívar yielded to popular pressure on only one point: Catholicism was given a monopoly position, despite the Liberator's plea for religious tolerance.

Thirty-three-year-old Sucre, as pure-hearted a patriot as graced those troubled years, was offered the life presidency. A sensible young man, wary of such generous grants of power (and eager to return to Quito for his postponed wedding), he accepted a two-year term, and proved an excellent administrator. In 1828, his term uncompleted, he was forced out by a mutiny among his own troops, the uprisings of ambitious caudillos, and the invasion of a Peruvian army under Gamarra. Sucre's name continued to adorn the capital city, but his moderate counsels did not prevail. Andrés Santa Cruz seized the presidency in 1829.

NINETEENTH-CENTURY CAUDILLOS

No other South American state, not even beggarly Paraguay, faced more initial handicaps than did Bolivia. There were few competent and patriotic leaders among the landed aristocracy, and there was virtually no middle class. The apathetic Indians and *cholos* were pawns in a game whose moves they did not comprehend. The military bosses, trained in the campaigns of San Martín and Bolívar, took over by default. They and their successors have ruled most of the time ever since.

Andrés Santa Cruz (1829–39), ablest of the early caudillos, was born about 1794, the son of a Spanish father and an Indian mother who boasted royal Inca blood. As a youth, he served under the Spanish flag, then joined San Martín, and later Bolívar. Serving a brief turn as president of Peru after Bolívar's withdrawal, Santa Cruz saw his opportunity in Bolivia. Quick-witted and competent, personally honest and tireless, he gave Bolivia the best government it would enjoy for half a century. It was a dictatorship, somewhat paternalistic, in which the vain ruler found comfort in collecting medals and honors, including the ribbon of the Legion of Honor conferred by Louis Philippe of France and the self-bestowed titles of "Captain-General," "Grand Marshal," and "Supreme Protector."

Santa Cruz, fancying himself as the Napoleon of the Andes and as heir of the Incas through his royal mother's line, conquered distraught Peru and created the Bolivian-Peruvian Confederation in 1836. Peru's resistance was slight; Santa Cruz was a better general than any of the novices mismanaging the City of the Kings; the numerous Masonic lodges served his cause; and many of the land barons accepted his strong rule as a pledge of security and peace. The Confederation, over which Santa Cruz presided as "Protector," was promptly recognized by Great Britain, the United States, and France. But the South American neighbors, fearful of such concentration of power, were hostile: Brazil, though in no position to fight, protested; Argentina sent troops which were easily repulsed; but Chile, dominated by able Diego Portales, sent an expeditionary force which delivered the *coup de grâce* to the Confederation at the battle of Yungay in 1839, and ended the life tenancy of the Protector.[1]

The ejection of Santa Cruz left Bolivia at the mercy of contentious rivals. Brief relief came under José Ballivián (1841–47), who repulsed an invasion by Peruvian troops, imposed order, and made some attempt to organize the government. He was followed by a demagogue named Manuel Isidoro Belzú, who incited the *cholos* to widespread attacks upon the great landlords. Under him and his inept successors, disorder spread during the 1850's and 1860's. The most lurid chapter was the rule of Mariano Melgarejo (1864–71), a *cholo* bastard who is remembered as "the scourge of God." Fearless, illiterate, physically powerful, Melgarejo commanded the

---

[1] Santa Cruz, like so many of his contemporaries in Latin American politics, found asylum in Europe, there to enjoy the friendship of Louis Philippe, and later, of Napoleon III. He continued to plot a triumphal return until his death in 1865.

feverish loyalty of the private army with which he imposed his will.[2] For six years he marched from city to city, putting down revolts with bestial cruelty. His debaucheries matched those of his contemporary, Francisco Solano López of Paraguay. His brutal mistress, Juana Sánchez, contributed to the sordidness of his ambulatory presidential court. While Melgarejo was devoting his energy to drink, women, and butchery, public business was at a standstill. In order to get money, he created a new currency, calling the new unit the *melgarejo;* and he indulged in illegal sales of Indian communal lands—a performance described by one Bolivian historian as "the first instance when a president did anything whatever about the Indian." In further search of profit, he sold debated border lands to Brazil and granted Chileans the right to exploit the nation's nitrate beds in Bolivia's Atacama province on the Pacific. The tyrant was finally dislodged in 1871 by a military uprising.

Hilarión Daza (1876–79), venal and incompetent, had the dubious distinction of leading the Bolivian army against the Chilean invaders of the Bolivian coastal region in the War of the Pacific. Long brewing, the war was finally provoked by Daza's demand for an increased tax upon the nitrates dug by Chileans. The Bolivian army was routed in a few weeks, but Peru—Bolivia's ally in the dispute—fought on for three years. An indefinite truce with Chile marked Bolivia's withdrawal and prepared the way for years of futile argument. But Bolivia had lost forever her Pacific province and the income from nitrates.[3]

Chastened by defeat, Bolivia rendered a somewhat better account of herself during the 1880's and 1890's. A few reasonably honest presidents, including some civilians, brought a glimmer of hope. Silver mining was revived, affording some relief to the treasury. A few schools were opened, chiefly for whites and ambitious *cholos.* Politics were enlivened by wordy contests between "Liberals" and "Conservatives." One of the chief Liberal demands was for transfer of the seat of government from inaccessible Sucre to the more populous and central La Paz. In 1899, Liberal José Manuel Pando won the presidency by a revolt, made La Paz the *de facto* capital, and inaugurated a period of comparative calm which lasted for almost twenty years.

EARLY-TWENTIETH-CENTURY BOLIVIA

Bolivia's fortunes improved under José Manuel Pando (1899–1904) and his successor Ismael Montes (1904–09, and again 1913–17). These Liberals, voicing a healthy skepticism of military control, placed a hopeful emphasis upon economic reforms. Somewhat anticlerical, they made a few cautious revisions of the Church's ancient prerogatives: in 1905, for the first time, toleration was decreed for religious worship other than Catholi-

---

[2] His complete ignorance is delightfully revealed by his reported debate with one of his ministers over the question as to whether Napoleon or Bonaparte was the greater general.
[3] See pp. 598 and 654–5 for further accounts of the War of the Pacific.

cism; in 1908 the control of cemeteries passed from the clergy to the municipalities; and in 1911 civil marriage was made obligatory. But there has never been in Bolivia—even up to the present time—any concerted attack upon the Church.

In international affairs, agreement was reached on obstinate territorial debates with Chile and Brazil. The first dispute, legacy of the War of the Pacific, involved the lost desert lands on the coast. By a treaty concluded with Chile in 1904, Bolivia surrendered all claims to that region; while Chile promised an indemnity of about $1.5 million, and agreed to build a railroad from coastal Arica to La Paz and to establish Arica as a free port for the passage of Bolivian products to the outer world. The pledges were redeemed and the railroad was completed in 1912. The second controversy involved the jungles of Acre in northern Bolivia, rich in rubber, accessible only by the Amazon river system. Unpoliced by Bolivia, Acre was occupied during the last years of the nineteenth century by a few Brazilian rubber prospectors, who in 1899 declared the region an independent republic. (Bolivia's experience with Acre had an earlier parallel with Mexico's troubles in Texas.) Two small Bolivian military expeditions sought to eject the interlopers, but did no more than increase the tension. In 1903 President Pando signed a treaty by which most of the disputed territory was conceded to Brazil, which, in return, promised to pay an indemnity of about $10 million and build a railroad from a port on the Mamoré River in Bolivia to the navigable waters of the Madeira in Brazil, to serve as an outlet for Bolivian commerce through the Amazon.

In an atmosphere of greater tranquillity, domestic and foreign, Bolivia's economy was fortified by the increased output of silver, the growing yield of tin, and the payment of indemnities by Chile and Brazil. Vigorous measures extended the inadequate lines of communication. Steamboats had been introduced on Lake Titicaca in the late nineteenth century. Now a considerable network of wagon roads was begun, most of the work being done by the unpaid labor of Indians. A beginning was made on railways linking La Paz, Oruro, and Potosí with the coast. Such ventures, small as they were, facilitated the shipping of foodstuffs to populous centers and the transfer of ores to the port of Arica.

The 1920's were years of "boom and bust." The Republicans—the label had no more meaning than had the earlier party designations—furnished presidents of indifferent quality culminating in arrogant Hernando Siles (1926–30). During this decade foreign capital, chiefly American, increased its stake in Bolivia. In 1924 a one-third interest in the Patiño tin properties (producers of about four-fifths of Bolivian tin) was bought by the United States National Lead Company. Oil also attracted American capital: in 1922 Standard Oil of New Jersey acquired the concessions of several companies which had been exploring and drilling in southeastern Bolivia near the borders of Argentina. Other companies got concessions to mine tungsten, lead, and copper. By 1930 American interests were the chief holders of mineral concessions.

The true arbiters of Bolivian destiny were now the New York bankers who thrust extravagant loans upon the La Paz government, increasing the foreign debt from $6 million to $60 million. The easy money had some useful results: railroads were built, linking La Paz with Buenos Aires; and better agriculture was encouraged, with some development of rubber and cacao in the lower *yungas* and *selvas*. But the largess of the bankers worked more harm than good, for their money led to reckless waste and wholesale corruption of public officials. Millions went into the purchase of guns and powder, and the building of a new army under a borrowed German general named Kundt. Meanwhile, the foreign bankers took a lien on export revenue, named agents to supervise its collection, and excited the outcry of fervid nationalists against "imperialistic Uncle Sam." However, the vendors of the engraved bonds served neither Bolivia nor the American investors. When the world depression hit Bolivia in 1930 and the price of tin—principal reliance for foreign exchange—plummeted, the entire national budget was little more than the fixed charges upon foreign-owned bonds. The fool's paradise collapsed, the treasury defaulted on its bonds, and unpopular President Siles was ousted.

The election of Daniel Salamanca in 1931 was a victory for the Patiño tin interests, which had again intervened in Bolivian politics. Salamanca was generally regarded as competent, and there were hopes that the country would now settle down. This optimistic mood was rudely interrupted by the outbreak of the insane war with Paraguay over the long-debated Gran Chaco (1932–35). When Bolivia lost her coastal province to Chile in the War of the Pacific, she began to look for an outlet to the Atlantic through the waterways of the Río de la Plata system. The no man's land of the Gran Chaco blocked access to the navigable waters of the Paraguay and Pilcomayo rivers, and it contained (or so the Bolivians thought) vast reservoirs of petroleum. The mixture of oil and patriotism proved explosive. A series of border clashes with the Paraguayans led to war in 1932.

The obvious advantages lay on Bolivia's side: she had more than three times Paraguay's population; her army was well trained by General Kundt; and she had abundant arms, bought with loans from American bankers. But Bolivia, as it turned out, never really had a chance. On the score of morale, there was striking disparity between the two armies: Paraguay's men thought that they were fighting for protection of their homeland; Bolivia's were chiefly conscripted Indians, often seized by force and sometimes transferred to the Chaco in chains. The physical setting favored Paraguay, whose soldiers moved in familiar terrain and climate; while Bolivia's men, with distended lungs adjusted to the thin air of the *altiplano*, sickened and died in the steaming lowlands. Paraguay's greater social egalitarianism also gave her clear advantage, as common soldier and officer fought side by side; while Bolivia's forces were divided by the deep chasm between Indians and the master class. The front line of the Bolivian army was often a ragged mass of apathetic Indians, foully housed and fed; and, several miles in the rear, there was a second line of defense where "gentlemen officers" lived comfortably, with ample food and drink, and often with the solace of their mistresses.[4] The war continued for three years, as fevers,

---

[4] The author bases his description on the testimony of three Bolivian officers, patriotic but disillusioned.

dysentery, malaria, and snakebites accounted for as many casualties as did Paraguayan gunfire. At least 60,000 Bolivians, and almost as many Paraguayans, died in contesting an area to which neither had clear title, and from which little value could come—unless, as is yet to be proved, there is oil. Meanwhile, Bolivia's internal situation steadily worsened; riotous inflation exacted heavy toll from workers and the middle class, and disillusion weakened the president's control. In 1934 Salamanca sought to dismiss Commander in Chief General Enrique Peñaranda, but was himself deposed by an army cabal.

By 1935 the war was virtually ended. The final treaty, signed in 1938, confirmed Paraguay in possession of most of the disputed region, although Bolivia was promised a corridor to the Paraguay River and the right to build a port. The national economy had been disrupted by the withdrawal of miners and farmers for service at the front. New voices added to the confusion. Returned soldiers, angered by their shabby treatment, demanded a hearing. University students for the first time interested themselves in politics. Labor agitators, hitherto easily cowed, denounced the conditions under which men labored in mine and field. These voices were loud and contradictory, and leadership was confused and immature. The targets of abuse were foreign imperialists (principally the United States), domestic caudillos, and the "tin barons." Three men—Patiño, Hochschild, and Aramayo—controlled the companies which had almost a complete monopoly on tin, owned or dominated numerous other enterprises, and dictated to presidents and cabinets.[5] This powerful alliance was popularly called the *rosco*—the word for the yoke on the neck of the oxen.

It was the logical setting for revolution, although agitators were vague in their demands. In May, 1936, in a bloodless coup, the current dictator was unseated by a junta under Colonel David Toro, a bewildered young man committed to "socialization," whose only tangible if somewhat Pyrrhic victory was the expropriation of the properties of the Standard Oil Company of New Jersey. Having thus bearded the Northern Colossus, he undertook to impose higher taxes upon the tin monopolists, a move which led to his overthrow in 1937. He was replaced by another army officer, Germán Busch, who pressed for larger payments from the tin interests and made veiled threats to nationalize the mines. In 1938 Busch, with the fervent

[5] The story of Simón Patiño deserves a place with the "success stories" of our times. Born in Cochabamba about 1868, a *cholo* of humble parentage, unschooled, Patiño acquired a small tin mine in the 1890's and expanded his holdings until by 1910 he was a millionaire. He moved to Europe, where he served for many years as a Bolivian diplomatic agent (thereby acquiring extraterritorial rights and dodging taxes). He extended his control over tin mines in Malaya, built smelters in Germany and England, had homes in Paris, Nice, and Biarritz, and married his son and two daughters to holders of French and Spanish titles. Meanwhile, controlling more than half of the tin output of Bolivia, he issued orders—through agents at home—to the La Paz government. He returned for a brief time in 1924 and built three great houses, including an extravagant palace in his native Cochabamba, at the cost of several million dollars. When the white aristocracy of Cochabamba snubbed him, he left Bolivia for the last time. Secretive, covering his tracks through subsidiary corporations in many lands, Patiño was probably one of the world's wealthiest men. When France fell in 1940, he retired to New York and died in 1947.

support of labor, promulgated a new constitution (to replace the instrument of 1880) which was reminiscent of the Mexican Constitution of 1917: it gave labor the right to organize and to bargain collectively, nationalized subsoil rights, provided schools for all children, and declared the supremacy of human rights over property interests. It was, in effect, a declaration of war against the great landowners, the "tin barons," and foreign capital. But in 1939 Busch committed suicide—or was murdered—and the propertied classes breathed more easily.

In 1940 Conservative army elements took control of the ballot boxes and elected General Enrique Peñaranda to the presidency. The new leader, a *cholo* of little education⁶ who had proved an inept commander in chief during the Chaco War, became—by encouraging the increased output of tin—a loyal friend of Messrs. Patiño, Hochschild, and Aramayo and a valiant ally of the United States. Labor outbreaks in the tin mines were put down by the army; the shooting of scores of strikers at Catavi in December, 1942, unloosed violent criticism of both the Bolivian president and the United States. Peñaranda's pro-Allied zeal continued unabated. He expelled the German minister in 1941, ousted the German operators of the air lines and turned the enterprise over to Pan American Airways; he severed relations with the Axis in early 1942 and persuaded his congress to declare war on Germany and Japan in 1943. He mollified Standard Oil by a settlement of $1.5 million for their expropriated claims. In return, the United States made loans for the rehabilitation of the railroads, the building of highways, the increase of hospitals and sanitation, and the development of agriculture in the lowlands.

A state visit by Peñaranda to Washington in 1943, suitably staged to advertise the cordiality of Bolivian-American relations, could not cloak the enmity of the Bolivian masses against the United States. The immediate target was the American ambassador in La Paz, who was charged with conspiring with Peñaranda and the "tin barons" to hold down miners' wages and to crush strikes. The "Catavi massacre" of 1942 became a *cause célèbre*. The 60,000 miners, according to Bolivian agitators, were worked cruel hours at low wages (half of them getting less than 60 cents a day), under conditions which induced silicosis and tuberculosis. Under Secretary of State Sumner Welles met the storm by organizing a joint United States–Bolivian Commission of labor experts whose report confirmed many of the charges and condemned the low wages, bad working conditions, inadequate medical care, and denial of collective bargaining. Peñaranda did nothing to correct the abuses.

In December, 1943, the unpopular Peñaranda was dislodged by a group calling themselves the *Movimiento Nacional Revolucionario* (MNR), who appealed to all the leftist elements that had been aroused by the

---

6 A common tale, undoubtedly apocryphal, had it that when the news of Peñaranda's election reached his mother, the old woman said: "Why, if I had known Enrique would be president, I would have sent him to school." But perhaps any lack of earlier booklearning was offset in 1943 when, on a visit to the United States, he was awarded an honorary Doctorate of Laws by Columbia University.

"Catavi massacre." Organized in 1941 by Víctor Paz Estenssoro, one-time professor of economics, Hernán Siles Zuazo, son of the ex-President, and other young intellectuals, the strongly nationalistic MNR included socialists of the Toro and Busch tradition, as well as some known Nazi sympathizers and others influenced by Argentina's Perón. Although allied briefly with the PIR (*Partido Izquierdista Revolucionario*), which was an aggregation of leftists and some Communists, the MNR was definitely not a Communist group. These strange confederates were bound by one tie: hatred of the tin barons and foreign capitalists. Installed in the presidency by the MNR was a Chaco War hero, Major Gualberto Villaroel, whose government immediately faced troubles from without and from within. Viewing Villaroel's presidency as no more than an extension of the Perón machine of Argentina, the United States withheld recognition for six months. The new President, while granting concessions to labor, alienated his left-wing supporters by rough handling of the PIR's leaders, by suppression of news and discussion and by attacks upon the civil and economic rights of the Jews.[7] Meanwhile the tin oligarchy heard ominous threats of expropriation. In July, 1946, after two and a half years of chaotic rule, Villaroel was lynched by a mob and his body was hung on a lamppost in front of the national palace. His admirers blamed the murder on foreign imperialists and tin masters, but most observers described it as the latest instance of political gangsterism. In any event, the brief power of the MNR was ended for the time being, and its leaders found it expedient to go into exile.

Ineffective rightist administrators brought no relief during the years 1946–52. Tin continued as the principal topic of debate, the United States serving as the convenient scapegoat. The defeat of Japan opened the sea lanes to the tin mines of Southeast Asia, and the United States lost interest in Bolivia's tin. There was acid argument over prices: by 1952 the United States was paying about $1.20 per pound for Indonesian tin, while offering Bolivia $1.215, but the Bolivians insisted upon the figure $1.50. Labor leaders won substantial wage increases and the right to appoint labor agents in the mines. Mining companies, caught between soaring production costs and low prices in the American market, watched their margin of profit disappear. Inflation laid heavy burdens on all wage earners.

THE NATIONAL REVOLUTION, 1952–64

Almost everyone in Bolivia was angry by 1951: sober citizens were weary of political anarchy; the peasants wanted lands of their own; the miners wanted more pay; and the tin oligarchy was distressed by the demands of agitators. In the elections of 1951, however, with the franchise limited to literate males, the government foresaw a hopelessly divided opposition and

---

[7] A major scandal of the Peñaranda administration had involved a cabinet minister who sold visas, at fees of $1,000 and more, to several thousand European Jews. The refugees settled in La Paz, Cochabamba, and other cities, set up businesses in competition with Bolivians, and excited considerable anti-Semitism.

expected to install its candidate easily. The MNR's choice for president was the soft-spoken ex-professor Víctor Paz Estenssoro, leader of the 1943 revolt, who since 1946 had enjoyed comfortable exile in Argentina (where, according to his critics, he had absorbed too much of the philosophy of dictator Perón). And for vice-president, the MNR put up Hernán Siles. When Paz and Siles surprised the country by polling 45 per cent of the votes, the army—regarding them as a dangerous team—installed a military junta which ruled awkwardly for eleven months.

In April, 1952, an MNR-inspired revolt broke out in La Paz, with labor boss Juan Lechín and politician Hernán Siles in command, backed by the *carabineros* (the national military police), the tin miners, and various student and civilian groups. (By one count, this was the 179th revolution of Bolivia's history.) After raging for three days, during which 2,000 or 3,000 were killed, the battle was won when the regular army was routed by the well-armed tin miners, who thereby became the most powerful single group in the country. The MNR took over the government, recalled Paz Estenssoro from Buenos Aires to serve as president, and named Siles as vice-president—thus preserving an aura of constitutionality, as both men were clearly the choice of the voters in the 1951 elections. Variously denounced as a Communist or a *peronista,* Paz seemed to be the ablest, the most honest—though perhaps in foreign eyes the most unpalatable—president in Bolivia's history. After hesitating for three months, Washington concluded that Paz would serve as a safety valve against more radical elements and granted him recognition. The "National Revolution"—committed to sweeping social and economic reforms—had arrived.

The twelve years of the National Revolution (1952–64) were dominated by the MNR, which, in turn, was dominated by Paz Estenssoro. When the MNR took power in 1952, four men shared the responsibility: Paz himself; Juan Lechín, the leftist boss of the miners; Hernán Siles Zuazo, a moderate dominated by Paz; and the right-wing Walter Guevara Arze. These unlikely confederates made a pact by which they would take turns in the presidency. Paz served from 1952–56, with Siles as his vice-president. Then Siles got his turn, 1956–60—but with Paz never far behind the scenes. With the approach of the 1960 elections, however, it became clear that Paz—probably convinced that he was the ablest of the lot—would hold onto the reins of the Revolution himself. Guevara Arze, who had confidently expected the top post himself, broke with Paz and the MNR, went into exile, organized forces in opposition to his erstwhile colleague. Paz was elected in 1960, and again in June, 1964 (we will have more to say on that irregular procedure later), and served until he was ousted from office in November, 1964. Thus the National Revolution, for better or worse, was Paz's revolution.

The Revolution made swift progress after Paz took over the government in April, 1952. The first edict, signed on August 2, granted suffrage to all men and women over the age of twenty-one (hitherto only literate males, about 7 per cent of the population, could vote). Henceforth voting in all elections was done with colored ballots for the sake of those who could not read. Local units of the MNR were promptly established in chief centers of population, on the great haciendas, and in the principal mines, for the guidance of the citizenry. Then came the complete dismantling of the regular army: all officers and enlisted men were dismissed and their arms distributed among the peasants. The new peasant militia and the already armed tin miners were expected to rise to the defense of the government in the event of counter-revolution—thus, supposedly, abolishing forever the military *coup d'état* as a political tool. In this fashion—Paz announced—the Revolution had transformed a feudal society into a civilian state dominated by the MNR, buttressed by the miners and the peasants, and the "rule of the people" was a reality.

The next objective was land for the landless peasants. Certainly the feudal latifundia pattern cried for redress: according to the 1950 census, holdings of 2,471 acres or more—some 92 per cent of all the usable land—were in the hands of 6.3 per cent of the *hacendados;* and the Indians who worked on the land were no more than serfs, overworked, half-starved, beaten at the will of their masters. Land reform had been a prime commitment in the MNR platform for years; and upon assuming office Paz appointed an Agrarian Reform Commission to study the problem and to make recommendations. But the peasants were not inclined to wait for any such gradual solution. To understand the mood of the peasants in 1952, one must look at least as far back as the Chaco War, when the Indian peasants were impressed into the service of their "nation"—a brand new concept for those bitterly poor souls who knew nothing but the subservient isolated life of drudgery on the haciendas. Fighting alongside *cholos* and university students, the Indians were exposed to ideas of nationhood and equality—ideas which they were never to forget. Furthermore, they met other Indians who shared their plight of serfdom; and their new awareness of being abused not as individuals but as a group led to attempts—as far back as the 1930's—to organize unions or *sindicados* through which they hoped to air their grievances against the landowners. Although suppressed by the *hacendados,* the *sindicados* developed strong leadership in the 1940's, and by 1952 they were ready to take full advantage of the Revolution. As soon as the MNR toppled the old regime, thousands of Indians simply took possession of the lands they wanted, using the guns allotted to them by the new government to drive off their masters. Thus a large measure of "land reform" was an accomplished fact by the time the Agrarian Commission was ready to act.

On August 2, 1953, a formal decree was issued legalizing the seizures already made and outlining procedure for further redistribution. The former owners were theoretically protected in possession of certain minimum holdings. Also, they were to be paid for confiscated lands with bonds: that was also purely theoretical, as the bonds were never issued—and they would have been worthless anyway, with the headlong drop in the value of the national currency. The formal distribution of land was pursued with vigor, incompetence, and riotous dishonesty. There were never enough surveyors and lawyers to assure a fair allotment of titles. Furthermore, the Indians who got their land and the tools to work it were unprepared for the responsibility, and they were almost immediately subjected to a new set of tyrants —self-appointed political bosses who organized the ignorant peasants for their own profit, imposing cruel levies upon all products moving in and out of the farming communities, exacting payments from their victims. Some peasants gained a new sense of dignity, others floundered, as poor, or poorer than they had been before. Reporting in 1963 on the first decade of land reform, Paz announced that titles to land had been granted to about 65 per cent of the 134,000 families who worked on the great haciendas—a figure which invites skepticism. But, at best, the hard fact remains that there never was land enough on the bleak and barren *altiplano.* The only clear hope for the landless lay in the transfer of thousands of families to the fertile *yungas* (the valleys draining northeast into the Amazon system) and to the Oriente (the eastern lowlands toward Brazil and Paraguay). Paz and his associates made honest efforts to carry out such a program of re-settlement, providing homesteads of 123 acres for each settler in the Oriente. But it was no easy task to transfer Indian peasants, who had never been more than exploited serfs, to their new status as freeholders. There was not capital enough, nor were there technicians enough, to arrange necessary financing and oversight of these many new farmers. Nor was it easy to uproot families who were accustomed to the thin air of the *altiplano,* 12,000 or more feet above the sea, and to move them down to such areas as the warm lush region of Santa Cruz, near sea level. In spite of the difficulties, estimates of the number of people actually resettled in the Oriente during the twelve years of the Revolution run as high as 200,000.

Meanwhile, in October 1952, the ax fell on the "Big Three" mining companies: Patiño, controlling 44 per cent of the tin output, of which 28 per cent was owned by American interests; Hochschild, producing 25 per cent of the tin, and largely Chilean-owned; Aramayo, accounting for 7 per cent of the tin, Swiss- and English-owned. There had been rising popular anger against the tin operators—especially against the Patiño family, of which three generations had been living in Europe superbly fed and housed by the money earned for them by the miners, who were lucky to get 60 cents a day, who lived in filth and worked under savagely primitive conditions. A luxurious palace, built (but never occupied) by Simón Patiño in the pleasant city of Cochabamba, at the comfortable altitude of 8,400 feet, stood as a bitter monument to the exploitation of the miners. (It was charged that Patiño's personal income was larger than the national budget.) A chief article of faith of the MNR and of Paz Estenssoro was seizure of the properties of the tin industry, long supplier of 15 to 20 per cent of the world's tin—and 60 to 70 per cent of Bolivia's government revenue. And now Paz—flanked by Juan Lechín, the rich and able boss of the miners—ordered the transfer of all tin-mining properties to the state. The signing of the expropriation was staged with effective pageantry at Catavi, the scene of Peñaranda's bloody massacre of miners in 1942. Paz promised full compensation to the companies (a promise partially fulfilled with money borrowed from the American government).

The tin properties were entrusted to a government monopoly, COMIBOL (*Corporación Minera de Bolivia*); but the true bosses of the mines were now the miners, and the boss of the miners was the redoubtable Juan Lechín. Lechín and the unions were more interested in wages and endless fringe benefits for the miners than they were in the solvency of the industry. The mines were hopelessly overstaffed, and Lechín not only insisted upon reinstating miners who had been laid off for political activity in the years before the Revolution, but continued to resist any effort on the part of COMIBOL to reduce the bulging ranks of the miners. Furthermore, he instituted a procedure called *Control obrero* whereby the unions participated in the management of the mines. The miners had their own "commissars" in every mine, to oversee the technicians, with the result that most of the foreign technicians, announcing that they could not work under such dictation, quit the job, leaving the mines in the woefully inexperienced hands of the miners themselves. During the twelve years of the National Revolution, Bolivia's tin industry floundered through crisis after crisis. Production fell off sharply,[8] and prices on the world market were almost always below the cost of mining the tin: the world price for tin in 1961, for example, was $1.20 per pound, while the cost of turning out that pound in Bolivia stood at about $1.27; and COMIBOL was losing about $9 million a year. Sporadic attempts to reduce the number of miners met with violent opposition from the unions and were only partly successful. Meanwhile mine equipment, always obsolete and unsafe, steadily deteriorated. In 1961, COMIBOL finally agreed to a rehabilitation plan, called *Operación triangular,* by which West German interests, the Inter-American Development Bank, and the United States government would furnish $38 million for modernization of equipment and for exploration for new mines. In return, COMIBOL agreed to lay off several thousand excess workers, to put an end to labor's dictation in the management of the mines, and to invite a German firm to reorganize mine operations. Serious strikes in 1963 protested the plan, but Paz was firm; and the program, partially fulfilled, brought a little improvement. But it was clear that tin mining offered slight hope to the ailing Bolivian economy.

Paz, a competent economist, sought to diversify Bolivia's economy. Modest experiments with new industries had limited success. A large sugar mill was constructed in the Santa Cruz area. Cement plants, food-processing plants, and factories for processing rubber were built. But industry seemed a remote hope in Bolivia, with its limited market, its lack of capital and technicians, its lack of power: Bolivia has no coal or iron, and the production of electric power, woefully inadequate in 1952, was increased only some 50 per cent by 1962. Furthermore, any attempts at mass production

[8] Output of the tin mines in 1948 before expropriation, was 37,935 metric tons (about 25 per cent of the world total); in 1958, after COMIBOL had been operating for six years, production fell to a low of 18,013 metric tons (about 13 per cent of the world total), after which there was some recovery.

awaited an increase in the domestic market. The most hopeful venture was the development of the petroleum industry, which was entrusted to the government monopoly company YPFB (*Yacimientos Petrolíferos Fiscales Bolivianos*). Production increased more than fivefold between 1952 and 1955, making the country self-sufficient in petroleum with some to spare for export. Lacking the financial resources to develop this potential, the government turned to the outside for help. Beginning in 1956, generous contracts were made with foreign oil companies for exploration and exploitation. The results of much of the exploration were unspectacular, but a Bolivian subsidiary of the Gulf Oil Corporation located promising new deposits in the Santa Cruz area, spending $80 million on exploration and drilling, and allotting an additional $25 million for extending the pipeline— already partially installed by YPFB—from Santa Cruz to Arica on the Pacific. Gulf was actually exporting petroleum by 1967.

Drawing up the balance sheet on twelve years of the National Revolution invites comparison with Mexico's Revolution in the 1910's and 1920's: it was revolution in a hurry, revolution by proclamation, revolution without blueprint. To be sure, it was a revolution from which there was no turning back: the *campesinos* would never again submit to serfdom; and Bolivians had become aware of their assets, and had gained some vision of what could be done to develop them. But the government paid dearly for giving too much power to the labor unions, especially those of the tin miners, who, understandably, were never minded to subordinate their interests to national goals. And the bold land reform program, badly handled and halting, aggravated the problem of inadequate food production: the peasants, endowed with land of their own, tended to produce more generously for their own needs, but—having no understanding of cash profits—produced less for sale in the cities than had their former masters. The increasing food shortages, causing prices to double and redouble, plus the waning productivity of the mines, accelerated the forces of inflation which was reflected in the dizzy fall of the national currency: in 1950, the boliviano sold for 60 to the American dollar; and by the end of 1956 it had reached the astronomical figure of 12,000. Thanks to the stabilization plan of Hernán Siles, put into effect on January 1, 1957, this riotous inflation was halted; and in January, 1960, with the help of the International Monetary Fund, the boliviano was steadied at 11,885.[9]

Furthermore, Bolivia's Revolution—again like Mexico's—was woefully short of honest and competent leaders. Plagued by *personalismo*, the MNR finally fell apart. Disillusionment, for many, came in Paz Estenssoro's first term in office (1952–56), when opponents of the MNR were brutally repressed. Hernán Siles (1956–60) brought some easing of the tyranny: the press was freer, critics spoke their mind, and there seemed some hope that the MNR would survive. However, with Paz's highhanded pushing aside of Guevara Arze in the presidential election of 1960, the ranks of the MNR

---

9 In 1963 the currency was reorganized: the new unit was the peso, worth 1,000 bolivianos, which has remained steady at 11.88 to the dollar.

were seriously weakened, and Paz slipped into the role of virtual dictator. Paz's vice-president was Juan Lechín, boss of the miners; but clashes between the two men over operations of the tin mines led to an open break by the end of 1963. Meanwhile, Paz continued to play the tyrant, repressing dissent by violence, punishing refractory aides by exile or imprisonment. The army—dismantled in 1952 but reorganized a year later as a tool of the MNR and liberally supported by the United States in recent years—had become Paz's chief reliance. Elections loomed again in 1964, and Paz, constitutionally blocked from reelection, compelled his subservient congress to amend the constitution, permitting him to run again. The election was conducted under the protecting cloud of martial law, with Paz supported only by the army, the police, and the peasants of the *altiplano*—to whom he sounded the familiar battle cry: It is my revolution, it is I who gave you land, vote for me or you will lose your land. (Paz was further fortified by the open and enthusiastic support of the United States: during his campaign he appeared again and again on platforms graced by the presence of the American ambassador and the representative of the U.S. AID Mission.) The rival parties, well subdued, refused to take part in the obviously rigged affair, and Paz was "unanimously" elected in June, 1964.

One by one Paz had lost his ablest allies. Guevara Arze had been dropped when he presumed to aspire to the presidency in 1960. Two days before the 1964 elections, Hernán Siles had shouted "*personalismo*" and joined the already disenchanted Juan Lechín in a hunger strike to protest the "dictatorship" of Paz. On the eve of the inauguration, Lechín was set upon in the open streets of La Paz by a mob which included members of the political police, and was beaten mercilessly. In September, Siles was exiled to Paraguay. Paz remained unperturbed: "Some people are necessary for the early part of a revolution," he said, "others for a later stage. When the revolution enters the constructive period, these people aren't necessary."

By October, 1964, President Paz Estenssoro was in deep trouble—and the core of the trouble was the army, which Paz himself had created but which now held him a virtual prisoner. He had been forced to accept as his vice-president air force General René Barrientos, but Barrientos turned on Paz within weeks after they took office. Criticism of Paz had brought press censorship, which in turn provoked student demonstrations and strikes by miners and factory workers. Barrientos—and the army—sided with the strikers; and Paz in desperation ordered the armed *campesinos* to enter the fray, and soon all Bolivia was in turmoil.

THE SECOND REPUBLIC, 1964–

The National Revolution ended on November 4, 1964, when General Alfredo Ovando Candia, commander in chief of the armed forces, summoned President Paz Estenssoro and said, "I am taking you either to the cemetery or to the airport." Paz chose the airport, and was shortly on his way to exile in Lima. The government was now in the hands of General Ovando and General René Barrientos, vice-president of the nation.

The brash Barrientos, famed for his skill as a dare-devil aviator, flew madly about the country, exhorting, captivating the peasants by speaking with them in their native Quechua and wearing Indian dress. He shoved Ovando aside, and played the presidential role unhindered. For six months he ruled by cajolery and coercion. The government was a shambles, as Paz's men were evicted from office. Strikes in the mines were violent, and in May, 1965, Barrientos decided to rid himself of the labor boss, Juan Lechín: that troublemaker and several of his aides were loaded on a plane bound for Paraguay. Barrientos promised stiff discipline of the miners. Then came fresh stoppages of work, the calling in of troops, with gunfire and bloody losses.

The armed forces, restive under all the confusion and bloodshed, were appeased somewhat in May, 1965, by the installation of a "co-presidency," with Barrientos and Ovando sharing presidential powers. Orders signed by both men now went out raising the salaries of the armed forces by 40 per cent, reducing the salaries of all miners, and giving COMIBOL the right to hire and fire at will. And to Washington went appeals—also signed by both presidents—for $5 million to put displaced miners at work on building roads, and for a long-term loan of $100 million. (And with these appeals they sounded the well-worn refrain: the Communists will get us if you don't bail us out.) By July, 1965, the co-Presidents were trumpeting news of "the Second Republic . . . a new fatherland . . . free from fear and poverty . . . archaic structures will be renewed with a new sense of social justice, political balance, and a just economic order."

At year's end, 1965, came the announcement that there would indeed be an election in July, 1966. And in January, 1966, René Barrientos resigned from the co-presidency and announced that he would be a candidate for the presidency in July. Then followed a six-month campaign, complete with bands and shouting, in which Barrientos flew from city to city and to the most remote villages, embracing *campesinos* and sharing their *chicha* (as corrosive a liquid as was ever brewed), and carrying the good news of higher wages, better houses, and all the gifts of revolution. Strikes still broke out in the mines, but the miners had lost their leaders, and they were no match for the armed soldiers.

The election of July, 1966, was a stunning success. No opposition candidates could stand out against the exuberant Barrientos, and he and his backers won not only the presidency but a majority in the congress. As Barrientos was installed in office on August 6, 1966, there were reminders from bystanders that since 1934 the batting average for four-year presidential terms had been about two years. But Barrientos's sense of humor did not fail him. "If the government does not succeed," he confided to reporters on election day, "then the military should intervene." And so it might. No one was placing or accepting any bets.

Trouble continued unabated in the bleak and battered nation during Barrientos's first year in office. The tin miners were angry. To be sure,

COMIBOL—the government tin monopoly which had lost money with dismal regularity since its founding in 1952—actually reported a small profit at the end of 1966. But it was profit bought by high-handed repression. The labor unions had been smashed, and the wages of the miners— whose rolls had been reduced from 40,000 to 23,000—had been drastically cut. In April and May, 1967, violence broke out in the mines, with workers demanding increased wages and the reinstatement of their unions; but the soldiers moved in with tear gas and gunfire, and the miners were subdued. Then, as agitators against Barrientos were hustled off to jail, the university students, recoiling against this praetorian rule, staged protest marches— but they were silenced by the police. Furthermore, the President was confronted by disaffection within his somewhat fictional Bolivian Revolutionary Front, as some of his hitherto faithful colleagues deserted him.

Fresh trouble came for Barrientos as bands of guerrillas (calling themselves The National Army of Liberation) appeared in the lowlands in March, 1956, 400–500 miles southeast of La Paz. One detachment operated within twenty miles of the city of Santa Cruz. There was no clear agreement as to the number of the troublemakers, and as to just who they were. Official spokesmen for the La Paz government talked of a total of 500 or more men, and asserted that the bands included Cubans, Argentines, Brazilians, Peruvians. But unofficial observers guessed that there were actually no more than five or six dozen disturbers, mostly Bolivian. Some 600 Bolivian troops pursued the interlopers without much success: the guerrillas seemed to have able leaders, and they also had more modern weapons than the Bolivian soldiers who hunted them down. Rumors spread that the guerrillas got their guns and money from Castro's Cuba, and it was widely believed that the operation was directed by Castro's Argentine lieutenant "Che" Guevara, who had disappeared from Cuba in 1965—but there was no evidence to support that theory by mid-1967. All that was clear was that slight progress had been made to wipe out the rebels. Operating as they were far from the capital city, they presented no immediate threat to the national government, unless they should indeed spark a revolt which might spread over the country. The running battle was a stalemate by September, 1967. (See note p. 425.)

Meanwhile, Barrientos's good friends in Washington continued in their generosity: not only did they send arms, food, helicopters, and trained jungle fighters to buttress the Bolivian military who were tracking down the guerrillas, but they continued—as they had since 1945—to supply dollars to bail out the chronically unbalanced national budget.

Despite the largess from Washington, Barrientos made a bold bid for independence by refusing to attend the summit meeting of American presidents in Punta del Este in April, 1967 (greatly to the chagrin of President Lyndon Johnson) because there was no place on its agenda for consideration of Bolivia's demand for access to the Pacific—and this stand of their President mollified Bolivian pride.

The nimble Barrientos seemed to live a charmed life. Eight attempts to assassinate him had failed, and he was still in office in September, 1967.

BOLIVIA'S PROSPECTS

What does the future hold for the people of this bleak country? Can it make the leap from its primitive and feudal past into the twentieth century? Out of Bolivia's 3.7 million people (1966), perhaps 500,000 can read a newspaper and are politically conscious. A few lucky Bolivians have money —a handful who have managed to retain their haciendas, a few entrepreneurs in business and mining, and some adroit politicians who turn their power to wealth. The middle classes are no more than a thin slice— and their "white collars" are definitely ragged. There are about 23,000 miners—whose wages are beggarly; whose recreation consists of two-cent movies and alcoholism; who die or are crippled by silicosis before they are thirty-five; and whose children—perhaps two out of five of them—die in their first year. And there are a few thousand workers in a few small and inefficient industries. But about two-thirds of all the people, almost all Indians, live from the soil. While many now take pride in their possession of a few acres of land, the Revolution has worked no miracles, least of all for the *campesino* on the high *altiplano,* whose thin rocky soil yields grudgingly. And the workers in the fields are still lucky to be paid with a little corn and potatoes and a handful of coca leaves which, chewed constantly, deaden the appetite. These are the Bolivian people, with an average per capita income of some $144, the lowest in all South America.

Statistics on Bolivia's population are meaningless: most Bolivians live and die unnoticed and uncounted in their scattered communities. But some conclusions are inescapable. The Bolivian population is probably as nearly stationary as that of any nation in the modern world. The birth rate on the *altiplano* seems to be low (although no accurate figures have been gathered) as compared with other areas of Latin America—some geneticists suggest that the cold of that inhospitable region does not encourage fecundity. In the lower stretches, breeding is more generous. Everywhere, the death rate is appalling. Infant mortality, infallible index to the well-being of a people, is among the highest in South America: unofficial estimates (sharply contradicting official figures) suggest that perhaps a third of the babies die in their first year. Bolivians are ill-housed, with virtually no sewers or sanitary facilities for more than a handful of city dwellers. Bolivians are ill-fed, consuming an average of less than 2,000 calories a day (the Latin American average, not high, is 2,570); it is a rare child who gets any milk, and the milk he gets is often lethal. And the Bolivians are a sick people: contaminated water spreads intestinal diseases; tuberculosis and malaria take cruel toll. Physicians and hospitals are reserved for the privileged few: in all Bolivia, there is 1 physician for every 3,700 people and 1 hospital bed for every 558. The illiterate masses take their sick to village *curanderos,* medicine men, and buy magical herbs and strange charms in the market— the dried foetus of a llama, stirred in milk, is warranted to perform mighty cures.

Culturally, Bolivia offers a meager exhibit. Some positive steps have

THE INDIAN LANDS OF THE ANDES

been taken in education; but while there are schools for some whites and *cholos,* there are only a few for the Indians in rural communities. The University of San Andrés boasts a fourteen-story building of glass and steel in the heart of La Paz, but it has few books and professors. The Church enjoys slight prestige. Although never persecuted as in some other nations, the Church has suffered under the general turmoil and poverty of the nation, and lacks a well-trained priesthood. The entrance of some foreign priests, notably the Maryknoll fathers, has been stimulating. A few Protestants, admitted after the turn of the century, have rendered good account of themselves. The Methodist schools in La Paz enjoy fine standing, and the hospitals of the Seventh Day Adventists are useful.

Economically, Bolivia is "a beggar sitting on a pile of gold." Assets include large untapped deposits of tin, tungsten, antimony, copper, lead, zinc, gold, silver, and petroleum; the rich soil of the *yungas* and the lower plains, capable of producing the meat, fruits, and grains which Bolivians lack; the fine woods, rubber, quinine, oils, and nuts in the *selvas;* and abundant water power to be turned into electric current. Exploitation of this varied wealth waits upon the services of trained technicians and engineers, upon man power, upon capital. It also depends upon the improvement of transportation, especially between the *altiplano* and the rich food-producing areas of the eastern lowlands, the Oriente, which comprise some 70 per cent of the nation's territory. Once virtually self-sufficient in foodstuffs, after World War I Bolivia became an importer of meat, rice, sugar, and other items necessary to feed her people. Ironically, this change was brought about largely by the building of railroads connecting La Paz on the *altiplano* with the outside world—to Arica and Antofagasta on the Pacific coast, to Jujuy in northern Argentina: for the goods produced in the lowlands, brought to the *altiplano* by llama or mule along tortuous mountain trails, could no longer compete with the cheaper goods brought in by rail; and, deprived of its markets, agricultural production in the Oriente stagnated. One of the more successful ventures of recent years has been the strategic 317-mile highway between Santa Cruz in the southern Oriente and Cochabamba (which is connected with La Paz by rail). This highway— completed in 1954 with United States aid—has not only opened up a hopeful area for the resettlement of landless *campesinos,* but has also made accessible the rich sugar-, cotton-, and rice-producing area of Santa Cruz. Also under construction is a road through the *yungas* to the province of Beni in the northern Oriente, which is rich in tropical hardwoods and wild rubber (said to have greater elasticity than any other substance in the world); and which has great potential as a cattle-raising—and perhaps meat-exporting—area.

The government, in the years of the National Revolution, made little progress in increasing food production. Even the supplies of grain from the United States reached high Bolivia only with difficulty: the railroads linking La Paz with ports on the Pacific, with inadequate and deteriorated rolling stock, were unable to furnish transport, and many of those supplies piled up on the wharfs. Another aggravating factor was the smuggling of foodstuffs: cattle were driven from the Beni into Peru; agricultural products of prime importance to Bolivia were smuggled into Brazil; and even foodstuffs sent as emergency aid by the United States were resold to outsiders.

Bolivia's relations with her near neighbors have not been greatly troubled since the days of the Chaco War. There was an angry quarrel with Chile in the 1950's over the waters of the Río Lauca: Bolivia claimed that Chile was exploiting that stream before it entered Bolivia, broke relations with Chile, and withdrew from the OAS in protest—but that minor unpleasantness was settled in 1965. Meanwhile, Bolivia watched Brazil and Argentina with a wary eye. Brazil, which in 1953 completed a railroad connecting her border city Corumbá with Santa Cruz, presented the threat of economic penetration of that rich area. Argentina, laying plans for a railroad spur connecting Santa Cruz with Salta, also aroused similar fears. But both Brazil and Argentina were too busy at home to indulge in imperialistic aggression.

Bolivia has enjoyed pleasant and lucrative relations with the United States, especially since 1952. Loans and grants in excess of $400 million have poured into the La Paz treasury—more dollars per capita than have gone to any other Latin American nation. Much of the money was well spent: a prime exhibit was the highway from Cochabamba to Santa Cruz; other millions went into hospitals, schools, health projects, technical aid to agriculture. But much of the money was used to balance budgets which suffered from unproductive mines, wasteful administration, and official corruption. In supporting Bolivia's National Revolution, Washington found itself in the unfamiliar role of extending financial relief to a nation which had expropriated land, oil properties, and tin mines with no more than a gesture toward compensation to the owners. But having decided in 1952 to back Paz Estenssoro, on the theory that he was the surest protection against the extremists of the left, Washington remained faithful. When Paz's government presented its ten-year plan to the Alliance for Progress in 1961 —boldly promising an end to economic stagnation, improved living standards for all Bolivians, and economic self-sufficiency by 1971—Washington applauded; and the plan, approved in early 1962, was the second (Colombia was the first) to receive the coveted accolade from the Alliance. Three presidents—Eisenhower, Kennedy, and Johnson—gave full-throated support to the Revolution, making it clear that Paz was "our man." Typical of this international esteem was President Kennedy's greeting to Paz when the Bolivian President visited Washington in October, 1963: "What you are attempting to do in your own country," said Kennedy, "is what I hope all of us in all our countries in this hemisphere would try to do for our people." But the United States proved elastic: no matter how much official unhappiness there may have been at another military takeover when Barrientos and Ovando toppled Paz in November, 1964, Washington speedily recognized the new regime; and when Barrientos was duly elected in mid-1966, President Johnson warmly welcomed the Bolivian President-elect to Washington in July. The American President lauded Barrientos for his country's efforts to improve the lot of the humble Indians. Barrientos responded in proper fashion, praising President Johnson for leading "the battle for liberty, justice, and progress." Barrientos, at luncheon, proposed the toast of *"Salud"* (good health) to Johnson. An unnamed guest audibly whispered the second part of the traditional toast ". . . *y pesetas*" (and money, too). It was a rude touch, but had pith. Bolivia, we may conclude, is an expensive friend. It will cost many more American *pesetas* to assure Bolivia of *salud*.

The reading of Bolivia's history and the scanning of her current dilemmas prompts pity rather than blame. Politically, Bolivia is an abyss. Parties are mythical: Paz's MNR disappeared in a cloud of dust when Paz was ejected. The rightist Falange is impotent. The "Second Republic" of Barrientos appears to be but one more bit of *personalista* trumpeting. As a government, Bolivia is unformed and chaotic. There is slight tradition of honest and competent officialdom. Even the casual visitor to La Paz, Cochabamba, or Oruro cannot escape the feeling of hopelessness: in the simplest dealings with government officials, he becomes involved in endless detail and much paper work, and feels like a clumsy Alice in a Wonderland which needs a city manager.

The indomitable Queen Victoria had one solution for this nation. In 1868, when braggart dictator Melgarejo insulted the British minister by tying him on a donkey, facing him backwards, and riding him around the public square of the capital, the Queen called for a map, drew rough lines across the offending country, and declared: "Bolivia no longer exists." But Bolivia does exist, and holds threat or promise for the entire company of American states. If she continues on her present course, her people will find no relief from their suffering, and the tranquillity of the hemisphere will be clouded.

PART VIII

Chile

Chile is a land of dramatic variety and contrast: in its geography, with swift passage from sea to towering mountains, from dense forests to arid desert; in its public life, where the usual orderliness of the people is sometimes marred by a violence characteristic of their Araucanian forebears; in its politics, where a fierce appetite for democracy battles Spanish feudalism; and in its cultural life, where the intellectual prowess of a few contrasts vividly with the ignorance of the masses.

 [*Chapter 34*]

CHILE: THE FORMATIVE YEARS,
1810–91

"The land where the earth ends," as the Indians of Upper Peru described Chile to conqueror Pedro de Valdivia, has the most grotesque geographical pattern of any nation on earth. Subercaseaux understates it when he writes of *Chile o una loca geografía* ("a crazy geography"). While it stretches lengthwise 2,600 miles from the tip of Cape Horn to the Peruvian border, it averages little more than 100 miles in width. If Chile were placed horizontally across the United States, it would connect New York and San Francisco, but it would slip easily between Chicago and St. Louis on the way; or, turned up on end, it would reach from Guatemala to Hudson Bay. Chile, with an area of 286,397 square miles, is somewhat larger than Texas.

This Chilean ribbon is ruffled on both edges: on the east by the towering cordillera of the Andes, on the west by the low coastal range. The Andes have 300 peaks higher than the highest peak in continental United States, 36 of them higher than Alaska's McKinley; and the most stately of all is Chile's (and Argentina's) Aconcagua, the highest mountain in the Western Hemisphere, which stands 23,834 feet above the sea. By contrast, Chile's western range seldom exceeds 3,000 feet. Some thirty rivers (all unnavigable) lace the country from east to west, carrying the mountains' melting snow to form the oases of the north, to irrigate the farm lands of the central valley, and to rush in torrents through the forests of the south. Of the total national area, only 3.5 per cent is arable.

There are four Chiles: the northern desert, where it never rains; the central valley, where it rains in winter; the forest lands in the south, where it rains all the time;[1] and "Atlantic" Chile, which spans the Strait of Magellan and embraces Tierra del Fuego and southern Antarctica. The northern desert, stretching from the Peruvian border to Coquimbo, a third of the national domain and rich in minerals, houses only 6.5 per cent of all Chileans. At the southern end, Atlantic Chile, with 7 per cent of the national territory, affords grazing land for sheep and a home for about 1 per

---

[1] A word for the literalist: there is an occasional raindrop in the north, and there are some sunny days in the south.

cent of the people. Forest Chile, reaching north from Tierra del Fuego to Concepción and the Bío-Bío River, comprises 40 per cent of the territory, with lakes as lovely as Switzerland's, fiords as fine as Norway's, and forests untouched by ax or fire; here live about 28 per cent of the people, almost all of them north of the island of Chiloé. Central or "Mediterranean" Chile, the heartland of the nation, embraces only 18 per cent of the total domain but includes the chief cities, the most productive farms, most of the industry, and about 65 per cent of the population. Perhaps a better breakdown would include Central Chile with that part of "forest" Chile which lies between the Bío-Bío River and the island of Chiloé, because this combined area is the productive Chile, with 30 per cent of the national domain and about 91 per cent of all Chileans. The regions to the north and the south are almost empty frontier lands.

The 8.6 million Chileans (1965), a homogeneous people, are chiefly a blend of Spaniard and Araucanian. A few old families boast pure Spanish blood. There are more than 50,000 survivors of the Araucanians, but they play little part in Chilean life. The few thousand Negro slaves inherited from colonial days have long since been assimilated. For more than a century, immigration from Europe has been steady but scant, bringing in, altogether, scarcely more than 100,000 English, Germans, Irish, French, Italians, Yugoslavs, and Arabs. However, the contribution of these foreigners to Chilean life has far outrun their numbers. For the most part, they have become Chileans, intermarried freely, and discarded their native languages. One finds Chileans with German names—umlauts and all—who speak no word of the tongue of their fathers. The process of assimilation is reminiscent of that in Minnesota or Wisconsin. Prominent Chilean families bear such names as Edwards, Cox, Körner, Braun, Swinburne, Balfour, Schnacke, Frei, and Müller. The one conspicuous exception to the incorporation of the foreigner into national life is the isolated colony south of Valdivia where some 30,000 to 40,000 first-, second-, and third-generation Germans maintain their thriving businesses and farms, and retain their German language and customs.

COLONY TO FREE REPUBLIC, 1810–17

After three centuries as colonial appendage to the Viceroyalty of Peru, Chile was in 1810 the least treasured of Spain's outposts in South America. Remote, yielding little mineral treasure, and with few tractable Indian slaves, Chile was neglected as a second-class colony. As the colonial period drew to a close, its total population was little more than 500,000, including some 100,000 unassimilated Indians in the south, about 150,000 creoles, 20,000 *peninsulares,* 250,000 mestizos, 4,000 Negroes, and a few British, French, Italian, German, and other peoples. A few powerful families, among whom Basques were conspicuous, owned the major share of the good land (as they still do in 1967).[2] The class structure was feudal:

[2] The reader will note how many of the chief figures in political, cultural, and business life bear names with *rr* and *ch,* which usually reveal a Basque inheritance—Larraín, Errázuriz, Lastarria, Echaurren, Echenique, Echeverría, and many others.

Chile and Argentina

the masters held the land, while their workers were hard-driven vassals.[3] The colonial Chileans were a rural people: Santiago was an unimpressive city of 30,000, while its nearest competitors were villages with populations of less than 5,000. City streets were unlighted and unpaved, and country roads were rutted trails. Cultural life had lagged. There were no printing presses, few schools, and no public libraries. The University of San Felipe, founded in 1758, chiefly a law school, was responsible for a few notable intellectuals. The Church had been weakened by the expulsion of the Jesuits in 1767. Economic life, long subservient to Lima, had improved somewhat after 1759 under the intelligent policies of Charles III. Royal governors, usually mediocre under the Hapsburgs, improved in quality under the Bourbons in the eighteenth century. The best of these was Ambrosio O'Higgins, the first famous Irishman in American politics, now chiefly remembered as the father of the hero of Chilean independence, Bernardo O'Higgins.

Chile's progress from colonial status to independence included four stormy periods between 1810 and 1818. The first was the brief rule of a junta appointed by a *cabildo abierto* in September, 1810, which, after the customary genuflection to "their most adored monarch, Ferdinand VII," decreed free trade, dissolved the royal *audiencia,* and entered into relations with the junta in Buenos Aires. Juan Martínez de Rozas, intellectual mentor of independence, was the most influential member of that first junta. An attractive figure among the early revolutionists was Juan Egaña, who, in 1811, boldly called for a federation of the liberated peoples of America—his declaration antedating by four years similar proposals by Simón Bolívar.

The second period, 1811 to 1814, was marked by internecine quarrels among Chilean patriots. A royalist plot to restore colonial rule was countered by José Miguel Carrera, a hot-headed aristocrat of twenty-six who seized dictatorial power, refused to accept edicts from Spain, set up a printing press, founded a secondary school called the National Institute, opened a few primary schools, organized a public library, and adopted a national flag—all the while continuing to profess allegiance to Ferdinand. His despotic course incited the first families of Santiago to revolt under the leadership of Bernardo O'Higgins. Meanwhile, the Spanish forces in the south, augmented by fresh troops, marched on Santiago and in the battle of Rancagua in October, 1814, routed the troops of both Carrera and O'Higgins, forcing these rivals to seek safety on the other side of the Andes in Argentine Mendoza.

With the third phase, 1814 to 1817, the restoration of Spanish power, exercised with ruthless disregard of Chilean pride, convinced the Chileans that they must go their separate way. After Rancagua, says a Chilean historian, "The proconsuls of Spain, with their brutal despotism and stupid excesses, demonstrated to the creoles . . . the unreasonableness of

---

[3] The feudal society of Chile resembled that of medieval Europe more closely than did that of any other Latin American people: in Chile, as in medieval Europe, master and man were of the same racial composition; elsewhere in Latin America, the lord was usually white, while the serf was Indian or Negro.

Spanish authority, and the respect for the motherland changed to bitter hatred." Arbitrary arrests, repeal of the mild reforms of Martínez de Rozas and Carrera, and suppression of free speech stiffened the determination of Chileans to be free.

The fourth period was opened by the triumph of the patriots in 1817. José de San Martín, assembling his forces in western Argentina for the final blow against the Spaniards in Chile and Peru, welcomed his Chilean allies, picking O'Higgins rather than Carrera as his second-in-command.[4] In February, 1817, after the incredible march over the Andes, San Martín and O'Higgins with 5,000 men defeated the Spanish troops at Chacabuco. On February 12, 1818, Chile's independence was formally proclaimed, and two months later the decisive victory at Maipú confirmed Chile's freedom.

DICTATORSHIP AND ANARCHY, 1817–30

In February, 1817, three days after the initial victory at Chacabuco, a *cabildo abierto* attended by 210 leading citizens in Santiago named forty-one-year-old Bernardo O'Higgins as supreme director, a post which San Martín had wisely refused for himself. Born in Chillán, O'Higgins was the illegitimate son of a creole mother and the Irish Ambrosio O'Higgins, who had served first as governor of Chile and then as viceroy of Peru. Sent to England for his education, Bernardo there met the agitator Francisco de Miranda and became a firm advocate of Spanish American independence, a stand which prompted his royalist father to cut off his allowance. After his father's death in 1801, the young man returned to care for his inherited properties and came under the influence of the brilliant Martínez de Rozas. Bernardo O'Higgins was short and pudgy but energetic, with blue eyes and fair skin which betrayed his Irish ancestry. Inferior to his father in imagination and administrative skill, with less intellectual range than Martínez de Rozas, nevertheless, thanks to San Martín's backing, he was the principal creator of the Chilean nation.

During his stormy five-year rule, O'Higgins's contributions to Chilean security included: eviction of the Spanish forces from Chile, except for one garrison on the southern island of Chiloé; creation of a navy to harry Spanish ships; and cooperation with San Martín in preparing the expeditionary force which sailed north against Peru in 1820. He enlisted the services of Lord Cochrane, Scottish knight-errant whose passion for liberty was linked with greed for personal aggrandizement. Cochrane accepted O'Higgins's commission in 1818, raided Spanish shipping from southern Chile to Ecuador, and finally ferried San Martín's troops to Peru in 1820.[5]

---

4 Carrera was banished to Buenos Aires and was never allowed to return to Chile. After an unsuccessful attempt to organize a force in Buenos Aires, he sailed to the United States, secured three ships and some volunteers, but was blocked by Argentine authorities when he returned to Buenos Aires. Carrera and his two brothers were executed in Mendoza, probably by O'Higgins's orders.

5 Thomas Cochrane (1775–1860), Lord Cochrane, after a stormy career in the British Navy, was convicted of fraud and jailed. On his release, he launched upon a series

O'Higgins's stubborn support of San Martín and Cochrane, which included enlisting Chilean soldiers and levying high taxes, contributed materially to the overthrow of Spanish power in Peru, although the final credit for that triumph went to Simón Bolívar.

O'Higgins's popularity ebbed as quickly as it had flowed. The patricians of Santiago, no matter how enthusiastically they had hailed him at first, could not stomach a bastard son of an Irishman as the standard-bearer for their new nation. Good Conservatives and Catholics, they deplored his innovations in government. He abolished the numerous titles of nobility which they cherished, describing them as mere hieroglyphics which had no place in a free nation. He organized a "Legion of Merit," which was a French innovation for honoring men of genius without regard to social position.

The clergy deplored his interference with the Church: his insistence upon the nation's right of patronage over ecclesiastical appointments; his demand for tolerance of dissenters; his opening of a cemetery for non-Catholics. Some explained his policy toward the Church by the fact that he was a Freemason. Conservatives generally feared his cultural excursions. Backed by such intellectuals as Manuel de Salas, O'Higgins reestablished the National Institute, enlarged the National Library, founded primary schools and imported teachers of the Lancasterian group from England, insisted upon free entry of books, and encouraged newspapers. The wealthy, deploring increased taxes, opposed his improvements in sanitation, paving, and lighting of the cities. The landholders were outraged by his proposal to abolish the *mayorazgos* (entailed estates passed intact from father to eldest son), a commendable but futile attempt to divide the good lands among a greater number of families. The partisans of José Miguel Carrera charged O'Higgins with responsibility for the execution of that hero and his brothers. The failure of the Peruvian campaign under San Martín, in which most of the soldiers were Chileans, further discredited O'Higgins. And finally, in 1822, when a disastrous drought and a severe earthquake, perennial scourge of Chile, brought general suffering, the populace turned against him.

The first uprising was organized in southern Concepción by Ramón Freire, a hero of San Martín's campaigns. Revolt spread; and in February, 1823, O'Higgins, who a few months earlier had been "elected" to a further term of ten years, was forced by the pressure of Santiago aristocrats to resign. By order of Freire, he was compelled to face a judicial review of his acts in office (after the fashion of the *residencia* of Spanish colonial days), and though cleared of guilt, O'Higgins sailed to Peru, where he remained until his death in 1842.

The years from 1823 to 1830 were chaotic. Although the young nation had declared itself free from Spain in 1818, it had not yet decided

of spectacular crusades in the service of Chile, Brazil, and Greece. By 1842 he was restored to his rank in the British service, and he was made an admiral in 1854. Although bad-tempered and grasping, he was capable of great bravery and occasional self-abnegation.

whether it was to be a free republic or a constitutional monarchy, whether its government should be a loose federation of autonomous provinces or a highly centralized state under a strong president, or under what formula Church and state would live together. O'Higgins, convinced that fundamental social issues were more important than forms of government, had given little direction to political life. He had ruled without a congress, naming his own cabinet and governing by decree. He had, to be sure, promulgated new constitutions in 1818 and 1822, but they were as vague as the dictator himself. Freire, inducted in 1823, followed the same course; he had a new constitution drafted, then promptly abandoned it, installing himself as supreme director. In 1826 still another constitution was promulgated; it divided the nation into eight provinces and assigned to each a large measure of autonomy. This excursion into federalism, lasting two years, was Chile's one departure from strong centralism. Meanwhile, Freire fell in 1827. Francisco Pinto, who took his place, dictated another constitution in 1828; he was formally elected in 1829, but resigned in the face of a Conservative uprising organized in Concepción by General Joaquín Prieto. The civil war which ensued was settled by the battle of Lircay in April, 1830, an event which delivered the nation into Conservative control for the next thirty years.

Significant events had taken place during the riotous seven years from 1823 to 1830. Freire had ended slavery and evicted the last Spanish garrison from the island of Chiloé in 1826. But the period was chiefly significant for the crystallization of the two political parties which would determine national destiny for the rest of the century. During the decade after the first defiance of Spain in 1810, political loyalties had been highly personal; men had followed O'Higgins, Carrera, or some lesser leader. Now, under Freire, citizens rallied to the banner of the Conservatives or the Liberals. The Conservatives, enlisting landholders, high clergy, and the military, regarded themselves as the party of order and authority. Monarchical in spirit, they sought to continue the social and political traditions of colonial days under a strong centralized republic with a president whom they could control. The Liberals, vaguely imbued with French liberalism and British parliamentary ideals, sought government by constitution, talked of reform rather than authority, favored limitations upon the Church (while remaining good Catholics), and argued hazily for land reform. Each party was promptly tagged with labels which stuck for many years: the Conservatives were *pelucones,* "the bigwigs"; the Liberals were *pipiolos,*[6] "novices." But the Liberals suffered from a lack of leaders, for neither Freire nor Pinto was strong enough to carry their banner. The Conservatives had most of the best-trained men of the republic, including the astute Diego Portales, whom we must now consider.

---

[6] The word *pipiolo* was applied to vagrant workers who drifted from *fundo* to *fundo* and were not competent enough to hold permanent positions.

THE DOMINATION OF
THE CONSERVATIVES, 1830–61

The rout of the Liberals at Lircay delivered Chile into the hands of the *pelucones,* the landed aristocracy of the central valley, who for thirty years enforced their will with little opposition, imposed order upon unruly factions, contributed largely to economic and cultural advance, and won for the nation a position of respect among the new republics of Spanish America. The Conservatives furnished three presidents, each of whom served for two five-year terms: Joaquín Prieto in the 1830's, Manuel Bulnes in the 1840's, and Manuel Montt in the 1850's. But the strong man of that period was Diego Portales, who, though he refused any post higher than a cabinet position (which he would hold only briefly), was the virtual dictator until he was assassinated in 1837. His doctrine of government has continued as a force in Chilean political life.

Diego Portales, thirty-seven when called to serve as minister of interior, foreign affairs, war, and navy in the stopgap Conservative regime of 1829, had little to commend him as a leader of the people. Arrogant and openly contemptuous of the ragged *inquilinos* (farm workers) and *rotos* (the "broken ones") who toiled in the fields and on the docks, he spoke for the rich landholders and traders. "The people," he said, "must be given both bread and blows." Nor had anything in his boyhood and young manhood prepared him for such leadership. The son of a prosperous family, he had shown no love for learning. When other young men were riding after O'Higgins, Carrera, and San Martín in the fight for a free Chile, Portales, then seventeen, took no interest in their brave battles for ideals, and was seeking personal profit. By the time he was twenty-three, he had a lucrative trading business in the port city of Valparaíso. In 1824 dictator Freire granted his firm the monopoly control of tobacco, teas, and liquors—as trustees for servicing the loan of £1 million advanced by British bankers. This concession, an early episode in Chilean national mercantilism, stirred up a storm of abuse against both Freire and Portales, and was terminated two years later. The cries of the angry *pipiolos*—"the harebrained novices"—persuaded him that it was high time sound businessmen took a hand in politics. He forthwith started a newspaper in Valparaíso, bought a second one in Santiago, and preached his doctrine of "the religion of government" with such zest and conviction that he was credited with the defeat of the Liberals in 1829–30.

The paradoxical young dictator who controlled Chile from 1830 to 1837 was not a popular leader. He was haughty and overbearing, "with a pallid face, finely chiseled features, and intense blue eyes," relentless in ridicule and invective. The Chilean historian, Sotomayor Valdés, notes his "mingling of sagacity and obstinacy, wisdom and absurdity, pride and abnegation, gravity and picaresque humor, moral severity and libertine tendencies, a desire for power and a contempt for wealth, honors, and all the usual fruits of office."

Portales's mission was to impose order and unity upon an anarchic people. Dedicated to his "religion of government," he was contemptuous of the shibboleths of democracy, republicanism, freedom. A monarchist at heart, he sought, says the astute Chilean writer Alberto Edwards, "the moral and material restoration of the monarchy—not in its dynastic forms . . . but in its basic genius as the conserving force of order." Royal autocracy was perpetuated in the all-powerful oligarchy. No Hapsburg or Bourbon prince ever did so thorough a job as did this man who ruled over the shoulder of President Prieto. Liberals were excluded from office, sometimes imprisoned, and often exiled. The critical press was silenced. The army, a hotbed of dissension, was subjected to the presidential will; officers of independent mind were demoted, imprisoned, exiled, or executed. The Church, although Portales himself was no more than a nominal Catholic, regained almost all her lost rights and privileges. The great landholders, angered by Liberal attempts to end the entailed estates, were soothed by Portales's assurance that the *fundos* (the Chilean word for hacienda) should pass undisturbed, from father to eldest son. Merchants and traders were gratified by Portales's vigorous improvement of the port of Valparaíso, his efforts to attract foreign capital, and his fiscal policies which promoted trade. By such measures, Portales won the gratitude of landlords, clerics, generals, and businessmen— the only people he reckoned worthy. He was not disturbed by the complaint that nine out of ten Chileans had no share in his bounty, no voice in government, no improvement in their lot. His formula was that of Alexander Hamilton: "The people is a great beast."

The Constitution of 1833, which embodied Portales's belief in the concentration of power in a highly centralized government, was destined to stand until 1925—next to Argentina's, the longest-enduring constitution in Latin American history. The president and the two houses of Congress were to be elected by an indirect vote (the president for a five-year term, with the privilege of one reelection). Suffrage was limited to males over twenty-five who could read and write and who owned a prescribed amount of property. Provincial and municipal authorities were subjected to presidential control. The Catholic Church was given full partnership with the state.

A three-year war with Peru and Bolivia (1836–39) was chargeable to Portales's bellicosity. The underlying issues were economic: Valparaíso was competing with Lima for trade, each country imposing punitive tariffs against the other. The immediate incitement to hostilities was Bolivian dictator Andrés Santa Cruz's move to federate his nation with Peru, a measure interpreted by Portales as a threat to Chile. Dilating upon the duty to win "the second independence of Chile," Portales mobilized the army and navy, refusing to explain his course to the people and mercilessly crushing the resistance of critics. The war was won, Santa Cruz was forced into exile, the federation was broken up, and Chilean military prestige was enhanced. But Portales was an early casualty of the war he had provoked; in 1837 he was assassinated while reviewing troops near Valparaíso on the eve of their departure for the war.

After the death of Portales, a general amnesty was declared, and the nation settled down during Prieto's second term to enjoy the material and cultural well-being that had made rapid progress since 1830. While Portales had been indifferent to popular education, he had stimulated intellectual activity by commissioning the Venezuelan émigré Andrés Bello to introduce classical studies and to draft a civil code for Chile. Andrés Antonio Gorbea, a Spanish mathematician, founded a school of engineering. William Blest, an Irish surgeon, organized the first medical school; his son, Alberto Blest Gana, is remembered as "the Chilean Balzac," the first novelist of Chile. Claudio Gay, a French naturalist, made a survey of Chile's flora and fauna.

Chileans were generally satisfied in 1841 when the elections gave the presidency to Manuel Bulnes, the hero of the Peruvian war. Pride in their nation's military prowess was matched by satisfaction over triumphs at home. Trade was booming; Valparaíso was overtaking Callao as the principal port of the west coast. The American William Wheelwright's project for a steamship line on the Pacific, originally encouraged by Portales, was realized in 1840 when the first vessel cleared Valparaíso's harbor. Mines were being opened; coal was being dug from the veins south of Concepción; there was copper in the north, and by 1840 Chile was the chief world producer; silver and a little gold were being extracted. Foreign technicians had introduced new methods of mining and smelting. The old families came into new wealth, and there was money with which to build finer houses and even a few public buildings; new wealthy families were beginning to challenge the old landed aristocracy.

Chilean nationalism, spurred by triumphs in war, now led to a wave of expansion and to controversy with Argentina. In 1843 President Bulnes laid claim to the territory around the Strait of Magellan, Tierra del Fuego, and much of Patagonia on the Atlantic. In 1847 he founded the city of Punta Arenas on the Strait. Bulnes then opened for settlement the rich lands of the lake country south of Valdivia, long the Araucanian stronghold and still fitfully defended by those warriors. German immigrants began to arrive in the late 1840's.

Economic triumphs were matched by an intellectual advance which gave the 1840's distinction in Chilean history. Profiting from the Rosas tyranny in Argentina, Chile offered asylum to Domingo Faustino Sarmiento, Bartolomé Mitre, and others. Cultural life was given impetus by Manuel Montt, who was to become president in 1851. Montt was an enlightened Conservative, and his political ideas were in the Portales tradition, but his varied interests made him hospitable to new ideas. Under Prieto, he had headed the National Institute, the secondary school founded in revolutionary days; he became minister of education under Bulnes, and was responsible for the organization of the Chilean school system, the most exciting in South America.

Alberto Edwards writes of this period: "The great silence was about to be broken." Credit for breaking it goes to what Chileans call "the generation of 1842." In that year the National University of Chile was built on the foundation of the colonial University of San Felipe. The Venezuelan Andrés Bello, named its rector, made it a center for new and stimulating ideas. There was vigorous clashing of opposing opinions. Sarmiento denounced Bello's devotion to classicism and argued for creation of an indigenous American literature. José Victorino Lastarria added his impetuous voice in favor of a break with colonial habits of thought. Francisco Bilboa gave a spirited defense of democracy. These and others spoke for a new generation of Liberals, more mature and determined than the impetuous *pipiolos* of the 1820's. Their attacks upon "colonialism in politics" and demands for "a true republic, popular and representative" aroused the fears of the aristocrats and high clergy. For a time debate was unchecked. But by 1850, with the approach of another presidential election, the lines tightened. Bilboa, who had organized the Sociedad de la Igualdad, was forced to leave the country by Conservatives who did not care to hear about equality. Lastarria, more restrained in expression, went to Lima.

Manuel Montt, chosen by Bulnes as his successor, was elected to the presidency in 1851. Opposed to Montt as representing the tradition of Portales, the Liberals denounced the election as fraudulent and instigated an armed revolt which lasted three months and cost 2,000 or 3,000 lives. Montt, a martinet, ruled with a heavy hand, stifling many of the free voices which he had earlier encouraged. However, his was an enlightened despotism which brought improved agriculture, enlarged foreign trade, and the building of railroads, telegraph lines, and water systems. Schools and libraries increased. A second normal school was founded under the direction of the Argentine Sarmiento. Andrés Bello's civil code, the work of twenty years, was published.

While Montt failed to mollify the Liberals with these modest benefits, neither could he satisfy the Conservatives. The great landholders deplored his railroads, complaining that engineers were slashing through their lands, destroying the isolation of the long faithful farm workers, the *inquilinos*. The Conservatives' chief protest was against his abolition of the *mayorazgos* (the entailed estates). But the crowning indignity at his hand was suffered by the Church. Montt, asserting the government's right of patronage in ecclesiastical appointments, became involved in a dispute with the Archbishop over the removal of a sacristan in the cathedral of Santiago. When the Archbishop refused to yield, Montt threatened to expel him from the country. The incident aroused an immense storm. The pious first ladies of the capital swore that they would cover the city streets with their bodies rather than see the Archbishop leave. Montt and the Archbishop arranged a tactful compromise, the ladies did not have to carry out their threat, and peace was restored. But the "affair of the sacristan" turned many of Montt's supporters against him and embittered relations between Conservatives and Liberals.

As the nation prepared for the elections of 1861, it became clear that the Conservatives must reckon with the power of the Liberals. Montt first proposed a man of his own dictatorial temper but was met by an armed uprising which persuaded him to accept a more moderate candidate, José

Joaquín Pérez. That acceptance ended the thirty years of absolute rule by the *pelucones*.

FROM AUTOCRACY TO CONFUSION, 1861–91

Chilean politics, like the French, are infinitely confusing to the American who does not understand why law-abiding people cannot be content with two parties. When he sees the figures for the 1949 Chilean Congress, in which fifteen separate parties had representatives, the outsider asks the reason for such a babel of political opinions. The thirty-year period beginning with the election of José Joaquín Pérez in 1861 throws light upon that question. During those years both Conservatives and Liberals did much splitting; the segments of old parties entered into new alliances, and other segments took on new names. All had been neat and simple as long as the spell of Portales prevailed; in those days, Conservatives ruled, and Liberals complained. The change came in the late 1850's when Montt lost ultra-Conservative support by defying the Church, and by the same token won a limited support of moderate Liberals. Then two strange alliances emerged: the moderates of both parties formed a pro-Montt coalition, while the extremists of both parties joined forces under the name of Nationalists. Thus the *pipiolos* and the *pelucones* at last lay down together. But, in the early 1860's, still another group appeared when the uncompromising Liberals, who cared neither for a dictator in Santiago nor a pope in Rome, began to call themselves Radicals. There now seemed to be three parties: Nationalists, Coalitionists, and Radicals. But it was never so simple as that. The shifting, the splintering, and the regrouping proceeded at a dizzy pace for the next thirty years. In general, there was a gradual triumph of the several varieties of Liberals over the Conservatives. The *pipiolos* had definitely overtaken the *pelucones*.

On the all-absorbing Church issue, the Liberals won consistently. In 1865 non-Catholics were granted freedom to worship as they pleased, but without public display, and were allowed to conduct their own schools. In 1874 a few cemeteries were set aside for non-Catholics. In 1875 Congress abolished the Church courts and gave the civil courts jurisdiction over priests—a measure which inspired the Archbishop to excommunicate congressmen who had voted for it. In the 1880's, under President Santa María, all cemeteries were nationalized. In 1883 civil marriage was legalized, whereupon the Archbishop excommunicated the president, members of his cabinet, and all congressmen who had approved the measure. Throughout this period there were intermittent demands for the complete severance of Church and state, but Chileans were not ready for that drastic action.

The Liberals also scored victories in curtailing presidential powers and increasing democratic controls. The constitution was amended in 1868 to forbid the immediate reelection of a president. In 1871, under

Federico Errázuriz Echaurren, presidential powers were further limited by granting proportional representation in Congress to minority parties. In 1885, under Santa María, the suffrage was liberalized by abolition of the property qualification for voters; but the literacy test continued to exclude more than half of all Chileans from the polls. Another measure increased the home rule of municipalities, hitherto subject to officials appointed by the president. Congress also won the power to override a presidential veto on legislation.

Education and intellectual life flourished during these years. Distinguished men of letters, notably historians, brought well-earned credit to the nation. Diego Barros Arana, an intellectual of varied interests and the greatest of Chilean historians, served secondary education as head of the National Institute, and higher education as rector of the University. A potent force was the Positivist "religion of humanity," with José Lastarria its most spirited protagonist. Schools—primary, secondary, and normal—multiplied, and there were increased educational opportunities for girls. A new vigor throughout the educational system reflected the enthusiasm for free inquiry and scientific method.

Economic life matured and prospered in the 1860's. Agriculture, despite the handicap of concentration of land in a few large *fundos,* made substantial gains. New machinery was introduced; new techniques were adopted. The Agricultural Society held fairs which spurred the improvement of stock and crops. Railroad building now became the chief national concern. William Wheelwright, the American who had earlier introduced steam navigation, in 1851 opened a stretch of less than fifty miles of railroad connecting the northern mining city of Copiapó with the coast. In 1863 a blatant American, Henry Meiggs, completed the railroad from Santiago to Valparaíso.[7] During the late 1860's and the early 1870's, the city of Santiago was beautified and modernized. The jagged hill of Santa Lucía rising abruptly from the city's center (this hill recalls the story of conquistador Valdivia and his mistress Inés de Suárez) was transformed from a dumping ground into a lovely park. But by the mid-1870's, prosperity was halted by a severe economic depression, chargeable in part to overextension at home, in part to the world doldrums to which the American Civil War and the European Franco-Prussian War had contributed. Meanwhile, Chile faced wars of its own. It was in these gloomy days that the cautious Liberal, Federico Errázuriz (1871–76), turned over the presidency to the moderate Liberal, Aníbal Pinto (1876–81).

Chile now fought one small, and one large war. In 1864 Spain launched the last futile attack upon her former American vassals. A naval expedition was sent to Peru with orders to collect some dubious debts, and seized the Chincha Islands with their heaps of guano. On the imperial

[7] Henry Meiggs, whom we met in our discussion of Peru's history, had made a fortune out of the California gold rush by overcharging the gold-hunters for transportation, and when his money was gone, he had fled from his creditors, reaching Chile in 1855. Thirteen years in Chile, building bridges and railroads, brought him new fame and fortune. In 1868 he moved to Peru, and within nine years performed greater wonders. See Watt Stewart: *Henry Meiggs: Yankee Pizarro* (Durham, N.C.: Duke University Press; 1946).

theory that two wars are as cheap as one, the Spaniards appeared off the Chilean coast, pounded Valparaíso with their cannon, killed a few people, inflicted some damage to property, and withdrew. The net effect was to convince Chileans of their need for ships and men with which to protect their long exposed coast.

The War of the Pacific (1879–83) was a contest for possession of the bleak Atacama Desert reaching 600 miles from Chilean Copiapó to Peruvian Arica. This parched wasteland lies between the jagged coastal range on the west and the high Andes on the east. Upon much of it scarcely a raindrop has ever fallen. No single blade of grass grows, except on the few oases, no desert flower, not even a struggling cactus. The coast is stark, with mountain crags rising from the water's edge, and with no natural harbors. In disdain for this sorry land, Spain had never bothered to establish a boundary between Peru (which in colonial days included Bolivia) and Chile. But by 1830 it was discovered that these valleys, basins of old lakes in other geologic ages, were thick inlaid with deposits of mineral salts, chiefly sodium nitrate, preserved through the ages by the rainlessness of the region. These deposits, ranging from a depth of a few inches to many feet, were worked after 1830, fortifying exhausted farm lands in Europe and North America; and they furnished the base for the nitroglycerine which Alfred Nobel started to produce in 1860, and for the smokeless powder derived from it.

This desert waste was divided among three countries: Peru claimed Tarapacá; Bolivia, the province of Atacama whose port was Antofagasta; while Chile clung to the southern fringe at Copiapó. Both Peruvians and Chileans, backed by considerable English and some German capital, actively exploited this buried treasure. The Chileans, the most energetic and possessed of the most ample labor force, took the lead, operating in both Bolivian and Peruvian territory and paying a royalty on the ore mined. In 1873 Peru and Bolivia made a secret alliance against their encroaching southern neighbor. In 1874 Chile signed a treaty with Bolivia fixing their common boundary at 24° south latitude, just below the port of Antofagasta, pledging Bolivia to reduce taxes upon any Chilean operations north of that new boundary. The arrangement did not pacify the rivals. In 1875 Peru took steps to seize Chilean nitrate works in Tarapacá; and in 1878 Bolivia imposed increased taxes upon the Chilean operations in Atacama and then laid claim to all Chile's installations in that region. The government of Pinto in Chile, confronted with an acute economic crisis at home, decided to fight. In February, 1879, 200 Chilean soldiers landed at Bolivian Antofagasta, and the war was on.

The people of Chile, though unprepared to fight two nations with double her population, united enthusiastically in this new crusade for honor and golden pesos. After some initial reverses, the Chilean navy and army gained quick victories. Iquique, port of Peruvian Tarapacá, was captured in 1879. Tacna and Arica were occupied in 1880. Chilean forces marched into Lima in 1881 and occupied it until 1884. In 1883 Chile dictated victor's terms, got Antofagasta from Bolivia and Tarapacá from Peru. Tacna and Arica were assigned to her for a term of ten years, but with the pledge that a plebiscite would then decide their permanent status. (The pledge, never redeemed, led to a bitter quarrel, which was not finally settled until 1929 when, with the United States' arbitration, Tacna was assigned to Peru and Arica was retained by Chile.)

The war had momentous results for the three contestants. Bolivia, deprived of her territory on the Pacific, nursed a helpless wrath and finally sought to redress her landlocked position by securing an outlet through the La Plata river system to the Atlantic; the later Chaco War was thus the logical consequence of the War of the Pacific. Peru, beggared and embittered, was reduced to a subordinate position. Chile, her territory enlarged, entered upon an era of unequaled prosperity from the sale of nitrates, copper, and other minerals. Nitrates alone furnished the major share of her national budget requirements for forty years—as much as 68 per cent in the 1890's. This new-found wealth had a profound effect upon her political and social life. A new plutocracy, rich from nitrates and copper, joined the Liberals and Radicals in opposition to the old Conservatives of Santiago and Valparaíso. The workers in the northern mines, augmented by a few immigrants from Europe, discovered their new power and gave impetus to the organization of labor unions. And the abundance of money in the national treasury now made politics lucrative and brought new corruption into public administration.

Meanwhile, the tough Araucanians, never completely quieted, blocked consolidation of the national territory. Entrenched in the forest and lake country south of Valdivia, they had raided the German settlements that took shape during the late 1840's and after. These attacks increased after 1859 and retarded further settlement. With the outbreak of the War of the Pacific, the Indians took advantage of the withdrawal of federal troops from the south by attacking and burning the farm houses on that sparsely settled frontier. After the peace of 1883, the Araucanians were finally subdued and driven further south. Treaties were signed with the Indian chieftains; the aborigines were assigned certain lands in perpetuity (after the fashion of the reservations of the United States), and there has since been little trouble from the hardiest survivors of Indian America.

The Liberal José Manuel Balmaceda, inducted in 1886, had reason for satisfaction as he viewed the nation over which he was called to preside. Chileans now had no doubts as to the splendor of their destiny. They were victorious over their enemies, their territory was expanded, and they had wealth beyond all expectation. The new president seemed every inch the man to lead a triumphant nation. Handsome, rich, generous, and one of the great orators of the day, Balmaceda was greatly admired. There was substance and deep conviction in his liberalism: unlike many Liberals, he was not content with baiting the Church and working for popular and representative government. Balmaceda's liberalism took account of the misery of the Chilean masses, the poverty which made the common man the victim of selfish landowners. His lively social concern—and he was the first Chilean president to possess such concern—was combined with a stern sense of the responsibility of a president to lead the nation; on that last point he was as inflexible as was the great Conservative Diego Portales. Balmaceda embarked upon an ambitious program of public works, the building of railroads and highways, the assurance of safe water systems for cities and towns, the provision of better sanitation, health services, and schools for all—including the *rotos,* whose interests had been slighted by the Liberals of earlier days. His program met violent opposition in Congress. The Liberals, not ready for such radical digressions, turned upon him angrily; the Conservatives, who resented his humanitarian measures even more than they deplored his anticlericalism, blocked him. Taxpayers generally accused him of extravagance.

By 1890 Balmaceda had few supporters in Congress, which challenged his cabinet choices and finally refused to approve his budget. He was denied respect which he deserved; an honorable Liberal, he stood firmly against the Spanish colonial tradition and resisted the intransigent oligarchy of landowners, clergy, and naval officers. These powerful forces fought him because his liberalism was honest and therefore inimical to their interests. In January, 1891, he defiantly announced that he would proceed without congressional approval, would set his own budget and name his own aides. A week later Congress voted to depose him and appointed a naval officer named Jorge Montt (no kin to the earlier president) to head a provisional government. Montt, with the help of the navy, occupied the northern mining ports and financed his operations by collecting taxes on nitrates and copper. Balmaceda, exercising dictatorial powers with the support of the army, jailed critics, silenced the press, and attempted to impose a successor. After eight months of civil war, which resulted in 10,000 killed and many millions of pesos in property damage, both Valparaíso and Santiago fell to Montt. In September Balmaceda, after months of asylum in the Argentine legation, wrote an eloquent political testament defending his course as dictated by "love of my country" and pleading for mercy for his supporters, and then shot himself.

Chapter 35

CHILE'S EVOLUTION SINCE 1891

The republic had now come full circle from the days of Portales. The strong executive, given power by the Constitution of 1833 to dominate elections and congresses, had finally been made subservient to political factions and to Congress. The defeat and death of Balmaceda marked the beginning of a new era in which parties, segments of parties, and shifting blocs would reduce the president to little more than a presiding officer over an unruly mass meeting.

THE TUMULT OF PARLIAMENTARY RULE, 1891–1920

The political tumults of the three decades after the civil war and the fall of Balmaceda reveal a striking resemblance to French parliamentary contests. Cabinets designed to mollify the warring congressional blocs lasted a few weeks or a few months—there were almost a hundred major reshufflings. None of the six presidents in this period,[1] each serving his five-year term, had a chance to govern in the fashion contemplated by the authors of the Constitution of 1833.

Jorge Montt, inducted in 1891, quieted the bitterness of the civil war by declaring a general amnesty. Confronted by the flood of paper money issued by Balmaceda, Montt approved a law in 1895 which recognized the worthless peso at par (36.5 cents in United States currency), a reckless move which enriched a few dozen speculators who had bought up the notes for trifling sums.

One unhappy legacy from the civil war was the ugly dispute with the United States over the "*Baltimore* affair." The American cruiser U.S.S. *Baltimore* had put into Valparaíso harbor and her captain had unwisely permitted his sailors to disembark. The United States, openly favorable to

---

[1] Jorge Montt, 1891–96; Federico Errázuriz Echaurren, 1896–1901; Germán Riesco, 1901–06; Pedro Montt (son of Manuel), 1906–11; Ramón Barros Luco, 1911–15; Juan Luis Sanfuentes, 1915–20.

Balmaceda, was already in bad odor with the Chilean people. The visiting sailors, tongues loosed by rum, soon were involved in a street fight. Two Americans were killed, several were wounded, while the police looked on. The result was an ultimatum from Secretary of State James G. Blaine demanding apologies, the firing of guns in salute to the American flag, and indemnity for the victims. Montt refused to comply, and the Chilean populace demanded war with the United States. (The idea was not regarded as preposterous: Chile had a fine navy, well organized by the British.) However, being a realistic man, Montt ordered $75,000 paid to the families of the dead, and the incident was officially closed; but Chile long remembered it as an affront to national dignity.

Meanwhile, the party system grew more tangled. Conservatives continued to represent the special interests of the big *hacendados* and traders of the central valley. The Liberals, mellowed by age and wealth, made common cause with the Conservatives, although they continued to demand the separation of Church and state. The Radicals were the party of the center, neither so impressive as the parties on the right nor so belligerent as the parties on the left. They became the most numerous and vocal opposition party, increasing in strength as the middle class expanded. The northern mining and business interests, impatient with the political dominance of Santiago and the central valley, supported the Radicals against the Conservatives. The energetic southerners, established in the old Araucanian domain south of Valdivia, joined the Radicals for the same reason. The Radicals were a strange conglomerate, a catch-all party enlisting underpaid clerks, rich mine operators, entrepreneurs, new businessmen, little farmers as well as successful commercial farmers (especially in the south and the north), and numbering among their ranks many Freemasons and anticlericals. These disparate elements were united by their biting distrust of *la fronda aristocrática* ("the aristocratic branch"), who insolently assumed that superior wisdom was based upon birth, land, and social position. And the Radicals—whose ideas on economics were not far removed from their Conservative-Liberal foes—had an equal dislike of the far left, and their opposition to the old oligarchy of the central valley failed to satisfy the militant labor leaders. In 1912 the Socialist Labor Party was organized by miners and other industrial workers. In 1920 the Communist Party was added to the general political confusion.

Chile scored some diplomatic triumphs during these years. The long-standing Argentine boundary dispute, bitter since 1843 when President Bulnes occupied Tierra del Fuego and laid claim to southern Patagonia, was finally settled. The earlier settlement of 1881, which had averted war with Argentina, had provided for division of Tierra del Fuego between the two claimants and had set a vague international boundary along the line of the "highest peaks" of the Andes. The debate was revived in the late 1890's, during the presidency of Errázuriz Echaurren, and hotheads on both sides began to oil their guns. But cooler counsels prevailed: the northern line of demarcation was settled in 1899, with an American as arbiter; the more difficult southern allotment of territory was completed in 1902, with the good offices of England's king. A heroic statue of Christ the Redeemer was erected under the shadow of Mount Aconcagua to celebrate the "perpetual accord." And in 1904 the long smoldering quarrel with Bolivia was temporarily quieted by a treaty which made Arica a free port for the landlocked mountain republic, with Chile pledged to construct a railroad from Arica to La Paz.

These were prosperous years for the public treasury, with royalties from nitrates alone furnishing more than half the national budget. After 1900 there was lavish spending on public buildings, paved streets, highways and bridges, and enlarged port installations for the booming trade. The national railways, begun in 1851, reached their triumph in 1914, when the 1,600-mile north-south span was completed, linking the nitrate fields on the Peruvian border with Puerto Montt in the southern forest lands. National industry, given impetus by protective tariffs after 1904, produced textiles, shoes, clothing, and other consumer goods. But easy money corrupted the politicians, who took their toll from the fat contracts which they voted. Congressmen, serving without salary as they had from the beginning, spent hundreds of thousands of pesos in order to get and to hold their lucrative posts. The corruption spread to lesser officials. The selling of votes was a general practice.

Behind the façade of national prosperity, the common man of Chile lived in misery, with little share in the bounty which was enriching the aristocracy and creating new fortunes from mines and farms. *Inquilinos*, virtually bound to the land of their masters, still worked from sunup to sundown for a few cents a day. Miners sweated under the blinding sun of the Atacama Desert, or choked in the deep shafts of the coal mines, for as little as 20 cents a day, and had no insurance against industrial accident, disease, and death. Factory workers fared no better. Domestic servants and other menials served interminable hours at wages of a few cents a day. The luxuries of the golden age were reserved for two or three out of every hundred people; the reasonable comforts of modern society were shared by a few more; but more than nine-tenths of the people were packed into huts or tenements, wore rags, ate scant and poor food, and had no security against disaster. More than half the people could neither read nor write.

Such was the sorry state of Chilean citizens in 1914, when World War I brought an unprecedented demand for Chile's nitrates and copper. Prices skyrocketed, while wages lagged. The takings of the rich increased, and the poor became even more miserable. Strikes broke out in mining communities and there was rioting in city streets. In 1915 the right-wing parties forced the election of Juan Luis Sanfuentes, an arrogant speculator whose fortune had been made in the currency scandal after the civil war of 1891 and a Conservative who believed with his political comrades that social change was not only bad for business but an insult to Almighty God. But not even Sanfuentes and his unenlightened congress could cow the starving populace; they were forced to grant higher wages, limited measures for employers' liability for occupational accidents, and a pension plan for railway workers. Such peace offerings to an aroused people were too little and too late. By 1920, when the war's end brought unemployment, the starving masses were in rebellion, demanding a messiah who would right their intolerable wrongs. They found him, or so they thought, in Arturo Alessandri Palma.

THE RESTORATION OF PRESIDENTIAL POWER, 1920–38

The election of Arturo Alessandri Palma in 1920 had all the aspects of social revolution, albeit a bloodless one. The bitter middle class made common cause with laborers in mine and factory to unseat the aristocracy. When the counting of the ballots failed to give a majority to Alessandri, the Conservative senate prudently decided in favor of this man, who was the clear popular choice. The *pelucones* bowed to the *pipiolos*.

There was little in Alessandri's first fifty years of life to alarm the rich and wellborn. Son of an Italian immigrant, trained in the law, he had settled in northern Iquique, capital of the province of Tarapacá, and had grown rich in the service of the nitrate corporations. He had entered politics as a Liberal (the Liberals, let us repeat, were now far to the right), served in Congress, and had said no word to frighten businessmen. It was not until the eve of the 1920 campaign that he became the spokesman of the ill-treated masses. Not since Balmaceda had Chileans been offered a candidate of such vigor and popular appeal. Strong-framed, shaggy-headed, with a clear and powerful voice, the "Lion of Tarapacá" carried his message to vast crowds, promising everything to everybody. As a cure for the parliamentary deadlock, he proposed enlarged powers for the president. As a brake upon the dictatorial power of the central valley's aristocracy, he demanded greater self-rule for the outlying provinces. For relief of the public treasury, he advocated an income tax on corporations and individuals and a high tax on land. To aid the nation's workers, he urged laws that would increase wages, shorten hours, and provide insurance against illness, accident, old age, and death. To satisfy the Liberals, he called for the separation of Church and state. The common people wept with joy on the day of his inauguration.

The promised miracles were not so easily performed. For almost four years Alessandri was blocked by the Conservatives in the congress. The "Lion of Tarapacá" roared, wheedled, appeased, and denounced; he reshuffled his cabinet sixteen times but failed to win any reform beyond the imposition of a moderate income tax. Meanwhile, economic distress, aftermath of World War I and the drop in demand for nitrates, brought increased misery to an already beggared people. In early 1924, with congressional elections approaching, he carried his magic appeal to the populace, pleading for and winning a clear majority in both the Senate and the Chamber of Deputies. But the triumph was illusory. His supporters fell to quarreling and failed to unite in support of his measures. His sole victory, won by pressure of army and labor groups, was the enactment of a labor code which was the basis for an ambitious body of social legislation (comparable to contemporary measures in Mexico and Uruguay). It provided for full recognition of labor unions, freely organized with leaders of their own choice, collective bargaining, restrictions on child labor, and a health insurance plan.

Alessandri's voice had lost its magic by mid-1924. Congress was out of hand, unemployment was increasing, the pay of soldiers and other public servants was in arrears, and the masses were hungry and angry. At that inopportune time the congressmen decided to vote themselves salaries—a luxury hitherto regarded as superfluous. The army, whose pay was badly overdue, rose in wrath, forced Alessandri to resign and to seek safety in Italy, and installed a military junta to administer the nation's affairs. The failure of the new junta to quiet the confusion led to another coup by which two army officers—Carlos Ibáñez and Marmaduque Grove—seized power, and in March, 1925, they recalled Alessandri from Italy.

Alessandri's six months in office in 1925 were stormy but fruitful. With the threat of military intervention hanging over them, the members of congress forgot their wrangles long enough to accept a new constitution which redeemed some of the president's campaign pledges of 1920. Like the ninety-two-year-old instrument promulgated by Portales, the new constitution increased presidential powers, making the chief executive virtually independent of Congress. But, unlike the Constitution of 1833, the new one prescribed direct election of the president for a six-year term and barred immediate reelection. No longer could Congress unseat a cabinet by a vote of censure, although it retained the right to impeach a president or any of his ministers. Church and state were separated and a subvention was pledged to the Church for five years; "the free exercise of all religions not opposed to morality, good customs or public order" was guaranteed. It was a moderate charter, with no such frightening revolutionary doctrine as Mexico had accepted in 1917, although large landholders and foreign mining corporations worried a little over one article which read: "The exercise of the right of ownership is subject to the limitation or precepts necessary for the maintenance and progress of social order; and in that sense the law will be able to impose obligations on services of public utility in behalf of the general interests of the State, the health of the people and the public well-being." Some critics suggested that these words opened the way for socialistic excursions in the future.

The final severance of the organic ties between Church and state was consummated with less acrimony than had been anticipated, thanks to the conciliatory spirit of Archbishop Crescente Errázuriz, who quieted angry churchmen. A zealous exponent of the social principles of Pope Leo XIII, the Chilean patriarch of eighty-six had also won the gratitude of the masses by his support of Alessandri's labor laws. He and his successors, notably Archbishop José Caro, who became a cardinal in 1946, deserve major credit for the prestige of the Church in modern Chile.

Despite his substantial triumphs, Alessandri was again forced into exile. Under fire from Conservatives who thought he had gone too far in reform and from leftists who thought he had not gone far enough, and unable to alleviate the general misery in the continuing economic crisis, he was evicted in October, 1925, by a *coup d'état* headed by Carlos Ibáñez del Campo who had made his return possible, and whom he had rewarded with the ministry of war. Once again he took refuge in Mussolini's Italy.

From late 1925 to 1931 the nation returned to the dictatorial rule which democratic Chileans hoped they had outgrown. Carlos Ibáñez, continuing as minister of war under the well-meaning but ineffective Emiliano Figueroa Larraín—nominal president for a little over a year—was the ruler in fact if not in name. When Figueroa resigned in disgust, Ibáñez was formally elected in his place and held office until 1931. Able, personally honest, and indefatigable, Ibáñez proved to be a Diego Portales in modern dress. With the army behind him, he imposed a rigid discipline upon lawmakers and public servants. Congress ceased its debate, the press was obedient, labor leaders made few demands; those who resisted his will found themselves in jail or in exile. "It is true," Ibáñez later admitted, "that I was guilty of many arbitrary acts . . . but all were inspired by the sincere desire of serving my country better."

Ibáñez had the good fortune to rule during the years of the "Coolidge prosperity" in the United States, when New York bankers lent about $2 billion on dubious security to governments in Latin America. All told, over $300 million of this easy money went into Chile's treasury during the 1920's. Despite the continuing distress of Chile's principal export product, nitrates, Ibáñez had the money with which to create the illusion of prosperity. He kept his army and navy contented by increasing the pay of officers and men and by giving them more and better guns, ships, and planes. He launched costly public works: railroads, docks, irrigation projects, and government buildings. Ibáñez, seeking revival of the ailing nitrate industry, made a bold venture into state capitalism by creating—in conjunction with American interests—the Compañía de Salitre de Chile, the Chilean Nitrate Company (COSACH). The company, with a monopoly of nitrates and their by-product, iodine, was owned share and share alike by the foreign operators and the Chilean nation. But COSACH proved a dismal failure, for there were not sales enough to pay interest and dividends on the overcapitalized corporation. Ibáñez sought to rescue the unemployed nitrate miners by settling them on land in the far southern Araucanian country, but that plan also miscarried; miners did not want to exchange the sunshine of the desert for the wet gloom of the forests—and besides, they were miners, not farmers. By 1931, Ibáñez's time was up. The world depression had reduced the flow of goods to a mere trickle. The chastened New York bankers were making no more reckless loans. The Chilean government now defaulted on its bonds. Dismissed public servants, unpaid soldiers, and the starving unemployed rioted under the windows of the presidential offices. University students added to the tumult. It was now Ibáñez's turn for exile. In July, 1931, he escaped over the Andes to Argentina.

Leaderless, overwhelmed by the economic crisis, Chile floundered through 1931 and 1932, the most chaotic period she had known since the 1820's. There were several army revolts, a navy mutiny, a series of juntas and short-term presidents, and the hundred-day "Socialist Republic." There were unwise issues of paper pesos, and prices soared. By the end of 1932, under widespread demand for orderly rule, the Chief Justice of the Supreme Court declared the Constitution of 1925 to be in full force and called for an election which returned Arturo Alessandri to the presidency in December, 1932.

It was a subdued Alessandri who was installed for the term 1932–36, not the "Lion of Tarapacá," the popular idol who had been carried on the shoulders of the *rotos* in 1920. Now a convert to the Conservative cause, Alessandri spoke in careful tones of order rather than of justice. Abandoning his erstwhile political companions, he chose safe Conservatives for his cabinet, the most conspicuous of whom was the astute and wealthy Gustavo Ross, the best-hated man in Chile. Thus slighted, the Radicals gradually withdrew their support and by 1937 were plotting with Socialists and Communists to form the *Frente Popular* (Popular Front). The cleavage between Alessandri and the partisans of democracy was widened by his quasi-dictatorial suppression of the press, his exile of political critics, and his highhandedness with Congress. Many Chileans charged that Alessandri unduly admired Mussolini, whom he had visited when in Italy.[2]

No matter how miserably Alessandri failed to honor the pledges of his own constitution, even his critics found much to applaud in his vigorous grappling with the economic distresses of his nation. When Alessandri came to office in 1932, business, public and private, was at a standstill. Mineral production in 1932 was but one-half, income from nitrates one-twentieth, export revenue one-eighth of the 1927 figures.[3] Building activities were only one-third of those in 1929. Neither soldiers, clerks in government offices, nor policemen had been paid for months. Bands of jobless roamed the streets, jeering, threatening. Even the rich were denied their accustomed luxuries: in 1932 only 42 automobiles were imported, compared with more than 10,000 in 1929.

The impressive record of Chile's economic recovery during the years 1932–38, while reflecting the upturn in world prosperity, also testified to the ability of Alessandri and his finance minister, Gustavo Ross. Their handicaps in meeting the crisis were heavy. They could not borrow a centavo in the world markets. They could not increase taxes, for their political backers were the only men who had money. They could not dismiss public servants without swelling the mobs of unemployed. Neverthe-

---

[2] The author, who interviewed Alessandri in 1941, remembers the autographed portrait of Mussolini on the ex-President's desk.

[3] P. T. Ellsworth: *Chile, An Economy in Transition* (New York: The Macmillan Co.; 1945), says on page 9: "While the League of Nations index of world trade fell from 100 in 1929 to 74.5 in 1932, Chile's index of the physical volume of exports (1927–29 = 100) dropped to an average of 32 for 1932 and the comparable index of imports to 25." Chile's figures for 1929–32, he notes, were the worst exhibit among the thirty-nine nations with which the League's report dealt.

less, the skillful management of these two men pulled Chile out of its doldrums. Building activity was stimulated by subsidies and tax exemptions. Reserves of foreign currency were conserved by Spartan limitation of imports. Within six years, nitrate sales doubled. The depressed peso was rescued and its price was lifted from 1.5 to 4 cents in United States currency. By 1937 the national budget was balanced, but without provision for service on the foreign debt. Ross, who had made a fortune as a speculator, found funds with which to redeem about one-fourth of the outstanding bonds at bargain rates of from 10 to 17 cents on the dollar. Meanwhile, national industry was strengthened and expanded and by 1938 was turning out scores of articles for everyday use—shoes, woolen cloth, glassware, soap, paper, cement, plumbing fixtures, electric light bulbs. The output of electrical energy more than doubled.

Alessandri and Ross excited fears abroad that Chile was about to emulate the example of Mexico in dealing with foreign-owned enterprise. They took over, and paid for, the British-owned trans-Andean railroad connecting the Chilean national system with the Argentine at Mendoza. More alarming was their treatment of the Chilean subsidiary of the American and Foreign Power Corporation, which operated various street railways and other utilities. Charging the corporation with defying the exchange laws and transferring profits abroad by dealings in the black market, they compelled it to reorganize, placing seven Chileans on its board of eleven directors, and requiring its net earnings to be distributed on the ratio of one-third to the government, one-third to the holders of common stock, and one-third to the reduction of rates to consumers. In dealing with the nitrate industry, in which the American Guggenheim interests held the largest stake, Alessandri was more conciliatory. COSACH, Ibáñez's unsuccessful enterprise, was replaced by the Chilean Nitrate and Iodine Sales Corporation, to which was given monopoly control of all sales and exports; the government took one-fourth of all profits and named five of the eleven-member board of directors. As for the copper industry, in which 96 per cent of the output was controlled by American interests, there was slight interference.

Although he had rescued Chile from political chaos and economic collapse, Alessandri had few supporters by the end of his term. While the right-wing parties still upheld him, the more numerous parties of the center and the left united against him under the banner of the Popular Front. This new political creation was a misalliance of privilege and misery, a catchall for every manner of man from rich mining operator to noisy Communist, who were for the moment united in distaste for Alessandri's denial of constitutional government, civil liberties, and fair elections. The Popular Fronters interpreted their campaign against the background of Europe's struggle against fascism; they identified Alessandri with the terror under Mussolini and Hitler; they disliked the parading of Alessandri's "Republican Militia" and the demonstrations of the Chilean *nacistas* (Nazis) led by the fanatical German-Chilean Jorge González von Marées; and they profoundly resented the flood of propaganda which poured from the German Embassy. Alessandri, consorting with archreactionaries, did little to reassure believers in democratic institutions. When the railroad workers struck for better wages and living conditions in 1936, Alessandri suppressed the outbreak with brutality. And in 1938, by attempting to impose the detested Gustavo Ross as his successor, Alessandri finally solidified the ranks of the Popular Front against him.

Gustavo Ross had clear advantages in the election of 1938: control of the political machinery and of the numerous office holders, supervision of the ballot boxes, and the support of an intimidated press. Betting men laid their wagers on a resounding victory for Ross over the Popular Front's Pedro Aguirre Cerda, but a curious episode upset all calculations. In September, 1938, on the eve of the election, there was an armed uprising organized by the *nacista* leader, González von Marées; a few hundred young hotheads occupied two public buildings in Santiago, sixty-two of them were shot by Alessandri's troops after they had surrendered, and the two leaders were jailed. The incident turned the support of the few thousand *nacistas* to the Popular Front. There was flagrant corruption in the elections, and the wealthy coterie around Gustavo Ross bought votes freely; nonetheless Pedro Aguirre Cerda won by the thin margin of 4,000 votes out of a total of almost 450,000.

THE POPULAR FRONT, 1938–42

There was nothing in the record of Pedro Aguirre Cerda, the Popular Front's successful candidate in 1938, to excite the fears of businessmen. Fifty-nine when he took office, he had won his way in teaching, the law, farming, and politics without the advantage of inherited wealth. The people called him *Don Tinto* (Mr. Red) for the good red wine his *fundo* produced, and for the swarthiness of his complexion. A Radical in politics, he represented the energetic businessmen who were supplanting the landed aristocracy of the central valley. In his spirited electoral campaign, he voiced the demands of his strange assortment of bedfellows in the Popular Front. In government, he called for a return to constitutional rule, free and honest elections, full civil liberties. In economics, he promised national planning for the increase of mineral, industrial, and agricultural production; the curbing of foreign interference; progressive land reform designed to establish more people upon their own farms; and increased taxation of those best able to carry the load. In social policy, he promised extension of safeguards to laborers in mines, factories, and farming. In international policy, he pledged cooperation with the republics of the Western Hemisphere in defense of peace. His slogan was *pan, techo y abrigo* (bread, roof and overcoat).

When Aguirre Cerda took office, the Conservatives and their allies set out to make life intolerable for the Popular Front president. Deprived by the Constitution of 1925 of their older right to unseat cabinets by a vote of censure, the die-hards made repeated efforts to impeach Aguirre's ministers—on what seemed solid grounds in at least one case, in which a cabinet member was charged with selling visas to Jewish refugees from Germany. In August, 1939, a revolt led by the perennial troubler, Carlos Ibáñez, was quickly crushed. Conservative tactics blocked most of Aguirre's legislative program.

Thus harassed by the gentlemen of the irreconcilable right, Aguirre was no less vexed by his comrades of the unteachable left. The Communists, having refused to accept any post in the cabinet, exercised their well-known skill as obstructionists to destroy the Popular Front to which they had pledged allegiance. Never their own masters, the Communist leaders slavishly followed the lead of their Moscow tutors. In August, 1939, when Stalin and Hitler signed their nonagression pact, Stalin's Chilean henchmen quickly got into step with the new political line, denouncing Radicals, Socialists, and other erstwhile allies in the Popular Front as "Trotskyites" and "social fascists."

After the outbreak of World War II, when Aguirre declared his support of all-American solidarity against the Axis powers, the Communists loosed tirades against the United States as the "ringleader of international capitalism"; the Socialists were divided, and some joined the Communists; and the Radicals, Aguirre's principal supporters, split between those who favored joint action with the leftists and those who would travel alone. Aguirre, a moderate reformer at most, became increasingly identified with his more cautious colleagues, and drafted cabinet members from that segment of the Radicals.

In January, 1941, the Popular Front, after two years of tenuous existence, was formally disbanded; first the Socialists and the Chilean Federation of Labor withdrew, and then the Radicals voted to pursue independent political action. Two months later the congressional elections brought new victories to all the erstwhile partners—Radicals, Socialists, and Communists. In June, 1941, when Hitler's armies invaded Russia, Chilean Communists rediscovered their affection for their "democratic allies" and demanded the resuscitation of the Popular Front for the defense of "freedom and democracy." In November, 1941, the death of Aguirre ended further talk about the Popular Front.

The actual achievements of the Popular Front were not brilliant. Public schooling was somewhat extended. Social services to workers were expanded: wages of industrial workers and government employees rose about 42 per cent, the salaries of white-collar workers increased about 24 per cent—but inflated prices canceled out much, if not most, of these gains. The most significant measure was the chartering in 1939 of the Corporación de Fomento, the Development Corporation, for the fostering of industry, mining, agriculture, and fisheries. Fomento was partly financed by the national treasury, but its major funds were supplied by the United States Export-Import Bank. It was denounced by some as an unwarranted attack upon private enterprise and by others as a plot to increase the wealth of those who were already rich. Although its principal successes would be scored after Aguirre's death, it served the nation by increasing industrial output, especially in chemicals, metallurgy, and textiles.[4] A minor but dramatic success was the expansion of fisheries. Provided by Fomento with nets and boats, fishermen who had hitherto depended upon hooks and lines so increased their catch as to make fresh fish available for the first time to the markets in Santiago. Stagnant Chilean agriculture, sleepily content with cheap labor and outmoded methods, was given fresh impetus by the introduction of American farm machinery and better strains of cattle and sheep, generously financed on easy terms. But this largess, as Socialists and Communists prophesied, went chiefly to the owners of great *fundos* in the central valley.

In the presidential election of 1942, domestic questions were over-shadowed by the exigencies of World War II. The United States was al-ready involved, and the Latin American nations were being asked to honor their promises of hemispheric solidarity. For Chile, it meant picking sides between the Axis and the Allies. The Conservatives and other right-wing elements chose as their candidate the durable Carlos Ibáñez, arch-reactionary in domestic policies and open sympathizer with the Axis. The Radicals named a wealthy fifty-four-year-old lawyer and businessman from southern Concepción, Juan Antonio Ríos. Dislike of Ibáñez, whom they knew so well, led most of the splinter-parties of the left (but not the Communists) to rally behind the Radical candidate, who was easily elected.

JUAN ANTONIO RÍOS AND WORLD WAR II, 1942–46

Juan Antonio Ríos was another of the vigorous sons of the frontier to whom modern Chile looks for leadership. A Radical, as were most of his wealthy colleagues in Concepción, he had never believed in the Popular Front; and he now made no attempt to appease even the mild Socialists but appointed a cabinet dominated by Radicals of his own stripe, with the addition of four Liberals. It was a businessman's government, moderate and intelligent.

The fortunes of World War II determined much of Chile's course during the Ríos administration. The entrance of the United States into the war, after the Japanese attack on Pearl Harbor in December, 1941, di-rectly involved Chile and all the American republics as they were pledged to "consult" whenever the sovereignty of any American nation was threat-ened. In January, 1942, a few weeks before Ríos assumed office, the for-eign ministers of the twenty-one republics met in Rio de Janeiro and agreed upon a weak resolution to "recommend" that all of the American republics sever relations with the Axis powers. The Chileans, who had given lukewarm support to that resolution, were fearful of being stam-

4 Taking the average production of 1927–29 as a base of 100, the production of 1938 stood at 159.6; 1939, at 158.4; and 1940, at 175.8. Cited by J. R. Stevenson: *The Chilean National Front* (Philadelphia, Penna.: University of Pennsylvania Press; 1942), p. 125.

peded into any action which might invite attack upon their vulnerable coast line. The outlook for Allied victory was not bright; Germany was triumphant in Europe, and the Japanese were unchecked in the Pacific. Although Ríos could not ignore his countrymen's fear of being entangled, his sympathies were clearly with the Allied cause; and one of his first decisions was to accept President Roosevelt's invitation to Washington. That visit was abandoned, however, when Under Secretary Sumner Welles made a speech exposing Axis plots in Chile and Argentina, and expressing the hope that those nations would not permit their American neighbors "to be stabbed in the back by Axis emissaries." Although Welles's charges were well founded, the anger they aroused among Chileans made it politically unwise for Ríos to visit the White House. But the pro-Allied convictions of Ríos and his cabinet were proved by Chile's diplomatic break with Japan and Germany a year later, in January, 1943, and by Ríos's statement that his country had "an essential interest in this fight. . . . We are fighting so that all men and nations may live in peace."

Chile's compact with the United States after 1943 paid both nations handsomely. Washington included Chile in its Lend-Lease arrangements, and the Export-Import Bank made fresh loans to Chile's Fomento. Chile, for her part, increased her vigilance in tracking down the Nazi agents whose information relayed to German submarines from clandestine radio stations had led to the sinking of ships; in February, 1944, more than a hundred such agents were arrested. Chilean nitrates and copper were allotted to the United States on fair terms, and production increased satisfactorily. Washington, as a reciprocal favor, undertook to buy all of Chile's gold production—for storage in the vaults of Fort Knox. This teamwork, animated by both expediency and conviction, was denounced by numerous Chileans who disliked the United States and who prophesied that the true test of the United States' good intentions would come when Chilean products were no longer needed. President Ríos, asserting his country's sovereignty, did not accept Washington's counsels in the case of Argentina, and recognized Farrell—the alter ego of Juan Domingo Perón—in early 1944. In October, 1945, Ríos made his deferred visit to Washington, where he was accorded all honors by President Truman. He laid a wreath on the tomb of Franklin D. Roosevelt and conferred the Chilean Order of Merit upon Eleanor Roosevelt. Columbia University gave him an honorary doctorate, and the Export-Import Bank promised him larger loans. He returned to Santiago with enhanced prestige.

Juan Antonio Ríos, an excellent man of business, sincerely believed that industrialization was Chile's path to salvation. The nation, he thought, would not be free from foreign influence until her soil and mines and forests produced more abundantly and until her products were processed in her own factories and mills; her liberation would be won when she made her own motor cars and tractors and cast her own steel rails. With money from Washington, Fomento's program was expanded. A mill for making copper wire was established. A national hydroelectric program, calling for the eventual investment of $100 million, was drafted. The street railway systems of Santiago and Valparaíso were bought from their American owners. Blueprints were drawn and work was begun on an ambitious new steel mill, Huachipato, near Concepción. Prospectors financed by Fomento struck oil in the far south, and hopes were kindled that the nation would not have to depend much longer upon foreign sources for petroleum products. Nor was Ríos indifferent to the social ills of his people. The school system was expanded, a little was done to extend measures for public health, and a small beginning was made in low-rent housing to relieve the crowded slums. Ríos, like his predecessor, failed to live to the end of his elected term, and died in June, 1946.

CHILE'S POSTWAR RECORD, 1946–58

Gabriel González Videla, installed for the term 1946–52, was received with general approval. His inauguration was graced by the presence of Admiral William D. Leahy, President Truman's personal envoy, escorted by five American warships.[5] The new President, a forceful white-haired man of forty-seven and perhaps the most adroit politician since Alessandri, was another of the successful businessmen whom Chileans admire. Born in northern La Serena, González was a lifelong Radical who, unlike Ríos, believed in the Popular Front. Against the advice of his chief supporters (and to repay the Communists who had helped to elect him), he included three Communists in his eleven-man cabinet, one of them in the critical post of public works, but they proved troublesome and were dropped after five months.

González Videla's principal difficulties came from the Communists whom he had hoped to woo and win. Their leaders were a continuing nuisance, inciting strikes in mines and factories, organizing demonstrations in cities and villages. Such tactics were simply an extension of Russia's postwar policy of making life miserable for moderate rulers everywhere. Within a year after assuming office, González broke off relations with Russia and her satellite Czechoslovakia. He then expelled Marshal Tito's Yugoslavian diplomats for their meddling in local affairs, whereupon Tito denounced Chile as "the puppet of the United States," and Chile retorted by calling Yugoslavia "the puppet of Russia." Early in 1948 González began to oust Communists from his congress; the unseating of Senator Pablo Neruda, one of Latin America's finest poets, led to the resignation of the octogenarian Arturo Alessandri as president of the senate and his denunciation of the President's act as "political betrayal." In September, 1948, the Communist Party was outlawed, and its 30,000 to 50,000 members were driven underground. The "soft appeaser of the Reds," as his opponents described González, now became their most vocal enemy. When the Ninth Pan American Conference met in Bogotá in March, 1948, the Chilean delegates were among the lustiest advocates of united action against the Com-

---

[5] Chileans liked the Admiral but were not enthusiastic over the warships. The martial display was probably intended as a reminder to Chile's truculent neighbor, Argentina's Perón.

munists. But there was trouble from the right as well: a small contingent of ultrareactionary nationalists supported a barracks-revolt led by ex-dictator Carlos Ibáñez in December, 1949; quickly quashed, the affair was generally described as "made in Argentina." Meanwhile, González Videla's government was maintained in power by the Radicals, with various allies from the right, the center, and the left.

González Videla's political legerdemain was displayed in his dramatic claim to a slice of the frozen Antarctic. It was not a new argument: both Chile and Argentina asserted rights to shares in those piles of ice and rock. Great Britain had long held the Falkland Islands, and had proclaimed its sovereignty over uncharted lands to the south. Shortly after his inauguration, González Videla sent a naval expedition to plant the Chilean flag in the Antarctic. In early 1948 the energetic President himself sailed south to raise a flag over Graham Land, which he renamed O'Higgins Land, to the annoyance of both Argentina and Great Britain. Some bystanders viewed the episode as high comedy, but Chileans regarded it as patriotic.

Argentina, dominated by Perón, added to González's perplexities. That more powerful neighbor had not only beef and wheat to offer but also credit, and postwar Chile needed all of these. In late 1946 a pact was drafted under which the two nations would lower tariff barriers and accord each other reciprocal free port privileges, Chile agreeing to favor Argentina in her buying, and Argentina promising a credit of $150 million to finance Chile's purchases in Argentina and to expand her public works. The United States was assured by González that the pact had "no political significance." But the Chilean congress delayed ratification, and it soon became clear that Argentina, whose currency was rapidly depreciating, could not furnish the motors, tools, and machinery required by an expanding Chilean industry. Chile needed dollars, and those were minted in the United States, not in Argentina. The Chilean-Argentine pact was not ratified.

Industrialization, more than ever the word of promise to Chile with its vast mineral resources and little fertile land, led to continued dependence upon the United States. Fomento received repeated loans from the Export-Import Bank, which made possible many industrial and agricultural projects. The processing of copper increased. Some petroleum from Tierra del Fuego was actually delivered in Valparaíso. A sugar-beet industry was established, in the hope that Chile would be freed from paying Peruvian and other producers some $20 million each year for sugar. Hydroelectric plants multiplied. The chief exhibit of national pride was the new $88 million Huachipato steel plant near Concepción, formally opened in 1950, for which the Export-Import Bank lent $48 million. This project had been planned by American technicians and its management was entrusted to a Pittsburgh firm. Smaller than Brazil's Volta Redonda—and tiny by United States standards—Huachipato promised not only to release Chile from dependence upon imported steel but to furnish a surplus for sale to neighboring nations. Utilizing iron ore from Bethlehem Steel's northern El Tofo mines and others, power from new hydroelectric plants, and coal from the nearby Lota mines (supplemented by some higher grade coal from

England, Germany, and the United States), Huachipato aspired to an annual quota of 350,000 tons of steel. Chileans looked with understandable pride upon the modern industrial city built around the new plant, with decent housing for workers, fifteen by-product plants, and modern port installations to accommodate the freighters that served the enterprise.

Chile's postwar years brought increased domestic and international tensions. She was short on foodstuffs, and there was a constant drain on her foreign exchange for purchases from Argentina and Peru. Demand for copper and nitrates fell off, and unemployment provoked strikes, with new opportunity for the Communists to make trouble. By 1949 the price of copper, now the principal source of government revenue, was dropping disastrously; between April and June of that year the price fell from about 23 cents to 16 cents a pound. Anaconda, chief producer, began to lay off men. Chilean economists reported that each one-cent drop in the price of copper cost the national treasury $5 million in royalties. Further fear was excited by reports that the United States would reimpose the copper tariff of 4 cents a pound which had been suspended during the war. Impartial observers suggested that the United States, with copper reserves for a bare twenty years, would be wise to conserve its scant supply and depend upon Chile, whose reserves were adequate for a hundred years or more. The Chilean government resorted to new issues of paper money, which increased inflation without a corresponding increase in wages. In 1950 the situation was somewhat eased by the renewed demand for copper from the United States, because of the war in Korea. Chile contracted to furnish copper at 27.5 cents a pound; however, because of rising production costs and the need for revenue for the national treasury, by 1952 the government raised the asking price to 36.5 cents a pound.

In the presidential contest of 1952, the hardy seventy-five-year-old Carlos Ibáñez del Campo offered to save his nation from the "false democracy" of González Videla. He had counts against him: his dictatorship of 1927–31; his repeated plots; and his frank admiration for Argentina's Perón. But the grievances against the administration in power served Ibáñez: the nation's workers were striking everywhere; inflation was making the cost of living intolerable; the financial dependence upon the United States was irksome, and many Chileans were saying that González was "the servant of American imperialism." Furthermore, the Radicals in power were split into hostile factions. The 30,000 to 50,000 Communists, resentful of the outlawing of their party, were ready to support the archreactionary Ibáñez in order to defeat González. Elected by an easy margin, Ibáñez was welcomed, somewhat ironically, as a savior.

Chief of the handicaps under which the assiduous Ibáñez labored was the general conviction, in and out of Chile, that he was a stooge for the Argentine dictator Perón; in fact, many Chileans believed that Perón had been a generous contributor to Ibáñez's campaign funds. In early 1953, Ibáñez gave Perón an enthusiastic reception in Santiago and received a fine ovation in Buenos Aires on a return visit. A trade agreement was then drafted under which customs barriers were to be lowered,

Chilean copper was to be exchanged for Argentine cattle, and steel and iron were to be traded for wheat and vegetable oils. But within a year the Chileans discovered that Perón had driven a hard bargain, demanding a ton of steel for two tons of wheat, a ton of copper for three head of cattle. When Perón had eloquently announced, "We will erase the boundary between Chile and Argentina," Chileans rejoined, "The Andes should be twice as high." The Chilean electorate had put Ibáñez into office for a variety of reasons, good or bad, but they had not voted for Perón. When the Argentine dictator was ignominiously ejected in September, 1955, the news was joyously received in Santiago.

To the surprise of onlookers, Ibáñez showed no sign of reverting to the dictatorial role which he had played so unpleasantly in the 1920's. His conduct in office was conciliatory and reasonably competent, considering the immense obstacles he faced. The price of copper continued to drop, the deficit in food production became more grave as population increased, there were angry strikes, and inflation ran its bitter course—the Chilean peso which had sold in the free market for about 300 to the dollar in early 1955, had sunk to more than 1,200 to the dollar within three years. Ibáñez invited an American firm of economic advisers to study the Chilean situation; their recommendations for thrift in government and for austerity in imports of luxury goods were put into effect. There was some slight improvement in the economy by mid-1957; but then there was a sudden drop of about 38 per cent in the world price of copper, and the central valley suffered a severe drought. Meanwhile, Ibáñez initiated many promising measures, promoting industry, opening new petroleum fields, reclaiming unused land, and increasing hydroelectric power; but his administration was so chaotic and frenetic as to make his best intentions futile. Cabinet officers were appointed and dismissed at the dictator's whim; 150 men filed in and out of his inner circle; on one occasion, he appointed his personal dentist to the post of minister of agriculture. He rounded out his term of office in 1958 at the age of eighty-one.

JORGE ALESSANDRI, 1958-64

As Chileans approached the election of 1958, there was clamor from almost all sectors for a change. It was uncertain whether it would be a change to the left or to the right. The Conservative-Liberal coalition supported Jorge Alessandri. The coalition of Socialists, Communists, and other leftists—the FRAP (*Frente de Acción Popular*)—backed the erratic Salvador Allende. The Christian Democrats (formerly called the Falange, but without links to the Spanish group of the same name) proposed the able Eduardo Frei Montalva. A hard-fought campaign culminated in as honest an election as Chile had ever had; Alessandri got about 32 per cent of the votes, with Allende a close second. Congress declared Alessandri elected. There was general relief among all Conservatives and most moderates.

Jorge Alessandri, sixty-two-year-old bachelor son of Arturo (The "Lion of Tarapacá"), an engineer and industrialist with varied experience and much financial success, was highly respected by the Chilean people. He made his appeal to men of all parties and all regions, and the response of almost all groups—except those of the far left—was approving. Upon assuming the presidency he chose his cabinet for ability rather than party affiliation, and even critics had to admit that his cabinet was able and honest. Stoutly conservative in his economic theories, Alessandri stressed the virtues of private enterprise; and his answer for all troubles was austerity—this was the prescription of the Klein-Saks analysts in 1955–56, and it was the central emphasis in the advice of the International Monetary Fund. We must live on what we have, said Alessandri in effect: we must tighten our belts, work hard, and we will win. But the belts that were tightened were, of course, the belts of the lower middle class and the poor.

One of Alessandri's first moves was to stabilize the currency and to create a new monetary unit, the escudo (equal to 1,000 pesos), which was pegged at the somewhat artificial rate of 1.053 to the United States dollar. After the riotous inflation of the 1950's, this was a welcome relief to the Chilean people: the air was charged with optimism, and there was a sudden rush of capital to the savings banks. Alessandri's competence as an administrator and his vigorous housekeeping further inspired confidence: in 1959 the national budget was actually balanced (at $440.6 million)—for the first time since 1950, when Alessandri was minister of finance in the cabinet of González Videla. In March, 1960, the President asked for and was granted by Congress dictatorial power for one year to make economic decisions. He used this power to drop 5 per cent of all government employees, to pay off long overdue accounts to private contractors, and to bring suits against delinquent taxpayers. He also lifted tax rates, a measure which had political risks for his administration; and he sought to speed up the launching of new copper companies in order to increase production.

In May, 1960, Chile was struck by a series of earthquakes and resultant tidal waves, which took several thousand lives and inflicted property damage estimated at more than $200 million. Aside from the human tragedy of the cataclysm, it brought new perplexities for the President. In addition to laying upon the government the burden of rebuilding cities and villages, and caring for the victims, it also released forces disruptive to the general economy. President Alessandri sought—and received—new loans from the United States for the reconstruction of the stricken areas.

The stability of the national currency was, of course, too good to be true. By heroic efforts, and by drawing on the scant reserves of foreign exchange, the escudo was held at 1.053 to the dollar for more than three years—the longest such period in recent history. But this unrealistically high valuation of the escudo put strain on the economy. Imported machinery bought with the dollar—which had become "the cheapest commodity in Chile"—was far less expensive than hiring local labor to do the job. And exports, overpriced in dollar terms, met ruinous competition on the world market. The result was an increasing trade deficit, and a disastrous drop in foreign exchange reserves. From early in 1962 there was grudging recognition of a free rate for the escudo as well as an official rate. And in October, 1962, the inevitable devaluation came: after that date both the "bank" rate and the "money-changers' " rate were free to fluctuate (the latter slipping to 3.27 to the dollar by the end of Alessandri's term in 1964); and a new round of rising prices, wage demands, and speculation was triggered.

The economy as a whole continued to stagnate: the per capita product increased scarcely more than 1 per cent a year between 1958 and 1964. To be sure, there were some hopeful developments: during those years, industrial production was up 44 per cent, and the production of electric power increased 50 per cent. However, industry—the magic key to the modern world—had flourished at the expense of agriculture. Confronted upon assuming office by the continued inadequacy of farm production, Alessandri had told the owners of the great *fundos*, in effect, that they must modernize their methods to produce more food and that they must put their profits back into the land. But this admonition produced no tangible results: per capita agricultural production actually decreased during 1958–64.

As Alessandri approached the end of his term it became clear that although few questioned his integrity and his patriotism, he had had no magic cure for the nation's ills. There was an uneasy awareness that the poor still did not receive their fair share of the economic bounty: in fact, Alessandri, in pushing his program of austerity, had asked the greatest sacrifice of the workers, whose wages did not keep pace with the cost of living: prices increased fourfold in the six-year period. In the words of the moderate economist, Daniel Armanet, "To maintain salaries almost unalterable when the level of prices has risen, is mathematically the same as to lower them when prices have remained stable. This, in a country of low living standards, is an intolerable measure"[6]

Alessandri took satisfaction in the relative calm which had prevailed during his presidency. "I am proud," he said, "that there were no social disorders in my regime, no state of siege." But Chileans were restless.

THE ELECTION OF 1964: REVOLUTION BY BALLOT

The Chilean election of 1964 was watched with fascination and anxiety by the entire world. It was the first open contest on American soil between the ideologies of the Western World and of Moscow. And there was a real chance that Chile might be the first nation anywhere to vote a Communist-dominated regime into power.

The traditionally conservative groups of Chile—for the first time

[6] Cited by Fredrick B. Pike: *Chile and the United States* (Notre Dame, Ind.: University of Notre Dame Press; 1963), p. 275.

in the nation's history—were scarcely represented in the test of strength: the one rightist candidate—Julio Durán, nominee of Alessandri's *Frente Democrática*—obviously had no chance at all, for Chilean experience with Alessandri had persuaded the voters that the old guard offered no ray of hope. The choice lay between two leftist contingents: the FRAP, a Socialist-Communist agglomeration with Salvador Allende as its candidate, and the Christian Democrats headed by Eduardo Frei Montalva. Washington, discreetly feigning neutrality, put all its hopes on Frei. Moscow, less discreet, cheered Allende.

The issues were clear-cut. Salvador Allende, tough, demagogic, able, was the Communist standard-bearer—perhaps a simplified description, for he was a practical man who could not quite be pigeonholed as a minion of Moscow. His promises were explicit: the seizure and partition of the great *fundos*; the nationalization of the copper mines (largely American-owned); the expropriation of all utility companies; and loyalty to his ally, Fidel Castro of Cuba. Eduardo Frei, calm, assured—and never demagogic—had been one of the founders in the 1930's of the National Falange, forerunner of the Christian Democratic Party, and was a firm friend of the United States. Frei's promises were as explicit as Allende's: land for the landless, but only by fair legal process, and with full payment to the owners; the "Chileanization" of the copper mines, a process whereby the government would buy into the American-owned companies, share the risks and the profits, expand production, and provide funds which would finance the program of agrarian reform. Both Allende and Frei were talking of a Chilean revolution, but their accents were different. Allende's voice had a Marxist ring, evoking visions of violence, swift action after the Mexican or Bolivian fashion in revolution. Frei's was the persuasive, quiet voice of a lawyer pleading for an amicable settlement of old disputes, for an orderly and just arrangement under which the rights of all would be assured.

The results of the election of September, 1964, were dramatic: Frei won, with a clear 56 per cent of the votes; Allende got 38 per cent: the other contenders had but 6 per cent between them. The analysis of the vote was illuminating. Allende's FRAP won most of organized labor's votes—but only 20 per cent of Chile's industrial workers are organized. Frei won by a wide margin among the miners in the more efficient copper mines, suggesting that those aristocrats of the industrial labor force had done some quiet thinking about issues—Allende's nationalization by seizure as against Frei's halfway nationalization by quiet agreement. It was significant that Frei had strong support from two of the most economically depressed groups: the dwellers in squalid city slums, the *callampas*; and the farm laborers, the *inquilinos*, who are still held in quasi-feudal fashion on the great *fundos*. And Frei had solid support from conservative and moderate groups, suggesting that many more were simply voting against Allende and Communism, while others were drawn to Frei and the Christian Democrats because of the constructiveness of their social and economic program. Beyond all other considerations the vote for Frei was a tribute to the integrity and solid ability of the man himself.

But the landslide for Frei was a dramatic vote of confidence for the Christian Democratic Party, which had had its beginnings in the 1930's when sons of the privileged conservatives had broken from their traditional political allegiances and formed the National Falange, dedicated to a bold new program of national renovation. The movement had grown slowly, and in 1957 had been rechristened the Christian Democratic Party, loosely aligned with movements of the same name in Europe, and later in Latin America (notably in Venezuela and Peru). The men who had founded the Falange in the 1930's, among whom Eduardo Frei was preeminent, were men of deep religious conviction, who had drawn inspiration from their Catholic tutors: from the encyclicals of Leo XIII (*Rerum Novarum*) and of John XXIII (*Mater et Magistra*) with their bold pleas for social justice; from Catholic philosophers who were the spokesmen of an awakening Church—such as the French Neo-Thomist Jacques Maritain, and the Belgian Jesuit Roger Vekemans, who worked long in Chile. Not a confessional party, not confined to adherents of the Catholic Church, and in no way the instrument of Catholic clergy and laity, the Christian Democratic movement was profoundly religious. Despite its aristocratic and conservative springs, it had aligned itself as left of center in the Chilean political spectrum. Definitely anti-Communist, the Christian Democrats had assumed much the same positions as were held by the Socialists (some called them "Socialists who pray"): they would be content with nothing short of a "Revolution in Liberty" (Frei's slogan in the presidential campaign). They would reject both capitalism and Communism in favor of a middle way—somewhat after the order of a Denmark or a Sweden—in which social renewal could come to pass by peaceful and legal means. Traditionally drawing support from upper- and middle-class families, their base had broadened rapidly to include the *inquilinos* of the countryside and the lowliest *rotos* in the city slums. Their winning of the presidency, the first such success of any Christian Democratic party in Latin America, was an event of the greatest importance for partisans of democracy everywhere.

EDUARDO FREI MONTALVA, 1964–

Inaugurated in November, 1964, President Frei was confronted with grave problems. The economy was tottering. "The facts cannot be cloaked," said Frei. "The nation ought to be told that there is not a single cent in the national treasury to meet the November and December payrolls." The interest and amortization on the $2.3 billion foreign debt— the highest per capita debt load of any Latin American country—took about one-half of all export earnings. Inflation continued to cancel out the best measures that could be devised: during the year before Frei assumed office, the cost of living had increased about 46 per cent. Education demanded attention: Chilean schools had long enjoyed an enviable reputation, but there were schools for only some 60 to 75 per cent of the children; Chile had some of the best teachers in all Latin America, but there were not enough of them. The housing situation called for redress: the slums of the chief cities (the *callampas*) were a melancholy exhibit of filth and misery, and Frei proposed to build 60,000 new housing units each year, 360,000 in his six years of office. The farming picture was depressing. The baronial landholdings, the *fundos* (comprising only about 4 per cent of all holdings but more than 75 per cent of the fruitful land), were not only an affront to any claim to equal opportunity for all citizens, but they were laggard in meeting the clamor for food: many of them were incompetently cultivated, and great stretches of the good land were not cultivated at all. There were fewer cattle in Chile than there had been in 1910. Before 1930, Chile had exported a substantial volume of foodstuffs; by 1964, Chile was buying grain and meat from Argentina, Peru, and elsewhere at a cost of more than $100 million each year. For more than thirty years, the Chilean population had been increasing at an annual rate of 2.5 per cent or more; during those same years, the increase in food production had averaged only about 1.6 per cent each year. Chile was running a losing race with hunger, as any observer wandering through the slum areas could tell at a glance.

Frei set out with vigor to tackle these problems and to fulfill the promises of the campaign. But he inherited a hostile lame-duck congress, a holdover from the election of 1961: the Christian Democrats held only 23 of the 192 seats in the Chamber of Deputies and 4 out of 45 in the Senate; and they faced the granite opposition of the intransigent rightists, who regarded Frei's program as too radical, and the equally intransigent FRAP, who swore that it was not radical enough—these extremists became strange bedfellows as they waged their united war on the President. Frei's early bouts with his congress were discouraging. His program, discussed for many months, included large housing projects, hospitals and health services, expanded education—and beyond all these the controversial plans for reorganization of the copper industry and extensive agrarian reform. The immediate crisis for the Frei administration was to get money enough to pay wages and salaries which were in arrears, and to make possible long-range planning. Proposals to increase taxes—especially on the large landholders, who had always been the chief tax-dodgers in Chile—were met by stubborn opposition. For four months there was an angry deadlock between the President and the Congress. There were gloomy forecasts that the Christian Democratic program would not get off the ground.

The March, 1965, congressional elections were fought on but one issue: Frei's program. The overwhelming victory of the Christian Democrats answered the question posed by the presidential election of November, 1964: Did Frei's victory represent the solid support of the Chilean people, or did it simply reflect fear of the Marxist-minded FRAP? The landslide vote in March—an "earthquake," Frei called it—increased the seats of the Christian Democrats in the 147-seat Chamber of Deputies from 23 to

82, the first clear majority for a ruling party since 1851; and it gave them 12 of the 21 seats at stake in the Senate, for a total of 13 out of the 45 seats in that body. The victory reflected the enormous charm and persuasiveness of Frei himself, and was a clear mandate for the government to launch one of the most fundamental and far-reaching programs of social and economic reform ever to be initiated in Latin America.

The cornerstone of Frei's economic program was the "Chileanization" of copper. Copper had long been Chile's chief reliance for export income, providing over 60 per cent of the nation's sales in the world market. The copper industry was almost entirely American-owned, controlled by Anaconda and Kennecott, with the Cerro Corporation a latecomer. But, curiously enough, Frei's chief opposition did not come from the foreign operators but from the obstinate owners of great estates and big businesses, who wanted no trifling with property values. And this Chilean aristocracy was now aligned against Frei's program with the FRAP, who would be content with nothing short of outright confiscation of the mines in the fashion which Mexico had adopted with the petroleum companies in 1917.

Frei and his inner circle of economists and technicians had been working on his "Chileanization" formula for many months before his election. The plan bore striking similarity to Mexico's newly adopted policy in handling foreign corporations, whereby Mexican capital enjoys majority control, with foreigners increasingly limited to a minority position. Frei's plan called for a one-quarter Chilean interest in the subsidiaries of Anaconda and Cerro, with careful provisions for control, and for special handling of Kennecott, of which the Braden Company was a subsidiary. The Kennecott properties included the great El Teniente mine, the world's largest underground copper mine, producer of about 40 per cent (180,000 tons per year) of Chile's copper. Ownership of this mine would be transferred to a new corporation, *Sociedad Minera El Teniente, SA,* in which the Chilean government would have a 51 per cent interest, and Kennecott 49 per cent. In return, the Chilean government would pay Kennecott $80 million over a twenty-year period, and Kennecott would put back that amount to help finance enlarged production. Further funds for expansion, some $100 million, would come from international lending agencies. Frei's experts forecast that copper output would be doubled in six years (from 685,000 tons in 1964 to 1.2 million tons in 1970), making Chile the chief world producer, ahead of the United States.

This bold plan won prompt approval from the American corporations, which recognized its advantages. Psychologically, it was dramatic insurance against the threat of confiscation (which was exactly what Allende and the FRAP had advocated), for under its workings the companies and the government of Chile would be yoked in a profitable partnership. Economically it would enable Chile to take advantage of the rising demand, at increased prices, for copper in the world market. Also important, the plan would enable Chile to bypass the United States effort to hold the price of copper at the unrealistically low price of 36 cents per pound. And there would be lowered taxes for the companies. Furthermore, the international lending agencies approved the plan and promised funds to support it. Frei's new congress debated the measure through 1965 and finally accepted it in early 1966. The timing was fortunate, for world demand for copper was forcing the price up.

By the end of 1966, in spite of bitter opposition from both extreme rightists and extreme leftists, the plan was beginning to take shape. In November, Frei's government reached an accord with Zambia, the Congo, and Peru—the four chief copper producers—for enlarged output and for higher prices: the atmosphere was buoyant, with copper in short supply and world demand increasing. But six months later when the representatives of the four countries met again in Lusaka, Zambia, on June 1, 1967, danger signs had appeared. The threat of higher prices for copper had provoked a search for cheaper substitutes; copper production had outrun world demand—and prices of copper were dropping. In April, 1967, the price had fallen from 54 cents a pound to 42 cents—and Frei's budget had been reckoned at a minimum of 48 cents, with 70 per cent of that budget based upon copper. Thus the fair hopes for "national salvation by copper" were dimmed. However, Chile's arrangements with the United States-owned copper interests were being completed with no more than minor friction, and the Chileanization program was a victory for Frei and the Christian Democrats.

Frei's land reform measures encountered much fiercer opposition than had his copper program. The little company of owners of *fundos,* especially in the central valley, had long been the dominant force in Chilean life; slowly stripped of their political power, they were not prepared to yield control of their broad acres. Frei's proposal called for the expropriation of all privately owned properties larger than 200 acres, but exempted those which were efficiently operated. Owners would be compensated, given 10 per cent in cash upon expropriation, the balance to be paid in bonds maturing over a twenty-five-year period. *Fundo* owners, organized in the powerful National Farmers Association, let out a cry of rage at this scheme, pointing out with some plausibility that payment over a twenty-five-year period was certain confiscation, as the currency had been depreciating at a rate of more than 30 per cent each year, and if that process continued today's escudo would not be worth the paper it was printed on by the time the final payment was made. In January, 1966, while this debate was under way, the American Ambassador to Chile injected a tactless note into the discussion. Commenting on Frei's agrarian measure, the Ambassador said that "from a social viewpoint, private property is not an unlimited right." "Busybody" was the response of various spokesmen for the *gente decente* of the central valley: a reaction which might have been echoed by some "decent people" in the Imperial Valley of California. But no matter what the land barons may have thought about Frei's proposals, there was rejoicing by the landless *inquilinos* and *rotos*: some of them exuberantly decided to take matters into their own hands and proceeded to seize some *fundos* near Santiago. Frei dealt summarily with these enterprising crusaders and made it clear that any land distribution would be regulated by orderly processes of law.

In May, 1966, the agrarian reform law was passed by the Chamber of Deputies. But there followed more than fourteen months of bitter debate before the Senate yielded to national pressure and approved the bill. In the meantime, there was some token distribution of land, utilizing state lands, a few private *fundos* whose owners had voluntarily come to terms with the government, and some lands turned over by the Church.

Victory for Frei's land program finally came on July 16, 1967, when his land reform law, which had been buffeted in Congress for two and a half years, was signed before a jubilant crowd of 12,000. It had been a bitter fight: the proud aristocracy of the landholders had denounced the measure as a swindle, and the noisy Communist-Socialist FRAP had shouted that it was a sellout to the owners of the *fundos,* who would find a way to circumvent its provisions. But for the moment, despite the reverses of Frei and his followers, the way was cleared for the nation to take over some 15 million acres of privately held land, and by 1972 some 100,000 farm families would have their own small holdings. The signing of the land law left deep bitterness in many sectors. Frei had won a great victory, but all bystanders knew that it would tax the courage and ability of their crusading president to carry out the provisions of the bold venture.

One of Frei's inner circle gave indication of the direction which the nation would follow under the leadership of the Christian Democrats: "Our goal is to turn Chile into a modern, socially progressive state like Denmark or Sweden." Frei's copper program and land reform program suggested the lines to be followed: no confiscation, no high-handed coercion. Frei carried on this same program in dealing with various foreign-owned utility companies, which were nationalized amicably, with satisfactory compensation for those whose interests were affected. One such, the Chilean subsidiary of American and Foreign Power, providing about one-third of Chile's power, was nationalized. Another, a subsidiary of International Telephone and Telegraph Company, also yielded gracefully to Frei's overtures.

Frei's energy and prestige went far toward lifting the level of performance of public officials. Some of his measures had a quixotic reformer's coloration: a titillating sample was his effort to change the working habits of Chileans. The historic working day of a Chilean had been made up of a morning spent in office or shop, a leisurely trip home for luncheon and a siesta, and then a return to work for an evening stretch of three or four hours. In December, 1965, Frei made the startling proposal that ten cities try out the experiment of an eight-hour day, from 8:30 to 5:00, with a half hour out for luncheon. He also urged that all bars be closed from 4 P.M to 7 P.M. to discourage those who would stop in for a drink or two. These parochial reforms were not enthusiastically received. Then, in 1966, he ordered a ban on movies after midnight, and the closing of television stations at 11:45 P.M. The government explained its point: "A nation that goes to bed late cannot work well the next day." Also, measures were taken to curb prostitution, with partial success.

Frei took time to strengthen Chile's lines of cooperation abroad. In 1965, after outbreak of fresh clashes on the Argentine border, he met with Argentine President Illia to discuss pacific measures for settling that old and angry source of discord. Frei proposed to Illia that attention be given to measures for linking the two countries in more profitable trade: one proposal was for the building of four highways over the Andes (in addition to the one already there); another was for a program for exchange of goods—for example, Chilean newsprint for Argentine auto parts; in still another Frei proposed that fruit from Mendoza should enter without duty into Chile.

Frei gave warm encouragement to an enlarged and more effective OAS. He was forthright in criticizing the United States' armed intervention in the Dominican Republic in April, 1965, and opposed Washington's plan for an Inter-American Force which could be summoned to intervene when other emergencies arise. He reflected the general Latin American dislike of interventions which might defeat the will of the people of any nation. While Frei urged that Cuba be "reintegrated into the American family," he was no lackey of Fidel Castro. In March, 1966, on the eve of a general strike called by FRAP to protest the government's tough handling of refractory miners, Fidel called Frei "a reactionary and a coward," giving force to Frei's denunciation of the strike as a "premeditated act of subversion." Nationalistic Chileans rallied behind the President, and the strike was a fiasco, undermining the influence of FRAP and its Castroite hangers on. As for Russia, one of Frei's first acts as president had been to resume relations with Moscow, becoming the sixth nation in Latin America to do so. "I prefer to have the Russians operating openly as diplomats," said Frei.

In August, 1965, Frei made a fruitful trip to Italy, France, England, and West Germany, was received warmly, and was given encouragement to hope for new trade pacts. After all, Chile had copper to sell—and, hopefully, would soon have more—and industrialized Western Europe was an important market. Frei proposed an "Alliance for Progress" between Europe and Latin America. He pleased De Gaulle by referring to the "hegemony" of the United States. "We Latin Americans," he said "want a system without hegemonies." But he hastened to add that this meant no lessening of his affection for the United States. "The discrepancy that exists in important matters—such as the U.S. intervention in the Dominican Republic—does not signify anything of the kind. Democracy functions with discrepancies."[7]

But in spite of the considerable prestige of Eduardo Frei and in spite of his victories in the copper and land programs, the year 1967 brought severe setbacks for the President and his followers. Although Frei still had

[7] *Time* (August 6, 1965), p. 36.

firm control in the lower house of Congress, his enemies in the Senate brought repeated embarrassment. An irritating insult came in January, 1967, when the Chilean Senate refused by a 23 to 15 vote to grant Frei permission to travel to Washington for talks with President Johnson and American leaders. It was a deliberate slap in the face for the man who was generally regarded throughout the Americas as one of the most eminent statesmen of these critical years.

And the municipal elections of April, 1967, were a major rebuff for Eduardo Frei and his Christian Democrats. Frei had banked on the elections to express popular support for his program, and the results turned out to be a massive repudiation. His Christian Democrats won but 36.5 per cent of the votes (as compared with 42.3 per cent in the 1965 elections). Communists, Radicals, and Nationalists (the merger of Conservatives and Liberals) all gained handsomely. The adverse vote did not affect the national Congress (which, as we have seen, passed the land reform law in July), but it indicated the widespread disenchantment of the middle classes, which had been hit by rising taxes and the increase in the cost of living.

The scoreboard for Eduardo Frei in mid-1967, despite growing resistance from both right and left, still revealed substantial progress. The copper program had indeed lagged, but there was faith that it would rally. The land reform campaign was under way. Inflation was lessened, industrial projects were being expanded, new school rooms had been built, hospitals were being modernized and increased, substantial progress had been made in building new housing units. And an interesting item—in light of the strong Catholic sentiment which animated the administration—was the establishment of a chain of birth control clinics. Frei's leadership had done more to give substance to the Alliance for Progress than anything that had happened since Punta del Este in 1961.

CHILE: PROBLEMS AND PROMISES

Modern Chile has three times the area and seventeen times the population of the Spanish colony which took the first steps toward independence in 1810. Straggling villages have become modern cities: Santiago had 2,184,149 people in 1964; Valparaíso, 273,158; Concepción, 170,034. The mining regions of the north and the forest lands of the south are linked by 6,000 miles of railroads. Steel mills, copper plants, textile factories, oil refineries, and other industrial enterprises promise escape from dependence upon foreign sources. Second—hopefully soon to become first—among world producers of copper, first in reserves of natural nitrates, Chile also yields iron, coal, gold, silver, some petroleum, and numerous other minerals.

Politically, Chile has a record of stability and democracy unique in Latin America. Since 1830 presidents have served their allotted terms, with few of the uprisings, unseatings, or dictatorships which have marred the record of most of the other countries. Since 1833, Chile has lived under two constitutions, while several of her neighbors have had a dozen or more. To be sure, García Calderón's characterization of Chile as "a false democracy governed by absolute overlords" sums up most of the nation's history, but since 1920, the "overlords" have been losing their strangle hold. The Chilean Congress has the best record of any in Latin America for unbroken continuity and vigorous independence. Elections have long been relatively honest and free. And the rolls of the electorate have increased sharply in the past two decades: less than 9 per cent of the population voted in the presidential election of 1946; but in 1964 the figure was increased to over 30 per cent.[8]

But that fair record is marred by a stubborn feudalism, inherited from Spain, which still casts its shadow over Chile. There were but two social classes in colonial times, writes the author of one of the most penetrating books ever written about the nation:

> There was a landholding aristocracy, well educated, far-traveled, highly cultured, in full control of the national life; and quite apart from them, a lower class, often spoken of with mixed disdain and affection as the *rotos* [the broken ones], constituting the fixed tenantry of the rural estates. This distinction . . . gave its cast to the nation. . . . Whatever might be a man's occupation or wherever he might live, he belonged to one or the other of these two classes. He was either Master or Man.[9]

The proud members of *la fronda aristocrática,* still described by some as *gente decente* ("decent" people), are those who *tienen fundos, son católicos y conservadores* (own land, are Catholics and Conservatives). The stronghold of this aristocracy is still the *fundo,* the baronial plantation, whose thousands of acres are a mark of superior status in the Chilean world—but a continuing affront to the democratic faith of thoughtful citizens.[1]

Socially, the *fundo*—sometimes extending 100,000 acres or more— crowds out the little farmer. It perpetuates a rural labor pattern which includes the *inquilino*—the farm worker who is bound to his master by custom if not by law, paid a few cents a day, allotted a windowless hut with a dirt floor, provided a little food, and the right to graze upon his master's land; and the *afuerino*—the outsider, the casual laborer who drifts into the countryside for a few weeks or months, earns a few centavos a day, then retreats to the city slums. Economically, the large *fundo* is usually inefficient—the abundance of cheap labor discouraging scien-

---

[8] This increase was largely due to the participation of women, who were given the franchise in 1949. Registration and voting are compulsory for those who are eligible, which now includes all literate citizens over the age of twenty-one.

[9] George McCutcheon McBride: *Chile: Land and Society* (New York: American Geographical Society; 1936), p. 12.

[1] The Agricultural Census of 1955 revealed that in the nation as a whole some 39 per cent of the landholders owned less than 3 per cent of the total land utilized; while fewer than 3 per cent owned 37 per cent. The central valley provinces of Santiago, Valparaíso, and Aconcagua—the best land of the country—offers an even less equitable exhibit, with 7 per cent of the landholders in control of 92 per cent of the land. And equally serious is the monopoly by a few of the irrigation water without which possession of land means little.

tific processes—and thus contributes to the declining productivity of the land.

The cruel disparity between the gracious prosperity of the rich and the stark poverty of the masses is also evident in the overcrowded cities. Chile suffers (as do Peru and other countries) from increased urbanization: today metropolitan Santiago alone houses more than 2 million people, about a quarter of the total national population. The rush to the cities is largely due to the increase in industry and to the stagnation of agriculture. The poor farm laborers drifting into the cities usually fail to find the decent jobs they hope for, and they swell the ranks of the city poor: the large body of the unemployed; the menial workers and those with jobs at the bottom of the industrial ladder, who may earn fifty cents a day on the average. The cities are ill-equipped to take care of these depressed groups: in Santiago, for instance, the housing of some 30 per cent of the people is inadequate, with serious lack of sanitary facilities; of these about 60,000 live in *conventillos,* or tenements; and about 75,000 live in *poblaciones callampas* (literally "mushroom towns"), the worst of Chile's slums, where the "houses" are so mean and beggarly as to defy description.

The proletariat of Chile—the city poor and the country poor, ill-fed, ill-clad, ill-housed—presents as bleak an exhibit as any in all America. It is in this submerged group of perhaps 2 million souls that alcoholism flourishes, that the incidence of tuberculosis is among the highest in South America. The chief line of demarcation is economic. But it is also racial: those with Indian blood are disadvantaged, no matter how vigorously most Chileans would deny it.

But if there are still only two classes in Chile—"Master and Man"— it is also true that the "Masters" are increasing in number: the gulf between the proletariat and the growing middle class is deep; but as that middle class grows more prosperous and apes the "Masters," the line between them blurs. And so, from lower middle class to upper-upper aristocracy there are perhaps 6 million Chileans—some two-thirds of the total population—who have an effective share in the life of the republic: these are the people who read the newspapers; who vote, organize, advance in schools and universities; and who—though their economic health is uneven—at least taste the pleasures of life. And this Chilean body politic, by and large, is intelligent, moderate, aware of social issues, proud of the nation's high place among the democracies of the world.

Among Chile's achievements is its social security system, which stands second only to that of Uruguay in the benefits it offers. It is a complicated system of some forty-two autonomous *cajas* (funds) which insure about 80 per cent of the labor force against sickness, accident, and unemployment, with generous old age and family allowances. Employees contribute 8 per cent of their wages, which theoretically covers one-fourth of the cost of the program, while the national treasury makes up the balance. The Chilean *cajas* have usually been honestly operated, but their administration has been bogged down by a top-heavy bureaucracy which takes too large a toll of the available revenue. The chief weakness of the system, however, lies in the continued and paralyzing inflation which waters down the national currency, eroding benefits. The resulting increases in the levies both upon the employees and upon the state have added to the general poverty, provoking further disastrous wage demands. Admirable in scope and purpose, the social security system has become a heavy burden on the nation—suggesting that such generous protection is viable only in a state whose economy can carry the load.

In the broad spectrum of Latin American nations, the Chile of 1967 presents a luminous exhibit of hope for democratic practice. Chile, of course, has a long tough road to travel, but she has started down that road with courage. Her assets are impressive. Government is competent. Public business, on the whole, is handled with honesty and efficiency. The dedication to legality is deeply rooted. Education, while still inadequate, is imaginative and inspiring. The armed forces, so anarchic in some Latin American nations, are professional in temper, and do not presume to dictate to the civilian authorities. The press is unshackled, and often useful.

Not the least among the assets of modern Chile is the Church, which is preeminent in Latin America in its faithfulness to the liberal counsels of the popes from the days of Leo XIII to the present. The Catholic clergy in Chile have served for more than four decades as a leaven of democratic progress: bishops, parish priests, and members of the religious orders—notably the Jesuits—are demanding social justice. Typical of such leadership is Cardinal Raúl Silva Henríquez, who is openly aligned with the Christian Democrats, and who warned in 1966: "We shall either achieve rapid evolution or confront social catastrophe. . . . Social reform is the only answer to Communism."

Over a period of a century or more Chile has had rather more than its share of distinguished historians and essayists, attesting the vigor of the nation's intellectual life. And of late years two Chilean poets have won worldwide acclaim: Pablo Neruda (*Residencia in la tierra, Canto general*) a stylist of great skill who has influenced writing in Spain and Latin America for nearly thirty years; and Gabriela Mistral (*Desolación, Ternura*) who was awarded the Nobel Prize in Literature in 1945.

As of 1967, it may be put down with assurance that Chile under the leadership of Eduardo Frei has done more than any other Latin American nation to give substance to the hope that a true social revolution can come without gunfire. And, as of 1967, a bystander dares to suggest that Eduardo Frei has done as much as any living man to undercut the threat of Communism in the Western Hemisphere.

PART IX

The Republics
of the Río de la Plata

The Spanish Viceroyalty of La Plata broke up, after 1810, into the modern nations of Bolivia, Paraguay, Uruguay, and Argentina. The first of these, despite its inclusion in the Viceroyalty, belongs ethnically and historically with Peru and has been treated in Part VII with the Indian lands of the Andes. We here consider independent Argentina, Uruguay, and Paraguay. The first, Argentina, richly endowed with fertile soil and peopled by European migrants, had a spectacular development in the last half of the nineteenth century and in the first decades of the twentieth, but lost its momentum after 1930. The second, Uruguay, is also European in extraction and has developed as a stoutly democratic state. The third, Paraguay, is a backward and isolated nation, of slight importance on the larger canvas of Latin America.

Chapter 36

ARGENTINA: LAND AND PEOPLE

Nature was benign in her endowment of the land which was to be Argentina. There was, to be sure, neither silver nor gold—although the first explorers named the estuary the Río de la Plata, river of silver, and the area around it Argentina, land of silver (after the Latin, *argentum*). Nor was Argentina granted such varied natural beauty as were Ecuador, Chile, and Mexico; she has little scenic grandeur save on her northern and western borders. Argentina's bounty was more practical: the expanse of alluvial soil, once the bed of an inland sea, is the most fertile and best-watered stretch of tillable land in all Latin America.

Argentina, spreading north to south some 2,300 miles, east to west at its widest more than 800 miles, covers over a million square miles, an area roughly equivalent to the United States east of the Mississippi, plus Iowa and California. In the south, Cape Horn reaches toward the cold waters of the Antarctic, and in the north, Argentine territory embraces the subtropics on the slopes of the Bolivian Andes; this north-south span is comparable to that of North America between the southern shores of Hudson Bay and the central Mexican plateau. Argentina boasts a wide variety of climate and terrain. North of Buenos Aires is the Littoral (described by Preston James as "the Argentine Mesopotamia") lying alongside the Paraná and Uruguay rivers, with the fingerlike province of Misiones (the name is a reminder of the Jesuit missions of colonial days) reaching up between Paraguay and Brazil. Northwestern Argentina shares the forests and sugar fields of the Gran Chaco with Bolivia and Paraguay. The corrugated semiarid region in the west, from the worn mountains of Córdoba to the granite wall of the Andes, is not unlike southern California, where irrigation gives life to vineyard and orchard. Beyond the Río Negro in the south lies Patagonia with its 1,000-mile stretch of wind-swept canyons and dry wastelands where the sheepman is king.

The Pampa is the heartland of Argentina; its plains comprise almost 250,000 square miles radiating in a semicircle from the capital. About 22 per cent of the national domain, the Pampa is the home of almost three-fourths of the 22.7 million Argentines; upon its pastures graze more than 60 per cent of the country's cattle; its fields yield more than 80 per cent of all the corn, wheat, and flax. Within its boundaries are laid about 70 per cent of the railroad tracks; and its factories and mills turn out more than 85 per cent of all industrial production. The Pampa *is* Argentina. The balance of the nation remains an undeveloped colonial empire.

God was good to those Argentines who live on the Pampa. Here is the planter's and stockman's paradise, where the plowman for mile after mile can cut a deep straight furrow into black soil free of pebbles, crossing few gulleys and making only occasional detour around a massive ombú tree. The cattleman glories in the wild lush grass which grows high enough to hide man and beast. The climate of the Pampa is as bracing as that of the plains of Wisconsin or Iowa, though not so extreme; it is hot in summer and cold in winter, with adequate rainfall in almost the entire area. The settlers in this region, corrupted neither by quick profit from precious metals nor by slave labor of docile Indians, repeated the experience of the frontiersmen of the United States and became self-reliant, tough, resourceful.

The 22.7 million people of modern Argentina (1966) are mostly of Spanish and Italian extraction and constitute (with the Uruguayans) the most homogeneous white population of any nation of Latin America. There is some Indian blood in the people of the interior, especially in the piedmont area against the Andean wall, and in the far northwest there is a continual drifting of Indians from Bolivia, most of whom work as seasonal laborers in the sugar fields (these may be compared with the migrant laborers who came from Mexico to the United States' southwest). However, only 20,000 to 30,000 Argentines can accurately be described as Indians. A little Negro blood has been absorbed in the national blood stream, but few reveal an African past. Argentine statisticians make much of the whiteness of their population; Alejandro Bunge, for example, cites figures for 1939 which report 77.4 per cent of European origin, 19.5 per cent of European birth, 3.1 per cent with some Indian blood—but there is little basis for such exactness. And there are probably more Negroes and mulattoes than some Argentine nationalists admit.

The population pattern of 1810, when a handful of Buenos Aires creoles took the first step toward separation from Spain, was quite different from that of the mid-twentieth century. In that year there may have been about 400,000 people in the area now comprising Argentina; half or more of these were Indians, 20,000 Negroes, 60,000 mulattoes, many thousand mestizos, and no more than 9,000 whites. We may hazard the guess that the effective literate section of the Argentine population of 1810 was not greater than the present population of such towns as Darien, Connecticut, or Grinnell, Iowa.

The creation of the present-day Argentine people began after 1850, when the gates were opened to immigrants. As late as 1852 the white population was only 22,000. During the eighty-five-year period, 1857–1940, a total of some 6,600,000 immigrants entered: about 3,000,000 from Italy, more than 2,000,000 from Spain, and more than 100,000 each from Poland, Turkey, France, Russia, Austria-Hungary, and Germany. Of these,

The Argentine Provinces

almost half returned to their homelands after working for short periods in Argentina, but not without leaving numerous progeny in the New World. Latin Americans call such migratory workers *golondrinas,* swallows.

The colonial background of this region was quite different from that of more populous Mexico and Peru. Long little-regarded by Spain, its original settlement was an afterthought of the Conquest; settlers from Peru spilled over the mountains to found Santiago del Estero in 1553, Tucumán in 1564, and Córdoba in 1573; others from Santiago de Chile established Mendoza in 1561 and San Juan in 1562; an expedition from inland Asunción founded Buenos Aires in 1580 (the earlier settlement of 1536 had been short-lived). During most of the colonial period the entire region was a political and economic dependency of far-off Lima. Such arrangement favored the interior cities to the disadvantage of Buenos Aires. Not only was the port city virtually padlocked against trade by sea and its population compelled to buy and sell through Lima, 3,000 miles over the Andes, but it was also blocked from free traffic with the interior. In 1622 a customs boundary was established at Córdoba (moved in 1695 to Jujuy), and goods from Buenos Aires were required to pay a toll of 50 per cent *ad valorem.* This *aduana seca,* "dry customhouse," encouraged smuggling and retarded the growth of Buenos Aires, which at the end of the seventeenth century was a straggling village of some 400 houses, eking out a bare living by its illicit dealings with freebooters. Not until 1776, when the Viceroyalty of La Plata was erected and the restraints upon trade were relaxed, did the city of Buenos Aires begin to prosper. Its population of about 25,000 in 1776 expanded to some 40,000 in the first years of the nineteenth century.

Spain's long bypassing of Buenos Aires had fixed a pattern of disunity which remained to plague independent Argentina for many decades. The *provincianos* had been taught to distrust Buenos Aires, and this incited the *porteños* (people of the port city, Buenos Aires), in turn, to look to Europe for inspiration—to England for their economics and to France for their culture—while they viewed with unconcealed contempt the pastures and the fields that gave them life. But it was the *porteño* who led the way to independence for all the people of the La Plata area, not only for those who lived in what is now Argentina but also for those in Uruguay and Paraguay.

Argentina's story as an independent nation falls into seven chapters: the years of tumult, 1810–29; the era of Rosas, 1829–52; the period of national organization, 1852–90; the rise and fall of the Radicals, 1890–1930; the rule of the oligarchy, 1930–43; the era of Perón, 1943–55; and the period since Perón, 1955–.

Chapter 37

ARGENTINA: THE YEARS OF TUMULT, 1810–29

The Argentine people celebrate May 25 as the natal day of their republic, since it was on this day in 1810 that 251 first citizens of Buenos Aires gathered in an open town meeting (*cabildo abierto*) to create a caretaker government in the name of deposed Ferdinand VII. However, their true Independence Day is July 9, the anniversary of the day in 1816 when a handful of delegates from a few provinces of what is now Argentina, with some from Upper Peru (now Bolivia), assembled in Tucumán to make the unequivocal break with Spain; "invoking the Eternal who rules the Universe," they declared the independence of the "United Provinces of South America," an area theoretically embracing all of the Viceroyalty of La Plata, although various groups in that domain refused to accept the leadership of Buenos Aires. It had taken six years for the independence movement to crystallize—years in which a little group of *porteño* creoles won a few allies in outlying provinces; years in which one junta, two triumvirates, and four supreme directors had taken brief turns at ruling; years in which some remained faithful to Ferdinand, some clamored for a king of their own, and others argued for a free republic.

The Congress of Tucumán in 1816, attended by thirty-two delegates, assembled at an unpropitious hour. The viceregal domain of La Plata, despite bold appeals from Buenos Aires, was falling apart. Paraguay had gone its separate way. Uruguay (the Banda Oriental del Uruguay, "the eastern bank of the river Uruguay") was the subject of contention between Artigas, whom we will discuss later, and his Brazilian opponents, neither of whom proposed to accept the domination of Buenos Aires. Upper Peru was strongly held by Spanish royalists, with armies poised to resist *porteño* forces. The "river provinces" of Santa Fe, Corrientes, and Entre Ríos (the Littoral) sided with Artigas and sent no delegates to Tucumán. Córdoba and Salta gave only lukewarm support to the congress. And the smoldering mutual dislike of *porteños* and *provincianos* continued as a divisive force. The United Provinces were sadly disunited. In Spanish American history, 1816 was also a dark year of retreat for the liberating forces in Mexico, Venezuela, New Granada, and Chile.

The delegates at Tucumán could no longer temporize on the issue of independence. Both Manuel Belgrano, hero of lost battles in Paraguay and Upper Peru, and José de San Martín, preparing his campaign against the Spanish forces in Chile, added their powerful voices in favor of a break with Spain. Twenty-eight delegates signed the declaration of independence and then revealed their monarchist sentiments by naming the royalist Juan Martín Pueyrredón as supreme director and by continuing their search for a king. That search had been going on ever since "the revolution of May" in 1810. An early project had called for crowning Princess Carlota Joaquina, sister of Spain's Ferdinand VII and wife of Portuguese Prince Regent John, as Queen of La Plata. Then Belgrano and Bernardino Rivadavia, envoys to Europe in 1814, had approached a younger son of Charles IV; but Ferdinand's restoration put an end to that idea. Rivadavia then cast about for an unemployed French prince suitable for the nonexistent throne and toyed with the idea of drafting the Prince of Lucca, nephew of Ferdinand. Meanwhile, Belgrano urged upon the Congress of Tucumán a fatuous scheme for joining the United Provinces with Peru in one constitutional monarchy ruled from Cuzco by a prince of Inca descent. The Inca scheme was laughed off, while England, whose economic control gave weight to her advice, vetoed either a Portuguese or French prince. Further opposition to all royalist projects came from the provincial bosses, the caudillos, whose power was increasing during this anarchic period. It soon became clear that these petty lords would oppose not only a king but even a supreme director or a president.

Despite such cacophony, Supreme Director Pueyrredón did remarkably well in his difficult office, actually holding it until 1819. A *porteño* himself, he promptly returned to Buenos Aires, and the congress followed him. He supported General San Martín, who was in western Cuyo organizing his campaign against the Spanish garrisons in Chile. In 1818 San Martín, after his victory at Maipú in Chile, returned to Buenos Aires, where he was hailed as a liberator. Eager to pursue his advantage north to Peru, he begged for money and supplies, but Pueyrredón could give little help. Meanwhile, Congress drafted a constitution, highly centralist and royalist, which was promulgated in 1819. Pueyrredón and his conservative backers had moved too far and too fast toward centralized authority and monarchism, and had failed to reckon with their unlettered countrymen of the backlands. These were the Gauchos; and their leaders were the provincial caudillos, who unseated Pueyrredón in 1819, undid what little unity the United Provinces possessed, and determined the destiny of Argentina for more than three decades.

GAUCHOS AND CAUDILLOS

The ubiquitous horseman of the Pampa called the Gaucho—southern cousin of the North American cowboy—is the hero of the Argentine people, celebrated in song and legend. By the mid-eighteenth century, the

Gauchos, who were usually half-breeds of Spanish and Indian blood (though some were whites and a few were Negroes), were a numerous and virile force, and they maintained their hold for a hundred years.[1] The Gauchos were dirty, illiterate, superstitious—and contented. They lived as nomad hunters of the wild horses and cattle which had multiplied on the high grasses of the Pampa after the coming of the Spaniards. They hunted with the knife, the lasso, and the *boleadoras*—a weapon made of three stones or iron balls lashed together with leather thongs, which was hurled to entangle the legs of the horse or steer, throwing the animals to the mercy of its captor. They broke the horses for their use and slaughtered the cattle, trading the hides for silver spangles, cotton and woolen cloth, knives, and raw rum from sugar cane. They devoured meat in vast quantities, brewed tea from yerba maté, and raised some corn to supplement their odd diet. Their dress consisted of long underdrawers, the *chiripá* around the loins, a long woolen poncho over the shoulders, and high boots of leather from horse or cow. Living in one-room mud huts shingled with grass mats, with heaps of hides for bedding, they drank profusely, gambled recklessly on the throw of the bone of a cow or sheep, played the guitar, and sang doggerel ballads celebrating their battles, their hunts, and their loves. Family life was casual, seldom requiring the blessing of a priest. The religion of the Gauchos was a patchwork of ancient superstition overlaid with a thin patina of Catholicism.

The true creator of the new world of Argentina, the Gaucho has been celebrated in a vast body of verse and prose. Domingo Faustino Sarmiento, writer, educator, and later president of Argentina, published, in 1842, his *Life of Facundo, or Civilization and Barbarism,* which gave that frontiersman a malodorous immortality. He quoted Sir Walter Scott's bad-tempered description of the Gauchos who evicted the English invaders in 1807: "The immense plains surrounding Buenos Aires," wrote Scott, "are in fact peopled by a sort of Christian savages called Gauchos whose principal furniture is the skulls of horses, whose only food is raw beef and water . . . and whose chief amusement is to ride wild horses to death. Unhappily they were found to prefer their national independence to cottons and muslins." And Sarmiento commented: "It would be interesting to make the offer to England just to know how many yards of linen and how many pieces of muslin she would give to own these plains of Buenos Aires."[2]

The oral tradition of the Gaucho himself, and the folk ballads composed by the *payadores,* or traveling minstrels, gave birth to a purely indigenous body of writing, *la literatura gauchesca,* which sang the glories

[1] The rise of the Gaucho in the eighteenth century was due to the brisk contraband trade in hides and tallow with Dutch, English, French, and Portuguese traders; this profitable business drew recruits to the frontier, and transformed the *vaquero,* the cattleman, into the Gaucho. The illegal activities of the Gaucho excited Spain to pay belated attention to the region, and furnished one of the reasons for establishing the Viceroyalty of La Plata in 1776.

[2] Allison Williams Bunkley, ed.: *A Sarmiento Anthology,* translated by Stuart Edgar Grummon (Princeton, N.J.: Princeton University Press; 1948), p. 109.

of the plainsman's history and mourned his passing. One of the most delightful examples is Estanislao del Campo's *Fausto,* the description of a Gaucho's visit to the Teatro Colón in Buenos Aires. Here he witnesses a production of Gounod's opera *Faust,* believing all of the events on the stage to be quite real. In 1872 José Hernández published his epic poem, *El gaucho Martín Fierro,* a defense of the rapidly disappearing nomads who struck back at presumptuous settlers for fencing in the open plains, confident that the land and the blue sky above it belonged to those who would use it. Martín Fierro, fresh incarnation of "the Conquering Cid" of Spanish tradition, fought lawmakers, judges, police, and settlers; he was finally conscripted into the army and forced to fight against the Indians whose blood he shared. The epic is a treasured heritage of Argentines.[3]

The Gauchos, "orphans of the pampas" as Torres Rioseco calls them, were the perfect instruments of the caudillos, who held almost absolute sway over their several regions during Argentina's first stormy years. The Gauchos were anarchical, fearless, and ready to fight for their rights or their opinions. There was no obsequiousness in their souls, and they had (wrote Sarmiento) only "pitying disdain for the sedentary city man who may have read many books, but cannot throw or kill a wild bull, nor catch a horse alone and on foot in the open country." The caudillos knew how to rally such men to their banners. The Gauchos' scorn for cultured city people made them eager recruits for the battles for freedom (or for anarchy)—freedom not only from the domination of kings from across the seas, but freedom also from Buenos Aires.

The caudillos, typical product of the Spanish American revolutions, were nowhere more aggressive and crafty than on the plains of La Plata. They were giants after their own fashion, vengeful, cunning, and ruthless, but generous in rewarding the Gauchos who served their cause. Sarmiento uses Facundo Quiroga, "Jaguar of the Plains," master of the province of La Rioja, as the symbol of all caudillos who scourged the land during the first tempestuous decades. "The Argentine *caudillo,*" wrote Sarmiento, "is a Mohammed who could change the dominant religion at will and set up a new one in its stead. He is omnipotent. His injustice is a misfortune for his victim, but it is not considered an abuse, because the *caudillo* is permitted to be unjust; further, he must necessarily be unjust. He has always been so."[4]

By 1819 the caudillos, supported by their Gaucho bands, were the true lords of much of the countryside. Estanislao López was master in Santa Fe, Ramírez in Entre Ríos, Güemes in Salta, and Aráoz in Tucumán; these four, hating each other cordially, were united only by common detes-

---

[3] Many changes had taken place during the quarter century between the writing of the work by Sarmiento and that by Hernández. The wire fence had doomed the Gaucho, and Argentina's economy had shifted from the pastoral to the agricultural. Hernández, a defender of federalism ("states' rights"), used the disappearing Gaucho to belabor Sarmiento, apologist for strongly centralized government. Hernández's sentimental nostalgia was the Argentine counterpart of the United States' romanticizing about the heroic cowboys of the wild West.

[4] Allison Williams Bunkley, *op. cit.,* p. 138.

tation of the king-makers in Buenos Aires. The caudillos unseated Pueyr-redón in 1819 and refused to accept Rondeau, who succeeded him as supreme director of the United Provinces. In February, 1820, Gaucho armies from the Littoral provinces of Santa Fe and Entre Ríos defeated the *porteño* forces of Rondeau in the battle of Cépeda. Their victory confirmed the autonomous character of the provinces and temporarily quieted the clamor for a king, blocked for a time the dominance of Buenos Aires, and silenced the *unitarios,* protagonists of centralism. It was followed by a treaty between the port city and the Littoral, which promised a federated nation in which the several provinces would maintain their separate powers. The caudillos and the Gauchos had won the first round against Buenos Aires and the creoles; the *porteños* were forced to think realistically about the life and the politics of La Plata.

The "terrible year of 1820"—as Argentine historians call it—brought increased anarchy. The *cabildo* of Buenos Aires, under the lash of the victorious caudillos, organized the provincial government of Buenos Aires, which was empowered to conduct diplomatic relations on behalf of all the disunited United Provinces. Within seven months after the battle of Cépeda, not less than seven governors moved in and out of office; some were radical reformers swayed by the provincial federalists; others were diehard conservatives who had the support of like-minded men in the outlying cities. In September, the storm somewhat spent, General Martín Rodríguez was named governor and held his post for four years. Though able and honest, he was overshadowed by his minister Bernardino Rivadavia, later described by historian-President Bartolomé Mitre as "the greatest civilian of Argentina . . . father of its free institutions . . . disinterested patriot, wise statesman . . . belonging to that company of the select who revivify the nations."

BERNARDINO RIVADAVIA

Bernardino Rivadavia, the ablest early leader, was forty-one when he returned from Europe in 1821 and was installed as Rodríguez's minister of government and foreign affairs. He was an unimpressive little man, heavy-featured and swarthy, big-bellied and stubby-armed, a dandy who had taken his clothes from the English and his manners from the French, a civilian who clung to his ceremonial sword, a man heartily disliked by many men but regarded as *precioso* by the women. He was ambitious yet capable of patriotic self-abnegation, pompous and overbearing yet eager for new ideas, "humorless as an old Castilian" but with the sparkling curiosity of a child. His philosophy of life and government had been shaped by admiration of Charles III, the French utopians, and Jeremy Bentham, at whose feet he had sat. He had fought in the patriot militia which evicted the British in 1807, had shared in the decisions of the *cabildo abierto* of 1810, and had agreed with Mariano Moreno's ideas on free trade, although his relations with that clear-eyed hero were unfriendly.

After the collapse of the first junta in 1811, Rivadavia came to power with the first triumvirate and dominated its counsels. The range of his activities was immense: he organized a military staff, built a foundry for cannon, a powder factory, a gun works; he signed the decree creating the blue and white national cockade, the emblem of Argentine nationality; he was responsible for disbanding the *audiencia,* symbol of royal authority, and for creating a national judiciary; he had a hand in liberalizing commerce, ending the slave trade, promoting immigration, decreeing liberty of the press, standardizing the currency—all within a period of less than thirteen months. In 1814, after two years of inactivity, Rivadavia was sent to Europe with Belgrano to secure British aid in persuading Spain to abandon her claims to the region of La Plata, and to search out a king for the chimerical throne. His royalism, incompatible with his liberal enthusiasms, was inspired by admiration for British ways in government, by prudent desire to appease the kings of Europe, and by conviction that only a firm hand could stave off anarchy in his turbulent homeland.

Rivadavia's activities as minister (1821–24) and as president (1826–1827) attest his energy and many-sided ability. Although in his first post his jurisdiction was limited to the province of Buenos Aires and in the presidency his national power was challenged by the regional caudillos, he succeeded in making his province a model for all the others, installing a provincial parliament (*junta de representantes*), extending the suffrage to all free males of twenty, and organizing the judiciary, a postal service, and a statistical office. The laws he originated reflected his liberalism: they included measures for the protection of property rights, individual security, and liberty of the press, and a "law of forgetfulness" (*ley de olvido*) granting amnesty to all political dissidents. Rivadavia's sound economic sense was revealed in his attempts to increase immigration, although his measures had little success. His financial policies dealt with taxation, tariffs, an organized treasury, and an accounting office. The Discount Bank which he organized fared badly and was replaced in 1826 by a national bank. He promoted loans abroad; Baring Brothers in London floated a bond issue for £1 million, yielding the Buenos Aires government a net return of only £600,000.

Rivadavia laid bold plans for stimulating the cultural life of the nation. In 1821 he founded the University of Buenos Aires, brought scholars from Europe to teach mathematics, chemistry, physics, and other subjects, and installed the first chemical laboratory. He was tireless in extending the public schools, drawing upon the Lancaster group in England for leaders. In 1823 he enlarged the museum of natural sciences which he had founded in 1812 (the modern Argentine Museum of the Natural Sciences bears his name). He strengthened and enlarged the national library, founded by Mariano Moreno in 1810, and supported the new Literary Society.

Rivadavia did not overlook the Church, which, since 1810 had been demoralized as most of the hierarchy and many of the priests left for Spain. The Vatican, under pressure from Catholic Spain, had excommunicated priests who joined the revolutionary cause. Rivadavia, whose orthodoxy was questionable, sought to inject new vigor into the Church. In 1822 he abolished ecclesiastical *fueros,* which gave priests the protection of their own courts, and ended the *diezmo,* the tithes collected by the state for the support of the Church. He confiscated the properties of a few orders and suppressed others whose zeal he thought was flagging, notably the Sisters of Charity who were responsible for orphanages, hospitals, and other agencies of mercy. By his decree, no one under twenty-five could assume monastic vows, and no convent or monastery could admit more than thirty members or exist with fewer than sixteen. These laws excited the wrath of priests and faithful followers, who organized fighting bands called *Las tropas de la fe,* troops of the faith. In 1823 there were bloody encounters between *porteño* armies and defenders of the Church. In distant La Rioja, the caudillo Facundo Quiroga raised a black banner bearing the legend "Religion or Death." Rivadavia was denounced as "the scourge of the deluge."[5]

Rivadavia, a humanitarian, created La Sociedad de Beneficencia with jurisdiction over hospitals, orphanages, and other agencies of mercy. Modeling it after the Philanthropic Society he had known in France, he entrusted its direction to a group of prosperous matrons of Buenos Aires society.[6] Rivadavia thereby encouraged the novel idea that women are capable of managing enterprises outside the walls of their sheltered homes.

As minister of foreign affairs for the United Provinces, Rivadavia won the recognition of the United States in 1822 and of England in 1824,[7] but faced continued threats from Spain and Brazil. Although he was eager to propitiate Spain and received Ferdinand's agents with courtesy, he refused to compromise on any measure short of full recognition of the independence of the United Provinces. Meanwhile, San Martín, with a soldier's distaste for diplomacy, pressed for decisive victory in Peru—a triumph reserved for Bolívar's forces at Ayacucho in 1824. Rivadavia counseled patience with Brazil, which had seized the Banda Oriental by 1820, but his attempts at conciliation were nullified by the belligerence of the provincial caudillos (notably Estanislao López of Santa Fe) who loved a fight almost as much as they relished their uncooked beef. All signs pointed toward war with Brazil.

Rivadavia was disqualified as a national leader by his ignorance of the Argentine hinterland, which he never visited, and his contempt for the

[5] His ways with the Church evoked both wrath and ridicule. One popular attack was in the form of a litany:
> From the marvelous future, Deliver us, O Lord!
> From the Jacobin reform, Deliver us, O Lord!
> From suppression of the religious, Deliver us, O Lord!
> From freedom of conscience, Deliver us, O Lord!
> From Rivadavia, Deliver us, O Lord!

C. Galván Moreno: *Rivadavia, el estadista genial* (Buenos Aires: Editorial Claridad; 1940), p. 326.

[6] The ladies did an excellent job and, with some interruptions, continued in charge for over 125 years, until in the mid-twentieth century a president's wife took over the business of organized charity and incorporated it into the Eva Duarte de Perón Foundation.

[7] France and the Vatican recognized Argentina in 1829, but resentful Spain held off until 1860.

provincianos, their semisavage Gauchos and brutal caudillos. He ruled as a *porteño,* for the benefit of the *porteños,* and had little comprehension of the problems of the interior. He was not indifferent to the demands of agriculture, for his own province of Buenos Aires was the richest of all the provinces in pasture and grain lands. He imported seeds, plants, and plows, and introduced better strains of sheep and cattle. But such matters were not his prime concern: his real preoccupation was with European trade.

Rivadavia's most important effort to serve the nation's agriculture was in the distribution of public lands. His apologists call him "the patron saint of land reform" and avow that his agrarian measures were designed to protect the national patrimony, to block creation of such distended latifundia as had cursed Spain, and to create a large body of self-respecting little farmers. His formula was the ancient emphyteusis, under which a nation retains full dominion over its lands but concedes their use under careful safeguards. Rivadavia's land law of 1824 for the province of Buenos Aires, extended to all the provinces in 1826, provided for rental of public lands to corporations and individuals for a twenty-year term, rent to be paid at the yearly rate of 8 per cent on the value of pasture lands and 4 per cent on cultivated lands. It further provided that rentals might be revised at the end of ten years by juries drawn from the neighborhood. Rivadavia's admirers have called him "the Argentine Henry George," but Miron Burgin discounts the utopian scope of his reforms and suggests that all he hoped for was to utilize the land rents and the direct taxes to bolster national finances and to "make the treasury less dependent upon customs duties, and so insure greater financial stability."

Rivadavia's land program, no matter how excellent his intentions, was directly responsible for fixing upon Argentina the pattern of latifundia which had long crippled Spain. From 1824 when the law was enacted until its repeal in 1869, vast public lands passed into the hands of a few people. These new masters of pasture and grain field became the political and economic dictators of the nation. Their monopoly of the soil retarded settlement of European immigrants on their own farms, provoked the unhealthy growth of cities, and delayed the development of democratic institutions.

Rivadavia's land reform paid off neither in tax return to the nation nor in social contribution to the citizenry. The rentals paid to the public treasury were negligible, as the new land barons became adept in dodging their obligations. By 1827 over 6.5 million acres had been rented to 112 corporations and individuals; of these, 10 received more than 133,000 acres each; an additional 16, more than 66,000 acres each. The lavish distribution continued after the fall of Rivadavia. By 1830, 538 individuals and corporations had received 20 million acres; an average of 37,000 each —but one man had received 880,000 acres, and another, 735,000. Rivadavia had failed to reckon with the rapacity of human nature, failed also to take account of how easily temporary concessions are made permanent— a lesson which might have been drawn from Spanish American experience with the *encomiendas* granted to deserving soldiers in the sixteenth century.

Rivadavia helped to create the oligarchy of baronial landholders whose names and influence were still conspicuous a century later.

When the governorship of Buenos Aires was shifted from Rodríguez to Juan Gregorio de las Heras in 1824, Rivadavia undertook a mission to Europe in the hope of persuading England to intervene in the impending fight with Brazil over the Banda Oriental. He was an eloquent supplicant, although Foreign Secretary George Canning was annoyed by his arrogance, confiding that he "demanded as a right that which he was entitled to only as a privilege." Meanwhile, a constituent congress of the United Provinces, convened in Buenos Aires at Rivadavia's suggestion, made plans to block the Brazilians, who not only showed no signs of evacuating Uruguay but were suspected of planning to cross the Río de la Plata into the heartland of the United Provinces.

The war with Brazil was hastened by the dramatic *coup de main* of thirty-three *orientales* (Uruguayans), political refugees in Buenos Aires, who suddenly crossed the estuary in April, 1825, and landed at Colonia near Montevideo, where they summoned patriots to revolt against Brazil and convened an assembly which pledged allegiance to the United Provinces. The congress in Buenos Aires declared the Banda Oriental restored to its rightful place with the United Provinces, thereby starting the war, which dragged on for three years with inconclusive battles on land and sea. Buenos Aires carried most of the burden, although some troops came from the other provinces. In 1828 England, solicitous for her South American trade, persuaded the belligerents to accept a peace treaty creating Uruguay as a buffer state, its independence guaranteed by Brazil and the United Provinces.

The war with Brazil, bravely fought but inconclusive, had a salutary effect upon the leaders in Buenos Aires, persuading them of the need for a government strong enough to cope with foreign troublers. In February, 1826, they elected Bernardino Rivadavia president of the United Provinces.[8] But the United Provinces were not ready to accept *porteño* leadership. Rivadavia's seventeen months in the presidency were unpleasant both for him and for his people. Everything he had said and done was used against him. Churchmen attacked him for his alleged infidelity. The interior provinces denounced his Banco Nacional (successor to his earlier Discount Bank) as designed to serve the port at the expense of the provinces; its monopoly of national currency angered the caudillos, who continued to issue their own worthless notes. Others deplored his pledging of the national domain as security for British loans. Almost all assailed his decision to dissolve the provincial government of Buenos Aires and to make that area the "federal district," in the manner of the District of Columbia.

The promulgation of a new constitution in 1826 incited revolt against him and against the deputies who had drafted it. The deputies, divided between centralists and federalists, were prudent men who sought national

---

[8] The congress, to be sure, had no legal right to elect a president. It had been convened to draft a constitution and had no authority to take further steps, but all seemed fair under the stress of war.

safety in a strong central power. Rivadavia, primarily concerned for efficient housekeeping in government, deplored the anarchic political institutions of the provinces and sought a constitution which would end confusion.[9] The constitution, centralist in spirit but assuring considerable autonomy to the provinces, evoked general anger. The caudillos refused to accept the new instrument. The reaction of redoubtable Facundo Quiroga was typical: refusing to break the seals on the document delivered to him by Rivadavia's messenger, he announced that he would not "submit to the chains that would bind me to the pompous chariot of despotism." The quasi dictatorship of Rivadavia was confronted by the tyrannies of regional chieftains: "The caudillos ruled the country," writes Gandía, "The people understood the meaning neither of federalism nor of centralism, but simply obeyed their local bosses."

Rivadavia, faced with general revolt, resigned in July, 1827.[1] The ill-fated congress named Manuel Dorrego governor of the reconstituted province of Buenos Aires, made him responsible for the foreign relations of the nation at large, dissolved the central government, and adjourned *sine die*. The several provinces conducted their affairs in their own disorderly fashion. Dorrego did what he could, concluding the peace with Brazil under British pressure and welcoming Uruguay as a sovereign neighbor in 1828. The returning soldiers, angry at the terms of the peace and the shabby treatment accorded them, organized a rebellion which in 1828 unseated Dorrego in favor of General Lavalle. Meanwhile, the country was torn by civil wars, and popular demand grew for a leader who could quiet the storm, for a caudillo of caudillos who could outthink, outshoot, and outwit all opponents. That leader appeared in 1829, and for twenty-three years the story of Argentina would be the story of Juan Manuel de Rosas.

---

[9] Administration of justice was farcical. In Córdoba the governor named a new judge for each case that arose. In Santa Fe, Entre Ríos, and Misiones there was not a single lawyer; in Corrientes there was one; in Entre Ríos a Franciscan friar was the sole arbiter in civil and criminal cases. Enrique de Gandía: *Historia de la república argentina en el siglo XIX* (Buenos Aires: A. Estrada y Cía; 1940), p. 371.

[1] The discredited Rivadavia went to Paris; he returned to Buenos Aires in 1834 but was not permitted to disembark, lived for a few years in Rio de Janeiro, and in 1841 retired again to Europe, dying in Cádiz in 1845. Like his contemporary José de San Martín, he was not honored by his nation until long after his death.

 [*Chapter 38*]

ARGENTINA: THE TYRANNY OF JUAN MANUEL DE ROSAS, 1829–52

All kinds of dictators have ruled in Latin America, but none has been more vigorous than the man who became governor of Buenos Aires in 1829 and who in 1835 was acclaimed as "the Restorer of the Laws." For more than two decades Juan Manuel de Rosas ruled the province of Buenos Aires as his private preserve and extended his power over the outlying provinces as well, consigning dissidents to imprisonment, death, or exile; imposing his will upon rival caudillos; and, in arrogant xenophobia, involving the Argentine people in futile wars with their American neighbors and eventually with France and England. He entered office as a federalist, upholder of provincial autonomy, and was finally unseated in 1852 because he had imposed on all the provinces a centralist rule more inflexible than the *unitarios* had ever proposed.

Juan Manuel de Rosas, thirty-six in 1829, was hard-muscled, blue-eyed, and fair, a man whom other men envied, but followed. The wellborn accepted him (at first), for there was no better family than his. The Gauchos respected him, for none of them were more expert than he with the knife, the lasso, or the *boleadoras*. The Negroes revered him for the grave courtesy he accorded his humblest workers. Even the Indians whom he had fought trusted his word. All accorded him the respect due the self-made man who owed neither fortune nor power to anyone.

Born in Buenos Aires in 1793, he was a volunteer against the British invaders at the age of thirteen; three years later he was entrusted with the care of his father's *estancia*. His boyhood and youth were spent on the open range of the Pampa, where his companions were the Gauchos, whose sports he shared. He broke away early from the iron-willed discipline of his mother, and he refused any share in the considerable patrimony which was his due. At twenty, he married María de la Encarnación Escurra, a headstrong girl of a family as proud as his own, securing the necessary consent of his parents (according to some accounts) by circulating the rumor that the girl was with child. At twenty-two, he joined two young men in building one of the first *saladeros* (meat-salting plants) in the province; they organized a monopoly of cattle breeders and processors, brought salt from

[*703*]

the Río Negro, cured their meat, and loaded it on their own ships anchored off the southern coast, to avoid paying the imposts of the Buenos Aires customhouse. This bit of private enterprise prompted Supreme Director Pueyrredón to decree an end to the *saladeros,* an edict illegally circumvented by Rosas. At twenty-five, Rosas owned thousands of acres on which he had demonstrated his skill in cattle breeding and grain production. Moreover, he held the loyal support of his Gauchos, whom he ruled with a strong but just hand. In the chaotic year 1820 Rosas, now a powerful caudillo, helped Governor Rodríguez to power, then broke with him and also with Rivadavia, for whom he had hearty contempt. In 1825, when Rodríguez quit office and Rivadavia was in Europe, Rosas was commissioned to negotiate a new demarcation line with the Indians in the south, a task which he performed with tact. A year later, when Rivadavia was made president, Rosas was brusquely ignored. After supporting Dorrego's election in 1828, Rosas was again commissioned to deal with the Indians and to establish new forts on the frontier, but these plans were interrupted by the uprising of Lavalle and the murder of Dorrego. Rosas took to the field with his Gauchos, speeded the flight of Lavalle into exile, and was installed as governor in late 1829. The junta of representatives, dissolved by Rivadavia and now reconvened, decided that Rosas was the only man who could suppress the anarchy.

FEDERALISTS AND UNITARIOS

Rosas's first task as governor in 1829 was to crush opposition and make himself master of Argentina's troubled house. He took office as the standard-bearer for the federalists in the mutually suspicious provinces. His opponents were the *unitarios,* who had failed so unhappily under Rivadavia. But the issues dividing them were not easily defined. The stand of the *unitarios* was clear enough: they wanted national unity under the leadership of Buenos Aires. The stand of the federalists was not so clear: there was not one federalist party; there were several. There were the federalists of the various provinces, commanded by caudillos who demanded not only local autonomy but also full recognition by Buenos Aires of their rights in the national partnership. The federalists of Buenos Aires also demanded autonomy but were as loath as the *unitarios* to make political or economic concessions to the provinces of the Littoral and the interior. "Federation," writes Carlos Pereyra, "was a word without meaning. The reality was the tyrannical power of the Buenos Aires customhouse." The Littoral provinces demanded free access to world markets through the river Paraná. The interior provinces demanded protection for their industries, crippled by the influx of cheap goods from Europe. But Buenos Aires controlled the tollgates and devoted to her own purposes the money rightly regarded by the provinces as national revenue.

Rosas's attacks upon the *unitarios,* continued throughout his years of power, were swift and thorough. His enemies were numerous and influential, including most of the wealthy and cultured families of Buenos Aires, who had turned against him after his first months in office. Hundreds of the ablest citizens were shot down in cold blood, and other hundreds were committed to filthy prisons.[1] Some escaped into exile in Montevideo, Santiago, Rio de Janeiro, or Europe. "Rosas," noted Sarmiento later, "might easily have been drowned in the blood of his victims." In spite of such terror, an American observer could write in 1832 that Rosas's "disposition . . . is not bad, and his intentions are honest."[2]

A master demagogue, Rosas proved the efficacy of the "big lie," which with repetition batters through the armor of timid souls. He rang the changes upon "Long live the federation! Death to the savage *unitarios*"; press, pulpit, and signboard repeated the lesson. Through the years the slogans were amplified, and even school children learned to denounce "the loathsome, filthy, savage *unitarios*." Travelers today may see toppling headstones in the cemeteries of Córdoba and Santa Fe with reverent inscriptions to fathers and mothers "resting in the Lord," and at the bottom of the stones the phrase: "Death to the savage *unitarios*." The blue-and-white banners of revolutionary years were banned, and blood-red ribbons took their place. Rosas's soldiers wore red uniforms. Doña Encarnación, intrepid First Lady, dressed in bright scarlet, and her example was prudently followed by other women. Scarcely a man, woman, or child failed to wear a red sash or a red ribbon. Rosas's portrait was displayed by the grocer, hardware merchant, prostitute, lawyer, and physician. The Church fell into line: priests welcomed his likeness with the ringing of bells and hung it close to the altar; and on occasion his portrait was escorted through the streets in carriages draped in red silk. A few priests resisted such servility, notably the Jesuits, whom Rosas had invited to return in 1836; his expulsion of the Jesuits in 1847 was a dictator's tribute to their fidelity to their vows.

While the *unitarios* were being harassed in Buenos Aires, the fight was on to eliminate them in the country at large. Early in 1829 General José María Paz, a man of letters and the ablest military leader of the

---

[1] An American resident in Buenos Aires reported later on the terror: "I have seen [his private] guards at mid-day enter the houses of citizens and either destroy or bear off the furniture and effects of their occupants, turning the families into the streets, and committing other acts of violence too horrible to mention." He described the central market place where "all popular rejoicings, gatherings and executions were held. It was in the market place that Rosas hung the bodies of his many victims; sometimes decorating them in mockery, with ribands of the unitarian blue and even attaching to the corpses, labels, on which were inscribed the revolting words 'Beef with the hide.' " J. Anthony King: *Twenty-Four Years in the Argentine Republic* (New York: D. Appleton and Company; 1846), pp. 241, 323.

[2] So wrote Francis Baylies, United States chargé d'affaires in Buenos Aires, to Secretary of State Edward Livingston in July, 1832; and he added: "But the tremendous power with which he is clothed would transform a patriot into a Tyrant and an angel into a demon." He then described summary executions and deportations and said: "Such, Sir, is the unhappy condition of society in this *Sister Republic* of ours, whose free and liberal principles and hatred of despotism have so often been themes for the panegyrics of our mistaken, romantic and imaginative politicians. I think one week's residence here would cure them of this hallucination." William R. Manning, ed.: *Diplomatic Correspondence of the United States; Inter-American Affairs, 1831–1860* (Washington: Carnegie Endowment for International Peace; 1932), Vol. I, pp. 132–3.

unitarios, seeing that power was passing into the hands of Rosas, assembled an army of 2,000 and marched inland, capturing the city of Córdoba and pressing on to defeat Facundo Quiroga; Paz shortly controlled nine western and northwestern provinces, uniting them in the Liga Unitaria.[3] For two years control of the nation was divided among Paz in the interior, Estanislao López in the Littoral, and Rosas in Buenos Aires. In 1831 Rosas signed the Federal Pact with López, uniting Buenos Aires and the Littoral in a pledge to destroy the *unitarios,* to create a Federal Commission with a seat in Santa Fe, and to take further steps toward organization of the nation on a federal basis at some unspecified future time. The situation was paradoxical. López wanted an Argentine nation; Rosas, it soon became clear, did not, but wanted a weak confederation dominated by Buenos Aires—or, rather, by himself. Fortune favored Rosas. In May, 1831, General Paz, while leading his troops into the Littoral, was unhorsed by *boleadoras* thrown by a common soldier, captured, and turned over to Rosas, who jailed him for seven years. By 1832 the Liga Unitaria was disrupted, federal troops had imposed their will on the provinces, and *unitario* resistance was for the moment quieted. The promises of the Federal Pact were not fulfilled. The Federal Commission, interim agency until federal organization was consummated, was disbanded in 1832; this action proved, according to Gandía, "that Rosas had no other political idea than to keep the country in disorder and poverty to maintain his own supreme power."

INTERLUDE, 1832–35

In late 1832, when his first term as governor of Buenos Aires ended, Rosas refused reelection by the junta because of its unwillingness to extend his dictatorial powers. For two and a half years there was a stormy interlude under three weak governors of Buenos Aires who could control neither the city nor the province. Meanwhile, Rosas, with sure sense of drama, accepted appointment to lead a campaign against the marauding Indians in the south. This was no new activity for Rosas, for he had led earlier expeditions to settle border lines and to erect frontier forts. He now pushed the frontier farther south and west, building new forts, manning them with garrisons, granting land to soldiers with families, and consigning to each fort "some of the unworthy women in which the capital abounds." His campaign reached south to the Río Colorado; and, despite the sabotage of a jealous governor in Buenos Aires, he effectually opened up a vast new area for settlement and laid out more definite border lines between Buenos Aires and the other provinces. His troops killed some 6,000 hostile Indians and freed about 2,000 captive Christians. It was during this southern campaign that Rosas received a guest named Charles Darwin, who was exploring the Pampa before rejoining his ship at Buenos Aires. Darwin described Rosas's camp near the Río Colorado:

[3] The League included Córdoba, Mendoza, San Luis, San Juan, Salta, Tucumán, Santiago del Estero, Catamarca, and Jujuy.

It consisted of a square formed by waggons, artillery, straw huts, etc. The soldiers were nearly all cavalry; and I should think such a villaneous, banditti-like army was never before collected together. The greater number of men were of mixed breed, between Negro, Indian and Spaniard. I know not the reason, but men of such origin seldom have a good expression of countenance.[4]

Darwin found Rosas "enthusiastic, sensible, very grave," remarked on his fine horsemanship and his great popularity with his men.

During Rosas's absence in the south, Buenos Aires politics were disturbed. The federalists, temporarily relieved of Rosas's strong hand, split between "moderates" loyal to Governor Balcarce and the die-hard partisans of Rosas. The "moderates" believed in the orderly development of national institutions, but the *rosistas* denounced them as *cismáticos* (schismatics) and called themselves *apostólicos*. Doña Encarnación, left behind by Rosas to safeguard his interests, directed a campaign to discredit Governor Balcarce and to prepare the way for the triumphant return of her husband. Her house became the headquarters from which attacks were launched upon honest Balcarce and his cabinet. She and her aides enlisted a network of spies, including Negro servants, to discover those who were hostile to Rosas. She organized the Sociedad Popular Restauradora, dedicated to the recall of Rosas, and which prudent men, whether bankers, lawyers, or horsethieves, found it expedient to join. This group was called the *mazorca*, literally, "ear of corn," the symbol of unity, although its enemies claimed that it should be spelled *más horca*, "more gallows." The agents of the *mazorca*, terrorists whose obscene brutalities increased during Rosas's later years, carried out the orders of Doña Encarnación. She was engaged, she wrote her husband, in "arming the rabble who would deliver the *cismáticos* to the devil"; again, referring to a minister of government, she confided her wish "to cut off his ears"; and, reporting the liquidation of an impudent priest, she described him as "a villainous knave." In October, 1833, her well-drilled mob staged the uprising that unseated Balcarce. We have Charles Darwin's firsthand account of Doña Encarnación's *coup d'état:*

> This revolution was supported by scarcely any pretext of grievances . . . seventy men left the city and with the cry of *Rosas,* the whole country took arms. The city was then blockaded, no provisions, cattle or horses were allowed to enter; besides, there was only a little skirmishing, and a few men killed daily. The outside party well knew that, by stopping the supply of meat, they would certainly be victorious. . . . The warfare on both sides was avowedly protracted till it was possible to hear from Rosas . . . on the bare reception of his views, the Governor, ministers, and part of the military . . . fled the city. The rebels entered, elected a new governor. . . . From these proceedings it was clear that Rosas ultimately would become dictator.[5]

4 P. P. King, Robert Fitzroy, and Charles Darwin: *Narrative of the Surveying Voyages of His Majesty's Ships* Adventure *and* Beagle (London: 1839–40), Vol. III, p. 83.
5 *Ibid.,* p. 166.

Governor Viamonte, elected in Balcarce's place, lasted less than a year, and he was plagued by the *rosistas* at every turn. The desperate junta begged Rosas to resume office but still refused to grant him dictatorial powers. In October, 1834, they placed Governor Maza in office, where he ruled unhappily for five months. Then the chastened junta—beaten down by Doña Encarnación's schemings, the failure of three governors, and the tumult of the city's mob—again begged Rosas to return. After repeated appeals they finally offered him acceptable terms, and in April, 1835, he was installed with "*toda la suma del poder público de la provincia, por todo el tiempo que a su juicio fuere necesario*"; certainly no dictator could ask more than "total power . . . for as long as he thinks necessary." Rosas, on his part, was pledged "to defend the Apostolic Roman Catholic Religion, and the national cause of the Federation." Rosas, however, as a last gesture toward legality, did not accept this endowment of regal power as final until a popular plebiscite persuaded him that it was the will of the people: the vote was 9,315 ayes and 5 noes.

THE RETURN OF ROSAS, 1835

Rosas resumed office with a pious genuflection: "Divine Providence," he proclaimed, "has placed us in this terrible situation to test our virtue and constancy. We will hound to death the infidel, the blasphemer, the thief . . . and all who dare scoff at our Holy Faith . . . until not one such monstrous person survives among us. . . . The All-Powerful will direct our steps." His consecration was rewarded by slavish adulation. Charles Darwin described the splendor of the demonstration on the Restorer's return to the port city—the flower-festooned triumphant arches under which Rosas's carriage was drawn with red silken ropes by 200 men, while the bells tolled, the bands played, and the blood-red banners of federalism waved. Rosas's picture was again paraded through the city streets and was restored to its place near the altars, so that priests, giving thanks to God, might gaze upon the face of the Restorer of the Laws. Men of high and low estate bowed fervently, some in fanaticism and some in terror. Rosas's spies reported the slightest word of disloyalty, and suspects were visited by *mazorca* agents with swift reprisal. Hundreds of public employees and army officers were dismissed; many were shot without pretense of a trial. Many others fled into exile.

Meanwhile, Rosas had been rid of his ambitious ally, Facundo Quiroga, the tyrant of La Rioja who was immortalized by Sarmiento. During the interregnum of 1832–35, Facundo had extended his power over the province of Córdoba and had evicted the four Reinafé brothers who ruled there. This prompted Rosas's good friend, Estanislao López of Santa Fe, to warn the Restorer that Facundo "aspired to chief power in the nation." Facundo had long annoyed Rosas with pleas for a national constitution, congress, president, and capital. By 1835 he had organized a league in the northwest which threatened the Rosas-López coalition. Despite his disloyalty to Rosas, Facundo was received in Buenos Aires as the dictator's friend and ally; then venturing north into the province of Córdoba he was waylaid and murdered by agents of the Reinafés. There was general relief over the death of the most savage of the caudillos. Rosas, beneficiary of the assassination, mourned loud for his fallen comrade, ordered a costly funeral, and sentenced the Reinafé brothers to death. Bystanders guessed that the true culprit was Rosas himself. Rosas later wrote from his exile in England: "They say I ordered the assassination of the illustrious General Quiroga. But have they proved it?"

The pattern of Rosas's government, set during his first term, was little modified during his last seventeen years of dictatorship. He continued to pay lip service to federalism by assuming no greater title than Governor of Buenos Aires and by repulsing all arguments for a national government. Meanwhile, he exercised a more absolute power over the scattered provinces than any *unitario* had ever ventured to hope for. As governor of Buenos Aires, entrusted by the United Provinces with power to represent all of them in foreign relations and general finance, he held the whip hand over the anarchic provincial caudillos. One by one his rivals died, sometimes at the hands of assassins, occasionally from natural causes. His rule by terror continued, with occasional intervals of relief for his badgered subjects, and then with redoubled fury. We have the testimony of an American observer in 1846:

> Such is the terror—the crushing fear—which is inspired by one man over that multitude, which now submits to his decrees with a zeal, apparently as ardent, as it is certainly abject and submissive. There is not a complaint heard. The calm and dark waters of despotism are never disturbed by the slightest ripple. Not a breath of free thought or manly speech passes over them, but they lie dead and deep, into which every vestige of the people's liberty and freedom has sunk and disappeared. Yet Gen'l. Rosas is the only man who could keep them together for twenty-four hours; and this he does by the extraordinary energy of his character, and the unqualified fear with which he has inspired them.[6]

ROSAS'S DOMESTIC POLICIES

Rosas's internal social and economic measures were as capricious as his political practices. He failed to reckon with the fact that the lightly populated Argentine countryside needed farmers with knowledge of soils, seeds, and fertilizers; stockmen with scientific techniques; artisans and industrial workers with modern skills. Rivadavia had devised plans for attracting European immigrants, but the nation could not understand his vision. When Rosas came to power, there were only about 600,000 people in all the nation, a quarter of them in the province of Buenos Aires. Rosas abolished the Immigration Commission created by Rivadavia and put nothing in its place; few outsiders entered Argentina before 1852, and her population did not increase more than 200,000 in twenty years. Rosas's

6 William A. Harris, United States chargé d'affaires at Buenos Aires, to Secretary of State James Buchanan, October 10, 1846. Manning, *op. cit.*, Vol. I, p. 400.

hostility to immigration reflected his deep suspicion of all foreigners and perhaps his fear that he could not control a more numerous people.

Nor did Rosas prove wiser than Rivadavia in his distribution of public lands. He first continued the program of emphyteusis; when he failed to collect the rents due the state, he abandoned the scheme and permitted tenants to acquire permanent titles on easy terms. Then, as the national domain was enlarged by successful campaigns against the Indians in the south and west, Rosas allowed these new lands to be added to the holdings of the great *estancieros* (of which he himself was one of the mightiest) with slight return to the national treasury or no return at all. The net result of Rosas's land policy, as of Rivadavia's, was to concentrate land ownership in the hands of a few thousand *estancieros,* who supported him throughout his years of power.

Rosas's economic policies—if, indeed, they may be so dignified—were no more than grudging compromises. Himself a stockman and grain producer, he favored the earlier *porteño* doctrine of free trade, confident of the profits from the sale of grain, meat, hides, and wool to industrial Europe. But as an avowed federalist, he was pledged to make concessions to the provinces which demanded protection for their halting industries. He granted those claimants sporadic measures of protection which were generally ineffective. Most of his policies were contrived to serve the *estancieros* of the province of Buenos Aires and to disregard the Littoral and the interior.[7]

He abolished Rivadavia's Banco Nacional, which had checked reckless borrowing and excessive issuance of paper currency; and he encouraged an inflation which benefited the *estancieros* by furnishing them with cheap money to pay their laborers and bringing increased profits from their sales in foreign markets. The customhouses on the Río de la Plata, taking toll from all ships entering or leaving the Paraná and Uruguay rivers, yielded the bulk of the income of the provincial treasury of Buenos Aires; in 1840 customs receipts furnished about 70 per cent of the total provincial budget, and in 1850 the figure reached almost 93 per cent. Rosas, thus relieved of financial pressure by the easy flow of money from the customhouses, was able to reward his fellow *estancieros* by taxing them lightly. Miron Burgin cites one *estancia* boasting 19,000 head of cattle which paid annual taxes of only 540 paper pesos ($100, more or less, in modern terms). Meanwhile, in spite of Rosas, Argentina was maturing economically. The lawless cattlemen, grown rich from Gaucho labor, the abundance of cheap land, and access to roaming herds of wild cattle and horses, were gradually yielding to the organized grain farmers and stockbreeders. An important milestone in this shift in agricultural economy was the introduction by an Englishman in 1844 of wire fencing: the fencing of the Pampa introduced a new period in Argentine life.

---

[7] Rosas's tariff exactions fluctuated, but during most of his rule there was an export duty on all goods from the provinces which passed through the Río de la Plata. In order to assure a monopoly to Buenos Aires, an additional 20 per cent import duty was levied on ships which first docked at any other Argentine port or at Montevideo.

ROSAS AND FOREIGN POWERS

Rosas's distrust of foreigners involved Argentina in endless disputes and costly wars. He shared the Gaucho's hatred of the city creoles, with their soft lives and their aping of French and English ways; this disdain, perhaps rooted in his early revolt against his parents, was increased by his experience with Rivadavia and other creole *unitarios* in the 1820's. His raucous belligerence led to disputes and wars with the one-time members of the La Plata viceregal family—Bolivia, Paraguay, and Uruguay—whose defection he never accepted as final. His political course in the La Plata basin, as well as his highhanded economic exactions, finally involved him in wars with France and England. His first major military excursion was an attack upon Bolivia in 1837. The immediate excuse was a border dispute, but his real target was dictator Santa Cruz, who was uniting Peru and Bolivia, plotting invasion of the La Plata area, and welcoming *unitario* refugees from Rosas's terror. The war on that upstart, chiefly conducted by Chile, ended with Santa Cruz's exile in 1839.

Rosas's meddling in Uruguay continued throughout the 1830's and 1840's and was largely responsible for Argentina's foreign troubles. Rosas, contemptuously rejecting the independence of Uruguay, repeatedly intervened in its affairs. He was the perennial ally of the Conservative Manuel Oribe against Liberal Fructuoso Rivera, who in turn had support from Brazil, Paraguay, the Argentine Littoral, and finally from France and England. During the 1840's Rosas's troops maintained an intermittent blockade of Montevideo. These futile adventures embroiled Rosas with France and England.

In 1838 the French, currently ruled by Louis Philippe, attacked. The ostensible excuse was Rosas's brusque treatment of a consular agent who had protested the drafting of French nationals into the *porteño* army; the real motive was protection of French commerce in the disturbed La Plata region. A French fleet captured the island of Martín García, which controls the entrance to the Paraná River. The effects were disastrous: customhouse receipts fell off; the trade of Buenos Aires, the Littoral, and the interior was reduced. A revolt in the city of Buenos Aires, followed by an uprising in the south of the province, was crushed at considerable cost in money and lives. López of Santa Fe, caudillo of the Littoral, took steps to break his covenant with Rosas and make terms with the French, a project ended by López's death in 1838. The French, finding neither glory nor profit in their crusade, withdrew in 1840 and agreed to arbitrate their claims. Meanwhile, the Uruguayans, with help from the Littoral and Paraguay, continued to resist Rosas's forces until 1842, when Rosas won a temporary mastery in their country, although never capturing Montevideo.

The joint Anglo-French blockade of the Río de la Plata in 1845, provoked by desire to protect their nationals, to safeguard their commercial interests, and to preserve Uruguay as a buffer state, again brought European ships into the estuary. English and French troops, joined by anti-Rosas

THE REPUBLICS OF THE RÍO DE LA PLATA

elements from Uruguay, occupied the island of Martín García and established a base in the Uruguayan city of Colonia, opposite Buenos Aires.

Meanwhile, the United States, now at war with Mexico, could do no more than protest this new assault upon the principles of the Monroe Doctrine;[8] it was in no position to police such a distant center of confusion as the Río de la Plata. However, Anglo-French efforts to humble Rosas were inconclusive. The British began to withdraw in 1847 and the French in 1848. By 1850 both powers had signed agreements with Rosas, who was hailed by his partisans as the defender of Argentine honor against two major European powers.[9] Besides such applause from the living, there was the last will of the hero, José de San Martín, who died in European exile in 1850; it directed that "the saber that has accompanied me throughout the entire war of South American independence will be presented to . . . Juan Manuel de Rosas, as a token of the satisfaction . . . I have felt on seeing the firmness with which he has sustained the republic's honor against . . . the foreigners who sought to humiliate her."

THE LAST YEARS OF ROSAS

It remained for the Argentines themselves to do what England and France had failed to do. When Rosas finally fell in 1852, the credit could be divided among the young intellectuals who fought the tyrant with their ideas, the *estancieros* who strove to retain their principal market in England, the *provincianos* who rose against his betrayal of federalism, and a rival caudillo who marshaled Rosas's numerous enemies against him.

No other nation of Latin America had more intellectual vigor than Argentina during the era of Rosas. A new generation of intellectuals reached maturity in the 1830's, and Rosas's assumption of plenary powers in 1835 stirred these young men to action. Their first move was to organize the Salón Literario, where they might listen to each other's poems. This disarming performance was followed by organization of "Young Argentina," modeled after Mazzini's "Young Italy." In 1837 the same company of poets and essayists organized "The Association of May" (the name invoking the events of 1810), dedicated to the overturn of Rosas. Some were

8 Secretary of State James Buchanan sent the American chargé d'affaires in Buenos Aires a note dated March 30, 1846, whose substance was delivered to Rosas's foreign office. He spoke of ". . . the great American doctrine in opposition to the interference of European governments in the internal concerns of the nations of this continent. . . . That Great Britain and France have flagrantly violated this principle by their armed intervention on the La Plata is manifest to the whole world. . . . The President desires that the whole moral influence of this Republic should be cast into the scale of the injured party. We cordially wish the Argentine Republic success in its struggle against foreign interference." Manning, *op. cit.*, Vol. I, p. 31.

9 Argentine historians generally agree that Rosas's martial role as defender of Argentine sovereignty was blemished by failure to take a strong stand against the British when they seized the Falkland Islands off the coast of Patagonia in 1833. Rosas, while repeatedly protesting, actually offered to sell England all rights to these islands. The acrid debate over these islands (called Las Islas Malvinas by Argentines) has continued to the present hour.

not only bold polemicists against Rosas but also effective builders of the nation after his fall.

Esteban Echeverría, romantic poet, wrote *El Matadero* (The Slaughter House) in which the crimes of the tyrant were epitomized. José Mármol, "the poetic hangman of Rosas," wrote an amateurish but eagerly read novel, *Amalia,* describing the same melancholy events. Bartolomé Mitre would later win distinction as general, historian, founder of the newspaper *La Nación,* and president of the republic. Juan Bautista Alberdi, jurist and penetrating political· analyst, wrote *Bases and Points of Departure for the Political Organization of the Argentine Republic,* whose arguments shaped the Constitution of 1853. Fervid admirer of the United States and England, Alberdi was instrumental in persuading his countrymen to open the gates to European immigrants, who, no matter how servile their previous condition, would become good citizens in the free air of the New World; *gobernar es poblar* (to govern is to populate) was the burden of his message. And to these should be added the name of Domingo Faustino Sarmiento, a *provinciano* of western San Juan and therefore not included in the *porteño* group, who gave international currency to the iniquities of Rosas in his torrential *Life of Facundo, or Civilization and Barbarism,* published in Chile in 1845.

These, and others associated with them, had been profoundly influenced by the European liberals, principally French. Some had lived in Europe; a few (notably Echeverría) had come under the spell of the cult of Saint-Simon, with its passionate plea for a scientific reordering of society for protection of the disinherited. Some had been influenced by the social fervor of the French cleric Lamennais. Others had been fired by Byron's gallant aid to the patriots of Italy and Greece. A few were influenced by the republican ideas of the United States. The brutish air of Buenos Aires made it expedient for such defenders of liberty to seek asylum beyond the reach of the tyrant. They became the leaders of groups of anti-Rosas Argentines in foreign centers, notably in Montevideo and Santiago, from which they continued their plottings and polemics against Rosas.

The honor of unseating the "boss of Buenos Aires" fell to another caudillo, Justo José de Urquiza, governor of Entre Ríos, long a faithful henchman of Rosas. His refusal to renew his compact with Rosas in 1851 was a declaration of independence for which Argentines had been waiting. *Estancieros,* businessmen, farmers in the interior provinces, intellectuals, and a host of other citizens joined Urquiza in striking against the man who had retarded the trade of the interior, who had denied them a true national government, and who had involved them in costly foreign wars. Urquiza had an army of some 10,000 men and this was quickly reinforced by volunteers: some 5,000 from Corrientes, 4,000 from the province of Buenos Aires, 2,000 from Uruguay, 4,000 from Brazil; his total force was about 25,000.

Urquiza's first act was to lift the siege imposed by Rosas upon Montevideo. Rosas moved north with his federal forces, a conscript army riddled with discontent, and the two armies met in the battle of Monte Caseros

717] THE REPUBLICS OF THE RÍO DE LA PLATA

on February 3, 1852. "The battle was won before it was fought," Mitre later reported, for Rosas had lost the support of the groups which had so long sustained him; the Gauchos had lost their fervor; the city riffraff was no longer ready to shout for him; even the prosperous landholders, long beholden to him, had discovered how suicidal his policies were.[1] Urquiza's victory was complete. Rosas resigned as governor of Buenos Aires; he was secretly put aboard the English steamboat *Centaur* and carried to exile in England.[2]

The verdict of history upon Juan Manuel de Rosas is not unanimous. His detractors wrote freely and passionately, describing his cruelty, his capriciousness, his vengefulness. Long after his death apologists arose to condone his offenses and to dwell upon his services to the nation. Such protagonists found confirmation in the words of the Peruvian García Calderón, who concluded that: "Rosas made federal unity a reality. . . . Without him anarchy would have been perpetuated, and the vice-kingdom of La Plata would have been irremediably disintegrated. Like the Roman deity Janus, Rosas had two faces; he closed one epoch and opened another; a past of warfare and terror and a future of unity, peace, democratic development, and industrial progress. . . . Rosas brought about the final harmony of the forces of Argentine politics. . . . His cruelty was effectual, his barbarism patriotic."[3] Such conclusions delight the Argentine *rosistas* of the mid-twentieth century, who suggest that had it not been for Rosas, Argentina might have been a colony of Great Britain, and who argue the need of a strong leader for their nation today. But few historians, either in or out of Argentina, regard Rosas with such enthusiasm. There is no monument to Rosas in all Argentina, no plaza or street bearing his name.

---

[1] On January 2, 1852, one month before the battle of Monte Caseros, John S. Pendleton, United States chargé d'affaires at Buenos Aires, wrote to Secretary of State Daniel Webster: "The only thing here which can with any propriety be call'd public sentiment is the feeling and judgement of foreign Society. . . . They almost entirely compose the Commercial class of the better sort. Taking counsel of what seem'd to be their interest . . . their sympathies have been heretofore . . . generaly [sic] with the Government of Rosas . . . [but now] they are all or nearly all against Rosas. Their money influence is in itself a most potent element, and it is telling every day, most effectively against the existing authority." Manning, *op. cit.*, Vol. I, p. 519.

[2] Rosas settled in Southampton, where he bought a little farm and wrote tracts condemning liberalism and democracy and advocating a league of Christian nations presided over by the Pope. There he lived on meager funds and a subvention from Urquiza to the age of eighty-four, dying in 1877 from "indigestion" according to one Argentine account. This double luxury, to die in ripe old age and from natural causes, Rosas had seldom vouchsafed his enemies.

[3] F. García Calderón: *Latin America, Its Rise and Progress*, translated by Bernard Miall (London: T. F. Unwin; 1913), pp. 145-6.

Chapter 39

CREATION OF THE ARGENTINE
NATION, 1852–90

On February 20, 1852, Justo José de Urquiza marched into Buenos Aires, quieted the anarchy provoked by the unpaid soldiers of Rosas, and declared a general amnesty. During the next four decades the republic found unity in a constitution, a congress, a chief executive—and, after stormy debates, a national capital removed from the control of the province of Buenos Aires. It was a period of economic progress: railroads were pushed north, west, and south, opening up empty frontier lands; the Pampa and the cities were peopled by European immigrants; herds of cattle and flocks of sheep multiplied; fields of grain expanded; commerce doubled and redoubled. It was a period of peace such as Argentina had not known since the days of the viceroys; the few military revolts did minor damage and were soon ended. It was a period in which political power passed from the caudillos to the electorate. It was not democracy, for the electorate was manipulated by the *estancieros* and traders; but these economic lords of Argentina wisely supported some able leaders, the best in any Latin American nation (with the possible exception of Brazil) during the last half of the nineteenth century.

JUSTO JOSÉ DE URQUIZA AND THE
SECESSION OF BUENOS AIRES

The arrival of Urquiza in 1852 evoked mixed emotions in the *porteños*. Grateful to their liberator, they accorded him high honors and in their exuberance kindled bonfires with the crimson banners and ribbons of Rosas, decking streets and houses with the blue-and-white of earlier revolutionary days. But the hero of Monte Caseros appeared wearing a blood-red hatband, disconcerting reminder that he was but another federalist caudillo.[1] He did not ingratiate himself with the *porteños;* by forbidding

[1] Charles S. Stewart: *Brazil and La Plata: The Personal Record of a Cruise* (New York: G. P. Putnam and Company; 1856), p. 326, notes that "The red hatband, besides its demi-savage look, gave offense . . . to the Buenos Ayreans, by reminding them of the thraldom of which it had been a badge under Rosas . . . they had indignantly and with abhorence thrown off [the red] the moment they found themselves free to do so."

popular demonstrations, he cast a chill over what should have been a happy hour. The *porteños*—who were still *unitarios*—began to murmur that they had been quit of one tyrant only to fall into the clutches of another; and they were confirmed in their unhappiness by the warnings of Bartolomé Mitre and Domingo Faustino Sarmiento.

But Buenos Aires had misjudged Urquiza, who revealed an unexpected spirit of conciliation and sound sense for the future of the nation. Urquiza's federalism had been subdued and matured; he believed now that the old cry for the autonomy of the provinces would serve neither them nor the nation. Convening the governors in May, he won their agreement to the Pact of San Nicolás, which called for a constituent congress, denounced interprovincial trade barriers, and named Urquiza provisional director of the nation. Urquiza, in exercise of the powers granted him, decreed nationalization of customs revenue and the opening of the rivers Paraná and Uruguay to free navigation, and negotiated trade treaties with the United States, Great Britain, and France.

But the leaders of Buenos Aires were not ready to accept such Spartan measures, which threatened their monopoly of customs receipts and subordinated them to a national government removed from their control.[2] The provincial legislature, aroused by Mitre's denunciation of this new "irresponsible dictatorship," refused to adhere to the Pact of San Nicolás, unseated the governor imposed by Urquiza, named the firebrand Valentín Alsina in his stead, and seceded from the nation. Urquiza, thus repudiated by Buenos Aires, moved his headquarters to Paraná, 300 miles from the port city, and for eight years ruled over the rest of the country while the province of Buenos Aires maintained an angry aloofness. It was the old quarrel of *unitarios* versus federalists, of Buenos Aires against the other provinces; and, within Buenos Aires, the conflict between those who wished complete isolation for themselves and those who, like Rivadavia in earlier days, would unite the nation under *porteño* rule.

The first fruits of secession were "war, anarchy, confusion, danger," according to an American who was there in January, 1853, and who wrote: "All business, foreign and domestic, is suspended; streets deserted; citizenry under arms. There is no intercourse with the rest of the country, and troops shoot people who defy their rule."[3] But Buenos Aires, with more advantages than the other provinces, quickly rallied. She had most of the money, the richest pastures and grain fields, the lucrative customhouse, and the best brains in the nation. Her *estancieros,* extending their domains at each

[2] The American chargé d'affaires reported to Secretary of State Edward Everett on December 28, 1852: "The city of Buenos Ayres has for the full period of twenty years absorbed the entire surplus production of the Fourteen Argentine States. . . . That City has *now* probably *Nine tenths* at the least, of all the money Capital of the Confederacy—possibly a much larger disproportion. . . . The Confederation of the States upon fair terms, breaks down the ascendency of Buenos Ayres. The free navigation of the rivers distributes the trade all along the line of the river, and its tributaries; and both measures therefore tend to the destruction of that monopoly on which these gentlemen have thriven, and are now thriving." William R. Manning, ed.: *Diplomatic Correspondence of the United States; Inter-American Affairs, 1831–1860* (Washington: Carnegie Endowment for International Peace; 1932), Vol. I, p. 539.

[3] Stewart, *op. cit.,* p. 418.

turn of the political wheel, fenced and cultivated their fields, bred their herds, and increased their trade. During this period of secession her promoters even completed the first railroad—only six miles of tracks, but enough to stimulate a sharp rise in land values. Cultural life, under the spur of the returned intellectuals, blossomed handsomely. Theaters, museums, libraries, and schools increased in number. Sarmiento, an imaginative schoolmaster who drew upon his experience in Chile and borrowed from his friend Horace Mann in the United States, directed the provincial schools. The province of Buenos Aires, self-sufficient in natural endowment, might have continued indefinitely as a separate nation, but for the good sense of sound patriots.

While Buenos Aires was thus traveling alone, Urquiza was busily organizing the rest of the nation. Despite forebodings of his capricious tyranny, Urquiza was faithful to his promises. The constituent congress, convened on his initiative, met in Santa Fe in late 1852. His appeal to its delegates was direct:

> I concern myself with one task . . . the creation of a nation. . . . Out of love for the people of Buenos Aires, I grieve over their absence from this assembly. But their absence does not mean permanent alienation, it is no more than a passing phase. Geography, history and old covenants bind Buenos Aires to the nation. Buenos Aires cannot live without her sister provinces, nor can her sisters live without her. There is room on the Argentine flag for more than fourteen stars, but no one of them can eclipse the others.[4]

The new constitution, promulgated in May, 1853, showed powerful influences from home and abroad: the patterns of the American Constitution were clearly reflected, as were those of the earlier Argentine constitutions of 1819 and 1823; the lessons of the hard-fought battles between federalists and *unitarios* were kept in mind; but most important was the influence of Juan Bautista Alberdi (although Alberdi was absent in Chile at the time, and, so far as we know, wrote not a single line of the new instrument). That constitution, destined to serve for almost a century, must be read with Alberdi's political theories in mind.

Alberdi, most penetrating political thinker in Argentine history, was born in Tucumán in 1810, a creole of Basque inheritance. In the late 1820's he was in Buenos Aires studying law, the classics, and French philosophy, and making friends among the young liberals of the capital. He was admitted to the bar in Córdoba and returned to Buenos Aires, where he shared the excitements of the Salón Literario and in 1837 helped found the Association of May. He excited the wrath of Rosas and in 1839 escaped to Montevideo, where he penned furious polemics against that tyrant. Sensitive to criticism, he could not work effectively with other people and lived much to himself, writing eagerly, reading hungrily. In 1843 he journeyed to France and Italy and then returned to a lonely exile of al-

---

[4] Quoted by Enrique de Gandía in *Historia de la república argentina en el siglo XIX* (Buenos Aires: A. Estrada y Cía; 1940), pp. 659–60.

718] THE REPUBLICS OF THE RÍO DE LA PLATA

most ten years in Chilean Valparaíso. From there he continued his verbal bombardment of Rosas, sharing honors with his fellow expatriate, Domingo Faustino Sarmiento—though neither man could abide the other.

When Urquiza struck in 1852, Alberdi wrote in furious haste a little book designed for the draftsmen of the new constitution, giving it the unwieldy title, *Bases y puntos de partido para la organización política de la república argentina,* "Bases and Points of Departure for the Political Organization of the Argentine Republic." He rushed it through the press and sent copies to the delegates in Santa Fe. One copy went to Urquiza himself, with a letter from its author felicitating the General upon his "heroism in restoring the liberty of the fatherland" and expressing fervent hope that his triumphs might be consolidated in a wise constitution "resting upon firm foundations. . . . The great buildings of olden times have not survived unless they were built on granite. . . . But history, Sir, all that has gone before, all our common experiences . . . are the granite upon which must rest any enduring constitution."[5] Despite his devotion to Argentina, Alberdi, disliking the storms of politics, did not return but lingered in Chile until 1854, when Urquiza appointed him as minister to France and England. When Urquiza fell from power in 1860, Alberdi remained in Europe, a recluse who loved his country but would not expose himself to its excitements, meanwhile living on in frail health, piling up manuscripts, which were printed after his death. After one last unhappy visit to Buenos Aires in 1880, he returned to Europe, where he died in 1884.

The Constitution of 1853, closely patterned after the instrument drafted in Philadelphia in 1787, reflected Alberdi's chief convictions. The presidential term was set at six years, with a ban on immediate reelection. In the protracted debate between *unitarios* and federalists, Alberdi upheld the just demands of both sides, making it clear that only a strong central government could guarantee the national unity so imperatively needed, but making it equally clear that the rights of the several provinces must be protected. The drafters of the new charter, like those in Philadelphia, sought to assure local self-government to the provinces while conferring large powers upon the president. The most formidable weapon given the federal government was the right of the president, with the approval of congress, to intervene in any province where republican government was threatened by internal disorders or foreign invasion. That grant of power, justified by long experience with anarchical caudillos, became an implement of tyranny in the hands of many presidents during the ensuing century.[6]

5 *Ibid.,* pp. 666–7.

6 There were over 200 such interventions, justified or unjustified, between 1853 and 1966. Ysabel F. Rennie: *The Argentine Republic* (New York: The Macmillan Co.; 1945), p. 92, pertinently reminds us that the United States Constitution, Art. 4, Sec. 4, provides that: "The United States shall guarantee to every State in the Union a republican form of government, and shall protect each of them against invasion; and, on application of the legislature, or of the executive (when the legislature cannot be convened), against domestic violence." The major difference between the Argentine and the United States provisions on this subject is that in the United States the state authorities must ask for intervention, while in Argentina the federal government may make the first move.

The economic and social prescriptions of Alberdi profoundly influenced the authors of the constitution. In his *Bases*, Alberdi argued that his people had moved too quickly from colonialism to independence and had been denied the long schooling in self-government enjoyed by the English colonists in North America. At last, after the wasted years under Rosas, they had opportunity to make up for lost time. Turning to analysis of Argentina, he painted the deadening misery and the appalling illiteracy of the sparsely occupied land; his prescription was: *gobernar es poblar,* "to govern is to populate." He bade his countrymen draw upon the surplus population of Europe, confident that even those of "servile mind," ground down by old tyrannies, would rise to new moral and physical stature in the free air of America. Let Argentina invite farmers with sound ideas on soils, seeds, and fertilizers; stockbreeders with modern techniques; artisans skilled with tools; industrial workers trained in shops and factories of the Old World. "The minister of government who does not double the population every decade" is a failure. There must be no religious discrimination against immigrants; Protestants as well as Catholics must be secure in their faith. But immigration, Alberdi continued, is not enough. There must be investment of capital, domestic and foreign, to build railroads which will open the frontier and to string telegraph wires so that the provinces may be linked together. He called for elimination of artificial trade barriers between provinces. The nation must have schools, universities, and technical institutes in order to raise up a trained citizenry. He urged modernization of the schools and the substitution of English for Latin as the second language.

The delegates at Santa Fe, thus counseled by Alberdi, charged the president and congress with responsibility for providing whatever "will lead to the prosperity of the country, to the advance and welfare of all the provinces and to the progress of learning, dictating plans of general and university instruction, and promoting industry, immigration, the construction of railroads and navigable canals, the colonization of public lands, the introduction and establishment of new industries, the importation of foreign capital, and the exploration of interior rivers, by laws which protect these ends and by temporary concessions of privileges and rewards."[7]

In 1853 the Argentine capital was established at Paraná, a pleasant little town on the river's edge, almost 300 miles upstream from Buenos Aires. There Urquiza, duly elected president, undertook the impossible task of consolidating a nation from which the heart had been cut. The nation was an underpopulated[8] wilderness, without railways or roads, with few schools, an empty treasury, and almost no lawyers, technicians, or trained administrators. Urquiza's control still depended upon the capricious loyalty of the caudillos. He had one appreciable advantage over the rival gov-

[7] Article 67 of the Constitution of 1853, cited by Ysabel F. Rennie in *The Argentine Republic*, p. 91. Copyright 1945, reprinted with the permission of The Macmillan Company, New York.

[8] The population of the area controlled by Urquiza was probably less than 1 million, with many of Indian blood, and largely illiterate; that of the province of Buenos Aires was about 400,000, including most of the better-trained artisans and farmers and almost all the professional men of the nation.

ernment in Buenos Aires—the recognition of the United States, England, France, and other powers.

Urquiza's efforts were valiant but futile. His government launched a bank which gasped and died within a few months; it sought to issue currency, but finally fell back upon use of Bolivian pesos. Bold immigration schemes were devised but few immigrants arrived. The port of Rosario was developed as an offset to Buenos Aires, and Urquiza imposed a heavy tariff penalty against ships that did not make it their exclusive port of call; this measure, patterned after Rosas's monopolistic favors to Buenos Aires, laid the foundation for Rosario's greatness as a grain port and bolstered the Paraná government. Urquiza was plagued by stubborn caudillos who were not persuaded that the age of Rosas was over. But despite long schooling in caudillo tactics, he was faithful to his constitutional pledges, and when self-appointed assassins murdered his most formidable rival in San Juan, he turned in wrath upon the men who thus used murder as an instrument of government. By 1859 Urquiza knew that there could be neither tranquillity nor prosperity until the nation was reunited.

In Buenos Aires the intransigent leaders had been preparing for a test of strength with their rivals in Paraná. In excessive exuberance, they opened up the old quarrel with Uruguay and sent troops against Montevideo; the *orientales* (the Uruguayans), without calling upon the proffered aid of Urquiza, repelled the invaders. Undaunted, *porteño* troops under Bartolomé Mitre marched north in 1859 and met and were defeated by the forces of Urquiza in the battle of Cépeda. Urquiza then marched toward Buenos Aires, a threat which persuaded the *porteños* to accept the constitution and unite with Urquiza's federated provinces, stipulating that the instrument of 1853 be amended to give a larger voice to Buenos Aires. The year 1860 brought two political changes which seemed to clear the air: Mitre was installed as governor of Buenos Aires, and Urquiza yielded the presidency of the federated provinces to the newly elected Santiago Derquí. A constitutional convention in Santa Fe amended the constitution to give larger representation to Buenos Aires and adjourned in confidence that national unity was assured. However, the fears of Buenos Aires were only temporarily eased:[9] there was one more battle to be fought. Urquiza remained the power behind Derquí in the provinces; and in September, 1861, forces commanded by Mitre and Urquiza met in the battle of Pavón. Although this battle was indecisive, it persuaded Urquiza that he was no match for his rivals, and he finally withdrew from the contest. His decision contributed to national serenity and left Bartolomé Mitre the logical leader of the united nation.

[9] *Porteño* fears of Urquiza, earlier denounced by Mitre as an "irresponsible dictator," were described by the United States minister in Paraná, writing to Secretary of State Lewis Cass: "From all the lights before me—I judge she [Buenos Aires] will never únite with the Confederation during the life of Gen'l. Urquiza. I say *life*—instead of *Presidency,* of Gen'l. Urquiza . . . it is regarded, that in this country he will be practically, if not nominally, the President—this Buenos Ayres fears. . . . It is certainly to be hoped, for the welfare of his country & the regard due to a Republican Constitution, that, as he is proud of the appellation of 'The Washington' [of the South]; he will manifest somewhat of the spirit and Patriotism of our Noble Washington." Manning, *op. cit.,* Vol. I, p. 683.

BARTOLOMÉ MITRE, 1862–68

Bartolomé Mitre won national power by default. Urquiza was out of the way, tending his cattle, preparing to reassume his governor's office in Entre Ríos. Derquí, now rejected by both Urquiza and Mitre, had resigned. In late 1861 Mitre assumed the provisional presidency and moved the capital from Paraná to Buenos Aires. A congress, convened in May, 1862, confirmed Mitre's irregular course and floridly acclaimed him *Benemérito de la Patria,* "well-deserving of the fatherland." The now bitter Alberdi wrote from his Paris exile that Mitre had "delivered the Argentine nation to Buenos Aires"; but the citizens of Argentina were in no mood to cavil: they were tired of battles. Mitre was elected and installed as the first constitutional president of a united Argentina.

The gaunt figure of Bartolomé Mitre, forty-one when he reached the presidency, had become the symbol of the *porteño* spirit. Born in Buenos Aires in 1821, he passed his boyhood amid the confusions that brought Rosas to power. At sixteen, he joined the impetuous Echeverría in founding the Association of May. At eighteen, he began an exile which carried him to Montevideo, Bolivia, Peru, and Chile, sometimes fighting and always writing. He was back in Buenos Aires again at thirty, serving under Urquiza in the battle of Monte Caseros. A year later he broke with Urquiza and became a leader in the secessionist government of Buenos Aires.

No Argentine of his time, except perhaps Sarmiento, possessed such generous gifts: he was a soldier of proved courage, an orator who could win assent either in Congress or public assembly, and a politician who could outplay his fellows. He was a writer of some distinction, his works including biographies of San Martín and Belgrano, hundreds of polemical articles, one mediocre novel, poetry of indifferent merit, and, for good measure, translations of Horace, *The Divine Comedy,* and *Ruy Blas.* His style was rotund, rococo. He was never so profound as Alberdi nor so colorful as Sarmiento, but his words recalled his fellow citizens to a sense of their national destiny. His patriotism was unassailable, although conviction of his own indispensability prevented him from giving due credit to such patriots as Urquiza and Sarmiento. His personal honesty was beyond question, his private life austere, his fidelity as a husband and father exemplary. He lived thirty-eight years after retiring from the presidency and, according to one Argentine historian, "governed the nation until the day of his death [in 1906]. His great prestige, his vast popularity, founded on his distinguished services to the state, made him . . . the oracle to whom both leaders and masses turned in moments of national anxiety."

Mitre's task was to bind together an unruly nation, to organize a government which would fulfill the pledges of the constitution, to quiet the last caudillos, to promote the social, economic, and cultural well-being of his nation, and finally to fight a senseless war with a power-drunk dictator in Paraguay. It was incredibly complicated: "On one side," writes an

Argentine, "he faced the roaming Indians and the haunted desert; on the other, the world of railroads, fleets, historical and geographical studies. Out in the provinces were the last of the caudillos, men who had overstayed their time; in the outer world, there was war and intrigue. And yet Mitre created the republic, building a new and strong nation out of the wreckage of civil war."[1]

The first problem to be faced was the location of the capital: a national government must have a capital, but the sticky question *Where?* had plagued the nation from the first days of independence. Rivadavia and the *unitarios* had wanted it in Buenos Aires; Artigas and like-minded caudillos had insisted that it be anywhere except in Buenos Aires. The Congress of 1853 had sought to "federalize" the province of Buenos Aires —to set it apart as the common possession of the nation; but that discussion had been ended by the secession of the province. Now, in 1862, with the nation reunited, the congress reverted to the idea of federalizing Buenos Aires, suggesting a new capital city on the Pampa; this proposal was beaten by *porteño* opposition. And now, under Mitre, the city's leaders split into two camps on the issue: the President's Nationalists proposed to detach and federalize the city of Buenos Aires as a national capital (they were dubbed *cocidos,* "the well cooked," by the rabble), while the Autonomists, led by Adolfo Alsina, demanded autonomy for the province (they were called *crudos,* "the raw ones," by the mob). There was immense excitement, with parades, banners, and shouting. The result was a compromise: for five years the national government and the provincial government would live side by side in Buenos Aires. When that compromise expired in 1867 and no wiser solution had appeared, the arrangement continued until 1880, when Mitre's original plan was accepted: Buenos Aires was detached from its province, a federal district was carved out, and the provincial government moved to the new city of La Plata.

Mitre's organization of the national government was skillful. Despite lack of trained administrators and technicians, especially in the outlying provinces, he found numerous excellent men who, inspired by his own example of honest zeal, created the necessary instruments for enforcing the laws. The postal service and the telegraph lines were extended, and a cableline was laid under the Río de la Plata to Montevideo. Public finance was organized, customs receipts were federalized, a national credit bank was created, and foreign banks were welcomed. Courts, including the Supreme Court, were installed, and a juridical code was formulated. The army and navy were strengthened, and the first steps were taken toward professional training of officers. Diplomatic and consular services were organized. The friendship of the Vatican was cultivated, and an archbishop was appointed to Buenos Aires. Railroads were projected with new energy, and the Rosario-Córdoba line was completed. Immigration was encouraged, and more than 100,000 Europeans entered Argentina during Mitre's term. Public education was expanded. Trade increased; the combined export-import figure was 45 million pesos in 1862, 72 million in 1868. Country

[1] Gandía, *op. cit.,* p. 729.

roads, long harassed by bandits, became more secure than they had been since the days of the viceroys.

Not least of Mitre's services was elimination of many troublesome caudillos, of whom the most stubborn was Angel Vicente Peñaloza, nick-named *El Chacho,* "little boy," by his affectionate followers. Mitre treated these outmoded tyrants with the grave patience a wise parent accords bad boys, and then with swift punishment. El Chacho, famed for his paternal care of his numerous followers, could not understand the objections raised as he extended his hold over the provinces of San Luis, La Rioja, Córdoba, Catamarca, Salta, Tucumán, and San Juan. Pursued by federal troops, he appealed to the President: "I do not believe that I deserve the name of traitor." He was finally overtaken and shot in 1863, almost the last of the caudillos.

Mitre's first three years were constructive, but the balance of his term was wasted on the Paraguayan War, in which for almost five years (1865–70) weak Paraguay was hammered by the armies of Argentina, Brazil, and Uruguay. When the Paraguayan dictator, Francisco Solano López, decided to intervene in Uruguay's perennial contests, his armies set out across Argentine territory to reach Montevideo; whereupon Mitre cried "invasion," made an alliance with Uruguay and Brazil, and himself headed the troops which started north to punish López. The explanations of Mitre's actions vary. Alberdi wrote from Paris that the President was trying to prove himself another San Martín or Belgrano. Pelham Box suggests that Mitre thought the hour auspicious for reuniting the one-time sectors of the Viceroyalty of La Plata under the banner of Buenos Aires—a theory born out by Mitre's aggressive nationalism. No matter what his motives, Mitre spent the rest of his presidential term fighting the Paraguayans. His absence from the capital, as well as the drain upon money and man power, cooled the ardor of the Argentines for their president; they complained that he was waging a war of conquest rather than of national defense.

Meanwhile, the nation prepared for the election of 1868. Mitre, con-stitutionally ineligible for reelection, had repeatedly avowed his purpose "to prepare my country for a free election," assuring citizens that they were free to pick whom they would although making clear his disapproval of Urquiza. Except for that bit of counsel, Mitre stood aside and permitted a free election. The electors chose Domingo Faustino Sarmiento, Mitre's rival for national eminence, who was as firmly convinced of his claim upon immortality as was Mitre of his own. Mitre retired to the home which his grateful fellow citizens had bought for him, as poor and as proud as when he took office.[2]

2 His retirement was nominal. He was soon seated in the Senate, where he usually opposed his successor's measures. In 1870 he founded *La Nación,* "the correct, conservative, Catholic spokesman for the rural society and landed gentry of Buenos Aires," in which he voiced his opinions with force, and which has continued to be one of the best newspapers of Latin America.

DOMINGO FAUSTINO SARMIENTO, 1868-74

Domingo Faustino Sarmiento, the most baffling, exasperating, and versatile man in Argentine history, took on a tough assignment in 1868. He was a man without a party, under fire from the Nationalists led by Mitre on one side, and from the Autonomists led by his own vice-president, Adolfo Alsina, on the other. On the frontier the Indians still harassed peaceful farmers. In the interior a few caudillos still disturbed national tranquillity. In the far north the expensive Paraguayan War ground on. And, to add further complication, the new president, for all his many-faceted brilliance, was an egotist with little skill in conciliation.

Sarmiento had traveled rough roads in his first fifty-seven years. He was born in western San Juan in 1811, of parents who despite their poverty had prodded him to study. He was a precocious child. "At five," he later recalled, "I read fluently, in a loud voice . . . with complete understanding. . . . I was taken from house to house to display my reading, reaping a great harvest of cakes, embraces and praises which filled me with vanity." Of his boyhood, he wrote: "I never knew how to spin a top, to bat a ball, to fly a kite . . . [but] I read every book that fell into my hands." The autobiography of Benjamin Franklin was his favorite; "I felt myself to be Franklin—and why not? I was very poor like him, I studied like him, and following in his footsteps, I might one day come, like him, to be a *doctor ad honorem,* and to make my place in letters and American politics."

Political matriculation came early for young Domingo. At sixteen, he was drafted into the local militia and promptly protested his induction; refusing to doff his hat to his superior, he was jailed for his impudence. He shortly joined the guerrillas who were fighting the caudillo Facundo Quiroga, did much marching and some shooting—and during a six weeks' lull learned French from a wandering soldier of Napoleon. Finding life under Facundo unbearable, he chose exile to Chile in 1831.

Sarmiento's first years in Chile (1831–36) were uneventful. He taught school in a village under the shadow of Mount Aconcagua. He clerked in Valparaíso—and paid half his wages to a teacher who roused him at two every morning for an English lesson. He was next a mine foreman—and at night translated Sir Walter Scott into Spanish. In 1836, receiving the good news of Facundo Quiroga's death, he returned to his native San Juan; founded "a school for young ladies"; learned Italian and Portuguese; started a newspaper whose outspoken editorials angered the new caudillo; and was jailed again. In 1840 he returned to Chile.

His second stay in Chile (1840–45) brought friendships and recognition. The generous Manuel Montt, soon to be president, welcomed him, saying: "Ideas, Sir, have no country." He became editor of *El Mercurio* in Valparaíso and founded *El Nacional* in Santiago. He turned his energy to the schools, prepared the first spelling book for classroom use, wrote and persuaded others to write textbooks, founded an educational journal, and organized the first Normal School. "It was living instruction such as we can hardly boast in our days of textbooks," Mrs. Horace Mann wrote later. He now wrote *The Life of Facundo, or Civilization and Barbarism,* the torrential analysis of the ills of his native Argentina, with its portrayal of the barbarous Gauchos and tyrannical caudillos; despite its unconventional form, the work had such dramatic power as to give its author a firm place in South American letters. But many Chileans could not stomach the egotistical Sarmiento (*Don Yo,* "Mister I," they called him). Manuel Montt, Sarmiento's devoted friend, found his presence embarrassing. Rosas was demanding Sarmiento's extradition, but Montt steadfastly refused to accede. As a way out of this uncomfortable situation, Sarmiento was persuaded to leave Chile to study education in Europe and the United States.

Sarmiento visited Spain, France, and England, talking with educators, scientists, and men of letters. In Algiers he found resemblances between the dress and habits of the Arabs (he himself had Arab blood) and the Gauchos of his homeland. He then crossed to the United States, where he became a fast friend of Horace Mann, the pioneer educator.[3] He returned to Chile for his third stay (1848–51), wrote profusely on all that he had seen and heard, continued his attacks on Rosas in the press, and wrote spirited pleas for European immigration as the panacea for underpopulated South America. His panegyrics on immigration reached Rosas and stirred that tyrant to fresh denunciations of the troublemaker upon whom he could not lay his hand. In Chile, the vain Sarmiento shared honors with two other émigrés, Bartolomé Mitre and Juan Bautista Alberdi; but the three men, although united in detestation of Rosas, had no liking for each other.

In 1851 the news of Urquiza's revolt called Sarmiento to Montevideo, where he joined the insurgents and served as a colonel at Monte Caseros. Urquiza, distrusting all intellectuals and discounting Sarmiento's claims to credit for his attacks upon Rosas, assigned him to the unspectacular task of editing the army's bulletin. Despite this slight, Sarmiento applauded Urquiza's triumphal entry into Buenos Aires, but later withdrew for a fourth period of exile in Chile. Meanwhile, the *porteños* seceded, setting up their own successful government; and Sarmiento returned to Buenos Aires in 1855 to edit a newspaper, to act as a senator in the provincial legislature, and to direct the provincial school system to such good effect that 17,000 children were enrolled by 1860. In 1862, with Urquiza eliminated and Mitre installed as president, Sarmiento became governor of his native province of San Juan, putting its government to rights, building schools, sharing the campaigns against the caudillo El Chacho. Mitre, perhaps hoping to banish his rival from sight and mind, assigned him to diplomatic service, first in Chile, then in Peru, and in 1865 as minister to the United States. Sarmiento spent three years in Washington eagerly collecting new ideas and creating warm friendships for himself and his country.

---

[3] Sarmiento's delight over the United States, his humorous and naïve reports on American life and customs, set his writings on the northern republic in pleasant contrast to the sour observations of Mrs. Trollope and Charles Dickens in that same period.

In 1868 he took ship for home, and when he stepped ashore in Rio de Janeiro he learned that he had been elected to the presidency.

Sarmiento entered office with the prestige of his long and spirited opposition to Rosas, and of his knowledge of the world. He also suffered handicaps: a graceless egotism cut him off from his fellows; a tedious emotionalism weakened his appeal to the thoughtful; and a snobbishness toward common men, especially those of "inferior" blood, belied his protestations of democracy. Perhaps as a reaction against his own rude beginnings, he proposed to "polish" his countrymen, to get them into city clothes; his naïve comment upon the farmers of the United States—that they wore frock coats and carried gold watches—was revealing. Although impressive in civic virtues, he lacked domestic virtues, eating and drinking immoderately and making a failure of his one brief marriage. His was a striking but not pleasing figure, obese, heavy-featured, his great head on a bull-like neck. But he had one gift rare in South American statesmen, a sense of humor which made it possible for him to ridicule his own ugliness and gaucherie. A Chilean, meeting him in 1855, tartly described his attempt to dress like a gentleman, then dismissed him in these words: "Sarmiento is the Dumas of South American literature. Never perhaps has the sun of our continent nourished such a fantastic, ardent, brilliant person, who is, at the same time, a blunderer and a liar. He has a marvelous imagination . . . with little true talent, no common sense, and his vanity overflows the pampas. . . . This absurd vanity is a perpetual cloud that obscures a sun that occasionally emits splendid rays."[4]

But no matter how many disabilities he suffered, Sarmiento's presidency was successful. The Paraguayan War was won, and Mitre was sent to Rio de Janeiro to settle territorial disputes with the government of Emperor Pedro II. Sarmiento ordered the first census in 1869, which counted a total population of about 1.8 million; of these, almost 500,000 were in the province of Buenos Aires, 178,000 in the capital city; of the total, 212,000 were of foreign birth, chiefly Italians and Spaniards; and about 71 per cent of those over five years of age could neither read nor write. He completed the work of Mitre in liquidating the caudillos. He made peace with Urquiza, paying him a friendly visit on his Entre Ríos *estancia*. In 1870 General López Jordán, a rival of Urquiza, sent assassins who murdered Urquiza at his own fireside. Sarmiento, aroused by this fresh instance of caudillo barbarism, sent troops against López and drove him into exile in 1871; but that last stubborn contender made two more attempts to gain a foothold in the Littoral and was not finally silenced until 1876.

The activities of Sarmiento's domestic administration were as varied as his own interests. Immigration, his cure-all for barbarism, was given systematic encouragement, 280,000 came from Europe during his six-year term, over 70,000 in 1874, his last year of office. Railroads, opening the way for settling the unoccupied lands, were extended until there were 826

4 Benjamin Vicuña Mackenna: *La Argentina en el año 1855* (Buenos Aires: La Revista Americana de Buenos Aires; 1936), pp. 91, 94.

miles of track in 1874. Telegraph lines increased to 3,100 miles, and a trans-Atlantic cable linked Buenos Aires and Europe. Highways were improved, bridges built, and postal services doubled. Business and trade increased: total exports and imports were valued at 74 million pesos in 1869, over 102 million in 1874. The modernization of the port of Buenos Aires was begun. Agriculture was stimulated by the introduction of new varieties of grain; the eucalyptus tree was introduced. Fisheries were expanded. Ambitious exploration brought new knowledge of the national domain. Scientific interests were served by organization of the Academy of Science, the founding of a national observatory, the bringing of natural history exhibits from Europe, and the establishment of chemical laboratories. The city of Buenos Aires was beautified with new parks. Humanitarian interests were served by new hospitals and an institute for deaf mutes. Sarmiento founded the first society for the protection of animals. The army and navy were given training schools, and there was a decided growth of professionalism in the armed forces. A national library commission distributed books to free public libraries, almost a hundred of which were established under Sarmiento. The organization of the national treasury was fortified by a national accounting office. The new Banco Nacional was organized. Lighthouses were erected.

But Sarmiento was first and always the schoolmaster, intent upon injecting new life into the Argentine masses, whom he called in contempt, "loafers, drunkards, useless fellows." It was significant that he should write a book, based on his years in the United States, called "The School, Basis of the Prosperity and Democracy of the United States." Now that he was president, school building and teacher training became his obsession. He assured Congress in 1869: "If I do not advance [popular education], all of my earlier words and deeds stand as vain ostentation. . . . Failure to do so, now that the way is open, will mean that this Government is impotent to break the tradition of ignorance which is our colonial heritage." An effective ally was frail undersized Nicolás Avellaneda, who was barely thirty when Sarmiento made him minister of education, and whose zeal for salvation through books was as ardent as his master's. School facilities and enrollment almost doubled during Sarmiento's term, reaching a total of 1,645 schools and over 100,000 pupils, an achievement outstripping that of any other nation in contemporary Latin America. Sixty-three women teachers, chosen by Mrs. Horace Mann, were brought from the United States to start normal schools. Among the educational innovations were evening classes for adults and school gymnasiums.

In 1871 the capital city suffered a plague of yellow fever. The cries of the dying echoed through the deserted streets. Thieves sacked empty houses. Heroic volunteers, including members of the first families, tended the sick and dying, dug trenches by torchlight in which to lay the bodies; 13,614 died within five months. It is remembered against Sarmiento that he, like many others, fled to the country. The ordeal, which the science of that day could not blame on the mosquito, stirred the government to improve sanitation, end the casual dumping of garbage, pave the streets, and improve the water supply. In 1874 the first sewer was constructed in Buenos Aires.

The election of 1874 was a test of strength between Sarmiento and Mitre, each convinced that he was indispensable. Mitre announced his candidacy for the presidency. Sarmiento, disbarred from reelection by the constitution, supported Minister of Education Nicolás Avellaneda, who was generally regarded as too young and unimpressive. Adolfo Alsina, Sarmiento's sulky vice-president, entered the race but finally threw his support to Avellaneda, whom he evidently disliked less than he did his old rival Mitre. Sarmiento, by controlling patronage and the election machinery, had his way: Avellaneda was elected and was inaugurated in October, 1874. Meanwhile, Mitre, claiming that Sarmiento had employed "every manner of fraud" in foisting his protégé upon the nation, rallied volunteers for attack from the north and south, and the revolt lasted three months. Mitre was jailed, threatened with the death penalty, but finally pardoned by Avellaneda after five months in the Luján jail, where he wrote some fine pages of history. The incident reflected credit upon neither Sarmiento nor Mitre; there was clear fraud on both sides. Sarmiento, by his arbitrary methods, and Mitre, by his resort to arms, had both cast disrespect upon orderly institutions. But Argentina was still young in republican ways, and would not have a clean election for another forty years.[5]

EXPANSION AND CONVULSION, 1874–90

The sixteen years from 1874 to 1890 brought final consolidation of the country under a national capital, rapid increase in population and wealth, and a major political convulsion. Nicolás Avellaneda, inaugurated in 1874, proved a much better leader than his detractors would admit. The unimpressive little man was tireless and sagacious. But in 1880 he disappointed friends of democracy by imposing Julio A. Roca as his successor, using the customary electoral coercion. Under Roca (1880–86) and Juárez Celman, who succeeded him (1886–90), official corruption and riotous speculation undermined public confidence and prepared the way for the upheaval of 1890.

Avellaneda won credit for settling two irritating border arguments. Paraguay, defeated by 1870, was forced to accept a redrawing of its boundaries with substantial territorial gains for Argentina. Chile, now rich from its nitrates and robustly nationalistic, laid claims to the southern areas of Patagonia and Tierra del Fuego; this region, long regarded as Argentine territory, had been neglected by the government of Buenos Aires, while Chileans had been moving in since the days of Rosas. In the 1870's Chilean

---

[5] Neither Sarmiento nor Mitre, despite their stature, would again reach the presidency. Sarmiento served as senator during Avellaneda's term, directed the provincial schools of Buenos Aires, and edited *El Nacional*. Later, under Roca, he directed the schools of the nation. Meanwhile, he continued his writing; and his complete works, brought out by the nation during his last years, filled fifty-three volumes. He died in 1888 at the age of seventy-seven.

bands raided Argentine fisheries, attacked a few ships flying the British flag, and claimed Chilean sovereignty over Patagonia. In 1878 Avellaneda dispatched a weak naval unit of fifty men to evict the intruders. But Chile was then involved in war with Bolivia and Peru and abandoned the contest with Avellaneda's tiny navy.

The frontier Indians in the south, perennial disturbers of the nation, renewed their activities during Avellaneda's presidency. The tough Ranqueles, an Araucanian tribe, enraged by the constant extension of the white man's wire fences, struck back: they burned crops, killed or enslaved Christian farmers, and seized cattle and sheep for sale in Chile. Avellaneda first sought to appease the warring chieftains by guarantees of security and offers of larger tribute—the devices of every leader since Rivadavia. Such appeasement was denounced by General Julio A. Roca, the minister of war. With an appropriation of 1.5 million pesos, Roca organized a force of some 8,000 men and in 1879 started south. "For the Argentine Republic," he announced, "there is no other frontier in the West and the South than the peaks of the Andes and the Ocean." It was a formidable crusade, in which soldiers and priests marched together, "representatives of the Sword and the Cross, traveling by train against savages riding their bareback horses." The virtually unarmed Indians—there were but 2,000 of them—made slight resistance, were captured and shipped to Buenos Aires. The pagans "arrived like animals"; some were jailed, others were confined on the island of Martín García, while young boys and girls were indentured as domestic servants to *porteño* families, their masters duly pledged to instruct them in the Christian faith. "It was civilization," writes historian Gandía, "with all its virtues and vices that had finally crushed the last sons of the American earth." The histrionic adventure paid the nation richly; Indians were no longer troublesome, and millions of acres were opened for settlement. And, parenthetically, it rewarded Julio Roca by making him a hero—"the Conqueror of the Desert"—and president of the republic.

In 1880 the stormy capital question was settled by federalizing the city of Buenos Aires as the property and capital of the nation. Not less than thirty-five different solutions had been advanced during the years since independence, but all had been unacceptable. During the turmoil of the presidential campaign of 1880, the issue was brought to the fore by a senator who told Congress: "Let us quit fooling ourselves . . . Buenos Aires is the capital. . . . It is [the nation's] brain and heart." There was general assent; the only opposition came from the province of Buenos Aires, which resisted the loss of the port city. A brief but bloody civil war ensued, with Mitre and Avellaneda leading the opposing forces. But popular will prevailed; a federal district was carved from the province, and the creation of a national capital marked the official end to more than a half century of controversy. The dominance of the city of Buenos Aires was thus established, and national organization was no longer an issue.[6]

[6] In 1882 the new city of La Plata, capital of the province of Buenos Aires, was founded on the Pampa, fifty miles southeast of the chief city. By 1884 it was well equipped with public buildings, schools, banks, and over a thousand houses, and its population exceeded 10,000.

The development of free political institutions continued to fall short of the generous promises of the Constitution of 1853. Mitre, reasonably faithful to those promises at least in the election of 1868, had spoiled his record by resorting to arms in 1874. Sarmiento, for all his admiration of United States ways, had proved dictatorial in imposing Avellaneda in 1874. Then in 1880 Avellaneda used his control of the ballot boxes to seat Roca, while six years later Roca, in turn, placed his brother-in-law Miguel Juárez Celman in the presidency by long-familiar caudillo methods.

The conduct of public business improved under Avellaneda and then deteriorated sadly under his two successors. Avellaneda inherited the deficits and foreign debts accumulated during the Paraguayan War. In 1875, his first year in office, the national treasury collected 17.2 million pesos and spent 28.5 million. By reducing salaries, cutting personnel, and other economies, he actually balanced the budget in 1878. But Roca, after 1880, poured money into railroads, telegraph lines, bridges, public buildings, and the enlargement of the port of Buenos Aires; he permitted his intimates to collect exorbitant profits from government contracts, authorized the printing of much unsupported paper currency, and increased foreign loans at usurious rates. Under his brother-in-law Juárez Celman, installed in 1886, extravagance and corruption were unrestrained. The public debt, 117 million pesos in 1886, increased to 355 million in 1890.

Meanwhile, the Argentine land was being peopled by European immigrants. The silencing of the Indians, the opening of new lands on the frontier, the extension of railroads, and the rapid increase in stock raising and grain culture offered eloquent inducements. In 1880 the country welcomed 26,000, and in 1889 almost 219,000, chiefly Italians and Spaniards. About half of these were farmers,[7] but they discovered that their land of promise had been largely preempted by the *estancieros*. A few got their own plots, especially in the Littoral provinces, but many became sharecroppers, tenant farmers, or farm hands on the *estancias*. Lack of intelligent planning led many to settle in the cities, where they swelled the ranks of industrial workers, artisans, and shopkeepers. Buenos Aires had some 300,-000 people in 1890, about nine-tenths of them foreign born. There was thus created a numerous and vocal middle class which would soon transform the social, economic, and political life of the nation.

Concentration of land in a few hands, the blunder for which every leader since independence shares the blame, reached new extremes after the wars with the Indians. Roca and his intimates acquired great blocks of the liberated areas in the south and west, their seizures ratified by a congress whose members had been bribed. Other tracts, allotted to the bondholders who had financed the Indian wars, went to speculators who made quick profits without regard for national well-being. The small farmer had little chance in this land orgy, and his plea for a few acres was overlooked as the political chieftains got hundreds of thousands, or even millions, of acres. In

[7] After 1890 there was generous influx of Poles, Turks and Turkish-dominated peoples, Russians, and others, including many Jews. See Carl C. Taylor: *Rural Life in Argentina* (Baton Rouge, La.: Louisiana State University Press; 1948), pp. 97, 103.

1886 public lands in northern Chaco (part of the region annexed from Paraguay) were offered at about twelve American cents an acre, and went mostly into new *estancias*. During Juárez Celman's last months in office, 134 land corporations were chartered and new fortunes were made by trafficking in the national domain. In 1889 about 150 million acres in southern Patagonia and in the far north—unsurveyed and with vague limits—were put on sale through agents in European capitals; and again the large operators gained the advantage. When the ministry of agriculture was belatedly established in 1898, writes Ysabel Rennie, "it found that, though the government had given away more than 60 million hectares [150 million acres], it had no idea what lands were left, where they were, or what they were worth."

The speculative boom, which created a few millionaires with fine houses in Buenos Aires and Paris, and on the Riviera, had a solid base in the generous profits from cattle, sheep, and grain. By 1890 Argentina was a principal supplier of foodstuffs to the world. Certain steps in its progress toward this end are worth noting. In 1844 an Englishman strung the first wire fence around his *estancia*, and gradually progressive owners followed his example. The results were profound: with confinement of herds came selective breeding; with protection of planted fields, grain production increased; with barriers raised against intruders, the Gauchos ceased their lawless roaming; with the fixing of boundaries, land values became stable and increased. In 1848 another Englishman introduced the first Durham bull, a pioneer attempt to improve the quality of stock. In 1857 the tide of immigration began. In 1866 the Sociedad Rural was launched by enterprising *estancieros* who were familiar with the stockbreeding practices of England and North America; from then on the Rural Society took the lead in introducing better strains of cattle, sheep, hogs, chickens, and other animals; their annual stock shows, inaugurated in 1875, became proud exhibits of progress. In 1876 the first refrigerated ship, the *Frigorifique,* crossed the Atlantic and proved that fresh meat could reach the hungry markets of England and the Continent; now fabulous profits were assured to Argentine *estancieros* hitherto dependent upon the sale of hides, wool, and tallow. By 1878 refrigerated ships were a proved success; within the next decade, fifty-seven were shuttling back and forth between the Río de la Plata and the Thames; and by 1890 the number had increased to 278. By 1884 the first packing house, or *frigorífico* (the name was derived from the first refrigerated ship), was built with English capital; and other plants were built during the years that followed. In the 1880's the use of alfalfa, prime fattener of cattle and sheep, was extending over the Pampa. The stock raiser was the economic lord of Argentina.

But the economic overlords had overreached themselves. A few hundred made vast fortunes and won new land in the speculative boom, but many thousands lost all they had in the frantic national gamble. This recklessness led to the ruinous collapse of 1890. The nation had borrowed too much at excessive interest rates, and there seemed no solution other than a repudiation of the nation's debts. The gold reserves were almost exhausted, and the speeding printing presses poured out a flood of paper pesos, whose solid value all but disappeared. Prices of foodstuffs shot up each day, and wages increased hardly at all. The result was misery for the masses.

The first open challenge to Juárez Celman's spoilsmen and speculators was a mass meeting called in 1889 to demand political house cleaning and free suffrage. The instigators were largely young men, quite unknown to the general public. Their chief spokesman was the forty-seven-year-old Leandro N. Alem, an unsuccessful lawyer and a minor politician whose bitterness toward the world was partially explained by his long persecution as the son of a hated lieutenant of the dictator Rosas. His associates included men who would live to play major roles in national life for a full half century. This company of political unknowns, within a few months after their first protest, formed *La Unión Cívica de la Juventud,* the "Civic Union of Youth," which attracted numerous middle-class adherents. The seventy-year-old Bartolomé Mitre joined them, perhaps hoping to regain his lost power or perhaps honestly desiring to help rescue his nation (or for both reasons); but he met with a cool welcome. Alem became president of the new organization and pleaded eloquently for honest government, equitable taxation, protection of civil rights, "protection for fruitful enterprise, and an end to the speculative orgies from which political parasites enrich themselves." It was a national uprising; Juárez Celman's cabinet understood its purport and resigned in a body in April, 1890, but the President clung to his post. In July the insurgents, supported by some contingents of the army and navy, fought inconclusively and then agreed to an armistice. A senator reported to Congress: "The revolution is crushed, but the government is dead." Juárez Celman was at last convinced; he resigned, turning over the office which he had dishonored to Vice-President Carlos Pellegrini.

 [*Chapter 40*]

ARGENTINA: THE RADICALS,
1890–1930

The year 1890 marks the opening of a new political era. For thirty years the oligarchy of landlords, merchants, and bankers had ruled the nation for their own profit—and often, in justice let it be added, for the nation's profit. Under such leadership, some of it able and even brilliant, the nation had been unified and had prospered. To be sure, the promises of the constitution were not fulfilled; the aristocracy controlled elections and permitted no interference by the masses. The popular uprising of 1890 (the *Noventa,* Argentines call it) was a body blow, but not a knockout, for the oligarchy. It initiated a forty-year contest between, on the one hand, the established masters of Argentina who had preempted the national domain, built their fine houses, and controlled the political life of the nation; and, on the other, the newcomers from Italy, Spain, and other parts of Europe[1] who were creating a new middle class which, given its first effective voice by Leandro Alem and his colleagues, would emerge as members of the *Unión Cívica Radical,* the "Radicals"[2] of subsequent history. For the first twenty-six years of the period 1890–1930, leaders of the old regime continued to impose their will in dictatorial fashion, seating presidents of limited ability, in a vain attempt to curb Radicals, Socialists, and other dissenters. Then, in 1916, the Radicals finally came to power, scored some successes and made more blunders, and were finally ejected in 1930.

---

[1] The steady and substantial flow of European immigrants was making Argentina the land of the foreigner. The 1895 census reported a total population of 3,954,911; of these, 2,950,000 were first or second generation Europeans; of the foreign born, 493,000 were Italians, 199,000 Spanish, 94,000 French, 22,000 English, 17,000 Germans, 15,000 Swiss, 12,800 Austrians.

[2] The word "radical" calls for a note on the political nomenclature not only of Argentina but of other Latin American lands. The careful reader will bear in mind that, while "conservatives" are always conservative, "liberals" are seldom liberal, and "radicals" are never radical. The relation to French political labels is clear.

THE OLIGARCHY IN CONTROL, 1890-1910

The ousting of Juárez Celman in 1890 automatically brought Vice-President Carlos Pellegrini to power, but that abler statesman refused to accept the presidency until his conditions were met. He summoned a group of wealthy men and gave them details on the national bankruptcy and the default on British loans and railroad contracts. He said: "If we do not pay, Argentina is entered on the Black Book of insolvent nations." The bankers, merchants, and *estancieros* heeded his appeal to their patriotism and agreed to lend 17 million pesos to the national treasury. Pellegrini, thus fortified, assumed office, to the general relief of worried Argentines. An English eye-witness to the overthrow of Juárez Celman and the installation of Pellegrini described the popular approval:

> The streets, the houses, the squares, the public offices, the whole city, nay, the whole country were in an uproar. The *Junta* [of the *Unión Cívica*] raised its head and lifted his colours—*it claimed the victory for its own!* It harangued the people . . . the masses went mad . . . the weak voices of the orators scarcely penetrated beyond the windowsills . . . far above all other crys . . . rose the cry *Ya se fué el burro!* [The donkey is gone!] . . . the frenzy, it was nothing less, lasted six days and nights.[3]

But the general public gave credit to the true hero of the hour, the gloomy Leandro Alem, whose *Unión Cívica* had called at least a temporary halt to the excesses of the old regime.

A *porteño* and wealthy *estanciero,* Pellegrini represented the wisest and most generous traditions of his class. He had been a fearless critic of Juárez Celman while serving in his cabinet. Although convinced of the right of the wellborn to rule, he desired a more equitable sharing of the national wealth. He denounced "public thieves" as lustily as did Alem, although his zeal did not embrace free and effective suffrage—and certainly not Alem's *Unión Cívica.* He sought to conciliate the disgruntled by declaring a general amnesty and improving public administration, and he brought his nation through its severe political and economic crisis. An admirer writes that he "belonged to the maimed and crippled group [the "oligarchy"] which completed national organization and established a sense of national destiny, giving it security and well-being. Himself a *porteño* of 'the little fatherland' [*patria chica*], he preferred the greater fatherland [*patria grande*]; that stand, today taken as a matter of course, was then quite novel."[4]

The election of 1892, conducted by men of the old regime well trained in circumventing the wishes of the electorate, furnished the first harsh lesson in political realism to the leaders of the *Unión Cívica.* Seventy-

[3] Thomas A. Turner: *Argentina and the Argentines . . . 1885-1890* (London: S. Sonnenschein and Company; 1892), pp. 313-14.
[4] Octavio R. Amadeo: *Vidas Argentinas* (Buenos Aires: Editorial La Facultad; 1938), p. 6.

year-old Bartolomé Mitre returned from Europe in 1891 an avowed adherent of Alem's new party, and was chosen as its candidate in the coming election. The enthusiasm for the returned hero roused ex-President Julio A. Roca and his Conservative allies to action. They quickly convinced Mitre of the folly of entrusting his hopes for political resurrection to such an untested leader as Leandro Alem; they persuaded him to join his forces with Roca's, promising him the presidency, while the vice-presidency was to go to a follower of Roca. Mitre's defection split the *Unión Cívica.* Some of its members stayed with him under the banner of the *Unión Cívica Nacional,* while others, including Alem and the principal leaders, formed the *Unión Cívica Radical.* Mitre shortly paid for his infidelity by being himself eliminated, and he had to content himself with joining Roca to elect Luis Sáenz Peña, an elderly lawyer of aristocratic traditions, as a bulwark against the dangerous new ideas of Alem.[5]

Luis Sáenz Peña, honorable standard-bearer for the old order, entered office in 1892 under serious handicaps. He was old, sick, and without taste for public office. He was a man without a party, caught in the cross fire of Roca, Mitre, and Alem. The clamoring factions forced repeated shuffling of his cabinet. In 1893 a quickly silenced revolt of the Radicals gave fresh notice of the determination of that opposition party. In 1895 the weary Sáenz Peña resigned his office. The vice-president who succeeded him, unable to cope either with his Conservative supporters or the Radicals, served uneasily until 1898, when he stepped out in favor of the veteran Julio A. Roca.

While victories at the polls had been won by the old regime, it daily became more clear that the Argentine populace preferred the *Unión Cívica Radical.* Meanwhile, the fortunes of that new party were influenced by three events: the death of its founder Alem; the rise of Alem's nephew, Hipólito Irigoyen; and the defection from the party of numerous able leaders.

The suicide of Leandro Alem in 1896 ended the brief public career of a patriot whose record was unsullied by personal ambition. In six short years he had inspired the Argentine people to fight again for the free institutions of a constitutional republic. He had been betrayed by Mitre, fought by Roca, and deserted by trusted lieutenants. His chief humiliation was at the hands of Hipólito Irigoyen, the nephew whom he had nurtured as boy and man, educated in the law, trained in politics, and made a partner in the adventure of faith which was born of the *Noventa.* Although Irigoyen had been tireless in organizing the Radical Party, he had been faithless to the man who had created that party. In Alem's last written words, he seems to refer to Irigoyen: "A viper feeds in my breast, biting at my heart." In his last testament to his fellow Radicals he wrote: "It is better to die than to live sterile, useless and humiliated." He prophesied the triumph of the Radical cause: "I myself gave the initial impulse, but my work is done. . . .

---

[5] The choice of Luis Sáenz Peña was also designed to silence the presidential aspirations of his son, Roque Sáenz Peña, of whom we shall happily hear more.

Now may those who remain press on!" His death left Irigoyen the master of the party.

Hipólito Irigoyen, who had taken over the *Unión Cívica Radical* which his uncle had created, and developed it as a national party, and who would finally be twice elected to the presidency, is the baffling enigma of modern Argentina. Born in 1850, he had little education (the doctorate in law, a title he cherished, seems to have been self-conferred). He served without distinction in minor public posts, read law under his uncle's tutelage, dabbled in ward politics, and taught in a girls' school. Delving into philosophy and spiritualism, he spun vague mystical theories. He had a small patrimony in land, with income enough to support him modestly; his meager earnings were devoted to charity. In 1890 he followed his uncle into the *Unión Cívica*. His unsmiling austerity, his obvious devotion to the Radical cause, and his utter indifference to money inspired wide respect. The defrauded masses saw in him the living embodiment of democratic faith, as he refused to accept public office, insisted upon government based upon "the will of the people," sought to avoid bloodshed, and dealt magnanimously with his political opponents. But despite such restraint, Irigoyen proved as thorough as any caudillo in creating political blocs, distributing favors to the faithful and discipline to the ungrateful. He first created a political machine in the province of Buenos Aires, organizing it ward by ward, with trained subalterns in command; and from there the organization was extended to cover the provinces. But Irigoyen's arrogance alienated many of the founders of the party. The idealistic physician, Juan B. Justo, broke with Irigoyen and founded the Socialist Party, which attracted many European immigrants. The impetuous and honest Lisandro de la Torre, an early colleague of Alem, denounced Irigoyen as a caudillo in the Gaucho tradition, withdrew to his native state of Santa Fe, and founded the Democratic Progressive Party. Meanwhile, Irigoyen, seemingly unmoved by Alem's death and by these desertions, continued to build the Radical Party around himself.

Roca's second term (1898–1904) was an effective dictatorship under which spoilsmen profited, rivals were circumvented by crooked elections, and the will of the provinces was overridden by frequent interventions. During this period Argentina prospered, railroads were extended, commerce was increased, irrigation projects were installed, public buildings erected, and ports improved. Roca won just credit for his handling of international affairs. He settled boundary disputes with Brazil and exchanged state visits with its president. The long-smoldering argument with Chile over lines of demarcation was finally settled in 1902, and a heroic statue of the Christ of the Andes was erected on the pass above Mendoza, with the inscription later added to its base: "Sooner shall these mountains crumble to dust than Argentines and Chileans break the peace sworn to at the feet of Christ the Redeemer." Roca's foreign minister Luis María Drago was a credit to his administration. In 1902, when naval units of Italy, Germany, and England were dispatched to collect unpaid debts from the irresponsible dictator of Venezuela, Drago sent a note to the Argentine minister in Washington:

"There can be no territorial expansion in America on the part of Europe. . . . The public debt cannot occasion armed intervention, nor even the actual occupation of the territory of American nations by a European power." The "Drago Doctrine" contributed to the growing United States emphasis upon the Monroe Doctrine and its demand that Europe keep its hands off the New World.

In 1904 Roca, in the face of angry denunciation by the Radicals, imposed Manuel Quintana, another old-guard henchman, as president. In 1905 the Radicals attempted to overturn the government by a revolution which was promptly crushed. Quintana died in 1906 and was succeeded by Vice-President Figueroa Alcorta, one of the more able and honest of the Conservative oligarchy, whose four years were disturbed by constant changes in cabinets, growing protests from Radicals, and increased labor agitation inspired by immigrants who introduced current varieties of European anarchism and socialism.

THE OLIGARCHY YIELDS TO THE RADICALS, 1910–30

In 1910 Figueroa Alcorta presided over the celebration of Argentina's first hundred years of independence. Guests from many nations praised the most powerful, prosperous, and modern of all the states that had taken shape out of the one-time American empire of Spain. The Argentina of 1910 showed signs of a maturing political life. Some intelligent Conservatives, wealthy enough to visit Paris and wise enough to admire British methods of governing, were growing ashamed of the tawdry devices by which their politicians ruled the nation. Perhaps more important, the blows of the Radicals, directed by Irigoyen, made them fear a violent revolution unless the opposition could be quieted by peaceful change.

Roque Sáenz Peña, who, it will be recalled, had been sidetracked by Mitre and Roca in 1892, was elected by the Conservatives in 1910. Liberals admired his uncompromising stand for free suffrage and political decency during the turgid years since 1890. Conservatives accepted him because of his social standing, wealth, Parisian education, and prestige in the law. Citizens liked his record as a soldier in suppressing Mitre's *coup d'état* of 1874, as a volunteer in Peru's army against Chile in 1879, as an honored diplomat in various critical posts, and as the spokesman for Argentina against the United States during its war with Spain in 1898.[6] Upon being installed, Sáenz Peña announced that he stood for honest elections, effective suffrage, and the participation of all political sectors in the government. He offered a cabinet post to Irigoyen, who refused it.

The need for electoral reform had long been clearly evident. Argentine citizens had never been permitted free expression of their convictions and desires. Caudillos of early decades had ruled by guns. The intelligent

---

[6] Argentine sympathy for Spain in 1898 was prompted by lingering nostalgia for the mother country and by growing hostility toward the United States, whose imperialistic ambitions were feared.

presidents of the 1860's and 1870's had ruled by patronage and control of the ballot boxes. The indifferent presidents of the 1880's, 1890's, and the first decade of the 1900's used their agents to buy the votes of immigrants and peons. The oligarchy had a political machine not unlike that of Tammany Hall in contemporary New York, in which henchmen were given posts as policemen, school teachers, customs officials, street cleaners, tax collectors, and so on.[7] Furthermore, the *Unión Cívica Radical* and Irigoyen (by 1910 the terms were synonymous) had adopted the tactics of their opponents, creating a political machine fully as powerful as that of the old guard.

Sáenz Peña stated his case to Congress: "I propose, gentlemen . . . that the representatives of minorities shall be fully protected in their rights. To be sure the majority will rule, but the minority will be heard, and its counsels weighed." In 1912 he presented his law for electoral reform, which was passed by Congress after heated debate. The law stipulated that the party which got a plurality, even though less than a majority, of the votes would get two-thirds of the seats in the Chamber of Deputies, while the party running second would get the other third of the seats—a procedure designed to encourage the two-party system. Furthermore, the law guaranteed all males over eighteen a vote "free, secret and obligatory." The prospective voters, who had heard fine words before, remained skeptical. Then followed a provincial election, carefully policed against fraud, in which Radical candidates won large majorities. Other elections followed and other Radicals with unknown names came to office. "I promised a free government," said the President, "and I have kept my word." There were angry Conservative demonstrations against him, as members of the long-despised middle class took their seats in provincial and federal congresses. The government's problems were complicated by a financial panic, which was blamed on Sáenz Peña. Argentina's trade was threatened when World War I broke out in July, 1914. Sáenz Peña died in August, yielding his office to the Vice-President, who honored the pledges of his predecessor and permitted a fair election in 1916 which finally gave the presidency to Hipólito Irigoyen.

When Irigoyen was informed of his nomination, he brusquely refused to run, actually barricading himself in his house against all visitors, and it was with difficulty that he was finally persuaded to enter the race. The election returns gave him less than the required majority of electoral votes, and his victory was not assured until his long-time rival, Lisandro de la Torre of Santa Fe, threw support to him as the lesser of possible evils.

The rule of Irigoyen was a strange interlude in Argentine history. The morose, unsmiling political veteran of sixty-six was paradoxically the best loved and the most soundly hated of the nation's presidents. He was tall,

---

[7] An Argentine historian, not without malice, notes: "In our country, no matter how corrupt our politics might be, we never reached such extremes [as Tammany]." He cites the "tariff" under which Tammany's gangsters operated—a beating for $2, a pair of black eyes for $4, a broken arm for $20, an assassination for $100. Enrique de Gandía, *Historia de la república argentina en el siglo XIX* (Buenos Aires: A. Estrada y Cía; 1940), p. 942.

erect, his swarthiness confirming his Indian blood, his eyes glowing but troubled. His style in writing and speech was abstruse and confused, colored by a strange mysticism. His personal life was screened from public view. He continued to live as he had always lived, in a poor house, badly dressed, eating meagerly, and giving his salary to the unfortunate. He never married, and the various women in his life were from the simple poor; a servant girl who bore him at least one child seems to have been by his side through most of his years of struggle and of triumph. He was contemptuous of the frippery of politicians; when a friend asked him for a personal memento, Irigoyen pointed to a cardboard box holding the golden and jeweled decorations with which statesmen delight themselves, and said: "Help yourself."

The official conduct of President Irigoyen was capricious. Most of his subordinates were unknown men; some were both able and honest, but many were neither. Demanding blind loyalty, adulation, and instant agreement, he dismissed those who refused such servility. He was suspicious of his aides, delegated little authority, made all major and most minor decisions, and even insisted upon signing personally the appointments of porters in public buildings and teachers in rural schools. Letters, communiqués from foreign governments, and congressional bills were piled up unread and unsigned. Important offices went unfilled for months. Although he exercised almost absolute power, there is no evidence that he used his position for private profit. Many of his less conscientious subordinates raided the treasury, collecting commissions from supplicants who sought interviews with the President, gratuities for appointment to public posts, and presents from businessmen requiring presidential approval of their contracts. The Argentine Felix Weil suggests that "Irigoyen's case illustrates . . . that an honest president may be much more expensive for the country in the course of time than a 'run-of-the-mill' politician."

The presidential office was always open to the poor. A young Italian bootblack, whose stand was opposite Irigoyen's house, was one of the few who had instant access to the President. Sweaty stevedores, bent farm women, hungry lads from the waterside crowded into his anteroom, were received with grave courtesy, and were usually given what they asked. A place on the public payroll was open to almost all who reached him, without reference to need or ability. Irigoyen saw no incongruity in such wasteful course, for was he not "the father of the poor"?

Meanwhile, the *gente decente,* respectable people—the sweet-smelling who spoke French, owned lands, ran businesses, sold grain and heavy beef—found it all but impossible to see their president on business. Their requests for audiences were ignored for months. The concessions they sought or the licenses they required were only obtained by the favoritism of someone in the President's inner circle or by bribery. Their initial contempt solidified into bitter hatred. They called his house "the cave," referred to him as "the armadillo." The responsible press, which he seldom read, notably *La Prensa* and *La Nación,* denounced him. The Socialists, the most ably led minority, bitterly attacked him. Lisandro de la Torre's Progressive Democrats repented their last-minute help in his election.

Irigoyen's economic course was vacillating. When he assumed office, Argentina was enjoying unprecedented profits from the sale of meat and grain to the warring nations of Europe, and her industry was expanding in order to make up for the scarcity of finished goods from foreign makers. But the waste and corruption of a chaotic administration led to unbalanced budgets, increased debt, and delays in paying public servants. Irigoyen's ignorance of national and international economic forces was profound. When the grain interests were ordered to pay more for wheat, their spokesmen argued that world supply and demand set their prices, to which the President answered (according to Felix Weil): "I don't believe you. The law of supply and demand is an old fairy tale. I know for sure that you can pay the farmer more if you really want to, and you are going to do it, or else."

Irigoyen's international course during World War I reflected his ignorance of the world and his contempt for foreigners. He announced Argentina's neutrality and stuck to it despite sinkings of Argentine ships by German U-boats and widespread public sympathy for the Allied cause. He was accused of pro-German sentiment, but his course is more accurately explained as tough pro-Argentine nationalism. Although he led his country into the League of Nations, he withdrew Argentina's support when that body refused to admit Germany and Austria. His neutrality paid off: Argentina emerged as a creditor nation for the first time in her history.

Irigoyen's sympathies for the poor were genuine and were expressed in generous social legislation and in aid to the labor unions, which gained new power. However, his attempts to conciliate labor were marred by the ruthless handling of strikers in January, 1919, which culminated in a week of anarchic and bloody confusion—*la semana trágica,* the Tragic Week— which brought Argentine life to a standstill. First came the wanton shooting of a few striking workers. Then as the mourners for these victims paraded through the streets of Buenos Aires, the police fired into the crowd, and general panic ensued. Then followed rioting and indiscriminate shooting by the police; and the conflict broadened to include assaults upon the Jews and supposed Communists, with the virtual collapse of law enforcement throughout the city and most of the nation. Estimates of the number killed during this cruel week run into the hundreds or even the thousands. The failure of Irigoyen's government to handle this sad affair went far toward undermining his influence with the masses.[8]

Irigoyen, for all his lifelong protestations of democratic faith, imposed a dictatorial rule. Unlike Rosas, he ordered no murders of dissenters, but he had more actual power than Rosas ever boasted. The political ills he had long denounced—wasteful political patronage, fraudulent elections, intervention in provincial affairs—flowered with new luxuriance.

At the command of Irigoyen, the elections of 1922 gave the presidency to Marcelo T. de Alvear. The choice was a relief to the rich, for Al-

---

[8] For a vivid account of *la semana trágica,* see Ysabel F. Rennie: *The Argentine Republic* (New York: The Macmillan Co.; 1945), pp. 214–19.

vear was one of them. His solid family tradition, his landed wealth, his Parisian culture, his world outlook all commended him. He had, to be sure, married an opera singer who was not received by the first ladies of society; but she stopped her singing, and they accepted her. The choice pleased faithful Radicals, for Alvear had stood with Leandro Alem in 1890 and had remained reasonably faithful to the cause. Furthermore, he could smile, a relief after the sulky Irigoyen. He was a gentleman *and* a Radical, an irresistible political combination.

Alvear's six-year term was amiable, reasonably efficient—and quite corrupt. Less dictatorial than his predecessor, he intervened only ten times in the provinces. He improved Argentine prestige among the nations by sending able ambassadors and ministers. Federal administration was tightened; thousands of Irigoyen's appointees were ejected; official peculation was restricted to those in high places. But his inevitable break with Irigoyen split the Radical ranks: he became titular chief of the anti-*personalistas,* while Irigoyen headed the *personalistas.*

Irigoyen's reelection in 1928, tribute of his loyal followers, introduced the last tragic era of his life. He was now seventy-eight, quite senile, and more irresponsible than before. His aides shut him off from all contact with the affairs of the nation, robbed the treasury openly, and made all decisions. The public treasury was disorganized, as debts mounted and unpaid wages increased. University students demonstrated against him, businessmen conspired, the press clamored, and army officers plotted; even his friends knew that a change was imperative. By early 1930 provincial elections began to go against the Radicals. In September Buenos Aires streets were filled with mobs shouting: "Down with the armadillo!" Irigoyen, a sick old man confined to his home, delegated his powers to the Vice-President, who declared a state of siege, naming a new cabinet of honorable men. But it was too late. General José F. Uriburu was the center of a group of angry ultrarightists who believed that only the army could save Argentina from the politicians and the Radicals. Chief intellectual mentor of this group was the poet Leopoldo Lugones, who—impressed by Mussolini—called for *la hora de la espada,* the hour of the sword. Uriburu and his cabal, seizing the Casa Rosada, the presidential palace, demanded the resignation of the Vice-President, who was charged with responsibility for any blood spilled in defense of "a government unanimously repudiated by public opinion." Both the President and the Vice-President resigned. Irigoyen died three years later, as poor as when he was born, still venerated by many as "the father of the poor."

The year 1930 marked a tragic turning point in Argentine history. The dismal failure of the Radicals was a calamity not only for the party but for the nation. Born in the genuine idealism of Leandro N. Alem, the movement had been wrecked by the incompetence and arrogant nationalism of Hipólito Irigoyen. And the failure of the middle class to assert itself as a political force had postponed any true national renovation.

Chapter 41

ARGENTINA: THE OLD REGIME
RETURNS, 1930–43

The power wrested from Irigoyen in 1930 was restored to the old Conservative oligarchy. For thirteen years a bloc of generals and *estancieros,* supported by bankers, merchants, and high clergy, ruled the country in their own behalf, crushing dissidents, staging fraudulent elections, and intervening arbitrarily in the affairs of the provinces. They viewed their war against the Radicals as a crusade for the fatherland—but these new knights proved singularly devoid of knightliness, furnishing neither new men nor new ideas. Their arrogance and their neglect of the just demands of the lower middle class and the underpaid masses paved the way for another overturn in 1943.

JOSÉ F. URIBURU, 1930–32

The installation of José F. Uriburu as president in 1930—the work of a few generals and 10,000 soldiers—brought relief to the wellborn. The new leader was also hailed by the city mobs who, long loyal to Irigoyen, now sacked the poor house of the old caudillo, smashed his meager furniture, and dragged his sculptured bust through the mire of the city streets. Uriburu quickly imposed order, assuring the loyalty of the army by distributing 7 million pesos among the officers.

Uriburu took over a bankrupt and confused government, which was suffering not only from the effects of the ousted president's senile rule but also from the world's economic crisis: Argentina's beef, wheat, corn, wool, and hides were selling at ruinous prices in the world market. Uriburu met the challenge with a ruthless dictatorship. He cut governmental costs by removing thousands from the public payroll. Opposition leaders, mostly Radicals and Socialists, were dismissed from office; some were jailed, many exiled. The broken Irigoyen was confined on the island of Martín García, and Alvear found refuge in Uruguay. Democratic resistance still showed itself: an election in the province of Buenos Aires resulted in victory for Radical candidates—but Uriburu canceled the election, and other Radical victories in outlying provinces were similarly disposed of. Labor unions were generally suppressed. The press was subjected to strict censorship, and rebellious editors found it expedient to conform—or flee. But Ezequiel Paz, publisher of *La Prensa,* threatened with closure by Uriburu, replied that on the day his paper was silenced he would resume publication in Paris, with a daily reminder to the world of the tyranny under which Argentina was groaning. Uriburu capitulated, and the great newspaper continued to roll from the presses.

Public sentiment turned against Uriburu when he advocated the abolition of Congress and the substitution of an authoritarian state modeled after Mussolini's Italy. Numerous army and navy officers, *estancieros,* and business leaders repudiated Uriburu's methods. Within six months after seizing power, the dictator found it wise to announce an election for November, 1931. The Radicals, aware of the frauds to be perpetrated, refused to participate. Socialists and Progressive Democrats nominated Lisandro de la Torre, the last survivor of the leaders of the *Noventa.* The Conservatives, together with some seceding Radicals, formed a coalition called *la concordancia,* and named and elected Agustín P. Justo.

AGUSTÍN P. JUSTO, 1932–38

Agustín P. Justo was a rich man with social and political prestige. Variously a civil engineer, army general, and a cabinet member under Alvear, he had also been an able administrator of public works. His record showed undeviating loyalty to friends in high places and a willingness to accept personal profit, but he was also a skillful public servant. At his inauguration he asked an end to all clamor "that may kindle or perpetuate hate, and incite to violence." His rule was a dictatorship, but a gentlemanly one, in which political foes were neither murdered, jailed, nor exiled; they were even permitted to make speeches and, in some instances, to sit in Congress. Political opposition became a myth, however, as electoral frauds multiplied, as provincial governments were subjected to repeated interventions, and as political dissidents were systematically barred from public employment. The business community and the *estancieros* found comfort in this happier political climate; public affairs were conducted with efficiency, trade increased, prices rose, national credit improved, and corruption was confined largely to those in top posts.

Argentina's relations with other nations, so long hampered by Irigoyen's dislike of foreigners, improved under an astute minister of foreign affairs, Carlos Saavedra Lamas, who revived Argentina's participation in the League of Nations. Representing Argentina at the Seventh Pan American Conference, which convened in Montevideo in December, 1933, Saavedra shared honors with the United States secretary of state, Cordell Hull. Hull, intent upon winning Argentine support for all-American cooperation, paid assiduous court to Saavedra, supporting his Antiwar Pact and encouraging his attempts to stop the Chaco War between Paraguay and Bolivia. Argentina, chief investor in Paraguayan real estate, had more than a platonic interest in the outcome of that savage contest, and her foreign minister was serving his national interest in arranging a settlement. Saavedra had first liquidated the commission of "neutrals" which had been seeking a solution, quite ineffectually, since 1928; then had helped turn over the dispute to a League of Nations commission; and finally, after blocking the League's commission, had succeeded in having the whole affair entrusted to a commission of "neighbors," in which he could play the stellar role. This arrangement, sanctioned by Hull, assured Saavedra principal credit when a truce of exhaustion was signed in 1935. The vain but able Argentine, thus honored in American circles, was further beholden to the American secretary of state for helping to persuade the Norwegian Storting to award him the Nobel Peace Prize. Meanwhile, Britain pleased Saavedra Lamas by securing his election as president of the Assembly of the League of Nations. In this fresh contest for Argentine favor, Washington finally lost to Downing Street, for the British bought Argentine beef, while the Americans did not. When Hull and Saavedra next met at the Pan American Conference of 1936 in Buenos Aires, the Argentine's lack of enthusiasm for Hull's measures for the lowering of trade barriers provoked harsh words between the two statesmen and increased the unpleasantness between Washington and Buenos Aires.

Argentina's rapid economic recovery in the 1930's, in contrast to other Latin American republics, attested both the solid resources of the nation and the considerable skill of her president. Justo faced a situation not unlike that of the United States under Franklin D. Roosevelt: diminished world demand for goods; ruinous prices (grain prices reached the lowest level in more than thirty years); farmers in distress, with widespread foreclosures; bank clearings down 40 per cent since 1928; artificially high land values, and an excessive mortgage load. Justo's measures, similar to Roosevelt's, were to devalue the currency, to establish fixed prices on some commodities, to create a quasi-governmental monopoly on grain exports, to control exchange operations, and to cut down on foreign imports. Recovery was swift, aided by rising prices on world markets. Meanwhile, Argentina stood almost alone among Latin American states in maintaining service on external loans. Treasury surpluses made possible retirement of some foreign issues, a start in purchasing British-owned railroads and other foreign-owned industries, and expansion of national petroleum production. (There had been some oil pumped since 1907, when the first well was drilled; and the national petroleum monopoly company, YPF—*Yacimientos Petrolíferos Fiscales*—had been organized under Irigoyen.)

Justo's program of economic recovery was supplemented by such generous concessions to foreign capital as to provoke a fresh surge of nationalism in the country. European and North American investments were heavy; but the British interest was by far the greatest, controlling about three-fourths of the railroad mileage, most of the street railway systems, and much of the meat-packing industry, and having a large stake in chemical works, tire factories, and other concerns.[1] Britain, leading investor, was

---

[1] The total foreign investment in Argentina stood at about $2.5 billion in 1942, of which about 60 per cent was British (more than three-fifths of it in railroads), about 20 per cent American, and the balance chiefly French and Belgian. See George Wythe: *Industry in Latin America* (New York: Columbia University Press; 1945), p. 94.

also the chief buyer of meat and grain. Argentines had long accepted Bartolomé Mitre's description of England as "the principal factor in the country's political, social and economic progress." Resentment against Great Britain's overshadowing economic power had grown steadily, but Justo did much to increase it.

Anglo-Argentine relations were reshaped under the shock of world depression. At the Ottawa Conference in 1932, Great Britain pledged trade preference to the grain- and meat-producing dominions of the Empire, chiefly Australia and Canada. That action aroused grave fears in Argentina. A trade commission headed by Julio A. Roca (son of the "Conqueror of the Desert") went to London, where in May, 1933, the Roca-Runciman pact was signed, installing for a three-year period a rigid bilateral trade agreement reminiscent of Spanish colonial mercantilism of the sixteenth century. The British slogan, "Buy from those who buy from us," basis of the Ottawa agreements, was extended to Argentina. Britain pledged herself not to reduce her purchases of chilled beef below the level of late 1932, and Argentina reciprocated by promising that money earned by such sales would be spent on British goods.[2] Thus the two nations, under the duress of the world crisis, had, in effect, reverted to the barter system of the primitive Indian: from now on it would be a cow for a plow, and a sheep for a keg of nails. There was grumbling in both London and Buenos Aires. Argentine nationalists complained that their nation had been granted "dominion status" and repeated the hoary tale of the hypothetical Englishman who said to the equally hypothetical American: "You may take Canada from us, but you will never take Argentina." And in Washington, Secretary of State Cordell Hull's dream of a world in which trade would flow with a minimum of restraint was given another rude setback.

The Roca-Runciman pact, whose immediate effects were salutary for the Argentine economy, also carried an Argentine pledge to all British interests in the La Plata area. The British-owned railroads, obsolete in equipment and service, were a major Argentine grievance. In the face of decreasing profits to British shareholders, the foreign managers had sought to protect their interests by lobbying against the building of highways which would parallel the railways and compete with them. But Justo, regardless of the fair promises made through Roca, disappointed the British by launching a vast network of new highways, almost doubling their mileage during the 1930's. On that point, at any rate, Justo had not sold out to the British.

On other occasions, however, Justo earned a reputation as an over-zealous ally of foreign interests. A major tempest involved the British-owned street railway system of Buenos Aires, whose trolleys were hopelessly outdated, inadequate in number, and badly operated. The management pleaded extenuating circumstances—high taxes, uneconomic restriction on fares, and ruinous assessments. The shareholders complained at the lack of dividends, while the *porteños* simply knew that they were crowded like cattle, jounced unmercifully, and delayed interminably. Meanwhile, the British company was subjected to the competition of thousands of *colectivos*,

---

[2] There was prudential hedging on both sides. Ysabel F. Rennie: *The Argentine Republic* (New York: The Macmillan Co.; 1945), pp. 236–7.

small, rude, privately owned buses which scurried around the lumbering trolleys, taking the cream of the traffic and paying no more than a token tax. The British demanded a charter for a new monopoly, Corporación de Transportes, with tax exemptions, a guaranteed return of 7 per cent to investors, and elimination of the *colectivos.* The *porteños,* using the *colectivos* as a symbol of their war against foreign capital, denounced the British proposal. But Justo, confronted by British threats to refuse renewal of the Roca-Runciman pact in 1936, yielded; and his congress created the new transport company in 1935, delivering the straphangers to the mercies of the British operators. It was a Pyrrhic victory for the British, and loosed a general protest against foreign control of railroads, trolleys, and other public services.[3]

Other foreign interests enjoyed Justo's favors. A French company had held since 1902 the concession for developing and operating the principal grain port of Rosario; its shares, widely held in Europe, had sold at prices sixty, seventy, and even eighty times their original cost. By the terms of its charter, all its properties would revert to the nation in 1942, when all foreign ownership would be terminated. In 1935, after negotiations in which critics smelled corruption, Justo's congress voted an extension to the concessionaires on highly favorable terms. (However, public clamor compelled President Castillo to cancel their contract in 1942.) Another instance was the Belgian-owned light and power monopoly in Buenos Aires, whose charter ran until 1957, when all its installations would revert to the city. In 1936 this franchise was extended to 1971, at which date the city was pledged to *pay* for the properties. By such measures Justo was responsible for the hardening of the antiforeign nationalism which would henceforth be a major factor in Argentine life.

ROBERTO M. ORTIZ AND RAMÓN S. CASTILLO, 1938–43

The shamelessly corrupt election of 1937 gave the presidency to Roberto M. Ortiz, whom Justo had chosen as a safe deputy not likely to forget his benefactor. A corporation lawyer, wealthy by inheritance and from fees paid by British railroad companies, Ortiz seemed a logical choice for a party dedicated to the interests of the first families. To be sure, as a young man he had shouted for Irigoyen and had been jailed for his Radical activities, but such indiscretions had been forgotten. Once installed in the Casa Rosada in 1938, however, Ortiz announced that the Roque Sáenz Peña electoral law was still in force, that from then on elections would be free and secret. Then, to the general surprise, there were several provincial elections in which the voting *was* free and secret. In other instances, especially in the province of Buenos Aires, old-line politicians conducted dis-

---

[3] The acceleration of protest against British economic penetration of Argentina began at this time. See Raúl Scalobrini Ortiz: *Política británica en el Río de la Plata,* 2nd ed. (Buenos Aires: Editorial Reconquista; 1940).

honest elections, only to be overtaken by presidential intervention and the calling of new elections under federal policing. Such measures, described as "treason to his class," were followed in 1939 and 1940 by an open display of sympathy for England and her allies, which alienated the pro-Axis group among Argentine army officers and their nationalistic supporters. By early 1940 Ortiz had been abandoned by those who had chosen him, but he had won new support from those who favored democracy and wanted to align Argentina with the Allies against the Axis powers.

Ortiz was a sick man, and was forced to turn over his office in mid-1940 to Vice-President Ramón S. Castillo. Worn by diabetes and almost blind, Ortiz retired to his home, powerless to stop the wrecking of the program he had launched. Castillo, long the dean of the law faculty of Buenos Aires, represented the ultranationalists and isolationists. As vice-president, he had watched Ortiz's course in sullen contempt. Now, as acting president, Castillo reverted to the old pattern of political repression, corrupt elections, and the overriding of provincial decisions. Surrounded by admirers of Hitler and Mussolini, Castillo permitted German agents to work unmolested and allowed the pro-Axis press to blare out its propaganda, while he suppressed expression of popular sympathy for the Allied cause. Such was the situation in Argentina when the Japanese attack on Pearl Harbor brought the war to the Western Hemisphere in December, 1941.

The Argentines split sharply on the question of their nation's stand on the war. Castillo's "neutrality," so useful to the Axis, had the support of influential and vocal elements: young nationalists who proved their devotion to the fatherland by hating England, the United States, Jews, and democracy; *soi-disant* intellectuals who called themselves *rosistas* in honor of the old caudillo; army officers trained by German tutors, admirers of fascist ways who were convinced of inevitable German victory; and numerous high clergy, many Spanish by birth, who were partisans of Franco. Castillo's foreign minister, Enrique Ruiz Guiñazú, was the logical leader of such foes of democracy. His principal article of faith was *hispanidad,* "Spanishness," the current rallying call of all illiberal sons of Spain. These pro-fascist groups were opposed by numerous other elements which sincerely hoped for Allied victory: the cultured minority who mourned the fall of France and looked to her liberation; *estancieros* whose economic and social ties were with England; the able and predominantly pro-Allied press; the organization called *Acción Argentina,* dedicated to friendship with Great Britain, and numbering several hundred thousand adherents; the women of La Junta de la Victoria, whose 40,000 members prepared and shipped first-aid supplies to Allied forces; some parish priests and one member of the hierarchy, Bishop Miguel de Andrea; and many Socialists and Radicals.

The conference of foreign ministers which met in Rio de Janeiro in January, 1942, a month after the Japanese attack on Pearl Harbor, was a test of strength between the great majority of the American republics, who stood for immediate and unanimous rupture of relations with the Axis, and Argentina, whose sole active ally was Chile. A compromise resolution "recommended" that all American republics break with the Axis, but Castillo announced that Argentina would not recall its ambassadors from Rome, Berlin, and Tokyo.

Castillo's pro-Axis course excited continued criticism in Argentina, but his path was smoothed by the death of three leading rivals—Alvear, Justo, and Ortiz, whose funerals were scenes of vast demonstrations with much shouting of *Viva democracia*. There was continued denunciation of flagrant thievery in high places, corruption of elections, and interventions in the provinces. Although record sales of meat and grain brought the highest prices in national history, the cost of living also skyrocketed, and wage earners were not sharing in the nation's prosperity. The first days of 1943 found Castillo unloved and unhonored, even by the quasi-fascist nationalists whom he had sought to serve.

As the nation prepared for the presidential election of 1943, no political party offered commanding leaders or convincing principles—neither the discouraged Radicals, nor the weak Socialists, nor the unimportant Progressive Democrats. They knew that the election, dominated by Castillo's henchmen, would be corrupt. There was talk of impending revolution, but by whom and for what end none seemed to know. Castillo's choice for the presidency, Robustiano Patrón Costas, owner of extensive sugar lands in northern Salta, angered the opposition and united numerous sectors, right and left, against Castillo and his nominee. Nationalists disliked Patrón Costas, describing him as the cat's-paw of British interests. The *estancieros* detested him as an upstart monopolist. Liberals despised him for his brutality toward his ill-paid peons, his importation of Bolivian Indians, and his drain upon the funds of the Banco de la Nación.

Castillo had made revolt inevitable. The democratic elements, quarreling and leaderless, could do nothing. The army, abetted by the nationalists, could. On June 4, 1943, some generals and a few thousand soldiers marched upon the Casa Rosada, ended the inglorious rule of Ramón Castillo, and opened a new chapter in the history of the nation.

Chapter 42

ARGENTINA: THE ERA OF JUAN DOMINGO PERÓN, 1943–55

The upheaval of June, 1943, delivered the nation into the hands of the military. The bungling generals who executed the coup proved unimportant, but out of the confusion emerged a new caudillo: one who ruled neither by grace of the Conservative oligarchy nor of the middle class, as had presidents since the time of Rosas; but a demagogue who held power by favor of the sweaty masses. This was the beginning of the era of Juan Domingo Perón.

The prosperous upper classes had themselves to thank for the latest turn of events. They had controlled Argentina, with one brief interval, for ninety years; they had named presidents and had often contributed to the building of the nation. But they had failed to serve the Argentine people; they had denied them free political institutions, monopolized the land, and perpetuated the colonial abuses of the workers. The middle class had also failed; despite its dominance from 1916 to 1930, the Radical Party had caused further strife, falling apart into warring factions; in 1943 it was powerless to block the upstart generals. The oligarchy and the Radicals shared responsibility for the emergence of Perón and *peronismo*.

THE RISE OF PERÓN

The march upon the Casa Rosada on June 4, the flight of Castillo to the safety of a mine sweeper on the Río de la Plata, the installation of General Arturo Rawson as president, the shift three days later to General Pedro Ramírez—these events seemed to the average citizen to augur happier days, for any change was welcome; and the streets echoed with shouts of *Viva Rawson! Viva Ramírez! Viva democracia!* Within a week the new government was recognized by the principal powers, including the United States. A few critics warned that the coup was not a victory for democracy; and their gloomy prophecies were speedily confirmed by the actions of Ramírez, who dismissed Congress and proceeded to rule by decree.

The election scheduled for September, 1943, was canceled. Cabinet and other appointments with rare exceptions went to blatant admirers of the Axis. Critics were jailed or exiled. Influential spokesmen for the Allies were silenced. Newspapers hostile to the new regime were generally suppressed, although *La Nación, La Prensa,* and the bellicose *Crítica* (whose publisher was currently described as "the Hearst of South America") continued to criticize the usurpers. The Jewish press was banned, while numerous German-subsidized dailies and weeklies, anti-Semitic and antidemocratic, were published without hindrance. Pro-Allied organizations such as *Acción Argentina* and La Junta de la Victoria were proscribed. The German Embassy continued to turn out tons of propaganda. Secret police haunted streets, cafés, hotel lobbies, theaters. Suspects were arrested, jailed, and held without trial.

In October a manifesto signed by some 150 intellectual, professional, and business leaders was printed in a few brave newspapers; it called for freedom of the press, "effective democracy . . . solidarity with the other American republics . . . fulfillment of international pledges," and abandonment of the idea that Argentina could stand aloof from those who "are fighting in the cause of democracy." The government's answer was fresh repression. Ramírez appointed as minister of education Gustavo Martínez Zuviría, a novelist who, under the pen name of "Hugo Wast," had written more than thirty tales of indifferent quality filled with venom against democracy, Communism, foreigners, and Jews. Martínez Zuviría was ordered to purge the nation's schools and universities, and the professors who had signed the manifesto were the first to go. There were bold protests. Alfredo Palacios, veteran Socialist and rector of the University of La Plata, defied the government by refusing to dismiss his professors, but he was himself forced from office. University students demonstrated but were soon quieted. The ejected professors included outstanding intellectuals such as Dr. Bernardo Houssay, a physiologist of world reputation (later honored with a Nobel prize) who bade farewell to his students with the words: "And now I have delivered my last lecture. . . . The next will be given by a colonel." The patriarchal Bishop Miguel de Andrea, beloved champion of democracy, announced a lecture on "Liberty in the Face of Authority"; when the police locked the meeting place, his words were printed and scattered widely, carrying their appeal to Ramírez: "To dominate slaves is doubly ignoble; to reign over the free is doubly glorious! Your Excellency, Mr. President: let your authority be the guarantee of our liberty." Meanwhile, Martínez Zuviría placed compliant puppets in university chairs, introduced nationalistic propaganda into the public schools, and added religious instruction, barred since 1884, to the school curriculum.

Ramírez aided the Axis powers by permitting German agents to carry on their propaganda and to furnish information on sailings of ships to U-boats at sea. The protests of the Allies were ignored. In August Foreign Minister Storni addressed a naïve note to Secretary of State Cordell Hull, arguing that Argentine "neutrality" really served the all-American cause, hinting at the imbalance caused by the United States' arming of Brazil, and suggesting that President Roosevelt make "a gesture of genuine friendship" to Argentina by sending airplanes, parts, and arms. Hull's sarcastic refusal was well deserved, but its principal effect was to discredit and unseat Storni, probably the one member of Ramírez's inner circle who favored the Allies. Hull's heavy-handed ridicule of the Ramírez regime united many Argentines behind the government they detested. In January, 1944, the United States and Great Britain confronted Ramírez with specific evidence of German espionage under the cloak of Argentine diplomatic immunity. The Argentine congress then "discovered" what every newsboy knew, that German and Japanese agents were conspiring on Argentine soil, and relations with the Axis powers were severed. As a face-saving gesture, army officers forced Ramírez to resign in February, 1944, and he was replaced by Vice-President Edelmiro Farrell, a blundering nonentity.

The true ruler was now Juan Domingo Perón, leader of the *Grupo de Oficiales Unidos* (the GOU), who henceforth directed the floundering revolution over which Ramírez had presided for eight months. Ramírez had given the Argentine masses no slogans to stir them to action. He had, in effect, told them to hate the United States, England, democracy, Communism, and Jews; and to love Hitler, Mussolini, and Franco. Such hating and loving meant little to the average citizen. It remained for Perón to furnish a fighting issue: the emancipation of the common man.

Those who dismissed Juan Domingo Perón as an insignificant upstart in 1944 lived to change their minds. He was forty-nine, *muy macho* (very much a male) in his six feet of hard flesh, with his quick smile and clear eyes and his easy command of men. His earlier years had been unspectacular. Born in 1895 in the south of the province of Buenos Aires, a son of poverty, he was trained in the military academy and then rose slowly in the ranks of the army. In 1930, as a captain, he took part in the Uriburu revolt. In the late 1930's he spent two years in Europe, studying tactics in Italy, France, Germany, and Spain. In 1943 he supported Ramírez, who appointed him chief of staff in the war ministry. While Ramírez and his colleagues vacillated, Perón determined that he would rise to power as the spokesman of the proletariat—the badly paid industrial worker in factory and *frigorífico*, the friendless peon on the *estancia*.

The times played into Perón's hand. The cities were crowded with sons and grandsons of Italian and Spanish immigrants, now loyal Argentines. Alongside them was a host of workers who had moved into the cities from the back country, an ill-paid company who had quit the quasi-feudalism of the *estancias* for the larger wages in industry. Crowded into the distended cities, these workers in *frigoríficos* and factories were ready for a leader who promised better pay, better living conditions, and a voice in government. And of like mind were the middle-class workers, little better off than the industrial workers. Perón offered himself to these groups as guide and savior. He moved astutely, picked a job no one else wanted, the head of the weak Labor Department, and cultivated the labor unions which had hitherto lived by sufferance at the hands of both Conservatives and

Radicals. By November, 1943, Perón had won *de facto* cabinet rank as secretary of labor and was creating a political machine around the labor unions he controlled. There was no question as to who ruled Argentina after the ousting of Ramírez and the seating of Farrell in early 1944. In May Perón was named minister of war; and in July, vice-president. In October of the following year an army coup forced him to withdraw from these offices, but the ouster was brief: in February, 1946, he was elected president; and in November, 1951, he was reelected.

PERÓN'S ALLIES

Not the least of the confederates who helped Perón to seize and hold power was María Eva Duarte, perhaps the shrewdest woman yet to appear in public life in South America. The glittering Evita, object of boundless affection as well as endless abuse, was the heroine of a success tale in a land where success is avidly worshiped. Of illegitimate birth, reared in poverty and with little schooling, ostracized by the "nice" people of her little town in the south of the province of Buenos Aires, she was early drilled in dislike for the favored upper classes and was perhaps inspired with some genuine desire to aid others whom society had scorned. Living by her wits, by 1943 she had a minor position in the principal radio station of Buenos Aires—at a wage of $1 a day. After the coup of 1943, she won friends among the Ramírez coterie, and within six months her pay was increased thirtyfold. During the last months of 1943 she met Perón and became his mistress as well as his partner in rallying the masses behind his banner. When the movement to unseat Perón two years later almost succeeded, Evita had a part in organizing the labor demonstration which restored him to power. Their marriage followed, and the twenty-six-year-old Evita shared the honors of the election of February, 1946.

From then on Evita, who in her fine clothes and costly jewels outshone any woman of the republic, exercised an authority scarcely second to that of her husband. She became the virtual minister of labor, dispensing and withholding favors with alternate wisdom and petulance. Political heads fell before her displeasure, while favorites rose to high place. She became the owner of principal newspapers, bought with funds whose source was never explained. In 1947 she took a hand in international affairs, making a triumphant state visit to Spain, Italy, and France, where she was accorded honors by Franco, received by the Pope, and fêted by the French president. At home Evita grew in favor with the *descamisados,* "the shirtless ones," who saw in the comely First Lady a model for all good *peronistas.* The wealthy matrons of the capital, guardians of morality and manners, showed their contempt for this young woman of humble parentage who had defied their standards. But Doña Evita paid them off by a humiliating *tour de force.* For 125 years the leading women of *porteño* society had enjoyed a monopoly of organized charity in the Sociedad de Beneficencia, managing hospitals, orphanages, and related charities with stately gravity.

When they snubbed Evita, she retaliated by organizing the Eva Perón Foundation, to which a presidential decree committed control of all charities hitherto directed by the virtuous ladies. The Foundation, Evita's alter ego, became the corporate well of mercy from which flowed waters of healing for widows and orphans, for the sick and the maimed, for the poor and disconsolate. Its treasury overflowed with offerings from grateful labor unions, prudent employers, wise foreign corporations, and public employees. It became a multimillion-peso enterprise, dwarfing banks and *frigoríficos.* No accounting was made, and the suggestion that organized charity should be subjected to the rude hands of a certified public accountant was received with shocked displeasure. Evita was then given supervision of the ministry of health, in which capacity she conducted the first effective campaign against tuberculosis and malaria and established hospitals and clinics.

Evita's monopoly over matters of labor, charity, and health was exercised with much energy, with due regard to advancing the political fortunes of her master, and—in fairness to the lady let it be added—with considerable benefit to the poor and the sick. The irreverent described her exploits as solely designed to promote *peronismo,* but the humble Argentine whose child's life had been saved by Evita's blood bank was in no mood to quibble. When the *descamisados* demanded that Evita should be nominated for the vice-presidency in 1951, they were voicing the genuine devotion of the masses. But that promotion for the First Lady was blocked by the army leaders, who knew, as all proper Argentine males know, the woman's place, and who proposed to keep her in that place.

Organized labor, whether persuaded or coerced, continued as Perón's firm ally. Despite resistance by a few honorable leaders, the General Federation of Labor (CGT) and the independent unions became instruments of his power. The workers were rewarded with wages, bonuses, and social legislation such as Argentina had never known before; they paid for these favors with fervid devotion to *peronismo.*

Perón's success with labor was dramatically proved in October, 1945, when his enemies assembled their forces against him. The opposition included substantial contingents of right-wing businessmen and *estancieros,* middle-class Radicals, left-wing Socialists, and some union leaders. The disaffection spread to the army and the navy, many of whose officers deplored Perón's failure to make terms with the victorious Allies. On October 9 an army coup forced Perón's resignation as vice-president, secretary of labor, and minister of war. Perón broadcast an appeal to labor, whereupon the military junta imprisoned him on the island of Martín García. For a week the issue was uncertain, as no new leader appeared. Meanwhile, under the skillful manipulation of faithful labor henchmen and the eloquent Evita, the packing-house workers from the suburbs converged upon the capital. By October 17 they filled the streets, shouting *Viva Perón! Viva Argentina!* The General Federation of Labor called a general strike for October 18. The contest was over, and puppet President Farrell announced that Perón was free. Thus the way was cleared for

Perón's campaign and for his election in 1946. It was labor's victory as well as Perón's, and both shared in the spoils. Wages were increased; but they ran a race with inflation, and the workers had only an illusion of prosperity.

All Perón's promises to labor were incorporated in his new constitution, promulgated in 1949. This instrument reaffirmed Perón's social program, guaranteeing rights and privileges to all sectors of society; it reaffirmed the right of the nation to intervene in economic affairs, including control of foreign trade. It was a document as revolutionary as the Mexican Constitution of 1917. But the joker was the provision permitting Perón's reelection—a clear contradiction to the provisions of the Constitution of 1853.

The military, without whose support few Latin American presidents last a fortnight, was held in line by Perón. Those officers who had taken part in the coup against Perón in October, 1945, were eliminated. Most officers found it profitable to serve their strong-arm president, and many were rewarded with political posts. The pay of all officers, from second lieutenants to generals, was repeatedly increased until by 1950 they were receiving more, grade for grade, than their counterparts in the United States. The budgets for the army and the navy increased handsomely, accounting for about one-quarter of all national expenditures in 1950. Modern guns, tanks, and planes replaced the obsolete equipment of other days. Skeptics asked the purpose of all this martial display. Was it for use against marauding neighbors? But only Brazil had guns and powder enough to challenge Argentina, and she exhibited no bellicose intentions. Or was it for excursions overseas? But when the United Nations, to which Perón avowed allegiance, invited Argentina to join in policing Korea, Perón found it unwise to send troops so far from home. Or was it, by chance, designed to extend Argentine dominion over such weakly held lands as Uruguay, Paraguay, and Bolivia?[1] But the tough-minded knew full well that such imperialistic advances would meet overwhelming opposition from the other American republics, including the United States; that had been made clear by successive Pan-American agreements since 1936. The true purpose of Perón's strengthened army and navy was the preservation of national order —which, in the lexicon of dictatorship, means keeping the dictator in power.

Perón was helped by the clergy. His presidential campaign of 1946 was aided by a pastoral letter signed by Cardinal Copello and the bishops, admonishing the faithful to withhold their votes from any candidate who advocated separation of Church and state, divorce, or exclusion of religious instruction from the schools. Perón, on all such counts, was the one untainted candidate. One bishop, Miguel de Andrea, refused to sign the letter, commenting: "It is tragic to sell liberty for a few social and economic

[1] Argentines had not forgotten that the officers' organization, the GOU, had distributed a manifesto in early 1943 which promised such happy conquests: "Paraguay," it stated, "is already with us. We will get Bolivia and Chile. Together and united with these countries, it will be easy to exert pressure on Uruguay. These five nations can easily attack Brazil. . . . Once Brazil has fallen, the South American continent will be ours." Robert J. Alexander: *The Perón Era* (New York: Columbia University Press; 1951), p. 13.

advantages." One parish priest refused to read the pastoral letter to his congregation and was dismissed by the Cardinal. Several hundred Catholic laymen signed a protest against the hierarchy's aid to Perón. Meanwhile, Perón, following the example of Franco in Spain, included priests in all party councils.

THE ECONOMICS OF PERÓN

Perón's bold and initially successful economic panaceas confuted the charges that he was simply another roughriding caudillo in the familiar Latin American pattern. From his first days of power, he preached "economic emancipation" from foreign masters, especially Great Britain and the United States; he demanded recapture of foreign-owned railroads, telephones and other public utilities, port installations, and grain elevators; he insisted upon the retiring of all foreign debt. The end of World War II found Argentina in an excellent position to capitalize on the world's woes: she had large reserves of blocked sterling piled up in London; and she had the meat and grain which Europe needed.

Determined to exact top prices from the starving millions and to divert major profits to the Argentine treasury, Perón created in 1946 the *Instituto Argentino de Promoción del Intercambio* (Argentine Institute for Promotion of Exchange), IAPI, which was a national monopoly corporation for handling all wheat (and later, other principal products) in the world markets. Commissioned to buy in Argentina and to sell abroad, the IAPI angered foreign buyers who resented the outrageous prices exacted for meat and grain, as well as the domestic producers who were paid a third, a fourth, or even less, of the receipts from foreign sales. The IAPI realized substantial gains during its first three years of operation, although no exact reckoning was ever made public. Its initial success was followed by economic disasters: denied fair prices, farmers sowed less grain and stockmen allowed their herds and flocks to be depleted; farm laborers crowded into the industrial centers. During the 1950–51 season the wheat farmers, partly because of a drought and partly because of the low prices allotted them, could not profitably harvest more than 80 per cent of the reduced acreage they had planted. By 1952 the government was decreeing "meatless days," an innovation unheard-of in the Argentine land of plenty. Although Perón's meddling with prices and production had made him the target for new discontent, his promise to remove "foreign shackles" from the economy was substantially fulfilled. In 1946 the Central Bank, until then semiautonomous, was nationalized and given control of all the nation's banks, including powerful institutions owned by American, British, French, Belgian, and other foreign interests. In that same year the national telephone system, a subsidiary of International Telephone and Telegraph Company, was acquired by the Argentine government on terms acceptable to its North American owners. In 1948, after negotiations involving use of the blocked sterling reserves in London and exchange of Argentine commodities for English coal, oil, and machinery, Argentina had acquired full title to the British-owned railways for the sum of £150 million, an event which caused rejoicing in Argentina and humiliation in England. Meanwhile, by drawing upon sterling reserves and profits from the IAPI, Perón had retired the entire outstanding foreign debt of some 12.5 billion pesos. But Perón had overreached himself: the peso was declining in value, and commercial debts piled up. In 1950 the United States allotted $125 million from the Export-Import Bank to ease Argentina's strained economy, and in deference to Perón's distaste for the word "loan," called it instead a "credit" to certain Argentine banks, thereby enabling the Argentine president to continue his claim that his nation owed not a centavo to any foreign power. It was a distinction without a difference, for the credit was guaranteed by the Argentine Republic.

Industrialization became a magic word for the *peronistas*. Argentina, they said, could produce every variety of finished goods and machinery and could thus escape the colonial status of a country obliged to sell cheap raw materials to the industrial nations and buy back manufactured goods at crippling prices. The argument was not new. Factories and mills for consumer goods had multiplied rapidly since 1920. The blocking of trade with Europe during World War I had encouraged the creation of a national industry. Having once lived almost entirely from its agriculture and stock raising, the nation by 1942 had reached the point where the returns from industry equaled those from the soil. Pessimists argued that industry was an exotic hope in a land which had little coal and iron, inadequate hydroelectric plants, and was producing little more than half enough petroleum; but the fact remained that the Argentina of 1942 seemed to be about one-half industrialized. *Industria Argentina,* symbol of self-respect, included shoes, electrical equipment, textiles, soap, dishes, processed foods, and almost everything the ordinary citizen bought from week to week. World War II and renewed interference with the free passage of goods brought further expansion of the national industrial plant.

Perón launched his first five-year plan in 1947, after he was legally established in the presidency. The plan was ambitious, covering everything from votes for women to the installation of hydroelectric plants, but its heart was industrialization. The framers of the document astutely allotted almost one-half the contemplated funds to construction of power plants. The chief hindrance to development of factories and mills was the chronic shortage of power and fuel. The coal used to drive locomotives, to generate electric current, and to stoke the furnaces of industry had long been imported from England and Germany, and in later years from Chile and Brazil. At times wood, corn, and linseed were burned. The national petroleum supply had never met more than 60 per cent of the national demand. Perón launched some forty-five big and little hydroelectric projects, loudly promising that the power needs of the nation would soon be met. Most of these schemes got little beyond the blueprint stage, for revenue from sales of meat and grain dropped, and there was not money enough to build dams and install generators. Perón's legacy to his successors included half-finished power plants, involving commitments beyond the reach of the national economy.

Manufacturing of all sorts had been given impetus in 1944 by the newly created Bank of Industrial Credit. By 1947 Perón could boast a five-fold increase in industrial production since 1943 and could say that Argentina had its own "iron and steel industry, coal mines and various other raw materials; makes all powder and explosives needed in the country and makes all its arms, munitions and vehicles." But these claims had little validity. To be sure, Argentina's factories and foundries turned out some farm machinery, tractors, guns, structural steel, and various other items; but phony bookkeeping concealed the price the nation was paying for this façade of industrial strength. The experience did not prove that Argentina could not be industrialized; it simply showed that Perón's program was only hocus-pocus.

Although Perón had preached industrialization as the cure for Argentine ills, by 1950 he was rudely reminded that his country's prosperity rested upon its pastures and grain fields. His early digressions in fixing farm prices should have taught him that cattle are not bred by presidential decree, that wheat is not harvested by political oratory. The output of wheat, for example, dropped from 8,150,000 metric tons in 1941 to a mere 2,300,000 in 1950. Beginning in 1952, he raised farm prices, and offered subsidies for the increase of herds and the expansion of grain fields, but it was too late. There is no evidence that Perón listened to the economists who warned in 1954 that there had been a 70 per cent decline in the rate of capital investment since 1943, that total production had actually gone down, and that labor's buying power had improved little, if any.

THE FOREIGN RELATIONS OF PERÓN

Perón's conduct of foreign relations through the stormy postwar years entitled him to oblique credit. When he entered the scene in late 1943, Argentina was in worse odor in the chancelleries of the democratic nations than at any time since the days of Rosas. Ten years later his government was recognized by the powers; it was represented in the United Nations, and held a seat in its Security Council. Perón had won almost every round against his foreign detractors.

Argentine relations with the United States, which had long been strained, became more difficult under Perón. The traditional complaint against the powerful northern nation was the fact that it sold much to Argentina and bought little. For example, during the fifteen-year period 1924–38, the United States sales to Argentina had exceeded its purchases by a total of $486.9 million. Furthermore, the successive tariff acts of the American Congress had blocked the profitable exportation of Argentine hides, skins, tallow, casein, and linseed. The crowning indignity in Argentine opinion was the exclusion from the American market of the beef of the Pampa, a step justified by Washington as defense against the hoof-and-

753] THE REPUBLICS OF THE RÍO DE LA PLATA

mouth disease which is endemic in Argentine herds, but resented by Argentines as an affront to their nation. Meanwhile, the British continued to buy, and enjoy, the beef spurned by the United States. Such accumulated resentments had created the anti-United States nationalism under which Perón carried on his quarrel with Washington.

The wartime confusions of Washington worked to Perón's advantage. When Secretary of State Cordell Hull castigated the Ramírez government in late 1943 and early 1944, then cracked the whip over Farrell and Perón throughout 1944,[2] Perón used the incidents to prove American contempt for Argentine sovereignty. When Argentina was admitted to the United Nations in 1945, Perón gloated over his outwitting of the "imperialistic United States," despite the fact that Assistant Secretary of State Nelson Rockefeller was responsible for the invitation to Argentina. And when Spruille Braden came to Buenos Aires as ambassador in mid-1945 and directed his fervent appeals on behalf of democracy against the current tyranny of Farrell and Perón, the dexterous Colonel again rallied his supporters against the intruding Yankees. The slogan "Perón or Braden" was plastered on the walls of city and village, and all the reserves of anti-United States sentiment were tapped to assure the Perón victory in February, 1946. Finally, after Perón's induction into office, the Washington winds shifted again. George Messersmith was sent as ambassador in the spring of 1946 to make peace with Perón, under instructions to speak softly, to argue mildly, and to praise tactfully. This more amiable American policy continued throughout Perón's days in office. Meanwhile, Perón countered by blowing first hot and then cold upon his newly discovered friends in the north. His controlled press continued to thunder against conspiracies hatched in Wall Street and other spots. He ignored mild suggestions to soften his ways. The United States maintained its conciliatory course, granting Argentina a $125 million "credit" in 1950. But Perón persisted in his repressive policies and also permitted highly placed Axis refugees to find asylum in his country.

Throughout his years of power, Perón found comfort in his friend Franco of Spain, whose political convictions and ways of governing resembled his own. Perón used Argentina's position in the United Nations to press for inclusion of Spain in the councils of the free nations. Substantial credits to Franco facilitated purchase of Argentine meat and grain. Doña Evita's dramatic visit to Spain cemented ties between the nations. By 1952, when it had become doubtful whether Spain could pay her debts, the flow of foodstuffs from the Río de la Plata had almost stopped, but praise of Franco continued in the *peronista* press.

Perón prided himself on being a mediator in world affairs, offering "a middle way" between Communism and capitalism—a policy which he called *justicialismo,* a word whose meaning was never clarified. His dra-

---

[2] Hull's measures included the verbal whipping of Storni already described; pressure upon Ramírez which forced a break with the Axis; withholding of recognition of Farrell; freezing of Argentine funds in New York; banning of shipping to Argentine ports; recall of the American ambassador—all accompanied by well-deserved but ineffective preachments.

matic appeal to the great powers in 1947 for a return to the paths of peace may not have greatly impressed London and Washington (or Moscow), but it had fine propaganda value in Buenos Aires, where the ragged *peronistas* learned to revere their leader as a world statesman of the first magnitude.

Perón's dealings with Great Britain brought him further renown. He seized the maximum advantage from the Empire's postwar tribulations, negotiated successive agreements under which Argentine meat and grain were exchanged for British machinery, coal, and petroleum, and acquired the British-owned railways. Argentina at last held the whip hand, and used it to exact ever higher prices for the beef that Englishmen craved. "Blackmail" was the comment of at least one British statesman, but there was little to be done about it, except to speed up cattle breeding in the British dominions. By 1954, England's purchases of Argentine beef were about one-third of what they had been in 1943.

In dealings with the Latin American republics, Perón wore the mantle of good-neighborliness. He became the self-anointed protector of weak nations against "the imperialistic *norteamericanos.*" In 1947 his ambassador in Washington chatted happily of a "little Marshall Plan" to be financed by Argentina to aid the defenseless nations of South and Central America. Negotiations were initiated with Argentina's nearest neighbors, and there was much discussion of customs unions, Argentine loans, subsidies and investments in Chile, Bolivia, Peru, and Paraguay. Perón's overtures met considerable resistance, especially from democratic Chile and Uruguay —and he was outbid by the United States, which had more money to offer. Perón's avid courting of his neighbors' affections was also clouded by the pressures he applied. When Bolivia's Villarroel, a Perón favorite, was hanged on a lamppost, Perón blockaded the Argentine-Bolivian border. When Uruguay persisted in welcoming refugees from Perón's discipline, Argentine wheat was withheld and the free passage of Argentine tourists to Montevideo was impeded.

Throughout his years in office, Perón's emissaries conducted an adroit anti-United States campaign in the other Latin American republics. His spokesmen played upon every grievance: they reminded Haiti, the Dominican Republic, and Nicaragua of the long interventions by American marines; they condemned the "gigantic North American plot" to seize monopoly control of Cuban sugar, Bolivian tin, Chilean copper, and Central American bananas. They prompted Guatemala to assert her sovereignty over British Honduras. Argentine labor leaders, appointed as attachés in Argentine embassies and consulates, carried the Perón gospel to the organized labor movements of almost all the republics. By 1952 widely scattered labor unions of *peronista* hue were organized into an inter-American federation under Argentine leadership—as an offset to the Communist-tinted Latin American labor federation (CTAL) directed by Lombardo Toledano of Mexico. There was suspicion, supported by some evidence, that these emissaries of Perón played more than a passive role in the military coups which dislodged democratic regimes in Peru, Venezuela, and

Cuba. They were charged with helping Velasco Ibarra to power in Ecuador, Carlos Ibáñez in Chile, and Laureano Gómez in Colombia. Perón's role in the Western Hemisphere may be described as a variation on the Holy Alliance of Napoleonic days in defense of rulers by divine right.

THE DEATH OF EVA PERÓN AND THE FALL OF PERÓN

The death of the beloved Evita in July, 1952, provoked mad hysteria: hundreds of thousands crowded around her body as it lay in state; eight were trampled to death, and over a thousand were seriously injured. The ragged *descamisados* saw nothing incongruous in petitions to the Pope that she be canonized; to them, she was *la madona de América*. They found it fitting that her likeness should appear on postage stamps, that a perpetual flame be lit in the headquarters of her Foundation, that the broad Avenida 9 de Julio be renamed Avenida Eva Perón, that the city of La Plata be rechristened in the same fashion, and that every province have at least one school bearing her name. Her autobiography, *La razón de mi vida,* was made required reading in every school; and when the unfounded rumor spread that the United States government had prohibited publication of a translation of that book, a mob bombed the Lincoln Library maintained in Buenos Aires by the American government.

The loss of this symbol of the hopes and prayers of the ragged masses worked a profound change in public sentiment. There were signs of restlessness, vague rumors of revolt. Faithful *peronistas* wondered whether the golden days promised by Evita could be realized by Juan Domingo alone. There were murmurings when Perón dropped a score of men whom Evita had put into high posts; notably, when her brother Juan Duarte was dismissed as secretary to the President—an anxiety not relieved when Duarte was found dead in his apartment, a bullet in his heart. But the resourceful Perón turned to his old magic; summoning the *peronistas* to a mass meeting in April, 1953, he was greeted by the shouts of some 100,000 people. He began to speak, but was interrupted by the explosion of two bombs, whose reverberations did more to rally support than all his words. With the cry, "We will hang the guilty on trees," the mob moved through downtown Buenos Aires, gutting with fire the headquarters of the Socialists, Radicals, and other opposition parties. It then sacked and burned the Jockey Club, proud citadel of wealthy *porteños,* destroying valuable books and paintings. The violence continued throughout the night, while the police and the army stood by. The next day, a *peronista* newspaper referred to "the flames of purification," and several scores of prominent citizens were arrested and jailed without bail or trial.

The death of Evita was the beginning of the end of Perón's rule: by 1952 there were abundant signs of the bankruptcy of his regime. It was an economic bankruptcy: figures on production, public contracts, and the growing debt had been falsified, but Argentines began to guess that his fair promises of prosperity had not been fulfilled. It was a moral bankruptcy: there was fear in men's eyes, and shame. Not least of the symptoms of moral collapse was the absence of a free and able press. One by one, the excellent newspapers of the nation had been silenced. *La Prensa,* one of the world's great newspapers, had been expropriated in April, 1951. Belonging to the Paz family since its founding in 1870, the paper had always served the ends of honorable government, speaking out against tyranny and corruption. Ramírez and Perón had repeatedly sought to silence it by bribery, by withholding newsprint, and by mob attacks. Finally, a government-fomented strike of news vendors provoked violence which furnished excuse for seizure by the government. Resuming publication under the aegis of the subservient General Federation of Labor, the once-great *La Prensa* became another mouthpiece for the dictator. *La Nación,* lone survivor of the responsible press, continued to appear, but its criticism of Perón's regime was no more than a whisper. The decay of national morale appeared everywhere—in conversation in coffee shops, in the public schools, and in the universities. Free Argentina was silenced and humiliated, but behind locked doors men were plotting.

The year 1955 brought hardening of the opposition to Perón. Businessmen and landowners, confronted with the wreckage of the national economy, were grim and determined. The leaders of the armed forces— partly out of desire to save their necks in the inevitable collapse of *peronista* power, partly out of patriotic desire to save the nation—were conspiring; those of the navy and the air force were the first to strike.

An important area of disaffection was the Church. Though Cardinal Copello and many bishops had supported Perón during his earlier years, after the death of Evita, Perón had repeatedly offended churchmen: he legalized divorce, lifted the ban against prostitution, proposed to end the Church's participation in public education, threatened complete separation of Church and state, and advocated the taxation of Church property. In June, 1955, some 100,000 Catholics demonstrated in the Plaza de Mayo in front of the Casa Rosada, and then marched to the Capitolio, over which some zealous youth had raised the papal flag.

This protest in June, 1955, set off the long-planned revolt. Naval planes roared over the capital city, actually dropping bombs on the Casa Rosada. But the plot foundered, and the attacking planes found safety in Uruguay. Perón's retaliation was swift: gangs of *peronistas* attacked some of the finest churches in Buenos Aires, setting fires, gutting the sanctuaries, smashing statues. When two of the higher clergy protested to Perón, they were put on a plane bound for Rome, whereupon the Vatican excommunicated Perón and all associated with him for "trampling on the rights of the Church." The influential Catholic journal *Commonweal* in New York commented: "The Church has made terrible compromises with tyranny through the centuries . . . but . . . the Church is the final, uncompromising enemy of any state that demands a total obedience of its citizens."

It was now clear that Perón's time was running out. One indication was his desperate attempt to save YPF by signing a contract for the development of petroleum reserves with Standard Oil of California—which was a complete repudiation of his nationalistic economic program. July and August of 1955 brought more plots and riots which were countered by police violence. Perón offered to resign, addressing his letter to the Argentine Federation of Labor; whereupon, in a nationwide strike, labor affirmed its loyalty to Perón. Perón even toyed with the idea of arming the CGT, which of course brought new resistance from the armed forces. *The New York Times* editorially called Perón's offer to resign "the convulsive reaction of a frightened man who is playing a losing game." On September 16, revolts broke out in army barracks in Córdoba, Rosario, Santa Fe, and Paraná; General Eduardo Lonardi was proclaimed "chief of the liberating movement." On September 19, Perón resigned and sought safety on a Paraguayan gunboat lying in the Río de la Plata. On September 23, Lonardi assumed the provisional presidency. Ecstatic mobs toppled hundreds of statues of Perón and Evita, ripping their photographs from walls. The era of Perón was ended: the chief actor found asylum first in Paraguay, then in Panama, Venezuela, the Dominican Republic, and finally in Spain.

 [*Chapter 43*]

ARGENTINA AFTER PERÓN,

1955–

THE LEGACY OF PERÓN

"*Peronismo* will survive me," warned the deposed dictator. And he was right: "*Peronismo* without Perón" is still a powerful force in Argentina today, with about one-third of the voters still to be described as *peronistas*. Perón himself, for more than a decade after his flight from the Casa Rosada, remained the single most formidable figure in Argentine political life, and his threat to return from exile hung like a dark shadow over the country. Even after his abortive attempt to reach Argentine soil in 1964, he did not cease his meddling in the politics of the nation. Although sober citizens hoped that they had seen the last of *el lider,* his name was still magic for millions of *descamisados,* for whom there had been born a dream of a better life which would outlive all vilification of their benefactor. They remembered the cheap meat, the generous wages, the health care for their families and themselves, and many remained faithful to the man who had worked these miracles. Labor, never a force in political life before, had learned from Perón and Evita how to organize trade unions, had become self-confident and articulate.

However, most of the people listened and were disenchanted— momentarily—when, in the fall of 1955, the Lonardi government told them the truth about their erstwhile hero, opened for public inspection the luxurious homes that Perón and Evita had filled with costly baubles, and spread the word that Perón had made off with millions of pesos stolen from the people. Perhaps the most damning charge in the eyes of the admiring Argentines was that Perón had taken as his mistress a thirteen-year-old girl, showering upon her many of Evita's costly jewels. That slight upon *la madona de América* was the most effective indictment, striking deeper than all the charges of wholesale robbery. But the pillaging offered a depressing exhibit: the treasury was almost empty; gold and foreign exchange reserves were down from $1,682 million in 1946 to $450 million in October, 1955, thanks largely to Perón's ill-advised purchase of the British-owned railroads and American utilities, and the retirement of the national debt;

[*763*]

the many millions of dollars of profit from IAPI (and no one knows what that figure was), while theoretically allocated to economic measures of the first five-year plan, had been dissipated on frantic consumer subsidies, on industrial subsidies to cover uneconomic wage increases, on budget deficits —and also on Evita's diamonds and Perón's prudential savings accounts in Swiss banks. Furthermore, in spite of Perón's proud boast that the nation owed not one centavo to any creditor, the external debt had climbed back up to $757 million[1] and the total public debt in pesos was almost eight times that of 1945. Reckless printing of paper currency had increased five-fold since 1946, and the free rate for the peso had dropped from 5.13 to the dollar in 1946 to 30.48 in 1955. Perón's lid on prices had discouraged production. Figures on economic growth during the Perón years were meaningless, as they made no allowance for depreciation: farm machinery had broken down and was rusting in the fields; automobiles and trucks were hopelessly overage; industrial and power equipment was outmoded and in bad repair; the state-owned railroads, suffering from reckless featherbedding, deterioration of equipment, and lack of technical skill, were a shambles. Perón had treated his *descamisados* with a lavish hand, but the cost was too high: the underpinnings of the economy were almost completely destroyed. Federico Pinedo, a former minister of finance, wrote in 1960 that Perón's handling of the Argentine economy "projects its malevolent shadow over the present and it will be difficult to prevent that shadow from continuing to darken the future."

THE PROVISIONAL GOVERNMENT: EDUARDO LONARDI AND PEDRO EUGENIO ARAMBURU, 1955–58

The two generals who ruled during the two and a half years following Perón's ouster were high-minded and patriotic men, and both made a conscientious effort to bring order and tranquillity to their troubled nation. General Eduardo Lonardi, leader of the revolt against Perón and the first provisional president, appointed a fairly competent cabinet, but his choices were denounced as including too many who had complacently accepted Perón. He abolished censorship and offered amnesty to *peronistas,* although few dared to return from exile. He restored amicable relations with the Church. He joined battle with the corruption and plunder which had been rampant in the Perón administration. Perhaps his most constructive move was to name as his financial and economic adviser, the eminent Argentine economist, Dr. Raúl Prebisch. Comparing the "crisis of unparalleled gravity" which confronted the nation in 1955 to the crises of 1890 and 1930, Dr. Prebisch said: "In those days the country's productive potential was intact. Such is not the case today. With the dynamic factors of the economy seriously endangered, an intensive and persistent effort will be required to restore a vigorous rate of development." But Lonardi had no chance to take on any long-term overhauling of the economy: after two

[1] Not including an estimated 2 billion pesos in frozen or delayed remittance payments.

months in office he was quietly unseated by elements in the military who felt that he was too tolerant of *peronista* influences in the government.

In November, 1955, the presidency went to General Pedro Eugenio Aramburu, one-time military attaché to the United States and also to Brazil, who commanded the respect of almost all Argentines. Aramburu tackled the job of reconciling the dissident factions and promised free elections for May, 1958. He was more thorough than his predecessor in dismantling the trappings of Perón's rule. He restored the Constitution of 1853, discarding Perón's instrument of 1949. He restored the autonomy of the Central Bank. He outlawed the *peronista* party. He restored *La Prensa* to its owner, Gainza Paz. He revoked Perón's law legalizing divorce and banned prostitution. In January, Dr. Prebisch issued a report giving his recommendations for the restoration of the economy: Argentines must tighten their belts; labor must no longer be pampered by consumer subsidies and uneconomically high wages; "excessive and inefficient state intervention" must be ended, giving freer reign to private industry; the peso should be devalued, the multiple exchange rates scrapped; and the country must be reequipped (at an estimated cost of some $1.2 billion) with pipelines, machinery, rolling stock, and all the tools necessary to get agriculture and industry back into full-scale production. It was a large order. Aramburu, aware that Argentina would need help in carrying out any such program, sought to bolster the nation's prestige abroad, secured membership for Argentina in the World Bank and the International Monetary Fund. He also made advantageous trade agreements with West Germany, Great Britain, Austria, Belgium, France, Italy, Holland, Norway, Sweden, and Switzerland. But his honest efforts at home were hampered by intermittent strikes inspired by Perón's agents, by bombings and terrorism, by plots in the army. Although Aramburu was open to criticism because of his "caretaker psychology," he could at least take pride in having fulfilled his pledge to return the country to constitutional government.

AN EXPERIMENT WITH CIVILIAN GOVERNMENT: ARTURO FRONDIZI, 1958–62

In February, 1958, the long-promised free elections were held (the first since 1916), and the jubilant Argentine people, heartily sick of dictators and revolutions, turned out in record numbers: ballots were cast by 90 per cent of the registered voters. By an overwhelming majority they gave the presidency to fifty-nine-year-old Arturo Frondizi, leader of the left wing of the *Unión Cívica Radical* (UCR). Frondizi won the office by wooing the *peronistas,* who voted for him on orders from the exiled dictator himself—Perón had probably extracted promises from Frondizi to restore the *peronista* party to full legal status and perhaps even to make possible his own eventual return to Argentina. But when Frondizi moved into the Casa Rosada on May 1, it soon became clear that he would not keep these promises, nor had he any intention of carrying out

his campaign pledges of social legislation, nationalism, and state control—
at least not for the time being. He announced that he would seek private
—even foreign—investment to rescue the sinking oil industry; that he would
welcome the help of private enterprise in spurring production; that a
period of austerity would be necessary to get the economy rolling again.
Such an about-face would seem to indicate that Frondizi had indulged in
demagoguery to get himself elected. But it is more likely that his campaign
utterances represented his real political and social philosophy, and that the
program he embarked upon in 1958 was a concession—probably intended
as a temporary concession—to the immediate economic and political realities
of the situation. Frondizi had been active in the Radical Party for more than
two decades, although he did not run for office himself until 1946, when
he became a member of the token minority in Perón's Chamber of
Deputies. Highly critical of the dictator's pilfering and authoritarian ways,
Frondizi believed in Perón's stated aims of social revolution for the masses,
as his writing and speeches for more than a decade before his election
testify; and the eventual incorporation of "peronismo without Perón" into
the political fabric of the nation was a consistent element of his philosophy.
The divergent factions in Frondizi's UCR crystallized after the fall of Perón,
and in 1957 formally split into the Unión Cívica Radical Intransigente
(UCRI) and the Unión Cívica Radical del Pueblo (UCRP). Frondizi
emerged as the undisputed leader of the more leftist UCRI, and Ricardo
Balbín headed the more conservative UCRP. The contest in 1958 was between these two parties, and the scales were tipped to Frondizi and the
UCRI, with their platform of nationalism and state control, by Perón's
last-minute endorsement.

The convulsive reactions of various sectors to Frondizi's election, then
to his sudden about-face, presaged the tumultuous years ahead. The armed
forces were outraged at the installation of a seemingly leftist, pro-peronista
president, but, faithful to their commitment to constitutional procedures
—and having a healthy respect for Frondizi's awesome majority at the polls
—they refrained from immediate takeover. Then, when Frondizi revealed
his real intentions, the labor unions, in which the peronistas still held the
whip hand, bedeviled him with strikes and violence. Frondizi soon realized
that he would need the support of the military to keep labor in hand—
and this meant concessions in matters of policy and personnel. Also, the
new administration's overtures to the United States and the International
Monetary Fund, whose help would be essential in carrying out the proposed
economic program, provoked angry cries from militant nationalists. Furthermore, the President had to do some fast talking to keep his own party,
the UCRI, in line, for he continued to repudiate, almost completely, the
platform on which he had been elected.[2] Thus Frondizi embarked upon
a four-year balancing act which proved him to be a nimble politician.
His government was threatened by some thirty-five "crises"—strikes, riots,
threats from the military—which he adroitly resolved by cabinet shifts,

[2] In December, 1960, the UCRI rewrote its platform, eliminating all mention of a
state-planned economy, national ownership and operation of industry, and agrarian reform,
affirming instead its devotion to private enterprise and foreign capital.

reshuffling of military posts, wage concessions to labor, promises (a few of which he fulfilled) to the *peronistas*. The only consistent applause for Frondizi came from abroad: Eisenhower held up his economic stabilization program as a model for all Latin America, and Frondizi's Argentina was the darling of the Kennedy Administration and the Alliance for Progress.

Frondizi was dogged, almost fanatical, in the constancy with which he pushed his program for economic recovery. It was his unswerving conviction that orthodox fiscal stability was a prerequisite to social and political health. To get his country on a sound economic footing he would —and did—make almost any sacrifice; he set aside his own predilection for social reform, pleaded with hostile workers to be patient, assuring them that his program of economic development would lead eventually to "the social justice you demand, need, and deserve." He gave up his popularity at the polls—after one bitter defeat he said, "I can afford to lose elections now, but I cannot afford to lose the economic campaign." He yielded time and time again to the military, dropping many of his most valued ministers and advisers. Perhaps his most painful concession was in foreign relations—and his reluctance to make this one cost him the presidency: he finally bowed to the demand of the military that he break relations with Cuba, a move which betrayed his innermost convictions against intervention in the politics of his neighbors. Did such juggling of principle stem from a desire for power? The constancy of his economic battle would belie the critics who said so.

Frondizi's first frontal attack was on the oil industry, and it was here that he achieved his most spectacular success. The oil monopoly, YPF (*Yacimientos Petrolíferos Fiscales*), had long been a chief pride of nationalistic Argentines. But by 1958, far from yielding any profits, it was a drag on the national budget. Furthermore, it was producing only 100,000 barrels out of the 250,000 barrels per day which the country consumed— which meant that Argentina had to spend each year some $200 million of its scant foreign exchange reserves to meet the shortage. Upon assuming office, Frondizi quickly abandoned the nationalistic oil policy which he had proclaimed in his campaign. In July, 1958, he announced that contracts had been negotiated with various American, British, and Dutch operators.[3] Some of these contracts called for the development of oil fields in the Comodoro Rivadavia area of Patagonia, in Neuquén, and in the region around Mendoza; others were contracts to search for oil in large unexplored areas, especially in northern Argentina. The foreign companies, however, were not allowed to control the oil: they could explore, drill, and in some cases produce the oil—but they were required to sell it to the YPF. Contracts were also let for the installation of pipelines connecting Buenos Aires with the Bolivian border, which, when completed, were utilized not only for oil but also for natural gas. These projects for making Argentina self-sufficient in petroleum products were denounced as a "sellout" by extreme na-

---

[3] In 1955, when Perón signed a contract with Standard Oil of California in a last ditch attempt to save the YPF, Frondizi was his most vociferous critic, charging him with deserting the cause of "economic sovereignty," a charge which was not the least among the causes of Perón's downfall.

tionalists, *peronistas,* and Communists. But petroleum production increased until by the end of 1961 Argentina was producing 260,000 barrels of oil a day—over two and a half times the output in 1958—which left her a slight exportable surplus. This record would seem to be vindication enough for Frondizi's courting of foreign capital. But the man on the street cared not at all that the gasoline he needed was produced from his native soil, only complained that it cost him more than it had in "the good old days," and refused to be impressed by the burgeoning national coffers.

Frondizi's stabilization and development program, formally launched in January, 1959, was chiefly dictated by the International Monetary Fund: the peso was devalued, multiple exchange rates scrapped; rigid credit restrictions were installed; tight limitations were placed on luxury imports; most consumer subsidies were eliminated; wage increases not tied to production rise were to be discouraged; a determined effort would be made to balance the budget. This head-on attack on inflation was immediately backed by generous loans and grants from the United States and the international lending agencies. In July, 1959, the President named as minister of economy Alvaro Carlos Alsogaray, a tough exponent of private enterprise. Only forty-three years old, Alsogaray had proved himself a competent businessman and able administrator; and, ironically, he had run against Frondizi in the election of 1958, attacking the leftist, nationalist platform of the very man who now named him as virtual economic czar and assigned him the task of imposing austerity and courting private capital. Alsogaray pushed the economic program with vigor. Determined to balance the budget he streamlined government costs, fired many useless workers on the public payrolls. He made progress in the dismantling of state-operated industries. Tackling the problem of the state-owned railway system he raised fares, tried to persuade the workers that there could be no change in wage scales until the railroads were reorganized on a profitable basis—a plea, however, which fell on deaf ears. Alsogaray restored the nation's credit among the bankers of the world, was personally responsible for securing substantial loans from abroad. In November, 1960, Alsogaray announced that "the basic work of economic stabilization can be considered as completed," and there was ample evidence to back up such optimism. But after a year and a half Alsogaray was under fire from various sectors: labor was hostile to his austerity program; Frondizi was impatient with the slow pace of production; and industrialists and businessmen, feeling the pinch of his tight credit restrictions, persuaded the military that he had to go. Alsogaray was ousted in April, 1961. Frondizi, appointing a new economics minister, announced that the stabilization program would continue, but that fresh impetus was needed for the development program.

In the meantime, Frondizi continued to play one group against another in a desperate attempt to salvage the support he needed to stay in office. He appeased the Church by returning to Catholic schools and colleges many of the privileges that had been curtailed during the Perón days —thus incurring the wrath of Communists and *peronistas.* He appeased labor by periodic wage boosts—but this angered the business community.

He appeased the Communists by repeated insistence on nonintervention in Cuba—but this provoked the wrath of the military. While industrialists grumbled over tight credit restrictions, Frondizi could point to his success in securing funds from abroad to further industrial expansion. The first Argentine president to set foot on American soil (in January, 1959), Frondizi made frequent and extensive trips to the United States, Europe, and Asia, in generally successful search for loans, investment capital, new markets; he could talk convincingly with the American Congress, business-men and bankers throughout the world; he charmed President Kennedy, proclaiming his undying devotion to Western democracy. Such performance could not help but impress his Conservative compatriots—but leftists and nationalist elements did not applaud.

Frondizi's most ticklish problem was to keep in the good graces of the military, without whose support no Argentine president could stay in power a week. Although united in hatred of Perón, the top brass were split between the *golpistas,* who favored outright military takeover until the country was cleansed of all vestiges of *peronismo,* and the *legalistas,* who believed in constitutional government and favored allowing Frondizi to complete his six-year term. There was constant jockeying for position between these groups, with the President caught in the middle. Frondizi's first major clash with the military was in the spring of 1959, when Admiral Isaac Rojas led a drive to oust all *peronistas* from the government—the chief victim this time was Rogelio Frigerio, Frondizi's economic adviser, who was a long-time friend of the hated Perón. In September, 1959, Frondizi was involved in a dispute with the army high command: he had unseated the formidable *golpista* General Carlos Toranzo Montero as commander in chief, thereby incurring the wrath of the most vocal anti-*peronista* generals. The argument was stilled only when Frondizi yielded and restored Toranzo Montero to his post. Plagued by a wave of terrorism surrounding the congressional elections of March, 1960, Frondizi survived only because the military—with the *golpistas* still dominant—imposed virtual martial law on the country. The elections were a bitter repudiation of the beleaguered President, especially in the provinces of Córdoba and Buenos Aires. Frondizi yielded to pressure from the army for federal inter-vention[4] in Córdoba, where the elected governor, allegedly a coddler of *peronistas* and Communists, was replaced by an interventor. Frondizi deplored the severe treatment of captured terrorists by the military, but he had to capitulate on this point as well. Following a week-long crisis in October, 1960, set off by an army memorandum demanding drastic changes in the personnel and policies of the administration, Frondizi was forced to replace his war minister; but he rejected the suggestion by Toranzo Montero and other generals that he oust some civilian members of his cabinet, insisting that he would not give up his right as president to "direct policies in the economic and social area, international affairs, and in those matters that are properly in the Presidential dominion."

In March, 1961, Frondizi made two moves which provoked fresh out-

4 See p. 718 for a discussion of "intervention."

cry from his right-wing critics, and caused bitter dispute among the factions of the armed forces. First, his offer to mediate United States–Cuban differences (an offer declined by both governments) enraged many generals. Then, after several false starts which ended in bitter disagreement on terms, Frondizi finally gave control of the powerful CGT back to the unions. This long-overdue fulfillment of a campaign pledge drew cheers from the *peronistas,* who promptly gave the President and his UCRI their first victory at the provincial polls in three years—but the military was not amused. In the ruckus that followed, crackling notes and memoranda shot back and forth among admirals and generals, bitterly attacking Frondizi, his cabinet—and each other. General Toranzo Montero resigned as commander in chief of the army—only as a gesture, was the report. But it soon became clear that this tough-fisted *golpista* no longer had the support of the majority of the army garrisons, and—to the relief of many—he was forced to step down, leaving the *legalistas* as victors in the paper skirmish.[5]

As Frondizi neared the end of his fourth year in office the record was mixed, but with some evidence that the nation was coming out of its long recession. While inflation had not been halted, it had been slowed down: the peso was stable at about 83 to the dollar; prices rose only 14 per cent in 1961 (compared to 114 per cent in 1959). Gold and foreign exchange reserves, which increased from a precarious $101 million in mid-1959 to a peak of $589 million in March, 1961, stood at $386 million at the end of the year. The crushing foreign trade deficit of $496 million in 1961, the largest in the nation's history, was due partly to a severe drought which caused the worst wheat harvest in ten years, reducing export income; partly to increased imports of raw materials and machinery, needed to get industry rolling. Over-all production figures were not impressive, in spite of the speedup in the oil industry, expanding steel production, a sharp increase in the manufacture and assembly of motor vehicles. And the state-owned enterprises—chiefly the national railway system—continued to operate at a crippling loss to the national economy: all efforts to reduce personnel and to raise rates triggered strikes among the workers. However, Frondizi had improved the Argentine image in the eyes of the world: during his regime the United States alone authorized some $150 million in loans to his government, and United States direct investments in Argentina about doubled.

On the diplomatic front there loomed the sticky question of Cuba. The attempts of the Kennedy administration to extract from the Latin American nations a denunciation of Fidel Castro culminated in plans for a meeting of the foreign ministers of the OAS at Punte del Este, Uruguay, in January, 1962. Frondizi had been cool to the idea from its inception. Any strong stand on Castro—for or against—would place him squarely between extremist groups in his own country: if he yielded to pressure from the United States to cut all ties with Cuba he would bring down upon his head the wrath of the Communists and the *peronistas;* if he refused to denounce Castro, once the question was formally posed, he would have to

---

[5] It was during this "crisis" that Alsogaray was ousted as economics minister.

answer to the military. Frondizi was not in a mood to commit himself on this problem; he urged caution in talks with Adlai Stevenson lest "the inter-American system . . . be driven to a crisis." However, the meeting was held, and Frondizi straddled the issue: he joined the standing ovation given Secretary Rusk after his plea "to take action to guard our own continent and our programs of democratic reforms against those who seek to replace democracy by dictatorship," voted with twenty states (all but Cuba) for a resolution declaring the "Marxist-Leninist" Cuban regime "incompatible" with the inter-American system—but abstained from the vote to oust Cuba from the OAS. On his return from the conference, Frondizi faced the combined wrath of all three branches of the armed forces: the ministers of the army, the navy, and the air force, with rare unanimity, joined in demanding not only that Frondizi reverse his OAS vote on the Cuban ouster, but also that he immediately break diplomatic relations with Cuba. Even though Frondizi finally gave in on both points, his reluctance cost him the confidence of the military, and his head was on the block.

Perhaps in an effort to quiet the stormy reaction of the *peronistas* to his capitulation in the Cuba affair, perhaps in belated fulfillment of a campaign pledge, certainly in a gross miscalculation of UCRI strength, Frondizi made the most fateful decision of his career: he allowed the *Frente Justicialista*[6] to present candidates for the general elections in March, 1962. The results startled the nation and touched off Frondizi's worst—and last—crisis: the *Frente* polled about 35 per cent of the total vote (to some 28 per cent for the UCRI);[7] *peronistas* captured 45 of the 86 seats in the Chamber of Deputies that were up for election, won 9 of the 14 governorships at stake, including that of the province of Buenos Aires, where the *peronista* labor leader, Andrés Framini, was the victor. There followed eleven tumultuous days during which Frondizi battled for his political life against formidable odds. The irate military forced him to order federal intervention in key provinces to block Framini and other *peronistas* from assuming control; whereupon more than a million members of *peronista* unions went on strike to protest their loss of franchise, and idle workers stood on street corners reminiscing about Perón and the "good old days."[8] There were angry shouts against the United States, who

6 *Peronistas* had been seeking recognition for a *Partido Justicialista* since 1958.

7 To the wrath of Communists and *peronistas* over the Cuba affair, the continuing anger of the workers who felt shortchanged by Frondizi's economic program, a further irritant was added when the United States, just two weeks before the elections, announced substantial new Alliance for Progress credits—a move which was interpreted by nationalistic Argentines as a reward for the administration's break with Cuba, as well as a bribe to the electorate to back up Frondizi, the good and loyal friend of the Kennedy administration and the Alliance for Progress.

8 *The New York Times* of March 24, 1962, reported the gist of these random remarks: "Why shouldn't we remember him? He was loyal to us and we are loyal to him. . . . We won Sunday and we will win again whenever there is an election in which we can vote for our candidates. . . . They [the Frondizi administration] have done nothing for us. . . . What they have done is to take away lots of things that we had. . . . Before Perón there was no retirement plan and you grew old working. There was no family wage bonus. I have four children. Why shouldn't we remember Perón? . . . He always provided seed and the crop purchase was guaranteed by the state. . . ."

seemed to be condoning the invalidation of some 2.5 million Argentine votes. "The Alliance for Progress is doomed," Framini was quoted as saying, "if the verdict of the people at the polls is not respected. The Alliance cannot speak about democracy if it supports any government that does not respect the election results." The armed forces were torn by bitter disagreement: the *golpistas,* led by such extremists as General Raúl Poggi, demanded immediate takeover of the government by the military for at least five years, until every trace of *peronismo* could be stamped out; while *legalista* military leaders, chiefly General Pedro Aramburu, struggled to work out a constitutional solution. Frondizi, with the help of Aramburu, attempted to assemble a coalition cabinet, but was rebuffed on every side. Even the UCRP, which in 1958 had branded Frondizi's platform as "too radical," now joined the *peronistas* in crucifying Frondizi for his "sellout" to the United States and refused to take part in any coalition. This failure of the two large middle-of-the-road parties— the UCRP and the UCRI—to get together in this crisis is ironic, for their combined strength could easily have prevented either a military takeover or the victory of *peronista* candidates.[9]

The moderates in the armed forces, aware that the world was watching, were frustrated by Frondizi's firm refusal to resign—even in the face of Aramburu's plea that Argentine democratic institutions were "in your hands and only your hands, but only on the basis of your voluntary resignation." Frondizi stood firm, stating that "only my person stands between order and chaos." It was a coup—but a reluctant coup—as Frondizi was physically removed from the Casa Rosada on March 29 and José María Guido, president of the Senate and constitutional successor to the presidency, was prevailed upon to take his place. The military chiefs subscribed to the paradox that the ouster of Frondizi was necessary to maintain democratic procedures; and many observers gave credence to their statement that "we Argentine military of today believe in civilian rule."

Arturo Frondizi had lost his gamble, and was soon on the way to exile on Martín García Island.

A PUPPET OF THE MILITARY: JOSÉ MARÍA GUIDO, 1962–63

For eighteen turbulent months (March 30, 1962, to October 12, 1963), José María Guido sat uneasily in the presidential chair, issuing decree after decree dictated by one or another of the warring military factions. For the first half year the *golpistas,* now called the *colorados,* held the reins, threatening outright military dictatorship if necessary to quash the *peronistas.* The March elections were formally annulled: a court ruling that such invalidation was unconstitutional prompted a perfunctory appeal,

---

[9] In the March elections the UCRP polled about 1.7 million votes, the UCRI about 2 million, which, added together, far exceeded the *peronistas'* 2.5 million.

was then ignored. When Congress was forced into a year's recess, defiant deputies entered the Congress building in a futile protest—but elected *peronistas* were dispersed in the streets by tear gas. In September Congress was formally dissolved. Alarmed at such threats to democratic procedures, the *legalistas*—now called *azules*—led by General Juan Carlos Onganía, rebelled against the army high command. After a brief shooting war on September 21, during which terrified citizens fled the streets and locked their doors, the victorious but somewhat shamefaced *azules*, now in control of the armed forces—and, hence, the government—issued their "Communiqué 150," promised early elections which would embrace "all sections of Argentine life," and the retirement of the military from politics. President Guido promptly switched his allegiance to his new masters, reorganized his cabinet, announced elections for mid-1963.

There followed ten months of wrangling over the ground rules for the upcoming elections. General Onganía, who became the commander in chief of the army after his victory in September, led the moderate *azules* in an effort to make the elections truly democratic, even favored allowing *peronistas* to participate. But concession after concession had to be made to the *colorados*. The military tension, the plots and counterplots, the wording and rewording of election rules—all this added up to the impression that Argentina was engaged in an elaborate face-saving maneuver to hold "democratic" elections without allowing *peronistas*—still some one-third of the electorate—to present candidates. Guido shuffled and reshuffled his cabinet, as plan after plan was discarded. The Sáenz Peña electoral law of 1912[1] was replaced by a system of proportional representation, which would prevent *peronistas* from winning more than their share of electors or deputies—but the *colorados* were adamant: *any* share was too much. When Guido issued a new decree banning the *peronista* party and all *peronista* propaganda, the followers of the exiled dictator formed a new party, the *Unión Popular*, which gained legal recognition by promising not to mention Perón in campaign speeches. But when it was discovered that the party was taking orders directly from Perón in Madrid, the UP was forbidden to put up candidates for the presidency or the provincial governorships. *Peronista* hopes then centered in the *Frente Nacional y Popular*, an unlikely coalition of several parties of varied stripe, including the UP and Frondizi's faction of the badly split UCRI. The presidential candidate of the *Frente* was conservative businessman Vicente Solano Lima—Perón's own surprising choice, dictated in a secret telephone call relayed from Madrid through Montevideo. Solano Lima was duped into saying Perón's piece—in public: *el lider*'s regime had been "marked by a profound political and social content," and if he, Solano Lima, were elected president, he would welcome both Frondizi and Perón back to their native Argentine soil. Frustrated in its attempts to erase Perón from the political scene, the government issued a last-minute decree giving itself the power to declare invalid the entire electoral slate of any party in any way associated with *peronismo*. This was the final

1 See p. 738.

blow: hard-core *peronistas* voted blank ballots in the July 7 elections.

Thus the contest for the presidency in July, 1963, was a "free" election—with the minor exception that the largest and most cohesive body of voters were prevented from casting ballots for candidates of their own choosing. The election was chiefly a contest between the UCRP candidate, Arturo Illia; the UCRI's Oscar Alende; and General Pedro Aramburu, candidate of the newly formed UDELPA (*Unión del Pueblo Argentino*). Illia received 27 per cent of the votes, which put him well ahead of either Alende or Aramburu. But since this was not a majority, and all efforts to form a coalition broke down, the outcome was decided by the electoral college, which voted overwhelmingly for Illia.

ANOTHER TRY AT CIVILIAN RULE: ARTURO ILLIA, 1963–66

The inauguration in October, 1963, of Arturo Illia, a small-town doctor from the province of Córdoba, was welcomed with relief if not with enthusiasm by most Argentines. A modest, little-known man with no powerful political foes, his quiet and slow-moving ways (the cartoonists dubbed him *la tortuga*, the turtle) were soothing to the raw nerves of the nation, which had suffered almost constant political turmoil since 1930. To be sure, he had been elected by a slim 27 per cent of the voters, and upon assuming office he took no steps to make alliances with other minor parties. His rule in the name of the UCRP was at best a precarious base, but almost everyone was disposed to give him a fair trial.

Most hopeful for Illia's chances for stability was the attitude of the military. All sectors of the armed forces were on their best behavior as Illia received the sash of office. General Juan Carlos Onganía, leader of the *azules* (the moderate faction of the military) and chief engineer of the July elections, announced that "the government must be left to run the country." And he seemed to mean what he said: for two years, as commander in chief of the armed forces, Onganía imposed stern discipline to keep the military out of politics.

Illia had made two definite promises during his campaign, each an appeal to extreme nationalists: he would cancel the foreign oil contracts negotiated by Frondizi, and he would sever the ties of the Argentine government with the World Bank and the International Monetary Fund—"economic intruders," he called these agencies. Both promises he promptly fulfilled, and both proved disastrous to the economy. Since the end of 1961, Argentina had been nearly self-sufficient in petroleum products,[2] thus saving the nation some $200 million a year in scarce foreign exchange.

---

[2] It should be noted that technically Argentina can never be "self-sufficient" in petroleum products, because the type of oil found in Argentina does not furnish some needed derivatives, and there will always be the need to import some special kinds of crude oil (especially for lube oil and asphalt). Argentina, therefore, continued to import around $70 million to $90 million in petroleum products annually.

Now Illia abruptly annulled those contracts, pronouncing them "unconstitutional." The cancellation was a tedious process, undermining the confidence of all foreign investors. Production immediately fell off, renewing Argentine dependence upon foreign supplies: this nationalistic gesture was one which the nation could ill afford. Illia's second positive step was the cancellation of an agreement with the World Bank by which $95 million was to have been made available for enlarging the electric power plants of Buenos Aires—a badly needed improvement. And Illia turned his back on the International Monetary Fund, preferring to solve the nation's fiscal problems by the increased printing of paper money, which aggravated the already acute problem of inflation. Relations with the vitally important IMF remained bad throughout Illia's stay in office: in the spring of 1965, with reserves precariously low and $500 million due on the $2.5 billion foreign debt, Illia was forced to turn to that agency for help. But this about-face of the President was short-lived: Illia announced that the government could not accept the conditions imposed—curtailed government spending, less printing of paper money—"without prejudicing its own plans for the gradual deceleration of the inflationary process."

Illia's economic policy was a policy of drift. Everything about Argentina's economy was out of order. The nation owed too much to the outer world; it was deep in debt to internal creditors; after cancellation of the foreign oil contracts, the decline in oil production made necessary increased import of petroleum products, causing a heavy drain on foreign exchange; the overstaffed and creaky railroads required an annual subsidy of $200 million to $300 million each year. The government's continued recourse to the printing presses to increase the money supply led to repeated devaluations of the peso (seven by May, 1966), which in turn brought higher prices, new demands for wage increases, higher deficits. Argentina was the last major nation to present a program to the Alliance for Progress: Illia's five-year plan, announced in October, 1964, was vague and unambitious, and was never really put into effect. To be sure, Illia's government had one turn of good luck, thanks to the gods or to the pampas: two near-record wheat crops, those of 1963–64 and 1964–65, tempered the economic pains of the nation—there was actually a favorable trade balance for two years, the first time (except for 1959) that Argentina had been so lucky since the overthrow of Perón in 1955. This bounty of nature brought temporary relief to the sick economy, and, together with the quiescence of the military, lulled the nation into a false sense of well-being. But sober citizens were aware that the wheat boom reflected no technical improvement in the earning power of the nation, as production as a whole continued to stagnate. By early 1966 the government faced an annual deficit variously reckoned between $400 million and $700 million—the exact figure hung upon the amount to be paid off on the foreign debt. In other words, Argentina was bankrupt—and the villain, of course, was Arturo Illia, the quiet little doctor from the hills of Córdoba.

And Illia had the *peronistas* to reckon with, just as had all governments since 1955. Juan Domingo Perón, seventy in 1965, living in exile in Madrid, was still a lively ghost hovering over the fruitful lands of the Río de la Plata. To be sure the ranks of his followers had tended to fracture: there were now rival factions of *peronistas*—one which would settle for *"peronismo* without Perón," one which vowed to link its fortunes with *el líder* until his triumphal return. Perón had indeed tried to return in December, 1964: he got as far as the airport in Rio de Janeiro, but the Brazilians packed him up and sent him back to Madrid, where the Spanish authorities exacted a promise that he would indulge in no more political campaigning from Spanish soil (a promise he did not keep). Then, in October, 1965, Perón sent his latest wife, Isabelita, to Buenos Aires as an emissary to reunite the *peronistas* into an effective political force: she was greeted with much applause, but achieved no tangible results—Isabelita was no Evita. In other words, the *peronistas*, like their leader, were ageing: the earlier careless rapture had lost its sheen. But if the *peronistas* were fragmented, they nevertheless remained a powerful force. In every test of strength those troublemakers commanded more than 30 per cent of the electorate.

Arturo Illia's ways with *peronismo*, while never explicitly spelled out, were quite different from those of his predecessors: the military had thought to extirpate the disease by outlawry; Frondizi had sought to placate the troublemakers, in the hope of luring them into his UCRI; Illia's formula was a gentle amiability which would hold the *peronistas* on a long leash, in the pleasant hope that they would quiet down into a respectable opposition party. This policy was given an impressive test in the congressional elections of March, 1965: the military, still in a pliant mood, acquiesced in the decision to allow the *Unión Popular*, the chief *peronista* party, to enter its own candidates—the first such concession to the *peronistas* in nine years. While Illia's UCRP ran on a platform of "peace and tranquillity," the *peronistas* waged a spirited campaign: pictures of the long-dead Evita were paraded through the streets; cries of "Bastard or thief, we want Perón!" echoed through the countryside. The results—37 per cent of the vote for the *peronistas*, only 28 per cent for the UCRP—were no less surprising than the seemingly unperturbed reaction of the military, the lack of panic on the part of Illia's forces. As the UP went on to win local and provincial elections through 1965 and early 1966—and as it proceeded to behave like a responsible opposition party, conferring with opponents, discussing measures of cooperation—it seemed like possible success for Illia's ambition to integrate the *peronistas* and to create something like a two-party system. But as the elections in the powerful province of Buenos Aires, scheduled for March, 1967—not to mention the presidential elections of 1969—loomed on the horizon, there were signs of jitters on the part of the military.

The honeymoon with the military was, of course, too good to be true. As early as May, 1965, Illia aroused the displeasure of General Onganía, chief of the armed forces, by his refusal to participate in the Inter-American Peace Force in the Dominican Republic: Onganía and others of like mind wanted Argentina to join the military government of Brazil in backing up the United States' forceful stand in that beleaguered island republic, but Illia quashed the military's hostile stance. And then, in November, 1965, Illia appointed as war minister a man charged with *peronista* sympathies, whereupon Onganía resigned his post as commander in chief. There followed a rash of rumors that a coup was in the making, with the military again turning out an elected president. A statement by the top brass in April, 1966, while expressing deep concern over the worsening economy and the do-nothing policies of Illia, disavowed any intention of staging a *golpe*. But the fine promises of the military that "no problems will be solved by breaking the constitutional order" soon proved to be quite without substance.

AGAIN, THE MILITARY: JUAN CARLOS ONGANÍA, 1966–

On June 28, 1966, a three-man military junta ejected Arturo Illia from office and replaced him with Lieutenant General Juan Carlos Onganía as provisional president. The house-cleaning, as its proponents called it, was swift and thorough: Congress was dismissed, Supreme Court judges were replaced, all political parties were abolished, provincial governors were deposed. No promise of elections was made. The junta would decide everything—and the junta, in effect, was Onganía.

It was a new and surprising role for General Onganía, who had long been the army's most ardent proponent of orderly constitutional government. It was Onganía who—after leading his moderate *azules* to victory over the militant *colorados* in September, 1962—had pushed through the elections of July, 1963, over the battering opposition of the *colorados,* who favored outright military takeover. It was Onganía who, as commander in chief of the armed forces, had prevented interference by the military in political affairs during the first two years of Illia's regime. But it was now Onganía who led the most sweeping displacement of civilian and constitutional government since the days of Perón.

The first reaction in Argentina was not hostile. Almost all sectors had lost faith in the do-nothing Illia. And even those who deplored a break in constitutional continuity admitted privately that Onganía was one of the ablest and most honest of the military leaders.

The reaction from the outer world was one of dismay—although formal recognition was not long withheld: in Latin America, only Venezuela and little Costa Rica remained aloof; and the United States, after waiting eighteen days, resumed relations. Onganía did not understand the reluctance of Washington to embrace him. His group had been close to the Castello Branco government in Brazil, which had been welcomed promptly and joyfully by the United States. A man close to Onganía said mournfully: "We thought the Pentagon favored a grand anti-Communist alliance between the military governments of Brazil and Argentina." This reasoning might indeed have had cogency if Illia, like Goulart, had associated openly with the Communists—but Illia was under no such charge.

Meanwhile the new government made half-hearted gestures toward easing the economic strain. The peso was devalued—for the seventh time since 1964. A wage boost of 35 per cent appeased labor: "Coddling the *peronistas*" was the verdict of business. But Onganía's most bold and positive steps caused deep apprehension among sober onlookers. One of his first moves was the shutting down of some 1,500 credit union cooperatives, controlling about one-fifth of the nation's lending power—in the case of one Jewish-controlled credit union, six directors were arrested on vague charges. These steadily expanding credit unions, first founded by Jewish settlers, were anathema to the commercial banks; and in closing them Onganía at once aligned himself with the nation's financial interests, and laid himself open to the charge of anti-Semitism—and attention was focused on many of Onganía's close associates, who were well-known anti-Semites.

Even more shocking was the attack, on July 29, upon the eight state universities, enrolling some 150,000 students, of which half were in the University of Buenos Aires. Traditionally enjoying autonomy, these institutions had long been exempt from police and army interference. Now, with the announced purpose of "improving the level of scholarly life" and the ostensible excuse that the universities were hotbeds of Communism, Onganía decreed an end to their autonomy, placing them under the control of the National Ministry of Education. The most blatant attack was upon the University of Buenos Aires. The police struck at this prestigious institution, rounded up several hundred professors and students, clubbed them unmercifully, herded many of them into trucks and took them off to jail. An ominous note in this chapter was the obvious venom directed against the large Jewish contingent—some 12 per cent of the student body: "Run, you Commie-Jew, SOB," was the refrain of the police. A Jew, it seems, was always a Communist. Bystanders were reminded of the days of Hitler.

In August, 1966, Onganía came under fire from high prelates of the Catholic Church. Although Onganía made much of his devout Christian faith, churchmen struck back against any attempt to identify his regime with the Church. One bishop had a letter read in all the parishes under his jurisdiction: "The persistent attitude that the present government is linked to the holy Church is false. . . . Let me make it clear once and for all that this government has no claim on the faithful." Another bishop, writing in the Uruguayan weekly *Marcha*, was even more explicit: "President Onganía is an honest man of good faith but with the mentality and outlook of a soldier. . . . He wants to run the country as if it were an army barracks." Significant, too, was the reaction of the four Roman Catholic universities whose faculties rallied to the support of the national universities.

Onganía continued to enlarge upon the repressive measures of his first days in office. In November, 1966, his forces raided the offices of all the former political parties, made off with their files and office equipment, and for good measure seized all their bank accounts. Onganía also closed the electoral courts, which were now useless as there were no elections to be supervised. To be sure, six months later he intimated that political parties might some day be revived—but he named no date.

Onganía carried on a running battle with organized labor. A critical item was the bankrupt national railways, which cut into the national budget at the rate of some $325 million a year. In December, 1966, Onganía issued a decree calling for bold overhauling of the railroads, but with nothing said about eliminating the 10,000 or more useless employees. Then in March, 1967, the railroad workers staged a one-day strike, whereupon Onganía announced that the 116,449 men who had participated in the strike would be "demoted or suspended." By this time, union members— including most *peronistas*—were thoroughly disenchanted with their president.

The universities continued as targets for Onganía's reforming zeal. After the violent purge of July, 1966, several hundred university professors were on their way to exile in other Latin American nations, in the United States, and in Europe—and many of these were men and women of international reputation in the sciences. Sporadic and ineffective student protests were brushed aside. Then in April, 1967, Onganía settled the question with a new university law under which students and graduates no longer had a voice in determining university policies. The law banned all propaganda and all political activity in the universities, and provided that the government could intervene in any university whenever it willed.

Onganía's cabinet continued to be reshuffled. Some men of pronounced fascist hue were eliminated when warnings came that the image of Argentina was being blackened over the world by the arrogant dictatorship which prevailed in Buenos Aires. (One such warning came in January, 1967, from Alvaro Alsogaray, ambassador to the United States—but in August that able man was relieved of his Washington post.) There was a great deal of talk about the "liberalization" of the Onganía regime, but there was scant evidence of such leavening. In June, 1967, a new Secretariat of Broadcasting and Tourism was installed to choke off criticism in the press or over the air waves. And in August a new law directed against Communism and Communist sympathizers called for the listing of all who would preach dangerous doctrine. Onganía seemed intent upon creating a national state of mind in which a Joe McCarthy would feel at home. There would be a blacklist of dangerous fellows, their unfitness to be decided by the military, who would forthwith be barred from voting (if, indeed, anyone should be permitted to vote), holding office, or having any share in public education.

Upon completion of his first year in office in June, 1967, Onganía had few admirers among the *peronistas,* the labor unions, or the intellectuals, but he had won friends in the business community—and, also important, among the dispensers of public and private funds in Washington, New York, and Europe. These all applauded his devaluation of the peso in March, 1967, from 250 to the dollar to 350. They credited him with a slight reduction of inflation, with increased reserves in the Central Bank, with more efficient tax collection. They liked his relaxing of the ban on foreign oil companies, permitting them to explore and drill for oil (although foreigners would be limited to the less promising areas). In May, the IMF (always admiring policies of austerity) granted a $125-million credit, and a group of American, European, and Japanese banks made loans aggregating $400 million. Onganía could comfort himself with the friendship of the bankers, no matter what the professors thought about him.

So matters stood for Onganía in mid-1967. The applause for him was not deafening, but he still wore the sash of office. No one was laying any bets as to the next turn in Argentina's fortunes.

THE PROSPECTS FOR ARGENTINA

That flavour of militarism which was so strong in former years has now virtually disappeared. The administration is conducted by civilians, and is pervaded by a legal spirit. In short, Argentina is now . . . a constitutional republic, whose defects, whatever they may be, are the defects of a republic, not of a despotism disguised under republican forms. . . . All is modern and new; all belongs to the prosperous present and betokens a still more prosperous future. . . . In this immense fertile and temperate country with hardly six people to the square mile, what limit can we set to the growth of wealth and population? . . . Men now living may see this nation, what with its growing numbers and its wealth, take rank beside France, Italy, and Spain. It may be, in the New World, the head and champion of what are called the Latin races.[3]

The year was 1912, and the words were those of the sagacious English analyst, James Bryce. Optimism was in the air in Buenos Aires. For a half century Argentina had registered progress such as few other nations could boast. She had had some able and devoted public servants who had led her to a position of strength. Her men of letters had made their mark in the intellectual world.[4] She had been well served by good schools, and the literacy rate was the highest in Latin America. Her wheat fields and herds of cattle had expanded until she was one of the chief providers for hungry Europe. Railroads yoked the interior with the ports. Immigrants poured in.

[3] James Bryce: *South America, Observations and Impressions* (New York: The Macmillan Co.; 1912), pp. 315, 337, 347, 545.

[4] This was true in 1912, as it had been throughout Argentine history—and is true today in 1967. We have noted (pp. 712-3) the significant work of the literary protestors against Rosas—Esteban Echeverría, Bartolomé Mitre, Juan Bautista Alberdi, and Domingo Faustino Sarmiento. We also mentioned (pp. 695-6) the importance of the literature which commemorated the Gaucho's role in national history, including such writers as Estanislao del Campo and José Hernández. The Gaucho continued as a subject for novelists in the twentieth century: perhaps the finest such work is Ricardo Güiraldes's *Don Segundo Sombra* (1926). Among other highly respected writers since 1900 are the poet Leopoldo Lugones, whose influence has been widespread in Latin America; Ezequiel Martínez Estrada, whose interpretation of his country in *Radiografía de la pampa* (1933) is profound and devastating; Eduardo Mallea, whose novels carry on the dissection of Argentine life; and the poet-essayist Jorge Luis Borges, the best known and most widely translated of all Argentine writers.

Foreign capital, almost $4 billion, had spurred the prosperity. The phrase "rich as an Argentine" was heard in Paris and London and Madrid. The streets of Buenos Aires were crowded with fine carriages, splendid horses, and a well-dressed populace whose faces revealed the sure pride they felt in their nation. "The breeze which blows from Argentina," reported another English traveler, "is one of prosperity." And still another foreign observer wrote: "It may safely be said that for stability and liberality, the government of the Argentine Republic may compare with any other in the world." There was no looking back for the citizen of Argentina, the future was rich with promise.

But that was 1912. In 1967, there were still Argentines who knew that they lived in one of the finest nations in the world—but now there was fear in their eyes. Too much had gone wrong. Their government, whose constitutional stability had developed so impressively, had faltered: since 1930 there had been a melancholy record of military coups, ousters of presidents, rigged elections (or no elections at all), and 1967 saw the country once again ruled by the generals. Economically, there had been a series of disasters. The pastures and grain fields, true source of Argentine wealth, had been increasingly neglected as successive governments turned to the building of national industry. The steady trek of farm laborers to the cities had drained away the man power needed to grow wheat and tend cattle, had swelled the population of the cities and increased the slums— some 75 per cent of all Argentines now lived in urban centers, more than a third of them in Greater Buenos Aires alone. To be sure, Argentina still stood second only to Venezuela among Latin American nations in per capita output. But in spite of that proud claim, economic stagnation reigned. Consider wheat: during the years 1874 to 1912, the acreage devoted to raising that profitable crop had multiplied fifty-seven times; there were fluctuations in the intervening years, but in 1963 there were actually 17 per cent fewer acres under wheat than there had been in 1912. Or cattle, Argentina's other great source of wealth: there were fewer cattle in the pastures in 1962 than there had been forty years earlier. Argentines should be reminded that their country was once the world's leading exporter of wheat, corn, flaxseed, and meat, and the second most important exporter of wool. Today it often has trouble meeting its own domestic needs. Or, for over-all economic growth, consider the per capita national product, which increased at an average annual rate of less than four-tenths of 1 per cent during the years 1945 to 1964. Proud Argentina's march to prosperity had slowed down to a crawl by the 1960's.

How can one explain Argentina's poor showing? How can one resolve the paradox of potential opulence and actual stagnation? How can one solve the riddle of a modern and literate people who allow their political institutions to slip back into chaos? Ask these questions of the Argentines at random and you get a variety of responses. Try a taxi driver: "Crooked politicians," he may tell you, "they are all for sale." Try a shopkeeper, and his answer may be: "It is all the fault of the Jews. There are half a

million of them in Argentina, and they are ruining honest businessmen."
From others you may hear that everything is the fault of the Italians, or
of the Gallegos (the Galicians of Spain), or of the Basques. There is nothing novel about these alibis: one can hear the same sort of nonsense in
other lands.

A popular rejoinder is to blame the nation's ills on Perón. Many an
Argentine, explaining the doldrums of his country since 1955, winds up
with a sobbing account of the sins of Perón and Evita. There is, of course,
meat to the argument. Perhaps it would be rude, but apposite, to suggest
that at least three other countries—West Germany, Japan, and Italy—lay
prostrate after the far more devastating experience of World War II, but
that with hard work, determination, and skill they wrought miracles of
reconstruction. It would seem that it was now high time for Argentines to
exorcise the ghost of Juan Domingo Perón, and to get on with the nation's
business.

A more plausible explanation of the nation's ills involves the role
of the armed forces. Wise men shake their heads and say: "The generals
are to blame for everything. They have usurped the role of the civilian
authorities, assumed that they alone have the political and economic wisdom to make decisions. They have ousted presidents who did not bow to
the military as the final arbiter—or they have seized power themselves."
This is an important indictment—but what does it prove? Perhaps the
highhandedness of the generals does not prove the power of the soldiery
so much as it does the helplessness and apathy of the citizenry. But then
we must ask: How could so able a people as the Argentines fall under
the heel of the generals and the admirals? Is this a nation of sheep, without wit or will, to be bullied by men in uniform?[5]

The question must be pressed. During the first half century of Argentina's independent life—the years after 1862—the army usually acted in a
professional fashion, yielding precedence to civilian rulers. Since 1930 the
generals have had their way. But why? It may be argued that Argentine
rightists, including many of the top brass in the armed forces, have been
too much influenced by the tyrannies which bedeviled Europe: the Primo
de Rivera and Franco dictatorships in Spain; the fascist arrogance of
Mussolini in Italy; the Nazi terror in Germany. The argument has substance. Of all the Latin American republics, Argentina has been the most
closely tied to European political trends. The steady flow of Italian, Spanish, and (in lesser numbers) German migrants brought to Argentina the
ideas which prospered in their homelands. For more than forty years,
proto-fascist groups have flourished in Argentina—most of them clearly
traceable to European fascist influences. Beginning in 1919, there was the
Liga Patriótica Argentina, anti-Communist, anti-Semitic, antiliberal. After

[5] Barnard Collier tells a pertinent story in *The New York Times* of February 19, 1967.
It seems that a skinny dog from Chile and a fat dog from Argentina met on the 12,000-foot
pass in the Andes. The skinny dog admitted that he was going to Argentina because there
was much to eat in that land. "Ah, yes," said the Argentine dog, "we have filet mignon three
times a day. . . ." On parting, the Chilean dog asked the Argentine dog: "Why on earth
are you going to *Chile*?" The Argentine dog replied softly: "I'm going to Chile to *bark*."

the Uriburu coup of 1930, other kindred rightist groups took shape, such as the Legión de Mayo, Liga Republicana, and the Legión Cívica Argentina. The Uriburu regime in 1930–31 was openly modeled on the Mussolini pattern. Thereafter, considerable elements in the armed forces felt the influence of both the Mussolini and Hitler ideologies, and when World War II broke out in 1939, there was a solid core of Axis sympathizers among the military who strongly backed the Argentine policy of pro-Axis neutrality. Even after the United States had virtually forced the Argentine break with Germany, Italy, and Japan in 1944, the ultrarightists continued to give comfort to the Axis. During more recent years, there has been a rash of neo-fascist groups such as Tacuara and Guardia Restauradora Nacional, with shock troops and much clamor, calling for suppression of Communism and the driving out of the Jews. Not impressive in numbers, but ominous in revealing an underlying mood, these excrescences tell much about what is wrong with Argentina. The military indeed must share the blame.

A further clue to the Argentine malaise is this: the nation has never had a thoroughgoing *social* revolution. Thomas Jefferson, writing to James Madison in 1787, said: "A little rebellion now and then . . . is a medicine necessary for the sound health of government." Argentina's "rebellions" have been numerous, to be sure, but they have never reached far enough or deep enough to bring social renovation. Certainly the revolt of the Radicals after 1890 was little more than a middle-class revolt: their conspicuous leader, Irigoyen, may have been the "father of the poor," but he did little to fulfill their hopes. Juan Domingo Perón may have been the patron of the *descamisados*, but their shirts remained as shabby as ever. To be sure, Perón changed the political structure of the nation by giving the urban proletariat a voice. But the workers beyond the outskirts of the cities remained as ill-served as they had always been.

Furthermore, the complete and disastrous failure to deal with the inequitable distribution of land is evidence that no profound social renewal has taken place. The latifundia pattern, inherited from colonial days, had been firmly entrenched throughout the nineteenth century—by Rivadavia, then by Rosas, further by the landgrabbers of the 1880's. The unwise concentration in a few hands of the richest lands of the pampas had worked marked disservice to the expanding republic: it had given slight chance to the migrants from Spain and Italy to establish themselves as self-respecting independent farmers in the fashion foreseen by the wise Alberdi; it had driven farm laborers from their unprofitable and lonely life in the interior to the cities, distending the slums. On this score, Argentina's course had differed markedly from that of the United States where the fine lands of the Mississippi Valley were opened to homesteading migrants from the eastern states and from Europe, creating a widely based middle class of independent farmers, with permanence of tenure and incentives to the investment of brawn and capital. No one—certainly not Irigoyen or Perón—did anything about this inequity, which left *estancias* of thousands or hundreds of thousands of acres in the hands of the favored few. The national census of 1960 told that tale: the little farmers with average holdings of less than 12.4 acres (about 15 per cent of all farm units) held a mere 0.1 per cent of the total farm acreage; while at the other extreme, the holders of farms averaging more than 2,471 acres (less than 6 per cent of all farm owners) commanded a princely three-fourths of all utilized farm lands. Surely this feudal pattern, which survives today, is incompatible with a democratic national life.

Perhaps the discussion can be narrowed to a consideration of the Argentines themselves. First, as a people they lack cohesiveness. Despite the homogeneity of the population, which suffers no serious racial lines, Argentina is curiously a "conglomeration of peoples" rather than an organic community. There is, of course, the deep cleavage between social classes: the vast distance between the rich and wellborn, on the one hand, and the workers in field and factory, on the other, follows the familiar pattern of almost all Latin America. Then there is the rift between the capital city and the provinces, which has persisted throughout Argentine history: the people of Buenos Aires still rule the nation and control the economy of the land; and their culture—which they regard as French— cuts them off effectively from the countryside. But this lack of cohesiveness also exhibits itself in the absence of any true cooperative spirit among the Argentine people. The vested interests of industry, agriculture, and labor, by their intransigent insistence upon their special rights, block progress. There is little consensus on national goals; there is slight sense of common purpose even among groups of seemingly like-minded citizens: consider the proliferation of political parties—the inability of the Radicals, for instance, to rally their dissident factions to any semblance of unity.

The Argentine people pay slight homage to the institutions of government. The presidency is not accorded the general respect of citizens: witness the almost universal apathy in the face of the unseating of a Frondizi or an Illia. Nor is the national Congress held in high esteem: scarcely a ripple of protest greets the overriding of its powers by president after president. The periodic dismantling of the Supreme Court causes scant concern among the citizenry. Nor does the constitution serve as a rallying point for national loyalty as it does in the United States. The average Argentine citizen seems unable or unwilling to accept a duly elected government as the final arbiter in national affairs.

The Argentine people, perhaps, are prone to oversimplification. There has been no lack of proffered panaceas for the nation's problems, but they all seem a bit too neat. In the years after 1955, the military—and those of like mind—were obsessed with the idea that Argentina would prosper if only she could be rid of the scourge of *peronismo*. Frondizi and his followers thought to cure all ills by economic reforms and industrialization. Illia offered salvation by "tranquillity," and believed that a freely elected government was in itself a solution. It is not yet clear what Onganía—and his successors—will have to offer.

The Argentines are perhaps more apt than some to place their own personal needs ahead of the common good (although any claim to distinction on this score could easily be overstated). They have developed some financial habits which do not improve the economic health of the nation: tax evasion has long been flagrant, especially among the large landholders; during recent unsettled days there has been a disastrous export of capital to banks in Switzerland and elsewhere; and the "flight from the peso"—the intricate maneuverings to capitalize upon the rampant inflation—have further undermined the economy. Still another drain upon Argentine capital—this time its intellectual capital—has been the steady exodus of physicians, engineers, technicians to other lands which offer better jobs.

It has been suggested by more than a few observers that the typical Argentine is not a hard worker. Those who should provide creative leadership in the nation today have come by wealth and position too easily. The speculative boom of the late nineteenth and early twentieth centuries brought fortunes to those who owned land: hard work was not required of the masters of the great *estancias*, and the sons of those masters grew up soft and undisciplined, and have not been willing to expend time and energy to assure the stability and success of the nation.

On the score of the Argentine character there is no dearth of rude remarks. The Argentine economist, Alejandro E. Bunge, writing in 1930, impolitely suggests that there are three basic traits in all Argentines— "arrogance, sadness, and laziness." The Spaniard Ortega y Gasset writes that "the Argentine is a marvellously gifted man . . . who has never devoted himself to the activity he carries out, who has never accepted it as his vital goal, who never considers it to be definitive but rather a transitory stage on the way to his ideal: advancement in wealth and social status."[6] The Argentine novelist Eduardo Mallea suggests that the Argentine motto is "God will provide," and adds that the Argentines "wait and hope and expect the attainment of the promised future not by their own effort but by 'magic' or divine grace."

But whatever the diagnosis or the prescription may be, it is clear that it will require a liberal visitation of divine grace to set Argentina back on the road to wealth.

6 Cited by Tomás Roberto Fillol: *Social Factors in Economic Development: The Argentine Case* (Cambridge, Mass.: The M.I.T. Press; 1961), p. 20.

◆:◆:◆:◆:◆:◆:◆:◆:◆:◆: [*Chapter 44*]

URUGUAY

Little Uruguay,[1] created in 1828 as a buffer state between Argentina and Brazil, has been, since the turn of the century, the most faithful to constitutional forms and democratic practice of all the nations of Latin America. With an area of 72,172 square miles (little more than the state of Washington), it has a 120-mile seaboard on the Atlantic, a 235-mile shoreline on the Río de la Plata, and a 270-mile frontage on the river Uruguay. Its grassy plains, extension of the Argentine Pampa, are fringed in the north by rolling hills, at their highest only 1,644 feet above the sea. Rainfall is adequate and dependable; climate is equable.

There are today (1966) 2.7 million Uruguayans, of whom at least nine out of every ten either were born in Europe or have parents or grandparents who were; most of these are of Italian or Spanish extraction (including numerous energetic Basques), and a few are of German, French, or English descent. Thus the population of Uruguay, like that of Argentina, is the result of European immigration. When the republic was formally launched in 1828, there were about 60,000 people; fifty years later, there were about half a million. Almost half of the people of modern Uruguay live in the capital city of Montevideo (the largest concentration of population in one city of any nation in the world).

Uruguay has been called the "Switzerland of South America." Although the analogy breaks down under close inspection (a point to which we will return on pp. 809–11), there are likenesses between the two countries. Uruguay is like Switzerland in its compactness and in its stout resistance to pressure from powerful neighbors. In the last half century Uruguay has emulated the Alpine republic in governmental practices and socialistic economic excursions. Like Switzerland, it has long served as a retreat for political refugees: thousands of Argentines found safety there from Rosas's wrath; numerous Brazilians and Paraguayans have at various times sought its hospitality; and, from 1944 to 1955, it was a haven for thousands who could not abide Perón.

---

[1] Properly La República Oriental del Uruguay, a name derived from its location on the Banda Oriental, the eastern shore of the river Uruguay.

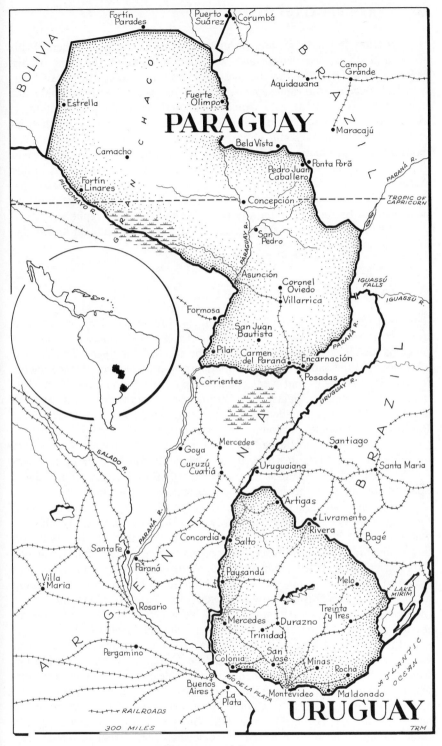

Uruguay and Paraguay

Uruguay is like Argentina on many counts, unlike it on others. With about a tenth of the people and less than a tenth of the area of her neighbor to the south, Uruguay, like Argentina, is a white European land, with few Negroes and almost no Indians. It is literate, with probably not more than 10 per cent who cannot read and write. Like Argentina, it aspires to industrialization, but has achieved far less on this score than its greater neighbor, and is still almost completely dependent on imports for manufactured products. Uruguay devotes about 74 per cent of its area to grazing cattle and sheep and only 12 per cent to cultivated fields, while Argentina's stock raising has long since become secondary to grain production. Both countries lack iron and coal. Uruguay and Argentina are better served by railways than any other South American republic.

The understanding of this freedom-loving state depends on knowledge of its stormy past.

COLONY AND REPUBLIC

The area now called Uruguay was long a hotly debated no man's land between Portuguese Brazil and Spanish La Plata. Remote and lacking precious metals, it was the last region to be claimed for Spain. The Jesuits, who gathered the Indians in mission villages, were effective advance agents for the Spanish kings and were chiefly responsible for holding both Uruguay and Paraguay against the Portuguese. Montevideo, last Spanish stronghold, was not founded until 1726—and then as a bastion against Portugal. Meanwhile, Colonia del Sacramento (the modern city of Colonia), had been established by the Portuguese on the Río de la Plata opposite Buenos Aires in 1680, to be repeatedly fought over until it was finally occupied by Spanish forces in 1776. That capture consolidated Spanish control over the Banda Oriental, at least for a time.

With the outbreak of revolt in 1810, the fever spread to the Banda Oriental. In 1811 José Gervasio Artigas, a thirty-seven-year-old Gaucho who had spent his youth as smuggler and cattle rustler and his manhood as an officer in the Spanish forces, offered his services to the junta in Buenos Aires, which had defied Spain in 1810. Artigas enlisted his Gauchos and struck at Montevideo, but the Buenos Aires junta blocked him by signing a truce with the Spanish viceroy in Montevideo. Artigas, refusing to accept the decision of Buenos Aires, continued his guerrilla attacks and then retreated across the river to the Argentine province of Entre Ríos.

In 1813 he was back in the Banda Oriental, hammering at Spanish garrisons and raising the banner of a free Uruguay. Then, on invitation from the Buenos Aires government, he sent delegates to the congress convened in the capital; he demanded a federal union of the lands of the Viceroyalty of La Plata, a capital not in Buenos Aires, and complete autonomy for the Banda Oriental. The Buenos Aires contingent rejected these demands and refused to seat his delegates—an affront which decided the Gaucho against any project for union with Buenos Aires. In 1814 a *porteño* army under Belgrano captured Montevideo but lost it the following year to Artigas, who for more than a year exercised authority over a chaotic but independent Banda Oriental. In 1816 Portuguese troops entered from the north and in January, 1817, captured Montevideo. For three more years Artigas continued to harass Portuguese forces, but finally in 1820 "the Father of Uruguayan independence" was compelled to withdraw across the river to Entre Ríos, never again to return to the Banda Oriental.[2]

The Portuguese-Brazilians, rid of Artigas, were now masters of the debated region, but their hold was soon contested. Determined Uruguayan refugees plotted in Buenos Aires; and in 1825 "the immortal thirty-three" under the leadership of Juan Lavalleja crossed the Río de la Plata, called patriots to arms, and precipitated the three-year war between Argentina and the now independent empire of Brazil. Brave fighting on land and sea resulted in no clear decision for either contestant. In 1828, under pressure from Great Britain (whose trade gave weight to her diplomacy), Brazil and Buenos Aires came to terms, agreeing to recognize Uruguayan independence and to defend its sovereignty forever. The separate status of the Republic of Uruguay, promised in 1828, was confirmed by the adoption of a constitution in 1830.

YEARS OF CONFUSION, 1830–1903

Uruguay, today one of the most democratic of Latin American republics, suffered almost unrelieved turbulence during her first seventy-three years of independent life. The nation's meager population was composed mostly of lawless frontiersmen, and she had less able urban leaders than Argentina had in that period. Uruguay was still, despite the pledges of the treaty of 1828, a target for interference by both Argentina and Brazil.

The first election in 1830 gave the presidency to Fructuoso Rivera, who had been first an aide of Artigas and then an ally of Brazil. His four years in office were marked by violence and revolts. In 1835 Manuel Oribe, friend of the hero Lavalleja, was elected. The people now split between two rival political parties. On Rivera's side were the *colorados*, supported by the followers of Artigas, the persecuted *unitarios* of Buenos Aires, and Brazil. On Oribe's side were the *blancos,* the *estancieros,* merchants, and high clergy, supported by the boss of Buenos Aires, Juan Manuel de Rosas. The political lines drawn in the mid-1830's hardened into the two parties which have persisted, at least in name, to the present day. Nowhere else in Latin America (except perhaps in Colombia) has the two-party system, with numerous lapses, prevailed so long or so angrily. The National Library in Montevideo has many shelves crowded with the polemics of the rival groups. The *colorados* have preened themselves on being the

2 Artigas, after ineffectual attempts to establish a hold in the Littoral, found refuge under the protection of dictator Francia in Paraguay, where he died in 1850 at the age of seventy-six.

party of liberalism and the common man, the defender of Uruguayan sovereignty. The *blancos* consider themselves the party of order, the protector of the faith, the instrument of conservatism. But the performance of neither party justifies its claims. During the nineteenth century neither the *colorados* nor the *blancos* stood consistently for liberalism or for order—or for anything else.

Until the fall of Rosas in 1852, Uruguay was agitated by the sorties of the Argentine dictator, who armed Oribe against Rivera. The last phase of the contest was the nine-year (1843–52) siege of Montevideo in which the *blanco*-Rosas allies bombarded the allied *colorados* and Brazilians. The Argentine attack upon Uruguay was in part responsible for the intervention of France and England, described earlier (see pp. 711–2). The clash was given further international character by the "red shirts" of the Italian patriot Giuseppe Garibaldi who entered the fight against Rosas. In 1852, when Urquiza lifted the siege of Montevideo and unseated Rosas, Uruguay was caught in Argentine confusions: Urquiza, ruling from Paraná, favored the *blancos,* while Mitre and the *porteños* favored the *colorados.*

In the 1860's the internal political strife in Uruguay furnished the immediate cause of the five-year war in which Paraguay was confronted by allied Argentina, Brazil, and Uruguay. In 1865 the Brazilians helped a *colorado* despot named Venancio Flores to unseat his *blanco* rival, whereupon the Paraguayan dictator, Francisco Solano López, rushed to the aid of the *blancos*; this act led to the tripartite alliance against Paraguay. The crushing of Paraguay left the *colorados* in control of Uruguay, a control they exercised continuously until 1958.

The end of the Paraguayan War in 1870 marks a turning point in Uruguayan history. By that time the older type of caudillo had lost his hold, for the same reasons as in Argentina; lands had been fenced, putting an end to the lawless ranging of the Gauchos; railroads had begun to link the national territory; Italian, Spanish, and other migrants had settled in the cities, creating a new middle class of lawyers, doctors, and traders. These changes had brought neither democracy nor peace, but they had created a substantial body of citizens who thought in national terms.

Politics continued to be tempestuous during the last decades of the nineteenth century. There were repeated clashes between *blancos* and *colorados,* and between rival factions of the *colorados* themselves. Three *colorado* despots ruled dictatorially for sixteen years (1875–90). In the 1890's two *colorado* presidents governed with disregard of democratic niceties and wanton looting of the public treasury. In 1897 the *blancos,* led by a half-Brazilian Gaucho, Aparicio Saravia, initiated a civil war which was settled by an awkward compromise under which the *blancos* (now calling themselves "nationalists") were given full control of 6 of the 19 departments, or provinces, and minority representation in the Chamber of Deputies.[3] This divisive arrangement was in force in 1903 when José Batlle y Ordóñez, most brilliant of Uruguay's leaders, was elected to the presidency.

---

[3] For the first time a major Uruguayan dispute was settled without foreign mediation.

The beginning of the twentieth century found Uruguay far behind Argentina in social and economic progress. Political instability (there had been about forty armed revolts between 1830 and 1903) and foreign interference had hindered the orderly development of national resources, frightened off foreign capital, discouraged investment by Uruguayans themselves, and deterred immigration. However, almost 400,000 immigrants had helped to increase the population from some 60,000 in 1830 to 915,000 in 1900. The new middle class created by these immigrants was chiefly urban, as in Argentina.

Economically, Uruguay had lagged far behind Argentina. Stock farms occupied about 96 per cent of the utilized area in 1900, and were dominated by a few hundred great *estancieros*. Both pastoral and agricultural progress was slower than in Argentina. The intermittent political warfare, more serious than Argentina's, had retarded such measures as the introduction of better stock and attention to soils and seeds. Uruguay got her first packing house, or *frigorífico*, in 1904, twenty-one years later than Argentina. Industry had made some progress after 1875, with slow increase in domestic production of textiles, clothing, shoes, and processed foods. Railroads, built by the British, grew from 192 miles in 1875 to 1,075 miles in 1895. Public utilities, foreign-owned, served the capital city but most of the country was without electricity or adequate water supply.

The public treasury had been drained—and looted—since 1830. The warring politicians consistently overspent on maintenance of extravagant military forces; during the 1880's and 1890's the army and navy, whose sole function was to keep one or another regime in power, consumed from a third to a fifth of the national budget. Such financial recklessness had prevented national investment in public works and had piled up foreign debt—chiefly to England. By 1902, as Hanson points out, £14.8 million was invested in railroads, utilities, and meat processing. The public debt stood at £24 million, the largest per capita debt of any South American nation. Service on foreign debts consumed 31 per cent of the national budget in 1879, 40 per cent in 1901.[4]

Socially, Uruguay's exhibit in 1900 was unimpressive. Almost half of her citizens were still illiterate. In the 1870's, despite the chaos in government, a brave start toward a national school system had been made under the leadership of José Pedro Varela, who had been influenced by his Argentine contemporary Sarmiento and by the educators of the United States. The University of Montevideo, founded in 1849, was enlarged and improved. But up to the end of the nineteenth century the cultural advantages of the nation were largely reserved for the capital city. Seldom was more than 5 per cent of the budget allotted to education.

---

[4] Simon G. Hanson: *Utopia in Uruguay, Chapters in the Economic History of Uruguay* (New York: Oxford University Press; 1938), pp. 14, 17.

THE ERA OF JOSÉ BATLLE Y ORDÓÑEZ, 1903–29

In no other Latin American republic has one man exercised so profound an influence upon his nation's thought and policies as has José Batlle y Ordóñez. Born in 1856, educated in Montevideo and in Europe, he founded in 1886 the newspaper *El Día,* through which he voiced his opinions for the remaining forty-three years of his life. President from 1903 to 1907, and again from 1911 to 1915, Batlle dominated the *colorado* party— and the life of Uruguay—until his death in 1929, and his influence is still powerful. Batlle was a crusader from the first, intent upon creating "a moral force for the regeneration of the country." Staunch democrat and firm constitutionalist, he persuaded his little nation to embark upon quasi-socialistic economic ventures and to adopt much of the political pattern of Switzerland. In effect a caudillo himself, he proposed to end *caudillismo* in Uruguay. Editorially, he lashed both *blancos* and *colorados.* Nominally a *colorado,* he castigated his party's presidents, demanding honest elections and administration. There was constant danger that his outspoken editorials would bring him imprisonment, exile, or sudden death. He rallied the support of the inarticulate middle class, fortified by European immigrants, and created a body of liberal sentiment within the *colorado* party, forcing cohesion, discipline, and leadership upon it. In 1898 he was elected senator and in 1903, president of the republic.

Inaugurated in early 1903, Batlle was confronted with the senseless division of the nation inherited from the civil war of 1897, with the *blancos* ("nationalists") in control of 6 of the 19 departments, and virtually free from any check by the *colorado* government over which Batlle presided. Although there were no fundamental issues dividing *blancos* and *colorados,* not even any deep rooted dislike, the forces of the opposing factions glowered at each other and armed themselves with more new weapons than any Uruguayan army had previously possessed. The *blanco* guerrilla forces—entrenched in the north and receiving aid and comfort from Brazil —were commanded by the tough and able Aparicio Saravia, the Gaucho chieftain of the *blanco* uprising in 1897. War finally broke out in January, 1904, with savage bloodletting on both sides. After eight months of this ridiculous civil war, Saravia himself was killed. When the news of his death reached Batlle, with tears in his eyes the President murmured, *"Un gaucho bueno. . . ."* With the loss of their most respected leader the *blancos* fell apart and the war was over.

In dictating the terms of the peace, Batlle was as surely animated by a desire for the unity of his country as had been Abraham Lincoln four decades earlier. The *blancos,* who had been fighting for almost complete autonomy for their six departments, now found themselves with no departments at all. Furthermore, Batlle quickly put through a new electoral law, including reallotment of congressional seats among the departments. While paying lip service to the principle of proportional representation implicit in the agreement of 1897,[5] the intricate new law actually worked to the advantage of the *colorados,* assuring *colorado* control of the country in the foreseeable future. The war's end left men of both parties in chastened mood and ready to consider long-overdue economic and social reforms. But the remainder of Batlle's first term was devoted to bringing peace to a now reunited Uruguay.

After turning over the presidential office to a trusted ally in 1907, Batlle sailed for Europe to spend four years of fruitful observation. Switzerland's government made a deep impression upon him: its assignment of executive responsibility to the Bundesrat, or Federal Council, and the subordination of the president suggested a panacea for the ills of *caudillismo* in his own troubled homeland. Its social legislation and national monopolies of railroads, telephones, and hydroelectric power offered further ideas for application in Uruguay.

The campaign for the 1911 presidential election was conducted without the presence of the chief actor: on March 1—just sixteen days after his return from Europe—Batlle was elected for his second term. His prestige was immense: as leader of the *colorados,* he had defeated the *blancos*; as protagonist for social legislation, he had the firm support of the workers; as an eloquent foe of corruption and waste, he had won respect from many outside his own party. He immediately made known his proposals, political and economic, measures so new and drastic that he frightened many within his own party and aroused violent opposition from the *blancos.* Numerous *colorados* withdrew their support and formed the *riveristas* (named after Uruguay's first president, Fructuoso Rivera), who remained the most powerful opposition faction of the *colorado* party, putting up their own candidates and fighting *batllistas* on many issues. However, Batlle, though he left the presidency in 1915, continued to dominate his party, and was the chief mentor of his successors, until his death in 1929.

From the editorial page of *El Día,* Batlle pleaded his case. His terse prose, undecorated with the oratorical trimmings so common to politicians everywhere, drove home his meaning to the simplest citizen. Drawing upon his observation of Swiss democracy in action, and convinced that executive power leads to dictatorship, he urged that Uruguay do away with the office of president and substitute a *colegiado* ("collegiate executive" or National Council) whose membership should be fairly representative of all sectors of political opinion. His suggestion that the nation be ruled "by a committee" rather than by one man was derided. It was debated from 1912 to 1917, when a constitutional convention was assembled to draft an instrument of state to take the place of the outdated Constitution of 1830. The drafters, few of whom favored Batlle's scheme in its entirety, agreed upon a compromise: in the new Constitution of 1917 the presidency was retained,

---

[5] The principle of proportional representation, actually a prime article of faith in Batlle's political philosophy ("the last word in science," he called it), was destined to play a large and sometimes curious role in Uruguay's politics. The basic idea—which has undergone shifting forms—has been that the majority party should control two-thirds, and the leading minority party one-third, of the congressional seats. We shall see how this principle has worked in later elections.

but its powers were limited to administration, foreign relations, and national defense; a nine-member *colegiado* was to have jurisdiction over education, health, commerce, industry, public works, and finance (except for the budget, which was made a presidential responsibility). Free suffrage and fair elections were assured by legislation similar to the Argentine Roque Sáenz Peña law of 1912. The president—formerly chosen by the congress —was to be elected by direct popular vote. Two-thirds of the seats on the *colegiado* were to go to the party with the largest popular vote, and one-third to the leading minority party. The congress and the departmental (state) officers were also to be elected by proportional representation—a device giving both *blancos* and *colorados* a voice in national and provincial decisions. Church and state were completely separated, a measure "enacted without rancor."

Batlle's social and economic program, announced step by step through *El Día,* was radical for its time. He demanded, and won, full freedom of press and speech; effective and free suffrage; compulsory free rural schools, primary and secondary; and university education for women. He made labor's cause his own; insisted upon the right of workers to organize freely and to strike; and argued for and finally won laws providing for the eight-hour day, minimum wages, old-age pensions, compensation for industrial accidents, and the regulation of working conditions. He sponsored and secured high tariffs for the protection of national industry as an offset to "foreign economic imperialism."

His proposals for the active participation of the state in enterprises hitherto handled by private companies excited heated debate throughout his term of office, and after. Some were defeated, but many were adopted before his death in 1929. His bold plans reflected his firm conviction that "modern industry must not be allowed to destroy human beings. The State must regulate it to make more happy the life of the masses." But he did not allow himself to be stampeded by his more radical advisers. Some of his disciples urged expropriation of the great landholdings in order to provide a more equitable sharing of the soil, but Batlle saw its unwisdom: "There is no pressing agrarian problem requiring the attention of the government," he said in 1910; "the division of the landed estates will take place in response to natural forces operating in our rural industries."

In facing foreign investors, he was less restrained. "The sphere of state intervention is expanding in every civilized country," he said in 1911. "Modern conditions have increased the number of industries that fall under the heading of public services. . . . Competition has ceased to mean something invariably beneficial, monopoly is not necessarily condemnable. . . .The modern state unhesitatingly accepts its status as an economic organization. It will enter industry when competition is not practicable, when control by private interests vests in them authority inconsistent with the welfare of the State, when a fiscal monopoly may serve as a great source of income to meet urgent tax problems, when the continued export of national wealth is considered undesirable."[6]

6 *Diario de sesiones de la H. Cámara de Representantes,* 1911, p. 79. Cited by Hanson, *op. cit.,* pp. 24–5.

The Banco de Seguros del Estado (State Insurance Bank), established in early 1912, was the first major excursion of the government into business. The Bank was given the power to write fire, life, and workmen's compensation insurance, but private companies were left free to compete if they could. Its scope was gradually enlarged, and its business grew until in 1934 it was writing two-thirds of the fire insurance, three-fourths of the life and marine insurance, and all the workmen's compensation, as well as various lesser lines in which it held a monopoly. The results were spotty. Administration was honest and efficient, but British, American, and other foreign companies argued that settlements were less generous than those offered by old-line companies. Furthermore, the government's insurance agency had the unfair advantage of tax exemptions denied commercial companies. After taking into account the loss of taxes to the nation, Hanson concludes that the nation was "losing considerable revenue on its four-fifths of the insurance business." Nor did the people benefit by lower rates. In the final reckoning, the measure was neither the dismal failure its enemies had prophesied, nor the brilliant success its author had predicted.

Other projects followed in rapid succession. In 1912 a government monopoly company took over the light and power business of the nation. Service improved and rates were lowered in Montevideo, but the extension of its facilities to other parts of the republic was slow. Then Batlle sought to create a government-owned railway system. The 1,800 miles of tracks were owned by the British, but in 1915 the government bought 220 miles of the lines. The government failed to lower rates, and the project was not generally popular. However, in 1948 the government completed the purchase of all the British railways.

In 1916 the government installed a state corporation to manage the port facilities of Montevideo; by cutting rates for lighterage and stevedore service, the measure encouraged commerce, but the experiment brought continued deficits to the state. After 1911, by successive steps, the National Bank (Banco de la República Oriental del Uruguay) was brought completely under government control, and its functions were enlarged to include rural credit and small savings accounts. In 1912 a State Mortgage Bank was added. State control of banking brought a lowering of interest rates, extension of banking services to outlying towns, and substantial profits to the national treasury. In 1928 a nationally owned packing house, a project long urged by Batlle, was opened as a check upon the foreign companies operating plants in Uruguay; but the enterprise was not well administered. The municipality of Montevideo even went into the hotel business, and it still owns and operates three of the largest tourist hotels on the outskirts of the city.

These innovations, while working no miracles for the average citizen, were not failures. The public corporations charged with responsibility for these various undertakings were usually directed by men of probity who resisted both political pressures and exorbitant labor demands, and often returned a modest profit to the national treasury. One of the most common criticisms of the directors was that they showed more zeal for profit than for extending service to the less privileged regions of the republic.

Although embarked on what was essentially a socialistic program, executives tended toward a conservative caution which commended itself to many who feared radical innovations. Batlle, the inspirer of these projects, got much of what he wanted, but all his plans were greatly modified by the pressure of the opposition. This was a fortunate check upon Batlle's rashness, for he had, says Hanson, "a weakness for trying out new ideas. . . . He was inclined to propose innovations without working out the details of enforcement and without considering if the experiment was suited to the peculiar Uruguayan conditions."

One vexing result of these quasi-socialistic measures was to discourage entrance of foreign capital. Nevertheless, the conservative British *South American Journal* had to admit in 1936: "Compared with the average return which British investors have received on the money placed in the Latin American countries, their experience in Uruguay is fortunate. . . . The return is, and practically always has been, relatively greater than in any other country of Latin America."[7]

THE COLORADOS AFTER THE DEATH
OF BATLLE, 1929–58

Batlle's reforms did not create an economic paradise. They failed to satisfy those on the left, who mourned that he did not subdivide the great *estancias* and make farm homes for thousands of families from Europe. They antagonized conservatives, who deplored the check upon foreign capital and resented attack upon private enterprise. The moderate success of the state monopoly companies was due to the prosperity of the 1920's, when almost any business made money. The test finally came with the world depression after 1929, when the nations of the world cut their buying and prices plummeted. Uruguay, lacking any sizable industrial development, and dependent upon the sale of wool, hides, and meat, was at the mercy of world markets in which prices were not set for the protection of weak nations.

In 1930, when the national economy was thus beset, Gabriel Terra was elected president.[8] A conservative *colorado* who had opposed many

7 Quoted by Hanson, *op. cit.,* p. 186.

8 Terra, representing only one faction of the *colorado* party, received fewer votes than the *blanco,* Luis Alberto de Herrera. Terra's victory is explained by a curious quirk in the Uruguayan electoral law called the "law of the *lema,*" according to which "two or more political parties could agree to use the same *lema* [party label or title] during elections. In the case of elections of presidents of the nation, in the days before the *colegiado,* this meant that the adherents of one presidential candidate could use the same *lema* as the followers of another presidential candidate. With their united votes they could beat another candidate who alone had more adherents than either of the other two. If this law had existed in the United States, it would have meant that Wilson would never have become president in 1912—if Taft and Roosevelt had used a right laid down in a *lema* law to unite their votes under the same *lema* and let the fight between them be decided by the number of votes cast for either *sublema*. It is almost as if the primary election were combined with the general election. Thus, let us say, if all the Blanco parties together get more votes than all the Colorado parties together, the Blanco candidate with more votes than his rivals

of Batlle's reforms, Terra faced strong opposition not only from the *blancos* but also from some *colorados* who wanted to speed up the program of socialization. Terra was able to maintain himself in office by making a pact with the militant *blanco* leader, Luis Alberto de Herrera, whom he rewarded by giving jobs to his numerous cohorts. Even this opportunistic compromise finally proved unworkable: Herrera was on the point of engineering a coup in 1933 when Terra forestalled him by dissolving Congress and the *colegiado* and assuming a moderate dictatorial rule. In 1934 Terra called a constitutional convention, which drafted a new constitution doing away with the controversial *colegiado* and concentrating executive power in the presidency. Batlle's voice, however, was far from stilled: all of his social legislation was accepted, his state corporations continued, and proportional representation of the two major parties in the new congress and the president's cabinet was retained. Terra's rule, extended by another term in 1934, was one of the gentler despotisms. Communists and other left-wing agitators were handled somewhat roughly, but there was only fitful interference with freedom of speech and press. Terra was illiberal in temper, but Uruguay's schooling under Batlle was not forgotten.

During the years after 1938, when Terra's brother-in-law, the *colorado* Alfredo Baldomir, was installed as president, there was a definite return to the Batlle tradition. Baldomir revived the *colegiado,* insisted upon full freedom for the press, and safeguarded free elections. In 1951 Uruguay's fidelity to the Batlle program of government was given dramatic proof when President Andrés Martínez Trueba proposed the outright abolition of the president's office, leaving the *colegiado* as the sole executive body. In December, 1951, the citizens accepted this innovation by a national plebiscite, and the republic was ruled by the nine-man council. Not all was sweet concord, however. The *blanco* party, refuge of die-hard conservatives, used its minority position[9] to fight all legislation sponsored by Batlle's disciples and to check their more impulsive measures. The lack of leadership was soon felt, and important decisions were often deadlocked.

Meanwhile, after 1938, the most obstinate issue dividing *blancos* and *colorados* was foreign policy. The *blancos* had long been dominated by Luis Alberto Herrera, whose admiration for Hitler, Mussolini, and Franco— and later Argentina's Perón—was as intense as his dislike of Great Britain

---

becomes president, even if one of the Colorado candidates has more individual votes." Goran G. Lindahl: "Uruguay: Government by Institutions," in Martin C. Needler, ed.: *Political Systems of Latin America* (Princeton: D. Van Nostrand Co. Inc.; 1964). As the *colorados* became more and more splintered, the *blancos* consolidated behind Herrera, and in two other elections, those of 1946 and 1950, Herrera won more popular votes than any single candidate; but, by the *lema* law, the victory in 1946 went to Tomás Berreta, and in 1950 to Andrés Martínez Trueba—each of whom represented only one faction of the *colorado* party.

9 The new *colegiado* retained Batlle's principle of proportional representation, with 6 of the 9 seats going to the party winning the majority of the popular votes, and the remaining 3 going to the leading minority party. The presidency of the *colegiado* was to rotate each year among the council members of the majority party.

and the United States.[1] He was a clerical extremist, hated by the *colorados* and distrusted by many of the Catholic clergy and laity for whom he presumed to speak. Under his leadership the *blancos* had supported Terra, applauding his praise of Franco in Spain; but they had violently opposed Baldomir when he showed clear sympathy for the Allied cause upon the outbreak of World War II in 1939, when he granted naval and air bases to the United States in 1941, and when he broke relations with the Axis in January, 1942, after Pearl Harbor. Baldomir's successor continued to antagonize the *blancos* by declaring war on the Axis in 1945.

Uruguay's chief international concern during the years 1944–55 was the constant threat to its free institutions from the strong-arm government of Juan Domingo Perón. Like his earlier prototype, Juan Manuel de Rosas, Perón cherished the dream of gathering together the scattered segments of the colonial Viceroyalty of La Plata in an Argentine sphere of influence. When Uruguay made it clear that she did not care to be a satellite of Argentina, Perón retaliated by blocking shipments of wheat and petroleum and by restricting the passage of tourists who had long contributed to the Uruguayan economy. The United States, through shipments of wheat and the extension of loans, helped the nation meet that attempt at coercion. Meanwhile, Perón's agents flooded Uruguay with *peronista* propaganda. There was no truckling to Perón; Uruguay continued to receive fugitives from that strong man's wrath and her newspapers reported faithfully and competently on events in Argentina. This brave independence reflected the stout spirit of democracy in the little republic, and it was fortified by the stand of the spokesmen of the American nations at the conference at Chapultepec in 1945; there it was clearly stated that the republics of the New World would unite their forces to meet aggression against any one of them—a declaration inspired by Uruguay. Argentina's retaliatory measures against Uruguay continued and increased; until Perón fell in 1955 it was almost impossible for an Argentine citizen to visit the Banda Oriental.

Perón's bedevilment of the Uruguayans led to better understanding with the United States. The agreement for mutual military aid, proposed by Washington, after being blocked for months by the opposition of Herrera and his die-hard *blancos,* was finally ratified in 1953. Uruguayans were fast forgetting the harsh appraisal of the United States in which they had been tutored by their greatest writer, José Enrique Rodó. In 1900 that brilliant essayist wrote *Ariel,* which has been sacred writ for generations of youth in Uruguay (and elsewhere in Latin America), and which relegated the North Americans to the unflattering role of Caliban—symbol of base materialism—in contrast to Latin America's Ariel—symbol of spirituality. Rodó assailed the United States for its efforts to win a "moral conquest" of the Americas. But by 1954 it became clear that as between the United States and Perón's Argentina, it was safer to trust the northern power.

By the late 1950's Uruguayans were sharply reminded that, with the shadow of Juan Domingo Perón safely banished, their fundamental prob-

[1] When the Japanese attacked Pearl Harbor on December 7, 1941, Herrera reportedly remarked: "We don't care whether the little yellow men beat the United States."

lem was the shaky economy of their little land. The price of wool, the commodity which had long furnished more than half their export revenue, had sunk steadily after World War II, dragging down the entire national economy with it. Quarreling politicians could not halt the inflation, with spiraling prices which in turn incited strikes for ever larger wages. Indicative of the weakness of the economy was the decline in the value of the peso, worth 50 American cents in 1950, but down to 7 cents by 1958. The collapse of the national currency was disastrous for all the socialistic state enterprises, whose success was dependent upon steady national income and stable money. The elaborate social-security system, with its generous provisions against accidents, sickness, and old age, was severely crippled as the peso depreciated. A victim of the economic collapse was the meat-packing industry, whose shipments had long accounted for almost 20 per cent of export revenue. American-owned *frigoríficos* (packing houses) of Swift and Armour, after losing money for several years, finally closed down in November, 1957, throwing 12,000 men out of work. The government took over these enterprises and united them into a cooperative, but it too lost money. Meanwhile, the state-owned national *frigorífico*—one of the Batlle projects —had a deficit every year, and was not even paying for cattle delivered by stockmen. A large factor in the bankruptcy of the meat-packing business was the activity of smugglers, who drove herds of cattle across the northern border into Brazil, where prices were higher and there were fewer controls —estimates on this contraband trading ran as high as 350,000 head of cattle each year. By 1959 there was such a shortage in Uruguay that beef was imported from Argentina.

THE BLANCOS IN POWER, 1958–67

The election in November, 1958, brought a revolution of sorts to Uruguay: the *colorados,* who had exercised almost undisputed control for ninety-three years, were decisively routed by the *blancos,* who thus won 6 of the 9 seats in the *colegiado* and a majority in the Congress. It was a crushing defeat for Luis Batlle Berres, leader of the *colorado* party, who had carried the banner for the ideals of his uncle, José Batlle, for more than a decade. The charges against the *colorados* were strident but justified: they had overspent, burdening the country with debt; they had refused to impose needed austerity upon the economy; they had loaded down the payrolls of state enterprises with superfluous employees; they were increasingly guilty of inefficiency and graft in the administration of state agencies; they had continued to liberalize the social security system, until many thousands of citizens in their fifties—and some even in their forties—were permitted to draw pensions in idleness; they had continued to subsidize beef, transportation, fuels, and luxury imports—fostering habits of consumption that the nation could ill afford; and they had given a clear green light to labor unions and their exorbitant demands. The *blancos,* long the spokesmen for the most conservative landholders, the bankers, the high clergy, and the chief businessmen, won the contest by promising to clean out the grafters and easy spenders, to spur lagging agricultural and live-stock production, and to restore the value of the peso. That last argument was all-powerful, as many thousands received pensions now worth only about one-fifth of their original value. The victory of the *blancos* was a personal triumph for eighty-five-year-old Luis Alberto de Herrera, but that veteran, after his half-century battle against the *colorados,* was not to taste the joys of victory: he died in April, 1959, just one month after his party had assumed control of the government.

With the death of Herrera, a new leader appeared: Benito Nardone, ambitious and erratic, son of an Italian immigrant, who had been a con-servative *colorado* until the mid-1950's, when he switched his allegiance and joined the *blancos.* Although a city man himself, born and raised in Montevideo (his father was a longshoreman), Nardone was a vigorous spokesman for the rural population of the country. He voiced the bitter anger of the men who worked the farms and pastures of the nation as opposed to the power of the capital city. For years he had broadcast a chatty radio program to the farmers, winning their hearts with such folksy observations as: "A pretty gal who works hard on a farm deserves a pretty dress to step out in as much as a city girl. We cannot keep on letting all the money come here to Montevideo so that a few can throw it away at roulette tables." Elected to the *colegiado* in the *blanco* landslide of 1958, Nardone continued, until his death in 1964, to be the country's most articulate spokesman for free enterprise and against Communism and the welfare state. Upon assuming office he promised: "The days of the robbers are over," and prescribed hard work and sound money as the cure for Uruguay's ills.

But "the days of the robbers" were far from over, "sound money" proved an elusive dream, and "hard work" had become almost foreign to the Uruguayan way of life. As the opposition party for almost a century, the *blancos* lacked practical experience in government, and they were soon uneasily aware that it was one thing to shout their disapproval from the sidelines, and quite another to direct the course of the people's fortunes from positions of power. Given a clear mandate in 1958 to set their country's house in order, the *blancos* proved quite unequal to the task. After their reelection by a narrow margin in 1962, the president of the council, Faustino Harrison, voiced the general mood when he announced that he would not deliver the customary New Year's address as there were only *cosas tristes* (sad things) to report. Indeed, *cosas tristes* continued to plague the *blancos* throughout two terms of office; and the affairs of the little nation were more chaotic in 1967 than they had been in 1958.

Faced with the crippling debts bequeathed them by the *colorados,* the new government was further confounded by the worst floods in the nation's history, which ravaged the countryside early in 1959; crops and livestock were seriously damaged, causing food shortages and decreasing export earnings; roads, bridges, and rail lines were washed out; the Rincon del Bonete hydroelectric plant, the country's chief source of electric power, was partly destroyed. In this atmosphere of crisis, with foreign exchange reserves dwindling and the trade deficit at an all-time high, Uruguay's harassed leaders looked for financial help to the United States and the International Monetary Fund, whose role in shaping the government's proposed economic reforms was bitterly resented by the *colorados,* who shouted their "outraged nationalism." The much-heralded stabilization program was finally launched in January, 1960: the peso was devalued; multiple exchange rates were scrapped (a reform which worked to the benefit of the farmers); and consumer subsidies and import privileges were removed. But the plea for "austerity"—companion piece to monetary reform—fell on deaf ears. As prices soared, the workers demanded commensurate wage hikes, and usually got them: the *blancos*—who had made a campaign issue of the recurrent strikes during the *colorado* administration—were faced with the same problem. Strike followed strike, month after month, year after year, with oppressive monotony. There were repeated strikes by the municipal workers, paralyzing the capital for days at a time. The newspapers went on strike in protest against the lifting of the subsidy on newsprint and ink. Industrial workers walked out from time to time, demanding not only pay increases up to 72 per cent, but also increased social security benefits. Teachers and students quit, demanding that a larger slice of the national budget be earmarked for education. Strikes in the meat-packing industry caused wasteful spoilage and disastrous delays in fulfilling foreign contracts. On one occasion the public utilities workers walked out demanding a salary increase of 94 per cent; when the government called in the armed forces to run the telephone and electric services, one rude observer pointed out that 1,000 army men were quite able to do the job of the 12,000 emloyees regularly engaged in the plants. As treasury funds were depleted and salaries fell into arrears, government workers struck for back pay. The teachers, at one point, threatened to strike regularly if their paychecks were not received by the tenth of each month. And strikes in the city transport system finally became a monthly tradition. Some pensioners, in the same mood, wistfully observed that the only strike possible for them would be a hunger strike—in which they were already involuntarily engaged, due to the nonpayment of their monthly checks.

In May, 1961, the *blanco* government announced "Operation Uruguay," a ten-year plan for social and economic development drafted with the help of an OAS mission under the Alliance for Progress. Financial help from abroad was, of course, essential to the program. But the ambivalence of Uruguayans in the matter of foreign aid was dramatized at the Punta del Este Conference launching the Alliance for Progress in August, 1961. Council President Eduardo Víctor Haedo, as chief dignitary of the host nation, welcomed the delegates with these words: "Those who think we are gathering here in a beggarly attitude are mistaken. We all feel capable of continuing the fight for democracy and the betterment of our peoples even without this conference." Whereupon the Uruguayan delegates hastened to outline projects—including the construction and improvement of housing, highways, schools, and power plants—requiring immediately some $200 million, which, they said, Uruguay would be happy to receive in the form of fifty-year loans at low interest, or even no interest at all. . . . The *blanco* government made repeated efforts to secure bounty from the international agencies—primarily the International Monetary Fund and the United States treasury. Some grants and loans were made, but Uruguay increasingly failed to live up to the conditions that were imposed, and the renewal of loans became more and more difficult.

Efforts of the government to halt inflation were futile. All but 3 of the 22 government business enterprises—including railroads, telephones, power systems, meat-packing plants, cement plants, and an oil refinery— operated at a loss. A government economic survey in 1963 warned that the costly welfare system was far beyond Uruguay's means unless production and exports could be increased. Investment capital, necessary to any development program, was in short supply—the ever-present threat of currency devaluation caused irresponsible and unprecedented flight of capital from the country, and the chronic labor unrest and general chaos held little attraction for the foreign investor. The government, desperate in the face of steadily dwindling funds, resorted from time to time to the printing of paper pesos, which added to the spiraling inflation. Efforts to improve taxation procedures were of no avail: an income tax was put on the books (effective in July, 1961) for the first time in history, but this affront to solid Uruguayan citizens was largely ignored. In June, 1963, the government lured the delinquent taxpayer by a moratorium on penalties, and announced that import permits in the future would be restricted to those who had met their tax obligations. But even these measures failed: tax evasion in 1964 was estimated at some 65 per cent. Furthermore, there was no effective control of smuggling, which became a major business enterprise, crippling local industries and causing staggering losses to the national treasury. Cheap textiles were brought in from Brazil, causing a slowdown in local textile mills; and there was a constant deluge of goods smuggled across the Río de la Plata—cigarettes, liquor, television sets, and all manner of necessary and unnecessary items. It has been estimated that in some years as much as one-fourth of all imports came into the country illegally. And there was smuggling out of, as well as into, the country. Cattle continued to be driven across the lightly patrolled northern border into Brazil, where they would bring higher prices. Sheep were herded to Brazil for shearing, in order to avoid the high export duties on wool.

As the economy worsened, there were periodic rumors of a military coup, which was angrily denied by citizens who believed stoutly—and with much justification—that military coups were quite un-Uruguayan. The *blancos,* looking for a scapegoat, blamed their failure on the clumsy *colegiado* system which they had inherited from the *colorados,* claiming that it had deprived the country of responsible leadership. Divided as they were within their own ranks on almost every issue, the *blancos* were single-minded in their determination to restore presidential rule. In barring *caudillismo,* they said, the *colegiado* system had simply assembled all of the would-be caudillos into one body, which was, according to one observer, "like a small senate complete with filibustering." One after another *blanco* leader worked for constitutional reform which would change the system—each one usually offering to resign his place on the Council in order to run for president. Benito Nardone proposed the change even before 1958; Eduardo Víctor Haedo (president of the Council 1961–62) complained that in his travels abroad he was unable to speak for his government; and in June, 1965, Washington Beltrán, the *blanco* president of the Council, announced his intention to abolish the "rule by committee," and restore the presidency to its former prestige. The *colegiado,* or National Council, he said, was "a well-intentioned experiment that has become totally inoperative and each day increases our administrative anarchy." And so it had. But, with the majority of the seats held by the *colorados* from 1951 to 1958, and by the *blancos* after 1958, it was not a party failure: the *blancos* were as feckless as the *colorados*. Under each party political control was a grab bag affair, as appointments were made on the basis of party merit. It was not even a clear contest of principle between the two parties, as there was constant shifting of position among the *blancos* themselves, as well as among the *colorados*. It was impossible to win a united stand for wiser fiscal measures, so desperately needed. Perhaps all might have gone well if the "nine wise men" had been wiser and a bit more competent. But the *colegiado* gained the reputation of being a "debating society," indulging in endless haggling over details, and vote-trading was the rule.

The mood of crisis deepened in 1965. The government was forced to announce, early in the year, that the treasury was exhausted, payrolls could not be met, and no more foreign exchange was available to importers. Then came a series of multi-millon-peso bank swindles involving officials of the Banco de la República which shook the financial and economic structure and further weakened the international position of the peso. The government was forced to default on scheduled payments of some $80 million on the foreign debt, which had soared to an unprecedented high. (It was estimated by some to be as high as $600 million—but, as *The Economist* of London observed, so great was the financial confusion that even the directors of the state bank did not know just what the figure was.) In July, the Council asked Congress for authority to print up to 5.6 billion new pesos—a third again as many as the 4.2 billion already in circulation. There were angry protests from the citizenry—in one demonstration a group of students distributed caricatures of the paper money, picturing the finance minister with a hole in his head and bearing the inscription "ten pieces of paper, payable to the swindled bearer." The congress authorized the printing of a mere 1.7 billion new pesos, which the finance minister scoffed at as "barely enough to cover our needs until September." In August, a delegation of Uruguayan officials descended upon New York to lay their predicament before a number of private banks. They then went to Washington, and presented their case to the World Bank, the International Monetary Fund, the Inter-American

Development Bank, and the Inter-American Committee for the Alliance for Progress. The case was clear: Uruguay was bankrupt. And it was also clear that further credits would not be forthcoming unless Uruguay could put a more effective rein on her economy. In addition to other woes, the year 1965 brought a severe drought which took its toll of grain and cattle.

When, in the fall of 1965, Beltrán announced a new ten-year economic program drafted with the help of the Alliance for Progress, it sounded at first like an old record. But this time there seemed to be a difference. Beltrán was determined upon a hard-line policy, and managed to unite the other five *blanco* members of the Council behind him. Social security was to be reorganized, there were to be further restrictions on imports, a massive drive for increased agricultural production for export, and the peso was devalued for the fifth time since 1958—this time from a basic rate of 24 pesos to the dollar to 59.90, drastic medicine for a people who had long regarded their currency as sound. Furthermore, the government, for the first time in history, took a firm stand against the inflationary demands of labor. A ceiling of 25 per cent was put on wage increases over the next year; strikes were declared illegal; and the country was placed under a mild state of siege—the first in twenty years. The orders aroused angry protests from the unions, and the battle lines were drawn. The fall of 1965 brought a new wave of strikes called in defiance of the emergency measures; and the armed forces were called in to operate the public services as civil servants staged intermittent walkouts during a three-month period. Hundreds of union leaders and demonstrators were arrested, and newspapers inciting the workers to strike were threatened with censorship. Such suspension of constitutional guarantees outraged democracy-proud Uruguayans.

Mid-1966 brought a little relief. Drastic restrictions on credit had slowed down the reckless purchases of imported goods such as automobiles and television sets. There was a more hopeful mood and the reluctant International Monetary Fund, which had denied help to Uruguay six months before, in June, 1966, granted a credit of $15 million—small in relation to the dire needs of the Uruguayan economy, but immensely stimulating to the beleaguered bankers and economists who were seeking a way out for their prostrate country. Furthermore, there was an upturn in the sales of wool, and meat exports increased a little. Also, the tourist season of 1965–66 had brought more Argentines across the Río de la Plata, and their spending had done much to offset the costly smuggling for which the Uruguayan officials have discovered no cure. In short, the financial climate had improved so greatly that the flow of foreign money to Uruguayan banks had been resumed.

In November, 1966, a national election was held which combined a thorough overhauling of the constitutional system with the naming of a president for a five-year term. The results of the vote were drastic: the Batlle *colegiado* was abandoned after fifteen years' trial; the provision giving the minority party proportional representation was canceled; and although these were reforms which the *blancos* had long demanded, and although the *blancos* had been largely responsible for some economic recovery in 1966, the *blancos* themselves were roundly defeated. A retired sixty-five-year-old air force general named Oscar Gestido, a *colorado*, was elected president for a five-year term. This radical overturn in Uruguay's political system was generally hailed with satisfaction. General Gestido was inaugurated on March 1, 1967, amid widespread optimism that, with the retirement of the awkward *colegiado,* the new government could cope more forcefully with the continuing scourge of inflation, labor unrest, and the incompetence of the state enterprises.

The first six months of General Gestido's administration brought no miracles. The honest president still had to deal with politicians, and the *colorado* breed were no more tractable than the *blanco.* And public confidence was crumbling as crippling strikes continued, political clamor increased, inflation persisted, and financial crises became more serious. Some gloomy observers expressed fear that the Communists, who held strong power in the labor unions (with perhaps 400,000 Communist members) might stage some manner of leftist coup—but thoughtful Uruguayans considered it likely that Uruguay would remain faithful to its historic constitutional course.

The outlook for Uruguay, as of September, 1967, was bleak. The facts were sobering. Inflation was riding high—at a rate close to 100 per cent for the year 1967. The New York bankers were due to collect $65 million on short term notes before the year's end—a sum which could be paid only by drawing upon the nation's almost exhausted gold reserves. The trade exhibit was dismal—sales of meat, wool, hides, and wheat were expected to drop by $40 million from 1966's figure of $186 million. Meanwhile labor, crushed by ever higher living costs, was demanding increases of 70, 80, and even 90 per cent. And the staggering social welfare program was fighting a losing battle to provide the benefits to the growing army of citizens entitled to aid. (See note p. 811.)

Uruguay's relations with other countries steadily deteriorated after 1958. We have noted the pleasantness which had marked relations with the United States when the northern republic took sides with Uruguay against Perón before 1955. But, as the economy of Uruguay broke down, resentment was revived against the United States, which was increasingly identified with the IMF demands for austerity. Uruguay, while quite ready to accept grants and loans from outsiders, took umbrage at suggestions from those outsiders that she put her own national economy in order—that, said the Uruguayans, was interference. Furthermore, as Castroism became an inter-American issue after 1959, Uruguay resisted pressure from the United States and the OAS to crack down on Cuba. There were sporadic demonstrations in favor of Fidel, reflecting the fact that there were substantial numbers of Castroites and Communists in Uruguay—but also suggesting that Uruguayan nationalists wished to use the Castro issue to slap the United States. The Uruguayan delegate to the OAS conference in July, 1964, while agreeing to condemn Cuban aggression, voted against imposing sanctions. However, two months later, Uruguay finally yielded to pressure from within and without and reluctantly severed diplomatic relations with Cuba. A further weakening of Uruguay's friendly relations with the United States came in 1965 in protest against Washington's unilateral handling of the Dominican crisis.

Meanwhile Uruguay's relations with her immediate neighbors followed an irregular course. There was a hopeful improvement in relations with Argentina when a long-standing conflict over boundary questions in the Río de la Plata area was peacefully settled in May, 1964. But relations with Brazil were troubled when deposed João Goulart and his brother-in-law, Leonel Brizola, together with numerous hangers-on, sought asylum in Uruguay in April, 1964. This unhappiness grew as refugees from Brazil continued to cross the border into Uruguay. But in January, 1965, the National Council voted to deny political asylum to two prominent members of the Goulart regime, and it became clear that Uruguay had no desire to serve as the launching pad for any plot against Brazil's Castello Branco. When Uruguay's financial troubles reached their peak in August, 1965, both Brazil and Argentina expressed willingness to give what help they could to their neighbor. However, as these two nations had their own economic troubles aplenty, there was little they could do but use their influence with the United States to the end that Uruguay's problems might have an early resolution.

Uruguay has little affection for Soviet Russia, although relations have been outwardly cordial. When President de Gaulle of France, visiting Montevideo in October, 1964, advised the Uruguayans to remain aloof from the cold war between the United States and Russia, he was politely reminded that Uruguay's fortunes were linked to the United States. And from time to time the Council expressed its discontent over the flamboyant propaganda campaign carried on by the Soviet Embassy in Montevideo, which had become a chief center for the distribution of propaganda in southern South America. Largely as a backlash against the flood of strikes, generally described as Communist-inspired, which had brought on open war between the government and the labor unions in late 1965, there was some talk of expelling the Russian Embassy and banning the Communist Party—but public sentiment was against such measures. The Uruguayans, no matter how upset their economy might be, clung to the conviction that all citizens, including the Communists, should be allowed to speak their minds.

APPRAISAL: 1967

A baffling nation, this. The general applause for Uruguay's democratic prowess has been deafening. While other republics flounder, Uruguay is praised for making democracy work. Votes are counted. The will of the people is reflected in national decisions. The citizenry is protected by an impressive system of social security: no one starves in Uruguay. Montevideo is the one large city in South America which has no rotting slums. In fact, the visitor to that capital city is impressed by the monotony of the social landscape: there is neither flagrant poverty nor flagrant ostentation. Communities for rich and poor look very much alike—not until one gets into the back country is this illusion shattered. Unlike most of her neighbors, Uruguay indulges in no riotous overproduction of babies: the annual increase in population is only 1.4 per cent. The press is free. The schools are good, and the literacy score is second only to Argentina in all Latin America. In short, there is "Utopia in Uruguay"—almost. In this atmosphere of euphoria, some may pray that if Heaven is denied them, they might at least be admitted to Uruguay.

But the buoyancy has been pricked. Flat broke in the 1960's, the little nation's messengers arrived in New York and Washington, presented their balance sheets speckled with red ink, and asked the bankers and the international lending concerns to bail them out. The spectacle was grim. After fifty years of democracy and full stomachs, the fine dreams of José Batlle were fading.

Politically, as of 1967, Uruguay was a question mark. The governmental pattern designed by Batlle had been discarded. A duly elected president—Oscar Gestido—was in office, endowed with ample power and prestige. Would he be able to unite his *colorado* associates into a working team? Would he be able to persuade the *blancos* to assume the role of "loyal opposition"? Could he quiet the clamor of labor without denying them their rights? Could he instill in the citizenry a new sense of common purpose?

Economically, the new president had troubles aplenty. "This country is in a mess," Gestido had told the voters in his election campaign, "but with common sense we can straighten it out." Mr. Gestido had not overstated the matter. Wages and salaries were far in arrears. For years Uruguay had been living beyond her means, selling too little and buying too much—there had been an almost continuous trade deficit for over a decade. Attempts at industrialization to reduce imports offered slight hope: the limited market made mass production impractical, costs were high, and management was ineffective. Furthermore, the new industries themselves needed foreign raw materials and equipment for their very survival, which placed an extra burden on imports (to say nothing of the expensive cars and television sets the people demanded). Just at a time when it was crucial for Uruguay to sell more on the world market, per capita exports, which had stood at about $94 annually before World War II, had dropped to about $70 in 1965. While in the early 1940's Uruguay exported almost half of its wool, meat, and hides, by 1960 this share fell to just over one-quarter. Wool, traditionally Uruguay's chief export, suffered not only from overproduction but from lessening world demand, as synthetic fibers were increasingly substituted for wool. The revenue from tourists, chiefly Argentine, has long been an important reliance for foreign exchange. But this tourist trade, discouraged by political and economic dislocations both in Argentina and in Uruguay, has failed to rally to the pre-Perón level. On the score of meat, the Uruguayans (among the largest meat eaters in the world) stepped up their own consumption of this prime exportable item, but did little to spur production, which has not increased appreciably in more than a decade. (It takes just twice as long to get a steer to market in Uruguay as it does in the United States.) It is estimated that improved techniques in the care of pastures plus a modest investment for silos and winter shelter for cattle could double beef production—but the son of the Gaucho has yet to display such foresight. Economic growth in any sector depends upon investment: but from 1955 to 1961 Uruguay consumed 87 per cent of its national income, leaving a scant 13 per cent for investment, almost half of which was put into unproductive dwellings—a significant element in the collapse of the country's economy.

The public payrolls were still overloaded in 1967: government agencies and the state-owned corporations, under constant pressure from labor unions and politicians to take care of their hangers-on, indulged in "make-work," multiplying jobs without regard to efficiency. The one-fourth of the nation's workers with government jobs led an easy life: holidays were plentiful and hours short—in summer the regular quitting time was 1 P.M., which made possible long afternoons on the beaches. Furthermore, the workers were well protected in their jobs: firing a public employee involved action by the Senate. (Private employees also, in effect, had tenure, due to the prohibitive severance pay guaranteed them.)

Of course, the elaborate social security measures rooted in the Batlle philosophy were blamed for much of the economic ills of the nation. Year after year, under pressure from various sectors, the provisions had been made more generous: unemployment insurance, old-age insurance, free medical care—the Uruguayan was theoretically protected against almost every untoward turn of fate from the cradle to the grave. By 1967, rough estimates indicated that for every two and one-half wage earners, one was retired in his fifties, or even his forties—often at full pay (even more in some instances, as the pensioner was released from most taxes). And as the average age of Uruguayans increased (due to the low birth rate and increase in life expectancy), the percentage of the population living on pensions (about 11 per cent in 1965) steadily went up. Thus, as pensions for more and more pensioners were adjusted to rising living costs, the burden on the workers increased, until between 28 per cent and 36 per cent of the average pay check was collected by the government in an attempt to pay the cost. This, in turn, brought repeated demands from the workers for higher wages—and the inflationary spiral was complete. But for all the generosity of this social security program, it was so badly administered that those entitled to pensions often had to spend months—or even years—sitting in line, filling out forms, blocked by bungling public servants, before getting the money to which they were legally entitled. (These delays, however, were often avoided by the payment of a *coima,* or bribe.)[2] By 1967, due to lack of funds as well as sloppy administration, payments on many

---

[2] One collector of stories on these unfortunate aspects of the welfare system tells of a man who had spent practically every day for several years sitting in line at the social security office. When at last he got his pension, the old man was so dependent upon the sociability of the waiting line, that he continued to go to the office each day.

of these social security accounts were seriously in arrears. The moral of the tale seems clear: the success of an economic paradise such as that envisioned by Batlle and his disciples depends upon economic programs wisely administered, thrift, and hard work—and an actuarial regard for the future.

Of all the Latin American republics, Uruguay shows the least fidelity to the Church. The Uruguayans are not noisy in their anticlericalism, but rather they seem quite indifferent; they do not persecute priests, they ignore them. This lack of allegiance to the Church is partially explained by the fact that the Spanish colonization of this area came late: the city of Montevideo was not founded until 1726; while the more devoutly religious countries such as Colombia, Peru, and Mexico were shaped during the sixteenth and seventeenth centuries. Another important factor in fixing agnosticism upon Uruguay was the influence of José Batlle y Ordóñez, who definitely disliked the Church, and whose newspaper, *El Día,* has always been frankly anticlerical. Batlle was responsible for the severing of all ties between Church and state, and for banning churchmen from any share in the conduct of the schools. As a result, the Catholic sector of the population is small. There is a Catholic newspaper, *El Bien Público,* but its circulation is the smallest of the newspapers of Montevideo. One rather ludicrous indication of the Uruguayan attitude toward the Church is the official changing of Holy Week into "the week of tourism," and the banishing of the word "Christmas" in favor of "the day of the family." (The Uruguayans, however, continue to wish each other a "Merry Christmas.")

Uruguay escapes one scourge which is common to almost all Latin American countries—the disastrous interference of the military in government affairs. The small Uruguayan army is, and almost always has been, completely professional. Military *coups d'état* are not a way of life in the Banda Oriental.

A continuing problem is that there are two Uruguays—not one. One is Montevideo, with almost half the population, with most of the social services and privileges of civilization. The other Uruguay is the back country, where life is ragged and mean, with the poorest of schools and the most meager facilities for health and welfare.

Numerous writers fasten the label of "Switzerland of South America" upon Uruguay. A charming idea—but the label must be unstuck. True, Uruguay and Switzerland are alike on several counts: both are small (Uruguay has about four and a half times the area of Switzerland, but only half as many people): both lack important mineral wealth; and both have experimented boldly with state socialism under a political system which subordinates the presidency to a council of state. Both Switzerland and Uruguay have been havens for fugitive capital: the numerous Uruguayan banks have provided shelters in their dollar accounts for runaway money from all Latin America. But the contrasts are far more numerous. Switzerland is crowded, with 379 persons to each square mile, while

Uruguay has but 38. Switzerland is a highly industrialized country; Uruguay depends almost entirely on the products of the soil. Switzerland's per capita national income is almost four times that of Uruguay. Switzerland has (as of the end of 1966) gold and foreign exchange reserves of some $3.3 billion; Uruguay has only $196 million.

Consider the history of the two nations. Switzerland—a federation of twenty-five independent cantons, each retaining its sovereign rights but yielding to the central government authority over foreign affairs—took shape over a period of six centuries. In this gradually assembled federation, the citizens developed a tradition of orderly self-government and a stout distaste for wars. There was little fighting after the early sixteenth century (aside from the disturbances of the Napoleonic days), and since 1815 no warring at all—except for a minuscule civil war in 1848. Remaining aloof from the world's battles in the nineteenth and twentieth centuries, Switzerland perfected her political system quite unmarred by incompetence and dishonesty, embarked upon quasi-socialist adventures in government ownership of railroads and utilities, launched sweeping social security legislation. Long a highly literate people, the Swiss have worked assiduously to make these ventures successful. Thus Switzerland came to its present estate, proud, independent, peaceful, and prosperous.

Then Uruguay. Independent only since 1828, Uruguay's nineteenth-century record was marred by footless civil wars, bloody brushes with Argentina, Brazil, Paraguay, France, England. Political strife was incessant, administration of public business slovenly and corrupt, the economy stagnant. Then came Batlle, whose fine dream was an anachronism: the Uruguayans—over 50 per cent illiterate in 1900, untrained in self-government, undisciplined in matters of economic life—were ill-prepared to handle the Swiss style of government and business which Batlle sought to impose. And so Uruguay arrives at the 1960's scarcely more viable as a sovereign state than the Uruguay of the early nineteenth century.

The Swiss and the Uruguayans are, of course, quite different people by racial inheritance: the Swiss are closer to the German tradition (about 69 per cent were German-speaking in 1960), while the Uruguayans are chiefly of Spanish or Italian background. James Bryce, writing in 1912, said:

> The Uruguayan is, of course, first and foremost a Colonial Spaniard, but a Spaniard moulded by the conditions of his life during the last ninety years. He has been a man of the country and the open air, strong, active, and lawless, always in the saddle riding after his cattle, handy with his lasso and his gun. Fifty years ago he was a Gaucho, much like his Argentine cousin beyond the river. Now he, too, like that cousin, is settling down, but he has retained something of the breezy recklessness and audacity, the frankness and free-handedness, of the older days. A touch of this Gaucho quality, in a milder form, is felt through all classes of Uruguayan society.[3]

[3] James Bryce: *South America; Observations and Impressions* (New York: The Macmillan Co.; 1912), p. 355.

The Englishman was astute: perhaps both the charm and the weakness of the Uruguayans can be traced to the "breezy recklessness and audacity" of the Gaucho. Perhaps that trait explains the slapdash quality of Uruguay's economic digressions—in contrast to the well-thought-out projects of the Swiss. Perhaps it explains the failure of the Uruguayans to use the rich land of the Banda Oriental to good advantage—while the Swiss made every patch of land yield its utmost. Perhaps it explains the unkempt Uruguayan countryside, where houses are mean and dingy and gardens are filled with weeds—in contrast to the grace and charm and neatness of the villages of Switzerland. Perhaps it explains the depressing exhibit of Uruguayan industrialization, which has been marked by lack of skilled technicians—while Swiss industries were expanded with ingenuity and precision. Perhaps it also explains the laxness in public administration, the lapses of honesty in business and banking enterprises, the flouting of the tax laws—all in sharp contrast to the hard-working, disciplined, and law-abiding people of Switzerland.

We submit that Uruguay is *not* Switzerland: it is Uruguay—a country whose people, in the words of one Uruguayan, "do not aspire to greatness. . . . The Uruguayan does not wish to be a very important man, or an insignificant one. He just wants to live in freedom. . . . Here, nothing is very rigorous. Everything is improvised, haphazard, and rather ineffectual. . . . With such a people one does not build empires or alter the course of history."[4]

NOTE: President Oscar Gestido died suddenly of a heart attack on December 6, 1967, after nine months in office. He was succeeded by his forty-seven-year-old vice president, Jorge Pacheco Areco, a former newspaper editor.

(President Gestido's death occurred after this book had been typeset.)

[4] Carlos Maggi in *Marcha* (Montevideo, November 24, 1961), quoted by George Pendle: *Uruguay* (Oxford: Oxford University Press; 1963).

Chapter 45

PARAGUAY

In the legends of primitive men who roamed the heart of South America, there was a Garden of Eden—a land of lush prairies, thick cedar forests, and broad rivers whose waters promised healing for man's ills. But modern Paraguay scarcely qualifies as a paradise. No country of South America has had a more bizarre history, or experienced greater suffering at the hands of domestic tyrants and foreign foes, than Paraguay. After four centuries as colony and free republic, it is still one of the most backward nations of the Western Hemisphere.

This land of Paraguay, about the size of the state of California, is well endowed: the rolling plains around the capital city of Asunción have rich heavy soil in pastures and grain fields; there are dense forests which yield yerba maté, favored beverage of South America, quebracho for tannin, and a variety of woods. In the northwest lies the almost empty wilderness of the Chaco, won by Paraguay in its latest war, with its scrub lands, forests, flooded jungles, and—it is hoped—oil deposits. The population of this least numerous of South American nations, reckoned at 2.1 million in a 1966 estimate, is concentrated around Asunción in the southwestern corner of the country; about 90 per cent of the people live in less than one-seventh of the national domain. The Paraguayans are a homogeneous people, almost entirely the product of interbreeding between Spaniards and the handsome Guaraní Indians. The few thousand Italians, Germans, Spaniards, and other Europeans exert an influence far beyond their numerical strength. The Italian-Swiss settlers have made a notable contribution. Paraguayans live from their cattle, their grain, and the products of their forests. Agricultural methods are primitive, and the country has not yet begun to produce as she could. Foreign interests, about three-fourths Argentine, control rail and river transportation, most of the industries, and much of the land. The nation sells the world woods, cotton, quebracho, yerba maté, hides, and meat products; but before World War II its total annual exports never reached the $13 million mark. In 1966 the total was $49 million.

Poor, illiterate, and sick, the people of Paraguay offer a melancholy contrast to their more prosperous neighbors in Uruguay and Argentina. Their hopes for a free and responsible national existence have been defeated by an inner weakness which has exposed them to dictatorships and continued coercion from without.

COLONY AND REPUBLIC

The Spaniards who founded Asunción in 1537 had little difficulty in subduing the 200,000—more or less—simple Indians of this area who lived by fishing, trapping, and a little planting. Those first Paraguayans were of many tribes, but principally of the Tupi-Guaraní linguistic group; they were an amiable people who shocked the newcomers by their occasional cannibalism, their plural wives, and their love for bathing. The community flourished and within twenty years boasted a Spanish population of 1,500, a cathedral, a textile mill, and the beginnings of a stock industry. For two centuries Asunción remained a principal center of Spanish power in the basin of the Río de la Plata, and from there went the expeditions that founded Santa Fe, Corrientes, and Buenos Aires. Neglected by the Crown, Asunción and its pleasant valley developed slowly during colonial years. Spain's best gift to Paraguay was the company of Jesuit missionaries who first reached Asunción in 1588 and who did more to shape the colony than all the governors and Spanish settlers. The Jesuits made the Indian cause their own. They gathered their charges, perhaps 100,000 of them, in *reducciones* or mission villages and taught them better methods of farming and stock raising and new skills in craftsmanship, while instructing them in the mysteries of the Christian faith. Obstinate and devoted, the Jesuits protected their wards against civil governors and Spanish landholders who sought the Indians' enslavement. Good Spaniards, the Jesuits fought a running battle with the slave-hunting *paulistas* of Portuguese Brazil and were largely responsible for holding Paraguay (and Uruguay) for the Spanish Crown. Their final expulsion from Paraguay—and all Spanish territory— by Charles III in 1767 was a sad loss for the struggling colony. The creation of the Viceroyalty of La Plata in 1776 reduced Paraguay to an unimportant outpost of Buenos Aires. By the first years of the nineteenth century, Asunción was a straggling town of seven or eight thousand people.

Paraguay's passage from colonial rule to independence was swift and almost painless. In July, 1810, two months after the creoles of Buenos Aires had taken half-measures toward independence, a *cabildo abierto* in Asunción took a similar stand but repudiated the leadership of Buenos Aires and prepared to fight any coercion by the port city. In January, 1811, a hastily improvised Paraguayan army defeated and drove back the forces of General Belgrano, sent to compel Paraguay's adherence to Buenos Aires' leadership. In June, 1811, a congress in Asunción declared Paraguay's independence; the most eloquent spokesman, José Gaspar Rodríguez de Francia, announced that his people had been "humiliated, oppressed, degraded and made the object of contempt by the pride and despotism of our rulers. . . . These unfortunate times of oppression and tyranny have ended at last. . . . The Province of Paraguay . . . is now completely free."[1] Paraguay was henceforth free—at least from Spain.

THREE DICTATORS, 1811–70

Dictatorship, the abiding curse of Latin America, found its archetype in the man whose will was absolute during the first three decades of Paraguay's independent life. Born in Córdoba in 1766, Dr. José Gaspar Rodríguez de Francia (president from 1811 to 1840), was first trained in theology (probably earning his doctorate in that discipline); but his religious ardor cooled under the influence of Jean Jacques Rousseau and other heretics, and he turned to the law. He settled in Asunción, taught, practiced law, and began to talk of an independent Paraguay. In 1811 he was one of the five-man junta elected to rule the new nation. Within two years, he had shaken off his colleagues, and in 1814 a quarreling congress voted him full dictatorial powers for three years, shortly extending this to a life term. Until his death in 1840, Francia was the undisputed master of the nation.

Austere, frugal, honest, and cruel beyond description, Francia thought only of service to his nation. He hated foreigners bitterly and was fearful of all entanglements. After a few attempts to encourage trade with England, he fell back upon the complete isolation of the nation, forbidding all river traffic to Buenos Aires and permitting few to leave or enter the country. In violent anticlericalism, he broke off relations with the Vatican and appointed his own bishops and clergy. Spaniards, owners of the best lands and businesses, were jailed, murdered, or exiled. Paraguay became a hermit nation, with *El Supremo* the unchallenged authority. In domestic matters, Francia imposed order, preached the gospel of hard work, and introduced improved methods in agriculture and stock raising. Under his rod, Paraguayans worked tirelessly, making the soil produce more than it ever had before. Critics guilty of a word or gesture against him were jailed, tortured, or murdered. Lacking freedom, Paraguay at least had bread and order. Peace, denied both Argentina and Uruguay during those stormy decades, was assured to Paraguay. Dr. Francia, seventy-four in 1840, could congratulate himself and his people upon their security.

There was no congress to take over the government when Francia died in 1840. After six months of disorder, Paraguay's second man of destiny seized power. Carlos Antonio López (president from 1841 to 1862), a vain, fat, incredibly ugly *estanciero,* ruled with a capriciousness equal to that of Francia but with more intelligence. Abandoning the monkish seclusion imposed by Francia, López opened the river trade with Buenos Aires and Europe and resumed normal relations with the Vatican. He was soon

[1] H. G. Warren: *Paraguay* (Norman, Okla.: University of Oklahoma Press; 1949), pp. 147–8.

involved in altercations with the Argentine dictator Rosas, and in 1845 joined the coalition against Buenos Aires. When Rosas was ousted in 1852, Paraguay shared the credit. López welcomed immigrants, and a few actually arrived. Preening himself as a statesman, López provoked a series of tragicomic disputes with the diplomatic agents of the United States, England, and France, while his relations with both Argentina and Brazil steadily worsened. Only Paraguay's remoteness and unimportance postponed a war.

Internally, López repressed his critics as Francia had, but with less cruelty. He showed commendable energy in promoting trade and building a few miles of roads and railways, and even a few schools. Meanwhile, he and his friends grew rich. Contemporary critics charged that he owned half the land of Paraguay, 300,000 cattle, sundry commercial enterprises, and the monopoly on yerba maté; but the modern reader is skeptical of such reports. Learning from Francia's mistakes, López did not leave the choice of his successor to chance. In 1845 he named his nineteen-year-old son Francisco Solano López commander in chief of the army. When the elder López died in 1862, there was no question as to who should assume the toga.

Francisco Solano López (president from 1862 to 1870), the thirty-five-year-old who inherited the presidency, proved even less pleasant than his predecessors. He was a bloated little man, who, when told that he resembled the great Napolean, promptly ordered uniforms like those the Corsican had worn and a replica of his crown. His father had sent him to Europe to study military tactics and statecraft, but he had busied himself with eating, drinking, and venery. Not least of the trophies which he brought to Asunción was Elisa Lynch, an Irish girl whom he had found in Paris, and who devoted herself to him until his death.

The second López was responsible for plunging his weak nation into a war with the combined forces of Argentina, Uruguay, and Brazil which began in the last days of 1864 and dragged on until 1870. The most savage and sanguinary war in all the records of Latin America, it was provoked by Francisco Solano López's intemperate dealings with his neighbors, which culminated in his seizure of a Brazilian steamer, the threat to intervene in Uruguayan politics, and an attempt to march his troops across Argentine territory in order to reach Uruguay. The armies of the three allies outnumbered Paraguay's by ten to one. López drafted men of all ages; boys of twelve fought side by side with their grandfathers. Any show of resistance to López's orders brought imprisonment, torture, lingering death. There were losses for all the nations involved, but for Paraguay the war meant virtual extinction. A cautious estimate suggests that her population was reduced from about 525,000 in 1865 to 221,000 in 1871—with only some 28,000 men among the survivors. In 1870 Brazilian soldiers caught the obese Francisco Solano López and ended his Napoleonic career with a bullet. Elisa Lynch, the mistress who had borne him various children, managed to escape from the country with money and jewels to comfort her in Parisian exile. Argentina and Brazil sliced off some 55,000 square miles of Paraguay's territory, levied a huge indemnity which was never paid, and maintained an occupation force until 1876.

INTERMISSION BETWEEN WARS, 1870–1928

The peace that came to Paraguay was the peace of a wind-swept graveyard: the women were widows; the children were orphans; the men were old and mutilated. Promiscuity was general; the Brazilian soldiers who occupied the land until 1876 fathered a new generation of Paraguayans. The country was broken and defenseless; Brazil and Argentina, had they reached accord, could have divided it between them, but for reasons good or bad they maintained it as a buffer state. Meanwhile, a few hundred adventurers from Europe and Argentina acquired rich lands by trickery or by marriage with Paraguayan women.

In politics, parties meaninglessly described as Conservative and Liberal took turns naming presidents. The Conservatives held power until 1904, when a popular uprising put the Liberals in control. Gunplay, not ballots, put man after man into high office; between 1870 and 1967 there were forty presidents, most of whom were jailed, exiled, or murdered before they had completed their terms. With two or three exceptions, they were outright dictators, although never in the grand manner of the first three "giants."

There was some progress. A few immigrants, not more than 40,000, came from Italy, Spain, Germany, and Argentina, and it was chiefly they who developed the stock industry, agriculture, and forest industries. Under pledge of perpetual military exemption, more than 5,000 pacifist Mennonites came from Europe and North America to settle on Paraguayan soil. A few schools and a National University were organized. By 1928 the population was over 800,000, but almost 90 per cent of the people were illiterate and the overwhelming majority lived meagerly, earning a few cents a day on the lands of others. The profits from Paraguayan fields, pastures, and forests were drained off by foreign owners, chiefly Argentine. Asunción, with less than 100,000 people, had no central water supply, sewers, fire department, or paved streets.

THE CHACO WAR AND AFTER, 1928–54

Unfortunately for Paraguay, and for Bolivia, there was the unsettled question of sovereignty over the Chaco Boreal, an uninviting and unpeopled wilderness of scrub land, dense forests, and swamps. At the conclusion of the Paraguayan War, Argentina had seized the area between the Bermejo and Pilcomayo rivers, while Brazil had taken the lands north of the Apa River. The greater part of the area of the Chaco Boreal was a desolate void between Paraguay and Bolivia, and the rivalry for its possession, begun in colonial days, was bitter. The polemicists of both nations used barrels of printer's ink to prove the validity of their claims. Cynics in Asunción and La Paz spoke derisively of the learned disputants as *doctores en Chaco*. Bolivians rested their case on the fact that the Spanish *Audiencia* of Charcas, created in 1559, had united the Gran Chaco with Upper Peru (Bolivia). Paraguayans argued that missionaries and settlers from Asunción had long maintained outposts in the disputed region. Bolivians countered by citing their own missionary and military activities. The outsider, viewing this empty wilderness, inclines to agree with Harris G. Warren: "Actually, neither country was right until the Chaco War decided the issue."

War had long been inevitable. Paraguay, profoundly humiliated by its losses in the 1860's, sought vindication of its national honor by extending its borders. Bolivia, cut off from access to the sea by the War of the Pacific (1879–84), now sought ports on the Paraguay River which would give her access to the Atlantic through the Río de la Plata. International rivalries played a part: Chile urged Bolivia on, while Argentina encouraged Paraguay. Furthermore, the unproved rumors of huge oil deposits in the Chaco excited both contestants. The lines of the conflict began to be drawn early in the twentieth century. By 1907 both nations were enlarging their frontier garrisons. Repeated efforts were made by outsiders to quiet the ominous rivalry. In 1927–28 President Alvear of Argentina made a futile effort to secure agreement between the claimants. In December, 1928, Paraguayan patrols attacked a Bolivian fort at Vanguardia, the first of a series of incidents. The interchange of charge and countercharge increased, and the arguments of neither side were impressive. Paraguayan spokesmen claimed that Standard Oil of New Jersey, holding a concession in Bolivia, was actively financing Bolivia's army. Bolivian apologists replied by accusing Argentina, in league with Great Britain, of inciting Paraguay to attack. The heights of absurdity were reached by Communist spokesmen: "At bottom," writes the long-time servant of Moscow, William Z. Foster, "it was a war between the Royal Dutch Shell [largely British-owned] and Standard Oil."

The Chaco War broke in full fury in 1932. Bolivia had the advantage of a population three times that of Paraguay but was handicapped by the general apathy of its people and by a weak and vacillating government. Furthermore, the Indians from the two-mile-high Bolivian *altiplano* were physically unfit for service in the lower lands of the drenched Chaco. Paraguay, on the other hand, had the support of its citizens, who regarded the struggle as the defense of their homeland. It also had the advantage of an able president, Eusebio Ayala, who had proved his worth in private business and public service, and an excellent chief of staff, General José Felix Estigarribía. Paraguay, regarded by many as the aggrieved party in the conflict, found it easier to get supplies of arms than did Bolivia. The senseless war ground on for three years. At times not less than 50,000 men were on the battle front of each nation, with an equal number serving the supply lines in the rear. Battles were fought in the heavy jungles and on the scrub lands; in the rainy seasons, soldiers floundered through flooded swamps; in the dry seasons, scarcely a drop of water was to be found. Malaria, dysentery, and other plagues killed as many men as did the guns of the enemy. The poisonous snakes which abound in that "green hell" took their toll. Paraguay gradually gained ground. In 1935 a truce of exhaustion was finally signed. The treaty of 1938 confirmed the victory of Paraguay, which (says Warren) had won "20,000 square miles . . . at the cost of about three Bolivians and two Paraguayans for each square mile." If it was a costly victory for Paraguay, it was a cheap one for Argentina, whose diplomacy won her the major credit for the final settlement. An enlarged Paraguay, in which Argentine investors would garner more profit, served the statesmen of Buenos Aires.

Paraguay's record since the Chaco War includes the rule of six war heroes who have taken their turns in the presidency. Ayala, the best president Paraguay ever had, was too fair and conciliatory in the peace settlement for the taste of strident nationalists; he was unseated in 1936. After two brief and ineffective dictatorships, General Estigarribía of well-earned war fame gave promise of rather better performance; but, after serving for a year, he was killed in an airplane crash. Higinio Morínigo ruled from 1940 to 1948 in a fashion unpleasantly reminiscent of earlier tyrants. Dissenters were jailed or fled into exile. World War II brought new demand for Paraguayan products, and the country prospered. Morínigo skillfully negotiated with foreign powers. Fortified with loans from Washington and Lend-Lease gifts of arms and planes, he was well equipped to crush uprisings that threatened his continuance in office. He faithfully did as Washington bade: he broke with the Axis in 1942, declared war and joined the United Nations in 1945—did everything except put an end to German activity in his own country.

When first Ramírez and then Perón came to power in Buenos Aires, Morínigo was more than willing to collaborate with the nation whose investors controlled three-fourths of the foreign interests in Paraguay. With fine impartiality, Morínigo journeyed to Rio de Janeiro for a visit with President Vargas, where he got the promise of free port privileges in Santos and an extension of the Brazilian railways from São Paulo to Concepción in Paraguay. He visited President Peñaranda in Bolivia, celebrated the happy amity now existing between the former foes, and made plans for a pipe line to carry Bolivia's oil to the Paraguay River. Having thus cemented cordial relations with his near neighbors, he traveled north, made a triumphal entry into Washington, was fêted by his "great and good friend," Franklin D. Roosevelt, and was given an honorary doctorate by a reputable university (at the suggestion of the United States Department of State). Meanwhile, political prisoners rotted in his jails, rivals lived angrily in Montevideo, the press was muzzled, schools languished, and labor unions were silenced.

After the retirement of Morínigo in 1948, the reins of government

Major Boundary Disputes Since 1830

passed through the hands of three men during the next year, no one of them able to rule the country or to maintain himself in power. When Federico Chávez was elected in 1949, he imposed a dictatorship much like that of Morínigo and managed to hold office until 1954, when another uprising brought a new president.

ALFREDO STROESSNER, 1954–

General Alfredo Stroessner, president by grace of an army coup in 1954, unanimously "reelected" in 1958, and again chosen by his grateful people in 1963, is the standard model of the Latin American tyrant. Son of a German immigrant, teutonic in appearance, but mild-mannered and resentful of being called a dictator, Stroessner has proved to be the most durable of Paraguayan chiefs of state in a century. His regime has been savage: his congress is meaningless, his courts bow to his orders, the press is shackled; his secret police—known as *pyragues,* a Guaraní word meaning "people with hairy feet"—pad noiselessly around, listening, reporting, seizing suspected critics. Intermittent revolts within the country and attacks from Argentina and Brazil averaged about two each year from 1954 to 1967; but the rebels were systematically jailed, tortured, and often murdered. "We are a geographically defenseless country," said Stroessner, explaining the almost permanent state of siege, which he claimed was necessary "to protect our democratic institutions against invasion by Communist-infiltrated expeditionaries."

Adlai Stevenson, who was unimpressed by Paraguay's "democratic institutions" when he visited the country in July, 1961, said unsmilingly upon his departure: "The protection of civil rights, free elections, and democratic procedures would greatly enhance international respect for Paraguay and confidence in her future development and prosperity." The message got through to dictator Stroessner, and he forthwith mended his ways: from then on, one or another newspaper was often permitted to headline a protest, in order to impress some visiting statesman; swift punishment for dissidents, if no less cruel, became less evident; arranging a "showcase election" in 1963, Stroessner prevailed upon an opposition leader to "run" for president, saw to it that he received a few votes, rewarded him with the ambassadorship to the Court of St. James's; and he welcomed a twenty-member token opposition in his sixty-seat congress "after years of stubborn and useless absence."

Stroessner was inaugurated for his third term in a three-day ceremony in August, 1963. Complete with tail coats, twenty-one-gun salutes, blood-red-shirted cavalry, bright-blue-uniformed police on new German motor-cycles, it was a lavish and flamboyant affair. "Were it not for an occasional headless body floating down the Paraná River," wrote one correspondent, "it might be possible to consider the gaudily uniformed and bemedaled dictator of Paraguay—the last of the breed in South America—a character out of Gilbert and Sullivan."

In spite of the savagery of the dictatorship, however, it must be grudgingly admitted that material progress has advanced during the years of Alfredo Stroessner. A hard-working and able administrator, Stroessner has imposed a considerable efficiency upon his subordinates; and he and his aides like to boast that Paraguay is a "showcase for the Alliance for Progress." Thanks to aid from international agencies—and a genuine effort on the part of the government—there are indeed some hopeful exhibits. The currency is stable—with the guaraní steady at 126 to the dollar since 1961—which is more than can be said for any of Paraguay's immediate neighbors. Inflation is mild—the cost of living increased less than 7 per cent a year between 1958 and 1966. Exports increased some 68 per cent between 1954 and 1965, and for the last three of those years there was a favorable balance of trade. Reserves in the Central Bank increased from less than $0.5 million in 1960 to over $10 million in 1965. Asunción has at last got a municipal sewer and water supply system. There are new schools, although most rural areas have none. Roads have been built: one from Asunción to Encarnación on the Argentine border; another stretch of 475 miles connects Asunción and the Bolivian border. Hydroelectric plants have been built or begun; the output may have increased by 60 per cent during Stroessner's regime. The river fleet connecting Asunción with the Río de la Plata and the Atlantic has been strengthened by thirty 1,000-ton ships.[2]

On the debit side of the ledger, over-all production is unimpressive, with per capita gross domestic product increasing by an average of only 1.2 per cent a year during 1960–65. The development of the potentially rich countryside has lagged—farm production is stagnant, yields are low. And a well-advertised land reform program has been little more than a paper promise. Gestures have been made toward colonization of government-owned virgin lands, especially in the fertile area of the northeast, near the Brazilian border. Immigrants have been invited, but the inflow of useful farmers has been slight. The government claims to have turned over 28,000 new plots comprising 1.7 million acres to new farmers—surely an optimistic figure. The pattern of land tenure remains feudal, with less than one half of 1 per cent of the landholders presiding regally over almost three-quarters of the farm lands—while the workers toil for pitiful wages. Tax reforms on the books are only fitfully enforced. And the public treasury is burdened by a military establishment which consumes more than half the national income, and whose sole function is to keep order—that is, to keep Stroessner in power.

Economically and politically, Paraguay is tied to Argentina—still a vassal and a puppet, just as she has always been. Much of the best land of Paraguay is still owned by Argentines. There have been serious strains

[2] There has even been an occasional word of praise for Stroessner's regime. In August, 1964, Felipe Herrera, president of the Inter-American Development Bank, visiting Asunción for the signing of loan agreements, had this to say: "I wish to pay homage to the institutional and financial system of Paraguay and to the honest vision of its leaders, who constitute an example to Latin America"—an appraisal which must have been as baffling to thoughtful Paraguayans as it was to outside observers.

between Asunción and Buenos Aires; and Paraguay stands to suffer further from the continued breakdown of Argentine stability.

This is a poor and frightened land. Its 2 million people are pocketed in the inner heart of a continent. At least 26 per cent can neither read nor write. The per capita income may be about $175 (the estimate for 1963). The trappings of modern civilization are reserved for those who live in the capital city, Asunción. And the country is caught in the vise of a tyranny. What are the avenues of hope? Opposition is sporadic and disorganized—and quickly crushed. A few courageous editors and army officers have protested, but they have seldom survived. Many able Paraguayans who dare to lift their voices against the dictator continue to find it wise to move to Buenos Aires, Montevideo, or São Paulo. These exiles—there are perhaps half a million of them—have so far failed in any concerted attempt to undermine Stroessner's grim power. The Church deserves credit for speaking out against the savagery of the dictatorship. In 1958 Father Ramón Talavera, a parish priest, publicly denounced the government for its torture of political prisoners. His stand was supported by the Catholic Vicar-General; then the Archbishop issued a pastoral letter to be read in all churches, which spoke of the "general misery" of the people and appealed for a more representative government "with genuine participation of the people in public life, and healthy freedom for public opinion." The twenty-eight-year-old priest paid for his presumption: he was assaulted by thugs and forced to leave the country. There have been other instances of criticism by churchmen. But the clergy, like everyone else, are captives of this police state.

What is the role of the United States in this drama? Stroessner continues to proclaim his deep affection and respect for his northern neighbor, but Stroessner's embrace is embarrassing. Washington has shamefacedly continued to extend financial aid to the dictator's regime—$44.1 million from 1961 to 1966. But much of official Washington is not happy over the affair. It is widely felt that it is hardly fitting that the democratic United States should lend even token support to a government which exists by torture. Nor is there much joy in Washington over the reiterated oratory of Stroessner on the subject of building Paraguay as a bulwark against Communism. In Stroessner's lexicon every dissenter is a Communist. The United States is put into the position of standing by consenting to the iniquity of Stroessner's rule. There is fresh discussion as to how the strongest nation in the Western Hemisphere could use its resources to aid the people of a poor land without fixing the hold of a despot more firmly upon them.

PART X

Brazil: Empire and Republic

I n the congeries of the twenty Latin American republics, Brazil is a
land apart. Its roots are in Portugal, which in the course of centuries
developed a culture quite unlike that of Spain, not only in language,
but also in religious attitudes, social customs, and economic habits.
More plastic than the Spaniards, the Portuguese transferred their
less rigid fashions to the land of Brazil. The result is a people whose personality and habits of thought set them in striking contrast to the Spanish
Americans.

Chapter 46

BRAZIL: LAND AND PEOPLE

Brazil is a study in superlatives. Largest of the Latin American nations and almost as large as the United States (including Alaska), Brazil, with an area of 3,286,478 square miles, occupies almost half of South America. It stretches some 2,700 miles from the Guiana highlands in the north to the plains of Paraguay and Uruguay; and it measures another 2,700 miles from the eastern hump across to the *yungas* and *selvas* of Bolivia and Peru. Brazil is an empire in which the homeland and the colonies are housed under one geographic roof. Almost half of this domain is wet, hot Amazonia, the scantily populated region of rain forest and brush land drained by the 3,900-mile-long Amazon (whose name is derived from the mythical women warriors of Grecian tales) with its thousands of tributaries, many still unmapped. In the Northeast, in the semiarid interior of the hump, is a region scourged by recurring droughts from which hundreds of thousands have fled. To the south and inland, in the states of Bahia and Minas Gerais, lies the plateau drained by the Rio São Francisco, a region of fine forests and plains which attract migrants from home and abroad. The effective Brazil, comprising about 29 per cent of the national territory but housing almost 90 per cent of all Brazilians, includes the southern area from Minas Gerais to Rio Grande do Sul, a region of tablelands and fine soil which is drained by the rivers of the Río de la Plata system; it also includes the narrow coastal plain south from Ceará, often crowded close to the sea by the high escarpment in the south, which contains many of the great cities and the fine harbors.

The almost 85 million Brazilians (1966), most numerous of all Latin Americans, are a composite of Portuguese, Indian, and Negro; to which in the last century have been added a few million Italians, Spaniards, Germans, other Europeans, and Japanese. No statistics on race tell much about the Brazilian people: no true reckoning has ever been made of the Portuguese who settled there, of the Indians whom they found, or of the Negroes who were brought from Africa. Perhaps 2 or 3 per cent of modern Brazilians are Indians; perhaps 50 per cent may be described as of white European inheritance; perhaps 10 per cent are mixed Indian and white; and perhaps 40 per cent, more or less, may be classified as Negro and mulatto—such figures are conjectural, and are warmly debated by Brazilians.

Who then is a Brazilian? He is the tough frontiersman in the backlands, whose name is Portuguese but whose ancestry may include the blood of Bantu and of Tupí. He is the sophisticated lawyer of Rio de Janeiro who speaks French as well as he speaks Portuguese. He is the Negro worker in the sugar fields of Pernambuco. He is the German banker and the Italian industrialist in São Paulo. He is the worn half-breed who has fled from poverty-stricken Ceará to live in a hut in the slums above the capital. He is the proud ranchman of the southern pasture country. He is the primitive Indian of the distant rain forest who has never heard of the emperors and presidents who have ruled his nation.

This great land and people are richly endowed. The Brazilian soil produces cotton, cacao, tobacco, grains, and more than half of the coffee sold in the world's markets. Its pastures are fertile and plentiful. Its forests yield hardwoods, oils, nuts, rubber, and many other items. Its mines are rich in iron, manganese, gold, diamonds, bauxite, chromium, molybdenum, nickel, uranium, thorium, mica, lead, and zinc; and perhaps in tin and mercury. The scarcity of good coal is partially offset by abundant sources of hydroelectric power. This wealth is still largely unexploited. Despite bold excursions into industry and agriculture, the development of the nation's wealth still awaits the investment of capital, the increase in technicians and man power, and the opening of railroads and highways.

Portuguese Brazil long followed a different course from that of its Spanish American neighbors. While the rest of Latin America was being fashioned into republics with presidents and constitutions after the pattern of the United States, Brazil followed the Iberian example and became an empire. The liberators of Spanish America had grave doubts as to the readiness of their new nations for free institutions: San Martín inclined toward monarchy; Bolívar, while founding republics, turned toward dictatorship. But Brazil, with little debate, formed an empire which lasted sixty-seven years (1822–89).

The story of independent Brazil falls into six chapters: Emperor Pedro I (1822–31); the regency (1831–41); Pedro II (1841–89); the first republic (1889–1930); the era of Getulio Vargas (1930–45); and the second republic (1945–   ). History credits the empire with having held Brazil together; had it not been for the cohesive power of the Crown, the nation might easily have split at its seams as did Gran Colombia, Peru, and the provinces of La Plata. But Brazil did not split; the secessionist movements which raged during the first decades were overcome; and even the abolition of slavery in 1888 did not break the unity of the nation. Thanks to the unifying force of the empire, the United States of Brazil exists today as the largest of the republics of Latin America.

Brazil

Chapter 47

THE EMPIRE OF BRAZIL:
PEDRO I, 1822–31

The twenty-four-year-old Pedro, having severed Brazil's ties with Portugal by his *grito do Ypiranga,* got off to a good start in 1822 and for a time bade fair to live down evil memories of Portuguese arrogance and greed. His chief good fortune was his prime minister, José Bonifácio de Andrada e Silva, who is revered as the father of the nation's independence. José Bonifácio,[1] fifty-seven in 1822, had a distinguished record. Born in the state of São Paulo and educated at the University of Coimbra, he worked and taught for thirty years in Portugal. He was recognized in Europe as a great mineralogist, and became the friend and colleague of the scientists Humboldt, Volta, Priestley, and Lavoisier; he was also a mediocre poet; and he was a critical observer of the political upheavals that were redrawing the maps of Europe and America.

In 1819 José Bonifácio returned to Brazil, where he had a decisive hand in shaping the events which led to peaceful separation from Portugal. Under no delusions as to his countrymen's fitness for democratic rule, he favored constitutional monarchy and staked his hopes on John's young son, Pedro, whom he persuaded to remain when Lisbon ordered him home. Then when Portugal sought to reduce Brazil to its older colonial status, he urged Pedro to declare Brazil's independence. José Bonifácio gave the young emperor stout support, and taught Brazil lessons which were not forgotten. He saw clearly the economic absurdity of slavery: "Twenty slaves require twenty hoes, all of which could be saved by one plow." He saw also its social corrosiveness: "He who lives on the earnings of his slaves lives in indolence, and indolence brings vice in its wake." He counseled patience and gradual abolition: "Make the Negroes free and proud, give them incentives, protect them, they will reproduce and become valuable citizens."

Meanwhile, young Pedro, despite his genuine desire to serve his country, encountered more obstacles than he could surmount. He bore the stigma of being Portuguese; Brazil—remembering Carlota's arrogance, the nobles' venality, John's final rifling of the Brazilian treasury—was weary of

---

[1] It is a common practice among Brazilians to use the given name when referring to their conspicuous leaders.

Portugal. The mother country was suspected of harboring ambition for a monopoly on Brazilian trade; of seeking continued linkage through the Crown as a way of involving Brazil in Portugal's European quarrels; and of preaching liberalism at home while imposing imperialism in America. Pedro angered the Brazilians by appointing Portuguese to high offices.

His prestige was early tested when a constituent assembly was convened in 1823 to draft a constitution. The able and patriotic members of the assembly, although predominantly monarchist in sentiment, were animated by current liberal ideas and were determined that there should be no truckling to Portugal. They assumed that they could impose their new instrument upon the emperor, but Pedro argued his royal right to dictate its terms; and when the assembly refused to accept these terms, Pedro disbanded it. José Bonifácio de Andrada e Silva and his two brothers, while eager to magnify royal authority, were stoutly Brazilian in their opposition to Portuguese interference and were forced into exile.

Pedro then entrusted the writing of a constitution to a council of state, whose members he named, and their document was promulgated in 1824. This constitution, under which Brazil would be ruled for sixty-five years, conferred the *poder moderador,* "the mediative power," upon the emperor: the right to nominate for life (from lists submitted by a group of electors) senators in the upper house of the parliament; the right to convoke the parliament and to veto its acts, but with the provision that the emperor's veto could be overridden if the parliament voted the same measure in three successive sessions. The lower house was made up of deputies popularly elected, but its powers were limited not only by the emperor's right of veto but also by his ability to dissolve it at will. The judiciary was declared independent of both emperor and parliament. The constitution was highly centralist; provincial and municipal assemblies were to be popularly elected, but they were subject to the control of presidents appointed by the emperor. Hardly democratic, the constitution was feared by liberals as a device by which an illiberal emperor might readily again subject Brazil to the dominance of Portugal.

Pedro had other troubles. He proved vigorous in quelling the civil wars which continued to threaten the unity of the empire. But a war with Argentina (1825–28), in which Brazil lost money, men, prestige, and the territory of Uruguay, brought discredit upon Pedro. Furthermore, the question of Brazil's relations with Portugal continued to plague him. When his father John died in 1826, Pedro inherited the throne of Portugal. The fears of Brazilians were somewhat quieted when Pedro renounced his rights to the Lisbon Crown, nominating his five-year-old daughter Maria da Gloria with the stipulation that she be betrothed to her uncle Miguel.

Further confusion was caused by Pedro's mismanagement in Rio de Janeiro. Immense sums were wasted on royal display, and his courtiers vied with one another in levying upon the national treasury. He treated his cabinet ministers as lackeys, dismissing them for an idle word of disrespect; and the members of the Chamber of Deputies were permitted slight share in governing. His effective counselors were the members of his unofficial "kitchen cabinet" headed by a much disliked royal favorite. The popular resentment against Pedro was increased by his open infidelity to his queen. Leopoldina, who combined liberal intelligence with a warm heart, reared their four children with love and wisdom—but she was not comely. Pedro was bored. The people revered their empress; and her cause became their own when the emperor took to himself as mistress Domitila de Castro Canto e Mello, built her a palace not far from his own royal residence, made her the Marchioness of Santos, admitted her to the inner councils of state, and all but forgot Leopoldina. The empress, whether of a broken heart or infection from a miscarriage, died. So great was the uproar that Pedro was forced to banish his Domitila, and he married again, this time the seventeen-year-old Princess Amelia de Leuchtenberg. But the people did not forgive him.

By 1831 the Brazilians had had enough of Pedro. He was too Portuguese for their taste, too arrogant, and too expensive. There were angry speeches in the parliament, demands for limitations upon his power and for more appointments of Brazilians to high office. Even José Bonifácio, finally restored to favor, could not save him from the wrath of the populace. He signed his abdication and sailed for Portugal where he died in 1834 in his thirty-sixth year.

 [*Chapter 48*]

THE EMPIRE: THE REGENCY AND PEDRO II, 1831–41

The empire was now in the soft hands of a blue-eyed, golden-haired boy of five. "Take him to your hearts, this crowned orphan," wrote his young stepmother to the Brazilian people. The record of almost sixty years tells how they took Pedro, child and boy and man, to their hearts.

Fortune endowed Pedro II with formidable ancestry: his forebears, Braganza, Bourbon, and Hapsburg, were kings and emperors of Spain, Portugal, France, England, and Austria. It was an impressive list for those concerned with heraldry; not so impressive for the geneticist, for the royal blood had run thin. Pedro II, in 1831, was a lonely small boy, with a mother whom he could not remember and a father who had sailed away. His tutor, stalwart old José Bonifácio, gathered him in his arms—"My emperor and my son." The child was paraded through the streets to the grateful shouts of the people; born on Brazilian soil, son of the beloved Leopoldina, this boy was their own "Pedro Segundo."

For nine years the education of Pedro was a national trust. José Bonifácio, his first tutor, served for two years, and was followed by the Marquis of Itanhaén, able, austere, and deeply religious. The boy was subjected to a strict regime: up at seven, mass in the royal chapel, breakfast, lessons, dinner, exercise, reading, prayers, bed. Numerous teachers took turns in instructing him. By the time Pedro was fourteen, he had ranged widely in history, geography, Latin, French, German, English, the natural sciences, art, piano, dancing, and horsemanship. He had little privacy; he was forever in the public eye, reviewing troops or presiding at state occasions. Despite such distractions, he read enormously and acquired firm habits of study which prepared him to be the best-educated ruler of nineteenth-century Latin America. And Pedro remained quite unspoiled.

The abdication of Pedro I had left the country in anarchy, and rival factions sought to take advantage of the chaos. Immediately after his departure, the parliament had appointed a temporary regency, but it was beset by clashing groups: the old-guard who favored recall of Pedro I, with strong power vested in the throne; the advocates of constitutional monarchy fashioned after the British model; the moderates who sought security on a compromise basis; and the few forthright liberals who wanted a republic. The principle of the monarchy was at stake while little Pedro II was learning his first lessons in spelling and arithmetic. The Crown was finally saved by the cool-headed moderates, who decided that it was wiser to reinforce the monarchists than to leave the decision to the disruptive liberals. But while decisions were being made in Rio de Janeiro, there were outbreaks of revolution: in 1831 in northern Pará; in 1833 in Minas Gerais; and in 1834 in Mato Grosso and Maranhão. In order to quiet these nagging civil wars, the regency modified the constitution in 1834 by creating provincial legislatures, through which disaffected minorities could make their voices heard; and, as a concession to republican sentiment, it was provided that the three-member regency be changed, in the interests of efficient government, to the rule of one regent. These reforms did not bring peace: there was a slave revolt in Bahia in 1835; a ten-year war of secession in Rio Grande do Sul (1835–45); and a new series of revolts in Maranhão.

Looking back to the nine years of Pedro II's minority (1831–40), the historian marvels that the succession of makeshift governments was able to prevent the dissolution of the empire. The first three-man regency lasted a few months; three new men then took over the onerous task for almost four years (1831–35); then, under the modified constitution, Father Diogo Antônio Feijó assumed office alone (1835–37); and he was followed by Pedro de Araújo Lima (later honored as the Marquis of Olinda) who served until 1840. The victory for order and unity, seriously threatened during this period, was largely due to the patriotism and sagacity of several remarkable men: the first was Evaristo da Veiga, the most influential editor of his time, who, while republican in conviction, supported the monarchy as protection against anarchy; the second, Father Feijó, introduced wise reforms in education and fought for preservation of the empire; the third, Araújo Lima, was a man of integrity who upheld the central authority; and the fourth, Bernardo Pereira de Vasconcelos, used his immense prestige to support Araújo Lima in subduing the various rebellious sectors. Meanwhile, the inherited conflict between the partisans and the critics of Portugal had been largely quieted by the death of the elder Pedro in Lisbon in 1834. From then on, the ostensible clash would be between monarchists and republicans—not between conservatives and liberals, as some contemporary writers described it, for many liberals continued to support the monarchy for another fifty years as the prudent offset to regional confusion.

Thanks to the good sense and solid patriotism of the men who ruled during the 1830's, Brazil was saved on the one hand from partition, and on the other from dictatorship. Time and again there seemed imminent a tearing apart of the empire, which could readily have created three Brazils: a northern sugar-raising state, a central mining and coffee-producing nation, and a southern cattle-raising land. Or, in line with the contemporary Spanish American experience, the nation might have fallen victim to such a military chieftain as Rosas of Argentina or Santa Anna of Mexico. Brazil's lucky escape from both of these catastrophes must be credited to the sensible men who were on hand to lead the empire while young Pedro was growing up.

In 1840 Pedro was almost fifteen, with two years to wait before he could be constitutionally crowned. By a curious paradox, it was the restless liberals who now insisted upon declaring the boy of age and ready for his throne. The Senate reluctantly agreed, and sent a deputation to young Pedro to ask whether he was ready to assume the throne. *"Quero já"* was Pedro's reply—"Yes, indeed, I wish it." That was in July, 1840. A year later he was crowned with the solemn pomp which has long proved potent in holding empires together.

[*Chapter 49*]

THE EMPIRE: PEDRO II, 1841–89

Pedro II had tasks enough. He had to grow up; he had to handle men; he had to win his right to rule. The royal court was alive with schemers ready to guide the boy emperor for their own selfish ends. His first ministry, with Antônio Carlos de Andrada e Silva (brother of José Bonifácio) as its chief, fell within a year. Pedro then restored the Council of State, an awkward government-by-committee, each of whose members pursued his own designs. In 1847 Pedro appointed a president for his council of ministers, a prime minister after the British model. This gave him a single helper to whom he could delegate authority, a pattern which prevailed until the end of the empire. By 1847 there was no question as to who was ruler of Brazil. Pedro, now twenty-two, was a man.

This fine figure of an emperor—six-feet-three and well shaped, robust after his earlier illnesses, his blue eyes direct and clear, and his hair and full beard a glowing brown—fulfilled for the Brazilian people the best promises of the Braganzas, Hapsburgs, and Bourbons. There was no doubting the deep patriotism, the profound concern for the welfare of the people, and the absorbing honesty of this young man. In 1843 he had acquired an empress. His ministers, in proper dynastic fashion, conducted the search. They asked the Austrian emperor to nominate a bride, but the Hapsburgs, remembering the fate of Leopoldina, did not respond. Negotiations for the hand of Princess Thereza of the Two Sicilies were successful, portraits were exchanged, the match was arranged, marriage by proxy was celebrated in Naples, and the bride reached Rio de Janeiro in 1843. Pedro was eighteen; Thereza was twenty-one. The meeting was painful; Thereza was charmed with Pedro, but Thereza was short, lumpy, and lame. The story runs that Pedro turned his back upon Thereza, appealed for sympathy to Dona Marianna, who had served as his foster mother, saying: "They have deceived me." But the contract had been made; Pedro accepted it and lived with Thereza in loyalty, respect, and growing affection for almost fifty years.

In 1850 the imperial stage was set. The emperor was twenty-five; Thereza had given him two sons, both had died—and Pedro wrote verses which ran: "Twice already I have suffered death, for the father dies who sees his son is dead." There were two daughters, Isabel and Leopoldina.

The Brazil of 1850 was smaller than the modern nation: boundary settlements, almost always favorable to Brazil, would add large debated areas at the expense of all her neighbors. The Amazon valley was uncharted and unoccupied. The narrow coastal plain had its plantations and small cities. Aggressive São Paulo, Minas Gerais, and the cattle-raising south were increasing in importance. Behind the Atlantic façade lay the backlands where frontiersmen lived a life without law, beyond the reach of the central power. Brazilians numbered about 7 million in 1850. There were between 1 million and 2 million whites—chiefly of Portuguese blood, with some Spaniards, Germans, and a scattering from other nations. Of Negro slaves, there were from 3 million to 4 million; of free Negroes, perhaps 1 million. Of Indians, more or less under the rule of the empire, there were probably half a million. Of mixtures of Indian, Negro, and white, there were 1 million or more. The chief centers of population were the provinces of Rio de Janeiro with about 1.4 million; Minas Gerais, with 1.1 million; São Paulo and Pernambuco, each with about 800,000. The city of Rio de Janeiro had a population of about 250,000; and Bahia had 150,000.

THE GOVERNMENT OF PEDRO II

There was never doubt as to Pedro's control. At times he was denounced as a dictator; at other times, jeered as "Pedro Banana," a term of contempt for the lazy. Both charges were unfair. Pedro ruled firmly, sometimes arbitrarily, always convinced that his people would never learn to rule themselves unless permitted to make their own mistakes. Even when overruling popular demands, he believed that he was educating his people for democracy. Mitre of Argentina would later describe Brazil as the "crowned democracy of America." Others, Brazilians and outsiders, have called Pedro's rule a dictatorship. The truth lies somewhere in between.

Pedro's administration had the outward forms of the English parliamentary system; a prime minister selected the cabinet, nominally answerable to the Chamber of Deputies, which was controlled by the emperor. Parties—usually called Liberal and Conservative—rose and fell. Over this system Pedro exercised "the mediative power" (the *poder moderador* of his father's Constitution of 1824), acting as a presiding ruler and conciliator between opposing factions. Actually, the underpinnings of the British system were lacking. There were no literate masses to voice the popular will. The inarticulate, illiterate proletariat was denied the franchise; and the electorate consisted of a few thousand landowners, lawyers, physicians, engineers, priests, officials, and businessmen.[1] Pedro held the whip hand. He could dissolve the assembly at will and did so on at least

1 Alan Manchester cites the election of 1881 as one of the fairest in the imperial period. There were but 142,000 qualified voters out of a total population of almost 14 million.

eleven occasions, in some instances, where no clear issue appeared. Not until the electoral reforms of 1876 were the emperor's powers somewhat abridged; after that the cabinet was generally responsible to the parliament, and only indirectly to the emperor. Pedro's appointive powers reinforced his authority. He named presidents of provinces and many lesser officials; he appointed senators for life terms, making his choice from lists submitted by the senate, each list naming three nominees for each post; and he named ministers. By the use of his appointive power, he effectively controlled the municipal councils, traditionally dominated by the *fazendeiros* (the great landholders); these councils in turn named representatives to provincial assemblies and the national parliament. It was an undemocratic system which, in the hands of a Rosas or a García Moreno, would have yielded dictatorship. In the generous hands of Pedro, it furnished as much democracy as immature Brazil could absorb. "Under the form of a constitutional monarchy," writes Alan Manchester, "he was in reality the absolute ruler of the empire, and Pedro presided over his tempestuous empire with rare benevolence and always with the greatest of conscience." Gilberto Freyre describes Pedro as "a sort of Queen Victoria in breeches . . . who watched his statesmen like a moral detective."

THE TASKS OF EMPIRE

Pedro's forty-nine-year rule falls roughly into three periods: the first decade, the 1840's, was given over to the suppression of civil wars and the consolidation of his power; the 1850's and 1860's were marked by quarrels with foreign nations; the last two decades, the 1870's and 1880's, saw growth in liberal and republican ideas which led to the abolition of slavery and the end of the empire.

Pacification was a problem inherited from the days of the regency. Revolts in Maranhão were suppressed in 1841; and there were brief revolts in Minas Gerais and São Paulo in 1842. The ten-year civil war in Rio Grande do Sul was finally quieted in 1845. The last serious threat to the unity of the empire was a liberal uprising in Pernambuco, which was put down in 1849. Chief credit for the suppressing of revolts against the empire goes to a young army officer, Luiz Alves de Lima e Silva, Baron of Caxias—later Count, then Duke, Brazil's most brilliant statesman-soldier under the empire, and Pedro's firm and able supporter for more than thirty years.

Pedro's next task was to establish Brazil's place among the nations. No contemporary ruler in Latin America knew more about the world than he did. His blood ties with Europe's kings had inspired wide reading which made him sensitive to international realities. But, despite his roots in Europe, Pedro was a Brazilian and had sworn to defend "the integrity and indivisibility of the empire," a pledge that involved him in disputes with England, the United States, Argentina, Uruguay, and Paraguay.

Pedro's troubles with England were part of his Portuguese inheritance. When John came to Rio de Janeiro in 1808, the British came with him, dominated his course and that of Pedro I, continued their suzerainty under the regency, and showed every intention of holding Pedro II in line. The chief issue was slavery. British recognition of Brazilian independence in 1825 had been bought with a Brazilian promise to end the slave trade by 1830, a humiliation forced upon Pedro I. The trade in Negroes, far from ending in 1830, increased. British pressure against the trade continued; inspired partly by the English abolitionists who were largely influenced by the Society of Friends, and partly by a sound economic sense which sought to end competition from slave-holding nations. In 1845 the British Parliament decreed that Brazilian slave ships seized upon the high seas would henceforth be subject to the arbitrament of British courts rather than of the mixed Anglo-Brazilian commissions provided by the earlier treaty. This was a clear affront to Brazil and to its emperor. Pedro had no love for slavery or for the slave trade, but he was of no mind to permit England to dictate. For five years the British repeatedly seized ships loaded with slaves bound for Brazil, refused to discuss the issue, and rejected all claims for damages. Meanwhile, shipments increased—over 50,000 new slaves were unloaded each year in 1847, 1848, and 1849.

In 1850 British cruisers entered Brazilian harbors and captured some slave ships. Brazil, unable to resist, capitulated and the parliament enacted measures to put a stop to the traffic—and to prevent Britain from interfering. This humiliation at British hands was followed by others, and the already tense relations worsened. In 1861 a British vessel was wrecked on the coast of Rio Grande do Sul; the arrogant British minister, W. D. Christie, charged that Brazilians had looted it and murdered some of its crew, but Pedro's government did not permit a free investigation. Then a few British sailors provoked a minor riot in Rio de Janeiro; Brazilian police handled the brawlers sternly, evoking violent protest from the British minister. When these protests were disregarded, British vessels blockaded the port of Rio de Janeiro, and Brazil was forced to accept British terms and to pay an indemnity. In June, 1863, Brazil broke off relations with England. These events convinced Pedro that Brazil must have an adequate army and navy.

During the United States Civil War, Brazil's relations with Washington were strained by Brazil's declaration of neutrality and by her concession of belligerent rights to the Confederate States. There were a few clashes in Brazilian waters between vessels of the contending American factions. Pedro made clear his sympathy for the Northern cause but maintained his nation's neutrality. The situation was needlessly embittered by the minister sent by Washington to Rio de Janeiro. A man of little intelligence and no tact, James W. Webb served as a constant irritant; however, Pedro kept his temper and paid little attention to the insults. When urged to accept arbitration between North and South, Abraham Lincoln (according to a seemingly accurate report) declared that Pedro II was the only monarch he would trust in such a matter.

While such arguments with distant powers plagued the empire, the perennial quarrel over the Banda Oriental (Uruguay) continued to trouble Pedro's government and finally led to a costly war. Uruguay's sovereignty had been pledged by both Brazil and Argentina in 1828, but the Brazilians had never been content with the settlement. During the 1830's the regents had had neither the money nor the men with which to assert Brazil's claims in that region; furthermore, the revolt in Rio Grande do Sul (1835–45) prevented any effective action. Brazil's irritation increased during the 1840's when the Argentine dictator Rosas took sides with the Uruguayan conservatives (*blancos*), besieged Montevideo, and threatened to take over the little buffer state. By the late 1840's, Brazilian businessmen who had a stake in Uruguay were demanding that the government in Rio de Janeiro intervene on their behalf.

By 1850, when Brazil's internal wars had been put down and the country was beginning to prosper, Pedro decided that it was time to strike. Then followed Brazil's alliance with the Uruguayan liberals (*colorados*), Paraguay, and the caudillos of the Argentine provinces of Corrientes and Entre Ríos against Rosas and the Uruguayan *blancos*. Brazil and her allies, with an army commanded by Entre Ríos' Urquiza, defeated Rosas in 1852 and lifted the siege of Montevideo. Meanwhile, Brazil pressed her advantage in Uruguay, forcing a treaty upon her in 1851 which transferred debated borderlands to the empire. By another treaty, Brazil made a loan which was guaranteed by Uruguay's customs receipts. Then in 1854 a Brazilian force was sent into Uruguay to strengthen the hold of the *colorados* (the party favoring Brazil); this action excited Urquiza, now president of all Argentina except the province of Buenos Aires. The argument was theoretically settled by a treaty with Argentina in 1859 by which both countries again underwrote the sovereignty of Uruguay. But the lawless *gaúcho* forces of Rio Grande do Sul (who had earlier attempted to detach their state from the empire) were encouraged by Brazilian business leaders who had properties in Uruguay to take matters into their hands; and there were repeated Brazilian raids into Uruguayan territory. These events provoked widespread fears, in the La Plata area, of imperialistic designs on the part of the Rio de Janeiro government.

Out of the clash of rival interests in Uruguay came the War of the Triple Alliance (Brazil, Argentina, and Uruguay) against Paraguay (1864–1870). The Uruguayan conservatives (*blancos*) persuaded Paraguay's *opéra bouffe* tyrant, Francisco Solano López, that Brazil and Argentina were about to take over control of Uruguay; their argument was substantiated by Brazil's sending an expeditionary force into Uruguay in 1864. Whereupon the foolhardy López seized a Brazilian steamboat on the Paraguay River in November, 1864, and a few weeks later sent troops to occupy Brazil's Mato Grosso. In January, 1865, López asked Argentina's permission to cross her territory for an attack upon Brazil's southern state, Rio Grande do Sul; when this was refused by Mitre's government, López's troops marched across the Argentine province of Corrientes. Paraguay was now at war with both Argentina and Brazil; Uruguay, under Brazilian pressure, was forced to enter the insane struggle. The war lasted five years, with Brazil furnishing the most men and money. At a cost of 50,000 dead and about $300 million, Brazil won some territory and prestige, and a new sense of the unity of the empire.

THE EXPANDING ECONOMY UNDER THE EMPIRE

The 1850's were marked by a burst of economic prosperity. There had been many changes since the beginning of the century. The south's cattle herds were increasing. Pernambuco and Bahia were producing more sugar, tobacco, and cotton; and São Paulo's coffee was now an important crop. Production of all commodities except gold and diamonds was on the increase. A few industries had been launched in the province of Rio de Janeiro. The *fazendeiros,* softened by the pleasures of Rio de Janeiro and Paris, were slowly losing their hold. The stage was set for vigorous advance. The founding of the Bank of Brazil and the adoption of a new commercial code in the early 1850's spurred private enterprise, and foreign trade doubled between 1849 and 1856. Economically, Brazil had come of age.

Chief leader of this new economic expansion was Irineu Evangelista de Souza, Baron of Mauá (1813–89). Mauá is Brazil's prime exhibit of the self-made man; the opening sentence of his autobiography is characteristic: "In the springtime of my life I had already won by tireless and honest labors a fortune which assured complete independence." Mauá's official biographer describes him as one of the three greatest men of the empire, bracketing him with Caxias the soldier and Pedro the emperor. "He personified his time," writes another Brazilian. José Jobim describes him as a "baron of industry" in a land already familiar with coffee barons, sugar barons, and cattle barons. Parallels may be drawn between Mauá and the elder Pierpoint Morgan. Like the New York financier, Mauá built a banking empire (it was centered in Rio de Janeiro, with branches in nine provincial capitals and also in Montevideo, Buenos Aires, London, and New York); and he helped to finance his country's wars—and collected generous toll for his patriotic service.

Mauá's ventures were scattered from the headwaters of the Amazon to the Río de la Plata. He built railroads, roads, ports, and canals and promoted shipping lines; he introduced gaslighting to Rio de Janeiro; he built textile mills; he laid telegraph lines and was chiefly responsible for the first transatlantic cable. He organized stock companies for his many enterprises and unloaded shares upon a speculation-hungry public. He organized a holding company which owned and operated vast farm lands in Brazil, Uruguay, and Argentina. His heavy stake in Uruguay was a factor in Brazil's intervention in the 1850's and 1860's. When war with Paraguay threatened, he regarded it as a poor business risk; for a time he used his influence against participation but finally helped to finance it. For twenty-five years, he dominated the money market; his speculative enterprises helped to bring on the financial crash of 1875, which ruined him, his companies, and thousands who had entrusted their money to him.

There are parallels between Mauá's Brazil and the contemporary

United States; the same bold building, the same riotous speculation, the same pushing back of the frontier by railroads, steamships, telegraph lines, canals, and roads. Mauá was convinced that Brazil must consume more of its own goods; hence his zeal for railroads which would link the farms and the city markets. Mauá's was the first effective voice against the colonial economy which made the country the producer and purveyor of cheap raw materials and the buyer of expensive finished goods. His, too, was the first voice for tariffs protecting industry, but he faced the opposition of the *fazendeiros* and of the English traders who had goods to sell. Pedro took little part in this controversy. He found no pleasure in the discussion of economic questions. While the industrialists argued about tariffs, Pedro studied botany and Arabic.

The expansion of the empire's business brought demand for new man power for the building of railroads, factories, and mills, and for the settlement of the frontier. Industrialists joined planters and stockmen in demanding more immigrants. There had been a thin trickle of new blood from the first days of the century, a few Germans, Swiss, Spaniards, and Portuguese. Beginning in the 1850's, the government offered fresh inducements to Europeans. A few thousand came each year during the 1850's and the 1860's, but not until 1874 did immigration begin in earnest. Between 1874 and 1889 over 600,000 came, chiefly from Italy, Germany, Spain, and Portugal; that total would rise by the mid-twentieth century to almost 5 million. Those who came brought technical skill to new industries, scientific methods to coffee culture and cattle breeding. Brazil unwisely permitted the Germans to create their own communities in the south, islands of an alien culture set apart from Brazilian life.[2]

The building of railroads had been discussed since the 1830's, when it was given impetus by news in 1831 that a steam locomotive had actually pulled a train from Albany to Schenectady. In 1840 the ever-zealous Lord Cochrane (whom we have already met in Chile and Brazil) landed in Rio de Janeiro, secured a concession to build a railroad, but failed to raise the necessary funds. In the 1850's Pedro's government offered subsidies to foreign railroad builders. In 1852, without subsidy, the Baron of Mauá began a railroad from the harbor of Rio de Janeiro to the foot of the escarpment crowned by Petropolis. This 9-mile railroad was opened to traffic in 1854. Other lines followed: a 19-mile road inland from Recife was opened in 1858; a 9-mile stretch in Bahia in 1860; the 49-mile cog railroad from Santos to São Paulo in 1867. By the end of the empire, Brazil had 6,193 miles of railroads.

Steamship lines multiplied. Regular services had been operating along the Atlantic coast and on the river systems of the Río de la Plata

---

[2] An item in this immigration, quite unimportant but interesting to Americans, was the flight of a thousand or more citizens of the defeated Confederate States to Brazil, where slavery still prevailed. Brazilian agents in the United States offered cheap land and tax exemptions. The Southerners settled in communities from the Amazon south to Rio Grande do Sul. Most of them, quickly disillusioned, returned home; but a few stayed. There is a town near the city of São Paulo, Villa Americana, settled by people from Alabama and Georgia whose livelihood was assured by the lowly watermelon.

and the Amazon since 1837. A shortsighted nationalism had restricted such navigation to Brazilian ships, but in 1867 the Amazon was opened to international commerce. The Amazon had a definite international character; it afforded access not only to interior Brazil but also to large but economically undeveloped areas of Venezuela, Colombia, Peru, and Bolivia. Pressure from Great Britain and the United States was effective in persuading Brazil to open her waterways to foreign ships.[3]

Other lines of communication were also expanded. A few roads were built and the postal service was increased. In 1852 the telegraph was introduced into Brazil; 116 miles of wires were in operation by 1864; 3,904 miles by 1875; and 11,752 miles by the end of the empire. In 1874 the first submarine cable was laid.

Foreign trade, mirror of growing production and improved communication, increased rapidly. By the middle 1870's, Brazil was importing about $84 million worth of goods per year, and selling the world about $104 million worth of coffee, sugar, tobacco, hides, and other commodities.

THE SOCIAL AND CULTURAL PATTERN OF THE EMPIRE

The social pattern of 1850 had changed little since colonial days. It was a slave society dominated by great landowners, who were the unchallenged lords of their domains. A few thousand owned the land; a few million worked it. The slaves, while still deprived of civil rights, usually lived under a tolerant paternal rule. They were permitted to buy their freedom, or were sometimes granted it by indulgent owners; and the free Negroes enjoyed the same rights as the whites, the line being economic rather than racial. "The Brazilian slave," writes Gilberto Freyre, "lived the life of a cherub if we contrast his lot with that of the English and other European factory workers."

In 1832 Charles Darwin had visited Rio de Janeiro and compared its unashamed filth to that which he had seen in Oriental cities. This situation was but little changed by 1850. Rio de Janeiro had no sewers—garbage was thrown into the streets and sewage found its own course. Buzzards were the chief scavengers. The water supply was scanty; leaking aqueducts carried it to central outlets. Vermin were accepted as an act of God; and women saw no social disgrace in having lice in their hair. Yellow fever and cholera were unchecked. Diet had not changed since colonial days: the poor still had their corn, manioc, a little jerked beef, and local fruit.

The Church, increasingly active in education and charity, furnished

---

[3] Americans played a considerable part in turning Pedro's attention to Amazonia. In 1851 William Lewis Herndon was sent by the United States navy on a journey of exploration; his report, *Exploration of the Valley of the Amazon,* recently reprinted, was a major contribution to knowledge of the region. In 1865 Louis Agassiz of Harvard University traveled far inland; the report by that scientist and his wife stirred further interest. The affection and respect of Pedro II for Louis Agassiz largely influenced the Emperor in decreeing the opening of the Amazon to foreign ships.

many notable priests, many of them educated in Europe. The Church held
high prestige. Every important family felt morally and socially bound to
contribute at least one son to the priesthood.

There had been slight cultural progress by 1850. Illiteracy had lessened but little; a few schools had been built but there was still no university. Education was reserved for the sons of the privileged. Rio de
Janeiro boasted a library, an academy of fine arts, and a botanical garden,
all founded by John VI. A start had been made toward creation of a national literature, though Gilberto Freyre remarks on "the lack of sap in
literature . . . the almost complete absence of critical thought." Few
Brazilians shared the scientific and intellectual thought of the world. A few
brilliant leaders had emerged such as the Marquis of Itanhaén, the Viscount of Rio Branco, and Nabuco de Araújo; but most Brazilians were still
living in the Middle Ages.

Education was one of Pedro's chief concerns. "If I were not an
emperor," he said as his reign neared its end, "I should like to be a school
teacher." Brazil continued to lag behind Spanish America in providing
schools. There are various explanations for the tardiness in providing schooling: the meager intellectual ardor of Portugal, the poverty of Brazil, the
vastness of its territory and the isolation of its scattered communities, the
drag of slavery, the fear of the *fazendeiros* that book learning would corrupt the workers. The hunger for popular education was revealed in the
constitutional convention of 1823, whose members agreed upon the stipulation that "each village or city should have a public school, each district a
high school"; but when Pedro I did not acquiesce, the words were deleted.
Law schools were established in Pernambuco and São Paulo in 1827; three
normal schools, in the 1830's; a high school, later named after Pedro II,
was built in Rio de Janeiro in 1838; an engineering school, in Rio de Janeiro
in 1847; a school of mines, in Minas Gerais in 1856. But Pedro was untiring in his pleas for more and better schools. When, at the close of the
war with Paraguay, it was proposed to erect a statue to him, he bade the
sponsors spend the money on schools. Later, when plans were laid to reno-
vate the national palace, he vetoed the project: "No—more school buildings." But his success was limited. At the end of his reign in 1889, when
the total population was almost 14 million, there were but 250,000 children
enrolled in primary classes. Nor was there a single great university, although
scattered faculties provided instruction in medicine, law, and engineering.

Pedro saw the need for trained leaders. Throughout his reign, he
sought out gifted boys and provided funds for their education in Paris,
London, Lisbon, and Coimbra. However, what little education was available was limited to boys; neither Brazil nor Pedro had learned that girls
might also have brains. An interesting contemporary report on the Brazilian
attitude toward women comes from the wife of the American scientist
Louis Agassiz, who visited Brazil at Pedro's invitation in 1865. Mrs. Agassiz reports that her husband was to lecture in Rio de Janeiro; she wished
to attend, but special permission from the emperor was required before
even one woman could be admitted. "Too great an innovation on national
habits," Mrs. Agassiz writes.

Pedro's enthusiasm for scholarship found outlet through the Brazilian Historical and Geographical Institute, which, under his generous patronage, became the most distinguished body of its kind in South America. Pedro encouraged writers. He fancied himself as a poet, turned out mediocre poetry of romantic vein, and enjoyed the cloying verse of Gonçalves Dias and Casimiro de Abreu. These were the popular writers of 1850, but, in Erico Verissimo's phrase, "they lacked sun, joy of living and fresh air." After 1850 Brazilian letters took on new life. Characteristic of the new and more realistic school were: Castro Alves, whose poems carried eloquent denunciation of slavery; José de Alencar whose novel *O guarany* interpreted the Indian; Aluizio de Azevedo, whose novel *The Mulatto* mirrored the social ills of the nation; and Machado de Assis, of Negro blood, the best loved of all Brazilian writers. His *Dom Casmurro* (*Mr. Peevish,* it has been translated) is best known to foreign readers. Here was "the novelist of the reign of Pedro II," writes Henríquez Ureña. Erico Verissimo adds: "We Brazilians are very proud of him."

PEDRO'S TRAVELS

Pedro felt a need to see the world known to him only through books—Europe, in which his own roots were sunk, many of whose rulers were his kin; and the United States, newcomer among the nations. In 1871, with the end of the Paraguayan War and with calm at home, he was free to go. He landed in Lisbon and spent ten months in Portugal, Spain, France, England, and Italy. Returning in 1872, he planned another trip; in 1876 he was in the United States for four months, then spent a full year in Europe. The record of his journeyings reveals the man. He had small interest in kings and princes, and avoided the honors of courts. He sought out philosophers, poets, novelists, and scientists: Pasteur, Victor Hugo, Herculano, Gobineau, Longfellow, Emerson, and Whittier. Pedro's interest in the work of the American writers led him to make Portuguese translations of a number of their poems. At the Centennial Exposition in Philadelphia, he was eager to meet a young man named Alexander Graham Bell, currently regarded as a crackpot, who had invented a gadget called the telephone. A devout Catholic, Pedro was curious about other faiths; he attended services in Jewish synagogues and discussed Hebrew syntax with rabbis; he sat on the platform at a Protestant revival service and listened with approval to evangelist Dwight L. Moody; and he went to a service in Salt Lake's Mormon Tabernacle. In Europe and the United States, he was indefatigable in visiting hospitals, clinics, schools, churches, and art galleries. And always, he was representing Brazil, gathering ideas for the enrichment of his country's life and inviting scientists to visit his land. The friends he made and the voluminous correspondence which followed served Brazil.

Pedro's was now a great name; he was one of the few South Americans known and respected outside their little-known lands. He was neither a great thinker, nor a scientist, nor a writer. García Calderón exaggerates in describing him as "a learned and skeptical Marcus Aurelius, a stoic who had read Voltaire." He was not a scholar but a dilettante driven to know something about everything under the sun—biology, astronomy, archaeology, history, philosophy, physics. His restless curiosity and his naïve dabbling in many subjects exposed him to the scorn of specialists, furnished a leaven to the empire over which he presided. Though his dreams outran his ability, Brazil profited by his dreams.

THE LAST YEARS OF THE EMPIRE, 1870–89

Even as Pedro explored the larger world, the forces which would unseat him were gathering momentum. For thirty years he had held the affectionate respect of his people; any fair plebiscite would have supported Pedro as emperor, president, or whatever title he might choose. Furthermore, the throne had powerful allies: the nobility ("Sons of the Kingdom," John VI had called them); the feudal *fazendeiros;* the Church; and the army. Now, within twenty years, he would lose their support and abdicate.

The first conflict was with the Church. Pedro was warmhearted in religious devotion, but his Catholicism was more akin to that of England and the United States than to the Church of Portugal and Spain. His fidelity was suspected by some of the more devout; his eclecticism was too pronounced for their tastes; he respected the sincerity of Protestants, Jews, and Mormons; he admired the heretics Renan and Herculano; he found inspiration in the Unitarians and Quakers of the United States. Joaquim Nabuco called Pedro a "limited Catholic." He had firm support from the Vatican in the earlier years, and especially in the 1850's when he undertook needed reform of some religious orders.

The controversy which finally embroiled his relations with Rome was the issue of Freemasonry. The Church in Brazil, unlike that in Spanish America, had seldom clashed with that secret order. José Bonifácio and many others had belonged to the lodges. The Church brotherhoods (*irmandades*), powerful throughout the colonial era and still influential under the empire, had usually included Freemasons. In fact, anticlericalism had never been so important in Brazil as it was in Colombia, Ecuador, or Mexico. When the Pope pronounced a ban upon Freemasonry in 1865, Pedro refused to have the encyclical published in Brazil—he had such authority under the concordat with the Vatican. However, without publication, the word spread and incited bitterness. Numerous Freemasons among the clergy obstinately insisted upon their right to continue as members of the lodges. This right was peremptorily denied by two bishops, who were forthwith convicted for defying the emperor, and were actually committed to jail. Pedro changed their sentences from imprisonment at hard labor to simple imprisonment; but his course mollified neither churchmen nor Freemasons. By punishing the bishops, he lost clerical support, but he did not punish them severely enough to please the Freemasons. In 1875 Pedro sought to appease the Church by granting full amnesty to the two bishops, but neither churchmen nor the members of the lodges forgave him.

Then there was the conflict over the army. Pedro's concern was the enlightenment and well-being of the people; guns and marching men bored him. However, the Paraguayan War had made clear the necessity of an army and a navy. The stormy figure who excited debate was the Duke of Caxias, chief military hero, stout Conservative, twice prime minister, who advocated stronger military power but was always loyal to Pedro. The issue was drawn between the Liberals, who demanded civilian rule, and the army, which saw itself neglected. Pedro, aware of the army's importance, sought to meet its fair demands, but he was determined to curb its political activities. Again, he finally satisfied neither side.

Meanwhile, sentiment for a republic increased. It was nourished by the fears of some, the hopes of others; churchmen saw in a republic release from Pedro's liberalism; generals hoped that a republic would give them greater power; Conservatives thought Pedro too gentle with Liberals; Liberals thought him too lenient with Conservatives. Then another element was injected, the Positivism of Auguste Comte, with numerous adherents in Brazil who called for rejection of the supernatural and the authoritarian, proclaiming a "religion of humanity" whose only saints are the servants of mankind. This movement clothed republican sentiment with fervor. In 1870 the crusade for a republic was formally launched with the founding, in Rio de Janeiro, of a newspaper, *A República,* carrying in its first issue a "Republican Manifesto" signed by many men who would live to see their hopes fulfilled. Pedro regarded this movement calmly, insisting that its leaders had a perfect right to press their case, and refused to permit reprisals against them. Positivism was freely taught in some schools. Pedro himself appointed as tutor for his grandsons one of the ablest leaders of the Positivists, a zealot for the republican cause, Benjamin Constant Botelho de Magalhães. Pedro's ministers protested the choice, but the emperor brushed their objections aside: "Let the country govern itself as it thinks best, and consider right whoever may be right."

Abolition of slavery finally brought an end to the empire. We have followed the fortunes of that tawdry institution; we have marked the tenacity of the slaveholders and the criticism which increased with each decade. Pedro's own convictions were clear. "No one," he said, "more ardently wishes abolition than I do." On assuming the throne in 1840, he freed his personal slaves, and he encouraged manumission on all occasions. In 1866, when the Benedictine Order in Rio de Janeiro freed 1,600 slaves, Pedro made a call upon their abbot to congratulate him. But Pedro was a realist and he knew that premature emancipation would ruin the *fazendeiros* and cripple the national economy. Meanwhile, as we have seen, British pressure, which dictated abolition of the slave trade in 1830 and led to effective enforcement of the laws against it in 1850, had affronted national pride and perhaps delayed rather than hastened abolition. Agitation against slavery was given new impetus by the victory of the American Union and Lincoln's Emancipation Proclamation. Pedro's daughter, Isabel, and her French husband were active abolitionists. In 1871 a movement led by the Liberal Nabuco de Araújo, the Conservative Viscount Rio Branco, and young Joaquim Nabuco took action. The emperor was in Europe; but no one doubted his support of the measure adopted by parliament and signed by Princess Isabel, Pedro's regent.

The Rio Branco law was a gradual and conciliatory measure, freeing slaves of the nation and the Crown, providing funds to buy the freedom of others, and declaring that all children born henceforth to slave mothers should be free—but, softening that blow to the planters, such children were to be apprenticed to their masters until they reached the age of twenty-one. This law affecting some 1.7 million slaves was received with popular enthusiasm, but it did not satisfy the abolitionists. The antislavery societies became more active under the guidance of Joaquim Nabuco. Local movements abolished slavery in the northern state of Ceará in 1883, and in Amazonas in 1884; many slaves were freed in Rio Grande do Sul. When the abolitionists demanded that a final deadline for slavery be fixed for 1890, the slaveholders were spurred to new attack. To both parties, Pedro counseled patience, but he satisfied neither. In 1885 a new measure strengthened the Rio Branco law of 1871, and agitation for complete and immediate emancipation continued. In 1888, while Pedro was in Europe for his health, the accumulated pressure of the abolitionists brought action from parliament and the last 700,000 slaves were freed, without compensation to the owners. Princess Regent Isabel signed the bill. The news was cabled to Pedro, desperately ill in Italy. Pedro wept, whispering: "What great people! What great people!"

The last pages of the chapter had been turned. The Church no longer supported the empire; the *fazendeiros,* many ruined by abolition, turned against Pedro; Liberals demanded a republic. It was a sick and prematurely aged Pedro who returned to Brazil in 1888. The heir to the throne was Isabel, a princess of character and ability, but not popular. Even less popular was her husband, the Count d'Eu, a man of solid virtues but described slightingly as "the Frenchman." A major cause of resentment was his failure to learn Portuguese. Brazilians would have no foreigner rule over them, and they could not believe that Isabel, when her turn came, would reign in her own right. Pedro did nothing to stem the tide which had turned against him. He did not cherish his royal prerogatives, although he favored the monarchy as a safeguard against the military dictatorships which were scourging Spanish America.

The army finally settled the question. Dominated by ambitious General Manoel Deodoro da Fonseca, the army was rife with mutinies and plots spread among the officers. The revolt came to a head in November, 1889, when Deodoro, Benjamin Constant, and Floriano Peixoto presented an ultimatum to Pedro. He agreed to abdicate and to sail for Europe. They offered him a pension, but he refused it. It was a lonely and broken man who reached Lisbon at the end of that year, and his loneliness was shortly deepened by the death of Thereza. He settled in France, where he died in 1891.

Chapter 50

THE FIRST REPUBLIC,
1 8 8 9 – 1 9 3 0

The break with the empire had been clean-cut. A barracks-revolt in the Latin American tradition, it had been the army's doing, not the people's. A contemporary eyewitness wrote: "The people stood by stupefied, dumfounded, without an inkling of what it all meant. Many honestly believed they were watching a parade." A parade it was, in which the military led by Deodoro da Fonseca and Floriano Peixoto took over the power from the civilian government of the empire. These generals, it seemed clear, cared little what sort of government they had so long as the army had its way. The propertied classes, nursing their grievances against the monarchy, stood by consenting. But if the generals were no more than expedient republicans, this was not true of their civilian partners in the enterprise; certainly not of that mercurial enthusiast Benjamin Constant Botelho de Magalhães, whose loyalty to the "religion of humanity" of the Positivist cult furnished crusading zeal to the new movement; nor of the brilliant but erratic Ruy Barbosa, who had worked so long for the realization of a republic.

The shift in government reflected a fundamental shift in the economy of the nation. The center of economic gravity had moved south, from the colonial sugar-cotton-tobacco-cacao plantations of Bahia and Pernambuco to the coffee-cattle-industrial lands of São Paulo, Minas Gerais, Rio de Janeiro, and Rio Grande do Sul. The abolition of slavery had dealt the *coup de grâce* to the north's hopes. The key was now coffee, and coffee meant São Paulo, major producer by the 1890's. Brazil was already producing more than 60 per cent of the world's coffee; by 1896 the figure would stand at 66 per cent, and by the first years of the new century, at 75 per cent. Rubber, rapidly growing in volume, would give brief importance to the Amazon basin, which at this time was simply the tropical colony of a nation whose economic heart was São Paulo.

DICTATORSHIP AND CONFUSION, 1889–98

The generals now ruled. Government was by decree—by the decrees of Deodoro da Fonseca, *de facto* dictator by grace of his control of the army. By decree, there was created the United States of Brazil, a federated republic of twenty states which "recognizes and respects" the pledges of the empire, an assurance which brought recognition from all major nations within a year. By decree, large powers were allotted the several states, but those powers were largely nullified by the interference of the executive. By decree, the ties between Church and state were severed; here we see the hand of Benjamin Constant and of Ruy Barbosa.

The new government inherited an empty treasury. The imperial regime, during its last months, had dissipated its funds in frantic efforts to rescue the *fazendeiros* from the woes of abolition, and had finally resorted to reckless issuing of paper currency. Ruy Barbosa, the new minister of finance, found no better solution than to print more money. This provoked dangerous inflation, as the abundance of paper milreis led to a speculative orgy of overcapitalized industries and high land prices. Brazil's credit in world markets fell disastrously; the value of her currency dropped by more than one-half between 1888 and 1891. Deodoro's government was incredibly wasteful; the number of army officers was more than doubled, and their paychecks were larger than they had ever been under the empire.

A commission chosen by the coterie in power was charged with writing a constitution, and in early 1891 the new charter was imposed upon the United States of Brazil without any pretense of popular referendum. On its face, this constitution was fashioned after that of the United States: there was the same distribution of powers and privileges among the executive, legislative, and judicial branches of the government. Under pressure from stout regionalists, it paid lip service to the principle of states' rights, granting to the states control of their local affairs and investing each with the right to impose import duties on goods from other states. But in reality it endowed the chief executive with almost dictatorial powers: the president could impose a "state of siege" at will, intervene in any state's internal affairs, and supplant elected governors. Theoretically democratic, the constitution gave less voice to the electorate than had the parliamentary system of Pedro.

The constituent assembly, largely hand-picked by the generals, promulgated the new constitution and then proceeded to the election of a president and vice-president. Civilian elements, scarcely represented, had no chance against the army groups, who named Manoel Deodoro da Fonseca and Floriano Peixoto to the top posts. Deodoro's luster as the hero of the republic was already tarnished by his arrogance during the months since Pedro's departure. As president, he proved inept and capricious, and after eight months disbanded his congress and again ruled by decree. The people, in no mood to accept dictatorship, rebelled, forcing his retirement in favor of Peixoto; but that opportunistic general proved even more irritating. Thirteen generals who demanded his resignation were jailed or exiled. Ruy Barbosa, speaking for the civilians, denounced him through his newspaper, the *Jornal do Brasil*. Barracks-revolts broke out in Rio de Janeiro, spread north and south, with the most formidable opposition coming from Rio Grande do Sul. In 1893 the navy rebelled under the leadership of Admiral de Mello, and for eight months the civil war continued. The United States, France, Italy, Great Britain, and Portugal kept their warships in Brazilian waters. When the rebellion had finally been crushed, Peixoto imposed a reign of terror such as Brazil had not hitherto experienced. Then, in 1894 to the surprise of everyone, the tyrant peacefully yielded his office to Prudente José de Moraes Barros.

The States of Brazil

Prudente's inauguration brought relief after the humiliating confusion of the first five years of the republic. A civilian from São Paulo and generally respected, he was caught in the angry schism between the military and the civilian factions. Governmental agencies had been demoralized under his predecessors, state administration was chaotic, and the nation's economy was at low ebb. Despite these handicaps, Prudente enjoyed a brief respite from armed revolts and made substantial progress during his first two years in office. The national treasury was reorganized, relations with foreign powers were improved, and progress was made in settling territorial disputes with Argentina, Great Britain, and France. But in 1897 his vice-president joined those who were plotting against him, and the country was again convulsed. The most disturbing uprising was in the *sertão,* the interior region behind the northern coastal zone of Bahia and Pernambuco; the struggle that ensued was immortalized in the chief classic of Brazilian literature, *Os sertões* by Euclides da Cunha.[1]

The *sertão* is a semiarid highland region, unlovely and unfruitful, peopled by frontiersmen of Portuguese-Indian blood whom Cunninghame Graham has described as "a race of Centaurs, deeply imbued with fanaticism, strong, honest, revengeful, primitive and refractory to modern ideas and life." Their stronghold was Canudos, 300 miles northwest of Bahia. They were led for thirty-five years by Antônio Maciel, a strange zealot called the *Conselheiro,* "the Counselor," by his followers. They formed a theocratic state dedicated to the Good Jesus (*Bom Jesús*), with the Counselor as its high priest and king. His faith was a strange mixture of Catholicism and fetishism, intertwined with vague appeal to the cult of Sebastianism.[2] The Counselor worked miracles of healing, and assumed paternal care of his subjects. About fifty-five in 1896, he was ambitious to restore the monarchy. In *Os sertões,* Euclides da Cunha tells the story of the federal armies which made their repeated attacks upon Canudos for almost three years; 6,000 soldiers were finally required to crush the Counselor and his disciples; the defenders of Canudos held out until the last man and boy were dead. Cunha's cry of protest immortalizes that inglorious campaign against brave men.

Prudente finished out his term in 1898. His last year was peaceful. Brazilians, shamed by the meager beginnings of their republic, had found in him a dim hope that they might learn to rule their national house in peace.

[1] Translated by Samuel Putnam as *Rebellion in the Backlands* (Chicago: University of Chicago Press; 1944. *Os sertões* appeared in 1902, and won recognition as "Brazil's greatest book," a work which is "lush and sensuous . . . rugged . . . intense . . . sculpturesque." Born in 1866, Cunha was a fervent republican during the last days of the empire, and suffered the disillusion of the first years of the republic. Like many other young intellectuals of his time he came under the spell of Positivism. By profession a military engineer, Cunha made his mark as an interpreter of social forces. "If," writes Erico Verissimo, "I had to choose just one book . . . as representative of my country and of my people, I would certainly pick *Os sertões.*

[2] King Sebastian of Portugal died in battle with the Moslems in 1578. For 300 years, his disciples in Europe and America swore that he still lived, and would return to vindicate his faith. See p. 90.

BUILDING THE REPUBLIC, 1898–1910

The twelve years which followed were the most constructive period in the history of the republic. Three men of ability and integrity served in the presidency: Manoel de Campos Salles, 1898–1902; Francisco de Paula Rodrígues Alves, 1902–06; and Affonso Penna, 1906–09—the first two were *paulistas,* the third a *mineiro. Paulistas* are the people of São Paulo; *mineiros,* those from Minas Gerais (these two states furnished all but two of the presidents who served during the first forty years of the republic); *cariocas,* the dwellers in Rio de Jáneiro; *gaúchos,* those of Rio Grande do Sul. It was a period of peace, of economic recovery, of constructive international agreements, of physical rebuilding of the capital, and of fight on disease. Constitutional forms were increasingly respected, and Brazil made use of some of her greatest sons.

In 1898 foreign loans were in default, the value of the currency continued to decline, and paper money flooded the market. Campos Salles, president-elect, was sent by Prudente to London to negotiate with the Rothschilds; his mission was successful; old loans were rewritten on generous terms and a new loan of £8.5 million granted. As security, the bankers were given a lien on customs receipts. Meanwhile, coffee and rubber exports were at a new peak. As president, Campos Salles had an able minister of finance, Joaquim Murtinho, whose methods were Spartan and effective: he withdrew and burned much paper money, imposed rigid controls on credit, encouraged industry, and imposed economies in government. In 1906 Brazil reestablished the gold standard.

In international relations, the policies of Prudente were continued, and settlements were reached on the more serious boundary disputes inherited from colonial and imperial days. The first, a dispute with Argentina over the region of Misiones, had long been stubborn. Spain and Portugal attempted to settle it by the Treaty of Madrid in 1750, but the pledges of that treaty had been honored by neither party. The dispute was arbitrated by President Grover Cleveland, and his decision in 1895, largely favoring Brazil, was a diplomatic triumph for the Baron of Rio Branco (son of the viscount whose name is fixed to the antislavery bill of 1871). Then, in 1900, a boundary argument with France over French Guiana was settled by the award of the president of the Swiss confederation. Again Rio Branco was credited with a favorable decision. The prestige won by these diplomatic successes led to Rio Branco's appointment as minister of foreign affairs in 1902, a post which he held with distinction until his death in 1912.

The third debate involved Acre, a triangular stretch in the headwaters of the Amazon claimed by both Bolivia and Brazil. Colonists had fled there from arid Ceará, and a few Brazilian contractors were collecting rubber. By 1899 both countries sought to establish their claims. There was serious tension, but in 1903 Rio Branco reached agreement with Bolivia, which relinquished its claims in return for £2 million sterling. Brazil also promised to build a railroad from the Amazon valley into the heart of Bolivia; and the Madeira-Mamoré railroad, affording Bolivia tenuous access to the navigable Madeira River, was finally completed at the cost of many lives. A fourth argument, with Great Britain, was over the boundary of British Guiana; in 1901 both accepted the arbitration of the King of Italy, but Brazil was disappointed by the award. A fifth dispute concerned the boundary between Dutch Guiana and Brazil; this was settled amicably by treaty in 1906. A sixth, with Colombia, involved title to about one-third of the state of Amazonas; in 1907 a treaty quieted the argument. A seventh concerned the line between Brazil and Venezuela; negotiations were begun in 1905, but agreement was not reached until 1929.

During these years Brazil won increased prestige in the family of nations, with chief credit going to the Baron of Rio Branco. He had spent thirty years in England and Germany, and his sympathies were strongly European and aristocratic. The Vatican's appointment of a Brazilian cardinal in 1905 was an important step in winning recognition of his nation's importance. Although Rio Branco looked to Europe for cultural inspiration, he recognized that all practical considerations dictated the value of close relations with the United States; he was successful in raising the status of his country's diplomatic post in Washington from a legation to an embassy, and was responsible for the appointment of Joaquim Nabuco as the first ambassador.

Rio Branco, unlike most contemporary South American statesmen, recognized the utility of the Monroe Doctrine and sought realization of the Bolivian dream of American unity. When Brazil entertained the Third Pan American Conference in 1906, Rio Branco addressed the delegates: "From Europe we come; Europe has been our teacher. . . . But [as for the United States] our interests are the same; they [the United States] consume on a large scale most of our important products." Secretary of State Elihu Root came from Washington to assure the Latin Americans that the United States "desired no sovereignties except the sovereignty over ourselves." The sessions were held in the Monroe Palace of Rio de Janeiro, a building erected at the Exposition in St. Louis, then moved stone by stone to Brazil's capital—the one Latin American monument to James Monroe. Rio Branco's enthusiasm for the United States was largely expedient, but not so Nabuco's. During his five-year term in Washington, ended by his death in 1910, Joaquim Nabuco was an eloquent and effective advocate of understanding with the United States, not a popular doctrine in the face of American indifference and much Brazilian suspicion. Ruy Barbosa also served Brazil by representing his country at the Second Hague Conference in 1907, where he made eloquent pleas for the rights of weak nations.

This period saw rebuilding of the nation's capital, now a city of 600,000 but still unformed and unkempt. Under Affonso Penna, the city was modernized and cleansed; broad boulevards were built, the impressive Avenida Rio Branco was cut through its heart, and "the most beautiful city in the world" won right to that description. But Rio de Janeiro needed more than face lifting. It was plague-ridden, sick. Yellow fever, brought from the Caribbean region, had taken tragic toll since 1850. In a half century, deaths from yellow fever had totaled not less than 15,000, and even in 1902 there were 982 deaths from that disease. In 1903 Dr. Oswaldo Cruz, disciple of Pasteur, organized the campaign against the stegomyia mosquito; he attacked the breeding spots of the guilty mosquito, and by 1909 had virtually ended yellow fever in the capital. He also eliminated bubonic plague and greatly lessened the incidence of smallpox. Oswaldo Cruz wrote the first notable chapter in Brazil's fight against disease; other Brazilians and outsiders (notably scientists of the Rockefeller Foundation) have added brilliantly to the story. In Rio de Janeiro a great laboratory, the Instituto Oswaldo Cruz, stands as a monument to this man.

This constructive period closed with the administration of Affonso Penna, a *mineiro* whose services to his state had been memorable. Affonso Penna's term was fruitful. He enlarged the harbor facilities of Rio de Janeiro, extended railroads, did much to restore national credit, and reorganized the army and the navy. Although he died before his term was completed, his vice-president carried on his policies; but Penna's last months in office were marred by political dissensions which boded no good for the future.

THE PERIOD OF TURMOIL, 1910–30

Two decades followed in which old ills were aggravated and new ills tested the stability of the republic. Five presidents served during this period: Hermes da Fonseca (the nephew of Deodoro), 1910–14; Wenceslau Braz, 1914–18; Epitácio da Silva Pessôa, 1919–22; Artur Bernardes, 1922–26; and Washington Luiz Pereira de Souza, 1926–30. Three perennial problems dogged them—the meddling of the military, anarchic regionalism, and the stumbling economy. A fourth complication was World War I.

The military were still untamed. Held in check for a dozen years, the generals were again out of hand by 1910. The presidential campaign of that year was a contest between soldiers and civilians: Hermes, the army's candidate, was opposed by Liberal Ruy Barbosa, who conducted Brazil's first popular political campaign. Hermes was elected, thanks to the army's manipulation of the elections and its bargains with political bosses. Hermes's dictatorial rule was countered by a grave outbreak by the navy, with much loss of life, followed by harsh reprisals. After Hermes's term was done, he and his son repeatedly provoked revolt. These upheavals convinced Brazilians of the evils of army rule. During this period the Club Militar exercised more power than is healthy in a democracy.

State loyalty still prevailed over allegiance to the nation. Elections were determined by shifting alliances between local political machines. The first truly national party, the *civilistas,* was launched in 1910 under eloquent Ruy Barbosa; he had the people behind him, but his party was helpless against the army-backed coalition which supported Hermes. Each state had a political machine and party chieftains; but those of São Paulo and Minas Gerais were dominant, passing the presidency back and forth between them like a football. The southern cattle state of Rio Grande do Sul offered the only effective challenge to these powerful states; its political boss, Pinheiro Machado, whom Lawrence Hill has called "the Mark Hanna of Brazil," dictated the choice of Hermes in 1910, and was a political force until his assassination in 1915. A constant source of trouble was the existence of state militia, used by the local bosses for their own purposes; that of São Paulo rivaled the federal army in strength.

Brazil's economy was buffeted by the shifting fortunes of rubber and coffee in world markets, but prosperity seemed assured in 1910. The Amazon valley was still yielding almost nine-tenths of the world's rubber, São Paulo and other areas about three-fourths of the world's coffee. Brazilians were confident of their future; their chief anxiety was the shortage of labor. Recruiting agents were seeking settlers from Italy, Spain, and Portugal; all records were broken—136,000 migrants came in 1911; 180,000 in 1912; 192,000 in 1913. Railroads were extended. Foreign loans increased through the lush 1920's, as the banking of Brazil shifted from London to New York. Caution vanished in public and private finance, the treasury was depleted, and the currency steadily deteriorated. Then two major blows crippled Brazilian economy.

The rubber bonanza collapsed. The "gold of the Amazon" was collected by a cruelly exploited labor force. For a half century, profits from rubber had lured men chiefly from Ceará, but also from the sugar, cotton, and tobacco plantations of Pará and Pernambuco and Bahia. By 1900, Brazil was providing almost all the world's rubber. Its generous profits built palaces in Belém and Manaus—and, in that inland city, the most fabulous opera house in South America. Meanwhile, untoward events had intervened. In 1875 a British scientist had taken seeds of the rubber tree (*hevea brasiliensis*) to England and planted them in the Kew Botanical Gardens; by 1895 the first rubber plantations were operating in the British and Dutch East Indies; in 1899 the first shipment of plantation rubber was made. The Brazilian monopoly was doomed. The Brazilian rubber industry suffered grave disabilities; the vast and remote areas involved, the inadequacy of communications, the scarcity of labor, the shortage of technicians, all resulted in high production costs. The East Indian plantations had numerous advantages—the scientific skills of England and Holland, rich land easily accessible, and an abundance of cheap labor. Brazil could not compete with the cleaner and better plantation rubber. In 1910 Brazil, furnishing nine-tenths of the world's rubber at about 34 cents a pound, received about $125 million. In 1921, furnishing less than one-tenth of the world's rubber at 6 cents a pound, she got about $5 million. When the efforts of Hermes failed to rescue the dying industry, his inept administration was further discredited.

Then coffee drifted into the doldrums. It had been of increasing importance in the Brazilian economy since its introduction in the early eighteenth century. By the 1870's Brazil was selling more than 50 per cent of the world's coffee; by 1900, more than 75 per cent. São Paulo had generous assets: rich red soil, enterprising foreign technicians, and the best labor supply in the republic. But São Paulo overreached itself, extending its production until it could meet the entire world demand—and forgetting its competitors in Central America, Colombia, Venezuela, Africa, and the East Indies. Before 1900, this competition had been negligible; by 1910, it was serious. In 1906, for example, Brazil produced 20 million bags (of 132 pounds each), a figure almost equal to world consumption for that year. Fitful and desperate efforts were made to limit plantings and to withhold surpluses from the market; the Coffee Institute, dominated by São Paulo, controlled production and marketing; federal support of the Institute was resented by other states. Riotous overproduction, cutthroat competition, and falling prices were destroying the coffee economy of the country.

The year 1914 brought the election of Wenceslau Braz Pereira Gomes, a Conservative civilian from Minas Gerais whose record of honesty and moderate ability made him welcome after the bad years under Hermes. But that same year saw the beginning of World War I and the further disruption of Brazil's economy. The prices of coffee and rubber fell in world markets; German submarines sank ships and blocked trade. Brazilian exports in 1914 were little more than half of what they had been the year before. Braz's government imposed higher taxes, cut the national budget, and imposed economy upon public officials, but he was finally forced to default on the national debt and to issue more paper money.

Brazil was sadly divided in its loyalties during World War I. Many influential people sided with the Allies: the cultured upper classes who regarded France as their second *Patria;* the many Italians in São Paulo; and numerous citizens who favored solidarity with the United States.. Other elements were frankly pro-German: those with German blood in southern Brazil, and some military men of strong nationalistic temper. But in 1917, after repeated sinkings of Brazilian ships by the Germans and after the entrance of the United States into the conflict, Brazil first revoked her neutrality, and then in October declared war on Germany—the only South American nation to take such action (seven of the little nations of Middle America also declared war). This gesture, involving no active share in the fighting, had a profound moral influence upon Brazil, giving her a sense of responsibility in world affairs.

The war years finally brought prosperity to Brazil. By 1917, in spite of German attacks upon shipping, she was selling foodstuffs to hungry Europe; between 1915 and 1917 her sales of beans increased over 400 times, and sugar sales multiplied almost 6 times; sales of chilled beef increased tenfold. When the war was over in 1918, Brazil took pride in being represented at the Versailles Peace Conference, where her spokesman Epitácio Pessôa asserted his country's place among the powers. And when the League of Nations was established by the signatories to the Versailles Treaty, Brazil adhered to the Covenant and contributed distinguished jurists (notably Afrânio de Mello Franco) to that ill-fated body. But in

1926, when the League refused to give Brazil a permanent seat on its Council—a slight not only to Brazil but to all Latin America—Brazil withdrew from the League.

In the last days of the war Brazil gave evidence of national maturity by electing as president Rodrígues Alves, whose earlier term in office, 1902–06, had been constructive, but he was too ill to assume office, and he died within a few months. In the special election called for 1919, the angry debate between the army candidates and the perennially eager Ruy Barbosa was settled by picking Epitácio Pessôa, who had won prestige at Versailles. In the presidency, with the support of substantial loans from England and the United States, Pessôa made a valiant effort to modernize the railroads and was the first leader to make generous plans to rescue the perpetually drought-ridden Northeast. But despite his integrity and ability, Pessôa was unable to quiet the storms caused by the continued economic crisis. Nor was there improvement under Artur da Silva Bernardes (1922–26); the refractory army elements led by the obdurate Hermes da Fonseca, having failed to impose their man as president, seemed intent upon preventing anyone else from ruling. Revolts in various states were put down by the imposition of a state of siege and by the intervention of federal troops.

The most dramatic episode of this stormy period was the revolt of the *tenentes* (lieutenants) at the Igrejinha fortress in Copacabana on July 5, 1922. It was significant that the rebels, lower middle class in origin, were inspired by lively concern for national renovation and social justice, ideals which their elder officers seldom shared. The revolt was stamped out in short order, and finally the tattered survivors (the "Eighteen of Copacabana") retreated to the beach where most of them died under gunfire. But the force of this revolt of the *tenentes* was not quelled. The few survivors[3] and their admirers continued to exert a disproportionate moral influence on into the days of Getulio Vargas.

In July, 1924, rebellious army elements still resisting the Bernardes government—including some survivors of the Copacabana revolt—held the city of São Paulo against federal forces for some weeks. And in October, the *tenentismo* movement was given impetus by a former army captain, Luiz Carlos Prestes, who recruited an expeditionary force of some 1,000 enthusiastic rebels for a march to dramatize their demand for regeneration of the nation. For two years they journeyed over the interior, south to the Paraná, north to the São Francisco, west toward the lowlands of Bolivia; finally overcome by federal troops, their leaders escaped into exile, not to appear again until the days of Vargas. The soil of Brazil was well cultivated and fertilized for the seeds of disorder—poverty, disease, and the inequities of a feudal system. Luiz Carlos Prestes and his followers seemed unimportant in 1924, but viewed from the perspective of the years, his march assumes fateful significance—for this was the beginning of Communism in Brazil.

[3] One of the survivors was Eduardo Gomes, later air brigadier, and in 1945 a candidate for the presidency.

. . .

There was brief relief under Washington Luiz Pereira de Souza (1926–30). That *paulista* had revealed competence and honesty in public service, and he now picked an able cabinet. Coffee prices improved in 1926 as the Coffee Institute limited production and regulated shipments into the world market. With a brief upturn in prosperity, political conditions improved and the military ceased their troubling. But Brazil was plagued with too much unsupported paper currency, which encouraged inflation, and an accumulated foreign debt of about $1,181,000,000. The service on foreign loans and investments called for annual payments of almost $200 million—four to five times the amount of the nation's favorable balance of trade. Then came two bumper crops of coffee in 1927–28 and 1928–29. The efforts of the Coffee Institute to restrict sales broke down, and there was reckless dumping of the coffee upon the world's overloaded exchanges; the price of coffee began to drop (in early 1929 the grade called "Rio No. 7" brought 15¾ cents a pound; by 1932, it was down to 8¹⁄₁₆ cents; by 1938, it was 5¼ cents). In 1930 São Paulo alone had 26.6 million bags piled up in its warehouses—more than the world could use in a year. Brazil had been caught in the worldwide depression.

With the approach of the 1930 election, Washington Luiz made a fatal political blunder by choosing a fellow *paulista,* Julio Prestes, as his successor, thereby defying the unwritten covenant under which São Paulo and Minas Gerais took turns in furnishing presidents. The indignant *mineiros* threw their support to Governor Getulio Vargas of Rio Grande do Sul. The election, firmly controlled by Washington Luiz's government, gave the verdict to Prestes; whereupon disaffected *mineiros, gaúchos,* and *paulistas* conspired to impose Vargas by force. The conspiracy, planned in Rio Grande do Sul, spread over the nation, and in October, 1930, a formidable body of army officers and politicians moved upon Rio de Janeiro, forced Washington Luiz from office, prevented the seating of Prestes, and placed Getulio Vargas in the presidential palace. His advent marked the end of the first republic, and the beginning of Vargas's fifteen-year rule.

Chapter 51

THE ERA OF GETULIO VARGAS,
1930-45

Getulio Vargas was forty-seven when he seized power. Born in Rio Grande do Sul in 1883, trained first for army life, then for the law, he had served in the national congress, as minister of the treasury under Washington Luiz, then as governor of his state—always with ability. There was nothing impressive, certainly nothing alarming about this compact little man of five feet, four inches who became president of Brazil in 1930; he met callers with a smile, walked unguarded, talked with any who accosted him, played poor golf on Sundays and smiled when people joked about it. His sedate home life reassured the Brazilians. He was usually described as an honest man who collected a modest thousand dollars a month salary and did not dip into the public treasury. Even critics admitted his loyalty to his country, while denouncing him as a dictator.

Vargas was certainly no kin to the rough tyrants who had often misruled nearby Spanish American nations. To be sure, some of his critics found it wiser to live abroad and a few went to jail for brief terms, but none were found in dark streets with bullets in their backs. The outcry against Vargas seemed incongruous to those who met him: he looked so mild and amiable. Vargas, says Gilberto Freyre, must be understood against the landscape and heritage of Rio Grande do Sul; he was spiritually kin to the Jesuit missionary fathers who had shaped that area. Like them he was "silent, introspective, subtle, realistic, distant, cold"; he was also a son of the *gaúchos* of Indian-Portuguese blood, "telluric, instinctive, fatalistic, proud, dramatic." Tavares de Sá speaks of Vargas's "shrewd, tortuous . . . sophistry." This was the man who for fifteen years played state against state, group against group, man against man—always with a smile—until at last he was retired—for a time—to his southern pastures.

The era of Vargas falls into two periods. First, the seven years during which he ruled under the check of Congress, with reasonable regard to constitutional niceties, but with noisy interruptions from both left and right. Then, after 1937, came dictatorship.

VARGAS: THE FIRST YEARS, 1930–37

Getulio Vargas's first months in office inspired the confidence of most Brazilians. His apologists blamed all ills upon the republic: the empty treasury, the defaulted foreign debts, the unhonored internal loans; the widespread unemployment; and the overproduction and underpricing of coffee. Brazilians accepted the explanation and hailed Vargas with relief. His first measures were reassuring. He made it clear that state loyalties must yield to national unity, a needed reproof to the arrogant bosses of São Paulo, Minas Gerais, and Rio Grande do Sul. With the consent of a frightened congress, Vargas imposed rigid censorship, removed elected state officials, and named his own men as governors and as mayors. The government was now in Rio de Janeiro—more accurately, in the hands of Getulio Vargas.

Vargas's economic measures were vigorous and often wise: he imposed new taxes, removed the ridiculous tariff barriers between the states, encouraged new industries, placed further checks on coffee production and marketing, and declared a moratorium on foreign loans. Public confidence in the central government increased, although there were rumblings of discontent as he failed to regularize his position by a legal election. The demand for constitutional government and democratic practices finally provoked the *paulistas* to revolt; the uprising of July, 1932, in São Paulo attracted support from factions in other states and led to a three-month defiance of federal troops, virtually a civil war. When the revolt was crushed, Vargas treated the rebels with moderation; a few were exiled, others were briefly jailed, and some were deprived of their civil rights—but there were no executions. When the city of São Paulo later dedicated the Avenida 9 de Julho, commemorating their unsuccessful revolution, Vargas himself participated in the ceremony, smiling amiably at his former enemies.

The Brazilians continued to demand a constitutional regime. In 1933 Vargas blandly convened a constituent assembly, which produced the Constitution of 1934. It was similar to the Constitution of 1891 but with economic provisions reminiscent of the Italian corporative state. The new instrument reinforced national unity by vesting larger powers in the federal government, provided for social legislation to safeguard laborers in field and factory, and granted the suffrage to women. The assembly then named Vargas president for a four-year term. Brazilians congratulated themselves upon their escape from dictatorship and return to legitimate government. The truce lasted a year. In November, 1935, there were barracks-revolts in Rio de Janeiro and Pernambuco, involving army and navy officers and many civilians. The rebellion was promptly crushed, and many were jailed or deported. Vargas pinned responsibility upon the Communists and declared a state of siege. Always quick to describe all critics as "Communists," Vargas was probably correct in naming them in this instance. The *Alliança Nacional Libertadora*, allied with the Third International, had been organized in 1934; its leader, able Luiz Carlos Prestes, was remembered for his spectacular march through the wilderness and respected by his bitterest critics. As an exile, Prestes had spent some years in Moscow and had been soundly converted to the gospel of Lenin. Brazil was ripe for Communist infiltration; its people were chiefly a hungry, angry proletariat. Prestes was arrested and, after a secret trial, was confined until 1945.

The threat from the Communist left was matched by no less a threat from the fascist right. A strange group called the *integralistas* had been growing rapidly since 1934, led by a neurotic zealot named Plinio Salgado. His language was a strange mumbo jumbo of sun worship, Italian Fascism, the corporative state, anti-Semitism, and the "leadership" principle. His devoted followers, several hundred thousand in all, wore green shirts, had a distinctive salute, used the Greek sigma as their identifying mark, exalted "God, Nation, Family," marched on all possible occasions, and staged bewildering ceremonies to the rising sun. Salgado had money to spend; some of it may have come from the German Embassy. *Integralismo* reached into the army, the navy, government offices, the best families of Brazil. It was clear that trouble was ahead.

VARGAS: THE DICTATORSHIP, 1937–45

Under pressure from his critics, Vargas early in 1937 set a presidential election for the following January. Three forces dominated the campaign: Vargas, who was constitutionally ineligible for reelection; the Communists, whose leader Luiz Carlos Prestes was in jail; and the *integralistas,* perhaps the most numerous of all the parties. The old-guard parties, representing coalitions of state machines, named their candidates. Vargas said nothing until October, when he announced that a Communist uprising was imminent and declared a state of war for ninety days, the exact period before election day. Plinio Salgado theatrically offered the services of 100,000 *integralistas* to protect the republic. In November, 1937, Vargas struck; he spoke to the nation over radio, proclaimed himself president for another term, dissolved Congress, and announced a new constitution for the *Estado Novo,* the "New State," a document written by Vargas himself with the help of his minister of justice, Francisco Campos. Vargas had outplayed the *integralistas,* perhaps forestalled an outright fascist state. Brazilians, happily quit of the preposterous Plinio Salgado, found it hard to stomach the *Estado Novo* and its "ghost constitution." Latin America has seen many fake constitutions, but this creation outfaked them all. It declared "a state of national emergency" and provided that so long as such emergency continued the constitution would not go into effect; it further provided that the constitution was without force until approved by a plebiscite, that only then could a congress be elected—and Vargas never mentioned the plebiscite again. So, concludes Karl Loewenstein, "a constitutional cat is chasing its legal tail, or vice versa . . . it is the Brazilian way of talking through his hat." However, Article 180 made all clear:

until Congress is elected "the president of the Republic shall be empowered to issue decrees on all matters of legislation for the union."

Vargas's dictatorship was now complete. He named all officials, high and low. His social program, launched by decree, guaranteed collective bargaining, but with trade unions controlled by the state; it also promised an eight-hour day, restriction on night work and child labor, medical assistance for workers and expectant mothers, and security from birth to death. Other decrees dealt with economic issues. The state theoretically assumed control of all national wealth. "Brazil for the Brazilians" was the slogan; foreign enterprise was caught in a tangle of new regulations.

In May, 1938, the *integralistas* made a last bid for power. Several hundred men, including army officers and civil servants, closed in upon the presidential palace where Vargas, his daughter, and a handful of servants held them off with a few guns until the army finally arrived. A few hundred were arrested, some were jailed briefly, but no one was executed for this bold treason. Plinio Salgado went into hiding and soon took refuge in Portugal. After 1938 there were no more armed revolts, and Vargas ruled uncontested for seven years.

Vargas called his government "a new kind of democracy," "a disciplined democracy." But the facts belie his phrases: there were neither congress nor elections; Vargas made all appointments and ruled by decree; labor unions were the tool of the state as in Mussolini's Italy; economic life was dominated by the state. Despite his arrogant rule, Vargas won credit by appointing some excellent men to office, by occasionally protecting the integrity of his courts, and by improving the administration of government throughout the nation. Karl Loewenstein, in his *Brazil Under Vargas,* found much to remind him of pre-Nazi Austria, "despotism mitigated by sloppiness." It was a dictatorship, but an amiable one—although its amiability lessened during the war years. Vargas had appointed himself father of his people, a role in which he delighted, and on the whole the people enjoyed it.

Civil liberties were curtailed. The press, radio, and schools came under the gloved hand of Getulio's press department, the DIP, presided over by the unsavory Lourival Fontes. A censor was assigned to each newspaper office. No unauthorized dispatch could be sent out by foreign correspondents. Foreign newspapermen who were "friendly and reasonable" were given generous privileges; and the unreasonable found it wise to leave. The case of *O Estado de São Paulo,* edited since the 1870's with stubborn independence, democratic zeal, and good taste, may be cited as an example of Vargas's ways with the press. Its owner-editor, Julio Mesquita Filho, grandson of the founder, supported Vargas in 1930, continued to support him in 1932 when the *paulistas* rebelled, but finally broke with the dictator in 1937. Mesquita went to jail for six months, then into exile. His editors continued to publish the paper under surveillance of the DIP. In March, 1940, police raided the newspaper's plant, "found" machine guns and ammunition. (This startling "discovery" was announced by the government three hours *before* the raid.) Seventeen members of the staff were jailed for two days, then released. The newspaper, a valuable property, was declared forfeited to the nation; publication was shortly resumed under an editor appointed by Vargas.[1]

Unlike the run-of-the-mill Spanish American dictator, Vargas made good use of able men, many of whom had scant sympathy with his methods. Afrânio de Mello Franco, Vargas's minister of foreign affairs during the first three years, belongs to the fine tradition of Brazilian international lawyers. Born in Minas Gerais in 1870, he entered public life as a congressman in 1906. After 1917, he represented Brazil in many international conferences, serving as a delegate to the League of Nations and as a judge of the Hague Court. In 1930 he became foreign minister and represented his country at the Seventh Pan American Conference in Montevideo in 1933. After his retirement in 1934, Mello Franco arbitrated the clash between Colombia and Peru over the Leticia area in the Upper Amazon. In 1938, at the Eighth Pan American Conference in Lima, he displayed wisdom in reconciling the stubborn divergence of opinion between the United States and Argentina.

Oswaldo Aranha, ambassador to Washington and then foreign minister, was another of Vargas's useful colleagues. Tall and fair, Aranha was the handsomest statesman to represent Brazil through the days of war and into the days of peace, when he became president of the Assembly of the United Nations. His skill was attested by his success in securing loans and grants of some $300 million from Washington. Candid, open, friendly, he was Vargas's most effective spokesman, persuading skeptical outsiders of the dictator's pure democratic intentions. While others in Vargas's circle made speeches which jarred democratic ears, Aranha was always on the side of the Allies and of the United States. Cynical bystanders described him as "Vargas's American Front."

There were others. A dictator needs a faithful army, and in his minister of war, Eurico Gaspar Dutra, and chief of staff, Góes Monteiro, Vargas had competent aides. Both seemed to waver on the issue of the Axis and Allies. Both were decorated by Hitler for "valued services by Brazil to Germany." This did not prove them pro-German, simply pro-Brazilian. They held the army together and kept Vargas in power.

Vargas is rightfully credited with efforts to improve the living conditions of his people. He made a little progress in providing better housing, more medical care, and increased wages. A fair appraisal of Vargas must take into account the economic burdens of the land, the load of foreign debt, and the low purchasing power of the people. In 1938 a government survey reported an average monthly wage of about $11.80 for all workers in agriculture, commerce, and industry, both rural and urban. José Jobim adds further testimony, citing figures on exports: in 1938 Brazil sold about

[1] For the further confusion of those who would paint Getulio Vargas in solid black, it may be added that when the newspaper plant was returned to Mesquita in 1945 he found it in better condition than when he had lost it and with more money in the tills.

$4.00 worth of goods per capita in world markets—a figure to be compared with Denmark's $56.30, Argentina's $20.50. Brazil's poverty appears in its federal budget which, in the years before the war, was not much more than $200 million—little more than New York City was spending on schools alone. The war brought brief prosperity, as the demand for Brazil's goods increased and American war expenditures in Brazil reached high levels. But it was a fictitious prosperity at best, canceled by disastrous inflation. Vargas had little to work with.

Industry, which had been enlarged during and after World War I, was given further stimulus by World War II. Total industrial production in 1907 was about $35 million; in 1920 it was $153 million; in 1940, almost $1.3 billion; by 1943, well over $1.4 billion. Industrial output had multiplied forty-three times in thirty-six years. The output of the textile mills, chiefly in São Paulo, was valued at about $30 million in 1926 and $209 million in 1942. In 1939 exports of textiles yielded about $1.5 million; in 1943, more than $66 million. In the paper industry the output was about $25,000 in 1938, almost $500,000 in 1943. There was expansion in the production of chemicals, leather products, rubber goods, cement, and machinery. The state of São Paulo was the chief producer of all these goods.

Vargas did much to develop Brazil's mineral resources. No one has computed these resources; scarcely a third of the nation has been scientifically explored. But Brazil has almost every mineral and metal—chromite, quartz crystals, mica, industrial diamonds, molybdenum, lead, vanadium, arsenic, and bauxite. Her manganese deposits may be the largest of any nation. She has perhaps 23 per cent of the world's known reserves of high-grade iron ore. The Itabira (iron mountain) in Minas Gerais is one of the largest deposits in the world. A beginning had already been made in building steel mills; two plants in Minas Gerais and one in the state of São Paulo had turned out some structural steel. Vargas sought to enlarge the steel industry and to keep its control in Brazilian hands. Foreign operators—United States Steel, the Krupps' interests, perhaps the Japanese—were more than willing to take a hand, but Vargas launched his National Steel Company in 1941, got loans from Washington's Export-Import Bank, and began construction of the Volta Redonda plant, 90 miles from Rio de Janeiro and 240 miles from Itabira. This operation necessitated railroads and ships to bring coal from Santa Catarina, manganese from Minas Gerais. Further loans from Washington speeded the work. The results were not spectacular when compared with operations elsewhere, but the Brazilian company could report output for the year 1948 of 224,000 tons of pig iron, 243,000 tons of bar steel, about 62,000 tons of rails, and numerous other items.

President Vargas's economic concerns ranged far afield; swamplands in the state of Rio de Janeiro were drained and opened to farming; highways and railroads were extended. In 1938 the National Petroleum Council was launched to survey and drill wells, and the Brazilians were hopeful of being rid of dependence upon foreign gasoline and lubricating oils. In

1939 the National Council of Hydraulic and Electrical Energy was organized to exploit the vast unharnessed power of the nation's rivers.

Under Vargas, Brazil's trade increased. During the years 1934–37, Brazil operated under a barter agreement with Germany. Locomotives, iron, coal, dyes, and chemicals were exchanged for Brazilian coffee, cotton, tobacco, and oils. By 1937 Germany was selling twice as much to Brazil as was Great Britain, half as much as the United States. After 1937 German trade fell off and the American increased. During World War II Brazil looked chiefly to Great Britain and the United States. In 1943 Brazil's exports were about $445 million, and she had a favorable balance of more than $135 million. At the war's end Brazil had a backlog of more than $500 million in balances abroad.

VARGAS AND WORLD WAR II

As the United States drew closer to war, Vargas's sympathies were unclear. His generals had been cultivated by Germany (the French had also sent military missions in the 1920's), and there was a queasy mistrust in the hearts of democrats that the *Estado Novo* resembled German and Italian models, and that a proto-fascist state was taking form on American soil. Vargas, it seemed, was sitting on the fence waiting to pick the victor. Perhaps his policy was symbolized by sending one son to the United States for schooling, another to Germany and Italy; prudence called for a crown prince in each camp. In the meantime, Vargas discouraged popular enthusiasm for the Allied cause. His DIP ruthlessly censored news which stressed Allied victories. As late as January, 1941, the newspaper *Diario Carioca* was closed for printing an article in praise of inter-American solidarity. When Russian armies were at last defeating Germany, the Brazilian press made it appear that Germany was still victorious. This ambiguity caused grave concern in Washington. In June, 1940, after the fall of France and the entrance of Italy on the Axis side, Franklin D. Roosevelt made a speech denouncing Mussolini's "stab in the back." The next day Vargas spoke on a battleship in Rio de Janeiro's harbor: "Virile peoples must follow the line of their aspirations. . . . We are marching toward a future different from all we know in economic, political and social organization, and we feel that old systems and antiquated formulas have entered a decline." Washington asked what Vargas meant. Meanwhile, there was no doubt that the majority of thoughtful Brazilians stood with the United States, with the Allies, and against the Axis. But they had no voice, no free press, no free platform. A popular doggerel of this period started out: "Don't speak; Getulio will do it for you—don't think; the DIP will do it for you."

By 1940 Washington was preparing for war, and Brazilian cooperation was important. Jefferson Caffery, ambassador to Rio de Janeiro, was assigned the task of persuading Getulio Vargas. It was not easy. Vargas and many of his aides were still uncertain as to the outcome; the pro-Allied populace had little outlet for their convictions. Foreign Minister Aranha gave invaluable aid to the Allies. Caffery, an able if somewhat crusty diplomat, won concession to build bases which later served American planes in the African campaign. By late 1940, the first permissions had been granted, and American engineers were laying out army, navy, and blimp bases from Amapá in the far north, south through Belém, São Luiz, Fortaleza, Natal, Maceió, Recife, Bahia, Caravellas, and Santa Cruz. Caffery had proved himself an excellent negotiator, Aranha a firm friend of the Allied cause.

After Pearl Harbor all the American nations were involved; Vargas knew it, but he was still cautious. In January, 1942, Rio de Janeiro was host to a conference of the foreign ministers of all the American republics. The almost unanimous stand of the delegates for American solidarity against the Axis was chiefly due to Aranha, the United States' Sumner Welles, Uruguay's Guani, and Mexico's Padilla, in the face of stubborn resistance from Argentina's Ruíz Guiñazú and Chile's Rossetti. Brazil was now officially on the Allied side, and on August 22 declared war. The United States furnished planes, ships, tanks, guns, and ammunition. A Brazilian expeditionary force of 25,000 fighting men was sent to Italy and acquitted itself with credit. The bases lent by Brazil contributed to the final victory.

One incident reveals Vargas's halfhearted commitment to the Allied cause. In August, 1944, when the war was all but won, Oswaldo Aranha was advertised to speak to the Society of the Friends of America (a pro-United Nations body); the police padlocked the doors of the meeting place. Vargas refused to support his foreign minister, and Aranha resigned.

THE END OF THE DICTATORSHIP

By the first days of 1945, there were clear signs of discontent with the dictatorship. Many politicians, generals, and professional people began to show their hands. For some, the stand reflected prudence; they knew that a dictator-bossed Brazil would have scant welcome at the peace tables. For others, it was simply a personal play for power. For many, it was a deeply rooted desire for democratic rule. In February came the "democratic breakthrough." Two newspapers suddenly began to talk of the election Vargas had promised, of the need for free discussion, and in favor of the candidacy of Air Brigadier Eduardo Gomes.[2] The DIP did not silence them; the inference was that Vargas had decided to loose his hold. The newspapers, such as were not owned by the government or the Communists, published vigorous discussions of Brazil's future.

National political parties took form. The National Democratic Union nominated Gomes; it had the support of most moderate Liberals, many Conservatives, and others intent upon striking at Vargas. The Social Demo-

---

[2] Eduardo Gomes, it should be recalled, was one of the few survivors of the ill-fated rebellion of *tenentes* (lieutenants) at the Copacabana fortress in July, 1922, a dramatic revolt of young idealists in the armed forces, and a movement which had profound influence on the early Vargas years.

cratic Party, backing Eurico Gaspar Dutra, Vargas's minister of war, made its chief appeal to those of the extreme right—with Vargas's blessing, they thought. The Communists, led by Luiz Carlos Prestes, finally released from prison, entered the contest. As the year wore on, it became clear that Vargas was not to be easily deposed. A mysterious movement sprang up with the slogan *Queremos Getulio,* "We want Getulio"; Brazil was plastered with the slogan on billboards, in the press, in pamphlets. It was then revealed that the promoter of this ostensibly spontaneous outburst was paying his printing bills from a loan of $14 million granted by the national Banco do Brasil (that is, by Vargas).

Meanwhile, elections were scheduled for December 2. By September political prophets knew that Vargas had no intention of quitting. Rumors spread that a military coup was planned, that prisons were readied. Now the American ambassador, Adolf A. Berle, Jr., took a hand. Berle had come to Brazil in January, 1945, and had made friends of those in power and in the opposition. Berle now decided to speak and on September 29 held a press conference for Brazilian reporters; he spoke eloquently of the long friendship between Brazil and the United States, and said that "the pledge of free Brazilian elections, set for a definite date, by a government whose word the United States has found inviolable, has been hailed with as much satisfaction in the United States as in Brazil itself." His point was clear; he hailed the election, knowing full well that Vargas proposed to continue himself in power. Berle's speech has been cited as another instance of American intervention in Latin America's internal affairs—if so, it was gentle and effective.

In October Vargas dismissed the capital's chief of police and installed his brother, Benjamin Vargas (nicknamed *O Beijo,* "The Kiss"), who was notorious for his pilferings and exploitation of prostitution and gambling. This affront to the dignity of the nation offended the generals, who demanded Vargas's resignation. Forthwith, tanks, guns, and troops surrounded public buildings. On October 29 Vargas resigned and flew to his farm in Rio Grande do Sul. Chief Justice José Linhares of the Supreme Court, who became provisional president, appointed an able cabinet. The political campaign continued. The *queremistas* were noisy; Vargas now ordered them to support Dutra. The election was held on schedule on December 2. Dutra won, 3 to 2 over Gomes. The Communists polled 10 per cent of the votes. Meanwhile, Vargas was tending his cattle, still smiling.

 [*Chapter 52*]

THE SECOND REPUBLIC, 1945−

The ending of the fifteen-year rule of Getulio Vargas brought a new era for Brazil. The people would now seek to atone for their apostasy from the republican faith and make a new beginning.

THE PRESIDENCY OF EURICO GASPAR DUTRA, 1946–50

General Eurico Gaspar Dutra took office on January 31, 1946, to the widespread relief of Brazilians. Heavy, taciturn, unsmiling, colorless, a good Catholic and a faithful family man, Dutra was welcomed by a people weary of the Getulio charm. But all was not easy for the new president. The Vargas dictatorship had corroded citizenship; a generation had come to maturity without a free press, without experience with the ballot box, without hope for an effective share in the building of the nation. Cynicism toward public service had spread like damp mold as evidence of official venality increased; Vargas, to his credit, had kept his hands technically clean; not so, his numerous friends. Garish symbol of this corruption was the wartime building of the $10-million hotel and gambling casino, Quitandinha, on the mountains above Rio de Janeiro. At a time when Brazilians were on short rations, Getulio's favorites were given priorities on man power, trucks, and scarce material for this sorry monument to bad taste and reckless waste.

Dutra the soldier proved an awkward politician. The men who had followed Brigadier Gomes in the election of 1945, while opposing many of Dutra's measures, inclined toward patriotic cooperation. But Getulio Vargas, angry over his repudiation, did all he could to embarrass his onetime loyal ally. Posing as the friend of labor, he courted the Communists at home and the *peronistas* in Argentina; and he revived old fears of the United States. The Communists were Dutra's chief troublers. In 1945 they had elected Luiz Carlos Prestes to the Senate and fourteen deputies to the lower house; in the congressional election of 1947 they increased their representation. Their spokesmen conducted an untiring campaign within the labor unions, and stirred up popular outcry against the United States. Senator Prestes brought down popular wrath upon himself and his party by announcing that Brazilian Communists, in the event of a war with Russia, would take up arms against their own government. By January, 1948, the Communist Party had been declared illegal, and its representatives in state and national government had been expelled from office. Such measures drove the leftists underground, and their agents continued to agitate. Despite the ban, numerous Communist newspapers and magazines continued to circulate.

In September, 1946, a new constitution—drafted by the constitutional assembly provided by the Linhares government—was promulgated. Based upon the first republic's Constitution of 1891, it included many of the social measures of the *Estado Novo;* it provided for the direct election of a president for a five-year term, forbade immediate reelection, and limited presidential powers. Ruling as a constitutional president, Dutra gave Brazil as democratic a government as it had ever enjoyed. The press was free, the arguments of political critics—including Communists—were voiced with vehemence, and there was less interference with the rights of the individual states than there had been at any time since the fall of the empire.

Dutra's most severe test came in his attempts to control the national economy. With the ending of World War II, Brazil had an accumulation of over $8 million in foreign credits; politicians and businessmen embarked upon reckless spending which increased the already serious inflation and exhausted the reserves. Neither an economist nor a statesman, Dutra was powerless to put a stop to the extravagance or to the inflationary spiral. Prices shot up, while wages lagged behind. Meanwhile, private enterprise, mostly foreign, was embarking upon all sorts of projects: textile mills, cement works, automobile assembly plants, farm machinery plants, chemical and drug concerns, and fertilizer plants. American, German, Italian, French, Japanese, and other foreign interests were investing funds and furnishing technicians. Expensive hotels, apartment houses, and private homes were going up in São Paulo and Rio de Janeiro—São Paulo was the fastest-growing city in the Western Hemisphere. São Paulo continued to dominate industry, as it had long dominated coffee (which continued to furnish from 60 to 70 per cent of the export revenue of the nation).

The expansion of private business was matched by enlarged federal investment in public works. Most of the foreign-owned railroad lines were taken over by the government and new mileage was added. A few highways were built. The steel plant at Volta Redonda was enlarged. A well-publicized beginning was made in development of the Amazon region; an investment of $50 million (a fourth of it from the United States) did much to improve health conditions in that area. There was new enthusiasm for hydroelectric installations; many projects were planned, and some were begun. The rich valley of the 1,800-mile Rio São Francisco, with abundant water power awaiting exploitation, attracted attention as a "Brazilian TVA." Many of these projects were admirable; but they lacked adequate capital, trained technical personnel, and man power. Perhaps the plans were over-pretentious; certainly this was true of Dutra's five-year plan, announced during the last months of his term, which called for an investment of 20 billion cruzeiros ($1 billion at the official rate of exchange) to be allotted to sanitation, food production, transportation, and power development. But by the time this plan was announced in 1950, the Brazilian economy had been so demoralized by overspending, corruption, and inflation as to make the promise empty. The fault, however, lay more in the recalcitrance of Congress than in Dutra, who made valiant efforts to resist extravagance and graft.

THE RETURN OF GETULIO VARGAS, 1950–54

Brazilians had tired of the unexciting Dutra by 1950, when they went to the polls to choose his successor. There were still no real national parties. The election narrowed down to a contest between Air Brigadier Eduardo Gomes, an honest democrat but no rabble-rouser, who was supported by the amorphous National Democratic Union; and sixty-seven-year-old Getulio Vargas, now eloquently defending free institutions and the common man, candidate of the fictitious Labor Party. Vargas made his appeal to a people who did not have enough to eat, who dressed in rags, and whose children had few schools. "The father of the people" (*O pai do povo*) was returned to the national palace.

But Vargas's voice had lost most of its magic, and his new term of office proved anticlimactic. The men around him were not impressive: some were incompetent, many were corrupt, and almost all were dull. The conduct of public business, never conspicuously capable in Brazil, became more sloppy. One of Vargas's cronies, mayor of the burgeoning city of São Paulo, was charged with taking a cut of 50 per cent or more on municipal contracts. Another, mayor of Rio de Janeiro, permitted the administration of the capital city to degenerate to a point where life on its beautiful streets was quite insecure. Chief target in Vargas's cabinet was João Goulart, the minister of labor, who was charged with coddling Communists in the labor unions and with attempting to create a labor bloc, in the manner of Perón, which would carry him to power as Vargas's successor in 1955. Almost as unpopular was the minister of war, variously accused of harboring Communists and of plotting for a return of dictatorship. The crisis was reached in early 1954 when eighty-two colonels presented a memorandum expressing the dissatisfaction of army leaders with these two men. As a result, both were dismissed.

Vargas's handling of the economic confusion was no more successful than his predecessor's. Superficially, business seemed promising when he took over the presidency: steel production had doubled within a year; foreign trade topped $1 billion; new factories, mills, and assembly plants were mushrooming in São Paulo. But by the end of his first year in office,

Brazil's traders were far in arrears in payments to their foreign creditors, the cost of living had increased about 30 per cent in twelve months, and strikes demanding increased wages were breaking out all through the nation. Even the mounting price of coffee, so irritating to customers in the United States, could not rescue the national economy. The cruzeiro, officially quoted at about 5 cents, was selling for 2 cents or less in the open market. Many Brazilian commodities would not sell in the world market on the basis of the overvalued cruzeiro. This was notably true of cotton, for many years second to coffee as a source of export revenue; at the official exchange rate, Brazil's cotton was, in 1953, 25 per cent above the world price. In June, 1953, Vargas turned in desperation to Oswaldo Aranha, who had helped him to power in 1930 and been his loyal aide during the period of dictatorship but who had finally turned against him to support Brigadier Gomes in 1945 and 1950. Appointed as minister of finance, Aranha warned Brazilian businessmen that they had rolled up about $1 billion worth of floating indebtedness; that the nation required rigorous economy, strict limitation on imports, and curbing of inflation. Meanwhile, the Export-Import Bank had extended a $300 million credit in order to liquidate commercial debts to American firms. Aranha's leadership brought a slight improvement in Brazil's trading position; a few new trade agreements were concluded with other nations, and by early 1954 the commercial debts had been canceled. But the internal economic situation remained desperate, as the currency sank in value, prices rose, and the inevitable clamor for higher wages continued.

The development of the nation's oil reserves, optimistically regarded as extensive although there had been little drilling, had long been a subject of debate. Finally, in October, 1953, a new law created the Brazilian Petroleum Corporation (Petrobras) and gave it monopoly of the exploitation of petroleum. The terms were ultranationalistic: only Brazilians could acquire stock in the new company; even Brazilians married to foreigners were barred from any share in its ownership. There had been offers from United States and other oil interests to invest money in developing the industry, but these were vigorously opposed by extreme nationalists and Communists. Inasmuch as about $200 million of foreign exchange was going each year into the purchase of petroleum products, self-sufficiency on this score was of great importance. But critics pointed out that oil exploration and drilling would cost hundreds of millions—or billions—of dollars and that Brazil had no such reserves of venture capital. The terms of the Petrobras charter threatened to keep Brazilian oil reserves (if indeed there are such) under ground; drilling had to wait until the way was opened for foreign investment.

By 1954 Brazilian relations with the United States had steadily deteriorated. Despite generous subventions from Washington, there was smoldering resentment against what was described as niggardly treatment by the United States. The Communists used the United States as the whipping boy in all their attacks upon governmental measures. There was a general outcry when the United States lent Perón's government $125 million; it was charged that Argentina would use the money to finance an attack upon Brazil. Vargas, who had been strengthened during his long dictatorship by loans and subsidies from the United States, did nothing to quiet the blasts against the northern neighbor.

By mid-1954, as discussion of presidential candidates for the election of 1955 began, widespread popular anger was directed at the one-time idol Getulio Vargas. Vargas was charged with reckless handling of the national economy and with responsibility for the riotous inflation which was laying an intolerable load upon all wage earners. He was blamed for the breakdown of government in the cities and states. He was condemned for the corruption which had spread from the smallest officeholder to top officials. A principal target was his bodyguard of thugs who enjoyed unprecedented favors from the treasury, enabling them to buy the finest foreign automobiles and maintain homes of fantastic luxury. By August there were abundant signs that both military and civilian elements were ready to oust the president.

The tinderbox was ignited by the attack of gunmen upon Carlos Lacerda, the fearless editor of the *Tribuna da Imprensa* of Rio de Janeiro, whose castigations of Vargas and his cronies had made him the effective voice of the opposition. The shots directed at him inflicted only a minor wound, but his companion, a major in the air force, was killed. Lacerda wrote a spirited editorial denouncing the "regime of corruption and terror" and fixing the responsibility for it upon Vargas himself. The officers of the air force, taking up the cause of their companion who had fallen to the assassins, pressed the inquiry with vigor and finally joined in an ultimatum demanding the withdrawal of Vargas. Evidence accumulated that directly implicated Vargas's bodyguard, perhaps even his unsavory brother Benjamin. The disaffection spread among army officers, and they, too, joined in demanding Vargas's retirement. Confronted with the evidence that those close to him were involved in the attack upon Lacerda, and with the demands of the air force leaders and other army men, Vargas shot himself on the night of August 24. He had penned a note: "To the wrath of my enemies, I leave the legacy of my death." Another note, typewritten and not signed (and whose authenticity has been questioned), laid the blame upon "international economic and financial groups."

INTERMISSION, 1954–56

The death of Vargas, who had dominated the nation most of the time for twenty-four years, brought a momentary resurgence of popular sympathy for the "martyred" president. The Communists utilized the fury for their own ends, leading attacks upon the American Embassy and lending their aid to the Vargas party, which sought vindication at the polls.

Meanwhile, Vice-President João Café Filho (*filho* is Portuguese for "Jr.") took over the office, dismissed some of the more disreputable of Vargas's cronies, and tried to restore order. Café was an honest public servant who had denounced the Vargas dictatorship before 1945, had been jailed, and had finally won the vice-presidency by a political fluke. He presided over an honest election in October, 1955, when Juscelino Kubitschek was named president, with the unsavory João Goulart (who, as Vargas's minister of labor, had done much of his chief's dirty work) as vice-president. After the election a heart attack forced Café to retire, and the government passed into the weak hands of another man. November and December brought rumors of a plot led by disgruntled politicians and army men to prevent the seating of Kubitschek; but General Henrique Teixeira Lott led a "countercoup" on November 11, imposed order, and made possible the inauguration of Kubitschek and Goulart in January, 1956.

JUSCELINO KUBITSCHEK, 1956–61

Juscelino Kubitschek, forty-four years old upon assuming office, was born in Diamantina, a mining town in the state of Minas Gerais. Partly of Czech descent, Kubitschek had earned his way through medical school, then turned to politics. As mayor of Belo Horizonte and later as governor of Minas Gerais, he had shown imagination and boundless energy in improvement of mining and farming, in construction of hydroelectric plants and other public works. He was a demagogue—but with solid achievement to his credit. His demagoguery was patent in the presidential campaign. By accepting the tawdry Goulart as his running mate, he invited the aid of the Communists. By capitalizing upon his loyalty to the dead Vargas, he won the votes of many disciples of that discredited leader. With the trumpeting of his slogan "Power, Transportation, and Food," he promised everything to everybody. When he became president, he airily promised "fifty years of progress in five years."

Even such a worker of miracles as Kubitschek might well have been appalled as he undertook to tame the anarchic economy and politics of Brazil. Inflation was running an angry course; the reasons were various. Wages were repeatedly boosted. Bank credit—especially to industrialists—was reckless. The price of coffee (which accounted for 55 per cent of Brazil's export revenue in 1958) dropped from 95 cents a pound in 1954 to 42 cents in 1958. Federal bonuses to exporters increased from year to year. Application of preferential exchange rates to the purchase of such luxury items as automobiles resulted in fantastically high prices (an American car cost from ten to twenty times as much as it did in the United States); but the wildly optimistic Brazilians bought such items anyway, paying interest rates of 12 per cent and more. Budgets—federal, state, and municipal—were in perpetual imbalance, and all units of government were virtually bankrupt. Government, in all its branches, was appallingly incompetent. A case in point was the rich state of São Paulo: a corrupt governor, Adhemar de Barros, plundered on every contract for road building and other public works; when he was replaced by Jânio Quadros, there was a brief period of honesty and efficiency; but in 1962 Adhemar was reelected, after publicly boasting: "I steal, but I get things done." In many cities and states, however, there was more stealing than doing. All these factors contributed to the growing chaos of the economy.

Never had Brazil had a more ubiquitous president: Kubitschek went everywhere, spoke repeatedly upon all subjects, announced innumerable programs for "national redemption"—while prices shot up and national income went down. Under pressure from the right and the left, he clung to the suicidal nationalism of the government oil monopoly, Petrobras. Although, due to inefficient operation of Petrobras, almost one-fourth of Brazil's import budget was spent on purchases of petroleum products, Kubitschek refused aid from foreign capital to fortify the industry.

Shortly after his inauguration in January, 1956, Kubitschek visited Washington, where he assured President Eisenhower that he had made no commitments to the Communists, that he was the faithful friend of the United States and of the Organization of American States. Whether or not he himself was sincere, he could not control his unruly congressmen, who had other ideas. When mining interests in Minas Gerais protested against giving the United States a monopoly on atomic minerals, Kubitschek had to yield to nationalistic sentiment. When the United States sought a lease on the seven-square-mile island of Fernando de Noronha, 200 miles east of the bulge, to be used as a tracking station for American missiles, there was angry debate for a year, before the United States got its lease. Meanwhile, abuse of Washington came from editors and politicians of various hues.

While Brazil was thus floundering under inflation and governmental incompetence, industry continued to expand. The state of São Paulo continued far in the lead, with the state of Rio de Janeiro second. Automobile assembly plants—branches of American, German, and French companies —were turning out more cars and trucks every year: more, some economists said, than Brazilians could afford to buy. Factories, steel mills, and textile mills were producing almost every item, big or little, that the market demanded. Brazil was a land of miracles, and although hard-headed bankers and economists predicted doom, energetic Italian, German, Spanish, American, and Brazilian promoters continued to build plants and install machinery, borrowing money at high interest rates. Real estate speculators vied with each other in buying fine lots in Rio de Janeiro and São Paulo at prices as absurd as those in American boom towns, and built high office buildings and apartment houses. Meanwhile, electric current was inadequate, the water supply faltered, public services limped along, and there were not enough police to make the streets safe.

For Juscelino Kubitschek, there was one chief joy and pride—the new capital, Brasília, 600 miles northwest of Rio de Janeiro in the almost empty state of Goiás. Undeterred by the financial doldrums of the nation, Kubitschek went ahead with unflagging nerve. The city was built, with a presidential palace, halls for congress, and housing for workers. Brilliant Brazilian architects—the most imaginative in Latin America—drew the plans, and artists added murals and sculptures. Before highways were built connecting the new capital with São Paulo and Rio de Janeiro, much material had to be flown in at great expense. Workmen labored in three shifts around the clock, and the city was dedicated in April, 1960. It had cost $700 million or more (no one knows). The arguments for the creation of this new capital were of long standing: it would serve to open up the inland empire of the nation, so that farmers and industrialists could expand; it would remove the seat of the government from the enervating climate of Rio de Janeiro. Arguments against the project were numerous: it cost too much, and it provoked further inflation which robbed the poor. But Kubitschek got his Brasília, and it remains a monument to his energy.[1]

During the hectic years under Kubitschek, with inflation galloping madly (during the one year of 1959, the cost of living increased 37 per cent), with federal budgets always out of balance (the budget deficit in 1959 was $212 million), with bills paid by reckless running of the printing presses, there were repeated requests for loans from the United States. Washington had bailed out Brazil three times since 1953, but by 1959 the United States took a firm stand toward Kubitschek's appeals. Requests for a $300-million credit from the Export-Import Bank and for a $37.5-million credit from the International Monetary Fund were countered by the suggestion that Brazil first set her own house in order. The advice was explicit: reduce the national budget, put a brake on bank credit, and adopt realistic exchange rates for the cruzeiro. Thereby, said the bankers, inflation can be stemmed, and the deficit in international balance of payments be ended. But Kubitschek and his congress found these conditions unacceptable and decided to go it alone. There was considerable anti-American outcry in Brazil, and Communists and others denounced "Uncle Shylock."

Juscelino Kubitschek had troubles enough during his last months of office in 1959 and 1960. The only bright spot was a sudden burst of coffee-selling during the last few months of 1959: despite the low prices, Brazil actually set a record by collecting almost $750 million from sales of coffee in 1959. But overproduction still plagued the economy, and by mid-1960, more than 34 million bags of coffee were piled up in government warehouses—all paid for by the nation with paper money on which the ink was hardly dry. The increased cost of living provoked many strikes. There were angry riots, put down with gunfire. Such was the atmosphere in which the presidential campaign of 1960 was conducted.

The contest culminating in the election of October, 1960, was between Henrique Teixeira Lott, sixty-five, and Jânio Quadros, forty-three. Retired Field Marshal Lott, an ultranationalist who invoked the name of Vargas and welcomed Communist support, was Kubitschek's candidate. Quadros, who enjoyed large prestige based on his honest and effective service as mayor of São Paulo and then as governor of the state of São Paulo,

[1] The much criticized Brasília venture may soon entitle Kubitschek to unstinted praise. The new capital is actually effecting a minor miracle in opening up Brazil's central west. Population of that area increased from 1.7 million in 1950 to 3 million in 1960—and the Brazilian Census Bureau projects its 1970 population at 5 million. The United States Department of Commerce, in its Brazilian Investment Guide, notes the acceleration of the economy of the state of Goiás—and of Mato Grosso as well.

had convincing words for all sectors: to the conservatives, he promised an end to inflation and a balanced budget; he assured leftists of his admiration for Cuba's Castro and the U.S.S.R.; and he gave eloquent pledges to ultra-nationalists that he would curb the threats from "foreign exploiters." Quadros's histrionics were offset by his constructive record, and he won the election by the largest plurality in Brazilian history.

JÂNIO QUADROS, JANUARY–AUGUST, 1961

Shortly after the inauguration of Jânio Quadros on January 31, 1961, the President confided to a colleague: "By August I will not have a friend left in this country." His prophecy proved accurate—by August he was out. His seven-month rule was an enlivening interlude: it might have been impressive if he had only kept his temper.

The ebullient Quadros inherited a "tropical nightmare." Everything was about as desperate as it could be. The reckless Kubitschek had made a shambles of the Brazilian economy: during his five-year term inflation was the highest in Brazilian history; the budget deficit skyrocketed (it was more than $300 million in 1960); the foreign debt passed the $3-billion mark; the printing of paper cruzeiros tripled; some $700 million, more or less, was squandered on the ambitious new capital of Brasília.

Jânio Quadros—"the man with the broom," he styled himself—seemed cut out for his job. Brazil was overdue for vigorous sweeping, and Quadros was honest and energetic. He promptly used his broom to flail those who had enriched themselves from the public treasury, sparing neither his predecessor nor his vice-president, João Goulart—both of whose records included graft on a princely scale. Congress, dominated by Kubitschek's Social Democrats and Goulart's Labor Party, was of no mind to be intimidated. But in spite of determined opposition, Quadros managed to force through some measures of economic austerity: an end to consumer subsidies, especially those on wheat and petroleum products; the reform of exchange controls; a halt to irresponsible wage increases; deep cuts in the national budget; an end to reckless printing of paper money; and, perhaps most important, a new coffee program designed to discontinue governmental purchases of poor grades of coffee—this "refuse" was stored at great expense in warehouses, and much of it was finally burned. But the congress, hostile to this drastic austerity program, grew angrier week by week, and Quadros was no mollifier. With all of his good intentions, inflation continued to mount.

Quadros was well aware of Brazil's dependence on the United States for major financial aid. But his determination to steer a neutralist course in foreign policy made him a bitter pill for Washington to swallow. The first Latin American chief of state (except for Fidel Castro) to challenge the United States policy on China—openly favoring debate on China's admission to the United Nations—Quadros also sought to reestablish ties with the U.S.S.R. and her European satellites. And when President Kennedy sent Adolf Berle as his special emissary to persuade Quadros to relax his embrace of Castro's Cuba—whose "right of self-determination" the Brazilian President heartily defended—Quadros treated Berle with scant courtesy. The argument over Cuba was not helped when Quadros received Ernesto "Che" Guevara, conferring upon him Brazil's Order of the Southern Cross. And when John Moors Cabot, the American ambassador, obliquely criticized Quadros's boast that Brazil was "uncommitted" in the cold war between West and East, Quadros snapped to newsmen that Brazil had a "positive independent international position and will not tolerate meddling from anybody whoever it might be."

But President Kennedy decided that Quadros—whose domestic policies were to the liking of Washington and the IMF—could be trusted, and in June the United States assumed a major share of a $2-billion package of loans, grants, and loan deferments for Brazil.

But Quadros was hopelessly deadlocked with Congress, and there seemed slight hope of pushing through such fundamental reforms as tax increases and land reform. Furthermore, there was rising controversy even among his associates on his foreign policy. On August 25 the bad-tempered President submitted his resignation—probably expecting a popular uprising in his defense. But his followers did not rally, Congress joyfully accepted his resignation, and Quadros took ship and sailed away. Thoughtful Brazilians and outsiders denounced the "man with the broom" as a petulant reformer.

JOÃO GOULART, 1961–64

The abdication of Quadros left his shabby vice-president, João Goulart, as legal heir to the presidency. The forty-three-year-old "Jango," as he was called with mingled derision and affection, was a complete demagogue. In 1950, at age thirty-two, he joined his Rio Grande do Sul neighbor and mentor, Getulio Vargas, as minister of labor in Vargas's last ill-fated term, and did much of the dirty work for his master—rounding up corrupt labor leaders, appeasing and rewarding Communists for their support. In 1953 he agitated for the doubling of the national minimum wage, in the face of fantastic inflation, and was booted out of office at the insistence of the generals. In 1954, when Vargas committed suicide, Jango inherited control of the Labor Party, which of course was no party at all, but simply the political tool of Vargas, and now of Jango. In 1955 he helped to rally labor and Communist support for the election of Juscelino Kubitschek, and was rewarded with the vice-presidency. And in 1960, by a quirk in the electoral machinery, he continued as vice-president under Quadros, whose contempt for his underling was complete. In all these meanderings, he fattened from the public treasury, borrowed large sums from the Bank of Brazil (which he did not repay), used his labor aides as bullies to intimidate his critics, and courted the Communists.

The prospects of having Jango as president aroused an instant and well-nigh unanimous cry of alarm. The three chiefs of staff of the armed forces demanded that Jango be barred from the office, calling him "an agent of disorder, of disunion, of anarchy." The majority of state governors and leading newspapers opposed him. He was a Communist at heart, many said. In fact, he was just starting home from a love feast in Peking on the day Quadros resigned; there he had announced loudly that "People's China, under the leadership of the great Mao Tse-tung, is an example that shows how a people can emancipate themselves from the yoke of their exploiters." For several days, the rumble of civil war was in the air, but calmer councils prevailed. In Brasília, Congress decided that the dispute could be quieted by amending the constitution to provide for a prime minister who would share honors and powers with the president. That settled, Goulart flew to Brasília and was inducted into office. At his side stood the newly elected prime minister, Tancredo Neves, lawyer and banker, and long-time crony of Getulio Vargas. They would rule together.

But the troubles of Brazil were not thus lightly exorcised. Neither Goulart nor Neves commanded national respect or enthusiasm, and their quarrelsome congress paid little heed to either of them. When Neves warned that the budget deficit for 1961 stood at some $380 million, and that it might rise to $600 million unless drastic action were taken, Congress blithely refused to listen.

Relations with the United States, meanwhile, ran a tortuous course. Stunned by the abrupt departure of Quadros from his post, Washington viewed Goulart with a wary eye. The new President continued to dally with Communism, but without his predecessor's honesty of purpose and responsible handling of his nation's housekeeping. Increased pressure by the United States and the International Monetary Fund for fiscal reform as a condition for further aid made slight impression. The uneasy friendship between the two nations was strained when, in February, 1962, Governor Leonel Brizola of Rio Grande do Sul (Jango's brother-in-law) expropriated his state's telephone system, a subsidiary of International Telephone and Telegraph, offering $400,000 for a property valued by its American owners at twenty times that figure. (He had already taken over the electric power facilities of American and Foreign Power.) President Kennedy was conciliatory, saying that Brazil should not be penalized for Brizola's highhandedness. But these events, and the general political turmoil in Brazil, served to chill the ardor of foreign investors. Then in August, 1962, Congress ruled that foreign companies in Brazil must limit their remittances of profits to 10 per cent of their capital, and could not reinvest their remaining profits as new capital. By this time, the influx of foreign capital had been reduced to a trickle. Numerous foreign companies steadily withdrew funds from Brazil, and even Brazilian concerns managed to transfer large sums to Swiss or American banks—no one knew the volume of this flight of capital, but it was substantial. The financial climate of Brazil deteriorated sadly as Brizola orated upon "the occupation of our nation by the United States," and suggested that the entire $1.5 billion of American investments should be nationalized. His attack was cheered by Luiz Carlos Prestes and his Communists.

The American financial community was also worried by what

appeared to be Communist agitation in the poverty-ridden Northeast of Brazil.[2] Then came Brazilian resumption of diplomatic relations with the U.S.S.R., which renewed fear as to the Communist leanings of the government. United States aid to Brazil was greatly reduced—from $355 million in fiscal 1962 to $174 million in 1963—although money was still going to the state of Guanabara (Rio de Janeiro) where Governor Carlos Lacerda was doing good work on low-cost housing, schools, and health projects; and subsidies for projects in the Northeast, already committed, were continued. In December, 1962, President Kennedy sent his brother Robert to warn Goulart that Brazilian inflation (about 65 per cent in 1962) "eats up our aid"—and that the "eating" had amounted to some $1.4 billion during the past ten years. The American Congress and bankers were obviously wearied of dropping large sums into the bottomless Brazilian purse.

But Jango had an answer for his critics: all will be well, he said, if you will oust the Prime Minister and return full presidential powers to me. And so a national plebiscite was held in January, 1963, and by a 5 to 1 vote Jango had his way. He promptly announced a three-year economic program calling for reduction of government spending, increase of taxes, elimination of further consumer subsidies—all to cost some $1.5 billion in loans, grants, and debt postponements. It all had a familiar sound to Washington. But under pressure from Kennedy, the United States government, on the frightening theory that Brazil must be bolstered under Goulart or it would sink into the Communist abyss, agreed in March, 1963, to a further credit to Brazil of $398.5 million—but with all the old strings attached: cuts in the budget, a cut in inflation, less printing of paper money, reform of money-losing state enterprises, tax reform. The money would be doled out as performance was assured, and as funds were secured from other outside sources. But Goulart would not, or could not, deliver. He could not hold his labor support in line without wage increases —so wages increased. He could not pay his bills without printing money— so tons of paper money were shipped in from English printing presses. He could not control his congress and his cabinet—so there was constant shuffling in top posts, with no improvement.

By March, 1964, it was clear that Goulart's time was up. The top brass of the armed forces were against him, almost to a man. Their fury was increased when the President made a dramatic appeal to non-commissioned officers and enlisted men to take his side against their superiors. In Rio de Janeiro, 1,425 sailors and marines, encouraged by Goulart's words, actually mutinied against their officers; and when the officers sought to discipline the men, Goulart pardoned the mutineers, and forestalled punishment. That senseless performance settled Goulart's fate so far as the military were concerned. Army revolts against the President sprang up over the country. There was little resistance, and by April 2 the army officers were in control. Goulart flew from Brasília to his ranches in Rio Grande do Sul, and on April 4 he crossed over to the safety of Uruguay.

2 See pp. 887–9 for a discussion of this area.

In Brasília, in the meantime, Congress had declared the presidency vacated and installed Paschoal Ranieri Mazzilli, president of the Chamber of Deputies, as acting president. So ended the reign of Jango.

During this bloodless revolution (and it is well to remember that Brazilian revolutions are usually bloodless), the United States played a curious role. So happy was Washington to be rid of the despised Goulart that the American Embassy in Rio served as a cheering bleacher even while the ouster was taking place. On April 2 (two days before Jango drove off to Uruguay), President Johnson cabled his "warmest wishes" to Mazzilli. A day later, Secretary of State Dean Rusk expressed his delight over the turn of events. *The New York Times* commented on April 7: "To make such a public show of rejoicing, even before the situation had clarified, has given the world the impression—an entirely wrong one—that the United States had something to do with the coup."

The record of Jango's thirty-one months of presidential rule was sobering. The cost of living had shot up about 300 per cent, the value of the cruzeiro (in relation to the American dollar) had dropped 83 per cent, the foreign debt had increased to $3.7 billion, and the inflow of foreign capital was halted. All his boasted reforms, especially his promise to recast the unjust land pattern, had proved no more than empty words. But—as Roberto Campos (Goulart's ambassador to Washington, and now to be minister of planning) wryly remarked—Jango had indeed had a program of land reform: he had personally inherited some 3,400 acres in Rio Grande do Sul; then, in eight years as vice-president and as president, he had increased his holdings to about 1.5 million acres (not to mention twenty-five fine apartment houses and other odd bits of real estate)—all on a salary of $350 a month. *The New York Times*, on April 2, 1964, editorialized: "[Goulart's] enemies cannot prove that he has been turning the country over to Communism, but they can prove that he has been turning Brazil over to chaos."

HUMBERTO CASTELLO BRANCO, 1964–67

The "revolution" of April, 1964, was Brazil's most drastic repudiation of civilian government since the 1890's. Opposition was almost non-existent—most of the leaders of the political parties accepted military rule as the only alternative to chaos. On April 11, Marshal Humberto Castello Branco, army chief of staff, was elected president by the Chamber of Deputies to serve out Goulart's term—that is, until January 31, 1966—and the mood of the country was one of relief.

Castello Branco, largely unknown to the general public, was held in high regard by his fellow officers as a scholarly, thoughtful, moderate leader who had always upheld constitutional rule. He had served with the Brazilian forces in Italy during World War II. His previous excursions into politics had been limited to joining the demand for Vargas's resignation in 1954. When the outcry against Goulart took shape, Castello Branco was slow to join the rebels. But his final decision that their course was sound helped to persuade others—and in the end he was largely responsible for the success of the uprising.

Even before Castello Branco was inducted into office on April 15, the military had proclaimed the Institutional Act, which empowered the three chiefs of the armed forces—and later the president—to arrest whomever they chose for "subversive activities," without recourse to civil courts, and to suspend their political rights for as long as ten years. The witch hunt that followed was a graceless affair, with the tracking down of "subversives," "Communists," and "grafters"—all in the name of the "economic, financial, political, and moral reconstruction of Brazil." Local officials saw the opportunity to pay off political or personal scores, and this they did with a vengeance. Thousands of men and women went to jail—no one knows how many—though most of them were shortly freed. Some 400 people were stripped of their political rights for a ten-year period: included were three ex-presidents—Juscelino Kubitschek, Jânio Quadros, and João Goulart (all of whom were unlikely targets for such abuse: Kubitscheck, no matter what grafting he had done in the building of Brasília, was certainly no "Communist"; nor was Quadros, for all his silly performances; and even Goulart, according to some, might more accurately be described as a swindler). Also included in the blanket proscription were six state governors, fifty-five congressmen, numerous labor leaders, army officers, public officials, and respected intellectuals. One of the first to be seized and flown to an island prison was Governor Miguel Arraes of Pernambuco, whose diatribes against Washington and the Alliance for Progress had angered many. Soon to suffer the same fate was the zealous Francisco Julião, organizer of the Peasant Leagues in the Northeast—a leftist of the Fidel Castro persuasion, but probably not a Communist. The most unlikely victim of the purge was Celso Furtado, an astute economist who had organized and directed with considerable success the project called SUDENE (the Superintendency for the Development of the Northeast)—an imaginative rehabilitation program for the bitterly poor Northeast, which had been partially financed by the United States. A permanent National Service of Information was installed, headed by a general with cabinet rank, and was assigned the task of watching "national security." It had an unpleasant sound.

The powers conferred upon the president by the Institutional Act were generous: beside the right to dismiss public servants at will, he was given almost complete control of the budget, and the right to declare a state of siege without the consent of Congress. Furthermore, any measure proposed by the president was to be automatically effective if Congress did not act upon it within thirty days. In short, it was a dictatorship. However, believers in democracy took comfort in the fact that Castello Branco seemed moderate and intent upon a rule of law. He assured his friends that "the evils of the extreme left" could not be cured by the "birth of a reactionary right." Castello Branco's appointments to his cabinet were on the whole reassuring—among them were two of Brazil's ablest economists: Octavio

Bulhões became minister of the treasury, and Roberto Campos, minister of planning. Campos had been Goulart's ambassador in Washington, but had quit that post as a protest against Goulart's "financial irresponsibility."

Among the early actions of the new government were a number of constitutional amendments. Castello Branco's term was extended for fourteen months, until March 15, 1967. Other changes provided that the election of both the president and the vice-president should be by an absolute majority of votes (something which had not happened since 1946), and also, wisely, that the vice-president must come from the same party as the president. While these provisions obviously had no immediate application, they held promise when and if regular elections should be held.

The economic plight was clear: the inflation rate for 1964 was almost 100 per cent; and the budget deficit for the year exceeded $600 million. Castello Branco imposed austerity and held the line with remarkable fidelity—but his program, which cut into the living standards of all, brought few shouts of popular acclaim. The ending of exchange subsidies on wheat and gasoline, which meant sharp increases in the price of bread and of transportation, penalized everyone. The national minimum wage remained frozen at a theoretical $26.25 a month—and many did not get even that beggarly sum. (Resentment on this score was not lessened when Castello Branco, in order to hold the military in line, increased the salaries of the armed forces by 100 per cent.) Consider the plight of the ill-paid workers: with the increase in bus fares, due to the rising price of gasoline, many of the poorest of them—living far out on the edges of Rio de Janeiro and São Paulo—had to pay out a fourth of their wages on transportation. And reliable estimates showed that the average worker receiving the minimum wage was spending about 60 per cent of his earnings on food. So the Castello Branco government was denounced as antilabor. Of course organized labor—in the hands of racketeers in the Goulart days—had earned its bad reputation; and now the government in effect took over the unions, appointing "interventors" to run them. Castello Branco was simply making the best of an impossibly bad situation, and the little man was hardest hit.

But Castello Branco's tough measures pleased the international bankers and the dispensers of aid in Washington. He slowed the printing presses, which had been grinding out paper cruzeiros. He made solid reforms in tax collection: in São Paulo alone some 150 tax inspectors were dismissed for corrupt practices. He tightened credit at the Bank of Brazil, which had long made fat loans to Vargas, Kubitschek, and Goulart without proper collateral and often without more than a token repayment. In June, 1964, he announced his agrarian reform program which called for widespread expropriation of lands which were not usefully exploited, payment to be made in bonds. Castello Branco also improved relations with foreign capital. In August, 1964, he eased the strict rules against remittance of profits by foreign companies: while still holding to the principle of limiting such remittances to an amount not larger than 10 per cent of invested capital, it permitted the foreign companies to add the balance of profits to their total investment. In October, agreement was reached with foreign utilities companies, principally American and Foreign Power, by which those concerns (some of which had been taken over by Governor Leonel Brizola in Rio Grande do Sul) would be purchased by the Brazilian government on fairly satisfactory terms: payment of some $135 million was promised—10 per cent down and the balance over a period of forty-five years. Then in December, 1965, the long dispute with foreign mining companies seeking iron-mining concessions was settled: there would be no state monopoly, and private concerns could get to work. This chiefly affected two concerns, The Hanna Company of Cleveland and the Antunes Mining Company, a Brazilian concern with large interest held by Bethlehem Steel. The December decree also permitted the companies to build shipping ports in Sepetiba Bay (forty miles south of Rio de Janeiro) and to build spurs of railroads to carry the ore mined in Minas Gerais. (Carlos Lacerda, an active campaigner for the presidency in 1967, denounced the decision as unconstitutional.)

Castello Branco further ingratiated himself with the United States by breaking off relations (in May, 1964) with Castro's Cuba. And in the spring of 1965 he gave warm support to Washington's military action in the Dominican Republic by sending the only sizable detachment of troops to participate in the Inter-American Peace Force—this in the face of general disapproval of the whole venture throughout Latin America. The Brazilian President was amply rewarded for his cooperation with the United States, as well as for his conservative fiscal policies: he could take personal credit for securing a bundle of almost $1 billion in extended loans and further credits from Washington, the World Bank, the International Monetary Fund, and from private banks in the United States and Europe.

But if Castello Branco pleased the international financial community, he made enemies at home. Certainly he brought no happiness to Brazilian intellectuals. University faculties and students denounced his measures as dictatorial, deplored his rough treatment of political leaders, and claimed that he was doing little about education. The university situation was aggravated by the zeal of the security police, who interfered repeatedly with student organizations and arrested student leaders, all on the somewhat vague charge of "Communist activity." There may indeed have been some Communists—but the whole atmosphere resembled that of the days of Joe McCarthy in the United States. Added to the discomfort of the intellectuals was the genuine misery of the poorly paid workers, and the growing poverty of the threadbare middle class. In fact no one liked Castello Branco very much, but he could say with truth: "I have not become the president of Brazil to win a popularity contest."

By October, 1965, it was obvious that all was not clear sailing for Castello Branco. Congressional elections in eleven states revealed something short of unanimity in the support for his government. In five of the state elections for governor, Castello Branco's candidates were duly chosen; but in four states the winning candidates were neutrals, and in the two most important states—Guanabara (Rio de Janeiro) and Minas

Gerais—there was clear opposition, and antigovernment men won. Then Juscelino Kubitschek returned from his travels abroad and was given a tumultuous hero's welcome, in spite of the ten-year proscription against him. Hard upon these events, the government struck back with its Second Institutional Act, promulgated on October 27. This measure made a clean sweep of the old political parties, including the machines set up by Vargas, Goulart, and Kubitschek. The Labor Party, the Social Democrats, and the Democratic National Union, together with some ten minor parties, were all discarded. In their place was fashioned a government party, the National Renovating Alliance, ARENA; and for good measure the Act also set up an "official" opposition party, MDB, the Brazilian Democratic Movement. The hard-line army men—who had brought pressures on Castello Branco to permit no debate and to crack down upon all dissidents—had finally triumphed. A cynical observer remarked: "We have our two-party system all right, the party of *Yes,* and the party of *Yes, Sir.*" The comments from abroad and from within the country were to the point. *The Economist* of London wrote: "President Castello Branco has finally torn it. Brazil's Constitution of 1946 lies in tatters. A second Constitutional Act . . . just about demolishes what was left of the country's democratic processes." From Rio de Janeiro, the *Correio da Manhã* editorialized: "The new Act is a dry and arrogant announcement of the establishment of a dictatorial order."

There was further tightening of the "dictatorial order" in February, 1966, with the promulgation of the Third Institutional Act, which laid down new ground rules for all elections in the foreseeable future. Henceforth, the president and all federal and state officials would be chosen, not by the people, but by the state and national legislatures. The congressmen alone would be freely elected by popular vote. This procedure was in full force by the end of 1966. ARENA's candidate for the presidency, General Artur da Costa e Silva—who had been given the green light months before —was unanimously elected by the national Congress on October 3 (the opposition boycotted the election), and would take office on March 15, 1967. Meanwhile, the state legislature had safely elected the official candidates for governor in eleven states. Thus, it would seem, the military had sewed up the political life of Brazil for some time to come, and it was clear that there would be no trifling with the decisions made by the government.

Further proof of the praetorian role of the military government was the press bill which Castello Branco announced in December, 1966. Heavy fines and imprisonment were prescribed for reporting which could "provoke lack of confidence in the banking system," and for the publishing of news prejudicial to the national security. The measure brought strong protests from the International Press Institute in Geneva and the Inter-American Press Association. And the able *Jornal do Brasil* of Rio de Janeiro, which is generally pro-government, warned editorially that the bill would "destroy, without doubt, whatever is left of the concept of Brazil as a democratic country."

ARTUR DA COSTA E SILVA, 1967–

The inauguration of Artur da Costa e Silva as president on March 15, 1967, continued the rule of the nation by the military: one half of his twenty-two cabinet members were military men—and while Costa was now subject to a constitution, he still had the right to rule by decree. But there seemed to be a change in mood as the new government took over. There was a difference between the groups around Costa e Silva and those who had surrounded Castello Branco: perhaps most significant was the retirement of Castello's minister of planning, the able Roberto Campos, who had been responsible for the more spartan austerity measures of Castello, and his replacement by an economist who said that Castello's stiff measures should be relaxed. And Costa himself said that "social humanism will be the most profound root of my government." Costa vowed that he would be as adamant as Castello in fighting inflation, but that ways must be opened for more homes, hospitals, schools, and "comforts" for the poor. Warnings against any softening of the lines against inflation came from Castello's Roberto Campos: he pointed out that, with inflation still mounting at more than 40 per cent a year, "premature humanization [of economic policy] can turn into future cruelty." But these warnings were ignored as Costa's minister of labor rehired 1,500 men dropped from the government payroll by Castello. "My principal job," he said, "will be to free the labor unions so that they can counter the pressure of employers. If only one side is strong, there is no justice." There was comfort for the intellectual community in assurances from Costa that the ban on student demonstrations would be abolished, and that more funds would be found to strengthen and enlarge the universities. And for believers in democracy there was a welcome promise that Castello Branco's press law would not be enforced. "The new president," remarked the *Jornal do Brasil* in grateful response to this new note, "makes us feel comfortable."

By mid-1967 there was considerable enthusiasm for Costa e Silva, under the conviction that he would be tough enough to battle inflation, but not too tough to consider the fundamental human needs of his people. The President had worked no miracles by September, 1967, after six months in office, but he had the continued support of Washington (which committed a total of $450 million to Brazil in 1967). And there had been a slight decrease in inflation.

BRAZIL: PROBLEMS AND PROMISES

The story of Brazil—we repeat—must be told with superlatives. In land area, it is larger than any nation on earth except the U.S.S.R., Canada, the United States, and China. Its population (84.7 million in 1966) is second only to that of the United States in the Western Hemisphere. In natural resources, it is one of the richest nations in the world: it has vast stretches of potentially productive land still untouched; forests with fine stands of hardwoods; and a bewildering variety of other products—buried veins of iron (an estimated 23 per cent of the world's supply) and almost every other metal and mineral, rushing streams to be harnessed for the generation of electricity. And Brazil has the most impressive industrial development of any nation in Latin America: by 1960 almost half of its capital goods were produced domestically.

But rich Brazil houses a poor people. There are few trustworthy statistics to tell how the Brazilian people fare. The riotous inflation makes it impossible to arrive at even a reasonably accurate figure for per capita national income in dollar terms, but it is certainly safe to say that it is under $300. This, however, involves an unrealistic averaging of the princely incomes of the rich with the pittances of the poor. A few are fabulously wealthy: those who own fine coffee lands, mills, factories, mines. Others live comfortably from good posts in industry, trading, and politics. Then there is the rapidly increasing middle class, aggregating some 20 to 25 per cent of the population, which includes professional people, technicians, teachers, white-collar workers in government and business: only a favored slice of this new middle class receives incomes which by any standard can be described as adequate. But what of those who tend the crops, herd the cattle, work in the mills and factories, dig in the mines, perform the menial tasks of towns and cities? What of the impoverished millions in the stricken Northeast? It may safely be guessed that more than half the Brazilian people live in filthy shacks, barely surviving on an income of less than $100 a year: largely illiterate, with few of their children able to attend school, these people are cut off from any effective share in the national life and bounty. (That is not a statistic. There is no accurate accounting of misery in Brazil.)

This poverty means a meager diet. "We do nothing well," writes Afrânio Peixoto, "because we are on a diet—a perpetual diet." The poor live on manioc flour, beans, a little jerked beef, corn, fish, very little fresh fruit and vegetables, and almost no milk. Ruy Coutinho characterizes this diet as "insufficient in calories . . . with a low percentage of proteins . . . deficient in vitamins and mineral salts." And, adds Coutinho, "Even the Brazilian of the middle class is badly nourished . . . he uses cereals and sweets in excess."

Brazil's health services are lamentably inadequate. Hospitals are chiefly reserved for the larger cities, and there are never enough beds. The shortage of physicians is tragic: if 1 physician to each 1,000 people is considered adequate, Brazil has a doctor shortage of at least 40,000. But even the few doctors available are badly distributed: while the cities of São Paulo and Rio de Janeiro are fairly well served, there is perhaps only 1 doctor to each 20,000 or more persons in the state of Maranhão in the Northeast. Infant mortality, sure index to misery and disease, may only be guessed: according to official figures (unreliable and probably low), in 1960, out of every 1,000 babies born alive 70 died in their first year in Rio de Janeiro, 125 in Recife, 201 in Fortaleza (as against 16.6 in Sweden, 26 in the United States).

Brazil's dire poverty is directly and tragically linked to its reckless population explosion. Despite the high death rate (perhaps 11–13 per 1,000), the astronomical number of births (perhaps 40–43 per 1,000) puts the rate of population increase today at 3.0 per cent—a rate almost twice that estimated for the entire world; a rate which would double the population every twenty-three years. And it must be noted that this increase is not chiefly among the literate and more competent sectors of the population: the most prolific breeding is among the least secure and the least literate—in the misery of the city slums, which are expanding and multiplying in frightening fashion; in the desperate Northeast, where life and death are scarcely tabulated. As a result, far too many of the new Brazilians added each year simply distend the company of the more defenseless citizens.

In any recounting of misery and poverty in Brazil, attention must be given to the problem of race. The Negro, descendant of the slaves brought to this land of promise during the sixteenth, seventeenth, eighteenth, and nineteenth centuries, accounts for at least a third of the nation's population. The Brazilian Negro has never suffered the thinly disguised savagery which has been the rule in some sections of the United States; and he has been free to break from his place among the miserable masses and to find new status as a responsible or even an honored citizen—indeed many have made that transition. True, Brazil's Negroes are chiefly to be found in the most depressed classes. But there has been no such open clash between races as today complicates life in the United States. There have been no Lester Maddoxes or George Wallaces or Ku Klux Klans breathing hate against the man of black skin. Neither have there been such evangelists for racial decency as Martin Luther King. But the evidence of the existence of race lines is abundant. Only 3 per cent of Brazil's army officers are Negro, and the navy officials are lily-white. Only one member of the diplomatic corps is a Negro. In the newspapers, applicants for jobs are usually warned, "Only the light-skinned need apply," and notices of apartments for rent often carry the caution "Whites only." So Brazil increasingly shares the racial tension which grips the world in the mid-twentieth century.

The malaise of Brazil is deepened by the flocking of country people into the cities. The figures are eloquent and depressing: between 1900 and 1960 the population of Rio de Janeiro grew from 629,000 to 4,700,-000; that of São Paulo from 240,000 to 4,400,000; and that of Recife from 113,000 to 1,100,000. It is the open country which ejects the people rather than the city which attracts them: the wretched life of farm workers drives men to the mean refuge of the overcrowded cities. The slums in all Brazilian cities are appalling. Rio de Janeiro, high candidate for the world's most beautiful city, is an unholy yoking of wealth and bitter poverty. There it rests in its cradle of mountains which reach down to the sea, with its eloquent boulevards and its fine houses—all enlaced by miles of silver beaches. On the hilltops which rise above this beauty and luxury are the *favelas,* shanty towns of squatters who have moved in from the parched Northeast and the lonely countryside: here some 700,000 people, more or less, are crowded into 297 desolate communities, living in huts of scrap iron, sticks, and cardboard held together with wires. The *favelas* have scant water supply, little electricity, practically no sewers or sanitary facilities, virtually no police protection. And yet—curiously enough—the *favelados* have the choice building lots of Rio de Janeiro, with the broad sweep of vision which embraces the breathtaking loveliness of the city, its mountain peaks, its unending beaches, and the islands and the distant sea. Thus Brazil, with its proud metropolis rotting at its very heart, shares the burdensome problems of the cities which so grievously afflict almost every nation on earth.

Brazil presents a frightening exhibit of poor housekeeping. The confusion of national government, the corruption and incompetence of municipal government, the neglect of the rural communities, the almost total lack of planning—all this produces a tangled and gloomy picture. Brasília, for example, flaunts its bold new buildings; but no housing has yet been provided for the ill-paid workers, so new slums spring up in the hapless fashion so familiar in Rio de Janeiro, São Paulo, Recife. In Rio, which presents such a handsome façade to the visitor, there is shortage of almost everything—police, firemen, taxis, buses, sewers. There is not enough electric current to run the elevators in the tall new apartments. There is not water enough for comfort or decency. Theoretically, there is a daily quota of forty gallons per day for each inhabitant (that is less than one-third of the standard accepted in American cities), but even that meager amount is not certain. Now and then, the city of Rio de Janeiro has a brief turn of good fortune. One such came with Carlos Lacerda, whose term as governor of Guanabara ended in 1966. That versatile and exasperating gentleman, although engaged in a frantic—and futile— effort to win the presidency, worked some major miracles in the housekeeping of the erstwhile capital. He built new tunnels to ease the traffic jams. He planned and started building a forty-mile aqueduct to bring water from the Guandu River. He tightened up city administration, police, and all services. His success, however, only served to highlight the sorry plight of Brazil's cities and rural communities. But Brazilians are philosophical: one of them remarks, "We don't brood over dried up faucets. We are surrounded by the world's most beautiful scenery, and the world's most beautiful women. We have the sea to wash off our worries, and the sun to dry our tears."

The Brazilian national conscience has belatedly been stirred by the tragic plight of the Northeast. Here, in nine states[3] comprising about 18 per cent of the national area, are housed over 24 million people, some 30 per cent of all Brazilians, most of whom live as miserably as the most impoverished people of India or of Haiti. The Northeast consists of two parts. The *sertão* of the interior is a sterile and parched land, where the sun beats down and the rains fail—a land cursed with extended periods of

3 Bahia, Piauí, Maranhão, Ceará, Rio Grande do Norte, Paraíba, Pernambuco, Alagôas, Sergipe.

drought from which thousands flee to the precarious refuge of the cities. The trek of these desperate peasants—some of whom travel as far south as Rio de Janeiro, São Paulo, or Pôrto Alegre—has been portrayed by Cândido Portinari in his memorable murals in Washington's Library of Congress. In the coastal area, where there is plenty of rain and the soil is fertile, are the great sugar plantations—but even here the land has suffered the ravages of monoculture. Also along the coast are the cities —Recife, Fortaleza, Salvador, São Luis, Maceió, and João Pessoa—which have become the dumping ground for the wretched and bitter peasants from the countryside. Upon the entire region of the Northeast is fixed the pattern of latifundia inherited from the early Portuguese colonists: today some three-fourths of the land belongs to a scant 2 per cent of the landholders. The great majority of the people are farm laborers, share-croppers, or squatters—virtual slaves whom Josué de Castro calls "sad half humans crushed like cane between rollers that leave only juiceless husks behind."[4] Half starved, housed in shacks or caves, these poor souls have almost no medical care and few schools for their children. The per capita income for the rural population of this area may be less than $50 a year.

In this sick land there is no true tally of those who are born and those who die. Perhaps as many as half the babies do not live out their first year. For those who survive, death is the one welcome release. It was to give dignity to death—not to life—that the first Peasant League was founded in 1955: the reform hopefully sought for was no more than the right of the poor to a decent burial in a proper coffin.

There soon emerged as the champion of the landless peasants the lawyer and political leader, Francisco Julião, who—outraged at the general wretchedness and degradation—organized Peasant Leagues throughout the area. Condemned as a rabble rouser, Julião styled himself as a "simple social agitator," and appealed to the people with such words as "We are not interested in anybody's religion or ideology: let's just get together, everybody, and free the peasant from oppression. . . . This struggle is nobler than the abolition of slavery. . . . We will put through agrarian reform either by law or by struggle. . . . Pope John XXIII was the first Pope of peasant origin. His recent encyclical is proof that the Pope supports the Peasant Leagues."[5] And it should be noted that there is a new generation of clergy who have taken to heart the Pope's admonition on social justice, and who have helped to organize farm workers for collective action.

In 1959, official recognition was given to the problems of the beleaguered Northeast: in that year the project called SUDENE was launched. Planned and directed by the competent and devoted Celso Furtado, financed by the Brazilian government and by a $131-million grant from Washington, SUDENE finally got under way in 1962. Solid progress has been made in improving sanitary conditions—installing sewers, and establishing safe water supplies. Power plants have been built, furnishing more generous

4 Josué de Castro: *Death in the Northeast* (New York: Random House; 1966), p. 7.
5 Cited by Josué de Castro, *op. cit.*, pp. 176–7.

supply of electric current. Streams have been dammed to extend irrigation. Roads have been built, including feeder roads to open up the interior. Farmers have had instruction in better farming methods, plows have been distributed for better preparation of the soil, and some tractors and other mechanized equipment have been supplied. A plan for opening up the state of Maranhão, a largely unoccupied jungle area about the size of Italy, facing north onto the Atlantic, promises thousands of new farms. To attract industry to the Northeast, the Castello Branco administration offered tax reductions to industrialists who would open plants in that area—and many are doing so, especially in the state of Pernambuco.

Celso Furtado and his colleagues pressed for bold new agrarian reform, for the transfer by peaceful means of many broad acres now monopolized by the favored few. But such proposals aroused the fierce resistance of the large landholders and led to the reckless use of the word "Communist"—the Castello Branco regime attached the label to Celso Furtado and many of his colleagues, stripping them of their citizenship. Furtado left Brazil for a professorship at Yale University, and many other competent economists and engineers were dropped from SUDENE. The situation was further embroiled when the zealous Francisco Julião—whose Peasant Leagues had seized some lands in an amateur agrarian program of their own—journeyed to Cuba and to China and returned with glowing enthusiasm for similar reforms to be instituted in the Brazilian Northeast. Julião was of course denounced as a Communist (which he may or may not be), and he was jailed in the purge of the early Castello Branco days, but was later released.

Aside from the issue of social justice, Brazil is uncomfortably aware that the Northeast is a deficit area in the Brazilian economy: its people depend upon the steady import of foodstuffs from central Brazil—the state of Rio Grande do Norte alone imports about 70 per cent of its food. Although the efforts of SUDENE have brought some improvement on this score, much of the money put in by the Brazilian government and by the United States has gone into dams and power plants which have been useful chiefly in enriching those who are already rich by increasing the value of their land.

Brazil must be understood as a land in the turmoil of revolution: a revolution inchoate and amorphous if you will, but a revolution which is shaking the life of the nation. It is this revolution which explains the passionate appeal of nationalism, which strikes back at all detractors, seeking to prove that Brazil is mighty. This revolution appears in the shift from agriculture to industry, as millions desert the open country for the crowded misery of the cities: out of this migration emerges the new urban industrial labor segment—which, organized or not, is the most powerful political force in the nation—offering the chief target to demagogues both of the right and the left. This revolution appears in the new and irresistible demand for agrarian reform, for the shifting of economic power from a few great masters of the nation to the landless and the depressed.

It is not a revolution which is carefully charted, or well conducted, but it has within it the buried power which could tear the nation apart—and hopefully perhaps to rebuild it.

The salvation of Brazil may be prescribed in terms of politics, education, or what you will: but all yield to the primary need for a viable economy. Empty stomachs and rotting bodies do not make sound citizens. What are the answers?

First and most important, is improvement in the use to which Brazil puts its land: it must be more equitably distributed; and it must be made to yield enough food for today's 85 millions—and, looking ahead, for the more than 230 millions who, if present trends continue, may occupy Brazil in the year 2000. The maldistribution of Brazil's farm lands (a blemish, as we have seen, common to most of Latin America) is shown in the figures for 1960, when 1 per cent of the landholdings, each more than 2,471 acres in extent, accounted for almost one-half of the entire farm land of the nation, and at the other extreme, some 31 per cent of the landholdings—occupying only 1 per cent of the land—were in plots of less than 12.4 acres. The chief victims of this land pattern are some 15 million completely landless tenant farmers, squatters, and day laborers—whose perpetual hunger, bad health, and illiteracy are an affront to all sense of national decency.

There is nothing to justify such niggardly treatment of present and prospective farmers. Pushing back the frontiers can open up millions of acres of potential farm and pasture lands which now lie untouched. We can only guess as to the possible future use of the Amazon basin for migrants from the crowded Northeast or from abroad. A hundred and sixty years ago Baron von Humboldt visited this unoccupied region (there are still only 1.2 persons to the square mile in the state of Amazonas) and expatiated upon the cities and farms which would one day prosper here. Scientists hold little hope for the agricultural development of the lowlands of Amazonia, where the heavy rains leach out the soil when the forests are cleared and the land is planted, and the yield is scant. But there are great and promising plateaus reaching northward from the highlands of Mato Grosso and Goiás. Conquest of this area awaits the builders of railroads and highways, the sanitary engineers who will overcome the scourges which attack man, his animals, his crops.

The United States secretary of agriculture, Orville Freeman, visiting Brazil in April, 1966, announced the grant to Brazil of a million tons of wheat—the proceeds from its sale to go into development projects for Brazil, with emphasis on transportation and on agriculture. It has long been true that surplus food piles up and rots within 100 miles of Rio de Janeiro and other cities, because there are not railroads enough, or highways enough, nor trucks enough to move the food into the suffering cities. And Brazil's agriculture, he said, must be modernized. In all Brazil there are but 63,500 tractors (compared with 4.6 million in the United States), and most of Brazil's fields are still cultivated with a hoe. The supply of fertilizers is scant, and the price is high: the lack of ships makes it cheaper to bring fertilizer from the United States or Africa to São Paulo than to move it from Recife. There is no reason, continued Secretary Freeman, why Brazil should not produce more generously: Brazil has abundant land, plenty of water, and in much of the nation, a favorable climate. With scientific methods, many areas could turn out three crops of rice each year. The nation as a whole could produce enough sugar, rice, corn, fruits, and potatoes to feed not only all Brazilians, but all South Americans as well. The American Secretary offered some sobering facts on Brazilian production: Brazil's per-acre yield of corn stands at 21 bushels (the United States figure is 73.1 bushels); Brazil's rice production is but 1,340 pounds per acre (in the United States the yield is 4,000 pounds). In Brazil, 40 per cent of the cows have a calf each year (compared to 90 per cent in the United States). Mr. Freeman also had wise counsel on beef prodution, which has been slowed down by unrealistic price controls: he suggested that it would be better for Brazil to encourage the production of beef than to maintain state supports for coffee, of which there was an unsold stock of 50 million bags in 1966—a year's supply for the entire world. He called attention to the monopoly of the sugar industry in the Northeast, where some forty-two big plantations collect the lion's share of the profits—not to mention the four cents a pound premium paid by the United States on the Brazilian quota of 340,000 tons of sugar. (Mr. Freeman offered other wholesome but unpalatable truths. He remarked on the failure to enforce payment of the small minimum wage provided by law, about $25 per month.)

Furthermore, increased diversity of products will serve the nation. Overdependence upon one or two products has made Brazil a slave of world markets for four centuries: sugar, cacao, cotton, gold, rubber, and coffee have each had their day of glory. In 1965 coffee was still in the lead, furnishing 44 per cent of export revenue. Cotton was second with 6 per cent. Cacao (in the world export of which Brazil is second only to Ghana), was third with 1.8 per cent of Brazil's exports. Brazil also exported timber and lumber, hides and skins, vegetable oils, waxes, fibers, tobacco, rice, iron ore, fruits, nuts, yerba maté, menthol; small quantities of tungsten, manganese, and mica; some sugar and wool; a little rubber and starches. And the possibility of further diversification seemed almost unlimited. Again, only capital, technicians, and man power were lacking.

The second cure for Brazil's ills, already vigorously pursued, is industrialization. Today, Brazil is making cars and trucks, steel rails, farm machinery, electrical equipment, textiles, and almost all its consumer goods. When Sears, Roebuck and Company built its new stores in Rio de Janeiro and São Paulo, they appealed to national pride by announcing that at least 70 per cent of their wares would come from Brazilian factories and mills; by 1966 about 99 per cent of the articles sold were made in Brazil. To promote the fortunes of industry, there must be exploitation of the varied mineral wealth, which has scarcely been touched, as well as continued development of hydroelectric plants.

The third imperative is to bring Brazil's inflation under control. At the end of 1966 the free cruzeiro was worth, in dollar terms, about one-thirtieth of its 1954 value; and during that same period (1954–66), the cost of living increased some sixtyfold. Although this inflation serves the purposes of industry, it involves the great bulk of the population in a spiral of deepening poverty. It piles up foreign debts. It devours the aid which is generously poured in by the United States and other foreign agencies. To block inflation, production must be increased and the fruits of production more equitably distributed. And some way must be found to keep wages and prices in line without penalizing the most defenseless.

The fourth great need is the extension of railroads and highways. Brazil has 24,531 miles of railroads, chiefly in the south, with only a few short spurs along the northern coast. (The United States has 234,351 miles of railroads; Argentina, with about one-third Brazil's area and population, has 27,770 miles of tracks.) Some states have no railroad connection with the others. Brazil's waterways, to be sure, partially compensate for lack of railroads: about 40,000 miles of navigable streams are utilized. Highways are being rapidly extended: these are used by some 1.8 million automobiles, trucks, and buses. Some observers believe that highways and motor vehicles will furnish the answer to Brazil's communication needs, and that the nation will pass over the age of railroads. Corwin Edwards suggests that "Brazil's resources and geography are better suited to an economy of light metals, electric power and transportation by automobile and airplane than they are to the age of steel, coal and railroads which is passing." Although Brazil leads South America in air transportation, primitive communications still rule. Most of the people move themselves and their goods on muleback and oxcart. The dearth of communications defers development of the frontier, delays realization of national unity, retards cultural advance, and creates scarcity of commodities and high prices in the populous centers.

Fifth, Brazil's welfare calls for increased immigration. This is a paradox in view of the fact that the population is already increasing at a dizzy rate. But this increase is among the most illiterate and poorly served of the Brazilian population. The nation's farms, factories, mines, and forest industries need a further injection of foreign settlers such as those who arrived before World War II. The 4,390,519 people who entered between the years 1874 and 1940 (34 per cent from Italy, 29 per cent from Portugal, 14 per cent from Spain, 4.5 per cent from Japan, and 4.1 per cent from Germany) brought new vigor and skill, introduced better farming and stock breeding, increased coffee and cotton culture, and built and manned the factories and mills. Most of them settled in the region south of Minas Gerais—about 55 per cent in the one state of São Paulo. The Japanese (of whom there are now about 500,000—first-, second-, and third-generation) have rendered fine account of themselves. Concentrated in the state of São Paulo, they have introduced the best methods of irrigation, fertilization, seed selection. According to figures from the Japanese Embassy, the Japanese constitute only six-tenths of 1 per cent of the

Brazilian farm population, but account for 6 per cent of the total farm production. The Japanese have also made signal contribution to industrialization—building the largest shipyard in all Latin America; producing steel in Minas Gerais; building factories which turn out automobiles, farm machinery, and a long list of consumer goods. The Japanese introduced jute, pepper, and green tea—all of which are now on Brazil's export list. It is obvious that Brazil would be wise to welcome more West Europeans and Japanese, but few have come since 1940. World War II blocked migration; the ineptness of Brazilian agencies prevented effective recruiting and settling of immigrants; the unavailability of good lands discouraged prospective farmers; a low standard of pay and poor living conditions offered little lure.

Sixth, Brazil needs doctors, hospitals, clinics. Brazil is finally learning that sick men do not dig in the fields, mine iron, cultivate coffee, tend cattle. Writes Dr. Miguel Pereira: "Brazil is a vast hospital." But, ironically, Brazil is a hospital without hospitals. Such luxuries are reserved for larger centers; the country as a whole has scant medical care. The universities train physicians, but few leave the cities, where life is pleasant. Thousands of towns and villages depend upon their local druggists who double as doctors, upon midwives, and upon untrained *curanderos* whose pragmatic knowledge of *materia medica* often enables them to render valiant—though scarcely scientific—service to their neighbors. During recent years the government-financed Prophylaxia Rural, with its floating hospitals and scattered clinics, has served well in the Amazon valley.

Seventh, Brazil needs schools and teachers. Despite official optimism, it is still probably true that at least half of all Brazilians can neither read nor write; that there are schools for not more than 40 per cent of the children and that not one out of ten children goes beyond the first three grades. The high schools are mostly in the favored south. While the national budget of 1963 alloted 45 per cent to the armed forces, a scant 2.6 per cent was assigned to education.

Eighth, Brazil's promise of greatness awaits a sense of national unity. It is still a land of loosely linked regions which do not yet make common cause in the solution of national problems. The city and state of São Paulo produce more than half the agricultural and industrial goods of the nation. São Paulo, together with the other states south of Minas Gerais, continues to be the effective Brazil. The arid Northeast, the interior lands of the Amazon, of the Brazilian highlands, and of Mato Grosso are the colonial outposts of an empire whose political capital is Rio de Janeiro (or, in theory, Brasília) and whose economic stronghold is São Paulo. There is, as yet, little disposition on the part of the more favored regions to accept full responsibility for the nation as a whole.

Ninth, the creation of a true Brazilian nation still waits upon the emergence of national leaders. The history of republican Brazil since 1889 has been the record of rival political machines in the important states— São Paulo, Minas Gerais, Rio de Janeiro, and Rio Grande do Sul—and of their various agreements to place aspiring *caudilhos* in the presidency. The full panoply of fine-sounding parties, far from representing any broad national conviction, have usually been the tools of the bosses: yesterday, there was Vargas; then Kubitschek, Quadros, Goulart. Today, in the mid-sixties, the armed forces have taken over, liquidated the old parties, installed two new ones of their own invention. President Costa e Silva does not command truly national support—nor did his predecessor, Castello Branco (who was killed in an airplane crash four months after quitting office). A tough and even competent military rule is no answer to Brazil's political ills. The hope for an effective democracy, in which popularly chosen leaders would speak for all, still seems dim.

Culturally, Brazil presents a pleasant exhibit. Her writers, painters, architects, and musicians have won enthusiastic praise from critics everywhere. In São Paulo in 1922, the *Semana de Arte Moderna*—a gathering of self-appointed representatives of the arts in Brazil—set out to make the arts truly Brazilian in inspiration rather than copies of foreign models. Among modern writers whose work is read eagerly at home and abroad are the novelists José Lins do Rêgo, who portrayed the sugar-cane aristocracy of the Northeast; Jorge Amado, the most widely translated of Brazilians, who wrote with broad scope and great gusto; Graciliano Ramos, a careful stylist, with psychological insight; Rachel de Queiroz, who wrote of Brazilian social life from a woman's point of view; Erico Verissimo, sophisticated novelist and critic; João Guimarães Rosa; Clarice Lispector; Dalton Trevisan; and the poets Manuel Bandeira, the dean of living Brazilian poets, a biting observer of life who praises the lyricism of madmen and Shakespeare's fools; Carlos Drummond de Andrade, whose early concern was the brotherhood of man but who has recently become disenchanted, who always writes with irony and honesty; Cecília Meireles, considered to be the finest woman poet in the Portuguese language; Jorge de Lima, a poet of tremendous range, whose themes include Christian mysticism and the Negro; Murilo Mendes; João Cabral de Melo Neto; and Cassiano Ricardo, who is important both as a poet and as the author of an interpretive and historical study of the *bandeirantes;* the essayists Afrânio Coutinho, Alceu Amoroso Lima, Antônio Cândido, and Eduardo Portella; the dramatists Ariano Saussuna, Dias Gomes, Pedro Bloch, and Jorge Andrade; and the sociologist-historian Gilberto Freyre, whose *Casa-grande e senzala* (translated as *The Masters and the Slaves*) is one of the finest works of social analysis to come out of Latin America.

There have been scores of excellent painters, especially in Rio de Janeiro and São Paulo. The most greatly honored was Cândido Portinari (1903–62), a son of Italian immigrants, trained in Europe, but whose work was robustly Brazilian. His range of expression and of interest was immense; he could paint the portrait of a child with simplicity and grace, and he could pour out his wrath against God and man on his savage canvases depicting the flight of the starving refugees from barren Ceará. He drew his inspiration from the Brazilian countryside, and from its people;

some of his greatest works deal with the Negro. Some rank him with José Clemente Orozco of Mexico as the greatest of modern painters in Latin America.

On the score of modern architecture, Brazil offers the most distinguished exhibit in South America. While the Argentines, Peruvians, and many others have been content to make poor copies of French buildings, Brazil's new architects have been building exciting skyscrapers and houses in the finest of modern design. Inspired largely by Le Corbusier, a group of Brazilian architects have been attracting international attention by their daring and imagination. Oscar Niemeyer, the best known, has excellent buildings to his credit in Rio de Janeiro, São Paulo, Belo Horizonte, Ouro Preto, and Brasília. The Ministry of Education in Rio de Janeiro was one of the earliest of these new creations; its builders devised external blinds to control the heat and glare of the sun, and it is built massively and simply, combining grace and power.

In music, Brazil stands with Mexico in the forefront of all the Latin American nations. Interest in music is of long standing in Brazil; the National Institute of Music, founded in 1848, was one of the first in South America. Among numerous distinguished composers the name of Antônio Carlos Gomes (1836–96) is conspicuous; his opera *Il guarany,* first presented in 1870, was hailed as the harbinger of a genuinely Brazilian art. But Gomes, influenced by Verdi, was more Italian than Brazilian. The prime exponent of truly national music was Heitor Villa-Lobos (1887–1959). Self-taught as a composer, he drew his inspiration from his own land and people. The folk music of the Negro and the backwoodsman furnished the materials from which he contrived his *chôros,* with their synthesis of the songs from the sugar cane fields and the forests. Of restless and ranging enthusiasm, Villa-Lobos wrote more than 2,000 compositions—symphonies, operas, chamber music, songs—the best of which won praise for their lustiness, sensitivity, and imagination.

PART XI

Latin America and the United States

The sovereign nations of Latin America assumed independence and developed as free states under the shadow of the greater powers of Europe and North America. A candid appraisal of their history and present status must reckon with the intermittent economic, military, and diplomatic meddling in their affairs by Spain, France, England, the United States, the U.S.S.R., and China. The repeated interventions of one or another of these powers—especially the United States—have exerted decisive influence on the course of the southern republics.

Chapter 53

LATIN AMERICA AND THE
UNITED STATES, 1810–95

The Latin Americans won independence in the third round of revolutionary struggles which tore the Western world during the last years of the eighteenth and the first years of the nineteenth centuries. First came the American Revolution, then the French, and finally the Latin American. By 1824, the year of the decisive battle of Ayacucho in Peru, the Spaniards, the Portuguese, and the French had yielded their control over most of the area from the Golden Gate to the Strait of Magellan. Spain still held Cuba and Puerto Rico; the French and English and Dutch retained islands in the Caribbean and unimportant areas on the mainland, but the way was cleared for the creation of eighteen of the twenty Latin American nations. The severance of Cuba would wait until 1898, and Panama would not be detached from Colombia until 1903.

The broils of Europe served the patriots of Latin America as they had earlier served those of the United States. England, Spain, France, Austria, Prussia, and Russia had been pursuing their various ambitious courses; uniting in successive coalitions, and then finding new alignments; making of Europe a cockpit which drained the man power and the treasure of all the contestants. The final torment of Europe was released by the storming of the Bastille in 1789, and for a quarter of a century the continent was involved in costly bloodletting; even when Napoleon Bonaparte was finally locked away on his lonely island, the event did not bring peace. The French Revolution had unloosed new and frightening ideas—the rights of man, the folly of kings, the uselessness of priests. Out of the mad convulsion had emerged the ambitious Napoleon, who turned the revolution into a campaign for imperial conquest. Against such affront, the royal masters of England, Austria, Prussia, and Russia united in the Quadruple Alliance; and then in 1815, with Great Britain dissenting, in the Holy Alliance in defense of kings-by-divine-right. Thus preoccupied with troubles at home, there was little that France, Spain, and Portugal could do to crush the uprisings in their American colonies; Haiti finally broke from France in 1804; the Spanish Americans fought from 1810 to 1824 until the last important peninsular army was routed at Ayacucho; while Brazil had peacefully severed her ties with Portugal in 1822.

THE UNITED STATES AND THE
INDEPENDENCE OF LATIN AMERICA

While Europe was passing through the agonies of the Napoleonic era and the patriot armies of Spanish America were battling Spanish troops, the United States was slowly extending its power in the north. The new republic was an inconsiderable power in 1800, its national domain confined between the Mississippi and the Atlantic, but the leaders of its virile people were dreaming of a glorious destiny which would expand the American union from sea to sea. The purchase of Louisiana and the Mississippi valley in 1803 was the earnest of greater successes to come: the addition of the Floridas in 1821; the annexation of Texas in 1845; the victory over Mexico, and the extension of national territory to California in 1848; the establishment of American sovereignty in the northwest by treaty with Great Britain in 1846; the purchase of the Mesilla valley from Mexico in 1853; the purchase of Alaska from Russia in 1867; the seizure of Cuba and Puerto Rico, and the purchase of the Philippines from Spain in 1898; the annexation of Hawaii in 1898.

It was a United States already possessed of a sense of Manifest Destiny that watched the brave fighting for independence in the south: Hidalgo's and Morelos's sorties in Mexico; Bolívar's in Venezuela, Colombia, Ecuador, Peru, and Bolivia; San Martín's in La Plata, Chile, and Peru—as well as the earlier struggle in Haiti. The response of the North Americans to these Latin American campaigns for liberty was sympathetic; the southern patriots were seeking an independence from Europe which the United States had already won. To be sure, there were few ties between the Anglo-Saxon Protestant north and the Latin Catholic south; traffic in goods and ideas between the two areas had never been important. In fact, the general attitude of the northerners toward the Spanish- and Portuguese-speaking peoples of the south was usually a blend of indifference and ill-disguised contempt; the "black legend" of Iberian perfidy, carefully insinuated by the writers of history books, had persuaded the North Americans that those who spoke Mediterranean tongues—and were Catholics—could not be accepted as first-class citizens of the world. But a sense of good-sportsmanship prevailed, and Americans applauded the efforts of the Latin Americans to be free. Furthermore, the hard-headed leaders of the United States saw that their country would be better served by free Latin American nations than by colonies whose trade would be monopolized by European masters.

The weak United States of 1810—the year in which the first important revolts broke out, from Mexico to Buenos Aires—was cautious in its attitude toward the struggles of the southern patriots. Great Britain's navy controlled the seaways, and the American leaders were not courting fresh involvement in Europe's turmoils. Nevertheless, gallantry—and hopes for profit—dictated a generous course toward the revolutionary juntas installed in 1810; agents of the patriots of Mexico, New Granada, and Venezuela were permitted to buy guns, powder, and even ships, to recruit American soldiers of fortune, and to sail from American ports. The agents of the rebel juntas, while denied official recognition, were received informally and in friendly fashion. In 1810 Washington went further by sending "agents for seamen and commerce" to the areas in revolt; consuls were sent in 1811, a step just short of recognition.

The year 1812 brought a change in official American policy toward the aspiring southern patriots, and for almost a decade the United States moved warily, professing and usually exercising a cautious neutrality in the struggles between Spain and her colonies. The War of 1812 with England dictated restraint; the poorly armed United States could not afford to risk involvement with Spain as well. The war also pricked the dreams of expansionists who hoped for new territory in Canada at England's expense; the United States was fortunate to get out of the tangle by the Treaty of Ghent in 1814.

Then relations with Spain, where shabby Ferdinand VII had been returned to the throne in 1814, became important as the United States sought to acquire the Floridas. It was obviously unwise to give comfort to Spain's rebellious subjects while carrying on negotiations for that territory. Furthermore, by 1815 the prospects of the Spanish American patriots were bleak: both Hidalgo and Morelos had failed in Mexico; Simón Bolívar had been defeated and was resting in Jamaica; Chile was again under Spanish control; only in Buenos Aires were the rebels unchallenged. Washington prudently received Ferdinand's minister in 1815, recalled its consuls from Spanish America, and contented itself with retaining "agents for seamen and commerce" in southern centers. This scrupulous neutrality was enforced with vigor by John Quincy Adams, who became President Monroe's secretary of state in 1817. Adams's policy, grounded in determination to get the Floridas, also reflected his lack of faith in the future of the southern peoples. He later admitted to Henry Clay that he had "little expectation of any beneficial result to this country from any future connection with them, political or commercial." The Latin Americans, he thought, were devoid of "the first elements of good or free government. . . . Arbitrary power, military and ecclesiastical, is stamped upon their education, their habits, and upon all their institutions." President Monroe, who had represented the United States in Spain, seems to have acquired more respect for the Spanish character.

In 1817 Adams's policy of neutrality was sharply challenged by Henry Clay who sought to accord recognition to the "United Provinces of South America"—the title covered only Buenos Aires and the limited area dominated by that port city. Clay, an archexpansionist who had helped provoke the War of 1812, now found in the Latin American cause an outlet for his enthusiasm for liberty and a promising source of political prestige for himself. "At the present time," he told the Senate in 1818 when pressing for funds with which to send a minister to Buenos Aires, "the patriots of the South are fighting for liberty and independence, for precisely what we fought for. . . . I ask . . . the patriot of '76 how the heart rebounded with joy, on the information that France had recognized us! The moral influence of such a recognition on the patriots of the South will be irresistible." But Adams, his eyes fixed upon Florida, won the argument, and no minister was then sent to Buenos Aires.

The Florida question was finally settled to Washington's satisfaction; a treaty signed in 1819 was ratified in 1821, and the United States boundary extended along the coast from the Atlantic to the Gulf of Mexico as far west as Texas. That triumph, and the almost complete victories of the independent forces in Spanish America, cleared the way for recognition of the new states. In May, 1822, Congress authorized Monroe to name ministers "as the President might deem proper." One by one, the new nations were formally recognized: the United Provinces (La Plata), Gran Colombia, and Mexico in 1822; Chile in 1823; Brazil and the United Provinces of Central America in 1824; Peru in 1826; Uruguay in 1834; Venezuela in 1835; Ecuador in 1838; Bolivia in 1848. The clash over slavery in the United States postponed recognition of Haiti until 1862. The Dominican Republic was recognized in 1865.

THE MONROE DOCTRINE, 1823

The steps which led to President Monroe's declaration of 1823, one of the most fateful and durable utterances in the history of American diplomacy, involved events in both America and Europe. On the American side there had been the growing desire that European meddling in the Western Hemisphere be ended. This sentiment had been crystallized in 1811 when the United States Congress, confronted with rumors that the Floridas might be transferred by Spain to England, had adopted a joint resolution declaring that "the United States . . . cannot without serious inquietude see any part of the said territory pass into the hands of any foreign power." This "No Transfer" resolution stands as the first official statement of the principle later enunciated by Monroe.

European statesmen also had ideas as to the future of Spanish and Portuguese America. But, fortunately for the Americas, England parted company with her allies of the Quadruple Alliance when they formed the Holy Alliance to halt all attacks upon monarchical government and dallied with the idea of restoring the lost rights of the Bourbons in America. The British, already heavily industrialized, were more concerned about their markets than European thrones, and sought a balance of power in Europe which would serve their trading interests abroad. Lord Castlereagh, foreign minister from 1812 to 1822, good royalist though he was, had no stomach for his continental allies' adventures on behalf of threatened monarchs—the Austrian intervention in Piedmont and Naples, the French interference in Spain in 1822 on behalf of Ferdinand, or the rumored projects for the recapture of Spain's American realm. Committing suicide on the eve of the Conference of Verona, Castlereagh was succeeded by George Canning, foreign minister from 1822 to 1827, who set about restoring the balance of power in Europe to England's advantage. And for Canning, much of that advantage lay in Latin America, by then well lost to Spain and Portugal.

Cuba, the only important colony whose fidelity to Spain was as yet unshaken, was of lively interest to both England and the United States. John Quincy Adams had long been convinced that it was only a question of time until, "by the law of political gravitation," the island would fall into the lap of the United States. England was equally insistent that it should not so fall. Thanks to the common sense of Canning and Adams, it was tacitly agreed that neither nation should seek its possession, but that both would be content to let it rest in the feeble hands of Spain. Canning's diplomacy went far toward healing old wounds in Anglo-American relations. "The course which you have taken," wrote the British minister in Washington to Canning, "has had the effect of making the English almost popular in the United States. . . . Even Adams has caught something of the soft infection."

In this more serene atmosphere of 1823, George Canning approached Richard Rush, the American minister in England. He confided that Britain could not countenance French efforts to block the emancipation of Spain's American colonies and asked: "What do you think your government would say to going hand in hand with England in such a policy?" There were further conversations between the two men in August and September, and finally Canning handed Rush a statement which he proposed as the basis for a joint declaration by England and the United States:

1. We conceive the recovery of the colonies by Spain to be hopeless.

2. We conceive the question of the recognition of them, as independent states, to be one of time and circumstances.

3. We are, however, by no means disposed to throw any impediment in the way of an arrangement between them and the mother country by amicable negotiations.

4. We aim not at the possession of any portion of them ourselves.

5. We could not see any portion of them transferred to any other power with indifference.

Rush, after failing to get a clear answer as to when and how England would recognize the new nations of Latin America (the United States had already recognized Gran Colombia, Mexico, and Chile), astutely decided that Canning was more interested in the European balance of power than in the freedom of the New World and forwarded the memorandum to Adams in Washington. Meanwhile, Canning persuaded France to take the pledge of abstinence known as the Polignac Memorandum of October 9, 1823, by which she stated for the record that it was "utterly hopeless" for Spain to recapture her lost colonies in America, disclaimed for herself all intention of seizing any part of Spain's lost empire, and "abjured" any attack upon those colonies. This was France's official admission that the case of the Holy Alliance against Spanish America was closed.

The scene then shifts to Washington. Monroe, with Rush's reports before him, considered England's willingness to make common cause with the United States in dealing with the new Latin American states. There were practical considerations: the new states might prove profitable customers for New England as well as for Old England. There were moral issues: the fate of people seeking freedom hung in the balance. There were possible threats in the offing: the Holy Alliance might find guns and powder and troops with which to suppress the pitifully weak nations which were emerging from Mexico to La Plata—a groundless threat as later became clear. Monroe had not yet heard of the Polignac Memorandum, which meant the end of such transatlantic adventures. Monroe appeared ready to accept Canning's overture. He consulted Thomas Jefferson and James Madison, and they, too, agreed that it might be wise to go along with England. At this point there came two disturbing notes from Russia, warning that the Czar's government would not recognize the rebellious Spanish colonies, expressing satisfaction over the routing of liberal revolts in Naples, Piedmont, and Spain, and giving assurance that Russia proposed to restore tranquillity everywhere—which, it was inferred, included Spanish America.

At this point John Quincy Adams spoke words which proved decisive: "It would be more candid, as well as more dignified, to avow our principles explicitly to Russia and France, than to come in as a cock-boat in the wake of the British man-of-war." Adams won over those who favored inclusion of advice to Europe: "The ground I wish to take is that of earnest remonstrance against the interference of European power by force in South America, but to disclaim all interference on our part in Europe; to make an American cause, and adhere inflexibly to that." The upshot was Monroe's message to Congress on December 2, 1823—a purely American statement, delivered as such, without consultation with or concession to England. It carried neither threats nor promises, but simply conveyed the convictions of the leaders of the United States. Though it bears Monroe's name, as is proper, behind Monroe stood one of the greatest of American statesmen, John Quincy Adams.

The Monroe Doctrine—as it would later be called—was a declaration of neutrality as regards Europe and its own affairs; the people of the United States stand as "anxious and interested spectators," but they have "never taken any part, nor does it comport with our policy, so to do." On European designs against America, it was a declaration of Hands Off: "We should consider any attempt on their part to extend their system to any portions of this Hemisphere, as dangerous to our peace and safety." On existing holdings of Europe and America: "We have not interfered, and shall not interfere." On attempts to recapture lost colonies: they will be viewed as "the manifestation of an unfriendly disposition to the United States."

Monroe's message evoked mixed reactions. For Canning, it meant lost prestige; the United States had not only been the first to recognize the new nations, but had also been forthright in warning Europe against trespassing. The British minister seized what advantage he could; he cited the Polignac Memorandum to prove that he had indeed blocked the schemings of the Holy Alliance, and he told Parliament in 1826: "I called the New World into existence to redress the balance of the Old." Prince Metternich wrote in 1824 of "the indecent declarations" of the United States, which have "cast scorn on the institutions of Europe most worthy of respect." And the Russian Czar declared that "the document . . . merits only the most profound contempt." From France, Lafayette pronounced it "the best little bit of paper that God ever permitted any man to give to the world." As for the Latin Americans, who presumably stood to gain by the valiant stand of their northern neighbor, Monroe's words were little heeded, seldom praised, seldom—and not until much later—denounced. Not until the Doctrine had gathered accretions by the beginning of the twentieth century was the full force of Latin American scorn directed against it. The import of that later criticism was summed up by the wise James Bryce, who found the Latin Americans saying, in effect: "Since there are no longer rain-clouds coming up from the east, why should a friend, however well-intentioned, insist on holding an umbrella over us? We are quite able to do that ourselves if necessary."

Today, more than a century after Monroe's message, the Doctrine occupies a position of more dignity than ever before. Hiram Bingham wrote of it as an "obsolete shibboleth," and a Bolivian—under the pen name of Gaston Nerval—wrote "The Autopsy of the Monroe Doctrine," but both stand confuted by the testimony of the years. The Doctrine has been elaborated and distorted; alternately praised and damned. But after the accretions are stripped away, the Doctrine is as valid in today's world of arrogant Communism and braggart fascism as it was in yesterday's world of unyielding kings. It continues to proclaim that America's destiny will be determined by Americans, that the Western Hemisphere is out-of-bounds for those who would transplant their systems of government to these shores. Worth saying in 1823, it has even greater meaning in 1967.

QUIESCENCE, 1823–45

The two decades following Monroe's statement brought few incidents in the relations between the United States and the new Latin American states. The northern republic was preoccupied with organizing and settling its vast new domain, with setting its governmental house in order, with calming the strife between industrialized New England and the agricultural West, and with seeking some solution to the bitter contest between the slave-holding South and the abolitionist North. Meanwhile, the Latin Americans were struggling to create free nations; they adopted constitutions and elected presidents; they were split between strong-arm conservatives and angry liberals; and they fell under control of dictators who ruled by grace of their armies.

Europe did not stay out of Latin America during this period. Spanish forces made a futile landing in Mexico in 1829; the few men who did not die from yellow fever were captured by the redoubtable Santa Anna: France occupied Veracruz in 1838, but was forced out by the Mexicans; she also took a hand in La Plata, occupied the island of Martín García, harassed Rosas in Argentina, interfered in Uruguay.

Great Britain's interventions, military and diplomatic, were more

important. Brazil was coerced into granting trading favors to English merchants and decreeing an end to the slave trade in 1830 (not finally enforced
until 1850). Uruguay, long the bone of contention between Brazil and
Spain, was erected as an independent nation in 1828 by the diplomatic
intervention of England. In Mexico, both England and France busied themselves in warning the Mexicans against the dangerous ambitions of the
United States in Texas. In other instances, England's interference went
beyond diplomatic pressure. In 1833, British forces occupied the Falkland
Islands, more than 200 bleak piles of rock east of the Strait of Magellan,
and claimed by Argentina. In 1845 England joined France in blockading
the Río de la Plata. These incidents evoked no firm protest from the United
States—a fact which inspired Latin American critics to suggest that Monroe's message of 1823 was meaningless, that the United States had no real
intention of protecting the Latin Americans against Europe. The United
States position should have been clear: she had never promised to give
military force to Monroe's Hands Off policy; she could have done nothing
about it anyway—England, not the United States, ruled the waves.

TENSION, 1845–66

The election of President James K. Polk in 1845 marked the beginning
of a new chapter in the relations between the United States and Latin
America. There was a new aggressiveness in the northern republic, largely
excited by England's and France's efforts to block the annexation of
Texas. Polk had popular support when he cited Monroe's words of 1823
and affirmed that: "It should be distinctly announced to the world as our
settled policy that no future European colony or dominion shall without our
consent be planted or established in any part of the North American continent." He ruled out European attempts to maintain a balance of power
in America: "We must ever maintain that the people of this continent
alone have the right to decide their own destiny. Should any portion of
them, constituting an independent state, propose to unite themselves with
our Confederacy, this will be a question for them and us to determine without any foreign interposition."

Texas was, of course, the major issue. In December, 1845, the Lone
Star Republic was formally annexed to the United States; in the war which
ensued, the domain of the United States was extended to the Pacific; and
Mexico lost half of her territory. In 1853 Mexico's Santa Anna sold the
United States an additional 45,535 square miles of territory—the Gadsden
Purchase. England and France had been outplayed, Mexico had been humil-
iated, and the United States had again tasted the delights of expansion.

After these triumphs, the United States was ready to assert her
rights elsewhere. England's steady encroachment on the Caribbean coast
of Central America was a case in point. Not content with her hold on
Belize (British Honduras), England had annexed the Bay Islands, enforced her protectorate over the Mosquito Indians on the coast of Honduras and Nicaragua, and in 1848 seized San Juan del Norte (Greytown)

at the mouth of the Río San Juan. The United States, regarding that river as a likely route for a transisthmian canal, challenged the British seizure. The debate was intensified in 1849 and 1850 as many gold prospectors bound for California used the Nicaraguan route to reach the Pacific. Britain's Lord Palmerston proved conciliatory, the Clayton-Bulwer Treaty of 1850 was signed, and the two powers renounced all intention of exercising exclusive control over any canal that might be dug, or of seeking any domination of Central America's territory.

The continued hold of England upon the Bay Islands provoked further controversy (the debate in Congress in 1853 marked the first time that the term "Monroe Doctrine" was used); but again England yielded, and in 1860 returned the islands to the custody of Honduras. Meanwhile, the Nicaraguan waters had been muddied by the American filibuster William Walker, whose bizarre career we have already described (see pp. 488–9). Despite such distractions, the handling of the Central American crisis had brought fresh laurels to the Monroe Doctrine.

There were further tests of the principles of the Monroe Doctrine in the 1860's. In 1861, Spain, taking advantage of the United States Civil War, reoccupied her ancient colony of Santo Domingo and again raised her flag over the first permanent settlement in the New World. Spanish occupation, as we have already noted, lasted but four years when the garrison fled before the fury of the populace and the ravages of yellow fever. The French invasion of Mexico in 1862–67 was a more serious affront, designed by Napoleon III to impose "an insuperable barrier to the encroachments of the United States." The United States, although powerless to do anything, made its position quite clear in language reminiscent of Monroe. Secretary of State Seward warned in 1861 that the United States could not countenance any step which would "impair the right of the Mexican people to choose and freely to constitute the form of its government." In 1862 a further warning was sent. Washington continued to recognize Benito Juárez as the rightful president, and refused recognition to Emperor Maximilian. In 1865 the French were informed that the American people "are disposed to regard with impatience the continued intervention of France." By 1866 the French troops were on their way home, and in 1867 Maximilian was shot, despite appeals for clemency from the United States. The Monroe Doctrine had again been vindicated.

Meanwhile, Spain attacked Peru in 1864 and seized the Chincha Islands with their piles of guano; Seward countered by warning that the United States could not "regard with indifference an attempt to reduce Peru by conquest and reannex its territory to the Kingdom of Spain." Then the Spanish navy moved south to Chile, shelled the port of Valparaíso in 1866, and sailed away.

INTERLUDE, 1866–95

The three decades after the United States Civil War were a period of relative calm in Latin America's relations with the United States and the outer world. Britain made no fresh sorties, aside from intermittent arguments over the Venezuela–British Guiana boundary question. France, her force spent in the Franco-Prussian War, made no more attacks upon American soil, although continuing her meddling in Haiti. Spain put down the Ten Years' War in Cuba in 1868–78. Russia, never truly a threat in the nineteenth century, was finally banished from America by the United States purchase of Alaska in 1867. A minor threat to American interests was the activity of the French Canal Company headed by Ferdinand de Lesseps which dug fitfully in Panama after 1881 and collapsed ignominiously in 1889. The most ridiculous episode of this period was President Ulysses S. Grant's scheme for annexing the Dominican Republic. The most hopeful venture was the launching of the official Pan American movement in 1889, with a conference of representatives of most of the New World republics called in Washington on the initiative of Secretary of State James G. Blaine. Its accomplishment was slight, but it opened the way for the creation of the Pan American Union, and today's Organization of American States.

Chapter 54

LATIN AMERICA AND THE UNITED STATES, 1895–1946

The year 1895 marks a radical shift in the United States attitude toward Latin America and the world. A new mood had laid its spell upon the Americans of the north. It was a mood born, in part, of an exultant sense of power: the smokestacks were belching clouds of smoke and flame, and thousands of factories, mills, and plants were turning out everything from carpet tacks to locomotives. The United States, men said, had everything: the finest of man power from England, Germany, Scandinavia, and all Europe; soil for raising every crop and for the pasturing of herds; mines with vast reserves; wells tapping lakes of petroleum. Yet with all this treasure, there was a sense of inadequacy. The land had been staked out from Maine to California; cities and towns were growing unwieldy; a great population (about 69 million in 1895) was crowding this fruitful land. Gloomy prophets said that shortly there would be too many people, too great an industrial output, and an inadequate market. The United States—they said—must enter the lists of empire, capture new lands and markets. The British, French, Italians, and Russians had already extended their lines; the Germans and the Japanese were following their example; the Americans could not be left behind. The prophet most reverently heeded was an American naval officer, Alfred T. Mahan, who was preaching the gospel of sea power for the salvation of nations. And just in the background were the emissaries of religion who had been carrying their message to far-off peoples, and who now persuaded many Americans of their divine appointment to enlighten dark places "from Greenland's icy mountains to India's coral strands."

THE RISE AND FALL OF AMERICAN IMPERIALISM, 1895–1933

The new imperial mood of the United States was dramatized by the dispute in 1895 over the Venezuela–British Guiana boundary. That British outpost had expanded enormously at the expense of Venezuela, as British surveyors pushed its boundaries almost to the delta of the Orinoco. (It had more than doubled in area since 1823.) The Venezuelans had made repeated protests, appealing unsuccessfully for American intervention, until President Cleveland decided that it was time to check England in the name of the Monroe Doctrine. In 1895 Secretary of State Richard Olney delivered his ultimatum, one of the most naïve and jejune boasts in the annals of American diplomacy. Olney wrote:

> Today the United States is practically sovereign on this continent, and its fiat is law upon the subjects to which it confines its interposition. Why? . . . It is because, in addition to all other grounds, its infinite resources combined with its isolated position render it master of the situation and practically invulnerable as against any or all other powers.

The message was greeted with delight by the American populace; editors praised it; Congress supported Olney; such spokesmen for American destiny as Theodore Roosevelt and Henry Cabot Lodge rejoiced. The British, confronted with war with the German-backed Boers in South Africa, yielded to Cleveland, submitted the issue to arbitration, and, in 1899, agreed to divide the disputed territory with Venezuela.

Symptomatic of the new imperial mood was the Republican platform of 1896, upon which William McKinley was elected. It called for American control of the Hawaiian Islands, an American canal across Nicaragua, purchase of the Danish West Indies, reaffirmation of the Monroe Doctrine and "the eventual withdrawal of European powers from this hemisphere," and American aid in freeing Cuba from Spain.

The Spanish-American War of 1898 was a popular little war. "This country needs a war," the ebullient Theodore Roosevelt had written Henry Cabot Lodge in 1895, and there were plenty of patriots to echo that sentiment. Cuba offered the perfect excuse: the sufferings of its people at Spanish hands appealed to American gallantry; the investment of American capital on the island and the hope for greater trade reinforced the argument. The war might easily have been avoided had McKinley been a stronger man, or had the yellow press of New York ceased its bellowing, or had Congress not been dominated by men of such bellicose energy. Spain was ready to make almost every concession, but the American people wanted to fight. The "splendid little war," as John Hay described it, had all the components of glory: dashing heroes, with Theodore Roosevelt the best advertised; fine little battles by land and sea; complete and irrefutable victory—the only thing lacking was an enemy worthy of the commotion. The victory over Spain profoundly affected American life: it excited new confidence in national power and destiny; it broke down the isolationism which had prevailed from the days of Washington; it convinced the people of their divine mission in a wicked world. The way was now cleared, said Dr. Lyman Abbott, a clergyman-journalist whose voice was powerful throughout the nation, "for the new Monroe Doctrine, the new imperialism, the imperialism of liberty."

The spell of the expansionists now lay upon the United States. Our "rightful supremacy in the Western Hemisphere" cannot be relinquished, said Henry Cabot Lodge. There must be a bigger and better navy, said Alfred T. Mahan. "God," announced Albert J. Beveridge, "has marked the American people as His chosen Nation to finally lead to the regeneration of the world. . . . We are trustees of the world's progress, guardians of its righteous peace." (The irreverent "Mr. Dooley"—Finley Peter Dunne—said of Beveridge's oratory: "Ye could waltz to it!") And Theodore Roosevelt, gaining the presidency by the death of McKinley, made it clear how he would deal with refractory Latin Americans: he would "show those Dagos that they will have to behave decently."

It was a brave new world for the United States. The American flag flew over Cuba, Puerto Rico, the Philippines. The Hawaiian Islands had been annexed in 1898. In 1900 American forces helped put down the Boxer Rebellion in China, and John Hay demanded "The Open Door" in the Far East. The most ominous threat to this vaulting ambition was Germany. This latest comer among world powers was rumored to be seeking to buy or capture sundry Danish, Dutch, and other islands in the Caribbean, to capture a foothold in Brazil or on the Galápagos Islands of Ecuador. The Old World in general, and Germany in particular, did not relish the new pretensions of the United States. Bismarck, shortly before his death, had stated the German position. The Monroe Doctrine, he said, is "a species of arrogance peculiarly American and inexcusable. . . . And how will you enforce it? And against whom? The powers most interested, now that Spain is out of the way, are England and France. . . . Will you drive them off American waters with your pygmy navy?" Roosevelt's answer was a bigger navy.

The Venezuela incident of 1902–03 provoked a minor clash between the United States and Europe. The local tyrant, Cipriano Castro, was playing fast and loose with his foreign creditors, whereupon German and British warships blockaded the coast. The United States protested, and the warships sailed away. Roosevelt later embellished the story by recounting the threats he made to the Europeans, but historians discount his racy version of the story. The incident prompted a statement from the Argentine foreign minister: "The public debt cannot occasion armed intervention nor even the actual occupation of the territory of American nations." This, the Drago Doctrine, found a place in the body of international law for the Western Hemisphere.

The dramatic events which led to the separation of Panama from Colombia, its recognition by Washington, and the conclusion of a treaty in 1903 permitting the United States to dig a canal brought new glory to Theodore Roosevelt of the Rough Riders. Again the United States had proved herself "practically sovereign" in American affairs, and England had tacitly admitted that perhaps it was well to accept the fact. It was not a pretty story, nor did it enhance the reputation of Roosevelt in the eyes of careful historians—but it served the interests of the United States.

In 1905 the Monroe Doctrine was embellished with what is called the Roosevelt Corollary. The immediate occasion was the misbehavior of the Dominican Republic, with which we have already dealt; but behind this was Theodore Roosevelt's continuing irritation with the Latin Americans generally: "These wretched republics cause me a great deal of trouble," he complained. And there was some excuse for his perturbation over the Dominicans, whose failure to pay their debts and keep the peace was inviting intervention by European creditors. These confusions inspired the irascible T. R. to write that, because the United States wished to "see all neighboring countries stable, orderly, and prosperous," when a nation shows "that it knows how to act with decency . . . it need fear no interference from the United States. . . . [But] brutal wrongdoing, or an impotence which results in a general loosening of the ties of civilized society, may finally require intervention by some civilized nation, and in the Western Hemisphere the United States cannot ignore this duty." Roosevelt, confronted wth the threats of Europeans to collect by force what was due them from the Dominicans, concluded that so long as the Monroe Doctrine prohibited European intervention it must also cover the right and duty of the United States to forestall such intervention by intervention of its own. "Under the Monroe Doctrine," Roosevelt informed the Senate, the United States "cannot see any European power seize and permanently occupy the territory of one of these republics; and yet such seizure of territory, disguised or undisguised, may eventually offer the only way in which the power in question can collect any debts, unless there is interference on the part of the United States." By this new interpretation, the Monroe Doctrine, which was devised as a warning of "Hands Off" to Europe, now became a proposal of the United States to lay "Hands On" whenever occasion prompted.

Thus was the new imperialism of the United States launched. In retrospect, it becomes clear that none of the leaders during the first years of the twentieth cenury, not even Theodore Roosevelt, had any serious intention of annexing any of the territory over which they extended American control. Cuba, entirely subject to the United States rule, was turned over to a legally elected government of her own in 1902—although tied to Washington by the Platt Amendment. Nor did Roosevelt have any intention of adding the Dominican Republic as another state of the Union (as had Grant). "As for annexing the island," wrote Roosevelt, "I have about the same desire . . . as a gorged boa constrictor might have to swallow a porcupine wrong-end-to."

Of the record of the United States during the administrations of William Howard Taft, Woodrow Wilson, Warren Gamaliel Harding, Calvin Coolidge, and Herbert Hoover, we have already considered the occupations of the Dominican Republic, of Haiti, and of Nicaragua. We have noted the blunders, the occasional successes, and the angers engendered—not only among the peoples who were subjected to the rule of American marines but also among all the nations of Latin America. We have described the fumbling with Cuba, the repeated diplomatic and military interventions under the authority of the Platt Amendment. We have watched the course of other interpositions by American armed forces in Panama. We have followed the tortuous course of American relations with Mexico after 1910, with American pressure sometimes applied by threats, sometimes by armed invasion of Mexican soil. These incidents constitute an unpleasant chapter in American history, productive neither of tranquillity nor of democracy in the nations affected, and leaving scars upon the body of inter-American understanding. "American imperialism," writes Dexter Perkins, "has been imperialism with an uneasy conscience."

With the return of the Republican Party to power in 1921, there was clear evidence of an uneasy conscience over the clumsy imperialism of Theodore Roosevelt, Taft, and Wilson. Charles Evans Hughes, Harding's secretary of state, voiced this new mood by stressing the United States' "deep interest in the prosperity, the independence, and the unimpaired sovereignty of the countries of Latin America." Hughes addressed himself to the liquidation of the earlier mistakes. He convened a conference in Washington in 1922–23 which led to new conventions between the quarreling Central American states. He sought to moderate the abuses involved in the occupation of Haiti and Nicaragua, and succeeded in terminating that of the Dominican Republic. He persuaded Mexico to accept peaceful settlement of oil and other disputes by the Bucareli agreements of 1923. His successor in office, Coolidge's secretary of state, Frank Kellogg, proved less flexible and needlessly aroused new fears in Mexico; in 1927 Coolidge himself intervened in the Mexican imbroglio and named Dwight W. Morrow as ambassador to Mexico. That appointment, so productive of good sense and good will in Mexican-American relations, may be said to mark the beginning of the new era in inter-American affairs. Meanwhile, Secretary Kellogg won credit by assigning his under secretary, J. Reuben Clark, Jr., to the restudy of the Monroe Doctrine. His "Memorandum on the Monroe Doctrine," published in December, 1928, is one of the epochal documents in American diplomatic history. Stripping away the excrescences (notably the Roosevelt Corollary) which had been attached to it, Clark restated the Doctrine in its original form—although without disavowing the right of intervention.

Herbert Hoover also deserves credit for improving the United States relations with her southern neighbors. His preinauguration trip around South America made friends for him and his country and led to the final arbitration of the Tacna-Arica dispute between Chile and Peru. He took steps to terminate the occupation of Haiti and Nicaragua, although the final withdrawal of American marines did not take place until after he had quit office.

FRANKLIN D. ROOSEVELT AND THE GOOD NEIGHBOR POLICY

In his inaugural address of 1933, the second Roosevelt spoke the felicitous words: "I would dedicate this nation to the policy of the good neighbor —the neighbor who resolutely respects himself, and because he does

so, respects the rights of others—the neighbor who respects his obligations and respects the sanctity of agreements in and with a world of
neighbors." The neighbors waited to see what these pleasant words might
mean. But the stage had been set for a more generous United States attitude toward Latin America—set largely by Roosevelt's predecessors; set
also by the United States need for allies against the looming danger from
Europe; and dictated by a genuine desire to create a zone of safety and
sanity in the New World. In this new climate inter-American relations improved immensely, and the name of the United States president became
an honored one throughout the Americas.

The Cuba offered the first test of the Good Neighbor policy. For eight
years Gerardo Machado had been pillaging and murdering, while the
United States government maintained an uneasy neutrality. Then Roosevelt named Sumner Welles as ambassador to the unhappy island, charging
him with the task of helping the Cubans rid themselves of their tyrant.
Welles did his unpleasant job with a minimum of interference and with
much good sense, and Machado found it expedient to flee in August, 1933.
Then the Cuban army, at that time headed by Batista, installed Grau San
Martín, whom Welles and Washington refused to recognize. This experience persuaded Welles of the absurdity of the Platt Amendment, and he
more than any other was responsible for the abrogation of that crippling
article in 1934. Welles got from Cubans little of the thanks which he
deserved.

The Seventh Pan American Conference in Montevideo in December, 1933, gave Secretary of State Cordell Hull a chance to interpret the
new policy of good neighborliness. He comported himself with skill and
imagination. Ignoring protocol, he was the first to make calls upon the delegations of the other countries. Disregarding the obstinate suspicions of the
Argentines toward the United States, he effectively courted the Argentine
foreign minister, Carlos Saavedra Lamas, supported his unimportant peace
compact, and won (for the time at least) that vain statesman's cooperation with the United States. He proposed an elaborate program for reciprocal
trade treaties, with provision for radical reduction in customs, and won
limited adherence to his proposals. After initial hesitation, and with some
hedging, he committed the United States to the Convention on the Rights
and Duties of States, in which were imbedded the words: "No state has
the right to intervene in the internal or external affairs of another."

Meanwhile, Roosevelt had fulfilled the promise of Hoover by recalling the last marines from Haiti, a step which went far toward persuading
the Latin Americans of the validity of the promises of the good neighbor.
This was reinforced in 1936 when Washington revised its treaty arrangements with Panama, abandoning the right to intervene in that nation's internal affairs.

The major test of the new policy came in 1938 when President Cárdenas
of Mexico expropriated the properties of American and British-Dutch
oil companies. There was immediate and understandable clamor from
stockholders in the unlucky companies. Secretary Hull inclined toward some

form of intervention, but Sumner Welles—then under secretary of state —stood firmly for keeping hands off. Welles was closer to Roosevelt than was Hull, and the President supported Welles. There was no intervention, diplomatic or otherwise. The Mexican government took over the properties, promised to pay for them in due course, and finally did so—although inadequately, according to the men who controlled the companies.

UNITED STATES–LATIN AMERICAN RELATIONS DURING WORLD WAR II

The outbreak of World War II in 1939 injected new problems into inter-American relations. The people of the United States, although predominantly on the side of the Allies, generally favored neutrality. The people of Latin America were badly divided in their convictions: the cultured classes, warmly sympathetic to France, were mostly pro-Allies; the large inarticulate masses were indifferent; a substantial minority took the Communist line, favoring the Axis as long as the Moscow-Berlin covenant prevailed and then shouting for the Allies; many of German and of Italian birth or parentage (in Brazil, Argentina, Chile, and elsewhere) were on the Axis side.

Three weeks after the Germans had invaded Poland, representatives of all the twenty-one American republics met in Panama. Agreement was quickly reached that the American republics would make a common stand for neutrality; it was provided that a zone of neutrality be declared around the United States and Latin America, and that all belligerents be warned against operating within it. An Inter-American Economic Committee was created to make a continuing study of the economic stresses caused by the war and to suggest remedies for the alleviation of these stresses. When Germany overran the Netherlands and France in June, 1940, a second conference was called in Havana to consider what steps the American nations should take in the event that Dutch and French possessions in America should be seized by the Germans. The United States proposed joint American occupation of such colonies when and if a clear threat appeared—a measure opposed by Argentina on the ground that the United States would use each intervention to gain new colonies for herself, but the American suggestion was finally accepted.

All-American cooperation proved increasingly effective during 1940 and 1941. German and Italian air lines, manned by reserve officers under control of the Axis powers, were either ousted or taken over by United States interests in Colombia, Ecuador, Peru, and Brazil. The United States "black list" of firms and individuals accused of trading with the enemy was enforced, usually with the generous help of the various southern republics. Prices of basic commodities sold to the United States were stabilized, often to the disadvantage of the producing country (a notable case was Brazil's coffee).

The Japanese attack on Pearl Harbor in December, 1941, furnished the supreme test of the genuineness of all-American solidarity. The principle that "an attack upon one American nation was an attack upon all" now received heartening confirmation. Nine nations—the Central American republics, Panama, Cuba, Haiti, and the Dominican Republic—immediately declared war upon the Axis. Mexico, Colombia, Venezuela, and Ecuador broke off relations with the enemy. At the instance of the United States and Chile, a meeting of foreign ministers was convened in Rio de Janeiro in January, 1942. Washington brought no pressure for declaration of war by the Latin American powers, but hoped for a unanimous severing of relations—useful for the blockading of the propaganda output of the German, Italian, and Japanese missions. This last proposal, urged by Sumner Welles on behalf of the American delegation, was vigorously opposed by only two countries, Chile and Argentina. After a long argument, a compromise resolution was finally adopted by which it was "recommended" that all the American republics break off diplomatic relations with the Axis powers. This somewhat weakened measure was accepted by the United States on the ground that only so could unanimity be assured—and as a concession to Brazil, many of whose army officers were still wavering between the Allied and Axis cause.[1] All the republics with the exception of Chile and Argentina broke relations immediately. Then followed a year in which steady pressure from the outside finally persuaded Chile to sever relations in January, 1943. Argentina under Castillo proved less tractable, and that country continued to give comfort to the enemy. Then came the coup of June, 1943, the installation of the Ramírez regime, and the rise of Perón. Subjected to increasing pressure from Washington, refusal to furnish Lend-Lease arms, and the threat to freeze Argentine assets in the United States, the new regime finally bowed to outside coercion and to internal persuasion and broke off diplomatic relations with the Axis in January, 1944.

Wartime cooperation of the American republics proved substantial and vital. Telegraphic communications with the Axis were cut off. Secret radio stations, used to relay word on sailings to U-boats at sea, were ferreted out. Air and naval bases were freely granted to the United States; those on the Brazilian coast were used by American planes in the attacks on North Africa. Brazil sent an expeditionary force to Italy, where it acquitted itself with honor. Mexico sent pilots who served in the Philippines, and later in Formosa. This direct participation in the fighting did more to increase the sense of being linked in a common cause than all the resolutions that had been passed by conferences. Countries other than Brazil and Mexico were eager to send men to the battle front, but such proposals were vetoed by the U.S. Army; such volunteers, it was said, would cost more to train and equip than they would be worth. From the technical point of view, the army may have been right. From the point of view of creating a great and glowing sense of all-American teamwork, the refusal to accept these volunteers was a grievous mistake.

[1] For light on this delicate bit of diplomatic maneuvering, see Laurence Duggan: *The Americas* (New York: Henry Holt and Company; 1949), pp. 87–8.

Economic collaboration was generous and intelligent. The United States, despite its shortage of consumer goods, strained itself to meet the demands from Latin America; between 1939 and 1944 the sales of civilian goods to Latin America more than doubled. The Latin Americans, in turn, speeded up the production and shipment of vital raw materials. The strategic importance of these materials can scarcely be overstated. The United States got practically all its balsa wood, kapok, quinine, rotenone, and quartz crystals from Latin America; most of its tanning materials, copper, sugar, manila fiber, vanadium, flax, mercury, tin, and henequen; and much of its tungsten, mica, and rubber.

United States diplomacy vis-à-vis Latin America during the war years suffered from the lack of consistent and continuing leadership. Secretary of State Cordell Hull had little liking for, and gave only grudging support to, Sumner Welles, who, first as assistant secretary and later as under secretary, directed the Latin American policy of the nation from January, 1934, to August, 1943. Welles and Roosevelt saw eye to eye, and most of the successes in the United States' dealings with Latin America are to be credited to Welles. After Welles was dropped in August, 1943 (on the insistence of Hull), the direction of Latin American diplomacy shifted four times within two years, resulting in costly confusion.

The case of the United States' dealings with Argentina offers prime instance of the folly of vacillation. Welles, confirmed exponent of nonintervention, watched the pro-Axis course of that republic from 1941 to 1943 with anxiety but blocked Hull from applying pressure upon the Castillo government—on the theory that external coercion only serves to unite people behind their government. In August, 1943, Welles was forced from office, and Hull at last had the chance to apply the type of coercion in which he believed: sharply written notes, one of which helped to unseat the only member of Ramírez's cabinet who inclined toward the Allied cause; the freezing of Argentine gold reserves in the United States; restrictions upon shipping to Argentine ports. Late 1944 brought another change. Hull was forced by ill health to retire; Edward Stettinius took his place, and Nelson Rockefeller became assistant secretary in charge of Latin American affairs. Then followed the Conference of Chapultepec, held in Mexico City in February and March, 1945, which was attended by spokesmen of all the American republics with the exception of Argentina; here a new United States policy appeared, which called for conciliation toward the Argentine regime; this was confirmed at the United Nations sessions in San Francisco, where the American republics forced the inclusion of Argentina in that body.

Meanwhile, the death of Roosevelt had brought a reshuffling in the Department of State and the sending of Spruille Braden as ambassador to Buenos Aires. Rockefeller's conciliatory program yielded to one of open hostility to the Perón government, as Braden delivered well-deserved but quite ineffective verbal attacks on that dictatorship. The net result of this policy of threat and pressure (reminiscent of the Hull policy) was to arouse general anger against the United States and to help elect Perón to the presidency in February, 1946. An unfortunate incident was the American publication of the Blue Book, with its valid charges of pro-Nazi activities in Argentina, on the eve of the 1946 election. Following Perón's election, Washington turned another somersault and appointed as ambassador George S. Messersmith, who was famed for his tact, and bade him make friends with Perón and discover ways in which the two countries could live peaceably together. And that policy of conciliation and official amiability remained in force until Perón fell in 1955. But the contortions of American diplomacy in relation to Argentina had inspired little respect either in or out of Buenos Aires. Perón had learned that bluster and abuse would be swallowed by the United States; Washington even lent his government $125 million without demanding any effective pledge of decent behavior. Meanwhile, American ambassadors continued to praise that strong man in a tasteless fashion which angered Argentines of strong democratic convictions.

LATIN AMERICA AND THE
UNITED STATES, 1946–

The weighing of today's relations between the United States and the Latin American republics calls for a candid summary of the United States' dealings with its southern neighbors since the early years of the nineteenth century. The period from 1810 to the present time falls roughly into six eras. The first, 1810–95, was marked chiefly by *indifference* on the part of the United States; it was a period in which the northern republic was so busy with her own affairs as to preclude any sustained interest in what was going on south of the border. To be sure, it was during these years that the Monroe Doctrine took shape and was invoked against various disturbers of the peace of the Western Hemisphere, but this doctrine was intended primarily to keep European countries out of the Americas. And it is also true that the United States took a lively interest in Mexico—and in acquiring Mexican territory. Furthermore, there were numerous and continued forays by enterprising North Americans into the southern republics. By the late 1820's, New York and New England merchants were pushing south to compete with the British for the markets in the nations newly separated from Spain and Portugal. And in the wake of the businessmen came the organizers and engineers, who were responsible for numerous useful projects, especially in the extension of transportation.[1] But in spite of the bold pronouncement of the Monroe Doctrine, the meddling of the United States in the Mexican War, and

---

[1] Merwin L. Bohan suggests that while the United States "contributed but an insignificant fraction of the investment funds made available by Great Britain for the financing of development during the first three-fourths of the nineteenth century, few countries supplied more in the way of enterprise and know-how than our own. We were the pioneers in establishing river transport on the Orinoco, the Guayas, the Magdalena, and many of the other great rivers of the area; we shared honors with Britain in providing international cable service throughout the hemisphere; and U.S. engineers and contractors built more miles of jungle and mountain railroads than those of any other nationality." ("United States Public and Private Investments in Latin America," *Proceedings of The 1962 Institute on Private Investments Abroad* (1962), p. 27). Mr. Bohan cites the records of North Americans who rendered conspicuous services. There was William Wheelwright, who installed gas lighting in Callao, Copiapó, and Valparaíso; organized the Pacific Steam Navigation Company; installed the first telegraph lines in Chile; built the first substantial railroads in Chile and Argentina. There was Henry Meiggs, a fugitive from California police, who was a pioneer in railroad building in Chile and Peru. There was W. R. Grace, who was responsible for a

the sporadic enterprises of American promoters, the fact remains that the man on the street in Boston and Kansas City during the nineteenth century viewed his southern neighbors with indifference.

The second period, 1895–1921, was that of the *policeman;* these were the years when the United States imposed its will upon various weak neighbors, sometimes to the good of those neighbors, but always to their annoyance. The third period, 1921–33, was the period of the *liquidation of American imperialism,* during which the United States gradually learned that marine rule solves no problems and only embitters the feelings of all concerned. The fourth, 1933–46, was the era of the *good neighbor.* In the face of the growing threat from Hitler's Germany, the United States—animated by the practical desire to further inter-American solidarity—first sought to dispel Latin American suspicions of their northern neighbor, then poured money and technicians and goods into Latin America in a remarkably successful effort to create a sense of common purpose.

The fifth period, 1946–61, might be called the era of the *good neighbor preoccupied,* when the threatening issues of Europe and Asia so absorbed the attention of Washington, that "neighborliness" was little more than a slogan. And the sixth, 1961– , carries the promise—and the frustration—of the *Alliance for Progress.*

The Alliance for Progress, launched in 1961, must be understood against the background of all that went before—the history of the inter-American system, which had its beginnings in the early nineteenth century; and most especially the developments in the dozen years after 1948.

THE CREATION OF THE INTER-AMERICAN SYSTEM

The movement popularly called "Pan Americanism"—a term disliked by many Latin Americans who regard it as coined in the United States— has its roots in the dream of Simón Bolívar for a fraternity of American states bound together by common hopes and ideals. The Congress of Panama, convened by him in 1826, was attended by representatives of only five of the new states, and the delegates from the United States failed to arrive. It was important chiefly as a gesture of recognition of the common interests of the Americas, and as the harbinger of the conferences which were finally inaugurated in 1889. During the course of the nineteenth century, seven other conferences, attended by representatives of some of the Latin American states, were held to discuss matters of common concern: commerce, the codification of international law, the control of yellow fever and cholera.

---

trading, manufacturing, and transportation empire on the west coast of South America. There was Minor C. Keith, who built railroads and laid the foundation of the banana culture in Central America. There was Percival Farquhar, who made daring plans for a transportation empire embracing Brazil, Argentina, Bolivia, Paraguay, and Uruguay—plans which almost succeeded. North American activity in Latin America was speeded up in the twentieth century and won notable success with Mexican petroleum and Chilean copper.

The official International Conferences of American States began with the Washington conference of 1889–90, attended by eighteen out of the nineteen American states then existing—the Dominican Republic was the only absentee. The second conference was held in Mexico in 1901–02; the third, in Rio de Janeiro in 1906; the fourth, in Buenos Aires in 1910; the fifth, in Santiago in 1923; the sixth, in Havana in 1928; the seventh, in Montevideo in 1933; the eighth, in Lima in 1938; the ninth, in Bogotá in 1948; and the tenth, in Caracas in 1954. In addition, various special conferences have been held, including meetings of the foreign ministers of the several republics. By 1910 the Pan American Union was created, with its seat in Washington. The successive conferences discussed and took action on a great variety of subjects, economic, cultural, juridical. But there was increasing lack of enthusiasm on the part of member nations as the resolutions passed were not ratified by enough nations to give them force— Argentina being the chief delinquent on this score.

The Seventh Conference at Montevideo in 1933 marked a turning point in the fortunes of organized Pan Americanism. There the United States at last accepted the principle of nonintervention, and that step did more to create faith in the cooperative process than anything that had gone before. Three years later, at the special Inter-American Conference for the Maintenance of Peace in Buenos Aires, the delegates accepted the principle that any act imperiling the peace of any one state is a matter of concern to all. In 1938, at Lima, they went further by affirming the intention of the American states to maintain their solidarity against all foreign intervention, with provision for consultation wherever a threat appeared. In 1945, at Mexico City, the Act of Chapultepec provided for joint defense of all the states in case of aggression against any one of them—a measure inspired by Uruguay's fear of Perón's Argentina. This principle was reaffirmed and enlarged at the special conference in Rio de Janeiro in 1947. By these successive enactments, all accepted by the United States, there was created a new sense of assurance that all the American states would stand together in guaranteeing the sovereignty of each state and the protection of that sovereignty against threats either from within or from without the Western Hemisphere.

THE OAS AND THE POSTWAR WORLD

Dissatisfaction had been growing with the machinery for inter-American cooperation in the Pan American Union, which had never had power enough, or will enough, to take decisive action. During its earlier years, the Union had been headed by a United States secretary-general and had been largely staffed by United States citizens; the secretary of state of the United States had automatically served as chairman of the governing board, which was made up of the various chiefs of missions from the several states in Washington. Some Latin American leaders derisively called the Union the "American Ministry of Colonies." The Ninth Conference of American States—a stormy session held in Bogotá in April, 1948—was dominated by the conviction that the Latin Americans should have a larger voice in making decisions. The Union was renamed the Organization of American States, the OAS, with a drastic realignment of personnel to give it a more representative character. At the Bogotá meeting and in succeeding conferences, provision was made for election of officials other than citizens of the United States, and for a governing board whose members would be appointed by the various states solely as ambassadors to the OAS.[2] This more truly representative arrangement has immeasurably strengthened the OAS. The staff is drawn from the constituent member nations, and the chairmanship of the governing board is passed around among representatives of the various states. The choice of Alberto Lleras Camargo of Colombia as the first secretary-general (1948–54) gave the reorganized body able leadership. His successor, José A. Mora of Uruguay, is respected, but his leadership has been less dynamic. Today the OAS enjoys a prestige throughout the Americas such as the Pan American Union never commanded.

The meeting in Bogotá in 1948, however, was marred by an incident which was ominous in its implications. On April 9, the eleventh day of the proceedings, Eliécer Gaitán, leader of the left wing of the Liberal Party of Colombia, was assassinated, an act which incited mobs to spread terror in the streets of the capital city. The scene in and around the Capitol building—where the sessions were being held—was described by a member of the United States delegation:

> Within minutes the mobs were surging through the plaza. The unarmed police were powerless to cope with the situation and were brushed aside by the rioters as they streamed into the building. Red flags were in profusion, and I personally saw hammer-and-sickle flags. Using stones, bricks, machetes, and boards, the mob commenced a methodical tour of destruction which was to render the first floor of the Capitol building a shambles within a matter of minutes.

The violence fanned out over Bogotá and some 1,500 persons were killed. The Conference was forced to suspend its sessions, but finally reconvened in a school building on the outskirts of the city. Some observers decided that international Communism had finally struck the Americas and that it was time to take swift countermeasures—a conclusion which seems to have been accepted by the U.S. Department of State. Many people in and out of government circles, however, skeptically rejected the Communist explanation, laying the blame for the event on more intricate forces. In any case, something had gone wrong.

Something had indeed gone wrong with "good neighborliness." After World War II the United States concern for Latin America declined, and

---

2 The importance of this shift in control can hardly be overstated. Under the older formula, the decisions of the Pan American Union were made by the ambassadors of the various countries to the United States government, and their chief responsibility was to get along amicably with Washington. Under the new formula, the men named specifically as ambassadors to the OAS were released from United States government pressures.

for at least a dozen years American policy in that area was halting and inept. The reasons were various. By 1945 the three principal architects of the Good Neighbor Policy—Franklin D. Roosevelt, Cordell Hull, and Sumner Welles—had disappeared from the national scene; and the men who took their places had neither their knowledge of nor their keen interest in the affairs of Latin America. Furthermore, the new emphasis was upon world rather than regional cooperation. Washington's attention was focused on the threats from the Communist powers toward Europe, the Middle East, and Asia. Financial aid to the Latin American nations fell off. And American policy in the area—notably that of John Foster Dulles—laid more emphasis upon a frontal attack on Communism than upon measures to eliminate the social ills which nurture Communism.

The Tenth Conference of American States, held in Caracas in March, 1954, furnished the Latin Americans an opportunity to air all of their grievances against the United States. Various Latin American spokesmen denounced the economic policies of Washington, pled for the stabilization of prices of raw materials, for greater aid in financing industrial and agricultural development, and more technical cooperation. These complaints reflected the widespread conviction that the United States, while pouring billions into economic cooperation and military aid to Europe and Asia, had dealt niggardly with Latin America after the close of World War II. In 1954, for example, United States aid to Latin America amounted to less than $100 million out of a total of almost $3.4 billion in foreign assistance, including over $600 million to Europe. But the chief objective of the American delegation, headed by Secretary of State John Foster Dulles, was to secure a clear statement of solidarity from the Latin American states against the intervention of international Communism—an aim inspired by recent events in Guatemala: well-marked Communists had gained positions of influence in that country, and their plottings had been fortified by a shipment of arms from behind the Iron Curtain. The heart of the resolution proposed by the United States was the declaration:

> That the domination or control of the political institutions of any American State by the international Communist movement, extending to this hemisphere the political system of an extracontinental power, would constitute a threat to the sovereignty and political independence of the American States, endangering the peace of America, and would call for a meeting of consultation to consider the adoption of appropriate action in accordance with existing treaties.

This proposal aroused angry opposition. It was widely interpreted as a demand on the part of the United States for the right to intervene in the internal affairs of other nations—especially Guatemala. It was also denounced as unworkable. Who would decide, the critics asked, just when and where "the international Communist movement" had staked out its claim? Would the agreement be invoked only in case of armed intervention by Russian troops? Or would "domination and control" be implied in trade treaties between American nations and the Soviet Union? Or in Communist penetration of the labor unions of any country? Would it be implied in the construction of an airstrip—by Cubans or Hondurans or Guatemalans—which *seemed* to be designed for use by a potential enemy of the United States? In spite of ambiguities, the Declaration of Caracas was finally adopted, with only one negative vote—Guatemala's—but with Argentina and Mexico abstaining. The Conference closed on a note of exasperation, much of which was directed against the United States Secretary of State.

Inter-American amity was further injured by the American role in Guatemala in 1954. Confronted by a weak and corrupt government in that republic, which was honeycombed with active disciples of Moscow, Washington (operating through the Central Intelligence Agency) had encouraged and furnished arms to rebels based in Honduras and Nicaragua; and when Carlos Castillo Armas occupied Guatemala City in July, 1954, the United States recognized him without delay and supported him with loans and grants. Washington blundered in this instance by encouraging Honduras and Nicaragua to violate the OAS charter, which prohibits interference by any nation in the affairs of another, and also by failing to consult the members of the OAS. It was a dismal performance on the part of the United States, arousing widespread criticism throughout Latin America and imposing upon Guatemala a president who was neither liked nor respected.

The failure of the Caracas conference to grapple with fundamental economic issues and its resort to a political solution, then the subsequent bungling by the United States in the Guatemalan affair, prompted the calling of a special economic conference in Rio de Janeiro in late 1954. But unfortunately this conference was dominated by men who had little appreciation of the deep-seated malaise of Latin America, and, according to Merwin Bohan, "the new policy was widely interpreted in Latin America as an effort on our part to make Latin America safe for American big business."

The Guatemalan episode of July, 1954, taught the United States a salutary lesson, and henceforth there was an increasing determination to work through the OAS. We have already told how the invasion of Costa Rica from Nicaraguan soil was ended quickly in January, 1955, when an OAS commission requested that the United States send fighting planes to reenforce Costa Rica (see p. 500). During the 1950's there were intermittent clashes in the Caribbean area, and the OAS convened a special conference in 1959 to consider that danger zone. In 1960, at the request of Venezuela, the peace committee of the OAS undertook a study of the denial of human rights in the Dominican Republic; the result was a vigorous indictment, issued in June, 1960, against the regime of Trujillo for "its denial of free assembly and free speech, arbitrary arrests, cruel and inhuman treatment of political prisoners, and the use of intimidation and terror as political weapons." This was inter-American cooperation at its best and its wisest.

The next important meeting of the OAS was held in San José, Costa

Rica, in August, 1960. Venezuela presented the evidence that Dominican agents had been responsible for an attempt to assassinate President Rómulo Betancourt in June; this overt act, coupled with the evidence already assembled by the peace committee of the OAS, led to an almost unanimous resolution calling for the severance of diplomatic relations with Trujillo's government. The charges and countercharges between Cuba and the United States were aired. The United States sought agreement upon a resolution which would condemn the introduction of "international Communism" into Cuba, but this was generally rejected by the Latin Americans. Washington finally accepted a vote deploring Communist activities in the Americas, but without naming Cuba.

The most disastrous lapse in reliance on the OAS for settling international disputes came with the Cuban invasion fiasco of April, 1961, when the unilateral action of the United States shook the confidence of the world in the wisdom of Washington (see pp. 414–6). This confidence was largely restored in the missile crisis of November, 1962, when President Kennedy called a meeting of the OAS and secured its blessing before issuing his ultimatum to Khrushchev (see pp. 417–8). Washington's handling of the Dominican revolution of April, 1965, when the OAS was called into conference with the United States *after* irrevocable commitment of American troops, was an ominous instance of unilateral action, exciting widespread fear and anger throughout Latin America (see pp. 455–60).

Further evidence of the difficulties confronting the OAS is offered by the fact that no full-scale session of the Conference of American States has been held since 1954; repeated efforts to stage such a conference in Quito were canceled because of political instability in Ecuador (the Ecuadorians built a new hotel to house the delegates who did not arrive). There was a conference of American presidents in Panama in 1956, called at the instance of President Eisenhower, but it proved futile. Then in 1966 the attempt to arrange such a meeting in Buenos Aires was abandoned because of the political overturn in Argentina. However, in April, 1967, a promising meeting of all the American presidents was finally held in Punta del Este, Uruguay (see pp. 941–3).

Meanwhile, by the late 1950's it had become clear that all was not well in relations between the United States and Latin America. The American people had optimistically assumed that the Good Neighbor Policy had created a firm sense of hemispheric solidarity and good will which nothing could disturb. But the grievances of the Latin Americans had been piling up—and had been largely ignored by Washington, or so said the Latin American critics. Most of the ill will was rooted in the fact that American grants and loans to Latin America had shrunk after World War II. As Washington devoted major attention to Europe and Asia, pouring billions of dollars into Japan, Korea, Formosa, Southeast Asia, India, and Western Europe in efforts to erect defenses against Communist Russia and China, Latin Americans regarded themselves as slighted in the allotment of funds. One analyst summarizes: "All the economic aid [direct grants, net, ex-

cluding military aid] furnished by the United States from public funds
($625 million) to all the Latin American countries, with their 175 million
people, from the end of World War II to the end of the calendar year 1958
was less than that furnished to Yugoslavia with only 20 million people
($795 million)."[3]

Another economic irritation came in 1958 when the United States
imposed a quota upon purchases of lead and zinc;[4] this policy was costly
to Mexico, Peru, and Bolivia, but its psychological impact was perhaps
even more serious—the United States, they said, had let them down. Another indictment of the United States was the dumping upon the world
market of surplus cotton, with the resulting drop in the price at which
Mexico and other cotton producers could sell. There was also complaint
that the United States had done nothing to stabilize the prices of chief
commodities; for example, the fourteen countries which produce coffee
joined in asking that something be done to give them security against violent
fluctuations in price. These and many other charges explained the restive-
ness of the Latin Americans.

The complacency of American public opinion was shaken, and the
image of generous Pan Americanism shattered by the ill-starred good will
mission of Vice-President Richard M. Nixon to South America in 1958.
Nixon was received with ill-concealed virulence in several countries, notably
in Peru and Venezuela, where he was stoned and cursed by noisy mobs.
Many dismissed the incident as Communist-inspired, but less emotional
bystanders found fresh and disturbing evidence of the Latin Americans'
deep-seated distrust of the United States.

By 1958 the United States was unpleasantly aware that she must mend
her fences in the Americas as well as in Europe and Asia. It was clear
that swift and bold action must be taken to halt the economic and political
deterioration in Latin America, and specifically to end the rising flood
of dislike for the United States. The spokesman for this conclusion was
the president of Brazil, Juscelino Kubitschek. After an exchange of correspondence with President Eisenhower, the Brazilian in late 1958 proposed
a new hemispheric plan for united action, *Operación Pan América*. This
Operación, forerunner of the Alliance for Progress, called for:

> Reaffirmation of the principles of hemispheric solidarity.
> Recognition of underdevelopment as a problem of common interest.
> Adaption of inter-American organs and agencies to wage the struggle
> against underdevelopment.
> Technical assistance for increased productivity.
> Measures to stabilize markets for basic commodities.
> Expansion of the resources of international financial institutions,
> and adaption to new needs.
> Reaffirmation of private initiative.
> Revision of local national economic policies to promote economic
> development.

[3] Donald M. Dozer: *Are We Good Neighbors?* (Gainesville: University of Florida
Press; 1959), p. 371.
[4] The quotas on lead and zinc were removed in 1965.

This proposal elicited quick approval from Washington, even though it was clear that it would be expensive for the United States. (It must be noted, parenthetically, that the prime mover of the project—President Kubitschek of Brazil—spoke for a country whose treasury had been drained almost to its last cruzeiro for the building of his dream city, Brasília.) The foreign ministers of all the American republics were invited to Washington in September, 1958, for the consideration and furthering of the Brazilian plan. Forthwith a "Committee of 21" was appointed by the OAS to take next steps. In early 1959, it was agreed to establish the Inter-American Development Bank (IDB), long sought by Latin American leaders. The United States had insisted that the World Bank and the Export-Import Bank were adequate agencies for providing Latin America with foreign capital. But the Latin Americans wanted a financial agency in the management of which they would have a substantial voice. In August, 1960, Washington entrusted to the IDB a $500-million appropriation voted by the American Congress for the newly established Inter-American Social Development Fund. In September, the "Committee of 21" met in Bogotá to consider ways and means for the economic development of the hemisphere. "The Act of Bogotá," there adopted, was the next step toward the Alliance for Progress.

Thus the machinery was set in motion for a bold new plan for hemispheric cooperation. But the knot linking the Americans in this common cause was made fast by the accession to power of Fidel Castro and his *barbudos,* who took over Cuba on January 1, 1959. In our earlier telling of the story of Castro and of his influence upon inter-American affairs, we made clear that the initial response to Fidel's bloodless victory over Batista was almost universally friendly: free men everywhere, including the United States, were glad that a tyrant had fallen before the attack of brave young men who loved their country. And then we saw this reservoir of good will dry up as Fidel Castro played the tyrant with his own people, making a travesty of justice in dealing with his enemies, betraying the loyalty of many of his own followers, and finally delivering his island home into the hands of men who would destroy the democracy which was a part of the American heritage. In the broad canvas of the Americas, *fidelismo* scarred and fractured the ideal of all-American unity. Troublemakers— honest zealots and opportunists—found it expedient to yoke their activities with Castro. The Alliance for Progress would be an eloquent answer to all who would disturb the peace.

THE ALLIANCE FOR PROGRESS: THE BLUEPRINT

President John F. Kennedy, addressing the Latin American diplomatic corps on March 31, 1961, announced the new move in inter-American relations:

> If we are going to meet a problem so staggering in its dimensions, our approach must itself be equally bold, an approach consistent with the

majestic concept of Operation Pan America. Therefore I have called on all the people of the Hemisphere to join in a new Alliance for Progress—*Alianza para el Progreso*—a vast cooperative effort, unparalleled in magnitude and nobility of purpose, to satisfy the basic needs of the American people for homes, work and land, health and schools—*techo, trabajo y tierra, salud y escuela.* . . . Let us once again transform the American continent into a vast crucible of revolutionary ideas and efforts —a tribute to the power of the creative energies of free men and women— an example to all the world that liberty and progress walk hand and hand.

The response to this evangelical appeal was varied. The Latin Americans generally rejoiced. The old-guard diplomats—both south and north— dismissed the words as fine oratory, little more. Five months later, in August, 1961, representatives of all the American nations were convened in the Uruguayan seaside resort of Punta del Este. President Kennedy's message to this group set the tone of the conference.

We live in a hemisphere whose own revolution has given birth to the most powerful forces of the modern age—the search for the freedom and self-fulfillment of man. We meet to carry on that revolution to shape the future. . . . There must be full recognition of the right of all the people to share fully in our progress. For there is no place in democratic life for institutions which benefit the few while denying the needs of the many, even though the elimination of such institutions may require far-reaching and difficult changes such as land reform and tax reform and a vastly increased emphasis on education and health and housing. Without these changes our common effort cannot succeed.

The provisions of the Charter of Punta del Este were bold and far-reaching. The drafters were not afraid of the word "revolution," although most of them represented nations which were far from revolutionary. Some American observers found the word disquieting—but not Secretary of the Treasury Douglas Dillon, erstwhile partner in Dillon, Read, and Company, most respectable bankers, now the chief American spokesman at the Conference. Said Dillon, who had been an eloquent defender of an enlarged and more generous Pan Americanism for a dozen years: "Throughout the hemisphere millions still live with hunger, poverty, and despair. . . . We cannot rest content until [their] just demands are met." Whereupon Ernesto "Che" Guevara—representing Cuba in her final appearance at any hemispheric meeting—reminded the delegates that they had Cuba to thank for this sudden generosity of the United States, and prophesied the failure of the whole enterprise.

A "Declaration to the Peoples of America" introducing the Charter proposed these goals:

To . . . strengthen democratic institutions through application of the principle of self-determination by the people.

To accelerate economic and social development. . . .

To carry out urban and rural housing programs to provide decent homes for all our people.

To encourage programs of comprehensive agrarian reform. . . .

To assure fair wages and satisfactory working conditions to all our workers. . . .

To wipe out illiteracy. . . .

To press forward with programs of health and sanitation. . . .

To reform tax laws. . . .

To maintain monetary and fiscal policies which . . . will protect the purchasing power of the many, guarantee the greatest possible price stability, and form an adequate basis for economic development.

To stimulate private enterprise. . . .

To find a quick and lasting solution to the grave problem created by excessive price fluctuations in the basic exports. . . .

To accelerate the integration of Latin America so as to stimulate the economic and social development of the Continent.

After outlining these ambitious goals, the Declaration affirmed "the conviction . . . that these profound economic, social and cultural changes can come about only through the self-help efforts of each country." But it recognized that such self-help "must be reinforced by essential contributions of external assistance." Then followed the pledge of the United States "to provide a major part of the minimum of $20 billion" over a ten-year period, and "over a billion dollars" during the first year of the Alliance. With this, there was the promise of the participating nations "to devote a steadily increasing share of their own resources to economic and social development, and to make the reforms necessary to assure that all share fully in the fruits of the Alliance for Progress." The Declaration closed with a brave peroration:

Conscious of the overriding importance of this declaration, the signatory countries declare that the inter-American community is now beginning an era when it will supplement its institutional, legal, cultural and social accomplishments with immediate and concrete actions to secure a better life, under freedom and democracy, for the present and future generations.

Thus was the Alliance born in ecstasy—and with a fairly precise budget. The financial goals were explicit: a total investment in Latin American development during the 1960's of at least $100 billion; of this total, 80 per cent or $80 billion would come from the Latin Americans themselves; this left 20 per cent or $20 billion to come from external sources. This last slice of the total budget was roughly allocated as follows:

About half from United States public funds—that is, about $1.1 billion per year, $11 billion for the decade.

About $300 million each year from United States private capital.

About $300 million each year from Western Europe and Japan.

About $300 million each year from the World Bank and other international agencies.

In August, 1965, President Johnson celebrated the fifth anniversary of Punta del Este with a glowing report which included this appraisal: "The Alliance is a revolution at work. It is creating; it is building; it is transforming; it is reaching forward; it is touching the lives of hundreds of millions of our fellow citizens." But there was no lack of gloomy critics in the United States and Latin America who rudely argued that such optimism was based on false claims and phony statistics; that too many dollars had gone down the drain in bolstering incompetent governments, in paying their bills for inflation by propping up their weak currencies; that the United States had lived up to its end of the bargain but that the Latin Americans had not; that far from "transforming . . . the lives of millions," in Latin America the rich were growing richer and the poor were growing poorer. Sober analysts were quick to point out, however, that the record was neither all black nor all white; that there had been both bleak failures and solid successes; that five years was too short a period in which to prove or disprove the rosy promises of which the Alliance was born. Such criticisms were repeated in 1966 and in 1967. And today we may ask how successfully the Alliance has functioned, and what progress has been made toward the goals so bravely announced.

THE ALLIANCE FOR PROGRESS: THE PERFORMANCE

Almost from the beginning the fundamental working arrangement of the Alliance went awry. In theory, the Alliance was a multilateral affair: a panel of economists, the "Nine Wise Men," drawn from Latin America as well as the United States, were appointed to study all plans, and the final allocation of loans and grants was to be a joint decision of all the member states. In practice, the United States increasingly assumed the right to decide upon the projects into which its considerable dollars were going. The handling of American money for the Alliance was entrusted to AID, the Administration for International Development. And the chief officer for the allotment of funds became the American Coordinator for the Alliance for Progress, Teodoro Moscoso, who held this post until 1964, and made a brave effort to be loyal to the multilateral ideal; but there was constant pressure from Congress and the Department of State for firm American control. This issue was faced at a meeting of the representatives of all the nations in São Paulo in November, 1963, and it was decided to appoint an Inter-American Committee for the Alliance for Progress (CIAP), headed by the respected Carlos Sanz de Santamaría, who had at various times held posts in his native Colombia, including that of minister of economy and foreign minister. (One casualty of this struggle for dominance of the Alliance was the resignation, early in 1966, of the "Nine Wise Men," who found themselves supplanted by the new committee.) CIAP was empowered to analyze the various projects proposed by the several countries, and to make recommendations for the assignment of funds. The injection of this new voice in the decision-making councils of the Alliance had a tonic effect, making way for more multilateral pressure as an offset to the preponderant influence of the United States. Of course the fact that Washington was supplying the lion's share of the funds made United States approval of any project necessary. But CIAP at least helped to return the Alliance to a more broadly based all-American effort.

The protest of Latin Americans against what they considered the excessive control of the Alliance by the United States is illustrated by the "tie-in" policy, under which recipients of American loans and grants were obligated to purchase substantial amounts—usually 60 per cent—of the equipment and machinery involved in a given project from the United States, when in fact they could save money by making the purchases elsewhere. For example, when Bolivia was granted a loan to modernize her mining equipment, there was bitter resentment that she was not entirely free to save money by making the purchases in Japan or Germany. Such criticism of Washington's policies did not give due weight to the United States balance-of-payments quandary—the United States, powerful as she is, must protect her monetary position. Another source of irritation was the decision of the U.S. Congress in January, 1964, to impose conditions for all aid projects: no project would be approved which would have any adverse effect on the United States economy, which would discourage private enterprise, or which would bar the participation of small American business; furthermore, no grants would be made to any country which did not sign an investment-guarantee agreement with the United States. (This last stipulation was a safeguard against such expropriation of American utility companies as occurred in Brazil under Goulart.)

The administration of the Alliance has called for the drafting of a numerous company of executives and managers of the varied projects. But men with the required skills are not easily found, whether in the United States or in Panama or anywhere else. The obvious and the sobering fact is that many of the men chosen to deal with the sensitive and complicated situations have not been competent. So far as the United States is concerned, the administration of AID and other agencies has suffered from the shifting fortunes of the Latin American section of the Department of State, where there has been little continuity, with assistant secretaries coming and going, and with shifting policies on Alliance projects. Excellent men have often been named to key positions, and have labored bravely, but have finally resigned out of frustration. And everywhere—north and south—the men concerned with Alliance programs have been beaten down by the harassments of those who hold political power.

Perhaps the most effective instrument of Alliance policy has been the Inter-American Development Bank, whose president, Felipe Herrera, has exercised strong leadership. Theoretically, Herrera and his aides have been free to pursue the multilateral ideal which was basic to the original Alliance philosophy. But in practice they have been subject to pressure from the United States, and bilateral considerations have influenced their operations.

Private capital, both domestic and foreign, has failed to behave according to the bold prospectus of Punta del Este. Latin American capital was expected to stay at home, to be plowed back into the economic development of the several countries. That was the theory. But in practice, many of the

Latin Americans who made profits and built up surpluses found it expedient to move their funds (legally or illegally) to the shelter of United States or Swiss banks. How much money fled? Senator Wayne Morse was perhaps only guessing when he wrote in January, 1964, that "as much local capital has left Latin America as the United States has put in since the Alliance began, because the wealthy classes there are not willing to invest in the future of their own countries." But, sadly enough, Morse's guess was confirmed by official and unofficial reports from Colombia, Chile, Argentina, Brazil, and elsewhere.

United States investors, for their part, were expected to put at least $300 million of new money into Latin America each year. But in actual practice the net annual flow of new American capital to Latin America for the first five years of the Alliance averaged only $91 million.[5] Furthermore, the net increase in total United States direct investments in Latin America from 1961 to 1965 was only 13.8 per cent—the lowest percentage of increase of investments in any major area of the world in that period.[6] David Rockefeller, president of the Chase Manhattan Bank, said in Caracas in February, 1964, that the Alliance was faltering "because private investors have been reluctant to put their funds to work." John T. Connor, when he was president of Merck and Company[7] (whose pharmaceutical plants are in Argentina, Brazil, Colombia, Mexico, Peru, and Venezuela) posed the question: "Would you invest in an atmosphere of rising anti-Americanism, unpredictable new taxes, revolutions that occur at the rate of two or three every few months, falling profits, and runaway inflation?"

However, there are numerous instances in which American corporations have not been afraid to invest in Latin America, and have won the respect of Latin American economists. Conspicuous among these is the case of Sears, Roebuck and Company. Sears has more than sixty stores in Latin America, with annual sales of over $100 million. One of its fundamental aims, and one which has been carried out with notable success, has been to sell an ever larger share of the products of the country in which it is operating. By 1966, for example, 99 per cent of the merchandise sold in Sears stores in Brazil and Colombia was made in Brazilian and Colombian factories. The figure for Mexico was 98 per cent; for Peru, 71 per cent; and for Venezuela, 51 per cent. Or consider Ecuador: in 1950 Ecuador sold about $6 million worth of Panama hats made in Cuenca. Then, as fashions changed, sales dropped to $400,000 annually. In January, 1964, a Sears agent persuaded a New York millinery to push the hats. Now Cuenca is two months behind schedule.

In 1961 the framers of the Alliance had set the goal for annual per capita economic growth at 2.5 per cent. But the fact is that the rate for

[5] This low figure of $91 million is due in part to the large net outflow from Venezuelan petroleum. The annual inflow to other industries in Latin America (excluding Cuba) has averaged some $161 million. This over-all figure does not include reinvestment of earnings.

[6] Between 1961 and 1965, United States direct investments in Asia increased 45.8 per cent; in Africa, 78.9 per cent; and in Europe, 79.5 per cent.

[7] Mr. Connor later became U.S. Secretary of Commerce.

1960–65 averaged only 1.7 per cent a year—and was actually less than it had been in the decade before the Alliance was born.[8] Perhaps the greatest single obstacle to increased productivity is the population explosion. With an average annual increase of 2.9 per cent—the highest for any major region in the world—the population of Latin America may exceed 600 million before the year 2000. This is ominous enough, but also serious is the fact that almost half of Latin America's population is under fifteen years of age, and therefore not only unproductive, but a drag on the economy. Also the highest birth rate is among groups of the untrained and economically deprived, especially in parts of Central America, the Northeast of Brazil, and the slums of the great cities. The poor take first honors—or chief blame—for riotous breeding. Furthermore, increased productivity involves mechanization, improved techniques of farming, and the training of technicians—all of which requires capital. And it also requires time, which suggests that critics of the Alliance hold their fire; the hemisphere cannot be remade in five years or even ten.

Tax reform, earnestly prescribed by the founders of the Alliance, proved to be a knotty problem. The proposal that tax systems be altered so that those who earn the most would pay their honest share was, of course, received as an affront by the more affluent. Ex-President Alberto Lleras Camargo of Colombia wrote in the October, 1963, issue of *Foreign Affairs:* "To indicate how outlandish this situation is, it is enough to say that not a single Latin American, whether of high standing or of the underworld, has ever been imprisoned for not paying his taxes or for sending in a fraudulent income tax report." Mr. Lleras continued that "tax evasion is widespread . . . taxes are very low and exemptions are large." Under the pressure of the Alliance program, there has been some lifting of tax levels, some improvement in collection; but thorough programs of tax reform have been little more than token improvements, and they have been fought with vigor at each step—just as, for that matter, any reform of tax procedures is fought in the United States.

The Alliance had dedicated its members to "improve and strengthen democratic institutions"—but this gesture toward free elections, legally installed governments, and an end to *coups d'état* proved idle. Not only did the savage dictatorships of Stroessner in Paraguay and Duvalier in Haiti continue to plague the hemisphere, but there was a fresh series of overturns of constitutionally installed regimes—each a body blow to all that the Alliance stood for. Here are the presidents who were evicted by the military in the years 1961–66: Frondizi in Argentina in March, 1962; Prado in Peru in July, 1962; Bosch in the Dominican Republic in December, 1962; Ydígoras in Guatemala in March, 1963; Arosemena in Ecuador

[8] The average annual per capita growth rate for the years 1950–55 was 2.2 per cent; and for 1955–60 it was 1.8 per cent. While figures on individual years are misleading, it is worth noting that in 1964 and 1965 the rate reached 3.3 per cent and 2.3 per cent respectively, figures which are heartening. For the period 1960–65, seven countries exceeded the 2.5 per cent goal—Panama, Nicaragua, Guatemala, El Salvador, Peru, Mexico, and Bolivia. At the other extreme three countries—the Dominican Republic, Haiti, and Uruguay—actually showed a decline in per capita production for those years. (See table p. 966.)

in July, 1963; Villeda Morales in Honduras in October, 1963; Goulart in Brazil in April, 1964; Paz Estenssoro in Bolivia in November, 1964; the junta in Ecuador in March, 1966; and Illia in Argentina in June, 1966. Of these eight countries only Peru and the Dominican Republic have made a start toward constitutional ways in 1967.

Then there are the cases of Panama and Nicaragua, which—although they had no military overturns—were scarcely in the democratic column. (Of course Cuba, which is outside the Alliance, does not even aspire to being a democracy.) In El Salvador, whose last military ouster was in January, 1961, a relatively stable constitutional regime holds promise in 1967—although there has not been time for a true test. In Mexico, although the dominance of one official party can scarcely be called democratic by any United States definition of the word, all the forms of constitutional procedure have been faithfully followed, and Mexico has achieved remarkable stability while at the same time relegating the military to its proper subordinate position. But only five of the twenty Latin American republics—Chile, Venezuela, Colombia, Uruguay, and Costa Rica—were firmly democratic in the 1960's.

The most revolutionary doctrine of the Alliance—and the most frightening to the economic overlords of Latin America—was the promise to recut the agrarian pattern. This was spelled out in the "Declaration" of Punta del Este:

> To encourage . . . programs of comprehensive agrarian reform, leading to the effective transformation, where required, of unjust structures and systems of land tenure and use; with a view to replacing latifundia and dwarf holdings by an equitable system of property so that, supplemented by timely and adequate credit, technical assistance, and improved marketing arrangements, the land will become for the man who works it the basis of his economic stability, the foundation of his increasing welfare, and the guarantee of his freedom and dignity.

This proposal was greeted by some with hope—by others with anger. Hope was the exultant response of the millions of landless throughout Latin America. And anger, mixed with disbelief, was the reaction of the large landholders, who could not comprehend that anyone would be so foolish as to upset the normal and proper balance of society. But the reactions from the great landowners in Peru, Chile, Argentina, Brazil, and other nations should not be viewed with such naïve surprise as some critics assume. After all, they were responding in exactly the same fashion that holders of great farms in Texas or the Central Valley of California would respond if Washington should suddenly decreè that 80 acres or 160 acres or 320 acres were enough for any man.

The proposals on land reform led to investigations, discussions, and some definite steps. There has been progress toward giving substance to the promise in Chile, Venezuela, Colombia, Peru, and Brazil. Meanwhile, there has been much rather smug satisfaction in Mexico, Bolivia, and Cuba who are sure that they have settled the question finally and admirably. But for most of Latin America land reform remains a pious aspiration.

Chief Exports from Latin America

THE ALLIANCE FOR PROGRESS: WHERE DID THE MONEY GO?

During the first six years of the Alliance, United States assistance to Latin America (commitments and obligations) averaged almost $1 billion a year.[9] And of course much more came from public and private sources in the countries involved. Where did the money go?

The Alliance was pledged to "provide decent homes for all our people," and during the first five years almost all the nations, with outside help, have made token steps to that end. Grants and loans from the Inter-American Development Bank, from the United States, from international agencies, from private sectors, have gone into new housing projects. The results have been important—as first steps. One difficulty encountered everywhere is that new housing, even though planned and executed with an eye on economy, has usually cost too much for the depressed people of the city slums. Another difficulty is typified by the experience of Rio de Janeiro, where the low cost housing planned to relieve the hardships of the *favelas* has often been located too far from the city's center, burdening the *favelados* with increased cost of transportation to and from their jobs. But, for all the difficulties, the brave beginning on housing is on the plus side of the ledger. The magnitude of the problem, however, was made clear by a report in 1965 of the Inter-American Development Bank, which estimated that almost 40 per cent of urban dwellers—or about 45 million people—lived in substandard houses, packed in three or more to a room, lacking running water and sewage systems; also that half of the rural population—another 45 million people—lived in similar conditions. The Bank estimated that the housing shortage ranged between 15 and 19 million units; and that to meet this deficit, and to meet new needs created by population growth and housing deterioration, would require the construction of 2.5 million to 3.3 million units annually for 30 years.

Another objective of the Alliance was to "wipe out illiteracy." And almost everywhere, there has at least been token improvement—in multiplying schools, in training teachers, in providing textbooks. A heartening project in Central America and Panama—which enjoys a subsidy of some $4 million from the United States AID—is turning out 10 million textbooks for the primary grades. Chile has taken the lead in improvement and extension of schooling, and there has been encouraging progress in Mexico, Venezuela, Peru—all with substantial help from Alliance funds.

The Alliance was further committed "to press forward with programs on health and sanitation in order to prevent sickness, combat contagious diseases, and strengthen our human potential." Again, at this point, there have been token attempts. New hospitals have been built in almost all the countries. In Brazil's blighted Northeast, a beginning has been made in providing safe water supplies and sewers for people who have long lived like animals. In Central America, mobile health teams traveling on land, on water, and by air are serving some 2 million people who have hitherto been without any medical services whatever. In Peru, with a loan from the Social Progress Trust Fund, improved water systems are being installed in 100 rural communities. In Bolivia, a small beginning has been made in training rural leaders for introducing programs in hygiene, nutrition, and environmental sanitation. These are but random samplings—almost every-

---

[9] For the six calendar years 1961–66, total United States commitments and obligations were $5,743,800,000. Actual disbursements during that period were $4,731,300,000.

where such projects are under way. There have been constructive measures by various agencies to meet the problem of malnutrition, especially of children. The World Health Organization reports that "among children aged one to four, half the deaths are attributable to malnutrition." Pioneering in providing more food, and better food, is the United States "Food for Peace" operation. Distributing food from the surpluses built up in the United States, its *Operación Niños* is today feeding some 13 to 15 million school children in eighteen Latin American nations. One happy result of this program is that ample school lunches are bringing many children to school for the first time: for example, those lunches are credited with doubling rural school attendance in Peru, and cutting absenteeism in Bolivia by more than one-third. (A *Time* reporter comments that "students now make sure to be on time, since latecomers go to the end of the lunch line.") During the years 1961–66 the total contribution of the United States in its "Food for Peace" program was $931 million.

The Alliance proposed to devise measures to check excessive price fluctuations in basic exports. The chief target was coffee—a commodity long afflicted by riotous rise and fall in prices—which was the principal reliance of Brazil, Colombia, and much of Central America, and a concern of fourteen countries in all. The United States took a hand in launching the International Coffee Agreement, under which the signatories agreed to a quota system designed to bring production and consumption into balance. The measure was vigorously opposed in the United States, where fears were held that it would result in unpopular higher prices to the housewives. But in May, 1965, with approval by Congress, President Johnson signed the controversial measure. The agreement has had success in holding coffee prices within a range of 38 to 44 cents a pound. The chief peril to the success of the plan comes from reckless overproduction of coffee in some countries, with resulting pressure to increase the export quotas fixed under the agreement. There is a threat to its success also from the smuggling of coffee.

The Alliance's objective of accelerating "the integration of Latin America so as to stimulate the economic and social development of the continent" has gained impetus from the creation of the Central American Common Market, CACM, and the larger Latin American Free Trade Association, LAFTA. The basic purpose of these common markets is to make possible the development of industries in the several countries by enlarging their markets through the progressive lowering of tariff barriers—thus freeing the Latin American nations from their traditional status as economic colonies of the industrial powers. The common market idea proceeds from the assumption that a given country might successfully manufacture farm machinery, for instance, if it could sell its product duty free in several countries—the first country would then, in exchange, permit its neighbors free access for its textiles. Such concentration in the production of shoes, plows, and machetes, or television sets would spur the economic development of the whole area.

CACM has made solid progress. Since its founding in 1960, trade within the area has risen an average of 32 per cent each year, and by 1965 amounted to some 20 per cent of the area's total exports. In 1965, AID loaned $42 million to the Central American Bank for Economic Integration. Major emphasis was to be placed on roads linking the various countries, upon electrical power plants whose service would extend beyond national boundaries, and upon intraregional communications. The CACM is now looking toward a customs union which would permit free movement of both goods and people within the area; and a monetary unit which would eventually provide a common currency for the whole region.

More aspiring, but to date far less successful than CACM, is LAFTA, created in 1960 and now including the ten South American republics plus Mexico. LAFTA's planning faced inevitable difficulties—the clash of national interests, the jockeying for position by individual industries, the reluctance to reach agreements for across-the-board tariff cuts, and the falling back on bilateral treaties. Chief apostle of the common market ideal is Felipe Herrera, president of the Inter-American Development Bank. Speaking at Georgetown University on June 22, 1966, Mr. Herrera ended his fervent plea for a common market for all of Latin America with these words:

> The trend toward "regionalization" is not an end in itself, but rather a transitional means—in many respects a measure of protection and self-defense—based on the irreversible process of internationalization of mankind; irreversible, that is, if we assume correctly that man wishes to escape the horrors of a nuclear holocaust. In the process of internationalization, those underdeveloped regions that are economically and politically integrated will be able to maintain their inherent identity and to make a positive, well-defined contribution; but those that fail to achieve the maturity essential for this purpose will continue to function as satellites of the real centers of political, economic and technological power in the present-day world.

The query "Where did the money go?" must also reckon with the continued inclusion of military aid in the foreign assistance program of the United States. It is a formidable and frustrating item in our dealing with Latin America. During the years 1946–63, the United States allotted a total of $790 million to the twenty nations of the south for munitions, planes, tanks, and the training of officers. The fiscal year 1963 alone brought an appropriation of almost $75 million. A few senators and others have continued to ask, "What is the purpose of this largess?" Certainly Washington would not encourage wars between the Latin Americans—anyway, as of recent decades, no such wars have been likely. The official answer, shaped during World War II, was that the security of the United States would be served by strengthening the armed forces of Latin America for the defense of the hemisphere. But the fact is that the armies, navies, and air forces of Latin America—scarcely formidable even to a third-rate power—actually serve but one clear purpose: to maintain internal order and stamp out subversion. ("The trouble is," as James Reston says, "that everybody wants to maintain 'order,' the bad guys as well as the good guys —both with our money.") For example, during the period under review, the United States gave Paraguay a total of $2.8 million in military aid. Why? The answer is simple and humiliating—to maintain the hold of General Stroessner. Against whom? Against the Communists, of course. And who are the Communists? The answer is obvious: anyone who opposes Stroessner. This is the way Onganía is talking in Argentina. This is the way Costa e Silva is talking in Brazil. This is the way Duvalier is talking in Haiti. In fact this argument is repeated with great tediousness around the entire Latin American circle—and it is an argument not without its appeal to Washington. The case for the military aid program is further bolstered by the warning that if Washington does not arm Latin America, other nations—including the U.S.S.R. and China—will. As for the training of military personnel in the United States, one Pentagon officer suggested, "I haven't heard anybody say they'd rather see Latin officers going to Russian service schools."

The irony of the situation is not pleasant. In the invasion of the Bay of Pigs in April, 1961, among the major weapons with which Fidel Castro defeated the patriotic invaders were fighting planes given Batista by the United States before Castro came to power. Again, when the armed forces of Peru unseated President Manuel Prado in July, 1962, the Sherman tank used to ram through the gates of the National Palace was made in the United States, and the officer who led the attack was trained at United States expense at Fort Benning, Georgia. Another sobering fact is that these military grants of the United States serve to speed up a costly arms race among countries that cannot even afford to feed and house their own people. There is sustained and general demand that Washington think again about the wisdom of speeding up the arming of Latin America, but the habit is well entrenched.

A large number of loans and grants must be put under the head of "money down the drain," money tragically wasted, money which fulfills virtually no purpose envisioned by the Alliance. It is a rough and discourteous description, but it is accurate. Any observer of the United States AID operations is aghast at the extravagant multiplication of personnel. In the technical assistance program, for instance, one wonders how much of the money gets to the grass roots of the problems involved, that is, to the face-to-face transfer of knowledge, and how much goes for programming, budgeting, negotiating, supervising, and administering—in the field and in Washington. Those who have watched the dispensing of aid to Latin America since President Truman launched the "Point Four" program in his inaugural address of 1949 have viewed with alarm the mushrooming bureaucracy: the mere machinery of AID has assumed monstrous size and incurred frightening expense. For example, in 1966 the directory of the AID offices in Rio de Janeiro—which occupy twelve floors of one of the newest and most flamboyant of Rio's office buildings—listed 804 individuals, each drawing pay for his share in the allotment of American dollars.

In Recife, center for directing the program of SUDENE in the Northeast, a five-story building is required for the American staff. But the problem of ill-advised distribution of funds poses more serious questions. How much AID money has gone into meeting the budget deficits of incompetent governments, and what has been the effect upon those governments? Is it possible that the easy loans and the failure to exact stiff conditions have simply saved them from having to take politically unpopular measures against inflation? Has this laxness saved them from affronting private enterprise with demands for increased production by farm and factory? The directive at Punta del Este was precise: "to maintain monetary and fiscal policies which, while avoiding the disastrous effect of inflation, will protect the purchasing power of the many, guarantee the greatest possible price stability, and form an adequate basis for economic development." Has the promise of this directive been fulfilled? What per cent of United States AID money goes into projects which meet the desperate situations of the poorest people? How much gets lost in the elaborate machinery of AID? There are no clear answers.

THE ALLIANCE FOR PROGRESS: THE LATIN AMERICAN RESPONSE

Critics of the Alliance in Latin America have been prone to lay the blame for all its failures upon the United States. For example, they point out that after Washington has made commitments of funds for a given project, the disbursement of such funds lags behind the commitment by about a fourth. The Latin Americans also charge the United States with the assumption of superior knowledge, with insistence upon making the final decisions, with ignoring the counsel first of the "Nine Wise Men," then of the Inter-American Committee for the Alliance for Progress. They say that the United States' self-righteousness has been a psychological block to Latin American cooperation. So, say critics, the United States is to blame. It is high time that a rejoinder be made: it is high time to say that the Latin Americans must accept a share in the responsibility for the frequent failures of the Alliance.

Take Brazil as an exhibit. João Goulart, president 1961–64, was demagogic, totally incompetent, and corrupt. Nevertheless, he proved persuasive with international lenders—the United States poured some $700 million into Brazil during his regime. How was the money spent? To stop inflation? No. To build schools and hospitals? Very few. To help the sick and the lowly? Not much. Aside from funds allotted to specific projects—notably SUDENE in the Northeast (see pp. 888–9)—it was a period of utter waste, rampant mismanagement, and scandalous pilfering. Of course, Goulart was not the first to overspend and endanger the nation's economy. Juscelino Kubitschek, president 1956–61, had neglected education and social services while pouring billions of cruzeiros (perhaps $700 million or more) into his dream city of Brasília.

Consider Bolivia, a country long dependent upon outside bounty. Bolivia has made brave efforts to step up agricultural production in the lower valleys to the north and to the east. But, crippled by inadequate transportation, by shortages of managerial and technical competence, and by the constant drain of smuggling into Brazil, Argentina, and Peru, Bolivia is still heavily dependent upon the import of food. Chronic trouble in the tin-mining industry, chief reliance for foreign exchange, adds its steady burden to the national economy. Year after year the United States and other international agencies seek to bail out this bankrupt nation: in 1963 the United States alone committed $56.1 million in aid to Bolivia—more than the $53.8 million expended by the La Paz government in that year. The reckless inflation which dogged Bolivia in the 1950's has been controlled only by the influx of foreign money. And in Bolivia, as elsewhere, the constant refrain is "If you do not help us out, the Communists will get us—and you." And as of 1967 there was no end in sight to that fevered appeal.

It may be put down with assurance that foreign aid has come nearer to realizing the goals of the Alliance for Progress in those countries in which leaders of stature have emerged. In Mexico, for example, an extraordinarily competent (although scarcely democratic) official party has rallied exceptional ability for meeting the economic demands of that prospering country. Colombia gave good account of herself under Alberto Lleras Camargo (1958–62), and after slipping miserably under Guillermo León Valencia (1962–66), again rallied under Carlos Lleras Restrepo (1966–   ). Venezuela, rich and competent, made a brilliant record under Rómulo Betancourt (1959–64), continued hopefully under Raúl Leoni (1964–   ). Little El Salvador, after repeated military turnovers, settled down to mind its business under Julio Adalberto Rivera (1962–67), and then under Fidel Sánchez Hernández (1967–   ). Peru, after sundry false starts and army meddling, found brilliant leadership in Fernando Belaúnde Terry (1963–   ). Chile, with the victory of the Christian Democrats under Eduardo Frei Montalva (1964–   ), grappled with its fundamental economic problems of copper and land, built solidly in education, and offers fair promise that social redemption can come to the Americas by ballots rather than by bullets.

THE ALLIANCE FOR PROGRESS:
THE PRESIDENTIAL RESCUE MISSION,
APRIL, 1967

The eager buoyancy of the Alliance for Progress was spent by 1967. For six years the courage of its devotees had been sustained by the now dimming memories of the gallant John F. Kennedy. While the old slogans were repeated by rote, few claimed any great victories or prophesied any splendid successes. But early 1967 brought a new word of hope. Thanks largely to the initiative of President Lyndon B. Johnson, a meeting of the presidents of all the American republics was arranged for April, 1967, in the Uruguayan resort of Punta del Este—the same spot where the Alliance had been formally launched in 1961. The purpose of the meeting was the uniting of CACM and LAFTA in a European-style common market for all Latin America. The response of the Latin American presidents was enthusiastic: all attended except Bolivia's President René Barrientos, who refused to come because there was no promise to discuss an access to the sea for his landlocked nation; Haiti's President François Duvalier, who dared not leave home for fear of what his enemies might do in his absence; and, of course, Cuba's Fidel Castro.

During the conference which began on April 11 the presidents, by common consent, kept attention focused upon the main purpose of the meeting by barring from the agenda such divisive issues as border disputes, offshore fishing rights, Castro's Cuba, the Inter-American Peace Force, and the exploding population. The discussions were devoted almost entirely to problems of international trade—the increase of exports, the leveling of trade barriers, and the eventual creation of a great common market which would free the Latin American nations from their dependence upon the large industrial powers.

The leading role was inevitably played by the United States' Lyndon Johnson. Of course the President came to Punta del Este with no money in his pocket. He had hoped to be able to make a commitment of an additional $1.5 billion in United States funds over a five-year period to back the new Latin American project, and had asked Congress for a resolution which would state that under certain conditions "Congress is prepared to support the allocation of significant . . . resources" toward the establishment of a Latin American Common Market. But Chairman J. W. Fulbright of the Senate Foreign Relations Committee succeeded in blocking that resolution, calling it a "blank check" and an "open-end commitment" which the President had no right to request. In spite of this awkward situation, however, President Johnson acquitted himself well: he cultivated the Latin American presidents with charm and deference (and just the right amount of "corn and candor," according to a *Newsweek* reporter). "I'm not here to say 'You do that and you do this,'" he told them. "I am just here to listen"—a course to which he was surprisingly faithful.

President Johnson's opening address contained these words:

> I represent a nation committed by history, by national interest, and by simple friendship to the cause of progress in Latin America. . . . [But] the role of the United States in Latin American problems is secondary. . . . The assistance of my nation will only be useful if it reinforces your determination and builds on your achievements. . . . Let us declare the next ten years the Decade of Urgency.

This blunt statement struck a responsive chord and set the mood for the conference. "No external aid can replace our own efforts," said President Eduardo Frei Montalva of Chile. "It is our effort, our imagination, and our resources," said President Gustavo Díaz Ordaz of Mexico, "that must carry out the tasks of economic integration." And Peru's President Fernando Belaúnde Terry exhorted his fellow heads of state to "appeal to our peoples in the conviction that the solution to their problems lies within themselves." It was a new mood of self-help and self-reliance—there was almost none of the persistent clamor for more American aid which had marked the presidents' conference called by Eisenhower in Panama in 1956.

After three days of discussions there was almost unanimous agreement upon the Declaration of the Presidents, which proposed to inaugurate a Latin American Common Market by 1970 which would be in "substantial operation" by 1985; to gradually lower protective tariffs among its members; to take steps toward eventually permitting both capital and labor to move freely among the member nations; and to work toward establishing a common currency for the entire region. The Declaration also expressed the determination to increase exports, to improve living conditions in rural areas, to modernize farms, to increase food production, to improve education, and to limit military expenditures. And these proposals were surrounded by the customary high-sounding phrases proclaiming "solidarity" and the desire for a "free, just, and democratic social order."

Only one of the presidents in attendance spoiled the unanimity of the occasion: President Otto Arosemena Gómez of Ecuador glumly complained that the United States had done more for its defeated enemies after World War II than it had for its friends and neighbors in the Western Hemisphere, loudly demanded more aid and better prices for Latin American products, and refused to sign the Declaration. But this one discordant note did not mar the general enthusiasm: Arosemena was vociferously shouted down by his colleagues.

The goal of Latin American integration seemed ultimately desirable and feasible. But those who were sensitive to the economic and political realities of the several countries foresaw the obstacles which would make its realization difficult. However, this latest and largely Johnson-inspired rescue mission for the Alliance for Progress was welcomed almost everywhere in the hemisphere.

INTER-AMERICAN RELATIONS: THE BALANCE SHEET

Where now does the United States stand in relation to its Latin American neighbors? The question is not readily answered in 1967. The fine careless rapture of the earlier dreams for the Alliance for Progress has disappeared, and we have noted some of the factors which have blocked its full success. An important element is the strident nationalism which flourishes everywhere. All the nations, big and little, have erected a wall of pride which encourages suspicion of others, and especially of the United States. Analysis of the anti-American sentiment in Latin America reveals a wide variety of grievances. In some cases it is a matter of wounded dignity: there have been real or fancied slights by American officials or private citizens. In other cases it may be explained by envy: it is difficult for bitterly poor peoples to live next door to the prosperous United States. In all inter-American planning, the anti-Americanism bred by nationalism makes life difficult at the conference table.

The three knottiest questions confronting Washington in 1967 were: What should be the American policy toward braggart dictatorships? What should the United States do to counter the inroads of the Communist powers, the Soviet Union and China, upon the immature nations of Latin America? How can the United States best use its resources to give substance to the just aspirations of the Alliance for Progress?

We have described the dictators who have dominated their several nations from the early nineteenth century down to the present time. It is an unpleasant story, studded with names of despots who have murdered, tortured, and pillaged. No single country has been free from these tyrants, and some have lived under them practically ever since independence. Americans have no grounds for pride in their record of dealing with those men. The government of the United States has repeatedly done things which it should not have done: it furnished arms to dictators when it was clear that the guns and power served no other purpose than to strengthen the dictatorship; it furnished funds when any bystander could guess that the dollars would fill the privy purses of the tyrants; it appointed witless ambassadors who betrayed the interests of the United States by graceless fawning at the feet of the dictators; it conferred ribbons and medals of honor upon rulers whose prisons were filled with citizens whose only crime was disrespect for the tyrant. These things Washington did, bringing shame to free American citizens and anger to Latin Americans.

What then should Washington do about dictators? Let us narrow the question to: What should Washington do about François "Papa Doc" Duvalier of Haiti? We need not labor the record of that most ruthless oppressor of a helpless people. Washington has cut off almost all aid to the Haitian government, and has from time to time expressed disapproval of Duvalier's dictatorial course. What more could Washington do? Send in the marines? It is to be hoped that it will not come to that. Apply economic boycotts? But the burden of such action would fall upon the innocent Haitian people. Or should Washington seek joint inter-American action against Duvalier? Perhaps that would be the wise course—but we must remember the almost unanimous condemnation of our Dominican venture in 1965.

Or, one might vary the theme by asking what the American attitude should be to the military dictatorship in Argentina. Does Washington have the right or the duty to protest the high-handed usurpation of power and the denial of the democratic rights of the Argentine people? Dr. Milton Eisenhower and Vice-President Richard M. Nixon, after trips to South America, prescribed: let there be a handshake for dictators and an *abrazo*, a warm embrace, for democratic rulers. A wise formula—but one which still leaves many questions dangling in the air.

As to the second main problem—the policy of the United States toward Russian and Chinese penetration of Latin America—no clear answer has yet appeared. It must be noted that Latin Americans—intelligent Latin Americans—quite generally regard the United States concern on that score as ill-advised, panicky, and intemperate. The Latin Americans say to the North Americans, in effect: Do not worry, we will work out our free institutions in our own way. The rejoinder of the United States is firm: There *are* grounds for alarm as the agents of the U.S.S.R. and China extend their trade pacts, increase their diplomatic representation, penetrate the labor movements, and conspire with national Communist parties —legal or outlawed—in the several nations of Latin America. For the fact remains that most of the Latin American republics offer fertile soil for the seeds of Communism; their bitter poverty makes them receptive to the promise of a Marxist heaven. The monopoly over land by a handful of men persuades landless people to reach for any utopia. When the wayfarer walks through the slums of Santiago, looks into the crowded tenements, watches the potbellied children, and learns the daily wage of a worker, he wonders that Chile has so few Communists. When he wanders among the hillside hovels above Lima or Caracas or Rio de Janeiro, he will have some understanding of the mobs who shout the slogans of rebellion.

Perhaps the mistake of the American government has been to place too great an emphasis upon the disruptive power of Communism in the Western Hemisphere, without devoting more wisdom to the analysis of the social illness which makes Communists. Fidel Castro's Cuba offers material for sober thought. Whether or not Castro and his colleagues are Communists of the Moscow breed is less important than the fact that their course bears family resemblance to Moscow's ways. Perhaps if Washington had given thought to a more equitable sharing of the Cuban soil forty, fifty, or sixty years ago, and if the American government had worked with the leaders of Cuba to end poverty—then, perhaps, we would not face the ghastly tragedy of today's bitterness between Cuba and the United States. Perhaps. . . . But it is impossible to write history with "ifs." The leaders of the United States will indeed do well to face the threat of Communism in Latin America—but rather than launching a head-on attack on Communism *per se,* major attention should be given to rooting out the disordered poverty of Bolivia, Chile, Brazil, Peru, and various other lands.

In considering the third fundamental question—how the United States shall spend its money to further the interests of the Western Hemisphere— we start from two assumptions (one or both of which will be disputed by some people): first, that the general aims enunciated by the Charter of Punta del Este are sound and practicable; and second, that in one form or another, American financial aid to Latin America will continue, and it will increase. If this giving is to be effective, it would seem most important that Washington return to the multilateral ideal upon which the Alliance for Progress was founded. Only thus can the United States escape the charge of sitting in final judgment upon the political, social, and economic ways of other peoples. The way of the village banker is hard—he loses friends whether he loans too little or too much—and the way of the international banker is even harder. Prudence would seem to dictate that Washington make greater use of the international agencies, especially those in which all of the American republics share control—such as the World Bank and the Inter-American Development Bank. There must be considerable latitude in the choice of projects: nations in the process of moving from underdevelopment to maturity must be free to make their own mistakes, and must not be forced to submit at each step to the dictates of the most powerful nation in the group. Perhaps the United States must be prepared to support revolutionary programs even though they run counter to the cherished ideals of the White House, the Pentagon, and the Department of State. It may be that this is asking too much of a nation whose revolution lies in the far past. But it is a prerequisite to the sort of giving and lending to which the Alliance for Progress was dedicated.

Perhaps the United States' most gracious, disinterested, and effective measure of international cooperation has been the Peace Corps. Launched in September, 1961, it now operates in fifty-two nations throughout the world, including all the Latin American countries except Argentina, Haiti, Nicaragua, Mexico—and, of course, Cuba. The Peace Corps is also the most economical of all of Washington's foreign excursions: the total budget for 1967 for Latin America (excluding Washington overhead) was only $8.8 million. Commanding the freely given services of hundreds of dedicated men and women (most of them youngsters just out of college), detachments of the Corps have gone into some of the poorest and most hopeless communities in Colombia, Bolivia, Chile, Brazil, and elsewhere. Paid only a subsistence wage, members of the Corps live and work in the city slums; and in remote villages they share the poor homes and the meager fare of the lowliest farm workers and laborers. They build schools and houses, dig wells and ditches, install sewers and latrines, teach the children, tend the sick—no job is too menial for them. Everywhere the Peace Corps has made friends. A chief reason for its success is that its members have not identified themselves with any political group. Two Corpsmen, commenting upon their experiences in Bolivia, said, "When we arrived, the Communists wanted to kill us. We then told them that we knew nothing about politics. Then they asked us which is better, the American way of life or Communism. We told them we couldn't say because we had no personal experience of Communism. We said we were Americans and loved America. After that, they left us alone."[1]

Denis Brogan, astute British analyst of the United States, warned in 1952 against "the illusion of American omnipotence." That warning is still timely. President Lyndon B. Johnson told a labor conference in May, 1965, that any effort of the Communists to "put Americans in danger" called for the caution that "where Americans go, their flag goes with them to protect them." Historians must remind the President that that is the language of Theodore Roosevelt and the Big Stick; that is the mood which inspired our

[1] Hugo Portisch, in *Kurier* (Vienna): *Atlas* (June, 1964), p. 361.

occupation of Nicaragua in 1909, of Veracruz in 1914, of Haiti in 1915, of the Dominican Republic in 1916. We thought that such clumsy digressions were ended in the days of the Good Neighbor. But the irresistible temptation to play God was reincarnated in Santo Domingo in 1965. No matter what short-term successes "American omnipotence" may have scored, the long-range fruits were melancholy.

Senator J. William Fulbright has been giving the same advice to the Johnson administration. Speaking at Johns Hopkins University in early 1966, Fulbright said:

> The question which I find intriguing is whether America can overcome the fatal arrogance of power. My hope and my belief are that it can, that it has the human resources to accomplish what few, if any, great nations have ever accomplished before: to be confident but also tolerant; and rich, but also generous; to be willing to teach but also willing to learn; to be powerful but also wise. I believe that America is capable of all these things; I also believe that it is falling short of them. Gradually but unmistakably we are succumbing to the arrogance of power. . . . Power also tends to take itself for omnipotence. Once imbued with the idea of a mission, a great nation easily assumes that it has the means as well as the duty to do God's work. The Lord, after all, surely would not choose you as His agent and then deny you the sword with which to work His will.

At long last the people of the United States seem aware that their happiness, prosperity, and security are linked with the well-being of the citizens of the twenty southern republics. The discussion of just and friendly relations between the United States and Latin America was once regarded as a pleasant elective; today it has become an imperious necessity.

Tables

Reading List

Index

Table 1. POPULATIONS AND AREAS

Country	Population							Area[e] (sq. mi.)	Density[f] (persons per sq. mi.)
	LATEST CENSUS[a]		MIDYEAR ESTIMATES (THOUSANDS)				AVERAGE ANNUAL INCREASE[d] (PER CENT)		1966
	Date	(thousands)	1937[b]	1948[b]	1958[c]	1966[c]	1958–66		
Latin America: The 20 Republics									
Mexico	6/ 8 /60	34,923	18,737	23,876	33,704	44,145	3.4%	761,602	58
Costa Rica	4/ 1 /63	1,336	599	814	1,076	1,486	4.1	19,575	76
El Salvador	5/ 2 /61	2,511	1,649	2,100	2,321	3,037	3.4	8,260	368
Guatemala	4/18/64	4,284*	2,088	2,642	3,584	4,575	3.1	42,042	109
Honduras	4/17/61	1,885	1,020	1,260	1,823	2,363	3.3	43,277	55
Nicaragua	4/25/63	1,536	926	1,160	1,330	1,655[g]	3.2[h]	53,938	31[g]
Panama	12/11/60	1,076	575	746	1,002	1,287	3.2	29,209	44
Total, Central American Republics			6,857	8,722	11,136	14,403[i]		196,301	

Cuba	1/28/53	5,829	4,359	5,164	6,548	7,833	2.3	44,218	177
Dominican Republic	8/7/60	3,047	1,586	2,214	2,826	3,750	3.6	18,816	199
Haiti	8/7/50	3,097		3,112^j	3,846	4,485	1.9	10,714	419
Total, Antillean Republics				10,490^i	13,220	16,068		73,748	
Argentina	9/30/60	20,006	14,100	16,311	19,980	22,691	1.6	1,072,070	21
Bolivia	9/5/50	2,704	3,237	3,922	3,360	3,748	1.4	424,163	9
Brazil	9/1/60	70,967	38,685	49,704	66,740	84,679	3.0	3,286,478	26
Chile	11/29/60	7,374	4,754	5,621	7,316	8,591^g	2.3^h	286,397	30^g
Colombia	7/15/64	17,482*	8,531	10,777	14,476	18,068^g	3.2^h	439,513	41^g
Ecuador	11/25/62	4,476	2,782	3,077^j	4,105	5,326	3.3	109,483	49
Paraguay	10/14/62	1,817*	934	1,270	1,687	2,094	2.7	157,047	13
Peru	7/2/61	9,907	6,695	8,078	9,483	12,012	3.0	496,223	24
Uruguay	10/16/63	2,593	2,080	2,329	2,464	2,749	1.4	72,172	38
Venezuela	2/26/61	7,524	3,415	4,496	6,830	9,030	3.6	352,143	26
Total, South American Republics			85,213	105,585^i	136,441	168,988^i		6,695,689	
Total, the 20 Latin American Republics				148,673^i	194,501	243,604^i		7,727,340	

(table continued)

Table 1. POPULATIONS AND AREAS (continued)

Country	Population							Area[e] (sq. mi.)	Density[f] (persons per sq. mi.)
	LATEST CENSUS[a]		MIDYEAR ESTIMATES (THOUSANDS)				AVERAGE ANNUAL INCREASE[d] (PER CENT)		
	Date	(thousands)	1937[b]	1948[b]	1958[c]	1966[c]	1958–66		1966
New States and Dependencies									
Bahama Islands	11/15/63	136	67	76	103	140	3.9%	4,403	32
Barbados	4/7/60	232	173	201	228	245	0.9	166	1,476
Bermuda	10/23/60	43	31	36	43	48[g]		20	2,400[g]
British Honduras	4/7/60	90	54	63	86	109	3.0	8,867	12
Falkland Islands	3/18/62	2	2	2	2	2[g]		4,618	0.4[g]
Guyana	4/7/60	560	333	397	532	662	2.8	83,000	8
Jamaica	4/7/60	1,610	1,123	1,351	1,566	1,839	2.0	4,232	435
Leeward Islands[k]	4/7/60	123	91	103	120	131[g]	1.3[h]	346	379[g]
Trinidad and Tobago	4/7/60	828	450	595	789	1,000	3.0	1,980	505
Virgin Islands (Br.)	4/7/60	7	6	7	7	9[g]		59	153[g]
Windward Islands[l]	4/7/60	315	247	264	315*	352[g]	1.6[h]	810	435[g]
Total, British Sphere			2,577	3,095	3,791*	4,537[i]		108,501	

	Date								
Netherlands Antilles	12/31/60	189	93	152	188	210	1.4	371	566
Surinam (Dutch Guiana)	3/31/64	324*	170	210	248	335g	4.4h	55,144	6g
Total, Dutch Sphere			263	362	436	545i		55,515	
French Guiana	10/9/61	34	25	30*	36g			35,135	1
Guadeloupe	10/9/61	283	282	258	319		2.7	687	464
Martinique	10/9/61	291	267	266	327		2.6	425	769
Total, French Sphere			574	554*	682i			36,247	
Canal Zone	4/1/60	42	48	53j	43	54g		553	98g
Puerto Rico	4/1/60	2,350	1,777	2,172	2,299	2,668	1.9	3,435	777
Virgin Islands (U.S.)	4/1/60	32	24	27	30	43*,g		133	323g
Total, U.S. Sphere			1,849	2,252i	2,372	2,765*,i		4,121	
United States	4/1/60	179,323	128,825	146,621	174,882	196,842	1.5	3,615,200	54

* Provisional or unofficial estimate.

a SOURCE: United Nations, *Statistical Yearbook*, 1965, Table 19.

b SOURCE: United Nations, *Statistical Yearbook*, 1951, Table 1.

c SOURCE: United Nations, *Monthly Bulletin of Statistics*, Vol. XXI, No. 7 (July, 1967), except: population estimates for Bermuda, Falkland Islands, Leeward Islands, Virgin Is. (Br.), Windward Is., Surinam, French Guiana, Canal Zone, and Virgin Is. (U.S.) from United Nations, *Statistical Yearbook*, 1966, Table 17.

d Annual rate of population increase computed (by formula for geometric mean rate given in United Nations, *Demographic Yearbook*, 1965, p. 16) from estimates of total populations in 1958 and 1966 (or 1965) as given in this table. Increase represents net change in population resulting from births, deaths, and in-and-out migration.

e SOURCE: United Nations, *Statistical Yearbook* 1965, Table 19. Areas reported in source in square kilometers have been converted to square miles by formula: 1 square kilometer equals 0.386101 square miles.

f Density computed by dividing 1966 population estimates by areas—both sets of figures as given in this table.

g 1965.

h 1958-65.

i The totals are additions of the figures presented here. Where a year other than that at the head of the column has been substituted for any of the countries in the group, the totals are necessarily inaccurate.

j 1950.

k Including Antigua, Montserrat, St. Kitts-Nevis-Anguilla.

l Including Dominica, Grenada, St. Lucia, St. Vincent.

For detailed qualifying notes see sources.

Table 2. GEOGRAPHIC CHARACTERISTICS

Country	Capital City							Highest Elevation[c]	
	NAME OF CITY	POPULATION[a]			Altitude (feet)	SETTING[b]		PEAK, RANGE	ELEVATION (FEET)
		Year	Inhabitants (thousands)	Per cent of total population		Average annual temperature (°F.)	Average annual precipitation (inches)		
Mexico	Mexico	1965	5,500*,d	13.4	7,555	60	23	Pico de Orizaba, Sierra Madre Oriental	18,701
Costa Rica	San José	1964	331[d]	23.9	3,844	69	74	Chirripó Grande, Talamanca	12,533
El Salvador	San Salvador	1963	281	10.3	2,230	74	70	Volcán de Santa Ana, Cadena Costera[e]	7,825
Guatemala	Guatemala	1963	439	10.5	4,927	64	49	Volcán Tajumulco, Sierra Madre	13,845
Honduras	Tegucigalpa	1965	171	7.5	3,303	71	37	Cerros de Culmi, Sierra de Agalta	8,497
Nicaragua	Managua	1964	249	15.6	100*	81	46	Cerro Saslaya, Cordillera Isabelia	6,560
Panama	Panama	1965	331	26.6	30	81	69	Volcán Chiriquí o Barú, Cordillera de Talamanca	11,410
Cuba	Havana	1964	1,518[d]	20.4	45*	76	46	Pico Turquino, Sierra Maestra	6,467
Dominican Rep.	Santo Domingo	1965	522	14.4	46	78	56	Pico Duarte, Cordillera Central	10,417
Haiti	Port-au-Prince	1960	240	5.8	164	79*	49	Mont la Selle, Massif de la Selle	8,793

Country	Capital city	Year	Population (city proper) (000)	%	Alt.	Temp.	Precip.	Highest point	Elevation
Argentina	Buenos Aires	1960	7,000^{d,f}	33.9	82	62	39	Aconcagua, Andes	22,834
Bolivia	La Paz^g	1962	353	9.9	11,920	49	22	Illampú, Andes	21,490
Brazil	Brasília^h	1961	131	0.2	3,809	70	55*	Pico da Bandeira, Serra de Caparaó	9,462
Chile	Santiago	1964	2,184^d	25.7	1,706	57	14	Nevado Ojos del Salado, Andes	22,539
Colombia	Bogotá	1964	1,681	9.6	8,397	58	37	Cristóbal Colón, Santa Marta	18,930
Ecuador	Quito^h	1965	402	7.9	9,250	56	49	Volcán Chimborazo, Andes	20,577
Paraguay	Asunción	1962	305	16.5	207	76	48	Cerro Villa Rica, Sierra de Amambay	2,231
Peru	Lima	1961	1,436^d	13.9	449	64	1	Huascarán, Andes	22,205
Uruguay	Montevideo	1963	1,154	43.6	72	62	41	Cerro Mirador Nacional, Sierra de las Animas	1,644
Venezuela	Caracas	1965	1,675^d	19.2	3,421	70	32	Pico Bolívar, Andes	16,411

* Estimate.
a SOURCE: United Nations, *Demographic Yearbook*, 1965, Table 5. Capital city is largest city in each country except Brasília (Brazil) and Quito (Ecuador); see note h. Per cent of national population in capital cities was computed for this publication, using midyear population estimates for the various countries for the appropriate years from the United Nations. *Demographic Yearbook*, 1965, Table 4.
b SOURCE: Pan American Union, *América en Cifras*, 1963, Vol. 1, Cuadro 102–01. Data refer to altitude, temperature, and precipitation at official weather stations in or near the capital cities; they are useful only as general indications of conditions near the capitals and are not necessarily typical of the entire country. Where seasonal variability is pronounced (chiefly in Buenos Aires, Santiago, Asunción, and Montevideo so far as temperature is concerned), the average yearly values fail to convey an adequate picture of the climate even at the reporting station.
c SOURCE: Pan American Union, *América en Cifras*, 1963, Vol. 1, Cuadro 101–03.

d Urban agglomeration.
e Conflicting claim for Pico Cayaguanca, said to be 9,199 feet (2,804 meters) high.
f Estimate of United Nations Economic Commission on Latin America.
g La Paz is the effective seat of government. But Sucre (population estimated at 54,270 in 1962) is legal capital.
h Data for largest cities in Brazil and Ecuador:

City	Year	Population (city proper) (000)	%	Setting Alt.	Temp.	Precip.
Rio de Janeiro, Brazil	1960	3,223	4.6	49	73	47
São Paulo, Brazil	1960	3,165	4.5	1,824	69	54
Guayaquil, Ecuador	1965	652	12.8	20	78	38

Table 3. POPULATION OF CHIEF CITIES[a]

Country and Year	City	Population	Country and Year	City	Population	Country and Year	City	Population
Argentina (1960)	Buenos Aires	7,000,000[b]	Chile (1964)	Santiago	2,184,149[i]	Mexico (1965)	Mexico	5,500,000[i,1]
	Rosario	671,852		Valparaíso	273,158		Guadalajara	1,048,351
	Córdoba	589,153		Concepción	170,034		Monterrey	821,843
	La Plata	330,310		Viña del Mar	131,479		Ciudad Juárez	385,082
	Tucumán	287,004		Antofagasta	107,828		Puebla	338,685
	Santa Fe	259,560		Talcahuano	102,323[j]		Mexicali	288,601
	Paraná	174,272	Colombia (1964)	Bogotá	1,680,758		León	275,335
	Bahía Blanca	150,354		Cali	812,810		Tijuana	244,290
	Mar del Plata	141,886[c]		Medellín	776,970		Torreón	212,900
	Mendoza	109,149		Barranquilla	521,070		Chihuahua	198,461
	San Juan	106,746		Bucaramanga	250,550		Mérida	187,015
Bolivia (1962)	La Paz[d]	352,912		Pereira	223,500		San Luis Potosí	180,881
	Sucre	54,270		Cartagena	197,590		Veracruz	173,347
Brazil (1960)	Rio de Janeiro	4,691,000[e]		Manizales	186,910		Aguascalientes	147,727
	São Paulo	4,367,000[f]		Ibagué	160,400		Hermosillo	143,215
	Recife	1,064,000[g]		Tuluá	151,370		Tampico	139,867
	Belo Horizonte	642,912		Palmira	148,510		Matamoros	131,576
	Salvador	630,878		Cúcuta	147,250		Morelia	127,816
	Pôrto Alegre	617,629		Pasto	130,130		Durango	124,472
	Belém	359,988		Buenaventura	110,660		Saltillo	117,827
				Montería	110,130		Nuevo Laredo	117,728

Country	City	Population
	Fortaleza	354,942
	Curitiba	344,560
	Santos	262,048
	Campinas	179,797
	Natal	154,276
	Manaus	154,040
	Maceió	153,305
	João Pessoa	135,820
	Goiânia	132,577
	Brasília	130,968[h]
	Juiz de Fora	124,979
	São Luís	124,606
	Pelotas	121,280
	Campina Grande	116,226
	Ribeirão Prêto	116,153
	Aracajú	112,516
	Sorocaba	109,258
	Teresina	100,006

Country	City	Population
	Armenia	107,150
	Sevilla	104,460
Costa Rica (1964)	San José	330,607[k]
Cuba (1964)	Havana	1,517,700[i]
	Santiago de Cuba	231,000
	Camaguey	153,100
	Santa Clara	120,600
Dominican Republic (1965)	Santo Domingo	522,490
Ecuador (1965)	Guayaquil	651,542
	Quito	401,811
El Salvador (1963)	San Salvador	281,122
Guatemala (1963)	Guatemala	439,081
Haiti (1960)	Port-au-Prince	240,000
Honduras (1965)	Tegucigalpa	170,535

Country	City	Population
Nicaragua (1964)	Managua	248,811
Panama (1965)	Panama	331,474
Paraguay (1962)	Asunción	305,160
Peru (1961)	Lima	1,436,231[k]
	Callao	155,953
	Arequipa	135,358
	Trujillo	100,130
Uruguay (1963)	Montevideo	1,154,465
Venezuela (1965)	Caracas	1,674,728[k]
	Maracaibo	530,182
	Barquisimeto	235,905
	Valencia	189,933[k]
	Maracay	159,671
	San Cristóbal	122,047
	Cabimas	117,734

[a] SOURCE: United Nations, *Demographic Yearbook*, 1965, Table 5, except: Rio de Janeiro, São Paulo, and Recife in Brazil, from Latin American Center, University of California at Los Angeles, *Statistical Abstract of Latin America*, 1965, Table 6. Populations of the following are census figures: cities in Argentina (other than Buenos Aires and Mar del Plata); cities in Brazil (other than Brasília), Bogotá in Colombia; cities in Paraguay, Peru, and Uruguay. All others are listed as "estimate" in source.

[b] Urban agglomeration, including cities of Avellaneda, San Martín, Lanús, Vicente López, Lomas de Zamora, Quilmes, Morón, San Isidro, La Matanza. United Nations estimate.

[c] 1958 estimate.

[d] La Paz is the effective seat of government, but Sucre is the legal capital.

[e] Urban agglomeration including cities of Nova Iguaçu, Niteroi, São Gonçalo, São João de Meriti, Duque de Caixas.

[f] Urban agglomeration including cities of Santo André, São Caetano Guarulhos, São Bernardo.

[g] Urban agglomeration including cities of Olinda and Jaboatão.

[h] 1961 estimate.

[i] Urban agglomeration.

[j] 1963.

[k] "Metropolitan area."

[l] Unofficial estimate.

Table 4. LAND USE AND LAND TENURE

Country	Land Use: Per Cent of Total Area^a						Persons^b Per Sq. Mile of Arable Land ca. 1966	Land Tenure^c				
	YEAR	AGRICULTURAL AREA		FORESTED LAND	OTHER AREA			YEAR	AGRICULTURAL LANDHOLDINGS OF 5 HECTARES OR LESS		AGRICULTURAL LANDHOLDINGS OF 1,000 HECTARES OR MORE	
		Arable land and land under permanent crops	Permanent meadows and pastures		Unused but potentially productive	Built-on area, wasteland and other			Per cent of total holdings	Per cent of total area utilized	Per cent of total holdings	Per cent of total area utilized
Mexico	1960	12.1%	40.1%	22.1%	5.7%	20.0%	479	1950	72.6%	0.9%	1.5%	79.4%
Costa Rica	1963	12.0	18.4	16.2		53.4	633	1963	43.2^d	3.0^d	0.6^e	31.2^e
El Salvador	1962	22.8	28.2	23.7		25.3	1,613	1961	85.2	14.9	—^f	15.7
Guatemala	1950	13.5	5.3	44.4		36.8	806	1950	88.4^d	14.3^d	—^g	—^g
Honduras	1963	7.3	30.4	26.9		35.3	748	1952	57.1	8.1	0.1	20.5
Nicaragua	1960	12.8		46.2	11.7	29.3	240	1963	50.9^d	3.6^d	1.4^h	40.0^h
Panama	1961	7.5	11.0	69.7		11.9	588	1961	46.2	5.2	0.1	15.4
Cuba	1946	17.2	34.0	11.4	.2	37.2	1,030	1952	14.3		0.9	
Dominican Rep.	1946	14.0	11.9	45.7		28.5	1,424	1960	86.2		0.2^i	
Haiti	1950	13.3	18.0	25.2	25.2	18.2	3,147	1950	93^j	70^j	—^k	

Argentina	1960	7.0	42.6	35.8	2.2	12.4	302	15.2	0.1	5.6	74.5
Bolivia	1950	2.8	10.3	42.8		44.1	316	59.3	0.2	6.3	91.9
Brazil	1957	2.2	12.6	60.8	4.0	20.2	1,171	30.9	1.0	1.0	47.2
Chile	1955	3.5	13.9	27.6		55.0	857	38.5^l	2.6^l	2.8	37.2
Colombia	1960	4.4	12.8	61.0		21.8	934	62.6	4.5	0.5^m	40.4^m
Ecuador	1961	10.7	8.1	54.8		26.3	455	73.1	7.2	0.2	19.2
Paraguay	1964	2.2	24.3	51.0		22.5	606	69.3^l	2.3^l	1.1	86.7
Peru	1962	1.4	14.2	54.5		29.9	1,729	87.9	5.2	0.2	72.6
Uruguay	1961	12.0	74.1	3.2		10.7	317	14.7	0.2	4.4	56.9
Venezuela	1961	2.7	18.3	20.8		58.1	950				
United States	1959	19.8	27.4	32.3	3.0	17.6	275	6.5^n		3.7^o	

a SOURCE: United Nations, Food and Agricultural Organization, *Production Yearbook.* 1965, Table 1.

b Computed for this publication using per cent of arable land given in this table together with areas and populations given in Table 1.

c SOURCE: Adapted from Latin American Center, University of California at Los Angeles, *Statistical Abstract of Latin America,* 1965, Table 37, except: data for Costa Rica, Guatemala, Nicaragua, Dominican Republic. Haiti, Argentina, Chile, Colombia, and Paraguay, adapted from Inter-American Development Bank, Social Progress Trust Fund, *Fifth Annual Report,* 1965, country chapters.

Note: One hectare (10,000 sq. meters) equals 2.47104 acres.

d Holdings of less than 6.9 hectares (10 *manzanas* or 17 acres).

e Holdings of 690 hectares (1,000 *manzanas*) or more.

f Less than 0.1 per cent.

g In Guatemala, 0.1 per cent of the holdings, comprising 40.8 per cent of the land, were in plots of 88.1 hectares (217.7 acres) or more in 1950.

h Holdings of 357 hectares or more.

i Holdings of 200 hectares (494.3 acres) or more.

j Holdings of less than 6 hectares.

k In Haiti, only 0.2 per cent of the holdings exceeded 26 hectares in 1950.

l Holdings of less than 10 hectares.

m Holdings of 500 hectares and over.

n Holdings of less than 4 hectares.

o Holdings of 404.5 hectares or more.

For detailed qualifying notes see sources.

Table 5. SOCIAL CHARACTERISTICS

Country	Vital Rates[a]				Medical Facilities				Illiteracy[d]		Urban Population[e]	
	YEAR	CRUDE BIRTH RATE	CRUDE DEATH RATE	INFANT MORTALITY RATE	YEAR	PERSONS[b] PER PHYSICIAN	PERSONS[b] PER DENTIST	PERSONS[c] PER HOSPITAL BED 1960	YEAR	PER CENT OF POP. 15 YRS. AND OVER	YEAR	PER CENT OF TOTAL POP.
Mexico	1965	44.2	9.5	60.7	1961	1,800	17,100	735[f]	1960	34.6%	1960	50.7%
Costa Rica	1965	40.5*	8.1	75.1	1963	2,600	6,600	204	1963	15.7	1963	34.5
El Salvador	1965	46.5*	10.5*	71.1*	1963	4,700	17,300	471	1961	51.0	1961	38.5
Guatemala	1965	43.5*	16.8*	94.6*	1963	3,600	23,900	359	1950	70.3[g]	1965	34.3
Honduras	1964	45.5*	9.3*	45.4*	1963		23,000	549	1961	55.0	1961	23.2
Nicaragua	1965	40.6*	7.2*	55.1*	1960	2,800	15,200	530	1963	50.4	1963	40.8
Panama	1965	39.1*	7.1*	43.5*	1964	3,100	23,600	268	1960	26.7	1960	41.5
Cuba	1964	35.6*	6.4*	37.7*	1963	1,200	5,700	437	1953	23.6[g]	1953	57.0
Dominican Rep.	1962	32.8*	6.9*	79.5*	1963		8,900	378	1950	56.8[g]	1960	30.5
Haiti	1961	45–50*	20–25*	171.6*,[h]	1961	10,600	25,500	1,723	1950	89.3[g]	1965	16.0
Argentina	1964	21.8*	8.3*	60.0*	1962	670	1,800	154[i]	1960	8.6[j]	1965	74.2
Bolivia	1965	18.4*	4.7*	—	1963	3,700	6,100	558	1950	68.9[k]	1965	35.0
Brazil	1961	40–43*	11–13*	—[l]	1960	2,700		328	1950	51.4[g]	1960	45.1

Chile	1964	32.8	11.2	114.2	1960	1,800	203	1960	16.4	1960	68.2
Colombia	1964	38.6*	10.0*	83.3*	1963	2,000	345	1951	38.5^g	1965	53.2
Ecuador	1964	46.9*	12.1*	89.9*	1962	2,800	481^i	1962	32.7	1965	38.2
Paraguay	1961	42–45*	14–17*		1962	1,700	1,253	1962	25.7	1965	35.7
Peru	1964	32.0*	8.9*	83.5*	1964	2,200	422^i	1961	39.9^m	1961	47.4
Uruguay	1962	25.1*	7.8*	47.4*,^{n}	1962	1,100	230	1963	9.7	1963	82.2
Venezuela	1964	43.4*	7.2*	49.3*	1963	1,300	281°	1961	34.2	1961	67.5
United States	1965	19.4	9.4*	24.7*	1963	690	111^p	1959	2.2^j	1960	69.9

* Provisional or estimate.

^{a} SOURCE: United Nations, *Demographic Yearbook*, 1965, Tables 12, 42, and 41, except: for Mexico, Costa Rica, El Salvador, Guatemala, and the United States, from United Nations, *Statistical Yearbook*, 1966, Tables 18, 19, and 20; and Infant Mortality for Haiti and Uruguay, from United Nations, *Demographic Yearbook*, 1964, Table 19.

Note: Birth rate is number of live births per 1,000 population. Death rate is number of deaths per 1,000 population. Infant Mortality rate is number of deaths of infants under one year of age per 1,000 live births.

^{b} SOURCE: United Nations, *Statistical Yearbook*, 1965, Table 193. Persons per dentist computed for this publication using data in source together with population figures for appropriate years from United Nations, *Monthly Bulletin of Statistics*, July, 1967.

^{c} SOURCE: Latin American Center, University of California at Los Angeles, *Statistical Abstract of Latin America*, 1965, Table 25. Persons per hospital bed computed for this publication using data in source together with population figures for appropriate years from United Nations, *Monthly Bulletin of Statistics*, July, 1967.

^{d} SOURCE: United Nations, *Demographic Yearbook*, 1964, Table 34, except: rates for Mexico, Panama, Argentina, Peru, and Venezuela from United Nations, *Statistical Yearbook*, 1964, Table 187; rates for Guatemala, Cuba, Dominican Republic, Haiti, Bolivia, Brazil, and Colombia, from United Nations, *Statistical Yearbook*, 1957, Table 180; and rate for the U.S. from U.S. Bureau of the Census, *Statistical Abstract of the United States*, 1966.

^{e} SOURCE: United Nations, *Demographic Yearbook*, 1964, Table 27, except: data for Mexico, Panama, Dominican Republic, Brazil, Venezuela, and the U.S., from United Nations, *Demographic Yearbook*, 1962, Table 9; data for Cuba, from United Nations, *Demographic Yearbook*, 1960, Table 9; and data for Guatemala, Haiti, Argentina, Bolivia, Colombia, Ecuador, and Paraguay, from Inter-American Development Bank, Social Progress Trust Fund, *Fifth Annual Report*, 1965, country chapters. Percentages have been figured for this publication where only totals were given in sources.

Note: Definitions of "urban" population vary greatly from country to country. With certain qualifications, Mexico and the U.S. count localities of 2,500 or more inhabitants as urban; Argentina and Guatemala, 2,000 or more; Colombia and Panama, 1,500 or more; Honduras and Venezuela, 1,000 or more. The other countries, in general, count administrative centers and capitals of provinces as urban providing they have essentially urban characteristics such as electricity and other municipal services.

^{f} 1958.
^{g} 10 years and over.
^{h} 1964.
^{i} 1959.
^{j} 14 years and over.
^{k} 5 years and over.
^{l} Infant mortality in the state of Guanabara (Rio de Janeiro) in 1960 was estimated at 70.0 per 1,000. SOURCE: United Nations, *Demographic Yearbook*, 1964, Table 19.
^{m} 1960.
^{n} 17 years and over.
^{o} 1961.
^{p} 1962.

For detailed qualifying notes see sources.

Table 6. COMMUNICATIONS: MOTOR VEHICLES AND MOTOR ROADS

Country	Motor Vehicles in Use[a]						Motor Roads[b]		
	Passenger Cars (Thousands)		Com'l. Vehicles (Thousands)		Total per Thousand Persons		Total Miles of Road[c]	Total Miles per 1,000 Sq. Mi. of Area	Miles Improved[d]
	1948	1964	1948	1964	1948	1964	1954	1954	1954
Mexico	167.9[e]	677.6	126.6[e]	388.6	11.4[e]	25.8	117,000	154	28,906
Costa Rica	3.7	20.0	2.1	10.7	3.2	22.1	4,659	238	931
El Salvador	5.2	22.9[f]	4.0	9.2[f]	3.5	11.8[f]	3,921	475	1,921
Guatemala	1.3[e]	28.0	1.9[e]	15.0	2.2[e]	10.0	8,100	193	6,616
Honduras	0.8	8.8	0.8	7.1	1.6	7.2	935	22	770
Nicaragua		12.9		5.0		11.2	4,700	87	500
Panama	17.1	24.7	4.0	12.1	27.5	30.5	1,384	47	885
Cuba	47.9	88.0	30.0	41.5	14.7	17.4			2,158
Dominican Rep.	3.1	27.5	2.9	11.3	3.0	11.1	2,017	107	1,636
Haiti		5.1		1.8		1.6	1,862	174	1,812
Argentina	304.4	725.0	204.1	530.0	31.3	57.0	89,090	83	34,384
Bolivia	3.7	14.5[f]	7.9	26.6[f]	3.9	11.4[f]	9,130	22	621
Brazil		906.4		898.2		22.6	190,300	58	57,269
Chile	36.8	89.1	32.1	98.9	11.8	22.4	30,202	105	27,214
Colombia	27.9	119.4	24.6	105.3	4.8	12.9	10,678	24	4,772
Ecuador	2.7	17.0	4.8	22.6	2.5	8.1	5,967	55	3,332
Paraguay	0.8	6.5[g]	1.3	3.8[g]	1.6	5.6[g]	4,600	29	470
Peru	22.8	124.3	18.3	96.8	5.3	19.6	22,285	45	14,730
Uruguay	35.2*[h]	112.0	21.0*[h]	81.4	26.0*[h]	72.1	6,342	88	6,200
Venezuela	40.6	352.4	45.1	145.6	18.3	59.1	10,674	30	6,174
United States	33,350.9[i]	71,635.7	7,734.6[i]	12,470.6	279.1[i]	437.8	3,418,000[j]	945	2,273,000[j,k]

* Provisional or estimate.

[a] SOURCE: United Nations, *Statistical Yearbook*, 1965, Table 154. Total per 1,000 persons computed by dividing total vehicles by official population estimates for the appropriate years as given in the United Nations, *Demographic Yearbook*, 1965, Table 4.

[b] SOURCE: U.S. Bureau of Foreign Commerce, *World Trade Information Service*, Part 3, No. 58-3, 1958 (Comparative Statistics on the American Republics), Table 7. Total miles per 1,000 sq. miles of area computed for this publication, using areas as given in Table 1.

[c] Total mileage includes all roads suitable for movement of motor vehicles. Some countries consider trails as part of their highway system, but as far as possible trail mileage has been excluded from the above list.

[d] Includes mileage graded and drained as well as mileage surfaced; in general, such roads are passable in all seasons.

[e] 1950.　[f] 1963.　[g] 1962.　[h] 1949.
[i] Excluding Alaska and Hawaii.
[j] 1955.　[k] Excluding graded and drained.
For detailed qualifying notes see sources.

Table 7. COMMUNICATIONS: RAILROADS, SHIPPING, AND TELEPHONES

Country	Railroads[a] TOTAL ROUTE MILES 1959	Railroads[a] MILES PER 1,000 SQ. MI. OF AREA 1959	Shipping[b] LOADED 1,000 METRIC TONS 1948	LOADED 1964*	Shipping[b] UNLOADED 1,000 METRIC TONS 1948	UNLOADED 1964*	Telephones in Use[c] TOTAL 1948	TOTAL 1964	PER 1,000 PERSONS[d] 1964
Mexico	12,760	16.8	2,840	8,293	708	1,725	246,426	725,072	18
Costa Rica	219	11.2	236e	492	106e	654	7,800*	21,559	16
El Salvador	385	46.6	82	492	113	1,060	5,972	22,000*	8
Guatemala	539	12.8	332	308f	388	750f	3,000*	23,370	5
Honduras	356	8.2	544g	612	356g	325	4,050	8,921	4
Nicaragua	216	4.0	88		113	215h	2,275	12,021	8
Panama	175	6.0		272h			10,280	41,658	35
Cuba	2,848	64.4	1,465g	2,244h	615g	876h	93,426	228,687	31
Dominican Rep.							4,888	30,375	9
Haiti	189	17.6	147e	3,646	165e	170	3,509	4,400	1
Argentina	27,770	25.9	8,759	13,251	14,333	8,360	684,739	1,472,132	67
Bolivia	2,039	4.8					8,500*	20,000*	5
Brazil	24,531	7.5	4,658	14,587	6,804	18,174	485,300	1,263,072	16
Chile	6,014	21.0	5,272	10,119	2,129	3,190	126,033	249,582	30
Colombia	3,417	7.8	2,965	5,970	816	1,462	67,626	409,589	23
Ecuador	1,392	12.7	423	1,471	124	774	18,882	43,499	9
Paraguay	660	4.2					4,986	13,566	7
Peru	2,262	4.6	1,726	9,490	507	2,063	42,400	132,367	12
Uruguay	1,853	25.7					77,686	189,500*	71
Venezuela	326	0.9	67,530	184,246	2,119	2,915	52,604	260,228	31
United States	234,351	64.8	80,115	156,155	61,159	225,348	38,205,000	88,787,000	462

* Provisional or estimate.

a SOURCE: Sampson, *World Railways*, London, 1960. Miles of railroad per 1,000 square miles of area computed for this publication using areas given in Table 1.

b SOURCE: United Nations, *Statistical Yearbook*, 1965, Table 157.

c SOURCE: United Nations, *Statistical Yearbook*, 1965, Table 164.

d Computed by dividing total number of telephones in 1964 by 1964 population estimates as given in United Nations, *Monthly Bulletin of Statistics*, Vol. XX, No. 11 (November, 1966), Table 1.

e 1949. f 1962. g 1957. h 1963.

Table 8. INDUSTRIAL INDICATORS

Country	Electric Energy						Consumption			
	INSTALLED CAPACITY[a] (THOUSAND KW)				PRODUCTION[b] (MILLION KWH)		ENERGY[c] (KG. PER CAP.)		STEEL[d] (KG. PER CAP.)	
	TOTAL		HYDROELECTRIC							
	1958	1963	1958	1963	1958	1963	1961	1964*	1960	1964
Mexico	2,560	4,193	1,184	1,597	9,058	13,567	963	1,029	50	65
Costa Rica	106.8	139.6	78.4	105.0	365	518	228	268		
El Salvador	76[e]	106			213	340	119	178		
Guatemala	55	89	30		219	364	172	175		
Honduras	26	38	4		74	108[f]	184	161		
Nicaragua	74.7	84.4	9.2	9.3	143	251	185	231		
Panama	53.5[g]	71.7[g]			195[g]	326[g]	531	907		
Cuba	854	976			2,589	3,057	889	931	32	29
Dominican Rep.					284	428[f]	146	209		
Haiti	25				47	74	34	32		
Argentina	2,947	4,686	278	363	9,418	12,449	1,180	1,242	76	93
Bolivia	143	158	96		264[g]	320[g]	143	173		
Brazil	3,993	6,355	3,224	4,480	19,766	27,869	339	364	41	43
Chile	1,014	1,336	522	683	4,146	5,623	928	1,078	70	74
Colombia	874	1,478	505	773	3,034	5,268	479	494	27	31
Ecuador	101	166	34	67	324	495	186	195		
Paraguay	28.7				82		94	105		
Peru	653	999	401	551	1,990	3,419	509	602	17	24
Uruguay	337[g]	432[f,g]	128[g]	224[f,g]	1,237[g]	1,578[g]	804	830	44	31
Venezuela	1,277*,[h]	1,977	130*,[h]	387	4,310[h]	6,771	2,640	3,000	76	119
United States	175,001[h]	228,756	31,884[h]	40,928	724,752	1,011,418	8,046	8,772	501	615

* Provisional or estimate.

[a] source: United Nations, Statistical Yearbook, 1965, Table 143. The data represent the nominal end-of-year capacity of all generators available for simultaneous operation in hydroelectric and thermoelectric plants. Data refer to total installed capacity unless otherwise noted.

[b] source: United Nations, Statistical Yearbook, 1965, Table 144. Data refer to total generation of electricity unless otherwise noted.

[c] source: United Nations, Statistical Yearbook, 1965, Table 142. Data for consumption of energy are based on apparent consumption of coal, lignite, petroleum products, natural gas and hydro and nuclear electricity. "Kilograms per capita" refers to kilograms of coal equivalent per capita.

[d] source: United Nations, Statistical Yearbook, 1965, Table 170. Data refer to the apparent consumption of crude steel in kilograms per capita.

[e] 1956.
[f] 1962.
[g] For public use only.
[h] 1959.

For detailed qualifying notes see sources.

Table 9. ECONOMICALLY ACTIVE POPULATION

Country	Year	Economically Active Population[a]			Percentage Distribution by Industry[b]								
		TOTAL (THOUSANDS)	LOWER AGE LIMIT[c]	PER CENT OF TOTAL POPULATION	AGRICULTURE[d]	MINING & QUARRYING	MANUFACTURING	CONSTRUCTION	UTILITIES[e]	COMMERCE[f]	TRANSPORT & COMMUNICATIONS	SERVICES[g]	INADEQUATELY DESCRIBED
Mexico	1960	11,332	8	32.4%	54.2%	1.2%	13.7%	3.6%	0.4%	9.5%	3.1%	13.5%	0.7%
Costa Rica	1963	395		29.6	49.4	0.3	11.4	5.5	1.1	10.2	3.5	17.4	2.2
El Salvador	1961	807	10	32.1	60.2	0.1	12.5	4.2	0.2	6.2	2.1	13.5	0.9
Guatemala	1955	1,130		34.7									
Honduras	1961	568	10	30.1	66.7	0.3	7.5	2.0	0.1	4.7	1.4	12.2	4.6
Nicaragua	1963	477	10	31.0	59.3	0.9	11.7	3.6	0.3	7.5	2.4	14.2	0.2
Panama	1960	337	10	33.3	46.2	0.1	7.5	4.3	0.5	9.1	3.0	20.1	9.2[h]
Cuba	1953	1,972	14	33.8	41.5	0.5	16.5	3.3	0.4	11.8	5.3	20.1	0.5
Dominican Rep.	1950	826	7	38.7	49.9	0.1	10.8	10.2	0.7	8.3	2.3	13.6	4.0
Haiti	1950	1,747	14	56.4	83.2	0.0	4.9	0.6	0.1	3.5	0.4	4.6	2.7
Argentina	1960	7,599	14	38.0	19.2	0.6	25.2	5.6	1.1	11.9	6.3	20.0	10.1
Bolivia	1950	1,361	10	50.3	63.5	4.1	10.3	2.5	3.8	5.4	2.0	6.6	1.8
Brazil	1950	17,117	10	33.0	58.0	2.6	——	13.0	——	6.3	4.1	15.8	0.3
Chile	1960	2,389	12	32.4	27.7	3.8	17.9	5.7	0.8	10.1	4.9	22.8	6.2
Colombia	1951	3,756	12	33.4									
Ecuador	1962	1,484	12	32.9	56.5	0.2	14.1	3.2	0.2	6.2	2.8	13.3	3.4
Paraguay	1950	437	12	32.9	53.8	0.1	15.6	2.9	0.1	6.9	2.2	15.5	3.4
Peru	1961	3,125	6	31.5	49.8	2.1	13.1	3.3	0.3	9.0	3.0	15.2	4.0
Uruguay	1963	1,016	10	39.2	17.9	0.2	21.8	4.8	1.7	13.0	6.1	28.3	8.0
Venezuela	1961	2,407	10	32.0	32.1	1.9	12.2	5.3	1.1	12.6	4.4	23.7	6.4
United States	1960	69,877	14	39.0	6.4	1.0	26.5	6.1	1.3	21.6	5.3	20.1[i]	11.5[i]

a SOURCE: United Nations, *Demographic Yearbook,* 1964, Table 8, except: data for Guatemala, Cuba, Dominican Republic, Haiti, Bolivia, Brazil, Colombia, Paraguay, from United Nations, *Demographic Yearbook,* 1960, Table 12.
b SOURCE: United Nations, *Demographic Yearbook,* 1964, Table 9, except: data for Cuba, Dominican Republic, Haiti, Bolivia, Brazil, Paraguay, from United Nations, *Demographic Yearbook,* 1956, Table 12.
c Persons younger than "lower age limit" are not tabulated in economically active population.

d Includes agriculture, forestry, hunting, and fishing.
e Includes gas, electric, water, steam, and sanitary services.
f Includes banking, insurance, and real estate.
g Includes government, community, business, recreation, and personal services.
h Includes Panamanians working in the Canal Zone.
i For the United States, persons employed in public administration and members of armed forces are included in "Inadequately described." For detailed qualifying notes see sources.

Table 10. NATIONAL ACCOUNTS: GROSS DOMESTIC PRODUCT

Country	Breakdown of Gross Domestic Product by Productive Sectors, 1965[a] (in percentages)								Share of Total GDP of Latin America 1965[b,c]	Average Annual GDP Growth Rates in Real Terms, 1960–65[b]	
	AGRICULTURE[d]	MINING	MANUFACTURING INDUSTRY	CONSTRUCTION	ELECTRIC POWER	TRANSPORT & COMMUNICATIONS	PUBLIC ADMINISTRATION	OTHER SERVICES[e]		TOTAL	PER CAPITA
Mexico	15.9%	5.3%[f]	25.2%[g]	3.5%	1.7%	4.3%	2.8%	41.3%	20.7%	6.1%	2.6%
Costa Rica	30.7	—[h]	15.1	2.8	2.8	4.7	9.6	34.2	0.7	6.0	1.9
El Salvador	29.5	0.1	16.9	3.7	1.4	4.1	7.1	37.2	1.0	6.6	3.3
Guatemala	28.3	0.1	14.9	1.7	0.9	5.2	4.3	44.6	1.8	6.6	3.6
Honduras	44.2	0.9	13.4	3.4	0.5	5.6	4.3	27.8	0.5	4.6	1.1
Nicaragua	38.5	1.8	14.2	3.1	1.6	5.2	6.1	29.5	0.7	8.3	4.6
Panama	20.5	0.3	15.9	5.3	2.4	5.9	2.3	47.4[f]	0.8	8.0	4.7
Dominican Rep.[i]	31.0	0.9	14.6	4.2	1.1	5.5	12.0	30.7	0.9	1.3	−2.0
Haiti	43.4	2.2	14.2	0.6	0.5	3.9	7.4	27.7	0.4	1.0	−1.3
Argentina	15.4	1.2	37.4	3.3	2.0	5.4	5.8	29.5	16.9	3.3	1.7
Bolivia	28.7	11.9	11.8	4.2	1.6	8.5	10.1	23.2	0.8	5.0	2.6
Brazil	29.6	0.7	21.6	1.3	1.1	7.9	6.9	31.1	28.3	4.4	1.5
Chile	10.1	6.9	18.9	3.4	1.2	7.9	8.7	42.9	4.9	4.2	1.8
Colombia	30.0	3.5	19.6	3.0	1.1	6.2	5.6	31.0	6.1	3.8	1.0
Ecuador	34.4	2.1	17.4	4.2	1.4	3.9	6.7	29.9	1.3	4.3	1.2
Paraguay	36.5	0.1	17.1	2.3	0.7	4.2	4.1	34.7	0.4	3.8	1.2
Peru	20.0	7.5	19.0	4.2	1.3	5.4	7.6	35.0	3.2	5.7	2.7
Uruguay	20.7	—[j]	21.1	3.9	1.7	7.3	8.2	37.1	1.4	1.1	−0.1
Venezuela	7.2	20.1	17.7	6.3	1.8	4.1	7.1	34.5	9.1	4.7	1.2
Total, Lat. Amer.[c]	21.1	4.3	23.7	3.1	1.4	5.9	6.3	34.1		4.6	1.7
United States	3.8[k]	6.2[k,l]	30.5[k]	—[k,l]	2.1[k,m]	6.1[k]	13.5[k]	37.9[k]		4.3[n]	2.7[n]

a SOURCE: Document prepared by the Secretariat for the eleventh meeting of CIAP (Inter-American Committee on the Alliance for Progress) held on March 27–31, 1967: *Summary Report on the 1966 Round of Country Reviews* (OEA/Ser. H/XIV, CIAP/120), Chapter I, "National Performance," Table 1–2, except figures for United States: see notes k and n.

b SOURCE: *Ibid.,* Table 1–1.

c Note that in this table "Latin America" does not include Cuba.

d Comprises agriculture, stock raising, forestry, hunting, and fishing.

e Comprises business, banking and finance, home ownership, and personal services.

f Includes petroleum refining.

g If petroleum refining were included, the contribution of this sector would be 27.2 per cent.

h Mining—of little importance in Costa Rica—is included under "manufacturing industry."

i 1964.

j Negligible.

k SOURCE: Adapted from U.S. Department of Commerce, *The National Income and Product Accounts of the United States, 1929–65* (Washington GPO, 1966). Note: Breakdown is for National Income rather than GDP.

l Construction is included under Mining.

m Includes electric, gas, and sanitary services.

n SOURCE: United Nations, *Statistical Yearbook,* 1965, Table 183. Rates are average annual rates of growth of real GDP at market prices for 1960–61

Estimates of National Income

Country	YEAR	NATIONAL CURRENCY[a] (MILLIONS)	U.S. DOLLARS[b] (MILLIONS)	U.S. DOLLARS[c] (PER CAPITA)	YEAR	NATIONAL CURRENCY[d] (MILLIONS)	U.S. DOLLARS[b] (MILLIONS)	EDUCATION[e] (PER CENT OF TOTAL)	PUBLIC HEALTH & WELFARE[e] (PER CENT OF TOTAL)	DEFENSE[e] (PER CENT OF TOTAL)
Mexico	1965	220,000	$17,614	$413	1965	17,372.8	$1,390.9	24%	16%	11%
Costa Rica	1965	3,350	504	352	1965	466.1	70.1	26	12	8[f]
El Salvador	1965	1,730	692	236	1965	249.8	99.9	18	9	10
Guatemala	1965	1,247	1,247	281	1964	106.6	106.6	——— 25 ———		10
Honduras	1965	884	442	194	1965	117.6	58.8	25	14	10
Nicaragua										
Panama	1964	480	480	398	1965	86.6	86.6	27	14	
Cuba	1965	4,038			1965	177.9	177.9	15	9	19
Dominican Rep.	1964	674	674	193	1966	141.0	28.2	11	11[g]	25
Haiti								11	6	12
Argentina					1965	387,022.0	207.2			
Bolivia	1965	6,320	532	144	1964	2,461.6		——— 14[i] ———		
Brazil	1960	1,879[h]			1964	3,775.0[h]		12	8	23
Chile	1965	17,134			1965	3,860.2		16	5[g]	10
Colombia	1964	44,200			1966	4,656.3		13	8	27
Ecuador	1965	17,400	940	185	1965	3,452.0	186.4			12
Paraguay	1963	42,100	334	175						
Peru					1964	17,418.2	649.4	18	26	12
Uruguay	1963	19,764			1966	7,585.0		12	22	10
Venezuela	1965	29,200	6,636	761	1965		1,723.9			
United States	1965	563,000	563,000	2,894	1966	127,398.0	127,398.0	2[j]	27[j]	41

[a] SOURCE: United Nations, *Monthly Bulletin of Statistics*, Vol. XX, No. 11 (November, 1966), Table 61.

[b] Converted to U.S. dollars using exchange rates for appropriate years as given in *ibid.*, Table 64. Conversions have been made only in the case of countries where the currency is relatively stable. The free rate has been used for Ecuador; the petroleum export rate for Venezuela; the other countries involved have single rates (see Table 13).

[c] Computed by dividing total in U.S. dollars by population estimates for appropriate years as given in *ibid.*, Table 1.

[d] SOURCE: United Nations, *Statistical Yearbook*, 1965, Table 192. All data are given as "estimate" except for Guatemala and Bolivia.

[e] Percentages computed from data given in *ibid.* Note that the share of national governments in expenditure for education and social welfare varies between countries. For example, in the United States education is largely in the hands of local and state governments. This must be considered when making international comparisons. See notes [i] and [j] below.

[f] Listed as "Justice, police, and other security forces."

[g] Listed as "Health" only.

[h] 1,000 million national currency units.

[i] Listed as "Education and health." The states and Federal District of Brazil reported a total expenditure for 1964 of 1,494,211 cruzeiros, of which 15 per cent was for education and 7 per cent was for health

[j] The state and local governments of the U.S. reported a total expenditure of $85,797 million, of which 39 per cent was education and 15 per cent was for public health and welfare.

Table 12. COST OF LIVING INDEX

Country	1938	1948	1955	1956	1957	1958	1959	1960	1961	1962	1963	1964	1965	1966
							Cost of Living Index (1958 = 100)ᵃ							
Mexico	15	47	81	84	89	100	102	108	109	110	111	114	118	123
Costa Rica	34	71	95	96	97	100	100	101	104	107	111	114	114	114
El Salvador	30	58	98	99	95	100	99	99	97	97	98	100	100	99
Guatemala		78	99	100	99	100	100	98	98	100	100	100	99	100
Honduras	47	75	103	99	97	100	101	99	101	102	105	110	114	115
Nicaragua					95	100	97	95	95	96	96	100	103	107
Panama			101	100	100	100	100	100	101	102	103	105	105	106
Cuba														
Dominican Rep.		95	96	97	102	100	100	96	93	102	110	112	110	119
Haiti		88	95	98	100	100	95	91	94	93	97	106	109	117
Argentina	6.8	14	54	61	76	100	214	272	309	395	491	600	771	1,020
Bolivia	0.2	0.9	16	45ᵇ	97	100	120	134	144	152	151	167	172	
Brazil	5.9ᶜ	25	60	73	87	100	137	185	256	390	684	1,270	2,050	3,000
Chile	1.2	5.2	40	63	79	100	139	155	167	190	274	400	512	632
Colombia	18	45	71	76	87	100	107	111	121	124	164	192	199	239
Ecuador			103	98	98	100	100	102	106	109	115	120	123	130
Paraguay			67	81	94	100	110	119	141	143	146	148	154	158
Peru	14	45	82	86	93	100	113	122	131	138	148	164	191	209
Uruguay	23	41	69	74	85	100	140	194	237	263	317	454	710	1,230
Venezuela		83	96	98	95	100	105	109	106	105	106	107	109	109
United States	49	83	93	94	97	100	101	102	103	105	106	107	109	112

ᵃ SOURCE: International Monetary Fund, *International Financial Statistics*, Supplement to 1966/67 issues, country pages; except: 1966 figures from *ibid.*, Vol. XX, No. 7 (July, 1967), country pages; 1938 indices adapted from United Nations, *Statistical Yearbook*, 1956, Table 160, to show "base 1958 = 100," using the year 1948 (given in *International Financial Statistics* cited above for "base 1958 = 100," and in *Statistical Yearbook* cited above for "base 1953 = 100") to link the two series. ᵇ Before December, 1956, controlled prices. ᶜ 1939.

National Currency Units per U.S. Dollar (end of year)

Country	Currency	Type of Rate	1961	1962	1963	1964	1965	1966
Mexico	Peso	Principal import	12.49	12.49	12.49	12.49	12.49	12.49
Costa Rica	Colón		6.65	6.65	6.65	6.65	6.65	6.65
El Salvador	Colón		2.50	2.50	2.50	2.50	2.50	2.50
Guatemala	Quetzal		1.00	1.00	1.00	1.00	1.00	1.00
Honduras	Lempira		2.00	2.00	2.00	2.00	2.00	2.00
Nicaragua	Córdoba	Selling	7.05	7.05	7.05	7.05	7.05	7.05
Panama	Balboa		1.00	1.00	1.00	1.00	1.00	1.00
Cuba	Peso							
Dominican Rep.	Peso		1.00	1.00	1.00	1.00	1.00	1.00
Haiti	Gourde		5.00	5.00	5.00	5.00	5.00	5.00
Argentina	Peso	Selling	83.02	134.10	132.50	150.90	188.50	247.30
Bolivia	Peso[b]		11,885[b]	11,885[b]	11.88[b]	11.88	11.88	11.88
Brazil	Cruzeiro	Coffee export	134.6	181.6	314.0	742.4	886.9	944.5
		Free	318.5	475.0	620.0	1,850.0	2,220.0	2,220.0
Chile	Escudo	Official market	1.053	1.64	2.15	2.70	3.47	4.37
		Free market		2.42	3.04	3.26	4.22	5.00
Colombia	Peso	Coffee export	5.72	6.96	7.01	7.42	8.50	9.94
		Principal selling	6.70	9.00	9.00	9.00	13.51	13.50
		Free	8.82	11.09	9.99	12.77	18.29	16.30
Ecuador	Sucre	Free	21.70	22.10	18.53	18.52	18.52	20.48
Paraguay	Guaraní		126.00	126.00	126.00	126.00	126.00	126.00
Peru	Sol		26.81	26.82	26.82	26.82	26.82	26.82
Uruguay	Peso	Free	10.98[c]	10.98[c]	17.35	24.35	69.20	76.50
Venezuela	Bolívar	Petroleum export	3.09	3.09	3.09	4.40	4.40	4.40
		Other export	3.33	3.33	3.33	4.48	4.48	4.48
		Selling	3.35	3.35	3.35	4.50	4.50	4.50

[a] SOURCE: International Monetary Fund, *International Financial Statistics*, Supplement to 1966/67 issues, country pages, except: 1966 figures from *ibid.*, July, 1967, country pages. In countries with multiple exchange rates, the most important rates have been selected. *Note*: While this table shows the serious inflation in some countries—notably Brazil—in the 1960's, it must be remembered that there was equally serious inflation in some spots in the 1950's: In Bolivia, for instance, the boliviano [see (b) below] dropped from 60 to the U.S. dollar in 1950 to 11,935 in 1958; and in Paraguay the guaraní dropped from 3.74 to the U.S. dollar in 1948 to 126 in 1960. While the inflation in Bolivia and Paraguay was halted, other countries have suffered continuous inflation: In Argentina the peso dropped from 4.81 to the U.S. dollar in 1948 to 82.70 in 1960; in Chile the free peso dropped from 65.55 to the U.S. dollar in 1948 to 1,053 in 1959 (on January 1, 1960, a new unit—the escudo, equal to 1,000 pesos—was introduced); in Brazil the free cruzeiro dropped from 55 to the U.S. dollar in 1953 to 205.1 in 1960; in Uruguay the free peso dropped from 2.38 to the U.S. dollar in 1948 to 11.18 in 1959; and in Colombia the free peso dropped from 2.678 to the U.S. dollar in 1948 to 7.23 in 1960—and these five countries have suffered continued inflation in the 1960's. Those who would look further at the fate of various currencies since 1948 may refer to the source cited above.

[b] On January 1, 1963, the Bolivian peso equal to 1,000 bolivianos was introduced. Rates for 1961 and 1962 are given in bolivianos; for 1963, 1964, 1965 and 1966, in pesos.

[c] Export-import rate.

Table 14. INTERNATIONAL TRADE

Country	Total Value of Trade[a] (millions of U.S. dollars)								Trade with U.S., U.S.S.R., and China[b]					
	IMPORTS				EXPORTS				SOURCE OF IMPORTS, 1965 (PER CENT OF TOTAL)			BUYERS OF EXPORTS, 1965 (PER CENT OF TOTAL)		
	1948	1958	1962	1966	1948	1958	1962	1966	U.S.	U.S.S.R.	China (Mainland)	U.S.	U.S.S.R.	China (Mainland)
Mexico	$561	$1,129	$1,143	$1,605	$484	$736	$930	$1,228	69%	.01%		58%	.01%	
Costa Rica	42	99	113	179	50	92	93	139	46			53		
El Salvador	41	108	125	220	45	116	136	192	35			26		.3
Guatemala	68	150	136	229[c]	67	108	118	187[c]	45			35		
Honduras	37	76	80	122[c]	55	70	81	127[c]	49			54		
Nicaragua	28	78	97	182	19	64	82	138	47			26		
Panama	73	110	171	254	24	33	48	87	43			61		
Cuba									4	53.1	10.5		30.1	13.4
Dominican Rep.	74	149	148	184	83	128	172	137	50			77		
Haiti	31	43	46	36[c]	30	39	42	36[c]						
Argentina	1,562	1,233	1,357	1,124	1,629	994	1,216	1,593	24	0.3	.02	7	1.9	6.5
Bolivia	79	80	92	126[c]	98	50	59	118	55			36		
Brazil	1,134	1,353	1,475	1,496	1,173	1,243	1,214	1,741	35	2.2	.05	33	2.6	.01
Chile	269	415	571	604[c]	327	386	530	685[c]	37			35		
Colombia	337	400	540	674	289	461	463	506	47			52		
Ecuador	60	105	97	171[c]	53	133	143	148[d]	47			56		
Paraguay	27	37	39	58	28	34	33	49	21			24		
Peru	168	382	534	817	157	281	538	763	41			31		
Uruguay	200	143	230	164	178	139	153	186	15	0.1		8	0.1	
Venezuela	814	1,599	1,096	1,331	1,040	2,321	2,594	2,713	53			34		.01
United States	8,081	14,619	17,783	27,729	12,666	17,920	21,687	30,450		0.1			0.6	

[a] SOURCE: Data for 1962 and 1966 (1965) from International Monetary Fund, *International Financial Statistics*, July, 1967, pp. 34–35; data for 1948 and 1958 from *ibid.*, Supplement to 1966/67 issues, pp. xvi-xvii.

[b] SOURCE: United Nations, *Yearbook of International Trade Statistics, 1964,* country tables. Percentages computed for this publication.

[c] 1965.

[d] 1964.

Country	Commodity	Per Cent of Total Exports 1958	Per Cent of Total Exports 1965
Mexico	Cotton	26%	19%
	Coffee	11	6
	Zinc	3	4
	Lead	5	2
	Copper	4	—b
Costa Rica	Coffee	55	42
	Bananas	29	25
	Cacao	6	2
El Salvador	Coffee	75	51
	Cotton	16	20
Guatemala	Coffee	72	49
	Cotton	5	18
	Bananas	12	2
Honduras	Bananas	54	42
	Coffee	16	17
	Wood	9	8
	Silver	4	3
Nicaragua	Cotton	39	46
	Coffee	38	18
	Cotton seed	6	6
	Meat		4
	Gold	11	4
	Sugar	3	4
	Sesame	3	1
Panama	Bananas	67	51
	Refined petroleum		30
	Shrimp	17	10
	Re-exports	6	1
	Cacao	3	—b

Country	Commodity	Per Cent of Total Exports 1958	Per Cent of Total Exports 1965
Cuba	Sugar	76%	
	Tobacco	7	
Dominican Rep.	Sugar	41	52c
	Coffee	19	17c
	Cacao	22	9c
	Tobacco	4	8c
Haiti	Coffee	74	48c
	Sisal	13	9c
	Sugar	3	6c
Argentina	Wheat	12	25
	Meat	27	22
	Corn	7	10
	Wool	11	8
	Hides	6	3
	Linseed	4	3
	Quebracho extract	1	1
Bolivia	Tin	57	72c
	Silver	8	6c
	Lead	9	4c
	Zinc	5	3c
	Tungsten	2	1c
Brazil	Coffee	55	44
	Cotton	2	6
	Cacao	7	2
Chile	Copper	63	66d
	Iron ore	6	11d
	Saltpetre	11	6d

Country	Commodity	Per Cent of Total Exports 1958	Per Cent of Total Exports 1965
Colombia	Coffee	77%	64%
	Petroleum	14	16
Ecuador	Bananas	55	57c
	Coffee	20	15c
	Cacao	15	10c
	Rice	3	—b,c
Paraguay	Meat	24	33
	Timber	29	17
	Cotton	11	8
	Tobacco	2	7
	Quebracho extract	10	6
	Oilseeds	4	6
	Hides	6	2
Peru	Fishmeal	4	22
	Copper	8	18
	Cotton	27	13
	Silver	7	6
	Lead	9	6
	Sugar	12	6
	Petroleum	6	6
	Zinc	4	
Uruguay	Wool	58	47
	Meat	11	32
	Hides	6	8
	Wheat	12	2
	Linseed oil	3	2
Venezuela	Petroleum	91	92c
	Iron ore	5	6c

a SOURCE: International Monetary Fund, *International Financial Statistics*, Vol. XIX, No. 12 (December, 1966), country tables, except: data for Chile, Cuba, Venezuela, and Peru (petroleum and zinc) from United Nations, *Yearbook of International Trade Statistics*, 1960, country tables (for 1958 data); and *ibid.*, 1964 (for 1963 and 1964 data). Percentages computed for this publication. b Less than 1 per cent. c 1963. d 1964.

Table 16. U.S. Economic Assistance: Commitments[a]

Recipients	Total U.S. Commitments for Six-Year Period 1961–66 (millions of U.S. dollars)						Average Annual Per Capita Commitments 1961–66	Per Capita Commitment for 1966
	AID	EXPORT-IMPORT BANK[b]	FOOD FOR PEACE[c]	SOCIAL PROGRESS TRUST FUND[d]	PEACE CORPS	TOTAL		
Mexico	$69.6	$279.4	$52.3	$35.5	$2.9	$436.8	$1.77	$2.24
Costa Rica	46.1	7.7	5.9	12.6	2.9	75.2	9.33	5.05
El Salvador	45.8	11.9	13.9	22.0	2.1	95.7	5.82	1.91
Guatemala	29.1	6.9	8.7	14.3	2.7	61.7	2.43	1.60
Honduras	38.6	0.4	3.1	7.6	2.9	52.6	4.02	3.22
Nicaragua	52.1	6.0	7.3	13.1		78.5	8.25	8.96
Panama	67.5	12.8	3.5	12.9	10.1	106.8	14.96	17.95
Dominican Rep.	206.1	28.7	51.3	10.2	4.6	300.9	14.18	19.63
Haiti	20.1	3.0	6.4			29.5	1.16	0.76

Country								
Argentina	142.3	57.5		43.5		243.3	1.87	0.07
Bolivia	187.2		55.2	14.5	8.7	265.6	12.24	9.93
Brazil	854.8	181.6	540.5	62.0	16.0	1,654.9	3.50	3.89
Chile	467.5	101.2	105.5	35.4	8.3	717.9	14.48	12.14
Colombia	305.5	89.4	82.7	49.9	18.3	545.8	5.33	2.33
Ecuador	96.9	16.0	24.0	27.8	9.6	174.3	5.95	3.92
Paraguay	34.3		20.8	7.8	0.2	63.1	5.45	7.02
Peru	95.4	82.7	46.4	45.2	12.4	282.1	4.23	3.16
Uruguay	21.9	7.1	5.1	10.5	1.4	46.0	2.89	2.51
Venezuela	60.3	80.9	37.5	73.0	9.3	261.0	5.39	2.02
Regional	113.8		0.9	19.3	27.3	161.3		
ROCAP[e]	87.9			2.9		90.8		
Total	$3,042.8	$973.2	$1,071.0	$520.0	$136.8	$5,743.8		

[a] SOURCE: Adapted from table furnished by the Office of Research and Analysis for American Republics, Department of State, Washington, D.C. Per capita commitments computed for this publication using population figures for the appropriate years from the United Nations, *Monthly Bulletin of Statistics*, July, 1967 (1966 projections used for Nicaragua, Chile, and Colombia). Data are for calendar year.
Note: Military assistance is not included.
[b] Long term.
[c] Less U.S. Uses, Title I of PL 480.
[d] SPTF technical assistance grants and administrative funds for various countries have not been computed by country and are included under Regional. Funds to Central American universities are included under ROCAP.
[e] Regional Office for Central America and Panama, established July 1, 1962, with headquarters in Guatemala City.

Table 17. U.S. Economic Assistance: Disbursements[a]

Recipients	Total U.S. Disbursements for Six-Year Period 1961–66 (millions of U.S. dollars)						Average Annual Per Capita Disbursements 1961–66	Per Capita Disbursements for 1966
	AID	EXPORT-IMPORT BANK[b]	FOOD FOR PEACE[c]	SOCIAL PROGRESS TRUST FUND[d]	PEACE CORPS	TOTAL		
Mexico	$47.6	$295.0	$53.6	$16.8	$ 2.2	$413.0	$1.71	$1.87
Costa Rica	34.0	6.5	5.3	5.8	2.6	53.8	6.52	7.60
El Salvador	34.3	9.7	12.5	15.6	1.8	74.7	4.41	6.26
Guatemala	34.4	9.8	7.5	5.9	2.2	59.4	2.34	1.62
Honduras	28.6	0.4	3.0	5.4	8.7	39.6	3.02	3.22
Nicaragua	26.3	9.1	6.9	8.7	2.7	51.0	5.37	7.03
Panama	48.5	20.1	3.8	11.4	4.0	86.5	11.96	16.24
Dominican Rep.	162.9	12.4	44.5	4.7		228.5	10.75	13.81
Haiti	26.6	3.0	6.3			35.9	1.43	0.71

Argentina	74.8	155.4		9.5		239.7	1.85	1.60
Bolivia	127.0	0.1	44.6	6.9	6.6	185.2	8.53	5.79
Brazil	532.5	248.3	455.9	44.6	12.7	1,294.0	2.74	3.53
Chile	390.5	167.8	107.5	25.5	6.6	697.9	14.06	10.54
Colombia	262.5	85.2	73.2	32.4	12.6	465.9	4.51	4.91
Ecuador	63.5	2.6	22.7	17.3	6.0	112.1	3.78	4.47
Paraguay	22.4	0.3	18.5	2.9	—e	44.1	3.81	3.01
Peru	66.8	75.9	37.4	29.9	10.0	220.0	3.24	4.38
Uruguay	17.2	4.7	4.6	2.3	0.9	29.7	1.86	1.67
Venezuela	49.6	125.5	22.6	50.0	6.8	254.5	5.12	5.35
Regional	73.4		0.6	19.1	20.2	113.3		
ROCAPf	31.6			0.9		32.5		
TOTAL	$2,155.0	$1,231.8	$931.0	$315.6	$97.9	$4,731.3		

a SOURCE: Adapted from table furnished by the Office of Research and Analysis for American Republics, Department of State. Washington, D.C. Per capita disbursements computed for this publication using population figures for the appropriate years from the United Nations, Monthly Bulletin of Statistics, July, 1967 (1966 projections used for Nicaragua, Chile, and Colombia). Data are for calendar year. Note: Military assistance is not included.

b Includes long and short term loans.

c Excludes U.S. Uses, Title I of PL 480.

d SPTF technical assistance grants and administrative funds for various countries have not been computed by country and are included under "Regional." Funds to Central American Universities are included under ROCAP.

e Less than $50,000.

f Regional Office for Central America and Panama, established July 1, 1962, with headquarters in Guatemala City.

Table 18. INTERNATIONAL LIQUIDITY^a

Country	Form of Liquidity	Total Reserves (millions of U.S. dollars: end of year)					
		1948	1955	1960	1964	1965	1966
Mexico	Gold holdings	$42	$142	$136	$169	$158	$109
	IMF Reserve Position		22	45	45	54	86
	Foreign Exchange	36	276	256	369	322	362
	Total	78	440	438	583	534	557
Costa Rica	Gold holdings	2.06	2.05	2.11	2.11	2.11	2.11
	IMF Reserve Position	3.10	1.25	1.38			
	Foreign Exchange		17.49	9.96	16.52	17.73	15.00
	Total	5.16	20.80	13.44	18.62	19.84	17.11
El Salvador	Gold holdings	14.5	28.4	30.0	17.8	19.3	18.0
	IMF Reserve Position	.6	.6		5.0	5.0	
	Foreign Exchange	15.2	10.3	3.1	30.6	32.0	38.9
	Total	30.3	39.3	33.0	53.4	56.3	56.9
Guatemala	Gold holdings	27.2	27.2	23.6	22.9	21.7	20.0
	IMF Reserve Position	1.3	1.3	3.8	3.8		
	Foreign Exchange	18.8	27.1	26.7	32.8	46.1	40.7
	Total	47.4	55.6	54.0	59.5	67.8	60.7

		1	2	3	4	5	6
Honduras	Gold holdings	.11	.11	.11	.12	.11	.11
	IMF Reserve Position		.63				
	Foreign Exchange	2.34	19.59	13.20	19.58	23.28	27.27
	Total	2.45	20.32	13.31	19.69	23.39	27.38
Nicaragua	Gold holdings	2.94	2.76	.35	.33	.38	.89
	IMF Reserve Position		.50	2.81			
	Foreign Exchange	.18	11.09	8.57	38.61	56.94	57.23
	Total	3.12	14.35	11.73	38.94	57.32	58.12
Panama	Gold holdings						
	IMF Reserve Position		.1	.1	.1		
	Foreign Exchange		42.1	34.5	18.6		
	Total	43.8	42.2	34.6	18.7		
Cuba	Gold holdings		136	1			
	IMF Reserve Position		12				
	Foreign Exchange		357	143			
	Total		505	144			
Dominican Rep.	Gold holdings	4.0	12.1	10.4	3.0	3.0	3.0
	IMF Reserve Position	1.2	1.2				
	Foreign Exchange	10.8	24.2	15.3	38.3	47.8	40.6
	Total	16.1	37.4	25.7	41.3	50.8	43.6
Haiti	Gold holdings	2.6	2.1	.7	.8	.8	.1
	IMF Reserve Position		.5				
	Foreign Exchange	6.6	6.7	4.3	2.1	1.4	2.2
	Total	9.3	9.4	5.0	2.9	2.2	2.3

(table continued)

Table 18. INTERNATIONAL LIQUIDITY^a (*continued*)

Country	Form of Liquidity	Total Reserves (millions of U.S. dollars: end of year)					
		1948	1955	1960	1964	1965	1966
Argentina	Gold holdings	143	372	104	71	66	84
	Foreign Exchange	561	85	422	82	170	132
	Total	704	457	525	153	236	216
Bolivia	Gold holdings	22.7	.1	.9	4.7	6.7	7.3
	IMF Reserve Position				.2	1.2	6.9
	Foreign Exchange	6.2	7.1	5.8	17.5	28.5	27.0
	Total	28.9	7.2	6.7	22.4	36.4	41.2
Brazil	Gold holdings	317	323	287	91	63	45
	IMF Reserve Position						13
	Foreign Exchange	441	168	58	161	442	352
	Total	758	491	345	252	505	410
Chile	Gold holdings	43.4	44.4	45.1	43.2	43.9	45.2
	Foreign Exchange	9.8	41.6	66.0	45.5	93.6	125.9
	Total	53.2	86.0	111.0	88.7	137.5	171.1
Colombia	Gold holdings	51	86	78	58	35	26
	IMF Reserve Position	12		25			
	Foreign Exchange	33	50	76	66	95	97
	Total	96	136	178	124	130	123
Ecuador	Gold holdings	20.6	22.9	20.0	11.2	11.2	11.0
	IMF Reserve Position	1.2	1.2	3.8	3.0		
	Foreign Exchange	7.2	10.8	17.0	37.4	34.8	50.1
	Total	29.0	34.9	40.8	51.6	46.0	61.1

Paraguay	Gold holdings	.23	.19	.10	.08	.08	.08
	IMF Reserve Position	.88	.38		2.32	2.81	3.76
	Foreign Exchange		5.37	.37	3.07	7.38	6.87
	Total		5.94	.47	5.47	10.27	10.71
Peru	Gold holdings	20.0	34.9	42.4	67.4	67.2	64.7
	IMF Reserve Position	3.2	6.2	7.5	9.4	9.4	11.8
	Foreign Exchange	24.3	17.0	26.2	83.4	98.1	78.4
	Total	47.5	58.1	76.1	160.2	174.7	154.9
Uruguay	Gold holdings	164	216	180	171	155	146
	Foreign Exchange	77	20	7	19	43	50
	Total	241	235	187	190	198	196
Venezuela	Gold holdings	323	404	401	401	401	401
	IMF Reserve Position	4	4	38	38	38	63
	Foreign Exchange	63	126	170	393	404	313
	Total	390	534	609	831	843	776
United States	Gold holdings	24,400	21,750	17,800	15,470	14,060	13,230
	IMF Reserve Position	1,360	1,040	1,550	770	600	330
	Foreign Exchange				430	780	1,320
	Total	$25,760	$22,800	$19,360	$16,670	$15,450	$14,880

ᵃ SOURCE: Data for 1960, 1964, 1965, and 1966 from International Monetary Fund, *International Statistics*, July, 1967, country pages; data for 1948 and 1955 from *ibid.*, Supplement to 1966/67 issues, country pages; except: data for Panama and Cuba from United Nations, *Statistical Yearbook*, 1965, Table 187.

Note: Totals not always equal to sum of the parts, due to rounding. Figures quoted as in source.

Reading List

This reading list is designed to introduce the student to the material on Latin America, and to indicate where he will find more. Emphasis is placed on books in English, although some sources in Spanish and Portuguese are cited. Monographs and articles are not included.

An asterisk (*) indicates that a paperback edition of the book was in print as of October, 1966.

BIBLIOGRAPHIES AND REFERENCE GUIDES

American Universities Field Staff, *A Select Bibliography: Asia, Africa, Eastern Europe, Latin America* (New York, 1960; supplement, 1961). D. H. ANDREWS, comp., *Latin America. A Bibliography of Paperback Books* (Washington, 1964). Council on Foreign Relations, *Foreign Affairs Bibliography* (New York 1952/62). CHARLES GIBSON, *The Colonial Period in Latin American History* (Washington, 1948). *Handbook of Latin American Studies* (published annually, Cambridge and Gainesville, 1936–   ). J. P. HARRISON, *Guide to Materials on Latin America in the National Archives* (Washington, 1961). RONALD HILTON, ed., *Who's Who in Latin America*, 3rd ed. rev. (Stanford, 1950–51). R. A. HUMPHREYS, *Latin American History: A Guide to the Literature in English* (New York, 1958). T. J. O'LEARY, *Ethnographic Bibliography of South America* (New Haven, 1963). J. R. WISH, *Economic Development in Latin America: An Annotated Bibliography* (New York, 1965).

CURRENT PUBLICATIONS

American Universities Field Staff, *Reports Service* (New York). *Américas* (Pan American Union, Washington). *The Americas*, quarterly (Academy of American Franciscan History, Washington). *Business in Brief* (Chase Manhattan Bank, New York). *Economic Survey of Latin America*, annual (UN, ECLA, New York). *The Economist* (London). *Finance and Development* (IMF, Washington). *Foreign Affairs*, quarterly (Council on Foreign Affairs, New York). *Foreign Policy Bulletin* (Foreign Policy Association, New York). *Foreign Policy Reports* (Foreign Policy Association, New York). *The Hispanic American Historical Review*, quarterly (Duke University Press, Durham, N.C.). *Hispanic American Report* (Stanford, Calif., 1948–64). *Inter-American Economic Affairs*, quarterly (Washington). *International Financial News Survey* (IMF, Washington). *Journal of Inter-American Studies*, quarterly (Gainesville). *Review of the River Plate* (Buenos Aires). *The Situation in Argentina* (First National Bank of Boston, Buenos Aires). *Social Progress Trust Fund Annual Report* (Inter-American Development Bank, Washington). *Statistical Abstract of Latin America*, annual (University of California, Los Angeles). *World Business*, quarterly (Chase Manhattan National Bank, New York).

See also documents published by the United Nations, the International Monetary Fund, the Organization of American States and various United States government agencies; also, occasional studies of elections in various countries published by the Institute for the Comparative Study of Political Systems (Washington).

GENERAL STUDIES

R. J. ALEXANDER, *Today's Latin America* (New York, 1962). J. F. BANNON and P. M. DUNNE, *Latin America: An Historical Survey* (Milwaukee, 1947). R. N. BURR, ed., *Latin America's Nationalistic Revolutions* (Philadelphia, 1961). J. J. CONSIDINE, *New Horizons in Latin America* (New York, 1958). J. A. CROW, *The Epic of Latin America* (New York, 1946). W. Z. FOSTER, *Outline Political History of the Americas* (New York, 1951), a Communist recital. LEWIS HANKE, *Do the Americas Have a Common History? A Critique of the Bolton Thesis* (New York, 1964); and *South America* (Princeton, 1959). R. A. HUMPHREYS, *The Evolution of Modern Latin America* (New York, 1946). J. J. JOHNSON, ed., *Continuity and Change in Latin America* (Stanford, 1964). BENJAMIN KEEN, ed., *Readings in Latin-American Civilization, 1492 to the Present* (Boston, 1955). F. A. KIRKPATRICK, *Latin America: A Brief History* (New York, 1939). JOSEPH MAIER and R. W. WEATHERHEAD, eds., *The Politics of Change in Latin America* (New York, 1964). GERARD MASUR, *Nationalism in Latin America; Diversity and Unity* (New York, 1966). D. G. MUNRO, *The Latin American Republics: A History*, 2nd ed. (New York, 1950). PETER NEHEMKIS, *Latin America, Myth and Reality* (New York, 1964). CARLOS PEREYRA, *Historia de la América Española*, 8 vols. (Madrid, 1920–26). J. FRED RIPPY, *Historical Evolution of Hispanic America*, 3rd ed. (New York, 1945); and *Latin America: A Modern History* (Ann Arbor, 1958). W. S. ROBERTSON, *History of the Latin American Nations*, 3rd ed. (New York, 1943). W. L. SCHURZ, *Latin America: A Descriptive Survey*, rev. ed. (New York, 1963); and *This New World: The Civilization of Latin America* (New York, 1954). TAD SZULC, *Latin America* (New York, 1966); and *The Winds of Revolution: Latin America Today—and Tomorrow* (New York, 1963). FRANK TANNENBAUM, *Ten Keys to Latin America* (New York, 1962). J. J. TEPASKE and S. N. FISHER, eds., *Explosive Forces in Latin America* (Columbus, 1964). CLAUDIO VÉLIZ, ed., *Obstacles to Change in Latin America* (New York, 1965). A. P. WHITAKER, *Nationalism in Latin America, Past and Present* (Gainesville, 1962). A. CURTIS WILGUS, *South American Dictators During the First Century of Independence* (Washington, 1937).

GOVERNMENT, POLITICS, AND JURISPRUDENCE: J. L. BUSEY, *Latin American Political Institutions and Processes* (New York, 1964). H. L. CLAGETT, *The Administration of Justice in Latin America* (New York, 1952). H. E. DAVIS, ed., *Government and Politics in Latin America* (New York, 1958). R. H. FITZGIBBON, ed., *The Constitutions of the Americas* (Chicago, 1948). R. A. GÓMEZ, *Government and Politics in Latin America* (New York, 1960). W. C. GORDON, *The Political Economy of Latin America* (New York, 1965). H. M. HAMILL, JR., ed., *Dictatorship in Spanish America* (New York, 1965). J. J. JOHNSON, *Political Change in Latin America: The Emergence of the Middle Sectors* (Stanford, 1958). J. D. MARTZ, ed., *The Dynamics of Change in Latin American Politics* (Englewood Cliffs, N.J., 1965). M. C. NEEDLER, *Latin American Politics in Perspective* (Princeton, 1963); and *Political Systems of Latin America* (Princeton, 1964). W. W. PIERSON and F. G. GIL, *Governments of Latin*

America (New York, 1957). TAD SZULC, *Twilight of the Tyrants* (New York, 1959).

SOCIAL AND ECONOMIC: R. N. ADAMS and others, *Social Change in Latin America Today: Its Implication for United States Policy* (New York, 1960). H. F. BAIN and T. T. REED, *Ores and Industry in Latin America* (New York, 1934). F. C. BENHAM and H. A. HOLLEY, *A Short Introduction to the Economy of Latin America* (New York, 1960). M. D. BERNSTEIN, ed., *Foreign Investments in Latin America: Cases and Attitudes* (New York, 1966). J. P. COLE, *Latin American Economic and Social Survey* (Washington, 1965). DANIEL COSÍO VILLEGAS, *American Extremes*, tr. by Américo Paredes (Austin, 1964). CELSO FURTADO, *Development and Underdevelopment*, tr. by R. W. de Aguiar and E. C. Drysdale (Berkeley, 1964). WENDELL GORDON, *The Economy of Latin America* (New York, 1950). S. G. HANSON, *Economic Development in Latin America: An Introduction to the Economic Problems of Latin America* (Washington, 1951). SEYMOUR HARRIS, ed., *Economic Problems of Latin America* (New York, 1944). P. M. HAUSER, ed., *Urbanization in Latin America* (New York, 1961). D. B. HEATH and R. N. ADAMS, eds., *Contemporary Cultures and Societies of Latin America: A Reader in the Social Anthropology of Middle and South America and the Caribbean* (New York, 1965). A. O. HIRSCHMAN, *Journeys Toward Progress: Studies of Economic Policy-Making in Latin America* (New York, 1963); and A. O. HIRSCHMAN, ed., *Latin American Issues: Essays and Comments* (New York, 1961). STACY MAY and G. PLAZA LASSO, *The United Fruit Company in Latin America* (Washington, 1958). D. M. PHELPS, *Migration of Industry to South America* (New York, 1936). F. B. PIKE, ed., *Freedom and Reform in Latin America* (Notre Dame, 1959). J. P. POWELSON, *Latin America: Today's Economic and Social Revolution* (New York, 1964). J. FRED RIPPY, *British Investments in Latin America: A Case Study in the Operations of Private Enterprise in Retarded Regions* (Minneapolis, 1959); and *Latin America and the Industrial Age,* 2nd ed. (New York, 1947). K. H. SILVERT, *The Conflict Society: Reaction and Revolution in Latin America*, rev. ed. (New York, 1966); and K. H. SILVERT, ed., *Expectant Peoples: Nationalism and Development* (New York, 1963); see chapters on Argentina, Brazil, and Bolivia. T. LYNN SMITH, ed., *Agrarian Reform in Latin America* (New York, 1965); and *Current Social Trends and Problems in Latin America* (Gainesville, 1951). United Nations, *The Economic Development of Latin America in the Post-War Period* (New York, 1964). V. L. URQUIDI, *The Challenge of Development in Latin America*, tr. by M. M. Urquidi (New York, 1964); and *Free Trade and Economic Integration in Latin America: The Evolution of a Common Market Policy*, tr. by M. M. Urquidi (Berkeley, 1962). RAYMOND VERNON, ed., *How Latin America Views the U.S. Investor* (New York, 1966). CHARLES WAGLEY and MARVIN HARRIS, *Minorities in the New World* (New York, 1958). GEORGE WYTHE, *Industry in Latin America,* 2nd ed. (New York, 1949); and *Outline of Latin American Economic Development* (New York, 1946).

LABOR: VÍCTOR ALBA, *Historia del movimiento obrero en América Latina* (Mexico City, 1964). R. J. ALEXANDER, *Labour Movements in Latin America* (London, 1947); and *Labor Relations in Argentina, Brazil and Chile* (New York, 1962). B. G. BURNETT and M. P. TRONCOSO, *The Rise of the Latin American Labor Movement* (New York, 1960). WALTER GALENSON, *Labor in Developing Economies* (Berkeley, 1962). G. C. LODGE, *Spearheads of Democracy: Labor in the Developing Countries* (New York, 1962). SINCLAIR SNOW, *The Pan-American Federation of Labor* (Durham, N.C., 1964).

THE MILITARY: W. F. BARBER and C. N. RONNING, *Internal Security and Military Power: Counter Insurgency and Civic Action in Latin America* (Columbus, 1966). S. E. FINER, *The Man on Horseback: The Role of the Military in Politics* (New York, 1962). J. J. JOHNSON, *The Military and Society in Latin America* (Stanford, 1964); and J. J. JOHNSON, ed., *The Role of the Military in Underdeveloped Countries* (Princeton, 1962). EDWIN LIEUWEN, *Generals vs. Presidents: Neomilitarism in Latin America* (New York, 1964); and *Arms and Politics in Latin America* (New York, 1960).

CULTURAL FORCES: ENRIQUE ANDERSON-IMBERT, *Spanish-American Literature: A History*, tr. by J. V. Falconieri (Detroit, 1963). MARGOT ARCE DE VÁZQUEZ, *Gabriela Mistral: The Poet and Her Work*, tr. by H. M. Anderson (New York, 1964). GERMÁN ARCINIEGAS, *Latin America: A Cultural History*, tr. from the Spanish by Joan MacLean (New York, 1966). H. R. BENJAMIN, *Higher Education in the American Republics* (New York, 1965). STEPHEN CLISSOLD, *Latin America: A Cultural Outline* (New York, 1965). W. R. CRAWFORD, ed., *A Century of Latin American Thought*, rev. ed. (Cambridge, Mass., 1961). PEDRO HENRÍQUEZ UREÑA, *A Concise History of Latin American Culture* (New York, 1965); and *Literary Currents in Hispanic America* (Cambridge, Mass., 1945). ARTURO TORRES-RIOSECO, ed., *Antología de la literatura hispanoamericana; selección, comentarios, notas y glosario*, 2nd ed. (New York, 1961); and *The Epic of Latin American Literature*, rev. ed. (New York, 1946). LEOPOLDO ZEA, *The Latin American Mind*, tr. from the Spanish by J. H. Abbott and Lowell Dunham (Norman, 1963).

THE CHURCH: W. J. COLEMAN, *Latin-American Catholicism: A Self-Evaluation* (Maryknoll, 1958). W. V. D'ANTONIO and F. B. PIKE, eds., *Religion, Revolution and Reform: New Forces for Change in Latin America* (New York, 1964). FRANÇOIS HOUTART and EMILE PIN, *The Church and the Latin American Revolution* (New York, 1965). J. L. MECHAM, *Church and State in Latin America: A History of Politico-Ecclesiastical Relations*, rev. ed. (Chapel Hill, N.C., 1966). MAGNUS MÖRNER, ed., *The Expulsion of the Jesuits from Latin America* (New York, 1965). RICHARD PATTEE, *Catholicism in Latin America* (Washington, 1945). F. B. PIKE, ed., *The Conflict Between Church and State in Latin America* (New York, 1964).

COMMUNISM: R. J. ALEXANDER, *Communism in Latin America* (New Brunswick, 1957). R. L. ALLEN, *Soviet Influence in Latin America, the Role of Economic Relations* (Washington, 1959). R. E. POPPINO, *International Communism in Latin America: A History of the Movement (1917–1963)* (New York, 1964).

GENERAL INTERPRETATIONS OF LATIN AMERICAN LIFE: GERMÁN ARCINIEGAS, *The State of Latin America* (New York, 1952); and GERMÁN ARCINIEGAS, ed., *The Green Continent: A Comprehensive View of Latin America by Its Leading Writers*, tr. by Harriet de Onís et al. (New York, 1944). JAMES BRYCE, *South America: Observations and Impressions*, new ed. (New York, 1917). GEORGES CLEMENCEAU, *South America Today* (New York, 1911). FRANCISCO GARCÍA CALDERÓN, *Latin America, Its Rise and Progress*, tr. by B. Miall (London, 1913). FRANK MACSHANE, ed., *Impressions of Latin America: Five Centuries of Travel and Adventure by English and North American Writers* (New York, 1963). LUIS QUINTANILLA, *A Latin American Speaks* (New York, 1943). ALFONSO REYES, *The Position of America and Other Essays*, tr. by Harriet de Onís (New York, 1950).

PART I *Foregrounds and Backgrounds*

GEOGRAPHY

G. J. BUTLAND, *Latin America: A Regional Geography* (New York, 1960). PRESTON E. JAMES, *Introduction to Latin America: The Geographic Background of Economic and Political Problems* (New York, 1964); and *Latin America*, 3rd ed. (New York, 1959). R. S. PLATT, *Latin America: Countrysides and United Regions* (New York, 1943). R. H. WHITBECK and F. E. WILLIAMS, *The Economic Geography of South America*, 3rd ed. (New York, 1940). A. CURTIS WILGUS, *Latin America in Maps, Historic, Economic, Geographic* (New York, 1943).

THE INDIAN BACKGROUND

A. L. KROEBER, ed., *Anthropology Today* (Chicago, 1953). GEORGE KUBLER, *The Art and Architecture of Ancient America: The Mexican, Maya, and Andean Peoples* (Baltimore, 1962). B. J. MEGGERS and CLIFFORD EVANS, eds., *Aboriginal Cultural Development in Latin America: An Interpretive Review* (Washington, 1963). SOL TAX, ed., *Acculturation in the Americas* (Chicago, 1942). H. M. WORMINGTON, *Ancient Man in North America*, 4th ed. (Denver, 1957).

MIDDLE AMERICA: IGNACIO BERNAL, **Mexico Before Cortez: Art, History, Legend* (New York, 1963). ALFONSO CASO, *The Aztecs, People of the Sun*, tr. by Lowell Dunham, ill. by Miguel Covarrubias (Norman, 1958). M. D. COE, **Mexico* (New York, 1962). MIGUEL COVARRUBIAS, *Indian Art of Mexico and Central America* (New York, 1957). FRAY DIEGO DURÁN, *The Aztecs: History of the Indies of New Spain,* tr. and ed. by Doris Heyden (New York, 1964). *Handbook of Middle American Indians,* ed. by Robert Wauchope (Austin, 1965); this multiple volume work is the chief reference on this subject. DIEGO DE LANDA, *Landa's Relación de las cosas de Yucatán,* ed. by A. M. Tozzer (Cambridge, 1941). S. G. MORLEY, *The Ancient Maya,* rev. by G. W. Brainerd (Stanford, 1956). W. H. PRESCOTT, **The Conquest of Mexico* (various eds., first pub. in New York, 1843). H. J. SPINDEN, *Maya Art and Civilization* (Indian Hills, 1957). J. L. STEPHENS, **Incidents of Travel in Central America, Chiapas and Yucatán* (New York, 1841, and various other eds.). SOL TAX, ed., *Heritage of Conquest: The Ethnology of Middle America* (Glencoe, Ill., 1952). J. ERIC THOMPSON, *The Rise and Fall of Maya Civilization* (Norman, 1956). G. C. VAILLANT, **The Aztecs of Mexico,* rev. by S. B. Vaillant (New York, 1962). E. R. WOLF, **Sons of the Shaking Earth* (Chicago, 1959), the best general guide to Meso-American anthropology.

SOUTH AMERICA: B. C. BRUNDAGE, *Empire of the Inca,* foreword by A. J. Toynbee (Norman, 1963). G. H. S. BUSHNELL, **Peru,* rev. ed. (London, 1963). PEDRO DE CIEZA DE LEÓN, *The Incas of Pedro de Cieza de León,* ed. by V. W. Von Hagen and tr. by Harriet de Onís (Norman, 1959). GARCILASO DE LA VEGA, *The Incas: Royal Commentaries of the Inca Garcilaso de la Vega, 1539–1616,* tr. by Maria Jolas from the French ed. of Alain Gheerbrant (New York, 1961). *Handbook of South American Indians,* ed. by J. H. Steward, 6 vols. (Washington, 1946–50). J. ALDEN MASON, **The Ancient Civilizations of Peru* (Baltimore, 1957). P. A. MEANS, *Ancient Civilizations of the Andes* (New York, 1931). S. F. MOORE, *Power and Property in Inca Peru* (New York, 1958). W.

H. Prescott, *The Conquest of Peru* (various eds., first pub. in New York, 1847).

THE SPANISH BACKGROUND

Rafael Altamira y Crevea, *Historia de España y de la civilización española*, 6 vols. (Barcelona, 1900–1930); and *History of Spain*, tr. by Muna Lee (New York, 1949). W. C. Atkinson, *A History of Spain and Portugal* (Baltimore, 1960). Miguel Cervantes Saavedra, *Don Quixote de la Mancha*, tr. by Samuel Putnam (New York, 1950). John H. Elliott, *Imperial Spain, 1469–1716* (New York, 1964). Havelock Ellis, *The Soul of Spain* (Boston, 1926). M. A. S. Hume, *The Spanish People: Their Origin, Growth and Influence* (New York, 1901). H. V. Livermore, *A History of Spain* (New York, 1958). John Lynch, *Spain Under the Hapsburgs, Vol. I: Empire and Absolutism, 1516–1598* (New York, 1964). Salvador de Madariaga, *Englishmen, Frenchmen, and Spaniards: An Essay in Comparative Psychology* (London, 1931); and *The Rise of the Spanish American Empire* (New York, 1947). J. H. Mariejol, *The Spain of Ferdinand and Isabella*, tr. and ed. by Benjamin Keen (New Brunswick, 1961). Ramón Menéndez Pidal, *The Spaniards in Their History*, tr. by Walter Starkie (London, 1951). R. B. Merriman, *The Rise of the Spanish Empire in the Old World and the New*, 4 vols. (New York, 1918–34). Miguel de Unamuno, *The Life of Don Quixote and Sancho*, tr. by H. P. Earle (New York, 1927).

THE PORTUGUESE BACKGROUND

W. C. Atkinson, *A History of Spain and Portugal* (Baltimore, 1960). W. J. Barnes, *Portugal, Gateway to Greatness* (London, 1950). H. V. Livermore, *Portugal and Brazil: An Introduction* (Oxford, 1953). J. P. de Oliveira Martins, *A History of Iberian Civilization*, tr. by A. F. G. Bell (London, 1930). C. E. Nowell, *A History of Portugal* (New York, 1952).

THE AFRICAN BACKGROUND

Henriette Alimen, *Préhistoire de l'Afrique* (Paris, 1955). S. M. Cole, *Prehistory of East Africa* (New York, 1963). Elizabeth Donnan, *Documents Illustrative of the Slave Trade to America*, 4 vols. (Washington, 1930); see especially Vols. I and II. Gilberto Freyre, *The Masters and the Slaves*, tr. by Samuel Putnam (New York, 1946). J. H. Greenberg, *The Languages of Africa* (Bloomington, 1963). M. J. Herskovits, *Dahomey: An Ancient West African Kingdom*, 2 vols. (New York, 1938); and *The Myth of the Negro Past* (New York, 1941). A. L. Kroeber, *Anthropology*, new rev. ed. (New York, 1958). J. G. Leyburn, *The Haitian People* (New Haven, 1941). D. P. Mannix and Malcolm Cowley, *Black Cargoes: A History of the Atlantic Slave Trade, 1518–1865* (New York, 1962). G. P. Murdock, *Africa: Its Peoples and Their Culture History* (New York, 1959). Fernando Ortiz, *Hampa afro-cubana—los negros esclavos* (Havana, 1916). Donald Pierson, *Negroes in Brazil* (Chicago, 1942). Arthur Ramos, *The Negroes in Brazil*, tr. by Richard Pattee (Washington, 1939). J. A. Saco, *Historia de la esclavitud de la raza africana en el nuevo mundo y en especial en los países americo-hispanos*, 4 vols. (Paris, 1875–79). Frank Tannenbaum, *Slave and Citizen: The Negro in the Americas* (New York, 1947). C. H. Wesley, ed.,

The Negro in the Americas (Washington, 1940). DONALD WIEDNER, **A History of Africa South of the Sahara* (New York, 1962).

PERIODICALS: *American Anthropologist. International Africa Institute, Bibliography Series. Hispanic American Historical Review. Journal of Negro History. Journal of African History. Sociological and Social Review.*

PART II *The Iberians in the New World*

DISCOVERY AND CONQUEST

J. F. BANNON, **The Spanish Conquistadores: Men or Devils?* (New York, 1960). E. G. BOURNE, **Spain in America, 1450–1580* (New York, 1904). R. B. CUNNINGHAME GRAHAM, *The Conquest of the River Plate* (New York, 1924). BERNAL DÍAZ DEL CASTILLO, **True History of the Conquest of New Spain* (New York, 1958, and various other eds.), an eyewitness account. H. E. DRIVER, **The Americas on the Eve of Discovery* (Englewood Cliffs, N.J., 1964). AUGUSTÍN EDWARDS, *Peoples of Old* (London, 1929). PATRICIA DE FUENTES, ed. and tr., *The Conquistadors: First-Person Accounts of the Conquest of Mexico* (New York, 1963). P. A. MEANS, *The Fall of the Inca Empire and the Spanish Rule in Peru, 1530–1780* (New York, 1932). BERNARD MOSES, *The Establishment of Spanish Rule in America* (New York, 1898). W. H. PRESCOTT, **The Conquest of Peru* (various eds., first pub. in New York, 1847); and, **The Conquest of Mexico* (various eds., first pub. in New York, 1843). S. A. ZAVALA, *The Political Philosophy of the Conquest of America* (Mexico, D.F., 1953).

BIOGRAPHY AND LETTERS: GERMÁN ARCINIEGAS, *Amerigo and the New World: The Life and Times of Amerigo Vespucci,* tr. by Harriet de Onís (New York, 1955). MORRIS BISHOP, *The Odyssey of Cabeza de Vaca* (New York, 1933). ALVAR NÚÑEZ CABEZA DE VACA, *Cabeza de Vaca's Adventures in the Unknown Interior of America,* ed. by Cyclone Covey (New York, 1961), a sixteenth-century account. STEPHEN CLISSOLD, *Conquistador: The Life of Don Pedro Sarmiento de Gamboa* (London, 1954). CHRISTOPHER COLUMBUS, **Four Voyages to the New World. Letters and Selected Documents,* bilingual edition (New York, 1961). HERNANDO CORTÉS, **Five Letters, 1519–1526,* tr. by J. B. Morris (London, 1928). R. B. CUNNINGHAME GRAHAM, *The Conquest of New Granada, Being the Life of Gonzalo Jiménez de Quesada* (London, 1922); and *Pedro de Valdivia, Conqueror of Chile* (London, 1926). BENJAMIN KEEN, tr. and ed., *Life of the Admiral Christopher Columbus by His Son Ferdinand* (New Brunswick, 1959). J. E. KELLY, *Pedro de Alvarado, Conquistador* (Princeton, 1932). F. A. KIRKPATRICK, **The Spanish Conquistadores* (New York, 1934). FRANCISCO LÓPEZ DE GÓMARA, **Cortés: The Life of the Conqueror of Mexico by His Secretary,* tr. and ed. by L. B. Simpson (Berkeley, 1964). S. E. MORISON, *Admiral of the Ocean Sea,* 2 vols. (Boston, 1942), a biography of Columbus. C. M. PARR, *Ferdinand Magellan, Circumnavigator* (New York, 1964). F. J. POHL, *Amerigo Vespucci, Pilot Major* (New York, 1944). KATHLEEN ROMOLI, *Balboa of Darién* (New York, 1953).

Three societies have concentrated on translating early chronicles, histories and narratives—the Hakluyt Society (founded in London in 1846 and named after the sixteenth-century geographer), the Cortés Society (New York), and the Quivira Society (Los Angeles and Albuquerque). Their publications are useful to the student of this period.

THE SPANISH COLONIAL PERIOD

E. G. BOURNE, *Spain in America, 1450–1580* (New York, 1904). S. F. COOK and L. B. SIMPSON, *The Population of Central Mexico in the Sixteenth Century* (Berkeley, 1948). B. W. DIFFIE, *Latin American Civilization: Colonial Period* (Harrisburg, 1945). THOMAS GAGE, *Travels in the New World* (Norman, 1958), a seventeenth-century account. CHARLES GIBSON, *The Aztecs Under Spanish Rule: A History of the Indians of the Valley of Mexico* (Stanford, 1964); *Spain in America* (New York, 1966); and *Tlaxcala in the Sixteenth Century* (New Haven, 1952). LEWIS HANKE, *The Spanish Struggle for Justice in the Conquest of America* (Philadelphia, 1949). C. H. HARING, *The Spanish Empire in America* (New York, 1947). ALEXANDER VON HUMBOLDT, *Political Essay on the Kingdom of New Spain*, tr. and ed. by John Black, 4 vols. (London, 1811–22). CECIL JANE, *Liberty and Despotism in Spanish America* (Oxford, 1929). SALVADOR DE MADARIAGA, *The Fall of the Spanish American Empire* (New York, 1948); and *The Rise of the Spanish American Empire* (New York, 1947). J. H. PARRY, *The Establishment of the European Hegemony: 1415–1715* (New York, 1961); and *The Spanish Seaborne Empire* (New York, 1966). ANTONIO VÁZQUEZ DE ESPINOSA, *Compendium and Description of the West Indies*, tr. by C. U. Clark (Washington, 1942), an early seventeenth-century eyewitness account. S. A. ZAVALA, *The Defense of Human Rights in Latin America, Sixteenth to Eighteenth Centuries* (Paris, 1964).

GOVERNMENT: C. H. CUNNINGHAM, *The Audiencia in the Spanish Colonies as Illustrated by the Audiencia of Manila, 1583–1800* (Berkeley, 1919). L. E. FISHER, *The Intendant System in the Spanish Colonies* (Berkeley, 1929); and *Viceregal Administration in the Spanish Colonies* (Berkeley, 1926). J. P. MOORE, *The Cabildo in Peru Under the Hapsburgs: A Study in the Origins and Powers of the Town Council in the Viceroyalty of Peru, 1530–1700* (Durham, N.C., 1954).

ECONOMIC AND SOCIAL: W. W. BORAH, *New Spain's Century of Depression* (Berkeley, 1951); and *Early Colonial Trade and Navigation Between Mexico and Peru* (Berkeley, 1954). FRANÇOIS CHEVALIER, *Land and Society in Colonial Mexico; The Great Hacienda*, tr. by Alvin Eustis and ed. by L. B. Simpson (Berkeley, 1963). E. J. HAMILTON, *American Treasure and the Price Revolution in Spain, 1501–1650* (Cambridge, 1934); and *American Treasure and the Rise of Capitalism, 1500–1700* (London, 1929). C. H. HARING, *Trade and Navigation Between Spain and the Indies in the Time of the Hapsburgs* (Cambridge, 1918). R. D. HUSSEY, *The Caracas Company, 1728–1784* (Cambridge, 1934). JORGE JUAN and ANTONIO DE ULLOA, *A Voyage to South America*, tr. from the Spanish by John Adams, 2 vols. (London, 1806); the paperback is an abridgement of the 4th ed. C. G. MOTTEN, *Mexican Silver and the Enlightenment* (Philadelphia, 1950). P. W. POWELL, *Soldiers, Indians, and Silver: The Northward Advance of New Spain, 1550–1560* (Berkeley, 1952). W. L. SCHURZ, *The Manila Galleon* (New York, 1939). L. B. SIMPSON, *The Encomienda in New Spain: Forced Native Labor in the Spanish Colonies, 1492–1550*, rev. and enl. ed. (Berkeley, 1950); and *Exploitation of Land in Central Mexico in the Sixteenth Century* (Berkeley, 1952). A. P. WHITAKER, *The Huancavélica Mercury Mine* (Cambridge, 1941). ALONSO DE ZURITA, *Life and Labor in Ancient Mexico: The Brief and Summary Relations of the Lords of New Spain*, tr. and ed. by Benjamin Keen (New Brunswick, 1964).

CULTURAL: P. J. BARTH, *Franciscan Education and the Social Order in Spanish North America (1502–1821)* (Chicago, 1945). J. T. LANNING, *Aca-*

demic Culture in the Spanish Colonies (New York, 1940). I. A. LEONARD, *Baroque Times in Old Mexico (Ann Arbor, 1959); and Books of the Brave (Cambridge, 1949). BERNARD MOSES, Spanish Colonial Literature in South America (New York, 1922). MARIANO PICÓN-SALAS, *A Cultural History of Hispanic America: From Conquest to Independence, tr. by I. A. Leonard (Berkeley, 1962). A. P. WHITAKER, ed., *Latin America and the Enlightenment, essays by A. P. Whitaker and others (New York, 1942).

THE CHURCH: C. S. BRADEN, Religious Aspects of the Conquest of Mexico (Durham, N.C., 1930). R. B. CUNNINGHAME GRAHAM, A Vanished Arcadia: Being Some Account of the Jesuits in Paraguay, 1607–1767, rev. ed. (New York, 1924). J. V. JACOBSEN, Educational Foundations of the Jesuits in Six-teenth-Century New Spain (Berkeley, 1938). MAGNUS MÖRNER, The Political and Economic Activities of the Jesuits in the La Plata Region: The Hapsburg Era, tr. by Albert Read (Stockholm, 1953).

BIOGRAPHY: A. S. AITON, Antonio de Mendoza, First Viceroy of New Spain (Durham, N.C., 1927). H. E. BOLTON, *Coronado, Knight of Pueblos and Plains (Albuquerque, 1949); and Rim of Christendom: A Biography of Eusebio Francisco Kino, Pacific Coast Pioneer (New York, 1936). HELMUT DE TERRA, Humboldt: The Life and Times of Alexander von Humboldt, 1769–1859 (New York, 1955). LEWIS HANKE, Bartolomé de las Casas: An Interpretation of His Life and Writings (The Hague, 1951); and Bartolomé de las Casas: Bookman, Scholar and Propagandist (Philadelphia, 1949). I. A. LEONARD, Don Carlos de Sigüenza y Góngora (Berkeley, 1929). H. I. PRIESTLEY, José de Gálvez, Visitor General of New Spain, 1765–1771 (Berkeley, 1916). AGNES REPPLIER, *Junípero Serra (Garden City, 1933). A. F. ZIMMERMAN, Francisco de Toledo: Fifth Viceroy of Peru, 1569–1581 (Caldwell, 1938).

THE PORTUGUESE IN THE NEW WORLD

C. R. BOXER, The Dutch in Brazil, 1624–1654 (Oxford, 1957). J. P. CALÓGERAS, A History of Brazil, tr. and ed. by P. A. Martin (Chapel Hill, N.C., 1939). A. N. MARCHANT, From Barter to Slavery: The Economic Rela-tions of Portuguese and Indians in the Settlements of Brazil, 1500–1580 (Balti-more, 1942). ROBERT SOUTHEY, History of Brazil, 3 vols. (London, 1817–22). F. A. VARNHAGEN, História geral do Brasil, 3rd ed., 5 vols. (São Paulo, 1927–30).

PART III   *The New World Breaks with the Old*

V. A. BELAÚNDE, Bolívar and the Political Thought of the Span-ish American Revolution (Baltimore, 1938). S. F. BEMIS, The Latin American Policy of the United States (New York, 1943). L. E. FISHER, The Background of the Revolution for Mexican Independence (Boston, 1934). C. C. GRIFFIN, The United States and the Disruption of the Spanish Empire, 1810–1822 (New York, 1937). ALFRED HASBROUCK, Foreign Legionaries in the Liberation of Spanish South America (New York, 1928). ALEXANDER VON HUMBOLDT, Personal Narrative of Travels to the Equinoctial Regions of the New Continent During the Years 1799–1804, tr. by H. M. Williams, 7 vols. (London, 1814–29). R. A. HUMPHREYS, ed., British Consular Reports on the Trade and Politics of Latin America, 1824–1826 (London, 1940). R. A.

HUMPHREYS and JOHN LYNCH, eds., *The Origins of the Latin American Revolution, 1808–1826 (New York, 1965). W. R. MANNING, Diplomatic Correspondence of the United States Concerning the Independence of the Latin American Nations, 3 vols. (New York, 1925). BARTOLOMÉ MITRE, The Emancipation of South America (London, 1893). BERNARD MOSES, The Intellectual Background of the Revolution in South America, 1810–1824 (New York, 1926); South America on the Eve of Independence (New York, 1908); and Spain's Declining Power in South America, 1730–1806 (Berkeley, 1919). J. FRED RIPPY, Rivalry of the United States and Great Britain over Latin America (1808–1830) (Baltimore, 1929). W. S. ROBERTSON, France and Latin American Independence (Baltimore, 1939).

BIOGRAPHIES: HILDEGARDE ANGELL, Simón Bolívar, South American Liberator (New York, 1930). SERGIO BAGÚ, Mariano Moreno: Pasión y vida del hombre de Mayo (Buenos Aires, 1939). THOMAS COCHRANE, Narrative of Services in the Liberation of Chile, Peru, and Brazil, 2 vols. (London, 1859). R. B. CUNNINGHAME GRAHAM, José Antonio Páez (London, 1929). BENJAMIN KEEN, David Curtis DeForest and the Revolution of Buenos Aires (New Haven, 1947). VICENTE LECUNA, comp., Selected Writings of Bolívar, tr. by Lewis Bertrand, 2 vols. (New York, 1951). SALVADOR DE MADARIAGA, Bolívar (New York, 1952). GERHARD MASUR, Simón Bolívar (Albuquerque, 1948). BARTOLOMÉ MITRE, Historia de San Martín y de la emancipación sudamericana, tr. by William Pilling, 2nd ed. (Buenos Aires, 1890). J. FRED RIPPY, Joel R. Poinsett, Versatile American (Durham, N.C., 1935). W. S. ROBERTSON, Iturbide of Mexico (Durham, N.C., 1952); The Life of Miranda, 2 vols. (Chapel Hill, N.C., 1929); and The Rise of the Spanish American Republics as Told in the Lives of Their Liberators (New York, 1918). RICARDO ROJAS, San Martín: Knight of the Andes, tr. by H. Brickell and C. Videla (New York, 1945). G. A. SHERWELL, Antonio José de Sucre (Washington, 1924).

PART IV   Mexico

LUCAS ALAMÁN, Historia de Méjico desde los primeros movimientos que preparan su independencia en el año 1808 hasta la época presente, 5 vols. (Mexico, D.F., 1849–52). H. H. BANCROFT, History of Mexico, 6 vols. (San Francisco, 1883–88). F. R. BRANDENBERG, The Making of Modern Mexico (Englewood Cliffs, N.J., 1964). ANITA BRENNER, Idols Behind Altars (New York, 1929); and, with G. R. LEIGHTON, The Wind That Swept Mexico (New York, 1943). W. H. CALLCOTT, Church and State in Mexico, 1822–1857 (Durham, N.C., 1926); and Liberalism in Mexico, 1857–1929 (Stanford, 1931). H. F. CLINE, *Mexico: Revolution to Evolution, 1940–1960 (New York, 1963); and *The United States and Mexico, rev. ed. (Cambridge, 1963). DANIEL COSÍO VILLEGAS, Changes in Latin America; The Mexican and Cuban Revolutions (Lincoln, 1961); and Historia moderna de México, ? vols. (Mexico, D.F., 1955–   ). MIGUEL COVARRUBIAS, Mexico South: The Isthmus of Tehuantepec (New York, 1946). MARIANO CUEVAS, S.J., Historia de la nación mexicana (Mexico, D.F., 1940). C. C. CUMBERLAND, Mexican Revolution, Genesis Under Madero (Austin, 1952). J. W. F. DULLES, Yesterday in Mexico: A Chronicle of the Revolution, 1919–1936 (Austin, 1961). W. P. GLADE, JR., and C. W. ANDERSON, The Political Economy of Mexico (Madison, 1963). GRAHAM GREENE, *Another Mexico (New York, 1939). ERNEST GRUENING, Mexico and Its Heritage (New York, 1940). LEWIS HANKE, *Mexico and the

Caribbean (Princeton, 1959). DANIEL JAMES, *Mexico and the Americans* (New York, 1963). BRANTZ MAYER, *Mexico: Aztec, Spanish and Republican* (Hartford, 1851). H. B. PARKES, *A History of Mexico,* 3rd ed. rev. and enl. (New York, 1960). OCTAVIO PAZ, **Labyrinth of Solitude: Life and Thought in Mexico* (New York, 1962). H. I. PRIESTLEY, *The Mexican Nation: A History* (New York, 1930). R. E. QUIRK, **The Mexican Revolution, 1914–1915: The Convention of Aguascalientes* (Bloomington, 1960). SAMUEL RAMOS, *Profile of Man and Culture in Mexico,* tr. by Peter G. Earle (New York, 1963). ROBERT RICARD, *The Spiritual Conquest of Mexico,* tr. by L. B. Simpson (Berkeley, 1966). S. R. ROSS, ed., **Is the Mexican Revolution Dead?* (New York, 1966). R. E. RUIZ, ed., **The Mexican War—Was it Manifest Destiny?* (New York, 1963). L. B. SIMPSON, **Many Mexicos,* 4th ed. rev. (Berkeley, 1966); the paperback is the 3rd ed. rev. and enl., 1952. O. A. SINGLETARY, **The Mexican War* (Chicago, 1960). FRANK TANNENBAUM, *Peace by Revolution; An Interpretation of Mexico* (New York, 1933). A. P. TISCHENDORF, *Great Britain and Mexico in the Era of Porfirio Díaz* (Durham, N.C., 1961). B. W. TUCHMAN, **The Zimmerman Telegram* (New York, 1958). JOSÉ VASCONCELOS, *Breve historia de México,* 4th ed. (Mexico, 1938).

SOCIAL AND ECONOMIC: TOM GILL, *Land Hunger in Mexico* (Washington, 1951). C. M. LESLIE, *Now We Are Civilized: A Study of the World View of the Zapotec Indians of Mitla, Oaxaca* (Detroit, 1960). OSCAR LEWIS, **The Children of Sánchez: Autobiography of a Mexican Family* (New York, 1961); **Five Families: Mexican Case Studies in the Culture of Poverty* (New York, 1959); **Life in a Mexican Village: Tepoztlán Restudied* (Urbana, 1951); *Pedro Martínez: A Mexican Peasant and His Family* (New York, 1964); and **Tepoztlán: Village in Mexico* (New York, 1960). G. M. MCBRIDE, *The Land Systems of Mexico* (New York, 1923). SANFORD MOSK, *Industrial Revolution in Mexico* (Berkeley, 1950). M. G. PARRA, *La industrialización de México* (Mexico City, 1954). ROBERT REDFIELD and ALFONSO VILLA ROJAS, **Cham Kom: A Maya Village* (Washington, 1934); the paperback is an abridgment. ROBERT REDFIELD, *The Folk Culture of Yucatán* (Chicago, 1941); *Tepoztlán: A Mexican Village* (Chicago, 1930); and **A Village that Chose Progress: Cham Kom Revisited* (Chicago, 1950). R. E. RUIZ, *Mexico: The Challenge of Poverty and Illiteracy* (San Marino, 1963). CLARENCE SENIOR, *Land Reform and Democracy* (Gainesville, 1958). JUSTO SIERRA, ed., *México: su evolución social,* 3 vols. (Mexico, D.F., 1900–1902). E. N. SIMPSON, *The Ejido: Mexico's Way Out* (Chapel Hill, N.C., 1937). FRANK TANNENBAUM, *Mexico: The Struggle for Peace and Bread* (New York, 1950); and *The Mexican Agrarian Revolution* (New York, 1929). RAYMOND VERNON, *The Dilemma of Mexico's Development: The Roles of the Private and Public Sectors* (Cambridge, 1963). D. A. WALKER, *The Nacional Financiera of Mexico* (Cambridge, 1961). NATHAN WHETTEN, *Rural Mexico* (Chicago, 1948).

BIOGRAPHY: CARLETON BEALS, *Porfirio Díaz, Dictator of Mexico* (Philadelphia, 1932). FRANCISCO BULNES, *El verdadero Juárez* (Mexico, D.F., 1904). W. H. CALLCOTT, *Santa Anna: The Story of an Enigma Who Once Was Mexico* (Norman, 1936). EGON CORTI, *Maximilian and Charlotte of Mexico,* tr. by C. A. Phillips, 2 vols. (New York, 1928). E. D. CRONON, **Josephus Daniels in Mexico* (Madison, 1960). F. A. KNAPP, JR., *Life of Sebastián Lerdo de Tejada, 1823–1889* (Austin, 1951). W. S. ROBERTSON, *Iturbide of Mexico* (Durham, N.C., 1952). RALPH ROEDER, *Juárez and his Mexico,* 2 vols. (New York, 1947). S. R. ROSS, *Francisco I. Madero, Apostle of Mexican Democracy* (New York, 1955). JUSTO SIERRA, *Juárez, su obra y su tiempo* (Mexico, 1905–

06). José Valadés, *Alamán, estadista y historiador* (Mexico, D.F., 1938). José Vasconcelos, *A Mexican Ulysses: An Autobiography*, tr. by W. R. Crawford (Bloomington, 1963). B. D. Wolfe, *The Fabulous Life of Diego Rivera* (New York, 1963).

IMPRESSIONS OF FOREIGNERS: Fanny Calderón de la Barca, *Life in Mexico: The Letters of Fanny Calderón de la Barca; with New Material from the Author's Private Journals*, ed. by H. T. and M. H. Fisher (Garden City, N.Y., 1966); the *Letters* were first published in Boston in 1843. C. M. Flandrau, **Viva Mexico* (New York, 1908). Edith O'Shaughnessy, *Diplomatic Days* (New York, 1917); *A Diplomat's Wife in Mexico* (New York, 1916); and *Intimate Pages of Mexican History* (New York, 1920). J. R. Poinsett, *Notes on Mexico Made in the Autumn of 1822* (Philadelphia, 1824). Waddy Thompson, *Recollections of Mexico* (New York, 1847). H. G. Ward, *Mexico in 1827*, 2 vols. (London, 1828).

PART V *The Caribbean and Central America*

R. N. Adams, *Cultural Survey of Panama-Nicaragua-Guatemala-El Salvador-Honduras* (Washington, 1957). Germán Arciniegas, *Caribbean: Sea of the New World*, tr. by Harriet de Onís (New York, 1946). J. J. Arévalo, *The Shark and the Sardines*, tr. from the Spanish by June Cobb and Raul Osegueda (New York, 1961). L. E. Bumgartner, *José del Valle of Central America* (Durham, N.C., 1963). J. E. Fagg, **Cuba, Haiti, and the Dominican Republic* (Englewood Cliffs, N.J., 1965). Lewis Hanke, **Mexico and the Caribbean* (Princeton, 1959). C. L. Jones, *The Caribbean Since 1900* (New York, 1936); and *The Caribbean Interests of the United States* (New York, 1916). T. L. Karnes, *The Failure of Union: Central America, 1824–1960* (Chapel Hill, N.C., 1961). C. D. Kepner, *Social Aspects of the Banana Industry* (New York, 1936); and, with Jay Soothill, *The Banana Empire* (New York, 1935). J. D. Martz, *Central America, The Crisis and the Challenge* (Chapel Hill, N.C., 1959); and *Justo Rufino Barrios and Central American Union* (Gainesville, 1963). Stacy May and Galo Plaza Lasso, *The United Fruit Company in Latin America* (Washington, 1958). D. G. Munro, *The Five Republics of Central America* (New York, 1918). F. D. Parker, *The Central American Republics* (New York, 1964). Dexter Perkins, *The United States and the Caribbean* (Cambridge, 1947). J. Fred Rippy, *The Caribbean Danger Zone* (New York, 1940). Mario Rodríguez, **Central America* (Englewood Cliffs, N.J., 1965). E. G. Squier, *Travels in Central America*, 2 vols. (New York, 1853). J. L. Stephens, **Incidents of Travel in Central America, Chiapas, and Yucatán*, new ed., ed. by R. L. Predmore (New Brunswick, 1949); the paperback is an abridgment. Sol Tax and others, *Heritage of Conquest: The Ethnology of Middle America* (Glencoe, Ill., 1952). A. Curtis Wilgus, ed., *The Caribbean at Mid-Century*, 8 vols. (Gainesville, 1951–58).

CUBA

Fulgencio Batista, *The Growth and Decline of the Cuban Republic*, tr. by B. M. Rocafort (New York, 1964). R. L. Buell and others, *Problems of the New Cuba* (New York, 1935). C. E. Chapman, *A History of the Cuban Republic* (New York, 1927). Erna Fergusson, *Cuba* (New York, 1946). R. H. Fitzgibbon, *Cuba and the United States, 1900–1935* (Menasha, Wis., 1935).

R. B. Gray, *José Martí: Cuban Patriot* (Gainesville, 1962). L. H. Jenks, *Our Cuban Colony: A Study in Sugar* (New York, 1928). Wyatt MacGaffey and C. R. Barnett, *Cuba: Its People, Its Society, Its Culture* (New Haven, 1962). Jorge Mañach, *Martí: Apostle of Freedom*, tr. by Coley Taylor (New York, 1950). Lowry Nelson, *Rural Cuba* (Minneapolis, 1950). Fernando Ortiz, *Cuban Counterpoint: Tobacco and Sugar*, tr. by Harriet de Onís (New York, 1947). Robert F. Smith, ed., *Background to Revolution: The Development of Modern Cuba* (New York, 1966); and *The United States and Cuba: Business and Diplomacy, 1917–1960* (New York, 1960). H. C. Wallich, *Monetary Problems of an Export Economy: The Cuban Experience, 1914–1947* (Cambridge, 1950).

CUBA UNDER CASTRO, 1959–   : Fidel Castro, *History Will Absolve Me*, tr. from the Spanish (New York, 1961). Theodore Draper, *Castro's Revolution: Myths and Realities* (New York, 1962); and *Castroism: Theory and Practice* (New York, 1965). Foreign Policy Association, *The Cuban Crisis: A Documentary Record* (New York, 1963). J. M. Gironella, *On China and Cuba*, tr. and prologue by J. F. Byrne (Notre Dame, 1963). Boris Goldenberg, *The Cuban Revolution and Latin America* (New York, 1965). Haynes Johnson and others, *The Bay of Pigs: The Leaders' Story of Brigade 2506* (New York, 1964). D. L. Larson, ed., *The Cuban Crisis of 1962: Selected Documents and Chronology* (Boston, 1963). H. L. Matthews, *The Cuban Story* (New York, 1961). K. E. Meyer and Tad Szulc, *The Cuban Invasion: The Chronicle of a Disaster* (New York, 1962). H. M. Patcher, *American-Soviet Confrontation: A Case Study of the Cuban Missile Crisis* (New York, 1963). Dudley Seers and others, *Cuba: The Economic and Social Revolution* (Chapel Hill, N.C., 1964). Robert F. Smith, *What Happened in Cuba? A Documentary History* (New York, 1963). W. A. Williams, *The United States, Castro and Cuba: An Essay on the Dynamics of Revolution and the Dissolution of Empire* (New York, 1962). Maurice Zeitlin and Robert Scheer, *Cuba: Tragedy in our Hemisphere* (New York, 1963).

HAITI

Stephen Alexis, *Black Liberator: The Life of Toussaint L'Ouverture*, tr. by W. Stirling (New York, 1949). Jonathan Brown, *The History and Present Condition of St. Domingo* (Philadelphia, 1837). Harold Courlander, *The Drum and the Hoe: Life and Lore of the Haitian People* (Berkeley, 1960). H. P. Davis, *Black Democracy*, rev. ed. (New York, 1936). Maya Deren, *Divine Horsemen: The Living Gods of Haiti* (New York, 1953). M. J. Herskovits, *Life in a Haitian Valley* (New York, 1937). M. A. Holly, *Agriculture in Haiti; With Special Reference to Rural Economy and Agricultural Education* (New York, 1955). C. L. R. James, *The Black Jacobins: Toussaint L'Ouverture and the San Domingo Revolution*, 2nd ed. (New York, 1963). J. G. Leyburn, *The Haitian People* (New Haven, 1941). R. W. Logan, *The Diplomatic Relations of the United States with Haiti, 1776–1891* (Chapel Hill, N.C., 1941). Alfred Métraux, *Haiti: Black Peasants and Voodoo*, tr. by Peter Lengyel (New York, 1960). L. L. Montague, *Haiti and the United States, 1714–1938* (Durham, N.C., 1940). Charles Moran, *Black Triumvirate: A Study of L'Ouverture, Dessalines, Christophe—the Men Who Made Haiti* (New York, 1957). J. W. Vandercook, *Black Majesty: The Life of Christophe, King of Haiti* (New York, 1928).

THE DOMINICAN REPUBLIC

JUAN BOSCH, *The Unfinished Experiment: Democracy in the Domin-ican Republic* (New York, 1965). R. D. CRASSWELLER, *Trujillo: The Life and Times of a Caribbean Dictator* (New York, 1966). A. R. ESPAILLAT, *Trujillo: The Last Caesar* (Chicago, 1963). JESÚS GALÍNDEZ SÚAREZ, *La era de Trujillo* (Santiago, 1956). A. C. HICKS, *Blood in the Streets: The Life and Rule of Trujillo* (New York, 1946). MELVIN KNIGHT, *The Americans in Santo Domingo* (New York, 1928). DAN KURZMAN, *Santo Domingo: Revolt of the Damned* (New York, 1965). JOHN BARTLOW MARTIN, *Overtaken by Events: The Dominican Crisis from the Fall of Trujillo to the Civil War* (New York, 1966). TAD SZULC, *Dominican Diary* (New York, 1965), an account of the 1965 inter-vention. SUMNER WELLS, *Naboth's Vineyard: The Dominican Republic, 1844–1924*, 2 vols. (New York, 1928).

CENTRAL AMERICA AND PANAMA

COSTA RICA: JOHN and MAVIS BIESANZ, *Costa Rican Life* (New York, 1944). J. L. BUSEY, *Notes on Costa Rican Democracy* (Boulder, 1962). C. L. JONES, *Costa Rica and the Civilization in the Caribbean* (Madison, 1935). WATT STEWART, *Keith and Costa Rica: A Biographical Study of Minor Cooper Keith* (Albuquerque, 1964).

GUATEMALA: ERNA FERGUSSON, *Guatemala* (New York, 1937). M. P. HOLLERAN, *Church and State in Guatemala* (New York, 1949). C. L. JONES, *Guatemala, Past and Present* (Minneapolis, 1940). VERA KELSEY and L. DE J. OSBORNE, *Four Keys to Guatemala* (New York, 1948). R. A. LABARGE, *Impact of the United Fruit Company on the Economic Development of Guatemala, 1946–1954* (New Orleans, 1960). MARIO ROSENTHAL, *Guatemala: The Story of an Emergent Latin American Democracy* (New York, 1962). R. M. SCHNEIDER, *Communism in Guatemala, 1944–1954* (New York, 1958). K. H. SILVERT, *A Study in Government: Guatemala* (New Orleans, 1954). N. L. WHETTEN, *Guatemala: The Land and the People* (New Haven, 1961).

HONDURAS: VINCENT CHECCHI and associates, *Honduras: A Problem in Economic Development* (New York, 1959). W. S. STOKES, *Honduras: An Area Study in Government* (Madison, 1950).

NICARAGUA: A. H. Z. CARR, *The World and William Walker* (New York, 1963). I. J. COX, *Nicaragua and the United States, 1909–1927* (Boston, 1927). W. O. SCROGGS, *Filibusters and Financiers: The Story of William Walker and His Associates* (New York, 1916).

PANAMA: JOHN and MAVIS BIESANZ, *The People of Panama* (New York, 1955). M. P. DUVAL, JR., *And the Mountains Will Move: The Story of the Building of the Panama Canal* (Stanford, 1947); and *Cádiz to Cathay: The Story of the Long Struggle for a Waterway Across the American Isthmus* (Stan-ford, 1940). L. O. EALY, *The Republic of Panama in World Affairs, 1903–1950* (Philadelphia, 1951). GERSTLE MACK, *The Land Divided: A History of the Panama Canal and Other Isthmian Canal Projects* (New York, 1944).

PART VI *Lands of the Spanish Main*

VENEZUELA

R. J. ALEXANDER, *The Venezuelan Democratic Revolution: A Profile of the Regime of Rómulo Betancourt* (New Brunswick, 1964). HARRY BERNSTEIN, **Venezuela and Colombia* (Englewood Cliffs, N.J., 1964). RÓMULO BETANCOURT, *Rómulo Betancourt: Pensamiento y acción* (Mexico, D.F., 1951); and *Venezuela: Política y petróleo* (Mexico, D.F., 1956). R. B. CUNNINGHAME GRAHAM, *José Antonio Páez* (Philadelphia, 1929). ERNA FERGUSSON, *Venezuela* (New York, 1939). EDWIN LIEUWEN, *Petroleum in Venezuela: A History* (Berkeley, 1954); and *Venezuela* (New York, 1961). W. D. and A. L. MARSLAND, *Venezuela Through Its History* (New York, 1954). GUILLERMO MORÓN, *A History of Venezuela*, tr. by John Street (New York, 1964). CARLOS PEREYRA, *Historia de la América Española*, Vol. VI of 8 vols. (Madrid, 1920–26). THOMAS ROURKE (pseud.), *Gómez, Tyrant of the Andes* (New York, 1948). MARY WATTERS, *A History of the Church in Venezuela, 1810–1930* (Chapel Hill, N.C., 1933). A. P. WHITAKER, *The United States and South America: The Northern Republics* (Cambridge, 1948). A. CURTIS WILGUS, ed., *South American Dictators During the First Century of Independence* (Washington, 1937); see articles by J. Fred Rippy on Páez, Guzmán Blanco, Castro, and Gómez. G. S. WISE, *Caudillo: A Portrait of Antonio Guzmán Blanco* (New York, 1951). R. A. WOHLRABE, *The Land and People of Venezuela* (Philadelphia, 1959).

COLOMBIA

R. C. ANDERSON, *The Diary and Journal, 1814–1826*, ed. by Alfred Tischendorf and E. T. Parks (Durham, N.C., 1964). HARRY BERNSTEIN, **Venezuela and Colombia* (Englewood Cliffs, N.J., 1964). DAVID BUSHNELL, *The Santander Regime in Gran Colombia* (Newark, 1954). V. L. FLUHARTY, **Dance of the Millions: Military Rule and the Social Revolution in Colombia 1930–1956* (Pittsburgh, 1957). W. O. GALBRAITH, *Colombia: A General Survey* (New York, 1953). W. M. GIBSON, *The Constitutions of Colombia* (Durham, N.C., 1948). J. M. HENAO and G. ARRUBLA, *A History of Colombia*, tr. by J. Fred Rippy (Chapel Hill, N.C., 1938). P. M. HOLT, *Colombia Today—and Tomorrow* (New York, 1964). J. M. HUNTER, *Emerging Colombia* (Washington, 1962). J. D. MARTZ, *Colombia: A Contemporary Political Survey* (Chapel Hill, N.C., 1962). RAFAEL NÚÑEZ, *La reforma política en Colombia*, 2 vols. (Bogotá, 1944). E. TAYLOR PARKS, *Colombia and the United States, 1765–1934* (Durham, N.C., 1935). KATHLEEN ROMOLI, *Colombia: Gateway to South America* (New York, 1941). A. P. WHITAKER, *The United States and South America: The Northern Republics* (Cambridge, 1948). A. CURTIS WILGUS, ed., *South American Dictators* (Washington, 1937); see essays by J. Fred Rippy on Mosquera, Núñez, and Reyes.

PART VII *The Indian Lands of the Andes*

ECUADOR

JOHN COLLIER, JR., and ANÍBAL BUITRÓN, *The Awakening Valley* (Chicago, 1949). CHARLES DARWIN, *The Voyage of the Beagle*, annotated and with an introd. by Leonard Engel (Garden City, N.Y., 1962). C. R. ENOCK,

Ecuador (New York, 1914). A. B. FRANKLIN, *Ecuador: Portrait of a People* (New York, 1943). F. HASSAUREK, *Four Years Among Spanish Americans* (New York, 1868). LILO LINKE, *Ecuador: Country of Contrast*, 3rd ed. (New York, 1960). M. C. NEEDLER, *Anatomy of a Coup d'Etat: Ecuador 1963* (Washington, 1964). E. W. PARSONS, *Peguche . . . Ecuador: A Study of Andean Indians* (Chicago, 1945). RICHARD PATTEE, *Gabriel García Moreno y el Ecuador de su tiempo* (Quito, 1941). O. E. REYES, *Breve historia general del Ecuador* (Quito, 1949). MOISÉS SÁENZ, *Sobre el indio ecuatoriano* (Mexico, D.F., 1933). J. V. D. SAUNDERS, *The People of Ecuador: A Demographic Analysis* (Gainesville, 1961). A. CURTIS WILGUS, ed., *South American Dictators* (Washington, 1937); see chapter on dictator Juan José Flores by N. A. N. Cleven. TEODORO WOLF, *Geografía y geología del Ecuador* (Leipzig, 1892). D. H. ZOOK, JR., *Zarumilla-Marañón: The Ecuador-Peru Dispute* (New York, 1964).

PERU

JORGE BASADRE, *Chile, Perú y Bolivia independientes* (Barcelona, 1948); and *Historia de la república del Perú, 1822–1908*, 2 vols., rev. ed. (Lima, 1949); and *Perú: Problema y posibilidad* (Lima, 1931). W. J. DENNIS, *Tacna and Arica* (New Haven, 1931). C. R. ENOCK, *Peru* (London, 1925). T. R. FORD, *Man and Land in Peru* (Gainesville, 1955). FRANCISCO GARCÍA CALDERÓN, *Entorno al Peru y América* (Lima, 1954). MANUEL GONZÁLEZ PRADA, *Figuras y figurones* (Paris, 1938); and *Propaganda y ataque* (Buenos Aires, 1939). V. R. HAYA DE LA TORRE, *Adonde va Indoamérica*, 2nd ed. (Santiago, 1935). HARRY KANTOR, *The Ideology and Program of the Peruvian Aprista Movement* (Berkeley, 1953). JOSÉ MARIÁTEGUI, *Siete ensayos de interpretación de la realidad peruana*, 2nd ed. (Lima, 1943). C. R. MARKHAM, *A History of Peru* (Chicago, 1892). HAROLD OSBORNE, *Indians of the Andes: Aymaras and Quechuas* (Cambridge, 1952). R. J. OWENS, *Peru* (New York, 1963). JAMES PAYNE, *Labor and Politics in Peru: The System of Political Bargaining* (New Haven, 1965). F. B. PIKE, *A History of Republican Peru* (London, 1967). EUDOCIO RAVINES, *The Yenan Road* (New York, 1951). MOISÉS SÁENZ, *Sobre el indio peruano* (Mexico, 1933). W. W. STEIN, *Hualcan: Life in the Highlands of Peru* (Ithaca, 1961). WATT STEWART, *Henry Meiggs, Yankee Pizarro* (Durham, N.C., 1946). A. P. WHITAKER, *The United States and South America: The Northern Republics* (Cambridge, 1948). A. CURTIS WILGUS, ed., *South American Dictators* (Washington, 1937); see chapters on Gamarra, Orbegoso, Salaverry, and Santa Cruz by N. A. N. CLEVEN.

BOLIVIA

R. J. ALEXANDER, *The Bolivian National Revolution* (New Brunswick, 1958). ALCIDES ARGÜEDES, *Historia general de Bolivia, 1809–1921* (La Paz, 1922). C. W. ARNADE, *The Emergence of the Republic of Bolivia* (Gainesville, 1957). JORGE BASADRE, *Chile, Peru y Bolivia independientes* (Barcelona, 1948). AUGUSTO CÉSPEDES, *Bolivia* (Washington, 1962). CARTER GOODRICH, *The Economic Transformation of Bolivia* (Ithaca, 1955). O. E. LEONARD, *Bolivia: Land, People, Institutions* (Washington, 1952). HAROLD OSBORNE, *Bolivia: A Land Divided*, 3rd ed. (New York, 1964). ALBERTO OSTRIA GUTIÉRREZ, *The Tragedy of Bolivia: A People Crucified*, tr. by Eithne Golden (New York, 1958). A. P. WHITAKER, *The United States and South America: The Northern Republics* (Cambridge, 1948). A. CURTIS WILGUS, ed., *South Amer-*

ican Dictators (Washington, 1937); see chapter on Mariano Melgarejo by N. A. N. CLEVEN. C. H. ZONDAG, *The Bolivian Economy, 1952–1965* (New York, 1966).

PART VIII *Chile*

D. B. ARAÑA, *Historia general de Chile,* 16 vols., 2nd ed. (Santiago, 1930). JORGE BASADRE, *Chile, Perú y Bolivia independientes* (Barcelona, 1948). C. G. BOWERS, *Chile Through Embassy Windows, 1939–1953* (New York, 1958). R. N. BURR, *By Reason or Force: Chile and the Balancing of Power in South America, 1830–1905* (Berkeley, 1965); and *The Stillborn Panama Congress: Power Politics and Chilean-Colombian Relations During the War of the Pacific* (Berkeley, 1962). G. J. BUTLAND, *Chile: An Outline of Its Geography, Economics and Politics,* 3rd ed. (New York, 1951); and *The Human Geography of Southern Chile* (London, 1957). STEPHEN CLISSOLD, *Chilean Scrapbook* (New York, 1952). AGUSTÍN EDWARDS, *My Native Land* (London, 1928); and *The Dawn* (London, 1931). ALBERTO EDWARDS, *La Fronda aristocrática* (Santiago, 1945). PAUL ELLSWORTH, *Chile: An Economy in Transition* (New York, 1945). F. A. ENCINA, *Portales,* 2 vols., (Santiago, 1934). ERNA FERGUSSON, *Chile* (New York, 1943). LUIS GALDAMES, *A History of Chile,* tr. and ed. by I. J. Cox (Chapel Hill, N.C., 1941). F. G. GIL, *Genesis and Modernization of Political Parties in Chile* (Gainesville, 1962); and **The Political System of Chile* (Boston, 1966); and, with C. J. PARRISH, *The Chilean Presidential Election of September 4, 1964: An Analysis* (Washington, 1965). MARIA GRAHAM, *Journal of a Residence in Chile, During the Year 1822; And a Voyage from Chile to Brazil in 1823* (London, 1824). ERNST HALPERIN, *Nationalism and Communism in Chile* (Cambridge, 1965); and, *Sino-Cuban Trends: The Case of Chile* (Cambridge, 1964). G. M. MCBRIDE, *Chile, Land and Society* (New York, 1936). JOAQUIM NABUCO, *Balmaceda* (Santiago, 1914). F. B. PIKE, *Chile and the United States, 1880–1962: The Emergence of Chile's Social Crisis and the Challenge to U.S. Diplomacy* (Notre Dame, 1963). K. H. SILVERT, *Chile, Yesterday and Today* (New York, 1965). J. R. STEVENSON, *The Chilean Popular Front* (Philadelphia, 1942). BENJAMIN SUBERCASEAUX, *Chile: A Geographic Extravaganza,* tr. by Angel Flores (New York, 1943). M. V. VALENZUELA, **La política económica del cobre en Chile* (Santiago, 1961). A. CURTIS WILGUS, ed., *Argentina, Brazil, and Chile Since Independence* (Washington, 1935); and *South American Dictators* (Washington, 1937); see chapters on Diego Portales and Balmaceda by Lewis Bealer. D. E. WORCESTER, *Seapower and Chilean Independence* (Gainesville, 1962).

PART IX *The Republics of the Río de la Plata*

ARGENTINA

R. J. ALEXANDER, *The Perón Era* (New York, 1951). SERGIO BAGÚ, *Argentina en el mundo* (Mexico, D.F., 1961). G. I. BLANKSTEN, *Perón's Argentina* (Chicago, 1953). J. H. FERGUSON and the editors of *Life, The River Plate Republics: Argentina, Paraguay, Uruguay* (New York, 1965). H. S. FERNS, *Britain and Argentina in the Nineteenth Century* (Oxford, 1960). ROBERT FITZROY, P. P. KING, and CHARLES DARWIN, *Narrative of the Surveying Voyages of His Majesty's Ships Adventure and Beagle,* 4 vols. (London, 1839).

ENRIQUE DE GANDÍA, *Historia de la república argentina en el siglo XIX* (Buenos Aires, 1940). JOSÉ INGENIEROS, *La evolución de las ideas argentinas* (Buenos Aires, 1946). J. J. KENNEDY, *Catholicism, Nationalism and Democracy in Argentina* (Notre Dame, 1958). F. A. KIRKPATRICK, *A History of the Argentine Republic* (Cambridge, 1931). RICARDO LEVENE, *A History of Argentina*, tr. and ed. by W. S. Robertson (Chapel Hill, N.C., 1937). V. F. LÓPEZ, *Historia de la república argentina*, 8 vols. (Buenos Aires, 1949–50). T. F. MCGANN, *Argentina, the United States, and the Inter-American System, 1880–1914* (Cambridge, Mass., 1957). ERNESTO PALACIO, *Historia de la Argentina, 1515–1957*, 3rd ed. (Buenos Aires, 1960). GEORGE PENDLE, *Argentina*, 3rd ed. (New York, 1963). H. F. PETERSON, *Argentina and the United States, 1810–1960* (Albany, 1964). Y. F. RENNIE, *The Argentine Republic* (New York, 1945). J. L. ROMERO, *A History of Argentine Political Thought* (Stanford, 1963). L. S. ROWE, *The Federal System of the Argentine Republic* (Washington, 1921). D. F. SARMIENTO, **Life in the Argentine Republic in the Days of the Tyrants: or, Civilization and Barbarism*, tr. from the Spanish, with a biographical sketch of the author by Mrs. Horace Mann (New York, 1868). J. R. SCOBIE, **Argentina: A City and a Nation* (New York, 1964). P. G. SNOW, *Argentine Radicalism* (Iowa City, 1965). A. P. WHITAKER, *Argentine Upheaval: Perón's Fall and the New Regime* (New York, 1956); and **Argentina* (Englewood Cliffs, N.J., 1964); and *The United States and Argentina* (Cambridge, 1954). A. CURTIS WILGUS, ed., *Argentina, Brazil, and Chile Since Independence* (Washington, 1935). J. C. ZURETTI, *Historia de la cultura argentina: arte y ciencia*, 10th ed. (Buenos Aires, 1964).

SOCIAL AND ECONOMIC: A. E. BUNGE, *Una nueva Argentina* (Buenos Aires, 1940). C. O. BUNGE, *Nuestra América* (Buenos Aires, 1905). MIRON BURGIN, *The Economic Aspects of Argentine Federalism, 1820–1852* (Cambridge, 1946). ALDO FERRER, *The Argentine Economy*, tr. by M. M. Urquidi (Berkeley, 1966). T. R. FILLOL, *Social Factors in Economic Development: The Argentine Case* (Cambridge, 1961). S. G. HANSON, *Argentine Meat and the British Market* (London, 1938). MARK JEFFERSON, *Peopling the Argentine Pampa* (New York, 1926). C. B. KROEBER, *The Growth of the Shipping Industry in the Río de la Plata Region, 1794–1860* (Madison, 1957). MADALINE NICHOLS, *The Gaucho* (Durham, N.C., 1942). V. L. PHELPS, *The International Economic Position of Argentina* (Philadelphia, 1938). C. C. TAYLOR, *Rural Life in Argentina* (Baton Rouge, 1948). FELIX WEIL, *Argentine Riddle* (New York, 1944).

BIOGRAPHY: OCTAVIO AMADEO, *Vidas argentinas*, 6th ed. (Buenos Aires, 1940). A. W. BUNKLEY, *The Life of Sarmiento* (Princeton, 1952). MARÍA FLORES, *The Woman with the Whip: Eva Perón* (Garden City, 1952). I. B. ESCOBAR, *Historia de los presidentes de Argentina*, enl. ed. (Buenos Aires, 1934). C. GALVÁN MORENO, *Rivadavia, el estadista genial* (Buenos Aires, 1940). MANUEL GÁLVEZ, *Vida de Hipólito Irigoyen*, 2nd ed. (Buenos Aires, 1939). CARLOS IBARGUREN, *Juan Manuel de Rosas*, 3rd ed. (Buenos Aires, 1930). J. M. NIÑO, *Mitre*, 2 vols. (Buenos Aires, 1906). EVA PERÓN, *My Mission in Life*, tr. by Ethel Cherry (New York, 1953). PABLO ROJAS PAZ, *Alberdi: el ciudadano de la soledad*, 2nd ed. (Buenos Aires, 1941). A. CURTIS WILGUS, ed., *South American Dictators* (Washington, 1937); see chapters on Rivadavia, Quiroga, Rosas, and Urquiza by Lewis W. Bealer. J. M. RAMOS MEJÍA, *Rosas y su tiempo*, 3 vols., 2nd ed. (Buenos Aires, 1907).

NINETEENTH-CENTURY TRAVELERS' DESCRIPTIONS: JOSEPH ANDREWS, *Journey from Buenos Ayres, etc.*, 2 vols. (London, 1827). J. A. KING, *Twenty-four*

Years in the Argentine Republic (New York, 1846). T. J. PAGE, *La Plata, the Argentine Confederation, and Paraguay* (New York, 1859). WOODBINE PARISH, *Buenos Aires and the Provinces of Rio de la Plata* (London, 1852). T. A. TURNER, *Argentina and the Argentines: Notes and Impressions, 1885–1890* (London, 1892). BENJAMÍN VICUÑA MACKENNA, *La Argentina en el año 1855* (Buenos Aires, 1936).

URUGUAY

PABLO BLANCO ACEVEDO, *Historia de la Republica Oriental del Uruguay,* 6 vols. (Montevideo, 1910). R. H. FITZGIBBON, *Uruguay: Portrait of a Democracy* (New Brunswick, 1954). J. H. FERGUSON and the editors of *Life, The River Plate Republics: Argentina, Paraguay, Uruguay* (New York, 1965). S. G. HANSON, *Utopia in Uruguay* (New York, 1938). W. H. HUDSON, *The Purple Land* (various eds., first pub. in London, 1885). W. H. KOEBEL, *Uruguay* (London, 1911). G. G. LINDAHL, *Uruguay's New Path: A Study in Politics During the First Colegiado, 1919–1933* (Stockholm, 1962). GEORGE PENDLE, *Uruguay, South America's First Welfare State,* 3rd ed. (New York, 1963). JOHN STREET, *Artigas and the Emancipation of Uruguay* (Cambridge, 1959). P. B. TAYLOR, *Government and Politics of Uruguay* (New Orleans, 1960). ALFREDO TRAVERSON, *Historia del Uruguay,* 2nd ed. (Montevideo, 1957). M. I. VANGER, *José Batlle y Ordóñez: Creator of His Times, 1902–1907* (Cambridge, 1963).

PARAGUAY

P. H. BOX, *The Origins of the Paraguayan War* (Urbana, 1930). R. F. BURTON, *Letters from the Battlefield of Paraguay* (London, 1870). GUILLERMO CABANELLAS, *El Dictador del Paraguay: Dr. Francia* (Buenos Aires, 1946). J. C. CHAVEZ, **La revolución paraguaya de la independencia* (Asunción, 1961). J. F. ESTIGARRIBIA, *The Epic of the Chaco: Marshal Estigarribia's Memoirs of the Chaco War, 1932–1935,* ed. by P. M. Insfran (Austin, 1950). J. W. FRETZ, *Pilgrims in Paraguay: The Story of Mennonite Colonization in South America* (Scottdale, 1953). G. F. MASTERMAN, *Seven Eventful Years in Paraguay,* 2nd ed. (London, 1870). GEORGE PENDLE, *Paraguay; A Riverside Nation* (New York, 1956). PHILIP RAINE, *Paraguay* (New Brunswick, 1956). J. RENGGER and I. LONGCHAMP, *The Reign of Doctor Joseph Gaspard Roderick de Francia in Paraguay* (London, 1827). J. P. ROBERTSON and W. P. ROBERTSON, *Letters on Paraguay,* 3 vols. (London, 1838–39). E. R. and H. S. SERVICE, *Tobatí: Paraguayan Town* (Chicago, 1954). G. THOMPSON, *The War in Paraguay* (London, 1869). H. G. WARREN, *Paraguay: An Informal History* (Norman, 1949). C. A. WASHBURN, *History of Paraguay,* 2 vols. (Boston, 1871). E. L. WHITE, *El Supremo* (New York, 1916). A. CURTIS WILGUS, ed., *South American Dictators* (Washington, 1937); see chapters on Francia, Carlos Antonio López, and Francisco Solano López by Lewis Bealer. D. H. ZOOK, JR., *The Conduct of the Chaco War* (New York, 1960).

PART X *Brazil*

JOHN ARMITAGE, *The History of Brazil* (London, 1836). J. M. BELLO, *A History of Modern Brazil, 1889–1964,* tr. from the Portuguese by J. L. Taylor with a new concluding chapter by R. E. Poppino (Stanford, 1966).

C. R. BOXER, *The Dutch in Brazil, 1624–1654* (Oxford, 1957); and *The Golden Age of Brazil, 1695–1750: Growing Pains of a Colonial Society* (Berkeley, 1962). E. B. BURNS, ed., *A Documentary History of Brazil* (New York, 1966); and *The Unwritten Alliance: Rio-Branco and Brazilian-American Relations* (New York, 1966). PEDRO CALMÓN, *História do Brasil,* 7 vols. (São Paulo, 1939–   ); and *History of Brazil: An Unpretentious Abridgement of the Brazilian History* by Doctor Pedro Calmón, with the collaboration of R. C. de Medeiros (Rio de Janeiro, 1939). J. P. CALOGERAS, *A History of Brazil,* tr. and ed. by P. A. Martin (Chapel Hill, N.C., 1939). J. A. CAMACHO, *Brazil: An Interim Assessment,* 2nd ed. (London, 1954). SERGIO CORRÊA DA COSTA, *Every Inch a King: A Biography of Dom Pedro I, First Emperor of Brazil,* tr. by Samuel Putnam (New York, 1950). EUCLIDES DA CUNHA, *Rebellion in the Backlands (Os sertões)* tr. by Samuel Putnam (Chicago, 1957). JOHN DOS PASSOS, *Brazil on the Move* (New York, 1963). J. W. F. DULLES, *Vargas of Brazil: A Political Biography* (Austin, 1967). GILBERTO FREYRE, *New World in the Tropics: The Culture of Modern Brazil* (New York, 1959). C. H. HARING, *Empire in Brazil: A New World Experiment with Monarchy* (Cambridge, 1958). W. L. HERNDON, *Exploration of the Valley of the Amazon,* ed. by Hamilton Basso (New York, 1952). L. F. HILL, *Brazil* (Berkeley, 1947); and *Diplomatic Relations Between the United States and Brazil* (Durham, N.C., 1932). SÉRGIO BUARQUE DE HOLANDE, ed., *História geral da civilização brasileira,* 3 vols. (São Paulo, 1960–62). H. W. HUTCHINSON, *Field Guide to Brazil* (Washington, 1960). H. G. JAMES, *Brazil After a Century of Independence* (New York, 1925); and *The Constitutional System of Brazil* (Washington, 1923). P. E. JAMES, *Brazil* (New York, 1946). DANIEL KIDDER and J. C. FLETCHER, *Brazil and the Brazilians* (Philadelphia, 1857). KARL LOEWENSTEIN, *Brazil Under Vargas* (New York, 1942). A. K. MANCHESTER, *British Preeminence in Brazil: Its Rise and Decline* (Chapel Hill, N.C., 1933). R. M. MORSE, ed., *The Bandeirantes: The Historical Role of the Brazilian Pathfinders* (New York, 1965); and *From Community to Metropolis: A Biography of São Paulo, Brazil* (Gainesville, 1958). JOAQUIM NABUCO, *Um estadista do Império: Nabuco de Araujo, sua vida, suas opiniões, sua epoca,* 3 vols. (Paris, 1898–1900). CAROLINA NABUCO, *The Life of Joaquim Nabuco,* tr. and ed. by Ronald Hilton (Stanford, 1950). ROY NASH, *The Conquest of Brazil* (New York, 1926). W. L. SCHURZ, *Brazil, the Infinite Country* (New York, 1961). T. LYNN SMITH, *Brazil: Peoples and Institutions,* rev. ed. (Baton Rouge, 1963). T. LYNN SMITH and ALEXANDER MARCHANT, eds., *Brazil: Portrait of Half a Continent* (New York, 1951). N. W. SODRÉ, *Formação histórica do Brasil* (Rio de Janeiro, 1962). HERNANE TAVARES DE SÁ, *The Brazilians: People of Tomorrow* (New York, 1947). HELIO VIANNA, *História do Brasil,* 2 vols. (Rio de Janeiro, 1961). CLODIMIR VIANNA MOOG, *Bandeirantes e pioneiros: Paralelo entre duas culturas,* tr. by L. L. Barrett (New York, 1964). CHARLES WAGLEY, *An Introduction to Brazil* (New York, 1963). A. CURTIS WILGUS, ed., *Argentina, Brazil and Chile Since Independence* (Washington, 1935). MARY W. WILLIAMS, *Dom Pedro the Magnanimous, Second Emperor of Brazil* (Chapel Hill, N.C., 1937).

SOCIAL AND ECONOMIC: JOSUÉ DE CASTRO, *Death in the Northeast: Poverty and Revolution in the Northeast of Brazil* (New York, 1966). GILBERTO FREYRE, *The Mansions and the Shanties: The Making of Modern Brazil,* tr. and ed. by Harriet de Onís (New York, 1963); and *The Masters and the Slaves,* tr. and ed. by Samuel Putnam, 2nd English language ed. rev. (New York, 1956); the paperback is an abridgment. CELSO FURTADO, *The Economic Growth of Brazil: A Survey from Colonial to Modern Times,* tr. by R. W. de Aguiar and

E. C. Drysdale (Berkeley, 1963). LINCOLN GORDON and E. L. GROMMERS, *United States Manufacturing Investment in Brazil: The Impact of Brazilian Government, 1946–1960* (Boston, 1962). MARVIN HARRIS, *Town and Country in Brazil* (New York, 1956). H. W. HUTCHINSON, *Village and Plantation Life in Northeastern Brazil* (Seattle, 1957). LILO LINKE, *People of the Amazon* (London, 1963). N. P. MACDONALD, *The Land and People of Brazil* (New York, 1959). J. F. NORMANO, *Brazil: A Study of Economic Types* (Chapel Hill, N.C., 1935). DONALD PIERSON, *Negroes in Brazil: A Study of Race Contact at Bahia* (Chicago, 1942). ARTHUR RAMOS, *The Negro in Brazil*, tr. by Richard Pattee (Washington, 1939). S. H. ROBOCK, *Brazil's Developing Northeast: A Study of Regional Planning and Foreign Aid* (Washington, 1963). R. C. SIMONSEN, *Brazil's Industrial Revolution* (São Paulo, 1939). FRANK TANNENBAUM, **Slave and Citizen: The Negro in the Americas* (New York, 1963). CHARLES WAGLEY, **Amazon Town: A Study of Man in the Tropics* (New York, 1953); and *Race and Class in Rural Brazil* (Paris, 1952). GEORGE WYTHE and others, *Brazil: An Expanding Economy* (New York, 1949).

CULTURE AND IDEAS: FERNANDO DE AZEVEDO, *Brazilian Culture: An Introduction to the Study of Culture in Brazil*, tr. by W. R. Crawford (New York, 1950). JOÃO CRUZ COSTA, *A History of Ideas in Brazil*, tr. by Suzette Macedo (Berkeley, 1964). F. P. ELLISON, *Brazil's New Novel. Four Northeastern Masters: José Lins do Rego, Jorge Amado, Graciliano Ramos, Rachel de Queiroz* (Berkeley, 1962). JOHN A. NIST, ed. and tr., *Modern Brazilian Poetry: An Anthology* (Bloomington, Ind., 1962). SAMUEL PUTNAM, *Marvelous Journey: Four Centuries of Brazilian Literature* (New York, 1948). ERICO VERISSIMO, *Brazilian Literature: An Outline* (New York, 1945).

NINETEENTH-CENTURY TRAVELERS' DESCRIPTIONS: PROFESSOR and MRS. LOUIS AGASSIZ, *A Journey in Brazil* (Boston, 1868). H. W. BATES, **The Naturalist on the River Amazon* (London, 1863). MARIA GRAHAM, *Journal of a Voyage to Brazil, and Residence There, During Part of the Years 1821, 1822, 1823* (London, 1824). R. WALSH, *Notices of Brazil, 1828–1829* (London, 1830).

PART XI   *Latin America and the United States*

VICTOR ALBA, *Alliance Without Allies: The Mythology of Progress in Latin America* (New York, 1965). S. F. BEMIS, *The Latin American Policy of the United States* (New York, 1943). A. A. BERLE, **Latin America: Diplomacy and Reality* (New York, 1962). J. P. DAVIES, JR., *Foreign and Other Affairs* (New York, 1966). ALEXANDER DECONDE, *Herbert Hoover's Latin American Policy* (Stanford, 1951); and *A History of American Foreign Policy* (New York, 1963). JOSÉ DE ONÍS, *The United States as Seen by Spanish American Writers, 1776–1890* (New York, 1952). D. M. DOZER, *Are We Good Neighbors? Three Decades of Inter-American Relations, 1930–1960* (Gainesville, 1959); and **The Monroe Doctrine: Its Modern Significance* (New York, 1965), a series of articles, addresses, editorials, and official policy statements. J. C. DRIER, ed., *The Alliance for Progress: Problems and Perspectives* (Baltimore, 1962); and *The Organization of American States and the Hemisphere Crisis* (New York, 1962). LAURENCE DUGGAN, *The Americas: In Search for Hemispheric Security* (New York, 1949). MILTON EISENHOWER, *The Wine is Bitter: The United States and Latin America* (Garden City, N.Y., 1963). HERBERT FEIS, **The Diplomacy of the Dollar: First Era, 1919–1932* (Baltimore, 1950); and *Foreign Aid and Foreign Policy* (New York, 1964). C. G. FENWICK, *The Organization of American States: The Inter-American Regional System* (Washington, 1963). J. W. GANTENBEIN, ed., *The Evolution of Our Latin American Policy; A Documentary Record* (New York, 1950). P. L. GEYELIN, *Lyndon B. Johnson and the World* (New York, 1966). LINCOLN GORDON, *A New Deal for Latin America: The Alliance for Progress* (Cambridge, 1963). E. O. GUERRANT, *Roosevelt's Good Neighbor Policy* (Albuquerque, 1950). J. A. HOUSTON, *Latin America in the United Nations* (New York, 1956). EDWIN LIEUWEN, **U.S. Policy in Latin America: A Short History* (New York, 1965). J. A. LOGAN, *No Transfer: An American Security Principle* (New Haven, 1961). G. S. McCLELLAN, ed., *U. S. Policy in Latin America* (New York, 1963). W. R. MANNING, ed., *Diplomatic Correspondence of the United States: Inter-American Affairs, 1831–1860*, 12 vols. (Washington, 1932–39). H. L. MATTHEWS, *The United States and Latin America*, 2nd ed. (Englewood Cliffs, N.J., 1963). J. L. MECHAM, *A Survey of United States–Latin American Relations* (Boston, 1965); and *The United States and Inter-American Security* (Austin, 1961). J. W. NYSTROM and N. A. HAVERSTOCK, *The Alliance for Progress* (Princeton, 1966). DEXTER PERKINS, *The Monroe Doctrine, 1823–1826* (Cambridge, Mass., 1927); *The Monroe Doctrine, 1826–1867* (Baltimore, 1933); *The Monroe Doctrine, 1867–1907* (Baltimore, 1937); and **Hands Off: A History of the Monroe Doctrine* (Boston, 1941). J. FRED RIPPY, *Latin America in World Politics*, 3rd ed. (New York, 1938). A. M. SCHLESINGER, JR., *A Thousand Days: John F. Kennedy in the White House* (Boston, 1965). J. B. SCOTT, ed., *The International Conferences of American States, 1889–1928* (New York, 1931). T. C. SORENSEN, **Kennedy* (New York, 1965). G. H. STUART, *Latin America and the United States*, 4th ed. (New York, 1943). A. F. TYLER, *Foreign Policy of James G. Blaine* (Minneapolis, 1927). A. P. WHITAKER, **The United States and the Independence of Latin America, 1800–1830* (Baltimore, 1941); *The United States and South America: The Northern Republics* (Cambridge, 1948); and **The Western Hemisphere Idea: Its Rise and Decline* (Ithaca, 1954). BRYCE WOOD, *The Making of the Good Neighbor Policy* (New York, 1961). GEORGE WYTHE, *The United States and Inter-American Relations: A Contemporary Appraisal* (Gainesville, 1964).

UNITED STATES RELATIONS WITH INDIVIDUAL COUNTRIES: With Argentina: C. H. HARING, *Argentina and the United States* (Boston, 1941). T. F. McGANN, *Argentina, the United States, and the Inter-American System, 1880–1914* (Cambridge, Mass., 1957). H. F. PETERSON, *Argentina and the United States: 1810–1960* (Albany, 1964). A. P. WHITAKER, *The United States and Argentina* (Cambridge, Mass., 1954). With Brazil: E. B. BURNS, *The Unwritten Alliance: Rio-Branco and Brazilian-American Relations* (New York, 1966). L. F. HILL, *Diplomatic Relations Between the United States and Brazil* (Durham, N.C., 1932). With Chile: F. B. PIKE, *Chile and the United States, 1808–1962* (Notre Dame, 1963). With Colombia: E. T. PARKS, *Colombia and the United States, 1765–1934* (Durham, N.C., 1935). With Mexico: J. M. CALLAHAN, *American Foreign Policy in Mexican Relations* (New York, 1932). E. D. CRONON, **Josephus Daniels in Mexico* (Madison, 1960). JOSEPHUS DANIELS, *Shirt-Sleeve Diplomat* (Chapel Hill, N.C., 1947). C. W. HACKETT, *The Mexican Revolution and the United States, 1910–1926* (Boston, 1926). J. FRED RIPPY, *The United States and Mexico*, rev. ed. (New York, 1931). G. L. RIVES, *The United States and Mexico, 1821–1848*, 2 vols. (New York, 1913). J. H. SMITH, *The War with Mexico*, 2 vols. (New York, 1919).

Index

Prepared by Margaret L. Mulhauser

[*i*]

A NOTE ON THE TYPE

The text of this book was set on the Linotype in a face called TIMES ROMAN, *designed by Stanley Morison for The Times (London), and first introduced by that newspaper in 1932.*

Among typographers and designers of the twentieth century, Stanley Morison has been a strong forming influence, as typographical advisor to the English Monotype Corporation, as a director of two distinguished English publishing houses, and as a writer of sensibility, erudition, and keen practical sense.

Composed and bound by The Haddon Craftsmen, Inc., Scranton, Pa. Printed by Halliday Lithograph Corporation, West Hanover, Massachusetts. Designed by Leon Bolognese.